KU-528-155

PROCEDURAL LAW
OF THE
EUROPEAN UNION

Second Edition

By

KOEN LENAERTS
Professor of European Law, Katholieke Universiteit Leuven,
Judge of the Court of Justice of the European Communities

DIRK ARTS
Advocaat, Member of the Brussels Bar

and

IGNACE MASELIS
Legal Secretary at the Court of First Instance of the
European Communities

ROBERT BRAY, EDITOR
Principal Administrator in the Secretariat of the
Committee on Legal Affairs of the European Parliament

LONDON
SWEET & MAXWELL
2006

Published in 2006 by
Sweet & Maxwell
100 Avenue Road
Swiss Cottage
London NW3 3PF

(*http://www.smlawpub.co.uk*)

Computerset by LBJ Typesetting Ltd of Kingsclere
Printed in England by CPI Bath

ISBN–10 0–421–94700–4
ISBN–13 978–0–421–88610–5

All rights reserved. U.K. statutory material in this publication is acknowledged as Crown copyright.

No part of this publication may be reproduced or transmitted in any form or by any means, or stored in any retrieval system of any nature, without prior written permission, except for permitted fair dealing under the Copyright, Designs and Patents Act 1988, or in accordance with the terms of a licence issued by the Copyright Licensing Agency in respect of photocopying and/or reprographic reproduction. Application for permission for other use of copyright material including permission to reproduce extracts in other published works shall be made to the publishers. Full acknowledgment of author, publisher and source must be given.

©
KOEN LENAERTS
DIRK ARTS
IGNACE MASELIS
ROBERT BRAY
2006

PREFACE

It is vital for practitioners and students to know how to enforce European Union law and to be aware of the mechanisms affording protection against unlawful action on the part of Union institutions. Hence, it seemed to us that there was even more need for an affordable book on European procedural law—the idea behind the first edition which came out in 1999—after the reforms of the European Union judiciary launched by the Nice Treaty and several crucial developments in the case-law of the European Courts over the past years. The present edition has not only been entirely revised but it is also more directly oriented towards legal practice. Accordingly, competition law, State aid and anti-dumping law are dealt with in special sections wherever it was thought appropriate to indicate how the available remedies work concretely in these fields.

Just as in the first edition, considerable importance has been given to the primary role played by the national courts in the Union legal order, by themselves as well as in dialogue with the Court of Justice under the preliminary ruling procedure. In addition, the various direct actions which can be brought in the Court of Justice, the Court of First Instance and the Civil Service Tribunal are considered.

The preliminary ruling procedure, in fact, permeates three parts of the book. Part I, which introduces the judicial machinery of the European Union, sets out the basic features of the reference for a preliminary ruling and reviews the influence of Community law on national procedural rules, the aim being to give an overall picture of the interaction between the national courts and the Court of Justice.

Part II—enforcement of Community law—deals with actions for infringement of Community law by a Member State together with preliminary rulings on the interpretation of Community law, in view of the fact that national courts often use that procedure to test the compatibility of national law and practice with Community law.

Part III—protection against unlawful action by the Union institutions—discusses preliminary references as a means of putting to the Court of Justice the question of the validity of acts of the institutions where it has been contested in a national court. This part also deals with actions for annulment and failure to act, actions for damages and the objection of illegality.

Part IV sets out a number of special forms of procedure, including a discussion of the jurisdiction of the European Courts in connection with interim relief, appeals, intellectual property rights, conventions concluded by the Member States and police and judicial cooperation in criminal matters.

Part V considers procedure before the Court of Justice and the Court of First Instance. The appendix sets out the Statute of the Court of Justice as well as the Rules of Procedure of the Court of Justice and the Court of First Instance.

Finally, for the reader's convenience all actions are described as far as possible on the same pattern: the subject-matter of the application, the identity of the parties, the special characteristics of the action and the effects of a judicial decision are dealt with in that order.

This work—which reflects the state of the law on January 1, 2006—is the companion volume to Koen Lenaerts and Piet Van Nuffel; Robert Bray (ed.), *Constitutional Law of the European Union*, Sweet and Maxwell, 2005 (second edition), which sets out to provide an overview of the institutional and substantive law of the European Union.

It only remains to thank Kathleen Gutman of the Institute of European Law (Leuven) for her most dedicated assistance with the finalisation of the tables and proofreading of the book. It goes furthermore without saying that all views expressed are our own and cannot be ascribed to the institutions to which we belong.

Koen Lenaerts
Dirk Arts
Ignace Maselis
Robert Bray (editor)
Luxembourg and Brussels, February 1, 2006

FOREWORD TO THE FIRST EDITION

There are already some very good books on European Union procedural law which give clear guidance to practitioners on the application of the basic rules.

This book is different in the sense that it really sets out to examine the principles on which such rules are based and to give a detailed exposition of the way in which the Court applies the rules. It will prove to be a valuable book from which to teach a course on litigation before the European Court and the Court of First Instance. Students will find it readable and stimulating—not here, to use Lord Wilberforce's famous phrase, mere "tabulated legalism" but a serious analysis of "how?" and "why?".

At the same time it is not only an "academic" book. It will give practitioners and judges a real understanding of the way things work not only at the Court itself but in the dialogue between national courts and the European Court through the reference procedure. There is, for example, a helpful discussion as to how the decision to refer should be taken and how the provisions of paragraph 3 of Article 234 of the Treaty (Final Courts) should be applied. (In the latter case the authors are generous about the judgment in *CILFIT*). The Court's jurisprudence dealing with the need for national remedies to be adapted so as effectively to protect Community law rights has developed considerably and sometimes controversially; at the time of *Francovich* it was plain (at any rate to me) that it was only the beginning of the story and that a lot of matters would have to be worked out in subsequent cases. The book deals valuably with such questions as these and the analysis of the cases, *e.g.* on what is a sufficiently serious breach to justify an order for compensation against the state in national courts is of considerably contemporary concern. There is still a long way to go in working out the parameters of this remedy and the chapter dealing with the subject will provide for practitioners and the courts a very useful starting point.

The actions for ingringement of Treaty obligations by a Member State and for annulment of Community Acts are dealt with in depth and, of particular relevance to practising lawyers, is the analysis of the right of individual challenge to the lawfulness of Community acts.

The concept of the scope of the "exception d'illégalité" ("objection of illegality") in Article 241 (ex 184) of the Treaty may be understood by civil lawyers but I have always found the subject difficult for a common lawyer. There is a helpful though brief analysis of this. Availability of interim measures, in many ways different from our interim forms of relief, the limits of appeals from the CFI and the detailed procedure before both the Court and the CFI are covered extensively.

The structure of the various sections follows a common pattern—contents of the form of action, the parties, procedural rules and the consequences of the judgment—which is helpful both to practitioners and students.

This is an excellent book which with its companion volume on the "constitutional law of the European Union" will be seen as one of the outstanding statements of European Union law and practice.

Slynn of Hadley

TABLE OF CONTENTS

PART I

THE JUDICIAL ORGANISATION OF THE EUROPEAN UNION

CHAPTER 1.   THE EUROPEAN COURTS

PART II

ENFORCEMENT OF COMMUNITY LAW

PART III

PROTECTION AGAINST ACTS OF THE INSTITUTIONS

CHAPTER 7. THE ACTION FOR ANNULMENT

PART IV

SPECIAL FORMS OF PROCEDURE

CHAPTER 13. PROCEEDINGS FOR INTERIM MEASURES BEFORE THE COURT OF JUSTICE AND THE COURT OF FIRST INSTANCE

PART V

PROCEDURE BEFORE THE COURT OF JUSTICE AND THE COURT OF FIRST INSTANCE

CHAPTER 23. INTRODUCTION

CHAPTER 24. PROCEDURE IN THE CASE OF DIRECT ACTIONS

LIST OF ABBREVIATIONS

ACP	African, Caribbean, Pacific
A.J.D.A.	*L'actualité juridique—droit administratif*
Anglo-Am.L.R.	*Anglo-American Law Review*
Cambridge L.J.	*Cambridge Law Journal*
Cambridge Y.E.L.S.	*Cambridge Yearbook of European Legal Studies*
C.D.E.	*Cahiers de droit européen*
CFI	Court of First Instance of the European Communities
C.M.L.R.	*Common Market Law Reports*
C.M.L.Rev.	*Common Market Law Review*
Col.J.E.L.	*Columbia Journal of European Law*
Coreper	Committee of Permanent Representatives
D.ö.V.	*Die öffentliche Verwaltung*
D.P.C.I.	*Droit et pratique du commerce international*
E.C. Bull.	*Bulletin of the European Communities*
E.Comp.L.Rev.	*European Competition Law Review*
ECJ	Court of Justice of the European Communities
E.C.R.	*European Court Reports*
E.For.Aff.Rev.	*European Foreign Affairs Review*
E.I.P.Rev.	*European Intellectual Property Review*
E.J.L.Ref.	*European Journal of Law Reform*
E.L.J.	*European Law Journal*
E.L.Rev.	*European Law Review*
E.Pub.L.	*European Public Law*
E.Rev.Priv.L.	*European Review of Private Law*
E.U. Bull.	*Bulletin of the European Union*
Eu.GR.Z.	*Europäische Grundrechte Zeitschrift*
Eu L.R.	*European Law Reporter*
EuR.	*Europarecht*
Eu.Z.W.	*Europäische Zeitschrift für Wirtschaftsrecht*
Fordham I.L.J.	*Fordham International Law Journal*
G.U.R.I.	*Gazetta Ufficiale della Repubblica Italiana*
I.C.L.Q.	*International and Comparative Law Quarterly*
Ir.J.E.L.	*Irish Journal of European Law*
J.B.L.	*The Journal of Business Law*
J.C.D.I.	*Jurisclasseur Droit international*
J.C.P.	*Jurisclasseur périodique—La semaine juridique*
J.D.I.	*Journal du droit international*
J.I.E.L.	*Journal of International Economic Law*
J.T.	*Journal des Tribunaux*
J.T.D.E.	*Journal des Tribunaux—Droit européen*
J.Z.	*Juristen—Zeitung*

L.I.E.I.	*Legal Issues of European Integration* (since 2000: *Legal Issues of Economic Integration*)
M.J.E.C.L.	*Maastricht Journal of European and Comparative Law*
Mich.L.Rev.	*Michigan Law Review*
Mod.L.R.	*Modern Law Review*
N.I.L.R.	*Netherlands International Law Review*
N.J.B.	*Nederlands Juristenblad*
N.J.W.	*Neue Juristische Wochenschrift*
N.T.B.	*Nederlands Tijdschrift voor bestuursrecht*
N.T.E.R.	*Nederlands Tijdscrift voor Europees Recht*
O.J.	*Official Journal of the European Union*
Pub.L.	*Public Law*
R.A.E.	*Revue des affaires européennes*
R.D.U.E.	*Revue du droit de l'Union européenne*
R.D.ULB	*Revue du droit de l'Université Libre de Bruxelles*
Rec. Dalloz	*Recueil Dalloz-Sirey*
R.G.D.I.P.	*Revue générale de droit international public*
R.I.D.C.	*Revue internationale de droit comparé*
Riv.D.E.	*Rivista di diritto europeo*
R.M.C.	*Revue du Marché Commun*
R.M.C.U.E.	*Revue du Marché Commun et de l'Union européenne*
R.M.U.E.	*Revue du Marché Unique européen*
R.S.C.D.P.C.	*Revue de science criminelle et de droit pénal comparé*
R.T.D.E.	*Revue trimestrielle de droit européen*
R.W.	*Rechtskundig Weekblad*
S.E.W.	*Sociaal-economische wetgeving. Tijdschrift voor Europees en economisch recht*
T.B.H.	*Tijdscrift voor Belgisch handelsrecht*
T.B.P.	*Tijdschrift voor bestuurswetenschappen en publiekrecht*
Texas I.L.J.	*Texas International Law Journal*
Tilburg For.L.Rev.	*Tilburg Foreign Law Review*
T.P.R.	*Tijdschrift voor privaatrecht*
Y.E.L.	*Yearbook of European Law*
Z.f.RV.	*Zeitschrift für Rechtsvergleichung, internationales Privatrecht und Europarecht*
Z.U.R.	*Zeitschrift für Umweltrecht*

ABBREVIATED FORMS FOR TREATIES AND ACTS

The following abbreviated forms for Treaties and legislative measures are used in this work:

Brussels Convention — Convention of September 27, 1968 on jurisdiction and the enforcement of judgments in civil and commercial matters (consolidated version, [1998] O.J. C27/1).

CFI Rules of Procedure — Rules of Procedure of the Court of First Instance of the European Communities of May 2, 1991 ([1991] O.J. L136/1, and [1991] O.J. L137/34 (corrigenda)), as amended on September 15, 1994 ([1994] O.J. L249/17), on February 17, 1995 ([1995] O.J. L44/64), on July 6, 1995 ([1995] O.J. L172/3), on March 12, 1997 ([1997] O.J. L103/6, and [1997] O.J. L351/72 (corrigenda)), on May 17, 1999 ([1999] O.J. L135/92), on December 6, 2000 ([2000] O.J. L322/4), on May 21, 2003 ([2003] O.J. L147/22), on April 19, 2004 ([2004] O.J. L132/3), on April 21, 2004 ([2004] O.J. L127/108), and on October 12, 2005 ([2005] O.J. L298/1).

Constitution — Treaty establishing a Constitution for Europe ([2004] O.J. C310/1).

Decision 2004/752 — Council Decision 2004/752/EC, Euratom of November 2, 2004 establishing the European Union Civil Service Tribunal ([2004] O.J. L333/7).

EAEC Treaty — Treaty establishing the European Atomic Energy Community.

EC Treaty — Treaty establishing the European Community (consolidated version, [2002] O.J. C325/33).

ECHR — European Convention for the Protection of Human Rights and Fundamental Freedoms.

ECJ Rules of Procedure — Rules of Procedure of the Court of Justice of the European Communities of June 19, 1991 ([1991] O.J. L176/7, and [1992] O.J. L383/117 (corrigenda)), as amended on February 21, 1995 ([1995] O.J. L44/61), on March 11, 1997 ([1997] O.J. L103/1, and [1977] O.J. L351/72 (corrigenda)), on May 16, 2000 ([2000] O.J. L122/43), on November 28, 2000 ([2000] O.J. L322/1), on April 3, 2001 ([2001] O.J. L119/1),

ECJ Rules of Procedure —cont.	on September 17, 2002 ([2002] O.J. L272/24, and [2002] O.J. L281/24 (corrigenda)), on April 8, 2003 ([2003] O.J. L147/17), on July 10, 2003 ([2003] O.J. L172/12), on April 19, 2004 ([2004] O.J. L132/2), on April 20, 2004 ([2004] O.J. L127/107), on July 12, 2005 ([2005] O.J. L203/19), and on October 18, 2005 ([2005] O.J. L288/51).
ECSC Treaty	Treaty establishing the European Coal and Steel Community.
EEA Agreement	Agreement on the European Economic Area.
EEC Treaty	Treaty establishing the European Economic Community.
EU Treaty	Treaty on European Union (consolidated version, [2002] O.J. C325/5).
Regulation No 17	Council Regulation No 17/62 ([1959–1962] O.J. English Spec. Ed. I, 87), First Regulation implementing Arts 85 and 86 of the Treaty, as amended and supplemented by Regulation No 59 ([1959–1962] O.J. English Spec. Ed. I, 249), Regulation No 118/63/EEC ([1963–1964] O.J. English Spec. Ed. I. 55) and Regulation No 2822/71/EEC ([1971] O.J. English Spec. Ed. III, 1035).
Regulation No 40/94	Council Regulation (EC) No 40/94 of December 20, 1993 on the Community trade mark ([1994] O.J. L11/1), as amended by Council Regulation (EC) No 422/2004 ([2004] O.J. L70/1).
Regulation No 384/96	Council Regulation (EC) No 384/96 of December 22, 1995 on protection against dumped imports from countries not members of the European Community ([1996] O.J. L56/1), as amended by Regulation No 2331/96 ([1996] O.J. L317/1), by Regulation No 905/98 ([1998] O.J. L128/18), by Regulation No 2238/2000 ([2000] O.J. L257/2), by Regulation No 1972/2002 ([2002] O.J. L305/1) and by Regulation No 461/2004 ([2004] O.J. L77/12).
Regulation No 659/1999	Council Regulation (EC) No 659/1999 of March 22, 1999 laying down detailed rules for the application of Art.93 of the EC Treaty ([1999] O.J. L83/1).
Regulation No 1049/2001	Regulation (EC) No 1049/2001 of the European Parliament and of the Council of May 30, 2001 regarding public access to European Parliament, Council and Commission documents ([2001] O.J. L145/43).

Regulation No 1/2003	Council Regulation (EC) No 1/2003 of December 16, 2002 on the implementation of the rules on competition laid down in Arts 81 and 82 of the Treaty ([2003] O.J. L1/1).
Regulation No 139/2004	Council Regulation (EC) No 139/2004 of January 20, 2004 on the control of concentrations between undertakings (the EC Merger Regulation) ([2004] O.J. L24/1).
Regulation No 773/2004	Commission Regulation (EC) No 773/2004 of April 7, 2004 relating to the conduct of proceedings by the Commission pursuant to Arts 81 and 82 of the EC Treaty ([2004] O.J. L123/18).
Regulation No 794/2004	Commission Regulation (EC) No 794/2004 of April 21, 2004 implementing Council Regulation (EC) No 659/1999 laying down detailed rules for the application of Art.93 [now Art.88] of the EC Treaty ([2004] O.J. L140/1); corrigendum in [2005] O.J. L25/74.
Regulation No 802/2004	Commission Regulation (EC) No 802/2004 of April 7, 2004 implementing Council Regulation (EC) No 139/2004 on the control of concentrations between undertakings ([2004] O.J. L133/1); corrigendum in [2004] O.J. L172/9.
Rome Convention	Convention of June 19, 1980 on the law applicable to contractual obligations (consolidated version, [1998] O.J. C27/34).
Statute	Protocol on the Statute of the Court of Justice annexed to the Treaty on European Union, to the Treaty establishing the European Community and to the Treaty establishing the European Atomic Energy Community, in accordance with Art.7 of the Treaty of Nice, amending the Treaty on European Union, the Treaties establishing the European Communities and certain related acts, signed at Nice on February 26, 2001 ([2001] O.J. C80/1), as amended by Council Decision of July 15, 2003 ([2003] O.J. L188/1), by Art.13(2) of the Act concerning the conditions of accession of April 16, 2003 ([2003] O.J. L236/37), Council Decisions of April 19 and 26, 2004 ([2004] L132/1 and 5, and [2004] O.J. L194/3 (corrigendum)) and Council Decision of November 2, 2004 establishing the European Union Civil Service Tribunal ([2004] O.J. L333/7) and by Council Decision of October 3, 2005 ([2005] O.J. L266/60).

References made in this work to the Advocate General apply in the case of the Court of First Instance only where a Judge has been designated to act as such.

TEXTBOOKS REFERRED TO THROUGHOUT

M. Brealey and M. Hoskins, *Remedies in E.C. Law* (2nd ed., Sweet & Maxwell, London, 1998), 632 pp.
  Brealey and Hoskins, *Remedies in E.C. Law*

R. Joliet, *Le droit institutionnel des Communautés européennes—Le contentieux* (Faculté de Droit, d'Économie et de Sciences sociales de Liège, Liège, 1981), 302 pp.
  Joliet, *Le contentieux*

K. Lenaerts and P. Van Nuffel, R. Bray (ed.), *Constitutional Law of the European Union* (2nd ed., Sweet & Maxwell, London, 2005), 969 pp.
  Lenaerts and Van Nuffel, *Constitutional Law of the European Union*

J. Rideau and F. Picod, *Code de procédures juridictionnelles de l'Union européenne* (2nd ed., Litec, Paris, 2002), 914 pp.
  Rideau and Picod, *Code de procédures juridictionnelles*

H.G. Schermers and D. Waelbroeck, *Judicial Protection in the European Communities* (6th ed., Kluwer, Deventer, 2001), 889 pp.
  Schermers and Waelbroeck, *Judicial Protection*

G. Vandersanden and A. Barav, *Contentieux communautaire* (Bruylant, Brussels, 1977), 722 pp.
  Vandersanden and Barav, *Contentieux communautaire*

M. Waelbroeck, D. Waelbroeck and G. Vandersanden, *La Cour de Justice*, in M. Waelbroeck, J.–V. Louis, D. Vignes, J.–L. Dewost and G. Vandersanden, *Commentaire Mégret* (2nd ed., Éditions de l'Université de Bruxelles, Brussels, 1993), Vol. 10, 666 pp.
  Commentaire Mégret

NUMERICAL TABLE OF EUROPEAN CASES

EUROPEAN COURT OF JUSTICE

LIVERPOOL JOHN MOORES UNIVERSITY
LEARNING SERVICES

EUROPEAN COURT OF HUMAN RIGHTS

ALPHABETICAL TABLE OF EUROPEAN CASES

TABLE OF NATIONAL CASES

TABLE OF EU AND EC TREATIES, PROTOCOLS AND DECLARATIONS

TABLE OF TEXTS RELATING TO PROCEDURE BEFORE THE COURT OF JUSTICE AND THE COURT OF FIRST INSTANCE

TABLE OF EUROPEAN UNION AND COMMUNITY ACTS

TABLE OF CONVENTIONS AND AGREEMENTS CONCLUDED BY THE EC OR THE EU

TABLE OF NATIONAL LEGISLATION

Part I

THE JUDICIAL ORGANISATION OF THE EUROPEAN UNION

CHAPTER 1

THE EUROPEAN COURTS

I. NATIONAL COURTS

General. National courts and tribunals are under an obligation to apply   **1–001**
Community law in all cases between national authorities and natural or
legal persons or between such persons[1] and to safeguard the rights
conferred by Community law.[2]

Primary role. The primary role played by national courts in applying   **1–002**
Community law is connected with the peculiar nature of that law. The
Community Treaties created a new legal order, directed at the Member
States and their nationals. The relationship between the Community legal
order and the national legal systems is characterised by the primacy of
Community law and the direct effect of a whole series of provisions of
Community law.[3] The question arises as to how individuals may assert the
rights which they derive from those provisions.

The system of legal protection formulated in the Treaties does not
provide for the creation of "Community courts" in the different Member
States. It starts from the premise that the national courts are the bodies to
which individuals may turn whenever action or failure to act on the part of
national authorities or other individuals infringes rights conferred on them
by Community law.[4] The national court is therefore the normal Community
court to hear and determine all cases which do not fall within the
jurisdiction of the Court of Justice, the Court of First Instance or a judicial
panel. Within the legal system of the individual's Member State, the
national courts are the bridgehead of the Community legal order and

---

[1] See 3–035 and 3–036, *infra*, with regard to whether the national court is under a duty to
raise a question of Community law of its own motion.

[2] ECJ, Case 106/77 *Simmenthal* [1978] E.C.R. 629, para.21; ECJ, Case C–224/97 *Ciola* [1999]
E.C.R. I–2517, paras 29–34; ECJ, Case C–290/00 *Duchon* [2002] E.C.R. I–3567, para.31.

[3] ECJ, Opinion 1/91 *Draft Agreement between the Community, on the one hand, and the
countries of the European Free Trade Association, on the other, relating to the creation of the
European Economic Area* [1991] E.C.R. I–6079, para.21. See Lenaerts and Van Nuffel,
Constitutional Law of the European Union (2nd ed., Sweet & Maxwell, London, 2005), § 17–
003–§ 17–050, at 660–703.

[4] ECJ, Case 26/62 *Van Gend & Loos* [1963] E.C.R. 1, third para. The second subpara. of
Art.I–29 of the Constitution provides: "Member States shall provide remedies sufficient to
ensure effective legal protection in the fields covered by Union law".

secure the enforcement of Community law through dialogue with the Court of Justice.[5]

The Court of Justice has defined the task of national courts in its case-law on the operation of the preliminary ruling procedure[6] and on the application of the principle of cooperation enshrined in Art.10 of the EC Treaty to national courts.[7]

II. The Court of Justice

1–003 **General.** The institution known as the "Court of Justice" consists at present of three courts, the Court of Justice, the Court of First Instance and the European Union Civil Service Tribunal which, within their respective spheres of jurisdiction, ensure that in the interpretation and application of the Treaties the law is observed.[8] In the future, new judicial panels may be attached to the Court of First Instance in order to exercise judicial competence in certain specific areas.[9]

A. Composition

1–004 **Judges and Advocates General.** The Court of Justice consists of one Judge per Member State,[10] assisted by eight Advocates General.[11] Should the Court so request, the Council may, acting unanimously, increase the number of Advocates General.[12] Judges and Advocates General are appointed for a term of six years by common accord of the governments of the Member States. They are chosen from persons whose independence is beyond doubt and who possess the qualifications required for appointment to the highest judicial offices in their respective countries or who are jurisconsults of recognised competence.[13] Every three years there is a

---

[5] Slynn, "What is a European Community Law Judge?" (1993) Cambridge L.J. 234–244; Kapteyn, "Europe's Expectations of its Judges", in Jansen, Koster and Van Zutphen (eds), *European Ambitions of the National Judiciary* (Kluwer Law International, The Hague/London/Boston, 1997), at 181–189.

[6] Ch.2, *infra*.

[7] Ch.3, *infra*.

[8] EC Treaty, Art.220, and EAEC Treaty, Art.136; Council Decision 2004/752/EC, Euratom of November 2, 2004, establishing the European Union Civil Service Tribunal ([2004] O.J. L333/7).

[9] EC Treaty, Arts 220 and 225a. At present only one judicial panel has been created, namely the European Union Civil Service Tribunal.

[10] EC Treaty, Art.221, first para.

[11] EC Treaty, Art.222, first para.

[12] *Ibid*. For the part played by Advocates General, see Borgsmidt, "The Advocate General at the European Court of Justice: A Comparative Study" (1988) E.L.Rev. 106–119 and Tridimas, "The Role of the Advocate General in the Development of Community Law: Some Reflections" (1997) C.M.L.Rev. 1349–1387. See Brealey and Hoskins, *Remedies in E.C. Law*, (2nd ed., Sweet and Maxwell, London, 1998) at 20, as regards the "persuasive value" of Opinions of Advocates General for national courts.

[13] EC Treaty, Art.223, first para.

partial replacement of Judges and Advocates General. Twelve and thirteen Judges are replaced alternately and four Advocates General.[14] Retiring Judges and Advocates General may be reappointed.[15] The Treaty does not require that Judges and Advocates-General must be nationals of Member States.[16]

Uneven number of Judges. The Court must always consist of an uneven number of Judges when it takes its decisions,[17] which is why in the past it always had an uneven number of Judges.[18] As far as Advocates General are concerned, there is one for France, Germany, Italy, Spain and the UK; the three remaining Advocates General come alternately from the other Member States.[19] If a Judge's or Advocate General's office falls vacant before the expiry of its term, a successor is appointed for the remainder of the normal term of office.[20]

1–005

---

[14] EC Treaty, Art.223, second para., and Statute, Art.9.

[15] EC Treaty, Art.223, fourth para.

[16] *Cf.* the Commission, of which only nationals of Member States may be members (EC Treaty, Art.213(1), third subpara) and which must include at least one national of each Member State, but may not include more than two members having the nationality of the same State (EC Treaty, Art.213(1), fourth subpara.).

[17] Statute, Art.17, first para.

[18] The need to have an uneven number of Judges stemmed from the rule that in principle the Court of Justice met in plenary session. Accordingly, the accession of new States in 1973 was to have increased the original number of Judges from seven to eleven (Art.17 of the 1972 Act of Accession, [1972] O.J., Spec. Ed. 14), but their number was reduced to nine on account of Norway's decision not to join the Community (Art.4 of the Council Decision of January 1, 1973, [1973] O.J. L2/1). Following the accession of Greece, the Court had only ten Judges (Art.16 of the 1979 Act of Accession, [1979] O.J. L291, and Council Decision of December 22, 1980 ([1980] O.J. L380/6), after which the Council raised the number to eleven by Decision of March 30, 1981 ([1981] O.J. L100/20). The number was increased to fifteen Judges by Art.10 of the Council Decision of January 1, 1995 adjusting the instruments concerning the accession of the new Member States to the European Union ([1995] O.J. L1/1), which amended Art.17 of the 1985 Act of Accession ([1985] O.J. L302). As from May 1, 2004, the Court of Justice consists of 25 Judges.

[19] When new Member States joined the Community in 1973, the original number of Advocates General was increased from two to four (Art.1 of the Decision of January 1, 1973, [1973] O.J. L2/29), which were to be shared among the four "large" Member States. After the accession of Greece, a fifth was added (Council Decision of March 30, 1981, [1981] O.J. L100/21) for a smaller Member State and, following the accession of Spain and Portugal, a sixth (Art.18 of the 1985 Act of Accession, [1985] O.J. L302). The accession of further Member States has raised the number of Advocates General to eight, and temporarily to nine (Art.11 of the Council Decision of January 1, 1995 amending Art.20 of the 1994 Act of Accession, [1995] O.J. L1/1): the five "large" Member States each put forward one person for appointment as Advocate General, whilst the other Member States share out in turn the remaining three posts. See the Joint Declaration on Art.31 of the Decision adjusting the instruments concerning the accession of the new Member States to the European Union, [1995] O.J. L1/221). In the case of the 2004 accessions, the number of Advocates General was kept at eight. Consequently, unlike the other large Member States, Poland has no "fixed" Advocate General. The Joint Declaration on the Court of Justice of the European Communities annexed to the Acts of Accession stated that "[s]hould the Court of Justice so request, the Council, acting unanimously, may increase the number of Advocates General" and added "[o]therwise, the new Member States will be integrated into the existing system for their appointment" ([2003] O.J. L236/971).

[20] Statute, Arts 7 and 8.

1–006 **Oath and immunity.** Before taking up their duties, Judges and Advocates General take an oath, in open court, to perform their duties impartially and conscientiously and to preserve the secrecy of the deliberations of the Court.[21] Judges and Advocates General are immune from legal proceedings. They continue to enjoy immunity after they have ceased to hold office in respect of acts performed by them in their official capacity, including words spoken or written. Their immunity may be waived only by the Court sitting in plenary session. Where immunity has been waived and criminal proceedings are instituted against a Judge or an Advocate General, the member concerned may be tried only by the court competent to judge the members of the highest national judiciary.[22]

Judges and Advocates General may not hold any political or administrative office or engage in any occupation unless exemption is granted by the Council. After their term of office, they must act with integrity and discretion as regards the acceptance of certain appointments or benefits.[23] A Judge or Advocate General may be deprived of his or her office or of his or her right to a pension or other benefits in its stead only if, in the unanimous opinion of the other Judges and Advocates General, he or she no longer fulfils the requisite conditions or meets the obligations arising from his or her office.[24]

1–007 **President.** Immediately after their partial replacement, the Judges elect one of their number as President of the Court for a term of three years. He or she may be re-elected.[25] The rule that if an office falls vacant before the normal expiry date of its term, a successor is to be elected for the remainder of the term, also applies to the President.[26]

1–008 **Registrar.** An election procedure is also used to appoint the Court Registrar for a term of six years.[27] He or she may be reappointed.[28] If the office of Registrar falls vacant before the normal expiry date, a new Registrar is to be appointed for six years.[29] The Registrar takes the same oath before the Court as the Judges and Advocates General.[30]

B. INTERNAL ORGANISATION

1–009 **Chambers.** In principle the Court of Justice sits in Chambers, each consisting of five (the most frequent case) or three Judges, or as the Grand Chamber when a Member State or an institution of the Communities that

---

[21] Statute, Art.2. By virtue of Art.8 of the Statute, the provisions of the Statute relating to the status of Judges (Arts 2–7) also apply to Advocates General.
[22] Statute, Art.3.
[23] Statute, Art.4.
[24] Statute, Art.6.
[25] EC Treaty, Art.223, third para.; ECJ Rules of Procedure, Art.7(1).
[26] ECJ Rules of Procedure, Art.7(2).
[27] EC Treaty, Art.223, fifth para.; ECJ Rules of Procedure, Art.12.
[28] ECJ Rules of Procedure, Art.12(4).
[29] ECJ Rules of Procedure, Art.12(7).
[30] Statute, Art.10.

is party to the proceedings so requests[31] or where the Court considers that a case before it has an important value as a precedent.[32] For specific cases listed in the Statute or where the Court considers that a case before it is of exceptional importance, the Court may sit as a Full Court.[33]

The Court forms Chambers consisting of three or five Judges.[34] The Judges elect the Presidents of Chambers from among their number. The Presidents of the Chambers of five Judges are elected for three years. They may be re-elected once.[35]

The Grand Chamber consists of thirteen Judges and is presided over by the President of the Court.[36] In order to avoid the important cases assigned to that chamber being heard always by the same Judges, its composition varies. Nevertheless, it consists of a fixed core, consisting of the President of the Court of Justice and the three Presidents of the Chambers of five Judges. In addition, the Judge-Rapporteur for the case at issue sits in that Chamber. Other Judges appointed, for each case, in accordance with the order laid down in the Rules of Procedure to make up the thirteen Judges also form part of the Grand Chamber.[37]

For each case, the Chambers of five Judges and three Judges are composed of the President of the Chamber, the Judge-Rapporteur and the number of Judges required to attain the number of five and three Judges respectively. The lists of Judges assigned to the Chambers of three and five Judges,[38] the order used to determine the composition of the Grand Chamber and the Chambers of three and five Judges and the appointments of Presidents of Chambers are published in the *Official Journal of the European Union*.[39]

Quorum. When the Court sits in Chambers, there is a quorum of three Judges in the case of three- or five-Judge Chambers and of nine Judges in the case of the Grand Chamber. Decisions of the Full Court are valid if fifteen Judges are sitting.[40]

1–010

---

[31] EC Treaty, Art.221, second para., and Statute, Art.16, first, second and third paras.

[32] See ECJ Rules of Procedure, Art.44(3), first subpara., which provides that "The Court shall assign to the Chambers of five and three Judges any case brought before it in so far as the difficulty or importance of the case or particular circumstances are not such as to require that it should be assigned to the Grand Chamber".

[33] EC Treaty, Art.221, third para., and Statute, Art.16, fourth and fifth paras.

[34] Statute, Art.16, first para., and ECJ Rules of Procedure, Art.11c. At present, the Court has three Chambers of five Judges and three Chambers of three Judges.

[35] Statute, Art.16, first para.

[36] EC Treaty, Art.221, second para., and Statute, Art.16, second para.

[37] ECJ Rules of Procedure, Art.11b.

[38] At present, eight Judges are assigned to each of the three Chambers of five Judges and seven Judges are assigned to each of the three Chambers of three Judges.

[39] ECJ Rules of Procedure, Arts 10(1), fifth subpara., 11b(2) and (3), and 11c(2).

[40] Statute, Art.17. It falls within the Court's power of internal organisation to assign the Judges from a Chamber which are to adjudicate a particular case (see ECJ, Case C–7/94 *Gaal* [1995] E.C.R. I–1031, para.13, in which the German Government argued that the criteria

1–011 **Assignment of a case to a Chamber.** At the end of the written procedure, the Court may at an administrative meeting assign any case to a Chamber of five or three Judges or to the Grand Chamber, upon consideration of the Judge-Rapporteur's preliminary report and after the Advocate General has been heard. The Court must comply with a request from a Member State or an institution of the Community that is party to the proceedings for a case to be assigned to the Grand Chamber.[41] A Member State or an institution which is a party to or an intervener in proceedings or which has submitted written observations in preliminary ruling proceedings is regarded as being a "party to the proceedings".[42] The Court meets as the Full Court in very exceptional cases exhaustedly listed in the Treaty (dismissal of the European Ombudsman, compulsory retirement of a Member of the Commission in breach of his or her obligations, etc.) and where the Court considers that the case before it is of exceptional importance.[43] A Chamber may, however, refer a case back to the Court at any stage in the proceedings in order that it may be reassigned to a formation composed of a greater number of Judges.[44] Parties are not entitled to require that a Judge of a particular nationality sit or not sit. The Court therefore constitutes a genuinely "supranational" court *vis-à-vis* the Member States and specifically national procedural interests.

1–012 **Roles of the Judge-Rapporteur and the Advocate General.** The primary responsibility for decision-making within the Court lies with the Judge-Rapporteur, who is designated for each case by the President immediately after proceedings have been brought.[45] At the same time, the First Advocate General[46] assigns an Advocate General to the case.[47] The Judge-Rapporteur and the Advocate General follow the procedural progress of the case with particular heed. The Judge-Rapporteur is responsible for

---

determining the composition of the Chamber adjudicating a case consisting of five Judges from a Chamber to which six Judges had been appointed had not been published in the *Official Journal of the European Union*). As far as the Court of First Instance is concerned, Art.32(4) of the CFI Rules of Procedure provides that if in a Chamber of three or five Judges the number of Judges assigned to that Chamber is higher than three or five respectively, the President of the Chamber is to decide which of the Judges will be called upon to take part in the judgment of the case.

[41] EC Treaty, Art.221, second para.; Statute, Art.16, third para.; ECJ Rules of Procedure, Art.44(3).

[42] ECJ Rules of Procedure, Art.44(3), second subpara.

[43] Statute, Art.16, fourth and fifth paras. Opinion 1/03 was assigned to the Full Court. The Court held that the conclusion of the new Lugano Convention on jurisdiction and the recognition and enforcement of judgments in civil and commercial matters fell entirely within the Community's exclusive competence: see ECJ (February 7, 2006), Opinion 1/03 *New Lugano Convention*, not yet reported.

[44] ECJ Rules of Procedure, Art.44(4).

[45] ECJ Rules of Procedure, Art.9(2).

[46] The First Advocate General is appointed for one year by the Court and has the rank of a President of Chamber. He is *primus inter pares* among the Advocates General (ECJ Rules of Procedure, Art.10(1)).

[47] ECJ Rules of Procedure, Art.10(2).

drawing up the preliminary report (see 24–060, *infra*) and the report for the hearing (see 24–064, *infra*). Lastly, it falls to the Judge-Rapporteur to draw up the draft judgment and subsequently to revise it so that it reflects the consensus of the Court or the Chamber (or the majority of the bench) (see 24–111 to 24–114, *infra*).

The Advocate General, acting with complete impartiality and independence, makes, in open court, reasoned submissions ("the Advocate General's Opinion") on each case assigned to him or her in order to assist the Court in the performance of its task.[48] Unlike the *Procureur Général* in some national legal systems, the Advocates General are not entrusted with the defence of the general interest and do not form a hierarchy. As members of the institution, the Advocates General take part in the process by which the Court reaches its judgment and in carrying out the judicial function entrusted to it.[49]

Where it considers that the case raises no new point of law, the Court may decide, after hearing the Advocate General, that the case shall be determined without a submission from the Advocate General.[50]

Role of the President. The President directs the judicial business and the administration of the Court[51]; he or she presides at hearings and deliberations of the Grand Chamber and when the Court sits as the Full Court. The President does not sit in the five- and three-Judge Chambers.   1–013

Staff. In performing its duties the Court has a variety of departments at its disposal. There is an interpreting service, a translation service, a research and documentation department, which also manages the Court's library, and internal administrative machinery (including personnel, finance and technical services departments). The registry staff assist the Registrar in the performance of his or her judicial duties. As far as his or her administrative tasks are concerned, the Registrar can have recourse to the various departments of the Court. The Judges and Advocates General are each served by three law clerks, known as *référendaires* or legal secretaries, who carry out the preparatory work for the Judges and Advocates General, and three secretarial staff members.   1–014

C. Basic Function

Constitutional and supreme court. The Court of Justice plays the role of the Community's constitutional court, that is to say, as the guardian of the   1–015

---

[48] EC Treaty, Art.222, second para.
[49] ECJ (order of February 4, 2002), Case C–17/98 *Emesa Sugar* [2000] E.C.R. I–665, para.10 *et seq.*, with a case note by Lawson (2000) C.M.L.Rev. 983–990.
[50] Statute, Art.20, fifth para.
[51] ECJ Rules of Procedure, Art.8.

objectives and rules of law laid down in the Treaties.[52] The Court rules in cases in which constitutional issues come to the fore,[53] such as the legality of Community secondary legislation, the preservation of institutional equilibrium, the demarcation of Community and national spheres of competence and the development of protection of fundamental rights.[54]

Alongside this, the Court plays the role of a supreme court where—on a request from a national court for a preliminary ruling—it ensures the uniform application of Community law. In a certain sense, there is also a constitutional aspect to that function performed by the Court inasmuch as disparate application of Community law in the Member States would run counter to achievement of the objectives laid down in the Treaties.

1–016 **Court of last resort for constitutional issues.** It is self-evident that constitutional issues of Community law may also arise in cases brought before national courts or the Court of First Instance. Consequently, the Court of Justice is not the sole guardian of the Community legal order. But national courts may (and, in some cases, must) still bring the constitutional issue before the Court by requesting a preliminary ruling (see Ch.2, *infra*). Likewise, an appeal may be brought or, in exceptional cases, a review procedure initiated against decisions of the Court of First Instance, which means that here again the Court of Justice can have the last word in determining legal questions with constitutional implications[55] (see 1–047 to

---

[52] Donner, "The Constitutional Powers of the Court of Justice of the European Communities" (1974) C.M.L.Rev. 127–140, and "The Court of Justice as a Constitutional Court of the Communities", in *Tussen het echte en het gemaakte*, (Tjeenk Willink, Zwolle, 1986), at 343–361; Due, "A Constitutional Court for the European Communities", in *Constitutional Adjudication in European Community and National Law. Essays for the Hon. Mr Justice T.F. O'Higgins* (Butterworths (Ireland), Dublin, 1992), 3, at 4–9; Gaudin, "La Cour de justice, juridiction constitututionnelle?" (2000) R.A.E. 209–222; Jacobs, "Is the Court of Justice of the European Communities a Constitutional Court?", in *Constitutional Adjudication in European Community and National Law. Essays for the Hon. Mr Justice T.F. O'Higgins* (Butterworths (Ireland), Dublin, 1992), at 25–32; Kapteyn, "The Role of the Court of Justice in the Development of the Community Legal Order", in *Il ruolo del giudice internazionale nell'evoluzione del diritto internazionale e comunitario* (CEDAM, Milan, 1995), at 157–173; Lenaerts, "Some Thoughts about the Interaction between Judges and Politicians" (1992) Y.E.L. 1–34; Mischo, "Un rôle nouveau pour la Cour de Justice?" (1990) R.M.C. 681–686; Pescatore, "Die Gemeinschaftsverträge als Verfassungsrecht—ein Kapitel Verfassungsgeschichte in der Perspektive des europäischen Gerichtshofs, systematisch geordnet", in *Festschrift Kutscher* (Nomos, Baden-Baden, 1981), at 319–338; Timmermans, "The European Union's Judicial System" (2004) C.M.L.Rev. 393–405.

[53] The constitutional dimension is clearly recognisable in the Court's case-law: see Lenaerts, *Le juge et la constitution aux Etats-Unis d'Amérique et dans l'ordre juridique européen* (Bruylant, Brussels, 1988), 817 pp. See also Weiler, "The Court of Justice on Trial. Review Essay of Hjalte Rasmussen: On Law and Policy in the European Court of Justice" (1987) C.M.L.Rev. 555–589.

[54] Rodríguez Iglesias, "Der Gerichtshof der Europäischen Gemeinschaften als Verfassungsgericht" (1992) EuR. 225–245. For the Court's jurisdiction to rule on the "constitutionality" of national law, see Rinze, "The Role of the European Court of Justice as a Federal Constitutional Court" (1993) Pub. L. 426–443.

[55] See Part IV, Chs 16 and 17, *infra*.

1–054, *infra*, concerning the distribution of heads of jurisdiction as between the various judicial bodies belonging to the Court of Justice).

III. THE COURT OF FIRST INSTANCE

A. COMPOSITION

Judges. The Court of First Instance consists of at least one Judge per   **1–017**
Member State[56] and, in its present composition, has twenty-five Judges.[57]
They are appointed for a term of six years by common accord of the
governments of the Member States.[58] They are chosen from persons whose
independence is beyond doubt and who possess the ability required for
appointment to judicial office. Membership of the Court is partially
renewed every three years, although retiring Judges are eligible for
reappointment.[59] As in the case of the Court of Justice, there is no
nationality requirement, but in practice there is one Judge from each
Member State. If a vacancy occurs during the term of office, the new Judge
is appointed for the remainder of his or her predecessor's normal term.[60]

Advocates General. At present, no separate Advocates General are   **1–018**
attached to the Court of First Instance, on the ground that cases brought
before it normally do not require the assistance of an Advocate General.
However, a Judge may be called upon to perform the task of Advocate
General in a given case.[61] In such case, he or she performs the same
function as an Advocate General in the Court of Justice and may not take
part in the judgment of the case.[62] The decision to designate an Advocate
General in a particular case is taken at an administrative meeting of the

---

[56] EC Treaty, Art.224, first para. The number of Judges is laid down in the Statute.
[57] Statute, Art.48.
[58] EC Treaty, Art.224, second para.
[59] *Ibid*.
[60] Statute, Art.7, applicable by virtue of Art.47, first para., of the Statute.
[61] Statute, Art.49. This rule is a "compromise" between the view that the Advocate General's
role principally consists of assisting the Court of Justice in its task of ensuring uniform
interpretation of Community law and that therefore there is no need for an Advocate
General in the Court of First Instance, and the view that the Advocate General's role is an
essential safeguard for the legal protection of individuals and that therefore it is important
for there to be an Advocate General in the first-instance court. See Christianos, "Le
Tribunal de première instance et la nouvelle organisation judiciaire des Communautés
européennes", in *Le Tribunal de première instance des Communautés européennes* (European
Institute for Public Administration, Maastricht, 1990), 17, at 23; Vandersanden, "Une
naissance désirée: le Tribunal de première instance des Communautés européennes" (1988)
J.T. 545, at 546. Art.224, first para., of the EC Treaty provides that the Statute may provide
that the Court of First Instance be assisted by Advocates General, which leaves the
possibility open to appoint permanent Advocates General and not just Judges as *ad hoc*
Advocates General.
[62] *Cf.* the second para. of Art.222 of the EC Treaty in conjunction with the second and fourth
subparas of Art.49 of the Statute.

Court of First Instance at the request of the Chamber dealing with the case or to which the case is assigned.[63] When the Court of First Instance sits in plenary session, it is assisted by an Advocate General.[64] In other cases, the Court of First Instance is under no obligation to have itself assisted by an Advocate General.[65] The Court may decide to appoint an Advocate General when sitting in a Chamber and the Chamber considers that the legal difficulty or the factual complexity of the case requires such appointment. The President of the Court of First Instance then designates the Judge called upon to perform the function of an Advocate General.[66] The consequence is that references to the Advocate General in the Rules of Procedure of the Court of First Instance apply only where a Judge has been designated so to act.[67]

1–019   **Oath and immunity.** Before taking up his or her duties, each Judge takes an oath before the Court of Justice (see 1–006, *supra*).[68] Judges of the Court of First Instance have the same status as Judges and Advocates General of the Court of Justice (see 1–006, *supra*)[69] and are subject to the same constraints and obligations as regards taking up political or administrative offices and engaging in other occupations.

A Judge may be removed from his or her office only by the Court of Justice, after seeking the opinion of the Court of First Instance.[70] Before that opinion—which must be reasoned—is given, the Judge concerned may make representations to the Court of First Instance in closed session.[71]

1–020   **President.** Immediately after their partial replacement, the Judges elect a President from among their number for a term of three years.[72] He or she may be re-elected. If the President gives up his or her office before the expiry of its term, a successor is to be elected only for the outstanding portion of the term.

---

[63] CFI Rules of Procedure, Art.19, first para.; Statute, Art.49, third para., provides that the criteria for selecting such cases, as well as the procedures for designating the Advocates General, are to be laid down in the CFI Rules of Procedure.

[64] CFI Rules of Procedure, Art.17. Where, following the designation of an Advocate General pursuant to Art.17 of the CFI Rules of Procedure, there is an even number of Judges in the Court of First Instance sitting in plenary session, the President is to designate, before the hearing and in accordance with a rota established in advance by the Court and published in the *Official Journal of the European Union*, the Judge who will not take part in the judgment of the case (CFI Rules of Procedure, Art.32(1), second subpara.).

[65] CFI, Rules of Procedure, Art.18. ECJ (order of July 18, 2002), Case C–136/01 P *Autosalone Ispra dei Fratelli Rossi v Commission* [2002] E.C.R. I–6565, paras 17–18.

[66] CFI Rules of Procedure, Art.19, second para.

[67] CFI Rules of Procedure, Art.2(2).

[68] CFI Rules of Procedure, Art.4(1).

[69] EC Treaty, Art.224, sixth para.; see also Statute, Art.47, first para., by virtue of which Arts 2 to 8 of the Statute are applicable to Judges of the Court of First Instance and its members.

[70] Statute, Art.47, first para.; CFI Rules of Procedure, Art.5.

[71] For further particulars, see Art.5 of the CFI Rules of Procedure.

[72] EC Treaty, Art.224, third para.

Registrar. The Court appoints its Registrar.[73] The provisions relating to **1–021**
the status of the Registrar of the Court of Justice apply *mutatis mutandis* to
the Registrar of the Court of First Instance.[74]

B. INTERNAL ORGANISATION

Chambers. As in the case of the Court of Justice, the Court of First **1–022**
Instance sits as a rule in Chambers of three or five Judges.[75] The Court of
First Instance has five Chambers of five Judges and five Chambers of three
Judges. Unlike in the case of the Court of Justice, the most common
formation is the three-Judge Chamber.

The Court of First Instance may also sit in plenary session,[76] as a single
Judge[77] or as the Grand Chamber.[78] The Grand Chamber consists of
thirteen Judges.[79] Under the second para. of Art.50 of the Statute and

---

[73] EC Treaty, Art.224, fourth para.

[74] Statute, Art.47, second para.

[75] Statute, Art.50, first para., and CFI Rules of Procedure, Art.10(1), first subpara.

[76] Statute, Art.50, second para., and CFI Rules of Procedure, Art.11(1), second subpara.

[77] Statute, Art.50, second para., and CFI Rules of Procedure, Art.11(1), third subpara. Under
Art.14(2), point 1, of the CFI Rules of Procedure, the Judge-Rapporteur of a Chamber of
three Judges may hear and determine the sort of cases described in that article as a single
Judge (Council Decision 1999/291/EC, ECSC, Euratom [1999] O.J. L114/5) if, having regard
to the lack of difficulty of the questions of law or fact raised, to the limited importance of
those cases and to the absence of other special circumstances, they are suitable for being so
heard and determined and have been delegated under the conditions laid down in Art.51 of
the CFI Rules of Procedure. However, as a result of Art.14(2), point 2, of the CFI Rules of
Procedure, it is not possible to delegate to a single Judge cases raising issues as to the
legality of an act of general application or cases concerning the implementation of the rules
on competition and on control of concentrations, relating to aid granted by States, relating
to measures to protect trade or relating to the common organisation of the agricultural
markets, with the exception of cases that form part of a series of cases in which the same
relief is sought and of which one has already been finally decided. Likewise, a single Judge
may not sit in proceedings brought against the Office for Harmonisation in the Internal
Market (Trade Marks and Designs) or against the Community Plant Variety Office
concerning the application of the rules relating to an intellectual property regime. For an
example, see CFI, Case T–68/99 *Toditec v Commission* [2001] E.C.R. II–1443. See also ECJ,
Case C–171/00 P *Libéros v Commission* [2002] E.C.R. 451, paras 25–39, where the judgment
of the Court of First Instance sitting as a single Judge was set aside on the ground that the
case raised an issue of the legality of an act of general application and therefore could not
be decided by a single Judge. See also Muñoz, "Le système de juge unique pour le
règlement d'un problème multiple: l'encombrement de la Cour de justice des Communautés
européennes et du Tribunal de première instance" (2001) R.M.U.E. 60–66 and Rinuy,
"L'incursion prudente du juge unique au Tribunal de première instance des Communautés
européennes" (2000) R.A.E. 267–274.

[78] Statute, Art.50, third para., and CFI Rules of Procedure, Arts 10(1), first subpara., and
11(1), second subpara. The first judgments of the Court of First Instance sitting in Grand
Chamber were given on December 14, 2005 (See CFI, Case T–69/00 *FIAMM and FIAMM
Technologies v Council and Commission*, not yet reported; CFI, Case T–151/00 *Laboratoire
du Bain v Council and Commission*, not reported; CFI, Case T–301/00 *Groupe Fremaux and
Palais Royal v Council and Commission*, not reported; CFI, Case T–320/00 *CD Cartondruck
v Council and Commission*, not reported; CFI, Case T–383/00 *Beamglow v European
Parliament and Others*, not yet reported; and CFI, Case T–135/01 *Fredon & Figli and Others
v Council and Commission*, not reported).

[79] CFI Rules of Procedure, Art.10(1).

Art.12 of the CFI Rules of Procedure, the Court of First Instance is to lay down criteria by which cases are to be allocated among the Chambers.[80] As soon as the application initiating proceedings has been lodged, the President of the Court of First Instance assigns the case to a three-Judge Chamber.[81] Each Chamber has a President of Chamber. The Presidents of the Chambers of five Judges are elected for three years. The President of the Court of First Instance himself or herself presides over a Chamber of five Judges. The Presidents of the Chambers of five Judges, with the exception of the President of the Court of First Instance, are also Presidents of two compositions of a Chamber of three Judges. The Presidents of the Chambers of five Judges may be reappointed once.[82] The composition of the Chambers and appointments of Presidents of Chambers are published in the *Official Journal of the European Union*.[83]

1–023 **Assignment of a case to a Chamber.** A case is immediately assigned to a Chamber of three Judges. Whenever the legal difficulty or the importance of the case or special circumstances so justify, a case may be referred to the Court of First Instance sitting in plenary session, to the Grand Chamber or to a Chamber consisting of a different number of Judges.[84] At any stage of the proceedings, the Chamber hearing the case may, on its own initiative or at the request of the parties, make a proposal to this effect to the Court sitting in plenary session. The Full Court then decides, after hearing the parties and the Advocate General, whether or not to refer the case.[85] Where a Member State or an institution of the European Union which is a party to the proceedings so requests, a case will be decided by a Chamber composed of at least five Judges.[86]

1–024 **Quorum.** A bench of the Court of First Instance can decide validly only when an uneven number of Judges is sitting in the deliberations. A quorum consists of three Judges in the case of three- or five-Judge Chambers,[87] nine Judges in the case of the Grand Chamber[88] and fifteen Judges where the Court sits in plenary session.[89]

---

[80] For the period from October 1, 2005 to September 30, 2006, see the decision of July 7, 2005 ([2005] O.J. C205/15).

[81] CFI, Rules of Procedure, Art.13(1) and decision of July 7, 2005 ([2005] O.J. C205/15); *cf.* ECJ Rules of Procedure, Art.9(2) (assignment only for preparatory inquiries) and ECJ Rules of Procedure, Art.44(2) and (3) (designation of a Judge-Rapporteur by the President of the Court; the administrative meeting assigns the case to a Chamber, at the proposal of the Judge-Rapporteur).

[82] Statute, Art.50, first para. The President of the Court of First Instance is not subject to this limitation.

[83] CFI Rules of Procedure, Arts 10(2) and 15, third para. See, for the period from October 1, 2005 to September 30, 2006, decision of July 7, 2005 ([2005] O.J. C205/15).

[84] CFI Rules of Procedure, Art.14(1).

[85] CFI Rules of Procedure, Art.51(1), first subpara.

[86] CFI Rules of Procedure, Art.51(1), second subpara.

[87] CFI Rules of Procedure, Art.32(3), first subpara.

[88] CFI Rules of Procedure, Art.32(3), second subpara.

[89] Statute, Art.17, fourth para., applicable to the Court of First Instance by virtue of Art.47, first subpara., of the Statute.

Procedure. The procedure before the Court of First Instance largely parallels that before the Court of Justice (see Part V, *infra*). 1–025

President and Registrar. The tasks of the President and the Registrar of the Court of First Instance are, to the extent of their powers, similar to those of their counterparts in the Court of Justice. 1–026

Staff. As far as the personnel of the Court of First Instance is concerned, the Statute of the Court of Justice provides as follows: "The President of the Court of Justice and the President of the Court of First Instance shall determine, by common accord, the conditions under which officials and other servants attached to the Court of Justice shall render their services to the Court of First Instance to enable it to function. Certain officials or other servants shall be responsible to the Registrar of the Court of First Instance under the authority of the President of the Court of First Instance."[90] 1–027

The last sentence of that passage applies, of course, to the staff of the Registrar and the *cabinets* of the Judges of the Court of First Instance (Judges are assisted by, among others, three legal secretaries or *référendaires*, who perform the same duties as the law clerks of the Judges and Advocates General of the Court of Justice, and two secretarial staff members). The aim is to bring the staff of the Court of First Instance who are directly and exclusively concerned with the performance of its judicial function under the President and the Registrar, which constitutes a guarantee of independence from the other court.

C. Basic Function

Purpose. The purpose of establishing the Court of First Instance, which was "attached"[91] to the Court of Justice in 1989, was to maintain and improve the quality and effectiveness of judicial protection in the Community legal order. In 1988 a steadily rising tide of cases had caused proceedings before the Court to become unacceptably protracted.[92] Furthermore, in cases requiring an appraisal of complex facts,[93] the Court of Justice could no longer provide the high quality of judicial protection which it was called upon to do.[94] 1–028

---

[90] Statute, Art.52.
[91] This term was employed in the pre-Nice version of Art.225(1) of the EC Treaty: "A Court of First Instance shall be attached to the Court of Justice . . .".
[92] The average duration of a direct action increased from 8.5 months in 1970 to 24 months. The average time taken to complete proceedings in a reference for a preliminary ruling was 17.5 months.
[93] Principally, competition and anti-dumping cases.
[94] For commentaries, see Biancarelli, "La création du Tribunal de première instance des Communautés européennes: un luxe ou une nécessité?" (1990) R.T.D.E. 1–25 and

The transfer in stages to the Court of First Instance of jurisdiction in all cases brought by natural or legal persons against any unlawful act or failure to act of a Community institution helped to allay those shortcomings.[95] At the same time, a two-tier court system was created for such cases, which can only improve the quality of legal protection.

1–029   **Treaty of Nice.** As a result of the Treaty of Nice, which entered into force on February 1, 2003, and the recent amendment on April 26, 2004 of Art.51 of the Statute,[96] the jurisdiction of the Court of First Instance has been extended to a considerable degree. The Court of First Instance is no longer confined to being an administrative court of the Community. The Court is incrementally becoming the Community Court of general jurisdiction at first instance (see 1–047 to 1–054, *infra*, concerning the distribution of heads of jurisdiction as between the various judicial bodies belonging to the Court of Justice).[97]

"Présentation générale du Tribunal de première instance des Communautés européennes" (1995) R.M.C.U.E. 564–567; Cras, "Zes jaar Gerecht van eerste aanleg" (1996) N.J.B 477–485; da Cruz Vilaça, "The Court of First Instance of the European Communities: A Significant Step towards the Consolidation of the European Community as a Community governed by the Rule of Law" (1990) Y.E.L. 1–56; Jung, "Das Gericht erster Instanz der Europäischen Gemeinschaften" (1992) EuR. 246–264; Kirschner and Klüpfel, *Das Gericht erster Instanz der Europäischen Gemeinschaften* (Carl Heymans Verlag KG, Cologne/Berlin/Bonn/Munich, 1998), 316 pp; Lenaerts, "Het Gerecht van eerste aanleg van de Europese Gemeenschappen" (1990) S.E.W. 527–548, "Le Tribunal de première instance des Communautés européennes: genèse et premiers pas" (1990) J.T. 409–415, "The Development of the Judicial Process in the European Community after the Establishment of the Court of First Instance", in *Collected Courses of the Academy of European Law* (Book 1, European University Institute Martinus Nijhoff, Florence/Dordrecht, 1991), Vol 1, at 53–113, and "Le Tribunal de Première Instance des Communautés européennes: regard sur une décennie d'activités et sur l'apport du double degré d'instance au droit communautaire" (2000) C.D.E. 323–411; Millett, *The Court of First Instance of the European Communities*, Butterworths, London-Edinburgh, 1990), 114 pp.; Neville Brown, "The First Five Years of the Court of First Instance and Appeals to the Court of Justice: Assessment and Statistics" (1995) C.M.L.Rev. 743–761; Palacio González, *El Sistema Judicial Comunitario* (Universidad de Deusto, Bilboa, 1996), at 87–94; Van der Woude, "Le Tribunal de première instance 'Les trois premières années'" (1992) R.M.U.E. 113–157; Vesterdorf, "The Court of First Instance of the European Communities after Two Full Years of Operation" (1992) C.M.L.Rev. 897–915; Van Ginderachter, "Le Tribunal de première instance des Communautés européennes. Un nouveau-né prodige?" (1989) C.D.E. 63–105.

[95] See Council Decision 88/591/ECSC, EEC, Euratom of October 24, 1988 establishing a Court of First Instance of the European Communities ([1988] O.J. L319/1; *corrigendum* in [1989] O.J. L 241/4), as amended by Council Decision 93/350/Euratom, ECSC, EEC of June 8, 1993 ([1993] O.J. L144/21) and Council Decision 94/149/ECSC, EC of March 7, 1994 ([1994] O.J. L66/29). Art.10 of the Treaty of Nice abrogated this Decision.

[96] Council Decision 2004/407/EC, Euratom of April 26, 2004 amending Arts 51 and 54 of the Protocol on the Statute of the Court of Justice ([2004] O.J. L132/5; *corrigendum* in [2004] O.J. L194/3).

[97] For a survey of the various heads of jurisdiction transferred, see Gautron, "Les compétences du Tribunal de première instance" (1995) R.M.C.U.E. 568–575; for the changes brought about by the Treaty of Nice, see Lenaerts and Desomer, "Het Verdrag van Nice en het "post Nice"-debat over de toekomst van de Europese Unie" (2001–2002) R.W. 73, paras 21–32. For the effects of the Treaty of Nice on the judicial organisation of the European

IV. JUDICIAL PANELS

General. As from the entry into force of the Treaty of Nice, the Council **1–030** has been empowered to create judicial panels to be attached to the Court of First Instance which will hear and determine at first instance certain classes of action or proceedings brought in specific areas.[98]

Appeal before the Court of First Instance. Decisions given by judicial **1–031** panels may be subject to a right of appeal before the Court of First Instance on points of law only or, when provided for in the decision establishing the panel, a right of appeal also on matters of fact.

Judicial panels set up and proposed. Recently, the European Union Civil **1–032** Service Tribunal was created which has taken over the staff cases previously falling within the jurisdiction of the Court of First Instance. The Commission has proposed that another judicial panel also be set up, namely the Court for the Community Patent. That Court would hear and determine cases which in the absence of the creation of the judicial panel would normally fall within the jurisdiction of the Court of First Instance.

A. EUROPEAN UNION CIVIL SERVICE TRIBUNAL

Creation. Declaration No 16 attached to the Nice Treaty called upon the **1–033** Court of Justice and the Commission "to prepare as swiftly as possible a draft decision establishing a judicial panel which has jurisdiction to deliver judgments at first instance on disputes between the Community and its

---

Union, see Andriantsimbazovina, "Le modè le juridictionnel de la Cour européenne des droits de l'homme et la réforme de la Cour de justice des Communautés européennes" (2000) R.A.E. 410–425; Coulon, "L'indispensable réforme du Tribunal de première instance des Communautés européennes" (2000) R.A.E. 254–266; Dyrberg, "What should the Court of Justice be doing?" (2001) E.L.Rev. 291–300; Dubos, "Quel avenir pour le Tribunal de première instance après le traité de Nice?" (2000) R.A.E. 426–440; Fierstra, "Een nieuw toekomstperspectief voor het Hof van Justitie; de tussenstand na het Verdrag van Nice" (2001) N.T.E.R. 95–103; Johnston, "Judicial Reform and the Treaty of Nice" (2001) C.M.L.Rev. 499–523; Kateyn, "De rechterlijke organisatie van de Europese Unie en de Intergouvernementele Conferentie 2000" (2001) N.J.B. 1–6; Lenaerts, "La réorganisation de l'architecture juridictionnelle de l'Union européenne: quel angle d'approche adopter?", in Dony and Bribosia (eds), *L'avenir du système juridictionnel de l'Union européenne* (Éditions de l'Université de Bruxelles, Brussels, 2002), at 49–64; Lenz, "Die Gerichtsbarkeit in der Europäischen Gemeinschaft nach dem Vertrag von Nizza" (2001) Eu.GR.Z. 433–441; Louis, "La Cour de justice après Nice", in Dony and Bribosia (eds), *L'avenir du système juridictionnel de l'Union européenne* (Editions de l'Université de Bruxelles, Brussels, 2002), at 5–17; Ruiz-Jarabo Colomer, "La réforme de la Cour de justice opérée par le traité de Nice et sa mise en oeuvre future" (2001) R.T.D.E. 705–726; Tambou, "Le système juridictionnel communautaire revu et corrigé par le traité de Nice" (2001) R.M.U.E. 164–170.

[98] EC Treaty, Arts 220 and 225a. The Council is to decide unanimously on a proposal of the Commission after consulting the European Parliament and the Court of Justice, or at the request of the Court of Justice after consulting the European Parliament and the Commission.

servants". On November 2, 2004, the Council adopted Decision 2004/752/ EC, Euratom establishing the European Union Civil Service Tribunal.[99] This decision inserts a new Art.62a in the Court's Statute which provides that the provisions relating to the jurisdiction, composition, organisation and procedure of the judicial panels are set out in an annex to the Statute. Council Decision 2004/752 adds a new Annex I to the Statute entitled "The European Union Civil Service Tribunal" (hereinafter "Civil Service Tribunal").

1–034 **Composition and jurisdiction.** The Civil Service Tribunal is attached to the Court of First Instance and has its seat in Luxembourg.[100] It exercises the jurisdiction previously exercised by the Court of First Instance in staff matters[101] and is composed of seven Judges appointed for a period of six years by the Council,[102] acting unanimously.[103] A selection committee composed of former members of the Court of Justice and the Court of First Instance and lawyers of recognised competence gives an opinion on the candidates' suitability to perform the duties of Judge at the Civil Service Tribunal.[104]

1–035 **Chambers.** The Civil Service Tribunal sits in chambers of three Judges. In certain cases determined by its rules of procedure, it sits in plenary session, as a chamber of five Judges, or as a chamber constituted by a single Judge.[105]

1–036 **Procedure.** Decision 2004/752 further lightens the existing procedure in staff cases with a view to settling disputes rapidly. Annex I to the Statute of the Court of Justice provides in principle for one exchange of written submissions between the parties.[106] When the Civil Service Tribunal deems that a second exchange is necessary, it may, with the agreement of the parties, decide to proceed to judgment without an oral hearing.[107] Furthermore, at all stages of the procedure the judicial panel may examine the

---

[99] [2004] O.J. L333/7.
[100] Council Decision 2004/752, Art.1.
[101] Statute, Annex I, Art.1.
[102] See Council Decision 2005/577/EC, Euratom of July 22, 2005 appointing Judges of the European Union Civil Service Tribunal ([2005] O.J. L197/28).
[103] EC Treaty, Art.225a and Statute, Annex I, Arts 2 and 3(1). The Council may, acting by a qualified majority, increase the number of Judges. The Council, when appointing Judges, will ensure a balanced composition of the Civil Service Tribunal on as broad a geographical basis as possible from among nationals of the Member States and with respect to the national legal systems represented.
[104] Statute, Annex I, Art.3(3) and (4).
[105] *Ibid.*, Art.4(2).
[106] *Ibid.*, Art.7(3).
[107] *Ibid.* At present, in proceedings before the Court of First Instance, a second exchange of written pleadings together with an oral hearing is the rule, with certain exceptions (see CFI Rules of Procedure, Arts 47(1) and 52 (1)).

possibility for an amicable settlement and may try to falicitate such settlement.[108]

Appeals. An appeal may be brought before the Court of First Instance against final decisions of the Civil Service Tribunal and decisions of the Civil Service Tribunal disposing of the substantive issues in part only or disposing of a procedural issue concerning a plea of lack of jurisdiction or inadmissibility. The appeal is to be lodged within two months of the notification of the decision appealed against by any party which had been unsuccessful, in whole or in part, in its submissions.[109]   1–037

Whereas Art.225a of the EC Treaty leaves the door open for appeals on points of law *and* fact, Decision 2004/752 clearly opts for an appeal limited to points of law.[110] If the appeal is well founded, the Court of First Instance will quash the decision of the Civil Service Tribunal and give final judgment in the matter. Only, where the state of the procedure does not permit the Court of First Instance to give final judgment is the case referred back to the Civil Service Tribunal, which will be bound by the decision of the Court of First Instance on points of law.[111]

B. THE COMMUNITY PATENT COURT

General. At present, the protection conferred by patents is governed by national law and in the event of a dispute patent rights have to be enforced before national courts. In order to increase the competitiveness of the Union's economy, the Commission put forward, on August 1, 2000, a proposal for a Council Regulation on a Community patent.[112] The holder of such a patent would enjoy protection based on Community law in all Member States of the Union.   1–038

Two stages. The establishment of a Community patent court intended to ensure uniform interpretation of Community patent legislation and give rulings enjoying Community-wide effect will take place in two stages. First, the Council will have to adopt a decision based on Art.229a of the EC Treaty conferring jurisdiction on the Court of Justice over disputes relating to the Community patent. Since patent litigation differs from proceedings normally brought before the Community courts in so far as it is between private parties, the relevant Council decision will also have to be adopted by the Member States in accordance with their respective constitutional   1–039

---

[108] Statute, Annex I, Art.7(4).
[109] *Ibid.*, Art.9.
[110] *Ibid.*, Art.11.
[111] *Ibid.*, Art.13.
[112] COM (2000) 412 final.

requirements.[113] The Commission has recently submitted to the Council a proposal for a decision conferring jurisdiction on the Court of Justice in disputes relating to the Community patent.[114]

As a second step, a Council decision based on Art.225a will have to be adopted to create a judicial panel and transfer to that panel the jurisdiction at first instance conferred upon the Court of Justice with respect to the Community patent. To that end, the Commission has prepared a proposal for a Council decision establishing the Community Patent Court (hereinafter referred to as the "CPC") and concerning appeals before the Court of First Instance.[115]

1–040 **Judges.** Under the Commission's proposal, the CPC will consist of seven Judges, appointed for a period of six years.[116] The Judges will be chosen from candidates presented by the Member States having an established high level of legal expertise in patent law. They are to be appointed by the Council on the basis of their expertise, after consultation of an advisory committee which will give an opinion on the adequacy of the candidates' profile.[117]

1–041 **Chambers.** The CPC will sit in chambers of three Judges. In special circumstances provided for in the Rules of Procedure, the CPC could sit in an enlarged composition, for example in cases where fundamental questions of patent law are concerned, or in a reduced composition (single Judge) in simple cases.[118]

1–042 **Assistant Rapporteurs.** The Judges will be assisted by seven technical experts named Assistant Rapporteurs[119] who will also be appointed for renewable periods of six years.[120] The Assistant Rapporteurs, who will be

---

[113] EC Treaty, Art.229a. Art.III–364 of the Constitution would simplify this procedure. Under that provision a "European law may confer on the Court of Justice of the European Union, to the extent that it shall determine, jurisdiction in disputes relating to the application of acts adopted on the basis of the Constitution which create European intellectual property rights". Such a European law would be adopted pursuant to the ordinary legislative procedure (Constitution, Arts I–34 and III–396).

[114] COM (2003) 827 final. Under this proposal, the Court of Justice would have jurisdiction in disputes relating to the infringement or the validity of a Community patent and a Community supplementary protection certificate, the use of the invention after the publication of the Community patent application, the right based on prior use of the invention, interim and evidence-protection measures in the subject matters conferred, damages or compensation in the situations referred to above and the ordering of a penalty payment in case of non-compliance with a decision or order constituting an obligation to act or to abstain from an act (Art.1).

[115] COM (2003) 828 final.

[116] COM (2003) 828 final, Art.2: Every three years there is to be a partial replacement of the Judges. Retiring Judges may be reappointed.

[117] COM (2003) 828 final: proposed Arts 2 and 3 of Annex II to the Statute of the Court of Justice.

[118] COM (2003) 828 final: proposed Art.8 of Annex II to the Statute of the Court of Justice.

[119] See Statute, Art.13.

[120] COM (2003) 828 final: proposed Art.7 of Annex II to the Statute of the Court of Justice and the legislative financial statement appended to the COM document.

specialised in different technical fields and have the "necessary legal qualifications",[121] will actively participate in the preparation, the hearing and the deliberation of cases. They will have the right to put questions to the parties but they will not be entitled to vote on the decision to be taken. Their input would be important in helping the Judges to focus from the start of proceedings on the essential technical questions involved.[122]

Procedure. The proposed decision would also modify the Statute and add   1–043
some specific provisions to it in order to take account of the special nature of litigation before the CPC. Accordingly, in contrast to other actions brought before the Community judicature, the competence of the CPC to prescribe any necessary interim measures will not be conditional upon main proceedings having already been instituted before it. Furthermore, where there is a demonstrable risk that evidence may be destroyed even before the commencement of proceedings on the merits of the case, the CPC may, in the event of an actual or imminent infringement of a Community patent, authorise in any place either the detailed description, with or without the taking of samples, or the physical seizure of the infringing goods, and, in appropriate cases, of the documents relating thereto. In the event that interim or evidence-protection measures are revoked, it is proposed that the CPC will order the applicant, at the defendant's request, to give the defendant adequate compensation for any injury caused by those measures.[123]

Costs. In contrast to other proceedings before the Community judicature,   1–044
it is proposed that proceedings before the CPC will not be free of charge. This is because the CPC will hear litigation in which parties seek to enforce their private rights against competitors and hence should adequately contribute to the court costs.[124]

Appeals. It is proposed that an appeal against a final decision of the CPC   1–045
may be brought before the Court of First Instance within two months of notification of the decision appealed against.[125] In contrast to other appeal procedures,[126] an appeal against a decision of the CPC will have suspensory effect.[127] Furthermore, under the proposal, appeals may be based on points of law *and* matters of fact.[128]

---

[121] See proposed Art.13 of the Statute of the Court of Justice; according to the Commission, "a thorough experience in patent law would seem necessary since the Assistant Rapporteur must have a good understanding of what technical aspects are relevant for a legally sound decision of the CPC" (COM (2003) 828 final).
[122] COM (2003) 828 final: proposed Art.7 of Annex II to the Statute of the Court of Justice.
[123] COM (2003) 828 final: proposed Art.14 of Annex II to the Statute of the Court of Justice.
[124] COM (2003) 828 final: proposed Art.23 of Annex II to the Statute of the Court of Justice.
[125] COM (2003) 828 final: proposed Art.26 of Annex II to the Statute of the Court of Justice.
[126] Appeals before the Court of Justice in cases for which the CFI has jurisdiction in first instance; appeals before the CFI against decisions of the Civil Service Tribunal.
[127] COM (2003) 828 final: proposed Art.22 of Annex II to the Statute of the Court of Justice.
[128] COM (2003) 828 final: proposed Art.27 of Annex II to the Statute of the Court of Justice.

Appeals against decisions of the CPC would be heard and determined by a specialised patent chamber within the Court of First Instance composed of three Judges and assisted by three technical experts (Assistant Rapporteurs).[129] As a result, the number of Judges in the Court of First Instance would be increased to 28.[130]

Under the proposal, if the appeal is well founded, the Court of First Instance will quash the decision of the CPC and give final judgment. The Court of First Instance may refer the case back to the CPC for judgment only in exceptional circumstances and in accordance with the Rules of Procedure. The *rationale* for this is that it is essential to avoid unnecessary referrals of cases back to the CPC in order to ensure efficient and swift patent proceedings. Where a case is referred back to the CPC, that court will be bound by the decision of the Court of First Instance on points of law.[131]

1–046 **Timeframe.** It is the intention of the Commission that the CPC will be operational by no later than 2010.

V. DISTRIBUTION OF HEADS OF JURISDICTION AS BETWEEN THE VARIOUS JUDICIAL BODIES BELONGING TO THE COURT OF JUSTICE

A. THE POSITION BEFORE THE TREATY OF NICE

1–047 **Court of First Instance.** Before the Treaty of Nice, the jurisdiction of the Court of First Instance was limited as follows. The Court had jurisdiction[132] to hear and determine actions for annulment,[133] actions for failure to act[134] and actions for reparation of non-contractual damage[135] brought by natural or legal persons against institutions and bodies of the Union and disputes between those institutions and bodies and their servants.[136] The Court of First Instance also had jurisdiction to entertain actions brought by natural and legal persons pursuant to an arbitration clause.[137] Lastly, the Court had jurisdiction in cases brought against the Office for Harmonisation in the

---

[129] COM (2003) 828 final: proposed Art.61a of the Statute of the Court of Justice and the legislative financial statement appended to the COM document.
[130] COM (2003) 828 final: proposed Art.48 of the Statute of the Court of Justice.
[131] COM (2003) 828 final: proposed Art.28 of Annex II to the Statute of the Court of Justice.
[132] See Council Decision 88/591/ECSC, EEC, Euratom of October 24, 1988 establishing a Court of First Instance of the European Communities ([1988] O.J. L319/1; *corrigendum* in [1989] O.J. L241/4), as amended by Council Decision 93/350/Euratom, ECSC, EEC of June 8, 1993 ([1993] O.J. L144/21) and Council Decision 94/149/ECSC, EC of March 7, 1994 ([1994] O.J. L66/29).
[133] EC Treaty, Art.230.
[134] EC Treaty, Art.232.
[135] EC Treaty, Arts 235 and 288, second para.
[136] EC Treaty, Art.236.
[137] EC Treaty, Art.238.

Internal Market relating to Community trademarks[138] and designs[139] as well as cases brought against the Community Plant Variety Office relating to Community plant variety rights.[140]

Court of Justice. The EC Treaty excluded preliminary references from the potential jurisdiction of the Court of First Instance.[141] They thus came within the reserved jurisdiction of the Court of Justice. That Court also had jurisdiction to decide actions for annulment or for failure to act and actions pursuant to an arbitration clause where those actions were lodged by a Member State, a Community institution, or, under certain circumstances, the European Central Bank. The Court of Justice was also competent to hear actions brought by the Commission or a Member State relating to the infringement of Community law by a Member State (infringement actions)[142] and actions relating to compensation for non-contractual damage brought by a Member State against the Community.[143] Lastly, as regards the jurisdiction of the Court of Justice, mention should be made of appeals which may be lodged on points of law only against rulings of the Court of First Instance.[144]

1–048

B. THE NICE TREATY: A FUNDAMENTAL REALLOCATION OF JURISDICTION IN EMBRYO

Role of Court of Justice. The Treaty of Nice contains in embryo a fundamental reallocation of jurisdiction as between the Community courts.[145] It appears from the Treaty of Nice that the Court of Justice's role should be confined to the examination of questions which are of essential

1–049

---

[138] Council Regulation (EC) No 40/94 of December 20, 1993 on the Community trademark [1994] O.J. L11/1.
[139] Council Regulation (EC) No 6/2002 of December 12, 2001 on Community designs [2002] O.J. L3/1.
[140] Council Regulation (EC) No 2100/94 of July 27, 1994 on Community plant variety rights [1994] O.J. L227/1, as amended by Council Regulation (EC) No 2506/95 of October 25, 1995 [1995] O.J. L258/3.
[141] Former Art.225(1) of the EC Treaty.
[142] EC Treaty, Arts 226–228.
[143] Such actions are, however, generally lodged by natural and legal persons and not by Member States. For completeness' sake the following actions falling within the jurisdiction of the Court of Justice should also be mentioned: actions based on Art.237 of the EC Treaty which concern the fulfilment by Member States of obligations under the Statute of the European Investment Bank (hereinafter "EIB"), the legality of measures adopted by the Board of Governors and of the Board of Directors of the EIB, and the fulfilment by national central banks of obligations within the framework of the monetary union; actions based on Art.239 of the EC Treaty concerning any dispute between Member States which relates to the subject-matter of the Treaty, submitted to the Court under a special agreement between the parties.
[144] EC Treaty, Art.225(1).
[145] See in this regard Louis, "La fonction juridictionnelle de Nice à Rome" (2003) J.T.D.E. 257; Vandersanden, "Le système juridictionnel communautaire après Nice" (2003) C.D.E. 3; Vesterdorf, "The Community court system ten years from now and beyond: challenges and possibilities", (2003) E.L.Rev. 303; Tizzano, "La Cour de Justice après Nice: le transfert de compétences au Tribunal de première instance" (2002) R.D.U.E 665.

importance for the Community legal order. In order to achieve this objective, the Treaty provides that the Court of Justice is to be the competent court for infringement actions,[146] for (the great majority of) preliminary references, for appeals against rulings of the Court of First Instance,[147] and, exceptionally, for the review of preliminary rulings of the Court of First Instance or of decisions taken by the Court of First Instance upon appeal in cases for which a judicial panel has jurisdiction at first instance.

1–050 **Transfer of jurisdiction to the Court of First Instance.** The Treaty of Nice introduced into the EC Treaty a legal basis for the transfer of jurisdiction to the Court of First Instance with regard to preliminary references in specific areas, which are still to be determined.[148] It is the intention of the Treaty of Nice[149] that the Court of First Instance, regardless of the status of the applicant, should have jurisdiction to hear at first instance actions for annulment[150] and for failure to act,[151] actions relating to compensation for non-contractual damage,[152] actions pursuant to an arbitration clause[153] and disputes between the Community and its staff.[154] There are two exceptions. First, judicial panels may be created. They are to hear and determine at first instance certain classes of action or proceeding brought in specific areas.[155] Secondly, the Statute of the Court of Justice may reserve certain actions at first and last instance to the Court of Justice.[156] However, the Statute attached to the Nice Treaty confirmed the pre-Nice *status quo* and, as far as the direct actions mentioned above are concerned, maintained— until a later amendment of the Statute[157]—the pre-Nice division of jurisdic-

---

[146] Under Art.225(1), first subpara., second sentence, of the EC Treaty, the Statute may provide for the Court of First Instance "to have jurisdiction for other classes of action or proceeding". This means that granting the Court of First Instance jurisdiction in infringement actions (based on Arts 226-228 of the EC Treaty) would not require a Treaty amendment: an amendment of the Statute would suffice.

[147] Art.225 of the EC Treaty allows for the introduction of a filter system for appeals in so far as Art.225 (1), second para., of the EC Treaty provides: "Decisions given by the Court of First Instance [. . .] may be subject to a right of appeal to the Court of Justice on points of law only, *under the conditions and within the limits laid down by the Statute*" (emphasis added).

[148] EC Treaty, Art.225(3).

[149] EC Treaty, Art.225(1).

[150] EC Treaty, Art.230.

[151] EC Treaty, Art.232.

[152] EC Treaty, Arts 235 and 288, second para.

[153] EC Treaty, Art.238.

[154] EC Treaty, Art.236.

[155] EC Treaty, Art.225(1), first subpara., and Art.225a, first para.

[156] EC Treaty, Art.225(1), first subpara.

[157] The Treaty of Nice introduced a simplified procedure for amending the Statute of the Court of Justice. Whereas until the entry into force of the Treaty of Nice the provisions relating to Treaty amendments applied, Art.245 of the EC Treaty now provides: "The Council, acting unanimously at the request of the Court of Justice and after consulting the European Parliament and the Commission, or at the request of the Commission and after consulting the European Parliament and the Court of Justice, may amend the provisions of the Statute, with the exception of Title I".

tion *ratione personae* between the Court of Justice and the Court of First Instance.

C. THE PRESENT ALLOCATION OF JURISDICTION

Present system. Council Decision 2004/407/EC of April 26, 2004, which amended Art.51 of the Protocol on the Statute of the Court of Justice,[158] (partly) implemented the principles of the Treaty of Nice by transferring jurisdiction from the Court of Justice to the Court of First Instance over direct actions, other than actions for infringement. The changes to the Statute, which aimed at leaving the Court of Justice with jurisdiction at first and last instance only in respect of basic legislative activity and in respect of the determination of interinstitutional disputes, may be summarised as follows.   **1–051**

First, actions which already fell within the jurisdiction of the Court of First Instance (see 1–047, *supra*) will continue to be heard and determined by that court.[159]

Secondly, all interinstitutional disputes (including those affecting the European Central Bank) are to be heard and determined at first and last instance by the Court of Justice.

Thirdly, as regards actions brought by Member States, the Statute favours the status of the defendant as the factor determining jurisdiction. The Court of Justice has jurisdiction to hear and determine actions brought by Member States *against* acts and failures to act of the European Parliament and/or the Council, either in the exercise of the powers vested in each of those institutions or pursuant to the co-decision procedure. In principle, therefore, actions brought by Member States against the Commission and the European Central Bank fall within the jurisdiction of the Court of First Instance, since such cases do not normally involve review of the basic legislative activity of the institutions.

Exceptions. Art.51 of the Statute contains two series of *exceptions*.[160] The first is based on the fact that the Council sometimes adopts acts which do not concern the basic legislative activity of the Community. Reserving   **1–052**

---

[158] [2004] O.J. L132/5; *corrigendum* in [2004] O.J. L194/3.

[159] This means that it cannot be ruled out that some cases involving basic legislative activity will be heard and determined at first instance by the Court of First Instance.

[160] Art.51 provides: "By way of derogation from the rule laid down in Art.225(1) of the EC Treaty and Art.140a(1) of the EAEC Treaty, jurisdiction shall be reserved to the Court of Justice in the actions referred to in Arts 230 and 232 of the EC Treaty and Arts 146 and 148 of the EAEC Treaty when they are brought by a Member State against:

(a) an act of or failure to act by the European Parliament or the Council, or by both those institutions acting jointly, except for:
– decisions taken by the Council under the third subpara. of Art.88(2) of the EC Treaty;
– acts of the Council adopted pursuant to a Council regulation concerning measures to protect trade within the meaning of Art.133 of the EC Treaty;
– acts of the Council by which the Council exercises implementing powers in

actions in relation to such acts to the Court of Justice would not be in conformity with the aim pursued by the changes made to the Statute. Art.51 of the Statute therefore provides that the Court of First Instance is to have jurisdiction to hear and determine at first instance actions brought by a Member State concerning acts or failures to act of the Council in the field of State aid (EC Treaty, Art.88(2), third subpara.), with respect to implementing measures to protect trade (within the meaning of Art.133 of the EC Treaty), as well as with respect to the Council's implementing powers reserved to it in the basic legislative act or which it has regained in the course of a "committee procedure" (EC Treaty, Art.202, third indent).

Conversely, action by the Commission may constitute basic legislative activity. The review of the legality of such acts or of a failure on the part of the Commission to adopt such an act would therefore logically fall within the jurisdiction of the Court of Justice at first and last instance. Accordingly, Art.51 of the Statute provides that the Court of Justice is to have jurisdiction to hear and determine actions brought by Member States against an act of or failure to act by the Commission under Art.11a of the EC Treaty (relating to enhanced cooperation).

1–053 **Infringement actions and preliminary references.** Since the recent changes to the Statute did not bear on infringement actions or preliminary references, the Court of Justice will continue to hear such actions (at first and last instance).

1–054 **Overview.** On the basis of the EC Treaty, as amended by the Nice Treaty, and the new Art.51 of the Statute, the current allocation of jurisdiction between the Court of Justice and the Court of First Instance is as follows:

The *Court of Justice* has jurisdiction in:

- infringement actions (EC Treaty, Arts 226–228);

- preliminary references (EC Treaty, Art.234);

- actions for annulment (EC Treaty, Art.230) lodged by

   o an institution or the European Central Bank against another institution or the European Central Bank;

   o a Member State against the European Parliament and/or the Council, with the exception of actions relating to decisions taken by the Council under Art.88(2), third subpara., of the EC Treaty;

---

accordance with the third indent of Art.202 of the EC Treaty;
(b) against an act of or failure to act by the Commission under Art.11a of the EC Treaty. Jurisdiction shall also be reserved to the Court of Justice in the actions referred to in the same articles when they are brought by an institution of the Communities or by the European Central Bank against an act of or failure to act by the European Parliament, the Council, both those institutions acting jointly, or the Commission, or brought by an institution of the Communities against an act of or failure to act by the European Central Bank."

acts of the Council adopted pursuant to a Council regulation concerning measures to protect trade within the meaning of Art.133 of the EC Treaty and acts of the Council by which the Council exercises implementing powers in accordance with Art.202, third indent, of the EC Treaty;

- ○ a Member State against an act by the Commission under Art.11a of the EC Treaty;

- actions for failure to act (EC Treaty, Art.232) lodged by

- ○ an institution or the European Central Bank against another institution or the European Central Bank;
- ○ a Member State against the European Parliament and/or the Council, with the exception of actions relating to the Council's failure to adopt a decision under Art.88(2), third subpara., of the EC Treaty, to the Council's failure to adopt an act pursuant to a Council regulation concerning measures to protect trade within the meaning of Art.133 of the EC Treaty and to the Council's failure to exercise its implementing powers in accordance with Art.202, third indent, of the EC Treaty;
- ○ a Member State against a failure to act by the Commission under Art.11a of the EC Treaty;

- actions based on Art.237 of the EC Treaty which concern the fulfilment by Member States of obligations under the Statute of the European Investment Bank ("EIB"), the legality of measures adopted by the Board of Governors and of the Board of Directors of the EIB, and the fulfilment by national central banks of obligations within the framework of the monetary Union;

- actions based on Art.239 of the EC Treaty concerning any dispute between Member States which relates to the subject-matter of the Treaty, submitted to the Court under a special agreement between the parties;

- appeals against rulings of the Court of First Instance (EC Treaty, Art.225(1));

- review of decisions which the Court of First Instance took on appeal against decisions of judicial panels.[161]

The *Court of First Instance* has jurisdiction in:

- actions for annulment (EC Treaty, Art.230) lodged by

---

[161] EC Treaty, Art.225(2), second subpara. Review of preliminary rulings given by the Court of First Instance will also be possible (EC Treaty, Art.225(3), third subpara.). Whilst one judicial panel has already been created (the European Union Civil Service Tribunal), a transfer of jurisdiction to the Court of First Instance over preliminary references is not envisaged for the time being.

○ natural or legal persons;
○ a Member State against the Commission (unless the action concerns an act by the Commission under Art.11a of the EC Treaty);
○ a Member State against the Council relating to decisions under Art.88(2), third subpara., of the EC Treaty;
○ a Member State against acts of the Council adopted pursuant to a Council regulation concerning measures to protect trade within the meaning of Art.133 of the EC Treaty;
○ a Member State against acts of the Council by which the latter exercises implementing powers in accordance with Art.202, third indent, of the EC Treaty;

– actions for failure to act (Art.232 of the EC Treaty) lodged by

○ natural or legal persons;
○ a Member State against the Commission (unless the action concerns a failure to act by the Commission under Art.11a of the EC Treaty);
○ a Member State against the Council relating to a failure to adopt a decision under Art.88(2), third subpara., of the EC Treaty;
○ a Member State against the Council relating to a failure to adopt an act pursuant to a Council regulation concerning measures to protect trade within the meaning of Art.133 of the EC Treaty;
○ a Member State against the Council relating to a failure to exercise its implementing powers in accordance with Art.202, third indent, of the EC Treaty;

– actions relating to compensation for non-contractual damage brought against the Community (EC Treaty, Arts 235 and 288, second para.);

– actions pursuant to an arbitration clause contained in a contract concluded by or on behalf of the Community, whether that contract be governed by public or private law (EC Treaty, Art.238);

– cases brought against the Office for Harmonisation in the Internal Market relating to Community trademarks[162] and designs[163] and cases brought against the Community Plant Variety Office relating to Community plant variety rights[164];

– appeals against decisions of judicial panels (EC Treaty, Art.225(2)).

---

[162] Council Regulation (EC) No 40/94 of December 20, 1993 on the Community trademark [1994] O.J. L11/1.
[163] Council Regulation (EC) No 6/2002 of December 12, 2001 on Community designs [2002] O.J. L3/1.
[164] Council Regulation (EC) No 2100/94 of July 27, 1994 on Community plant variety rights [1994] O.J. L227/1, as amended by Council Regulation (EC) No 2506/95 of October 25, 1995 [1995] O.J. L258/3.

The *Civil Service Tribunal* has jurisdiction in staff cases (EC Treaty, Art.236).[165]

Procedural document submitted to the wrong court. In addition, mention **1–055** should be made of Art.54 of the Statute of the Court of Justice of the EC, which deals with three complications regarding the allocation of jurisdiction as between the Court of Justice and the Court of First Instance.[166] First, there is *formal mistake*: if an application or other procedural document addressed to the Court of First Instance is lodged by mistake with the Registrar of the Court of Justice, or *vice versa*, it is to be transmitted immediately from one Registrar to the other.[167] Secondly, there is *substantive mistake*: if the Court of First Instance finds that it does not have jurisdiction to hear and determine an action in respect of which the Court of Justice has jurisdiction, it is to refer the action to the Court of Justice[168]; likewise, where the Court of Justice finds that an action falls within the jurisdiction of the Court of First Instance, it is to refer it to the Court of First Instance, whereupon that court may not decline jurisdiction.[169] As will be appreciated, the allocation of jurisdiction as between the Court of Justice and the Court of First Instance is based on objective grounds in so far as the court wrongly seised of a case falling within the jurisdiction of the other court is under an obligation to refer it to that other court. In case of doubt, the Court of Justice has the last word, since after it has referred a case to the Court of First Instance in that way, that court cannot decline jurisdiction. This system does not detract from the right of the Court of First Instance to decline jurisdiction where a case falls outside the sphere of action of the Community judiciary, regarded as a whole.

---

[165] Where the protocol establishing a Community institution or body provides that the Court of Justice should be the competent court to hear and determine disputes between that institution or body and its servants, the expression "Court of Justice" is to "be interpreted as referring to the Community judicature as a whole within the meaning of Art.7 EC and thus as including the Court of First Instance" (CFI, Case T–333/99 *X v ECB* [2001] E.C.R. II–3021, IA-199, II–921, para.41) as well as the European Union Civil Service Tribunal. If such a provision was interpreted "as precluding actions by certain servants against certain institutions or organs . . . from the improved system of legal remedies introduced by Decision 88/591 [which is characterised by a two-tier approach] for the same type of dispute, that departure from the general system of legal remedies, for which there is no objective justification, would be in breach of the principle of equal treatment and therefore of a fundamental principle of Community law." (*ibid.*, para.40).

[166] See Klinke, "Quelques réflexions à propos de la relation entre la Cour de justice et le Tribunal de première instance des Communautés européennes" (2000) R.A.E. 239–253.

[167] Statute, Art.54, first para.

[168] Statute, Art.54, second para. See, for example, CFI (order of November 25, 2003), Case T–85/01 *IAMA Consulting v Commission*, [2003] E.C.R. II–4973, para.62.

[169] Statute, Art.54, second para. For practical examples, see ECJ (order of May 23, 1990), Case C–72/90 *Asia Motor France v Commission* [1990] E.C.R. I–2181; ECJ (order of June 4, 1991), Case C–66/90 *PTT v Commission* [1991] E.C.R. I–2723; ECJ (order of May 3, 1993), Case C–424/92 *Ladbroke Racing v Commission* [1993] E.C.R. I–2213; ECJ (order of March 21, 1997), Case C–95/97 *Régione Wallonne v Commission* [1997] E.C.R. I–1787; ECJ (order of October 1, 1997), Case C–180/97 *Regione Toscana v Commission* [1997] E.C.R. I–5245, paras 9–12; ECJ (order of July 14, 2005), Case C–70/04 *Swiss Confederation v Commission*, not reported, para.52.

1–056   **Identical or similar object of cases pending before different courts.** Thirdly, there is the case where the two courts are validly seised of cases in which *the object is identical or similar*.[170] Identity of object will occur where a natural or legal person or a Member State brings an action before the Court of First Instance against a Community institution for annulment of an act or for failure to take a decision, and another Community institution brings an action against the same act or failure to act before the Court of Justice. Similarity of object will occur where a natural or legal person or a Member State brings an action for annulment of an act—*e.g.* of a Commission decision approving State aid—before the Court of First Instance, whilst a national court makes a reference for a preliminary ruling to the Court of Justice relating to the validity of the same act. Likewise, the same question of interpretation may be raised before both the Court of First Instance and the Court of Justice.

The third and fourth paras of Art.54 of the Statute[171] resolve the matter as follows:

> "Where the Court of Justice and the Court of First Instance are seised of cases in which the same relief is sought, the same issue of interpretation is raised or the validity of the same act is called in question, the Court of First Instance may, after hearing the parties, stay the proceedings before it until such time as the Court of Justice has delivered judgment or, where the action is one brought pursuant to Art.230 of the EC Treaty [. . .], may decline jurisdiction so as to allow the Court of Justice to rule on such actions. In the same circumstances, the Court of Justice may also decide to stay the proceedings before it; in that event, the proceedings before the Court of First Instance shall continue.

> Where a Member State and an institution of the Communities are challenging the same act, the Court of First Instance is to decline jurisdiction so that the Court of Justice may rule on those applications."

This solution calls for a number of observations. The Court of First Instance is obliged to decline jurisdiction only in one instance, namely where a Member State (before the Court of First Instance) and an institution (before the Court of Justice) contest the same act. For the rest, the Court of First Instance cannot be compelled to decline jurisdiction (*se dessaisir*) or to stay proceedings.[172] This is a reflection of the judicial

---

[170] Joliet and Vogel, "Le Tribunal de premiè re instance des Communautés européennes" (1989) R.M.C. 423, at 429. For an example, see CFI (order of November 16, 1998), Case T–310/97 *Nederlandse Antillen v Council* [1998] E.C.R. II–4131, para.7.

[171] [2004] O.J. L132/5; *corrigendum* in [2004] O.J. L194/3.

[172] The expression "decline jurisdiction" (*se dessaisir* in the French version) in the third para. of Art.54 of the Statute does not have the same meaning as it has in the second para. of

independence of the two courts, expressed by the words "the Court of First Instance may". But if that court decides to make use of that possibility, the Court of Justice can prevent it from doing so by staying proceedings on its part, thus causing the procedure to have to go through the Court of First Instance. In the event that the Court of First Instance has already declined jurisdiction, the Court of Justice can refer the case back to it by staying the parallel proceedings.

D. THE CONSTITUTION

Denomination of different courts. Under Art.I-29(1) of the Constitution, the Court of Justice of the European Union is to include the Court of Justice, the General Court and specialised courts.[173] Thus, the Constitution would put an end to the confusion which has existed ever since the creation of the Court of First Instance between the institution and the courts which it comprises. The envisaged change in the names of the courts can be attributed, on the one hand, to the fact that the abolition of the three pillars in the Constitution rendered any reference to the "European Communities" obsolete and, on the other hand, as far as the Court of First Instance is concerned, to the fact that that court could no longer be treated as a court of "first instance". The judicial panels, which constitue in reality fully fledged courts,[174] are to be called specialised courts.

1–057

Selection committee for Judges and Advocates General. As regards the composition, the internal organisation and the jurisdiction of the Court of Justice, the General Court and specialised courts, the Constitution reproduces the corresponding provisions of the EC Treaty. What is new,

1–058

Art.54 (where the French reads "décliner sa compétence"). Where the Court of First Instance stays proceedings, an appeal will not lie against that decision (ECJ (order of November 26, 2003), Joined Cases C–366/03, C–368/03, C–390/03, C–391/03 and C–394/03 P Associazione Bancaria Italiana and Others v Commission, not reported). Where the Court of Justice refers a case to the Court of First Instance pursuant to the second para. of Art.54 of the Statute, the Court of First Instance may no longer decline jurisdiction on account of the nature of the action, but it may refrain from deciding the case (se dessaisir), for example on jurisdictional grounds, and refer the case back to the Court of Justice. For examples, see ECJ (order of February 26, 2002), Case C–407/01 Netherlands v Commission, not reported; CFI (order of June 21, 1991), Case T–42/91 PTT v Commission [1991] E.C.R. II–273; CFI (order of February 1, 1995), Case T–88/94 Société Commerciale des Potasses et de l'Azote and Others v Commission [1995] E.C.R. II–221 (this case was decided by the Court of Justice: ECJ, Joined Cases C–68/94 and C–30/95 France and Others v Commission [1998] E.C.R. I–1375); CFI (order of February 23, 1995), Case T–488/93 Hanseatische Industrie-Beteiligungen v Commission [1995] E.C.R. II–469; CFI (order of February 23, 1995), Case T–490/93 Bremer Vulkan Verband v Commission [1995] E.C.R. II–477 (these cases, too, were decided by the Court of Justice: ECJ, Joined Cases C–329/93, C–62/95 and C–63/95 Germany and Others v Commission [1996] E.C.R. I–5151); CFI (order of November 16, 1998), Case T–41/97 Antillean Rice Mills v Council [1998] E.C.R. II–4117, para.7.

[173] On this subject, see Barents, "The Court of Justice in the Draft Constitution" (2004) M.J.E.C.L. 121–141.

[174] They will, however, remain "attached" to the General Court (Constitution, Art.III–359(1)).

however, is the envisaged creation of a panel which would give an opinion on candidates' suitability to perform the duties of Judge and Advocate General of the Court of Justice and the General Court before the national governments take their decision.[175]

1–059 **Amendment of Statute.** Another important innovation concerns the procedure to be followed for amending the Statute of the Court of Justice of the European Union. The Constitution provides that a European law may amend the provisions of the Statute.[176] The ordinary legislative procedure would apply with the particularity that either the Court of Justice or the Commission may take the initiative and that the other institution will be consulted.[177] As a result, amendments to the Statute would no longer require unanimity in the Council[178]: a qualified majority would suffice. Furthermore, whereas at present the European Parliament is only consulted on amendments to the Statute,[179] the Constitution would make the Parliament a co-legislator also in this area.

---

[175] Constitution, Art.III–357. The panel is to comprise seven persons chosen from among former members of the Court of Justice and the General Court, members of national supreme courts and lawyers of recognised competence, one of whom is to be proposed by the European Parliament. The Council is to adopt a European decision establishing the panel's operating rules and a European decision appointing its members. It is to act on the initiative of the President of the Court of Justice.

[176] Constitution, Art.III–381 (with the exception of Title I and Art.64 of the Statute). The Rules of Procedure of the Court of Justice will require the consent of the Council (Art.III–355, fourth para., of the Constitution). The Rules of Procedure of the General Court and of the specialised courts will be established in agreement with the Court of Justice and will be subject to the consent of the Council (see Constitution, Arts III–356, fifth para., and III–359(5), respectively). The Council is to act by a qualified majority (Constitution, Art.I–23(3)).

[177] Constitution, Arts I–34, III–381 and III–396.

[178] EC Treaty, Art.245.

[179] *Ibid.*

COOPERATION BETWEEN NATIONAL COURTS AND THE COURT OF JUSTICE: THE REFERENCE FOR A PRELIMINARY RULING

General. The primary responsibility of national courts for the correct application of Community law is rounded off by the preliminary ruling procedure, which, in the words of the Court of Justice, is "essential for preservation of the Community character of the law established by the Treaty and has the object of ensuring that in all circumstances this law is the same in all States of the Community".[180]

2–001

EC and EAEC Treaties. Art.234 of the EC Treaty and Art.150 of the EAEC Treaty, which are virtually identical, [181] empower the Court of Justice to "give

2–002

---

[180] ECJ, Case 166/73 *Rheinmühlen–Düsseldorf* [1974] E.C.R. 33, para.2.
[181] EC Treaty, Art.234:
    The Court of Justice shall have jurisdiction to give preliminary rulings concerning:
    (a) the interpretation of this Treaty;
    (b) the validity and interpretation of acts of the institutions of the Community and of the ECB;
    (c) the interpretation of the statutes of bodies established by an act of the Council, where those statutes so provide.
    Where such a question is raised before any court or tribunal of a Member State, that court or tribunal may, if it considers that a decision of the question is necessary to enable it to give judgment, request the Court of Justice to give a ruling thereon.
    Where any such question is raised in a case pending before a court or tribunal of a Member State against whose decisions there is no judicial remedy under national law, that court or tribunal shall bring the matter before the Court of Justice.
    EAEC Treaty, Art.150:
    The Court of Justice shall have jurisdiction to give preliminary rulings concerning:
    (b) the interpretation of this Treaty;
    (b) the validity and interpretation of acts of the institutions of the Community;
    (c) the interpretation of the statutes of bodies established by an act of the Council, save where those statutes provide otherwise.
    Where such a question is raised before any court or tribunal of a Member State, that court or tribunal may, if it considers that a decision of the question is necessary to enable it to give judgment, request the Court of Justice to give a ruling thereon.
    Where any such question is raised in a case pending before a court or tribunal of a Member State, against whose decisions there is no judicial remedy under national law, that court or tribunal shall bring the matter before the Court of Justice.

preliminary rulings" on the interpretation of Community law[182] and on the validity of acts of the Community institutions. [183] Any court or tribunal of a Member State is entitled to make a reference for a preliminary ruling to the Court of Justice. However, if a question regarding the validity or the interpretation of a Community act is raised in a case pending before a court or tribunal of a Member State against whose decisions there is no judicial remedy under national law, that court or tribunal is obliged to bring the matter before the Court of Justice.

Special provisions apply in the Title of the EC Treaty on visas, asylum and other policies related to free movement of persons, introduced by the Treaty of Amsterdam. [184] Art.68(1) of the EC Treaty confers on the Court of Justice jurisdiction to give preliminary rulings on the interpretation of the title in question or on the validity or interpretation of acts of the Community institutions based on that title. However, only national courts or tribunals against whose decisions there is no judicial remedy under national law may make such references for preliminary rulings. They are under a duty to make such a reference if they consider that a decision on the question is necessary to enable them to give judgment (see 2–041 to 2–058, *infra*).[185]

2–003 **EU Treaty.** Art.35(1) of Title VI of the EU Treaty "Provisions on police and judicial cooperation in criminal matters" gives the Court of Justice jurisdiction to give preliminary rulings on the validity and interpretation of framework decisions and decisions, on the interpretation of conventions established under that title and on the validity and interpretation of the measures implementing them. Under Art.35(2) of the EU Treaty, that jurisdiction to give preliminary rulings has to be accepted by Member States wishing to do so by a declaration made at the time of signature of the Treaty or at any time thereafter (see 22–004, *infra*).

2–004 **Former ECSC Treaty.** The ECSC Treaty contained no provision relating to the Court's jurisdiction to give preliminary rulings on interpretation, but did provide that "The Court shall have sole jurisdiction to give preliminary rulings on the validity of acts of the High Authority [Commission] and of the Council where such validity is in issue in proceedings brought before a national court or tribunal" (Art.41). Nevertheless, the Court held that it had jurisdiction to answer questions referred for a preliminary ruling on the

---

[182] Ch. 6, *infra*.
[183] Ch. 10, *infra*.
[184] [1997] O.J. C 340.
[185] See Girerd,"L'article 68 CE: un renvoi préjudiciel d'interprétation et d'application incertaines" (1999) R.T.D.E. 239–260; Labayle, "Les nouveaux domaines d'intervention de la Cour de justice: l'espace de liberté, de sécurité et de justice", in Dony and Bribosia (eds), *L'avenir du système juridictionnel de l'Union européenne* (Éditions de l'Université de Bruxelles, Brussels, 2002), at 73–105.

interpretation of ECSC law, on the ground that it would be "contrary to the objectives and the coherence of the Treaties if the determination of the meaning and scope of rules deriving from the EEC and EAEC Treaties were ultimately a matter for the Court of Justice, as is provided in identical terms by Art.177*[now Art.234]* of the E[E]C Treaty and Art.150 of the EAEC Treaty, thereby enabling those rules to be applied in a uniform manner, but such jurisdiction in respect of rules deriving from the ECSC Treaty were to be retained exclusively by the various national courts, whose interpretations might differ, and the Court of Justice were to have no power to ensure that such rules were given a uniform interpretation".[186]

Objective. As far as the Court of Justice is concerned, Art.234 of the EC Treaty and Art.150 of the EAEC Treaty "all express a twofold need: to ensure the utmost uniformity in the application of Community law and to establish for that purpose effective cooperation between the Court of Justice and national courts".[187] That cooperation requires "the national court and the Court of Justice, both keeping within their respective jurisdiction, and with the aim of ensuring that Community law is applied in a uniform manner, to make direct and complementary contributions to the working out of a decision".[188] **2–005**

Sole power of Court of Justice to declare a Community act invalid. That aim of the preliminary ruling procedure holds good no matter whether the ruling is sought on the interpretation of Community law or on the validity of a Community act.[189] This was the principal reason which prompted the Court to declare with regard to the application of Art.234 of the EC Treaty that it has the sole power to declare an act of a Community institution invalid.[190] This is because the uniform application of Community law is particularly necessary when the validity of a Community act is at stake. Divergences of view between courts in the Member States as to the validity of Community acts would be liable to place in jeopardy the very unity of the Community legal order and detract from the fundamental requirement of legal certainty.[191] Naturally, this does not alter the fact that reviewing the validity of acts of Community institutions is essentially a control of the **2–006**

---

[186] ECJ, Case C–221/88 *Busseni* [1990] E.C.R. I–495, para.16 (case notes by Arnull (1990) E.L.Rev. 321–326, and Bebr (1991) C.M.L.Rev. 415–427).

[187] *Busseni*, cited in the preceding n., para.13.

[188] ECJ, Case 16/65 *Schwarze* [1965] E.C.R. 877; ECJ, Case C–454/98 *Schmeink & Cofreth and Strobel* [2000] E.C.R. I–6973, para.36.

[189] ECJ, Case 66/80 *International Chemical* [1981] E.C.R. 1191, para.11.

[190] ECJ, Case 314/85 *Foto-Frost* [1987] E.C.R. 4199, para.17. See Bebr, "The Reinforcement of the Constitutional Review of Community Acts under Art.177*[now Art.234]* EEC Treaty (cases 314/85 and 133 to 136/85)" (1988) C.M.L.Rev. 667, at 672–684; Glaesner, "Die Vorlagepflicht unterinstanzlicher Gerichte im Vorabentscheidungsverfahren" (1990) EuR. 143–157; Goffin, "De l'incompétence des juridictions nationales pour constater l'invalidité des actes d'institutions communautaires" (1990) C.D.E. 216–226.

[191] *Foto-Frost*, cited in the preceding n., para.15.

legality of such acts, which is primarily designed to protect the rights of individuals.[192]

2–007 Topics to be discussed. A request for a preliminary ruling takes the form of a question put to the Court, which is subject to a number of rules. First, the *initiative* of referring the question must emanate from "a court or tribunal [*juridiction* in French] of a Member State", either of its own motion or acting on a request made by one of the parties in proceedings pending before it,[193] and national (procedural) law may not put impediments in the way of the right to seek a preliminary ruling (which every national court or tribunal has by virtue of Community law).[194] Consequently, the *relevance* of the question falls to be determined by the national court, albeit only within certain limits which the Court of Justice has placed upon its competence to answer questions referred for a preliminary ruling. Lastly, a "court or tribunal of a Member State against whose decisions there is no judicial remedy under national law" is in principle *obliged* to refer questions for a preliminary ruling which are raised in a case pending before it.

These matters will be considered below.

I. THE INITIATIVE FOR REQUESTING A PRELIMINARY RULING

A. WHAT IS A "COURT OR TRIBUNAL OF A MEMBER STATE"?

2–008 *Vaassen* criteria. Generally, the expression "court or tribunal or a Member State" does not raise any difficulties. Where a Member State regards a public body as a "court or tribunal", Community law normally accepts it as such. This is because in that case the body manifestly fulfils the criteria which the Court of Justice has formulated—which are known as the *Vaassen* criteria after the case in which they were first framed[195]—in order to confer on a body which is not considered a court or tribunal under national law that capacity under Community law with a view to the application of the articles of the Treaties relating to the preliminary ruling procedure.

---

[192] *Cf.* ECJ, Case 294/83 *Les Verts v European Parliament* [1986] E.C.R. 1339, para.23.

[193] For a critical appraisal of the exclusive right of initiative of national courts and tribunals, see Meilicke, "Hindernislauf zum gesetzlichen Richter" (2000) Steuerrecht 17–24.

[194] ECJ, Case 166/73 *Rheinmühlen–Düsseldorf* [1974] E.C.R. 33, para.2; ECJ, Case C–312/93 *Peterbroeck* [1995] E.C.R. I–4599, para.13. Note that where a potential question of Community law arises before a court not being a court of last resort, it has to decide whether a decision on the question is necessary in order to give judgment and, if so, whether the court should order a reference to be made. Matters taken into account in the UK include the importance of the point of law for the uniform interpretation of Community law; the question of delay and costs; the parties' wishes; the existence of parallel proceedings in other Member States and whether there is a need to consider a Community text in different languages; see Brealey and Hoskins, *Remedies in E.C. Law*, at 214–224.

[195] ECJ, Case 61/65 *Vaassen (née Göbbels)* [1966] E.C.R. 261, at 273, with case notes by Haardt (1966–67) C.M.L.Rev. 441–444; Storm (1967) C.D.E. 311–320.

A "court or tribunal" under Art.234 of the EC Treaty is (1) a body (2) which is established by law, (3) permanent and independent[196] and (4) charged with the settlement of disputes defined in general terms (5) which is bound by rules governing *inter partes* proceedings similar to those used by the ordinary courts of law,[197] (6) in so far as it acts as the "proper judicial body" for the disputes in question, which means that parties must be required to apply to the court or tribunal for the settlement of their dispute and its determination must be binding,[198] and (7) is bound to apply rules of law.[199]

Application of *Vaassen* criteria. In accordance with that test, the Nether-   2–009
lands *Commissie van Beroep Huisartsgeneeskunde* (Appeals Committee for General Medicine) was regarded as being a "court or tribunal" even though it was part of a professional body and not considered to be a court or tribunal under Netherlands law.[200] The crucial factor appeared to be that

---

[196] ECJ, Case C–54/96 *Dorsch Consult* [1997] E.C.R. I–4961, para.23.

[197] In the case of *Dorsch Consult* (*ibid.*, paras 22–38), the Court held that "the requirement that the procedure before the hearing body concerned must be *inter partes* is not an absolute requirement", after which it found that the adjudicating body, the Federal German *Vergabeüberwachungsausschuss*, a statutory administrative body supervising the award of procurement contracts, had to hear the parties before making any determination (see *ibid.*, para.31, at I–4994). The Court of Justice held on that ground that the board in question was a "court or tribunal" within the meaning of Art.234 of the EC Treaty. See also in this connection ECJ, Case C–18/93 *Corsica Ferries* [1994] E.C.R. I–1783, para.12; ECJ, Joined Cases C–110/98– C–147/98 *Gabalfrisa and Others* [2000] E.C.R. I–1557, para.47; ECJ, Case C–182/00 *Lutz and Others* [2002] E.C.R. I–547, para.13. For a more detailed analysis of the case-law, see Tridimas, "Knocking on heaven's door: fragmentation, efficiency and defiance in the preliminary reference procedure" (2003) C.M.L.Rev. 9–50.

[198] ECJ, Case C–54/96 *Dorsch Consult* [1997] E.C.R. I–4961, paras 27–29. In *Österreichischer Gewerkschaftsbund*, the Court of Justice held that the Austrian *Oberster Gerichtshof* [Supreme Court] was a court or tribunal within the meaning of Art.234 of the EC Treaty when adjudicating in a dispute between a union for public-sector employees and the Austrian Republic, although there were features of the procedure which were less characteristic of judicial proceedings, namely the fact that the *Oberster Gerichtshof* did not rule on disputes in a specific case involving identified persons, that it must base its legal assessment on the facts alleged by the applicant without further examination, that the decision was declaratory in nature and that the right to bring proceedings was exercised collectively (ECJ, Case C–195/98 *Österreichischer Gewerkschaftsbund* [2000] E.C.R. I–10497, paras 21–32).

[199] ECJ, Case 61/65 *Vaassen (née Göbbels)* [1966] E.C.R. 261, at 273; ECJ, Joined Cases C–9/97 and C–118/97 *Jokela and Pitkäranta* [1998] E.C.R. I–6267, para.18; see also ECJ, Case C–416/96 *Eddline El-Yassini* [1999] E.C.R. I–1209, paras 17–22 (Immigration Adjudicator in the UK held to be a court or tribunal within the meaning of Art.234 of the EC Treaty); ECJ, Case C–92/00 *HI* [2002] E.C.R. I–5553, paras 24–28 (the *Vergabekontrollsenat des Landes Wien* [Public-Procurement Review Chamber of the Vienna Region] held to be a court or tribunal within the meaning of Art.234 of the EC Treaty); ECJ, Case C–407/98 *Abrahamsson and Anderson* [2000] E.C.R. I–5539, paras 28–38 (the Swedish *Överklagandenämnden för Högskolan*, which undertakes an independent examination of appeals lodged against decisions on appointments taken in universities and higher educational institutions, held to be a court or tribunal within the meaning of Art.234 of the EC Treaty); ECJ (order of July 11, 2003), Case C–161/03 *CAFOM and Samsung Electronics France*, not reported, paras 10–17 (the French *Commission de conciliation et d'expertise douanière* held to be a court or tribunal within the meaning of Art.234 of the EC Treaty).

[200] ECJ, Case 246/80 *Broekmeulen* [1981] E.C.R. 2311, para.11.

the decisions delivered by the Appeals Committee, after an adversarial procedure, were "in fact recognised as final", since "in a matter involving the application of Community law" (registration of general practitioners) there was "in practice [no] right of appeal to the ordinary courts", with the result that the absence of any opportunity of seeking a preliminary ruling from the Appeals Committee would constitute a threat to "the proper functioning of Community law".[201]

The position was completely different when the Court, of its own motion,[202] refused to answer a question referred for a preliminary ruling by the *Directeur des Contributions Directes et des Accises* (Director of Taxation and Excise Duties) of the Grand Duchy of Luxembourg on the ground that he was not a "court or tribunal".[203] The Court emphasised that that expression, which had to be defined under Community law, referred by its nature to an authority acting as a third party in relation to the authority which adopted the decision forming the subject-matter of the proceedings.[204] This was clearly not so in the case of the *Directeur des Contributions*, who was in charge of the revenue departments which had made the contested assessment to tax. Furthermore, if the matter were to come before the Luxembourg *Conseil d'Etat* on appeal, the *Directeur des Contributions* would be the defendant, which was regarded as confirming that he was a party to proceedings and not an authority separating the parties to the proceedings as a neutral outsider.[205] In that respect, the Director should be compared with the British "Chief Adjudication Officer", who takes the administrative decision with regard to the grant of social security benefits. That "Officer" is not a judicial authority, but a party who, as such, defends

---

[201] *Ibid.*, paras 16 and 17.

[202] The Commission and the Luxembourg Government, which alone submitted observations to the Court pursuant to Art.23 of the Statute, did not take issue with the competence of the body requesting the preliminary ruling.

[203] ECJ, Case C–24/92 *Corbiau* [1993] E.C.R. I–1277, para.17. *Cf.* ECJ, Case C–17/00 *De Coster* [2001] E.C.R. I–9445, paras 9–22, in which the Court of Justice considered that the *Rechtsprekend College van het Brussels Hoofdstedelijk Gewest/Collège juridictionnel de la Région de Bruxelles-Capitale* [Judicial Board of the Brussels-Capital region], which adjudicates in disputes relating to the legality of municipal taxes, constituted a court or tribunal (Advocate General D. Ruiz-Jarabo Colomer reached the opposite conclusion). *Cf.* ECJ, Joined Cases C–110/98—C–147/98 *Gabalfrisa and Others* [2000] E.C.R. I–1577, para.40, relating to the Spanish Tribunales Económico-Administrativos.

[204] The criterion of independence implies that the authority may be held to be a court or tribunal within the meaning of Art.234 of the EC Treaty only if it "acts as a third party" in relation to the authority which adopted the contested decision. This assumes that there are no organisational (*e.g.* in terms of its composition) or functional links which preclude this (ECJ, Case C–516/99 *Schmid* [2002] E.C.R. I–4573, paras 34–44). The criterion of independence likewise implies in principle that members of the court or tribunal must be able to be challenged and that there must be circumstances in which members of the body in question must withdraw (ECJ, Case C–103/97 *Köllensperger and Atzwanger* [1999] E.C.R. I–551, paras 19–25). For a survey of this case-law, see Oliver, "La recevabilité des questions préjudicielles: la jurisprudence des années 1990" (2001) C.D.E. 15–43, in particular at 16–24.

[205] ECJ, Case C–24/92 *Corbiau* [1993] E.C.R. I–1277, para.16.

his decision on appeal before a "third party", namely the "Chief Social Security Commissioner", who is entitled, as a "court or tribunal" to make a reference to the Court for a preliminary ruling (not that there has been any dispute or doubt about this).[206]

Administrative bodies. Bodies which act in an administrative capacity, but   2–010
not as a judicial authority, or only submit opinions to the public authorities with a view to their taking a decision are not entitled to refer questions for a preliminary ruling. Examples are bodies of professional organisations deciding on admission to a profession[207] or a consultative committee whose duty is to submit reasoned—but not binding—opinions to the Treasury Minister on the sanctions to be imposed by that minister on persons infringing national legislation relating to transfers of foreign exchange.[208] In

---

[206] ECJ, Case 150/85 *Drake* [1986] E.C.R. 1995. See, to the same effect, ECJ, Joined Cases C–74/95 and C–129/95 *X* [1996] E.C.R. I–6609, paras 17–20, in which the Court held that the Italian *Procura della Repubblica* could not be regarded as being a court or tribunal within the meaning of Art.234 of the EC Treaty on the ground that its role in the main proceedings in the case in question was not to rule on an issue in complete independence but, acting as prosecutor in the proceedings, to submit that issue, if appropriate, for consideration by the competent judicial body. By contrast, a judge in charge of preliminary inquiries in criminal proceedings acts in a judicial capacity, so that he must be regarded as a "court or tribunal of a Member State": ECJ, Joined Cases C–54/94 and C–74/94 *Cacchiarelli and Stanghellini* [1995] E.C.R. I–391 (with respect to Art.234 of the EC Treaty); ECJ, Case C–105/03 *Pupino* [2005] E.C.R. I–5285, para.22 (with respect to Art.35 of the EU Treaty).

[207] ECJ, Case 65/77 *Razanatsimba* [1977] E.C.R. 2229, para.5; ECJ (order of June 18, 1980), Case 138/80 *Borker* [1980] E.C.R. 1975, para.4. See also ECJ, Case C–178/99 *Salzmann* [2001] E.C.R. I–4421, paras 11-22, in which it was held that the Austrian *Bezirksgericht* [District Court] does not constitute a court or tribunal where, acting as an administrative body, it considers an application for registration of a contract of sale of land in the land register. This is because, in that capacity, it does not decide a dispute but merely checks that applications for registration of titles to property in the land register comply with the conditions laid down by law. ECJ, Case C–182/00 *Lutz and Others* [2002] E.C.R. I–547, paras 11–15: when ruling on obligations to disclose annual accounts and the annual report, the Austrian *Landesgericht* [Regional Court] does not decide any dispute and therefore does not constitute a court or tribunal within the meaning of Art.234 of the EC Treaty when acting in that capacity (see the Opinion of Advocate General L.A. Geelhoed to the same effect).

[208] ECJ (order of March 5, 1986), Case 318/85 *Greis Unterweger* [1986] E.C.R. 955, para.4. But see ECJ, Case 36/73 *Nederlandse Spoorwegen* [1973] E.C.R. 1299, together with ECJ, Joined Cases C–69-79/96 *Garofalo and Others* [1997] E.C.R. I–5603, paras 17–27, in which the Court held that where the Italian *Consiglio di Stato* issues an opinion in relation to an extraordinary petition made to the President of the Republic for annulment of an administrative act, it constitutes a court or tribunal within the meaning of Art.234 of the EC Treaty. The Swedish *Skatterättsnämnden* [Revenue Board], which may give a preliminary decision on matters of taxation upon application by a taxable person, is not a court or tribunal within the meaning of Art.234 of the EC Treaty. The Court held that that board essentially performs an administrative function on the ground that it does not have as its task to review the legality of the decisions of the tax authorities but rather to adopt a view on how a specific transaction is to be assessed to tax. It therefore acts in an administrative capacity and is not called upon to decide a dispute (ECJ, Case C–134/97 *Victoria Film* [1998] E.C.R. I–7023). In contrast, the *Regeringsrätten* [Swedish Supreme Administrative

both cases, there was the possibility of an appeal after the final administrative decision to a judicial body which could, if necessary, make a reference for a preliminary ruling. In addition, none of the bodies concerned could be regarded as a "third party", either because they took the first—*ex hypothesi* subsequently contested—decision themselves or because they were directly involved in taking that decision. Judicial bodies which also perform non-judicial functions are likewise not entitled to make a reference for a preliminary ruling in connection with that administrative activity.[209]

2–011   National competition authorities. The question arises as to whether national authorities responsible for settling disputes relating to the application of competition law (domestic as well as European) are entitled to refer questions for a preliminary ruling. Do the authorities in question give a ruling in like manner to a court in proceedings brought by the prosecuting party (the public department responsible for ensuring that competition law is complied with) against a defendant undertaking or do they instead take an administrative decision after a procedure in which the other party is entitled to give its views which they must subsequently defend before a court or tribunal to which the undertaking concerned has appealed?

The answer to this question depends on a prior analysis of the legal position of the authorities concerned in each Member State and hence is liable to differ from one Member State to another.[210] The Court gave a ruling, without any reservation, on the questions referred for a preliminary ruling by the Spanish *Tribunal de Defensa de la Competencia*, after Advocate General Jacobs had pointed out that whilst, administratively, the "Tribunal" formed part of the Ministry of Trade, it nevertheless fulfilled the *Vaassen* criteria (see 2–006, *supra*).[211] In addition, the applicant in the proceedings was the "*Dirección General de Defensa de la Competencia*" suing a number of banks, with the result that the "Tribunal" did in fact come across as a third party.

Court] does constitute a court or tribunal within the meaning of Art.234 of the EC Treaty when seised of an appeal against a ruling of the *Skatterättsnämnden* (see ECJ, Case C–200/98 *X and Y* [1999] E.C.R. I–8261, paras 13–17); ECJ (order of November 26, 1999), Case C–440/98 *RAI* [1999] E.C.R. I–8597, paras 14–15 (the *Corte dei Conti* [Italian Court of Auditors] does not perform a judicial function when it plays an administrative role consisting in the evaluation and verification of the results of administrative action).

[209] ECJ, Joined Cases C–110/98—C–147/98 *Gabalfrisa and Others* [2000] E.C.R. I–1577, para.33 (see Maublanc, "La définition de la juridiction fiscale et la déduction de la TVA devant la Cour de justice" (2001) R.M.U.E. 208–212); ECJ, Case C–178/99 *Salzmann* [2001] E.C.R. I–4421, paras 15–17; ECJ (order of March 18, 2004) Case C–45/03 *Oxana Dem' Yanenko*, not reported, paras 26–283.

[210] See Komninos, "Article 234 EC and national competition authorities in the era of decentralisation" (2004) E.L.Rev. 106–114.

[211] Opinion of Advocate General F.G. Jacobs in ECJ, Case C–67/91 *Asociación Espanola de Banca Privada and Others* [1992] E.C.R. I–4785, at I–4809.

Recently, in a case concerning a reference for a preliminary ruling made by the Greek competition authority—the *Epitropi Antagonismou*—the Court of Justice adopted a more restrictive approach. According to the Court, in so far as there is an operational link between the *Epitropi Antagonismou*, a decision-making body, and its secretariat, a fact-finding body on the basis of whose proposal it adopts decisions, the *Epitropi Antagonismou* is not a clearly distinct third party in relation to the State body which, by virtue of its role, may be akin to a party in the course of competition proceedings.[212] Moreover, the Court stressed the fact that a competition authority such as the *Epitropi Antagonismou* may, pursuant to Art.11(6) of Council Regulation 1/2003, be relieved of its competence by a decision of the Commission initiating its own proceedings. After having recalled its case-law according to which a body may refer a question to the Court only if that body is called upon to give judgment in proceedings intended to lead to a decision of a judicial nature,[213] the Court of Justice concluded that the *Epitropi Antagonismou* is not a court or tribunal within the meaning of Art.234 of the EC Treaty since whenever the Commission relieves a national competition authority such as the *Epitropi Antagonismou* of its competence, the proceedings initiated before that authority will not lead to a decision of a judicial nature.[214] The question was thus declared inadmissible on grounds which make the admissibility of future references of national competition authorities very doubtful.

Arbitrators. An arbitrator who does not fulfil *all* the *Vaassen* criteria **2–012** cannot be regarded as a "court or tribunal of a Member State" within the meaning of Art.234 of the EC Treaty despite the fact that "there are certain similarities between the activities of the arbitration tribunal in question and those of an ordinary court or tribunal in as much as the arbitration is provided for within the framework of the law, the arbitrator must decide according to law and his award has, as between the parties, the force of *res judicata*, and may be enforceable if leave to issue execution is obtained".[215] Those characteristics were not sufficient to give the arbitrator the status of a "court or tribunal of a Member State" because the parties to the contract were "free to leave their disputes to be resolved by the ordinary courts or to opt for arbitration by inserting a clause to that effect in the contract".[216] Consequently, the arbitrator did not act as the "proper judicial body" designated by law, with the result that at least that *Vaassen* criterion was

---

[212] ECJ, Case C–53/03 *Syfait and Others* [2005] E.C.R. I–4609, para.33.
[213] ECJ, Case C–134/97 *Victoria Film* [1998] E.C.R. I–7023, para.14; ECJ, Case C–195/98 *Österreichischer Gewerkschaftsbund* [2000] E.C.R. I–10497, para.25; ECJ, Case C–53/03 *Syfait and Others* [2005] E.C.R. I–4609, para.35.
[214] ECJ, Case C–53/03 *Syfait and Others* [2005] E.C.R. I–4609, paras 35–37.
[215] ECJ, Case 102/81 *Nordsee* [1982] E.C.R. 1095, para.10 (see the extensive case note by Hepting, "Art. 177*[now Art.234]* EWGV und die private Schiedsgerichtsbarkeit" (1982) EuR. 315–333).
[216] *Nordsee*, cited in the preceding n., para.11,

not fulfilled. The parties were indeed under "no obligation, whether in law or in fact, to refer their disputes to arbitration".[217] Moreover, the Member State in which the arbitrator operated was not involved in the decision to opt for arbitration and was not called upon to intervene of its own motion in the proceedings before the arbitrator.[218] If questions of Community law arise in an arbitration resorted to by agreement, the Court reckons on the "ordinary courts" examining the issues and, where necessary, requesting a preliminary ruling. The ordinary courts will have an opportunity to do so "in the context of their collaboration" with arbitration tribunals, "in particular in order to assist them in certain procedural matters or to interpret the law applicable", or when they are called upon to conduct a "review of an arbitration award" in the case of "an appeal or objection, in proceedings for leave to issue execution or by any other method of recourse available under the relevant national legislation".[219]

In this context, it makes no difference that, in reviewing the arbitration award, the ordinary court has, pursuant to the arbitration agreement concluded between the parties, to rule *ex aequo et bono*: "It follows from the principles of the primacy of Community law and of its uniform application, in conjunction with Art.5*[now Art.10]* of the Treaty, that a court of a Member State to which an appeal against an arbitration award is made pursuant to national law must, even where it gives judgment having regard to fairness, observe the rules of Community law . . .".[220]

The Court of Justice likewise recognises that the review of arbitration awards is limited in scope and that annulment of or refusal to recognise an award is possible only in exceptional circumstances. However, the limited nature of that review may not preclude reviewing the award in the light of fundamental provisions of Community law, such as Art.81 of the EC Treaty, which prohibits agreements and concerted practices in restraint of competition.[221]

By declining jurisdiction to answer questions referred for a preliminary ruling by arbitrators, the Court sought to prevent contracting parties from creating "courts and tribunals" *of their own* and subsequently inducing (obliging) them to seek preliminary rulings. Indeed, Art.234 of the EC

---

[217] *Ibid.*, para.11; ECJ, Case C–125/04 *Denuit and Cordenier* [2005] E.C.R. I–923, para.13.

[218] This consideration was perhaps intended to distinguish the *Broekmeulen* situation (*ibid.*, para.12); *cf.* n.200, *supra*, and accompanying text. See also ECJ, Case 102/81 *Nordsee* [1982] E.C.R. 1095, para 11; ECJ, Case C–125/04 *Denuit and Cordenier* [2005] E.C.R. I–923, para.13.

[219] *Ibid.*, para.14. Where a point of Community law is raised before an arbitrator and leave to appeal is sought against the award, an English judge will normally grant leave to appeal where the point is "capable of serious argument": *Bulk Oil (Zug) AG v Sun International Ltd and Sun Oil Trading Co.* [1984] 1 W.L.R. 147, at 154–155F, *per* Ackner LJ.

[220] ECJ, Case C–393/92 *Almelo* [1994] E.C.R. I–1477, para.23.

[221] ECJ, Case C–126/97 *Eco Swiss China Time* [1999] E.C.R. I–3055, paras 33–40. This requirement is, however, subject to the proviso that it is not excessively difficult or impossible in practice for the national court to review the arbitration award in the light of the relevant provision of Community law. See also 3–035 and 3–036, *infra*.

Treaty is intended to bring about a dialogue between courts in the Member States and the Court of Justice. National courts which have the monopoly right to seek preliminary rulings submit to the Court for preliminary rulings only questions which are genuinely necessary in order to deliver a judgment with the authority of *res judicata*. In the Court's view, this mechanism would be endangered if parties to a contract could circumvent it by setting up an arbitration board whose organisation is in no way based on action on the part of the public authorities and which is not regarded as the obligatory legal authority for dealing with a particular class of disputes. Where there is a "sufficiently close connection" between the arbitration and the general system of legal protection in the Member State concerned, the "arbitrator" is deemed to be "a court or tribunal of a Member State" within the meaning of Art.234 of the EC Treaty (as in the case of the "arbitration tribunal" in the *Vaassen* case).[222]

Courts of a Member State. The court or tribunal must be "of a Member State". Although this is generally obvious, it should be noted that the following courts qualify as such: courts and tribunals established in the Member States[223]; in the "French overseas departments"[224]; in the "overseas countries and territories" listed in Annex II to the Treaty to which the special association arrangements set out in Part Four of the Treaty apply[225]; the "European territories for whose external relations a Member State is responsible"[226] and the Åland Islands[227] to which the Treaty applies; and

2–013

---

[222] ECJ, Case 109/88 *Handels- og Kontorfunktionærernes Forbund i Danemark* [1989] E.C.R. 3199, paras 7–9. See also Behr, "Arbitration Tribunals and Art.177*[now Art.234]* of the EEC Treaty" (1985) C.M.L.Rev. 489–504. For a critical commentary, see Kornblum, "Private Schiedsgerichte und Art.177*[now Art.234]* EWGV", in *Jahrbuch für die Praxis der Schiedsgerichtsbarkeit* (Verlag Recht und Wirtschaft GmbH, Heidelberg, 1988), at 102–110. See, however, Storm, "Quod licet iovi. The Precarious Relationship between the Court of Justice of the European Communities and Arbitration", in *Essays on International and Comparative Law in Honour of Judge Erades* (T.M.C. Asser Institute, The Hague, 1983), at 144–177, who approves of the Court's case-law on practical grounds.

[223] EC Treaty, Art.299(1). In England and Wales, references may be made, *e.g.* by magistrates' courts, the Crown Court, the High Court, the Court of Appeal, the House of Lords and specialist courts such as the Patent Court. The Social Security Commissioner, income tax commissioners, industrial tribunals, the Employment Appeal Tribunal and the VAT Tribunal have also made successful requests for preliminary rulings.

[224] EC Treaty, Art.299(2).

[225] EC Treaty, Art.299(3); for applications, see ECJ, Joined Cases C–100/89 and C–101/89 *Kaefer and Procacci* [1990] E.C.R. I–4647 and ECJ, Case C–260/90 *Leplat* [1992] E.C.R. I–643, in which the *Tribunal Administratif* and the *Tribunal de Paix*, respectively, of Papeete in French Polynesia, were held to be courts or tribunals "of a Member State". For the Netherlands Antilles and Aruba, see Mischo, "The Competence of the Judiciary of the Netherlands Antilles and Aruba to request Preliminary Rulings from the Court of Justice of the European Communities", in *Met het oog op Europa* (Stichting Tijdschrift voor Antilliaans Recht-Justicia, Curaçao, 1991), at 140–145.

[226] EC Treaty, Art.299(4); in practice, only Gibraltar.

[227] EC Treaty, Art.299(5). The Treaty applies in accordance with the provisions set out in Protocol 2 to the Act concerning the conditions of accession of the Republic of Austria, the Republic of Finland and the Kingdom of Sweden.

lastly "the Channel Islands and the Isle of Man"[228] in so far as courts and tribunals established there refer to the Court questions concerning the interpretation of "Protocol No 3",[229] the interpretation and validity of the Community legislation to which that Protocol refers, and the interpretation and validity of measures adopted by the Community institutions on the basis of Protocol No 3.

2–014 **International courts.** International courts, such as the International Court of Justice or the European Court of Human Rights, are not entitled to refer questions to the Court of Justice for a preliminary ruling, even though this might have been useful in some cases.[230] The position is different in the case of the Benelux Court of Justice. That court has the task of ensuring that the legal rules common to the three Benelux States are applied uniformly. The procedure before it is a step in the proceedings before the national courts leading to definitive interpretations of common Benelux legal rules. For those reasons, the Benelux Court of Justice is entitled— and, as a court against whose decisions there is no judicial remedy under national law, may be under a duty (see 2–041, *infra*)—to refer a question to the Court of Justice in Luxembourg for a preliminary ruling where it is faced with the task of interpreting Community rules in the performance of its function.[231]

2–015 **Third countries' courts.** Of course, courts and tribunals established in non-member countries do not come under Art.234 of the EC Treaty. In the event that it is nevertheless intended to confer on such courts and tribunals to a certain extent the right to refer questions for a preliminary ruling, that

---

[228] EC Treaty, Art.299(6)(c).
[229] Protocol No 3 constitutes the "arrangements for those islands set out" in the Accession Treaty signed on January 22, 1972. See ECJ, Case C–355/89 *Barr and Montrose Holdings* [1991] E.C.R. I–3479, paras 6–10; ECJ, Case C–171/96 *Pereira Roque* [1998] E.C.R. I–4607 and the Opinion of Advocate General A. La Pergola in that case at I–4610; Arnull, "The Evolution of the Court's Jurisdiction under Art.177*[now Art.234]* EEC" (1993) E.L.Rev. 129, at 132–133.
[230] *Cf.* Schermers and Waelbroeck, *Judicial Protection in the European Union* (6th ed., Kluwer, Deventer, 2001) § 531, at 258–259.
[231] ECJ, Case C–337/95 *Parfums Christian Dior* [1997] E.C.R. I–6013, paras 19–23. It would be hard to argue that proceedings brought against a Member State in the European Court of Human Rights constitute "a step in the proceedings" before a national court. Proceedings before the European Court of Human Rights do not fall within any national proceedings and hence the reasoning employed by the Court of Justice in the *Christian Dior* case in order to hold that the Benelux Court of Justice constitutes a court or tribunal within the meaning of Art.234 of the EC Treaty cannot be used so as to allow the European Court of Human Rights to make a reference for a preliminary ruling to the Court of Justice.

right must be enshrined in an international agreement concluded between the Community and the non-member countries concerned. An example is the EEA Agreement, which authorises courts and tribunals of EFTA States to refer questions to the Court of Justice on the interpretation of an EEA rule.[232]

B. Types of Proceedings in Which a Preliminary Ruling May Be Requested

Dispute must be pending before national court. The Court has no jurisdiction to entertain a request for a preliminary ruling when at the time when it is made the procedure before the court making it has already been terminated.[233] Art.234 of the EC Treaty in fact restricts the right to make a reference to a court or tribunal which considers that the preliminary ruling requested is necessary to enable *it* to give judgment.[234] A national court is empowered to bring a matter before the Court by way of reference for a preliminary ruling only if a dispute is pending before it in the context of which it is called upon to give a decision capable of taking into account the preliminary ruling.[235] The preliminary ruling must actually be intended to make a contribution to the decision which the referring court is to take. 2–016

Since this is a question of securing the very essence of the preliminary ruling procedure, the Court does not shrink from going back to seek further information about the course of the procedure before the referring court with a view to ascertaining whether the proceedings were still pending before that court at the time when the request for a ruling was made. In *Pardini* the Court held—contrary to its first impressions—that, in view of the explanations which it had obtained, it had to be assumed that "the interlocutory proceedings which gave rise to the reference to the Court must be regarded as still pending before the *Pretore* [Magistrate], who may take account of the preliminary ruling for the purposes of his own decision confirming, varying or discharging his original order".[236]

---

[232] EEA Agreement, Art.107 ([1994] O.J. L 1/26) and Protocol 34 annexed to the EEA Agreement on the possibility for courts and tribunals of EFTA States to request the Court of Justice of the European Communities to decide on the interpretation of EEA rules corresponding to EC rules ([1994] O.J. L 1/204); Arnull (n.229, *supra*), at 134. See also Lenaerts and Van Nuffel, *Constitutional Law of the European Union*, § 23–017, at 918–919.

[233] ECJ, Case 338/85 *Pardini* [1988] E.C.R. 2041, para.11, second sentence; ECJ, Case C–159/90 *Society for the Protection of Unborn Children Ireland* [1991] E.C.R. I–4685, para.12. Once an English court has given judgment and its order has been drawn up, it is *functus officio* and may no longer make a reference: *SA Magnavision v General Optical Council (No 2)* [1987] 2 C.M.L.R. 262, paras 14–16, *per* Wilkins LJ; *Chiron Corp. v Murex Diagnostics Ltd* [1995] All E.R. (EC) 88, at 92g–93e (per Balcombe LJ).

[234] *Pardini*, cited in the preceding n., para.10.

[235] *Ibid.*, para.11, first sentence. Accordingly, hypothetical questions are inadmissible: see, *e.g.* ECJ, Case C–315/02 *Lenz* [2004] E.C.R. I–7063, paras 52–54.

[236] *Pardini*, para.14.

2–017   **Types of proceedings.** All sorts of proceedings may give rise to a preliminary ruling: matters of civil law, criminal law,[237] commercial and economic law, social law, revenue law, constitutional[238] and administrative law, and so on. Neither the substantive law at issue nor the type of proceedings has any bearing. Questions may be referred by an examining magistrate[239] and in interlocutory proceedings.[240] Even *ex parte* proceedings, at which the other party is not represented, may result in a reference for a preliminary ruling if the body making the reference is exercising the functions of a court or tribunal.[241] Furthermore, it does not matter if the body making the reference performs other functions in addition to its functions as a court or tribunal. Accordingly, the Court held that "the *Pretori* [Italian magistrates] are judges who, in proceedings such as those in which the questions referred . . . were raised, combine the functions of a public prosecutor and an examining magistrate". Yet it declared that it had jurisdiction to reply to the questions referred since the request emanated from "a court or tribunal which has acted in the general framework of its task of judging, independently and in accordance with the law, cases coming within the jurisdiction conferred on it by law, even though certain functions of that court or tribunal in the proceedings which gave rise to the reference for a preliminary ruling are not, strictly speaking, of a judicial nature".[242]

However, if in given proceedings the national court simply acts as an administrative authority and performs a non-judicial function, the Court of Justice considers that it has no jurisdiction to rule on questions referred for a preliminary ruling in the proceedings in question.[243]

---

[237] A request for a preliminary ruling arising in the context of an inquiry in criminal proceedings which could result in an order that no further action be taken, a summons to appear, or an acquittal is admissible (ECJ, Case 14/86 *Pretore di Salò v X* [1987] E.C.R. 2545, paras 10 and 11; ECJ, Case C–60/02 *X* [2004] E.C.R. I–651, para.25).

[238] ECJ, Case C–93/97 *Fédération Belge des Chambres Syndicales de Médecins* [1998] E.C.R. I–4837, in which the *Cour d'Arbitrage*, the Belgian Constitutional Court, made a reference for a preliminary ruling. For the judgment of the *Cour d'Arbitrage* of February 19, 1997, see (1997) J.T. 430, with a case note by Delgrange and van Ypersele.

[239] ECJ, Case 65/79 *Chatain* [1980] E.C.R. 1345, para.1.

[240] ECJ, Case 29/69 *Stauder* [1969] E.C.R. 419, at 424; ECJ, Case 107/76 *Hoffmann-La Roche* [1977] E.C.R. 957, para.4; ECJ, Case C–176/96 *Lehtonen and Castors Braine* [2000] E.C.R. I–2681; ECJ, Case C–60/02 *X* [2004] E.C.R. I–651, para.26 (a preliminary question raised in proceedings concerning interim measures is admissible notwithstanding the fact that the measures may be confirmed, varied or revoked). See in addition, Korte, "Prejudiciële verwijzingen (art.177 EEC *[now Art.234])* in het kader van kort geding procedures door Nederlandse rechters (art.289–297 Rv.)" (1990) S.E.W. 103–118.

[241] For examples, see the Italian proceedings for a court order in ECJ, Case 70/77 *Simmenthal* [1978] E.C.R. 1453, paras 4–11; ECJ, Case C–18/93 *Corsica Ferries* [1994] E.C.R. I–1783, para.12, and the cases referred to therein, and the proceedings for the protective sequestration of assets in ECJ, Case 23/75 *Rey Soda* [1975] E.C.R. 1279.

[242] ECJ, Case 14/86 *Pretore di Salò v X* [1987] E.C.R. 2545, para.7; ECJ (order of January 15, 2004), Case C–235/02 *Saetti* [2004] E.C.R. I–1005, para.23 (a judge investigating a criminal matter or an investigating magistrate may make a reference for a preliminary ruling).

[243] ECJ, Case C–111/94 *Job Centre* [1995] E.C.R. I–3361, paras 8–11; *cf.* the Opinion of Advocate General M.B. Elmer. In contrast, a preliminary question raised by a national

Issues concerning jurisdiction. Questions of jurisdiction which are apt to arise before national courts in connection with the classification of legal situations based on Community law cannot be determined by the Court of Justice. This is because it is for the legal system of each Member State to determine which court has jurisdiction to hear disputes involving individual rights derived from Community law.[244] In such circumstances, a national court may make a reference for a preliminary ruling to the Court of Justice with a view to obtaining an explanation of points of Community law which may help to solve the problem of jurisdiction.[245]

2–018

C. TIME AND CONTENT OF A REQUEST FOR A PRELIMINARY RULING

Initiative. From the wording of Art.234 of the EC Treaty it merely appears that only the national court is entitled to apply to the Court of Justice for a preliminary ruling.[246] Parties to the main proceedings, including the public prosecutor, cannot compel the national court to make a reference.[247] The national court has the right to refer questions of its own motion,[248] a right which Community law confers on *every* "court or tribunal of a Member State" within the meaning of Art.234 of the EC Treaty. National (procedural) law cannot detract from this. Accordingly, the Court has held that "the existence of a rule of domestic law whereby a court is bound on points of law by the rulings of the court superior to it cannot of itself take away the power provided for by Art.177*[now Art.234]* of referring cases to the Court",[249] especially "if it considers that the ruling on law made by the

2–019

---

court in proceedings brought for judicial review of a decision made in such non-contentious proceedings will be admissible (*ibid.*, para.11; ECJ, Case C–55/96 *Job Centre* [1997] E.C.R. I–7119; see also ECJ, Case 32/74 *Haaga* [1974] E.C.R. 1201, para.2).

[244] It is not for the Court to determine whether the decision whereby a matter is brought before it was taken in conformity with the rules of domestic law governing the organisation of the courts and their procedure. The position is the same where international jurisdiction falls to be determined on the basis of the Brussels Convention, unless the provisions of that Convention are expressly made the subject of the reference for a preliminary ruling: ECJ, Case C–105/94 *Celestini* [1997] E.C.R. I–2971, para.20; ECJ (judgment of December 1, 2005), Case C–213/04 *Burtscher*, not yet reported, para.31.

[245] ECJ, Case 179/84 *Bozzetti v Invernizzi* [1985] E.C.R. 2301, para.17; ECJ, Case C–446/93 *SEIM* [1996] E.C.R. I–73, paras 32–33; ECJ, Joined Cases C–10/97—C–22/97 *IN.CO.GE.'90 and Others* [1998] E.C.R. I–6307, paras 14–17.

[246] ECJ, Joined Cases 31 and 33/62 *Wöhrmann and Others v Commission* [1962] E.C.R. 501. See *Portsmouth City Council v Richards and Quietlynn* [1989] 1 C.M.L.R. 673, at 708, where Kerr LJ stated that ". . . references by consent should not creep into our practice. All references must be by the court. The court itself must be satisfied of the need for a reference . . .". Nevertheless, it is the practice in the English courts for the parties to draft the questions for approval by the national court, but the necessity for a reference is for the court to determine.

[247] ECJ, Case 93/78 *Mattheus* [1978] E.C.R. 2203, paras 4–6.

[248] ECJ, Case 166/73 *Rheinmühlen–Düsseldorf* [1974] E.C.R. 33, para.3; ECJ, Case 126/80 *Salonia* [1981] E.C.R. 1563, para.7; ECJ, Case 283/81 *CILFIT* [1982] E.C.R. 3415, para.9; ECJ, Case C–261/95 *Palmisani* [1997] E.C.R. I–4025, para.20. For England and Wales, see Civil Procedure Rules, R.68.2(1): an order for reference may be made by the court of its own initiative at any stage of the proceedings.

[249] *Rheinmühlen-Düsseldorf*, cited in the preceding n., para.5.

superior court could lead it to give a judgment contrary to Community law".[250]

2-020 **Content determined by national court.** It is for the national court to determine the content of the preliminary questions.[251] Of course, the parties to the main proceedings are at liberty to make proposals, but it is the judge alone who determines whether he or she accepts them wholly or in part or completely deviates from them. The Court does not allow parties to the main proceedings to seek to extend the request for a preliminary ruling to cover questions which they suggested to the national court, but it did not wish to ask.[252] It is immaterial in this connection that the Commission or one or more Member States support parties in their attempt to alter the subject-matter of the preliminary ruling procedure. The Court will not go against the referring court's (express or implicit) refusal to refer a particular question because that court "alone is competent under the system established by Art.177*[now Art.234]* to assess the relevance of questions concerning the interpretation of Community law in order to resolve the dispute before it".[253]

2-021 **Court of Justice may reformulate questions.** This does not mean that the Court will shrink from giving a more precise definition of the subject-matter of the reference for a preliminary ruling or even from altering it where this appears necessary in order to obtain a helpful answer, namely an answer which the national court can use.[254] But the adjustment of the

---

[250] *Ibid.*, para.4.
[251] The questions referred for a preliminary ruling are considered within the factual and legal context as set out by the referring court. The Court of Justice does not take account of observations from interested parties within the meaning of Art.23 of the Statute of the Court of Justice which take issue with that context (ECJ, Case C–153/02 *Neri* [2003] E.C.R. I–13555, paras 33–36; see also ECJ, Case C–145/03 *Keller* [2005] E.C.R. I–2529, paras 32–34). But see ECJ, Case C–88/99 *Roquette Frères* [2000] E.C.R. I–10465, paras 18–19 and note 254 *infra*.
[252] ECJ, Case 247/86 *Alsatel* [1988] E.C.R. 5987, para.8; *Palmisani*, cited in n.248, para.31; ECJ, Case C–402/98 *ATB and Others* [2000] E.C.R. I–5501, para.29; ECJ, Case C–236/02 *Slob* [2004] E.C.R. I–1861, paras 29–30.
[253] *Alsatel*, cited in the preceding n., para.8.
[254] Bergerès, "La reformulation des questions préjudicielles en interprétation par la Cour de justice des Communautés européennes" (1985) Rec. Dalloz, Chronique 155–162. In the *Marks & Spencer* case, the Court stated that its task is to provide the referring court with an answer which will be of use to it and enable it to determine the case before it and that "to that end, the Court may have to reformulate the question referred to it" (ECJ, Case C–62/00 *Marks & Spencer* [2002] E.C.R. I–6325, para.32). See also ECJ, Case C–88/99 *Roquette Frères* [2000] E.C.R. I–10465, paras 18–19, where the Court of Justice reformulated the question referred to it because it appeared from the observations submitted to the Court that the interpretation given by the referring judge to the rule of national law at issue in the proceedings did not accord with the case-law of the highest court in the Member State concerned; see also ECJ, Case C–87/97 *Consorzio per la Tutela del Formaggio Gorgonzola* [1999] E.C.R. I–1301, para.16; ECJ (order of March 18, 2004), Case C–45/03 *Dem' Yanenko*, not reported, para.37; ECJ, Case C–387/01 *Weigel* [2004] E.C.R. I–4981,

questions referred must always be consonant with the actual objective of the referring court, which precludes any change running contrary to that court's intention. In a case in which the national court had not formulated *any* question, but had simply referred the parties to the Court, the Court itself defined the question of interpretation of Community law which had in fact arisen on the basis of the order for reference and the case-file directed to the Court through the registry.[255]

Furthermore, the Court has not drawn the demarcation line over strictly between interpretation of Community law and assessing the validity of acts of the institutions.[256] Questions which ostensibly relate to the interpretation of Community law, but, having regard to the whole content of the order for reference, rather probe the validity of a Community measure, are also answered as such.[257] Accordingly, the Court has gone so far as to expand a question of interpretation to cover the validity of a Commission decision which was not mentioned in the national court's order for reference and of which the national court was probably unaware. The Court nevertheless held that the requirement for a "useful" answer warranted its raising and answering the question of the validity of the decision in question. The Court also invoked reasons of procedural economy in so far as the question

---

para.44, in which the Court of Justice held that the national court can be provided with all those elements for the interpretation of Community law which may be of assistance in adjudicating on the case pending before it, whether or not that court has specifically referred to them in its questions. The Court of Justice can therefore take account of provisions of Community law not mentioned by the national court in formulating its questions. See also ECJ, Case C–271/01 *COPPI* [2004] E.C.R. I–1029, para.27; ECJ, Case C–456/02 *Trojani* [2004] E.C.R. I–7573, paras 38–40; ECJ, Case C–452/03 *RAL and Others* [2005] E.C.R. I–3947, para.25.

[255] ECJ, Case 101/63 *Wagner* [1964] E.C.R. 195, at 199–200. In this way, the Court has declared that "it is for the Court alone, where questions are formulated imprecisely, to extract from all the information provided by the national court and from the documents in the main proceedings the points of Community law which require interpretation, having regard to the subject-matter of those proceedings (ECJ, Case C–107/98 *Teckal* [1999] E.C.R. I–8121, para.34). See to the same effect ECJ, Case C–425/98 *Marca Mode* [2000] E.C.R. I–4861, para.21; ECJ, Joined Cases C–223/99 and C–260/99 *Agorà and Excelsior* [2001] E.C.R. I–3605, para.24. Furthermore, it is possible that the Court of Justice will examine of its own motion a question of interpretation (not raised by the national court) "in the context of the close cooperation which it is required to establish with national courts" (ECJ, Case C–295/97 *Piaggio* [1999] E.C.R. I–3735, para.25). The Court may sometimes also make supplementary "observations" with regard to questions of Community law not raised by the national court in its preliminary question to which parties have drawn attention in their observations (see, *e.g.* ECJ, Case C–131/97 *Carbonari and Others* [1999] E.C.R. I–1103, para.52 *et seq.*); but see ECJ (order of December 21, 1995), Case C–307/95 *Max Mara* [1995] E.C.R. I–5083, paras 5–10, in which the Court found that the order for reference did not contain specific questions addressed to the Court and that it did not allow the questions on which the national court wished the Court to give a preliminary ruling to be discerned. The national court's order also did not contain enough information to permit the Court to give a useful interpretation. Accordingly, the Court held that the national court's request was manifestly inadmissible.

[256] For a critical appraisal, see the Opinion of Advocate General D. Ruiz-Jarabo Colomer in ECJ, Case C–30/02 *Recheio* [2004] E.C.R. I–6053, points 23–36.

[257] ECJ, Case 16/65 *Schwarze* [1965] E.C.R. 877, at 886–887.

of the validity of the Commission decision in question had already been raised in an action for annulment brought by the Netherlands in relation to which proceedings had been suspended pending the Court's judgment in the preliminary ruling proceedings.[258]

The opposite situation may also arise. That is to say, the Court may consider whether the question of validity is based on a correct interpretation of the Community act at issue. It may then find—after interpreting the act in question—that it is no longer necessary to inquire into its validity inasmuch as the argument that superior Community law has been breached is founded upon a different interpretation of the relevant Community act. If it so finds, the Court will also not go into the consequences which would have ensued from a finding that the act was invalid.[259]

However, in the event that the questions referred for a preliminary ruling are concerned with the validity of an individual decision against which no action for annulment has been brought, the Court of Justice will refuse to alter the substance of the questions referred in so far as the validity of the contested decision can no longer be called in question (see 10–008, infra). In those circumstances, to alter the substance of the questions referred would be incompatible with the Court's function under Art.234 of the EC Treaty and with its duty to ensure that the governments of the Member States and parties concerned are given the opportunity to submit observations under Art.23 of the Statute of the Court of Justice, bearing in mind that only the order for reference is notified to interested parties.[260] In the light of the order for reference, they may therefore confine their observations to the validity of the contested decision by arguing solely that the questions raised no longer require an answer. To amend the scope of the order for reference would infringe the right conferred on them by Art.23 of the Statute.

The Court does not hesitate to supplement the provisions of Community law of which the national courts seek an interpretation by provisions—as revealed by the national court in the order for reference—which it regards as relevant in the context of the main proceedings.[261] This is because it is

---

258 ECJ, Case C–61/98 *De Haan Beheer* [1999] E.C.R. I–5003. See also ECJ, Case C–383/98 *Polo / Lauren* [2000] E.C.R. I–2519, para.23, in which the Court held that the question of interpretation also called the validity of the act of the Community institution in question and therefore ruled on its validity as well as on the question of interpretation.

259 ECJ, Case C–334/95 *Krüger* [1997] E.C.R. I–4517, paras 21 and 35.

260 ECJ, Case C–188/92 *TWD Textilwerke Deggendorf* [1994] E.C.R. I–833; ECJ, Case C–178/95 *Wiljo* [1997] E.C.R. I–585, para.30, and the Opinion of Advocate General F.G. Jacobs to the same effect; ECJ, Case C–239/99 *Nachi Europe* [2001] E.C.R. I–1197, paras 28–40; ECJ, Case C–241/01 *National Farmers' Union* [2002] E.C.R. I–9079, para.34. See for a critical analysis, Barav, "Déviation préjudicielle", in *Études en l'honneur de Jean-Claude Gautron, Les dynamiques du droit européen en début de siècle* (Éditions A. Pedone, Paris, 2004), at 227–247.

261 ECJ, Case 12/82 *Ministère Public v Trinon* [1982] E.C.R. 4089, para.5; ECJ, Case C–241/89 *SARPP* [1990] E.C.R. I–4695, para.8; ECJ, Case C–315/92 *Clinique Laboratoires and Estée*

the Court's duty to interpret all provisions of Community law which national courts need in order to decide the actions pending before them.[262] By the same token, the Court may even replace[263] or supplement[264] the provisions indicated by the national court in its preliminary question by those provisions of Community law which are actually relevant. The Court even referred to the relevant provision of the ECSC Treaty or the Euratom Treaty when it found that those Treaties were applicable in the main proceedings and not the EC Treaty to which the national court referred in its preliminary question.[265] This can be explained in terms of the Court's concern for efficient collaboration with the national courts, whilst leaving the initiative to seek a preliminary ruling with the national courts.

Timing. The decision at which stage a reference should be made for a preliminary ruling pursuant to Art.234 is dictated by considerations of procedural economy and efficiency to be weighed by the national court alone and not the Court of Justice.[266] The national court is "in the best position to appreciate at which stage of the proceedings it requires a preliminary ruling from the Court of Justice".[267] Nevertheless, the national court does not have unlimited latitude in this respect. It is only "in the best position" to appreciate the stage at which a reference should be made. In principle, the Court of Justice goes along with its assessment, unless it is manifestly premature. This will be clear from the content of the order for reference. If the national court has not yet sufficiently ascertained the

2–022

Lauder Cosmetics [1994] E.C.R. I–317, para.7; ECJ, Case C–87/97 *Consorzio per la Tutela del Formaggio Gorgonzola* [1999] E.C.R. I–1301, para.16. But see ECJ, Case C–124/97 *Läärä and Others* [1999] E.C.R. I–6067, para.23: in its preliminary questions the national court referred not only to specific Treaty provisions but also to "any other article of the EC Treaty" without providing any further details in that regard, either in the reasoning or in the operative part of its order. The Court was unable to rule on the question whether any provisions of the Treaty other than those specifically named precluded national legislation of the type at issue in the main proceedings.

[262] ECJ, Case C–280/91 *Viessmann* [1993] E.C.R. I–971, para.17; ECJ, Case C–42/96 *Società Immobiliare SIF* [1997] E.C.R. I–7089, para.28; ECJ, Joined Cases C–228/01 and C–289/01 *Bourrasse and Perchicot* [2002] E.C.R. I–10213, para.33 (and the case-law cited therein), in which the Court stated that, in order to provide a satisfactory answer to the national court which has referred a question to it, it may deem it necessary to consider provisions of Community law to which the national court has not referred in its question. See also ECJ, Case C–304/00 *Strawson and Gagg & Sons* [2002] E.C.R. I–10737, para.58; ECJ, Case C–456/02 *Trojani* [2004] E.C.R. I–7573, paras 38–40.

[263] ECJ, Case 294/82 *Einberger* [1984] E.C.R. 1177, para.6; ECJ, Case C–187/91 *Société Coopérative Belovo* [1992] E.C.R. I–4937, para.13.

[264] ECJ, Case C–190/00 *Balguerie and Others* [2001] E.C.R. I–3437, para.22.

[265] ECJ, Case C–200/97 *Ecotrade* [1998] E.C.R. I–7907, paras 29–30.

[266] ECJ, Case 14/86 *Pretore di Salò v X* [1987] E.C.R. 2545, para.11.

[267] *Ibid.*, para.11; see also an earlier case: ECJ, Case 43/71 *Politi* [1971] E.C.R. 1039, para.5, and also ECJ, Case C–176/96 *Lehtonen and Castors Braine* [2000] E.C.R. I–2681, paras 19–20. Accordingly, the choice of the most appropriate time to refer a question to the Court for a preliminary ruling lies within the exclusive jurisdiction of the national court (ECJ, Case C–60/02 *X* [2004] E.C.R. I–651, para.28). See Civil Procedure Rules, R.68.2(1): an order for reference may be made at any stage of the proceedings.

factual and legal context of the case and therefore does not say anything about it in the order for reference, it leaves the Court uncertain about the way in which the preliminary ruling sought is intended to help resolve the main action pending before the national court. In those circumstances, there is a great risk that the Court will not reach a "helpful" determination. The upshot would be that the preliminary ruling would be ignored as a purely hypothetical "opinion" and the collaboration between the national court and the Court of Justice would not achieve its aim.[268]

In order to avoid this the Court has gradually stepped up its requirements with regard to the content of the order for reference. As will become clear later, in order to satisfy those requirements the national court should make a request for a preliminary ruling to the Court only if it has determined the facts and non-Community aspects of the case to such an extent that it can indicate precisely how the preliminary ruling sought is to be applied. This inevitably restricts the national court's latitude to choose the stage at which the request for a preliminary ruling is made.

2–023 **Requirements for a reference.** What requirements are imposed as regards the content of the order for reference? In the 1979 judgment in *Union Laitière Normande*, the Court held in the first place that "the need to afford a helpful interpretation of Community law makes it essential to define the legal context in which the interpretation requested should be placed".[269] Although in that case the national court had not stated why it sought an interpretation of Community law, the reasons for the questions referred were sufficiently clear from the case-file submitted to the Court and it consequently appeared that a "helpful interpretation of Community law" was possible and that the Court could give a ruling.

Two years later, in the 1981 *Irish Creamery Milk Suppliers Association* case, the Court enlarged upon that basic requirement: "From that aspect it might be *convenient*, in certain circumstances, for the facts in the case to be established and for questions of purely national law to be settled at the time the reference is made to the Court of Justice so as to enable the latter to take cognisance of all the features of fact and of law which may be relevant to the interpretation of Community law which it is called upon to give".[270] This sounded like encouragement to formulate the order for reference in concrete terms, yet without taking away the national court's discretion to determine at what stage in the main proceedings it needed a preliminary ruling from the Court of Justice.[271] Plainly this is a compromise: the national court was given good advice in quite strong terms, but, at the same time, failure to follow it did not make the request for a preliminary ruling

---

[268] See, *e.g.* ECJ, Case C–380/01 *Schneider* [2004] E.C.R. I–1389, paras 20–31.
[269] ECJ, Case 244/78 *Union Laitière Normande* [1979] E.C.R. 2663, para.5.
[270] ECJ, Joined Cases 36 and 71/80 *Irish Creamery Milk Suppliers Association* [1981] E.C.R. 735, para.6 (emphasis added).
[271] *Ibid.*, paras 7–9.

inadmissible. Where the Court of Justice could fill the gaps in the order for reference by using information gleaned from the national court's case-file or adduced in the proceedings before the Court, it was still generally prepared to answer the questions referred on that basis. Nonetheless, the Court has intimated that it is not entirely happy about this on account of the risk that the quality of judicial debate will suffer if it is based on insufficiently informative orders for reference. Indeed, "the information furnished in the decisions making the references does not serve only to enable the Court to give helpful answers but also to enable the Governments of the Member States and other interested parties to submit observations in accordance with Art.20 [now Art.23] of the Statute of the Court . . . It is the Court's duty to ensure that the opportunity to submit observations is safeguarded, in view of the fact that, by virtue of the above-mentioned provision, only the decisions making the references are notified to the interested parties".[272]

Inadmissibility of a reference. In the 1993 judgment in *Telemarsicabruzzo*,   2–024
the Court converted the good advice to national courts into a genuine requirement which, if not complied with, will cause the preliminary reference to be inadmissible.[273] The Court held that the need to provide an interpretation of Community law which would be of use to the national court made it necessary that the national court define the factual and legislative context of the questions it was asking or, at the very least, explain the factual circumstances on which those questions were based.[274] In fact, to

---

[272] ECJ, Joined Cases 141-143/81 *Holdijk* [1982] E.C.R. 1299, para.6; ECJ (order of March 20, 1996), Case C–2/96 *Sunino and Data* [1996] E.C.R. I–1543, para.5; ECJ (order of June 25, 1996), Case C–101/96 *Italia Testa* [1996] E.C.R. I–3081, para.5; ECJ (order of July 19, 1996), Case C–191/96 *Modesti* [1996] E.C.R. I–3937, para.5; ECJ (order of July 19, 1996), Case C–196/96 *Lahlou* [1996] E.C.R. I–3945, para.5; ECJ, Case C–207/01 *Altair Chimica* [2003] E.C.R. I–8875, para.25; ECJ, Case C–145/03 *Keller* [2005] E.C.R. I–2529, para 30. *Cf.* ECJ, Case C–178/95 *Wiljo* [1997] E.C.R. I–585.

[273] See the Information note on references from national courts for a preliminary ruling [2005] O.J. C143/1.

[274] ECJ, Joined Cases C–320-322/90 *Telemarsicabruzzo and Others* [1993] E.C.R. I–393, para.5; ECJ, Case C–378/93 *La Pyramide* [1994] E.C.R. I–3999, para.17. It is, however, enough if the order for reference "contains the essential circumstances of the dispute in the main proceedings" (ECJ, Case C–181/97 *Van der Kooy* [1999] E.C.R. I–483, para.29). See also ECJ (order of March 21, 2002), Case C–447/01 *DLD Trading Company Import-Export*, not reported, paras 8–20, and ECJ (order of March 21, 2002), Case C–430/01 *Herbstrith*, not reported, paras 7–19, in which the Court declared the preliminary question inadmissible on the grounds that the national court had not given details of the legislative context of the main proceedings, had merely summarised arguments of the parties to the main proceedings which described the dispute in contradictory ways and failed to specify the necessity for the preliminary ruling and its relevance. Moreover, the questions were formulated in general terms and did not refer to a specific provision of Community law on which an interpretation was requested. A subsequent new reference for a preliminary ruling from the national court was also declared inadmissible (ECJ (order of April 1, 2004), Case C–229/03 *Herbstrith*, not reported). See also ECJ (order of April 21, 1999), Joined Cases C–28/98 and C–29/98 *Charreire and Hirtsmann* [1999] E.C.R. I–1963, in which the Court held that the

a limited extent the Court had previously refused to consider particular parts of preliminary references, where they were insufficiently precise, but this had never resulted in the whole of the request for a ruling being declared inadmissible.[275] The reason for this change was that the Court considered it unrealistic—in particular in the light of the complex factual and legal situations arising in competition law, which was the subject of the main proceedings—to expect it to fill the *lacunae* in the order for reference (which was virtually unreasoned) with sufficient certainty from the information in the file provided by the national court and the observations submitted to the Court by the parties to the main proceedings, the Italian Government and the Commission pursuant to what is now Art.23 of the Statute of the Court.[276] The risk that the Court's judgment would be of no assistance to the national court was too great and hence cooperation with the referring court could not serve its purpose. The Court declined to give potentially ineffective rulings which would merely serve as an "opinion" for a hypothetical case and not contribute towards the determination of the main proceedings. In subsequent cases, the Court has even gone so far as to decide that the preliminary reference was *manifestly* inadmissible for the same reasons (in orders given pursuant to Art.92(1) of the ECJ Rules of Procedure).[277] The Court has recognised, however, that the requirement for

---

order for reference contained contradictory information and that it was therefore impossible to form a clear picture of the legal situation. But see ECJ, Case C–116/02 *Gasser* [2003] E.C.R. I–14693, paras 21–27, in which the Court held that a preliminary question was admissible even though it was based on the submissions of a party to the main proceedings, the merits of which the national court had not yet assessed.

[275] ECJ, Case 52/76 *Benedetti* [1977] E.C.R. 163, paras 20–22; ECJ, Joined Cases 205–215/82 *Deutsche Milchkontor* [1983] E.C.R. 2633, para.36; *cf.* ECJ, Case 222/78 *ICAP* [1979] E.C.R. 1163, paras 19 and 20; ECJ, Case 14/86 *Pretore di Salò v X* [1987] E.C.R. 2545, para.16.

[276] See also ECJ, Case C–134/03 *Viacom Outdoor* [2005] E.C.R. I–1167, paras 23-29. *Cf.* ECJ, Joined Cases C–180/98-C–184/98 *Pavlov and Others* [2000] E.C.R. I–6451, paras 54–55, in which the Court found that the information provided in the order for reference was amplified by the case-file forwarded by the national court, by the written observations and by the answers given to the questions asked by the Court, which were summarised in the Report for the Hearing and had been made available to the governments of the Member States and the other interested parties for the purposes of the hearing, at which they had an opportunity to amplify their observations. For those reasons, the Court rejected the argument that the preliminary question was inadmissible. See also ECJ, Case C–67/96 *Albany International* [1999] E.C.R. I–5751, para.43; ECJ, Case C–56/99 *Gascogne Limousin Viandes* [2000] E.C.R. I–3079, para.31; ECJ, Case C–176/96 *Lehtonen and Castors Braine* [2000] E.C.R. I–2681, para.26; ECJ, Case C–109/99 *ABBOI* [2000] E.C.R. I–7247, para.43.

[277] ECJ (order of March 19, 1993), Case C–157/92 *Banchero* [1993] E.C.R. I–1085; ECJ (order of April 26, 1993), Case C–386/92 *Monin Automobiles* [1993] E.C.R. I–2049; ECJ (order of March 23, 1995), Case C–458/93 *Saddik* [1995] E.C.R. I–511, para.19; ECJ (order of April 7, 1995), Case C–167/94 *Grau Gomis and Others* [1995] E.C.R. I–1023, para.12; ECJ (order of February 2, 1996), Case C–257/95 *Bresle* [1996] E.C.R. I–233, paras 16–18; ECJ (order of March 13, 1996), Case C–326/95 *Banco de Fomento e Exterior* [1996] E.C.R. I–1385; ECJ (order of March 20, 1996), Case C–2/96 *Sunino and Data* [1996] E.C.R. I–1543, paras 6 and 7; ECJ (order of June 25, 1996), Case C–101/96 *Italia Testa* [1996] E.C.R. I–3081, para.4; ECJ (order of July 19, 1996), Case C–191/96 *Modesti* [1996] E.C.R. I–3937, para.4; ECJ

the national court to define the factual and legislative context of the questions referred is less pressing where they relate to specific technical points and enable the Court to give a useful reply even where the national court has not given an exhaustive description of the legal and factual situation.[278]

The Court of Justice may also hold that a preliminary question is admissible in part. In *FDV* the Court accepted the admissibility of a preliminary question relating to the interpretation of Arts 28 and 30 of the EC Treaty, but observed that the national court had given no explanation of the reasons for which it raised the question of the interpretation of Arts 81 and 82 of the EC Treaty in connection with the matters of fact and law in the main proceedings. In the absence of such information the national court had failed to put the Court in a position to give an interpretation of those articles which could be of use to it. That question was therefore declared inadmissible.[279]

Clear description of the factual and legal context. It follows from the abovementioned overview that it is essential[280] for the national court, in order to enable the Court to give a useful interpretation of Community law, to provide a sufficiently clear description in its order for reference of the factual and legal context of the main proceedings.[281] Where the Court does

2–025

(order of July 19, 1996), Case C–196/96 *Lahlou* [1996] E.C.R. I–3945, para.4; ECJ (order of June 30, 1997), Case C–66/97 *Banco de Fomento e Exterior* [1997] E.C.R. I–3757, para.19; ECJ (order of April 30, 1998), Joined Cases C–128/97 and C–137/97 *Italia Testa and Modesti* [1998] E.C.R. I–2181, paras 12–18; ECJ (order of July 8, 1998), Case C–9/98 *Agostini* [1998] E.C.R. I–4261, paras 4–10; ECJ (order of March 2, 1999), Case C–422/98 *Colonia Versicherung and Others* [1999] E.C.R. I–1279; ECJ, Case C–325/98 *Anssens* [1999] E.C.R. I–2969; ECJ (order of December 6, 2000), Case C–252/00 *Vandeweerd*, not reported; ECJ, Case C–123/00 *Bellamy and English Shop Wholesale* [2001] E.C.R. I–2795, para.52; ECJ (order of October 8, 2002), Case C–190/02 *Viacom* [2002] E.C.R. I–8287, paras 13–26; ECJ (order of March 12, 2004), Case C–54/03 *Austroplant Arzneimittel*, not reported, paras 10–22. See also Arnull, case note in (1994) C.M.L.Rev. 377; *cf.* Bergerès, "La CJCE et la pertinence de la question préjudicielle" (1993) Rec. Dalloz, Chronique 245; Wooldridge, "Disguised Contributions in Kind; the European Court refuses a Preliminary Ruling on Hypothetical Questions" (1993) 2 L.I.E.I. 69.

[278] ECJ, Case C–316/93 *Vaneetveld* [1994] E.C.R. I–763, para.13; ECJ (order of March 13, 1996), Case C–326/95 *Banco de Fomento e Exterior* [1996] E.C.R. I–1385, para.8.

[279] ECJ, Case C–61/97 *FDV* [1998] E.C.R. I–5171, paras 9–10; For a similar situation, see ECJ, Case C–399/98 *Ordine degli Architetti and Others* [2001] E.C.R. I–5409, paras 105–107. See also ECJ, Case C–258/98 *Carra and Others* [2000] E.C.R. I–4217, paras 19–20; ECJ, Case C–123/00 *Bellamy and English Shop Wholesale* [2001] E.C.R. I–2795, para.52; ECJ, Case C–341/01 *Plato Plastik Robert Frank* [2004] E.C.R. I–4883, paras 37–39; ECJ, Case C–72/03 *Carbonati Apuani* [2004] E.C.R. I–8027, paras 12–14.

[280] This is also stressed in the Information note on references from national courts for a preliminary ruling [2005] O.J. C143/1.

[281] This must also afford the national governments and other interested parties the possibility to submit observations under Art.23 of the Statute: ECJ, Case C–67/96 *Albany International* [1999] E.C.R. I–5751, para.40; ECJ, Joined Cases C–480/00 to C–482/00, C–484/00, C–489/00 to C–491/00, C–497/00 to C–499/00 *Azienda Agricola Ettore Ribaldi and Others* [2004] E.C.R. I–2943, para.73. It should be noted that only the order for reference is served

not have the necessary factual and legal information to enable it to give a useful answer to the question referred, it will declare the question inadmissible.[282]

2–026 **National court's discretion.** The *Telemarsicabruzzo* requirement as to the precision of the order for reference in terms of its content does not completely negate the national court's discretion in determining at what stage in the proceedings pending before it should make a reference to the Court of Justice. It is sufficient for the national court to set out in the order for reference the factual and national legal premises or hypotheses underlying the questions referred so as to enable the Court of Justice to arrive at a helpful answer. In contrast, the national court is not in principle required to have chosen between the premises or hypotheses at the time when it seeks the preliminary ruling. It may still be influenced by "considerations of procedural organisation and efficiency"[283] and await the Court's answer to a preliminary question before making a definitive ruling on the factual and national legal aspects of the case. The only condition is that the national court's order for reference should interpret the various premises or hypotheses and explain the reasons why it is seeking a preliminary ruling so as to make it clear in what way Community law is relevant in the case of *each* of those premises or hypotheses. It goes without saying that the national court must have fully apprised itself of the case in order to fulfil this condition. This is at the heart of the *Telemarsicabruzzo* requirement, which is designed to give rise to a genuine dialogue between courts.

In one situation the order for reference has to contain more than an exposition of the various factual and national legal premises or hypotheses underlying the case, together with the reasons for seeking the preliminary ruling. This is where it appears that Community law is not relevant in every eventuality to the decision in the main proceedings. In such a case, it is the national court's task first to narrow down the legal debate to only those premises or hypotheses in which Community law is relevant *in any event*. In order to do so, it will perhaps have to make a full or partial determination

---

on the Member States. A preliminary question will be declared inadmissible if it merely refers as regards the factual context to a judgment of another court and to a decision of a national competition authority (ECJ (order of February 11, 2004), Joined Cases C–438/03, C–439/03, C–509/03 and C–2/04 *Cannito and Others* [2004] E.C.R. I–1605, paras 8–12).

[282] ECJ, Case C–415/93 *Bosman* [1995] E.C.R. I–4921, paras 59–61; ECJ, Case C–36/99 *Idéal Tourisme* [2000] E.C.R. I–6049, para.20; ECJ, Case C–137/00 *Milk Marque and National Farmers' Union* [2003] E.C.R. I–7975, para.37; ECJ, Joined Cases C–480/00 to C–482/00, C–484/00, C–489/00 to C–491/00, C–497/00 to C–499/00 *Azienda Agricola Ettore Ribaldi and Others* [2004] E.C.R. I–2943, para.72; ECJ, Case C–286/02 *Bellio Fratelli* [2004] E.C.R. I–3465, para.28; ECJ (order of February 22, 2005), Case C–480/04 *D'Antonio*, not reported, paras 5–8.

[283] ECJ, Joined Cases 36 and 71/80 *Irish Creamery Milk Suppliers Association* [1981] E.C.R. 735, para.8.

of the facts and national legal aspects of the case before it makes a reference to the Court, which certainly restricts its discretion to determine at what stage the reference is made. The intention behind this restriction is to avoid a fruitless judgment from the Court in the event that the national court should subsequently find that Community law has no part to play at all, having regard to the facts or the relevant national law. The 1992 judgment in *Meilicke* illustrates this.[284] A German court had referred a long series of involved questions concerning the interpretation of the Second Company Law Directive in order to be able to rule on the compatibility with the directive of a principle of German company law enshrined in case-law. However, the parties to the main proceedings did not agree whether that principle was applicable to the facts of the case. The national court had elected not to rule on that issue and first to submit the question of compatibility to the Court. Its idea was that if it should become clear from the Court's interpretation of the Second Company Law Directive that the principle of German company law conflicted therewith, the question as to the applicability of that principle to the facts of the case would be of no account, given that the principle would have in any event to yield to Community law, which took precedence. The Court of Justice was unable to accept the sequence of the national court's decision-making on the ground that if, conversely, it were to appear from the preliminary ruling that the principle of German company law was compatible with the Second Company Law Directive, the judgment of the Court of Justice would have no practical effect as a contribution to the resolution of the main proceedings, if at that stage the national court were to decide that under national law the principle laid down by case-law was not applicable to the facts of the case. The only way of eliminating the risk of a hypothetical ruling from the Court was to oblige the German court to determine the facts and rule on the applicability of the principle of national law at issue before considering making a reference to the Court for a preliminary ruling.

It should be borne in mind that, in preliminary ruling proceedings, any assessment of the facts in the case is a matter for the national court. The Court of Justice is empowered to rule on the interpretation or validity of Community provisions only on the basis of the facts which the national court places before it.[285]

---

[284] ECJ, Case C–83/91 *Meilicke* [1992] E.C.R. I–4871 (case note by Arnull (1993) C.M.L.Rev. 613-622). See also ECJ, Case C–153/00 *Der Weduwe* [2002] E.C.R. I–11319; ECJ, Case C–318/00 *Bacardi-Martini and Cellier des Dauphins* [2003] E.C.R. I–905.

[285] ECJ, Case C–30/93 *AC-ATEL Electronics* [1994] E.C.R. I–2305, paras 16–17; ECJ, Case C–352/95 *Phytheron International* [1997] E.C.R. I–1729, paras 11–14; ECJ, Case C–235/95 *AGS Assedic Pas-de-Calais* [1998] E.C.R. I–4531, para.25; ECJ, Joined Cases C–175/98 and C–177/98 *Lirussi and Bizzaro* [1999] E.C.R. I–6881, paras 36–39; ECJ, Case C–9/02 *De Lasteyrie du Saillant* [2004] E.C.R. I–2409, para.41; ECJ, Case C–267/03 *Lindberg* [2005] E.C.R. I–3247, paras 41–42.

D. ANNULMENT OF A REQUEST FOR A PRELIMINARY RULING

2–027 General. The Court considers that a request for a preliminary ruling made pursuant to Art.234 continues "so long as the request of the national court has not been withdrawn by the court from which it emanates or has not been quashed on appeal from a superior court".[286] Consequently, the Court refuses to go into objections to its jurisdiction raised in observations submitted pursuant to Art.23 of the Statute of the Court claiming that the questions are no longer relevant, for example on the ground that the national legislative provisions whose compatibility with Community law the preliminary reference seeks to assess have in the meantime been declared unconstitutional[287] or that the request for a preliminary ruling was the outcome of a decision which was not taken in accordance with the applicable national (procedural) law.[288] "[I]n view of the distribution of functions between itself and the national court, it is not for the Court to determine whether the decision whereby a matter is brought before it was taken in accordance with the rules of national law governing the organisation of the courts and their procedure. The Court is therefore bound by a decision of a court or tribunal of a Member State referring a matter to it, in so far as that decision has not been rescinded on the basis of a means of redress provided for by national law".[289] However, the Court may find that the main proceedings are to no purpose and that for it to reply to the

---

[286] ECJ, Case 127/73 *BRT* [1974] E.C.R. 51, para.9; ECJ, Case 106/77 *Simmenthal* [1978] E.C.R. 629, para.10; for examples, see ECJ, Case 65/77 *Razanatsimba* [1977] E.C.R. 2229, paras 5–6; ECJ (order of June 24, 1997), Case C–184/95 *Lores Guillín*, not reported.

[287] *Simmenthal*, cited in the preceding n., paras 8–12.

[288] ECJ, Case 65/81 *Reina* [1982] E.C.R. 33, para.7; *cf.* the Opinions of Advocate General M. Lagrange in ECJ, Case 13/61 *Bosch and Others* [1962] E.C.R. 45, at 56, and of Advocate General H. Mayras in ECJ, Case 127/73 *BRT* [1974] E.C.R. 51, at 68; ECJ, Joined Cases C–332–333 and C–335/92 *Eurico Italia and Others* [1994] E.C.R. I–711, para.13; ECJ, Case C–472/93 *Spano and Others* [1995] E.C.R. I–4321, para.16; but see the Opinion of Advocate General C. Gulmann in ECJ, Joined Cases C–320–322/90 *Telemarsicabruzzo and Others* [1993] E.C.R. I–393, at I–410–415.

[289] *Reina*, cited in the preceding n., para.7; ECJ, Case C–39/94 *SFEI and Others* [1996] E.C.R. I–3547, para.24; ECJ, Case C–371/97 *Gozza and Others* [2000] E.C.R. I–7881, para.30; ECJ, Case C–309/02 *Radlberger Getränkegesellschaft and S. Spitz* [2004] E.C.R. I–11763, para.26. If, however, the Court of Justice finds that, after making a reference for a preliminary ruling, the national court considers that it cannot terminate the main proceedings even though the defendant has acceded to the plaintiff's claims, on the ground that Community law debars it from doing so, it considers itself entitled to inquire into the reasons given by the national court. If it appears that Community law does not preclude the national court from terminating the main proceedings under national law, the Court considers that it has no jurisdiction to answer the questions referred for a preliminary ruling as long as the national court has not found that in national law the acts of the parties have not terminated the main proceedings: ECJ, Joined Cases C–422, C–423 and C–424/93 *Zabala Erasun and Others* [1995] E.C.R. I–1567; ECJ, Case C–343/96 *Dilexport* [1999] E.C.R. I–597, para.19.

questions referred would therefore be of no avail to the national court. In those circumstances, it will hold that the reference is to no purpose and that there is no need to reply to the questions referred.[290]

Appeal brought against the order for reference. In order for a request for a preliminary ruling to be admissible, it is not necessary that the order for reference should have the force of *res judicata* under national law.[291] Community law does not restrict the remedies available under national law against the order for reference.[292]

2–028

Where an appeal brought against the order for reference under national law has suspensory effect and the Court is officially notified of this by the national courts concerned, it will defer its ruling until it has received notification that the appeal has been decided.[293] If the appeal results in the annulment of the order for reference, the Court will order the case to be removed from the register.[294] In this way, the Court avoids giving a ruling which is no longer of any assistance for the purposes of making a determination in the main proceedings.[295]

---

[290] ECJ, Case C–314/96 *Djabali* [1998] E.C.R. I–1149, paras 17–23; ECJ, Case C–225/02 *Garciá Blanco*, [2005] E.C.R. I–523, paras 28-32. Where, after the national court has made a reference for a preliminary ruling, the Court of Justice gives a preliminary ruling in another case involving the same question of interpretation, the national court should consider whether it should maintain its reference. If that court subsequently makes it known that it withdraws its request, the case will be removed from the register of the Court (for an example, see ECJ (order of the President of April 30, 1999), Case C–26/97 *Giolfo and Others*, not reported).

[291] ECJ, Case 13/61 *Bosch and Others* [1962] E.C.R. 45, at 49–50; ECJ, Joined Cases 2-4/82 *Delhaize Frères and Others* [1983] E.C.R. 2973, paras 8–9.

[292] ECJ, Case 146/73 *Rheinmühlen-Düsseldorf* [1974] E.C.R. 139, third subpara. of para.3; such a restriction may, however, ensue from national law itself, see for example Walsh, "The Appeal of an Art.177*[now Art.234]* EEC Referral" (1993) Mod.L.Rev. 881, n.9, at 885. See also Pfeiffer, "Keine Beschwerde gegen EuGH-Vorlagen?" (1994) N.J.W. 1996, at 1998–2002.

[293] See, by way of example, ECJ (order of the President of December 8, 1993), Case C–269/92 *Bosman*, not reported. *Cf.* ECJ, Case C–405/98 *Gourmet International Products* [2001] E.C.R. I–1795, para.12, in which the Court noted the fact that an appeal against the order for reference had been rejected.

[294] See ECJ (order of June 3, 1969), Case 31/68 *Chanel* [1970] E.C.R. 403, at 403–404, and ECJ (order of June 16, 1970), Case 31/68 *Chanel* [1970] E.C.R. 404, at 405–406; ECJ (order of the President of January 16, 1996), Case C–310/94 *Garage Ardon*, not reported, paras 2–3. By an order, the President of the Court instructed a case to be struck out where an appeal against the order for reference had been blocked for seven years because one of the parties to the main proceedings had been declared insolvent. The President took the view that in the circumstances it was no longer necessary to reply to the questions set out in the order for reference (ECJ (order of the President of February 20, 1997), Case C–205/90 *Les Assurances du Crédit Namur*, not reported).

[295] *Cf.* the Opinion of Advocate General K. Roemer in *Chanel*, cited above, 406, at 408–409.

II. Determination of the Relevance of the Request for a Preliminary Ruling

A. Task of the National Court

2–029 **National court's responsibility for assessing relevance.** Ever since the 1978 judgment in the *Pigs Marketing Board* case, it has been settled case-law that *"[a]s regards the division of jurisdiction between national courts and the Court of Justice* under Art.177*[now Art.234]* of the Treaty the national court, which is alone in having a direct knowledge of the facts of the case and of the arguments put forward by the parties, and which will have to give judgment in the case, *is in the best position* to appreciate, with full knowledge of the matter before it, the relevance of the questions of law raised by the dispute before it and the necessity for a preliminary ruling so as to enable it to give judgment".[296] Consequently, the national court's responsibility for assessing the relevance of the questions referred for a preliminary ruling has a dual basis.

In the first place, that assessment falls to it as part of its *jurisdiction* to hear and determine the main proceedings, which is left intact by Art.234. This aspect of the national court's task was stressed above all during the first twenty years of preliminary rulings from the Court, when it repeatedly stated that, under Art.234 of the EC Treaty, which enshrines the principle of the mutual independence of the national and the Community courts, the Court of Justice has no jurisdiction to pronounce on the considerations which prompted the request for an interpretation or for the assessment of the validity of an act.[297] When the questions referred by the national court relate to the interpretation of a provision of Community law or to the

---

[296] ECJ, Case 83/78 *Pigs Marketing Board v Redmond* [1978] E.C.R. 2347, para.25 (emphasis added); see also, among other cases, ECJ, Joined Cases C–399, C–409 and C–425/92, C–34, C–50 and C–78/93 *Helmig and Others* [1994] E.C.R. I–5727, para.8; ECJ, Case C–134/94 *Esso Española* [1995] E.C.R. I–4223, para.9; ECJ, Joined Cases C–320, C–328, C–329, C–337, C–338 and C–339/94 *RTI and Others* [1996] E.C.R. I–6471, para.21. The judgment in ECJ, Case C–193/94 *Skanavi and Chryssanthakopoulos* [1996] E.C.R. I–929, paras 17–18, affords a good example. The facts material to the main proceedings had occurred three days before the EU Treaty entered into force. The question submitted for a preliminary ruling related in part to Art.18 of the EC Treaty, a new provision introduced by the EU Treaty, which, according to the national court, might preclude application of the national rules at issue in the criminal proceedings pending before it. The Court of Justice found that the national court could apply the principle, recognised by its national law, that the more favourable rule of criminal law should take retroactive effect and, consequently, set aside national law to the extent to which it was contrary to the provisions of the Treaty. For those reasons, the Court did not contest the need for the preliminary ruling or the relevance of the questions referred. To like effect, see ECJ, Joined Cases C–163, C–165 and C–250/94 *Sanz de Lera and Others* [1995] E.C.R. I–4821, para.14; ECJ, Case C–200/97 *Ecotrade* [1998] E.C.R. I–7907, para.25; ECJ, Case C–167/01 *Inspire Art* [2003] E.C.R. I–10155, para.43.
[297] ECJ, Case 13/68 *Salgoil* [1968] E.C.R. 453, at 459–460; ECJ, Case 5/77 *Tedeschi* [1977] E.C.R. 1555, paras 17–19.

validity of an act of a Community institution, "the Court is, *in principle*, bound to give a ruling".[298]

Secondly, it is for the national court to determine the relevance of the request for a preliminary ruling on account of its special *ability* to make the relevant assessment. This signifies that the national court's competence to determine the relevance of the preliminary questions constitutes the starting point, but is not absolute or subject to no possible correction in any circumstances (the Court is only obliged "in principle" to reply). The Court accordingly points out that, in the event of questions having been improperly formulated or going beyond the scope of the powers conferred on the Court of Justice by Art.234, it is free to extract from all the factors provided by the national court and in particular from the statement of grounds contained in the reference, the elements of Community law requiring an interpretation—or, as the case may be, an assessment of validity—*having regard to the subject-matter of the dispute*.[299]

The ruling must contribute to resolving the dispute before the national court. In other words, the national court's jurisdiction to adjudge the relevance of the questions referred for a preliminary ruling and, in that light, to determine their content is not exclusive. The Court of Justice itself must take heed that the questions do not go beyond the scope of its powers and, where necessary, adapt the questions, "having regard to the subject-matter of the dispute", so that the preliminary ruling achieves its aim of making an effective contribution towards resolving the dispute before the national court.[300]

2–030

---

[298] ECJ, Case C–231/89 *Gmurzynska-Bscher* [1990] E.C.R. I–4003, para.20 (emphasis added); see also para.19; ECJ, Joined Cases C–480/00 to C–482/00, C–484/00, C–489/00 to C–491/00, C–497/00 to C–499/00 *Azienda Agricola Ettore Ribaldi and Others* [2004] E.C.R. I–2943, para.72. If the request for a preliminary ruling has nothing to do with the interpretation of the Treaty or the validity or interpretation of an act of the institutions, it will be inadmissible. The Court of Justice may then declare the request inadmissible by an order given pursuant to Art.92(1) of the ECJ Rules of Procedure. See ECJ (order of June 12, 1996), Case C–95/96 *Clinique de la Pointe Rouge*, not reported, paras 6–7; ECJ (order of June 12, 1996), Case C–96/96 *Clinique Florens*, not reported, paras 6–7.

[299] ECJ, Case 83/78 *Pigs Marketing Board v Redmond* [1978] E.C.R. 2347, para.26 (emphasis added).

[300] On those grounds, the Court may, in exceptional circumstances, examine the conditions in which the case was referred to it by the national court (ECJ, Case C–390/99 *Canal Satélite Digital* [2002] E.C.R. I–607, paras 18–20). In *Mazzoleni* (ECJ, Case C–165/98 *Mazzoleni and ISA* [2001] E.C.R. I–2189, paras 16–17), the Court held that it was "not necessary" to give an interpretation of Directive 96/71/EC on the grounds that the period prescribed for the implementation of the directive had not expired and it had not been transposed into national law at the time of the facts of the main proceedings. In the light of the observations submitted by the parties or the national governments, the Court may sometimes add a question which does not appear expressly in the order for reference on the ground that it has "jurisdiction to provide the national court with all the guidance of interpretation . . . for the purposes of deciding the case before it": ECJ, Joined Cases C–441/98 and C–442/98 *Michaïlidis* [2000] E.C.R. I–7145, paras 20–21; ECJ, Case C–387/01 *Weigel* [2004] E.C.R. I–4981, para.44.

Consequently, in its subsequent case-law, the Court has emphasised that the national court's power to determine the relevance of questions referred for a preliminary ruling is constrained by its aim.

"[I]n the use which it makes of the facilities provided by Art.177 [*now Art.234*] [the national court] should have regard to the proper function of the Court of the Justice in this field",[301] which is not that of "delivering advisory opinions on general or hypothetical questions but of assisting in the administration of justice in the Member States".[302] The Court of Justice must always examine whether the questions raised are connected with its own task in order—just as in the case of any other court—not to exceed the limits of its jurisdiction. That limit would be exceeded if it would be impossible for the ruling requested to contribute towards the resolution of the dispute pending before the national court because of a manifest error in assessing the relevance of the questions of Community law referred to the Court.[303]

2–031 **The relevance of questions must appear from the order for reference.** In order to enable the Court to ascertain whether it has jurisdiction, "it is essential for national courts to explain, when the reasons do not emerge beyond any doubt from the documents, why they consider that a reply to their questions is necessary to enable them to give judgment".[304] Failure to fulfil that duty to state reasons does not automatically mean that the request for a preliminary ruling is inadmissible,[305] but it does cause the Court to adopt a more critical attitude when it makes its substantive review

---

[301] ECJ, Case 244/80 *Foglia v Novello* (*Foglia v Novello II*) [1981] E.C.R. 3045, para.20 *in fine*; ECJ, Case C–167/01 *Inspire Art* [2003] E.C.R. I–10155, para.45.

[302] *Foglia v Novello II*, para.18; *Inspire Art*, para.45; *cf.* ECJ, Case 149/82 *Robards* [1983] E.C.R. 171, para.19; ECJ, Case C–116/02 *Gasser* [2003] E.C.R. I–14693, para.24; ECJ, Case C–314/01 *Siemens and ARGE Telekom & Partner* [2004] E.C.R. I–2549, para.35; ECJ, Case C–315/02 *Lenz* [2004] E.C.R. I–7063, paras 52–54.

[303] See, however, ECJ, Case C–343/98 *Collino and Chiappero* [2000] E.C.R. I–6659, paras 19–24, in which the Court did not question the admissibility of a preliminary question even though it was not certain whether the provisions of the directive at issue could be invoked against one of the parties to the main proceedings; see also ECJ (order of January 15, 2004), Case C–235/02 *Saetti* [2004] E.C.R. I–1005, paras 24–30. In ECJ, Case C–315/01 *GAT* [2003] E.C.R. I–6351, paras 38–39, the Court declared inadmissible a preliminary question relating to the award of compensation for infringement of Community law—or the conditions therefore—on the ground that the question had been referred by a court which, under national law, had no power to award damages.

[304] ECJ, Case 244/80 *Foglia v Novello* (*Foglia v Novello II*) [1981] E.C.R. 3045, para.17. See also Case C–325/98 *Anssens* [1999] E.C.R. I–2969, para.14, in which the Court declared a preliminary question inadmissible, in particular because the referring court had not given reasons justifying the need for the preliminary reference even though one of the parties to the main proceedings had drawn the national court's attention to a judgment of the Court giving a preliminary ruling on an identical question. It appears from recent case-law that the Court will declare a preliminary question inadmissible only where it is obvious that the interpretation of Community law requested is not necessary for resolving the dispute before the national court (ECJ, Case C–448/98 *Guimont* [2000] E.C.R. I–10663, para.23; ECJ, Case C–71/02 *Herbert Karner Industrie-Auktionen* [2004] E.C.R. I–3025, para.21).

[305] ECJ, Joined Cases 98, 162 and 258/85 *Bertini* [1986] E.C.R. 1885, paras 6 and 7.

of the assessment of relevance which the national court is implicitly deemed to have carried out.[306]

The assessment of relevance which the Court of Justice expects the national court to carry out in order to ensure that it does not exceed the limits of its jurisdiction in answering questions referred for a preliminary ruling is very close to the description given by Lord Denning MR:

> "The judge must have got to the stage when he says to himself: 'This clause of the Treaty is capable of two or more meanings. If it means this, I give judgment for the plaintiff. If it means that, I give judgment for the defendant.' In short, the point must be such that, whichever way the point is decided, it is conclusive of the case. Nothing more remains but to give judgment".[307]

B. THE LIMITS SET BY COMMUNITY LAW

1. Obviously irrelevant questions

The reference bears no relation to the dispute before the national court. The 2–032 Court will not follow the national court's assessment of relevance where "it is quite obvious that the interpretation of Community law or the examination of the validity of a rule of Community law sought by that court bears no relation to the actual nature of the case or to the subject-matter of the main action".[308] The request for a preliminary ruling is then inadmissible and will be dismissed, wholly[309] or in part,[310] on that account.

---

[306] 2–032 to 2–035, *infra*.

[307] *Bulmer v Bollinger* [1974] C.M.L.R. 91, [1974] Ch 401.

[308] ECJ, Case 126/80 *Salonia* [1981] E.C.R. 1563, para.6. See in particular also ECJ, Case C–368/89 *Crispoltoni* [1991] E.C.R. I–3695, para.11; ECJ, Case C–186/90 *Durighello* [1991] E.C.R. I–5773, para.9; ECJ, Case C–343/90 *Lourenço Dias* [1992] E.C.R. I–4673, para.18; ECJ, Case C–67/91 *Asociación Española de Banca Privada and Others* [1992] E.C.R. I–4785, para.26; ECJ, Joined Cases C–332–333 and C–335/92 *Eurico Italia and Others* [1994] E.C.R. I–711, para.17; ECJ, Case C–18/93 *Corsica Ferries* [1994] E.C.R. I–1783, para.14; ECJ, Case C–62/93 *BP Supergaz* [1995] E.C.R. I–1883, para.10; ECJ, Case C–143/94 *Furlanis* [1995] E.C.R. I–3633, para.12; ECJ, Case C–415/93 *Bosman* [1995] E.C.R. I–4921, para.61; ECJ, Case C–118/94 *Associazione Italiana per il WWF and Others* [1996] E.C.R. I–1223, para.15; ECJ, Case C–129/94 *Bernáldez* [1996] E.C.R. I–1829, para.7; ECJ, Case C–85/95 *Reisdorf* [1996] E.C.R. I–6257, para.16; ECJ, Joined Cases C–320, C–328, C–329, C–337, C–338 and C–339/94 *RTI and Others* [1996] E.C.R. I–6471, para.23; ECJ, Case C–104/95 *Kontogeorgas* [1996] E.C.R. I–6643, paras 10–11; ECJ, Case C–261/95 *Palmisani* [1997] E.C.R. I–4025, para.18; ECJ, Case C–373/95 *Maso and Others* [1997] E.C.R. I–4051, para.26.

[309] See, *inter alia*, ECJ (order of May 16, 1994), Case C–428/93 *Monin Automobiles* [1994] E.C.R. I–1707, paras 13–16; ECJ (order of May 2, 2002), Case C–129/01 *Condominio Facchinei Orsini*, not reported, paras 17–23; ECJ (order of July 24, 2003), Case C–44/03 *Horn*, not reported, paras 12–16.

[310] ECJ, Case C–421/97 *Tarantik* [1999] E.C.R. I–3633, paras 33–37; ECJ, Joined Cases C–430/99 and C–431/99 *Sealand Service and Nedlloyd Lijnen* [2002] E.C.R. I–5235, paras 46–47; ECJ, Case C–315/02 *Lenz* [2004] E.C.R. I–7063, paras 52–54.

In the words of the Court, it must be "obvious" that the preliminary questions are irrelevant.[311] The question arises, however, as to how far the Court will take its examination of the facts and national legal aspects of the main action in order to ascertain whether the preliminary ruling sought has some chance of making an actual contribution towards the decision in the case. Is it not the case that the Court must exercise a degree of restraint, given that determining the facts and the national law comes under the national court's jurisdiction? The answer to that question is yes in so far as the Court may not pronounce upon facts or aspects of national law which are in issue between the parties and on which the national court has not yet made any determination.[312] In contrast, where the facts and national legal aspects of the case have been determined in the order for reference or are clear from the case-file submitted to the Court, there is nothing to prevent the Court from having regard to them in testing the national court's assessment of the relevance of the preliminary questions against the requirements which arise out of the aims of the Court's jurisdiction under Art.234 of the EC Treaty. Two examples will serve to clarify the Court's approach.

2–033   *Vlaeminck*. In the 1982 judgment in *Vlaeminck* the Court undertook an in-depth appraisal of the facts set forth in the order for reference of the *Arbeidshof* [Labour Court], Ghent, and reached the following conclusion: "In view of that factual situation the preliminary question appears to lack any purpose. It is not possible to glean from it the factors necessary for an interpretation of Community law which the national court might usefully apply in order to resolve, in accordance with that law, the dispute before it. It follows that in the light of the factual and legal circumstances of the main proceedings no question of Community law is raised in the present case, so that the Court is unable to give a ruling, in the context of proceedings under Art.177*[now Art.234]*, on the question referred to it by the *Arbeidshof*, Ghent".[313] This judgment is noteworthy in that the facts and aspects of national law relating to a pension scheme applicable to a married couple where the husband and wife had worked in France and Belgium were particularly complicated. Nevertheless, the Court felt that it was in a position to decide on the basis of the particulars set out in the order for reference and the case-file submitted by the national court that the decision

---

[311] That will be the case where it is quite obvious that the questions of interpretation referred for a preliminary ruling are not necessary for the national court (ECJ, Case C–71/02 *Herbert Karner Industrie-Auktionen* [2004] E.C.R. I–3025, para.21; ECJ, Case C–286/02 *Bellio Fratelli* [2004] E.C.R. I–3465, para.28). A question will be regarded as relevant where the Court's answer may be of use to the national court in finding whether a provision of national law is compatible with Community law (*ibid.*).

[312] ECJ, Case C–153/02 *Neri* [2003] E.C.R. I–13555, para.34.

[313] ECJ, Case 132/81 *Vlaeminck* [1982] E.C.R. 2953, paras 13–14.

in the main proceedings could be reached without Community law having any part to play.[314]

Falciola. Matters were even more clear-cut in the 1990 order in *Falciola*.[315]   **2–034**
The Court declined jurisdiction to answer a number of questions referred by an Italian court. The questions arose in proceedings purportedly relating to the award of a road works contract. According to the order for reference, the contract was subject to two Council directives by reason of its value. However, the questions referred exclusively to the compatibility with Community law of several aspects of Italian Law No 117/88 of 13 April 1988 on compensation for damage caused in the exercise of judicial functions and the civil liability of the judiciary.[316] The Court plainly had no difficulty in finding that the questions bore no relation to "the subject-matter of the [main] action" since the request for a preliminary ruling was not concerned with the interpretation of the two Council directives; instead, it was clear "from the actual wording of the order for reference" that the national court was only in doubt "as to the possible psychological reactions of certain Italian judges as a result of the enactment of the Italian Law of 13 April 1988". Accordingly, the Court held that "the preliminary questions submitted to the Court do not involve an interpretation of Community law objectively required in order to settle the dispute in the main action".[317]

Lourenço Dias. Where the order for reference taken as a whole does not   **2–035**
state the reasons why the national court considers that a preliminary ruling is necessary in order to determine the case before it, the Court gives itself greater latitude in testing the relevance of the questions referred. Such a situation occurred in the 1992 judgment in *Lourenço Dias*.[318] A Portuguese court had referred eight questions concerning the interpretation of Art.25 and Art.90 of the EC Treaty. The questions sought to ascertain the compatibility with Community law of various aspects of a new Portuguese law on motor-vehicle taxation. The public prosecutor, who was a party in the main proceedings, the Portuguese and British Governments and the Commission claimed that the Court had no jurisdiction on the ground that the questions, or at least some of them, bore no relation to the actual nature of the case or to the subject-matter of the main action.[319] The case

---

[314] In *Der Weduwe* (ECJ, Case C–153/00 *Der Weduwe* [2002] E.C.R. I–11319), the Court considered that the referring court had not provided the Court with all the necessary information to determine whether an interpretation of Community law would serve a useful purpose in the main proceedings. It therefore declared the request for a preliminary ruling inadmissible. In fact, the relevance of the preliminary question depended upon the interpretation of the national law at issue in the proceedings. The Court did not rule on the relevance of the question, but found that it did not have sufficient information to be certain about its relevance.

[315] ECJ (order of January 26, 1990), Case C–286/88 *Falciola* [1990] E.C.R. I–191.

[316] (1988) GURI, No 88, 3.

[317] ECJ (order of January 26, 1990), Case C–286/88 *Falciola* [1990] E.C.R. I–191, para.9; for another example, see ECJ (order of July 24, 2003), Case C–44/03 *Horn and Schelling*, not reported, paras. 12–16.

[318] ECJ, Case C–343/90 *Lourenço Dias* [1992] E.C.R. I–4673.

[319] This is the *Salonia* test: ECJ, Case 126/80 *Salonia* [1981] E.C.R. 1563, para.6.

was concerned with a vehicle which, upon importation into Portugal, was converted for goods transport, thus enjoying tax exemption. When a check was carried out some months later, it transpired, however, that the conversion had been reversed in order that passengers could be carried as well as goods. Consequently, the tax authorities claimed the tax, which the owner of the vehicle, *Lourenço Dias*, contested before the national court. The Court of Justice observed that the national court had expressed doubts about the compatibility with Community law of certain provisions of the Portuguese law, but had omitted to inform the Court how those provisions were to be applied to the facts of the main proceedings. The Court itself then proceeded to identify the provisions of the Portuguese law to which each of the eight preliminary questions referred and related them to the characteristics of the vehicle involved and the other factual circumstances which emerged, not only from the order for reference and the case-file submitted by the national court, but also—a much more radical step—from the observations submitted pursuant to what is now Art.23 of the Statute of the Court, including those presented by an "outsider", the British Government. Having conducted that exercise, the Court held that the provisions of Portuguese law to which six of the eight preliminary questions referred, expressly or impliedly, were manifestly inapplicable to the facts of the main proceedings and that there was therefore no need to answer them. Whatever the Court's answer to them, it would have had no bearing on the outcome of the main proceedings.[320] This was because purely hypothetical questions were involved.[321]

At first sight, that judgment may suggest that the Court trespassed over the borderline between interpreting Community law and interpreting national law. Yet its approach was perfectly proper since it did not pronounce upon any factual or national legal aspect of the main proceedings which was in issue between the parties (see 6–021, *infra*). The Court regarded itself as being obliged simply to supply the *lacunae* which the national court had left in its order, namely its omission to give reasons why it considered it needed an answer to the preliminary questions so as to decide the main action, in order not to exceed its jurisdiction. If the Court had answered all eight questions, it is clear that it would have done so without a prior thorough judicial debate of questions which in actual fact were not relevant from the point of view of the positions argued for by the parties to the main proceedings. For this reason too it is undesirable that the Court should be compelled to give a ruling—as it were in a vacuum— on hypothetical questions whose answers would not contribute towards the resolution of a dispute.[322] In addition, it has to be borne in mind in this

---

[320] See also ECJ, Case C–297/93 *Grau-Hupka* [1994] E.C.R. I–5535, para.19.
[321] See also ECJ, Case C–315/02 *Lenz* [2004] E.C.R. I–7063, paras 52–54.
[322] See, *e.g.* ECJ, Case C–380/01 *Schneider* [2004] E.C.R. I–1389, paras 20–31; ECJ, Case C–314/01 *Siemens and ARGE Telecom & Partner* [2004] E.C.R. I–2549, para.37.

connection that a preliminary ruling has general value as a precedent in the Community legal order (see 6–027 to 6–034, *infra*), which makes the Court—in common with all courts—careful only to decide on what is necessary in order to bring a case to a conclusion and thereby to allow the whole mosaic of case-law to build itself up incrementally. A court is not a legislative body laying down abstract rules of general scope.

The dispute concerns the legislation of another Member State. The Court   2–036
will be particularly attentive where a question is referred to it in connection with proceedings between individuals which is intended to assess whether the legislation of another Member State is in conformity with Community law.[323] In those circumstances, the national court must take particular pains to explain why it considers that an answer to its questions is necessary in order to determine the dispute.[324] If it fails to do so, the preliminary question will be inadmissible.

Absence of cross-border elements in the national dispute. Finally, ques-   2–037
tions relating to the Treaty provisions on the fundamental freedoms may be declared inadmissible where the activities in question in the main proceedings are confined in all respects within a single Member State. However, the Court of Justice is rather reluctant to turn down requests for preliminary rulings simply because the main proceedings lack cross-border elements. It considers that a reply might be useful to the national court if its national law were to require that a citizen of the Member State concerned must be allowed to enjoy the same rights as those which a citizen of another Member State would derive from Community law in the same situation.[325]

2. Spurious disputes

General. The idea that the preliminary ruling should contribute towards   2–038
bringing a dispute to a conclusion also underlies the Court's refusal to answer questions raised by means of spurious main proceedings. This means that the Court will refuse to give a preliminary ruling "where it appears that the procedure of Art.177*[now Art.234]* of the Treaty has been misused and been resorted to, in fact, in order to elicit a ruling from the Court by means of a spurious dispute".[326]

---

[323] ECJ, Case 244/80 *Foglia v Novello* (*Foglia v Novello II*) [1981] E.C.R. 3045 (legality of French legislation raised by an Italian court); ECJ, Case C–153/00 *Der Weduwe* [2002] E.C.R. I–11319 (legality of Luxembourg legislation questioned by a Belgian court); ECJ, Case C–318/00 *Bacardi-Martini and Cellier des Dauphins* [2003] E.C.R. I–905 (legality of French legislation questioned by a UK court).

[324] ECJ, Case C–318/00 *Bacardi-Martini and Cellier des Dauphins* [2003] E.C.R. I–905, paras 45–46; see also ECJ, Case C–153/00 *Der Weduwe* [2002] E.C.R. I–11319, paras 31–40.

[325] ECJ, Case C–448/98 *Guimont* [2000] E.C.R. I–10663, para.23; ECJ, Joined Cases C–515/99, C–519/99—C–524/99 and C–526/99—C–540/99 *Reisch and Others* [2002] E.C.R. I–2157, para.26 (and Opinion of Advocate General L.A. Geelhoed in this case); ECJ (order of February 17, 2005), Case C–250/03 *Mauri*, not reported, para.21.

[326] ECJ, Case C–231/89 *Gmurzynska-Bscher* [1990] E.C.R. I–4003, para.23.

2–039 **Fictitious dispute.** It is not, however, an easy matter for the Court to decide that it "appears" that the main proceedings are spurious, without in so doing exceeding the limits of its jurisdiction. It is a slippery slope from finding that preliminary questions have been raised "within the framework of procedural devices arranged by the parties in order to induce the Court to give its views on certain problems of Community law which do not correspond to an objective requirement inherent in the resolution of a dispute"[327] to assessing facts and aspects of national law on which no definitive finding has yet been made by the national court, a task which falls outside the limits of the Court's jurisdiction.

In order to avoid this difficulty the Court will decide that the preliminary reference is inadmissible only where it is manifestly apparent from the facts set out in the order for reference that the dispute is in fact fictitious.[328] In this way, the Court confines its review to a species of "marginal review" of facts plainly set out in the order for reference, even without having regard to further particulars contained in the case-file from the national court or in observations submitted pursuant to what is now Art.23 of the Statute of the Court.[329]

2–040 ***Foglia v Novello.*** The only case to date in which the Court has declined jurisdiction on account of the spurious nature of the main proceedings was one in which the parties were concerned to obtain a ruling that a tax system in one Member State was invalid by the expedient of proceedings before a court in another Member State between two private individuals who were in agreement as to the result to be obtained and had inserted a clause in their contract in order to induce a court in another Member State to give a ruling on the point.[330] The Court held that the artificial nature of this expedient was underlined by the fact that the remedies available under the law of the first Member State to contest the tax in question had not been used.[331]

This judgment has been severely criticised by commentators on the ground that the Court exceeded its powers by going too deeply into the facts of the main proceedings, specifically with the intention of making the national court respect the limits of the Court's jurisdiction in so far as it is to give only preliminary rulings which actually contribute towards resolving

---

[327] ECJ, Case 244/80 *Foglia v Novello* (*Foglia v Novello II*) [1981] E.C.R. 3045, para.18.

[328] ECJ, Case 267/86 *Van Eycke* [1988] E.C.R. 4769, para.12; ECJ, Case C–118/94 *Associazione Italiana per il WWF and Others* [1996] E.C.R. I–1223, para.15; ECJ, Case C–129/94 *Bernáldez* [1996] E.C.R. I–1829, para.7; ECJ, Case C–36/99 *Idéal Tourisme* [2000] E.C.R. I–6049, para.22 (the documents in the case contained nothing to show that the parties to the main proceedings had colluded).

[329] *Cf. Van Eycke*, cited in the preceding n., Report for the Hearing, at 4774, second column.

[330] ECJ, Case 104/79 *Foglia v Novello* (*Foglia v Novello I*) [1980] E.C.R. 745, para.10. Where a court in one Member State makes a reference for a preliminary ruling relating to the legality of another Member State's legislation, the hurdle for admissibility will invariably be set high: see 2–036, *supra*.

[331] *Foglia v Novello I*, para.10.

the main dispute. It has been argued that this puts at risk the whole relationship of trust between the Court of Justice and the national courts on which the cooperation mechanism set in place by Art.234 of the EC Treaty is founded.[332] It is therefore not surprising that subsequently the Court has done everything to reduce the scope of this case-law to a hard core of exceptional cases[333]: where it is clear from the factual data set out in the order for reference that the main proceedings are manifestly spurious, the Court will decline jurisdiction on the ground that answering the national court's preliminary questions will not assist it in giving judgment (which is unnecessary if there is no "dispute"). Clearly, such a situation will arise only exceptionally.[334]

III. The Duty to Request a Preliminary Ruling

General. The third para. of Art.234 of the EC Treaty provides that where a question concerning the interpretation of Community law or the validity of acts of Community institutions is raised in a national court and it considers that a decision on the question is necessary to enable it to give judgment, it

2–041

---

[332] Audretsch, "Storm in een glas water?" (1981) S.E.W. 390–396; Barav, "Preliminary Censorship? The Judgment of the European Court in *Foglia v Novello*" (1980) E.L.Rev. 443–468; Barav, "Imbroglio préjudiciel" (1982) R.T.D.E. 431–483; Bebr, "The Existence of a Genuine Dispute: an Indispensable Precondition for the Jurisdiction of the Court under Art.177 [*now Art.234*] EEC Treaty" (1980) C.M.L.Rev. 525–537; Lenaerts, "Toegewezen bevoegdheden en prejudiciële evenwichtsoefeningen in de rechtsorde van de Europese Gemeenschap. Een perspectiefbeeld" (1983–1984) R.W. 129, at 143–149; Lipstein, "*Foglia v Novello*—Some Unexplored Aspects", in *Du droit international au droit de l'intégration— Liber amicorum Pierre Pescatore* (Nomos, Baden-Baden, 1987), at 373–385; Tizzano, "Litiges fictifs et compétence préjudicielle de la Cour de justice européenne" (1981) R.G.D.I.P. 514, at 524–525; Van Nuffel, case note in (1980–1981) S.E.W. 1247–1252.

[333] ECJ, Case 46/80 *Vinal* [1981] E.C.R. 77, paras 5–7, and the Opinion of Advocate General G. Reischl in that case, at 98, which refers to the exceptional nature of *Foglia v Novello*.

[334] Consequently, the case-law on this point is in fact reverting to the Court's former stance; *cf.* Case 20/64 *Albatros* [1965] E.C.R. 29, at 33–34; ECJ, Case 261/81 *Rau* [1982] E.C.R. 3961, paras 8–9; ECJ, Case 267/86 *Van Eycke* [1988] E.C.R. 4769, para.12; but the principle that spurious proceedings are inadmissible remains: ECJ, Joined Cases C–297/88 and C–197/89 *Dzodzi* [1990] E.C.R. I–3763, para.40; *cf.* ECJ, Case C–88/91 *Federconsorzi* [1992] E.C.R. I–4035, paras 6–10 (Community law applicable through a contractual provision); ECJ, Case C–412/93 *Leclerc-Siplec* [1995] E.C.R. I–179, para.14 (the fact that the parties to the main proceedings are in agreement as to the result to be obtained makes the dispute no less real); ECJ, Case C–408/95 *Eurotunnel and Others* [1997] E.C.R. I–6315, para.22 (the reality of the dispute may be inferred from the fact that all the arguments raised by the plaintiff in the main proceedings have been contested by the defendant in those proceedings); EJC, Case C–451/99 *Cura Anlagen* [2002] E.C.R. I–3193, para.27 (the preliminary question was admissible because the main proceedings related to a genuine contract the performance or annulment of which depended on a question of Community law, even if some of the information on the file might give rise to a suspicion that the situation underlying the main proceedings was contrived with a view to obtaining a decision from the Court on a question of Community law of general interest); ECJ, Case C–341/01 *Plato Plastik Robert Frank* [2004] E.C.R. I–4883, para.30 (the fact that the parties to the main proceedings were in agreement as to the interpretation of the Community provisions in question did not affect the reality of the dispute).

is bound to bring the matter before the Court of Justice where "there is no judicial remedy under national law" against the national court's decisions.

A. WHAT NATIONAL COURTS AND TRIBUNALS ARE INVOLVED?

2–042 **Highest courts.** In the first place, the highest courts in the hierarchy are under a duty to make a preliminary reference, irrespective as to whether they have general competence (House of Lords) or specialised jurisdiction (*e.g.* the *Tariefcommissie voor Belastingzaken*, a revenue court in the Netherlands[335]).[336]

The idea behind this is that in the national legal systems decisions of the highest courts bind lower courts (in one way or another) with the result that the most efficient way of securing uniformity of Community law in all the Member States is to oblige courts of last resort to refer questions to the Court of Justice for a preliminary ruling.[337] If that obligation were to be extended to all courts and tribunals, the Court of Justice would be overloaded and there would be no real additional gain in terms of the uniformity of Community law since the lower courts have to follow decisions of courts of last resort which are the outcome of collaboration with the Court of Justice. Naturally, this does not detract from the *right* of *any* court[338] to decide to refer a question to the Court of Justice of its own motion.

2–043 **No remedy available against the decision of a lower court.** Secondly, courts other than those of last resort may in certain circumstances take decisions against which there is no remedy. Are those courts then under a duty to make a reference for a preliminary ruling under the third para. of Art.234 of the EC Treaty? The Court of Justice appears to have answered this question in the affirmative in an *obiter dictum* in the leading case of *Costa v ENEL*, decided in 1964. It stated with regard to a request for a preliminary ruling from an Italian *Giudice Conciliatore* (magistrate) that "By the terms of [Art. 177*[now Art.234]*] national courts against whose decisions, *as in the present case*, there is no judicial remedy, must refer the matter to the Court of Justice so that a preliminary ruling may be given . . .".[339] Accordingly,

---

[335] ECJ, Case 26/62 *Van Gend & Loos* [1963] E.C.R. 1; ECJ, Joined Cases 28–30/62 *Da Costa en Schaake and Others* [1963] E.C.R. 31, at 38.

[336] Joliet, *Le droit institutionnel des Communautés européennes—Le contentieux* (Faculté de Droit, d'Économie et des Sciences Sociales de Liège, Liège, 1981), at 180. A survey of the highest courts may be found in Mayer, "Das Bundesverfassungsgericht und die Verpflichtung zur Vorlage an den Europäischen Gerichtshof" (2002) EuR. 239–257, in particular at 253–255.

[337] ECJ, Case 107/76 *Hoffmann-La Roche* [1977] E.C.R. 957, first subpara. of para.5: "[T]he particular object of the third para. [of Art.177 [*now Art.234*]] is to prevent a body of case-law not in accord with the rules of Community law from coming into existence in any Member State". See also ECJ, Joined Cases 35 and 36/82 *Morson and Jhanjan* [1982] E.C.R. 3723, para.8.

[338] See, however, EC Treaty, Art.68(1); 22–002, *infra*.

[339] ECJ, Case 6/64 *Costa v ENEL* [1964] E.C.R. 585, third para., at 592 (emphasis added).

where a lower court has the power to prevent an appeal from it, it must make a reference if it is minded to exercise its power not to allow an appeal (*e.g.* in England and Wales where a court such as the Divisional Court declines to certify a question of law as fit for consideration by the House of Lords).

Interim proceedings. A judge hearing an application for *interim relief*, where no judicial remedy is available against his order, is in a special position. In response to a preliminary question relating specifically to that situation the Court of Justice ruled that "a national court or tribunal is not required to refer to the Court a question of interpretation or of validity mentioned in [Art. 177*[now Art.234]*] when the question is raised in interlocutory proceedings for [interim relief], even where no judicial remedy is available against the decision to be taken in the context of those proceedings provided that each of the parties is entitled to institute proceedings or to require proceedings to be instituted on the substance of the case and that during such proceedings the question provisionally decided in the summary proceedings may be re-examined and may be the subject of a reference to the Court under Art.177*[now Art.234]*".[340] Subsequently, the Court refined this by stating that the requirements of the third para. of Art.234 are observed even if only the unsuccessful party may bring proceedings as to the substance and the action is tried "before courts or tribunals belonging to a jurisdictional system different from that under which the interlocutory proceedings are conducted, provided that it is still possible to refer to the Court under Art.177*[now Art.234]* any questions of Community law which are raised".[341]

2–044

Benelux Court of Justice. Lastly, the Benelux Court of Justice (see 2–014, *supra*), which gives definitive rulings on questions of interpretation of uniform Benelux law, may be obliged to make a reference to the Court of Justice under the third para. of Art.234 of the EC Treaty.[342] The Court of Justice has held, however, that if, before making a reference to the Benelux Court, a national court has submitted a question of Community law to the Court of Justice, the Benelux Court is released from its obligation to submit the question if it would be couched in "substantially the same terms" (see 2–050, *infra*).

2–045

B. DECISIONS AGAINST WHICH THERE IS NO JUDICIAL REMEDY UNDER NATIONAL LAW

Existence of a judicial remedy. The question as to against what decisions a "judicial remedy" exists is a matter of national law, as is clear from the actual wording of the third para. of Art.234. All the same, Community law

2–046

---

[340] ECJ, Case 107/76 *Hoffmann-La Roche* [1977] E.C.R. 957, para.6.
[341] ECJ, Joined Cases 35 and 36/82 *Morson and Jhanjan* [1982] E.C.R. 3723, paras 8 and 9.
[342] ECJ, Case C–337/95 *Parfums Christian Dior* [1997] E.C.R. I–6013, para.26.

does play a role, more specifically in ascertaining what type of possible "judicial remedy" precludes the obligation to make a reference for a preliminary ruling. The starting point for any inquiry should be the aim of the third para. of Art.234, which is to avoid the most authoritative case-law in any given Member State developing contrary to Community law, thus putting all courts in that State at risk of going off in the same—wrong—direction.

Consequently, the obligation to make a preliminary reference arises whenever the national court finds that there is no judicial remedy available against its decisions which can normally be deployed against judicial decisions, no matter how the remedy is described. Whether the remedy is termed "ordinary" or "exceptional" has no bearing in this regard. The only test is whether the legal issues which the lower court has decided may, as a matter of course, be subjected to a fresh judicial assessment. This is clearly the case with an appeal on a point of law or in cassation proceedings, which must accordingly be deemed to be a "judicial remedy" within the meaning of the third para. of Art.234.[343] Questions of Community law are in fact legal issues which are definitively settled in the highest courts.

2–047 **Wholly exceptional judicial remedies.** In contrast, the existence of wholly exceptional judicial remedies—even where they may be available against decisions of the highest courts—may not be invoked in order to avoid the obligation to seek a preliminary ruling. Examples are applications for the revision of a judgment or *tierce-opposition* proceedings. The *Verfassungsbeschwerde* (constitutional appeal) which may be brought before the Federal Constitutional Court against a judgment of a court of last resort (*e.g.* the *Bundesgerichtshof* or the *Bundesfinanzhof*) is an example from Germany. The existence of such an exceptional remedy—which, moreover, does not enable all the legal issues decided by the court of last resort to be reviewed, but relates only to the compatibility of the contested judgment with the German Basic Law—does not detract from the obligation of the ordinary German courts of last resort to request a preliminary ruling from the Court of Justice.[344]

C. LIMITS SET TO THE DUTY TO REQUEST A PRELIMINARY RULING

2–048 **Irrelevant questions.** First and foremost, courts coming within the scope of the third para. of Art.234 have a discretion to assess the *relevance* of a request for a preliminary ruling (see 2–029 to 2–031, *supra*). The Court of

---

[343] The fact that, as in Sweden, leave is required from the highest court in order to lodge an appeal does not have the effect of depriving the parties of a judicial remedy with the result that this must be regarded as an "exceptional remedy". Where appropriate, the question of Community law raised in a dispute may place the highest court under a duty to grant leave to appeal and, at a later stage, refer a question for a preliminary ruling to the Court of Justice (ECJ, Case C–99/00 *Lyckeskog* [2002] E.C.R. I–4839, paras 10–19).

[344] *Cf.* Lagrange, "L'action préjudicielle dans le droit interne des États membres et en droit communautaire" (1974) R.T.D.E. 268, at 284.

Justice enlarged upon this in the leading case of *CILFIT*, decided in 1982.[345] The mere fact that a party contends that the dispute gives rise to a question concerning the interpretation of Community law or the validity of an act of a Community institution does not mean that the court concerned is compelled to request a preliminary ruling.[346] The Court takes the view that "it follows from the relationship between the second and third paras of Art.177*[now Art.234]* that the courts or tribunals referred to in the third para. have the same discretion as any other national court or tribunal to ascertain whether a decision on a question of Community law is necessary to enable them to give judgment. Accordingly, those courts or tribunals are not obliged to refer to the Court of Justice a question concerning the interpretation of Community law [or the validity of an act of a Community institution] raised before them if that question is not relevant, that is to say, if the answer to that question, regardless of what it may be, can in no way affect the outcome of the case".[347] In such a case the Court of Justice would moreover dismiss the request for a preliminary ruling in any event on account of the irrelevance of the question referred (see the *Salonia* and *Lourenço Dias* cases) (see 2–032 to 2–035, *supra*).

Limits to the duty to refer with respect to relevant questions. Next, it falls to consider the actual exceptions to the obligation to request a preliminary ruling where the question is manifestly relevant for the purposes of reaching a decision in the main proceedings. There are three instances in which the Court of Justice has tempered the obligation to seek a preliminary ruling in the interests of more efficiently achieving the aim of the third para. of Art.234, namely "to prevent the occurrence within the Community of divergences in judicial decisions on questions of Community law".[348]   2–049

Identical question. *First*: in the 1963 judgment in *Da Costa en Schaake*, the Court ruled that "the authority of an interpretation under Art.177*[now Art.234]* already given by the Court may deprive the obligation [to seek a preliminary ruling] of its purpose and thus empty it of its substance. Such is   2–050

---

[345] ECJ, Case 283/81 *CILFIT* [1982] E.C.R. 3415.
[346] *Cf. ibid.*, para.9. For the approach taken in the courts of England and Wales, see Brealey and Hoskins, *Remedies in E.C. Law*, at 218–224. In *R v International Stock Exchange, ex parte Else Ltd* [1993] QB 534, at 545C–G, Sir Thomas Bingham said, "If the national court has any real doubt, it should ordinarily refer". Advocate General F.G. Jacobs expressed the view in his Opinion of July 10, 1997 in Case C–338/95 *Wiener SI* [1997] E.C.R. I–6495, points 12–20, that national courts should show self-restraint in making references where there is no question of general importance or the ruling is not likely to promote the uniform application of Community law. In *Customs & Excise Commissioners v APS Samex* [1983] 1 All E.R. 1042, at 1056f–g, Bingham J. called on judges to have regard to the expense and time needed for a preliminary ruling.
[347] *Ibid.*, para.10. For a case in which leave to make a reference for a preliminary ruling was refused on grounds of lack of relevance, see *R v Licensing Authority, ex parte Smith-Kline* [1990] 1 A.C. 64.
[348] *Ibid.*, para.7.

the case especially when the question raised is materially identical with a question which has already been the subject of a preliminary ruling in a similar case".[349] The national court which is obliged in principle under the third para. of Art.234 to make a reference to the Court of Justice is released from its obligation provided that it follows the existing preliminary ruling. It is only the obligation to make a reference which ceases to apply, not the possibility of seeking a ruling. More specifically, where the national court would like the Court of Justice to amend, qualify or limit its earlier preliminary ruling—for instance, in the light of the particular facts of the main action—the only solution is for the national court to make use of that possibility.[350]

2–051 **The answer can be clearly deduced from the case-law.** *Secondly*: "The same effect, as regards the limits set to the obligation laid down by the third para. of Art.177*[now Art.234]*, may be produced where previous decisions of the Court have already dealt with the point of law in question, irrespective of the nature of the proceedings which led to those decisions, even though the questions at issue are not strictly identical".[351] This is an extension of the first exception: it is no longer a requirement for the earlier judgment of the Court to have ruled on a virtually identical preliminary question. In contrast, it is sufficient that the earlier decision should provide an answer to the question of Community law which has arisen in the main proceedings, regardless of the procedural context in which it came about. This also provides an explanation as to why the questions at issue need not be completely identical, which would appear to be out of the question where the earlier judgment was not given in answer to a request for a preliminary ruling. The only critical point is whether the decision is capable of being regarded as "settled case-law" or one of a number of "previous decisions" as the English translation has it, or, in other words, whether it can be definitely regarded as constituting the Court of Justice's answer to the question of Community law which has arisen. Thus, a judgment given pursuant to Arts 226 to 228 of the EC Treaty in which the Court declared that a Member State had failed to fulfil its obligations under Community law will generally contain an interpretation of provisions and principles of

---

[349] ECJ, Joined Cases 28–30/62 *Da Costa en Schaake and Others* [1963] E.C.R. 31, at 38, confirmed by ECJ, Case 283/81 *CILFIT* [1982] E.C.R. 3415, para.13, and ECJ, Case C–337/95 *Parfums Christian Dior* [1997] E.C.R. I–6013, paras 29–30 (where it was held that the question had to be in "substantially the same terms").
[350] *CILFIT*, cited in the preceding n., para.15.
[351] *Ibid.*, para.14.

that law.[352] In so far as that is so, national courts subject to the third para. of Art.234 can extract from the judgment what they need in order to answer the questions concerning the interpretation of Community law which are determinative of the main proceedings pending before them. In common with any court, they are even obliged to do this,[353] unless they opt to exercise their right to bring the matter before the Court of Justice anew, perhaps with a view to an adjustment of the case-law.[354]

Acte clair. *Thirdly*: "[T]he correct application of Community law may be so 2–052
obvious as to leave no scope for any reasonable doubt as to the manner in which the question raised is to be resolved. Before it comes to the conclusion that such is the case, the national court or tribunal must be convinced that the matter is equally obvious to the courts of the other Member States and to the Court of Justice". If that condition is satisfied, the national court may "refrain from submitting the question to the Court of Justice and take upon itself the responsibility for resolving it".[355] This exception is known as the *acte clair* doctrine.

The strict conditions to which implementation of the *acte clair* doctrine is subject are designed to prevent national courts from abusing the doctrine in order to evade their obligation to seek a preliminary ruling where they are disinclined to adhere to the Court's case-law. Both the French *Conseil d'Etat* and the German *Bundesfinanzhof* at one time abused the *acte clair* doctrine in this way.[356] According to those courts, the wording of the third para. of Art.249 of the EC Treaty was so clear that it was unnecessary to seek a preliminary ruling from the Court of Justice on the effect within a Member State's national legal system of a directive which had failed to be

---

[352] The fact that the Commission discontinues infringement proceedings under Art.226 of the EC Treaty against a Member State concerning a piece of legislation has no effect on the obligation upon a court of last instance of that Member State to refer to the Court of Justice a preliminary question on the interpretation of Community law so as to be able to assess the compatibility with that law of the national legislation which was the subject of the infringement proceedings. This is because the Commission is not empowered to determine conclusively, by opinions formulated pursuant to Art.226 or by other statements of its attitude under that procedure, the rights and duties of a Member State and hence determine the scope of Community law. The rights and duties of Member States may be determined only by a judgment of the Court of Justice (ECJ, Case C–393/98 *Gomes Valente* [2001] E.C.R. I–1327, paras 17–19).

[353] ECJ, Joined Cases 314–316/81 and 83/82 *Waterkeyn* [1982] E.C.R. 4337, paras 13–16.

[354] ECJ, Case 283/81 *CILFIT* [1982] E.C.R. 3415, para.15.

[355] *Ibid.*, para.16; ECJ, Case C–340/99 *TNT Traco* [2001] E.C.R. I–4109, para.35.

[356] France: Conseil d'Etat, December 22, 1978, *Ministre de l'Intérieur v Cohn-Bendit* (1979) R.T.D.E. 168–189, translated in [1980] 1 C.M.L.R. 543. Germany: Bundesfinanzhof, July 16, 1981, (1981) EuR. 442–444. See Bebr, "The Rambling Ghost of 'Cohn-Bendit': *Acte clair* and the Court of Justice" (1983) C.M.L.Rev. 439–472. An explanation of the position taken by the *Conseil d'Etat* is to be found in Genevois, "Der Conseil d'Etat und das Gemeinschaftsrecht: Antagonismus oder Komplementarität?" (1985) EuR. 355–367. For English examples, see *R v London Boroughs Transport Committee, ex parte Freight Transport Association Ltd* [1992] 1 C.M.L.R. 5 and *Kirklees Borough Council v Wickes Building Supplies Ltd* [1992] 3 W.L.R. 170, discussed in Brealey and Hoskins, *Remedies in E.C. Law*, at 227–228.

implemented within the prescribed period. By reference to the plain words of Art.249, however, they decided, completely contrary to the settled case-law of the Court of Justice,[357] that in the circumstances in question a directive could never have direct effect on account of its legal nature.

The *CILFIT* formulation of the *acte clair* doctrine is the expression of a particularly subtle compromise.[358] On the one hand, the Court sought to reinforce spontaneous collaboration on the part of the highest national courts by allowing them to take the responsibility upon themselves to decide questions of Community law where it is not reasonably conceivable that anyone would come to a different answer. A very limited category of extremely obvious questions of Community law is involved here. It would have been insensitive of the Court to have placed no trust in the judgment of the highest national courts with regard even to that sort of question. For other types of questions, the national courts have to place their trust in the Court of Justice once they realise that more than one answer is conceivable.[359] On the other hand, the Court seeks to constrain the judgment of the highest national courts as to the obvious nature of the—apparently only conceivable—answer to a question of Community law as much as possible in order to preclude *bona fide* inadvertence. To this end, the Court has listed three factors which the highest national courts have to take into account before they are entitled to consider that they may release themselves from their obligation to seek a preliminary ruling. Those factors have to do with the "characteristic features of Community law and the particular difficulties to which its interpretation gives rise".[360] These factors are as follows: (1) the interpretation of a provision of Community law involves a comparison of the various language versions, all of which are authentic; (2) given that Community law uses terminology peculiar to it, legal concepts do not necessarily have the same meaning as they do in the different national legal systems; (3) every provision of Community law must be placed in its context and interpreted "in the light of the provisions of Community law as a whole, regard being had to the objectives thereof and to its state of evolution at the date on which the provision in question is to be applied".[361]

It is self-evident that if these three factors were scrupulously taken into account, the number of cases in which "the correct application of Com-

---

[357] For the direct effect of directives, see Lenaerts and Van Nuffel, *Constitutional Law of the European Union*, § 17–124–§ 17–129, at 769–774.

[358] *Cf.* the opposite view taken in the Opinion of Advocate General F. Capotorti in ECJ, Case 283/81 *CILFIT* [1982] E.C.R. 3415, at 3442.

[359] See to this effect Mancini and Keeling, "From *CILFIT* to *ERT*: the Constitutional Challenge facing the European Court" (1991) Y.E.L. 1, at 4–5; Rasmussen, "The European Court's Acte Clair Strategy in *CILFIT* (Or: 'Acte Clair, of course! But what does it mean?')" (1984) E.L.Rev. 242.

[360] ECJ, Case 283/81 *CILFIT* [1982] E.C.R. 3415, para.17.

[361] *Ibid.*, paras 18–20. See also ECJ (judgment of September 15, 2005), Case C–495/03 *Intermodal Transports*, not yet reported, paras 26–45. The *CILFIT* case-law does not apply to questions relating to the validity of a Community act (ECJ (judgment of December 6, 2005), Case C–461/03 *Gaston Schul Douane-expediteur*, not yet reported, para.19).

munity law is so obvious as to leave no scope for any reasonable doubt"[362] would be reduced to an absolute minimum.[363]

D. Enforcement of the Obligation to Request a Preliminary Ruling

Infringement action. There is no remedy available from the Court of Justice to parties to the main proceedings against a refusal of a court of last resort to make a preliminary reference. The Commission or a Member State may, however, seek a declaration from the Court of Justice pursuant to Art.226 or 227 of the EC Treaty that, through its national court's refusal to seek a ruling, the Member State in question has infringed the third para. of Art.234. Courts and tribunals are in fact "institutions of the Member State concerned".[364]   2–053

The Commission acknowledges a duty to oversee the way in which national courts subject to the obligation to seek preliminary rulings make use of the *acte clair* doctrine enshrined in the judgment in *CILFIT*.[365]

Difficulties. The institution of proceedings for infringement of Community law on account of the failure of a national court to comply with its obligation under the third para. of Art.234 is not, however, an efficient way of enforcing that obligation. In the first place, the parties to the main proceedings are not directly assisted thereby. Secondly, whilst in such proceedings it is no defence for a Member State to plead the independence under its Constitution of the State institution responsible for the infringement of Community law,[366] in a "Community based on the rule of law"[367] the essential principle of the constitutional independence of the judiciary from the executive and the legislature nevertheless implies that a national government which is unsuccessful in an action brought against it under Art.226 can count on comprehension where it is not in a position to compel the offending court to change its position. Unlike other "independent"   2–054

---

[362] *CILFIT*, para.21.

[363] *CILFIT* may, however, also be abused: see Arnull, "The Use and Abuse of Art.177 [*now Art.234*] EEC" (1989) Mod.L.Rev. 622–639, in which the author cites a number of English cases which wrongly used the *CILFIT* judgment in order not to seek a preliminary ruling. For a general discussion of *CILFIT*, see Masclet, "Vers la fin d'une controverse? La Cour de justice tempère l'obligation de renvoi préjudiciel en interprétation faite aux juridictions suprêmes (art. 177 [*now Art.234*], alinéa 3, CEE)" (1983) R.M.C. 363–373.

[364] ECJ, Joined Cases 314–316/81 and 83/82 *Waterkeyn* [1982] E.C.R. 4337, para.14. See also ECJ, Case C–224/01 *Köbler* [2003] E.C.R. I–10239; ECJ, Case C–129/00 *Commission v Italy* [2003] E.C.R. I–14637.

[365] Answer given by President G. Thorn on behalf of the Commission on July 25, 1983 to a written question from A. Tyrrell MEP, [1983] O.J. C 268/25. In Germany, the *Bundesverfassungsgericht* held that the failure of the *Bundesverwaltungsgericht* to refer a preliminary question to the Court of Justice was in breach of Art.101(1)(2) of the Basic Law (see Bundesverfassungsgericht, January 9, 2001 (2001) Eu.GR.Z. 150, with a case note by Classen (2002) C.M.L.Rev. 641–652).

[366] Rideau and Picod, *Code de procédures juridictionnelles de l'Union européenne* (2nd ed., Litec, Paris, 2002), at 178.

[367] ECJ, Case 294/83 *Les Verts v European Parliament* [1986] E.C.R. 1339, para.23.

institutions of the State (e.g. legislative bodies, States forming part of a federation, etc.), in respect of which it is felt that the Member State should, where necessary, adjust its internal structure in such a way that it is always in a position to ensure that those institutions effectively comply with Community law, even if this is at the expense of their independence, a certain reluctance is—properly—felt in advocating that idea as far as the highest national courts are concerned. Commentators are also at one in taking the view that it would be inappropriate to enforce the obligation laid down in the third para. of Art.234 by means of proceedings under Arts 226 and 227 of the EC Treaty.[368]

The conclusion is that, as a matter of fact, the obligation to seek a preliminary ruling cannot be enforced directly. Instead, compliance with that obligation is based on the relationship of trust linking the highest national courts and the Court of Justice in a context of efficient collaboration.

2–055   **Claim in damages.** However, Community law requires Member States to recognise the possibility of a claim in damages against the public authorities where an infringement by a court of last resort of its obligation to make a reference for a preliminary ruling demonstrably thwarts a right conferred on individuals by Community law. The Court confirmed this in the case of Köbler.[369] Especially in cases where the acte clair doctrine is abused and the court of last resort shirks its obligation to seek a preliminary ruling in order to ignore the settled case-law of the Court of Justice on the interpretation of a particular provision on the purported ground that it is obvious, it may well be imagined that the interested individual may identify an individual right which is denied to him (loss or damage) as a result (causal link) of the national court's refusal to comply with the third para. of Art.234 of the EC

---

[368] Joliet, Le contentieux, at 186.
[369] ECJ, Case C–224/01 Köbler [2003] E.C.R. I–10239, paras 30–50; ECJ (judgment of September 15, 2005), Case C–495/03 Intermodal Transports, not yet reported, para.37. It is for the internal legal order of each Member State to designate the competent court to deal with such claims. According to the Court of Justice, the independence of the judiciary and the principle of res judicata do not preclude recognition of the principle of State liability stemming from a decision of a court adjudicating at last instance. See also Steyger, "De gevolgen van de aansprakelijkheid van de Staat voor rechterlijke schendingen van EG-recht" (2004) N.T.E.R. 18–22; Breuer, "State liability for judicial wrongs and Community law: the case of Gerhard Köbler v Austria" (2004) E.L.Rev. 243–254; Huglo, "La responsabilité des États membres du fait des violations du droit communautaire par les juridictions nationales: un autre regard" (2004) Gazette du Palais 33–40; Botella, "La responsabilité du juge national" (2004) R.T.D.E. 283–315; for a particularly critical view, see Wattel, "Köbler, CILFIT and Welthgrove: we can't go on meeting like this" (2004) C.M.L.Rev. 177–190: the author argues that the Court of Justice also ought to be able to be held liable for manifest breaches of Community law; he manifestly overlooks the fact that the Court of Justice, unlike courts of last resort in the Member States, is the highest court for the interpretation of Community law. By definition, the interpretation which the Court of Justice gives to provisions of Community law is correct.

Treaty (breach of Community law).[370] This development accords well with the right recognised by a number of Member States in connection with State liability in damages for loss or damage caused to individuals as a result of a breach of superior law on the part of the judiciary.[371]

E. OBLIGATION TO REQUEST A PRELIMINARY RULING *PRAETER LEGEM*

Invalidity of a Community act. Where a court or tribunal not subject to the 2–056 third para. of Art.234 perceives that an act of a Community institution is invalid, it may not make such a finding itself, but *must* seek a preliminary ruling thereon from the Court of Justice.[372] At first sight, this obligation detracts from the national court's freedom under the second para. of Art.234 to decide whether or not to make a reference to the Court of Justice. But the Court has held that "In enabling national courts, against whose decisions there is a judicial remedy under national law, to refer to the Court for a preliminary ruling questions on interpretation or validity, Art.177*[now Art.234]* did not settle the question whether those courts themselves may declare that acts of Community institutions are invalid".[373] Consequently, the relevant provision of the Treaty has a *lacuna* which the Court has filled by answering that question in the negative. In the Court's view, this is necessary for three reasons: *first*, divergences between courts in the Member States as to the validity of Community acts would be liable to place in jeopardy the unity of Community law; *secondly*, since the Court has exclusive jurisdiction to declare void an act of a Community institution (EC Treaty, Art.230), the coherence of the system of judicial protection established by the Treaty requires that where the validity of a Community act is challenged before a national court the power to declare the act invalid must also be reserved to the Court of Justice, since both proceedings are "designed to permit the Court of Justice to review the legality of measures adopted by the institutions"[374]; *thirdly*, the Court of Justice is in the best

---

[370] By analogy with ECJ, Joined Cases C–6 and C–9/90 *Francovich and Others* [1991] E.C.R. I–5357, paras 39–40. The Member State concerned may incur liability under Community law all the more readily inasmuch as the highest national court has no discretion in applying the third para.of Art.234; see 3–041, *infra*. See also Ter Kuile, "To Refer or not to Refer: About the Last Para. of Art.177 *[now Art.234]* of the EC Treaty", in Curtin and Heukels (eds), *Institutional Dynamics of European Integration. Essays in Honour of H.G. Schermers* (Martinus Nijhoff, Dordrecht, 1994), Vol.II, 381, at 388–389.

[371] Belgium: Cass., December 19, 1991 (1992) J.T. 142. Netherlands: In principle there is no recognition of State liability on account of judicial conduct amounting to fault: *Hoge Raad*, March 17, 1978 (1979) NJ 204, but in a judgment of October 11, 1991 ((1992) NJ 62), the *Hoge Raad* recognised that there may be State liability for the wrong interpretation of a provision of the Code of Criminal Procedure by the public prosecutor's office.

[372] ECJ, Case 314/85 *Foto-Frost* [1987] E.C.R. 4199 (with case notes by Arnull, "National Courts and the Validity of Community Acts" (1988) E.L.Rev. 125–131, and Bebr (cited in 2–006, n.190, *supra*), at 678, who identifies the autonomous nature of Community law as an additional reason for the exclusive jurisdiction of the Court of Justice to declare a Community measure invalid); see also ECJ, Case C–6/99 *Greenpeace France and Others* [2000] E.C.R. I–1651, para.55.

[373] *Foto-Frost*, para.13.

[374] *Ibid.*, paras 16 and 17.

position to decide on the validity of Community acts, since Community institutions whose acts are challenged "are entitled [under what is now Art.23 of the Protocol on the Statute of the Court of Justice to participate in the proceedings in order to defend the validity of the acts in question".[375]

2–057 **Limits to *Foto-Frost*.** What national courts not subject to the third para. of Art.234 may of course do is "consider the validity of a Community act and, if they consider that the grounds put forward before them by the parties in support of invalidity are unfounded, they may reject them, concluding that the measure is completely valid. By taking that action they are not calling into question the existence of the Community measure."[376] It is only where the validity of a Community act is contested before a court subject to the third para. of Art.234 that that court must seek a preliminary ruling from the Court of Justice, even if it itself does not share the view that the act is invalid.[377]

2–058 **Divergence from the case-law of Court of Justice.** According to some commentators,[378] the authority of the Court's case-law causes a second obligation to request a preliminary ruling *praeter legem* to arise: where national courts against whose decisions a judicial remedy exists under national law are minded to diverge from the interpretation which the Court of Justice has given to a provision or a principle of Community law, they must first attempt to obtain a change in the Court's case-law by making a request for a preliminary ruling.

It is only by so doing that such courts, as institutions of a Member State, can act in accordance with Art.10 of the EC Treaty (obligation to cooperate in good faith). It would indeed be illogical if national courts of last resort were bound by the "settled case-law" of the Court of Justice, subject to the

---

[375] *Ibid.*, para.18; in addition, under the second para. of Art.24 of the Statute the Court may require the Member States and institutions not being party to the case to supply all information which the Court considers necessary for the proceedings. See also n.361, *supra*.
[376] *Ibid.*, para.14.
[377] When the addressee of a Commission decision has, within the period prescribed in the fifth para. of Art.230 of the Treaty, brought an action for annulment of that decision pursuant to that article, it is for the national court to decide whether to stay proceedings until a definitive decision has been given in the action for annulment or in order to refer a question to the Court for a preliminary ruling. However, when the outcome of the dispute before the national court depends on the validity of the Commission decision, it follows from the obligation of sincere cooperation that the national court *should*, in order to avoid reaching a decision that runs counter to that of the Commission, stay its proceedings pending final judgment in the action for annulment by the Community Courts, unless it considers that, in the circumstances of the case, a reference to the Court of Justice for a preliminary ruling on the validity of the Commission decision is warranted (ECJ, Case C–344/98 *Masterfoods and HB Ice Cream* [2000] E.C.R. I-11369, paras 55 and 57).
[378] Joliet, "L'Art. 177 [*now Art.234*] du traité CEE et le renvoi préjudiciel" (1991) Riv.D.E. 591, at 606–607; Schockweiler,"L'exécution des arrêts de la Cour", in *Du droit international au droit de l'intégration—Liber amicorum Pierre Pescatore* (Nomos, Baden-Baden, 1987), 613, at 630.

possibility of their raising the content of the case-law afresh with the Court (see 2–051, *supra*), yet inferior courts were completely at liberty to diverge from that case-law without having to refer to the Court of Justice.[379]

The different treatment of inferior and superior courts in Art.234 only comes into its own, therefore, where there is not as yet any case-law of the Court of Justice on a question of interpretation of Community law. In such a case, the inferior court will be at liberty to answer the question itself, whilst the superior court will be under an obligation to make a reference to the Court of Justice.

IV. THE CONSTITUTION

Minor changes. Only minor changes are made to the provisions of the EC Treaty regarding preliminary references. First, the provisions of the Constitution reflect new realities and incorporate existing case-law. In this way, Art.III-369, first para., provides that the Court of Justice of the European Union has jurisdiction to give preliminary rulings concerning the interpretation of the Constitution (no longer "of this Treaty") and on the validity and the interpretation of acts of the institutions, bodies, offices and agencies of the Union. Art.III-369 thus incorporates the *acquis communautaire* by formally extending the Court's jurisdiction to give preliminary rulings to cover acts of bodies, offices and agencies of the Union. In fact, the Court's jurisdiction to examine the validity of such acts and to interpret them under the EC Treaty has never been questioned.[380] Since the ECB has been promoted to the status of an institution,[381] Art.III-369 no longer contains an explicit reference to it.

2–059

Proceedings relating to persons in custody. Moreover, since, under the Constitution, *any* national judge can decide to make a reference for a preliminary ruling concerning the interpretation or the validity of acts adopted in the field of police and judicial cooperation in criminal matters (as a result of the extension of the Community method to the third pillar),[382] a significant increase in preliminary references in national crimi-

2–060

---

[379] See to this effect the Opinion of Advocate General J.-P. Warner in ECJ, Case 112/76 *Manzoni* [1977] E.C.R. 1647, second column, at 1662. Moreover, the effect of s.3(1) of the European Communities Act 1972 is that, if no reference to the Court of Justice is made, the UK courts must follow "the principles laid down by and any relevant decision of the European Court".

[380] ECJ, Case 152/83 *Demouche and Others* [1987] E.C.R. 3833, para.19.

[381] Constitution, Art.I–30(3).

[382] Under Art.68(1) of the EC Treaty, *only* courts against whose decisions there is no judicial remedy under national law may make a reference for a preliminary ruling to the Court of Justice with respect to the interpretation or the validity of an act based on Part III, Title IV "Visas, asylum, immigration and other policies related to free movement of persons" of the EC Treaty.

nal proceedings may be expected once the Constitution enters into force. Since the preliminary ruling procedure inevitably results in national proceedings being stayed, the authors of the Constitution deemed it necessary to protect the interests of persons in custody. The fourth para. of Art.III-369 therefore provides that where a preliminary question "is raised in a case pending before a court or a tribunal of a Member State with regard to a person in custody, the Court shall act with the minimum of delay". The Court's Statute could prescribe a more precise period.

2–061 **No incorporation of *Foto-Frost*.** Lastly, it may be regretted that the provisions of the Constitution relating to preliminary references do not incorporate the *Foto-Frost* case-law, according to which a national court which considers a Community act to be invalid is under an obligation to refer a preliminary question to the Court of Justice concerning the validity of the act in question.[383]

---

[383] ECJ, Case 314/85 *Foto-Frost* [1987] E.C.R. 4199. For this case-law, see 2–056 and 2–057, *supra*.

CHAPTER 3

THE PRINCIPLE OF THE FULL EFFECTIVENESS OF COMMUNITY LAW AND ITS IMPACT ON NATIONAL LAW RELATING TO PROCEDURE AND SANCTIONS

National procedural law. As has already been mentioned, Community law falls to be applied principally by national courts. Since the Community does not have procedural law or law governing sanctions of its own,[384] it is for the domestic legal system of each Member State to designate the courts and tribunals having jurisdiction and to lay down the detailed procedural rules governing actions for safeguarding rights which individuals derive from Community law.[385]

3–001

Judicial supervision. The full effectiveness of Community law is achieved only if individuals can assert before their national courts the rights which

3–002

---

[384] What is meant is all those rules of law which come into play in order to apply Community law in the Member States' legal systems. They may have to do with the conduct of judicial proceedings, such as rules on admissibility, procedural time-limits and rules of evidence, or with the execution of judgments. However, concepts of civil law or other substantive law (for example, the concept of unjust enrichment) may sometimes be relevant.

[385] See, *e.g.* ECJ, Case C–231/96 *Edis* [1998] E.C.R. I–4951, para.19, which refers to the judgments in *Rewe* and *Comet* (ECJ, Case 33/76 *Rewe* [1976] E.C.R. 1989, third subpara. of para.5; ECJ, Case 45/76 *Comet* [1976] E.C.R. 2043, para.13). In *Rewe* and *Comet*, the Court referred to "actions at law intended to ensure the protection of the rights which citizens have from the *direct effect* of Community law" (emphasis added). But the duty for Member States to ensure effective legal protection may also require access to the national courts for individuals who seek protection against acts of national authorities infringing provisions of Community law which do not have direct effect (see, *e.g.* ECJ, Joined Cases C–6 and C–9/90 *Francovich and Others* [1991] E.C.R. I–5357). The Court further pointed out in *Rewe* (fourth and fifth subparas of para.5) and *Comet* (paras 14 and 15) that "[w]here necessary, Arts 100 to 102 and 235*[now Arts 94 to 97 and 308]* of the Treaty enable appropriate measures to be taken to remedy differences between the provisions laid down by law, regulation or administrative action in Member States if they are likely to distort or harm the functioning of the common market", but that "[i]n the absence of such harmonisation the rights conferred by Community law must be exercised before the national courts in accordance with the conditions laid down by national rules". This does not, however, preclude testing the national procedural rule against Treaty provisions relating to the four freedoms: see ECJ, Case C–412/97 *ED* [1999] E.C.R. I–3845.

they derive from Community law.[386] Accordingly, the Member States are under an obligation to designate the competent court or tribunal to which individuals may apply with a view to protecting the rights which they derive from the application of Community law.

3–003 **Constraints.** As far as the application of national rules relating to procedure and sanctions by national courts and tribunals is concerned, two difficulties arise. First, these national rules may impede the effective application of Community law, and thereby affect its primacy and direct effect.[387] Secondly, uniform application of Community law may be jeopardised as a result of diverging national laws.[388]

In order to deal with these difficulties, Art.10 of the EC Treaty places national courts and tribunals under a duty to ensure the "full effectiveness of Community law".[389] The Court of Justice has defined this duty by means of a number of Community constraints with which national procedural law and law relating to sanctions must comply.[390] Those constraints (the principles of equivalence and effectiveness) are a practical expression of the principles of the primacy and direct effect of Community law[391] and aim at

---

[386] See, on this subject, Eilmansberger, "The relationship between rights and remedies in EC law : in search of the missing link" (2004) C.M.L. Rev. 1199–1246.

[387] The national law may apply very short limitation periods or deal with the burden of proof or admissible evidence in such a way that the party relying on Community law is unable or has extreme difficulty in proving its claims.

[388] Bridge, "Procedural Aspects of the Enforcement of European Community Law through the Legal Systems of the Member States" (1984) E.L.Rev. 28–42. For examples of judgments in which the Court has expressed regret at the lack of Community provisions harmonising procedures and time-limits, see ECJ, Case 130/79 *Express Dairy Foods* [1980] E.C.R. 1887, para.12, and ECJ, Case 54/81 *Fromme* [1982] E.C.R. 1449, para.4.

[389] ECJ, Case C–213/89 *Factortame and Others* (*Factortame I*) [1990] E.C.R. I–2433, para.21. For a useful discussion of this topic, see Brealey and Hoskins, *Remedies in E.C. Law*, at 99–117. In *R v Secretary of State for the Home Department, ex parte Gallagher* [1996] 2 C.M.L.R. 951, Lord Bingham CJ referred to the "cardinal principle of Community law" that national laws should provide "effective and adequate redress for violations" of that law.

[390] The relevant case-law is remarkable in that the Court of Justice does not have jurisdiction to rule directly on questions of national procedural law (indeed, it systematically refuses to answer preliminary questions relating to the interpretation or validity of national law), yet will nevertheless seize upon the basis in Community law of national courts' obligation to achieve a particular result in order to provide very concrete guidance as to how that obligation must be complied with. For a critical appraisal, see the Opinion of Advocate General D. Ruiz-Jarabo Colomer in Case C–30/02 *Recheio* [2004] E.C.R. I–6053, points 23–36.

[391] Grévisse and Bonichot, "Les incidences du droit communautaire sur l'organisation et l'exercice de la fonction juridictionnelle dans les Etats membres", in *L'Europe et le Droit— Mélanges en hommage à J. Boulouis* (Ed. Dalloz, Paris, 1991), 297, at 309, observe in this connection that "La Cour ne fixe pas les règles de procédure nationale, elle énonce les exigences du droit communautaire qu'elles doivent satisfaire" [The Court does not fix national procedural rules, it sets forth the Community-law requirements which they must fulfil]. See also in this connection Kakouris, "Do the Member States possess Judicial Procedural 'Autonomy'?" (1997) C.M.L.Rev. 1389–1412, who argues that Member States do not possess "procedural autonomy", but that national procedural law is an "ancillary body of law" whose function is to "ensure the effective application of substantive

enabling individuals to claim before national courts the *full* enforcement and protection of the rights which they derive from Community law.[392]

I. The Need for Judicial Supervision

Access to a court. The full effectiveness of Community law can be attained only if individuals can assert the rights which they derive from Community law before a national court. Consequently, the Member States must provide them actual access to a court and to judicial proceedings.[393] Those obligations are not only connected with the full effectiveness of Community law but also reflect a general principle of law which underlies the constitutional traditions common to the Member States and is laid down in

3–004

Community law". He points out that where national courts apply Community law, they belong, functionally, to the Community legal order and therefore cannot be said to possess procedural autonomy. *Cf.* the approach taken by Prechal, "Community Law in National Courts: the Lessons from *Van Schijndel*" (1998) C.M.L.Rev. 681, at 686–687, who emphasises that Community law is part of the national legal order and that the primacy of Community law only applies within the realm of the substantive law.

[392] See also Barav, "La plénitude de compétence du juge national en sa qualité de juge communautaire", in *L'Europe et le Droit—Mélanges en hommage à J. Boulouis* (Ed. Dalloz, Paris, 1991), at 1–20; Borgsmidt, "Principles of Equivalence and Effectiveness" (2001) The EC Tax Journal, Vol. 5, 11–21; Curtin, "The Decentralised Enforcement of Community Law Rights. Judicial Snakes and Ladders", in *Constitutional Adjudication in European Community and National Law. Essays for the Hon. Mr Justice O'Higgins* (Butterworths (Ireland), Dublin, 1992), at 33–49; Girerd, "Les principes d'équivalence et d'effectivité: encadrement ou désencadrement de l'autonomie procédurale des Etats membres" (2002) R.T.D.E. 75–102; Jacobs, "Remedies in National Courts for the Enforcement of Community Rights", in *Liber amicorum Diez de Velasco* (Editorial Tecnos, Madrid, 1993), at 969–983; Michel, "La protection des droits conférés par l'ordre juridique européen", in Tercier, Volken and Michel (eds), *Aspects du droit européen* (Editions universitaires Fribourg Suisse, Fribourg, 1993), at 43–70; Oliver, "Le droit communautaire et les voies de recours nationales" (1992) C.D.E. 348–374; Röben, *Die Einwirkung der Rechtsprechung des Europäischen Gerichtshofs auf das Mitgliedstaatliche Verfahren in öffentlich-rechtlichen Streitigkeiten* (Springer Verlag, Berlin, 1998), 478 pp.; Rodríguez Iglesias, "Zu den Grenzen der verfahrensrechtlichen Autonomie der Mitgliedstaaten bei der Anwendung des Gemeinschaftsrechts" (1997) Eu.GR.Z. 289-295; Struys, "Le droit communautaire et l'application des règles procédurales nationales" (2000) J.T.D.E. 49–53; Szyszczak, "Making Europe more Relevant to its Citizens: Effective Judicial Process" (1996) E.L.Rev. 351–364; van Gerven, "Bridging the Gap between Community and National Laws: Towards a Principle of Homogeneity in the Field of Legal Remedies?" (1995) C.M.L.Rev. 679–702, and "Of Rights, Remedies and Procedures" (2000) C.M.L.Rev. 501–506; see also Ward, "Government Liability in the United Kingdom for Breach of Individual Rights in European Community Law" (1990) 1 Anglo-Am.L.R. 2–11.

[393] Provided that in any event the Member States must ensure effective protection for individual rights derived from Community law, Community law is not involved in resolving questions of jurisdiction to which the classification of certain legal situations based on Community law may give rise in the national judicial system (ECJ, Case C–446/93 *SEIM* [1996] E.C.R. I–73, para 32; ECJ, Case C–224/01 *Köbler* [2003] E.C.R. I–10239, para.47). See also ECJ, Case C–15/04 *Koppensteiner* [2005] E.C.R. I–4855, para.34.

Arts 6 and 13 of the ECHR.[394] That general principle of law is also enshrined in the first para. of Art.47 of the Charter of Fundamental Rights of the European Union.[395]

3–005 **Equal treatment.** In addition, it is a corollary of the prohibition of discrimination enshrined in Art.12 of the EC Treaty that nationals of a Member State carrying out an economic activity on the market of another Member State which falls within the scope of the Treaty must be able to bring actions in the courts of that Member State on the same footing as nationals of that State in order to resolve any disputes arising from their economic activities.[396] Consequently, a Member State is precluded from requiring provision of security for costs by a legal person established in another Member State or by a national of another Member State, even if the person concerned is also a national of a non-member country in which he or she is resident,[397] who has brought an action in its courts against one of its nationals or a company established in its territory where security for costs cannot be required to be provided by legal persons from the State in question[398] and the action is connected with the exercise of fundamental freedoms guaranteed by Community law.[399]

3–006 **Statement of reasons.** In addition, national law must provide for effective judicial review.[400] To that end, the court before which the case is brought should generally be empowered to require the competent authority to state the reasons for any national decision which is contested on the basis of Community law.

---

[394] ECJ, Case 222/84 *Johnston* [1986] E.C.R. 1651, paras 17–18; ECJ, Case C–97/91 *Oleificio Borrelli v Commission* [1992] E.C.R. I–6313, paras 13–14. Indirect confirmation of this is provided by ECJ, Case C–54/96 *Dorsch Consult* [1997] E.C.R. I–4961, para.40; ECJ, Case C–185/97 *Coote* [1998] E.C.R. I–5199, paras 20–21; ECJ, Case C–76/97 *Tögel* [1998] E.C.R. I–5357, para.22; ECJ, Case C–258/97 *HI* [1999] E.C.R. I–1405, para.28; ECJ, Case C–226/99 *Siples* [2001] E.C.R. I–227, paras 15–20. As far as Art.6 of the ECHR is concerned, see also the judgment of the European Court of Human Rights of September 24, 2002 in Case 27824/95 *Posti and Rahko v Finland*.

[395] [2000] O.J. C 364/1.

[396] ECJ, Case C–43/95 *Data Delecta Aktiebolag and Forsberg* [1996] E.C.R. I–4661.

[397] ECJ, Case C–122/96 *Saldanha and MTS Securities* [1997] E.C.R. I–5325, para.30.

[398] ECJ, Case C–323/95 *Hayes* [1997] E.C.R. I–1711, para.22.

[399] *Ibid.*, para.25. See Ackermann's case note to these three judgments (1998) C.M.L.Rev. 783–799. In *Fitzgerald v Williams* [1996] 2 QB 657, the Court of Appeal followed the emergent case-law of the Court of Justice on the ground that to require security for costs under what was then Rules of the Supreme Court, Ord. 23, from Irish nationals resident in Ireland would be discriminatory and not justified in view of the Brussels Convention on jurisdiction and the enforcement of judgments in civil and commercial matters. See now Civil Procedure Rules, R.25(2)(a)(ii).

[400] ECJ, Case 222/86 *Heylens and Others* [1987] E.C.R. 4097, paras 14–16; ECJ, Case C–340/89 *Vlassopoulou* [1991] E.C.R. I–2357, para.22; ECJ, Case C–104/91 *Aguirre Borrell and Others* [1992] E.C.R. I–3003, para.15; ECJ, Case C–111/97 *EvoBus Austria* [1998] E.C.R. I–5411, para.15; ECJ, Case C–228/98 *Dounias* [2000] E.C.R. I–577, para.63; ECJ, Case C–467/01 *Eribrand* [2003] E.C.R. I–6471, para.61.

Individuals must also be able to defend their rights in the best possible circumstances and be in a position to decide with a full knowledge of the facts whether they will benefit from going to court. The competent authority is therefore under a duty to inform them of the grounds for its decision, either in the decision itself or in a subsequent communication made at their request. The possibility of bringing legal proceedings and the duty to state reasons are designed, among other things, effectively to protect the fundamental rights conferred on individuals by Community law. These Community law requirements apply only to final decisions of national authorities, not to opinions or to measures taken at the preparatory or investigative stage.

Deficiencies of the system. The fact that Member States are under a duty to ensure effective legal protection may entail a national court's being obliged to hold that a particular claim based on a breach of Community law is admissible even though in normal circumstances—*i.e.* if it was based simply on an infringement of national law—such a claim would not be admissible[401] (*e.g.* a claim brought against a Member State for reparation of damage caused by a breach of Community law[402] or a claim for interim relief in the shape of the suspension of a provision of national law which is in breach of Community law[403]). The question arises as to whether a national court has to take account of the restrictive admissibility requirements prescribed by the fourth para. of Art.230 of the EC Treaty[404] where an individual seeks legal protection against the application in the national legal order of allegedly unlawful provisions of Community law which are of general application.[405]   **3–007**

The point of departure for the reasoning of the Court of Justice in this connection is that by Arts 230 and 241, on the one hand, and Art.234, on the other, the EC Treaty has established a complete system of legal remedies and procedures designed to ensure judicial review by the Community Courts of the legality of acts of the institutions. Under that system, where natural or legal persons, by reason of the conditions for admissibility laid down in the fourth para. of Art.230 of the EC Treaty, cannot directly

---

[401] See, *e.g.* ECJ, Case C–15/04, *Koppensteiner* [2005] E.C.R. I–4855, paras 30–39.
[402] ECJ, Joined Cases C–6 and C–9/90 *Francovich and Others* [1991] E.C.R. I–5357; ECJ, Joined Cases C–46 and C–48/93 *Brasserie du Pêcheur and Factortame* (*Factortame IV*) [1996] E.C.R. I–1029; see 3–041, *infra*.
[403] ECJ, Case C–213/89 *Factortame and Others* (*Factortame I*) [1990] E.C.R. I–2433; see 3–052, *infra*.
[404] See 3–008, *infra*.
[405] See Gilliaux, "L'arrêt *Unión de Pequeños Agricultores*: entre subsidiarité juridictionnelle et effectivité" (2003) C.D.E 177–202; Lenaerts and Corthaut, "Judicial review as a contribution to the development of European constitutionalsim" (2003/2004) Y.E.L. 1–43; Nihoul, "Le recours des particuliers contre les actes communautaires de portée générale. Nouveaux développements dans la jurisprudence" (2003) J.T.D.E. 38–43; Temple Lang, "Declarations, regional authorities, subsidiarity, regional policy measures, and the Constitutional Treaty" (2004) E.L.Rev. 94–105.

challenge Community measures of general application, they are able, depending on the case, either indirectly to plead the invalidity of such acts before the Community Courts under Art.241 of the EC Treaty or to do so before the national courts and ask them, since they have no jurisdiction themselves to declare those measures invalid, to make a reference to the Court of Justice for a preliminary ruling on validity.[406]

A complete system of legal remedies may not normally have any gaps. Nevertheless, the preliminary ruling procedure and the objection of illegality to which the Court of Justice refers in its case-law does not invariably afford a sufficient legal remedy for an individual who seeks to contest the validity of a Community act of general application.[407] The reason for this is that recourse to Arts 234 and 241 of the EC Treaty is conditional upon the existence of a national or a Community implementing measure, respectively, which will permit the individual to contest the validity of the Community act of general application before the national court or the Community Courts in an action brought against the implementing measure. Where a Community act requires no implementing measures at national level, as is often the case with regulations, and national law affords no form of declaratory relief, an individual must first infringe the Community act before he or she can challenge its validity in the national courts. The same problem arises where there are national implementing measures—*e.g.* where directives have to be implemented in national law—but those measures cannot be challenged directly under national law.

3–008 **Possible solutions.** If it is assumed that the system of legal remedies is already "complete",[408] two solutions are conceivable. Either the Court of Justice puts a more flexible construction on what is to be understood by "individual concern" within the meaning of the fourth para. of Art.230 of the EC Treaty so that individuals whose legal position is affected by a Community act of general application are entitled to contest that act directly in the Court of First Instance by means of an action for annulment or the national courts must fill the gap.

This question was raised in the *Unión de Pequeños Agricultores*[409] and *Jégo-Quéré*[410] cases. It appears from these cases, first, that the Court of

---

[406] ECJ, Case 294/83 *Les Verts v European Parliament* [1986] E.C.R. I–1339, para.23; ECJ, Case C–50/00 P *Unión de Pequeños Agricultores v Council* [2002] E.C.R. I–6677, para.40; ECJ, Case C–167/02 P *Rothley and Others v European Parliament* [2004] E.C.R. I–3149, para.46.
[407] See the case-law referred to in the preceding note.
[408] *Ibid*.
[409] CFI (order of November 23, 1999), Case T–173/98 *Unión de Pequeños Agricultores v Council* [1999] E.C.R. II–3357; ECJ, Case C–50/00 P *Unión de Pequeños Agricultores v Council* [2002] E.C.R. I–6677 (upheld on appeal).
[410] CFI, Case T–177/01 *Jégo-Quéré v Commission* [2002] E.C.R. II–2365, para.41; overturned on appeal in ECJ, Case C–263/02 P *Commission v Jégo-Quéré* [2004] E.C.R. I–3425.

Justice is entirely unwilling to embark upon the relaxation of the admissibility requirements set out in the fourth para. of Art.230 of the EC Treaty which had been proposed by the Court of First Instance in *Jégo-Quéré*.[411] Referring to its judgment in *Plaumann*,[412] the Court of Justice held that a measure is of individual concern to natural or legal persons "where the measure in question affects specific natural or legal persons by reason of certain attributes peculiar to them, or by reason of a factual situation which differentiates them from all other persons and distinguishes them individually in the same way as the addressee".[413] No other interpretation of this admissibility condition is possible, it held, "without going beyond the jurisdiction conferred by the Treaty on the Community Courts".[414] Consequently, an individual cannot bring an action for annulment before the Court of First Instance against an act of general application, such as a regulation which does not distinguish him or her individually in the same way as the addressee, even where it can be shown, following an examination by that Court of the particular national procedural rules, that those rules do not allow the individual to bring proceedings before a national court to contest the validity of the Community measure at issue.[415]

As far as the second solution is concerned, the Court of Justice repeatedly states that the right to effective legal protection is one of the general principles of law stemming from the constitutional traditions common to the Member States and that that right is enshrined in Arts 6 and 13 of the European Convention for the Protection of Human Rights and Fundamental Freedoms.[416] The Court of Justice draws the following conclusion from this: "Thus *it is for the Member States* to establish a system of legal remedies and procedures which ensure respect for the right to effective judicial protection".[417] Notwithstanding the wording used, what is involved here is only a commitment to make best endeavours and then it rests only on the hypothesis that there are national implementing measures for the unlawful Community act at issue. Accordingly, the Court of Justice

---

[411] See 7–086, *infra*.

[412] ECJ, Case 25/62 *Plaumann v Commission* [1963] E.C.R. 95, at 107.

[413] ECJ, Case C–50/00 P *Unión de Pequeños Agricultores v Council* [2002] E.C.R. I–6677, para.36.

[414] *Ibid.*, para.44; ECJ, Case C–167/02 P *Rothley and Others v European Parliament* [2004] E.C.R. I–3149, para.25; ECJ, Case C–263/02 P *Commission v Jégo-Quéré* [2004] E.C.R. I–3425, para.36.

[415] ECJ, Case C–50/00 P *Unión de Pequeños Agricultores v Council* [2002] E.C.R. I–6677, para.43; ECJ, Case C–263/02 P *Commission v Jégo-Quéré* [2004] E.C.R. I–3425, para.33.

[416] ECJ, Case 222/84 *Johnston* [1986] E.C.R. 1651, para.18; ECJ, Case C–424/99 *Commission v Austria* [2001] E.C.R. I–9285, para.45; ECJ, Case C–50/00 P *Unión de Pequeños Agricultores v Council* [2002] E.C.R. I–6677, para.39; ECJ, Case C–263/02 P *Commission v Jégo-Quéré* [2004] E.C.R. I–3425, para.29.

[417] ECJ, Case C–263/02 P *Commission v Jégo-Quéré* [2004] E.C.R. I–3425, para.31 (emphasis added); ECJ, Case C–50/00 P *Unión de Pequeños Agricultores v Council* [2002] E.C.R. I–6677, para.41. This wording is included virtually verbatim in Art.I–29(1) of the Constitution.

has held that "in accordance with the principle of sincere cooperation laid down in Article 10 EC, national courts are required, *so far as possible*, to interpret and apply national procedural rules governing the exercise of rights of action in a way that enables natural and legal persons to challenge before the courts the legality of any decision or other *national measure relative to the application to them of a Community act* of general application, by pleading the invalidity of such an act".[418]

The Court of Justice thus leaves two loopholes open in the system of judicial protection. On the one hand, the degree of judicial protection available to an individual is made dependent on the ability and creativity of the national judge to provide such a remedy. On the other hand, the Court provides no solution for those situations where no national implementing measures exist, despite the claim made by the applicants in *Jégo-Quéré* and *Unión de Pequeños Agricultores* that they were precisely in this kind of situation.[419] It cannot therefore be inferred from the case-law of the Court of Justice that a national court is *obliged* to declare admissible an action brought against the public authority's intention to apply a regulation or to transpose a directive into the national legal order where the procedural law of the Member State in question does not provide for such a form of "declaratory relief".[420] On the contrary, the Court of Justice is resigned to

---

[418] ECJ, Case C–263/02 P *Commission v Jégo-Quéré* [2004] E.C.R. I–3425, para.32 (emphasis added); ECJ, Case C–50/00 P *Unión de Pequeños Agricultores v Council* [2002] E.C.R. I–6677, para.42.

[419] Lenaerts and Corthaut, "Judicial Review as a contribution to the development of European constitutionalism" (2003/2004) Y.E.L. 1–43.

[420] In the judgment of December 10, 2002 in Case C–491/01 *British American Tobacco and Imperial Tobacco* [2002] E.C.R. I–11453, the Court of Justice ruled on the admissibility of a reference for a preliminary ruling made in proceedings for declaratory relief concerning the validity of a directive. The Court declared that the question was admissible on the ground that "The opportunity open to individuals to plead the invalidity of a Community act of general application before national courts is not conditional upon that act's actually having been the subject of implementing measures adopted pursuant to national law". Nihoul infers from this that there is an obligation for Member States to adapt their procedural rules so as to give individuals the opportunity to contest in the national courts the national authorities' intention to implement a directive. This would enable individuals to contest the legality of a directive in the national courts, which might then make a reference for a preliminary ruling to the Court of Justice (see Nihoul, "Le recours des particuliers contre les actes communautaires de portée générale. Nouveaux développements dans la jurisprudence" (2003) J.T.D.E. 38–43). In our view, such an obligation cannot be inferred from the *British American Tobacco* judgment. See Lenaerts and Corthaut, "Judicial review as a contribution to the development of European constitutionalism" (2003/2004) Y.E.L. 1–43; see also Gilliaux, "L'arrêt *Unión de Pequeños Agricoltores*: entre subsidiarité juridictionnelle et effectivité" (2003) C.D.E. 177–202; Temple Lang, "Declarations, regional authorities, subsidiarity, regional policy measures, and the Constitutional Treaty" (2004) E.L.Rev. 94–105. As far as declaratory relief and the validity of a regulation are concerned, see ECJ, Cases C–27/00 and C–122/00 *Omega Air and Others* [2002] E.C.R. I–2569, in which the Court of Justice did not even consider the admissibility of the reference for a preliminary ruling.

the fact that in some cases an individual must first infringe a Community act before he or she can challenge its validity.[421]

The Court of Justice therefore posits a third solution, which, however, boils down in practice to recognition of the incompleteness of the system of legal remedies. This is because it refers to the possibility for Member States to alter the existing system of legal protection under Art.48 of the EU Treaty.[422]

Constitution. The Member States have taken up this invitation. In the first place, Art.III-365 of the Constitution relaxes the conditions for the admissibility of actions brought by individuals for the annulment of regulatory acts which do not entail implementing measures.[423]   **3–009**

Then, as far as judicial review by national courts is concerned, Art.I-29 of the Constitution provides as follows: "Member States shall provide remedies sufficient to ensure effective legal protection in the fields covered by Union law." On the one hand, it may be objected that this provision adds nothing to the *acquis*, since it amounts to a virtually verbatim repetition of a passage from the Court's judgments in *Jégo-Quéré* and *Unión de Pequeños Agricultores*,[424] from which the Court merely inferred an obligation to make best endeavours. On the other hand, it cannot be ruled out that this provision, read against the background of the incorporation in the Constitution of the Charter of Fundamental Rights of the European Union, which confers on "everyone whose rights and freedoms guaranteed by the law of the Union are violated" the right to "an effective remedy before a tribunal",[425] and the recent case-law of the Court of Human

---

[421] ECJ, Case C–263/02 P *Commission v Jégo-Quéré* [2004] E.C.R. I–3425, para.34; CFI (order of June 28, 2005), Case T–386/04 *Eridania Sadam and Others v Commission*, not yet reported, para.43.

[422] ECJ, Case C–50/00 P *Unión de Pequeños Agricultores v Council* [2002] E.C.R. I–6677, para.45. See in this connection Gilliaux, "L'arrêt *Unión de Pequeños Agricultores*: entre subsidiarité juridictionnelle et effectivité" (2003) C.D.E. 177–202; Ginter, "Access to Justice in the European Court of Justice in Luxembourg" (2002) E.J.L.Ref. 381–445; Granger, "Towards a Liberalisation of Standing Conditions for Individuals Seeking Judicial Review of Community Acts: *Jégo-Quéré et Cie SA v Commission* and *Unión de Pequeños Agricultores v Council*" (2003) Mod.L.Rev. 124–138; Groussot, "The EC System of Legal Remedies and Effective Judicial Protection: Does the System Really Need Reform?" (2003) L.I.E.I. 221–248; Hanf, "Talking with the 'pouvoir constituant' in Times of Constitutional Reform: The European Court of Justice on Private Applicants' Access to Justice" (2003) 10 M.J.E.C.L. 3, 265–290; Köngeter, "Die Ambivalenz effektiven Rechtsschutzes Einzelner gegen EG-Verordnungen" (2003) Z.f.RV. 123–132; Mehdi, "La recevabilité des recours formés par les personnes physiques et morales à l'encontre d'un acte de portée générale : l'aggiornamento n'aura pas eu lieu . . ." (2003) R.T.D.E. 23–50; Usher, "Direct and individual concern—an effective remedy or a conventional solution?" (2003) E.L.Rev. 575–600.

[423] See 7–184 to 7–188, *infra*.

[424] See n. 417, *supra*.

[425] Constitution, Art.II–107.

Rights[426] will prompt the Court of Justice to transform the obligation to make best endeavours into an obligation to achieve a particular result. Effective legal redress would then mean that national courts would be obliged to interpret and apply their national rules of procedural law in such a way as to give natural and legal persons the possibility to act against the national authorities' intention to apply or implement a Community measure of general application where it appears that those persons cannot attack the measure directly in the Court of First Instance by means of an action for annulment. Only then would the system of legal redress enshrined in the Treaty be complete[427] in actual fact and not just on paper.

II. CONSTRAINTS: EQUIVALENCE AND EFFECTIVENESS

3–010 **General.** The Court of Justice laid down the two most important constraints at the same time as it held that, in principle, national procedural rules and rules on sanctions are to apply, namely (1) that those rules may not be less favourable than those governing similar domestic actions (principle of equivalence),[428] and (2) that they may not render virtually impossible or excessively difficult the exercise of rights conferred by Community law (principle of effectiveness).[429]

3–011 **Principle of equivalence.** Above all, there is the requirement for procedural equal treatment of claims based on Community law and those based on national law, for example as regards the effects of the expiry of a time-limit for bringing proceedings or of an error in drawing up the document originating proceedings. In addition, it must be possible for every type of

---

[426] In its judgment of September 24, 2002 in Case 27824/95 *Posti and Rahko v Finland*, the European Court of Human Rights ruled that the European Convention on Human Rights had been violated on acount of the fact that no remedy was available against a Finnish decree which curtailed the applicants' rights. The idea that one could obtain judicial review by first breaching the contested act was rejected by the European Court of Human Rights in the following terms: "no one can be required to breach the law so as to be able to have a 'civil right' determined in accordance with Article 6§1" (para. 64).

[427] See 3–007, *supra*.

[428] ECJ, Case 33/76 *Rewe* [1976] E.C.R. 1989, third subpara. *in fine* of para.5; ECJ, Case 45/76 *Comet* [1976] E.C.R. 2043, para.13 *in fine*; ECJ, Case 811/79 *Ariete* [1980] E.C.R. 2545, para.12; ECJ, Case 826/79 *MIRECO* [1980] E.C.R. 2559, para.13; ECJ, Case C–338/91 *Steenhorst-Neerings* [1993] E.C.R. I–5475, para.15, and ECJ, Case C–410/92 *Johnson* [1994] E.C.R. I–5483, para.21; ECJ, Case C–180/95 *Draehmpaehl* [1997] E.C.R. I–2195, para.29.

[429] *Rewe*, cited in the preceding n., sixth subpara. of para.5; *Comet*, para.16; *Ariete*, para.12 *in fine*, and *MIRECO*, para.13 *in fine*. See also ECJ, Case C–231/96 *Edis* [1998] E.C.R. I–4951, paras 19 and 34, ECJ, Case C–290/96 *Spac* [1998] E.C.R. I–4997, para.18, ECJ, Joined Cases C–279/96, C–280/96 and C–281/96, *Ansaldo Energia and Others* [1998] E.C.R. I–5025, para.27, and ECJ, Joined Cases C–52/99 and C–53/99 *Camarotto and Vignone* [2001] E.C.R. I–1395, para.21.

action provided for by national law to be available for the purpose of ensuring observance of Community provisions having direct effect.[430]

In order to decide whether procedural rules relating to a claim based on national law and those relating to claims based on Community law are equivalent, the national court must verify objectively, in the abstract, whether the rules at issue are similar taking into account the role played by those rules in the procedure as a whole, as well as the operation of that procedure and any special features of those rules.[431]

Principle of effectiveness. In addition, national procedural rules and rules relating to sanctions, albeit complying with the principle of equivalence, "may not be so framed as to render virtually impossible the exercise of rights conferred by Community law".[432]   3–012

Case-by-case approach. National procedural rules and rules relating to sanctions are assessed by the Court of Justice on a case-by-case basis in the light of the constraints they contain, which means that the categories described below must be regarded as being open to enlargement.   3–013

A. LOCUS STANDI AND INTEREST IN BRINGING PROCEEDINGS

Principle. The rules of national law relating to an individual's *locus standi* and interest in bringing proceedings may not detract from the full effectiveness of Community law. In a first attempt to define the Community law requirements from the point of view of the principles of equivalence and effectiveness, the Court of Justice has held that persons who do not come within the scope *ratione personae* of a provision of Community law may nevertheless have an interest in the provision being taken into account *vis-à-vis* the person protected.[433] In this way, they may have sufficient *locus standi* under Community law, which must be recognised in national law.   3–014

Thus, an undertaking which is not a competitor of the beneficiary of unlawful State aid may have an interest in relying before the national court on the direct effect of the prohibition on implementation referred to in the

---

[430] ECJ, Case 158/80 *Rewe* [1981] E.C.R. 1805, para.44. The Court of Justice specified in *Pasquini* that the principle of equivalence "must be applied not only with regard to provisions of national law on limitation of actions and recovery of sums paid though not due, but also to all procedural rules governing the treatment of comparable situations, whether administrative or judicial" (ECJ, Case C–34/02 *Pasquini* [2003] E.C.R. I–6515, para.62).

[431] ECJ, Case C–78/98 *Preston and Others* [2000] E.C.R. I–3201, para.63.

[432] ECJ, Case 199/82 *San Giorgio* [1983] E.C.R. 3595, para.12 (this phrase has tended to be rendered in English as "framed in such a way as *in practice* to make it impossible": ECJ, Joined Cases C–46/93 and C–48/93 *Brasserie du Pêcheur and Factortame (Factortame IV)* [1996] E.C.R. I–1029, para.74); in his Opinion in ECJ, Case 2/94 *Denkavit International* [1996] E.C.R. I–2829, point 75, Advocate General F.G. Jacobs suggests "unduly difficult".

[433] ECJ, Joined Cases C–87-89/90 *Verholen and Others* [1991] E.C.R. I–3757, paras 23–24 (with a case note by Prechal (1993) S.E.W. 163–169).

last sentence of Art.88(3) of the EC Treaty. This will be the case, for example, where the undertaking concerned is subject to a tax which forms an integral part of a measure implemented in breach of the prohibition referred to in that provision.[434]

B. LIMITATION PERIODS AND RULES OF EVIDENCE

3–015 **Limitation periods.** It may appear from a judgment of the Court of Justice giving a preliminary ruling that the imposition of a particular charge or the refusal to grant a particular social advantage conflicts with Community law. Where a person seeks recovery of the charge or payment of the advantage unlawfully denied before a national court, the national procedural rules should apply. Those rules may provide for limitation periods. According to a consistent line of cases, limitation periods are compatible with Community law, provided, of course, that the principles of equivalence and effectiveness are respected.[435] According to the Court of Justice, this does not amount to a temporal limitation of the effects of an interpretative judgment which falls outside the competence of a national court.[436] This is because national procedural rules providing for limitation periods do not detract from specific rights which individuals derive from Community law. It merely results in them having to bring their claim within a particular period.[437]

3–016 **Rules of evidence.** As far as the application of rules of evidence is concerned in proceedings in which an individual asserts rights derived from Community law, the Court of Justice considers that, in the absence of Community legislation, any type of evidence admissible under the procedural law of the Member States in similar proceedings is in principle admissible provided that the principles of equivalence and effectiveness are respected.[438]

1. Recovery of unlawful charges

3–017 **Heterogeneity of national systems.** The question of challenging charges unlawfully claimed or the recovery of charges unduly paid is dealt with in divergent ways in the various Member States and even within a given

---

[434] ECJ, Case C–174/02 *Streekgewest Westelijk Noord-Brabant* [2005] E.C.R. I–85, para.19 (with a case note by Jans and van de Gronden (2005) S.E.W. 234–238).

[435] ECJ, Case 45/76 *Comet* [1976] E.C.R. 2043, paras 17–18; ECJ, Case 61/79 *Denkavit Italiana* [1980] E.C.R. 1205, para.23; ECJ, Case C–90/94 *Haahr Petroleum* [1997] E.C.R. I–4085, para.48; ECJ, Case C–231/96 *Edis* [1998] E.C.R. I–4951, para.20.

[436] See 6–034, *infra*.

[437] ECJ, Case C–231/96 *Edis* [1998] E.C.R. I–4951, paras 15–19.

[438] ECJ, Joined Cases C–310/98 and C–406/98 *Met-Trans and Sagpol* [2000] E.C.R. I–1797, para.29. Accordingly, a provision of national procedural law under which, in judicial proceedings in which it is sought to establish State liability with a view to obtaining compensation for damage caused by a breach of Community law, witness evidence is admissible only in exceptional cases is permissible to the extent to which it does not infringe the principles of equivalence and effectiveness (ECJ, Case C–228/98 *Dounias* [2000] E.C.R. I–577, paras 68–72).

Member State depending on the sort of tax or charge concerned. In some cases, the law requires both complaints addressed to the tax office and appeals to comply with fairly strict requirements as to the form in which and the time-limits within which such legal claims or applications may be submitted. In others, actions for the recovery of unduly paid charges must be brought before the ordinary courts, for instance in the form of an action based on an undue payment; such actions are subject to varying time-limits which in some cases correspond to the normal limitation period laid down by the ordinary law.[439]

Constraints. The heterogeneity of the national systems is the upshot in particular of the lack of Community rules on the recovery of unlawfully imposed national charges. As has already been observed, this is because in such a situation it is for the national law of each Member State to designate the competent court and lay down the procedural rules governing legal claims for protecting the rights which individuals derive from Community law, provided that those rules are not more unfavourable than those that apply to similar national claims (principle of equivalence) and do not render the exercise of rights conferred by Community law virtually impossible or excessively difficult (principle of effectiveness).   **3–018**

Periods of limitation. It clearly appears from the case-law of the Court of Justice on the recovery of a charge levied under national law but undue under Community law,[440] that the setting of "reasonable periods of limitation of actions" satisfies in principle the test of the principles of equivalence and effectiveness.[441]   **3–019**

Principle of equivalence. In the first place, as far as the application of the principle of equivalence is concerned, a Member State may not lay down provisions for the repayment of a charge declared contrary to or incompatible with Community law by the Court of Justice which set conditions specifically relating to the charge in question that are less favourable than   **3–020**

---

[439] ECJ, Case 61/79 *Denkavit Italiana* [1980] E.C.R. 1205, paras 23-24; ECJ, Case 68/79 *Just* [1980] E.C.R. 501, paras 22–23, and Case C–231/96 *Edis* [1998] E.C.R. I–4951, para.36.

[440] A clear exposition of all these aspects of this doctrine is set out in ECJ, Joined Cases C–192/95 to C–218/95 *Comateb and Others* [1997] E.C.R. I–165, paras 19–34. See also Joined Cases C–397/98 and C–410/98 *Metallgesellschaft and Others* [2001] E.C.R. I–1727, paras 82–86; ECJ, Case C–147/01 *Weber's Wine World and Others* [2003] E.C.R. I–11365, paras 93–118; Opinion of Advocate-General L. A. Geelhoed in Case C–129/00 *Commission v Italy* [2003] E.C.R. I–14640, points 68–101; Opinion of Advocate-General D. Ruiz-Jarabo Colomer in Case C–30/02 *Recheio* [2004] E.C.R. I–6053, points 23–43.

[441] ECJ, Case 33/76 *Rewe* [1976] E.C.R. 1989, seventh and eighth subparas of para.5; ECJ, Case 45/76 *Comet* [1976] E.C.R. 2043, paras 17–18; ECJ, Case 61/79 *Denkavit Italiana* [1980] E.C.R. 1205, para.23; ECJ, Case C–261/95 *Palmisani* [1997] E.C.R. I–4025, para.28; ECJ, Case C–90/94 *Haahr Petroleum* [1997] E.C.R. I–4085, para.48; ECJ, Case C–228/96 *Aprile* [1998] E.C.R. I–7141, para.19; ECJ, Case C–343/96 *Dilexport* [1999] E.C.R. I–579, para.26.

those otherwise laid down for repayment of charges.[442] In contrast, Community law does not prohibit a Member State from resisting actions for repayment of charges levied in breach of Community law by relying on a time-limit under national law of three years, by way of derogation from the ordinary rules governing actions between private individuals for the recovery of sums paid but not due, for which the period allowed is more favourable, provided that that time-limit applies in the same way to actions based on Community law for repayment of such charges as to those based on national law.[443] Consequently, observance of the principle of equivalence hinges on correctly identifying what claims—based on Community law or based on national law—are of the same kind. It seems appropriate to use the most precise comparative criterion, namely the recovery of charges paid but undue (undue either under Community law or under national law).[444]

Accordingly, Community law does not preclude the legislation of a Member State from laying down, alongside a limitation period applicable under the ordinary law to actions between private individuals for the recovery of sums paid but not due, special detailed rules, which are less favourable, governing claims and legal proceedings to challenge the imposition of charges and other levies. The position would be different only if those detailed rules applied solely to actions based on Community law for the repayment of such charges or levies. The same test is applied where a Member State adopts rules which retroactively restrict the right to repayment of a sum levied but not due, in order to forestall the possible effects of a judgment of the Court of Justice.[445]

3–021 **Principle of effectiveness.** As far as the principle of effectiveness is concerned, the Court of Justice considers that it is compatible with Community law to lay down reasonable limitation periods for bringing proceedings.[446] A reasonable limitation period finds its justification in the fundamental principle of legal certainty which protects both the taxpayer

---

[442] See, *e.g.*, ECJ, Case 309/85 *Barra* [1988] E.C.R. 355, paras 18 and 19, in which the Court of Justice held that a Belgian law restricting the right to repayment of an enrolment fee imposed on students from other Member States contrary to Community law made it impossible to exercise the rights guaranteed by Art.12 of the EC Treaty (then Art.7 of the EEC Treaty). See also ECJ, Case C–343/96 *Dilexport* [1999] E.C.R. I–579, paras 37–43.

[443] It is a matter of national law whether, in the case of a claim for repayment of a charge which is contrary to Community law and therefore undue, the legal relationship between the national tax authorities and companies in a Member State is regarded as a fiscal relationship or whether the rules of the ordinary law govern that legal relationship. The primacy of Community law which caused the imposition of the charge to be undue has no bearing on the classification in national law of the claim to repayment (See ECJ, Joined Cases C–10/97 to C–22/97 *IN.CO.GE.'90* [1998] E.C.R. I–6307, paras 28–29).

[444] ECJ, Case C–231/96 *Edis* [1998] E.C.R. I–4951, paras 36–37; ECJ, Case C–260/96 *Spac* [1998] E.C.R. I–4997, paras 20–21.

[445] ECJ, Case C–343/96 *Dilexport* [1999] E.C.R. I–579, para.43; ECJ, Case C–147/01 *Weber's Wine World and Others* [2003] E.C.R. I–11365, para.92.

[446] ECJ, Case C–78/98 *Preston and Others* [2000] E.C.R. I–3201, para.43; ECJ, Case C–125/01 *Pflücke* [2003] E.C.R. I–9375, para.36.

and the administration concerned. Such time-limits are not liable to render practically impossible or excessively difficult the exercise of rights conferred by Community law.[447]

The Court of Justice has regarded a national limitation period of three years from the date of the contested payment as reasonable.[448] Of course, national limitation periods are assessed on a case-by-case basis.[449]

Reduction of a limitation period. If a Member State decides to reduce a limitation period, the new reduced period should itself be reasonable. Reducing a limitation period will infringe the principle of effectiveness where the legislation which effected the reduction does not include transitional arrangements allowing an adequate period after its enactment for lodging the claims for repayment which persons were entitled to submit under the original legislation.[450] As far as the duration of the requisite transitional period is concerned, the Court of Justice has further specified that it must be sufficient to allow taxpayers who initially thought that the old period for bringing proceedings was available to them a reasonable period of time to assert their right of recovery. The Court considered that a transitional period of 90 days prior to the retroactive application of a period of three years for initiating proceedings in place of a five-year period was clearly insufficient. If an initial period of five years was taken as a reference, 90 days left taxpayers whose rights accrued approximately three years earlier in a position of having to act within three months when they had thought that almost another two years were still available. Consequently, the Court of Justice considered that where a period of ten or five

3–022

---

[447] ECJ, Case C–231/96 *Edis* [1998] E.C.R. I–4951, para.35. The fact that the Court has given a preliminary ruling interpreting a provision of Community law without limiting the temporal effects of its judgment does not affect the right of a Member State to impose a time-limit under national law within which, on penalty of being barred, proceedings for repayment of charges levied in breach of that provision must be commenced (*ibid.*, para. 26).

[448] ECJ, Case C–231/96 *Edis* [1998] E.C.R. I–4951, para.35; ECJ, Case C–260/96 *Spac* [1998] E.C.R. I–4997, para.19; ECJ, Joined Cases C–279/96, C–280/96 and C–281/96 *Ansaldo Energia and Others* [1998] E.C.R. I–5025, paras 17–18; ECJ, Case C–343/96 *Dilexport* [1999] E.C.R. I–579, para.70; see also ECJ, Joined Cases C–216/99 and C–222/99 *Riccardo Prisco and CASER* [2002] E.C.R. I–6761, para.70. In *Roquette Frères* (ECJ, Case C–88/99 *Roquette Frères* [2000] E.C.R. I–10465), the Court of Justice considered that a national limitation period for a claim for the recovery of undue payment of up to a minimum of 4 years and a maximum of 5 years preceding the year of the judicial decision finding the rule of national law establishing the tax to be incompatible with a superior rule of law was reasonable.

[449] Assessment of the reasonableness of a limitation period is done on a case-by-case basis, taking account of each case's own factual and legal context as a whole. It is not possible to infer from such assessments a general rule which can be applied mechanically in every field (ECJ, Case C–473/00 *Cofidis* [2002] E.C.R. I–10875, para.37). The Court of Justice has held, *e.g.* that a short limitation period of two weeks to contest a decision to award a public procurement contract is reasonable (ECJ, Case C–470/99 *Universale-Bau and Others* [2002] E.C.R. I–11617, paras 71–78).

[450] ECJ, Case C–62/00 *Marks & Spencer* [2002] E.C.R. I–6325, paras 34–42 (where the Court of Justice held that a three-year limitation period was reasonable, but that the principle of effectiveness had been infringed because the new legislation did not provide for a transitional limitation period and was applicable immediately with retroactive effect).

years for initiating proceedings is reduced to three years, the minimum transitional period required to ensure that rights conferred by Community law can be effectively exercised and that normally diligent taxpayers can familiarise themselves with the new regime and prepare and commence proceedings in circumstances which do not compromise their chances of success can be reasonably assessed at six months.[451]

3–023   **Charge passed on to third parties.** In principle, a trader who has paid a charge which was levied unduly is entitled to recover the sum in question. The tax authorities may refuse to repay such a charge only where repayment would result in the trader being unjustly enriched.[452] Therefore, from the point of view of Community law, there is nothing to prevent national courts from taking account in accordance with their national law of the fact that it has been possible for charges unduly levied to be incorporated in the prices of the undertaking liable for the charge and to be passed on to the purchasers. In principle, therefore, national legislative provisions which preclude the repayment of taxes, charges and duties levied contrary to Community law are not to be regarded as being in breach of Community law where it is clear that the persons who had to pay them actually passed them on to others.[453]

3–024   **Burden of proof.** However, rules of evidence which render it virtually impossible or extremely difficult to recover a charge levied contrary to Community law are in breach of Community law.[454] A national provision which imposes on the taxpayer the—negative—burden of proving that the charge was not passed on to third parties or embodies a presumption that the charge was passed on does not satisfy the requirements of Community

---

[451] ECJ, Case C–255/00 *Grundig Italiana* [2002] E.C.R. I–8003, paras 36–42 (reducing a five- to ten-year limitation period to three years requires a minimum transitional period of six months). In contrast, in *Recheio* (ECJ, Case C–30/02 *Recheio* [2004] E.C.R. I–6051, para.21), a limitation period of 90 days was held to be compatible with the principle of effectiveness. In that case, however, there was not originally a longer limitation period which was subsequently reduced to 90 days.

[452] ECJ, Joined Cases C–192/95 to C–218/95 *Comateb and Others* [1997] E.C.R. I–165, paras 20–22; ECJ, Case C–147/01 *Weber's Wine World and Others* [2003] E.C.R. I–11365, para.109.

[453] ECJ, Case 61/79 *Denkavit Italiana* [1980] E.C.R. 1205, para.26; ECJ, Case 68/79 *Just* [1980] E.C.R. 501, para.26; ECJ, Case 130/79 *Express Dairy Foods* [1980] E.C.R. 1887, para.12; ECJ, Case 199/82 *San Giorgio* [1983] E.C.R. 3595, para.13; ECJ, Joined Cases C–192/95 to C–218/95 *Comateb and Others* [1997] E.C.R. I–165, para.12; ECJ, Case C–343/96 *Dilexport* [1999] E.C.R. I–579, para.47. For a critical commentary on this rule, see, *inter alia*, Hubeau, "La répétition de l'indu en droit communutaire" (1981) R.T.D.E. 442–470. The same principle is applied in respect of a claim for repayment of an invalid "Community charge": ECJ, Case 66/80 *International Chemical* [1981] E.C.R. 1191, paras 22–26.

[454] Similarly, rules of evidence which render it virtually impossible or extremely difficult to demonstrate that a provision of Community law having direct effect has been breached also violate Community law: ECJ, Case C–242/95 *GT-Link* [1997] E.C.R. I–4449, para.26.

law.[455] Accordingly, a national tax authority (or a national court) cannot merely state that a charge was passed on in the selling price to consumers, that the economic burden which the charge represented for the taxable person is neutralised and that, consequently, repayment would automatically entail unjust enrichment of the trader.[456]

Payment under protest. A Member State may not make the recovery of a sum which was paid to a public authority under a mistake of law and was not due under Community law depend upon the payment having been made under protest, since such a condition is liable to prejudice effective protection of the rights conferred by Community law on the individuals involved.[457]

3–025

Interest. As for the question as to whether interest is payable on wrongly levied charges, according to the case-law it is "for national law to settle all ancillary questions relating to the reimbursement of charges improperly levied, such as the payment of interest, including the rate of interest and the date from which it must be calculated".[458] However, the principles of equivalence and effectiveness must be complied with. Thus, Community law does not preclude, in the event of the repayment of charges levied in breach thereof, payment of interest calculated by methods less favourable than those applicable under the ordinary rules governing actions for the recovery of sums paid but not due between private individuals, provided that those methods apply in the same way to such actions brought under Community

3–026

---

[455] ECJ, Case 199/82 *San Giorgio* [1983] E.C.R. 3595, para.14; ECJ, Joined Cases 331, 376 and 378/85 *Bianco and Girard* [1988] E.C.R. 1099, paras 12–13; ECJ, Case C–343/96 *Dilexport* [1999] E.C.R. I–579, para.48; ECJ, Joined Cases C–441/98 and C–442/98 *Michaïlidis* [2000] E.C.R. I–7145, paras 40–41. See also ECJ, Case C–129/00 *Commission v Italy* [2003] E.C.R. I–14637, where the Court held that Italy had infringed Community law in so far as the case-law of the *Corte suprema di cassazione* was in breach of the principles enshrined in the judgments in *San Giorgio* and *Dilexport*. See, with regard to the proof of the abuse of law, ECJ, Case C–110/99 *Emsland-Stärke* [2000] E.C.R. I–11569, para.54, in which the Court of Justice held that it was necessary to prove the existence of two elements, namely a combination of objective circumstances in which, despite formal observance of the conditions laid down by the Community rules, the purpose of those rules had not been achieved, and a subjective element consisting in the intention to obtain an advantage from the Community rules by creating artificially the conditions laid down for obtaining it. It is for the national court to establish the existence of those two elements, evidence of which must be adduced in accordance with the rules of national law, provided that the effectiveness of Community law is not thereby undermined (see also Joined Cases C–418/97 and C–419/97 *ARCO Chemie Netherlands and Others* [2000] E.C.R. I–4475, para.41).

[456] ECJ, Case 199/82 *San Giorgio* [1983] E.C.R. 3595, para.14; ECJ, Case C–343/96 *Dilexport* [1999] E.C.R. I–579, paras 48, 52 and 54; ECJ, Joined Cases C–441/98 and C–442/98 *Michaïlidis* [2000] E.C.R. I–7145, paras 36–37; ECJ, Case C–147/01 *Weber's Wine World and Others* [2003] E.C.R. I–11365, paras 110–111. For an enlightening analysis, see the Opinion of Advocate General L.A. Geelhoed, in Case C–129/00 *Commission v Italy* [2003] E.C.R. I–14640, points 68–100.

[457] ECJ, Case C–212/94 *FMC and Others* [1996] E.C.R. I–389, para.72.

[458] ECJ, Joined Cases C–397/98 and C–410/98 *Metallgesellschaft and Others* [2001] E.C.R. I–1727, para.86.

law as to those brought under national law.[459] As far as the principle of effectiveness is concerned, the Court of Justice has made it clear that national law must enable interest to be paid where this is essential if the damage caused by a breach of the Treaty is to be repaired. This will be the case, for example, where the breach of Community law arises, not from the payment of the tax itself but from its being levied prematurely.[460]

2. Recovery of unlawful State aid

3–027 **Obligation to recover.** Where the Commission orders the recovery of State aid paid over unlawfully under Community law, applicable provisions of national law may not affect the scope and effectiveness of Community law.[461] The decision declaring the aid incompatible with the common market will generally require the authority which granted the aid to recover it in accordance with the rules of national law. But the application of those rules must not make it impossible in practice to recover the sums irregularly granted or be discriminatory in relation to comparable cases which are governed solely by national legislation.[462]

3. Claims for an advantage due under Community law

3–028 **Limitation period.** An individual who claims a certain advantage on the basis of Community law from a national authority will normally also have to assert his or her claim within a specific time-limit. Here, too, the case-law assumes that a reasonable limitation period finds its justification in the fundamental principle of legal certainty.[463]

3–029 **Claim based on a directive.** It may happen that individuals base their claim to a certain social advantage on the provisions having direct effect of a directive which the Member State concerned failed to implement in time.

---

[459] ECJ, Joined Cases C–279/96, C–280/96 and C–281/96 *Ansaldo Energia and Others* [1998] E.C.R. I–5025, paras 24–36.

[460] ECJ, Joined Cases C–397/98 and C–410/98 *Metallgesellschaft and Others* [2001] E.C.R. I–1727, paras 87–96.

[461] The same basic rules also apply to the recovery by national authorities of Community aid which has been unduly paid : ECJ, Case C–298/96 *Oelmühle Hamburg and Schmidt Söhne* [1998] E.C.R. I–4767 (specification of the requirements of Community law for the application of the principle of the loss of unjust enrichment on which the recipient of undue Community aid may possibly rely in order to avoid having to make repayment to the national authorities).

[462] ECJ, Joined Cases 205-215/82 *Deutsche Milchkontor* [1983] E.C.R. 2633, paras 17–24; ECJ, Case 94/87 *Commission v Germany* [1989] E.C.R. 175, para.12; CFI, Case T–459/93 *Siemens v Commission* [1995] E.C.R. II–1675, para.82. For an example in which various principles of national law were set aside, see ECJ, Case C–24/95 *Alcan Deutschland* [1997] E.C.R. I–1591. Nevertheless, it cannot be precluded that a recipient of illegally granted aid may rely on exceptional circumstances on the basis of which it had legitimately assumed the aid to be lawful and thus declined to refund the aid (ECJ, Case C–99/02 *Commission v Italy* [2004] E.C.R. I–3353, para.20).

[463] ECJ, Case C–78/98 *Preston and Others* [2000] E.C.R. I–3201, para.33; ECJ, Case C–125/01 *Pflücke* [2003] E.C.R. I–9375, para.36.

In such a case, is the national court entitled to apply the limitation period provided for in its national procedural law? The answer given initially by the Court of Justice was unqualifiedly in the negative. Accordingly, it held in *Emmott* that, in the light of the particular nature of directives, "Community law precludes the competent authorities of a Member State from relying, in proceedings brought against them by an individual before the national courts in order to protect rights directly conferred upon him by ... [a directive], on national procedural rules relating to time-limits for bringing proceedings so long as that Member State has not properly transposed that directive into its domestic legal system".[464] The rationale was that so long as a directive has not been properly transposed into national law, individuals are unable to ascertain the full extent of their rights.[465]

Subsequently, the Court of Justice has refined that case-law. It is only where it appears that, as a result of the application of a limitation period, an individual has no possibility at all of asserting the rights conferred upon him or her by a directive that the limitation period may not be applied.[466] A national rule which restricts the retroactive effect of a claim to an unpaid social security benefit is compatible with Community law, even where the claim is based on a provision with direct effect of a directive which has not been properly transposed into national law. This is because such a rule does not affect the individual's actual right to the relevant benefit. Furthermore, Community law does not preclude the application of a provision of national law whereby benefits for incapacity for work are payable not earlier than one year before the date of claim, in the case where an individual seeks to rely on rights conferred by a provision with direct effect of a directive which was not transposed into national law on time.[467]

---

[464] ECJ, Case C–208/90 *Emmott* [1991] E.C.R. I–4269, paras 17 and 24, at I–4298-4299 (case note by Szyszczak (1992) C.M.L.Rev. 604–612; for a very critical commentary, see Hoskins, "Tilting the Balance: Supremacy and National Procedural Rules" (1996) E.L.Rev. 365–377). For a good exposition of the criticism levelled against *Emmott* and of the way in which the Court of Justice has subsequently distinguished that case, see Brealey and Hoskins, *Remedies in E.C. Law*, at 115–117. As far as the "particular nature of directives" is concerned, see ECJ, Case C–91/92 *Faccini Dori* [1994] E.C.R. I–3325.

[465] ECJ, Case C–208/90 *Emmott* [1991] E.C.R. I–4269, para.21.

[466] ECJ, Case C–90/94 *Haahr Petroleum* [1997] E.C.R. I–4085, para.52; ECJ, Joined Cases C–114/95 and C–115/95 *Texaco and Olieselskabet Danmark* [1997] E.C.R. I–4263, para.48; ECJ, Case C–188/95 *Fantask and Others* [1997] E.C.R. I–6783, para.51.

[467] ECJ, Case C–338/91 *Steenhorst-Neerings* [1993] E.C.R. I–5475, para.24, with a case note by Adiba Sohrab (1994) C.M.L.Rev. 875–887; ECJ, Case C–410/92 *Johnson* [1994] E.C.R. I–5483, para.36, with a case note clearly summarising this question by Docksey (1995) C.M.L.Rev. 1447–1459. For the application of these principles to the recovery of unlawful charges, see *Edis* (n.448, *supra*), paras 40–49; *Spac* (n.448, *supra*), paras 24–32; *Ansaldo Energia and Others* (n.448, *supra*), paras 13–23. In each of those judgments, the Court of Justice held that having regard to the documents before the Court and the arguments presented at the hearing, it did not appear that the conduct of the Italian authorities, in conjunction with the existence of the contested time-limit, had the effect, as it did in *Emmott* (n. 464, *supra*), of depriving the claimants of any opportunity of enforcing their

3–030 **Principle of effectiveness.** In contrast, a national provision which is such as to render any action by individuals relying on Community law impossible in practice is incompatible with Community law. Thus, the Court of Justice held in *Magorrian and Cunningham*[468] that Community law precludes the application, to a claim based on Art.141 of the EC Treaty for recognition of the claimants' entitlement to join an occupational pension scheme, of a national rule under which such entitlement is limited to a period which starts to run from a point in time two years prior to commencement of proceedings in connection with the claim. Unlike rules which in the interests of legal certainty merely limit the retroactive scope of a claim for certain benefits and do not therefore strike at the very essence of the rights conferred by the Community legal order, a rule such as the one at issue in *Magorrian and Cunningham* was such as to render any action by individuals relying on Art.141 of the EC Treaty impossible in practice. In fact, the rule at issue meant that a large number of years of service were not taken into account in calculating the pensions to which those concerned would have been entitled in the future.[469]

3–031 **Deceit.** Lastly, the principle of effectiveness precludes the application of a national limitation period, which is *per se* reasonable, where the claim was brought out of time owing to the deceit of the other party. Accordingly, Community law precludes the application of a rule of national law which limits an employee's entitlement to arrears of remuneration or damages for breach of the principle of equal pay to a period of two years prior to the date on which the proceedings were instituted, there being no possibility of extending that period, where the delay in bringing a claim is attributable to the fact that the employer deliberately misrepresented to the employee the level of remuneration received by persons of the opposite sex performing like work.[470]

C. Assessment of the Legality of National Provisions in the Light of Community Law

3–032 **Inapplicability of conflicting national rules.** The national court's obligation to give full effect to Community law means that it must "if necessary, [refuse] of its own motion to apply any conflicting provisions of national

---

rights before the national courts. Community law does not preclude the application of a period of limitation or prescription laid down by a rule of national law which restricts the period prior to the bringing of the claim in the national court in respect of which reimbursement of undue payments may be obtained, where that rule is not discriminatory and does not prejudice the actual right conferred on individuals by a preliminary ruling on invalidity: ECJ, Case C–212/94 *FMC and Others* [1996] E.C.R. I–389, paras 63–64; ECJ, Case C–90/94 *Haahr Petroleum* [1997] E.C.R. I–4085, paras 45–53; ECJ, Joined Cases C–114/95 and C–115/95 *Texaco and Olieselskabet Danmark* [1997] E.C.R. I–4263, paras 44–49; ECJ, Case C–188/95 *Fantask and Others* [1997] E.C.R. I–6783.
[468] ECJ, Case C–246/96 *Magorrian and Cunningham* [1997] E.C.R. I–7153.
[469] *Ibid.*, paras 43–45.
[470] ECJ, Case C–326/96 *Levez* [1998] E.C.R. I–7835, para 34.

legislation, even if adopted subsequently, and it is not necessary for the court to request or await the prior setting aside of such provisions by legislative or other constitutional means".[471] By that ruling, the Court of Justice debarred Member States from placing any restriction on their courts in declaring inapplicable provisions or principles of national law which conflict with Community law. If there is nevertheless such a restriction, national courts must simply set it aside on the basis of Community law, which is binding upon the Member State of which they are institutions.[472]

Avoiding conflict. This principle can be respected without any difficulty where a provision of national law conflicts with a provision of the EC Treaty having direct effect, a regulation, or even a directive in proceedings between a private party and public authorities. The situation is, however, different in proceedings exclusively between private parties. Since a directive cannot of itself apply in proceedings exclusively between private parties, a national court cannot be obliged simply to set aside a provision of national law conflicting with a provision of a directive, even if it concerns a clear, precise and unconditional provision seeking to confer rights or impose obligations on individuals. Nevertheless, the national court is bound to interpret national law, so far as possible, in the light of the wording and the purpose of the directive concerned in order to achieve the result sought by it. Although the principle that national law must be interpreted in conformity with Community law concerns chiefly domestic provisions enacted in order to implement the directive in question, it does not require merely those provisions to be so interpreted but requires the national court to consider national law as a whole in order to assess to what extent it may be applied so as not to produce a result contrary to that sought by the directive. In that context, if the application of interpretative methods recognised by national law enables a provision of domestic law to be construed, in certain circumstances, in such a way as to avoid conflict with another rule of domestic law or the scope of that provision to be restricted to that end by applying it only in so far as it is compatible with the rule concerned, the national court is bound to use those methods in order to achieve the result sought by the directive. The principle of interpretation in conformity with Community law thus requires the national court to do whatever lies within its power, having regard to the whole body of rules of national law, to ensure that the directive is fully effective.[473]

3–033

---

[471] ECJ, Case 106/77 *Simmenthal* [1978] E.C.R. 629, operative part, at 645–646. With regard to the non-applicability of a technical provision which was not notified in accordance with Directive 83/189 as then applicable in the context of a dispute between individuals relating in particular to contractual rights and obligations, national law will determine what consequences (as regards the possible nullity or unenforceability of the contract) ensue from the non-applicability of the technical provision (ECJ, Case C–159/00 *Sapod Audic* [2002] E.C.R. I–5031, para.53).

[472] *Cf.* Carreau, "Droit communautaire et droits nationaux: concurrence ou primauté? La contribution de l'arrêt '*Simmenthal*'" (1978) R.T.D.E. 381–418.

[473] ECJ, Joined Cases C–397/01 to C–403/01 *Pfeiffer and Others* [2004] E.C.R. I–8835, paras 107–118, and the case-law cited therein.

3–034   **Timeframe.** The decisive *point in time* which the national court takes into account in order to assess the legality of an act in the light of Community law is determined by national law, provided that it does not detract from the principles of equivalence and effectiveness.[474]

D. Raising pleas derived from Community law of the court's own motion

3–035   **Principle.** The principle of the full effectiveness of Community law does not require the national court to raise applicable Community law in all circumstances of its own motion. The national court has the power to do so if it considers that Community law must be applied,[475] but it is only where the parties have failed to invoke mandatory rules of Community law having direct effect[476] that it may be obliged to raise those rules of its own motion.

3–036   **Bases of the principle.** Depending on the case, the Court of Justice has identified different bases for this principle. Where there is an obligation for the national court to raise mandatory rules of law of its own motion by virtue of domestic law, there will be the same obligation to raise Community rules by virtue of the principle of procedural equal treatment. Where domestic law merely confers on national courts a discretion to apply mandatory rules of law of their own motion, the same obligation to raise Community rules remains pursuant to the principle of cooperation laid down in Art.10 of the EC Treaty, which requires national courts to use all the possibilities afforded by national law in order to ensure the legal protection which persons derive from the direct effect of provisions of Community law,[477] or alternatively pursuant to the duty on the courts, as authorities of the Member States, under the third para. of Art.249 of the EC Treaty to take all the measures necessary to achieve the result prescribed by a directive.[478] It follows that, in the absence of any Com-

---

[474] ECJ, Case C–92/00 *HI* [2002] E.C.R. I–5553, para.67.

[475] ECJ, Joined Cases C–87-89/90 *Verholen and Others* [1991] E.C.R. I–3757, para.13.

[476] The mandatory (or public policy) nature of a provision of Community law does not depend on criteria stemming from national law, but is determined on the basis of Community law (see ECJ, Case C–126/97 *Eco Swiss China Time* [1999] E.C.R. I–3055, paras 34–39, with a case note by Komninos (2000) C.M.L.Rev. 459–578). See also Prechal and Shelkoplyas, "National Procedures, Public Policy and EC Law. From *Van Schijndel* to *Eco Swiss* and Beyond" (2004) E.Rev.Priv.L. 589–611.

[477] ECJ, Joined Cases C–430 and C–431/93 *Van Schijndel and Van Veen* [1995] E.C.R. I–4705, paras 13–14 (case note by Heukels (1996) C.M.L.Rev. 337–353). That judgment has been given a somewhat critical reception: see, *inter alia*, Hoskins (n.464, *supra*), but *cf.* Prechal (n.391, *supra*). For an application of the judgment in the French legal system, see Szyszczak and Delicostopoulos, "Intrusions into National Procedural Autonomy: The French Paradigm" (1997) E.L.Rev. 141–149.

[478] ECJ, Case C–72/95 *Kraaijeveld and Others* [1996] E.C.R. I–5403, paras 54–61, with a case note by Coppieters (1997–1998) R.W. 60–61. *Cf.* ECJ, Joined Cases C–240/98 to C–244/98 *Océano Grupo Editorial and Salvat Editores* [2000] E.C.R. I–4941, where the national court's power to declare of its own motion that it had no jurisdiction was inferred directly from Council Directive 93/13/EEC of April 5, 1993 on unfair terms in consumer contracts and from the objectives underlying that directive. See Prechal, "Ambtshalve toetsen van oneerlijke bedingen door middel van conforme uitleg" (2001) N.T.E.R. 104–108; see also Delicostopoulos, "Towards European Procedural Primacy in National Legal Systems" (2003) E.L.J. 599–613.

munity provision governing the matter, there will be a requirement for the national courts to raise provisions of Community law of their own motion only if there exists a requirement or a discretion to raise mandatory rules by virtue of domestic law.[479] Where national courts are precluded from so doing under national procedural law, there is in principle no requirement for them to do so, provided, however, that this does not cause national procedural law to conflict with Community law. National procedural law must comply with the constraints to which reference has already been made (see 3–003, *supra*),[480] in particular the requirement that it must not render the exercise of rights conferred by Community law virtually impossible or excessively difficult. In addition, it must not prevent the procedure laid down in Art.234 of the EC Treaty from being followed.[481] A rule of national procedural law which does not satisfy those conditions must be set aside,[482] with the result that the national court in question may nevertheless be subject to the requirement to raise rules of Community law of its own motion. In this regard, the Court of Justice tests the national procedural rules against Community law having regard to their role in the procedure, its progress and its special features, before the various national authorities. Frequently, the Court also has regard to the basic principles of the domestic legal system, such as protection of the rights of the defence, the principle of legal certainty and the proper conduct of the procedure.[483] Accordingly, the Court has held that civil courts are not required to abandon the passive role assigned to them by raising a rule of Community law of their own motion.[484] In contrast, a rule of the Belgian Income Tax

---

[479] ECJ, Joined Cases C-430 and C-431/93 *Van Schijndel and Van Veen* [1995] E.C.R. I–4705, para. 15. The Court did not explain exactly why a requirement for national courts to raise of their own motion rules of Community law having direct effect exists only where it is possible to raise mandatory national rules of their own motion. In his Opinion in that case, Advocate General F.G. Jacobs argued that if the view were taken that national procedural rules must always yield to Community law that would unduly subvert established principles underlying the legal systems of the Member States. It could be regarded as infringing the principles of proportionality and subsidiarity. It would also give rise to widespread anomalies, since the effect would be to afford greater protection to rights which are not, by virtue of being Community rights, inherently of greater importance than rights recognised by national law (Opinion of Advocate General F.G. Jacobs, point 27; see also the case note by Heukels, n.477, *supra*, at 349).

[480] *Van Schijndel and Van Veen*, para.17.

[481] *Van Schijndel and Van Veen*, para.18, and ECJ, Case 166/73 *Rheinmühlen–Düsseldorf* [1974] E.C.R. 33, paras 2–3, cited therein.

[482] See 3–032, *supra*.

[483] *Van Schijndel and Van Veen*, para.19. The criterion whereby the Court of Justice also considers the role of the procedural rule under national law seems to go further than the criterion in Case 33/76 *Rewe* (see 3–001, *supra*), whereby the Court of Justice considers only the effect of the relevant rule in a particular case: see Hoskins (n.464, *supra*), at 373.

[484] *Van Schijndel and Van Veen*, para.22: Community law does not require national courts to raise of their own motion an issue concerning the breach of provisions of Community law where examination of that issue would oblige them to abandon the passive role assigned to them by going beyond the dispute defined by the parties themselves and relying on facts and circumstances other than those on which the party with an interest in application of those provisions bases his or her claim.

Code (Art. 278, second para., in conjunction with Arts 279, second para., and 282) which prevented the national court from inquiring of its own motion into the compatibility of a tax assessment with a provision of Community law in proceedings relating to that assessment unless the taxpayer had raised the relevant provision within a specified time-limit was held by the Court to be contrary to Community law.[485]

E. EFFECTS OF INFRINGEMENTS OF COMMUNITY LAW

1. Imposition of sanctions

3–037 **Division of powers.** The division of powers as between the Community and the Member States as regards the imposition of sanctions is a controversial question.[486] The Community does not have a general power to impose criminal sanctions.[487] It can, however, impose other types of sanctions.[488] If it does not do so,[489] Member States are empowered to enforce compliance with Community law by imposing criminal sanctions or using sanctions available under other branches of the law.[490]

3–038 **Power of Member States.** The Member States' power to impose penalties or other sanctions for infringement of Community law must, pursuant to Art.10 of the EC Treaty, be exercised in order to guarantee the full

---

[485] ECJ, Case C–312/93 *Peterbroeck* [1995] E.C.R. I–4599 (with a case note by Heukels, n.477, *supra*). Characteristics and circumstances to which the Court of Justice has regard in finding that such a procedural rule is incompatible with Community law include the fact that the national court is the first judicial authority to have cognisance of the case and to be able to request a preliminary ruling, the fact that another judicial authority in a further hearing was precluded from raising the question of compatibility with Community law of its own motion and the fact that the impossibility for national courts to raise points of Community law of their own motion does not appear to be reasonably justifiable by principles such as the requirement of legal certainty or proper conduct of the procedure.

[486] For an extensive survey of the relevant *doctrine*, see Tesauro, "La sanction des infractions au droit communautaire" (1992) Riv.D.E. 477–509.

[487] ECJ, Case 203/80 *Casati* [1981] E.C.R. 2595, para.27; ECJ, Case 186/87 *Cowan* [1989] E.C.R. 195, para.19. But see, in the specific field of Community environmental legislation, ECJ (judgment of September 13, 2005), Case C–176/03 *Commission v Council*, not yet reported; compare Haguenau, "Sanctions pénales destinées à assurer le respect du droit communautaire" (1993) R.M.C. 351, at 359, who argues that the Community has the power to impose criminal sanctions under Arts 10 and 308 of the EC Treaty; and Zuleeg, "Der Beitrag des Strafrechts zur europäischen Integration" (1992) J.Z. 761–769.

[488] ECJ, Case C–240/90 *Germany v Commission* [1992] E.C.R. I–5383; for a commentary, see Stessens, "De bevoegdheid van de Europese Gemeenschap tot het vaststellen van sancties: op weg naar een communautair strafrecht?" (1993–1994) R.W. 137–153.

[489] If Community sanctions are imposed, the principle *nec bis in idem* would prevent the imposition of additional national sanctions for the same breach of Community law. Naturally, the position would be different where the same set of measures constituted an infringement of both Community and national law. In such case, penalties and other sanctions could be imposed for the infringement of national law alongside the sanctions provided for by the Community provision itself in respect of the infringement of Community law. See also Biancarelli, "Les principes généraux du droit communautaire applicables en matière pénale" (1987) R.S.C.D.P.C. 131–166; de Doelder and van der Hulst "EEG-sancties en ne bis in idem" (1993) S.E.W. 722–733.

[490] ECJ, Joined Cases C–58, C–75, C–112, C–119, C–123, C–135, C–140, C–141, C–154 and C–157/95 *Gallotti and Others* [1996] E.C.R. I–4345, paras 14–15.

effectiveness of that law.[491] This power constitutes the corollary of the Member States' obligation to impose Community law in their territory.[492]

Effectiveness and equivalence. The obligation to guarantee the full effec-   3–039
tiveness of Community law entails that the sanction imposed by a Member State in the event of infringement of a Community provision from which individuals derive rights be such as to guarantee real and effective legal protection and have a real deterrent effect.[493] To that end, not only the imposition, but also the enforcement, of the sanction is important. For example, it would appear not to be in accordance with Community law for an obligation to pay compensation imposed upon a Member State for infringement of a Community provision to be thwarted by a general executive immunity with regard to public goods.

Infringements of Community law must be penalised under conditions, both procedural and substantive, which are analogous to those applicable to infringements of national law of a similar nature. Penalties for infringements of provisions of Community law must be effective, proportionate and dissuasive.[494] When exercising their power to impose sanctions, Member States must comply with Community law and the general principles of law embodied therein.[495] Furthermore, control procedures must not be conceived in such a manner as to restrict the freedoms required by the Treaty and must not be accompanied by a penalty which is so disproportionate to

---

[491] ECJ, Case 68/88 *Commission v Greece* [1989] E.C.R. 2965, para.23; ECJ, Case C–326/88 *Hansen* [1990] E.C.R. I–2911, para.17; ECJ, Case C–7/90 *Vandevenne* [1991] E.C.R. I–4371, para.11; ECJ, Case C–382/92 *Commission v United Kingdom* [1994] E.C.R. I–2435, para.55; ECJ, Case C–383/92 *Commission v United Kingdom* [1994] E.C.R. I–2479, para.40.

[492] Temple Lang, "Art. 5*[now Art.10]* of the EEC Treaty: the Emergence of Constitutional Principles in the Case Law of the Court of Justice" (1987) Fordham I.L.J. 503, at 519–522.

[493] ECJ, Case 14/83 *Von Colson and Kamann* [1984] E.C.R. 1891, para.23; ECJ, Case 79/83 *Harz* [1984] E.C.R. 1921, paras 22–23 (where a Member State chooses to penalise a breach of the prohibition of discrimination by the award of compensation, the compensation must be adequate in relation to the damage sustained). See also ECJ, Case C–177/88 *Dekker* [1990] E.C.R. I–3941, paras 23–26; ECJ, Case C–271/91 *Marshall* [1993] E.C.R. I–4367, paras 24–26; ECJ, Case C–186/98 *Nunes and De Matos* [1999] E.C.R. I–4883, paras 10–11; ECJ, Case C–354/99 *Commission v Ireland* [2001] E.C.R. I–7657, para.46.

[494] ECJ, Case 68/88, *Commission v Greece*, [1989] E.C.R. 2965, paras 23 and 24; ECJ, Case C–326/88 *Hansen* [1990] E.C.R. I–2911, para.17; Case C–167/01 *Inspire Art* [2003] E.C.R. I–10155, para.62; ECJ, Case C–230/01 *Penycoed Farming Partnership* [2004] E.C.R. I–937, para.36; ECJ, Joined Cases C–387/02, C–391/02 and C–403/02 *Berlusconi and Others* [2005] E.C.R. I–3565, para.65.

[495] ECJ, Joined Cases 201 and 202/85 *Klensch* [1986] E.C.R. 3477, para.8; ECJ, Case 5/88 *Wachauf* [1989] E.C.R. 2609, para.19; ECJ, Case C–210/91 *Commission v Greece* [1992] E.C.R. I–6735, para.19. It may be noted that the penalties imposed by a Member State for non-compliance with formalities lawfully required in order to establish a right conferred by Community law may not be such as to constitute an obstacle to the exercise of that right. Such penalties are disproportionate and contrary to Community law: ECJ, Case C–193/94 *Skanavi and Chryssanthakopoulos* [1996] E.C.R. I–929, paras 36–39. The sanction imposed may not be contrary to provisions of the ECHR (ECJ, Case C–60/02 *X* [2004] E.C.R. I–651, paras 61–63).

the seriousness of the infringement that it becomes an obstacle to those freedoms.[496]

3–040 **Example.** In the field of criminal or disciplinary proceedings, the Court of Justice subscribes to the Commission's view that "the Member States are required by virtue of Art.5[now Art.10] of the E[E]C Treaty to penalise any persons who infringe Community law in the same way as they penalise those who infringe national law".[497] The Hellenic Republic was charged with having infringed Community law "by omitting to initiate all the criminal or disciplinary proceedings provided for by national law against the perpetrators of the fraud and all those who collaborated in the commission and concealment of it".[498] This certainly places a restriction on the public prosecutor's freedom in principle to decide whether or not to bring criminal proceedings for breaches of Community law. Yet that freedom does not disappear altogether. The Court of Justice simply held that "the national authorities must proceed, with respect to infringements of Community law, with the same diligence as that which they bring to bear in implementing corresponding national laws",[499] or, in other words, that the public prosecutor must be able to show the same strictness in respect of breaches of Community law pursued under the criminal law as he or she does in respect of similar breaches of national law. This is consistent with the general obligation for Member States to ensure that "infringements of Community law are penalised under conditions, both procedural and substantive, which are analogous to those applicable to infringements of national law of a similar nature and importance and which, in any event, make the penalty effective, proportionate and dissuasive".[500]

2. Claims for damages for an infringement of Community law by Member States

3–041 **Principle.** Community law obliges Member States to provide for the specific "sanction" of a right to reparation where, by their action or failure to act, national authorities infringe Community law (unlawful act or omission) and this results (causal link)[501] in damage to rights which individuals derive from Community law (loss or damage).[502] The Court of

---

[496] ECJ, Case 203/80 *Casati* [1981] E.C.R. 2595, para.27; ECJ, Joined Cases 286/82 and 26/83 *Luisi and Carbone* [1984] E.C.R. 377, para.34.

[497] ECJ, Case 68/88 *Commission v Greece* [1989] E.C.R. 2965, first sentence of para.22.

[498] *Ibid.* second sentence of para.22.

[499] *Ibid.*, para.25.

[500] *Ibid.*, para.24. See, to the same effect, Case C–326/88 *Hansen* [1990] E.C.R. I–2911, para.17; ECJ, Case C–36/94 *Siesse* [1995] E.C.R. I–3573, para.20; ECJ, Case C–213/99 *De Andrade* [2000] E.C.R. I–11083, para.19.

[501] The causal connection is determined in principle by the national court (see ECJ, Case C–140/97 *Rechberger and Others* [1999] E.C.R. I–3499, paras 72–73).

[502] ECJ, Joined Cases C–6 and C–9/90 *Francovich and Others* [1991] E.C.R. I–5357. See Vuye, "Overheidsaansprakelijkheid wegens schending van het Europees Gemeenschapsrecht" (2003) T.B.H. 713–763.

Justice takes the view that "the principle whereby a State must be liable for loss and damage caused to individuals as a result of breaches of Community law for which the State can be held responsible is inherent in the system of the Treaty".[503] "A further basis for the obligation of Member States to make good such loss and damage is to be found in [Art. 10] of the Treaty".[504]

The basic conditions "under which that liability gives rise to a right to reparation depend on the nature of the breach of Community law giving rise to the loss and damage".[505] This means that those conditions invariably have to be assessed in the light of the particular situation.[506] In determining those conditions, the Court of Justice has regard to its case-law on the non-contractual liability of the Community. First, this is because the second para. of Art.288 of the EC Treaty refers to the general principles common to the legal systems of the Member States, from which, in the absence of written rules, the Court also draws inspiration in other areas of Community law and, secondly, because the conditions under which the State may incur liability for damage caused to individuals by a breach of Community law cannot differ from those governing the liability of the Community in like circumstances.[507] Since the judgment in *Bergaderm*[508] the conditions for the Community to incur liability have been completely aligned with the criteria identified by the Court of Justice for Member States to incur liability.

Conditions. According to the established case-law of the Court of Justice, **3–042** it appears that a Member State must make good loss or damage sustained by individuals as a result of breaches of Community law attributable to it where three conditions are met: the rule of law infringed must be intended to confer rights on individuals; the breach must be sufficiently serious; and there must be a direct causal link between the breach of the obligation resting on the State and the loss or damage sustained by the injured parties.[509]

---

[503] *Ibid.*, para.35; ECJ, Case C–63/01 *Evans* [2003] E.C.R. I–14447, para.83.
[504] *Ibid.*, para.36.
[505] *Ibid.*, para.38.
[506] ECJ, Joined Cases C–178, C–179, C–188, C–189 and C–190/94 *Dillenkofer and Others* [1996] E.C.R. I–4845, para.24.
[507] ECJ, Joined Cases C–46 and C–48/93 *Brasserie du Pêcheur and Factortame (Factortame IV)* [1996] E.C.R. I–1029, paras 39–42 (case note by Oliver (1997) C.M.L.Rev. 635–680). Some commentators would have preferred it if the conditions for liability on the part of the Community had been equated with those for liability on the part of the Member States and not the other way around, while arguing for "clarification" of the interpretation of Art.288 of the EC Treaty in the light of the judgment in *Francovich* (see Caranta, "Judicial Protection against Member States: a New *Jus Commune* takes Shape" (1995) C.M.L.Rev. 703–726).
[508] ECJ, Case C–352/98 P *Bergaderm and Goupil v Commission* [2000] E.C.R. I–5291.
[509] ECJ, Joined Cases C–46 and C–48/93 *Brasserie du Pêcheur and Factortame (Factortame IV)* [1996] E.C.R. I–1029, para.51; ECJ, Case C–424/97 *Haim* [2000] E.C.R. I–5123, para.26; ECJ, Case C–224/01 *Köbler* [2003] E.C.R. I–10239, para.51; ECJ, Case C–63/01 *Evans*

As far as the second condition is concerned, namely whether the breach of Community law was sufficiently serious, all the factors which characterise the situation must be taken into account. Those factors include, in particular, the clarity and precision of the rule infringed, the measure of discretion left by that rule to the national or Community authorities, whether the infringement or the damage caused was intentional or involuntary, whether any error of law was excusable or inexcusable, and the fact that the position taken by a Community institution may have contributed towards the omission, and the adoption or retention of national measures or practices contrary to Community law.[510]

3–043 Margin of discretion. The decisive test for finding that a breach of Community law is sufficiently serious is whether the Member State concerned manifestly and gravely disregarded the limits on its discretion.[511] Where an institution of a Member State acts in a matter in which it had only considerably reduced or no discretion at all at the time when it committed the infringement, the mere infringement of Community law may be enough to establish the existence of a sufficiently serious breach.[512] Accordingly, failure to take any measure to transpose a directive into national law within the prescribed period in order to achieve the result sought constitutes a sufficiently serious breach of Community law.[513] Where conduct has persisted in spite of a preliminary ruling or a judgment of the Court of Justice finding a failure to fulfil obligations from which it appears that that conduct constitutes a breach of Community law, that will also amount to a sufficiently serious breach.[514]

3–044 Transposition of directives. As far as the actual transposition of the provisions of a directive is concerned, a Member State's margin of discretion may be broader, depending on its content. In this way, improper

---

[2003] E.C.R. I–14447, para.83. For the question as to whether a directive without direct effect confers "rights" on individuals breach of which may give rise to an obligation to make reparation, see ECJ, Case C–91/92 *Faccini Dori* [1994] E.C.R. I–3325, para.27; ECJ, Case C–192/94 *El Corte Inglés* [1996] E.C.R. I–1281, para.22.

[510] ECJ, Joined Cases C–46 and C–48/93 *Brasserie du Pêcheur and Factortame (Factortame IV)* [1996] E.C.R. I–1029, para.56; ECJ, Case C–424/97 *Haim* [2000] E.C.R. I–5123, para.26; ECJ, Case C–63/01 *Evans* [2003] E.C.R. I–14447, para.86.

[511] *Factortame IV*, para.55.

[512] For an example, see ECJ, Case C–5/94 *Hedley Lomas* [1996] E.C.R. I–2553, para.28, where the Court of Justice held that the mere infringement of Art.29 of the EC Treaty by the UK in refusing to grant an export licence constituted a sufficiently serious breach of Community law on the ground that at the time of the infringement the UK had considerably reduced discretion, if any (*ibid.*, para.28); see also ECJ, Case C–127/95 *Norbrook Laboratories* [1998] E.C.R. I–1531, para.109.

[513] ECJ, Joined Cases C–178, C–179, C–188, C–189 and C–190/94 *Dillenkofer and Others* [1996] E.C.R. I–4845. See, also ECJ, Case C–319/96 *Brinkmann* [1998] E.C.R. I–5255, para.29. See, with respect to the liability of the Spanish authorities for the incorrect transposition of a directive, Tribunal Supremo (Spanish Supreme Court), Administrative Law Chamber, judgment of June 12, 2003, *Canal Satélite Digital* (Case 46/1999) with case note by Castillo de la Torre (2004) C.M.L.Rev. 1717–1734.

[514] ECJ, Joined Cases C–46 and C–48/93 *Brasserie du Pêcheur and Factortame (Factortame IV)* [1996] E.C.R. I–1029, para.57; ECJ, Case C–118/00 *Larsy* [2001] E.C.R. I–5063, para.44.

transposition of a directive may not automatically constitute a sufficiently serious breach and give rise to liability on the part of the State. Accordingly in the *British Telecommunications* case, the Court of Justice held that the improper transposition of a particular directive into national law did not constitute a sufficiently serious breach of Community law on the ground that the directive at issue was imprecisely worded and was reasonably capable of bearing the interpretation given to it by the UK in good faith and on the basis of arguments which were not entirely devoid of substance and not manifestly contrary to the wording of the directive or its objectives.[515]

Court decisions. In *Köbler*, the Court of Justice ruled that a Member State 3–045 may be held liable for a breach of Community law as a result of a decision of a national court adjudicating at last instance only in the exceptional case where the court has manifestly infringed the applicable law.[516] In order to determine whether that condition is satisfied, the national court hearing a claim for reparation must take account of all the factors which characterise the situation put before it. Those factors include, in particular, the degree of clarity and precision of the rule infringed, whether the infringement was intentional, whether the error of law was excusable or inexcusable, the position taken, where applicable, by a Community institution and non-compliance by the court in question with its obligation to make a reference for a preliminary ruling under the third para. of Art.234 of the EC Treaty. In any event, an infringement of Community law will be sufficiently serious where the judicial decision concerned was taken in manifest breach of the case-law of the Court of Justice in the relevant matter.[517]

---

[515] ECJ, Case C–392/93 *British Telecommunications* [1996] E.C.R. I–1631, para.43. In ECJ, Joined Cases C–283, C–291 and C–292/94 *Denkavit and Others* [1996] E.C.R. I–5063, paras 51–54, the Court of Justice held that its case-law did not provide Germany with any interpretation as to how a provision of a particular directive had to be interpreted. Consequently, the erroneous interpretation which Germany had given to it, which had been adopted by almost all the other Member States following discussions within the Council, could not be regarded as a sufficiently serious breach of Community law. In contrast, in *Rechberger* the Court of Justice held that a national implementing provision which limited the time from which a right conferred by a directive entered into effect where the directive conferred no discretion on the Member States in this respect constituted a sufficiently serious breach of Community law (ECJ, Case C–140/97 *Rechberger and Others* [1999] E.C.R. I–3499, para.51). See also ECJ, Case C–150/99 *Stockholm Lindöpark* [2001] E.C.R. I–493, para.39.

[516] ECJ, Case C–224/01 *Köbler* [2003] E.C.R. I–10239, para.55. See, on this judgment, Gorton, "Staatshaftung im EWR nach *Köbler*—eine Zwischenbemerkung" (2004) Eu L.R.65–68; Krans, "Het arrest *Köbler*: aansprakelijkheid voor schending van EG-recht in rechterlijke uitspraken" (2004) N.J.B. 571–576; Kotschy, "Responsabilité de l'État : arrêt *Köbler*" (2003) R.D.U.E. 763–765; Breuer, "State liability for judicial wrongs and Community law : the case of *Gerhard Köbler v Austria*" (2004) E.L.Rev. 243–254; Classen, "Case C–224/01 *Gerhard Köbler v Republik Österreich*" (2004) C.M.L. Rev. 813–824; Wattel, "*Köbler*, *CILFIT* and *Welthgrove*: We can't go on meeting like this" (2004) C.M.L.Rev. 243–254. For the relationship between *Köbler* and *Kühne & Heitz*, see Komárek, "Federal elements in the Community judicial system: building coherence in the Community legal order" (2005) C.M.L. Rev. 9–34.

[517] ECJ, Case C–224/01 *Köbler* [2003] E.C.R. I–10239, para.56.

3–046 **Principle of effectiveness.** In the absence of Community rules, the procedural organisation of the legal proceedings is left to national law, but the provisions of national law must not be less favourable for actions for damages for breach of Community law than they are for other actions for damages, or be so framed as to make it "virtually impossible or excessively difficult to obtain reparation".[518] In addition, traditional concepts applying in some Member States must where appropriate yield to State liability under Community law.[519] Accordingly, the principle that the State cannot be held liable for an unlawful act or omission on the part of the legislature, which applies in some Member States' legal systems, cannot restrict the principle of State liability for breaches of Community law. The reason for this is that State liability holds good for any case in which a Member State breaches Community law, whatever be the organ of the State whose act or omission was responsible for the breach.[520] This applies not only to breaches of Community law by organs of the legislature or the executive,

---

[518] ECJ, Joined Cases C–6 and C–9/90 *Francovich and Others* [1991] E.C.R. I–5357, para.43; ECJ, Case C–66/95 *Sutton* [1997] E.C.R. I–2163, para.33; ECJ, Case C–224/01 *Köbler* [2003] E.C.R. I–10239, paras 46–50.

[519] See Arts, "Het *Francovich*-arrest en zijn toepassing in de Belgische rechtsorde" (1993) T.B.P. 495–510; Betlem and Rood, "*Francovich*-aansprakelijkheid: Schadevergoeding wegens schending van het gemeenschapsrecht" (1992) N.J.B. 250; Bok, "Het *Francovich*-arrest en onrechtmatige wetgeving naar Nederlands recht" (1993) T.P.R 37; Emiliou, "State Liability under Community Law: Shedding More Light on the *Francovich* Principle" (1996) E.L.Rev. 399–411; Gilliams, "Overheidsaansprakelijkheid bij schending van Europees gemeenschapsrecht" (1991–1992) R.W. 877–880; Rodríguez Iglesias, "Reflections on the general principles of Community Law" (1998/1999) Cambridge Y.E.L.S. 1–16; Tesauro, "Responsabilité des Etats membres pour violation du droit communautaire" (1996) R.M.U.E. 15–34; Vandersanden and Dony, *La responsabilité des Etats membres en cas de violation du droit communautaire* (Bruylant, Brussels, 1997), 413 pp.; van Gerven, "Bridging the unbridgeable: Community and National Tort Laws after *Francovich* and *Brasserie*" (1996) I.C.L.Q. 507–544; Wissink, "De Nederlandse rechter en overheidsaansprakelijkheid krachtens *Francovich* en *Brasserie du Pêcheur*" (1997) S.E.W. 78–90; Dantonel-Cor, "La violation de la norme communautaire et la responsabilité extracontractuelle de l'Etat" (1998) R.T.D.E. 75–91. For actions in damages against the State in English law, see Brealey and Hoskins, *Remedies in E.C. Law*, at 128–148; for damages actions against private parties, see *ibid.*, at 118–127.

[520] ECJ, Joined Cases C–46 and C–48/93 *Brasserie du Pêcheur and Factortame* (*Factortame IV*) [1996] E.C.R. I–1029, paras 32–36, and the Opinion of Advocate General G. Tesauro, at points 35–38. It appears from the same judgment that the Court of Justice considers that the condition imposed by German law where a law is in breach of higher-ranking national provisions, which makes reparation dependent upon the legislature's act or omission being referable to an individual situation, must be set aside in the case of a breach of Community law. The reason for this is that that condition would in practice make it impossible or extremely difficult to obtain effective reparation for loss or damage resulting from a breach of Community law, since the tasks falling to the national legislature relate, in principle, to the public at large and not to identifiable persons or classes of persons (*ibid.*, paras 71–72). The Court likewise held in *Factortame IV* that any condition that may be imposed by English law on State liability requiring proof of misfeasance in public office must be set aside because such an abuse of power is inconceivable in the case of the legislature and therefore the condition makes it impossible to obtain effective reparation for loss or damage resulting from a breach of Community law (*ibid.*, para.73).

but also to judicial bodies adjudicating at last instance.[521] In addition, the acts of a federated State or a territorial authority with a degree of autonomy and likewise public-law bodies[522] may cause the Member State itself, as well as themselves, to incur liability.

In Member States with a federal structure, reparation for damage caused to individuals does not necessarily have to be provided by the federal State (federal authority). It is sufficient that individuals' right to reparation for loss or damage flowing from an infringement of Community law by a federated State is effectively protected. If, however, there is no effective protection, a Member State (federal authority) cannot plead the distribution of powers and responsibilities between the bodies which exist in its national legal order in order to free itself from liability on that basis.[523] That is also true for those Member States in which certain legislative or administrative tasks are devolved to territorial bodies with a certain degree of autonomy or to any other public-law body legally distinct from the State.[524]

Compensation. The amount of the damages must be commensurate with the loss or damage sustained so as to ensure the effective protection of the rights of the injured parties.[525] In the case of late implementation of a directive, retroactive and proper application in full of the measures implementing the directive will suffice in principle, unless the beneficiaries establish the existence of complementary loss sustained on account of the fact that they were unable to benefit at the appropriate time from the financial advantages guaranteed by the directive, with the result that such loss must also be made good.[526] Limiting compensation to an upper limit or a prohibition on the national court's granting interest on that basic amount are contrary to Community law in so far as they make it impossible to make reparation in full for the damage sustained.[527] The national rules may

3–047

---

[521] See ECJ, Case C–224/01 *Köbler* [2003] E.C.R. I–10239: the principle of *res judicata* and the principle of the independence of the judiciary do not preclude State liability for breaches of Community law committed by courts adjudicating at last instance (paras 30–50). See also ECJ (order of June 3, 2005), Case C–396/03 P *Killinger v Germany, Council and Commission* [2005] E.C.R. I–4967, para.28. See also Blanchet, "L'usage de la théorie de l'acte clair en droit communautaire: une hypothèse de mise en jeu de la responsabilité de l'Etat français du fait de la fonction juridictionnelle" (2001) R.T.D.E. 397–438.

[522] ECJ, Case C–424/97 *Haim* [2000] E.C.R. I–5123, para.32.

[523] ECJ, Case C–302/97 *Konle* [1999] E.C.R. I–3099, paras 61–64.

[524] ECJ, Case C–424/97 *Haim* [2000] E.C.R. I–5123, paras 30–31.

[525] ECJ, Joined Cases C–46 and C–48/93 *Brasserie du Pêcheur and Factortame (Factortame IV)* [1996] E.C.R. I–1029, para.82.

[526] ECJ, Joined Cases C–94 and C–95/95 *Bonifaci and Others and Berto and Others* [1997] E.C.R. I–3969, para.54; ECJ, Case C–373/95 *Maso and Others* [1997] E.C.R. I–4051, para.41; ECJ, Case C–131/97 *Carbonari and Others* [1999] E.C.R. I–1103, para.53.

[527] ECJ, Case C–271/91 *Marshall* [1993] E.C.R. I–4367, paras 22–32. To limit compensation to an upper limit may, where the loss or damage exceeds that upper limit, conflict with the requirement for an effective, deterrent sanction. This is also true of the prohibition on

require the injured party to show reasonable diligence in order to avoid the loss or damage or limit its extent.[528] The setting of reasonable limitation periods for bringing an action for damages is compatible with the above requirements, provided that it does not make it virtually impossible or excessively difficult to obtain reparation.[529]

3. Claims for damages for an infringement of Community law by individuals

3–048   *Courage judgment.* Individuals who have infringed a Community provision with direct effect may be obliged to make reparation for the loss or damage caused thereby.[530] In its judgment in the *Courage* case[531] the Court of Justice held that Community law (and in particular Art.81 of the EC Treaty) precludes a rule of national law under which a party to a contract liable to restrict or distort competition is barred from claiming damages under national law for loss caused by performance of that contract on the sole ground that the claimant is a party to that contract. But national law can deny that right to a party which bears significant responsibility for the distortion of competition. The *Courage* judgment made a first approach, on the basis of the principles of effectiveness and equivalence, to define the contours of claims to damages under national law for breaches of Community law, without giving such claims a direct basis in Community law. However, the Court did state expressly that the practical effect of Art.81 of the EC Treaty would be put at risk "if it were not open to any individual to

---

adding interest to the basic amount. If account cannot be taken of the effluxion of time, reparation will not be made for the whole of the damage. Consequently, the grant of interest under the applicable national law is essential in order to satisfy the requirement of the full effectiveness of Community law. See Fitzpatrick and Szyszczak, "Remedies and Effective Judicial Protection in Community Law" (1994) Mod.L.Rev. 434–441. See to the same effect ECJ, Joined Cases C–397/98 and C–410/98 *Metallgesellschaft and Others* [2001] E.C.R. I–1727, para.4. Note that in *Marshall*, the Employment Appeal Tribunal held that the industrial tribunal had wrongly awarded interest on damages (for sex discrimination contrary to the Sex Discrimination Act 1975) under s.35A of the Supreme Court Act 1981 as it was not a court of record. On appeal the House of Lords restored the award. The question of jurisdiction to award such interest was subsequently catered for by the Sex Discrimination and Equal Pay (Remedies) Regulations 1993 (SI 1993/2798).

[528] ECJ, Joined Cases C–46 and C–48/93 *Brasserie du Pêcheur and Factortame* (*Factortame IV*) [1996] E.C.R. I–1029, paras 84 and 85. However, this rule must be applied having regard to the specific circumstances of the case. In the judgment in *Metallgesellschaft* (ECJ, Joined Cases C–397/98 and C–410/98 *Metallgesellschaft and Others* [2001] E.C.R. I–1727, paras 101–107), the Court of Justice considered that rejecting or reducing reparation for a financial disadvantage sustained because the claimants had not applied for a tax advantage which national law denied them, with a view to challenging the refusal of the tax authorities by means of the legal remedies provided for that purpose, would render the exercise of rights conferred on private persons by directly applicable provisions of Community law (in that case Art.43 of the EC Treaty) impossible or excessively difficult.

[529] ECJ, Case C–261/95 *Palmisani* [1997] E.C.R. I–4025, para.28.

[530] ECJ, Case C–453/99 *Courage and Crehan* [2001] E.C.R. I–6297. See also Opinion of Advocate General W. van Gerven in Case C–128/92 *Banks* [1994] E.C.R. I–1209.

[531] ECJ, Case C–453/99 *Courage and Crehan* [2001] E.C.R. I–6297.

claim damages for loss caused to him by a contract or by conduct liable to restrict or distort competition".[532]

4. Withdrawal of a decision of a national administrative body which has become final

Problem. It may appear from a judgment of the Court of Justice that earlier decisions taken by national administrative bodies are based on a wrong interpretation of Community law. The question then arises whether those national administrative bodies are obliged to reopen those decisions which have become definitive.

3–049

Kühne & Heitz judgment. The fact is that the interpretation which the Court of Justice gives to a rule of Community law in a preliminary ruling clarifies and defines where necessary the meaning and scope of that rule as it must be or ought to have been understood and applied from the time of its coming into force.[533] It follows that a rule of Community law interpreted in this way must be applied by an administrative body within the sphere of its competence even to legal relationships which arose or were formed before the Court gave its ruling on the question on interpretation.[534] However, it does not follow automatically that an administrative body has to reopen an administrative decision which has become final. On the contrary, the Court, referring to the principle of legal certainty, considers that, in principle, such a body is not required to reopen an administrative decision which has become final.[535] However, in very specific circumstances there may be an obligation to reopen a decision. This will be the case in

3–050

---

[532] *Ibid.*, para.26. For an extensive discussion, see Komninos, "New prospects for private enforcement of EC Competition Law: *Courage v Crehan* and the Community right to damages" (2002) C.M.L.Rev. 447–487; Kremer, "Die Haftung Privater für Verstösse gegen Gemeinschaftsrecht" (2003) EuR. 696–705; Mäsch, "Private Ansprüche bei Verstösse gegen das europäische Kartellverbot - *"Courage"* und die Folgen" (2003) EuR. 825–846; Reich, "The *'Courage'* doctrine: encouraging or discouraging compensation for antitrust injuries?" (2005) C.M.L.Rev. 35–66.

[533] ECJ, Case 61/79 *Denkavit Italiana* [1980] E.C.R. 1205, para.16; ECJ, Case C–50/96 *Deutsche Telekom* [2000] E.C.R. I–743, para.43; ECJ, Case C–453/00 *Kühne & Heitz* [2004] E.C.R. I–837, para.21.

[534] ECJ, Case C–453/00 *Kühne & Heitz* [2004] E.C.R. I–837, para.22. See on this judgment, Caranta "Case C–453, *Kühne & Heitz*" (2005) C.M.L.Rev. 179–188; Urlesberger "Zur Rechtskraft im Gemeinschaftsrecht" (2004) Z.f.R.V.99–104; Potacs, "Bestandskraft staatlicher Verwaltungsakte oder Effektivität des Gemeinschaftsrechts?" (2004) EuR., 595–602; Peerbux-Beaugendre, "Une administration ne peut invoquer le principe de la force de chose définitivement jugée pour refuser de reexaminer une décision dont une interprétation préjudicielle ultérieure a révélé la contrariété avec le droit communautaire" (2004) R.D.U.E. 559–567; Jans and De Graaf, "Bevoegdheid = verplichting? Enkele opmerkingen over de uitspraak van het Hof van Justitie in de zaak *Kühne & Heitz*" (2004) N.T.E.R., 98–102. For the relationship between *Köbler* and *Kühne & Heitz*, see Komárek, "Federal elements in the Community judicial system: building coherence in the Community legal order" (2005) C.M.L.Rev. 9–34.

[535] ECJ, Case C–453/00 *Kühne & Heitz* [2004] E.C.R. I–837, para.24.

particular where the following three conditions are satisfied: under national law, the administrative body concerned has the power to reopen the decision[536]; the administrative decision in question has become final as a result of a judgment of a national court ruling at final instance which was based on a misinterpretation of Community law which was adopted without a question being referred to the Court for a preliminary ruling; and the person concerned complained to the administrative body immediately after becoming aware of the decision of the Court of Justice from which it appears that the national decision is contrary to Community law.[537]

III. Legal Protection in Proceedings for Interim Relief

3–051 **Two situations.** The protracted nature of judicial proceedings may pose a threat to the actual enforcement of the rights conferred upon an individual by Community law. This explains the interest for the full effectiveness of Community law of a system of provisional legal protection which enables a real claim to those rights to be safeguarded by freezing a provision which is allegedly in conflict with (superior) Community law or by granting interim relief provisionally to settle or regulate disputed legal positions or relationships pending a judicial ruling in the main proceedings.[538] Two situations need to be distinguished. First, there is the situation where the national court grants interim relief in order to freeze the effect of a national provision which is allegedly in breach of Community law. Secondly, the national court may grant interim relief in order to freeze the implementation of a Community measure which is allegedly in breach of the superior law (and therefore unlawful) or provisionally to settle or regulate disputed legal positions or relationships with reference to a national administrative measure based on a Community act whose validity is under consideration in proceedings for a preliminary ruling.

3–052 **Allegedly illegal national measure.** As far as the first situation is concerned, the Court of Justice has held as follows: "Community law must be interpreted as meaning that a national court which, in a case before it concerning Community law, considers that the sole obstacle which precludes it from granting interim relief is a rule of national law must set aside

---

[536] See, by analogy, the question in connection with raising pleas derived from Community law of the court's own motion, 3–036, *supra*.

[537] ECJ, Case C–453/00 *Kühne & Heitz* [2004] E.C.R. I–837, paras 26–28.

[538] De la Sierra, "Provisional court protection in administrative disputes in Europe: the constitutional status of interim measures deriving from the right to effective court protection. A comparative approach" (2004) E.L.J. 42–60; Morlot-Dehan, "La protection provisoire devant les juridictions administratives dans l'Union européenne" (2004) R.I.D.C. 459–474.

that rule".[539] It is only in this way that the "full effectiveness of Community law" can be secured by "the judgment to be given on the existence of the rights claimed under Community law".[540]

This means that, where necessary, the national court can derive directly from Community law the power to suspend a provision of national law in interlocutory proceedings.[541] The nature of the measure whose suspension is sought is immaterial. Furthermore, Community law embodies no special requirements for the suspension of provisions of national law, although here too the principle applies that there must be equal treatment of suspension on grounds of domestic law and suspension on Community law grounds, together with the principle that the applicable domestic law must not subject the suspension to conditions such as to make it impossible in practice to obtain.

Allegedly illegal Community measure. As far as the second situation is concerned, the Court of Justice has held as follows: "In cases where national authorities are responsible for the administrative application of Community regulations, the legal protection guaranteed by Community law includes the right of individuals to challenge, as a preliminary issue, the legality of such regulations before national courts and to induce those courts to refer questions to the Court of Justice for a preliminary ruling. That right would be compromised if, pending delivery of a judgment of the Court, which alone has jurisdiction to declare that a Community regulation is invalid . . ., individuals were not in a position, where certain conditions

3–053

---

[539] ECJ, Case C–213/89 *Factortame and Others* (*Factortame*) [1990] E.C.R. I–2433, operative part. After the House of Lords had held that it could not give an interim injunction in judicial review proceedings seeking to set aside an Act of Parliament because courts had no such power under the Supreme Court Act 1981 and an Act of Parliament was presumed valid until declared otherwise (*R v Secretary of State for Transport, ex parte Factortame (no 2)* [1990] A.C. 603), the preliminary ruling in *Factortame I* was considered to give it the power to grant such an injunction (or at least to remove the common law rule that an interim injunction may not be granted against the Crown): see Brealey and Hoskins, *Remedies in E.C. Law*, at 106–107 and 154–155. For the injunctions available under English law to secure the full effectiveness of Community law, see *ibid.*, at 149–164.

[540] *Ibid.*, para.21. See also ECJ, Case C–226/99 *Siples* [2001] E.C.R. I–277, paras 17–20.

[541] Barav, "Omnipotent Courts", in Curtin and Heukels (eds), *Institutional Dynamics of European Integration. Essays in Honour of H.G. Schermers* (Martinus Nijhoff, Dordrecht, 1994), Vol.II, 265, at 277, and "The Effectiveness of Judicial Protection and the Role of the National Courts", in *Judicial Protection of Rights in the Community Legal Order* (Bruylant, Brussels, 1997), at 259–296; Simon and Barav, "Le droit communautaire et la suspension provisoire des measures nationales: Les enjeux de l'affaire Factortame" (1990) R.M.C. 591–597: "[L]'arrêt Factortame a le mérite d'établir, fût-ce d'une manière quelque peu indirecte, la compétence du juge national d'écarter, à titre provisoire, l'application d'une mesure nationale prétendue contraire au droit communautaire dans l'attente d'une décision définitive" [The *Factortame* judgment has the merit of establishing—albeit indirectly—jurisdiction on the part of a national court to set aside, provisionally, the application of a national measure alleged to be contrary to Community law pending a definitive decision]. See also case notes by Lauwaars (1991) S.E.W. 478–480; Toth (1990) C.M.L.Rev. 573, at 586, and Joliet, "Coopération entre la Cour de justice des Communautés européennes et les juridictions nationales" (1993) 2 J.T.D.E. 4–5.

are satisfied, to obtain a decision granting suspension of enforcement which would make it possible for the effects of the disputed regulation to be rendered for the time being inoperative as regards them".[542] For this reason, Art.249 of the EC Treaty does not preclude national courts from "granting interim relief to settle or regulate the disputed legal positions or relationships with reference to a national administrative measure based on a Community regulation which is the subject of a reference for a preliminary ruling on its validity".[543]

The question arises as to what is meant by "where certain conditions are satisfied". The Court of Justice has held that "the rules of procedure of the courts are determined by national law and . . . those conditions differ according to the national law governing them, which may jeopardise the uniform application of Community law".[544] In order to reduce this danger, the Court of Justice has held that suspension of enforcement of national administrative measures based on a Community regulation or the grant of other interim measures "must in all the Member States be subject to conditions which are uniform".[545] The Court identifies those "uniform conditions" with "the conditions which must be satisfied for the Court of Justice [itself] to allow an application to it for interim measures".[546] The parallel between the conditions for the grant of interim relief applicable before the national court and the Court of Justice (and the Court of First Instance) is due to the fact that an assessment of validity via a request for a preliminary ruling and an action for annulment constitute two aspects of a single system of judicial review of legality. The coherence of the system demands uniformity in the procedural rules for provisional suspension or limitation of enforcement of contested Community measures until such time as the Court of Justice or the Court of First Instance has carried out its review of legality, whether by a preliminary ruling (Court of Justice) or by a judgment on an application for annulment (Court of Justice or Court of First Instance). As a result, the national court must base itself, as far as the substantive conditions for suspension or limitation of enforcement of national administrative measures based on a Community regulation are concerned, on the case-law of the Court of Justice concerning interim

---

[542] ECJ, Joined Cases C–143/88 and C–92/89 *Zuckerfabrik Süderdithmarschen and Zuckerfabrik Soest* [1991] E.C.R. I–415, paras 16–17. See Mongin, "Le juge national et les mesures provisoires ordonnées en vertu du droit communautaire", in Christianos (ed.), *Evolution récente du droit judiciaire communautaire*, (European Institute of Public Administration, Maastricht, 1994), Vol.I, 125–131; Sinnaeve, "Voorlopige maatregelen tegen secundair gemeenschapsrecht: de bevoegdheden van de nationale rechter in kort geding" (1996-1997) R.W. 105–112.

[543] ECJ, Case C–465/93 *Atlanta Fruchthandelsgesellschaft and Others* [1995] E.C.R. I–3761, para.30; see Mehdi, "Le droit communautaire et les pouvoirs du juge national de l'urgence" (1996) R.T.D.E. 77–100.

[544] *Zuckerfabrik Süderdithmarschen and Zuckerfabrik Soest*, cited in n.542, para.25.

[545] *Atlanta Fruchthandelsgesellschaft and Others*, cited in n.543, paras 29 and 33.

[546] *Zuckerfabrik Süderdithmarschen and Zuckerfabrik Soest*, cited in n.542, paras 26–27.

measures, and no longer on national law.[547] National law governs only "the making and examination of the application".[548]

Interim measures may be granted by a national court only if:

- that court entertains serious doubts as to the validity of the Community regulation and, if the validity of the contested act is not already in issue before the Court of Justice, itself refers that question to the Court[549];

- there is urgency, in that interim relief is necessary to avoid serious and irreparable damage to the party seeking the relief;

- the national court takes due account of the Community interest;

- in its assessment of all those conditions, it respects any decisions of the Court of Justice or the Court of First Instance ruling on the lawfulness of the regulation or on an application for interim measures seeking similar interim relief at Community level.[550]

As far as the first requirement is concerned, the Court of Justice has held that "the national court cannot restrict itself to referring the question of the validity of the regulation to the Court for a preliminary ruling, but must set out, when making the interim order, the reasons for which it considers that the Court should find the regulation to be invalid. The national court must take into account here the extent of the discretion which, having regard to the Court's case-law, the Community institutions must be allowed in the sectors concerned".[551]

The Court has clarified the second requirement as follows: "With regard to the question of urgency, . . . damage invoked by the applicant must be liable to materialise before the Court of Justice has been able to rule on the validity of the contested Community measure. With regard to the nature of that damage, purely financial damage cannot, as the Court has held on

---

[547] See Arts 242 and 243 of the EC Treaty; for examples, see ECJ (order of the President of October 25, 1985), Case 293/85 R *Commission v Belgium* [1985] E.C.R. 3521; with a case note by Watson (1987) C.M.L.Rev. 93; and ECJ (order of July 12, 1990), Case C–195/90 R *Commission v Germany* [1990] E.C.R. I–3351. *Cf.* Pastor and Van Ginderachter, "La procédure en référé" (1989) R.T.D.E. 561–621. See also Joliet, Bertrand and Nihoul, "Protection juridictionnelle provisoire et droit communautaire" (1992) Riv.D.E. 253–284.

[548] ECJ, Joined Cases C–143/88 and C–92/89 *Zuckerfabrik Süderdithmarschen and Zuckerfabrik Soest* [1991] E.C.R. I–415, para.26 (with a case note by Schermers (1992) C.M.L.Rev. 133–139, who emphasises that that judgment places the interest of the protection of the individual above the interest of the primacy of Community law).

[549] *Ibid.*, para.33. See also ECJ, Case C–334/95 *Krüger* [1997] E.C.R. I–4517, para.47. These conditions also apply where the interim measures are directed against an authority of an overseas country or territory (OCT): ECJ, Case C–17/98 *Emesa Sugar* [2000] E.C.R. I–675, paras 69–73.

[550] ECJ, Case C–465/93 *Atlanta Fruchthandelsgesellschaft and Others* [1995] E.C.R. I–3761, para.51.

[551] *Ibid.*, paras 36–37.

numerous occasions, be regarded in principle as irreparable. However, it is for the national court hearing the application for interim relief to examine the circumstances particular to the case before it. It must in this connection consider whether immediate enforcement of the measure which is the subject of the application for interim relief would be likely to result in irreversible damage to the applicant which could not be made good if the Community act were to be declared invalid".[552]

As far as the third requirement is concerned, the Court of Justice has observed that the national court "must first examine whether the Community measure in question would be deprived of all effectiveness if not immediately implemented"[553] and, "if suspension of enforcement is liable to involve a financial risk for the Community, the national court must also be in a position to require the applicant to provide adequate guarantees, such as the deposit of money or other security".[554] In assessing the Community interest, the national court is free to decide, in accordance with its own rules of procedure, which is the most appropriate way of obtaining all relevant information on the Community act in question.[555]

The fourth requirement signifies that if the Court of Justice has dismissed an action for annulment of the act in question or has held, in the context of a reference for a preliminary ruling on validity, that the reference disclosed nothing to affect the validity of that act, the national court can no longer order interim measures or must revoke any existing measures, unless the grounds of illegality put forward before it differ from the pleas in law or grounds of illegality rejected by the Court in its judgment. The same applies if the Court of First Instance, in a judgment which has become final and binding, has dismissed on the merits an action for annulment of the act or an objection of illegality.[556]

3–054　**Appeal against a national decision.** National procedural rules allowing an appeal to be brought against a decision granting interim measures in the form of suspension of enforcement of a national administrative measure are compatible with Community law, provided that they do not affect the national court's obligation in such a case to make a reference for a preliminary ruling on the validity of the Community act on which the suspended national administrative implementing measure is based and that they do not restrict the right conferred by Art.234 on every court or tribunal to make a reference to the Court of Justice.[557]

---

[552] ECJ, Joined Cases C–143/88 and C–92/89 *Zuckerfabrik Süderdithmarschen and Zuckerfabrik Soest* [1991] E.C.R. I–415, para.29.
[553] *Ibid.*, para.31.
[554] *Ibid.*, para.32.
[555] ECJ, Case C–334/95 *Krüger* [1997] E.C.R. I–4517, para.46.
[556] ECJ, Case C–465/93 *Atlanta Fruchthandelsgesellschaft and Others* [1995] E.C.R. I–3761, para.46.
[557] ECJ, Case C–334/95 *Krüger* [1997] E.C.R. I–4517, paras 49–54.

Counterpart of interim relief of the Community judicature. National 3–055
courts' power to grant interim relief under Community law in the two
situations described above (see 3–052 and 3–053, *supra*) is also based on the
consideration that the supervision of the legality of Community acts which
the Court of Justice carries out in the preliminary ruling procedure needs
to retain its full effectiveness.[558] In both situations, the national court has
the power or even a duty to make a reference to the Court of Justice for a
preliminary ruling. In the first situation, it may, by referring a question on
the interpretation of the applicable provision of Community law, indirectly
determine whether the national provision at issue is, as alleged, contrary to
Community law. In the second, it is under a duty, if the question concerning
the validity of the disputed Community act has not yet been submitted to
the Court, to raise that question with the Court itself (see 2–056, *supra*).
Consequently, the interim relief granted by national courts in those two
situations is the precise counterpart of the interim relief which the Court of
Justice or the Court of First Instance grants under Arts 242–243 of the EC
Treaty in order to ensure the effectiveness of the judicial supervision which
it carries out in direct actions.[559] The Court of Justice has held, in full
accord with its concern to guarantee the coherence of the system of legal
protection outlined in the Treaty, that the national courts are not
empowered to grant interim relief in situations in which, by virtue of a
Community regulation, the existence and scope of traders' rights must be
established by a Commission measure which that institution has not yet
adopted. This is because the Treaty makes no provision for a reference for
a preliminary ruling by which the national court asks the Court of Justice to
rule that an institution has failed to act.[560] The Court of Justice and the
Court of First Instance may only make such a ruling in a direct action
brought pursuant to Art.232 of the EC Treaty.[561]

---

[558] ECJ, Joined Cases C–143/88 and C–92/89 *Zuckerfabrik Süderdithmarschen and Zuckerfabrik Soest* [1991] E.C.R. I–415, para.19.
[559] For further particulars, see Lenaerts, "The Legal Protection of Private Parties under the EC Treaty: a Coherent and Complete System of Judicial Review", in *Scritti in onore di Giuseppe Federico Mancini* (Giuffrè editore, Milan, 1998), Vol.II, at 591–623.
[560] ECJ, Case C–68/95 *T. Port v Commission* [1996] E.C.R. I–6065, paras 52–53.
[561] *Ibid.*, para.24. See, to the same effect, ECJ, Case C–326/88 *Hansen* [1990] E.C.R. I–2911, para.17; ECJ, Case C–36/94 *Siesse* [1995] E.C.R. I–3573, para.20; ECJ, Case C–213/99 *De Andrade* [2000] E.C.R. I–11083, para.19.

Part II

ENFORCEMENT OF COMMUNITY LAW

CHAPTER 4

INTRODUCTION

Three pillars. The original version of Art.L of the EU Treaty limited the **4–001** exercise of powers by the Community judicature[1] to the Treaty establishing the European Community, the Treaty establishing the European Coal and Steel Community, the Treaty establishing the European Atomic Energy Community, the former third subpara.of Art.K.3(2)(c) of the EU Treaty and the former Arts L to S of that Treaty.[2] Accordingly, the jurisdiction of the Court of Justice covered Community law, certain agreements concluded by the Member States outwith Community law (see Ch.21, *infra*) and the final provisions of the EU Treaty. The Treaty of Amsterdam introduced a new Art.46 into the EU Treaty (which has been further amended by the Treaty of Nice) replacing the former Art.L and considerably extending the jurisdiction of the Court of Justice in the field of police and judicial cooperation in criminal matters[3] and expressly empowering the Court of Justice to review acts of the institutions in the light of fundamental rights protected by Art.6(2) of the EU Treaty in so far as the Court has jurisdiction under the Community Treaties or the EU Treaty.[4]

Art.46 of the EU Treaty does not prevent the Court of Justice itself from delimiting the scope of its jurisdiction. For instance, a measure which was purportedly adopted in connection with a pillar other than the Community pillar of the Union (*e.g.* sanctions imposed under the common foreign and security policy) may in fact be ascribable to a Community competence (*e.g.* the common commercial policy referred to in Art.133 of the EC Treaty), which would mean that the Court of Justice would be competent to review the measure for compatibility with the Community Treaties. In the event of a dispute, it is the task of the Court of Justice or the Court of First Instance to define the pillars of the Union in relation to each other. That task cannot be undertaken by any other institution, since it is a matter of interpreting

---

[1] For an application of Art.L of the EU Treaty, see ECJ (order of April 7, 1995), Case C–167/94 *Grau Gomis and Others* [1995] E.C.R. I–1023, para.6.

[2] For a discussion of the structure of the Union, see Lenaerts and Van Nuffel, *Constitutional Law of the European Union*, § 3–012–§3–015, at 49–55.

[3] As far as the Court's jurisdiction in this connection is concerned, see Ch.22, *infra*.

[4] For further details, see Lenaerts, "Le respect des droits fondamentaux en tant que principe constitutionnel de l'Union européenne", in *Mélanges en homage à Michel Waelbroeck* (Bruylant, Brussels, 1999), Vol.I, 423–457.

and applying the Community Treaties and hence within the jurisdiction of the Court of Justice and the Court of First Instance within the Community legal order, which, by virtue of the judicially enforceable Art.47 of the EU Treaty, is not affected by any other provision of that Treaty.[5]

4–002 **Community based on the rule of law.** The Community is a Community based on the rule of law in which each legislative, executive or implementing act of an institution or a Member State must be compatible with the "constitutional charter" on which the Community is based.[6] The preamble to the Charter of Fundamental Rights of the EU[7] states that the Union is based in particular on the "principle of the rule of law". The substance of that principle is fleshed out in the first para.of Art.47 of the Charter, which provides that "Everyone whose rights and freedoms guaranteed by the law of the Union are violated has the right to an effective remedy before a tribunal. . .". The Treaties set out to establish a complete system of legal remedies, whereby any act or failure to act on the part of an institution or a Member State can be subjected to review by the Community court,[8] which has to ensure that in the interpretation and application of the Treaties the law is observed.[9]

---

[5] ECJ, Case C–170/96 *Commission v Council* [1998] E.C.R. I–2763, paras 12–18; ECJ (judgment of September 13, 2005), Case C–176/03 *Commission v Council*, not yet reported, paras 38–40. In connection with litigation on access to documents of the Community institutions, it follows from the scope of Council Decision 93/731/EC of December 20, 1993 (now replaced by Regulation (EC) No 1049/2001 of the European Parliament and of the Council of May 30, 2001 regarding public access to European Parliament, Council and Commission documents, [2001] O.J. L145/43) that the Community judicature is competent to review the legality of any decision made pursuant to that Council decision, even if the documents to which access is sought relate to a sphere of activity of the Council which is not subject to judicial review by the Court of Justice (CFI, Case T–14/98 *Hautala v Council* [1999] E.C.R. II–2489, paras 40–42).

[6] ECJ, Case 294/83 *Les Verts v European Parliament* [1986] E.C.R. 1339, para.23; ECJ, Opinion 1/91 *Draft Agreement between the Community, on the one hand, and the countries of the European Free Trade Association, on the other, relating to the creation of the European Economic Area* [1991] E.C.R. I–6079, para.21; CFI (order of January 17, 2002), Case T–236/00 *Stauner and Others v European Parliament and Commission* [2002] E.C.R. II–135, para.50; CFI, Case T–231/99 *Joynson v Commission* [2002] E.C.R. II–2085, para.32. As far as Community law is concerned, there is an exception under Art.68(2) of the EC Treaty. That article provides that the Court of Justice shall not have jurisdiction to rule on any measure or decision taken pursuant to Art.62(1) relating to the maintenance of law and order or the safeguarding of internal security. See also Schwarze, "Judicial Review in EC Law—Some Reflections on the Origins and the Actual Legal Situation" (2002) I.C.L.Q. 17–33.

[7] [2000] O.J. C364/1.

[8] For a concise review of the Community's system of legal remedies, See Lenaerts, "Rechtsbescherming en rechtsafdwinging: de functies van de rechter in het Europees gemeenschapsrecht" (1992–1993) R.W. 1105–1118; Lenz, "Rechtsschutz im Binnenmarkt: Stand und Probleme" (1994) N.J.W. 2063-2067; Van der Wal and Prechal, "Aspecten van Europese rechtsbescherming" (1990) Advocatenblad 604–612.

[9] EC Treaty, Art.220; EAEC Treaty, Art.136.

Two-fold task of the judiciary. The judiciary has a two-fold task in   **4–003** connection with the Community system of legal remedies. First, it is responsible for enforcing *all* the rules of Community law. As a result, it affords protection against any act or failure to act on the part of national authorities and persons which offends against such provisions. In this respect, Community law acts as a sword for safeguarding the rights deriving from that law (see Chs 5 and 6, below). In addition, the judiciary secures the enforcement of written and unwritten *superior* rules of Community law[10] and affords protection against any act or failure to act of institutions and other bodies of the Community in breach of those rules. In this respect, Community law acts as a shield (see Part III, below).

---

[10] For a survey of the hierarchy of norms in Community law, see Lenaerts and Van Nuffel, *Constitutional Law of the European Union*, § 17–052–§ 17–055, at 703–705.

CHAPTER 5

ACTION FOR INFRINGEMENT OF COMMUNITY LAW BY A MEMBER STATE

I. SUBJECT-MATTER

A. GENERAL

5–001 **Objective nature.** The action for failure to fulfil obligations (or infringement proceedings)[11] is for the purpose of obtaining a declaration that the conduct of a Member State infringes Community law and of terminating that conduct.[12] The action is objective in nature and the only question raised is whether or not the defendant Member State has breached Community law.[13] In determining whether the alleged infringement took place, the Court of Justice takes no account of subjective factors invoked to justify the Member State's conduct or omission, the frequency or the scale of the circumstances complained of[14] or of the fact that there is no evidence that the infringement of Community law was intentional.[15] No reasonable-

---

[11] EC Treaty, Art.226; EAEC Treaty, Art.141. A somewhat similar procedure under the third pillar may be found in Art.35(7) of the EU Treaty (see Ch.22, *infra*).

[12] ECJ, Joined Cases 15 and 16/76 *France v Commission* [1979] E.C.R. 321, para.27.

[13] See, *inter alia*, ECJ, Case 7/68 *Commission v Italy* [1968] E.C.R. 423, at 428; ECJ, Case 415/85 *Commission v Ireland* [1988] E.C.R. 3097, paras 8–9; ECJ, Case 416/85 *Commission v United Kingdom* [1988] E.C.R. 3127, paras 8–9; ECJ, Case C–140/00 *Commission v United Kingdom* [2002] E.C.R. I–10372, para.34. See also ECJ, Case 301/81 *Commission v Belgium* [1983] E.C.R. 467, para.8: the well-foundedness of an action under Art.226 of the EC Treaty depends only on an objective finding of a failure to fulfil obligations and not on proof of any inertia or opposition on the part of the Member State. See further ECJ (judgment of September 9, 2004), Case C–383/02 *Commission v Italy*, not reported, paras 12–20; ECJ (judgment of September 16, 2004), Case C–248/02 *Commission v Italy*, not reported, para.25.

[14] ECJ, Case C–404/99 *Commission v France* [2001] E.C.R. I–2667, para.51.

[15] See, for instance, the case-law rejecting the following as pleas in justification: difficulties in the domestic decision-making process (ECJ, Case 96/81 *Commission v Netherlands* [1982] E.C.R. 1791, para.12; ECJ, Case 97/81 *Commission v Netherlands* [1982] E.C.R. 1819, para.12; ECJ, Case 301/81 *Commission v Belgium* [1983] E.C.R. 467, para.6; ECJ, Joined Cases 227–230/85 *Commission v Belgium* [1988] E.C.R. 1, para.9; ECJ, Case C–33/90 *Commission v Italy* [1991] E.C.R. I–5987, para.24); the fact that other Member States are also guilty of the infringement (ECJ, Case 52/75 *Commission v Italy* [1976] 277, para.11; ECJ, Case 78/76 *Steinike & Weinlig* [1977] E.C.R. 595, para.24; ECJ, Case 232/78 *Commission v France* [1979] E.C.R. 2729, para.9; ECJ, Case 325/82 *Commission v Germany*

ness test may be applied. The objective nature of the action for failure to fulfil obligations does not mean, however, that the Court of Justice does not subject the relevant conduct of the Member State concerned to thorough examination, from the point of view of both the law and the facts. In contradistinction to the action for annulment (see Ch.7, *infra*), the Court of Justice does not confine its examination to a number of "grounds" on which the application must be based. Any infringement of Community law may be "found" pursuant to Arts 226-228 of the EC Treaty.[16]

Purpose. The "finding" of an infringement serves principally to enforce the actual application of Community law by the Member State in breach. In the first place, since *Francovich*,[17] a Member State may incur liability under Community law for a breach of a Community provision. The judgment finding the infringement may ground liability.[18] In addition, Art.228 of the EC Treaty provides for options for enforcing such a judgment.[19]

    5-002

The action may also be used as a means of determining the exact nature of the obligations of a Member State in the event of differences of interpretation of Community law.[20] After the Court of Justice has given judgment, the Member State concerned may no longer contest the extent of its Community obligations. If the Member State continues to be in breach of its obligations, this will constitute a sufficiently serious breach of

---

[1984] E.C.R. 777, para.11; ECJ, Case C–38/89 *Blanguernon* [1990] E.C.R. I–83, para.7). See also Dashwood and White, "Enforcement Actions Under Arts 169 and 170[*now Arts 226 and 227]* EEC" (1989) E.L.Rev. 388, at 400–401; Joliet, *Le contentieux*, at 20; Nafilyan, "La position des États membres et le recours en manquement des Arts 169[*now Art.226]* CEE et 141 CEEA" (1977) R.T.D.E. 214, at 215; Waelbroeck, Waelbroeck and Vandersanden, *La Cour de Justice*, in Waelbroeck, Louis, Vignes, Dewost and Vandersanden, *Commentaire Mégret* (2nd ed., Éditions de l'Université de Bruxelles, Brussels, 1993), Vol.10, at 74–76. See, however, Mertens de Wilmars and Verougstraete, "Proceedings against Member States for Failure to Fulfil their Obligations" (1970) C.M.L.Rev. 385, who at the time of the "breakthrough" of the action for failure to fulfil obligations in the Court's case-law still advocated, with certain reservations, merging the objective nature of the action with full powers on the part of the Court to take account also of subjective factors. This does not seem to have been followed.

[16] For a wide-ranging discussion of Art.226 of the EC Treaty, see Ebke, "Les techniques contentieuses d'application du droit des Communautés européennes" (1986) R.T.D.E. 209–230.

[17] ECJ, Joined Cases C–6 and C–9/90 *Francovich and Others* [1991] E.C.R. I–5357 (see 3–041, *supra*).

[18] See the settled case-law since ECJ, Case 39/72 *Commission v Italy* [1973] E.C.R. 101, para.11, in which it was held that "a judgment by the Court under [Arts 169 and 171[*now Arts 226 and 228]*] may be of substantive interest as establishing the basis of a responsibility that a Member State can incur as a result of its default, as regards other Member States, the Community or private parties". See also 3–041 to 3–047, *supra*.

[19] The procedure provided for in Art.228 of the EC Treaty may be applied only where the Court has determined pursuant to Art.226 or Art.227 of the EC Treaty that the Member State has failed to fulfil an obligation under the Community law (ECJ (order of the President of May 30, 2001) Case C–334/97 R-EX *Comune di Montorio al Vomano v Commission* [2001] E.C.R. I–4229, para.19).

[20] ECJ, Case 7/71 *Commission v France* [1971] E.C.R. 1003, para.49.

Community law, which may cause it to incur liability *vis-à-vis* injured individuals.[21]

5–003 **Procedure.** The procedure is set forth in Arts 226, 227 and 228 of the EC Treaty[22] (Arts 141, 142 and 143 of the EAEC Treaty are identical).[23] The action for failure to fulfil obligations is the only procedure—apart from some special procedures (5–016 to 5–024, *infra*)—which allows the Court of Justice to measure the conduct of a Member State *directly* against Community law.[24]

B. Failure of a Member State to fulfil an obligation under the Treaty

1. What rules are covered by the expression "an obligation under this Treaty"?

5–004 **All rules of Community law.** The expression "an obligation under this Treaty" covers all rules of Community law which are binding on the Member States. These are all the Treaty provisions, binding acts of Community institutions,[25] international agreements concluded by the Community[26] and the general principles of law recognised by the Court of

---

[21] See 3–041, *supra*.

[22] Under Art.237(d) of the EC Treaty actions may be brought against a national central bank for failure to fulfil obligations. Proceedings are to be brought by the European Central Bank, which has the same powers as the Commission has under Art.226 of the EC Treaty. Under Art.237(a) of the EC Treaty, the Board of Directors of the European Investment Bank may bring an action in the Court of Justice against a Member State in relation to the fulfilment of its obligations under the Bank's Statute. In this connection, the Board of Directors enjoys the powers conferred upon the Commission by Art.226 of the EC Treaty: see CFI (order of April 10, 2000), Case T–361/99 *Meyer v Commission* [2000] E.C.R. II–2031, para.12). For an extensive discussion of legal protection within the framework of the European System of Central Banks, see Gaiser, "Gerichtliche Kontrolle im Europäischen System der Zentralbanken" (2000) EuR. 517–539. Art.104(10) of the EC Treaty rules out the possibility of bringing an action against a Member State for failing to fulfil its obligations under Art.104(1)–(9) by failing to avoid an excessive government deficit.

[23] See, *e.g.* ECJ, Case C–61/03 *Commission v United Kingdom* [2005] E.C.R. I–2477.

[24] ECJ, Case 28/83 *Forcheri v Commission* [1984] E.C.R. 1425, para.12; CFI, Case T–13/93 *Cordier v Commission* [1993] E.C.R. II–1215, para.52. Since *Van Gend & Loos* (ECJ, Case 26/62 *Van Gend & Loos* [1963] E.C.R. 1, at 10–13), however, the Court of Justice has held that it can use the procedure for a preliminary ruling on interpretation in order to appraise a Member State's conduct *indirectly* against Community law.

[25] ECJ, Case C–205/98 *Commission v Austria* [2000] E.C.R. I–7367, para.43. The infringement of a directive which has been annulled but whose effects the Court of Justice preserved in the judgment until such time as it had been replaced by a new directive in compliance with the Court's judgment may form the subject of an action for failure to fulfil obligations. It made no difference that the Council and the European Parliament did not adopt the new directive until four years had elapsed.

[26] EC Treaty, Art.300(7); ECJ, Case 104/81 *Kupferberg* [1982] E.C.R. 3641, para.11; ECJ, Case C–61/94 *Commission v Germany* [1996] E.C.R. I–3989, para.15; ECJ, Case C–13/00 *Commission v Ireland* [2002] E.C.R. I–2943, para.20, in which the Court held that Ireland's failure to accede to the Berne Convention as required by Art.5 of Protocol 28 to the EEA

Justice. A finding that those rules have been infringed may be made as a result of an action brought pursuant to Arts 226 to 228 of the EC Treaty.[27]

General principles of law. A finding that a Member State has infringed 5–005 general principles of law, including fundamental rights, may be made only in so far as the national conduct falls within the scope of Community law. This will be so in particular where the Member State justifies its conduct on one of the grounds provided for in the Treaty.[28]

Conventions pursuant to Art.293 of the EC Treaty. It is an open question 5–006 whether a Member State may be brought before the Court of Justice for infringing a convention concluded pursuant to Art.293 of the EC Treaty. Some commentators have argued that this is possible on the ground that Art.293 puts the Member States under a duty to enter into negotiations with each other in order to achieve clearly defined Community objectives.[29] Others contend that a distinction should be made between the obligation to conclude the convention under Art.293 and the obligations ensuing out of such a convention for Member States. They maintain that the latter obligations are not part of Community law.[30] The Court of Justice has not yet had to rule on the question.[31]

Agreement (a mixed agreement concluded by the Community, its Member States and non-member countries and related to an area covered in large measure by the Treaty) came within the Community framework. This therefore constituted a failure to fulfil obligations within the meaning of Art.226 of the EC Treaty. See also ECJ, Case C–465/01 *Commission v Austria* [2004] E.C.R. I–8291; ECJ, Case C–239/03 *Commission v France* [2004] E.C.R. I–9325, paras 22–31: provisions of a mixed agreement come within the Community framework if they—even in the absence of specific Community legislation regarding the issue covered by these provisions (*e.g.* discharges of fresh water and alluvia into saltwater marsh)—concern a field (*e.g.* environmental protection) in large measure covered by Community law; if this is the case, the Court of Justice has jurisdiction to assess a Member State's compliance with the provisions concerned of the mixed agreement in proceedings brought before it under Art.226 of the EC Treaty.

[27] For a discussion of the sources of Community law, see Lenaerts and Van Nuffel, *Constitutional Law of the European Union*, Part V, at 663 *et seq.*, and Brealey and Hoskins, *Remedies in E.C. Law*, at 3–26.

[28] ECJ, Case C–260/89 *ERT* [1991] E.C.R. I–2925, para.42; ECJ, Case C–159/90 *Society for the Protection of Unborn Children Ireland* [1991] E.C.R. I–4685, para.31.

[29] See Dashwood and White (n.15, *supra*), at 390; *cf.* Pescatore, "Remarques sur la nature juridique des 'décisions des représentants des Etats membres réunis au sein du Conseil'" (1966) S.E.W. 579, at 583–584.

[30] See Schwartz, "Voies d'uniformisation du droit dans la CEE: règlements de la Communauté ou conventions entre les Etats membres" (1978) J.D.I. 751, at 781.

[31] However, the Court has held in its case-law on the Brussels Convention—which has since been replaced except so far as Denmark is concerned by Council Regulation (EC) No 44/2001 of December 22, 2000 on jurisdiction and the recognition and enforcement of judgments in civil and commercial matters ([2001] O.J. L 12/1; *corrigendum* in [2001] O.J. L307/28), which manifestly forms part of Community law—that the provisions of that convention were "linked to the E[E]C Treaty" and that this allowed the Court of Justice to assess the compatibility of those provisions with Art.12 of the EC Treaty (prohibition of discrimination on grounds of nationality) (ECJ, Case C–398/92 *Mund & Fester* [1994] E.C.R

In any event, it is agreed that compliance with conventions concluded by the Member States outside Art.293 cannot be enforced by proceedings under Arts 226 and 227 of the EC Treaty, even if they do contribute to the attainment of the objectives of the EC Treaty.[32]

2. What is meant by "failure to fulfil"?

5–007 **Any shortcoming.** Since the action for failure to fulfil obligations is objective in nature, *any* shortcoming by a Member State in respect of its obligations under Community law will ground a claim for a declaration that it is in breach. The frequency or scale of the shortcoming is irrelevant, likewise the fact that the failure had no adverse effects.[33] A minimum, isolated and negligible infringement of Community law is sufficient for the action to be declared well founded.[34] It lies with the Commission or the applicant Member State (see 5–025 and 5–029, *infra*) to assess whether it is appropriate to bring an action. Once the action is pending, the Court of Justice has to consider whether or not the alleged infringement was committed.[35]

5–008 **Administrative practice.** Not only the exercise by a Member State of its regulatory powers can constitue a failure to fulfil an obligation of the Treaty.[36] An administrative practice can also be the subject-matter of an action for failure to fulfil obligations when it is, to some degree, of a consistent and general nature.[37]

I–467, paras 11–12). Admittedly, the Court has not provided any answer to the question whether infringements on the part of Member States of the Brussels Convention can be the subject of proceedings brought under Arts 226 and 227 of the EC Treaty. It may be considered, however, that the answer must be in the negative, given that the Court of Justice mentioned the Brussels Convention and the national provisions to which it refers on an equal footing when it stated that they are linked to the EC Treaty and therefore "within the scope of application of this Treaty" within the meaning of Art.12 of the EC Treaty. As a result, the Brussels Convention came over as a joint measure of the Member States, which, in common with unilateral national measures, must be compatible with Community law, but does not form part of it.

[32] See Dashwood and White (n.15, *supra*), at 390, who refer to the Convention for the European Patent for the Common Market, which provides for a special procedure for failure of Member States to fulfil their obligations in Art.101(2) and (3) ([1976] O.J. L 17/1).

[33] ECJ, Case C–150/97 *Commission v Portugal* [1999] E.C.R. I–259, para.22; ECJ, Case C–348/97 *Commission v Germany* [2000] E.C.R. I–4429, para.62.

[34] Thus, the Commission may ask the Court of Justice to find that, in not having achieved, in a specific case, the result intended by the directive, a Member State has failed to fulfil its obligations (ECJ, Joined Cases C–20/01 and C–28/01 *Commission v Germany* [2003] E.C.R. I–3609, para.30; ECJ, Case C–157/03 *Commission v Spain* [2005] E.C.R. I–2911, para.44).

[35] ECJ, Case C–209/89 *Commission v Italy* [1991] E.C.R. I–1575, para.6.

[36] ECJ, Case 8/70 *Commission v Italy* [1970] E.C.R. 961, paras 8–9; ECJ, Case 94/81 *Commission v Italy* [1982] E.C.R. 739, para.4; ECJ, Case 41/82 *Commission v Italy* [1982] E.C.R. 4213, para.15; ECJ, Case 309/84 *Commission v Italy* [1986] E.C.R. 599, para.9.

[37] ECJ, Case 21/84 *Commission v France* [1985] E.C.R. 1355, paras 13 and 15; ECJ, Case C–387/99 *Commission v Germany* [2004] E.C.R. I–3751, para.42; ECJ, Case C–494/01 *Commission v Ireland* [2005] E.C.R. I–3331, para.28. The Commission does not prove the existence of an administrative practice—which must be, to some degree, of a consistent and general nature—by making reference to a single complaint (ECJ, Case C–287/03 *Commission v Belgium* [2005] E.C.R. I–3761, paras 29–30).

It will be easier to make a finding that there has been a failure to fulfil an obligation where it ensues from the existence of a provision of national law which infringes Community law[38] than where it ensues out of a so-called "administrative practice" of a Member State, which assumes that a particular pattern of behaviour can be discerned on the part of the authorities of the defendant Member State.[39]

Case-law. A rule established by case-law in a Member State may also constitute a failure to fulfil obligations.[40]   **5–009**

International agreements. The conclusion by a Member State of an agreement with a third State constitues a violation of the EC Treaty if such conclusion infringes Community law, *e.g.* where it infringes the exclusive external competence of the Community.[41] Even the negotiation of a bilateral agreement may constitute such infringement.[42]   **5–010**

Similarly, a Member State may not invoke as a justification for an infringement of Community law the existence of an international agreement with other Member States to which it was a party prior to its accession to the Union. Indeed, Art.307 of the EC Treaty does not

---

[38] However, the scope of national laws, regulations or administrative provisions must be assessed in the light of the interpretation given to them by national courts: ECJ, Case 300/95 *Commission v United Kingdom* [1997] E.C.R. I–2649, para.37.

[39] See, for example, ECJ, Case 21/84 *Commission v France* [1985] E.C.R. 1355; ECJ, Case 35/84 *Commission v Italy* [1986] E.C.R. 545; ECJ, Case C–150/00 *Commission v Austria* [2004] E.C.R. I–3887; ECJ, Case C–41/02 *Commission v Netherlands* [2004] E.C.R. I–11375.

[40] ECJ, Case C–129/00 *Commission v Italy* [2003] E.C.R. I–14637, para.33 (case note by Rossi and Di Federico (2005) C.M.L.Rev. 829–849): Where national legislation has been the subject of different relevant judicial constructions, some leading to the application of that legislation in compliance with Community law, others leading to the opposite application, it must be held that, at the very least, such legislation is not sufficiently clear to ensure its application in compliance with Community law. See also ECJ (order of June 3, 2005), Case C–396/03 P *Killinger v Germany, Council and Commission* [2005] E.C.R. I–4967, para.28; ECJ, Case C–289/02 *AMOK Verlags* [2003] E.C.R. I–15059, para.41. See also 5–032, *infra*.

[41] ECJ, Case C–266/03 *Commission v Luxembourg,* [2005] E.C.R. I–4805 paras 34–52.

[42] *Ibid., Commission v Luxembourg*, not yet reported, paras 57–67: the adoption by the Council of a decision authorising the Commission to negotiate a multilateral agreement on behalf of the Community marks the start of a concerted Community action at international level and requires, for that purpose, if not a duty of abstention on the part of the Member States, at the very least a duty of close cooperation between the latter and the Community institutions in order to facilitate the achievement of the Community tasks and to ensure the coherence and consistency of the action and its international representation. Therefore, if a Member State negotiates and/or concludes and ratifies a bilateral agreement in the field concerned without cooperating or consulting with the Commission, that Member State compromises the achievement of the Community's task and the attainment of the objectives of the Treaty and violates Art.10 of the EC Treaty. Even the willingness of the Member State concerned to denounce the contested bilateral agreement on the entry into force of a multilateral agreement binding the Community does not demonstrate compliance with the obligation of genuine cooperation laid down in Art.10 of the EC Treaty. See also ECJ (judgment of July 14, 2005), Case C–433/03 *Commission v Germany*, not yet reported, paras 60–74.

authorise Member States to exercise rights under international agreements which conflict with Community law in intra-Community relations.[43]

5–011 **Act or failure to act.** The failure to fulfil obligations can arise both out of an act and out of a failure to act on the part of the Member State.[44] The classic example of the latter is failure by a Member State to implement a directive in national law.[45] Failure to respond to a request from the

---

[43] ECJ (judgment of July 7, 2005), Case C–147/03 *Commission v Austria*, not yet reported, paras 71–75.

[44] ECJ, Case 31/69 *Commission v Italy* [1970] E.C.R. 25, para.9 (when the application of Community regulations requires a modification of certain public services or of the rules governing them, the failure of the authorities concerned to take the necessary measures constitutes a failure within the meaning of Art.226). The French authorities' failure to adopt all necessary measures to prevent the free movement of fruit and vegetables from being obstructed by actions by private individuals constituted a failure to fulfil obligations under Art.28, in conjunction with Art.10 of the EC Treaty, and under the common organisations of the markets in agricultural products (ECJ, Case C–265/95 *Commission v France* [1997] E.C.R. I–6959). The failure of the French authorities to take penal or administrative action pursuant to Regulation No 2241/87 against those responsible in cases of infringement of Community rules on the conservation and control of fishery resources constituted a failure to fulfil obligations (ECJ, Joined Cases C–418/00 and C–419/00 *Commission v France* [2002] E.C.R. I–3969, paras 60–64).

[45] A few examples: ECJ, Case 386/85 *Commission v Italy* [1987] E.C.R. 1061; ECJ, Case 116/86 *Commission v Italy* [1988] E.C.R. 1323; ECJ, Case C–290/89 *Commission v Belgium* [1991] E.C.R. I–2851, paras 8–10. Each of the Member States to which a directive is addressed is obliged to adopt, within the framework of its national legal system, all the measures necessary to ensure that the directive is fully effective, in accordance with the objective it pursues (see ECJ, Case C–336/97 *Commission v Italy* [1999] E.C.R. I–3771, para.19; ECJ, Case C–97/00 *Commission v France* [2001] E.C.R. I–2053, para.9; ECJ, Case C–478/99 *Commission v Sweden* [2002] E.C.R. I–4147, para.15). A provision of a directive which concerns only relations between a Member State and the Commission or the other Member States need not, in principle, be transposed. However, given that the Member States are obliged to ensure that Community law is fully complied with, it is open to the Commission to demonstrate that compliance with a provision of a directive governing those relations requires the adoption of specific transposing measures in national law (ECJ, Case C–296/01 *Commission v France* [2003] E.C.R. I–13909, para.92; ECJ, Case C–429/01 *Commission v France* [2003] E.C.R. I–14355, para.68; ECJ, Case C–410/03 *Commission v Italy* [2005] E.C.R. I–3507, paras 38–39 et 52–58). For the purposes of the implementation of a directive conferring rights on individuals in a Member State, it is essential for national law to guarantee that the directive is effectively applied in full, that the legal position under national law should be sufficiently precise and clear and that individuals are made fully aware of their rights and obligations: ECJ, Case C–365/93 *Commission v Greece* [1995] E.C.R. I–499, para.9; ECJ, Case C–429/01 *Commission v France* [2003] E.C.R. I–14355, para.83. It is not invariably necessary formally to incorporate the provisions of a directive in an express, specific legislative provision. Depending on the content of the directive, a general legal framework may suffice. In particular the existence of general principles of constitutional or administrative law may render implementation by specific legislation superfluous, provided however that those principles guarantee that the national authorities will in fact apply the directive fully and that, where the directive is intended to create rights for individuals, the legal position arising from those principles is sufficiently precise and clear and the persons concerned are made fully aware of their rights and, where appropriate, afforded the possibility of relying on them before the national courts: ECJ, Case C–29/84 *Commission v Germany* [1985] E.C.R. 1661, paras 22–23; ECJ, Case C–296/01 *Commission v France* [2003] E.C.R. I–13909, para.55; ECJ, Case C–410/03 *Commission v*

Commission for information will also constitute a failure to fulfil obligations, namely of the obligations ensuing for Member States from Art.10 of the EC Treaty.[46] An example of conduct contrary to Community law is the imposition of administrative formalities restricting the import of goods and therefore infringing Art.28 of the EC Treaty.[47]

Legal provision which is no longer applied. The existence of a legal 5–012
provision conflicting with Community law may also be categorised as a "failure", even if it is not or no longer being applied by the national authorities. The fact that such a provision exists is liable to create uncertainty in those subject to the law about the possibility of relying on Community law. That uncertainty impedes the operation of Community law and is regarded as a "failure to fulfil" an obligation.[48] Only where such a provision can have no effect at all which conflicts with Community law, will its mere existence be insufficient to constitute an infringement of Community law.[49]

Conversely, a failure to fulfil obligations may arise owing to the existence of an administrative practice which infringes Community law, even if the applicable national legislation itself complies with that law.[50]

Italy [2005] E.C.R. I–3507, para.60. The obligation to transpose directives into national law requires a "positive act of transposition" if the directive in question expressly requires the Member States to refer to it in adopting provisions or when officially notifying the provisions adopted: ECJ, Case C–137/96 *Commission v Germany* [1997] E.C.R. I–6749, para.8; ECJ, Case C–360/95 *Commission v Spain* [1997] E.C.R. I–7337, para.13.

[46] ECJ, Case C–82/03 *Commission v Italy* [2004] E.C.R. I–6635, para.15; ECJ, Case C–494/01 *Commission v Ireland* [2005] E.C.R. I–3331, paras 195–200.

[47] A few examples: ECJ, Case 154/85 *Commission v Italy* [1987] E.C.R. 2717, para.12; ECJ, Case C–80/92 *Commission v Belgium* [1994] E.C.R. I–1019, para.18.

[48] ECJ, Case 167/73 *Commission v France* [1974] E.C.R. 359 (see Barav, "Failure of Member States to Fulfil Their Obligations Under Community Law" (1975) C.M.L.Rev. 369, at 374–376); ECJ, Case 159/78 *Commission v Italy* [1979] E.C.R. 3247, para.22; ECJ, Case 168/85 *Commission v Italy* [1986] E.C.R. 2945, para.14; Case 104/86 *Commission v Italy* [1988] E.C.R. 1799, para.12; ECJ, Case 74/86 *Commission v Germany* [1988] E.C.R. 2139, para.10; ECJ, Case 38/87 *Commission v Greece* [1988] E.C.R. 4415, para.9; ECJ, Case C–197/96 *Commission v France* [1997] E.C.R. I–1489, para.14; ECJ, Case C–358/98 *Commission v Italy* [2000] E.C.R. I–1255, para.17; ECJ, Case C–145/99 *Commission v Italy* [2002] E.C.R. I–2235, paras 30 and 37; ECJ (judgment of July 7, 2005), Case C–214/04 *Commission v Italy*, not reported, para.13.

[49] ECJ, Case 28/69 *Commission v Italy* [1970] E.C.R. 187, paras 14–17. The excise duty which Italy imposed on cocoa shells and husks differed depending on whether they were imported or produced by the Italian processing industry. Nevertheless, they were exempt from the duty if they were used for certain specified purposes. The high level of duty made it impossible in practice to use the products for purposes other than those to which the exemption applied. The existence of differential taxation was therefore insufficient to constitute an infringement of Art.90 of the EC Treaty.

[50] ECJ, Case C–212/99 *Commission v Italy* [2001] E.C.R. I–4923, para.31; ECJ, Case C–278/03 *Commission v Italy* [2005] E.C.R. I–3747, para.13.

5–013 **Non-binding acts.** Even acts of a Member State which are not binding under the domestic legal system, may result in a failure to fulfil obligations under Community law in so far as their potential effects are comparable with those resulting from binding measures. A large-scale campaign launched by the Irish Government to promote the sale of Irish goods on the home market was accordingly held to be a measure of equivalent effect contrary to Art.28 of the EC Treaty.[51]

5–014 **Acts affecting the jurisdiction of the Court of Justice.** Acts of a Member State which affect the jurisdiction of the Court of Justice will invariably contravene Community law. For instance, a Member State is prohibited from transposing a regulation, which has direct effect, into national law, thereby concealing its Community origin, which would be liable to jeopardise the making of preliminary references on the interpretation or validity of the regulation.[52]

5–015 **National rules allegedly violating the Treaty but complying with a directive.** A failure to fulfil obligations under Community law will, however, not be found in case a national rule, which at first sight conflicts with a provision of the EC Treaty, expressly complies with a provision of secondary Community legislation. The Court thus dismissed an infringement action brought against Greece with respect to the reduced rate of excise duty applicable in this Member State for ouzo. The Commission considered that this reduced rate was incompatible with Art.90 of the EC Treaty prohibiting discriminatory internal taxes. The Court, however, found that a provision of Directive 92/83 explicitly allowed Greece to apply a lower rate of excise duty for ouzo. Since that provision had not been declared invalid or annulled by the Court of Justice and since it could also not be considered to be non-existent, its legal effects were presumed to be lawful. Greece therefore did not fail to fulfil its obligations under Community law by maintaining in force a national measure complying with that provision of a directive.[53]

---

[51] ECJ, Case 249/81 *Commission v Ireland* [1982] E.C.R. 4005, para.27.
[52] ECJ, Case 39/72 *Commission v Italy* [1973] E.C.R. 101, paras 16–17; ECJ, Case 34/73 *Fratelli Variola* [1973] E.C.R. 981, para.11; ECJ, Case 50/76 *Amsterdam Bulb* [1977] E.C.R. 137, paras 4–7.
[53] ECJ, Case C–475/01 *Commission v Greece* [2004] E.C.R. I–8923, paras 16–24. An individual who cannot bring an action directly against a directive before the Community judicature may, however, raise the unlawfulness of the directive before a national court, which may (or must) make a reference for a preliminary ruling to the Court of Justice.

C. Relationship with special legal procedures to obtain a declaration that a Member State has failed to fulfil its obligations under Community law

1. Relationship between Arts 226 and 227 of the EC Treaty and Art.88(2) of the EC Treaty

Procedure under Art.88(2) of the EC Treaty. Under Art.88 of the EC Treaty, the Commission is empowered to rule on the compatibility of State aid with the common market.[54] Both existing aid and the introduction or alteration of aid are subject to supervision by the Commission.[55] Any plans to grant or alter aid must be notified to the Commission pursuant to Art.88(3) of the EC Treaty.[56]

5–016

The Commission may take action against aid which it considers, on the basis of Art.87 of the EC Treaty, to be incompatible with the common market in accordance with the procedure laid down in Art.88(2). It makes a finding that the aid is incompatible and orders the Member State concerned to abolish or alter the aid within a specified period. If the Member State fails to comply with the decision within the prescribed period, the Commission or any other interested party may, by way of derogation from Arts 226 and 227, refer the matter directly to the Court of Justice.[57]

Art.88(2) of the EC Treaty secures all interested parties the right to submit observations.[58] In addition, on application by a Member State, the Council may, acting unanimously and by way of derogation from Art.87, decide that the aid must be considered to be compatible if such a decision is justified by exceptional circumstances.[59]

Relationship with Arts 226 and 227 of the EC Treaty. The question arises as to whether, despite the existence of the special procedure provided for in Art.88(2), the general procedure set out in Art.226 may still be used by the Commission to find infringements of Art.87.

5–017

---

[54] For a survey of the case-law of the Court of Justice, see Winter, "Supervision of State Aid: Art.93[now Art.88] in the Court of Justice" (1993) C.M.L.Rev. 311–329.

[55] For the distinction between "existing" and "new" aid and an explanation of the respective powers of the Commission and the national courts in supervising aid for compatibility with the common market, see ECJ, Case C–44/93 Namur—Les Assurances du Crédit [1994] E.C.R. I–3829, paras 10–17; CFI, Joined Cases T–195/01 and T–207/01 Gibraltar v Commission [2002] E.C.R. II–2309; see also Council Regulation (EC) No 659/1999 of March 22, 1999 laying down detailed rules for the application of Art.[88] of the EC Treaty ([1999] O.J. L83/1).

[56] The applicable procedural requirements are laid down in Regulation No 659/1999 (see preceding n.). For a survey of the procedural requirements existing prior to that regulation, see Slot, "Procedural Aspects of State Aids: the Guardian of Competition versus the Subsidy Villains?" (1990) C.M.L.Rev. 741–760.

[57] EC Treaty, Art.88(2), second subpara.

[58] ECJ, Case C–294/90 British Aerospace and Rover v Commission [1992] E.C.R. I–493, para.13.

[59] EC Treaty, Art.88(2), third subpara. For the powers of the Council under this provision, see ECJ, Case C–110/02 Commission v Council [2004] E.C.R. I–6333, paras 28–51.

In the first place, the procedure provided for in Art.88(2) affords all interested parties guarantees commensurate with the specific problems raised by State aid for competition in the common market; those guarantees are much more extensive than those afforded by the pre-litigation procedure under Art.226, in which only the Commission and the Member State concerned take part. Accordingly, if the Commission wishes to make a finding that a State aid is incompatible with the common market, it is obliged to follow the procedure set out in Art.88(2).[60]

However, the existence of the procedure laid down in Art.88(2) does not preclude an aid measure being found incompatible with rules of Community law other than Art.87 by means of the Art.226 procedure.[61]

Lastly, in the event of an infringement of a decision made pursuant to the first subpara. of Art.88(2), the Commission may elect either to bring the matter directly before the Court of Justice under the second subpara.of Art.88(2) or to initiate the Art.226 procedure.[62]

5–018   **Violation of the obligation to notify aid.** The Commission also often has a choice between the Art.88(2) procedure and that provided for in Art.226 where a Member State fails to inform the Commission in time, contrary to Art.88(3), of a plan to grant new aid or altered aid.[63] The fact that the duty to notify the Commission has been infringed, however, does not make the aid incompatible with the common market. Accordingly, the Commission must initiate an examination of the compatibility of the non-notified aid with the common market under Art.88(2). In that event, it may require the aid to be suspended pending the outcome of its examination and order the Member State to provide information under a procedure pursuant to Art.88(2).[64] If the Member State refuses to suspend the aid, the Commis-

---

[60] ECJ, Case 290/83 *Commission v France* [1985] E.C.R. 439, para.17.

[61] ECJ, Case 72/79 *Commission v Italy* [1980] E.C.R. 1411, para.12; ECJ, Case 73/79 *Commission v Italy* [1980] E.C.R. 1533, para.9 (for these two judgments, see Gilmour, "The Enforcement of Community Law by the Commission in the Context of State Aids: the Relationship Between Arts 93 and 169 *[now Arts 88 and 226]* and the Choice of Remedies" (1981) C.M.L.Rev. 63–77); ECJ, Case 290/83 *Commission v France* [1985] E.C.R. 439, para.17; ECJ, Case C–35/88 *Commission v Greece* [1990] E.C.R. I–3125, para.11.

[62] ECJ, Case 70/72 *Commission v Germany* [1973] E.C.R. 813, paras 8–13 (action based on the second subpara. of Art.88(2)); ECJ, Case 130/83 *Commission v Italy* [1984] E.C.R. 2849 (action based on Art.226); *cf.* ECJ, Case C–294/90 *British Aerospace and Rover v Commission* [1992] E.C.R. I–493, para.12 (the Commission may also take the approach that the infringement of its decision constitutes new aid within the meaning of Art.88(3); if so, it must start up the special procedure under the first subpara.of Art.88(2) afresh and if necessary take a fresh decision after having put interested parties on notice to submit observations, *ibid.*, para.13); ECJ, Case C–404/00 *Commission v Spain* [2003] E.C.R. I–6695, para.25. See the case notes by Joris (1993) S.E.W. 698–703 and Blumann, "Régime des aides d'Etat: jurisprudence récente de la Cour de justice (1989–1992)" (1992) R.M.C. 721, at 732–733.

[63] ECJ, Case 173/73 *Italy v Commission* [1974] E.C.R. 709, para.9; see also Biancarelli, "Le contrôle de la Cour de justice des Communautés européennes en matière d'aides publiques" (1993) A.J.D.A. 412, at 428.

[64] ECJ, Case C–301/87 *France v Commission* [1990] E.C.R. I–307, paras 18–23; ECJ, Case C–142/87 *Belgium v Commission* [1990] E.C.R. I–959, paras 15–19.

sion may bring the matter directly before the Court of Justice pursuant to the second subpara.of Art.88(2)[65] or bring an action against the Member State under Art.226.[66]

A finding by the Commission, after carrying out an examination, that the non-notified aid measure is compatible with the common market does not retroactively remedy the infringement of the Treaty caused by the failure to notify. Since Art.88(3) of the EC Treaty has direct effect, national courts are obliged to regard as unlawful any acts performed to implement the non-notified aid before the Commission made its finding that the aid was compatible with the common market, and impose the appropriate sanctions.[67]

Aid to agriculture. Since "the Council is entitled to lay down, within the context of the regulations establishing the common organisation of the markets in agricultural products, provisions prohibiting wholly or partially certain forms of national aids for the production or marketing of the products in question and . . . an infringement of such a prohibition may be dealt with within the specific framework of such an organisation", the procedure laid down by Art.226 is to be used in order to determine the infringement.[68] Under Art.36 of the EC Treaty, all the provisions of Arts 78 to 89 are applicable to production of and trade in agricultural products only to the extent determined by the Council within the framework of measures adopted for the organisation of agricultural markets. This explains why recourse by a Member State to Arts 87 to 89 on aid cannot receive priority over the provisions of a regulation on the organisation of a sector of the agricultural market.[69] Consequently, the fact that there is a special procedure in Art.88 of the EC Treaty for appraising the compatibility of State aid with the common market cannot preclude recourse to the Art.226 procedure in the event that the Commission considers that an aid measure of a Member State infringes the provisions of a regulation organising a sector of the agricultural market, even though the aid measure is also open to criticism under Art.87 of the EC Treaty.

5–019

2. Relationship between Arts 226 and 227 of the EC Treaty and Art.86(3) of the EC Treaty

Procedure under Art.86(3) of the EC Treaty. Art.86(3) of the EC Treaty charges the Commission with supervising Member States' compliance with their obligations with regard to public undertakings and undertakings to

5–020

---

[65] ECJ, Case C–301/87 *France v Commission*, cited in the preceding n., para.23.
[66] *Ibid.*, para.23. See also Arts 11 and 12 of Regulation No 659/1999 ([1999] O.J. L83/1).
[67] ECJ, Case 120/73 *Lorenz* [1973] E.C.R. 1471; ECJ, Case C–354/90 *Fédération Nationale du Commerce Extérieur des Produits Alimentaires and Others* [1991] E.C.R. I–5505; ECJ, Joined Cases C–261/01 and C–262/01 *Van Calster and Cleeren* [2003] E.C.R. I–12249, para.53.
[68] ECJ, Case 72/79 *Commission v Italy* [1980] E.C.R. 1411, para.12. See also Case C–61/90 *Commission v Greece* [1992] E.C.R. I–2407.
[69] ECJ, Case 177/78 *McCarren* [1979] E.C.R. 2161, paras 11 and 21; see also Biancarelli (n.63, *supra*), at 428.

which they have granted special or exclusive rights, and expressly confers on it the power to use two legal instruments to this end, namely directives and decisions.

The Commission is empowered to use *directives* to specify in general terms the obligations arising under Art.86(1) of the EC Treaty. It exercises that power where, without taking into consideration the particular situation existing in the various Member States, it defines in concrete terms the obligations imposed on them under that provision of the Treaty. In view of its very nature, such a power cannot be used to make a finding that a Member State has failed to fulfil a particular obligation under the EC Treaty.[70]

The powers exercised by the Commission under Art.86(3) by *decision* are different from those which it exercises by directive. Decisions are adopted in respect of a specific situation in one or more Member States and necessarily involve an appreciation of the situation in the light of Community law. They specify the consequences arising for the Member State concerned, regard being had to the requirements which the performance of the particular tasks assigned to an undertaking imposes on it where it is entrusted with the operation of services of general economic interest (Art.86(1) and (2)).[71] If the power to adopt decisions conferred on the Commission by Art.86(3) is not to be deprived of all practical effect, the Commission must be empowered to determine that a given State measure is incompatible with the rules of the Treaty and to indicate what measures the State to which the decision is addressed must take in order to comply with its obligations under Community law.[72] Even though there is no express provision to this effect in Art.86(3)—unlike in Art.226 and Art.88(2)—the general principle of respect for the rights of the defence requires that the Member State concerned must receive an exact and

---

[70] ECJ, Case C–202/88 *France v Commission* [1991] E.C.R. I–1223, para.17; ECJ, Case C–163/99 *Portugal v Commission* [2001] E.C.R. I–2613, para.26. *Cf.* for the use of directives in specific cases, Arts 38 and 82 of the EAEC Treaty. See also Lenaerts, "Nuclear Border Installations: A Case-Study" (1988) E.L.Rev. 159, at 171–179. In *Commission v Portugal*, the Portuguese government argued that the Commission was wrong to commence an action for failure to fulfil obligations under Art.226 of the EC Treaty and that it ought to have followed the procedure provided for in Art.86(3) of the EC Treaty and adopted a harmonisation directive. The Court rejected this argument, holding that, notwithstanding its other powers under the Treaty to ensure that Member States comply with Community law, the Commission enjoyed a discretion in deciding whether or not to commence an action for failure to fulfil obligations. It was not required to justify its decision, nor would the admissibility of the action be dependent upon the circumstances dictating its choice (ECJ, Case C–70/99 *Commission v Portugal* [2001] E.C.R. I–4845, para.17).

[71] ECJ, Joined Cases C–48 and C–66/90 *Netherlands and Others v Commission* [1992] E.C.R. I–565, para.27; ECJ, Case C–163/99 *Portugal v Commission* [2001] E.C.R. I–2613, para.27.

[72] *Netherlands and Others v Commission*, para.28. The fact that other Member States also infringe the Treaty by granting similar exclusive rights does not oblige the Commission to bring proceedings under Art.226 of the EC Treaty and exercise its power to address a decision to those Member States under Art.86(3) of the EC Treaty: ECJ, Case C–163/99 *Commission v Portugal* [2001] E.C.R. I–2613, para.31 *et seq.*

complete statement of the objections which the Commission intends to raise against it. It must also be placed in a position in which it may effectively make known its views on the observations submitted by interested third parties.[73]

Commission's discretion. The Commission's power to appraise, in a decision adopted pursuant to Art.86(3), the conformity with the Treaty of measures adopted or applied by Member States with regard to undertakings referred to in Art.86(1) does not run counter to the powers conferred on the Court of Justice by Art.226 of the EC Treaty. If the Member State does not comply with the decision, this may form the basis for infringement proceedings under Art.226.[74]

Whether the Commission may bring an action for failure to fulfil obligations before it has adopted a decision pursuant to Art.86(3), depends in all likelihood on the requirements of the rights of the defence. The procedure which affords the strongest guarantees for the Member State concerned should probably take precedence at the stage of the initial examination of the compatibility of a national measure with Art.86(1) and (2) of the EC Treaty by analogy with the aforementioned case-law on Art.88(2) (see 5–017, *supra*).[75] In any event, it is certain that Member States may invariably bring an action under Art.227 of the EC Treaty against a Member State for failure to fulfil its obligations under Art.86(1) and (2), even if the Commission has not yet exercised its powers under Art.86(3) to address a decision to the Member State concerned.

5–021

3. Relationship between Arts 226 and 227 of the EC Treaty and special procedures relating to the improper use of derogating provisions

Other procedures. Apart from Art.88(2), the EC Treaty provides for other cases in which, by way of derogation from the procedure laid down in Arts 226 and 227, the Commission or a Member State may bring a Member State directly before the Court of Justice, namely where the derogating provisions provided for in the Treaty are misused (EC Treaty, Art.95(4) and Arts 296 to 298). The opportunity afforded to the Commission by Art.95(9)[76] of the EC Treaty in order to bring a matter directly before the Court of Justice without incurring the delay of a pre-litigation procedure is

5–022

---

[73] *Netherlands and Others v Commission*, paras 45–46.

[74] ECJ, Case 226/87 *Commission v Greece* [1988] E.C.R. 3611 (it appears from this judgment that if the Member State to which the Commission's decision is addressed contests its legality, it must bring an action for annulment within the time-limit laid down by Art.230; thereafter, the Member State may not plead the unlawfulness of the decision as a defence in proceedings for failure to fulfil obligations).

[75] Besides, the Court of Justice itself has strongly emphasised the parallel between Art.86(3) and Art.88; see ECJ, Joined Cases C–48 and C–66/90 *Netherlands and Others v Commission* [1992] E.C.R. I–565, paras 31–33.

[76] This was formerly part of Art.100a(4) of the EC Treaty.

intended to serve the Community interest of protecting in full the establishment of the internal market. However, this does not preclude the Commission from opting to bring proceedings under Art.226 of the EC Treaty in the interests of the defendant Member State.[77]

The action that the Commission or any Member State may bring against a Member State pursuant to the second para.of Art.298 if it considers that that State is making improper use of the powers provided for in Arts 296 and 297 does not involve a pre-litigation stage (which is precisely the difference compared with proceedings under Arts 226 and 227), but does afford the guarantee that the Court of Justice is to give its ruling *in camera*, this being essential in the case of a politically charged dispute.[78]

4. Relationship between Arts 226 and 227 of the EC Treaty and special procedures relating to public procurement contracts

5–023   **Special procedures relating to public procurement contracts.** The Commission is empowered to order the suspension of the award of a public procurement contract under Art.3 of Council Directive 89/665/EEC of December 21, 1989 on the coordination of the laws, regulations and administrative provisions relating to the application of review procedures to the award of public supply and public works contracts[79] or under Art.8 of Council Directive 92/13/EEC of 25 February 1992 coordinating the laws, regulations and administrative provisions relating to the application of Community rules on the procurement procedures of entities operating in the water, energy, transport and telecommunications sectors.[80]

5–024   **Commission's discretion.** Even if it were it preferable that the Commission should use the procedure for direct intervention established by those directives, such a procedure is a preventive measure which can neither derogate from nor replace the powers of the Commission under Art.226 of

---

[77] It is argued that proceedings should have to be brought under Art.226 of the EC Treaty against a failure of a Member State to notify the Commission of the application of a national measure conflicting with a harmonising measure adopted pursuant to Art.95(1) of the EC Treaty. If proceedings under Art.95(9) were to be allowed, this might also mean that a Member State would in some cases have the power not to notify the Commission of a national measure (although it is considered that this is not the case) on the ground that such proceedings relate only to "improper use of the powers provided for in this Article" (see Flynn, "How will Art.100a*[now Art.95]*(4) work? A Comparison with Art.93*[now Art.88]*" (1987) C.M.L.Rev. 689, at 700–701). For the Commission's handling of a complaint on account of the grant of State aid to a manufacturer of military goods and the application of Arts 296 and 298 of the EC Treaty, see CFI, Case T–26/01 *Fiocchi Munizioni v Commission* [2003] E.C.R. II–3951.

[78] See ECJ (order of the President of March 19, 1996), Case C–120/94 *Commission v Greece* [1996] E.C.R. I–1513. A case brought under Art.226 or 227 of the EC Treaty is heard in principle in public, although the Court of Justice may decide otherwise of its own motion or on application by the parties for serious reasons (Statute, Art.31).

[79] [1989] O.J. L395/33.

[80] [1992] O.J. L76/14.

the EC Treaty.[81] The fact that the Commission used or did not use that procedure is therefore irrelevant where it is a matter of deciding on the admissibility of infringement proceedings. The Commission alone is competent to decide whether it is appropriate to bring proceedings under Art.226 of the EC Treaty for failure to fulfil obligations. Thus, the choice between the two procedures is within its discretion.[82]

II. Identity of the Parties

A. The applicant

Commission. Under Art.226 of the EC Treaty, only the Commission may bring an action against a Member State.[83] That power is consistent with its task of ensuring that Community law is applied.[84] The Commission exercises its supervisory task of its own motion in the general interest of the Community[85] and does not have to show the existence of a specific interest in bringing proceedings.[86] It itself assesses whether it is appropriate to bring proceedings under Art.226 and has therefore no obligation to do so in the event of an alleged infringement of the Treaty.[87] In view of the objective

5–025

---

[81] See, in the context of Directive 89/665, ECJ, Case C–359/93 *Commission v Netherlands* [1995] E.C.R. I–157, para.13; ECJ, Case C–79/94 *Commission v Greece* [1995] E.C.R. I–1071, para.11; ECJ, Case C–353/96 *Commission v Ireland* [1998] E.C.R. I–8565, para.22; ECJ, Case C–328/96 *Commission v Austria* [1999] E.C.R. I–7479, para.57 and, in the context of Directive 92/13, ECJ, Case C–394/02 *Commission v Greece* [2005] E.C.R. I–4713, paras 25–29.

[82] ECJ, Case C–394/02 *Commission v Greece* [2005] E.C.R. I–4713, paras 25–29.

[83] For the (lack of) capacity of the Court of Auditors to bring an action for failure to fulfil obligations, see Inghelram, "The European Court of Auditors: current legal issues" (2000) C.M.L.Rev. 129–146, at 140.

[84] EC Treaty, Art.211, first indent. ECJ, Case C–422/92 *Commission v Germany* [1995] E.C.R. I–1097, para.16.

[85] ECJ, Case 167/73 *Commission v France* [1974] E.C.R. 359, para.15; ECJ, Case C–191/95 *Commission v Germany* [1998] E.C.R. I–5449, para.35 ; CFI, Case T–209/00 *Lamberts v Ombudsman* [2002] E.C.R. II–2203, para.55. See also Goffin, "Le manquement d'un État membre selon la jurisprudence de la Cour de Justice des Communautés européennes", in *Mélanges Fernand Dehousse, La construction européenne* (Nathan/Labor, Paris/Brussels, 1979), Vol.II, 211; and Lenaerts and Van Nuffel, *Constitutional Law of the European Union*, § 10–057, at 427.

[86] ECJ, Case C–422/92 *Commission v Germany* [1995] E.C.R. I–1097, para.16; ECJ, Case C–182/94 *Commission v Italy* [1995] E.C.R. I–1465, para.5; ECJ, Case C–333/99 *Commission v France* [2001] E.C.R. I–1025, para.5; ECJ, Joined Cases C–418/00 and C–419/00 *Commission v France* [2002] E.C.R. I–3969, para.29; ECJ, Case C–476/98 *Commission v Germany* [2002] E.C.R. I–9855, para.38.

[87] ECJ, Case C–87/89 *SONITO and Others v Commission* [1990] E.C.R. I–1981, paras 6–7; ECJ, Case C–200/88 *Commission v Greece* [1990] E.C.R. I–4299, para.9; ECJ, Case C–209/88 *Commission v Italy* [1990] E.C.R. I–4313, para.13; ECJ, Case C–243/89 *Commission v Denmark* [1993] E.C.R. I–3353, para.30; ECJ, Case C–353/96 *Commission v Ireland* [1998] E.C.R. I–8565, para.22; ECJ, Case C–333/99 *Commission v France* [2001] E.C.R. I–1025, para.24; ECJ, Case C–383/00 *Commission v Germany* [2002] E.C.R. I–4219, para.19; ECJ,

nature of the action, the Court must consider whether or not there has been a failure to fulfil obligations as alleged, without its being part of its role to take a view on the Commission's exercise of its discretion.[88] The decision to apply to the Court of Justice for a declaration that a Member State has failed to fulfil its obligations cannot be described as a measure of administration or management and hence may not be delegated; it must be taken by all the members of the college of Commissioners, who should bear collective responsibility for it.[89] The formal requirements for effective compliance with that principle of collegiate responsibility are less strict in this case than in the case of the adoption of decisions affecting the legal position of individuals.[90] The reason for this is that, whilst the decision to commence proceedings for failure to fulfil obligations before the Court constitutes an indispensable step for the purpose of enabling the Court to give judgment by way of a binding decision on the alleged failure to fulfil obligations, it does not *per se* alter the legal position of the Member State in question. Consequently, it is sufficient that the decision to bring an action was the subject of collective deliberation by the college of Commissioners and that the information on which the decision was based was available to the members of the college. However, it is not necessary for the college itself formally to decide on the wording of the acts which give effect to the decision and put them in final form.[91]

The involvement of the Court is not always necessary or appropriate in order to ensure that the Member States effectively apply Community law.

Case C–471/98 *Commission v Belgium* [2002] E.C.R. I–9681, para.39; ECJ, Case C–472/98 *Commission v Luxembourg* [2002] ECJ I–9741, para.37. See also the second para. of Art.226 of the EC Treaty, which provides that the Commission *may* bring the matter before the Court of Justice if the Member State concerned fails to comply with the reasoned opinion within the period laid down: ECJ, Case C–152/98 *Commission v Netherlands* [2001] E.C.R. I–3463, para.20. See Evans, "The Enforcement Procedure of Art.169*[now Art.226]* EEC: Commission Discretion" (1979) E.L.Rev. 442–456. The controversy in academic writings as to whether or not the Commission has a discretion to bring an action and the allegedly different implications of the first and second paras of Art.226 of the EC Treaty (see, for example, Smit and Herzog (now Campbell and Powers), *The Law of the European Community* (Matthew Bender & Co., New York, 1976), 5–321) has been overtaken by case-law. For a survey of the use of Art.226 of the EC Treaty, see Thomas, "Infractions et manquements des États membres au droit communautaire" (1991) R.M.C. 887-892.

[88] ECJ, Case C–191/95 *Commission v Spain* [2002] E.C.R. I–5293, para.25.

[89] ECJ, Case C–191/95 *Commission v Germany* [1998] E.C.R. I–5449, paras 35–37, and ECJ, Case C–272/97 *Commission v Germany* [1999] E.C.R. I–2175, paras 13–22, in which the Court justified this position in terms, *inter alia*, of "the discretionary power of the institution", which "[i]n its role as guardian of the Treaty ... is competent to decide whether it is appropriate to bring proceedings against a Member State for failure to fulfil its obligations".

[90] See Lenaerts and Van Nuffel, *Constitutional Law of the European Union*, §10–068, at 436–438.

[91] Case C–191/95 *Commission v Germany*, paras 47–48. See also ECJ, Case C–272/97 *Commission v Germany* [1999] E.C.R. I–2175, paras 13–22; ECJ, Case C–198/97 *Commission v Germany* [1999] E.C.R. I–3257, paras 19–21. The decision to bring an action is therefore not a challengeable act within the meaning of Art.230 of the EC Treaty (CFI, Joined Cases T–377/00, T–379/00, T–380/00, T–260/01 and T–272/01 *Philip Morris International and Others v Commission* [2003] E.C.R. II–1, para.79).

The Commission is therefore also free to determine the time when it brings any proceedings.[92] In contrast, the Commission is not empowered to determine conclusively whether given conduct of a Member State is compatible with the Treaty. The rights and duties of Member States may be determined and their conduct appraised only by judgment of the Court of Justice.[93] Consequently, a decision by the Commission not to bring proceedings against a Member State does not mean that it is not in breach of Community law.[94]

No standing for individuals. Individuals may not bring actions for failure   **5–026** to fulfil obligations before the Court of Justice (or the Court of First Instance).[95] If the need arises, they must contest the conduct of the Member State in a national court.[96] The latter may (or must) request a preliminary ruling from the Court of Justice in order indirectly to have the conduct complained of reviewed in the light of the requirements of Community law (see Chs 2 and 6).[97] Furthermore, persons considering that a Member State is infringing Community law may lay a complaint before the Commission.[98] The Commission, however, is under no obligation to act on the complaint.[99]

---

[92] ECJ, Case 7/68 *Commission v Italy* [1968] E.C.R. 423, at 428; ECJ, Case 7/71 *Commission v France* [1971] E.C.R. 1003, para.5; ECJ, Case 324/82 *Commission v Belgium* [1984] E.C.R. 1861, para.12; see also ECJ, Case C–422/92 *Commission v Germany* [1995] E.C.R. I–1097, paras 17–18. Although the Court was surprised at the Commission's having brought an action more than six years after the national legislation at issue had entered into force, it held that the Commission was not obliged to act within a specified period.

[93] ECJ, Joined Cases 142 and 143/80 *Essevi and Salengo* [1981] E.C.R. 1413, para.16.

[94] Where it subsequently appears that the Member State is indeed infringing Community law, the fact that the Commission did not bring an action for failure to fulfil obligations may, in certain circumstances, constitute a reason for limiting the temporal effects of a judgment of the Court on a reference for a preliminary ruling which brings the infringement to light (see 6–034, *infra*). This may also be relevant in assessing whether the breach of Community law was sufficiently serious as to cause the Member State to incur liability *vis-à-vis* individuals who suffered loss or damage as a result of it, see 3–041, *supra*.

[95] See, *e.g.* CFI (order of July 8, 2004), Case T–213/04 *Ascione*, not reported. Individuals may also not have the Court of First Instance review the legality of national measures through an action for annulment brought against the Commission (CFI, Case T–148/00 *Panhellenic Union of Cotton Ginners and Exporters v Commission* [2003] E.C.R. II–4415, para.66).

[96] The fact that individuals have brought proceedings before a national court cannot prevent the bringing of an action by the Commission under Art.226 of the EC Treaty, since the two procedures have different objectives and effects: ECJ, Case 31/69 *Commission v Italy* [1970] E.C.R. 25, para.9; ECJ, Case 85/85 *Commission v Belgium* [1986] E.C.R. 1149, para.24; ECJ, Case C–87/02 *Commission v Italy* [2004] E.C.R. I–5975, para.39.

[97] ECJ, Case 1/82 *D* [1982] E.C.R. 3709, para.8. See also ECJ, Joined Cases C–106/90, C–317/90 and C–129/91 *Emerald Meats v Commission* [1993] E.C.R. I–209, para.40. For further discussion of this point, see Timmermans, "Judicial Protection against the Member States: Arts 169*[now Art.226]* and 177*[now Art.234]* revisited", in Curtin and Heukels (eds), *Institutional Dynamics of European Integration. Essays in Honour of H.G. Schermers* (Martinus Nijhoff, Dordrecht, 1994), Vol.II, at 391–407.

[98] See Muñoz, "La participation du plaignant à la procédure en infraction au droit communautaire diligentée par la Commission" (2003) R.M.C.U.E. 610–616.

[99] CFI (order of January 14, 2004), Case T–202/02 *Makedoniko Metro Michaniki v Commission* [2004] E.C.R. II–181, paras 42–47 and the case-law cited therein. Consequently, the position

5–027   **Rejection of a complaint.** The Commission's decision rejecting a complaint cannot be challenged by an action for annulment,[100] since the Commission does not adopt any binding legal act in the course of the pre-litigation stage[101]: it does not determine the rights and duties of the Member State or afford any guarantee that a given line of conduct is compatible with the Treaty. Accordingly, an opinion of the Commission cannot release a Member State from its Treaty obligations and certainly does not give it a licence to restrict rights which individuals derive from the Treaty.[102] Consequently, the Commission's decision rejecting a complaint from individuals does not affect their legal position since the Commission is simply refusing to take measures which in no event would have legal effects for them.

5–028   **Failure of the Commission to bring an infringement action.** If the Commission leaves the complaint unanswered, an action for failure to act will not lie, since the Commission has not infringed any duty to act.[103] The same is true where the Commission fails to bring proceedings in the Court in the event of a Member State's infringing a decision adopted pursuant to Art.88(2) of the EC Treaty.[104] In addition, natural or legal persons may bring such an action against the Commission only if it failed to adopt an act

---

of an individual who makes a complaint against an undertaking for infringement of Art.81 and/or Art.82 of the EC Treaty (see 7-033 and 8-015, *infra*) differs fundamentally from that of an individual who brings a complaint against a Member State for infringement of Community law (CFI (order of September 19, 2005), T–247/04 *Aseprofar and Edifa v Commission*, not yet reported, paras 40–61).

[100] ECJ, Case C–87/89 *SONITO and Others v Commission* [1990] E.C.R. I–1981, paras 5–9; CFI, Case T–16/91 *Rendo and Others v Commission* [1992] E.C.R. II–2417, para.52; CFI, Case T–575/93 *Koelman v Commission* [1996] E.C.R. II–1, para.71; CFI, Case T–111/96 *ITT Promedia v Commission* [1998] E.C.R. II–2937, para.97. Since the Commission likewise has a broad discretion in carrying out the function conferred on it by Art.86 of the EC Treaty of ensuring that Member States fulfil their obligations in respect of public undertakings and undertakings to which Member States grant special or exclusive rights, individuals who requested the Commission to intervene pursuant to that article may not bring an action for annulment against the decision by which the Commission refuses to act against a Member State infringing Art.86(1) and (2) of the EC Treaty : ECJ, Case C–107/95 P *Bundesverband der Bilanzbuchhalter v Commission* [1997] E.C.R. I–947, paras 26–30 (*cf.*, however, the Opinion of Advocate General A. La Pergola, paras 14–21, who took a different view); CFI (order of January 23, 1995), Case T–84/94 *Bundesverband der Bilanzbuchhalter v Commission* [1995] E.C.R. II–101, para.23; ECJ, Case C–141/02 P *Commission v T-Mobile Austria* [2005] E.C.R. I–1283, para.70 (annulling the CFI's judgment in Case T–54/99 *max.mobil Telekommunication Service v Commission* [2002] E.C.R. II–313, in which the CFI had found that the rejection of an Art.86 complaint constituted a reviewable act).

[101] ECJ, Case 48/65 *Lütticke v Commission* [1966] E.C.R. 19, at 27: the Court held that "[n]o measure taken by the Commission during [the pre-litigation] stage has any binding force"; CFI (order of September 6, 2005), Case T–209/05 *Gisti v Commission*, not reported, paras 4–11.

[102] ECJ, Joined Cases 142 and 143/80 *Essevi and Salengo* [1981] E.C.R. 1431, paras 16–18.

[103] CFI (order of February 19, 1997), Case T–117/96 *Intertronic v Commission* [1997] E.C.R. II–141, para.32; CFI (order of June 5, 2002), Case T–143/02 *Olive v Commission and Others*, not reported, para.11.

[104] CFI, Case T–277/94 *AITEC v Commission* [1996] E.C.R. II–351, paras 65–72.

addressed to them, other than a recommendation or an opinion.[105] Since in a procedure pursuant to Art.226 of the EC Treaty the Commission addresses to the Member State concerned only a reasoned "opinion", natural or legal persons are precluded from bringing an action for failure to deliver such an opinion.[106]

A failure on the part of the Commission to bring an action for failure to fulfil obligations will not ground an action for damages either.[107] The reason for this is that the Commission's inaction does not infringe Art.226 of the EC Treaty and therefore cannot be regarded as constituting fault.[108] In such a case, the source of any damage lies in the Member State's infringement of the Treaty and not in any shortcoming of the Commission.

Member States. Under Art.227 of the EC Treaty, a Member State may also bring a matter before the Court of Justice if it considers that another Member State has failed to fulfil an obligation under Community law. The Member State must first submit a complaint to the Commission. The Commission delivers a reasoned opinion, after giving each of the States concerned the opportunity to submit its own case and its observations on the other party's case both orally and in writing. The opinion sets out the Commission's view as to whether or not the alleged infringement of Community obligations under the Treaty is made out. If the Commission has not delivered an opinion within three months of the date of receipt of the complaint, the matter may be brought before the Court of Justice. 5–029

The Commission may also bring the matter before the Court itself pursuant to Art.226 of the EC Treaty. If it does so, it does not prevent the Member State from also bringing an action. In the event that the Commission's reasoned opinion falls short of the Member State's expectations, it may add to it in its application.

---

[105] ECJ, Case 247/87 *Star Fruit v Commission* [1989] E.C.R. 291, paras 10–14; ECJ (order of May 23, 1990), Case C–72/90 *Asia Motor France v Commission* [1990] E.C.R. I–2181, para.11; CFI (order of December 14, 1993), Case T–29/93 *Calvo Alonso-Cortès v Commission* [1993] E.C.R. II–1389, para.55; CFI (order of May 27, 1994), Case T–5/94 *J v Commission* [1994] E.C.R. II–391, para.16; CFI (order of July 4, 1994), Case T–13/94 *Century Oils Hellas v Commission* [1994] E.C.R. II–431, para.13.

[106] ECJ (order of March 30, 1990), Case C–371/89 *Emrich v Commission* [1990] E.C.R. I–1555. Individuals may possibly take up the matter with the European Ombudsman. For examples, see the decision in complaint 472/6.3.96 against the European Commission ([1999] O.J. C300/105) and the decision in complaint 176/97/JMA against the European Commission available from *www.euro-ombudsman.eu.int*.

[107] ECJ (order of May 23, 1990), Case C–72/90 *Asia Motor France v Commission* [1990] E.C.R. I–2181, para.13; CFI (order of July 3, 1997), Case T–201/96 *Smanor and Others v Commission* [1997] E.C.R. II–1081, para.30; CFI (order of May 5, 1999), Case T–190/98 *Gluiber v Council and Commission*, not reported, para.13.

[108] However, the Commission's conduct may possibly infringe other Treaty provisions and hence potentially make it liable in damages if all the necessary conditions are fulfilled (see Ch.11, *infra*). The Court of Justice has declared actions for damages for infringement of the second para.of Art.97 (since repealed) of the EC Treaty and Arts 88(2), 211 and 226, respectively, admissible but unfounded (ECJ, Case 4/69 *Lütticke v Commission* [1971] E.C.R. 325; ECJ, Case 40/75 *Produits Bertrand v Commission* [1976] E.C.R. 1).

To date, only four actions have been brought under Art.227 of the EC Treaty, and only two of them resulted in a judgment.[109]

B. The defendant

5–030   **Member State.** An action under Arts 226–227 may be brought in the Court of Justice only against a Member State.

5–031   **Notion of Member State.** By "Member State" is meant the entity under international law which acceded to the Treaties. Any act or failure to act by any agency of the State or constitutionally independent bodies or institutions which are to be regarded as public bodies may potentially cause the Member State to become liable under Community law.[110] The domestic organisation of a Member State may not detract from the full effect of Community law.

Consequently, it may be that a Member State is found guilty of infringing Community law even though the infringement was committed by a sub-entity and the national government, which represents the "Member State" before the Court of Justice, was not at fault and has no defence under domestic law.[111] The rationale of the Court's case-law is that the Member State is under a Community-law duty to construct its constitutional structure in such a way as to avoid that evil.

5–032   **Legislature, executive and judiciary.** An act or omission of the legislative authority of a Member State can certainly give rise to an action for failure to fulfil obligations.[112] The same is true for shortcomings of the executive branch. Shortcomings in the way in which national courts apply Community

---

[109] ECJ, Case 141/78 *France v United Kingdom* [1979] E.C.R. 2923; ECJ, Case C–388/95 *Belgium v Spain* [2000] E.C.R. I–3123.

[110] ECJ, Case 77/69 *Commission v Belgium* [1970] E.C.R. 237, para.15; ECJ, Case 169/82 *Commission v Italy* [1984] E.C.R. 1603; ECJ, Case 1/86 *Commission v Belgium* [1987] E.C.R. 2797; ECJ, Joined Cases 227–230/85 *Commission v Belgium* [1988] E.C.R. 1; ECJ, Case 45/87 *Commission v Ireland* [1988] E.C.R. 4929; ECJ, Case C–58/89 *Commission v Germany* [1991] E.C.R. I–4983; ECJ, Case C–33/90 *Commission v Italy* [1991] E.C.R. I–5987. See also the definition of the expression "Member State" in ECJ (order of March 21, 1997), Case C–95/97 *Région Wallonne v Commission* [1997] E.C.R. I–1787, paras 16–17.

[111] ECJ, Case 239/85 *Commission v Belgium* [1986] E.C.R. 3645, paras 13–14. In Belgium, there is a system of substitution whereby the federal authorities may, subject to certain conditions, invest themselves with powers of a sub-entity in order to give effect to a judgment of the Court of Justice finding Belgium guilty of an infringement of Community law by that entity (Belgian Constitution, Art.169 and Art.16(3) of the Special Law on Institutional Reform); for a commentary, see Ingelaere, "De Europeesrechtelijke raakvlakken van de nieuwe wetgeving inzake de internationale betrekkingen van de Belgische Gemeenschappen en Gewesten" (1994) S.E.W. 67–82.

[112] ECJ, Case 8/70 *Commission v Italy* [1970] E.C.R. 961, paras 8–9; ECJ, Case 94/81 *Commission v Italy* [1982] E.C.R. 739, para.4; Case 41/82 *Commission v Italy* [1982] E.C.R. 4213, para.15; Case 309/84 *Commission v Italy* [1986] E.C.R. 599, para.9.

law may also be imputed to the Member States.[113] In all likelihood, an ordinary judicial error is not sufficient.[114] If a (supreme) national court deliberately ignored or disregarded Community law, this could certainly bring the Community liability of the relevant Member State into play.[115]

Private companies controlled by public authorities. Lastly, acts of legal   5–033
persons governed by private law which are controlled by the public authorities may result in an infringement of Community law on the part of the Member State concerned.[116] An example is the Irish Goods Council which was set up to organise the "Buy Irish" campaign in Ireland. The acts of the Irish Goods Council had to be imputed to the Irish State, since its membership, funding and aims were determined by the Irish government.[117]

III. Special Characteristics

A. The pre-litigation stage of the procedure

Objective. The aim of the pre-litigation stage of the procedure is to give   5–034
the Member State an opportunity (a) of remedying the infringement before the matter is brought before the Court of Justice and (b) of putting forward

---

[113] ECJ, Case C–129/00 *Commission v Italy* [2003] E.C.R. I–14637, paras 29–41 (with case notes by Peerbux-Beaugendre in (2004) R.T.D.E. 208–215 and by Rossi and Di Federico in (2005) C.M.L.Rev. 829–849): an Italian law, which in itself was not contrary to Community law, was interpreted by a large part of the Italian judiciary, including the *Corte suprema di cassazione*, in a way which was incompatible with Community law. This led to the finding that Italy was in breach of its obligations under the EC Treaty. See also ECJ, Case C–224/01 *Köbler* [2003] E.C.R. I–10239 as regards State liability for infringements imputable to the judiciary. See also De Bellescise, "L'Art.169 du traité de Rome, et l'efficacité du contrôle communautaire sur les manquements des Etats membres" (1977) R.T.D.E. 173, at 178.

[114] ECJ, Case C–129/00 *Commission v Italy* [2003] E.C.R. I–14637, para.33 (with case notes by Peerbux-Beaugendre in (2004) R.T.D.E. 208–215 and by Rossi and Di Federico in (2005) C.M.L.Rev. 829–849): where national legislation has been the subject of different relevant judicial constructions, some leading to the application of that legislation in compliance with Community law, others leading to the opposite application, it must be held that, at the very least, such legislation is not sufficiently clear to ensure its application in compliance with Community law. See also ECJ (order of June 3, 2005), Case C–396/03 P *Killinger v Germany, Council and Commission* [2005] E.C.R. I–4967, para.28.

[115] Opinion of Advocate General J.-P. Warner in Case 30/77 *Bouchereau* [1977] E.C.R. 1999, at 2021. See also 2–053 and 2–054, *supra*, for the possibility of bringing proceedings under Arts 226–227 of the EC Treaty against a Member State where one of its courts infringes the obligation to seek a preliminary ruling under the third para. of Art.234.

[116] ECJ, Case 249/81 *Commission v Ireland* [1982] E.C.R. 4005, para.15; ECJ, Case C–325/00 *Commission v Germany* [2002] E.C.R. I–9977, paras 14–21.

[117] ECJ, Case 249/81 *Commission v Ireland* [1982] E.C.R. 4005, para.15; see also Dashwood and White (n.15, *supra*), at 391. ECJ, C–353/96 *Commission v Ireland* [1998] E.C.R. I–8565, para.23: the State is liable for acts of an individual undertaking which is State-owned and acts as a contracting authority within the meaning of the directives on public contract awards. See also CFI (order of 29 September 1997), Case T–83/97 *Sateba v Commission* [1997] E.C.R. II–1523, para.36.

its defence to the Commission's complaints.[118] Moreover, during the pre-litigation stage the Commission and the Member State may come to an accommodation, thus rendering a court hearing unnecessary.[119] Lastly, the proper conduct of the pre-litigation procedure constitutes an essential guarantee, not only in order to protect the rights of the Member States concerned, but also so as to ensure that any contentious procedure will have a clearly defined dispute as to its subject-matter.[120] The scope of the dispute is defined in the pre-litigation procedure. As a result, in the contentious proceedings the Court may only judge the merits of the pleas in law put forward by the Commission in the pre-litigation procedure.[121]

1. Letter of formal notice

5–035   **Content and purpose.** The Art.226 procedure formally commences on receipt of a letter before action from the Commission giving the Member State formal notice. As a rule, the letter will have been preceded by informal contacts between the Commission and the Member State by which the former starts its investigation into the possible infringements of Community law.[122]

The purpose of the letter of formal notice or letter before action is to delimit the subject-matter of the dispute and to provide the Member State, which is asked to submit observations, with the information necessary in order for it to prepare its defence.[123]

Consequently, the letter of formal notice must precisely specify the obligation which the Commission maintains the Member State has failed to

---

[118] ECJ, Case 74/82 *Commission v Ireland* [1984] E.C.R. 317, para.13; ECJ, Case C–287/00 *Commission v Germany* [2002] E.C.R. I–5811, para.16.

[119] Consequently, the Commission is justified to refuse to disclose a letter of formal notice and a reasoned opinion requested under the right of access to documents by an individual who lodged a complaint. This is because the Member States are entitled to expect the Commission to guarantee confidentiality during investigations which might lead to an infringement procedure and also after proceedings are brought in the Court. This enables discussions to continue between the parties even after proceedings have been brought with a view to reaching a speedy resolution (CFI, Case T–191/99 *Petrie and Others v Commission* [2001] E.C.R. II–3677, paras 61–69).

[120] ECJ (order of July 11, 1995), Case C–266/94 *Commission v Spain* [1995] E.C.R. I–1975, para.17; ECJ, Case C–362/01 *Commission v Ireland* [2003] E.C.R. I–11433, para.18.

[121] ECJ, Case C–158/94 *Commission v Italy* [1997] E.C.R. I–5789, paras 59–60; ECJ, Case C–159/94 *Commission v France* [1997] E.C.R. I–5815, paras 106–107.

[122] For a more extensive survey of the Commission's activities in this "administrative stage", see Rideau and Picod, *Code de procédures juridictionelles*, at 168–174, and Brealey and Hoskins, *Remedies in E.C. Law*, at 250–254.

[123] ECJ, Case 274/83 *Commission v Italy* [1985] E.C.R. 1077, para.19: ECJ, Case 229/87 *Commission v Greece* [1988] E.C.R. 6347, para.12.

fulfil and the grounds on which the Commission takes this view.[124] Any vagueness in the letter of formal notice depriving the Member State of the opportunity of submitting observations to good effect may be remedied by the Commission's sending a new letter of formal notice setting out in time additional particulars or information.[125] At that point in the pre-litigation stage, it is sufficient if the Member State receives an initial brief summary of the complaints.[126] The test is whether the Member State was placed in possession of all the relevant information needed for its defence.[127]

Formal notice must be complete. The Member State must be put on notice   5–036 of the whole of the alleged infringement of Community law. The complaints may not be subsequently extended in the reasoned opinion, since that would be in breach of the Commission's duty to give the Member State concerned a fair hearing.[128] The illegality cannot be regarded as cured even by the fact that the Member State put forward a defence in its observations on the reasoned opinion to the new complaints enlarging the scope of the dispute.[129]

Essential procedural requirement. Because it gives the Member State   5–037 concerned the opportunity to submit prior observations, the letter of formal notice constitutes an essential procedural requirement for the legality of the procedure for a declaration that a Member State has failed to fulfil its

---

[124] ECJ (order of September 13, 2000), Case C–341/97 *Commission v Netherlands* [2000] E.C.R. I–6611. A detailed opinion within the meaning of Art.9(1) of Directive 83/189 (procedure for the provision of information in the field of technical standards and regulations) informing a Member State that a national measure notified to the Commission did not comply with Community law cannot be regarded as a letter of formal notice within the meaning of Art.226 of the EC Treaty. At the time when such a detailed opinion is delivered, the Member State to which it is addressed cannot have infringed Community law, since the measure exists only in draft form.
[125] ECJ, Case 211/81 *Commission v Denmark* [1982] E.C.R. 4547, paras 10–11.
[126] ECJ, Case 274/83 *Commission v Italy* [1985] E.C.R. 1077, para.21; ECJ, Case C–289/94 *Commission v Italy* [1996] E.C.R. I–4405, para.16; ECJ, Case C–279/94 *Commission v Italy* [1997] E.C.R. I–4743, para.15; ECJ, Case C–225/98 *Commission v France* [2000] E.C.R. I–7445, para.70. If, in the letter of formal notice, the Commission wrongly refers to Art.226 of the EC Treaty instead of to Art.141 of the EAEC Treaty where the failure to fulfil an obligation relates to the latter Treaty, that irregularity cannot result in the application being inadmissible if, in the circumstances of the case, the rights of defence of the Member State concerned are not affected.
[127] ECJ, Case 229/87 *Commission v Greece* [1988] E.C.R. 6347, para.13.
[128] ECJ, Case 51/83 *Commission v Italy* [1984] E.C.R. 2793, para.6; ECJ, Case C–145/01 *Commission v Italy* [2003] E.C.R. I–5581, paras 17–18 (the reasoned opinion and the application made to the Court pursuant to the second para. of Art.226 of the EC Treaty were flawed with regard to the rights of the defence (i) since they referred to rules of Community law other than those cited in the letter of formal notice and (ii) since a change in the legal situation was likely to have affected the assessment of the compatibility of the national legislation in question with Community law).
[129] Case 51/83 *Commission v Italy*, para.7.

obligations.[130] Even if the Member State does not wish to make any observations, the Commission must comply with that requirement.[131]

5–038 **Sufficient time for lodging observations.** The Member State must have a reasonable time in which to make its observations. The reasonableness of the period prescribed by the Commission has to be assessed in the light of the particular circumstances. Thus, the urgent nature of the case or the fact that the Member State was fully apprised of the Commission's position even before the letter of formal notice may warrant setting a short period.[132] However, the urgency of the case may not be brought about by the Commission itself, for instance because it was tardy in bringing proceedings for failure to fulfil obligations. Moreover, a Member State cannot be regarded as having been fully apprised of the Commission's position before the letter of formal notice where the Commission did not make any clear view known to it.[133]

2. Reasoned opinion

5–039 **Content and purpose.** If the Member State fails to remedy the failure to fulfil obligations under Community law, the Commission may issue a reasoned opinion. That document describes the infringement of Community law in detail and prescribes the time within which the Member State must put an end to it. As in the case of the letter of formal notice, delivery of a reasoned opinion is an essential procedural requirement for the purposes of the legality of the proceedings and the admissibility of any proceedings brought against the Member State in the Court of Justice.[134]

The issue of a reasoned opinion constitutes a preliminary procedure, which does not have any binding legal effect for the addressee. It is merely a pre-litigation stage of a procedure which may lead to an action before the Court. The purpose of that pre-litigation procedure provided for by Art.226 of the EC Treaty is to enable the Member State concerned to comply of its own accord with the requirements of the Treaty or, if appropriate, to justify its position. If that attempt at settlement is unsuccessful, the function of the reasoned opinion is to define the subject-matter of the dispute. However, the Commission is not empowered to determine conclusively, by reasoned

---

[130] ECJ, Case C–306/91 *Commission v Italy* [1993] E.C.R. I–2133, paras 22–24; ECJ, Case C–243/89 *Commission v Denmark* [1993] E.C.R. I–3353, para.13.
[131] ECJ, Case 31/69 *Commission v Italy* [1970] E.C.R. 25, paras 13–14; ECJ, Case 124/81 *Commission v United Kingdom* [1983] E.C.R. 203, para.6; ECJ, Case 274/83 *Commission v Italy* [1985] E.C.R. 1077, para.21.
[132] ECJ, Case C–473/93 *Commission v Luxembourg* [1996] E.C.R. I–3207, para.22; ECJ (judgment of November 15, 2005), Case C–320/03 *Commission v Austria*, not yet reported, paras 33–34.
[133] ECJ, Case 293/85 *Commission v Belgium* [1988] E.C.R. 305, paras 10–20.
[134] *Commentaire Mégret*, at 70. ECJ, Case 325/82 *Commission v Germany* [1984] E.C.R. 777, para.8; ECJ, Case C–152/89 *Commission v Luxembourg* [1991] E.C.R. I–3141, para.9.

opinions formulated pursuant to Art.226, the rights and duties of a Member State or to afford that State guarantees concerning the compatibility of a given line of conduct with the Treaty. According to the system embodied in Arts 226 to 228 of the EC Treaty, the rights and duties of Member States may be determined and their conduct appraised only by a judgment of the Court. The reasoned opinion therefore has legal effect only in relation to the commencement of proceedings before the Court so that where a Member State does not comply with that opinion within the period allowed, the Commission has the right, but not the duty, to commence proceedings before the Court.[135]

Collegiate responsibility of the Commission. A decision to issue a reasoned opinion is subject to the principle of collegiate responsibility, since it is not a measure of administration or management and therefore may not be delegated. Here too, however, a less stringent approach to effective compliance with the principle of collegiate responsibility applies, having regard to the legal consequences attaching to reasoned opinions in that it is not necessary for the college itself formally to decide on the wording of the act which gives effect to the decision to issue a reasoned opinion and put it in final form. It is sufficient that the decision was the subject of collective deliberation by the college of Commissioners and that the information on which the decision was based was available to the members of the college.[136]   **5-040**

Reasoned opinion must be coherent and detailed. The opinion is sufficiently reasoned if it contains a coherent and detailed statement of the reasons which led the Commission to believe that the Member State in question has failed to fulfil an obligation under the Treaty.[137] The opinion may only relate to shortcomings of the Member State which were mentioned in the letter of formal notice.[138]   **5-041**

Relationship with the formal notice. The reasoned opinion must be clear in itself.[139] A general reference to the letter of formal notice is not sufficient. Whilst the formal letter of notice, which comprises an initial succinct résumé of the alleged infringement, may be useful in construing   **5-042**

---

[135] This summary is based on ECJ, Case C–191/95 *Commission v Germany* [1998] E.C.R. I–5449, paras 44–36, and the case-law cited therein.

[136] *Ibid.*, paras 34–36 and 48.

[137] ECJ, Case 7/61 *Commission v Italy* [1961] E.C.R. 317, at 327; ECJ, *Commission v Germany*, cited in the preceding n., para.8; ECJ, 74/82 *Commission v Ireland* [1984] E.C.R. 317, para.20; ECJ, Case C–279/94 *Commission v Italy* [1997] E.C.R. I–4743, para.19; ECJ, Case C–350/02 *Commission v Netherlands* [2004] E.C.R. I–6213, para.20; ECJ, C–340/02 *Commission v France* [2004] E.C.R. I–9845, para.27.

[138] ECJ, Case C–145/01 *Commission v Italy* [2003] E.C.R. I–5581.

[139] In case of doubt as to the clarity of a reasoned opinion, the reply of the government concerned to the opinion can be taken into account in order to assess whether the grounds of complaint raised by the Commission were comprehensible (ECJ, Case C–463/01 *Commission v Germany* [2004] ECR I–11705, para.31).

the reasoned opinion, the Commission is none the less obliged to specify precisely in that opinion the grounds of complaint which it already raised more generally in the letter of formal notice and alleges against the Member State concerned, after taking cognisance of any observations submitted by it under the first para. of Art.226 EC. That requirement is essential in order to delimit the subject-matter of the dispute prior to any initiation of the contentious procedure provided for in the second para. of Art.226 and in order to ensure that the Member State in question is accurately apprised of the grounds of complaint maintained against it by the Commission and can thus bring an end to the alleged infringements or put forward its arguments in defence prior to any application to the Court by the Commission.[140]

In the reasoned opinion, however, the Commission may set out the complaints contained in the letter of formal notice in more detail and refine them.[141] The Commission takes account in the reasoned opinion of the observations submitted by the Member State in response to the letter of formal notice.[142] If, nevertheless, the reasoned opinion contains new complaints, the Court of Justice will have regard in the subsequent judicial proceedings only to those contained *both* in the letter of formal notice and in the reasoned opinion.[143] This is because the Member State was in a position to submit observations only on those complaints in accordance with the first para. of Art.226 of the EC Treaty before the Commission delivered its reasoned opinion.

5-043 **Reasoned opinion may propose measures to be taken.** The Commission also may—but is not obliged to[144]—set forth the measures which need to be taken in order to bring the infringement to an end. To this extent, the

---

[140] ECJ, Case C–350/02 *Commission v Netherlands* [2004] E.C.R. I–6213, para.21.

[141] ECJ, Case 274/83 *Commission v Italy* [1985] E.C.R. 1077, para.21; ECJ, Case C–358/01 *Commission v Spain* [2003] E.C.R. I–13145, para.29; ECJ, Case C–185/00 *Commission v Finland* [2003] E.C.R. I–14189, paras 79–81.

[142] If the Commission takes no account in the reasoned opinion of the observations submitted by the Member State concerned in response to the letter of formal notice, this may mean that the nature and scope of the dispute are not precisely defined at the time when the case is brought before the Court. If so, the Court will hold that the pre-litigation procedure was not properly conducted and declare the application manifestly inadmissible: ECJ (order of July 11, 1995), Case C–266/94 *Commission v Spain* [1995] E.C.R. I–1975, paras 16–26. Although, in principle, the Commission is required to state in its reasoned opinion how it assesses the Member State's observations, even if they are received late, a failure to do so will not result directly in the inadmissibility of the application if it did not make it impossible for the Member State to put an end to its infringement, did not compromise its rights of defence and had no effect on the definition of the subject-matter of the dispute (ECJ, Case C–362/01 *Commission v Ireland* [2002] E.C.R. I–11433, paras 14–22).

[143] ECJ, Case 51/83 *Commission v Italy* [1984] E.C.R. 2793, paras 6–8; ECJ, Case C–159/99 *Commission v Italy* [2001] E.C.R. I–4007, para.54.

[144] ECJ, Case C–247/89 *Commission v Portugal* [1991] E.C.R. I–3659, para.22. It is only where the Commission intends to make failure to adopt measures to enable the infringement complained of to be remedied the subject-matter of its action for failure to fulfil obligations that it has to specify those measures in the reasoned opinion (ECJ, Case C–328/96

Member State's freedom to determine the manner in which it terminates the relevant infringement of Community law is restricted. The fact that the Court of Justice is confined to making a "finding" that there has been a failure to fulfil an obligation does not affect this power of the Commission. This is because the aim of Art.226 proceedings is to achieve the practical elimination of infringements.[145] Where the Commission indicates in its reasoned opinion the measures required to this end and the Member State does not act on it, the "finding" made by the Court of Justice refers both to the actual infringement of Community law and to the measures which could have been taken in order to bring the infringement to an end. As a result, the Member State then knows—from the reasoning of the Court's judgment finding the infringement—what measures indicated in the reasoned opinion are capable of bringing the failure to fulfil obligations to an end.

Prescribed period. The Commission must prescribe in the reasoned opinion the time within which the Member State must comply with it. The period must be reasonable having regard to the circumstances of the case.[146] The Court of Justice has no power to alter the period prescribed by the Commission.[147] An action for failure to fulfil obligations brought after the expiry of a period which was too short to enable the Member State to take the necessary measures or, as the case may be, to prepare its defence will be declared inadmissible.[148] The application may be declared admissible, however, if in the actual case the aims of the pre-litigation procedure were nevertheless achieved in spite of the unreasonably short period of time allowed to the Member State.[149]

5–044

B. THE STAGE OF THE PROCEDURE HELD BEFORE THE COURT OF JUSTICE

1. Conditions of admissibility

a. The requirement for the pre-litigation stage of the procedure to be properly conducted

Objective. The proper conduct of the pre-litigation stage of the procedure is, as noted above, an essential guarantee required by the Treaty not only in order to protect the rights of the Member State concerned, but also so as to

5–045

Commission v Austria [1999] E.C.R. I–7479, para.39; ECJ, Case C–394/02 Commission v Greece [2005] E.C.R. I–4713, para.23).
[145] ECJ, Case 70/72 Commission v Germany [1973] E.C.R. 813, paras 10–13.
[146] ECJ, Case 74/82 Commission v Ireland [1984] E.C.R. 317, paras 9–12; ECJ, Case 293/85 Commission v Belgium [1988] E.C.R. 305, para.14; ECJ, Case C–56/90 Commission v United Kingdom [1993] E.C.R. I–4109, para.18; ECJ, Case C–328/96 Commission v Austria [1999] E.C.R. I–7479, para.51; ECJ (judgment of November 15, 2005), Case C–320/03 Commission v Austria, not yet reported, paras 33–34 (one week was deemed to be sufficient). See also 5–038, supra, in relation to the time prescribed for submitting observations on the letter of formal notice.
[147] ECJ, Case 28/81 Commission v Italy [1981] E.C.R. 2577, para.6; ECJ, Case 29/81 Commission v Italy [1981] E.C.R. 2585, para.6.
[148] ECJ, Case 293/85 Commission v Belgium [1988] E.C.R. 305, para.20.
[149] For an example, see Case 74/82 Commission v Ireland [1984] E.C.R. 317, para.13.

ensure that any contentious procedure will have a clearly defined dispute as its subject-matter.[150] For those reasons, the Commission must take account in the reasoned opinion of the observations submitted by the Member State concerned in response to the letter of formal notice so that the Court may judge, when proceedings are brought, what specific obligations the Commission claims the Member State concerned has breached. If the Commission fails to satisfy this requirement, this may mean that the subject-matter of the dispute is not precisely defined. Such an irregularity in the conduct of the pre-litigation stage of the procedure may result in the application being declared manifestly inadmissible.[151]

b. The requirement for the letter of formal notice and the reasoned opinion to accord with the application by which an action for failure to fulfil obligations is brought before the Court

5-046   **Consistency between the pre-litigation stage and the application.** Since the subject-matter of the proceedings is defined in the pre-litigation stage, the application by which the action for failure to fulfil obligations is brought before the Court of Justice must accord both with the reasoned opinion and with the letter of formal notice.[152] Where necessary, the Court will take up this point of its own motion.[153] This means that the alleged infringement of Community law must be defined in both the application and in the reasoned opinion in consistent, sufficiently precise terms, and that the application must be based on the same pleas and arguments as the reasoned opinion.[154] For example, the Commission cannot extend an action brought against a Member State for failing to implement a directive in national law to cover the infringement of failing in practice to comply with provisions of the directive where that complaint was not raised during the

---

[150] ECJ, Case C-1/00 *Commission v France* [2001] E.C.R. I-9989, para.53; ECJ, Case C-287/00 *Commission v Germany* [2002] E.C.R. I-5811, para.17; ECJ, Case C-350/02 *Commission v Netherlands* [2004] E.C.R. I-6213, para.19.

[151] ECJ (order of July 11, 1995), Case C-266/94 *Commission v Spain* [1995] E.C.R. I-1975.

[152] ECJ, Case C-340/96 *Commission v United Kingdom* [1999] E.C.R. I-2023, para.36; ECJ, Case C-350/02 *Commission v Netherlands* [2004] E.C.R. I-6213, paras 19-20. It goes without saying that the application must accord with the general requirements of Art.21 of the Statute and Art.38(1)(c) of the ECJ Rules of Procedure (see ECJ, Case C-52/90 *Commission v Denmark* [1992] E.C.R. I-2187, para.17) (24-003 to 24-028, *infra*).

[153] ECJ, Case C-417/02 *Commission v Greece* [2004] E.C.R. I-7973, paras 15-16.

[154] ECJ, Case C-157/91 *Commission v Netherlands* [1992] E.C.R. I-5899, para.16; ECJ, Case 306/91 *Commission v Italy* [1993] E.C.R. I-2133, para.22; ECJ, Case C-243/89 *Commission v Denmark* [1993] E.C.R. I-3353, para.13; ECJ, Case C-296/92 *Commission v Italy* [1994] E.C.R. I-1, para.11; ECJ (judgment of September 7, 2004), Case C-469/02 *Commission v Belgium*, not reported, paras 17-21.

pre-litigation stage.[155] However, the statement of the subject-matter of the proceedings in the reasoned opinion does not invariably have to be exactly the same as the form of order sought in the application if the subject-matter of the proceedings has not been extended or altered but simply restated in greater detail[156] or if the subject-matter—compared to the pre-litigation proceedings—has been limited.[157]

Moreover, an application will be admissible only in so far as the Commission adduces matters of fact and law which support the conclusions set out in general terms in the reasoned opinion and the application.[158]

Infringement relates to a cluster of acts. Where an action for failure to fulfil obligations relates, not to a single act, but to a cluster of acts, each involving a separate infringement, the Member State must have been given an opportunity in the pre-litigation stage to set forth its defence to each breach of which it stands accused. If the letter of formal notice referred only to certain isolated cases, the action cannot extend to the whole collection of acts categorised as infringements. In this event, the application will be admissible only to the extent to which the acts complained of in the application were also dealt with in the pre-litigation stage.[159]

5–047

---

[155] ECJ, Case C–237/90 *Commission v Germany* [1992] E.C.R. I–5973, paras 20–22. Where the Commission has given a Member State formal notice of a failure to transpose a directive and the Member State adopts some implementing measures after the pre-litigation stage but not all those necessary in order to transpose the directive, the Commission may restrict the form of order sought in the application made to the Court to those provisions not yet implemented at that time: ECJ, Case C–132/94 *Commission v Ireland* [1995] E.C.R. I–4789, paras 7–9, but see ECJ, Case C–274/93 *Commission v Luxembourg* [1996] E.C.R. I–2019, paras 12–13.

[156] ECJ, Case C–185/00 *Commission v Finland* [2003] E.C.R. I–14189, para.87: the fact that in the application the Commission set out in detail the complaints it had already made in a more general way in the letter of formal notice and the reasoned opinion has no effect on the scope of the proceedings; ECJ, Case C–279/94 *Commission v Italy* [1997] E.C.R. I–4743, para.25; ECJ, Case C–52/00 *Commission v France* [2002] E.C.R. I–3827, para.44; ECJ, Case C–139/00 *Commission v Spain* [2002] E.C.R. I–6407, para.19: the Commission can reword the complaints in the application to take account of additional evidence produced after notification of the reasoned opinion; ECJ, Case C–256/98 *Commission v France* [2000] E.C.R. I–2487, paras 29–33: where, in its reply, the Commission amends its grounds of complaint so as to go beyond a mere restatement, albeit in greater detail, of the initial complaints or thereby raises submissions before the Court which were not put forward during the pre-litigation procedure or in the application initiating the proceedings, the Court will hold that the Commission must be deemed to have withdrawn its original complaints and declare the application inadmissible.

[157] ECJ, Case C–117/02 *Commission v Portugal* [2004] E.C.R. I–5517, paras 52–55: the Commission can base its application on a complaint which was raised only in the alternative in the pre-litigation procedure in so far as the complaint was set out in the reasoned opinion; ECJ, Case C–203/03 *Commission v Austria* [2005] E.C.R. I–935, para.29: limitation of the subject-matter of the proceedings in the application as a result of a modification of the national legislation concerned.

[158] ECJ, Case C–429/97 *Commission v France* [2001] E.C.R. I–637, para.56.

[159] ECJ, Case 309/84 *Commission v Italy* [1986] E.C.R. 599, paras 15–16.

5–048   Modification of national legislation. If, in both the pre-litigation stage (the letter of formal notice and the reasoned opinion) and in its application, the Commission complains of a specific shortcoming on the part of the Member State, the latter cannot claim that the application is irregular on the ground that the same shortcoming was due in the pre-litigation stage to a different national provision than the one to which it was attributable at the time when the action was brought. This is because the shortcoming with which the Member State is charged is not the existence of a specific provision incompatible with Community law, but the specific shortcoming arising as a result of such provision. As a result, a change in the national provision in the course of or after the pre-litigation procedure does not jeopardise the admissibility of the action for failure to fulfil obligations.[160] Neither does the opposite situation affect the admissibility of the application. Where Community law changes in the course of the pre-litigation procedure (after the submission of a letter of formal notice and of the reasoned opinion), the Commission may still bring, for example, an admissible application for a declaration of failure to fulfil obligations in respect of an original version of a subsequently amended or withdrawn directive if the obligations are retained in the new provisions.[161]

5–049   Infringements committed after the notification of the reasoned opinion. The requirement that the reasoned opinion and the application must accord with each other does not preclude infringements committed by the Member State after notification of the reasoned opinion from nevertheless being covered by the application provided that the conduct at issue is of the same kind as that complained of in the opinion. Accordingly, the Court of Justice was entitled to take account of administrative practices which were applied after the reasoned opinion was given but were substantively the same as those referred to in the reasoned opinion.[162] Factual circumstances referred to in the reasoned opinion which continued after it was given may unquestionably be reviewed by the Court of Justice for the whole of their duration.[163]

---

[160] ECJ, Case 45/64 *Commission v Italy* [1965] E.C.R. 857, at 864–865; ECJ, Case C–42/89 *Commission v Belgium* [1990] E.C.R. I–2821, para.11; ECJ, Case C–105/91 *Commission v Greece* [1992] E.C.R. I–5871, para.13; ECJ, Case C–11/95 *Commission v Belgium* [1996] E.C.R. I–4115, para.74; ECJ, Case C–375/95 *Commission v Greece* [1997] E.C.R. I–5981, para.38; ECJ, Case C–203/03 *Commission v Austria* [2005] E.C.R. I–935, paras 27–32. However, in *Commission v France* (ECJ, Case C–177/03 *Commission v France* [2004] E.C.R. I–11671, para.21) the Court ruled that where the relevant national provisions have fundamentally changed between the expiry of the period laid down for compliance with the reasoned opinion and the lodging of the application, that change in circumstances may render the judgment to be given by the Court otiose. According to the Court, in such situations, it may be preferable for the Commission not to bring an action (which would, however, be admissible) but to issue a new reasoned opinion precisely identifying the complaints which it intends pursuing, having regard to the changed circumstances.
[161] ECJ, Case C–365/97 *Commission v Italy* [1999] E.C.R. I–7773, para.36.
[162] ECJ, Case 42/82 *Commission v France* [1983] E.C.R. 1013, para.20; ECJ, Case 113/86 *Commission v Italy* [1988] E.C.R. 607, para.11.
[163] *Commission v France*, cited in the preceding n., para.20.

Measures taken in order to comply with the reasoned opinion. An   5–050
infringement arising where a Member State takes measures in order to
eliminate an infringement complained of by the Commission may be the
subject of an action for failure to fulfil obligations only if a new pre-
litigation stage is held. This is because the infringement resulting from the
measures in question is not the same as the breach originally complained
of. It is therefore impossible to bring a new action on the basis of the
original pre-litigation procedure without infringing the requirement that
the subject-matter of the reasoned opinion and the application must be the
same.[164]

New application may remedy defects. If the Court declares an application   5–051
inadmissible on the ground that the application does not square with the
reasoned opinion, the Commission may remedy the defects by submitting a
new application based on the same complaints, pleas in law and arguments
as the reasoned opinion. If it does this, it is not under a duty to start the
pre-litigation stage afresh or to issue a supplementary reasoned opinion.[165]

c. Existence of a failure to fulfil obligations

Infringement no longer exists on the expiry of the period prescribed in the   5–052
reasoned opinion. In principle, an action for failure to fulfil obligations is
admissible only if the infringement complained of exists on the expiry of the
period prescribed by the reasoned opinion.[166] The action is to no purpose if
the Member State has taken measures in time in order to eliminate the
infringement at issue.[167]

Similarly, the application will be to no purpose where all the legal effects
of the national conduct at issue had been exhausted on the expiry of the
period prescribed by the reasoned opinion.[168] Thus, as far as concerns the

---

[164] ECJ, Case 7/69 *Commission v Italy* [1970] E.C.R. 111, paras 4–5; for further examples, see
Case 391/85 *Commission v Belgium* [1988] E.C.R. 579 and ECJ, Case C–207/97 *Commission
v Belgium* [1999] E.C.R. I–275, para.25.
[165] ECJ, Case C–57/94 *Commission v Italy* [1995] E.C.R. I–1249, para.14.
[166] ECJ, Case C–166/97 *Commission v France* [1999] E.C.R. I–1719, para.18; ECJ, Case C–
384/99 *Commission v Belgium* [2000] E.C.R. I–10633, para.16; ECJ, Case C–147/00
Commission v France [2001] E.C.R. I–2387, para.26; ECJ, Case C–119/00 *Commission v
Luxembourg* [2001] E.C.R. I–4795, para.14; ECJ, Case C–29/01 *Commission v Spain* [2002]
E.C.R. I–2503, para.11; ECJ (judgment of October 27, 2005), Case C–525/03 *Commission v
Italy*, not yet reported, paras 8–17. Where the Commission brings an action under Art.88(2)
of the EC Treaty on the ground that the Member State concerned has not complied with a
decision requiring unlawful State aid to be repaid, the reference date for determining the
failure to fulfil obligations is that provided for in the decision or, where appropriate, that
subsequently fixed by the Commission: ECJ, Case C–378/98 *Commission v Belgium* [2001]
E.C.R. I–5107, para.26; ECJ, Case C–99/02 *Commission v Italy* [2004] E.C.R. I–3353,
para.24.
[167] ECJ, Case 240/86 *Commission v Greece* [1988] E.C.R. 1835, para.16; ECJ, Case C–439/99
Commission v Italy [2002] E.C.R. I–305, paras 16–17.
[168] ECJ, Case C–362/90 *Commission v Italy* [1992] E.C.R. I–2353, paras 11–13.

award of public procurement contracts, an action for failure to fulfil obligations will be inadmissible if, when the period prescribed in the reasoned opinion expired, the contract in question had already been completely performed.[169]

5–053   **Infringement ceases after the prescribed period.** If the Member State has not taken measures in time, the application will be admissible. Even if the Member State remedies the infringement after the prescribed period has expired but before the action is brought, the application will still be admissible. In the light of the potential liability on the part of the Member State, there remains an interest for the Community, other Member States and individuals in the Court's making a finding that there has been an infringement. The finding may then serve as the basis for claims for damages.[170]

The Commission is always presumed to have an interest. Nevertheless, the Court of Justice will inquire into that interest in a case where the action was brought at a time when the infringement of Community law with which the Member State was charged had in fact come to an end.[171]

5–054   **Acknowledgement of the infringement by the Member State.** The fact that the Member State acknowledges that it has failed to fulfil its obligations and its resultant liability during the pre-litigation stage of the procedure or after the action has been brought before the Court of Justice does not mean that the application is to no purpose. Otherwise, the Member State would be at liberty, at any time during the proceedings, to have them brought to an end without any judicial determination of the breach of obligations and of the basis of its liability and the exclusive jurisdiction of the Court of Justice to make a determination—after an action has been

---

[169] ECJ (judgment of September 9, 2004), Case C–125/03 *Commission v Germany*, not reported, paras 12–13 (action was admissible since the contracts were not completely performed); ECJ, Case C–394/02 *Commission v Greece* [2005] E.C.R. I–4713 paras 18–19 (action was admissible since only 85 per cent of the works had been completed when the period prescribed by the reasoned opinion expired).

[170] ECJ, Case 39/72 *Commission v Italy* [1973] E.C.R. 101, para.11; ECJ, Case 309/84 *Commission v Italy* [1986] E.C.R. 599, para.18; ECJ, Case 103/84 *Commission v Italy* [1986] E.C.R. 1759, para.8; ECJ, Case 154/85 *Commission v Italy* [1987] E.C.R. 2717, para.6; Case 240/86 *Commission v Greece* [1988] E.C.R. 1835, para.14; ECJ, Case 283/86 *Commission v Belgium* [1988] E.C.R. 3271, para.6; ECJ, Case C–249/88 *Commission v Belgium* [1991] E.C.R. I–1275, para.41; ECJ, Case C–361/88 *Commission v Germany* [1991] E.C.R. I–2567, para.31; Case C–59/89 *Commission v Germany* [1991] E.C.R. I–2607, para.35; ECJ, Case C–29/90 *Commission v Greece* [1992] E.C.R. I–1971, para.12; ECJ, Case C–280/89 *Commission v Ireland* [1992] E.C.R. I–6185, para.7; ECJ, Case C–317/92 *Commission v Germany* [1994] E.C.R. I–2039, para.3; ECJ, Case C–289/94 *Commission v Italy* [1996] E.C.R. I–4405, para.20; ECJ, Case C–119/00 *Commission v Luxembourg* [2001] E.C.R. I–4795, para.17; ECJ, Case C–299/01 *Commission v Luxembourg* [2002] E.C.R. I–5899, para.11; ECJ, Case C–209/02 *Commission v Austria* [2004] E.C.R. I–1211, paras 16–19; ECJ, Case C–168/03 *Commission v Spain* [2004] E.C.R. I–8227, para.24. See also Goffin (n.85, *supra*), at 215.

[171] ECJ, Case 26/69 *Commission v France* [1970] E.C.R. 565, paras 9–13 (the Court held that the Commission did have an interest in bringing the proceedings).

brought—as to whether or not Community law has been infringed would be impaired.[172]

d. Time-limits

Commission's discretion. In exercising its powers in connection with an action for failure to fulfil obligations, the Commission does not have to comply with any time-limits. It is free to judge at what time it starts the pre-litigation stage and at what time after the expiry of the period prescribed by the reasoned opinion it brings an action before the Court of Justice.[173] Yet the Commission may not abuse its discretion.[174] For instance, if the pre-litigation procedure is excessively long, the Member State may find it more difficult to refute the Commission's arguments and this may constitute an infringement of the rights of the defence. The Member State has to prove that the unusual length of the pre-litigation procedure had adverse effects on the way in which it conducted its defence.[175] Only if it succeeds in proving this, will the application be declared inadmissible. However, the burden of proof is difficult for the Member State to discharge, since there will generally be factors justifying the unusually long lapse of time between the "infringement" and the commencement of the procedure or the

5–055

---

[172] ECJ, Case C–243/89 *Commission v Denmark* [1993] E.C.R. I–3353, para.30; ECJ (judgment of March 3, 2005), Case C–414/03 *Commission v Germany*, not reported, paras 8–9. An application from a Member State for the proceedings to be stayed in order to allow it to put an end to the infringement and hence in the expectation of a hypothetical withdrawal of the action by the Commission cannot be granted, since a failure to fulfil obligations must be determined by reference to the situation prevailing in the Member State at the end of the period prescribed in the reasoned opinion (ECJ, Case C–366/00 *Commission v Luxembourg* [2002] E.C.R. I–1749, paras 10–12).

[173] ECJ, Case 7/68 *Commission v Italy* [1968] E.C.R. 423, at 428; ECJ, Case 7/71 *Commission v France* [1971] E.C.R. 1003, paras 2–8; ECJ, Case 324/82 *Commission v Belgium* [1984] E.C.R. 1861, para.12; ECJ, Case C–56/90 *Commission v United Kingdom* [1993] E.C.R. I–4109, para.15; ECJ, Case C–317/92 *Commission v Germany* [1994] E.C.R. I–2039, paras 4–5; ECJ, Case C–333/99 *Commission v France* [2001] E.C.R. I–1025, para.25 (in that case the Commission brought an action seven years after it had received the observations of the Member State concerned on the reasoned opinion); ECJ, Case C–40/00 *Commission v France* [2001] E.C.R. I–4539, para.23; it would appear, however, that the principle *nec bis in idem* precludes the Commission from bringing an action for failure to fulfil obligations where the Court has already given a judgment in respect of that failure: ECJ, Case C–127/99 *Commission v Italy* [2001] E.C.R. I–8305, para.29 (where the Court held that the principle *nec bis in idem* had not been violated as regards the question whether the Member State concerned had implemented the directive within the prescribed period, since the earlier judgment of the Court related to provisions other than those at issue in the new proceedings). Where it determines that a Member State has not taken the measures necessary to comply with a judgment finding an infringement, the Commission can apply to the Court to impose a lump sum or a penalty payment pursuant to Art.228 of the EC Treaty.

[174] ECJ Case C–177/03 *Commission v France* [2004] E.C.R. I–11671, para.17.

[175] ECJ, Case C–96/89 *Commission v Netherlands* [1991] E.C.R. I–2461, paras 14–16; ECJ, Case C–475/98 *Commission v Austria* [2002] E.C.R. I–9797, paras 34–39.

unusual duration of the pre-litigation stage and causing them not to be regarded as excessive.[176]

2. Aspects of the treatment given to the substantive claim

a. Burden of proof

5–056 **Commission bears the burden of proof.** The burden of proof has to be discharged by the Commission.[177] It has to adduce evidence to the Court of Justice that the infringement existed at the time when the period prescribed by the reasoned opinion expired.[178] The Commission may not rely on any presumptions (of law) in this connection.[179] It is settled case-law that the scope of national laws, regulations or administrative provisions must be assessed in the light of the interpretation given to them by national courts. Therefore, if a national provision can be interpreted in two ways—one

---

[176] In Case 7/71 *Commission v France* [1971] E.C.R. 1003, the Commission applied to the Court of Justice in 1971 to find an infringement which had existed since 1965. The infringement did not come to light until 1968 and the Commission formally started the procedure in April 1970 following informal contacts with the Member State. In Case 324/82 *Commission v Belgium* [1984] E.C.R. 1861, the Commission waited until the directive concerned had been implemented in all the Member States before investigating the contested Belgian measures. In Case C–96/89 *Commission v Netherlands* [1991] E.C.R. I–2461, the Commission waited for the Court of Justice to give judgment in another case and for the reaction of the Netherlands government. See also ECJ (judgment of December 2, 2004), Case C–42/03 *Commisson v Spain*, not reported, paras 21–25.

[177] ECJ, Case 96/81 *Commission v Netherlands* [1982] E.C.R. 1791, para.6; ECJ, Case C–249/88 *Commission v Belgium* [1991] E.C.R. I–1275, para.6; ECJ, Case C–210/91 *Commission v Greece* [1992] E.C.R. I–6735, para.22; ECJ, Case C–375/90 *Commission v Greece* [1993] E.C.R. I–2055, para.33; ECJ, Case C–68/99 *Commission v Germany* [2001] E.C.R. I–1865, para.38; ECJ (judgment of July 15, 2004), Case C–419/03 *Commission v France*, not reported, paras 7–8. See also Louis, "Le rôle de la Commission dans la procédure en manquement selon la jurisprudence récente de la Cour de justice", in *Du droit international au droit de l'intégration—Liber amicorum Pierre Pescatore* (Nomos, Baden-Baden, 1987), 387, at 397–405. However, it is not sufficient for the Commission, in order to claim that the defendant Member State has not complied with a provision of Community law, merely to cite that provision in the section of the reasoned opinion or of the application which covers the legal context and which is purely descriptive and lacking of any explanatory character (ECJ, Case C–202/99 *Commission v Italy* [2001] E.C.R. I–9319, para.21).

[178] ECJ, Case 121/84 *Commission v Italy* [1986] E.C.R. 107, paras 10–12; ECJ, Case 188/84 *Commission v France* [1986] E.C.R. 419, paras 38–39; ECJ, Case 298/86 *Commission v Belgium* [1988] E.C.R. 4343, para.15; ECJ, Case C–157/91 *Commission v Netherlands* [1992] E.C.R. I–5899, para.12; ECJ, Case C–166/97 *Commission v France* [1999] E.C.R. I–1719, para.40; ECJ, Case C–337/98 *Commission v France* [2000] E.C.R. I–8377, para.45; ECJ, Case C–347/98 *Commission v Belgium* [2001] E.C.R. I–3327, para.39; ECJ, Case C–263/99 *Commission v Italy* [2001] E.C.R. I–4195, para.27; ECJ (judgment of September 16, 2004), Case C–248/02 *Commission v Italy*, not reported, para.28 (in assessing whether or not there has been an infringement, the Court takes no account of information provided to the Commission by the Member State after the expiry of the period prescribed in the reasoned opinion).

[179] ECJ, Case 290/87 *Commission v Netherlands* [1989] E.C.R. 3083, para.11; ECJ, Case C–61/94 *Commission v Germany* [1996] E.C.R. I–3989, para.61; ECJ, Case C–214/98 *Commission v Greece* [2000] E.C.R. I–9601, para.42; ECJ, Case C–147/00 *Commission v France* [2001] E.C.R. I–2387, para.27.

consistent with and another one inconsistent with Community law—the Commission will have to prove that the national courts interpret the domestic provision at issue inconsistently with Community law.[180]

An application from the Commission for an expert's report to be commissioned by the Court will be refused, since if it were granted the Commission itself would not be providing evidence of the alleged failure to fulfil obligations.[181]

It is only when the Commission has produced sufficient evidence of the failure to fulfil obligations that the defendant Member State has to adduce its counter-arguments.[182]

Duty of Member States to cooperate in good faith. Member States are under a duty, by virtue of Art.10 of the EC Treaty, to facilitate the achievement of the Commission's tasks, which consist in particular, in accordance with Art.211 of the EC Treaty, in ensuring that the measures taken by the institutions pursuant to the Treaty are applied.[183] It follows that the Member States are required to cooperate in good faith with the inquiries of the Commission pursuant to Art.226 of the EC Treaty, and to provide the Commission with all the information requested for that purpose.[184] A failure to comply with this obligation may result in a finding of a failure to fulfil an obligation under the Treaty.[185]   5–057

Many directives incorporate that duty to cooperate in good faith and to provide information in a specific provision. Such a provision will require Member States to provide clear, accurate information about the legal and administrative provisions adopted in order to implement the directive in question which enables the Commission to ascertain whether the Member State has effectively and completely implemented it.[186]

When a directive imposes upon the Member States an obligation to provide information, the information which the Member States are thus obliged to supply to the Commission must be clear and precise. It must indicate unequivocally the laws, regulations and administrative provisions

---

[180] ECJ, Case C–382/92 *Commission v United Kingdom* [1994] E.C.R. I–2435, para.36; ECJ, Case C–300/95 *Commission v United Kingdom* [1997] E.C.R. I–2649, para.37; ECJ, Case C–287/03 *Commission v Belgium* [2005] E.C.R. I–3761, paras 28–30.

[181] ECJ, Case 141/87 *Commission v Italy* [1989] E.C.R. 943, para.17.

[182] ECJ, Case 272/86 *Commission v Greece* [1988] E.C.R. 4875, para.21.

[183] ECJ, Case C–33/90 *Commission v Italy* [1991] E.C.R. I–5987, para.18; ECJ, Case C–494/01 *Commission v Ireland* [2005] E.C.R. I–3331, para.197.

[184] ECJ, Case C–65/91 *Commission v Greece* [1992] E.C.R. I–5245, para.14. A Member State cannot therefore claim that the Commission's application is inadmissible because the details of the national law and practice are not specific enough (ECJ, Case C–408/97 *Commission v Netherlands* [2000] E.C.R. I–6417, para.17). Failure to cooperate in good faith with the Commission will constitute a breach of the obligation imposed on the Member State by Art.10 of the EC Treaty (ECJ, Case C–82/03 *Commission v Italy* [2004] E.C.R. I–6635).

[185] ECJ, Case C–82/03 *Commission v Italy* [2004] E.C.R. I–6635, para.15; ECJ, Case C–494/01 *Commission v Ireland* [2005] E.C.R. I–3331, paras 195–200.

[186] See, for example, ECJ, Case 274/83 *Commission v Italy* [1985] E.C.R. 1077, para.42.

LIVERPOOL JOHN MOORES UNIVERSITY
LEARNING SERVICES

by means of which the Member State considers that it has satisfied the various requirements imposed on it by the directive. In the absence of such information, the Commission is not in a position to ascertain whether the Member State has genuinely implemented the directive completely. The failure of a Member State to fulfil that obligation, whether by providing no information at all or by providing insufficiently clear and precise information, may of itself justify recourse to the procedure under Art.226 of the EC Treaty in order to establish the failure to fulfil the obligation.[187]

5–058 **Member State complies with secondary Community law.** The Commission cannot make reference directly to a provision of the EC Treaty in order to prove an infringement where a provision of a directive explicitly allows the Member State concerned to adopt the act allegedly violating the EC Treaty. A directive is indeed presumed to be lawful. A Member State which complies with the provisions of such Community act cannot be held not to fulfil its obligations under Community law.[188]

b. **Substantive defence of the Member State**

5–059 **Objective nature of the action.** The chances of success of defence pleas which a Member State wishes to raise are determined first by the objective nature of actions for failure to fulfil obligations (see 5–001, *supra*). The Court of Justice pays no regard to the underlying reasons for the breach or to circumstances which in fact limited its adverse effects or explain the breach. It is virtually certain that a defence based on such pleas will fail. Accordingly, a Member State may not plead provisions, practices or situations existing in its internal legal system (such as those resulting from its federal organisation)[189] in order to justify a failure to comply with Community obligations.[190] Moreover, the fact that the failure to fulfil obligations had no adverse effects is irrelevant.[191] Neither does the fact that

---

[187] ECJ, Case 96/81 *Commission v Netherlands* [1982] E.C.R. 1791, para.8; ECJ Case C–456/03 *Commission v Italy* [2005] E.C.R. I–5335, para.27.

[188] ECJ Case C–475/01 *Commission v Greece* [2004] E.C.R. I–8923, paras 16–24. See 5–015, *supra*.

[189] ECJ, Case C–236/99 *Commission v Belgium* [2000] E.C.R. I–5657, para.23; ECJ, Case C–358/03 *Commission v Austria* [2004] E.C.R. I–12055, paras 12–13: the fact that Austrian constitutional law precludes the Federal State from adopting transposition measures in the place of a Land and that only censure by the Court of Justice confers the power on the Federal State to undertake the transposition cannot justify an infringement for which the Federal State bears responsibility under Community law. Although each Member State may freely allocate areas of internal legal competence as it sees fit, the fact remains that it alone is responsible to the Community under Art.226 of the EC Treaty for compliance with obligations arising under Community law.

[190] ECJ, Case 52/75 *Commission v Italy* [1976] E.C.R. 277, para.14; ECJ, Case C–166/97 *Commission v France* [1999] E.C.R. I–1719, para.13; ECJ, Case C–473/99 *Commission v Austria* [2001] E.C.R. I–4527, para.12. The argument that the rule of Community law infringed is incompatible with national public policy is therefore also inadmissible (ECJ, Case C–52/00 *Commission v France* [2002] E.C.R. I–3827, para.33).

[191] ECJ, Case C–150/97 *Commission v Portugal* [1999] E.C.R. I–259, para.22.

a directive with direct effect produces the same result in practice as if the directive had been implemented properly and in time justify a failure to fulfil the obligation to implement it.[192] What is more, a Member State cannot rely on the principle of protection of legitimate expectations—in so far as that principle can be invoked by a Member State at all—because that defence is incompatible with the objective nature of these proceedings.[193]

Secondly, the special nature of Community law prevents a Member State from relying on a number of common defences in international law. For instance, a Member State cannot justify its failure to perform its obligations by reference to the shortcomings of other Member States, since the Treaty did not merely create reciprocal obligations between the Member States, but also established a new legal order governing the procedures necessary for the purposes of having any infringement of Community law "declared and punished".[194]

Illegality of the Community act. It appears from the case-law that a Member State can plead the illegality of a regulation in proceedings for failure to fulfil obligations.[195] In contrast, a Member State is not entitled to raise the claim that a directive or a decision addressed to it is unlawful

5–060

---

[192] ECJ, Case 102/79 *Commission v Belgium* [1980] E.C.R. 1473, para.12; ECJ, Case 301/81 *Commission v Belgium* [1983] E.C.R. 467, para.13; ECJ, Case C–433/93 *Commission v Germany* [1995] E.C.R. I–2303, para.24; ECJ, Case C–253/95 *Commission v Germany* [1996] E.C.R. I–2423, para.13. The obligation to ensure the full effectiveness of a directive, in accordance with its objective, cannot be interpreted as meaning that the Member States are released from adopting transposition measures where they consider that their national provisions are better than the Community provisions concerned and that the national provisions are therefore more likely to ensure that the objective pursued by the directive is achieved. According to the Court's case-law, the existence of national rules may render transposition by specific legislative or regulatory measures superfluous only if those rules actually ensure the full application of the directive by the national authorities (see, ECJ, Case C–103/02 *Commission v Italy* [2004] E.C.R. I–9127, para.33).

[193] ECJ, Case C–83/99 *Commission v Spain* [2001] E.C.R. I–445, paras 22–27; ECJ, Case C–99/02 *Commission v Italy* [2004] E.C.R. I–3353, paras 20–21, in which the Court held that a Member State whose authorities have granted aid contrary to the procedural rules laid down in Art.88 of the EC Treaty may not plead the legitimate expectations of recipients in order to justify a failure to comply with the obligation to take the steps necessary to implement a Commission decision instructing it to recover the aid. If it could do so, Arts 87 and 88 of the EC Treaty would be deprived of all practical force, since national authorities would thus be able to rely on their own unlawful conduct in order to render decisions taken by the Commission under those provisions of the Treaty ineffectual.

[194] ECJ, Case 52/75 *Commission v Italy* [1976] E.C.R. 277, para.11; ECJ, Case C–11/95 *Commission v Belgium* [1996] E.C.R. I–4115, paras 36–37; ECJ, Case C–163/99 *Portugal v Commission* [2001] E.C.R. I–2613, para.22; ECJ (judgment of July 15, 2004), Case C–118/03 *Commission v Germany*, not reported, para.8.

[195] ECJ, Case C–11/00 *Commission v ECB* [2003] E.C.R. I–7174, paras 74–78. Art.241 of the EC Treaty provides, without exception, that an objection of illegality may be raised "in proceedings in which a regulation of the kind referred to in Art.241 is at issue". As a result, the objection of illegality expressly constitutes part of the system of legal remedies provided for in the Treaty and does not threaten the stability of that system (see also Schermers and Waelbroeck, *Judicial Protection*, § 1266, at 624 who likewise argue in favour of the admissibility of the objection; Goffin (n.85, *supra*), at 217).

where it is accused of breaching such a measure and the time-limit for applying for its annulment has expired or even where it has brought an action for annulment and not at the same time a (successful) application for interim measures to suspend the contested act pending the judgment in the main proceedings.[196] The Court of Justice takes the view that to allow this defence would jeopardise the stability of the system of legal remedies established by the Treaty and the principle of legal certainty on which it is based.[197]

In the exceptional case where the directive or decision infringed contained such serious and manifest defects that it could be deemed non-existent, the Court of Justice may be asked to declare it non-existent, thereby making the claim of an infringement to no purpose.[198]

5–061　**Violation of the Treaty but compliance with Community legislation.** Where the Commission deems that a national rule violates a Treaty provision, the Member State concerned can justify its national legislation by referring to the fact that it expressly complies with a provision of secondary Community law. Provisions of secondary Community law are indeed presumed to be lawful (as long as they are not annulled or declared unlawful by the Community judicature).[199]

5–062　**Pleas refuting the breach in an objective manner.** The Member State's defence is not restricted to a limited number of pleas. Any plea, of law or fact, which refutes the alleged breach in an objective manner is admissible. In addition, the Member State may raise defences not relied upon in the

---

[196] In Case C–261/99 *Commission v France* [2001] E.C.R. I–2537 the Court held in connection with an action brought under Art.88(2) of the EC Treaty that France had failed to fulfil its obligations by not implementing a Commission decision requiring it to recover unlawful State aid. That decision was deemed to be lawful despite the action for annulment already brought by France (ECJ, Case C–17/99 *France v Commission* [2001] E.C.R. I–2481).

[197] ECJ, Case 156/77 *Commission v Belgium* [1978] E.C.R. 1881, paras 15–25; ECJ, Case 52/83 *Commission v France* [1983] E.C.R. 3707, para.10; ECJ, Case 52/84 *Commission v Belgium* [1986] E.C.R. 89, para.13; ECJ, Case 226/87 *Commission v Greece* [1988] E.C.R. 3611, para.14; ECJ, Case C–74/91 *Commission v Germany* [1992] E.C.R. I–5437, para.10 (concerning a directive); ECJ, Case C–183/91 *Commission v Greece* [1993] E.C.R. I–3131, para.10; ECJ, Case C–404/97 *Commission v Portugal* [2000] E.C.R. I–4897, para.34 (this also applies to an action brought on the basis of Art.88(2) of the EC Treaty); ECJ, Case C–1/00 *Commission v France* [2001] E.C.R. I–9989, para.101; ECJ, Case C–52/00 *Commission v France* [2001] E.C.R. I–3827, para.28; ECJ, Case C–194/01 *Commission v Austria* [2004] E.C.R. I–4579, para.41; ECJ (judgment of July 15, 2004), Case C–118/03 *Commission v Germany*, not reported, para.7. See 9–008, *infra*.

[198] ECJ, Case 226/87 *Commission v Greece*, cited in the preceding n., paras 15–16; ECJ, Case C–404/97 *Commission v Portugal* [2000] E.C.R. I–4897, para.35. The beginnings of this case-law can be found in Joined Cases 6 and 11/69 *Commission v France* [1969] E.C.R. 523, paras 11–13.

[199] ECJ, Case C–475/01 *Commission v Greece* [2004] E.C.R. I–8923, paras 18–26. See 5–015, *supra*. An act of secondary Community law is presumed to be lawful unless it is tainted by an irregularity whose gravity is so obvious that it cannot be tolerated by the Community legal order so that the act must be regarded as legally non-existent (*ibid*. para.19).

pre-litigation procedure.[200] The pleas must, however, be raised timeously in the defence.[201]

Thus, a Member State may claim that it was "absolutely impossible" for it to have adopted measures capable of eliminating the infringement or, in proceedings based on Art.88(2) of the EC Treaty,[202] to implement the decision properly (see 5–016, *supra*). In such case it would have to prove the existence of such a situation of *force majeure*[203] but may plead it only for the period necessary in order to resolve the difficulties.[204] In compliance with the duty of cooperation imposed by Art.10 of the EC Treaty, the Member State must inform the Commission of the difficulties arising in applying a Community provision, with a view to their seeking a solution together. If the Member State does not do so, its *force majeure* defence will fail because the Member State will in any event be in breach of that obligation to cooperate.[205]

IV. CONSEQUENCES

A. RESULT OF THE ACTION

Declaratory judgment. The Court of Justice either finds the infringement made out or dismisses the application.[206] The judgment finding the failure to fulfil obligations is purely declaratory. The infringement existed before the Court made its finding. It does not have the power to require specific measures to be taken in order to give effect to the judgment. At the most, it may indicate such measures as it considers necessary in order to eliminate

5–063

---

[200] ECJ, Case C–414/97 *Commission v Spain* [1999] E.C.R. I–5585, paras 18–19.
[201] ECJ, Case C–519/03 *Commission v Luxembourg* [2005] E.C.R. I–3067, para.22: plea raised for the first time in the rejoinder was inadmissible.
[202] See, *e.g.* ECJ, Case the C–415/03 *Commission v Greece* [2005] E.C.R. I–3875, paras 42–43.
[203] ECJ, Case 52/84 *Commission v Belgium* [1986] E.C.R. 89, para.14; ECJ, Case 213/85 *Commission v Netherlands* [1988] E.C.R. 281, paras 22–25.
[204] ECJ, Case C–1/00 *Commission v France* [2001] E.C.R. I–9989, para.131.
[205] ECJ, Case 52/84 *Commission v Belgium* [1986] E.C.R. 89, para.16. See also ECJ, Case C–349/93 *Commission v Italy* [1995] E.C.R. I–343, para.13; ECJ, Case C–348/93 *Commission v Italy* [1995] E.C.R. I–673, para.17; ECJ, Case C–99/02 *Commission v Italy* [2004] E.C.R. I–3353, paras 16–18 and ECJ, Case C–415/03 *Commission v Greece* [2005] E.C.R. I–3875, para.43, in which the Court held that the condition that it be absolutely impossible to implement a decision is not fulfilled where the defendant government merely informs the Commission of the legal, political or practical difficulties involved in implementing the decision, without taking any real step to recover the aid from the undertakings concerned, and without proposing to the Commission any alternative arrangements for implementing the decision which could have enabled the difficulties to be overcome. For an example of a breach of the duty to cooperate in good faith, see ECJ, Case C–82/03 *Commission v Italy* [2004] E.C.R. I–6635.
[206] If the Court does not have sufficient information to find that the act of the Member State constitutes a failure to fulfil obligations, it may ask the parties to resume examination of the question at issue and report to it, after which the Court will give final judgment (see ECJ, Case 170/78 *Commission v United Kingdom* [1980] E.C.R. 417, para.24).

the infringement found.[207] In addition, the Court may not set a period of time for compliance with its judgment, since Art.228 of the EC Treaty does not confer a power on it to do so.[208] Equally, the Court may not declare acts (or failures to act) on the part of a Member State unlawful, void or not applicable. Only the national courts have the power to do so under national law.[209] The Court of Justice may find only that the act (or failure to act) was or was not contrary to Community law.

B. LEGAL FORCE OF THE JUDGMENT DECLARING THAT A MEMBER STATE HAS FAILED TO FULFIL ITS OBLIGATIONS

5–064   **Duty for the Member State to take the necessary measures.** Art.228(1) of the EC Treaty puts the Member State which has been found by the Court of Justice to have failed to fulfil its Treaty obligations under a duty to take the necessary measures to comply with the Court's judgment. That duty, which also arises because the judgment has the force of *res judicata*, entails a prohibition having the full force of law against applying a national rule held to be incompatible with Community law and an obligation to take every measure to enable Community law to be fully applied.[210] The duty to give effect to the Court's judgment is borne by all institutions of the Member State concerned within the fields covered by their respective powers. The legislative and executive authorities have to bring the offending provisions of domestic law into conformity with the requirements of Community law. The courts of the Member State concerned have to disregard those provisions in determining cases.[211]

Because the judgment has the force of *res judicata*, the Commission may not make an application for interim measures pursuant to Art.243 of the EC Treaty in order to require the Member State to desist from an infringement of Community law which has already been found by judgment of the Court of Justice. This is because the Member State is required to take the necessary measures under Art.228(1) of the EC Treaty. No further decision of the Court, in interlocutory or other proceedings, is required.

---

[207] In the reasoned opinion, the Commission may prescribe the measures which it deems necessary in order to eliminate the infringement. In addition, in a procedure under Art.88(2) of the EC Treaty, the Commission may adopt a decision finding that a measure constitutes aid incompatible with the common market and requiring the unlawfully granted aid to be repaid. If the Member State concerned fails to comply with that decision, the Commission may bring an action in the Court for failure to fulfil the specific obligation to obtain repayment of the aid (ECJ, Case 70/72 *Commission v Germany* [1973] E.C.R. 813, para.13) (see 5–016, *supra*).

[208] ECJ, Case C–473/93 *Commission v Luxembourg* [1996] E.C.R. I–3207, para.52.

[209] Opinion of Advocate General G. Reischl in Case 141/78 *France v United Kingdom* [1979] E.C.R. 2923, at 2946.

[210] ECJ, Case 48/71 *Commission v Italy* [1972] E.C.R. 527, para.7; ECJ (order of March 28, 1980), Joined Cases 24 and 97/80 R *Commission v France* [1980] E.C.R. 1319, para.16; ECJ, Case C–101/91 *Commission v Italy* [1993] E.C.R. I–191, para.24.

[211] ECJ, Joined Cases 314–316/81 and 83/82 *Waterkeyn* [1982] E.C.R. 4337, para.14.

Where the Commission sought such interim measures, the Court held that they were not necessary within the meaning of Art.243 of the EC Treaty.[212]

Court may limit the temporal effects. Exceptionally, by virtue of the general principle of legal certainty inherent in the Community legal order, the Court may limit the effects in time of a judgment given on the basis of Art.226 of the EC Treaty.[213] The declaratory nature of the judgment does not preclude the Court from deciding, in application of that general principle, to restrict the right to rely upon a provision it has interpreted with a view to calling in question legal relations established in good faith. The Court will only take such a step in exceptional circumstances. The fact that a finding of failure to fulfil obligations (which is invariably coupled, explicitly or implicitly, with an interpretation of the applicable provision of Community law) will have serious financial consequences for the Member State concerned is not sufficient in itself to justify limiting the scope of the judgment.[214]   **5–065**

Position of individuals. The judgment finding the infringement of Community law does not as such confer any rights on individuals. Individuals may not rely directly on such a judgment before the national courts, but only on the "provision" of Community law having direct effect which the judgment finds has been infringed by the Member State.[215]   **5–066**

In the event that an individual pleads a provision of Community law in his defence which does not have direct effect, but which has been found by the Court of Justice to have been infringed by the Member State concerned, the national court, as an institution of that Member State, must ensure in the exercise of its functions that it is complied with by applying national law in such a way that it is compatible with the obligations that — according to the judgment of the Court—ensue from Community law for that Member State.

Judgment may constitute the basis for State liability. The finding of a failure to fulfil obligations may potentially form the basis for liability on the part of the Member State concerned.[216] However, it appears from the case-   **5–067**

---

[212] ECJ (order of March 28, 1980), Joined Cases 24 and 97/80 R *Commission v France* [1980] E.C.R. 1319, para.19.

[213] ECJ, Case C–426/98 *Commission v Greece* [2002] E.C.R. I–2793, para.43. *Cf.* ECJ, Case C–359/97 *Commission v United Kingdom* [2000] E.C.R. I–6355, paras 91–96, in which the Court avoided this question of principle.

[214] ECJ, Case C–35/97 *Commission v France* [1998] E.C.R. I–5325, paras 49–52; ECJ, Case C–426/98 *Commission v Greece* [2002] E.C.R. I–2793, paras 42–44.

[215] ECJ, Joined Cases 314–316/81 and 83/82 *Waterkeyn* [1982] E.C.R. 4337, paras 15–16.

[216] ECJ, Case 39/72 *Commission v Italy* [1973] E.C.R. 102, para.11; ECJ, Case 309/84 *Commission v Italy* [1986] E.C.R. 599, para.18; ECJ, Case 240/86 *Commission v Greece* [1988] E.C.R. 1835, para.14; ECJ, Case C–287/87 *Commission v Greece* [1990] E.C.R. I–125; ECJ, Case C–249/88 *Commission v Belgium* [1991] E.C.R. I–1275, para.41.

law that a Member State may incur liability only in the case of a sufficiently serious breach of Community law.[217] A judgment finding a failure to fulfil obligations is in itself not enough, certainly not for loss or damage which arose before judgment was given. The requirement for a "sufficiently serious breach" of Community law does not square completely with the strict or objective nature of an action for failure to fulfil obligations,[218] since the Court of Justice also takes other factors into account where the Member State had a discretion in applying Community law, such as whether or not the breach was intentional and whether any mistake of law was excusable. It is self-evident that if the failure to fulfil obligations continues after delivery of the judgment declaring the Member State concerned to be in breach of its obligations, that itself will constitute a sufficiently serious breach of Community law and cause the Member State to incur liability to make good any loss or damage which occurred in that period (see 3–043, *supra*).

In addition, it must be noted that the Community provision infringed must confer a "right" on individuals in order for the issue of State liability to arise.[219] It follows that a finding of an infringement in proceedings under Arts 226–227 of the EC Treaty does not automatically result in the Member State concerned incurring liability under Community law. Yet it may well be that the Member State will incur liability in damages under national law for loss or damage caused by an infringement of a Community provision even though that provision does not directly confer any "right" on individuals.

5–068   **Period within which the Member State must comply with the judgment.** The Treaty itself does not specify the period within which the judgment must be complied with, but the Court of Justice has held that the process must be initiated at once and completed as soon as possible.[220]

---

217 ECJ, Joined Cases C–46 and C–48/93 *Brasserie du Pêcheur and Factortame* (*Factortame IV*) [1996] E.C.R. I–1029, para.93.
218 Moreover, there is no need for the Court of Justice to have made a finding that the Member State is in breach in order for the Member State to incur liability. The national courts may themselves find that the Member State has infringed Community law. If difficulties arise in this connection, they may always enlist the help of the Court of Justice by making a reference for a preliminary ruling. This power of the national courts is important. Since the Commission has a discretion whether to bring proceedings under Art.226 of the EC Treaty, individuals may play a major, complementary role in enforcing Community law by invoking *Francovich* liability in national courts (*cf.* ECJ, Case C–91/92 *Faccini Dori* [1994] E.C.R. I–3325, paras 27–29); see in particular Curtin, "De rechtstreekse werking van richtlijnen" (1993) S.E.W. 93, at 96.
219 Schockweiler, "La responsabilité de l'autorité nationale en cas de violation du droit communautaire" (1992) R.T.D.E. 27, at 48.
220 ECJ, Case 69/86 *Commission v Italy* [1987] E.C.R. 773, para.8; ECJ, Case 169/87 *Commission v France* [1988] 4093, para.14; ECJ, Case C–345/92 *Commission v Germany* [1993] E.C.R. I–1115, para.6; ECJ, Case C–334/94 *Commission v France* [1996] E.C.R. I–1307, para.31; ECJ, Case C–387/97 *Commission v Greece* [2000] E.C.R. I–5047, para.82.

C. Sanctions for failure to comply with the judgment

Art.228(2) of the EC Treaty. The Commission is responsible for ensuring   5–069
that the judgment finding a breach of Community law is complied with. If
the Member State fails to take the necessary measures, under the first para.
of Art.228(2) of the EC Treaty the Commission must first give it written
notice, giving it an opportunity to submit any observations. It then issues a
reasoned opinion "specifying the points on which the Member State
concerned has not complied with the judgment of the Court of Justice". If
the Member State then fails to take the necessary measures within the
time-limit laid down by the Commission, it may be brought before the
Court of Justice again with a view to a finding that it has failed to comply
with the original judgment (or to give effect to it in time or correctly). In
bringing the case before the Court, the Commission may specify such lump
sum or penalty payment to be paid by the Member State as it considers
appropriate in the circumstances.[221]

In proceedings under Art.228(2) of the EC Treaty, the Court of Justice
has jurisdiction to assess the suitability and effectiveness of any measures
which the Member State has taken in compliance with the original
judgment. The Commission must provide the Court with the information
necessary to determine the extent to which a Member State has complied
with a judgment declaring it to be in breach of its obligations.[222] As that
judgment has the force of *res judicata*, the dispute as to the original failure
to fulfil obligations may not be reopened in proceedings under Art.228(2)
of the EC Treaty. The only matter in issue is the alleged failure to give
effect to the original judgment.

Lump sum or penalty payment. The Court may impose a lump sum or   5–070
penalty payment pursuant to the third subpara. of Art.228(2) of the EC
Treaty in the event that it finds that the original judgment has not been
complied with. Whilst the imposition of a penalty payment seems particularly suited to inducing a Member State to put an end as soon as
possible to a breach of obligations which, in the absence of such a measure,
would tend to persist, the imposition of a lump sum is based more on an
assessment of the effects on public and private interests of the failure of the
Member State concerned to comply with its obligations, in particular where
the breach has persisted for a long period since the judgment which initially

---

[221] In the "Communication from the Commission—Memorandum on applying Art.171 *[now Art.228]* of the EC Treaty" (96/C 242/07; [1996] O.J. C 242/6), the Commission expresses a preference for penalty payments on the ground that this is the most appropriate instrument for securing compliance with the judgment as rapidly as possible. The amount of the payment should be calculated in the light of the seriousness of the infringement, its duration and the need to ensure that the penalty itself is a deterrent to future infringements. See on this subject, Masson, ""L'obscure clarté" de l'article 228 § 2 CE" (2004) R.T.D.E. 639–668.

[222] ECJ, Case C–387/97 *Commission v Greece* [2000] E.C.R. I–5047, para.73.

established it. Even where the Commission has in its application asked only for the imposition of a daily penalty payment, the Court of Justice may have recourse to both types of penalty provided for in Art.228(2) of the EC Treaty. The imposition of such a "double" penalty is appropriate in particular where the breach of obligations has continued for a long period and tends to persist.[223]

5–071 **Court's discretion.** Where the Court imposes a penalty payment, its amount (which must ensure that penalty payments have coercive force and that Community law is applied uniformly and effectively) must be determined having regard to the duration of the infringement, its degree of seriousness and the ability of the Member State to pay. Regard should also be had to the effects of failure to comply on private and public interests and to the urgency of getting the Member State concerned to fulfil its obligations.[224] Where a Member State has taken certain measures—but not all that are needed—to comply with the Court's judgment finding that it has failed to fulfil its obligations, the amount of the penalty payment will take account of the progress which it has made in complying with its obligations.[225]

5–072 **New failure to comply with the judgment.** Failure to comply with a judgment constitutes an infringement of Art.228 of the EC Treaty and may therefore give rise in its turn to a finding of liability on the part of the Member State concerned.

V. The Constitution

5–073 Arts III-360 and III-361 of the Constitution reproduce the provisions of Arts 226 and 227 of the EC Treaty *verbatim*.[226] However, with respect to the Court's jurisdiction to impose a lump sum or a penalty payment on a Member State, the rather inefficient procedure at present provided for in

---

[223] ECJ (judgment of July 12, 2005), Case C–304/02 *Commission v France*, not yet reported, paras 80–86 and 89–95. According to the Court (para.83), the conjunction 'or' in Art.228(2) of the EC Treaty to link the financial penalties capable of being imposed may, linguistically, have an alternative or a cumulative sense and must therefore be read in the context in which it is used. In light of the objective pursued by Art.228 of the EC Treaty, the conjunction 'or' in Art.228(2) must be understood as being used in a cumulative sense.

[224] *Ibid.*, para.92; ECJ, Case C–278/01 *Commission v Spain* [2003] E.C.R. I–14141, para.52. For an exhaustive discussion of whether a judgment of the Court of Justice imposing a penalty payment on a Member State is or is not "enforceable", see Härtel, "Durchsetzbarkeit von Zwangsgeld-Urteilen des EuGH gegen Mitgliedstaaten" (2001) EuR. 617–630.

[225] ECJ, Case C–278/01 *Commission v Spain* [2003] E.C.R. I–14141, para.50.

[226] Regrettably, Art.III–360 of the Constitution mentions a failure of a Member State to fulfil "an obligation *under the Constitution*" (italics added). It would have been possible to incorporate the *acquis communautaire* by mentioning instead a failure to fulfil "an obligation under the law of the Union".

Art.228 of the EC Treaty has been modified. Indeed, as the law stands at present it is only when a Member State fails to comply with a judgment of the Court of Justice finding an infringement that the Commission can initiate new proceedings before the Court—after having completed another two-stage pre-litigation procedure (letter of formal notice and reasoned opinion)—in which it asks the Court to impose a pecuniary sanction upon the Member State concerned. As a result, Art.228 of the EC Treaty has so far been applied on only a few occasions since it was incorporated into the Treaty in 1993.[227]

Changes. Art.III-362 of the Constitution provides that where a Member State has failed to fulfil its obligation to notify[228] measures transposing a European framework law,[229] the Commission may bring a case before the Court asking the latter to find an infringement *and* to impose a pecuniary sanction. The obligation to make payment would take effect on the date set by the Court in its judgment. By contrast, as far as other infringements are concerned, *e.g.* incorrect implementation of European framework laws and other violations of Union law, the imposition of a pecuniary sanction would still be conditional upon a first judgment of the Court of Justice finding against the Member State and non-compliance with the judgment by the Member State concerned. However, the Constitution renders the second action somewhat less onerous by doing away with the need for a reasoned opinion in the pre-litigation stage. So, if in the future—when the Constitution has entered into force—the Commission considers that a Member State has not taken the necessary measures to comply with a judgment of the Court finding an infringement, it will be able to bring an action before the Court in which it asks for the imposition of a pecuniary sanction, after having invited the Member State concerned to submit its observations.[230]

5–074

Retroactive pecuniary sanctions. The authors of the Constitution did not consider it necessary explicitly to grant jurisdiction to the Court to impose pecuniary sanctions retroactively (as from the first day of the infringement). A provision in that regard was not necessary since the current Art.228(2) of the EC Treaty allows the Court to impose, not only a penalty payment to be paid per day of infringement as from the day the judgment is given, but also a lump sum which can be determined having regard to the gravity of the infringement in the period preceding the judgment.[231]

5–075

---

[227] ECJ, Case C–387/97 *Commission v Greece* [2000] E.C.R. I–5047; ECJ, Case C–278/01, *Commission v Spain* [2003] E.C.R. I–14141; ECJ (judgment of July 12, 2005), Case C–304/02 *Commission v France*, not yet reported.
[228] According to document CONV 734/03, this is where the Member State has not taken any implementing measure.
[229] Constitution, Art.III–362(3).
[230] Constitution, Art.III–362(2).
[231] CONV 734/03; see also the Opinion of Advocate-General L. A. Geelhoed of April 29, 2004 in ECJ (judgment of July 12, 2005), Case C–304/02 *Commission v France*, not yet reported, paras 81–108.

CHAPTER 6

INTERPRETATION OF COMMUNITY LAW BY WAY OF PRELIMINARY RULING

6–001 **Topics to be discussed.** The request for a preliminary ruling[232] on the interpretation of Community law raises three specific questions. The first relates to the *subject-matter* of the preliminary ruling on interpretation, in other words, to what provisions and principles may be interpreted by the Court of Justice. The second relates to the *content* of the preliminary ruling on interpretation and the related limits set to the jurisdiction of the Court of Justice. Thirdly, there is the question of the *consequences* of a preliminary ruling.

These three questions will be considered in turn.

I. SUBJECT-MATTER OF AN INTERPRETATION BY WAY OF PRELIMINARY RULING

6–002 **General.** According to Art.234 of the EC Treaty, the jurisdiction of the Court of Justice to give preliminary rulings on interpretation extends to "this Treaty" and "acts of the institutions of the Community and of the ECB [European Central Bank]". The wording of Art.150 of the EAEC Treaty is similar.

The upshot is that, as far as the subject-matter of a reference for a preliminary ruling is concerned, the Court has parallel jurisdiction to give preliminary rulings on interpretation under the two Treaties. This covers the Treaties themselves, acts of the Community institutions, including international agreements concluded by the Community and acts of bodies set up by such agreements, and provisions of Community law to which national law refers.

---

[232] For the mechanism of cooperation between national courts and the Court of Justice and the general requirements which requests for preliminary rulings have to satisfy, see Ch.2, *supra*. Art.234 is the only form of action provided for in the EC Treaty allowing the Community judicature to rule on the interpretation of a Community act: CFI (order of February 28, 2005), Case T–108/03 *Von Pezold v Commission*, not yet reported, paras 56–58.

A. THE TREATIES

Notion of Treaty. The Treaties establishing the European Communities **6–003** (EC and EAEC Treaties) constitute the "basic constitutional charter".[233] They are the written constitution surmounting the hierarchy of Community norms and consequently are the first instruments whose interpretation may form the subject-matter of preliminary rulings by the Court of Justice.

What is meant is the Treaties establishing the Communities and all amendments thereto, the treaties and acts relating to the accession of new Member States, complementary "treaties", such as the former (1957) "Convention on certain institutions common to the European Communities"[234] and the former (1965) "Treaty establishing a Single Council and a Single Commission of the European Communities" (the "Merger Treaty"; see Art.30 thereof),[235] and all the annexes and protocols annexed to the Treaty, which have the same legal force as the Treaties themselves.[236]

Not all of the Single European Act (1986) and the Treaty on European Union (1992) relate to the European Communities. Consequently, only those parts of them relating to Community law fall within the Court's jurisdiction to give preliminary rulings on interpretation under Art.234 of the EC Treaty (EU Treaty, Arts 46 to 53; see also Ch.4, *supra*, and Ch.22, *infra*).

Treaty status also has to be given to such provisions, adopted by the Council by means of a special procedure, as it "shall recommend to the Member States for adoption in accordance with their respective constitu-

---

[233] ECJ, Case 294/83 *Les Verts v European Parliament* [1986] E.C.R. 1339, para.23.

[234] Convention on certain institutions common to the European Communities, in *European Union. Selected instruments taken from the Treaties* (Book I, Office for Official Publications of the European Communities, Luxembourg, 1995), Vol.I, at 683–696.

[235] *Ibid.*, 697–737. This Treaty and the Convention cited in the preceding n. have been repealed by Art.9(1) of the Treaty of Amsterdam ([1997] O.J. C340/76-77). Most of their provisions had been incorporated in the Community Treaties. As for the remainder, Art.9(2) to (7) of the Treaty of Amsterdam set out to retain their essential elements (*ibid.*).

[236] EC Treaty, Art.311; EAEC Treaty, Art.207. The principal protocols are those on the Statute of the European Investment Bank, on the Statute of the Court of Justice, and on the Privileges and Immunities of the European Communities, together with the seventeen protocols appended to the EC Treaty by the EU Treaty. For the text of the protocols, see *European Union. Selected instruments taken from the Treaties* (Book I, Office for Official Publications of the European Communities, Luxembourg, 1999), Vol.I. See also the further protocols annexed by the Treaty of Amsterdam to the EC Treaty ([1997] O.J. C340/103–110), to the EU Treaty and the EC Treaty (*ibid.*, 93–102) and to the EU Treaty and the three Community Treaties (*ibid.*, 111–114). For a practical example, see ECJ, Case C–147/95 *Evrenopoulos* [1997] E.C.R. I–2057, in which the Court of Justice gave a ruling on the interpretation of the Protocol on Art.114 of the EC Treaty. At the same time, a whole series of declarations of intergovernmental conferences relating to various provisions of the Treaties accompany the Treaties (especially the Single European Act, the EU Treaty, the Treaty of Amsterdam and the Treaty of Nice as well as a series of declarations on various provisions of the Treaties). Although those declarations do not have the status of legislation (and hence certainly not the status of treaties), their content may be taken into account in interpreting the provisions to which they relate (for the text of the declarations, see the references cited above).

tional requirements".[237] The provisions decided upon by the Council do not enter into force until they have been adopted by all Member States (by act of parliament or after a referendum, depending on the "constitutional requirements" of each Member State). Once they have been so adopted, they obtain Treaty status in the hierarchy of norms of Community law.[238]

6–004 **General principles of Community law.** The unwritten general principles of Community law, including fundamental rights, may also be the subject of a reference for a preliminary ruling on interpretation. Those principles form part of the "law" which the Court of Justice has to ensure is observed in the interpretation and application of the Treaties (EC Treaty, Art.220; EAEC Treaty, Art.136). Examples are the principles of equal treatment, proportionality and *nec bis in idem* and the rights of the defence prior to the adoption of an individual decision having adverse effect.[239] Naturally, a preliminary ruling on the interpretation of those principles may be sought only in connection with the application of substantive Community law, that is to say, in connection with main proceedings relating (at least to some extent) to Community law.[240]

B. Acts of Community institutions

6–005 **All acts of Community institutions.** All acts of Community institutions may be the subject of a request for a preliminary ruling on their interpretation, irrespective of whether the act is specifically mentioned in the Treaties[241] or

---

[237] See, *inter alia*, Art.22 of the EC Treaty (adding to rights arising out of citizenship of the Union); Art.190(4) of the EC Treaty (determining a uniform procedure for elections to the European Parliament; see the Act concerning the election of the representatives of the Assembly by direct universal suffrage, annexed to the Council Decision of September 20, 1976, [1976] L 278/1, as amended by Council Decision of February 1, 1993, [1993] O.J. L33/15); Art.229a of the EC Treaty (conferring jurisdiction on the Court of Justice in disputes relating to the application of acts creating Community industrial property rights) and Art.269 of the EC Treaty (determining the system of the Community's own resources).

[238] See Isaac, *Droit communautaire général* (Masson, Paris, 1990), at 281; *cf.* Joliet, *Le contentieux*, at 190–191.

[239] The "interpretation" of the principle concerned is concealed behind the appraisal of the "validity" of an inferior provision of Community law. See ECJ, Joined Cases 41, 121 and 796/79 *Testa* [1980] E.C.R. 1979, para.21; ECJ, Case 265/87 *Schräder* [1989] E.C.R. 2237, paras 20–24; ECJ, Case C–331/88 *Fedesa and Others* [1990] E.C.R. I–4023, paras 12–14.

[240] ECJ, Case C–144/95 *Maurin* [1996] E.C.R. I–2909, paras 12–13; ECJ, Case C–299/95 *Kremzow* [1997] E.C.R. I–2629, paras 15–19. For further particulars, see Lenaerts and Van Nuffel, *Constitutional Law of the European Union*, §17–065–§ 17–090, at 711–739. See also 6–024, *infra*.

[241] In Art.249 of the EC Treaty or elsewhere in the Treaties, such as the Rules of Procedure of the institutions (EC Treaty, Arts 199, 207(3) and 218(2)), the Financial Regulation (EC Treaty, Art.279) or the measures provided for in the third indent of Art.202 of the EC Treaty ("Comitology Decision": Council Decision 1999/468/EC of June 28, 1999 laying down the procedures for the exercise of implementing powers conferred on the Commission [1999] O.J. L184/23).

not,[242] whether it is binding or non-binding[243] or whether or not it has direct effect.[244]

Act must be attributable to Community institution(s). The sole criterion is whether the act may be ascribed to a Community institution. The Court of Justice has held that no such act was involved in the case of an agreement concluded between national central insurance bureaux relating to the Green Card Scheme pursuant to Council Directive 72/166 on insurance against civil liability in respect of the use of motor vehicles. The agreement could not be considered an act of a Community institution on the ground that "no Community institution or agency took part in its conclusion", even though the conclusion of the agreement was a precondition for the entry into force of the directive and the length of time for which the directive was applicable was determined by the agreement's duration. It made no difference that the Commission had consistently stated, in a recommendation and in successive decisions, that the agreement complied with the directive's requirements or that it was annexed to a Commission decision and published with it in the *Official Journal*. This did not mean that the agreement itself was the work of a Community institution.[245]

6–006

The test that a Community institution or body must have "taken part" in the conclusion of the act in order for it to be amenable to interpretation by the Court of Justice in Art.234 proceedings is, in all likelihood, open to flexible application. There are many ways in which a Community institution or body might conceivably "take part" in the conclusion of an act. Thus, the test is satisfied in the case of international agreements concluded by the

---

[242] *E.g.* a Council resolution: ECJ, Case 9/73 *Schlüter* [1973] E.C.R. 1135, para.40.

[243] *E.g.* a recommendation (or opinion) within the meaning of Art.249 of the EC Treaty: ECJ, Case 113/75 *Frecassetti* [1976] E.C.R. 983, paras 8–9; ECJ, Case C–322/88 *Grimaldi* [1989] E.C.R. 4407, paras 7–9. As a result of the principle of cooperation in good faith, national courts are bound to take recommendations into consideration in order to decide disputes referred to them, in particular where they cast light on the interpretation of national measures adopted in order to implement them or where they are designed to supplement binding Community provisions.

[244] *E.g.* ECJ, Case 32/74 *Haaga* [1974] E.C.R. 1201, para.1; ECJ, Case 111/75 *Impresa Costruzioni Comm. Quirino Mazzalai* [1976] E.C.R. 657, para.7–9; ECJ, Case 14/83 *Von Colson and Kamann* [1984] E.C.R. 1891, para.27; ECJ, Case C–261/95 *Palmisani* [1997] E.C.R. I–4025, para.21; ECJ, Case C–373/95 *Maso and Others* [1997] E.C.R. I–4051, para.28. Irrespective of whether the Community measure has direct effect, its interpretation will be useful to the national court, which, as a public body, is required under Art.10 of the EC Treaty to apply its domestic legislation in conformity with the requirements of Community law (see also ECJ, Case 31/87 *Beentjes* [1988] E.C.R. 4635, para.39; ECJ, Case C–106/89 *Marleasing* [1990] E.C.R. I–4135, paras 8–9; see the case note by Stuyck and Wytinck (1991) C.M.L.Rev. 205–223).

[245] ECJ, Case 152/83 *Demouche and Others* [1987] E.C.R. 3833, paras 15–21; see also an earlier case, ECJ, Case 116/83 *Fantozzi* [1984] E.C.R. 2481, para.11. *Cf.* ECJ, Case C–193/98 *Pfennigmann* [1999] E.C.R. I–7747, paras 16–20, in which the Court held that an Agreement of February 9, 1994 concluded pursuant to Directive 93/89/EC between the governments of certain Member States on the levying of charges for the use of certain roads by heavy commercial vehicles could not be regarded as Community law. As a result, the Court had no competence to interpret it.

Community and of (binding and non-binding) acts adopted by bodies set up by such agreements (since the Community participates in the operation of such bodies).

New forms of regulatory activity within the Community will make it necessary to take a creative approach to this test. An example may be found in the Title of the EC Treaty concerning social policy. Under Art.139 of the EC Treaty, management and labour may conclude agreements at Community level. The question is whether, in certain circumstances, such agreements may also be the subject of a reference for a preliminary ruling. Such agreements are intended to be an alternative to the Community legislation contemplated by Art.137 of the EC Treaty. In addition, before submitting proposals for legislation to the Council, the Commission has to consult management and labour and, if they express a wish to that effect, must give them the opportunity to conclude an agreement on the content of the proposal (EC Treaty, Art.138). Lastly, "[a]greements concluded at Community level shall be implemented . . . in matters covered by Art.137, at the joint request of the signatory parties, by a Council decision on a proposal from the Commission" (adopted by the voting method specified in Art.137) (EC Treaty, Art.139(2)). Although, strictly speaking, Community institutions or bodies do not play any part in drawing up the agreements to be concluded by management and labour at Community level, it may perhaps be accepted, in the light of the contribution they make, that they "take part" to a sufficient extent in the conferral of legal force on the agreements, as a result of the Council decisions implementing them, as to make them qualify for preliminary rulings by the Court of Justice.[246] The position will be different, of course, where the agreements are implemented, not by Council decision, but "in accordance with the procedures and practices specific to management and labour and the Member States" (the other alternative set out in Art.139(2) of the EC Treaty). The main reason for taking this view is that it is stated in Declaration No 27 annexed to the Treaty of Amsterdam that "the content of [such] agreements" is to be developed "by collective bargaining according to the rules of each Member State" and that there is therefore "no obligation on the Member States to apply the agreements directly or to work out rules for their transposition, nor any obligation to amend national legislation in force to facilitate their implementation". Precisely the opposite situation obtains where the agreements are implemented by Council decision, which means that the aim of the procedure of preliminary rulings on interpretation may be achieved in full in that case.

6–007 **Notion of Community institution.** The question also arises as to what is the precise meaning of the expression "institutions of the Community" in indent (b) of the first para.of Art.234 of the EC Treaty. The Court of

---

[246] An action for annulment may lie against such a Council decision: see CFI, Case T–135/96 *UEAPME v Council* [1998] E.C.R. II–2335.

Justice has interpreted it broadly by referring to a "Community institution or agency", which must have taken part in the conclusion of the relevant act.[247] It appears from this that the expression covers any Community body in addition to the "institutions of the Community" referred to in Art.7 of the EC Treaty.

It is self-evident that all measures adopted by the Council, the Commission or the European Parliament and the Council jointly may be the subject of a reference for a preliminary ruling on their interpretation. In the overwhelming majority of cases, Community decision-making results in such an act in one form or another (see EC Treaty, Art.249).

Acts of the European Parliament and the Court of Auditors also come under the jurisdiction of the Court of Justice to give preliminary rulings on interpretation,[248] albeit it is rarer for the interpretation of such acts to be relevant to the determination of main proceedings before a national court.[249]

Judgments of the Court of Justice. Preliminary rulings may also be sought   6–008
on the interpretation of judgments of the Court of Justice. For instance, an interpretation of a previous judgment may be sought in the event that the national court has difficulty in understanding or applying it.[250] The judgment to be interpreted does not have to be a preliminary ruling; it may have been given in any sort of proceedings.[251]

Commentators have long been divided on this issue. Those arguing that judgments of the Court could be the subject of a reference for a preliminary ruling did so chiefly on the basis of the wording of Art.234 of the EC Treaty: the Court of Justice is an "institution" of the Community and so its "acts" (judgments/orders) may be interpreted by way of preliminary ruling.[252] Those taking the opposite view contended that the subject-matter of a reference for a preliminary ruling on the interpretation of an earlier

---

[247] ECJ, Case 152/83 *Demouche* [1987] E.C.R. 3833, para.19.
[248] For acts of the European Parliament, see Dumon, "La Cour de justice: Questions préjudicielles", in *Les Novelles: Droit des Communautés européennes* (Larcier, Brussels, 1969), at 341–366; Vandersanden and Barav, *Contentieux communautaire* (Bruylant, Brussels, 1977), at 296; for acts of the Court of Auditors, see *Commentaire Mégret*, at 212.
[249] Rideau and Picod, *Code de procédures juridictionnelles*, at 291.
[250] ECJ (order of March 5, 1986), Case 69/85 *Wünsche* [1986] E.C.R. 947, para.15; ECJ, Case 14/86 *Pretore di Salò v X* [1987] E.C.R. 2545, para.12. For an example, see ECJ, Joined Cases C–363 and C–407–411/93 *Lancry and Others* [1994] E.C.R. I–3957; ECJ, Case C–280/94 *Posthuma-van Damme and Oztürk* [1996] E.C.R. I–179, para.13; ECJ, Case C–5/97 *Ballast Nedam Groep* [1997] E.C.R. I–7549, para.1; ECJ, Case C–219/98 *Anastasiou and Others* [2000] E.C.R. I–5241, paras 13–14; ECJ, Case C–224/01 *Köbler* [2003] E.C.R. I–10239.
[251] See, for example, ECJ, Joined Cases 314–316/81 and 83/82 *Waterkeyn* [1982] E.C.R. 4337: interpretation of the scope and legal effects of a judgment given pursuant to Art.226 of the EC Treaty.
[252] Chevallier and Maidani, *Guide pratique. Art.177* [now Art.234] (Office for Official Publications of the European Communities, Luxembourg, 1982), 121 pp.; Vandersanden and Barav, *Contentieux communautaire*, at 296.

judgment was in fact not the judgment as such but the provisions and principles of Community law applied or interpreted therein.[253]

The distinction is perhaps not as clear-cut as it seems. The Court of Justice allows national courts and tribunals to refer questions to it on the interpretation of its previous judgments, but in answering them, it inevitably falls back on the provisions and principles of Community law underlying those judgments. This is also true where national courts apply to the Court of Justice for an interpretation of a judgment of the Court of First Instance. The possibility of making such a reference is of great practical importance for national courts where they query whether a judgment of the Court of First Instance against which no appeal has been brought before the Court of Justice correctly interprets the principles and provisions of Community law with which it deals.

6–009 **Acts of European Central Bank.** Alongside acts of "institutions of the Community", since the EU Treaty entered into force, indent (b) of the first para.of Art.234 of the EC Treaty has expressly mentioned acts of the European Central Bank. Consequently, a preliminary ruling may also be sought from the Court of Justice on the interpretation of its acts.

6–010 **Acts of Community bodies and agencies.** The fact that only the European Central Bank is also mentioned in Art.234 of the EC Treaty does not mean that acts of other Community bodies may not be the subject of a reference for a preliminary ruling.[254] The correct position is that acts of bodies which have been established by Community institutions in the exercise of their powers and given specific executive tasks (and the associated power to take decisions) may form the subject of a request for a preliminary ruling. As has already been pointed out, the Court of Justice requires Community institutions or bodies to have taken part in the adoption of an act in order for it to be capable of being the subject of an Art.234 reference on its interpretation. That requirement is certainly fulfilled in the case of the

---

[253] Joliet, *Le contentieux*, at 193; Kovar, "Cour de justice. Recours préjudiciel en interprétation et en appréciation de validité—Examen de la question préjudicielle par la Cour de justice" (1991) J.C.D.I. Vol. 161–26–2, No 24, referring to ECJ, Case 135/77 *Bosch* [1978] E.C.R. 855 and ECJ, Joined Cases 87, 112 and 113/79 *Bagusat and Others* [1980] E.C.R. 1159; see also the Opinion of Advocate General J.-P. Warner in ECJ, Case 8/78 *Milac* [1978] E.C.R. 1721, at 1740–1741. Brealey and Hoskins, *Remedies in E.C. Law*, at 204, also take the view that judgments of the Court of Justice are not open to review in the context of preliminary ruling proceedings: they refer to ECJ (order of March 5, 1986), Case 69/85 *Wünsche* [1986] E.C.R. 947, paras 10–16.

[254] Art.III–369, first para., of the Constitution provides that the Court of Justice of the European Union has jurisdiction to give preliminary rulings concerning the interpretation of the Constitution, as well as the validity and the interpretation of acts of the institutions, bodies, offices and agencies of the Union. Art.III–369 thus incorporates the *acquis communautaire* by formally extending the Court's preliminary jurisdiction to cover acts of bodies, offices and agencies of the Union.

agencies, offices, foundations and other "bodies" established by the Community institutions.[255]

Acts of committees. The European Economic and Social Committee and the Committee of the Regions, which assist the Council and the Commission in an advisory capacity (EC Treaty, Art.7), are not institutions or bodies whose acts are amenable to interpretation by the Court of Justice pursuant to Art.234 of the EC Treaty. The Opinions which they deliver form part of the decision-making process carried out between the Commission, the Council and (generally) the European Parliament. They have no independent existence and could, at the most, be used to help interpret acts where they took part in the process of their adoption.[256]   **6–011**

Acts of European Council. The European Council is not an institution of the Community[257]; in principle, its acts fall outwith the Court's jurisdiction to give preliminary rulings on interpretation. Nevertheless, some have argued that it should be equated with the Community institutions for the purposes of Art.234 on the ground that it has to provide the Union (and hence the Community) with the necessary impetus for its development and to define general political guidelines (EU Treaty, Art.4).[258] Exceptionally, the European Council itself plays a formal role in the Community's decision-making process[259] or serves as the forum for the adoption of a decision of the Heads of State or Government meeting in the European Council.[260] As such, those acts do not give rise to references for preliminary rulings from national courts, although they may well have to be interpreted by the Court of Justice in conjunction with the Community acts or Treaty provisions to which they relate in order to determine the precise implications of those acts or provisions.   **6–012**

---

[255] See the list set out in Art.1 of the Decision taken by common agreement between the Representatives of the Governments of the Member States, meeting at Head of State or Government level, on the location of the seats of certain bodies and departments of the European Communities and of Europol, [1993] O.J. C323/1. See also Lenaerts, "Regulating the Regulatory Process: 'Delegation of Powers' in the European Community" (1993) E.L.Rev. 23, at 45–46.

[256] *Commentaire Mégret*, at 212–213.

[257] The Constitution promotes the European Council to the status of an institution. See Art.I–19. When the Constitution enters into force, the Court will therefore have jurisdiction also to give rulings on preliminary references concerning the interpretation and the validity of acts of the European Council.

[258] Rideau and Picod, *Code de procédures juridictionnelles*, at 291.

[259] EC Treaty, Art.99—adoption of a conclusion on the broad guidelines of the economic policies of the Member States and the Community, on the basis of which the Council is to adopt a recommendation.

[260] See with regard to the position of Denmark in the European Union, [1992] O.J. C348; see also Curtin and Van Ooik, "De bijzondere positie van Denemarken in de Europese Unie" (1993) S.E.W. 675–689.

C. International Agreements Concluded by the Community and Acts of Bodies Established by Such Agreements

6–013 **Agreements concluded by the Community.** Not only acts adopted by Community institutions autonomously, but also "contractual" acts, are covered by indent (b) of the first para.of Art.234. Thus, the Court of Justice has held that it has jurisdiction to give preliminary rulings on the interpretation of international agreements concluded by the Community.[261]

6–014 **Agreements concluded by the Community and the Member States.** The question arises as to whether in the case of a mixed agreement concluded by the Community and the Member States jointly with a third country the jurisdiction of the Court extends to rulings interpreting provisions of the agreement by which the Member States enter into commitments *vis-à-vis* that country by virtue of their own powers. The Court of Justice first left this question expressly open.[262] It was able to do so because it could take the view that the provisions whose interpretation was sought fell partly within the Community's powers to guarantee commitments towards the non-member country concerned. The fact that the Member States had to carry out the commitments was irrelevant because in doing so they were simply fulfilling an obligation in relation to the Community[263] and did not

---

[261] ECJ, Case 181/73 *Haegeman* [1974] E.C.R. 449, paras 1–6; for examples, see ECJ, Case 87/75 *Bresciani* [1976] E.C.R. 129; ECJ, Case 65/77 *Razanatsimba* [1977] E.C.R. 2229; ECJ, Case C–18/90 *Kziber* [1991] E.C.R. I–199; ECJ, Case C–432/92 *Anastasiou and Others* [1994] E.C.R. I–3087; ECJ, Case C–113/97 *Babahenini* [1998] E.C.R. I–183; ECJ, Case C–321/97 *Andersson and Wåkerås-Andersson* [1999] E.C.R. I–3551, paras 23–33. It is clear from this judgment that the Court of Justice has jurisdiction to interpret the EEA Agreement. However, the interpretation is binding only on the Community and not on the EFTA States. The EFTA Court is empowered to give rulings on the interpretation of the EEA Agreement which are applicable in the EFTA States. See also ECJ, Case C–213/03 *Syndicat professionnel coordination des pêcheurs de l'étang de Berre et de la région* [2004] E.C.R. I–7357; ECJ, Case C–265/03 *Simutenkov*, [2005] E.C.R. I–2579.

[262] ECJ, Case 12/86 *Demirel* [1987] E.C.R. 3719, para.9; ECJ, Case C–53/96 *Hermès International* [1998] E.C.R. I–3603, paras 24–33; see also Bontinck, "The TRIPs Agreement and the ECJ: A New Dawn? Some Comments about Joined Cases C–300/98 and C–329/98, Parfums Dior and Assco Gerüste" available from *www.jeanmonnetprogram.org/papers*; Neframi, "La competence de la Cour de justice pour interpreter l'Accord TRIPs selon l'arrêt 'Parfums Christian Dior'" (2001) R.D.U.E. 491–519, who emphasises moreover that the Court can rule only on the direct effect of a provision of a mixed agreement in so far as the agreement falls within the substantive sphere of competence of the Community; Koutrakos, "The Interpretation of Mixed Agreements under the Preliminary Reference Procedure" (2002) E.For.Aff.Rev. 25–52; Snyder, "The gatekeepers: the European Courts and WTO Law" (2003) C.M.L.Rev. 313–367.

[263] EC Treaty, Art.10; ECJ, Case 104/81 *Kupferberg* [1982] E.C.R. 3641. See also ECJ, Case C–439/01 *Cipra and Kvasnicka* [2003] E.C.R. I–745, paras 23–24 with respect to the AETR Agreement (European Agreement concerning the Work of Crews of Vehicles engaged in International Road Transport). The Court held, after having recalled that in ratifying or acceding to that agreement, the Member States had acted in the interest and on behalf of the Community, that it forms part of Community law and hence that it has jurisdiction to interpret it: ECJ, Case C–439/01 *Cipra and Kvasnicka* [2003] E.C.R. I–745, paras 23–24.

assume, *vis-à-vis* the non-member country, the Community's responsibility for the due performance of the agreement.[264]

In *Parfums Christian Dior*[265] the Court held, however, that it had jurisdiction to interpret Art.50 of TRIPs[266] (a procedural provision conferring on the judicial authorities of the Contracting Parties the authority to order prompt and effective provisional measures to prevent a threatened or suspected infringement of any intellectual property right from occurring) both in situations falling within the scope of the national law of the Member States and in those coming under Community law. The Court inferred its interpretative jurisdiction from the finding that Art.50 of TRIPs constitutes a procedural provision which should be applied in the same way in every situation falling within its scope (both situations covered by national law and situations covered by Community law) and that that obligation requires the judicial bodies of the Member States and the Community, for practical and legal reasons, to give it a uniform interpretation.

Lately the Court of Justice seems to consider itself competent to interpret any provision of a mixed agreement if the agreement concerns a field in large measure covered by Community law.[267]

Pre-existing agreement in an area of Community competence. For the purposes of the Court's jurisdiction to give preliminary rulings on interpretation, international agreements by which the Community is bound by way of substitution for the Member States are treated in the same way as international agreements concluded by the Community. In this way, the Court of Justice has held that it has jurisdiction to give preliminary rulings on the interpretation of the GATT (General Agreement on Tariffs and Trade) of 1947 on the ground that, since the Common Customs Tariff entered into effect, the Community has been substituted for the Member

6–015

---

[264] Likewise the Court considers that it has no jurisdiction under Art.234 of the EC Treaty to interpret a provision of an agreement concluded between a number of Member States, not even if the agreement was concluded pursuant to a Community directive: ECJ (order of November 12, 1998), Case C–162/98 *Hartmann* [1998] E.C.R. I–7083, paras 8–10.

[265] ECJ, Joined Cases C–300/98 and C–392/98 *Parfums Christian Dior and Others* [2000] E.C.R. I–11307, paras 32–40, with a case note by Heliskoski (2002) C.M.L.Rev. 159–174. See also ECJ, Case C–89/99 *Schieving-Nijstad and Others* [2001] E.C.R. I–5851, para.30; ECJ, Case C–245/02 *Anheuser-Busch* [2004] E.C.R. I–10989, paras 40–46.

[266] On the WTO and the competence of the Community and the Member States for matters falling within the scope of the WTO, see Lenaerts and Van Nuffel, *Constitutional Law of the European Union*, § 20–002–§ 20–014, at 828–843.

[267] In the *Anheuser-Busch* case, the Court deemed itself competent to interpret Art.16 of TRIPs, a substantive provision concerning the rights conferred on the owner of a registered trade-mark, after having stressed, however, that the Community is under an obligation to interpret its trade-mark legislation, as far as possible, in the light of the wording and purpose of TRIPs : ECJ, Case C–245/02 *Anheuser-Busch* [2004] E.C.R. I–10989, paras 40–46. See also as far as actions under Art.226 of the EC Treaty are concerned, ECJ, Case C–239/03 *Commission v France* [2004] E.C.R. I-9325, paras 22–31.

States as regards fulfilment of the commitments laid down in the GATT, the result being that "the provisions of GATT should, like the provisions of all other agreements binding the Community, receive uniform application throughout the Community".[268]

It is striking that the Court of Justice assumed jurisdiction to give preliminary rulings simply by referring to the aim of that jurisdiction, namely "to ensure the uniform interpretation of Community law"[269] (thereby completely ignoring the lack of any actual connection between the GATT of 1947 and any act of a Community institution, whereas such a connection does, of course, exist in the case of international agreements concluded by the Community).

6–016 **Acts of bodies established by international agreements.** That same aim of the Court's jurisdiction to give preliminary rulings on interpretation has prompted it to hold that it may give preliminary rulings on the interpretation of binding and non-binding acts of bodies established by international agreements concluded by the Community. Thus, the Court has held that decisions of an Association Council form an integral part of Community law on account of their direct connection with the agreement itself.[270] Since the function of Art.234 of the EC Treaty is to ensure the uniform application throughout the Community of all provisions forming part of the Community legal system and to ensure that their effects do not vary according to the interpretation accorded to them in the various Member States, the Court of Justice must have jurisdiction to give preliminary rulings on the interpretation, not only of the agreement itself, but also of decisions of the body established by the agreement and entrusted with responsibility for its implementation.[271]

D. PROVISIONS OF COMMUNITY LAW TO WHICH NATIONAL LAW REFERS

6–017 **The *Dzodzi* case-law.** In 1990 the Court of Justice considerably extended its jurisdiction to give preliminary rulings on interpretation (after Advocate General M. Darmon had delivered an Opinion proposing that it should not

---

[268] ECJ, Joined Cases 267–269/81 *SPI and SAMI* [1983] E.C.R. 801, paras 14 and 15–19.

[269] *Ibid.*, para.15.

[270] ECJ, Case 30/88 *Greece v Commission* [1989] E.C.R. 3711, para.13.

[271] ECJ, Case C–192/89 *Sevince* [1990] E.C.R. I–3461, paras 9–11; see also ECJ, Case C–237/91 *Kus* [1992] E.C.R. I–6781; ECJ, Case C–188/91 *Deutsche Shell* [1993] E.C.R. I–363 (the latter case was concerned with the interpretation of a non-binding act, which was of interest to the national court because it wanted to apply its national law as consistently as possible with that act on account of the obligation of cooperation in good faith borne by the Member State of which that court was a body); ECJ, Case C–277/94 *Taflan-Met and Others* [1996] E.C.R. I–4085; ECJ, Case C–171/95 *Tetik* [1997] E.C.R. I–329; ECJ, Case C–351/95 *Kadiman* [1997] E.C.R. I–2133; ECJ, Case C–386/95 *Eker* [1997] E.C.R. I–2697; ECJ, Case C–285/95 *Kol* [1997] E.C.R. I–3069; ECJ, Case C–36/96 *Günaydin* [1997] E.C.R. I–5143; ECJ, Case C–98/96 *Ertanir* [1997] E.C.R. I–5179; ECJ, Case C–210/97 *Akman* [1998] E.C.R. I–7519; ECJ, Case C–1/97 *Birden* [1998] E.C.R. I–7747; ECJ, Case C–329/97 *Ergat* [2000] E.C.R. I–1487; ECJ, Case C–275/02 *Ayaz* [2004] E.C.R. I-8765.

do so): "It does not appear either from the wording of Art.177 [*now Art.234*] or from the aim of the procedure introduced by that article that the authors of the Treaty intended to exclude from the jurisdiction of the Court requests for a preliminary ruling on a Community provision in the specific case where the national law of a Member State refers to the content of that provision in order to determine rules applicable to a situation which is purely internal to that State".[272] The Court stated that it was "manifestly in the interest of the Community legal order that, in order to forestall future differences of interpretation, every Community provision should be given a uniform interpretation irrespective of the circumstances in which it is to be applied".[273]

Dzodzi remains within the confines of the interpretation of Community law, although it breaks new ground because it accepts that Community law is being applied, not by virtue of its own authority, but by virtue of that of national law, and that this does not prevent the Court ruling on its interpretation.[274] The Court of Justice also accepts jurisdiction to give preliminary rulings on interpretation on the same terms where provisions of Community law are applicable for the resolution of a dispute by virtue of a contractual relationship between the parties.[275]

Limits of *Dzodzi*. The Court has jurisdiction only to interpret Community law; it cannot "take account of the general scheme of the provisions of domestic law which, while referring to Community law, define the extent of

6–018

---

[272] ECJ, Joined Cases C–297/88 and C–197/89 *Dzodzi* [1990] E.C.R. I–3763, para.36. See also ECJ, Case C–28/95 *Leur-Bloem* [1997] E.C.R. I–4161, para.27; ECJ, Case C–130/95 *Giloy* [1997] E.C.R. I–4291, para.23; ECJ, Case C–247/97 *Schoonbroodt* [1998] E.C.R. I–8095, para.41; ECJ, Case C–2/97 *IP* [1998] E.C.R. I–8597, para.59 (where the Court found that the national legislature had not referred to Community law in order to treat a purely domestic situation in the same way as a situation governed by Community law. Whilst *Leur-Bloem* was referred to as "settled case-law", it did not apply to this case); ECJ (order of April 26, 2002), Case C–454/00 *Vis Farmaceutici Istituto Scientifico delle Venezie*, not reported, paras 21–24; ECJ, Case C–222/01 *British American Tobacco Manufacturing* [2004] E.C.R. I–4683, paras 40–41.

[273] *Dzodzi*, cited in the preceding n., para.37; ECJ, Case C–43/00 *Andersen og Jensen* [2002] E.C.R. I–379, para.18. By recognising its interpretative jurisdiction the Court avoids the provisions of Community law in issue taking on a life of their own. If the Court of Justice refused—in a case like *Dzodzi*—to accede to a request from the national court to provide the correct interpretation of the provisions in question, a national court could in a future case in which—by contrast to *Dzodzi*—Community law is applicable in its own right be more easily inclined to come to the (possibly wrong) conclusion that the answer to the question of interpretation is obvious (or already in existence) and that it is therefore under no obligation to seek a preliminary ruling. This would in turn put the uniform interpretation of Community law at risk. For an extensive discussion, see Lenaerts, "Prejudiciële uitlegging van het gemeenshapsrecht met het oog op toepassing van nationaal recht", *Mokaria*, Deventer, Kluwer, 2002, at 173–186. For a critical analysis, see Barav, "Une anomalie préjudicielle", in *50 ans de droit communautaire—Mélanges en hommage de Guy Isaac* (Presses de l'Université des Sciences sociales de Toulouse, Toulouse, 2004), at 773–801; see also Lefevre, "The interpretation of Community law by the Court of Justice in areas of national competence" (2004) E.L.Rev. 29, at 501–516.

[274] For other applications, see ECJ, Case C–231/89 *Gmurzynska-Bscher* [1990] E.C.R. I–4003; ECJ, Case C–384/89 *Tomatis and Fulchiron* [1991] E.C.R. I–127.

[275] ECJ, Case C–88/91 *Federconsorzi* [1992] E.C.R. I–4035.

that reference". The Court drew the demarcation line between its own jurisdiction and that of the national court in the following terms: "Consideration of the limits which the national legislature may have placed on the application of Community law to purely internal situations, to which it is applicable only through the operation of the national legislation, is a matter for domestic law and hence falls within the exclusive jurisdiction of the courts of the Member States".[276]

Indeed the Court has consistently held that it has no jurisdiction to rule on questions of national law which remain unanswered in the order for reference, even if this means that it has to consider different hypotheses in interpreting Community law.[277]

Moreover, it is on account of the same limitation of its jurisdiction to give preliminary rulings that the Court refuses to rule on the interpretation of provisions of international law (e.g. of an agreement) which are binding on Member States outside the confines of Community law.[278]

---

[276] *Dzodzi* (cited in n. 272), para.42. In *Leur-Bloem* and *Giloy* (cited in n. 272), the Court held, however, that in every case where it had held that it had jurisdiction to give preliminary rulings on questions concerning Community provisions in situations where the facts of the cases being considered by the national courts were outside the scope of Community law, the application of the provisions of Community law was manifestly not limited by provisions of domestic law or contractual provisions incorporating those Community provisions (*Leur-Bloem*, para.27, and *Giloy*, para.23). See also ECJ, Case C–1/99 *Kofisa Italia* [2001] E.C.R. I–207, paras 18–33; ECJ, Case C–267/99 *Adam* [2001] E.C.R. I–7467, paras 27–31. The position was different in *Kleinwort Benson* (ECJ, Case C–346/93 *Kleinwort Benson* [1995] E.C.R. I–615). In that case, the Court of Appeal made a reference to the Court of Justice pursuant to the Protocol of June 3, 1971 on a provision of the Brussels Convention. The Court of Justice held that it had no jurisdiction to answer the question on the ground that the dispute in the main proceedings was concerned with the interpretation not of the relevant provision of the Brussels Convention as such, but of a provision of domestic law (the Civil Jurisdiction and Judgments Act 1982) modelled on the Convention and partially reproducing its terms. The Court of Justice further found that the Act provided for the national authorities to adopt modifications designed to produce divergence between provisions of the act and corresponding provisions of the Convention. The Court properly inferred from this that the provisions of the Convention could not be regarded as having been rendered applicable as such in cases outwith the scope of the Convention by the law of the Contracting State concerned. The Court went on to observe that, in applying the provisions of national law modelled on the Brussels Convention, the national courts were not bound by its case-law but were required only to have regard to it (see also the case note by Betlem (1996) C.M.L.Rev. 137–147, who even argues that the Court lacks jurisdiction to give preliminary rulings on questions such as those referred in the *Dzodzi* case; a less extreme position is taken by Poilvache, "Compétence préjudicielle et dispositions nationales inspirées du droit communautaire" (1998) J.T.D.E. 121–125, who mentions some examples from Belgian law in which the legislature took over Community provisions expressly and unconditionally). See with regard to the question as to what extent national courts may request a preliminary ruling from the Court of Justice in applying national competition law—which is largely inspired by the relevant Treaty provisions—Attew, "National Competition Law and the Preliminary Ruling Procedure (2002) E.J.L.Ref. 241–257.

[277] See Wils, *Prejudiciële vragen van Belgische rechters en hun gevolgen* (Preadvies, Vereniging voor de vergelijkende studie van het recht van België en Nederland) (Tjeenk Willink, Zwolle, 1993), at 14–15.

[278] ECJ, Case 130/73 *Vandeweghe and Others* [1973] E.C.R. 1329, para.2; ECJ, Case 44/84 *Hurd* [1986] E.C.R. 26, para.20.

II. Content of a Preliminary Ruling on Interpretation

Interpretation v. application. The Treaty does not define precisely what is   **6–019**
meant by "interpretation" of Community law in the context of the
preliminary ruling procedure.[279] Initially, the Court of Justice strongly
emphasised the distinction between interpretation and application, which
was also to demarcate the respective functions of the Court of Justice and
the national courts.[280] At the same time, however, it referred to "the special
field of judicial cooperation under Art.177 [*now Art.234*] which requires the
national court and the Court of Justice, both keeping within their respective
jurisdiction, and with the aim of ensuring that Community law is applied in
a unified manner, to make direct and complementary contributions to the
working out of a decision".[281]

Judicial cooperation. Since then, the idea of "judicial cooperation" has got   **6–020**
the upper hand over the distinction between interpretation and application,[282] the aim being to ensure that the main proceedings are determined
in a way which secures the uniform "application" of Community law.

This is why the Court of Justice regularly refers to "the need to afford a
helpful interpretation of Community law".[283] Such an interpretation can be
confined very specifically to the facts and points of national law underlying
the national proceedings as they emerge from the "documents before the
Court".[284] The documents in the case from which the Court derives the
relevant facts and points of national law include not only the order for
reference and the file submitted by the national court, but also the
observations of the parties to the main proceedings, the Member States, the
Commission and the Council or the European Parliament (where an act of

---

[279] See ECJ, Case 13/61 *Bosch and Others* [1962] E.C.R. 45, where the Court of Justice held
that "since the question what is meant in Art.177 [*now Art.234*] by 'the interpretation of
Community law' may itself be a matter of interpretation, it is permissible for the national
court to formulate its request in a simple and direct way".

[280] ECJ (order of June 3, 1964), Case 6/64 *Costa v ENEL* [1964] E.C.R. 614, at 614–615; ECJ,
Case 20/64 *Albatros* [1965] E.C.R. 29, at 34; ECJ, Case 13/68 *Salgoil* [1968] E.C.R. 453, at
459–460.

[281] ECJ, Case 16/65 *Schwarze* [1965] E.C.R. 877, at 886; ECJ, Joined Cases C–260/00 to C–
263/00 *Lohmann and Medi Bayreuth* [2002] E.C.R. I–10045, para.26, where the Court stated
in connection with a preliminary question concerning a tariff classiciation in the Combined
Nomenclature that "its task is to provide the national court with guidance on the criteria
which will enable the latter to classify the products at issue correctly in the [Combined
Nomenclature], rather than to effect that classification itself".

[282] For a critical approach to the distinction between interpretation and application, see
Donner, "Uitlegging en toepassing", in *Miscellanea W.J. Ganshof van der Meersch*
(Bruylant, Brussels, 1972), Vol.II, at 103 *et seq.*; see also the Opinion of Advocate General
D. Ruiz-Jarabo Colomer in ECJ, Case C–30/02 *Recheio* [2004] E.C.R. I–6051, points 23–36,
at I–6053.

[283] ECJ, Case 244/78 *Union Laitière Normande* [1979] E.C.R. 2663, para.5.

[284] ECJ, Case 311/85 *VVR* [1987] E.C.R. 3801, para.11.

the Council or the Parliament is at issue in the proceedings) submitted pursuant to Art.23 of the Statute of the Court of Justice.

6–021 **The Court of Justice does not rule on facts and points of national law.** It is essential in this connection that the "matters disclosed by the documents before the Court" are not disputed,[285] since the Court is not entitled to find the facts and points of national law in *inter partes* proceedings,[286] or to verify whether they are correct.[287] Where, however, the facts and points of national law are agreed as between the "parties" (being all the parties participating in the legal debate before the Court under Art.23 of the Statute), there is nothing to prevent the Court from spelling out its understanding of the facts and points of national law as its starting point for its "useful" (*i.e.* specific) interpretation of the applicable provisions and principles of Community law.[288]

More specifically, in answering questions on interpretation which in fact are designed to bring to light a possible inconsistency of national law as compared with Community law,[289] it is important for the Court to be able to base itself on the undisputed facts and points of national law set out by the "defendant" government in its observations.[290]

The Court of Justice may also ask the national court or the government concerned to elucidate certain facts and points of national law and, if those explanations are not contested, take account of them in the judgment giving a preliminary ruling.[291] A request to the national court will be based on Art.104(5) of the ECJ Rules of Procedure. Generally, a request to the national government will be informal in the shape of a letter from the Registrar, but it may if necessary be made in the form of an order of the Court prescribing measures of inquiry within the meaning of Art.45(2) of the ECJ Rules of Procedure (request for information and production of documents).[292] Other measures of inquiry, such as taking oral testimony,

---

[285] It is for this reason that the Court refers to the fact that the observations submitted are "not disputed", see *ibid.*, paras 13–17. The Court disregards observations of interested parties within the meaning of Art.23 of the Statute which contradict information in the order for reference (ECJ, Case C–153/02 *Neri* [2003] E.C.R. I–13555, paras 33–36; ECJ, Case C–267/03 *Lindberg* [2005] E.C.R. I–3247, paras 41–42).

[286] ECJ, Case 17/81 *Pabst & Richarz* [1982] E.C.R. 1331, paras 10–12.

[287] ECJ, Case 104/77 *Oehlschläger* [1978] E.C.R. 791, para.4. See also ECJ, Joined Cases C–482/01 and C–493/01 *Orfanopoulos and Oliveri* [2004] E.C.R. I–5257, para.42: it is not for the Court, in the context of a reference for a preliminary ruling, to rule on the interpretation of national provisions or to decide whether the referring court's interpretation thereof is correct.

[288] See, for a very explicit example, ECJ, Case 311/85 *VVR* [1987] E.C.R. 3801, paras 16–18.

[289] This is an accepted feature of the preliminary ruling procedure, see ECJ, Case 26/62 *Van Gend & Loos* [1963] E.C.R. 1, at 10–11 and 13.

[290] See, for example, Case 33/88 *Allué and Others* [1989] E.C.R. 1591, para.12.

[291] ECJ, Case C–343/90 *Lourenço Dias* [1992] E.C.R. I–4673, para.52; ECJ (order of March 12, 2004), Case C–54/03 *Austroplant-Arzneimittel*, not reported, para.14.

[292] See, for example, ECJ, Case 148/77 *Hansen* [1978] E.C.R. 1787, at 1790, from which it

commissioning an expert's report and inspections of a place or thing, are not formally precluded in proceedings for a preliminary ruling on the interpretation of Community law, but probably go too far in practice because they are intrinsically intended to determine or verify contested facts and points of national law and the Court of Justice has indeed no jurisdiction to do this.[293]

Reformulation of questions. In order to arrive at a "useful interpretation", the Court of Justice often has to rework the questions to some extent before answering them (see 2–021, *supra*). It will do this where the questions referred are too vague, for instance where they do not refer specifically to any provision or principle of Community law,[294] or are deficient in other respects.[295] In such cases, the Court will specify and flesh out the questions in the light of the particulars set out in the order for reference and in the national case-file. Sometimes, too, a great many questions are referred and the Court prunes them back somewhat [296] or the questions are put in a very complicated way (divided into propositions and sub-propositions) and the Court has first to identify the core issue raised.[297] This exercise often makes it unnecessary to answer some of the questions referred.[298]

6–022

---

appears that the Court decided "to open the procedure without any preparatory inquiry", but "requested the Government of the Federal Republic of Germany, the Government of the French Republic and the Commission of the European Communities to provide written answers to a certain number of questions before the opening of the oral procedure". Germany had submitted observations to the Court pursuant to Art.23 of the Statute, but France had not, so that the questions were intended to involve that State in the proceedings, which is what happened; see *ibid.*, at 1798–1799.

[293] This is because, when ruling on the interpretation or validity of Community provisions, the Court of Justice is empowered to do so only on the basis of the facts which the national court puts before it (ECJ, Case C–418/01 *IMS Health and Others* [2004] E.C.R. I–5039, para.18). See Pescatore, "Art.177 [*now Art.234*]", in *Traité instituant la CEE. Commentaire article par article* (Economica, Paris, 1992), 1073, No 61, at 1115–1116.

[294] ECJ, Case 10/71 *Muller* [1971] E.C.R. 723; ECJ, Case 251/83 *Haug-Adrion* [1984] E.C.R. 4277, paras 6–11.

[295] ECJ, Joined Cases 141–143/81 *Holdijk* [1982] E.C.R. 1299; ECJ, Case C–237/94 *O'Flynn* [1996] E.C.R. I–2617, paras 24–25.

[296] See, for example, ECJ, Joined Cases 115 and 116/81 *Adoui and Cornuaille* [1982] E.C.R. 1665.

[297] See, for example, ECJ, Case 266/81 *SIOT* [1983] E.C.R. 731, paras 10–13; ECJ, Joined Cases C–297/88 and C–197/89 *Dzodzi* [1990] E.C.R. I–3763, para.11: "The questions submitted for a preliminary ruling by the Tribunal de première instance essentially seek to establish whether, and in what circumstances, the Community provisions . . ."; para.14: "The questions submitted by the Cour d'appel, Brussels, ask the Court to interpret Arts 8 and 9 of Directive 64/221/EEC of February 25, 1964 . . .". Paras 11 to 15 of the judgment contain, under the heading "The object of the questions submitted to the Court", a meticulous analysis of the orders for reference (and the associated case-files) showing which provisions and principles of Community law raise difficulty for the referring courts.

[298] See, for example, Case 352/85 *Bond van Adverteerders* [1988] E.C.R. 2085, paras 40–41.

6–023 **No jurisdiction to rule on the compatibility of national rules with Community law.** The Court sometimes reworks the wording of the questions referred on account of the limits placed by the Treaty on its jurisdiction to give preliminary rulings. It has to do so because the Treaty "neither expressly nor by implication prescribes a particular form in which a national court must present its request for a preliminary ruling" and it therefore falls to the Court of Justice itself to decide "on that request only in so far as it has jurisdiction to do so, that is to say, only in so far as the decision relates to the interpretation" of Community law.[299]

This has occurred principally where questions were referred by which the national court sought a ruling on whether or not national provisions were consistent with Community law. Commonly, the national court puts the question of compatibility with Community law directly to the Court of Justice, as indeed is its right precisely because of the lack of any requirements as to the form in which questions are to be referred. Moreover, formulating questions directly in this way affords the advantage that there is no doubt as to the scope of the request for a preliminary ruling. Consequently, the referring court should not be concerned if the Court of Justice, referring to its settled case-law,[300] prefaces its judgment with the words "although in proceedings brought under Art.177 [*now Art.234*] of the Treaty, it is not for the Court to rule on the compatibility of national rules with provisions of Community law, the Court is competent to give a ruling on the interpretation of Community law in order to enable the national court to assess the compatibility of those rules with the Community provisions".[301] That caveat which the Court enters as regards the limits placed on its jurisdiction, however, does not lead it to give a somewhat abstract interpretation of the Community law at issue. On the contrary, the Court will reformulate the national court's questions in a particularly concrete manner. As a result, although they are primarily based on the interpretation of provisions or principles of Community law, the answers given will nevertheless at the same time be determinative of the outcome of the question of compatibility.[302]

---

[299] ECJ, Case 13/61 *Bosch and Others* [1962] E.C.R. 45.
[300] For the first of those cases, see ECJ, Case 6/64 *Costa v ENEL* [1964] E.C.R. 585, at 592–593.
[301] ECJ, Case C–130/93 *Lamaire* [1994] E.C.R. I–3215, para.10; ECJ, Joined Case C–37/96 and C–38/96 *Sodiprem and Others* [1998] E.C.R. I–2039, para.22; ECJ, Case C–399/98 *Ordine degli Architetti and Others* [2001] E.C.R. I–5409, para.49.
[322] See, as an example, *Lamaire*, para.11: "The national court's question asks essentially whether Arts 9 and 12 [*now Arts 23 and 25*] of the Treaty preclude national legislation from levying a compulsory contribution, such as the charge of BFR 2 per 100 kg of potatoes exported [to other Member States], provided for in Art.4(4) of the [Belgian] Royal Decree of May 15, 1986, as amended by the Royal Decree of July 14, 1987, on exports of agricultural products to other Member States". In answering that question, the Court of Justice came to the conclusion that "a compulsory contribution levied in respect of the exportation of potatoes, such as the charge levied for the National Board pursuant to

The issues raised must fall within scope of Community law. Where the question of interpretation referred by the national court is intended to test the compatibility of a national measure with the Treaty provisions on free movement of persons, goods or capital, the Court ascertains that the issues raised in the main proceedings have points of connection with a situation coming under Community law. This is because if the issues raised in the main proceedings relate to activities which are confined in all respects within a single Member State, the Treaty provisions on free movement are not applicable to the main proceedings and the Court will leave the preliminary question without a substantive answer.[303] For the purposes of assessing whether or not an issue is confined within a single Member State, the facts of the main proceedings are not conclusive, but rather the content and scope of the measure under consideration. Accordingly, the Court held that a tax levied by the municipality of Carrara on the export of marble outside the confines of the city did not relate to an internal situation even though the main proceedings were concerned with a purely local tax imposed by an Italian municipality on an Italian undertaking. The Court held that "the marble tax is imposed on all marble from Carrara that crosses that municipality's territorial boundaries, no distinction being made between marble the final destination of which is in Italy and marble destined for other Member States". As a result, "by its nature and terms, the marble tax therefore impinges on trade between Member States".[304]

6–024

Reference back to the national court. Where the Court of Justice interprets Community law in a case where certain relevant facts or points of national law have not yet been established in the main proceedings, it will indicate very precisely what findings the national court has to make in order to

6–025

Art.4(4) of the Belgian Royal Decree of May 15, 1986, as amended, must be regarded as a charge having equivalent effect to a customs duty on exports and as such prohibited by Arts 9 and 12 [*now Arts 23 and 25*] of the [EC] Treaty" (para.20). It then gave the same answer, couched in somewhat more neutral terms, in the operative part. Sometimes, the Court does not formulate the operative part neutrally and refers expressly to the provisions of national law as being compatible or incompatible with Community law: ECJ, Case C–130/92 *OTO* [1994] E.C.R. I–3281. For a critical appraisal, see the Opinion of Advocate General D. Ruiz-Jarabo Colomer in ECJ, Case C–30/02 *Recheio* [2004] E.C.R. I–6051, points 23–36, at I–6053.

[303] ECJ, Joined Cases C–54/88, C–91/88 and C–14/89 *Nino and Others* [1990] E.C.R. I–3537, paras 11–12; ECJ, Joined Cases C–29/94 to C–35/94 *Aubertin and Others* [1995] E.C.R. I–301, para.9; ECJ, Case C–134/95 *USSL No 47 di Biella* [1997] E.C.R. I–195, para.19; ECJ (order of October 6, 2005), Case C–328/04 *Vajnai*, not reported, paras 12–15.

[304] ECJ, Case C–72/03 *Carbonati Apuani* [2004] E.C.R. I–8027, para.26. See, to the same effect, ECJ, Case 286/81 *Oosthoek's Uitgeversmaatschappij* [1982] E.C.R. 4575, para.9; ECJ, Joined Cases C–277/91, C–318/91 and C–319/91 *Ligur Carni and Others* [1993] E.C.R. I–6621, paras 36–37; ECJ, Case C–254/98 *TK-Heimdienst* [2000] E.C.R. I–151, paras 27–31; ECJ, Case C–448/98 *Guimont* [2000] E.C.R. I–10663, paras 21–23. See also the Opinion of Advocate General L.A. Geelhoed in ECJ, Case C–515/99 *Reisch* [2002] E.C.R. I–2157, points 77–101, at I–2161.

resolve the case in accordance with its interpretation.[305] However, the Court of Justice may not abuse this sort of reference back to the national court by evading its responsibility for making the necessary appraisals in interpreting Community law, especially the fundamental provisions and principles.[306] The Court is under a duty to give the national court an answer which, in principle, will lead directly to the resolution of the case (at least as far as Community law is concerned). Only where, in the concrete context of the main proceedings some specific facts or points of national law require clarification in order to make a "useful interpretation" of Community law, will that clarification have to be made by the national court after the Court of Justice has clearly identified which facts and points of national law must be elucidated.[307] Where, by contrast, the Court of Justice is itself apprised of the uncontested facts and points of national law which are necessary in order to reach a decision in the main proceedings, then it has to have regard to those facts and points of law as such in making the "useful interpretation" of Community law expected by the national court.[308]

6–026 **Jurisdiction of the national court.** Naturally, it falls in any event to the national court to dispose of the case. In that sense, the judgment giving a ruling on interpretation, no matter to what extent it determines the outcome of the main proceedings, is always "preliminary", that is to say, given before the national court gives final judgment in the main proceedings.[309] However, the Court of Justice does not shrink from giving guidance based on the case-file and the written and oral observations which have been submitted to it, with a view to enabling the national court to give judgment on the application of Community law in the specific case with which it is having to deal.[310] The Court went a step further in dealing with a request for a preliminary ruling in a factually complex case on State liability

---

[305] For examples, see ECJ, Joined Cases 286/82 and 26/83 *Luisi and Carbone* [1984] E.C.R. 377, para.36; ECJ, Case 171/88 *Rinner-Kühn* [1989] E.C.R. 2743, paras 14–15; ECJ, Joined Cases C–184 and C–221/91 *Oorburg and Van Messem* [1993] E.C.R. I–1633; ECJ, Case C–127/92 *Enderby* [1993] E.C.R. I–5535, paras 26–29.

[306] See, for instance, the criticism in learned articles of ECJ, Case C–145/88 *Torfaen Borough Council* [1989] E.C.R. 3851, paras 15–17: Gormley (1990) C.M.L.Rev. 141, at 148; Pisuisse (1990) S.E.W. 599, at 604.

[307] However, the Court may, after hearing the Advocate General, request clarification from the national court (ECJ Rules of Procedure, Art.104(5)). For an illustration, see ECJ (order of March 12, 2004), Case C–54/03 *Austroplant-Arzneimittel*, not reported, para.14.

[308] See also Lenaerts, "Form and Substance of the Preliminary Rulings Procedure", in Curtin and Heukels (eds), *Institutional Dynamics of European Integration. Essays in Honour of H.G. Schermers* (Martinus Nijhoff, Dordrecht, 1994), Vol.II, 355, at 364–370.

[309] *Cf.* ECJ, Case 1/80 *Salmon* [1980] E.C.R. 1937, para.6.

[310] ECJ, Case C–328/91 *Thomas and Others* [1993] E.C.R. I–1247, para.13, ECJ, Case C–278/93 *Freers and Speckmann* [1996] E.C.R. I–1165, para.24; see also the more cautious terms employed in ECJ, Joined Cases C–46 and C–48/93 *Brasserie du Pêcheur and Factortame (Factortame IV)* [1996] E.C.R. I–1029, para.58, and ECJ, Case C–319/96 *Brinkmann* [1998] E.C.R. I–5255, para.29; ECJ, Case C–381/99 *Brunnhofer* [2001] E.C.R. I–4961, para.53.

for an alleged breach of Community law. While recognising that it was in principle for the national courts to verify whether or not the conditions governing State liability for a breach of Community law are fulfilled, the Court held that in the case in question it had all the necessary information to assess the acts of the Member State concerned itself.[311]

III. Consequences of a Preliminary Ruling on Interpretation

A. As regards the national court deciding the case at issue in the main proceedings

Binding effect. A judgment given by the Court under Art.234 is binding on the national court hearing the case in which the decision is given.[312] This is to be understood as meaning that all courts and tribunals dealing with the case, also at a later stage of the proceedings, on appeal or upon an appeal on a point of law, are obliged to comply with the substance of the judgment giving the preliminary ruling.[313]

6–027

The binding effect attaches to the whole of the operative part and main body of the judgment, since the operative part has to be understood in the light of the reasoning on which it is based.[314]

Naturally, the fact that the judgment given by way of preliminary ruling is binding does not mean that the national court has invariably to apply the provisions or principles of Community law elucidated thereby in reaching its decision in the main proceedings. It may be that that judgment specifically indicates why those provisions or principles are not applicable.[315]

New reference possible. The fact that a judgment given by way of a preliminary ruling is binding does not preclude the court to which the judgment is addressed, or another court involved in deciding the case, from making a further reference for a preliminary ruling to the Court of Justice if it considers such a step to be necessary in order to give judgment in the main proceedings.[316] Such a request will be justified "when the national court encounters difficulties in understanding or applying the judgment,

6–028

---

[311] ECJ, Case C–392/93 *British Telecommunications* [1996] E.C.R. I–1631, para.41; ECJ, Joined Cases C–283, C–291 and C–292/94 *Denkavit and Others* [1996] E.C.R. I–5063, para.49. *Cf.* ECJ, Case C–302/97 *Konle* [1999] E.C.R. I–3099, para.59, and ECJ, Case C–140/97 *Rechberger and Others* [1999] E.C.R. I–3499, paras 72–73. See also Lenaerts, "De feiten in het recht: kanttekeningen vanuit de Europese rechtspraak", in *Liber Amicorum W. van Gerven* (Kluwer, Antwerp, 2000), at 41–61.

[312] ECJ, Case 29/68 *Milch-, Fett-, und Eierkontor* [1969] E.C.R. 165, para.2; ECJ, Case C–446/98 *Fazenda Pública* [2000] E.C.R. I–11435, para.49.

[313] Pescatore (n.293, *supra*), No 65, at 1118; see also the general wording of ECJ, Case 52/76 *Benedetti* [1977] E.C.R. 163, para.26.

[314] ECJ, Case 135/77 *Bosch* [1978] E.C.R. 855, para.4.

[315] ECJ, Case 222/78 *ICAP* [1979] E.C.R. 1163, paras 7–12.

[316] See ECJ, Case 29/68 *Milch-, Fett-, und Eierkontor* [1969] E.C.R. 165, para.3.

when it refers a fresh question of law to the Court, or again when it submits new considerations which might lead the Court to give a different answer to a question submitted earlier".[317]

The validity of the judgment delivered previously cannot be contested by means of a further reference for a preliminary ruling "as this would call in question the allocation of jurisdiction as between national courts and the Court of Justice under Art.177 [*now Art.234*] of the Treaty".[318]

Furthermore, the initiative for making a fresh request for a preliminary ruling lies with the national court dealing with the main proceedings alone. The parties to those proceedings are not entitled to ask the Court of Justice to interpret an earlier preliminary ruling.[319] More generally, moreover, the Court has held that "Arts 38 to 41 [*now Arts 41 to 44*] of the Protocol on the Statute of the Court of Justice list exhaustively the exceptional review procedures available for challenging the authority of the Court's judgments; however, since there are no parties to proceedings in which the Court gives judgment by way of a preliminary ruling, the aforesaid articles do not apply to such a judgment".[320]

6–029 **Sanction for non-compliance.** In the event that the national court fails to comply with its obligation to follow the judgment giving the preliminary ruling, that court, as an institution of its Member State, will be in breach of Community law. This means that proceedings may be brought against that Member State under Arts 226–228 of the EC Treaty.[321] This may also result in domestic remedies being taken with a view to reversing the infringement of Community law or at least its consequences.[322]

B. As regards national courts generally

6–030 **Binding on all national courts.** The binding effect of a judgment by way of preliminary ruling extends further than to merely what is necessary to determine the main proceedings. It also applies outside the specific dispute in respect of which it was given to all national courts and tribunals, subject, of course, to their right to make a further reference on interpretation to the Court of Justice.[323] In the United Kingdom, this has been given effect by section 3(1) of the European Communities Act 1972, under which ques-

---

[317] ECJ, Case 14/86 *Pretore di Salòv* [1987] E.C.R. 2545, para.12.
[318] ECJ (order of March 5, 1986), Case 69/85 *Wünsche* [1986] E.C.R. 947, para.15.
[319] ECJ (order of May 16, 1968), Case 13/67 *Becher* [1968] E.C.R. 196; ECJ (order of October 18, 1979), Case 40/70 *Sirena* [1979] E.C.R. 3169, at 3170–3171.
[320] ECJ (order of March 5, 1986), Case 69/85 *Wünsche* [1986] E.C.R. 947, para.14.
[321] Pescatore (n.293, *supra*), No 65, at 1118. See also 5–032, *supra*.
[322] For examples, see Rideau and Picod, *Code de procédures juridictionnelles*, at 307.
[323] For an example, see ECJ, Case 68/74 *Alaimo* [1975] E.C.R. 109. The Court of First Instance is bound by a preliminary ruling of the Court of Justice, unless it appears that the latter court "based its assessment on inaccurate or incomplete information" (CFI, Case T–43/98 *Emesa Sugar v Council* [2001] E.C.R. II–3519, para.73).

tions of Community law shall, if not referred to the Court of Justice, be decided "in accordance with the principles laid down by and any relevant decision" of that Court.[324]

Declaratory nature of the interpretation. There are two arguments in favour of the generalisation of the binding effect of judgments by way of preliminary rulings. First, there is the fact that the interpretation is declaratory; it does not lay down any new rule, but is incorporated into the body of provisions and principles of Community law on which it is based. Consequently, the binding effect of the interpretation coincides with the binding effect of the provisions and principles on which it is based and which all national courts must respect.[325] It is, moreover, precisely because the interpretation has, by its very nature, such effect *erga omnes* that there are no "parties to proceedings",[326] but in contrast a system in which, alongside the parties to the main proceedings, the Commission, the Council and the European Parliament (where one of their acts is at issue) and all the Member States are entitled to submit observations pursuant to Art.23 of the Statute of the Court of Justice (and to take part in the oral procedure before the Court). The compass of the legal discussion which takes place before the Court accordingly corresponds with the scope of the judgment to be given.[327] It would therefore be wrong to seize on the idea that a judgment given in preliminary ruling proceedings has effects only *inter partes* on the ground that it is designed primarily to help the national court reach its decision in the main proceedings in which the question referred for a preliminary ruling arose. The *inter partes* aspect attaches only to the judicial decision in the main proceedings, including the way in which that decision deals with the judgment given by way of preliminary ruling, but it does not extend to that judgment itself.[328]

6–031

Uniformity in the application of Community law. Secondly, the purpose for which the preliminary ruling procedure exists, which is to secure uniformity in the application of Community law throughout the Member States, would be defeated if it were to be considered that a ruling under Art.234 had "no binding effect at all except in the case in which it was

6–032

---

[324] This provision was cited by Advocate General J.-P. Warner in his Opinion in Case 112/76 *Manzoni* [1977] E.C.R. 1647, at 1663.

[325] See to this effect Trabucchi, "L'effet *erga omnes* des décisions préjudicielles rendues par la CJCE" (1974) R.T.D.E. 56, at 76; Jeantet, "Originalité de la procédure d'interprétation du traité de Rome" (1966) J.C.P. Doctrine No 1987.

[326] ECJ (order of March 5, 1986), Case 69/85 *Wünsche* [1986] E.C.R. 947, para.14.

[327] It would seem from ECJ, Joined Cases 141–143/81 *Holdijk and Others* [1982] E.C.R. 1299, para.6, that the Court of Justice takes the same view.

[328] See, for instance, Joliet, *Le contentieux*, at 212–213.

given".[329] The Court of Justice assumes that, with the exception of any new feature necessitating a refinement or even a reversal of the existing case-law, the preliminary ruling provides all national courts and tribunals with an answer to the question of Community law which gave rise to the interpretation given.[330] This is underscored by Art.104(3) of the ECJ Rules of Procedure: "Where a question referred to the Court for a preliminary ruling is identical to a question on which the Court has already ruled . . . the Court may, after hearing the Advocate General, at any time give its decision by reasoned order in which reference is made to its previous judgment or to the relevant case-law". That provision combines with the practice of many years standing by which the Court informs the national court by letter from the Registrar that an earlier judgment has answered its question, and requests it to let it know whether in the circumstances it still wishes to pursue its request for a preliminary ruling (very often the national court will then withdraw its request).[331]

C. TEMPORAL EFFECTS

6-033   *Ex tunc* effect. In principle, the interpretation simply expresses what was contained *ab initio* in the provisions and principles of Community law to which it relates. Consequently, its temporal effects are the same as the effects of those provisions and principles, in other words, it is effective as from their entry into force or *ex tunc*.[332] This is the starting point for the Court's case-law: "The interpretation which, in the exercise of the jurisdiction conferred upon it by Art.177 [*now Art.234*], the Court of Justice gives to a rule of Community law clarifies and defines where necessary the meaning and scope of that rule as it must be or ought to have been understood and applied from the time of its entry into force. It follows that the rule as thus interpreted may, and must, be applied by the courts even to legal relationships arising and established before the judgment ruling on the request for interpretation, provided that in other respects the conditions

---

[329] Opinion of Advocate General J.-P. Warner in ECJ, Case 112/76 *Manzoni* [1977] E.C.R. 1647, at 1662–1663, where he went on to say as follows: "This, it seems to me, is where the doctrine of *stare decisis* must come into play. . . . It means that all Courts throughout the Community, with the exception of the Court itself, are bound by the *ratio decidendi* of a Judgment of this Court". He then referred to German legislation and the UK European Communities Act 1972, which confirm this binding effect; *cf.* Toth, "The Authority of Judgments of the European Court of Justice: Binding Force and Legal Effects" (1984) Y.E.L. 1, at 24.

[330] ECJ, Joined Cases 76, 86–89 and 149/87 *Seguela and Others* [1988] E.C.R. 2397, paras 11–14. For an express reversal of the case-law prompted by a new reference for a preliminary ruling, see ECJ, Case C–10/89 *CNL-SUCAL* [1990] E.C.R. I–3711, para.10; ECJ, Joined Cases C–267 and C–268/91 *Keck and Mithouard* [1993] E.C.R. I–6097; *cf.* Arnull, "Owning up to Fallibility: Precedent and the Court of Justice" (1993) C.M.L.Rev. 247.

[331] See Arnull (preceding n.), at 252.

[332] See Pescatore (n.293, *supra*), No 70, at 1120.

enabling an action relating to the application of that rule to be brought before the courts having jurisdiction, are satisfied".[333]

The proviso set out in the last sentence of that passage refers to the national procedural rules which continue to govern the conditions in which such a dispute may be brought before the courts (*e.g.* time limits and other procedural requirements). Admittedly the procedural rules must accord with Community law (see 3–001 to 3–003, *supra*), but their relevance—and hence the fact that they may prevent the dispute from being brought back before the courts—is not necessarily defeated by the effects *ex tunc* of the preliminary ruling on interpretation.[334]

Limitation of temporal effects. The only exception to the *ex tunc* rule arises out of "the general principle of legal certainty inherent in the Community legal order".[335] Pursuant to that principle, the Court may "be moved to restrict for any person concerned the opportunity of relying upon the provision as . . . interpreted with a view to calling into question legal relationships established in good faith. As the Court has consistently held, such a restriction may be allowed only in the actual judgment ruling upon the interpretation sought".[336] The national legislature or the domestic courts have no power to restrict the effects *ratione temporis* of a judgment given by way of preliminary ruling if the Court of Justice itself has not done so.[337] In practice, the Court of Justice weighs the principle of legal certainty—which is applied to obviate the serious effects which its judgment might have, as regards the past, on legal relationships entered into in good faith—against the principle of the uniform application of Community law.

Where the scales fall in favour of the principle of legal certainty, the Court declares that no reliance may be placed in the provision as interpreted in order to support claims concerning periods prior to the date

6–034

---

[333] ECJ, Case 61/79 *Denkavit Italiana* [1980] E.C.R. 1205, para.16; ECJ, Joined Cases 66, 127 and 128/79 *Salumi* [1980] E.C.R. 1237, para.9; ECJ, Case C–137/94 *Richardson* [1995] E.C.R. I–3407, para.31.

[334] The fact that the Court has given a preliminary ruling interpreting a provision of Community law without limiting the temporal effects of its judgment does not affect the right of a Member State to impose a time-limit under national law within which, on penalty of being barred, proceedings for repayment of charges levied in breach of that provision must be commenced (ECJ, Case C–88/99 *Roquette Frères* [2000] E.C.R. I–10465, para.36).

[335] ECJ, Case 24/86 *Blaizot* [1988] E.C.R. 379, para.28; ECJ, Case C–72/03 *Carbonati Apuani* [2004] E.C.R. I–8027, para.37.

[336] *Blaizot*, cited in the preceding n., para.28.

[337] ECJ, Case 309/85 *Barra* [1988] E.C.R. 355, para.13, at 375: "[T]he Court has consistently held that such a restriction may be allowed only in the judgment ruling upon the interpretation sought. The fundamental need for a general and uniform application of Community law implies that it is for the Court of Justice alone to decide upon the temporal restrictions to be placed on the interpretation which it lays down." See also Alexander, "The Temporal Effects of Preliminary Rulings" (1988) Y.E.L. 11, at 25; Bebr, "Preliminary Rulings of the Court of Justice: Their Authority and Temporal Effect" (1981) C.M.L.Rev. 475, at 503; Bribosia and Rorive, "Le droit transitoire jurisprudentiel dans la pratique des juridictions européennes" (2002) R.D.ULB 125–152.

of its judgment, except in the case of persons who have before that date initiated legal proceedings or raised an equivalent claim under national law.[338]

The preliminary ruling on interpretation will be limited in time only where "Member States and the circles concerned" were reasonably entitled to assume that the relevant provision of Community law did not apply to their situation and it was only the Court's judgment which showed that it in fact did so apply. The Commission's conduct in the period prior to the judgment will have a decisive bearing on the Court's decision in this regard,[339] alongside the Court's earlier case-law[340] and any existing measures of other Community institutions[341] or other Member States.[342] The financial consequences which might ensue for a Member State from a preliminary ruling do not in themselves justify limiting the temporal effect of the ruling.[343]

---

[338] ECJ, Case 43/75 *Defrenne* [1976] E.C.R. 455, paras 69–75; ECJ, Case 24/86 *Blaizot* [1988] E.C.R. 379, para.35; ECJ, Case C–262/88 *Barber* [1990] E.C.R. I–1889, paras 44–45; ECJ, Case C–163/90 *Legros and Others* [1992] E.C.R. I–4625, paras 34–35; ECJ, Joined Cases C–485 and C–486/93 *Simitzi* [1995] E.C.R. I–2655, para.34; ECJ, Case C–126/94 *Société Cadi Surgelés and Others* [1996] E.C.R. I–5647, paras 32–34; ECJ, Case C–72/03 *Carbonati Apuani* [2004] E.C.R. I–8027, paras 37–42.

[339] See four of the six cases cited in the preceding n.: *Defrenne*, paras 72–73; *Blaizot*, paras 32–33; *Barber*, para.40; *Legros and Others*, para.32. See also ECJ, Case C–437/97 *EKW and Wein & Co* [2000] E.C.R. I–1157, para.58.

[340] Cited in favour of restricting the temporal effects of the preliminary ruling, ECJ, Case 24/86 *Blaizot* [1988] E.C.R. 379, para.31, and ECJ, Case C–262/96 *Sürül* [1999] E.C.R. I–2685, paras 106–113, and against ECJ, Case 61/79 *Denkavit Italiana* [1980] E.C.R. 1205, paras 19–21.

[341] ECJ, Case C–262/88 *Barber* [1990] E.C.R. I–1889, para.42. The Court of Justice will limit the effects of its judgment *ratione temporis* where, for example, there is a risk of serious economic repercussions owing in particular to the large number of legal relationships entered into in good faith on the basis of rules considered validly to be in force, or where it appears that both individuals and national authorities have been prompted to adopt practices which do not comply with Community law by reason of objective, significant uncertainty regarding the implications of Community provisions, to which the conduct of other Member States or the Commission may even have contributed (see, for instance, ECJ, Case C–163/90 *Legros and Others* [1992] E.C.R. I–4625, para.32; ECJ, Joined Cases C–197 and C–252/94 *Société Bautiaa and Société Française Maritime* [1996] E.C.R. I–505, paras 44–56; ECJ, Case C–294/99 *Athinaïki Zythopoïïa* [2001] E.C.R. I–6797, paras 34–40; ECJ, Case C–366/99 *Griesmar* [2001] E.C.R. I–9383, paras 73–78 (limitation not granted); ECJ, Case C–481/99 *Heininger* [2001] E.C.R. I–9945, para.52; ECJ, Case C–347/00 *Barreira Pérez* [2002] E.C.R. I–8191, paras 43–47 (limitation not granted). The fact that the interpretative judgment could result in the re-examination of numerous files and give rise to administrative and practical difficulties did not suffice in order to limit the temporal effect of the interpretative judgment: ECJ, Case C–372/98 *Cooke* [2000] E.C.R. I–8683, para.43.

[342] ECJ, Case C–184/99 *Grzelczyk* [2001] E.C.R. I–6193, para.53.

[343] ECJ, Case C–104/98 *Buchner and Others* [2000] E.C.R. I–3625, para.41; ECJ, Case C–184/99 *Grzelczyk* [2001] E.C.R. I–6193, paras 52–53; ECJ, Case C–209/03 *Bidar* [2005] E.C.R. I–2119, paras 68–69. However, in his Opinion of March 17, 2005 in ECJ, Case C–475/03 *Banca populare di Cremona* (not yet reported), Advocate General F.G Jacobs proposed to limit the temporal effects of the Court's ruling since "an unlimited temporal effect might 'retroactively cast into confusion the system whereby Italian regions are financed'" (point 80).

Lastly, it should be noted that the precise scope of the temporal limitation of the effects of a preliminary ruling may be the subject of a further request for an interpretation by way of preliminary ruling (see 6–008, *supra*).[344]

---

[343] See, for instance, ECJ, Case C–109/91 *Ten Oever* [1993] E.C.R. I–4879; ECJ, Case C–110/91 *Moroni* [1993] E.C.R. I–6591 (these two judgments interpret the restriction of the temporal effects of the judgment in *Barber* which the Court of Justice associated with its interpretation of Art.141 of the EC Treaty); see also ECJ, Joined Cases C–363 and C–407-411/93 *Lancry and Others* [1994] E.C.R. I–3957, paras 42–43.

PART III

PROTECTION AGAINST ACTS OF THE INSTITUTIONS

CHAPTER 7

THE ACTION FOR ANNULMENT

I. SUBJECT-MATTER

General. The action for annulment (*i.e.* for a declaration that an act is   7–001
void), which is provided for in Art.230 of the EC Treaty and Art.146 of the
EAEC Treaty, enables Community institutions, Member States and natural
and legal persons to protect themselves against unlawful binding acts of
Community institutions, provided that specific conditions as to admissibility
are fulfilled.[1] By this procedure, the Court of Justice or the Court of First
Instance reviews the contested act in the light of superior—written and
unwritten—Community law. In the event that an infringement of that
superior law is found, the action will result in the annulment of the
contested act.[2]

A. THE TERM "ACT"

1. The requirement for there to be a contested act

Existing act. An application for annulment is admissible only if it is   7–002
directed against an existing act.[3] A non-existent act may not be declared
void.

---

[1] Art.35(6) of the EU Treaty provides for a comparable, yet not identical, procedure in the
context of the third pillar (see Ch.22, *infra*; see also ECJ (judgment of September 13, 2005),
Case C–176/03 *Commission v Council*, not yet reported). It is for the applicant to choose the
legal basis of its action and not for the Community judicature itself to choose the most
appropriate legal basis. So, if an action is brought under Art.230 of the EC Treaty, the
Court will not examine whether it would be admissible under Art.35 of the EU Treaty even
if the contested act concerns the provisions of the EU Treaty relating to police and judicial
cooperation in criminal matters (see ECJ, Case C–160/03 *Spain v Eurojust* [2005] E.C.R. I–
2077, paras 35 and 38).
[2] An application for a declaratory judgment that the Commission has no power to adopt
certain measures, without seeking annulment of a specific act, will be inadmissible (ECJ
(order of December 9, 2003), Case C-224/03 *Italy v Commission* [2003] E.C.R. I–14751,
paras 20–22).
[3] ECJ (order of October 7, 1987), Case 248/86 *Brüggemann v ESC* [1987] E.C.R. 3963; CFI,
Case T–64/89 *Automec v Commission* [1990] E.C.R. II–367, para.41; CFI, Case T–16/91
Rendo v Commission [1992] E.C.R. II–2417, para.39; ECJ, Case C–27/04 *Commission v
Council* [2004] E.C.R. I–6649, para.34 (failure by the Council to adopt acts that are
recommended by the Commission cannot be regarded as giving rise to acts open to
challenge for the purposes of Art.230 of the EC Treaty). The Court of Justice (under
Art.92(2) of the ECJ Rules of Procedure) and the Court of First Instance (under Art.113 of
the CFI Rules of Procedure) may declare of its own motion that an act is non-existent.

7–003   **Identification of the act.** Consequently, the applicant must identify precisely the act which it is seeking to have annulled. If it fails to do so, the application will be inadmissible on the ground that its subject-matter is unknown.[4] However, it may be that an application for annulment which is formally directed against a particular act is in fact directed against other acts which are linked with the contested act in such a way that they constitute a single whole.[5]

7–004   **Act no longer in force.** An application for annulment of an act which is no longer in force is not necessarily devoid of purpose. If the applicant has an interest in the annulment of an act which is no longer in force and it is within the time-limit prescribed by the fifth para.of Art.230 of the EC Treaty, the application will be admissible (at least from this point of view).[6]

---

[4] ECJ, Case 30/68 *Lacroix v Commission* [1970] E.C.R. 301, paras 20–27; ECJ, Case 247/87 *Star Fruit v Commission* [1989] E.C.R. 291, para.9.

[5] ECJ, Joined Cases 25 and 26/65 *SIMET and FERAM v High Authority* [1967] E.C.R. 33, at 43–44. See also ECJ, Case 34/77 *Oslizlok v Commission* [1978] E.C.R. 1099, paras 5 and 6, where an application for annulment which was not expressly directed against a specific Commission decision was nevertheless regarded as being directed against that decision in view of the arguments put forward in one of the applicant's pleas raised against other decisions related to the first decision which were expressly mentioned as being the subject-matter of the application for annulment.

[6] For an example of a case where the applicant had an interest, see ECJ, Case 207/86 *APESCO v Commission* [1988] E.C.R. 2151, paras 15–16 (the interest which the Court of Justice considered sufficient was in preventing a repetition of the alleged illegality in similar future acts); for examples of cases in which the applicant was held not to have an interest, see ECJ, Joined Cases 294/86 and 77/87 *Technointorg v Commission and Council* [1988] E.C.R. 6077, paras 11–14 (the application for annulment of a regulation imposing a provisional anti-dumping duty became devoid of purpose where, in the course of the proceedings, it was replaced by a definitive regulation, against which a new action for annulment had been brought); ECJ, Joined Cases C–305/86 and C–160/87 *Neotype Techmashexport v Commission and Council* [1990] E.C.R. I–2945, paras 14–15; CFI, Case T–239/94 *EISA v Commission* [1997] E.C.R. II–1839, paras 34–35 (an action brought against a Commission decision authorising the grant of aid by a Member State pursuant to Art.95 of the ECSC Treaty which was withdrawn in the course of the procedure was held to be devoid of purpose because the contested decision had become "inapplicable"); CFI (order of July 31, 2000), Case T–31/00 *BSB-Fleischimport v Commission*, not reported, para.11 (application to no purpose following the withdrawal of the contested act); CFI (order of March 10, 2005), Case T–184/01 *IMS Health v Commission*, not yet reported, paras 34–49 (the Court of First Instance held that there was no need to give a decision in this case since no legal effect of the contested decision remained following its withdrawal). An action brought against a Commission decision implementing a "basic decision" of that institution will have no subject-matter if the decision which it implements has been declared void. If, pursuant to the judgment annulling the basic decision, the Commission adopts a new basic decision incorporating the original implementing decision, the applicant will lose any interest in continuing an action to obtain annulment of the original implementing decision. This is because the annulment of the original basic decision causes the implementing decision to lose its *raison d'être* with the result that the new decision cannot be regarded as a confirmatory act but as an "autonomous act creating or altering legal rights" which takes the place of the original implementing act (CFI (order of January 27, 2000), Case T-236/95 *TAT European Airlines v Commission* [2000] E.C.R. II–51).

This also applies where the contested act has already been implemented at the time when the action is brought.[7]

Act replacing a withdrawn act. In the interests of the due administration of justice and the requirements of procedural economy, an action for annulment of an act which is withdrawn in the course of the proceedings may be directed against a new, closely related act which replaces or simply revokes the contested act.[8] In such case, the new act is regarded as a new matter which has arisen in the course of the proceedings and the applicant may put forward new pleas in law.[9] Naturally, it is also possible to bring a new action for annulment. The new act is regarded as being of the same kind as the act which was withdrawn.[10]
 7–005

Non-existent act. The requirement that the contested measure must exist is applied in the special case of the doctrine of the non-existent act. Such a measure exhibits such particularly serious and manifest defects that it must be regarded as non-existent. If a measure is found to be non-existent, it loses the benefit of the normal presumption that an act is valid in so far as it has not been annulled or the institution which adopted it has not properly repealed or withdrawn it.[11] Moreover, the non-existent act cannot produce any legal effects at all. Consequently, an application for annulment of a non-existent act will invariably be declared inadmissible.[12] Furthermore, an act may be declared non-existent after the period prescribed for bringing an action for annulment has run out. The case-law, which shows every sign of
 7–006

---

[7] ECJ, Case 53/85 *AKZO Chemie v Commission* [1986] E.C.R. 1965, para.21; CFI, Case T–22/97 *Kesko v Commission* [1999] E.C.R. II–3775, para.59.

[8] ECJ, Case 14/81 *Alpha Steel v Commission* [1982] E.C.R. 749 (the withdrawal of an unlawful measure is permissible, provided that the withdrawal occurs within a reasonable time and that the Commission has had sufficient regard to how the applicant might have been led to rely on the lawfulness of the measure); CFI, Joined Cases T–46/98 and T–151/98 *CCRE v Commission* [2000] E.C.R. II–167, para.33. See also CFI (judgment of September 21, 2005), Case T–306/01 *Yusuf and Al Barakaat International Foundation v Council and Commission*, not yet reported, paras 71–77.

[9] ECJ Rules of Procedure, Art.42(2); CFI Rules of Procedure, Art.48(2).

[10] Schermers and Waelbroeck, *Judicial Protection*, § 711, at 355.

[11] Joined Cases 7/56 and 3–7/57 *Algera and Others v Common Assembly* [1957 and 1958] E.C.R. 39, at 60–61; ECJ, Case 15/85 *Consorzio Cooperative d'Abruzzo v Commission* [1987] E.C.R. 1005, para.10. The purpose of this exception to the principle that acts are presumed to be lawful is to "maintain a balance between two fundamental, but sometimes conflicting, requirements with which a legal order must comply, namely stability of legal relations and respect for legality". See also ECJ, Case C–199/92 P *Hüls v Commission* [1999] E.C.R. I–4287, para.85; ECJ, Case C–200/92 P *ICI v Commission* [1999] E.C.R. I–4399, para.70; ECJ, Case C–235/92 P *Montecatini v Commission* [1999] E.C.R. I–4539, para.97; ECJ, Case C–475/01 *Commission v Greece* [2004] E.C.R. I–8923, para.16.

[12] In view of the non-existence of the contested measure, the Court of Justice and the Court of First Instance may make an order for costs against the defendant in favour of the applicant while declaring that the application is inadmissible (ECJ Rules of Procedure, Art.69(3), second subpara.; CFI Rules of Procedure, Art.87(3), second subpara.).

reluctance,[13] affords only two instances in which a measure was actually declared non-existent (one of them being a case heard by the Court of First Instance, the judgment ultimately being set aside by the Court of Justice).[14]

2. The requirement for a binding act

7–007 **Definition.** It follows from Art.230 of the EC Treaty, which precludes the annulment of opinions and recommendations, that acts whose annulment is sought must be binding.[15] Binding acts are the outcome of "the exercise, upon the conclusion of an internal procedure laid down by law, of a power provided for by law which is intended to produce legal effects of such a nature as to affect adversely the interests of the applicant by modifying its legal position".[16] They must therefore have a legitimate legal basis, reflect the definitive position of a Community institution or body and be intended to have legal effects.

7–008 **Silence on the part of an institution.** When a party makes a request to a Community institution, mere silence on the part of that institution cannot be placed on the same footing as an implied refusal, except where that result is expressly provided for by a provision of Community law.[17] So, where in a legislative procedure, the Council does not act upon measures proposed by the Commission, that failure cannot be regarded as giving rise to a challengeable act within the meaning of Art.230 of the EC Treaty.[18]

---

[13] ECJ, Joined Cases 7/56 and 3–7/57 *Algera and Others v Common Assembly* [1957 and 1958] E.C.R. 39, at 60–61; ECJ, Joined Cases 15–33, 52–53, 57–109, 116–117, 123, 132 and 135–137/73 *Schots (née Kortner) and Others v Council and Others* [1974] E.C.R. 177, para.33; ECJ, Case 15/85 *Consorzio Cooperative d'Abruzzo v Commission* [1987] E.C.R. 1005, para.10; ECJ, Case 226/87 *Commission v Greece* [1988] E.C.R. 3611, para.16.

[14] ECJ, Joined Cases 1 and 14/57 *Société des Usines à Tubes de la Sarre v High Authority* [1957 and 1958] E.C.R. 105, at 112–113. It must be noted, however, that that judgment was not so much concerned with the non-existence of the measure in question, but to fathom its nature (Mathijsen, "Nullité et annulabilité des actes des institutions européennes", in *Miscellanea W.J. Ganshof van der Meersch* (Brussels, Bruylant, 1972), Vol. II, at 272–276); CFI, Joined Cases T–79, T–84–86, T–89, T–91–92, T–94, T–96, T–98, T–102 and T–104/89 *BASF and Others v Commission* [1992] E.C.R. II–315, set aside by ECJ, Case C–137/92 P *Commission v BASF and Others* [1994] E.C.R. I–2555 (case note by Le Mire (1994) A.J.D.A. 724).

[15] *Société des Usines à Tubes de la Sarre v High Authority*, cited in the preceding n., at 114; ECJ, Case 133/79 *Sucrimex v Commission* [1980] E.C.R. 1299, paras 12–19. For examples of acts which have been held open to review, see Brealey and Hoskins, *Remedies in E.C. Law*, at 271 *et seq.* A report drawn up by OLAF pursuant to Art.9 of Regulation No 1073/1999 contains only recommendations and is therefore not a challengeable act within the meaning of Art.230 of the EC Treaty (CFI (order of July 13, 2004), Case T–29/03 *Comunidad Autónoma de Andalucía v Commission*, not yet reported, paras 33–40).

[16] ECJ, Case 182/80 *Gauff v Commission* [1982] E.C.R. 799, para.18. In Community law there is no general obligation on the administrative or judicial authorities to inform the addressees of measures of the judicial remedies available or of the conditions for availing themselves thereof (ECJ (order of March 5, 1999), Case C–154/98 P *Guérin Automobiles v Commission* [1999] E.C.R. I–1451, para.15) and hence a Community institution is not obliged to indicate whether one of its acts is binding.

[17] ECJ, Case C–123/03 P *Commission v Greencore* [2004] E.C.R. I–11647, para.45.

[18] ECJ, Case C–27/04 *Commission v Council* [2004] E.C.R. I–6649, para.34. In the event of an unlawful failure to act, an action for failure to act may be brought under Art.232 of the EC Treaty (see Ch.8, *infra*).

The position would be different if, under Community law, the Council were deemed, after the expiry of a specific period of time, to have taken an implied decision whose content is determined by Community law.[19]

Contracts. Mere contractual acts of an institution cannot be regarded as acts exercising prerogatives of public authority and, as a result, such acts cannot be the subject of an action for annulment.[20] An application for the annulment of a letter by which the Commission demanded a party to a contract with it to repay certain sums on account of improper performance of the contract will therefore be inadmissible.[21] In the absence of an arbitration clause within the meaning of Art.238 of the EC Treaty,[22] the national courts have jurisdiction.

7–009

a. Content and not form determines whether the act is binding

Content. The binding nature of an act is inferred only from its content.[23] The form in which an act is cast cannot alter its nature.[24] Consequently, an act which does not satisfy the relevant requirements as to form does not cease to be binding as a result.[25] Thus, the Court of Justice held that it did not follow from non-compliance with the formal requirements prescribed by the High Authority "as a matter of obligation" for decisions within the

7–010

---

[19] ECJ, Case C–27/04 *Commission v Council* [2004] E.C.R. I–6649, para.32. See in this connection, ECJ, C–76/01 P *Eurocoton and Others v Council* [2003] E.C.R. I–10091, paras 54–65.

[20] CFI (order of October 3, 1997), Case T–186/96 *Mutual Aid Administration Services v Commission* [1997] E.C.R. II–1633, paras 50 and 51; CFI (order of January 9, 2001), Case T–149/00 *Innova v Commission* [2001] E.C.R. II–1, para.28; CFI (order of November 25, 2003), Case T–85/01 *IAMA Consulting v Commission* [2003] E.C.R. II–4973, paras 51–53; CFI (order of May 10, 2004), Joined Cases T–314/03 and T–378/03 *Musée Grévin v Commission* [2004] E.C.R. II–1421, paras 80–85.

[21] CFI (order of May 10, 2004), Joined Cases T–314/03 and T–378/03 *Musée Grévin v Commission*, [2004] E.C.R. II–1421.

[22] See Ch.19, *infra*.

[23] For applications, see ECJ, Case C–57/95 *France v Commission* [1997] E.C.R. I–1627, para.9; CFI, Joined Cases T–25/97 and T–127/97 *Coca-Cola v Commission* [2000] E.C.R. II–1733; CFI, Joined Cases T–222/99, T–327/99 and T–329/99 *Martinez and Others v European Parliament* [2001] E.C.R. II–2823, para.26; CFI, Case T–113/00 *Dupont Teijin Films Luxembourg and Others v Commission* [2002] E.C.R. II–3681, para.45; CFI (order of July 9, 2003), Case T–216/01 *Reisebank v Commission*, not reported, para.45.

[24] ECJ, Case 101/76 *Koninklijke Scholten Honig v Council and Commission* [1977] E.C.R. 797, para.7; CFI (order of April 28, 1994), Joined Cases T–452 and T–453/93 *Pevasa and Inpesca v Commission* [1994] E.C.R. II–229, para.29.

[25] ECJ, Joined Cases 53 and 54/63 *Lemmerz-Werke and Others v High Authority* [1963] E.C.R. 239. Once the Court has established that a measure contained in a letter satisfies the substantive requirements of a binding act, the application cannot be declared inadmissible on that count: ECJ, Joined Cases 15 and 29/59 *Société Métallurgique de Knutange v High Authority* [1960] E.C.R. 1, at 7; ECJ, Joined Cases 8–11/66 *Cimenteries CBR Cementbedrijven and Others v Commission* [1967] E.C.R. 75, at 90–91; ECJ, Case C–135/92 *Fiskano v Commission* [1994] E.C.R. I–2885, paras 21–26 (Commission letter to Sweden containing a binding act); ECJ, Case C–249/02 *Portugal v Commission* [2004] E.C.R. I–10717, paras 35–43 (letter from a Commission official to the Portuguese authorities containing a binding act).

meaning of Art.14 of the ECSC Treaty that a measure should not be considered a decision if it did not comply with those formal requirements, provided that it satisfied the substantive requirements which decisions had to fulfil under the Treaty.[26] In addition, the Court of First Instance has held that an action will lie against an act made simply orally—by means of a statement by the spokesman for the Commissioner responsible for competition matters, also reported by the press agency *Agence Europe*—on the ground that its contents were not contested by the parties and had subsequently been confirmed by the Commission itself, and that hence the Court of First Instance was in a position to investigate whether it had produced legal effects.[27] However, an action for annulment will not lie against a "practice" of the Commission.[28] Silence on the part of an institution cannot produce legal effects unless this is expressly provided for in a provision of Community law.[29]

7–011 **Form.** In the legal sphere of the EC Treaty the class of measures against which an action for annulment will lie is not confined to the binding acts mentioned in Art.249 of that Treaty. The Court of Justice has held that to confine that class of measures in that way would conflict with the obligation under Art.220 of the EC Treaty to ensure observance of the law in the interpretation and application of the Treaty, and that an action for annulment, as a means of fulfilling that obligation, "must therefore be

---

[26] ECJ, Joined Cases 23–24 and 52/63 *Usines Emile Henricot and Others v High Authority* [1963] E.C.R. 217, at 222, where the Court of Justice held, however, that these "fundamental conditions" were not met, namely "a decision must appear as a measure taken by the High Authority, acting as a body, intended to produce legal effects and constituting the culmination of a procedure within the High Authority, whereby the High Authority gives its final ruling in a form from which its nature can be identified", *ibid.*, at 224.

[27] CFI, Case T–3/93 *Air France v Commission* [1994] E.C.R. II–121, paras 55–60. In a staff case, the Court of Justice likewise accepted that a binding act could be communicated orally (ECJ, Joined Cases 316/82 and 40/83 *Kohler v Court of Auditors* [1984] E.C.R. 641, paras 8–13). See also ECJ (judgment of July 7, 2005), Case C–208/03 *Le Pen v European Parliament*, not yet reported, para.47. But see CFI (order of July 9, 2003), Case T–178/02 *WONUC and Others v Commission*, not reported, para.7, in which the Court of First Instance held that statements made by a Member of the Commission, Ms Loyola de Palacio, at a press conference did not have legal effects and therefore did not constitute an act which could be challenged before the Court.

[28] ECJ, Case C–159/96 *Portugal v Commission* [1998] E.C.R. I–7379, paras 23–24 (in this case, Portugal brought an action for annulment of the "practice" of exceptional flexibility allegedly followed by the Commission in the administration of quantitative limits on the importation into the Community of textile products originating in various non-member countries. The Court of Justice held that the application was inadmissible in so far as it was brought against this practice).

[29] CFI, Joined Cases T–189/95, T–39/96 and T–123/96 *SGA v Commission* [1999] E.C.R. II–3587, paras 26–27; CFI, Joined Cases T–190/95 and T–45/96 *Sodima v Commission* [1999] E.C.R. II–3617, paras 31–36. *Cf.*, however, ECJ, Case C–19/93 P *Rendo and Others v Commission* [1995] E.C.R. I–3319, para.29, where the Court of Justice held that where the Commission gives a ruling on only a part of a complaint, that act may be regarded as a partial, implicit dismissal of the part of the complaint to which it has not responded. Silence on the part of an institution which is obliged to act may constitute the subject-matter of an action for failure to act (see Ch.8, *infra*).

available in the case of all measures adopted by the institutions, whatever their nature or form, which are intended to have legal effects".[30]

In the judgment in the *AETR* case, the Court of Justice found that the Council's decision establishing a common negotiating position on the part of the Member States with a view to the conclusion of an international agreement fell within the competence of the Community and therefore laid down a course of action binding on the institutions as well as on the Member States. Accordingly, the Court held that the decision constituted a binding act and hence one against which an action would lie, even though it could not be brought within one of the classes of binding acts listed in Art.249 of the EC Treaty.[31]

Council conclusions holding the excessive deficit procedure brought against France and Germany in abeyance have been held to be challengeable because they have legal effects, even though such conclusions are not provided for as a instrument in the EC Treaty.[32]

In contrast, the Court of Justice did not find that a decision of the representatives of the Governments of the Member States meeting in the Council, made at the Commission's proposal, to grant special aid to Bangladesh was a binding act of the Council. The Court did not come to that view because of the name of the act in question,[33] but based its assessment on the precise content of the act and the context in which it was adopted.[34]

Refusal. An act of an institution amounting to a rejection must be appraised in the light of the nature of the request to which it constitutes a reply. The refusal by a Community institution to withdraw or amend an act may constitute an act whose legality may be reviewed under Art.230 of the EC Treaty only if the act which the Community institution refuses to withdraw or amend could itself have been contested under that provision.[35] Accordingly, the fact that a letter is sent by a Community institution to its

7–012

---

[30] ECJ, Case 22/70 *Commission v Council* (the *AETR* case) [1971] E.C.R. 263, para.42. See also ECJ, Case 60/81 *IBM v Commission* [1981] E.C.R. 2639, para.8; ECJ, Case C–25/94 *Commission v Council* [1996] E.C.R. I–1469, para.29; ECJ, Case C–27/04 *Commission v Council* [2004] E.C.R. I–6649, para.44.

[31] An action will even lie against an act by which the Commission concludes an international agreement on behalf of the Community: ECJ, Case C–327/91 *France v Commission* [1994] E.C.R. I–3641, paras 14–17.

[32] ECJ, Case C–27/04 *Commission v Council* [2004] E.C.R. I–6649, paras 44–51.

[33] Press release entitled "Aid for Bangladesh—Council conclusions" (reference 6004/91, Press 60-c).

[34] ECJ, Joined Cases C–181 and C–248/91 *European Parliament v Council and Commission* [1993] E.C.R. I–3685.

[35] ECJ, Case 42/71 *Nordgetreide v Commission* [1972] E.C.R. 105, para.5; CFI (order of April 18, 2002), Case T–238/00 *IPSO and USE v ECB* [2002] E.C.R. II–2237, para.45; CFI (order of July 13, 2004), Case T–29/03 *Comunidad Autónoma de Andalucía v Commission*, not yet reported, para.30. See also CFI, Case T–154/94 *CSF and CSME v Commission* [1996] E.C.R. II–1377, para.37 *et seq.* (the binding nature of a letter from the Commission was considered in the light of a letter from the applicants to which the Commission's letter replied).

addressee in response to a request from the addressee is not sufficient to make that letter a challengeable act within the meaning of Art.230 of the EC Treaty.[36]

A Commission decision to shelve a complaint from an individual in the course of a procedure brought pursuant to Art.226 of the EC Treaty does not have any legal effects as regards the complainant. This is because the act sought by the complainant, a decision to commence proceedings before the Court of Justice, is not *per se* a challengeable act.[37] In any event, the complainant has no entitlement to a Commission decision, since that institution has a discretion whether or not to bring proceedings for failure to fulfil obligations.[38]

7–013 **Legitimate legal basis.** Lastly, an institution may adopt a binding act only in so far as it has a legitimate legal basis which empowers the institution to adopt a binding act.[39] No such power may be presumed to exist in the absence of a specific Community provision.[40] As a result of that requirement, the Court of Justice and the Court of First Instance often take the view that they have to consider whether the application for annulment is admissible together with the substance.[41]

---

[36] CFI (order of April 9, 2003), Case T–280/02 *Pikaart and Others v Commission* [2003] E.C.R. II–1621, para.23; CFI (order of November 5, 2003), Case T–130/02 *Kronoply v Commission* [2003] E.C.R. II–4857, para.42; CFI (order of July 13, 2004), Case T–29/03 *Comunidad Autónoma de Andalucía v Commission*, not yet reported, para.29.

[37] See ECJ, Case C–191/95 *Commission v Germany* [1998] E.C.R. I–5449, para.47; see also CFI, Joined Cases T–377/00, T–379/00, T–380/00, T–260/01 and T–272/01 *Philip Morris International and Others v Commission* [2003] E.C.R. II–1, para.79: a Commission decision to bring legal proceedings—in the particular case before a US court—cannot be considered *per se* to be a decision which is open to challenge. See also 5–026, *supra*.

[38] CFI (order of September 29, 1997), Case T–83/97 *Sateba v Commission* [1997] E.C.R. II–1523, paras 32–40; CFI, Case T–148/00 *Panhellenic Union of Cotton Ginners and Exporters v Commission* [2003] E.C.R. II–4415, para.66; CFI (order of September 19, 2005), T–247/04 *Aseprofar and Edifa v Commission*, not yet reported, paras 40–61. Moreover, the complainant has no procedural rights on the basis of which it can require the Commission to inform it and give it a hearing.

[39] CFI, Case T–113/89 *Nefarma v Commission* [1990] E.C.R. II–797, para.68 *et seq.* (see 7–127, *infra*).

[40] ECJ (order of September 30, 1987), Case 229/86 *Brother Industries v Commission* [1987] E.C.R. 3757; *Nefarma v Commission*, cited in the preceding n., para.69.

[41] See ECJ, Case C–233/02 *France v Commission* [2004] E.C.R. I–2759, para.26, where the Court of Justice did not rule on the admissibility of an action for annulment of the decision by which the Commission concluded an agreement with the United States of America on Guidelines on Regulatory Cooperation and Transparency since the "form of order sought by the French Republic must in any event be dismissed on the substance". The question whether the contested act has a legitimate legal basis coincides with the question whether the institution was empowered to adopt it: ECJ, Joined Cases 358/85 and 51/86 *France v European Parliament* [1988] E.C.R. 4821, paras 13–15; ECJ, Case C–366/88 *France v Commission* [1990] E.C.R. I–3571; ECJ, Case C–303/90 *France v Commission* [1991] E.C.R. I–5315, with a case note by Van der Woude (1993) S.E.W. 522–527; ECJ, Case C–325/91 *France v Commission* [1993] E.C.R. I–3283, paras 8–11.

b. The act is intended to produce legal effects

Legal effects. Acts of a Community institution are binding in so far as **7–014**
they produce legal effects.[42] This means that they must be "capable of
affecting the interests of the applicant by bringing about a distinct change
in his legal position"[43] or adversely affect his legal position by restricting his
rights.[44] If this is not the case, such acts are not binding and an action will
not lie against them.[45] A proposal will therefore, in principle, not constitute
a challengeable act.[46]

---

[42] ECJ, Joined Cases 8–11/66 *Cimenteries CBR Cementbedrijven and Others v Commission*
[1967] ECJ 75, at 91; ECJ, Case 22/70 *Commission v Council* (the *AETR* case) [1971] E.C.R.
263, para.39; ECJ, Case C–312/90 *Spain v Commission* [1992] E.C.R. I–4117, paras 11–26,
and ECJ, Case C–327/91 *France v Commission* [1994] E.C.R. I–3641, paras 14–15 (the
application for annulment of an act by which the Commission purported to conclude an
international agreement "between the Commission of the European Communities and the
Government of the United States of America regarding the application of their competition
laws" was declared admissible on the ground that, "as is apparent from its actual wording,
the Agreement is intended to produce legal effects"); CFI, Case T–154/94 *CSF and CSME v
Commission* [1996] E.C.R. II–1377, para.37 *et seq.* (the binding nature of a letter from the
Commission was considered in the light of a letter from the applicants to which the
Commission's letter answered).

[43] ECJ, Case 60/81 *IBM v Commission* [1981] E.C.R. 2639, para.9; ECJ, Case 53/85 *AKZO
Chemie v Commission* [1986] E.C.R. 1965, para.16; CFI, Case T–112/99 *M6 and Others v
Commission* [2001] E.C.R. I 2459, paras 40–41, where the Commission decision to grant
clearance for a period shorter than that of the whole agreement was held to be a
challengeable act. See also ECJ, Case C–242/00 *Germany v Commission* [2002] E.C.R. I–
5603, paras 39–46: the decision by which the Commission approved a new definition of
areas eligible for aid under the Community action programme "scheme for improving
regional economic structures" in Germany did not constitute a challengeable act. The Court
of Justice held that it followed, both from the content of the contested decision and from
the context of its adoption, that that decision had neither the purpose nor the effect of
rejecting implicitly a request by Germany concerning an additional list of regions.

[44] For cases in which this was held not to be the case, see CFI, Case T–541/93 *Connaughton
and Others v Council* [1997] E.C.R. II–549 and CFI, Case T–554/93 *Saint and Murray v
Council and Commission* [1997] E.C.R. II–563.

[45] ECJ (order of May 17, 1989), Case 151/88 *Italy v Commission* [1989] E.C.R. 1255, paras 22–
23; ECJ (order of October 4, 1991), Case C–117/91 *Bosman v Commission* [1991] E.C.R. I–
4837, para.14; ECJ, Case C–476/93 P *Nutral v Commission* [1995] E.C.R. I–4125, paras 30–
31; ECJ, Case C–58/94 *Netherlands v Council* [1996] E.C.R. I–2169, para.27; ECJ, Case C–
180/96 *United Kingdom v Commission* [1998] E.C.R. I–2265, para.29; CFI, Case T–113/89
Nefarma v Commission [1990] E.C.R. II–797, paras 66–99; CFI, Joined Cases T–10–12 and
T–15/92 *Cimenteries CBR and Others v Commission* [1992] E.C.R. II–2667, para.28; CFI,
Case T–277/94 *AITEC v Commission* [1996] E.C.R. II–351, paras 49–56; CFI, Case T–
271/94 *Branco v Commission* [1996] E.C.R. II–749, para.32; CFI (order of September 15,
1998), Case T–54/96 *Oleifici Italiani and Fratelli Rubino Industrie Olearie v Commission*
[1998] E.C.R. II–3377, paras 50–51: it appeared from the wording of a letter from the
Commission to a Member State and from its legal context that it did not alter the
applicants' legal position; CFI, Joined Cases T–377/00, T–379/00, T–380/00, T–260/01 and
T–272/01 *Philip Morris International and Others v Commission* [2003] E.C.R. II–1, para.79: a
Commission decision to bring proceedings—in that case before a US court—did not
constitute a challengeable act.

[46] ECJ (judgment of December 1, 2005), Case C–301/03 *Italy v Commission*, not yet reported,
paras 21–24.

7–015 **Operative part and recitals.** Whether an act is capable of having adverse effect must be determined in the first place from its operative part.[47] But the explanations and recitals contained in the act in support of the operative part[48] as well as the context in which the act is adopted[49] may also mean that the act has adverse effect and is amenable to review. Where a measure against which an action for annulment has been brought comprises essentially distinct parts, only those parts of that measure which produce binding legal effects capable of bringing about a significant change in the applicant's legal situation can be challenged.[50]

(1) *Confirmatory acts*

7–016 **Act inadmissible in the absence of new legal effects.** An application for annulment of an act which merely confirms an irrevocable act which was previously adopted is inadmissible.[51] The confirmatory measure does not

---

[47] CFI, Case T–138/89 *NBV and NVB v Commission* [1992] E.C.R. II–2181, para.31; CFI, Joined Cases T–125/97 and T–127/97 *Coca-Cola v Commission* [2000] E.C.R. II–1733, paras 77–92.

[48] This is because the operative part of an act is indissociably linked to the statement of reasons for it, so that, when it has to be interpreted, account must be taken of the reasons which led to its adoption: ECJ, Case C–355/95 P *TWD Textilwerke Deggendorf v Commission* [1997] E.C.R. I–2549, para.21; CFI, Joined Cases T–213/95 and T–18/96 *SCK and FNK v Commission* [1997] E.C.R. II–1739, para.104, and the case-law cited therein. Whether the operative part has adverse effect consequently extends to the recitals, which constitute the necessary support for the operative part. The assessments made in the recitals to an act can be subject to judicial review by the Community judicature to the extent that, as grounds of an act adversely affecting a person's interests, they constitute the essential basis for the operative part of that act: CFI, Case T–16/91 *Rendo and Others v Commission* [1992] E.C.R. II–2417, paras 40–41 and 55: ECJ (order of January 28, 2004), Case C–164/02 *Netherlands v Commission* [2004] E.C.R. I–1177, para.21.

[49] ECJ (judgment of December 1, 2005), Case C–301/03 *Italy v Commission*, not yet reported, paras 21–24.

[50] CFI, Case T–184/97 *BP Chemicals v Commission* [2000] E.C.R. II–3145, para.34. In this case, BP Chemicals contested a Commission decision whereby aid was approved for two groups of bio-fuels which differed in point of their composition, use and the market for which they were of interest. The applicant had shown that it had *locus standi* only in so far as it was a producer of synthetic ethyl alcohol, a product which competes with bio-ethanol, but not with regard to the measures for the esters sector. The Court of First Instance therefore held that the applicants had not suffered a significant change in their legal situation as a result of the decision approving aid for esters and declared the application inadmissible in that regard. See also CFI (judgment of July 8, 2004), Case T–50/00 *Dalmine v Commission*, not yet reported, paras 134–135.

[51] ECJ, Case 56/72 *Goeth v Commission* [1973] E.C.R. 181, para.15; ECJ, Case 1/76 *Wack v Commission* [1976] E.C.R. 1017, para.7; ECJ, Case 26/76 *Metro v Commission* [1977] E.C.R. 1875, para.4; ECJ, Joined Cases 166 and 220/86 *Irish Cement v Commission* [1988] E.C.R. 6473, paras 1–16; ECJ (order of November 21, 1990), Case C–12/90 *Infortec v Commission* [1990] E.C.R. I–4265, para.10; ECJ, Case C–199/91 *Foyer Culturel du Sart-Tilman v Commission* [1993] E.C.R. I–2667, paras 20–24; ECJ, Case C–480/93 P *Zunis Holding and Others v Commission* [1996] E.C.R. I–1, para.14; CFI, Case T–514/93 *Cobrecaf and Others v Commission* [1995] E.C.R. II–621, para.44; CFI, Case T–275/94 *Groupement des Cartes Bancaires "CB" v Commission* [1995] E.C.R. II–2169, para.27; CFI (order of March 16, 1998), Case T–235/95 *Goldstein v Commission* [1998] E.C.R. II–523, paras 36–48; CFI

produce any new legal effects. If the Court of Justice or the Court of First Instance were to hold that an application for annulment of a confirmatory act was admissible despite the fact that the time-limit for bringing an action against the original act had run out, this would make it possible to circumvent that time-limit. An applicant who was out of time would then be able to reactivate the possibility of bringing proceedings by provoking the adoption of a confirmatory act, thereby jeopardising legal certainty.[52] So long as the time-limit for bringing an action against the original act has not expired, an action for annulment may be brought against the original act, the confirmatory act or both concurrently.[53]

An action against a confirmatory measure will be inadmissible only in so far as it is a genuinely confirmatory act.[54] Thus, from the point of view of procedural law, a measure will be regarded as confirmatory of an earlier measure only if the latter is or was amenable to appeal.[55] Furthermore, a new fact which is of such a character as to alter the essential circumstances and conditions which governed the adoption of the original act causes the new act no longer to be confirmatory even though it has the same content as the original act. An action brought against such an ostensibly confirmatory act will be admissible.[56] On those grounds, an act (decision) by which an institution refuses to amend an earlier decision—in spite of the new facts presented by the applicant—may be the subject of an action for annulment.[57]

(order of June 10, 1998), Case T–116/95 *Cementir v Commission* [1998] E.C.R. II–2261, paras 19–25; CFI, Case T–188/95 *Waterleiding Maatschappij "Noord-West Brabant" v Commission* [1998] E.C.R. II–3713, paras 88–141 (a complaint made against State aid which the Commission had already declared to be compatible with the common market does not, where the decision has become definitive, cause time to start running afresh in order to bring an action for annulment of the decision by which the Commission rejects the complaint while confirming its earlier decision); CFI (order of July 9, 2002), Case T–127/01 *Ripa di Meana v European Parliament* [2002] E.C.R. II–3005; CFI (order of February 23, 2005), Case T–478/04 *Campailla v Commission*, not reported, paras 21–22.

[52] ECJ, Joined Cases 166 and 220/86 *Irish Cement v Commission* [1988] E.C.R. 6473, para.16; ECJ, Case C–199/91 *Foyer Culturel du Sart-Tilman v Commission* [1993] E.C.R. I–2667, paras 23–24; CFI, Joined Cases T–121/96 and T–151/96 *Mutual Aid Administration Services v Commission* [1997] E.C.R. II–1355, para.50.

[53] ECJ, Joined Cases 193 and 194/87 *Maurissen and European Public Service Union v Court of Auditors* [1989] E.C.R. 1045, para.26.

[54] ECJ, Case 9/81 *Williams v Court of Auditors* [1982] E.C.R. 3301, para.15; CFI, Case T–321/01 *Internationaler Hilfsfonds v Commission* [2003] E.C.R. II–3225, para.31.

[55] ECJ, Joined Cases 193 & 194/87 *Maurissen and European Public Service Union v Court of Auditors* [1989] E.C.R. 1045, para.23.

[56] ECJ, Joined Cases 42 and 49/59 *SNUPAT v High Authority* [1961] E.C.R. 53, at 75–76; CFI, Case T–331/94 *IPK v Commission* [1997] E.C.R. II–1665, para.26; CFI, Case T–365/00 *AICS v European Parliament* [2002] E.C.R. II–2719, paras 28–40.

[57] ECJ, Case C–514/99 *France v Commission* [2000] E.C.R. I–4705, para.45, in which the Court of Justice declared an action brought by France inadmissible on the ground that the Commission had not taken any decision on the application to amend a former decision. France argued that the Commission had refused to amend or withdraw an earlier decision. The Court of Justice suggested that the applicant could have brought an action for failure to

213

(2) Resolutions

7–017 Act inadmissible if a mere declaration of intent. Resolutions often express a political declaration of intent which embodies no binding commitments and therefore produces no legal effects. Accordingly, an action will not lie against a resolution,[58] unless it appears from its content that it affects the legal position of a Member State or a person.[59]

(3) Internal instructions and guidelines

7–018 No legal effects vis-à-vis third parties. Internal instructions are usually simply guidelines for the adoption of acts of institutions. Generally, they do not produce legal effects.[60] Consequently, an internal instruction of the Commission indicating the manner in which it intended to exercise its provisional power to compile a list of candidates for service contracts concluded within the framework of the Lomé Convention was not an act producing legal effects. It was not the line of conduct set out in the internal instruction which produced legal effects and reflected the Commission's definitive position, but the drawing up of the list itself.[61]

---

act. See also CFI, Case T–186/98 *Inpesca v Commission* [2001] E.C.R. II–557, paras 45–51, and CFI (order of April 29, 2004), Case T–308/02 *SGL Carbon v Commission*, [2004] E.C.R. II–1363, paras 51–53, in which the Court of First Instance emphasised that the confirmatory nature of a decision cannot be assessed solely in the light of its content as compared with the previous decision which it purportedly confirms. The confirmatory nature of the decision must also be assessed having regard to the application to which the decision constitutes an answer. If the application in question is based on significant new facts of which neither the applicant nor the administration was aware when the earlier decision was taken and which are liable to bring about a significant change in the applicant's position which was the starting point for the original—now definitive—decision, the new decision can in that respect not be regarded as merely confirmatory, since it makes a determination on the new facts and so contains a new factor as compared with the earlier decision. See also ECJ (judgment of November 24, 2005), Joined Cases C–138/03, C–324/03 and C–431/03 *Italy v Commission*, not yet reported, paras 36–37; ECJ (judgment of December 1, 2005), Case C–46/03 *United Kingdom v Commission*, not yet reported, paras 23–26.

[58] ECJ, Joined Cases 90 and 91/63 *Commission v Luxembourg and Belgium* [1964] E.C.R. 625, at 631 (in that judgment, given pursuant to Art.226 of the EC Treaty, the Court of Justice held that a Council resolution was not a binding measure); ECJ, Case 9/73 *Schlüter* [1973] E.C.R. 1135, para.40 (in that judgment, given in response to a request for a preliminary ruling, the Court of Justice held that the resolution in question was "primarily an expression of the policy favoured by the Council and Government Representatives of the Member States" and could not, "by reason of its content, create legal consequences of which parties might avail themselves in court").

[59] ECJ, Case 108/83 *Luxembourg v European Parliament* [1984] E.C.R. 1945, paras 19–23; ECJ, Joined Cases C–213/88 and C–39/89 *Luxembourg v European Parliament* [1991] E.C.R. I–5643.

[60] See, *e.g.* ECJ, Case C–233/02 *France v Commission* [2004] E.C.R. I–2759.

[61] ECJ, Case 114/86 *United Kingdom v Commission* [1988] E.C.R. 5289; ECJ, Case C–443/97 *Spain v Commission* [2000] E.C.R. I–2415, para.34.

Even where internal instructions do have legal effects, they must create rights or obligations outside the institution concerned before third parties may bring an admissible application for their annulment.[62]

Binding on the institution concerned. Where the Commission notifies   **7–019**
guidelines for the exercise of its discretion (*e.g.* for the assessment of State aid under Art.87(3) of the EC Treaty or the determination of a fine on account of infringement of Art.81 and/or Art.82 of the EC Treaty), this entails a self-imposed limitation of that discretion in so far as it must comply with the indicative rules which it has itself laid down.[63] Such guidelines may be relied upon as against the Commission. In an action for annulment (brought, for instance, against a decision relating to State aid or a decision based on Art.81 and/or Art.82 of the EC Treaty), parties may therefore argue before the Community Court that the Commission has wrongly failed to apply the guidelines.[64]

(4) *Preparatory acts and measures laying down a definitive position*

Definitive statement of position. An action will lie against an act only if it   **7–020**
definitively lays down the position of the institution which adopted it.[65]

Measure concluding an internal procedure. Some acts of institutions are   **7–021**
adopted by means of a procedure comprising different stages. Only the measure which concludes the procedure expresses the definitive position of the institution. Measures paving the way for the final measure do not

---

[62] For examples of cases in which the internal instruction produced only internal effects, see ECJ, Case 20/58 *Phoenix-Rheinrohr v High Authority* [1959] E.C.R. 75; ECJ, Case 190/84 *Les Verts v European Parliament* [1988] E.C.R. 1017. For a case in which the internal instruction had effects outside the institution and could therefore be challenged before the Court of Justice, see Case C–366/88 *France v Commission* [1990] E.C.R. I–3571.

[63] For guidelines in connection with State aid: see CFI, Case T–380/94 *AIUFFASS and AKT v Commission* [1996] E.C.R. II–2169, para.57; CFI, Case T–214/95 *Vlaams Gewest v Commission* [1998] E.C.R. II–717, para.89; CFI (judgment of December 1, 2004), Case T–27/02 *Kronofrance v Commission*, not yet reported, para.79. For guidelines with regard to the amount of fines which may be imposed on account of infringement of Arts 81 and 82 of the EC Treaty, see CFI (judgment of July 8, 2004), Case T–44/00 *Mannesmannröhren-Werke v Commission*, not yet reported, paras 212 and 232.

[64] CFI, Case T–35/99 *Keller and Keller Meccanica v Commission* [2002] E.C.R. II–261, para.77; CFI (judgment of December 1, 2004), Case T–27/02 *Kronofrance v Commission*, not yet reported, para.79.

[65] ECJ, Joined Cases 23–24 and 52/63 *Usines Emile Henricot and Others v High Authority* [1963] E.C.R. 217, at 223–224; ECJ, Case 60/81 *IBM v Commission* [1981] E.C.R. 2639, para.10. For an instance in which the contested act did not definitively lay down a position and therefore had no legal effects, see ECJ (order of June 28, 1993), Case C–64/93 *Danotab and Others v Commission* [1993] E.C.R. I–3595, paras 13–14. It was possible to infer from additional questions put by the Commission with regard to a request for access to documents that the contested act was not a definitive decision and therefore produced no legal effects: CFI, Case T–123/99 *JT's Corporation v Commission* [2000] E.C.R. II–3269, para.25. See also CFI (order of June 2, 2004), Case T–123/03 *Pfizer v Commission* [2004] E.C.R. II–1631, paras 25–27.

determine a definitive position. Consequently, preparatory acts may not be the subject of an action for annulment.[66] This is because an action brought against such a measure would make it necessary for the Court of Justice or the Court of First Instance to "arrive at a decision on questions on which the [institution] has not yet had an opportunity to state its position and would as a result anticipate the arguments on the substance of the case, confusing different procedural stages both administrative and judicial".[67]

7–022 **Irregularities in preparatory acts.** Where an action for annulment is brought against the measure concluding the procedure, any irregularities in the preparatory acts may be raised in challenging the final act.[68]

B. THE CONCEPT OF A REVIEWABLE ACT: SOME FIELDS OF APPLICATION

1. Enforcement of Arts 81 and 82 of the EC Treaty

7–023 **Regulatory framework.** The processing of complaints relating to, inquiries into and the prosecution of infringements of Arts 81 and 82 of the EC Treaty are governed by Regulation No 1/2003[69] and Regulation No 773/2004,[70] which determine an administrative procedure in which the Commission and/or the national competition authorities adopt various acts. The acts adopted by the national authorities may be challenged only before the courts of the Member State concerned, which may—and in some cases must—refer a question for a preliminary ruling to the Court of Justice. Acts adopted by the Commission on the basis of Regulations Nos 1/2003 and 773/2004 can be challenged before the Court of First Instance,[71] provided that they produce binding legal effects.

---

[66] See, for instance, ECJ, Case 346/87 *Bossi v Commission* [1989] 303, para.23; ECJ, Case C–147/96 *Netherlands v Commission* [2000] E.C.R. I–4723, para.35; CFI, Case T–64/89 *Automec v Commission* [1990] E.C.R. II–367, para.42; CFI, Joined Cases T–17/90, T–28/91 and T–17/92 *Camara Alloisio and Others v Commission* [1993] E.C.R. II–841, para.39; CFI, Case T–95/99 *Satellimages TV5 v Commission* [2002] E.C.R. II–1425, paras 32–41; CFI, Case T–47/01 *Co-Frutta v Commission* [2003] E.C.R. II–4441, paras 28–33 (in connection with access to documents).

[67] ECJ, Case 60/81 *IBM v Commission* [1981] E.C.R. 2639, para.20.

[68] ECJ, Joined Cases 12 and 29/64 *Ley v Commission* [1965] E.C.R. 107, at 118; CFI, Joined Cases T–10–12 and T–15/92 *Cimenteries CBR and Others v Commission* [1992] E.C.R. II–2667; CFI (order of June 2, 2004), Case T–123/03 *Pfizer v Commission* [2004] E.C.R. II–1631, para.24. The unlawful act in the preparatory phase may even affect an institution other than the one against which the action for annulment is brought (ECJ, Case C–445/00 *Austria v Council* [2003] E.C.R. I–8549, paras 31–35: in an action for annulment of a Council regulation, it was argued that the Commission proposal was unlawful).

[69] Council Regulation (EC) No 1/2003 of December 16, 2002 on the implementation of the rules on competition laid down in Arts 81 and 82 of the Treaty ([2003] O.J. L1/1).

[70] Commission Regulation (EC) No 773/2004 of April 7, 2004 relating to the conduct of proceedings by the Commission pursuant to Arts 81 and 82 of the EC Treaty ([2004] O.J. L123/18).

[71] In the unlikely event that a Community institution would challenge such act, proceedings would have to be brought before the Court of Justice (see 1–054, *supra*).

Until April 30, 2004 Regulation No 17[72] and Regulation No 2842/98[73] were in force. It may be assumed that the case-law which has been built up with regard to acts adopted by the Commission on the basis of those regulations will apply *mutatis mutandis* to similar acts adopted on the basis of the new Regulations Nos 1/2003 and 773/2004.

Requests for information. Whenever the Commission becomes aware that **7–024** an infringement of Art.81 and/or Art.82 of the EC Treaty may have been committed, it may decide to address a request for information to the undertakings or associations of undertakings concerned in order to obtain "all necessary information".[74] A distinction has to be drawn between "simple requests" for information on the basis of Art.18(2) of Regulation No 1/2003 and requests "by decision" on the basis of Art.18(3) of that regulation. The addressees of a simple request are free to reply or not to reply to the questions put to them. Such requests for information do not bring about a distinct change in the legal position of the undertakings and associations concerned and cannot be challenged before the Court of First Instance.[75] By contrast, the addressees of a Commission decision based on Art.18(3) of Regulation No 1/2003 requiring them to supply information are obliged, on pain of penalties, to comply with such a request.[76] Such a decision is a reviewable act.[77] If the party to which such a decision is addressed wishes to challenge its legality, it will have to bring its action within the two-month time-limit imposed by the fifth para. of Art.230 of the EC Treaty. Indeed, an undertaking or association concerned which has not sought the annulment of such a decision within this two-month time-limit will be foreclosed from pleading the illegality of the decision requiring information in an action for annulment brought against the Commission decision finding an infringement.[78]

---

[72] Regulation No 17: First Regulation implementing Arts 85 and 86 *[now Arts 81 and 82]* of the Treaty, [1959–1962] O.J. English Spec. Ed. I, 8.

[73] Commission Regulation (EC) No 2842/98 of December 22, 1998 on the hearing of parties in certain proceedings under Arts 85 and 86 *[now Arts 81 and 82]* of the EC Treaty ([1998] O.J. L354/18). That regulation replaced the earlier Regulation No 99/63 ([1963–1964] O.J. English Spec. Ed. I, 47).

[74] Regulation No 1/2003, Art.18(1).

[75] Regulation No 1/2003, Arts 18(2) and 23(1)(a). A penalty may only be imposed where, having agreed to reply, the undertaking or association concerned provides inaccurate information.

[76] Regulation No 1/2003, Arts 18(3) and 23(1)(b). The Commission may not, however, compel an undertaking or an association to provide answers which might involve an admission on its part of the existence of an infringement which it is incumbent on the Commission to prove (ECJ, Case 374/87 *Orkem v Commission* [1989] E.C.R. I–3283, para.35; CFI, Case T–34/93 *Société Générale v Commission* [1995] E.C.R. II–545, para.74; CFI, Case T–112/98 *Mannesmannröhren-Werke v Commission* [2001] E.C.R. II–729, para.67).

[77] Under Art.18(3) of Regulation No. 1/2003 the Commission is even obliged to indicate in a request by decision the right of the parties concerned to have the decision reviewed by the Community Courts. See also ECJ, Case 374/87 *Orkem v Commission* [1989] E.C.R. 3282.

[78] CFI, Joined Cases T–305/94, T–306/94, T–307/94, T–313/94 to T–316/94, T–318/94, T–325/94, T–328/94, T–329/94 and T–335/94 *Limburgse Vinyl Maatschappij and Others v Commission* [1999] E.C.R. II–931, paras 441 and 442.

The decision by which, in a first stage, the Commission, acting on the basis of Art.24(1) of Regulation No 1/2003,[79] fixes a deadline by which an undertaking which has provided what the Commission considers to be an incomplete response to a decision requesting information[80] is required to give a full response and at the same time imposes a penalty payment is, however, not a challengeable act as regards the imposition of the penalty payment. This is because such a decision does not produce binding legal effects in so far as it only fixes a periodical penalty in terms of a specific amount for each day by which the deadline is exceeded. It is not enforceable because it does not fix the total amount of the penalty payable. The total amount is fixed in a second stage by a new decision when it is found that the undertaking has not provided the information in good time.[81]

7–025 **Inspections.** Art.20 of Regulation No 1/2003 draws a distinction between two forms of inspections, namely inspections carried out upon production of an authorisation in writing[82] ("inspections under authorisation") and inspections formally ordered by a decision of the Commission.[83] The former type of inspection may be carried out only on the premises, land and means of transport of the undertakings and associations concerned and only if the undertakings and associations concerned are prepared to cooperate. No fine may be imposed where an undertaking or association of undertakings refuses to submit to an inspection under authorisation. Where the Commission wishes to search other premises, land and means of transport, including the homes of directors, managers and other members of staff of the undertakings and associations concerned or where it expects the parties concerned not to adopt a cooperative attitude, it will order an inspection by a formal decision.[84] It should be stressed that the Commission may carry out such an inspection without first attempting an inspection by authorisation.[85] There is a legal obligation to submit to an inspection ordered by a decision.

Given its binding character, a decision ordering an inspection can be the subject of an action for annulment brought under Art.230 of the EC Treaty.[86] However, all persons subject to Community law are under an

---

[79] Formerly Art.16(1) of Regulation No 17.
[80] Regulation No 1/2003, Art.18(3).
[81] CFI (order of June 24, 1998), Case T–596/97 *Dalmine v Commission* [1998] E.C.R. II–2383, paras 27–34.
[82] Regulation No 1/2003, Art.20(3).
[83] Regulation No 1/2003, Arts 20(4) and 21(1).
[84] *Ibid*.
[85] ECJ, Case 136/79 *National Panasonic v Commission* [1980] E.C.R. 2033, paras 10–12.
[86] Art.20(4) of Regulation No 1/2003 requires the Commission to specify in such a decision that the right exists to have it reviewed by the Court of Justice/Court of First Instance. It should be noted, however, that reports, drawn up by the Commission's officials during an investigation into an undertaking and containing a summary of what was said by that undertaking's representatives in the course of the investigation, are not actionable measures: CFI (order of June 9, 1997), Case T–9/97 *Elf Atochem v Commission* [1997] E.C.R. II–909, paras 18–27.

obligation to acknowledge that measures adopted by the institutions are fully effective as long as they have not been declared invalid by the Court of Justice or the Court of First Instance and to recognise their enforceability unless one of those courts has decided to suspend the legal effects of the said measures.[87] Practically speaking, this means that an undertaking or association of undertakings will not be in a position to prevent an inspection ordered by a decision of the Commission from taking place. The party concerned will be able only to seek judicial redress before the Court of First Instance after the event by lodging an action for annulment against the decision ordering an inspection.[88] If such action were to be lodged within the two-month time limit laid down by the fifth para. of Art.230 of the EC Treaty and the Court of First Instance were to find that the inspection had been unlawful, the evidence obtained in the course of such inspection would also be unlawful. The Commission could then no longer find an infringement on the basis of that evidence.[89]

An addressee of a decision ordering an inspection who does not seek the annulment of that decision within the two-month time-limit laid down by the fifth para. of Art.230 of the EC Treaty will be foreclosed from pleading the illegality of the decision (as well as of the evidence obtained in the course of such inspection) in any subsequent action for annulment of the Commission decision finding an infringement of Art.81(1) and/or Art.82 of the EC Treaty.[90] Where, however, the applicant does not contest the legality of the decision ordering an inspection but only criticises the way in which that decision was implemented, such arguments may still be raised in the action for annulment brought against the final decision of the Commission finding the infringement.[91]

Before an inspection takes place, a national judicial authority will generally be asked to carry out a limited review of the Commission decision

---

[87] ECJ, Joined Cases 46/87 and 227/88 *Hoechst v Commission* [1989] E.C.R. I–2859, para.64.

[88] There remains the theoretical possibility of bringing an application for interim relief. However, it would be hard to prove irreparable damage as a result of an inspection. See CFI (order of the President of October 30, 2003), Joined Cases T–125/03 R and T–253/03 R Akzo *Nobel Chemicals and Others v Commission* [2003] E.C.R. II–4771.

[89] Opinion of Advocate General J.-P. Warner in Case 136/79 *National Panasonic v Commission* [1980] E.C.R. 2033, at 2069: "[The fact that the remedy can only be invoked] after the investigation has taken place, [. . .] does not make it an ineffective remedy. The Court may [. . .] if it holds the decision to have been unlawful, order the Commission to return to the undertaking any copies of documents obtained as a result of the investigation and to refrain from using any information so obtained". See also ECJ, Case 46/87 R *Hoechst v Commission* [1987] E.C.R. 1549, para.34, and ECJ, Case 85/87 R *Dow Chemical Nederland v Commission* [1987] E.C.R. 4367, para.17.

[90] CFI, Joined Cases T–305/94, T–306/94, T–307/94, T–313/94, T–316/94, T–318/94, T–325/94, T–328/94, T–329/94 and T–335/94 *Limburgse Vinyl Maatschappij and Others v Commission* [1999] E.C.R. II–931, paras 408–410.

[91] ECJ, Case 85/87 *Dow Benelux v Commission* [1989] E.C.R. I–3137, para 49; CFI, Joined Cases T–305/94, T–306/94, T–307/94, T–313/94, T–316/94, T–318/94, T–325/94, T–328/94, T–329/94 and T–335/94 *Limburgse Vinyl Maatschappij and Others v Commission* [1999] E.C.R. II–931, para 413.

ordering the inspection.[92] This will be the case where the Commission requests the assistance of the police in order to compel the undertaking or association concerned to submit to an inspection or where the Commission seeks to conduct an inspection in the homes of members of staff of the undertaking or association concerned. The national judicial authority will check whether the Commission decision is authentic. It will see to it that the coercive measures envisaged are neither arbitrary nor excessive having regard to the subject-matter of the inspection. In reviewing the proportionality of the coercive measures, the national judicial authority may ask the Commission, directly or through the Member State competition authority, for detailed explanations in particular of the grounds the Commission has for suspecting an infringement of Arts 81 and 82 of the EC Treaty, as well as of the seriousness of the suspected infringement and the nature of the involvement of the undertaking concerned. However, the national judicial authority may not call into question the necessity for the inspection or demand that it be provided with the information in the Commission's file. Only the Court of First Instance and the Court of Justice can review the legality of the Commission's decision.[93]

7–026 **Initiation of infringement proceedings and statement of objections.** If the Commission considers, on the basis of the information obtained during its investigation, that certain undertakings and/or associations of undertakings have infringed the EC competition rules, it may open a formal procedure against the parties concerned pursuant to Art.2 of Regulation No 773/2004. Shortly after the initiation of proceedings, it will send a statement of objections to these parties pursuant to Art.10 of Regulation No 773/2004. The initiation of an administrative procedure[94] and the communication of a statement of objections[95] are not acts against which an application for annulment may be brought. This is because they are preparatory acts. Any irregularities in such acts may be raised in an action brought against the decision concluding the procedure.

Accordingly, in *Woodpulp*, the Court of Justice annulled a number of paragraphs of the operative part of the Commission's final decision after finding that the infringements found in those paragraphs had not been

---

[92] Regulation No 1/2003, Art.20(7) and (8) and Art.21(3).

[93] *Ibid.* See in particular ECJ, Case C–94/00 *Roquette Frères* [2002] E.C.R. I–9011.

[94] Regulation No 773/2004, Art.2. The initiation of the administrative procedure requires "an authoritative act of the Commission, evidencing its intention of taking a decision [on the matter]" (ECJ, Case 48/72 *Brasserie de Haecht* [1973] E.C.R. 77, para.16). The undertaking addressed is aware of the fact that an administrative procedure is under way against it and knows its procedural position. Such notification does not constitute a definitive adoption of a position.

[95] Regulation No 773/2004, Art.10. See in this connection ECJ, Case 60/81 *IBM v Commission* [1981] E.C.R. 2639, para.21. The Commission is obliged to apprise the undertaking charged with an infringement of Art.81 or Art.82 of the EC Treaty of the facts and arguments underlying its charges. That statement secures the right of the undertaking concerned to a fair hearing.

clearly set out in the statement of objections. The parties concerned had therefore not been given an opportunity to defend themselves effectively during the administrative procedure against the objections raised against them.[96]

Notice pursuant to Art.27(4) of Regulation No 1/2003. It may be assumed that a Commission notice pursuant to Art.27(4) of Regulation No 1/2003 in which the Commission informs interested third parties either of its intention to adopt a decision making the commitments offered by the undertakings concerned binding on them or of its intention to adopt a decision finding the inapplicability of Art.81 of the EC Treaty to an agreement, a decision of an assocation of undertakings or a concerted practice, and invites third parties to submit their observations within a fixed time-limit, does not constitute a challengeable act.[97] The reason is that such notice is a preparatory act in a procedure which will normally result in the adoption of a challengeable act based on Art.9 or Art.10 of Regulation No 1/2003.   7–027

Commission's refusal to give access to its file to the parties under investigation. In the course of the administrative procedure the Commission has to give the parties under investigation access to its file. The Commission's obligation extends to its entire file, except for its internal   7–028

---

[96] ECJ, Joined Cases C–89/85, C–104/85, C–114/85, C–116/85, C–117/85 and C–125/85, C–129/85 *Ahlström and Others v Commission* [1993] E.C.R. I–1307, paras 52 and 154; see also CFI, Joined Cases T–39/92 and T–40/92 *Groupement des Cartes Bancaires "CB" and Europay International v Commission* [1994] E.C.R. II–49, paras 49–61.

[97] See, by analogy, CFI, Case T–74/92 *Ladbroke Racing v Commission* [1995] E.C.R. II–115, para.72, with regard to the notice given by the Commission pursuant to Art.19(3) of Regulation No 17 (notice indicating that the Commission intended to adopt a favourable position with regard to a notified agreement; under Regulation No 1/2003 agreements can no longer be notified to the Commission with a view to obtaining an exemption under Art.81(3) of the EC Treaty). By contrast, a communication pursuant to Art.15(6) of Regulation No 17 by which the Commission withdrew exemption from a fine from an undertaking which had notified an agreement was held to be an act against which an annulment action could be brought. The Commission took that decision where, after conducting a preliminary examination, it considered that the agreement notified was prohibited by Art.81 of the EC Treaty and that a declaration under Art.81(3) that the first para. of that article was inapplicable was unjustified. The Court of Justice ruled that if such a "preliminary measure" were excluded from all (direct) judicial review, there would be no alternative for the undertakings concerned than to "take the risk of a serious threat of a fine or to terminate against their own interests an agreement which, if proceedings had been instituted, might have had a chance of escaping the prohibition" (ECJ, Joined Cases 8–11/66 *Cimenteries CBR Cementbedrijven and Others v Commission* [1967] E.C.R. 75 at 92–93; CFI, Case T–19/91 *Vichy v Commission* [1992] E.C.R. II–415, para.5; CFI, Joined Cases T–213/95 and T–18/96 *SCK and FNK v Commission* [1997] E.C.R. II–1739, para.68). That dilemma for the undertakings concerned generally led to the termination of the notified agreement, with the result that the Commission often did not have to take a final decision in order to impose its views on the merits. If no action had been possible against a communication pursuant to Art.15(6) of Regulation No 17, the Commission could have effectually avoided any judicial review of its action.

documents and documents containing business secrets or other confidential information.[98] A refusal on the part of the Commission to accede to a request of a party under investigation to disclose some documents in its file does not constitute a challengeable act.[99] The possible illegality of such refusal may be raised in an application brought against the final decision of the Commission finding an infringement (and possibly imposing fines).

If a party demonstrates in the context of an action for annulment brought against the final Commission decision that it was not in a position to express its views with regard to one or more inculpatory documents in the course of the administrative procedure, the Court of First Instance will find that there has been a violation of the rights of the defence. The inculpatory documents will be excluded as evidence. Far from leading inevitably to the annulment of the decision in its entirety, the exclusion of such documents will lead to the annulment in whole or in part of the decision only in so far as the corresponding objection raised by the Commission can only be proved by reference to them.[100] In other words, if the Court of First Instance considers that the infringement has been sufficiently made out on the basis of other inculpatory documents which were made available to the applicant in the course of the administrative procedure and in respect of which the applicant was able to express its views, the violation of the rights of the defence will not affect the legality of the decision.[101]

---

[98] This rule was first developed in the case-law: CFI, Case T–7/89 *Hercules Chemicals v Commission* [1991] E.C.R. II–1711, para.54; CFI, Case T–65/89 *BPB Industries and British Gypsum v Commission* [1993] E.C.R. II–389, para.29; CFI, Joined Cases T–25/95, T–26/95, T–30/95, T–31/95, T–32/95, T–34/95, T–35/95, T–36/95, T–37/95, T–38/95, T–39/95, T–42/95, T–43/95, T–44/95, T–45/95, T–46/95, T–48/95, T–50/95, T–51/95, T–52/95, T–53/95, T–54/95, T–55/95, T–56/95, T–57/95, T–58/95, T–59/95, T–60/95, T–61/95, T–62/95, T–63/95, T–64/95, T–65/95, T–68/95, T–69/95, T–70/95, T–71/95, T–87/95, T–88/95, T–103/95 and T–104/95 *Cimenteries CBR and Others v Commission* [2000] E.C.R. II–491, para.144; CFI (judgment of October 25, 2005), Case T–38/02 *Groupe Danone v Commission*, not yet reported, para.34. This rule is now incorporated into Art.15 of Regulation No 773/2004, which adds that the right of access does not also extend to internal documents of the national competition authorities, to correspondence between the Commission and such authorities and to correspondence between national competition authorities where that correspondence is contained in the Commission's file.

[99] CFI, Joined Cases T–10–12 and T–15/92 *CBR Cementbedrijven and Others v Commission* [1992] E.C.R. II–2667, para.42; CFI (order of July 9, 2003), Case T–216/01 *Reisebank v Commission*, not reported, paras 49–51.

[100] ECJ, Case 107/82 *AEG v Commission* [1983] E.C.R. 3151, paras 24–30; CFI, Case T–30/91 *Solvay v Commission* [1995] E.C.R. II–1775, para.58; CFI, Joined Cases T–25/95, T–26/95, T–30/95, T–31/95, T–32/95, T–34/95, T–35/95, T–36/95, T–37/95, T–38/95, T–39/95, T–42/95, T–43/95, T–44/95, T–45/95, T–46/95, T–48/95, T–50/95, T–51/95, T–52/95, T–53/95, T–54/95, T–55/95, T–56/95, T–57/95, T–58/95, T–59/95, T–60/95, T–61/95, T–62/95, T–63/95, T–64/95, T–65/95, T–68/95, T–69/95, T–70/95, T–71/95, T–87/95, T–88/95, T–103/95 and T–104/95 *Cimenteries CBR and Others v Commission* [2000] E.C.R. II–491, para.364; CFI (judgment of October 25, 2005), Case T–38/02 *Groupe Danone v Commission*, not yet reported, para.35.

[101] It is therefore only exceptionally that the non-communication of incriminating documents during the administrative procedure will lead to the partial or total annulment of the decision finding the infringement. For an example, see ECJ, Joined Cases C–89/85, C–

If a party claims in the context of an action for annulment brought against the final Commission decision that a document in the Commission's file which might contain exculpatory evidence was not available to it during the administrative procedure, the Court of First Instance will find a violation of that party's rights of defence and annul the contested decision in whole or in part if the party concerned can show that there is even a small chance that the outcome of the administrative procedure might have been different if it had been able to rely on that document during that procedure.[102]

Therefore, when, in the context of an action seeking annulment of the Commission's final decision, an applicant challenges the Commission's refusal to disclose one or more documents during the administrative procedure, the Court of First Instance will require their disclosure in the proceedings before it.[103] The applicant will then be invited to inspect the documents and to substantiate its plea alleging infringement of its rights of

---

104/85, C–114/85, C–116/85, C–117/85 and C–125/85, C–129/85 *Ahlström and Others v Commission* [1993] E.C.R. I–1307, para.138, where the Court of Justice held that "in establishing the infringement relating to transaction prices, the Commission must have relied essentially on documents gathered after the statement of objections was drawn up. Since the members of KEA had no opportunity to make their views known on those documents, Art.1(3) of the contested decision must be annulled for disregard of the rights of the defence in so far as it concerns that infringement."

[102] See CFI, Case T–7/89 *Hercules Chemicals v Commission* [1991] E.C.R. II–1711, para.56; CFI, Case T–30/91 *Solvay v Commission* [1995] E.C.R. II–1775, para.68; CFI, Case T–36/91 *ICI v Commission* [1995] E.C.R. II–1847, para.78; CFI, Joined Cases T–25/95, T–26/95, T–30/95, T–31/95, T–32/95, T–34/95, T–35/95, T–36/95, T–37/95, T–38/95, T–39/95, T–42/95, T–43/95, T–44/95, T–45/95, T–46/95, T–48/95, T–50/95, T–51/95, T–52/95, T–53/95, T–54/95, T–55/95, T–56/95, T–57/95, T–58/95, T–59/95, T–60/95, T–61/95, T–62/95, T–63/95, T–64/95, T–65/95, T–68/95, T–69/95, T–70/95, T–71/95, T–87/95, T–88/95, T–103/95 and T–104/95 *Cimenteries CBR and Others v Commission* [2000] E.C.R. II–491, paras 241 and 247; CFI, Joined Cases T–191/98, T–212/98, T–213/98 and T–214/98 *Atlantic Container Line and Others v Commission* [2003] E.C.R. II–3275, para.340. The test applied by the Court of First Instance with respect to the non-disclosure of potentially exculpatory documents is fully in line with the case-law which the Court of Justice developed in *Distillers* (ECJ, Case 30/78 *Distillers v Commission* [1980] E.C.R. 2229, para.26) with respect to procedural defects, according to which an alleged procedural defect cannot be relied upon to annul a decision where that defect could not in any event have affected the content of the decision. The applicant does not have to show that, if it had had access to certain documents in the administrative proceedings, the Commission decision would have been different in content, merely that it would have been able to use those documents in its defence (ECJ, Case C–51/92 P *Hercules Chemicals v Commission* [1999] E.C.R. I–4235, para.81). The test applied by the Court of First Instance with respect to the non-disclosure of potentially exculpatory documents is therefore more favourable to the applicant than the test applied with respect to the non-disclosure of inculpatory documents. Indeed, if the Court of First Instance were to apply the same test in respect of potentially exculpatory documents as that laid down in its case-law in respect of the non-disclosure of inculpatory documents, it would have to assess whether the evidence adduced in the decision read in conjunction with the exculpatory documents which had not been disclosed in the administrative proceedings demonstrated the existence of the infringement concerned and the participation of the party concerned in that infringement.

[103] By way of a measure of organisation of procedure within the meaning of Art.64 or a measure of inquiry within the meaning of Art.65 of the CFI Rules of Procedure.

defence.[104] If the Court of First Instance did not order such disclosure, it would be impossible for an applicant which alleges that its rights of defence have been infringed during the administrative procedure because of the failure to disclose certain documents to it to demonstrate that the outcome of the administrative procedure might have been different had such access been granted.[105]

7–029   Commission's disclosure of documents to third parties. As has already been made clear, an action for annulment cannot be brought by undertakings under investigation by the Commission on the ground of its refusal to give them access to certain documents during the administrative procedure. In contrast, a decision by the Commission not to treat certain documents as confidential during the administrative procedure and to disclose them to third parties may form the subject-matter of an action for annulment.[106]

---

[104] CFI, Joined Cases T–305/94, T–306/94, T–307/94, T–313/94, T–316/94, T–318/94, T–325/94, T–328/94, T–329/94 and T–335/94 *Limburgse Vinyl Maatschappij and Others v Commission* [1999] E.C.R. II–931, para.1023; CFI, Joined Cases T–25/95, T–26/95, T–30/95, T–31/95, T–32/95, T–34/95, T–35/95, T–36/95, T–37/95, T–38/95, T–39/95, T–42/95, T–43/95, T–44/95, T–45/95, T–46/95, T–48/95, T–50/95, T–51/95, T–52/95, T–53/95, T–54/95, T–55/95, T–56/95, T–57/95, T–58/95, T–59/95, T–60/95, T–61/95, T–62/95, T–63/95, T–64/95, T–65/95, T–68/95, T–69/95, T–70/95, T–71/95, T–87/95, T–88/95, T–103/95 and T–104/95 *Cimenteries CBR and Others v Commission* [2000] E.C.R. II–491, paras 158 to 162 and 241.

[105] In CFI, Joined Cases T–25/95, T–26/95, T–30/95, T–31/95, T–32/95, T–34/95, T–35/95, T–36/95, T–37/95, T–38/95, T–39/95, T–42/95, T–43/95, T–44/95, T–45/95, T–46/95, T–48/95, T–50/95, T–51/95, T–52/95, T–53/95, T–54/95, T–55/95, T–56/95, T–57/95, T–58/95, T–59/95, T–60/95, T–61/95, T–62/95, T–63/95, T–64/95, T–65/95, T–68/95, T–69/95, T–70/95, T–71/95, T–87/95, T–88/95, T–103/95 and T–104/95 *Cimenteries CBR and Others v Commission* [2000] E.C.R. II–491, the Court of First Instance held that "Applicants who have raised a plea alleging infringement of their rights of defence cannot be required to set out in their application detailed arguments or a consistent body of evidence to show that the outcome of the administrative procedure might have been different if they had had access to certain documents which were in fact never disclosed to them. Such an approach would in effect amount to requiring a *probatio diabolica* . . . ." (para.161).

[106] ECJ, Case 53/85 *AKZO Chemie v Commission* [1986] E.C.R. 1965; CFI, Case T–353/94 *Postbank v Commission* [1996] E.C.R. II–921, paras 33–39: a letter by which the Commission removes the prohibition—mentioned when the statement of objections was sent to undertakings which were participating, but were not formal complainants, in a proceeding before the Commission—on using the statement of objections in national legal proceedings and by which it also gives its view as to the lack of any obstacle to production, in the national court, of that statement of objections and the minutes of the subsequent hearing, is in the nature of a challengeable decision. But see CFI (order of May 2, 1997), Case T–136/96 *Peugeot v Commission* [1997] E.C.R. II–663: an action will not lie against a letter addressed by the Commission to an undertaking in which it expresses its intention to communicate purported business secrets of that undertaking and giving it one month to submit any comments to the hearing officer pursuant to Art.9 of Commission Decision No 2001/462/EC, ECSC of May 23, 2001 on the terms of reference of hearing officers in competition procedures before the Commission ([2001] O.J. L162/21). Such an act is only a preparatory act forming part of the first stage of the procedure set out in Art.9 of Decision No 2001/462 (the order refers to the identically worded Art.5 of Decision No 94/810, which was replaced by Decision No 2001/462). A decision to transmit a non-confidential version of the statement of objections to the complainant is *prima facie* a challengeable act: CFI (order of the President of December 20, 2001), Case T–213/01 R *Österreichische*

Such a decision is independent of the final decision bringing the administrative procedure to an end. Moreover, the possibility of bringing an action for annulment of the final decision does not afford adequate protection. On the one hand, the administrative procedure does not always culminate in a final decision, which, at the same time, rules out any chance of bringing an action and would hence enable the right to confidential treatment of documents to be breached without any judicial sanction; on the other hand, an action against the final decision affords no guarantee of being able to prevent the disclosure of confidential documents from having irreparable consequences.

Interim measures. The Commission has the power to impose interim measures[107] in the course of the administrative procedure in order to avoid serious and irreparable damage to competition which could not be remedied by its final decision. The decision imposing interim measures must be "made in such a form that an action may be brought upon them . . . by any party who considers it has been injured".[108] However, it will have to be assessed whether an applicant still retains an interest in having the decision imposing interim measures annulled where the Commission has adopted a final decision withdrawing the decision imposing interim measures.[109]   **7–030**

Commitments. Where the Commission intends to adopt a decision requiring that an infringement be brought to an end and the undertakings concerned offer commitments to meet the concerns expressed to them by the Commission in its preliminary assessment, the Commission may by decision make those commitments binding on the undertakings.[110] It may be assumed that such a decision is a challengeable act within the meaning of Art.230 of the EC Treaty.[111]   **7–031**

Finding of infringement and imposition of fines. The decision by which the Commission finds an infringement of Art.81 and/or Art.82 of the EC Treaty   **7–032**

Postsparkasse v Commission [2001] E.C.R. II–3961, paras 49–52; CFI (order of the President of December 20, 2001), Case T–214/01 R *Bank für Arbeit und Wirtschaft v Commission* [2001] E.C.R. II–3993, paras 43–46.

107 The Commission will adopt interim measures only on its own initiative and not at the request of a party. Indeed, Art.8(1) of Regulation No 1/2003 provides: "In cases of urgency due to the risk of serious and irreparable damage to competition, the Commission, acting on its own initiative may by decision, on the basis of a *prima facie* finding of infringement, order interim measures".

108 ECJ, Case 792/79 R *Camera Care v Commission* [1980] E.C.R. 119, para.19; ECJ, Joined Cases 228 and 229/82 *Ford v Commission* [1984] E.C.R. 1129, para.10.

109 CFI (order of March 10, 2005), Case T–184/01 *IMS Health v Commission*, not yet reported, paras 34–49.

110 Regulation No 1/2003, Art.9(1).

111 See, by analogy, ECJ, Joined Cases C–89, C–104, C–114, C–116–117 and C–125–129/85 *Ahlström and Others v Commission* [1993] E.C.R. I–1307, para.181.

and, possibly, imposing a fine produces obligatory legal effects and is a challengeable act. However, an action will not lie against the Commission's refusal to accede to a request from one of the addressees of the decision to agree to their paying the fine in a particular way.[112] This is because such an act must be regarded as confirming the initial decision. The obligatory legal effects therefore arise out of the initial decision and not out of the refusal.[113]

7–033 **Position of complainant.** Acts adopted by the Commission during the administrative procedure *vis-à-vis* persons who have lodged complaints[114] alleging breaches of Art.81 and/or Art.82 of the EC Treaty are not all capable of forming the subject-matter of an action for annulment.

Accordingly, an action will not lie against the notification to be served on the complainants under Art.7 of Regulation No 773/2004[115] informing them that the Commission is not going to take up the complaint and fixes a time-limit for them to submit any further comments, following which it will take its final decision.[116] The notification must make it clear that the complainant is entitled to submit comments on the proposed rejection of its complaint. If the letter addressed to the complainant does not contain such an invitation to submit comments, the rejection of the complaint is final and, according to established case-law,[117] may be the subject of judicial proceedings.[118]

---

[112] CFI (order of April 29, 2004), Case T–308/02 *SGL Carbon v Commission* [2004] E.C.R. II–1363.

[113] There is a possibility of securing the suspension of the decision finding the infringement and imposing a fine provided that the conditions for the grant of interim measures are satisfied (see Ch.13, *infra*).

[114] On the basis of Art.7(2) of Regulation No 1/2003 (formerly Art.3(2) of Regulation No 17).

[115] Formerly Art.6 of Regulation No 99/63 and Art.6 of Regulation No 2842/98.

[116] ECJ, Case C–282/95 P *Guérin Automobiles v Commission* [1997] E.C.R. I–1503, para.34; CFI, Case T–64/89 *Automec v Commission* [1990] E.C.R. II–367, para.46.

[117] ECJ, Case 210/81 *Demo-Studio Schmidt v Commission* [1983] E.C.R. 3045; ECJ, Case 298/83 *CICCE v Commission* [1985] E.C.R. 1105; ECJ, Joined Cases 142 and 156/84 *British American Tobacco and R.J. Reynolds Industries v Commission* [1987] E.C.R. 4487.

[118] See ECJ, Case C–39/93 P *SFEI and Others v Commission* [1994] E.C.R. I–2681, paras 24–33, in which the Court of Justice set aside the order of the Court of First Instance in Case T–36/92 *SFEI and Others v Commission* [1992] E.C.R. II–2479. The judgment given on appeal by the Court of Justice links up with the analysis carried out by the Court of First Instance in Case T–64/89 *Automec v Commission* [1990] E.C.R. II–367 of the procedure to be applied where the Commission deals with a complaint alleging infringement of the Treaty competition rules. The Court of First Instance distinguished between three stages (*ibid.*, paras 45–47). During the first of those stages, the Commission collects the information needed to decide what action to take on the complaint. That stage may include an informal exchange of views and information between the Commission and the complainant. In the view of the Court of First Instance, preliminary observations made by Commission officials in the context of those informal contacts cannot be regarded as measures open to challenge. In the second stage, the Commission *either* informs the complainant, in accordance with Art.7(1) of Regulation No 773/2004, that it does not intend to take up the complaint and sets a time-limit within which the complainant is to submit its observations, *or* serves on the undertaking allegedly in breach of the competition

If the complainant makes known its views within the time-limit set by the Commission and the written submissions made by the complainant do not lead to a different assessment of the complaint, the Commission is to reject the complaint by decision. An action will lie against that act. If the complainant fails to make known its views within the time-limit set by the Commission, the complaint is deemed to have been withdrawn.[119]

An action will also lie against a decision of the Commission suspending an administrative procedure under Regulation No 1/2003 pending delivery of judgment in proceedings pursuant to Art.226 of the EC Treaty. This is because such a decision affects the procedural rights of persons who have submitted a complaint pursuant to Art.7(2) of Regulation No 1/2003, in particular the right to be informed beforehand of the Commission's intention not to uphold their complaint and to submit observations in that connection and the right to bring an action for annulment against the rejection of the complaint. In the case of proceedings under Art.226 of the EC Treaty, persons who have lodged a complaint do not have those rights. If some of the questions raised in the complaint pursuant to Regulation No 1/2003 are going to form the subject of infringement proceedings and the Commission therefore suspends judgement on the complaint as far as those questions are concerned, this deprives the complainant of its procedural rights. An action may consequently be brought against the decision suspending the administrative procedure.[120]

As far as access to the file is concerned, the principle that there must be full disclosure applies only to undertakings and associations on which a penalty may be imposed by a Commission decision finding an infringement

---

rules a statement of objections if it considers that the infringement raised in the complaint should be pursued. As already mentioned, neither of those acts may be challenged because they do not amount to a definitive position on the part of the Commission. If the Commission intends to reject the complaint, the Commission takes cognisance of the complainant's comments in the third stage. That stage may end with a final decision by which the Commission rejects the complaint (Regulation No 773/2004, Art.7(2)). The complainant may bring an action to annul that decision. In its order in *SFEI and Others v Commission*, the Court of First Instance took the view that the contested act formed part of the first stage of the investigation and was therefore not amenable to an action for annulment. On appeal, however, the Court of Justice held that the act constituted a final decision definitively rejecting the complaint, and set aside the order of the Court of First Instance. That judgment does not detract from the analysis of the Court of First Instance in *Automec*. It merely indicates—as also emerges from the judgment of the Court of First Instance in *Automec* (para.48)—that the breakdown of the processing of a complaint into three stages for analytical purposes does not mean that an action will lie against the rejection of a complaint only if all three stages of the procedure have been completed (see, however, Spinks, case note on *Automec v Commission* (1991) C.M.L.Rev. 453, at 461; see also CFI, Case T–37/92 *BEUC and NCC v Commission* [1994] E.C.R. II–285, paras 27–36 and CFI, Case T–241/97 *Stork Amsterdam v Commission* [2000] E.C.R. II–309, paras 49–69).

[119] Regulation No 773/2004, Art.7.

[120] CFI, Case T–16/91 *Rendo and Others v Commission* [1992] E.C.R. II–2417, paras 51–55 (those paras are not affected by the fact that the Court of Justice partially set aside that judgment in ECJ, Case C–19/93 P *Rendo and Others v Commission* [1995] E.C.R. II–3319).

of Art.81(1) or Art.82 of the EC Treaty.[121] Thus, complainants cannot claim to have a right of access to the file on the same basis as the parties under investigation.[122] In any event, the Commission's refusal to grant (partial) access to its file to a complainant cannot be held to be a challengeable act. However, when the Commission rejects the complaint, the complainant may challenge the Commission's final decision on the ground that it had insufficient access to the Commission's file during the administrative procedure. In this connection it must be borne in mind that Art.8(1) of Regulation No 773/2004 provides that the complainant may request access to the documents on which the Commission bases its provisional assessment that the complaint should be rejected.[123]

7–034 **Complaint relating to a breach of Art.86 of the EC Treaty.** Art.86(3) of the EC Treaty requires the Commission to ensure that the Member States comply with the obligations imposed on them in regard to the undertakings mentioned in Art.86(1), and expressly confers on it the power to take action for that purpose by way of directives and decisions. The Commission is empowered to determine that a given State measure is incompatible with the rules of the Treaty and to indicate what measures the Member State to which a decision is addressed must adopt in order to comply with its obligations under Community law.[124]

If an undertaking requests the Commission to find that a Member State has infringed the combined provisions of Arts 82 and 86(1) of the EC Treaty, an action will not lie against the Commission's rejection of that request. The Court of Justice considers that a letter to that effect cannot be regarded as producing binding legal effects.[125] As a result, complaints based on Arts 82 and 86(1) of the EC Treaty are treated in the same way as complaints that a Member State has infringed other provisions of Community law.[126]

2. Merger control

7–035 **Regulatory framework.** Until May 1, 2004, the Commission's supervisory competence with regard to mergers (or concentrations) and the administrative procedure which it had to follow in that area was laid down in Council

---

[121] CFI, Case T–65/96 *Kish Glass v Commission* [2000] E.C.R. II–1885, para 34; Case T–17/93 *Matra Hachette v Commission* [1994] E.C.R. II–595, para.34.
[122] *Ibid.*
[123] Access to the Commission's file cannot only be achieved through Regulations Nos 1/2003 and 773/2004. It can also be secured under Regulation (EC) No 1049/2001 of the European Parliament and of the Council of May 30, 2001 regarding public access to European Parliament, Council and Commission documents ([2001] O.J. L145/43). See 7–055, *infra*.
[124] ECJ, Case C–107/95 P *Bundesverband der Bilanzbuchhalter v Commission* [1997] E.C.R. I–947, para.23.
[125] ECJ, Case C–141/02 P *Commission v T–Mobile Austria* [2005] E.C.R. I–1283, para.70, setting aside CFI, Case T–54/99 *max.mobil Telekommunikation Service v Commission* [2002] E.C.R. II–313, in which the Court of First Instance had categorised the Commission's rejection of such a complaint as a formal decision addressed to the complainant.
[126] See 7–012, *supra*.

Regulation No 4064/89[127] and Commission Regulation No 447/98.[128] The applicable regulations now in force are Council Regulation No 139/2004[129] and Commission Regulation No 802/2004.[130]

Final decisions on notification. An action will lie against a decision by which the Commission declares a merger compatible or incompatible with the common market.[131] An action will also lie against a Commission decision finding that a joint venture does not constitute a concentration within the meaning of Regulation No. 139/2004 and therefore does not fall within the scope of that regulation.[132]

7–036

Ancillary restrictions. The assessment made by the Commission which is contained in the grounds of a concentration decision on whether ancillary restrictions mentioned by the notifying undertakings are permitted or not permitted is likewise a challengeable act.[133] This is because a decision declaring a concentration compatible with the common market is to be deemed to cover restrictions directly related and necessary to the implementation of the concentration.[134]

7–037

Finding of a dominant position. The mere finding in a concentration decision that an undertaking occupies a dominant position cannot be challenged. The reason for this is that such a finding does not produce binding legal effects.[135]

7–038

Referral to national authorities. An action will lie against the referral of a merger falling within the scope of Regulation No 139/2004 to the competition authorities of a Member State pursuant to Art.9 of that regulation.[136]

7–039

---

[127] Council Regulation (EEC) No 4064/89 of December 21, 1989 on the control of concentrations between undertakings ([1990] O.J. L257/13) as amended by Council Regulation (EC) No 1310/97 of June 30, 1997 ([1997] O.J. L180/1).

[128] Commission Regulation (EC) No 447/98 of March 1, 1998 on the notifications, time limits and hearings provided for in Council Regulation (EEC) No 4064/89 on the control of concentrations between undertakings ([1998] O.J. L61/1; *corrigendum* in [1998] L66/25).

[129] Council Regulation (EC) No 139/2004 of January 20, 2004 on the control of concentrations between undertakings ([2004] O.J. L 24/1).

[130] Commission Regulation (EC) No 802/2004 of April 7, 2004 implementing Council Regulation (EC) No 139/2004 on the control of concentrations between undertakings ([2004] O.J., L133/1; *corrigendum* in [2004] O.J. L 172/9).

[131] Regulation No 139/2004, Art.8(1)–(3).

[132] CFI, Case T–87/96 *Assicurazioni Generali and Unicredito v Commission* [1999] E.C.R. II–203, paras 37–44.

[133] CFI, Case T–251/00 *Lagardère and Canal+ v Commission* [2002] E.C.R. II–4825, paras 63–118.

[134] Regulation No 139/2004, Art.8(1) and (2).

[135] CFI, Joined Cases T–125/97 and T–127/97 *Coca-Cola v Commission* [2000] E.C.R. II–1733, para.92.

[136] CFI, Case T–119/02 *Royal Philips Electronics v Commission* [2003] E.C.R. II–1433, paras 267–300; CFI, Joined Cases T–346/02 and T–347/02 *Cableuropa and Others v Commission* [2003] E.C.R. II–4251, paras 47–82. A decision taken by such national authorities may be

7–040 **Commitments.** Commitments submitted by the undertakings concerned in the administrative procedure are as such not challengeable acts.[137] However, the conditions which the Commission imposes in its decision with a view to ensuring that the undertakings concerned comply with the commitments they have entered into *vis-à-vis* the Commission produce binding legal effects and may be reviewed by the Community courts.[138]

3. State aid cases

7–041 **Regulatory framework.** The Commission's supervisory competence and the administrative procedure which it must comply with in relation to State aid are laid down in Arts 87 and 88 of the EC Treaty and in Regulations Nos 659/99[139] and 794/2004.[140] This legal framework makes provision for separate procedures depending on whether the aid concerned is existing aid or new aid.

7–042 **Existing aid.** As far as existing aid[141] is concerned, Art.88(1) of the EC Treaty and Arts 17 to 19 of Regulation No 659/99 empower the Commission, in cooperation with the Member States, to keep aid under constant review. Where the Commission considers that existing aid is not, or is no longer, compatible with the common market, it informs the Member State concerned of its preliminary view and gives the Member State concerned the opportunity to submit its comments. Where the Commission, in the light of the information submitted by the Member State, concludes that the existing aid scheme is not, or is no longer, compatible with the common market, it will propose to the Member State concerned any appropriate measures required by the progressive development or by the functioning of the common market. Where the Member State concerned does not accept the proposed measures and the Commission, having taken into account the arguments of the Member State concerned, still considers that those measures are necessary, it will initiate the procedure provided for in Art.88(2) of the EC Treaty.

---

contested only before the national courts, although they may refer a question to the Court of Justice for a preliminary ruling on the interpretation of Regulation No 139/2004. A complaint made to the Commission about the handling of the case after referral is a complaint under Art.226 of the EC Treaty and the rejection of such a complaint is not a challengeable act (CFI (order of May 25, 2005), Case T–443/03 *Retecal and Others v Commission*, not yet reported, paras 34–46).

[137] See Regulation No 139/2004, Arts 6(2) and 8(2); Regulation No 802/2004, Art.20.

[138] See in this regard CFI, Joined Cases T–125/97 and T–127/97 *Coca-Cola v Commission* [2000] E.C.R. II–1733, paras 94–106.

[139] Council Regulation (EC) No 659/1999 of March 22, 1999 laying down detailed rules for the application of Art.93 [now Art.88] of the EC Treaty ([1999] O.J. L83/1).

[140] Commission Regulation (EC) No 794/2004 of April 21, 2004 implementing Council Regulation (EC) No 659/1999 laying down detailed rules for the application of Art.93 [now Art.88] of the EC Treaty ([2004] O.J. L140/1; *corrigendum* in [2005] O.J. L25 /74).

[141] For this concept, see Regulation No 659/1999, Art.1(b).

As far as existing aid is concerned, therefore, the initiative lies with the Commission.[142] If the Commission considers that there is existing aid whose compatibility with the common market it wishes to re-examine, it cannot require the Member State concerned to suspend that aid before it has taken a final decision holding it incompatible with the common market. For its part, the Member State is not under any obligation to suspend existing aid before such final decision.[143]

New aid. As far as new aid is concerned,[144] Art.88(3) of the EC Treaty provides that the Commission is to be informed, in sufficient time to enable it to submit its comments, of any plans to grant or alter aid. The Commission then proceeds to an initial examination of the planned aid. If, at the end of that examination, it considers that doubts are raised as to the compatibility with the common market of the measure concerned, it is to initiate the procedure provided for in Art.88(2).[145] In that event, the last sentence of Art.88(3) prohibits the Member State concerned from putting the proposed measures into effect until the procedure has resulted in a final decision.[146] New aid is therefore subject to preventive review by the Commission and in principle cannot be put into effect as long as that institution has not declared it compatible with the Treaty.[147]   **7–043**

Final decisions. Irrespective of whether existing aid or new aid is involved, Commission decisions by which national measures are held to be aid and compatible or incompatible with the common market produce binding legal effects and constitute challengeable acts.[148] The same is true of decisions by   **7–044**

---

[142] ECJ, Case C–44/93 *Namur-Les Aassurances du Crédit* [1994] E.C.R. I–3829, para.11.

[143] ECJ, Case C–400/99 *Italy v Commission* [2001] E.C.R. I–7303, para.48.

[144] ECJ, Case C–295/97 *Piaggio* [1999] E.C.R. I–3735, paras 47–48: the answer to the question whether aid is new cannot depend on a subjective assessment by the Commission. According to Art.1(c) of Regulation No 659/1999, new aid is aid which is not existing aid. Art.1(b) of Regulation No 659/1999 provides a list of all aid which must be regarded as existing aid.

[145] See Art.4(4) of Regulation No 659/1999. Proceedings must also be initiated where the Commission has doubts whether the measure should be categorised as aid unless, in the course of the initial examination, the Commission is able to satisfy itself that the measure at issue is in any event compatible with the common market, even if it is aid (CFI, Case T–11/95 *BP Chemicals v Commission* [1998] E.C.R. II–3235, para.166; CFI, Case T–46/97 *SIC v Commission* [2000] E.C.R. 2125, para.72). This case-law was confirmed by ECJ, Case C–400/99 *Italy v Commission* [2005] E.C.R. I–3657, para.47. The fact that the time spent on an initial examination under Art.88(3) of the EC Treaty considerably exceeds the time usually taken may, in addition to other factors, justify the conclusion that the Commission encountered serious difficulties of assessment necessitating initiation of the procedure under Art.88(2) of the EC Treaty (CFI, Case T–46/97 *SIC v Commission* [2000] E.C.R. II–2125, para.102).

[146] See also Regulation No 659/1999, Art.3.

[147] ECJ, Case C–44/93 *Namur-Les Assurances du Crédit* [1994] E.C.R. I–3829, para.12.

[148] A decision of the Council pursuant to Art.88(2), third subpara. of the EC Treaty by which aid is considered to be compatible with the common market by way of derogation from the provisions of Art.87 or from the regulations provided for in Art.89 is also a challengeable act (see ECJ, Case C–110/02 *Commission v Council* [2004] E.C.R. I–6333).

which the Commission determines that a measure of a Member State does not constitute aid within the meaning of Art.87(1) of the EC Treaty.[149]

7–045 **Initiation of the procedure.** Another question is whether the initiation of the formal investigation procedure provided for in Art.88(2) of the EC Treaty constitutes a challengeable act in itself. Under that provision, the Commission has to give notice to the "parties concerned" to submit their comments before it decides whether aid is compatible with the common market.

It is settled case-law that the initiation of that procedure produces no legal effects and therefore cannot be challenged before the Community Court where it relates to existing aid[150] since the Member State concerned may maintain the aid at that stage of the procedure.[151]

Where, in contrast, the procedure initiated relates to new aid the Member State concerned must not put its proposed measures into effect until the *inter partes* procedure has resulted in a final decision (EC Treaty, Art.88(3)). The obligation to suspend putting the aid into effect which arises out of the initiation of the procedure has autonomous legal effects which cannot be eradicated.[152] This is because the delay in putting the aid into effect caused by the suspensory effect of initiating the procedure is not offset by a decision by which the Commission declares the aid to be compatible with the common market or by a successful action for annulment of the Commission's finding that the proposed aid is incompatible with the common market. Any implementation of the new aid from the initiation of the procedure until the date of the final decision remains in any event unlawful. For those reasons, initiating a procedure under Art.88(2) of the EC Treaty cannot be regarded as a mere preparatory act.[153]

---

[149] ECJ, Case C–367/95 P *Commission v Sytraval and Brink's France* [1998] E.C.R. I–1719, paras 45–48. An action will not lie against a letter from the Commission informing the complainant about its decision addressed to a Member State with regard to State aid (CFI, Case T–82/96 *ARAP and Others v Commission* [1999] E.C.R. II–1889, para.28). As a result, the complainant should challenge the decision addressed to the Member State. The action will be admissible only if the decision is of direct and individual concern to the complainant within the meaning of the fourth para. of Art.230 of the EC Treaty.

[150] ECJ (order of the President of June 26, 2003), Joined Cases C–182/03 R and C–217/03 R *Belgium and Forum 187 v Commission* [2003] E.C.R. I–6887, para.119; CFI (order of June 2, 2003), Case T–276/02 *Forum 187 v Commission* [2003] E.C.R. II–2075. For a list of all measures to be regarded as being existing aid, see Art.1(b) of Regulation No 659/1999 ([1999] O.J. L83/1).

[151] As far as existing aid is concerned, the Commission's proposal of appropriate measures under Art.88(1) of the EC Treaty is also not a reviewable act. See CFI, Case T–330/94 *Salt Union v Commission* [1996] E.C.R. II–1475.

[152] ECJ, Case C–312/90 *Spain v Commission* [1992] E.C.R. I–4117, paras 14–20; ECJ, Case C–47/91 *Italy v Commission* [1992] E.C.R. I–4145, paras 22–26; ECJ, Case C–400/99 *Italy v Commission* [2001] E.C.R. I–7303, para.63. As a result, an action to annul the decision to initiate the formal procedure does not become devoid of purpose where the Commission adopts a final decision and that decision is not contested by the party which challenged the decision initiating the procedure (see ECJ, Case C–400/99 *Italy v Commission* [2005] E.C.R. I–3657, paras 15–18).

[153] ECJ, Case C–312/90 *Spain v Commission* [1992] E.C.R. I–4117, paras 21–24; ECJ, Case C–400/99 *Italy v Commission* [2001] E.C.R. I–7303, paras 62 and 69.

A decision to initiate a formal investigation procedure therefore has autonomous legal consequences, in particular with regard to the suspension of the measure under investigation, not only when the measure has already been put into effect by the authorities of the Member State concerned as existing aid, but also where the Member State considers that the measure to which the decision initiating the procedure relates does not fall within the scope of Art.87(1) of the EC Treaty.[154] In both cases, an action will lie against the decision.[155] A decision to initiate a formal investigation procedure in relation to a measure in the course of implementation which the Commission has classified as new aid necessarily alters the legal position of the measure under consideration and that of the undertakings which are its beneficiaries, particularly as regards the pursuit of its implementation. Until the adoption of such a decision, the Member State, the beneficiary undertakings and other economic operators may think that the measure is being lawfully carried out as a general measure which does not fall within the scope of Art.87(1) of the EC Treaty or as an existing aid. In contrast, after the adoption of such a decision there is at the very least a significant element of doubt as to the legality of that measure which, without prejudice to the possibility of seeking interim relief from the court with the power to grant it, must lead the Member State to suspend payment, since the initiation of the formal investigation procedure excludes the possibility of an immediate decision holding the measure compatible with the common market which would enable it to be lawfully pursued. Such a decision might also be invoked before a national court called upon to draw all the consequences arising from the infringement of the last sentence of Art.88(3) of the EC Treaty. Finally, it is capable of leading the undertakings which are beneficiaries of the measure to refuse new payments in any event, or to hold the necessary sums as provision for possible subsequent repayments. Businesses will also take account, in their relations with those beneficiaries, of the fragile legal and financial situation of the latter.[156]

---

[154] ECJ, Case C–400/99 *Italy v Commission* [2001] E.C.R. I–7303, paras 59, 60 and 69; CFI, Joined Cases T–269/99, T–271/99 and T–272/99 *Diputación Foral de Guipúzcoa and Others v Commission* [2002] E.C.R. II–4217, para.37.

[155] ECJ, Case C–400/99 *Italy v Commission*, [2005] E.C.R. I–3657) not yet reported, para.29: "In view of the legal consequences of a decision to initiate the procedure provided for in Art.88(2) EC, classifying the measures concerned as new aid even though the Member State concerned is unlikely to subscribe to that classification (. . .), the Commission must first broach the subject of the measures in question with the Member State concerned so that the latter has an opportunity, if appropriate, to inform the Commission that, in its view, those measures do not constitute aid or else constitute existing aid."

[156] ECJ, Case C–400/99 *Italy v Commission* [2001] E.C.R. I–7303, para.59; CFI, Joined Cases T–195/01 and T–207/01 *Gibraltar v Commission* [2002] E.C.R. II–2309, para.85; CFI, Joined Cases T–269/99, T–271/99 and T–272/99, *Diputación Foral de Guipúzcoa and Others v Commission* [2002] E.C.R. II–4217, para.38; CFI, Case T–190/00 *Regione Siciliana v Commission* [2003] E.C.R. II–5015 paras 42–53 (the right to contest a decision to initiate the procedure provided for in Art.88(2) of the EC Treaty does not affect the procedural rights of interested parties to challenge the final decision).

7–046 **Suspension and recovery injunctions.** An action will also lie against an injunction to suspend or recover aid that the Commission may address to a Member State by separate decision (before taking a final decision with regard to the compatibility of the aid with the common market) under Art.11(1) and (2) of Regulation No 659/1999.[157]

7–047 **Information injunction.** In the course of the administrative procedure, the Commission may address a request for information to the Member State concerned.[158] Where, despite a reminder, the Member State does not provide the information requested within the period prescribed by the Commission, or where it provides incomplete information, the Commission may by decision require the information to be provided. It remains an open question whether such an "information injunction" is a reviewable act.[159] In the event of non-compliance with an information injunction, the Commission will decide on the basis of the information available.[160]

7–048 **Right to file a complaint.** As regards the position of complainants,[161] Art.20(2) of Regulation No. 659/1999 provides that "[a]ny interested party may inform the Commission of any alleged unlawful aid and any alleged misuse of aid."[162] It follows from Art.20(1) and (2) of Regulation No 659/1999 that the interested parties entitled to file a complaint are those which may submit comments following a Commission decision to initiate the formal investigation procedure. They include "[. . .] the persons, undertakings or associations whose interests might be affected by the grant of the aid, in particular competing undertakings and trade associations [. . .]".[163]

---

[157] The Commission's power to issue such injunctions was already recognised by case-law: ECJ, Case C–301/87 *France v Commission* [1990] E.C.R. I–307, paras 19 and 22; ECJ, C–39/94 *SFEI and Others* [1996] E.C.R. I–3547, para.34. See also ECJ, Case C–400/99 *Italy v Commission* [2001] E.C.R. I–7303, para.51.

[158] Regulation No 659/1999, Art.10(2).

[159] Regulation No 659/1999, Art.10(3). See Soltész and Bielesz, "Judicial review of State aid decisions" (2004) E.Comp.L.Rev. 133, at 137, who consider that an information injunction constitutes a measure of a preparatory character which is not subject to judicial review.

[160] In the context of an action for annulment under Art.230 of the Treaty, the legality of a Community measure must be assessed on the basis of the elements of fact and of law existing at the time when the measure was adopted. In particular, the complex assessments made by the Commission must be examined solely on the basis of the information available to the Commission at the time when those assessments were made (ECJ, Case C–288/96 *Germany v Commission* [2000] E.C.R. I–8237, para.34; ECJ, Joined Cases T–371/94 and T–394/94 *British Airways and Others v Commission* [1998] E.C.R. II–2405, para.81; CFI, Case T–123/97 *Salomon v Commission* [1999] E.C.R. II–2925, para.42; CFI, Case T–296/97 *Alitalia v Commission* [2000] E.C.R. II–3871, para.86).

[161] On this issue, see Slot and Skudder, "The position of the complainant in EC State aid cases, in *Mélanges en hommage à Michel Waelbroeck* (Bruylant, Brussels, 1999), Vol. II, 1457–1476. See also Winter "The rights of complainants in State aid cases: judicial review of Commission decisions adopted under Art.88 (ex 93) EC" (1999) C.M.L.Rev. 521–568.

[162] For the form to be used for filing a complaint, see [2003] O.J. C116/3.

[163] See, *e.g.* ECJ, Case C–204/97 *Portugal v Commission* [2001] E.C.R. I–3175, para.31.

Decisions pursuant to a complaint. "In so far as the Commission has 7–049
exclusive jurisdiction to assess the compatibility of a grant of State aid with
the common market, it is required, in the interests of the sound administration of the fundamental rules of the Treaty relating to State aid, to conduct a
diligent and impartial examination of complaints reporting the grant of aid
which is incompatible with the common market [. . .]."[164] After examining the
complaint, the Commission takes in principle[165] one of the following
decisions, all of which will be addressed to the Member State concerned[166]:
(a) a decision by which the Commission finds that no aid within the meaning
of Art.87(1) of the EC Treaty is being granted, (b) a decision by which the
Commission finds that the aid is compatible with the common market or (c)
if it has doubts as to the compatibility with the common market of an aid
measure, a decision to initiate proceedings pursuant to Art.88(2) of the EC
Treaty, in which case all parties concerned, in particular the complainant and
the Member States may submit comments.[167] The first two decisions, which
are to be addressed to the Member State concerned,[168] may be contested by
the complainant, if it demonstrates that they are of direct and individual
concern to it within the meaning of the fourth para.of Art.230 of the EC
Treaty.[169] In our view, the complainant will have no interest in challenging
the initiation of proceedings under Art.88(2) of the EC Treaty. This is
because the complaint normally will aim at having the aid declared incompatible with the common market and this can only happen after the Commission
has gone through the procedure prescribed by Art.88(2) of the EC Treaty.[170]

---

[164] CFI, Case T–17/96 *TF1 v Commission* [1999] E.C.R. II–1757, para.73. See also Art.10(1) of
Regulation No 659/1999, which obliges the Commission to examine: "[. . .] information
from whatever source regarding alleged unlawful aid". Diligent and impartial examination
of the complaint may make it necessary for the Commission to examine matters not
expressly raised by the complainant. The Commission may therefore be obliged to extend
its investigation beyond a mere examination of the facts and the points of law brought to its
notice by the complainant (see ECJ, Case C–367/95 P *Commission v Sytraval and Brink's
France* [1998] E.C.R. I–1719, para.62).

[165] However, where the Commission considers that on the basis of the information in its
possession there are insufficient grounds for taking a view on the case, it has to inform the
complainant thereof (Regulation No 659/1999, Art.20(2)). It is unclear whether such a
decision will be susceptible of judicial review. It follows from Art.10(1) of Regulation No
659/1999, according to which the Commission has to examine any possible unlawful aid,
read in conjunction with Art.13(1), according to which "the examination of possible
unlawful aid shall result in a decision pursuant to Art.4(2), (3) or (4) [*i.e.* a decision finding
that the measure does not constitute aid, a decision finding that no doubts are raised as to
the compatibility with the common market, or a decision initiating proceedings pursuant to
Art.88(2)]" that the Commission has not much scope for responding to a complainant that
there are no grounds for taking a view on the case.

[166] Regulation No 659/1999, Art.25. See also ECJ, Case C–367/95 P *Commission v Sytraval and
Brink's France* [1998] E.C.R. I–1719, para.45.

[167] Regulation No 659/1999, Art.4. *See also* CFI, Case T–17/96 *TF1 v Commission* [1999]
E.C.R. II–1757, para.78.

[168] Regulation No 659/1999, Art.25.

[169] See 7–093 to 7–105, *infra*.

[170] The formal investigation procedure does not lead to an *inter partes* debate involving the

7–050   **Correspondence with complainants.** Any letters which the Commission may address to complainants are not acts amenable to judicial review. Only the formal decision addressed to the Member State concerned can be challenged.[171] Thus, an action for annulment lodged by a complainant against a letter from the Commission informing the complainant that a specific aid measure is covered by an approved general aid scheme will be inadmissible.[172] By contrast, a similar action brought against a decision addressed to a Member State in which the Commission raises no objections to an aid measure on the ground that it falls within the scope of an approved aid scheme will be admissible insofar as the complainant demonstrates that the contested act is of direct and individual concern to it within the meaning of the fourth para.of Art.230 of the EC Treaty.[173]

7–051   **Refusal to take appropriate measures.** Lastly, as regards existing aid, an action will not lie against the Commission's refusal to take appropriate measures within the meaning of Art.88(1) of the EC Treaty.[174] It should be borne in mind that when the Court is considering whether an action for the annulment of a negative decision of an institution is admissible, the decision must be appraised in the light of the nature of the request to which it constitutes a reply. Since, according to the wording of Art.88(1) of the EC Treaty, appropriate measures are merely proposals, which the State concerned is not bound to respect,[175] the Commission's refusal to take such measures does not constitute an act producing binding legal effects.

4. Anti-dumping cases

7–052   **General.** The final decision in an anti-dumping procedure normally lies with the Council. It imposes definitive anti-dumping duties or decides to terminate the anti-dumping procedure without imposing such duties. It also decides on the definitive imposition of provisional anti-dumping duties.

---

complainant or even the recipient of the aid. The comments received in the course of the formal investigation will only be submitted to the Member State concerned (Regulation No 659/1999, Art.6 (2)). See also CFI, Case T–613/97 *Ufex and Others v Commission* [2000] E.C.R. II–4055, paras 85–90; CFI (judgment of July 8, 2004), Case T–198/01 *Technische Glaswerke Ilmenau v Commission*, not yet reported, paras 193–198.
[171] See ECJ, Case C–367/95 P *Commission v Sytraval and Brink's France* [1998] E.C.R. I–1719, para.45; CFI (order of February 14, 2005), Case T–81/04 *Bouygues and Bouygues Télécom v Commission*, not reported, para 23.
[172] CFI, Case T–154/94 *CSF and CSME v Commission* [1996] E.C.R. II–1377; but see ECJ, Case C–313/90 *CIRFS and Others v Commission* [1993] E.C.R. I–1125.
[173] ECJ, Case C–321/99 *ARAP and Others v Commission* [2002] E.C.R. I–4287, paras 60 and 61.
[174] CFI, Case T–330/94 *Salt Union v Commission* [1996] E.C.R. II–1475.
[175] ECJ (order of the President of June 26, 2003), Joined Cases C–182/03 R and C–217/03 R *Belgium and Forum 187 v Commission* [2003] E.C.R. I–6887, para.119. However, where the Member State concerned accepts the proposed measures and informs the Commission thereof, it will be bound by its acceptance to implement the appropriate measures.

Such regulations and decisions produce legal effects and constitute challengeable acts.[176]

Preparatory measures. Regulation (EC) No 384/96[177] confers extensive   **7-053**
duties on the Commission in connection with the investigation of dumping
and the provisional control thereof. It receives complaints, directly or
indirectly, initiates investigations and decides whether or not protective
measures are needed. Various acts adopted by the Commission pursuant to
that regulation are preparatory and hence cannot be the subject of an
application for annulment, the reason being that sufficient protection is
afforded by bringing an action against the final decision. Examples of acts
against which an action will not lie are: a decision to initiate an anti-dumping
procedure[178]; a proposal submitted by the Commission to the Council,
following an objection raised in the Advisory Committee, to terminate the
procedure without imposing protective measures[179]; a decision of the Commission rejecting an undertaking offered by the company concerned in return
for the termination of the anti-dumping investigation[180]; a Commission
decision terminating an undertaking breached by an exporter.[181]

Definitive measures. Nevertheless, it should be noted that other acts   **7-054**
adopted by the Commission in anti-dumping procedures have definitive
legal effects and may be attacked by means of an action for annulment.
Examples of such acts include[182] a Commission decision to terminate the
anti-dumping procedure without imposing anti-dumping duties[183] and a
Commission regulation imposing provisional anti-dumping duties.
    As far as Commission regulations imposing provisional anti-dumping
duties are concerned, an action for the annulment of such a regulation will
become devoid of purpose when the Council takes a decision with regard to
the imposition of definitive anti-dumping duties.[184] This does not prevent

---

[176] ECJ, Case C–121/86 *Epicheiriseon Metalleftikon Viomichanikon kai Naftiliakon and Others v Council* [1989] ECI–3919; ECJ, Case C–76/01 *Eurocoton and Others v Council* [2003] E.C.R. I–10091, para.72.
[177] Council Regulation (EC) No 384/96 of December 22, 1995 on protection against dumped imports from countries not members of the European Community ([1996] O.J. L56/1).
[178] CFI (order of March 14, 1996), Case T–134/95 *Dysan Magnetics and Review Magnetics v Commission* [1996] E.C.R. II–181, para.23, and CFI (order of December 10, 1996), Case T–75/96 *Söktas v Commission* [1996] E.C.R. II–1689, paras 26–43.
[179] CFI, Case T–212/95 *Oficemen v Commission* [1997] E.C.R. II–1161, paras 45–54.
[180] ECJ, Joined Cases C–133 and C–150/87 *Nashua and Others v Commission and Council* [1990] E.C.R. I–719, paras 8–11; ECJ, Case C–156/87 *Gestetner Holdings v Council and Commission* [1990] E.C.R. I–781, para.8.
[181] CFI (order of July 10, 1996), Case T–208/95 *Miwon v Commission* [1996] E.C.R. II–635, para.31.
[182] Note that an action will also lie against a decision of the Commission denying a third party access to the non-confidential file: ECJ, Case C–170/89 *BEUC v Commission* [1991] E.C.R. I–5709, para.11.
[183] ECJ, Case C–315/90 *Gimelec and Others v Commission* [1991] E.C.R. I–5589; ECJ, Case C–76/01 *Eurocoton and Others v Council* [2003] E.C.R. I–10091, para.72.
[184] ECJ, Case 56/85 *Brother Industries v Commission* [1988] E.C.R. 5655; ECJ, Joined Cases 294/86 and 77/87 *Technointorg v Commission and Council* [1988] E.C.R. 6077, paras 10–14.

irregularities committed by the Commission in the course of the procedure leading to the imposition of provisional anti-dumping duties from being raised in order to claim that the Council regulation imposing definitive anti-dumping duties should be annulled, provided that the Council regulation takes the place of the Commission regulation. If, however, the defects are remedied in the course of the procedure resulting in the imposition of definitive anti-dumping duties, the unlawfulness of the Commission regulation will no longer affect the legality of the Council regulation.[185]

Not only the Council regulation imposing definitive anti-dumping duties may be contested in judicial proceedings. The tacit rejection by the Council (on account of failure to achieve the requisite majority in the Council) of the Commission's proposal for a regulation imposing definitive anti-dumping duties also constitutes a reviewable act.[186]

5. Access to documents pursuant to Regulation No 1049/2001

7–055 **Institutions' rejection of a confirmatory application is a reviewable act.** Regulation No 1049/2001[187] defines the principles, conditions and limits governing the right of access by the public to European Parliament, Council and Commission documents so as to enable citizens to participate more closely in the decision-making process, guarantee that the administration enjoys greater legitimacy and is more effective and more accountable to the citizen in a democratic system and strengthen the principles of democracy and respect for fundamental rights. A two-stage administrative procedure applies. If an initial application for access to documents is refused, the person concerned may make a confirmatory application asking the institution to reconsider its position. Only the institution's decision to reject a confirmatory application is a reviewable act.[188]

---

[185] CFI, Joined Cases T–159/94 and T–160/94 *Ajinomoto and NutraSweet v Council* [1997] E.C.R. II–2461, para.87, upheld by ECJ, Joined Cases C–76/98 P and C–77/98 P *Ajinomoto and NutraSweet v Council* [2001] E.C.R. I–3223, paras 65–72.

[186] ECJ, Case C–76/01 P *Eurocoton and Others v Council* [2003] E.C.R. I–10091, paras 54–65 (see also CFI (judgment of March 13, 2005), Case T–177/00 *Koninklijke Philips Electronics v Council*, not reported, paras 29–33). In a subsequent judgment, given in relation to an excessive-deficit procedure, the Court of Justice held that the Council's failure to adopt acts recommended by the Commission could not be regarded as giving rise to acts open to challenge for the purposes of Art.230 of the EC Treaty. The Court stressed, however, that in an excessive-deficit procedure—unlike in the case of an anti-dumping procedure—there is no provision of Community law prescribing a period on the expiry of which the Council is no longer empowered to adopt the measure proposed by the Commission (ECJ, Case C–27/04 *Commission v Council* [2004] E.C.R. I–6649, paras 32–34).

[187] Regulation (EC) No 1049/2001 of the European Parliament and of the Council of May 30, 2001 regarding public access to European Parliament, Council and Commission documents ([2001] O.J. L145/43).

[188] CFI (judgment of April 13, 2005), Case T–2/03 *Verein für Konsumenteninformation v Commission*, not yet reported.

II. IDENTITY OF THE PARTIES

A. DEFENDANTS: AGAINST WHICH INSTITUTIONS CAN AN ACTION FOR ANNULMENT BE BROUGHT?

1. Institutions

Acts of institutions. The first para.of Art.230 of the EC Treaty enables actions for annulment to be brought against acts adopted jointly by the European Parliament and the Council and acts of the Council,[189] the Commission and the European Central Bank. Acts of the European Parliament may also be reviewed if they are intended to produce legal effects *vis-à-vis* third parties.[190] This confirms the case-law on the EEC Treaty with regard to the admissibility of applications for annulment of acts of the European Parliament.[191]

7–056

---

[189] An application to annul an act of the European Council will be inadmissible since such acts do not fall within the jurisdiction of the Court of Justice or the Court of First Instance to conduct judicial review: CFI (order of July 14, 1994), Case T–179/94 *Bonnamy v Council*, not reported, para.10; CFI (order of July 14, 1994), Case T–584/93 *Roujansky v Council* [1994] E.C.R. II–585, para.12.

[190] A decision by which the European Parliament deprived some of its Members of the possibility of forming a political group affects the conditions under which the parliamentary mandate of the Members concerned are exercised, and thus produces legal effects in their regard and goes beyond an act confined to the internal organisation of the work of the Parliament (CFI, Joined Cases T–222/99, T–327/99 and T–329/99 *Martinez and Others v European Parliament* [2001] E.C.R. II–2823, paras 56–62). A framework agreement concluded by the Parliament with the Commission which applied a code of conduct governing relations between the two institutions is not an act affecting the legal position of individual Members of Parliament, in particular the right to put questions to the Commission under Art.197 of the EC Treaty. Consequently, an action brought by a number of Members of Parliament against that framework agreement was dismissed as inadmissible (CFI (order of January 17, 2002), Case T–236/00 *Stauner and Others v European Parliament and Commission* [2002] E.C.R. II–135, para.62). A decision of the European Parliament laying down the conditions in which OLAF can conduct an investigation in the Parliament goes beyond, in both its object and its effects, the internal organisation of the work of the Parliament and may therefore be the subject of an action for annulment (CFI, Case T–17/00 *Rothley and Others v European Parliament* [2002] E.C.R. II–579, paras 56–67, upheld on appeal by ECJ, Case C–167/02 P *Rothley and Others v European Parliament* [2004] E.C.R. I–3149).

[191] The first para. of the former Art.173 of the EEC Treaty confined actions for annulment to acts of the Council or the Commission. That limitation stemmed from the original institutional structure of the Community in which only the Council and the Commission were empowered to adopt binding acts. The gradual expansion of the European Parliament's competence which enabled it to adopt binding acts prompted the Court of Justice to give a broad interpretation to the first para. of the former Art.173 of the EEC Treaty in order to avoid acts of the Parliament not being subject to judicial review with regard to their compatibility with the Treaty (ECJ, Case 294/83 *Les Verts v European Parliament* [1986] E.C.R. 1339, confirmed by ECJ, Case 34/86 *Council v European Parliament* [1986] E.C.R. 2155, para.5).

2. Community bodies entrusted with the preparation or implementation of Community law

7–057   **Bodies, offices and agencies.** Community institutions may set up bodies (legal persons governed by private or public law) and delegate powers to them. Following on from the judgment in *Les Verts*, which made any binding act of any Community "institution" amenable to judicial review by the Court of Justice and the Court of First Instance, the question arises as to whether the Court of Justice and the Court of First Instance have jurisdiction under Art.230 of the EC Treaty to declare acts of such bodies void. As far as actions for damages are concerned, the Court of Justice has already held that "a Community body established by the Treaty and authorised to act in [the Community's] name and on its behalf" may be an "institution" of the Community for the purposes of the second para. of Art.288 of the EC Treaty[192] (see 11–011, *infra*). The same approach would not seem to be precluded in the case of actions for annulment.[193] It must nevertheless be emphasised that the legal procedure provided for in Art.230 of the EC Treaty cannot be used against bodies established on the basis of provisions of the EU Treaty[194] or of the EEA Agreement.[195]

---

[192] ECJ, Case C–370/89 *SGEEM and EIB* [1992] E.C.R. I–6211, paras 15–16.

[193] But naturally only in so far as the Community act establishing the body in question does not provide for an effective procedure organising supervision of the legality of acts of that body (see, *e.g.* CFI (order of June 8, 1998), Case T–148/97 *Keeling v OHIM* [1998] E.C.R. II–2217, paras 31–34); see also Lenaerts, "Regulating the Regulatory Process: 'Delegation of Powers' in the European Community" (1993) E.L.Rev. 23–49. For a survey of such bodies, see Lenaerts and Van Nuffel, *Constitutional Law of the European Union*, §10–109–§10–110, at 472–476 and §14–062, at 619–620. It has become clear from ECJ, Case C–25/94 *Commission v Council* [1996] E.C.R. I–1469, paras 21–28, that Coreper is not an institution, but an auxiliary body of the Council, in that it carries out preparatory work and tasks assigned to it by the Council (EC Treaty, Art.207(1)). Coreper's function of carrying out tasks assigned to it by the Council does not give it the power to take decisions which belongs, under the Treaty, to the Council. Acts adopted by Coreper in this context therefore cannot be regarded as binding acts of the Council. In an order of November 26, 1993, the Court of First Instance held that Art.237(c) of the EC Treaty did not afford a legal basis for individuals to bring an action for annulment of decisions of the Board of Directors of the European Investment Bank. The Court took this view because the European Investment Bank, unlike the European Parliament, had not increased its original powers and because acts of the EIB did not have legal effects *vis-à-vis* third parties. Consequently, there was no need to give a broad interpretation to Art.230 as the Court of Justice had done in the judgment in *Les Verts* in order to enable actions to be brought against acts of the European Parliament: CFI (order of November 26, 1993), Case T–460/93 *Tête and Others v EIB* [1993] E.C.R. II–1257. An action for annulment of a decision of the Management Committee of the European Investment Bank brought by the Commission under Art.237(b) of the EC Treaty has been declared admissible (and well founded) by the Court of Justice: ECJ, Case C–15/00 *Commission v EIB* [2003] E.C.R. I–7281.

[194] See ECJ, Case C–160/03, *Spain v Eurojust* [2005] E.C.R. I–2077, paras 35–40. Art.35 of the EU Treaty relates to the jurisdiction of the Court of Justice with regard to the provisions of Title VI of the EU Treaty.

[195] CFI (order of July 22, 2005), Case T–376/04 *Polyelectrolyte Producers Group v Council and Commission*, not yet reported, para.31.

3. What acts may be imputed to an institution?

Outcome of the institution's decision-making power. An action for annul-   **7–058**
ment will lie only against acts which may be imputed to a Community
institution.[196] It is not enough that an institution was involved in bringing
the act about in order for it to be imputed to that institution. The act must
be the outcome of the institution's decision-making power.

The classic example is a decision to award a tender in a public tendering
procedure for works in the ACP States which are financed by the
Community. The decision to award the tender is a sovereign decision of the
ACP State concerned.[197] The Commission's involvement, which is governed
by legislation, in preparing the decision does not mean that that decision
may be imputed to it.[198]

Act of a Member or staff member of an institution. An act of a Member or   **7–059**
of a staff member of an institution is not necessarily to be imputed to the
institution.[199] It will be so imputable only if the person who adopts the act
makes it clear that he or she does so pursuant to his or her power to act in
the name of the institution.[200] Furthermore, it must transpire from the
content of the act that the person in question intended to express the
position or the decision of the institution.[201]

Treaty amendments. Treaty amendments and Acts relating to the accession   **7–060**
of new Member States (adopted pursuant to Art.49 of the EU Treaty,
formerly Art.237 of the EEC Treaty) are not acts of Community institu-

---

[196] ECJ, Case C–201/89 *Le Pen and Front National* [1990] E.C.R. I–1183, para.14: acts of a
political group of the European Parliament cannot be imputed to the Parliament *qua*
institution; ECJ, Case C–97/91 *Oleificio Borelli v Commission* [1992] E.C.R. I–6313, paras
9–10; ECJ, Joined Cases C–181 and C–248/91 *European Parliament v Council and
Commission* [1993] E.C.R. I–3685: acts adopted by representatives of the Member States'
governments meeting in the Council cannot be imputed to the Council, a Community
institution.

[197] See, *e.g.* the former Lomé Convention [1991] O.J. L229/3.

[198] ECJ, Case 126/83 *STS v Commission* [1984] E.C.R. 2769; ECJ, Case 118/83 *CMC v
Commission* [1985] E.C.R. 2325; ECJ, Case C–257/90 *Italsolar v Commission* [1993] E.C.R.
I–9. For an application of this principle in the agricultural sector, see CFI, Case T–93/95
Laga v Commission [1998] E.C.R. II–195, paras 33–42; CFI, Case T–94/95 *Landuyt v
Commission* [1998] E.C.R. II–213, paras 33–42 (in which the Court of First Instance held
that the claim for annulment was essentially directed against the act of a national authority
and not against an act of a Community institution). But see ECJ, Case C–395/95 P
Geotronics v Commission [1997] E.C.R. I–2271.

[199] ECJ, Joined Cases 42 and 49/59 *SNUPAT v High Authority* [1961] E.C.R. 53, at 72.

[200] ECJ, Case 34/86 *Council v European Parliament* [1986] E.C.R. 2155, paras 7–8. A report
commissioned by an institution from a private consultancy firm cannot be imputed to the
institution. This is because such a report does not contain any act adopted by the institution
itself (ECJ (order of March 26, 1980), Case 51/79 *Buttner v Commission* [1980] E.C.R.
1201).

[201] CFI, Case T–113/89 *Nefarma v Commission* [1990] E.C.R. II–797, para.81 (a letter from the
Member of the Commission responsible for competition to the Netherlands Government
appeared to have been written in his own name and in the context of an exchange of views
between politicians, and could therefore not be regarded as an act of the Commission).

tions.[202] They are provisions of primary law which are not subject to the system of judicial review provided for in the Treaty. Even if modifications of acts of the institutions ensue out of those provisions, they still do not constitute acts of the institutions and are therefore not amenable to judicial review.[203]

B. APPLICANTS: WHO CAN BRING AN ACTION FOR ANNULMENT?

1. The European Parliament, the Council, the Commission and the Member States

7–061   **Privileged applicants.** The European Parliament, the Council, the Commission and the Member States derive from the second para.of Art.230 of the EC Treaty the right to bring actions for annulment. They are privileged applicants. They may, without proving that they have an interest in bringing proceedings,[204] bring an action for annulment against any binding act of a Community institution, whether general or individual, and may also rely on any plea in law permitted under Art.230 of the EC Treaty.[205] The right to bring an action for annulment is not dependent upon the position which they took up when the act at issue was adopted. Thus, the fact that an act was voted for in the Council by the representative of a Member State does not disentitle that Member State from bringing an application for its annulment.[206] Any Member State has a right to bring an action for annulment and that right is not dependent upon other Member States, the Council or the Commission participating in the proceedings before the Court of Justice.[207]

---

[202] ECJ, Case C–313/89 *Commission v Spain* [1991] E.C.R. I–5231, para.10.

[203] ECJ, Joined Cases 31 and 35/86 *LAISA and Others v Council* [1988] E.C.R. 2285, paras 1–18 (with a case note by Vandersanden (1989) C.M.L.Rev. 551–561).

[204] ECJ, Case 45/86 *Commission v Council* [1987] E.C.R. 1493, para.3. For the first case brought by the European Parliament as a privileged applicant, see ECJ, Case C–540/03 *European Parliament v Council* (pending case).

[205] ECJ, Case 41/83 *Italy v Commission* [1985] E.C.R. 873, para.30. One of the questions raised in that case was whether Italy could bring an action for annulment against a Commission decision finding that British Telecommunications, at that time a nationalised undertaking having a statutory monopoly in the UK over the running of telecommunications services, had infringed Art.82 of the EC Treaty. Italy argued, amongst other things, that the Commission had disregarded Art.86(2) of the EC Treaty and that undertakings entrusted with the operation of services of general economic interest were subject to Community competition law only in so far as its application did not impede the performance of their particular tasks. The Court of Justice allowed Italy to raise that plea despite the fact that what was involved was a balancing of interests—described by the Commission as difficult—which affected only the UK.

[206] ECJ, Case 166/78 *Italy v Council* [1979] E.C.R. 2575, paras 5–6.

[207] ECJ, Case 230/81 *Luxembourg v European Parliament* [1983] E.C.R. 255, paras 22–26 (interpretation of Art.38, first para., of the ECSC Treaty, which also held good for Art.230, second para., of the EC Treaty). Community law does not impose any obligation on a Member State to bring an action for annulment for the benefit of one of its citizens. As to the question whether national law may impose such an obligation, the Court of Justice

Local authorities. Local authorities (municipalities, federated States, etc.) are not equated to a Member State and are therefore not privileged applicants. If they have legal personality under national law, they may be regarded as legal persons within the meaning of the fourth para.of Art.230 of the EC Treaty and bring an action, provided that the admissibility requirements laid down in that provision of the Treaty are satisfied.[208]

7–062

2. The Court of Auditors and the European Central Bank

Semi-privileged applicants. In the judgment in the *Chernobyl* case, the Court of Justice granted the European Parliament a right not conferred by the former Art.173 of the EEC Treaty (now Art.230 of the EC Treaty) to bring an action for annulment against acts of the Council or the Commission "provided that the action seeks only to safeguard its prerogatives and that it is founded only on submissions alleging their infringement".[209] The

7–063

---

ruled that such obligation would, in principle, not infringe Community law but added that a Member State could, however, breach the obligation of sincere cooperation laid down in Art.10 of the EC Treaty if it did not retain a degree of discretion as to the appropriateness of bringing an action, thereby giving rise to a risk that the Community Courts might be inundated with actions, some of which would be patently unfounded, thus jeopardising the proper functioning of the Court of Justice (ECJ (judgment of October 20, 2005), Case C–511/03 *Ten Kate Holding Musselkanaal and Others*, not yet reported, paras 30–31).

[208] ECJ, Case 222/83 *Municipality of Differdange and Others v Commission* [1984] E.C.R. 2889, para.9; see also the Opinion of Advocate General C.O. Lenz in ECJ, Joined Cases 62 and 72/87 *Exécutif Régional Wallon and Glaverbel v Commission* [1988] E.C.R. 1573, at 1582; ECJ, Case C–298/89 *Gibraltar v Council* [1993] E.C.R. I–3605, para.14; ECJ (order of March 21, 1997), Case C–95/97 *Région Wallonne v Commission* [1997] E.C.R. I–1787, para.6, and ECJ (order of October 1, 1997), Case C–180/97 *Regione Toscana v Commission* [1997] E.C.R. I–5245, paras 6–8; CFI, Case T–214/95 *Vlaams Gewest v Commission* [1998] E.C.R. II–717, para.28; CFI (order of June 16, 1998), Case T–238/97 *Comunidad Autónoma de Catanbria v Council* [1998] E.C.R. II–2271; CFI, Case T–288/97 *Regione Autonoma Friuli Venezia Giulia v Commission* [1998] E.C.R. II–1871, paras 28 *et seq.*, in particular paras 46–48, in which the Court of First Instance held that the fact that a Member State is responsible in an action for failure to fulfil obligations for the acts of devolved bodies and cannot rely in its defence on the division of powers in effect nationally does not mean that the devolved body cannot bring an action for annulment where a decision addressed to a Member State is of direct and individual concern to it. This is because the two actions (action for failure to fulfil obligations and action for annulment) are autonomous procedures and, as a result, the admissibility of an action brought under Art.230 of the EC Treaty must be decided only in the light of "the objectives specific to that provision and of the principle of judicial protection according to which it must be open to every natural or legal person to apply to the courts on his own initiative, that is to say in the exercise of his own judgment, in order to obtain review of an act which adversely affects that person"; CFI, Case T–609/97 *Regione Puglia v Commission and Spain* [1998] E.C.R. II–4051, para.17; CFI, Joined Cases T–195/01 and T–207/01 *Gibraltar v Commission* [2002] E.C.R. II–2309, paras 52–55. For an extended discussion, see P. Van Nuffel, "What's in a Member State? Central and Decentralised Authorities before the Community Courts" (2001) C.M.L.Rev. 871–901.

[209] ECJ, Case C–70/88 *European Parliament v Council* [1990] E.C.R. I–2041, para.27. In the judgment on the substance of the case, moreover, the Court of Justice declared the European Parliament's second and third pleas inadmissible in that they did not allege any infringement of its prerogatives: ECJ, Case C–70/88 *European Parliament v Council* [1991]

primary intention of the Court in so ruling was to maintain the balance between the institutions laid down by the Treaties.[210] The Treaty of Nice has now raised the European Parliament to the status of a privileged applicant. The third para.of Art.230 of the EC Treaty confers a limited right of action on the Court of Auditors and the European Central Bank within the meaning of the *Chernobyl* judgment. Accordingly, the Court of Auditors and the European Central Bank must clearly show which of their prerogatives should have been respected and in what way the prerogative in question has been infringed.[211]

3. Individual applicants

7–064   **Conditions.** Under the fourth para.of Art.230 of the EC Treaty, any natural or legal person has the right to institute proceedings against a decision addressed to that person or against a decision which, although in the form of a regulation or a decision addressed to another person, is of direct and individual concern to the former.[212]

a. Requirements as to admissibility relating to the person

7–065   **Which persons?** Any natural or legal person may bring an action for annulment.[213] The applicant's nationality is irrelevant as far as the admissibility of the application is concerned. Moreover, the fourth para. of

---

E.C.R. I–4529, paras 19–20. That condition for admissibility has been confirmed in, for example, ECJ, Case C–295/90 *European Parliament v Council* [1992] E.C.R. I–4193, paras 8–10; ECJ, Case C–316/91 *European Parliament v Council* [1994] E.C.R. I–625, para.19; ECJ, Case C–187/93 *European Parliament v Council* [1994] E.C.R. I–2857, paras 14–16; ECJ, Case C–189/97 *European Parliament v Council* [1999] E.C.R. I–4741, paras 13–17.

[210] *Cf.* Bradley, "The Variable Evolution of the Standing of the European Parliament in Proceedings before the Court of Justice" (1988) Y.E.L. 27–57; Darmon, "Le statut contentieux du Parlement européen", in *L'Europe et le Droit—Mélanges en hommage à J. Boulouis* (Ed. Dalloz, Paris, 1991), at 75–96.

[211] The earlier case-law with regard to the European Parliament provides indications which will also apply to the Court of Auditors and the European Central Bank in assessing the admissibility of actions for annulment brought by those bodies: ECJ, Case C–316/91 *European Parliament v Council* [1994] E.C.R. I–625, para.16; ECJ, Case C–21/94 *European Parliament v Council* [1995] E.C.R. I–1827, para.8; ECJ, Case C–156/93 *European Parliament v Commission* [1995] E.C.R. I–2019, para.11 (infringement of the requirement laid down in Art.253 of the EC Treaty to state the reasons on which acts are based cannot be relied upon by the European Parliament on the ground that it is not clear how that breaches its prerogatives); ECJ, Case C–360/93 *European Parliament v Council* [1996] E.C.R. I–1195, para.18 (an action contesting the legal basis on which the action attacked is founded has a bearing on the protection of the Parliament's prerogatives); ECJ, Case C–392/95 *European Parliament v Council* [1997] E.C.R. I–3213, paras 14–15; ECJ, Case C–259/95 *European Parliament v Council* [1997] E.C.R. I–5303.

[212] The admissibility requirements for individuals must not be interpreted restrictively. See CFI, Case T–288/97 *Regione Autonoma Friuli Venezia Giulia v Commission* [1999] E.C.R. I–1871, para.40. For a recent analysis of the case-law, see Arnull, "Private Applicants and the Action for Annulment since *Codorníu*" (2001) C.M.L.Rev. 7–52.

[213] In all probability this includes third countries, *cf.* ECJ (order of February 23, 1983), Joined Cases 91 and 200/82 *Chris International Foods v Commission* [1983] E.C.R. 417, in which

Art.230 of the EC Treaty does not require the applicant to belong to a particular sector of the economy.

Notion of legal personality. In principle, national law determines whether the applicant has legal personality.[214] Sometimes lack of legal personality precludes access to the Court of Justice or the Court of First Instance.[215] Often, however, entities without legal personality may nevertheless be admitted to bring an action for annulment. In order for them to bring an action, they must be entitled and in a position to act as a responsible body in legal matters.[216] As a result, the expression "legal persons" has been given an independent, Community meaning which is not necessarily the same one it has in national law. The fact that the applicant was recognised by the defendant as a negotiating partner before the proceedings arose[217] and the fact that an *ad hoc* association was allowed to take part in a tendering procedure organised by the Commission[218] have helped applicants to be recognised as legal persons within the meaning of the fourth para.of Art.230 of the EC Treaty.

7–066

b. Requirements as to admissibility based on the type of act

(1) *The requirement that the contested act should be a decision*

Decision. The only Community acts which can, in principle, be challenged by natural or legal persons in an action for annulment are decisions addressed to them, decisions addressed to another person or decisions adopted in the form of a regulation.[219] In the last two cases, an action for

7–067

---

the Court of Justice gave a third country leave to intervene in the proceedings on the ground that it was an interested "person" within the meaning of the second para. of Art.40 of the Statute of the Court of Justice.

[214] ECJ, Case 18/57 *Nold v High Authority* [1959] E.C.R. 41, at 48–49; ECJ, Case 50/84 *Bensider v Commission* [1984] E.C.R. 3991, para.7; CFI, Case T–174/95 *Svenska Journalistförbundet v Council* [1998] E.C.R. II–2289, para.43; *cf.* ECJ, Case 294/83 *Les Verts v European Parliament* [1986] E.C.R. 1339, paras 13–18, in regard to merging associations and the assignment of a pending legal action to the new association.

[215] ECJ, Case 50/84 *Bensider v Commission* [1984] E.C.R. 3991, para.9; CFI (order of February 15, 2005), Case T–229/02 *PKK and Others v Council*, not yet reported, para.37.

[216] ECJ, Case 175/73 *Union Syndicale and Others v Council* [1974] E.C.R. 917, paras 7–17, at 924–925; ECJ, Case 18/74 *Syndicat Général du Personnel des Organismes Européens v Commission* [1974] E.C.R. 933, paras 3–11.

[217] *Union Syndicale and Others v Council*, para.12; *Syndicat Général du Personnel des Organismes Européens v Commission*, para.9, both cases cited in the preceding n.; CFI, Case T–161/94 *Sinochem Heilongjiang v Council* [1996] E.C.R. II–695, para.34; CFI, Case T–170/94 *Shanghai Bicycle v Council* [1997] E.C.R. II–1383, para.26.

[218] ECJ, Case 135/81 *Groupement des Agences de Voyage v Commission* [1982] E.C.R. 3799, paras 10–11.

[219] Some applicants have argued that the term "decision" used in the fourth para. of Art.230 of EC Treaty *[then Art.173, second para., of the EEC Treaty]* had a wider meaning than it does in Art.249 of the EC Treaty and covers any binding act. That argument has been

LIVERPOOL JOHN MOORES UNIVERSITY
Aldham Roberts L.R.C.
TEL. 0151 231 3701/3634

annulment of the "decision" will lie only if it is of direct and individual concern to the applicant. The expression "decision addressed to another person" also covers decisions addressed to a Member State.[220]

7–068 **Measure of general application.** The Court of Justice has held that "[t]he essential characteristics of a decision arise from the limitation of the persons to whom it is addressed, whereas a regulation, being essentially of a legislative nature, is applicable not to a limited number of persons, defined or identifiable, but to categories of persons viewed abstractly and in their entirety".[221] Consequently, a regulation differs on account of its general application.[222] In order to determine the scope of a measure, the Court of Justice and the Court of First Instance assess "[t]he nature of the contested [measure] . . . and in particular the legal effects which it is intended to or does actually produce".[223]

This requires a substantive analysis of the contested measure.[224] If a measure lays down generally applicable principles, applies to objectively defined situations and produces legal effects for categories of persons determined in an abstract manner, the measure will be regarded as a regulation.[225] A measure does not lose its general character because "it may be possible to ascertain with a greater or lesser degree of accuracy the

---

rejected by the Court of Justice (see ECJ, Joined Cases 16 and 17/62 *Confédération Nationale des Producteurs de Fruits et Légumes and Others v Council* [1962] E.C.R. 471, at 478–479). The *rationale* for confining actions brought by individuals to decisions is probably that regulations are legislative in character. Moreover, regulations, being the outcome of hard-won compromises, ought to be given greater protection against possible actions for annulment.

[220] ECJ, Case 25/62 *Plaumann v Commission* [1963] E.C.R. 95, at 106–107.

[221] ECJ, Joined Cases 16 and 17/62 *Confédération Nationale des Producteurs de Fruits et Légumes and Others v Council* [1962] E.C.R. 471, at 478; ECJ (order of April 24, 1996), Case C–87/95 P *Cassa Nazionale di Previdenza ed Assistenza a favore degli Avvocati e Procuratori v Council* [1996] E.C.R. I–2003, para.33. See also Greaves, "The Nature and Binding Effect of Decisions under Art.189*[now Art.249]* EC" (1996) E.L.Rev. 3–16.

[222] See, *e.g.* CFI (judgment of September 21, 2005), Case T–306/01 *Yusuf and Al Barakaat International Foundation v Council and Commission*, not yet reported, paras 186–188.

[223] ECJ, Case 101/76 *Koninklijke Scholten Honig v Council and Commission* [1977] E.C.R. 797, para.10.

[224] ECJ, Joined Cases 789 and 790/79 *Calpak v Commission* [1980] E.C.R. 1949, para.7: "the choice of form cannot change the nature of the measure". For a Commission decision which was held to be a "measure of general application", see ECJ, Case 231/82 *Spijker v Commission* [1983] E.C.R. 2559, para.9, and CFI, Joined Cases T–480/93 and T–483/93 *Antillean Rice Mills and Others v Commission* [1995] E.C.R. II–2305, para.65; CFI, Joined Cases T–198/95, T–171/96, T–230/97, T–174/98 and T–225/99 *Comafrica and Dole Fresh Fruit Europe v Commission* [2001] E.C.R. II–1975.

[225] ECJ, Joined Cases 36–38 and 40–41/58 *SIMET and Others v High Authority* [1959] E.C.R. 157, at 166; ECJ, Case 147/83 *Binderer v Commission* [1985] E.C.R. 257, paras 11–15; ECJ, Case C–244/88 *Usines Coopératives de Déshydratation du Vexin and Others v Commission* [1989] E.C.R. 3811, para.13; ECJ, Case C–229/88 *Cargill and Others v Commission* [1990] E.C.R. I–1303, paras 13–19; CFI (order of January 11, 1995), Case T–116/94 *Cassa Nazionale di Previdenza ed Assistenza a favore degli Avvocati e Procuratori* [1995] E.C.R. II–1, paras 21–25; CFI (order of June 19, 1995), Case T–107/94 *Kik v Council and Commission* [1995] E.C.R. II–1717, para.35; CFI, Case T–47/95 *Terres Rouges and Others v Commission* [1997] E.C.R. II–481, paras 40–41.

number or even the identity of the persons to which it applies at any given time as long as there is no doubt that the measure is applicable as a result of an objective situation of law or of fact which it specifies and which is in harmony with its ultimate objective".[226] Even the fact that a legal provision may have different practical effects for the various persons to whom it applies is not inconsistent with its nature as a regulation when the circumstances in which it applies are objectively determined.[227]

Finding that a measure is of general application does not lead to an automatic finding of inadmissibility. Although, in principle, a single provision cannot at one and the same time have the character of a measure of general application and of an individual measure,[228] the admissibility of an action for annulment brought by a natural or legal person will not turn directly on the mere finding that the contested act is legislative in nature.[229]

7–069

In the first place, some provisions of acts which, *per se*, are to be regarded as regulations may be decisions against which a natural or legal person can

---

[226] ECJ, Case 6/68 *Zuckerfabrik Watenstedt v Commission* [1968] E.C.R. 409, at 415. See also ECJ, Case 64/69 *Compagnie Française Commerciale and Financière v Commission* [1970] E.C.R. 221, para.11; ECJ, Joined Cases 789 and 790/79 *Calpak v Commission* [1980] E.C.R. 1949, para.9; ECJ, Case 242/81 *Roquette Frères v Council* [1982] E.C.R. 3213, para.7; ECJ, Case 307/81 *Alusuisse v Council and Commission* [1982] E.C.R. 3463, para.11; ECJ, Case 231/82 *Spijker v Commission* [1983] E.C.R. 2559, para.10; ECJ, Case 26/86 *Deutz and Geldermann v Council* [1987] E.C.R. 941, para.8; ECJ, Joined Cases C–15 and C–108/91 *Buckl and Others v Commission* [1992] E.C.R. I–6061, para.25; ECJ, Case C–213/91 *Abertal v Commission* [1993] E.C.R. I–3177, para.17; ECJ, Case C–264/91 *Abertal v Council* [1993] E.C.R. I–3265, para.16; CFI (order of October 28, 1993), Case T–476/93 *FRSEA and FNSEA v Council* [1993] E.C.R. II–1187, para.19; CFI, Case T–489/93 *Unifruit Hellas v Commission* [1994] E.C.R. II–1201; CFI (order of October 4, 1996), Case T–197/95 *Sveriges Betodlares and Henrikson v Commission* [1996] E.C.R. II–1283, para.28; CFI (judgment of February 3, 2005), Case T–139/01 *Comafrica and Others v Commission*, not yet reported, para.100. *Cf.* ECJ, Joined Cases 41–44/70 *International Fruit and Others v Commission* [1971] E.C.R. 411, in which the contested "regulation" applied to a number of applications for import licences which was known at the time when the "regulation" was adopted and no new application could be added. The Court of Justice regarded the act as a conglomeration of individual decisions which, albeit adopted in the guise of a regulation, affected the legal position of each of the applicants for a licence. This indicates that the condition of admissibility to the effect that the contested act must be a decision is particularly closely linked with the condition of admissibility requiring a contested act not addressed to the applicant to be of direct and individual concern to him. See also ECJ, Case C–354/87 *Weddel v Commission* [1990] E.C.R. I–3847, paras 16–23; CFI, Case T–70/94 *Comafrica and Dole Fresh Fruit Europe v Commission* [1996] E.C.R. II–1741, paras 40–41; set aside on appeal in ECJ, Case C–73/97 P *France v Comafrica and Others* [1999] E.C.R. I–185.

[227] ECJ (order of March 28, 1996), Case C–270/95 P *Kik v Council and Commission* [1996] E.C.R. I–1987, para.13.

[228] ECJ, Case 18/57 *Nold v High Authority* [1959] E.C.R. 41, at 50; ECJ, Case 45/81 *Moksel v Commission* [1982] E.C.R. 1129, para.18.

[229] Cf. Neuwahl, "Art.173*[now Art.230]* para.4 EC: Past, Present and Possible Future" (1996) E.L.Rev. 17, at 23; Waelbroeck and Verheyden, "Les conditions de recevabilité des recours en annulation des particuliers contre les actes normatifs communautaires" (1995) C.D.E. 399–441; CFI (order of April 29, 1999), Case T–120/98 *Alce v Commission* [1999] E.C.R. II–1395, para.19.

bring an action for annulment.[230] However, it will be possible to separate out provisions of a regulation only in so far as they do not constitute an indissoluble whole together with the remaining provisions of the regulation.[231] This will be so only where the intended aim of the regulation can be equally well attained after the provisions alleged to be decisions have been severed.[232]

Secondly, sometimes the dual nature of the contested act as a whole or of some of its provisions will nevertheless be recognised. Then, the act or some of its provisions will operate as a "decision" *vis-à-vis* some natural or legal persons, whilst remaining for others a regulation.[233] The reason for this is that it appears from the case-law that the fact that an act is of a legislative nature does not prevent it in certain circumstances from affecting some of the market participants concerned individually.[234] The requirement is that the market participants in question must be affected by the Community act by reason of attributes peculiar to them or by reason of factual circumstances differentiating them from all other persons as if it was a decision addressed to them (see 7–078, *infra*). In such a case, the determination of the nature of the act coincides with the review as to whether the requirement is met for the act, albeit not addressed to the

---

[230] ECJ, Joined Cases 16 and 17/62 *Confédération Nationale des Producteurs de Fruits et Légumes and Others v Council* [1962] E.C.R. 471, 479, first para.

[231] It will be hard to separate out transitional provisions from the legislative measure without this causing adverse effects as far as achievement of the intended objective is concerned. Generally, therefore, they will have the same nature as the contested measure: see, for example, ECJ, Case 64/80 *Giuffrida and Campogrande v Council* [1981] E.C.R. 693, paras 4–7.

[232] For some cases in which any severing of provisions appeared impossible, see Case 45/81 *Moksel v Commission* [1982] E.C.R. 1129, paras 16–19, and ECJ, Case 276/82 *Roomboterfabriek "De beste boter"* [1983] E.C.R. 3331, paras 12–17.

[233] ECJ, Case 264/82 *Timex v Council and Commission* [1985] E.C.R. 849, paras 8–17; CFI, Joined Cases T–481 and T–484/93 *Exporteurs in Levende Varkens and Others v Commission* [1995] E.C.R. II–2941, para.50. See, *e.g.* CFI (judgment of February 3, 2005), Case T–139/01 *Comafrica and Others v Commission*, not yet reported, para.107: "It should be noted that a measure of general application such as a regulation may, in certain circumstances, be of individual concern to certain natural or legal persons and thus in the nature of a decision in their regard".

[234] ECJ, Case C–152/88 *Sofrimport v Commission* [1990] E.C.R. I–2477, paras 8–13; ECJ, Case C–309/89 *Codorníu v Council* [1994] E.C.R. I–1853, paras 14–23; ECJ (order of November 24, 1995), Case C–10/95 P *Asocarne v Council* [1995] E.C.R. I–4149, para.43; ECJ (order of April 24, 1996), Case C–87/95 P *Cassa Nazionale di Previdenza ed Assistenza a favore degli Avvocati e Procuratori v Council* [1996] E.C.R. I–2003, para.36; ECJ, Case C–451/99 P *Antillean Rice Mills v Council* [2001] E.C.R. I–8946, para.46; CFI, Joined Cases T–480 and T–483/93 *Antillean Rice Mills and Others v Commission* [1995] E.C.R. II–2305, para.66; CFI (order of October 4, 1996), Case T–197/95 *Sverige Betodlares and Henrikson v Commission* [1996] E.C.R. II–1283, para.31; CFI, Case T–298/94 *Roquette Frères v Council* [1996] E.C.R. II–1531, para.37; CFI (order of December 10, 1996), Case T–18/95 *Atlanta and Internationale Fruchtimport Gesellschaft Weichert v Commission* [1996] E.C.R. II–1669, para.47; CFI (order of May 6, 2003) Case T–45/02 *DOW AgroSciences and Others v European Parliament and Council* [2003] E.C.R. II–1973, para.34; CFI (order of July 8, 2004), Case T–338/03 *Eridania Sadam and Others v Commission*, not reported, para.32. See also Nihoul, "La recevabilité des recours en annulation introduits par un particulier à l'encontre d'un acte communautaire de portée générale" (1994) R.T.D.E. 173–174.

traders in question, nevertheless to be of individual concern to them.[235] Only those traders who are individually concerned may bring an action for annulment against the contested "decision". For others, the regulation preserves its general legislative character and will not be amenable to an action for annulment. Anti-dumping cases afford striking illustrations. Undertakings which can prove that their identity is apparent from the contested regulation or that the investigation which resulted in the imposition of anti-dumping duties related to them may bring an action for annulment of the regulation or of the provisions of the regulation which imposed anti-dumping duties on them.[236]

Examination whether a measure is of general application may be super-   7–070
fluous. Ascertaining whether the act is of individual concern closely resembles the criteria that are employed in order to determine whether the contested act is essentially a decision. Both questions—that is to say, whether a given act is a decision or whether an act, albeit not addressed to the applicant, is of individual concern to it—are directed towards the legal effects produced by the act in question and imply a similar investigation of the content of the act. For those reasons, there is increasingly often no express determination of the nature of the contested act. In such cases, the Community Court considers only whether the contested act is of direct and individual concern to the applicant, after observing that the fact that a

---

[235] ECJ, Case 123/77 *UNICME v Council* [1978] E.C.R. 845, para.7, and ECJ, Case 64/69 *Compagnie Française Commerciale and Financière v Commission* [1970] E.C.R. 221, para.3 *et seq.*; ECJ, Case C–264/91 *Abertal v Council* [1993] E.C.R. I–3265, para.16; see also CFI, Case T–489/93 *Unifruit Hellas v Commission* [1994] E.C.R. II–1201, para.21; for a wide-ranging discussion, see Schermers and Waelbroeck, *Judicial Protection*, § 861–§ 866, at 424–428; Harding, "The Review of EEC Regulations and Decisions" (1982) C.M.L.Rev. 311–323. See also Bleckmann, "Zur Klagebefugnis für die Individualklage vor dem Europäischen Gerichtshof", in *Festschrift für C.F. Menger—System des verwaltungsgerichtlichen Rechtsschutzes* (Carl Heymanns Verlag KG, Cologne/Berlin/Bonn/Munich, 1985), 871, at 883; Parkinson, "Admissibility of Direct Actions by Natural or Legal Persons in the European Court of Justice: Judicial Distinctions Between Decisions and Regulations" (1989) Texas I.L.J. 433, at 445–449.

[236] ECJ, Case 113/77 *NTN Toyo Bearing v Council* [1979] E.C.R. 1185, paras 10–11; ECJ, Case 118/77 *ISO v Council* [1979] E.C.R. 1277, paras 17–27; ECJ, Case 119/77 *Nippon Seiko v Council and Commission* [1979] E.C.R. 1303, paras 12–15; ECJ, Case 121/77 *Nachi Fujikoshi v Council* [1979] E.C.R. 1363, paras 7–13; ECJ, Joined Cases 239 and 275/82 *Allied Corporation v Commission* [1984] E.C.R. 1005, paras 7–16; ECJ, Case 53/83 *Allied Corporation v Council* [1985] E.C.R. 1621, paras 2–5; ECJ, Case 240/84 *NTN Toyo Bearing v Council* [1987] E.C.R. 1809, paras 4–7; ECJ, Joined Cases C–133 and C–150/87 *Nashua and Others v Commission and Council* [1990] E.C.R. I–719, paras 12–21; ECJ, Joined Cases C–305/86 and C–160/87 *Neotype Techmashexport v Commission and Council* [1990] E.C.R. I–2945, para.19; ECJ, Case C–358/89 *Extramet Industrie v Council* [1991] E.C.R. I–2501, paras 13–14. See also Greaves, "Locus Standi under Art.173*[now Art.230]* EEC when Seeking Annulment of a Regulation" (1986) E.L.Rev. 119, at 131; Nihoul, "La recevabilité des recours en annulation introduits par un particulier à l'encontre d'un acte communautaire de portée générale" (1994) R.T.D.E. 171–194. For a critical note, see Von Heydebrand und der Lasa, "Die Nichtigkeitsklage von Unternehmen aus Drittländern vor dem EuGH gegen 'Verordnungen' im Bereich des Antidumpingsrechts" (1985) N.J.W. 1257, at 1259.

measure is of general application does not mean that it cannot be of direct and individual concern to certain economic operators.[237]

Accordingly, the Court of Justice has declared admissible an application brought by a legal person for annulment of an intrinsically legislative regulation laying down general rules for the description and presentation of sparkling wines. The Court of Justice treated the regulation as far as the applicant was concerned as a decision of individual concern to it on the ground that the regulation prohibited use of a graphic trade mark which the applicant had officially registered before the regulation entered into force.[238] As a result, the contested regulation adversely affected "specific rights" of the applicant, which, as the Court held, the latter must be able to challenge by means of an action for annulment.[239]

(2) *The requirement that, if the contested act is not addressed to the applicant, it should be of direct and individual concern to him*

7–071   **Avoiding the risk of an *actio popularis*.** Under the fourth para. of Art.230 of the EC Treaty, an application brought by natural or legal persons against decisions adopted in the form of a regulation or addressed to another person will be admissible only in so far as they are of direct and individual concern to them. The justification for the restriction lies in the far-reaching consequences of the annulment of a Community act. Annulment applies *erga omnes* and is retroactive. To make the action for annulment generally available might mean permanent litigation on Community regulations and open the way to an *actio popularis*.[240]

---

[237] ECJ, Case C–309/89 *Codorníu v Council* [1994] E.C.R. I–1853, para.19; ECJ, Case C–142/00 P *Commission v Netherlands Antilles* [2003] E.C.R. I–3483, para.64; ECJ, Case C–263/02 P *Commission v Jégo-Quéré* [2004] E.C.R. I–3425.

[238] ECJ, Case C–309/89 *Codorníu v Council* [1994] E.C.R. I–1853, paras 14–23.

[239] See the interpretation of the judgment in *Codorníu* to this effect in ECJ (order of November 23, 1995), Case C–10/95 P *Asocarne v Council* [1995] E.C.R. I–4149, para.43 (from which it also appears that the Court considers this to be an absolutely exceptional situation). See also CFI (order of September 9, 1998), Case T–269/97 *Azienda Agricola Tre e Mezzo and Bazzocchi v Commission* [1998] E.C.R. II–3105, paras 12–17; CFI (order of September 15, 1998), Case T–100/94 *Michailidis and Others v Commission* [1998] E.C.R. II–3115, paras 57–70; CFI (order of September 15, 1998), Case T–109/97 *Molkerei Grossbraustein and Bene Nahrungsmittel v Commission* [1998] E.C.R. II–3533, paras 57–73; CFI, Case T–17/96 *TF1 v Commission* [1999] E.C.R. II–1757, para.30.

[240] Opinion of Advocate General A. Dutheillet de Lamothe in ECJ, Joined Cases 9 and 11/71 *Compagnie d'Approvisionnement, de Transport et Crédit and Others v Commission* [1972] E.C.R. 391, at 411; Opinion of Advocate General H. Mayras in ECJ, Case 43/72 *Merkur Aussenhandels v Commission* [1973] E.C.R. 1055, at 1078. See, to the same effect, Harding, "The Private Interest in Challenging Community Action" (1980) E.L.Rev. 354, at 358. For an example where a measure was held not to be of direct concern to the applicants, see CFI, Case T–96/92 *CCE de la Société Générale des Grandes Sources and Others v Commission* [1995] E.C.R. II–1213, para.45.

(i) Direct concern

Definition. The requirement that a decision not addressed to the applicant   7–072
must be of direct concern to it expresses the rule that an applicant may
bring an action for annulment only against acts of Community institutions
which, as such, have legal effects on it.[241] By contrast, Community acts
which are to be implemented by national authorities and in respect of
which the latter have a discretion do not obtain their precise scope until
they have been implemented. Interested individuals are entitled to challenge the implementing measures before the national courts when they
have been adopted. If it is argued that the implementing measures are
unlawful on the ground that the Community act purported to be implemented is invalid, the national court may (or must) make a reference to the
Court of Justice for a preliminary ruling (see Ch.10, *infra*). In this way, the
structure of legal protection reflects the structure of Community law-
making.

Measure affecting the applicant's legal position. In order for it to be found   7–073
that an act is of direct concern to the applicant, the question whether the
contested measure confers a discretion on the national authorities or on its
addressee[242] with regard to its implementation must be answered in the
negative.[243] The Court of Justice has further specified that the requirement
that the measure must be of direct concern will be satisfied only if the
contested act is capable of directly producing effects on the applicant's legal
position.[244] The Court therefore held that an interpretative note, adopted in

---

[241] ECJ, Case 294/83 *Les Verts v European Parliament* [1986] E.C.R. 1339, para.31: the
contested measures are of direct concern to the applicant because they "constitute a
complete set of rules which are sufficient in themselves and . . . require no implementing
provisions". See also the Opinion of Advocate General K. Roemer in ECJ, Case 25/62
Plaumann v Commission [1963] E.C.R. 95, at 114–115.

[242] The fact that the Commission declares a concentration notified to it pursuant to Regulation
No 4064/89 compatible with the common market on condition that the notifying parties
implement "commitments" set forth in the notification does not prevent a third undertaking, which is affected by the implementation of those commitments, from being directly
concerned by the Commission's decision. This is because there is no doubt that parties to
the concentration have undertaken to implement those commitments, given that the
Commission declared it compatible with the common market in return for compliance with
those commitments and the Commission may always revoke its decision under Art.8(5)(b)
of the regulation if the undertakings concerned commit a breach of an obligation attached
thereto (ECJ, Joined Cases C–68/94 and C–30/95 *France and Others and EMC v
Commission* [1998] E.C.R. I–1375, para.51).

[243] For examples, see ECJ, Joined Cases 41–44/70 *International Fruit and Others v Commission*
[1971] E.C.R. 411, paras 23–28; ECJ, Joined Cases 87 and 130/77, 22/83, 9 and 10/84
Salerno and Others v Commission [1985] E.C.R. 2523, paras 31–32; ECJ, Case 207/86
APESCO v Commission [1988] E.C.R. 2151, para.12.

[244] ECJ, Case C–486/01 P *Front National v European Parliament* [2004] E.C.R. I–6289, paras
34–43. See in this connection also CFI, Case T–96/92 *CCE de la Société Générale de
Grandes Sources and Others v Commission* [1995] E.C.R. II–1213, para.26; CFI (order of
February 18, 1998), Case T–189/97 *Comité d'entreprise de la Société française de production
and Others v Commission* [1998] E.C.R. II–335, para.48.

plenary session on September 13, 1999, to Rule 29(1) of the Rules of Procedure of the European Parliament[245] which no longer permitted a political group to be formed where the group openly rejected any political character and all political affiliation between its Members did not directly affect the *Front National* as a political party. As a result, the *"Groupe technique des députés indépendants"*, to which the Members of the *Front National* belonged, could no longer function as a political group. Since, in accordance with the wording of Rule 29 of the Rules of Procedure, only Members of the European Parliament could form political groups, the *Front National* as a political party was affected only indirectly with the result that the application brought by that party for annulment of the interpretative note was declared inadmissible.[246] By contrast, a regulation relating to the funding of European political parties[247] was of direct concern only to the political parties in question and not to individual Members of the European Parliament.[248]

7–074 **Discretion with regard to implementation.** The contested act will not be of direct concern to the applicant where, in implementing the act, the authorities entrusted with the task of implementation, have a *genuine* discretion.[249] Where implementation is "purely automatic", no discretion on the part of the national authorities (or other authorities entrusted with the task of implementation) is involved and the Community act to be implemented is of direct concern to the applicant, provided, of course, that the act is capable of actually affecting the applicant's legal position.[250] Accord-

---

[245] [1999] O.J. L202/1.

[246] ECJ, Case C–486/01 P *Front National v European Parliament* [2004] E.C.R. I–6289, paras 34–43 and 47. In contrast, the interpretative note did have a direct effect on Members of the European Parliament; see CFI, Joined Cases T–222/99, T–327/99 and T–329/99 *Martinez and Others v European Parliament* [2001] E.C.R. II–2823, para.65, upheld on appeal in ECJ (order of November 11, 2003), Case C–488/01 P *Martinez v European Parliament* [2003] E.C.R. I–3355.

[247] Regulation (EC) No 2004/2003 of the European Parliament and of the Council of November 4, 2003 on the regulations governing political parties at European level and the rules regarding their funding ([2003] O.J. L297/1).

[248] CFI (order of July 11, 2005), Case T–40/04 *Bonino and Others v European Parliament and Council*, not yet reported, paras 39–59.

[249] For examples, see ECJ, Case 123/77 *UNICME v Council* [1978] E.C.R. 845, para.11; ECJ, Case 55/86 *ARPOSOL v Council* [1988] E.C.R. 13, paras 11–13; CFI (order of October 21, 1993), Joined Cases T–492/93 and T–492/93 R *Nutral v Commission* [1993] E.C.R. II–1023, paras 26–29; CFI, Case T–54/96 *Oleifici Italiani and Fratelli Rubino Industrie Olearie v Commission* [1998] E.C.R. II–3377, para.56; CFI (order of March 15, 2004), Case T–139/02 *Institouto N. Avgerinopoulou and Others v Commission* [2004] E.C.R. II–875, paras 62–70.

[250] ECJ, Case 113/77 *NTN Toyo Bearing v Council* [1979] E.C.R. 1185, para.11; ECJ, Case 118/77 *ISO v Council* [1979] E.C.R. 1277, para.26; ECJ, Case 119/77 *Nippon Seiko v Council and Commission* [1979] E.C.R. 1303, para.14; ECJ, Case 120/77 *Koyo Seiko v Council and Commission* [1979] E.C.R. 1337, para.25; ECJ, Case 121/77 *Nachi Fujikoshi v Council* [1979] E.C.R. 1363, para.11; ECJ, Case C–386/96 P *Dreyfus v Commission* [1998] E.C.R. I–2309, para.43; CFI, Case T–155/94 *Climax Paper v Council* [1996] E.C.R. II–873, para.53; CFI, Case T–170/94 *Shanghai Bicycle v Council* [1997] E.C.R. II–1383, para.41; CFI, Joined Cases T–198/95, T–171/96, T–230/97, T–174/98 and T–225/99 *Comafrica and Dole Fresh Fruit Europe v Commission* [2001] E.C.R. II–1975, para.96; ECJ, Case C–486/01 P *Front National v European Parliament* [2004] E.C.R. I–6289, paras 34–43.

ingly, an undertaking was found to be directly concerned by a Commission decision on State aid where there was no doubt as to the national authorities' intention to put the aid measure into effect.[251] An interested third party will also be directly affected by a Commission decision referring the examination of a concentration to the authorities of a Member State pursuant to Art.9 of Regulation No 4064/89 (now Regulation No 139/2004). This is because the effect of the contested decision is to deprive the applicant of a review of the concentration by the Commission on the basis of Regulation No 4064/89, of the procedural rights provided therein for third parties and of the judicial protection provided for by the Treaty. That effect is direct because the contested decision requires no additional implementing measure in order to render the referral effective.[252]

Directives. In principle, an application brought by a natural or legal person   **7–075** for annulment of a directive is inadmissible because a directive cannot be of direct concern to such persons. This is because, in transposing the directive, the Member States remain free to choose the form and method of implementing it in national law and achieving the result to be attained. In that context, a directive cannot in itself impose obligations on individuals. For those reasons, a directive is not capable in itself, independently of the adoption of implementing measures, of affecting the legal position of market participants.[253]

Authorisation by the Commission of an act of a Member State. A decision   **7–076** by which the Commission authorises Member States in some areas of Community law to diverge from the applicable general provisions may be of

---

[251] CFI, Case T–435/93 *ASPEC and Others v Commission* [1995] E.C.R. I–1281, para.60; CFI, Case T–17/96 *TF1 v Commission* [1999] E.C.R. II–1757, para.30.

[252] CFI, Joined Cases T–346/02 and T–347/02 *Cableuropa and Others v Commission* [2003] E.C.R. II–4251, paras 64–65.

[253] CFI (order of September 10, 2002), Case T–223/01 *Japan Tobacco and JT International v European Parliament and Council* [2002] E.C.R. II–3259, paras 45–50, CFI, Joined Cases T–172/98 and T–175/98 to T–177/98 *Salamander and Others v European Parliament and Council* [2000] E.C.R. II–2487, para.54; CFI (order of May 6, 2003) Case T–45/02 *DOW AgroSciences and Others v European Parliament and Council* [2003] E.C.R. II–1973, paras 35–40. See also ECJ (order of December 7, 1988), Case 138/88 *Flourez v Council* [1988] E.C.R. 6393, paras 10–12; ECJ (order of December 7, 1988) Case 160/88 *Fédération Européenne de la Santé Animale and Others v Council* [1988] E.C.R. 6399, paras 12–14; ECJ, Case C–298/89 *Gibraltar v Council* [1993] E.C.R. I–3605, paras 14–24; CFI (order of October 29, 1993), Case T–463/93 *GUNA v Council* [1993] E.C.R. II–1206, para.13; CFI (order of October 20, 1994), Case T–99/94 *Asocarne v Council* [1994] E.C.R. II–871, paras 17–19; ECJ (order of November 23, 1995), Case C–10/95 P *Asocarne v Council* [1995] E.C.R. I–4149, paras 29–34. *Cf.* CFI, Case T–135/96 *UEAPME v Council* [1998] E.C.R. II–2335, para.90, from which it appears that, exceptionally, it is possible that an applicant may be directly and individually concerned by a directive if it can prove that it has a right which the Community institutions should have taken into account when they adopted the directive. This is because the mere existence of such a right means that its holder should be afforded legal protection. *Cf.* Schneider, "Effektiver Rechtsschutz Privater gegen EG-Richtlinien nach dem Maastricht-Urteil des Bundesverfassungsgerichts" (1994) Archiv des öffentlichen Rechts 294.

direct concern to individuals, depending on the circumstances. This will be so where, before they were given authorisation, the national authorities limited their discretion themselves. The Court of Justice has therefore held that where the Member State concerned makes it known beforehand that it will implement an authorising decision, that decision will be of direct concern to individuals.[254] The Member State's position does not have to be express, it may be inferred from all relevant factors.[255] If a Member State does not make its position known beforehand with regard to an authorising decision, it reserves its power of discretion and the decision is not of direct concern to individuals.[256]

If an application from a Member State for authorisation is refused and this adversely affects an individual's interests, the requirement that the contested act must be of direct concern to the applicant is assessed just as if the authorisation had been granted.[257] Authorisation from the Commission of a protective measure already adopted by a Member State is of direct concern to individuals.[258]

7–077 **Aid programmes financed by the Commission.** In the context of aid programmes financed by the Community or the grant of Community loans to non-member countries, one and the same division of powers is generally instituted between the authorities of the beneficiary State and the Community institutions. The authorities of the beneficiary State have the power to select a contractual partner to carry out a particular project, to negotiate the contractual conditions and to conclude the agreement. The Commission is given the task only of examining whether the conditions for Community financing are met. Undertakings competing for the grant of a particular project are in a legal relationship only with the authorities of the beneficiary State. For its part, the Commission has legal relations only with the authorities of the beneficiary State. This pattern of legal relations means that the decision by which the Commission approves the financing of

---

[254] ECJ, Case 62/70 *Bock v Commission* [1971] E.C.R. 897, paras 6–8; *contra*: ECJ, Joined Cases 10 and 18/68 *"Eridania" Zuccherifici Nationali and Others v Commission* [1969] E.C.R. 459. A decision by which the Commission declares, pursuant to Directive 89/552/EEC (television-without-frontiers directive), that an autonomous decision by a Member State to impede reception of a television broadcaster established in a another Member State on the ground that it is likely to impair the development of minors is compatible with Community law is not of direct concern to the broadcaster. The reason for this is that the Commission decision does not replace the national measure and cannot be regarded as a prior authorisation, with the result that the national measure does not implement the Commission decision (CFI, Case T–69/99 *DSTV v Commission* [2000] E.C.R. II–4039).

[255] ECJ, Case 11/82 *Piraiki-Patraiki v Commission* [1985] E.C.R. 207, paras 7–10.

[256] *Cf.* ECJ, Case 123/77 *UNICME v Council* [1978] E.C.R. 845 (where derogating rules were provided for a Member State in a Council regulation).

[257] ECJ, Case 69/69 *Alcan v Commission* [1970] E.C.R. 385, para.15: "The decision rejecting the request does not . . . concern the applicants in any other way than would the positive decision which they wish to obtain".

[258] ECJ, Joined Cases 106 and 107/63 *Toepfer and Getreide-Import v Commission* [1965] E.C.R. 405, at 411.

a contract concluded by the beneficiary State is not of direct concern to undertakings to which the contract is not granted.[259] This is because the Commission's decision to finance the project does not take the place of the decision of the beneficiary State granting the contract in question.[260] However, it is possible for the undertaking to which the beneficiary State awarded a contract to be directly concerned by the Commission decision refusing financing. This depends on the circumstances in which the Commission decision was adopted.[261] If it appears that the Commission decision refusing Community financing deprived the applicant of any real possibility of performing the transaction entered into with the beneficiary State or of obtaining payment of the goods supplied on the agreed terms, the applicant's "legal situation" will be directly concerned. This will be the case where the contract with the beneficiary State was concluded on account of the commitments which the Commission would enter into in its capacity as "financing authority" once it found that the contract was in conformity with the Community rules.[262]

(ii) *Individual concern*

Definition. An act not addressed to natural or legal persons will be of individual concern to them if it "affects them by reason of certain attributes which are peculiar to them or by reason of circumstances in which they are differentiated from all other persons and by virtue of these factors distinguishes them individually just as in the case of the person addressed

7–078

---

[259] ECJ, Case 126/83 *STS v Commission* [1984] E.C.R. 2769, para.18; ECJ, Case 118/83 *CMC v Commission* [1985] E.C.R. 2325, para.28.

[260] But a Commission act which, by reason of its context, may be isolated from the procedure for the conclusion of a contract between the beneficiary State and an undertaking inasmuch as the Commission adopted it in the exercise of its own powers and specifically directed it to an individual undertaking, which loses any chance of actually being awarded the contract simply because that act is adopted, does give rise to binding legal effects as regards the undertaking in question and may therefore be regarded as an act adversely affecting it against which the undertaking concerned may bring an action for annulment: ECJ, Case C–395/95 P *Geotronics v Commission* [1997] E.C.R. I–2271, paras 12–15.

[261] The assessment is not always easy to make. See, *e.g.* two cases with similar factual settings but which led to different results: CFI (order of July 8, 2004), Case T–341/02 *Regione Siciliana v Commission*, not yet reported (no direct concern; under appeal: ECJ, Case C–417/04 P *Regione Siciliana v Commission*) and CFI (order of October 18, 2005), Case T–60/03 *Regione Siciliana v Commission*, not yet reported (direct concern).

[262] ECJ, Case C–386/96 P *Dreyfus v Commission* [1998] E.C.R. I–2309, paras 40–56; ECJ, Case C–391/96 P *Compagnie Continentale v Commission* [1998] E.C.R. I–2377, paras 38–54; ECJ, Case C–403/96 P *Glencore Grain v Commission* [1998] E.C.R. I–2405, paras 40–56; ECJ, Case C–404/96 P *Glencore Grain v Commission* [1998] E.C.R. I–2435, paras 38–54: the Court of Justice set aside the judgments given by the Court of First Instance in these cases in which the latter court held that the applicants were not directly concerned. In comparison with the approach taken by the Court of Justice, the Court of First Instance made a formal juridical analysis of the question whether the applicants' "legal situation" was affected, whereas the Court of Justice based its reasoning more on the "objective economic" finding that the third country could not execute the contracts concluded with the applicant for the supply of grain in the absence of Community aid.

[by the act]".[263] This means that the applicant must prove that the contested act, which, in terms of form, is not addressed to him, affects him substantively as if the act was a decision addressed to him.[264] This is a particularly strict requirement and it extensively curtails natural or legal persons' ability to bring actions for annulment.[265]

7–079 **Contested act constitutes a decision.** Where the contested measure is a "decision",[266] it is sufficient for the applicant to show that, at the time when that decision was adopted, he or she was part of a closed class of persons concerned by that act.[267] It makes no difference whether the class is large or small or whether its members are known by name. Various sets of circumstances may bring about a closed class.

Accordingly, a closed class is involved where the contested decision affects only persons who satisfied certain conditions before it was adopted. This is a situation in which the decision has completely retroactive effect. Because the number of persons who satisfied the conditions laid down for the application of the decision in the past can no longer change, the act is applicable to a closed class. Accordingly, a Commission decision approving a national decision refusing to grant import licences concerns the closed class of importers who were refused an import licence before the Commission decision was taken. That group was known (or at least ascertainable) when the decision was adopted.[268] The contested decision may be intended

---

[263] ECJ, Case 25/62 *Plaumann v Commission* [1963] E.C.R. 95, at 107.

[264] ECJ (order of December 12, 2003), Case C–258/02 P *Bactria Industriehygiene-Service v Commission* [2003] E.C.R. I–15105, paras 34, 36 and 50: the time for assessing whether the individual was individually concerned is the date of adoption of the contested act; CFI, Case T–112/97 *Monsanto v Commission* [1999] E.C.R. II–1277, paras 48–60: a parent company is individually concerned by a decision addressed to its wholly-owned subsidiary.

[265] In recent years, commentators have been pressing for a broad interpretation to be placed on the admissibility requirements to be satisfied by applicants who are individuals: see, for instance, Moitinho de Almeida, "Le recours en annullation des particuliers (Art.173, deuxième alinéa*[now Art.230, fourth para.]*, du traité CE): nouvelles réflexions sur l'expression 'la concernent . . . individuellement'", in *Festschrift für Ulrich Everling* (Nomos, Baden-Baden, 1995), at 849–874. An attempt by Greenpeace to have this requirement less strictly interpreted in environmental cases was rejected by both the Court of First Instance and the Court of Justice (sitting as the Full Court): CFI (order of August 9, 1995), Case T–585/93 *Greenpeace v Commission* [1995] E.C.R. II–2205 and ECJ, Case C–321/95 P *Greenpeace Council and Others v Commission* [1998] E.C.R. I–1651. For a critical case note, see Wegener, "Keine Klagebefugnis für Greenpeace und 18 andere. Anmerkung zu EuGH, Rs C–321/95 P (*Greenpeace*)" (1998) Z.U.R. 131–135. Some years ago, the Court of First Instance attempted to make the admissibility requirements more flexible, but this attempt was rejected by the Court of Justice (see CFI, Case T–177/01 *Jégo-Quéré v Commission* [2002] E.C.R. II–2365 & ECJ, Case C–50/00 P *Unión de Pequeños Agricultores v Council* [2002] E.C.R. I–6677, not following the Opinion of Advocate General F.G. Jacobs).

[266] That is to say, an act, irrespective of its name or form, which is *not* of general application, see 7–067 and 7–068, *supra*.

[267] ECJ, Case 97/85 *Deutsche Lebensmittelwerke v Commission* [1987] E.C.R. 2265, para.11. The Court of Justice uses the expression "closed circle". See also ECJ (order of May 24, 1993), Case C–131/92 *Arnaud and Others v Council* [1993] E.C.R. I–2573, para.8, where the applicant used the expression "closed class".

[268] ECJ, Joined Cases 106 and 107/63 *Toepfer and Getreide-Import v Commission* [1965] E.C.R. 405, at 411–412.

to cover both events in the past and events to come about in the future. If provisions can be found in the contested decision which are applicable solely to events in the past, those provisions concern a closed class of persons.[269]

Contested act is a measure of general application. Where, in contrast, the contested act is a measure of general application, it is not enough for the applicant to show that it belongs to a closed class in order to show that it is individually concerned by it.[270]   **7–080**

The fact that the persons to whom a regulation is applicable are identifiable is not determinative in itself.[271] Also the fact that an act of general application is applicable only to a small number of individuals,[272] that certain market participants are affected more harshly in economic terms than their competitors[273] or that different specific consequences may ensue for the various persons to whom the contested measure applies[274] is

---

[269] ECJ, Case 62/70 *Bock v Commission* [1971] E.C.R. 897, paras 2–5.
[270] CFI, Case T–482/93 *Weber v Commission* [1996] E.C.R. II–609, para.65.
[271] ECJ, Case 6/68 *Zuckerfabrik Watenstedt v Council* [1968] E.C.R. 409; ECJ, Case 63/69 *Compagnie Française Commerciale and Financière v Commission* [1970] E.C.R. 221, para.11; ECJ, Case 123/77 *UNICME v Council* [1978] E.C.R. 845, para.16; ECJ, Case 242/81 *Roquette Frères v Council* [1982] E.C.R. 3213, para.7; ECJ, Case 26/86 *Deutz and Geldermann v Council* [1987] E.C.R. 941, para.8; ECJ, Joined Cases 97, 193, 99 and 215/86 *Asteris v Commission* [1988] E.C.R. 2181, para.13; ECJ (order of the President of July 13, 1988), Case 160/88 R *Fédération Européenne de la Santé Animale and Others v Council* [1988] F.C.R. 4121, para.29; ECJ, Joined Cases C–15 and C–108/91 *Buckl and Others v Commission* [1992] E.C.R. I–6061, para.25; ECJ (order of May 24, 1993), Case C–131/92 *Arnaud v Council* [1993] E.C.R. I–2573, paras 13–17; ECJ, Case C–213/91 *Abertal v Commission* [1993] E.C.R. I–3177, paras 17–24; ECJ (orders of June 21, 1993), Case C–256/93 *Pacific Fruit Company and Others v Council and Commission*, not reported; Case C–257/93 *Van Parijs and Others v Council and Commission* [1993] E.C.R. I–3335; Case C–276/93 *Chiquita Banana and Others v Council* [1993] E.C.R. I–3345; Case C–282/93 *Comafrica and Others v Council and Commission*, not reported, and Case C–288/93 *CO.MA.CO v Council*, not reported; ECJ, Case C–298/89 *Gibraltar v Council* [1993] E.C.R. I–3605, para.17. For the possibility that the contested act is also applicable to situations in the future, see ECJ, Case 231/82 *Spijker v Commission* [1983] E.C.R. 2559, paras 8–11; CFI (order of May 11, 2001), Case T–178/96 *Eridania and Others v Council*, not reported, para.53. For the possibility that the regulation is also applicable to individuals established in another Member State, see ECJ, Case 1/64 *Glucoseries Réunies v Commission* [1964] E.C.R. 413, at 417. Also the fact that the applicant is the largest undertaking in the sector in question does not individualise its position sufficiently: CFI (order of April 29, 1999), Case T–120/98 *Alce v Commission* [1999] E.C.R. I–1395.
[272] ECJ, Case C–263/02 P *Commission v Jégo-Quéré* [2004] E.C.R. I–3425, para.46.
[273] ECJ, Case C–312/00 P *Commission v Camar and Tico* [2002] E.C.R. I–11355, paras 69–83: the chief importer of Somalian bananas was not individually concerned by the Commission's refusal to adjust the tariff quota for such bananas; CFI (order of September 15, 1999), Case T–11/99 *Van Parijs and Others v Commission* [1999] E.C.R. II–2653, para.50; CFI (order of July 8, 2004), Case T–338/03 *Edidania Sadam and Others v Commission*, not reported, para.35.
[274] ECJ (order of December 18, 1997), Case C–409/96 P *Sveriges Betodlares Centralförening and Henrikson v Commission* [1997] E.C.R. I–7531, para.37; CFI (order of the President of February 15, 2000), Case T–1/00 R *Hölzl and Others v Commission* [2000] E.C.R. II–251, para.21; CFI (order of July 6, 2004), Case T–370/02 *Alpenhain-Camembert-Werk and Others v Commission*, not yet reported, para.62.

not sufficient to show that the persons in question are individually concerned by the measure.[275]

If the situation to be regulated is such that, in order to attain its aim, the regulation must be held to be applicable without distinction to facts which existed at the time when it entered into effect and to similar facts which arose thereafter, an applicant cannot rely on its partial retroactive effect in order to claim that it is individually concerned by the act in question.[276]

7–081   Exceptional circumstances in which the applicant is individually concerned by a measure of general application. An applicant can show in only limited ways that it is individually concerned by a legislative act.

In the first place, an applicant will be individually concerned where the act adversely affected specific rights of the applicant or its members.[277] This is exceptional and there is only one instance to be found in the case-law. In *Codorníu*[278] the Court of Justice held that a provision of a Council regulation which reserved the use of the term *"crémant"* to sparkling wine produced in France and Luxembourg prevented the Spanish undertaking concerned from continuing to sell its wine under the trade mark *"Gran Cremant de Codorníu"*. It had registered this trade mark in Spain as long ago as 1924. It was therefore in a position which differentiated it, from the point of view of the said provision, from all other market participants.

Secondly, the applicant may argue that, in adopting the legislative act, the Community institution was under a duty to take account of its specific circumstances. Such specific protection distinguishes it sufficiently from other market participants' to which the act applies. In addition, there is the

---

[275] ECJ, Case 38/64 *Getreide-Import v Commission* [1965] E.C.R. 203, at 208. In that case, the contested act was a decision addressed to all Member States valid for one day and laying down the basis for an import levy. The applicant was the only individual who had applied for an import certificate.

[276] ECJ, Case C–244/88 *Usines Coopératives de Déshydratation du Vexin and Others v Commission* [1989] E.C.R. 3811, paras 11–14; ECJ, Case C–229/88 *Cargill and Others v Commission* [1990] E.C.R. I–1303, paras 13–18.

[277] ECJ, Case C–309/89 *Codorníu v Council* [1994] E.C.R. I–1853; ECJ (order of November 23, 1995), Case C–10/95 P *Asocarne v Council* [1995] E.C.R. I–4149, para.49 (no specific right infringed); CFI (order of March 26, 1999), Case T–114/96 *Confiserie du TECH and Biscuiterie Confiserie LOR v Commission* [1999] E.C.R. II–913, para.33 (no specific right infringed); CFI (order of July 6, 2004), Case T–370/02 *Alpenhain-Camembert-Werk and Others v Commission*, not yet reported, paras 65–66 (no specific right infringed; an application for annulment brought by manufacturers of Feta cheese established in Denmark against a regulation that made it impossible for them to go on making cheese under that denomination was declared inadmissible); CFI (order of September 6, 2004), Case T–213/02 *SNF v Commission*, not yet reported, paras 65–71; CFI (order of December 10, 2004), Case T–196/03 *European Federation for Cosmetic Ingredients v European Parliament and Council*, not yet reported, paras 56–62 (no specific rights infringed despite the fact that the applicant complained that its intellectual property rights had been impaired by the contested general measure).

[278] ECJ, Case C–309/89 *Codorníu v Council* [1994] E.C.R. I–1853.

fact that such a market participant must be able to assert that specific protection and therefore to bring an action.[279]

The fact that a person intervenes in some way in the procedure leading to the adoption of a Community act can only cause that person to be individualised with regard to that act within the meaning of the fourth para. of Art.230 of the EC Treaty if the applicable Community rules confer on that person specific procedural guarantees,[280] such as the right to be heard.[281]

Thirdly, an applicant will be individually concerned when the contested act mentions it by name (although it is not the addressee of the act) and a situation specific to it is directly governed by the act.[282] What is involved, therefore, is a situation in which the legislator adopts an act with the aim of

---

[279] ECJ, Case 11/82 *Piraiki-Patraiki v Commission* [1985] E.C.R. 207, paras 17–32; ECJ, Case C–209/94 P *Buralux and Others v Council* [1996] E.C.R. I–615, paras 30–35; ECJ, Case C–152/88 *Sofrimport v Commission* [1990] E.C.R. I–2477, paras 8–13; ECJ, Case C–390/95 P *Antillean Rice Mills v Council* [1999] E.C.R. I–769, paras 25–30; ECJ, Case C–167/02 P *Rothley and Others v European Parliament* [2004] E.C.R. I–3149, paras 32–38. *Cf.*, however, ECJ, Case C–451/98 *Antillean Rice Mills v Council* [2001] E.C.R. I–8949, paras 56–68, and ECJ, Case C–452/98 *Nederlandse Antillen v Council* [2001] E.C.R. I–8973, paras 54–77, in which the Court of Justice stated in relatively strong terms that the requirement for the Council to take account of the effects of an intended safeguard measure based on the OCT Decision (Decision on the association of the overseas countries and territories) on the OCTs concerned was not sufficient to individualise the OCT in question. *Cf.* CFI, Joined Cases T–32/98 and T–41/98 *Nederlandse Antillen v Commission* [2000] E.C.R. II–201, in which the Court of First Instance declared an action brought by the Netherlands Antilles for annulment of a safeguard measure relating to the import of sugar from OCTs admissible and well founded. The Court of First Instance considered that the Commission was required to take account of the adverse effects for the Netherlands Antilles of a safeguard measure adopted pursuant to Art.109(2) of the OCT Decision. However, that judgment was set aside by the Court of Justice on the ground that the factual situation of the Netherlands Antilles did not differentiate them from all other OCTs. Other OCTs, too, suffered the effects of the safeguard measure. Consequently, the Netherlands Antilles were not individually concerned by the safeguard measure and the Court of First Instance should have declared the claim inadmissible (ECJ, Case C–142/00 P *Commission v Nederlandse Antillen* [2003] E.C.R. I–3483). See also CFI, Joined Cases T–480/93 and T–483/93 *Antillean Rice Mills and Others v Commission* [1995] E.C.R. II–2305, paras 67–78 (with a case note by Waelbroeck and Fosselard (1996) C.M.L.Rev. 811–829); CFI, Case T–47/00 *Rica Foods v Commission* [2002] E.C.R. II–113, para.41. But see CFI, Joined Cases T–38/99 to T–50/99 *Sociedade Agrícola dos Arinhos and Others v Commission* [2001] E.C.R. II–585, paras 49–51; CFI, Case T–43/98 *Emesa Sugar v Council* [2001] E.C.R. II–3519, paras 54–56.

[280] CFI, Joined Cases T–38/99 to T–50/99 *Sociedade Agrícola dos Arinhos v Commission* [2001] II–585, para.48; CFI, Case T–47/00 *Rica Foods v Commission* [2002] E.C.R. II–113, para.55; CFI, Case T–70/99 *Alpharma v Council* [1999] E.C.R. II–3495, paras 73–98; CFI, Case T–13/99 *Pfizer Animal Health v Council* [2002] E.C.R. II–3305, paras 81–106; CFI (order of May 25, 2004), Case T–264/03 *Schmoldt and Others v Commission* [2004] E.C.R. II–1515, para.100; CFI (order of July 6, 2004), Case T–370/02 *Alpenhain-Camembert-Werk and Others v Commission*, not yet reported, paras 67–68.

[281] ECJ, Case C–263/02 P *Commission v Jégo-Quéré* [2004] E.C.R. I–3425, para.47.

[282] ECJ, Case 138/79 *Roquette Frères v Council* [1980] E.C.R. 3333, paras 13–16; ECJ, Case 139/79 *Maizena v Council* [1980] E.C.R. 3393, paras 13–16; ECJ, Joined Cases 239 and 275/82 *Allied Corporation v Commission* [1984] E.C.R. 1005, paras 4 and 12.

obtaining a specific result in favour of[283] or to the disadvantage[284] of specific persons.

7–082 Refusal of an institution. An action for annulment may be brought by a natural or legal person against an institution's refusal to adopt an act only if an application brought against the act refused would have been admissible.[285]

7–083 Judgment in *Les Verts*. In exceptional circumstances, the requirement that the contested act must be of individual concern to the applicant discriminates against persons who find themselves in a similar position. In such a case, the Court of Justice, applying the principle of equal treatment—part of superior Community law—will, if necessary, lower the hurdle of admissibility. The judgment in *Les Verts v European Parliament*[286] provides an illustration. The decision of the Bureau of the European Parliament determining the allocation of financial assistance to political parties with a view to preparing for the European elections applied both to political parties which were represented in the Parliament at the time when the decision was adopted, which were therefore identifiable, and to parties which were not so represented at that time and therefore were not identifiable, but which would be taking part in the elections. According to the wording of the judgment, there was no doubt that parties represented in the Parliament, which were identifiable, were individually concerned.[287] The question arose whether this was also true of parties not represented in the Parliament, who were therefore not identifiable. The Court of Justice held that the fact that the decision applied to all parties taking part in the elections placed the second class of parties in a similar position to the first, with the result that both classes had to be regarded as individually concerned by the decision in the same way.[288]

7–084 Associations. The question whether trade associations are individually concerned is arising increasingly frequently. It appears from the case-law that trade associations may be deemed to be sufficiently individually

---

[283] CFI (judgment of February 3, 2005), Case T–139/01 *Comafrica and Dole Fresh Fruit Europe v Commission*, not yet reported, para.110.
[284] ECJ, Case 100/74 *CAM v Commission* [1975] E.C.R. 1393, para.16.
[285] ECJ, Case 42/71 *Nordgetreide v Commission* [1972] E.C.R. 105, para.5; ECJ, Joined Cases 97, 193, 99 and 215/86 *Asteris and Others v Commission* [1988] E.C.R. 2181, paras 17–18; ECJ, Case C–87/89 *SONITO and Others v Commission* [1990] E.C.R. I–1981, para.8; ECJ, Joined Cases C–15 and C–108/91 *Buckl and Others v Commission* [1992] E.C.R. I–6061, para.22; CFI, Case T–83/92 *Zunis Holding and Others v Commission* [1993] E.C.R. II–1169, para.31; CFI (order of March 15, 2004), Case T–139/02 *Institouto N. Avgerinopoulou and Others v Commission* [2004] E.C.R. II–875, paras 56–57; CFI (order of July 13, 2004), Case T–29/03 *Comunidad Autónoma de Andalucía v Commission*, not yet reported, para.30.
[286] ECJ, Case 294/83 *Les Verts v European Parliament* [1986] E.C.R. 1339.
[287] Commentators point to the specific character of the contested measure (Kovar (1987) C.D.E. 300–332; *cf.* Jacqué (1986) R.T.D.E. 500–511).
[288] See, however, CFI (order of January 10, 2005), Case T–357/03 *Gollnisch and Others v European Parliament*, not yet reported, paras 69–70; CFI (order of July 11, 2005), Case T–40/04 *Bonino and Others v European Parliament and Council*, not yet reported, paras 73–74.

concerned in three types of situation.[289] First, a trade association may be individually concerned if it can show that a provision of Community law expressly grants it a series of procedural rights.[290] Secondly, this may be so where the association represents the interests of natural or legal persons who would be entitled to bring proceedings in their own right.[291] Thirdly, a trade association will be sufficiently individually concerned where it is differentiated because its own interests as an association are affected by the contested measure, especially where its position as negotiator of the act in question is affected.[292] In those three situations, the Court of Justice and the Court of First Instance also take account of the participation of the association in question in the decision-making procedure.

Effective judicial protection. The Court of Justice is not prepared to relax   7–085
the criteria developed in its case-law for individual concern depending on the legal protection enjoyed by individuals before their national courts.[293] The Court has pointed out that, in the complete system of legal remedies and procedures established by the EC Treaty with a view to ensuring

---

[289] For a clear survey of the case-law, see CFI (order of September 30, 1997), Case T–122/96 *Federolio v Commission* [1997] E.C.R. II–1559, para.60 *et seq.*; CFI (order of November 23, 1999), Case T–173/98 *Unión de Pequeños Agricultores v Council* [1999] E.C.R. II–3357, para.62; CFI, Case T–157/01 *Danske Busvognmænd v Commission* [2004] E.C.R. II–917, paras 40–41; CFI (order of May 10, 2004), Case T–391/02 *Bundesverband der Nahrungsmittel- und Speiseresteverwertung and Kloh v European Parliament* [2004] E.C.R. II–1447, paras 44–59; CFI (order of December 10, 2004), Case T–196/03 *European Federation for Cosmetic Ingredients v European Parliament and Council*, not yet reported, paras 41–42.

[290] ECJ, Case 191/82 *Fediol v Commission* [1983] E.C.R. 2913; CFI, Case T–12/93 *CCE de Vittel and Others v Commission* [1995] E.C.R. II–1247.

[291] CFI, Joined Cases T–447, T–448 and T–449/93 *AITEC and Others v Commission* [1995] E.C.R. II–1971; CFI, Case T–380/94 *AIUFASS and AKT v Commission* [1996] E.C.R. II–2169, para.50; CFI (order of February 15, 2005), Case T–229/02 *PKK and KNK v Council*, not yet reported, para.45.

[292] See, for instance, ECJ, Joined Cases 67/85, 68/85 and 70/85 *Van der Kooy and Others v Commission* [1988] E.C.R. 219; CFI (order of January 14, 2002), Case T–84/01 *ACHE v European Parliament and Council* [2002] E.C.R. II–99, para.25. The test is that the position as negotiator is clearly defined and must be related to the subject-matter of the contested act and that that position must have been affected by the adoption of the contested act (CFI (order of May 10, 2004), Case T–391/02 *Bundesverband der Nahrungsmittel- und Speiseresteverwertung and Kloh v European Parliament* [2004] E.C.R. II–1447, para.48; CFI (order of May 25, 2004), Case T–264/03 *Schmoldt and Others v Commission* [2004] E.C.R. II–1515, paras 131–143). The fact that an association has communicated information to the Community institutions or has tried to influence the position adopted by the national authorities in the Community legislative procedure does not suffice in itself to show that the act adopted at the end of that procedure affects the association in its position as negotiator: CFI (order of May 10, 2004), Case T–391/02 *Bundesverband der Nahrungsmittel- und Speiseresteverwertung and Kloh v European Parliament* [2004] E.C.R. II–1447, paras 48–50; see also CFI (order of May 25, 2004), Case T–264/03 *Schmoldt and Others v Commission*, [2004] E.C.R. II–1515, paras 137–143); CFI (order of July 11, 2005), Case T–40/04 *Bonino and Others v European Parliament and Council*, not yet reported, para.70.

[293] ECJ, Case C–321/95 P *Greenpeace Council and Others v Commission* [1998] E.C.R. I–1651, paras 33–34; see also CFI (order of March 12, 1998), Case T–207/97 *Berthu v Council* [1998] E.C.R. II–509, para.29; CFI (order of September 15, 1999), Case T–11/99 *Van Parijs and Others v Commission* [1999] E.C.R. II–2653, para.54.

judicial review of the legality of acts of the institutions, where natural or legal persons cannot, by reason of the conditions for admissibility laid down in the fourth para. of that article, directly challenge Community measures of general application, they are able, depending on the case, either indirectly to plead the invalidity of such acts before the Community judicature under Art.241 of the EC Treaty or to do so before the national courts and ask them, since they have no jurisdiction themselves to declare those measures invalid, to make a reference to the Court of Justice for a preliminary ruling.[294]

7–086   **Acts which do not entail implementing measures.** There are cases, however, in which an individual has no remedy for contesting a provision of Community law before a national court.[295] This may occur in particular where a regulation does not require Member States to adopt any implementing measures. The question arises as to whether the Community Court will take a more flexible approach to the admissibility requirements laid down in the fourth para. of Art.230 of the EC Treaty in such circumstances. In its judgment of May 3, 2002 in *Jégo-Quéré*,[296] the Court of First Instance recalled that the Treaty established a complete system of legal remedies and procedures designed to permit the Court of Justice to review the legality of acts of the institutions.[297]

The right to an effective remedy before a court of competent jurisdiction is based on the constitutional traditions common to the Member States, Arts 6 and 13 of the ECHR and Art.47 of the Charter of Fundamental

---

[294] ECJ, Case C–491/01 *British American Tobacco and Imperial Tobacco* [2002] E.C.R. I–11453, paras 39–40; ECJ, Case C–167/02 P *Rothley and Others v European Parliament* [2004] E.C.R. I–3149, para.46.

[295] CFI, Case T–138/98 *ACAV and Others v Council* [2000] E.C.R. II–341: the Court of First Instance held that the lack of a legal remedy at national level or the fact that such remedies are in any event ineffective do not enable an action for annulment to be declared admissible where it does not satisfy the conditions laid down in the fourth para. of Art.230 of the EC Treaty. To declare such an application admissible would result in a wrongful amendment by judicial interpretation of the system of remedies and procedures laid down in the Treaty; CFI, Joined Cases T–172/98 and T–175/98 to T–177/98 *Salamander and Others v European Parliament and Council* [2000] E.C.R. II–2487, para.75; CFI (order of April 29, 2002), Case T–339/00 *Bactria v Commission* [2002] E.C.R. II–2287, para.54: the Court of First Instance held that the possible absence of remedies cannot justify an amendment by way of judicial interpretation of the system of remedies and procedures laid down in the Treaty (upheld on appeal in ECJ (order of December 12, 2003), Case C–258/02 P *Bactria Industriehygiene-Service v Commission* [2003] E.C.R. I–15105, paras 57–60); CFI (order of June 28, 2005), Case T–386/04 *Eridania Sadam and Others v Commission*, not yet reported, paras 42–43; CFI (order of July 11, 2005), Case T–40/04 *Bonino and Others v European Parliament and Council*, not yet reported, para.77. See also Lenaerts, "The Legal Protection of Private Parties under the EC Treaty: a Coherent and Complete System of Judicial Review", in *Scritti in onore di Giuseppe Federico Mancini* (Giuffrè editore, Milan, 1998), Vol.II, at 591–623.

[296] CFI, Case T–177/01 *Jégo-Quéré v Commission* [2002] E.C.R. II–2365, para.41; set aside on appeal by ECJ, Case C–263/02 P *Commission v Jégo-Quéré* [2004] E.C.R. I–3425.

[297] *Ibid.*, para.41; ECJ, Case 294/83 *Les Verts v European Parliament* [1986] E.C.R. 1339, para.23.

Rights of the European Union proclaimed at Nice on December 7, 2000.[298] The Court of First Instance therefore considered that the strict interpretation of the notion of a person individually concerned according to the fourth para. of Art.230 of the EC Treaty had to be reconsidered in order to ensure effective judicial protection for individuals.[299] It took the view in the *Jégo-Quéré* case that "a natural or legal person is to be regarded as individually concerned by a Community measure of general application that concerns him directly if the measure in question affects his legal position, in a manner which is both definite and immediate, by restricting his rights or by imposing obligations on him".[300]

Less than three months later, the Court of Justice made it very clear in its judgment in the *Unión de Pequeños Agricultores* case[301] that it would not follow the approach of the Court of First Instance.[302] Referring to the *Plaumann* case,[303] the Court of Justice declared that natural or legal persons may be individually concerned by a measure where "the measure in question affects [them] by reason of certain attributes peculiar to them, or by reason of a factual situation which differentiates them from all other persons and distinguishes them individually in the same way as the addressee".[304] The Court considered that no other interpretation of this condition for admissibility was possible "without going beyond the jurisdiction conferred by the Treaty on the Community Courts".[305] As a result, only

---

[298] *Ibid.*, paras 41 and 42; ECJ, Case 222/84 *Johnston* [1986] E.C.R. 1651, para.18; CFI (judgment of September 21, 2005), Case T–306/01 *Yusuf and Al Barakaat International Foundation v Council and Commission*, not yet reported, paras 260–283 and 332–347 (as regards the question whether there exist any structural limits, imposed by general international law or by the EC Treaty itself, on the judicial review which it falls to the Court of First Instance to carry out with regard to a Community regulation putting into effect a decision of the UN Security Council).

[299] *Ibid.*, paras 50 and 51.

[300] *Ibid.*, para.51.

[301] ECJ, Case C–50/00 P *Unión de Pequeños Agricultores v Council* [2002] E.C.R. I–6677.

[302] The Opinion of Advocate General F.G. Jacobs in Case C–50/00 P *Unión de Pequeños Agricultores v Council* [2002] E.C.R. I–6681 was closer to the view taken by the Court of First Instance in *Jégo-Quéré*.

[303] ECJ, Case 25/62 *Plaumann v Commission* [1963] E.C.R. 95, at 107.

[304] ECJ, Case C–50/00 P *Unión de Pequeños Agricultores v Council* [2002] E.C.R. I–6677, para.36.

[305] *Ibid.*, para.44; ECJ, Case C–167/02 P *Rothley and Others v European Parliament* [2004] E.C.R. I–3149, para.25; ECJ, Case C–263/02 P *Commission v Jégo-Quéré* [2004] E.C.R. I–3425, para.36; CFI (order of April 2, 2004), Case T–231/02 *Gonnelli and AIFO v Commission* [2004] E.C.R. II–1051, paras 53–54; CFI (order of May 25, 2004), Case T–264/03 *Schmoldt and Others v Commission* [2004] E.C.R. II–1515, paras 151–159. In ECJ, Case C–312/00 P *Commission v Camar and Tico* [2002] E.C.R. I–11355, para.78, the Court of Justice declared that "the condition that natural or legal persons may bring an action challenging a regulation only if they are concerned individually must be interpreted in the light of the principle of effective judicial protection by taking account of the various circumstances that may distinguish an applicant individually". See in this connection Lenaerts and Corthaut "Judicial Review as a contribution to the development of European constitutionalism" [2003/2004] Y.E.L. 1–43, point 39: a measure of flexibility in the actual assessment whether the *Plaumann* test is satisfied may make a great difference. Neverthe-

an amendment to the Treaty could make the admissibility requirements set out in the fourth para. of Art.230 of the EC Treaty more flexible.[306] At the same time, the Court of Justice called on national courts "so far as possible, to interpret and apply national procedural rules governing the exercise of rights of action in a way that enables natural and legal persons to challenge before the courts the legality of any decision or other national measure relative to the application to them of a Community act of general application, by pleading the invalidity of such an act"[307] (see also 3–007 and 3–008, *supra*).

c. The concept of individual concern: some fields of application

(1) *Application of Arts 81 and 82 of the EC Treaty*

7–087 **Decisions finding an infringement or rejecting a complaint.** Where the Commission finds that certain undertakings or associations of undertakings have infringed Art.81 and/or Art.82 of the EC Treaty and possibly imposes fines on them, the undertakings or associations of undertakings concerned may bring an action for the annulment of the decision in question. As addressees of the decision, they derive that right from the fourth para. of Art.230 of the EC Treaty. Similarly, when a natural or legal person showing a legitimate interest lodges a complaint with the Commission on account of

---

less, it is not clear whether the Court of Justice sought to create an opening by that *dictum* in the *Camar* case: see, *e.g.* ECJ, Case C–263/02 P *Commission v Jégo-Quéré* [2004] E.C.R. I–3425, paras 43–48.

[306] ECJ, Case C–50/00 P *Unión de Pequeños Agricultores v Council* [2002] E.C.R. I–6677, para.45. See in this connection Borowski, "Die Nichtigkeitsklage gem. Art.230 Abs. 4 EGV" (2004) Eu.R. 879–910; Brown and Morijn, "Case C–263/02 P, *Jégo-Quéré & Cie*" (2004) C.M.L.Rev. 1639–1659; Corthaut, "Case CFI May 3, 2002, *Jégo-Quéré v Commission* T–177/01 and C–50/00P ECJ July 25, 2002, *Unión De Pequeños Agricultores v Council*" (2002) Col.J.E.L. 141–166; Gilliaux, "L'arrêt *Unión de Pequeños Agricultores*: entre subsidiarité juridictionnelle et effectivité" (2003) C.D.E. 177–202; Ginter, "Access to Justice in the European Court of Justice in Luxembourg" (2002) E.J.L.Ref. 381–445; Granger, "Towards a Liberalisation of Standing Conditions for Individuals Seeking Judicial Review of Community Acts: *Jégo-Quéré et Cie SA v Commission* and *Unión de Pequeños Agricultores v Council*" (2003) Mod.L.Rev. 124–138; Groussot, "The EC System of Legal Remedies and Effective Judicial Protection: Does the System Really Need Reform?" (2003) L.I.E.I. 221–248; Hanf, "Talking with the 'pouvoir constituant' in Times of Constitutional Reform: The European Court of Justice on Private Applicants' Access to Justice" (2003) 10 M.J.E.C.L. 3, 265–290; Köngeter, "Die Ambivalenz effektiven Rechtsschutzes Einzelner gegen EG-Verordnungen" (2003) Z.f.R.V 123–132; Martin, "Ubi ius, ibi remedium?—Locus Standi of Private Applicants under Article 230(4) EC at a European Constitutional Crossroads" (2004) M.J.E.C.L. 3, 233–261; Mehdi, "La recevabilité des recours formés par les personnes physiques et morales à l'encontre d'un acte de portée générale: l'aggiornamento n'aura pas eu lieu . . ." (2003) R.T.D.E. 23–50; Schwarze, "The Legal Protection of the Individual against Regulations in European Union Law" (2004) E.Pub.L. 285–303; Usher, "Direct and individual concern—an effective remedy or a conventional solution?" (2003) E.L.Rev. 575–600.

[307] ECJ, Case C–50/00 P *Unión de Pequeños Agricultores v Council* [2002] E.C.R. I–6677, para.42; ECJ, Case C–263/02 P *Commission v Jégo-Quéré* [2004] E.C.R. I–3425, para.32.

an alleged infringement of Art.81 and/or Art.82 of the EC Treaty,[308] such persons will be entitled—as addressees of the Commission decision—to bring an action for the annulment against the full or partial rejection of their complaint.[309]

Decisions making commitments binding and decisions finding Art.81 and/ or Art.82 of the EC Treaty inapplicable. Under the rules of Regulation No 17, under which the Commission had exclusive competence to declare that Art.81(1) of the EC Treaty was inapplicable, persons who submitted objections in writing to the Commission during the investigation in regard to a proposed declaration that Art.81(1) of the EC Treaty was not applicable to the practices of a competitor or supplier, or persons who participated in the hearing organised by the Commission, were individually concerned by such declaration.[310] The Court of Justice and the Court of First Instance considered that those classes of person had been sufficiently involved in the procedure whereby the contested decision was adopted in order to constitute a closed class in the light of the act.[311] This case-law will

7–088

---

[308] Regulation No 1/2003, Art.7, and Regulation No 773/2004, Art.5.

[309] ECJ, Case 26/76 *Metro v Commission* [1977] E.C.R. 1875; ECJ, Case 210/81 *Demo-Studio Schmidt v Commission* [1983] E.C.R. 3045, paras 10–16; CFI, Case T–37/92 *BEUC and NCC v Commission* [1994] E.C.R. II–285, para.36; CFI, Case T–114/92 *BEMIM v Commission* [1995] E.C.R. II–147, para.27; CFI (judgment of January 26, 2005), Case T 193/02 *Piau v Commission*, not yet reported, para.38.

[310] ECJ, Case 75/84 *Metro v Commission* [1986] E.C.R. 3021, paras 18–23; CFI, Case T–19/92 *Leclerc v Commission* [1996] E.C.R. II–1851, paras 53–63 and Case T–88/92 *Leclerc v Commission* [1996] E.C.R. II–1961, paras 49–50. In these judgments, the Court of First Instance based its finding that the applicant—a cooperative society—was individually concerned also on the fact that it had taken part in the administrative procedure as a representative of its members, who, as potential competitors of the traders belonging to the selective distribution system to which Art.81(1) of the EC Treaty had been declared inapplicable, could have taken part in the administrative procedure, and been individually concerned thereby, as "interested third parties" under Art.19(3) of Regulation No 17.

[311] Sometimes the case-law went even further: see CFI, Joined Cases T–528, T–542, T–543 and T–546/93 *Métropole Télévision and Others v Commission* [1996] E.C.R. II–649, where the Court of First Instance held that it is sufficient for the applicant to be able to be regarded as an interested third party within the meaning of the first sentence of Art.19(3) of Regulation No 17 which was entitled to be associated by the Commission with the administrative procedure for the adoption of the decision in order for it to be individually concerned thereby within the meaning of the fourth para.of Art.230 of the EC Treaty. The Court considered it irrelevant that the applicant had not availed itself of its procedural rights under Art.19(3) of Regulation No 17. It considered that to make the capacity to bring proceedings of such interested third parties subject to their actually taking part in the administrative procedure would be tantamount to introducing an additional condition of admissibility in the form of a compulsory pre-litigation procedure not provided for in Art.230. *Cf.*, however, CFI, Case T–87/92 *Kruidvat v Commission* [1996] E.C.R. II–1931, paras 61–67. The Court of Justice upheld the judgment of the Court of First Instance in *Kruidvat*, holding that the fact that a trade organisation participated in the administrative procedure before the Commission cannot relieve their members of the need to establish a link between their individual situation and the action of the organisation. In other words, the organisation's participation was not sufficient to individualise one of its members which had not participated in the administrative procedure: ECJ, Case C–70/97 P *Kruidvat v*

likely be relevant for the purpose of assessing the admissibility of actions for annulment brought by third parties against decisions making commitments binding on undertakings or finding that there are no longer grounds for action by the Commission (Regulation No 1/2003, Art.9(1)) and against decisions in which the Commission finds that Art.81 and/or Art.82 of the EC Treaty are inapplicable to a certain practice or agreement (Regulation No 1/2003, Art.10).

(2) Merger control

7–089 **Addressees.** Where the Commission finds that a concentration is incompatible with the common market, the addressees of the relevant decision have standing, pursuant to the fourth para. of Art.230 of the EC Treaty, to bring an action for annulment of that decision.

7–090 **Competitors.** A competitor of undertakings involved in the concentration which has actively participated in the administrative procedure (by submitting observations and criticisms, clarifying, among other things, the effects of the concentration on its competitive position) will be individually concerned by a Commission decision declaring the concentration compatible with the common market.[312] It would appear to be sufficient that the applicant is a potential competitor on most of the markets affected.[313]

7–091 **Referral to national authorities.** An undertaking is individually concerned by a decision to refer the matter to the national competition authorities pursuant to Art.9 of Regulation No 139/2004 if the undertaking would have

---

Commission [1998] E.C.R. I–7183, para.23. An undertaking which participated in the administrative procedure before the Commission and which started proceedings in the national courts for compensation for having had obligations contrary to Art.81 of the EC Treaty imposed on it under an agreement to which Art.81(1) was declared inapplicable was held to be individually concerned by the decision exempting the agreement (CFI, Case T–131/99 *Shaw and Falla v Commission* [2002] E.C.R. II–2023, paras 25–27).

[312] CFI, Case T–2/93 *Air France v Commission* [1994] E.C.R. II–323, paras 40–48 (the Court of First Instance also took account in this case of the fact that the Commission had judged the competitive structure of the market in question above all in the light of the applicant's competitive position and that some months before the concentration came about, the applicant undertaking had given up its interest in one of the undertakings concerned pursuant to an agreement concluded with the Commission); ECJ, Joined Cases C–68/94 and C–30/95 *France and Others and EMC v Commission* [1998] E.C.R. I–1375, paras 54–58 (the Court of Justice also took account in this case of the fact that the conditions attached to the declaration by which the concentration was stated to be compatible with the common market primarily touched the applicant's interests); CFI, Case T–114/02 *BaByliss v Commission* [2003] E.C.R. II–1279, paras 87–117. *Cf.* Heidenhain, "Zur Klagebefugnis Dritter in der europäischen Fusionskontrolle" (1991) Eu.Z.W. 590–595. For a thorough analysis of admissibility problems in the case of actions against Commission decisions pursuant to Regulation No 4064/89, see Langeheine, "Judicial Review in the Field of Merger Control" (1992) J.B.L. 121, at 121–131.

[313] *Ibid.*, paras 99–100.

been individually concerned by the Commission's final decision had the Commission not referred the case to the national authorities.[314]

Representatives of employees. The Court of First Instance has held in connection with Regulation No 4064/89 that recognised employees' representatives of an undertaking involved in a concentration were individually concerned by a Commission decision adopted pursuant to that regulation on the ground that Regulation No 4064/89 mentioned them expressly and specifically among the third persons showing a "sufficient interest" to submit observations to the Commission during the administrative investigation of the concentration's compatibility with the common market.[315] The Court of First Instance regarded it as irrelevant whether the employees' representatives of the undertaking had actually taken part in the administrative procedure.[316]   **7–092**

(3) *State aid cases*

Decisions addressed to Member States. State aid decisions are addressed to the Member State concerned.[317] It is settled case-law that persons other than those to whom a decision is addressed may claim to be individually concerned only if the decision affects them by reason of certain attributes peculiar to them or by reason of circumstances in which they are differentiated from all other persons and if, by virtue of those factors, it distinguishes them individually in the same way as the person addressed.[318]   **7–093**

(i) *Position of beneficiaries of State aid and their competitors*

General. As regards the position of beneficiaries of State aid and their competitors, a distinction has to be drawn between decisions relating to general aid regimes and decisions relating to individual aid measures.   **7–094**

---

[314] CFI, Case 119/02 *Royal Philips Electronics v Commission* [2003] E.C.R. II–1433, paras 291–298; CFI, Joined Cases T–346/02 and T–347/02 *Cableuropa and Others v Commission* [2003] E.C.R. II–4251, paras 78–79.

[315] Representatives of employees and representatives of management enjoy the same right under Art.18(4) of Regulation No 139/2004.

[316] CFI, Case T–96/92 *CCE de la Société Générale des Grandes Sources and Others v Commission* [1995] E.C.R. II–1213, para.37; CFI, Case T–12/93 *CCE de Vittel and Others v Commission* [1995] E.C.R. II–1247, para.48. In those cases, the Court of First Instance subsequently held that the applicants were directly affected by the contested decision only in so far as their procedural rights during the administrative procedure had been affected. Consequently, it considered only the plea alleging that those rights had been breached. For a critical note on that limited admissibility, see Arnull (1996) C.M.L.Rev. 319–335.

[317] Regulation No 659/1999, Art.25.

[318] ECJ, Case 25/62 *Plaumann v Commission* [1963] E.C.R. 197; ECJ Case C–321/95 P *Greenpeace Council and Others v Commission* [1998] E.C.R. I–1651, paras 7 and 28; ECJ, Joined Cases C–15/98 and C–105/99 *Italy and Sardegna Lines v Commission* [2000] E.C.R. I–8855, para.32.

* *Decisions relating to general aid regimes*

7–095 **Measures of general application.** Commission decisions which declare general aid regimes compatible or incompatible with the common market are considered to be measures of general application. By and large, actions brought by undertakings against such decisions will be inadmissible since they will generally fail to satisfy the "individually concerned" condition laid down in the fourth para. of Art.230 of the EC Treaty. In this respect it seems to be immaterial whether the decision was taken on the basis of the preliminary procedure laid down by Art.88(3) of the EC Treaty[319] or upon completion of the procedure provided for in Art.88(2) of the EC Treaty.[320] Similarly, a Commission decision to initiate the procedure laid down in Art.88(2) of the EC Treaty relating to general aid regimes should be deemed to be of general application.

7–096 **Competitors of beneficiaries of the aid.** An undertaking which is a competitor of a potential beneficiary of aid authorised under a general aid scheme does not have *locus standi* to challenge a Commission decision authorising that scheme.[321] This is because the contested decision affects such an undertaking only by virtue of its objective capacity in the same manner as any other undertaking which is, or might be in the future, in the same situation.[322] The fact that the applicant made a complaint to the Commission (and in that connection corresponded and even had meetings with the Commission) does not constitute sufficient circumstances peculiar to the applicant by which it can be distinguished individually from all other persons, thus conferring on it standing to bring proceedings against a decision of the Commission relating to a general aid scheme.[323]

7–097 **Beneficiaries of the aid.** Similarly, potential beneficiaries of a general aid scheme are not individually concerned by a Commission decision relating to that scheme. The Court has therefore consistently held that an undertaking

---

[319] CFI, Case T–398/94 *Kahn Scheepvaart v Commission* [1996] E.C.R. II–477; CFI, Case T–69/96 *Hamburger Hafen- und Lagerhaus and Others v Commission* [2001] E.C.R. II–1037. But see CFI, Case T–188/95, *Waterleiding Maatschappij "Noord-West Brabant" v Commission* [1998] E.C.R. II–3713, paras 55–86, and CFI, Case T–114/00 *Aktionsgemeinschaft Recht und Eigentum v Commission* [2002] E.C.R. II–5121, paras 41–60, in which the Court of First Instance held that the applicants were individually concerned by the contested decision on the sole ground that they were (or represented) "parties concerned" within the meaning of Art.88(2) of the EC Treaty. The latter judgment was annulled on appeal (ECJ (judgment of December 13, 2005), Case C–78/03 P *Commission v Aktionsgemeinschaft Recht und Eigentum*, not yet reported).

[320] ECJ, Cases 67–68 and 70/85 *Van der Kooy v Commission* [1988] E.C.R. 219, paras 13–16; ECJ, Cases C–15/98 ct C–105/99 *Italy and Sardegna Lines v Commission* [2000] E.C.R. I–8855, para.33; ECJ, Case C–298/00 P *Italy v Commission* [2004] E.C.R. I–4087, para 37; CFI, Case T–86/96 *Arbeitsgemeinschaft Deutscher Luftfahrt-Unternehmen v Commission* [1999] E.C.R. II–179, paras 45–46; CFI, Case T–9/98 *Mitteldeutsche Erdöl-Raffinerie v Commission* [2001] E.C.R. II–3367, para.77.

[321] CFI, Case T–398/94 *Kahn Scheepvaart v Commission* [1996] E.C.R. II–477.

[322] *Ibid.*, para.41.

[323] *Ibid.*, para.42.

cannot, in principle, contest a Commission decision prohibiting a sectoral aid scheme if it is concerned by that decision solely by virtue of belonging to the sector in question and being a *potential beneficiary* of the scheme. *Vis-à-vis* the undertaking should it seek to contest the decision, such a decision is a measure of general application covering situations which are determined objectively, and entails legal effects for a class of persons envisaged in a general and abstract manner.[324]

Where, however, the applicant undertaking is concerned by the contested decision not only by virtue of its being potential beneficiary of the aid scheme in question, but also by virtue of its being an actual recipient of individual aid granted under that scheme, the recovery of which has been ordered by the Commission, the Court will find that the *Plaumann* test[325] is satisfied. Thus, an *actual beneficiary* of individual aid granted under a general scheme is individually concerned by the Commission decision declaring the aid incompatible with the common market in the case of a decision ordering the recovery of the aid.[326] It should be recalled that as a result of the *TWD Textilwerke Deggendorf* case a person who undoubtedly has the right under Art.230 of the EC Treaty to seek the annulment of a Community act may not plead the illegality of that act in subsequent proceedings before the national courts.[327] That case-law, however, only applies where there is absolutely no doubt that the recovery order applies to the undertaking concerned.[328]

---

[324] ECJ, Cases 67/85, 68/85 and 70/85 *Van der Kooy and Others v Commission* [1988] E.C.R. 219, para.15; ECJ, Case C–6/92 *Federmineraria and Others v Commission* [1993] E.C.R. I–6357, para.14; ECJ, Joined Cases C–15/98 and C–105/99 *Italy and Sardegna Lines v Commission* [2000] E.C.R. I–8855, para.33; CFI (order of March 10, 2005), Case T–273/00 *Unione degi industriali della provincia di Venezia v Commission*, not reported, para.25.

[325] See 7–078, *supra*.

[326] ECJ, Joined Cases C–15/98 and C–105/99 *Italy and Sardegna Lines v Commission*, [2000] E.C.R. I–8855, para.34; ECJ, Case C–298/00 P *Italy v Commission* [2004] E.C.R. I–4087, paras 37–39; CFI, Case T–55/99 *CETM v Commission* [2000] E.C.R. II–3207. See, with respect to existing aid, ECJ, Joined Cases C–182/03 R and C–217/03 R (order of the President of June 26, 2003) *Belgium and Forum 187 v Commission* [2003] E.C.R. I–6887, paras 104–107; CFI (order of March 10, 2005), Case T–266/00 *Confartigianato Venezia and Others v Commission*, not yet reported, paras 13–26.

[327] ECJ, Case C–188/92 *TWD Textilwerke Deggendorf* [1994] E.C.R. I–833, paras 24–26; ECJ, Case C–241/95 *Accrington Beef* [1996] E.C.R. I–6699, paras 15–16. See also 10–008, *infra*.

[328] When the national authorities consider that the recovery order does not apply to the undertaking having brought an action for annulment before the Court of First Instance, that court will declare the action inadmissible and the *TWD Textilwerke Deggendorf* case-law will not apply: see CFI (order of March 10, 2005), Joined Cases T–228/00, T–229/00, T–242/00, T–243/00, T–245/00 to T–248/00, T–250/00, T–252/00, T–256/00 to T–259/00, T–265/00, T–267/00, T–268/00, T–271/00, T–274/00 to T–276/00, T–281/00, and T–287/00 to T–296/00 *Gruppo ormeggiatori del porto di Venezia and Others v Commission*, not yet reported, paras 24 and 30–32; CFI (order of March 10, 2005), Case T–266/00 *Confartigianato Venezia and Others v Commission*, not yet reported, paras 21–23; CFI (order of March 10, 2005), Case T–273/00 *Unione degli industriali della provincia di Venezia v Commission*, not reported, paras 21–23. See also the Opinion of Advocate General D. Ruiz-Jarabo Colomer of April 28, 2005 in Joined Cases C–346/03 and C–529/03 *Atzeni and Others*, not yet reported, paras 86–90 and 98.

* *Decisions relating to individual aid measures*

7–098   Decisions taken on the basis of the preliminary procedure provided for in Art.88(3) of the EC Treaty. As far as new aid[329] is concerned, the Commission is empowered to take decisions at two stages of its investigation into its compatibility with the common market.[330]

First, there is the preliminary stage for reviewing aid pursuant to Art.88(3) of the EC Treaty. Where, at the conclusion of its investigation, the Commission decides to initiate the procedure under Art.88(2) of the EC Treaty, that decision is of individual concern to undertakings which are the envisaged beneficiaries of the proposed aid.[331] Where, in contrast, the Commission considers at the end of the preliminary stage that the proposed aid is compatible with the common market and therefore decides not to initiate a procedure pursuant to Art.88(2), that decision is of individual concern to all the parties concerned which could have submitted observations in the course of that procedure.[332] Indeed, judicial review is the only means whereby those parties concerned can enforce their procedural rights.[333] "Parties concerned" within the meaning of Art.88(2) do not

---

[329] For a definition, see n.144, *supra*.

[330] For an extensive discussion, see Coulon and Cras, "Contentieux de la légalité dans le domaine des aides d'État: les récentes évolutions dans l'application des articles 173 et 175 du traité CE" (1999) C.D.E. 90–129.

[331] The Member State concerned may not put the measure into effect before the procedure has resulted in a final decision.

[332] ECJ, Case C–198/91 *Cook v Commission* [1993] E.C.R. I–2487, paras 13–26; ECJ, Case C–225/91 *Matra v Commission* [1993] E.C.R. I–3203, paras 15–20. The same applies where the Commission considers that there is no question of State aid with the result that competing undertakings which have submitted complaints about it are deprived in any event of their procedural rights under Art.88(2) of the EC Treaty. They are directly and individually concerned by such a Commission decision and may enforce their procedural rights before the Community Court: ECJ, Case C–367/95 P *Commission v Sytraval and Brink's France* [1998] E.C.R. I–1719, para.47; CFI, Case 11/95 *BP Chemicals v Commission* [1998] E.C.R. II–3232, paras 164–166.

[333] See, *e.g.* CFI, Case T–158/99 *Thermenhotel Stoiser Franz and Others v Commission* [2004] E.C.R. II–1, para.69. In its application, an applicant must not confine itself to pleading a breach of the procedural rights provided for in Art.88(2) of the EC Treaty. It may invoke all the grounds of illegality mentioned in the second para.of Art.230 of the EC Treaty: CFI, Case T–157/01 *Danske Busvognmaend v Commission* [2004] E.C.R. II–917, paras 39–42). However, where an applicant does not seek the annulment of a decision taken on the basis of the preliminary procedure laid down by Art.88(3) of the EC Treaty on the ground that the Commission was in breach of the obligation to initiate the procedure provided for in Art.88(2) or on the ground that the procedural safeguards provided for by Art.88(2) were infringed, the mere fact that the applicant may be considered to be a party concerned within the meaning of Art.88(2) does not render it individually concerned for the purposes of the fourth para.of Art.230 of the EC Treaty. In such a case, the action will be admissible only if the applicant is affected by the contested decision by reason of other circumstances distinguishing it individually in like manner to the person addressed, in accordance with the *Plaumann* test (CFI, Case T–266/94 *Skibsvaerftsforeningen and Others v Commission* [1996] E.C.R. II–1399, para.45; CFI, Case T–188/95, *Waterleiding Maatschappij "Noord-West Brabant" v Commission* [1998] E.C.R. II–3713, para.54). See also ECJ (judgment of December 13, 2005), Case C–78/03 P *Commission v Aktionsgemeinschaft Recht und Eigentum*, not yet reported.

comprise only the undertaking or undertakings in receipt of aid (which in this event naturally have no interest in bringing an action for annulment), but also such persons, undertakings or associations whose interests might be affected by the grant of the aid, for instance, competing undertakings and trade associations.[334]

Decision taken upon completion of the procedure provided for in Art.88(2) **7–099** **of the EC Treaty.** In addition, the Commission may also take a decision after the *inter partes* procedure provided for in Art.88(2) of the EC Treaty has been completed. Such a decision is likewise addressed to the Member State concerned. If the Commission declares the aid incompatible with the common market, *the undertaking for which the aid was intended* will be individually concerned.[335] Furthermore, a recipient of aid will likewise be individually concerned by a Commission decision declaring aid compatible with the common market subject to the express condition that the recipient of the aid fulfils a number of obligations. It will also have an interest in the annulment of such a decision.[336] In contrast, it will have no interest such as

---

[334] ECJ, Case 323/82 *Intermills v Commission* [1984] E.C.R. 3809, para.16; CFI, Case T–17/96 *TF1 v Commission*, [1999] E.C.R. II–1757, para.31; CFI, Case T–158/99 *Thermenhotel Stoiser Franz and Others v Commission* [2004] E.C.R. II–1, para.69. It is not enough for the competitive position of an undertaking to have been affected by the aid measure approved only potentially and incidentally in order for it to be regarded as a "party concerned" within the meaning of Art.88(2) of the EC Treaty. See also CFI, Case T–398/94 *Kahn Scheepvaart v Commission* [1996] E.C.R. II–477, paras 47–49; CFI, Case T–188/95 *Waterleiding Maatschappij Noord-West Brabant v Commission* [1998] E.C.R. II–3713, paras 50–87; CFI, Case T–69/96 *Hamburger Hafen- und Lagerhaus and Others v Commission* [2001] E.C.R. II–1037, para.42, and CFI (order of June 25, 2003), Case T–41/01 *Pérez Escolar v Commission* [2003] E.C.R. II–2157, paras 34–47. A taxpayer *per se* is not a party concerned within the meaning of Art.88(2) of the EC Treaty. This is because if this were admitted to be the case it would deprive the notion of a person individually concerned within the meaning of the fourth para. of Art.230 of the EC Treaty of any legal meaning in the context of actions for annulment brought against decisions taken on the basis of Art.88(3) of the EC Treaty by making that remedy into a species of *actio popularis*. The fact that a person has submitted a complaint to the Commission is not sufficient in itself for that person to be regarded as a party concerned within the meaning of Art. 88(2) of the EC Treaty. A complainant has to show that it has a legitimate interest, consisting, for instance, in the protection of its competitive position on the market *vis-à-vis* the measures complained of (CFI (order of June 25, 2003), Case T–41/01 *Pérez Escolar v Commission* [2003] E.C.R. II–2157, paras 36–40).

[335] ECJ, Case 730/79 *Philip Morris v Commission* [1980] E.C.R. 2671, para.5; ECJ, Case 323/82 *Intermills v Commission* [1984] E.C.R. 3809, para.5; ECJ, Joined Cases 296 and 318/82 *Netherlands and Leeuwarder Papierwarenfabriek v Commission* [1985] E.C.R. 809, para.13; CFI, Case T–358/94 *Air France v Commission* [1996] E.C.R. II–2109, para.31. Works councils and trade unions of undertakings in receipt of aid were, however, not held to be individually concerned by a Commission decision declaring the aid incompatible with the common market. Such works councils and trade unions are parties concerned within the meaning of Art.88(2), but that is not sufficient to render them individually concerned, not even if they submitted comments during the administrative procedure: CFI (order of February 18, 1998), Case T–189/97 *Comité d'entreprise de la Société française de production and Others v Commission* [1998] E.C.R. II–335, paras 42–44, upheld by ECJ, Case C–106/98 P *Comité d'entreprise de la Société française de production and Others v Commission* [2000] E.C.R. I–3659.

[336] CFI, Case T–296/97 *Alitalia v Commission* [2000] E.C.R. II–3871.

to entitle it to claim annulment of a decision which simply declares a specific aid measure compatible with the common market. Accordingly, it cannot contest the classification of a measure as aid where the aid is declared unconditionally compatible with the common market.[337]

As regards an undertaking which is *not the beneficiary of the aid measure*, the Court has consistently held that a decision closing a procedure under Art.88(2) of the EC Treaty is of individual concern to those competitors of the beneficiary which have played a significant role in the investigation procedure, provided that their position on the market is significantly affected by the aid which is the subject of the decision at issue.[338] However, that does not preclude the possibility that an undertaking may be in a position to demonstrate by other means—by reference to specific circumstances distinguishing it individually as in the case of the person addressed—that it is individually concerned.[339]

Nevertheless, an undertaking which is not a recipient of aid will have difficulty in showing that it is individually concerned by a Commission decision approving the aid after completion of the procedure provided for in Art.88(2) of the EC Treaty where it did not take part or played only a negligible role in that procedure.[340] Unlike in the case of an action for annulment of a decision taken after the preliminary investigation pursuant to Art.88(3) of the EC Treaty, an undertaking cannot simply rely on its status as a competitor of the recipient of aid in order to demonstrate that it is individually concerned by the Commission's decision.[341] Where the undertaking has not exercised its right to submit comments in the course of the procedure provided for in Art.88(2) of the EC Treaty, it must prove

---

[337] CFI (judgment of April 14, 2005), Case T–141/03 *Sniace v Commission*, not yet reported, paras 20–41.

[338] This will be the case, for instance, where the applicant undertaking was at the origin of the complaint which led to the initiation of the Art.88(2) procedure and where the views of that undertaking were heard during that procedure and largely determined the conduct of that procedure. See in this respect ECJ, Case 169/84 *Cofaz v Commission* [1986] E.C.R. 391, paras 22–25 (for critical comments, see Gyselen, "La transparence en matière d'aides d'Etat: Les droits des tiers" (1993) C.D.E. 417, at 433–434); see also CFI, Joined Cases T–447/93, T–448/93 and T–449/93 *AITEC and Others v Commission* [1995] E.C.R. II–1971, paras 33–42 and 75–80; CFI, Case T–149/95 *Ducros v Commission* [1997] E.C.R. II–2031, paras 30–43; CFI (judgment of October 21, 2004), Case T–36/99 *Lenzing v Commission*, not yet reported, para.90: the fact that the position on the market of the person concerned is substantially affected does not necessarily mean that its profitability falls, that its market share is reduced or that operating losses are incurred. The question in that connection is whether the person concerned would be in a more favourable situation in the absence of the decision which it seeks to have annulled. That may validly cover the situation in which the applicant loses the opportunity to make a profit because the public authorities confer an advantage on one of its competitors.

[339] CFI, Case T–435/93, ASPEC *and Others v Commission* [1995] E.C.R. II–1281, para.64; CFI, Case T–11/95 *BP Chemicals v Commission* [1998] E.C.R. II–3235, para 72.

[340] CFI (judgment of April 14, 2005), Case T–141/03 *Sniace v Commission*, not yet reported, para.59.

[341] ECJ, Case C–106/98 P *Comité d'entreprise de la Société française de production and Others v Commission* [2000] E.C.R. I–3659, para.41; CFI (judgment of April 14, 2005), Case T–141/03 *Sniace v Commission*, not yet reported, para.70.

that it is in a distinct competitive position which differentiates it, as regards the State aid in question, from any other trader.[342] Accordingly, the Court of First Instance has accepted that undertakings which had not taken part in the formal investigation pursuant to Art.88(2) of the EC Treaty could nevertheless be directly and individually concerned on the ground that the market in which the aid was granted was characterised by a limited number of producers (the applicants had a market share of 95 per cent) and by the significant increase in production capacity involved in the investments planned by the company in receipt of the aid in question. That special situation distinguished them from every other market participant as far as the aid in issue was concerned.[343]

(ii) *Position of regions and devolved authorities*

Not privileged applicants under the second para. of Art.230 of the EC Treaty. As regards the position of regions, the term Member State employed in the second para. of Art.230 refers, for the purposes of the institutional provisions and, in particular, those relating to judicial proceedings, only to government authorities of the Member States of the European Communities and cannot include the governments of regions or autonomous communities, irrespective of the powers they may have.[344] Regions and other devolved bodies are therefore not entitled to bring proceedings pursuant to the second para. of Art.230 of the EC Treaty. By contrast, where devolved bodies have legal personality under national law they must, on that basis, be treated as legal persons within the meaning of the fourth para. of Art.230 of the EC Treaty.[345]

7–100

Individually concerned if the authority concerned is the author of the aid measure. A region or other devolved body will be deemed to be individually concerned by a Commission decision declaring a general aid scheme[346]

7–101

---

[342] CFI, Case T–435/93 *ASPEC and Others v Commission* [1995] E.C.R. p. II–1281, para.70; CFI, Case T–266/94 *Skibsvaerftsforeningen and Others v Commission* [1996] E.C.R. II–1399, para.47; CFI Case T–11/95 *BP Chemicals v Commission* [1998] E.C.R. II–3235, para.77; CFI (order of May 27, 2004) Case T–358/02 *Deutsche Post and DHL v Commission* [2004] E.C.R. II–1565, para.36.

[343] CFI, Case T–435/93 *ASPEC and Others v Commission* [1995] E.C.R. I–1281, para.70.

[344] ECJ (order of March 21, 1997), Case C–95/97 *Région Wallonne v Commission* [1997] E.C.R. I–1787, para.6; ECJ (order of October 1, 1997), C–180/97 *Regione Toscana v Commission* [1997] E.C.R. I–5245, para.6; CFI, Case T–214/95 *Vlaams Gewest v Commission* [1998] E.C.R. II–717, para.28.

[345] ECJ (order of March 21, 1997), Case C–95/97 *Région Wallonne v Commission* [1997] E.C.R. I–1787, para.11; ECJ (order of October 1, 1997), C–180/97 *Regione Toscana v Commission* [1997] E.C.R. I–5245, para.11; CFI, Case T–214/95 *Vlaams Gewest v Commission* [1998] E.C.R. II–717, para.28; CFI (judgment of October 5, 2005), Joined Cases T–366/03 and T–235/04 *Land Oberösterreich and Austria v Commission*, not yet reported, paras 25–30 (with respect to a decision taken under Art.95(5) of the EC Treaty).

[346] CFI, Case T–288/97 *Regione Autonoma Friuli-Venezia Giulia v Commission* [1999] E.C.R. II–1871, para.31; CFI, Joined Cases T–269/99, T–271/99 and T–272/99 *Diputación Foral de Guipúzcoa and Others v Commission* [2002] E.C.R. II–4217, para.41.

or an individual aid measure[347] adopted by the region or body concerned incompatible with the common market. Indeed under such circumstances, the contested decision directly prevents the authority concerned from exercising its own powers as it sees fit.[348] However, where the applicant is not the author of the aid scheme, reliance by a regional or other devolved authority of a Member State on the fact that the application or implementation of the contested Community measure is capable generally of affecting socio-economic conditions within its territorial jurisdiction is not sufficient to render an action brought by that authority admissible.[349]

(iii) *Position of associations*

7–102 **General.** An action for annulment brought by an association of undertakings against a Community decision relating to State aid will be admissible in two sets of circumstances. The first is where the association has a particular interest in acting, especially because its negotiating position is affected by the measure which it seeks to have annulled. The second is where the association, by bringing its action, has substituted itself for one or more of the members whom it represents, on condition that those members were themselves in a position to bring an admissible action.

7–103 **Association representing the interests of undertakings which are directly and individually concerned.** The defence of common interests is not enough to establish the admissibility of an action for annulment brought by an association. An association will, however, be able to bring an action where it defends the individual interests of certain of its members before the Court of First Instance in accordance with the powers conferred on it by its statutes if it can be demonstrated that those members are directly and individually concerned by the decision concerned. Such collective action brought by the association presents procedural advantages, since it obviates the institution of numerous separate actions against the same decision, whilst avoiding any risk of Art.230 of the EC Treaty being circumvented by means of such a collective action.[350]

---

[347] CFI, Case T–214/95 *Vlaams Gewest v Commission* [1998] E.C.R. II–717, para.29; CFI, Joined Cases T–132/96 and T–143/96 *Freistaat Sachsen and Others v Commission* [1999] E.C.R. II–3663, para.84.

[348] CFI, Case T–214/95 *Vlaams Gewest v Commission* [1998] E.C.R. II–717, para.29; CFI, Joined Cases T–132/96 and T–143/96 *Freistaat Sachsen and Others v Commission* [1999] E.C.R. II–3663, para.84; CFI, Case T–288/97 *Regione Autonoma Friuli-Venezia Giulia v Commission* [1999] E.C.R. II–1871, para.31; CFI, Joined Cases T–269/99, T–271/99 and T–272/99 *Diputación Foral de Guipúzcoa and Others v Commission* [2002] E.C.R. II–4217, para.41.

[349] CFI, Case T–238/97 *Comunidad Autónoma de Cantabria v Council* [1998] E.C.R. II–2271, para.50.

[350] ECJ, Case 282/85 *DEFI v Commission* [1986] E.C.R. 2469, para.16; ECJ, Case C–6/92 *Federmineraria and Others v Commission* [1993] E.C.R. I–6357, para.17; CFI, Joined Cases T–447/93, T–448/93 and T–449/93 *AITEC and Others v Commission* [1995] E.C.R. II–1971, paras 60 and 62; CFI, Case T–55/99 *CETM v Commission* [2000] E.C.R. II–3207, para.23.

The association's position as negotiator is affected. An association will be 7–104
considered to be individually concerned by a Commission decision relating
to State aid if it is capable of demonstrating that its position as a negotiator
is affected by that decision.[351]

A trade organisation which was closely involved in the development of
the Commission's policy on aid in a particular sector will be individually
concerned by a Commission decision which is allegedly at odds with the
policy outlined. This is because such a decision affects the trade organisation in its capacity as a negotiator of the policy.[352]

Thus, in the *CIRFS* case, the Court of Justice held that the *Comité
International de la Rayonne et des Fibres Synthétiques* (International Rayon
and Synthetic Fibres Committee) was individually concerned by a Commission decision which allegedly violated the Commission's "discipline" with
respect to aid to the synthetic fibre industry, after noting that the
association concerned had been the Commission's interlocutor with regard
to the adoption of this "discipline" and to its later extension and adaptation
and had actively pursued negotiations with the Commission during the pre-
litigation procedure, in particular by submitting written observations to it
and by keeping in close contact with the responsible departments.[353]

Similarly in the *Van der Kooy* case, the *Landbouwschap* (a body
established under public law of the Netherlands to protect the common
interests of agricultural undertakings) had negotiated with a public undertaking a preferential gas tariff which was considered by the Commission to
constitute State aid. It was also one of the signatories of the agreement
establishing that tariff. The Court of Justice held that the *Landbouwschap*
was individually concerned by the Commission decision declaring the
preferential gas tariff incompatible with the common market. The Court
stressed that the association's position as negotiator of gas tariffs in the
interests of the growers concerned was affected by the contested decision
and that in that capacity the association had taken an active part in the
procedure under Art.88 (2) of the EC Treaty by submitting written
comments to the Commission and by keeping in close contact with the
responsible officials throughout the procedure.[354] Accordingly, the *Van der
Kooy* and *CIRFS* cases concerned particular situations in which the
applicants occupied a clearly circumscribed position as negotiators which

---

[351] ECJ, Joined Cases 67/85, 68/85 and 70/85 *Van der Kooy and Others v Commission* [1988]
E.C.R. 219, paras 19–25; ECJ, Case C–313/90 *CIRFS and Others v Commission* [1993]
E.C.R. I–1125, paras 29 and 30; CFI, Case T–380/94 *AIUFFASS and AKT v Commission*
[1996] E.C.R. II–2169, para.50; CFI, Case T–55/99 *CETM v Commission* [2000] E.C.R. II–
3207, para.23.
[352] ECJ, Case C–313/90 *CIRFS and Others v Commission* [1993] E.C.R. I–1125, paras 28–31;
CFI, Case T–380/94 *AIUFASS and AKT v Commission* [1996] E.C.R. I–2169, para.51.
[353] ECJ, Case C–313/90 *CIRFS and Others v Commission* [1993] E.C.R. I–1125, paras 24–31.
[354] ECJ, Joined Cases 67–68 and 70/85 *Van der Kooy v Commisson* [1988] E.C.R. 219, paras
20–24. The position of the association as a negotiator at both national and Community
level is taken into account.

was closely linked to the actual subject-matter of the Commission decision, thus placing them in a factual situation which distinguished them from all other persons.[355]

7–105 Trade unions. A trade union will not normally be individually concerned by a decision of the Commission declaring an aid measure incompatible with the common market. The status of negotiator with regard to the social aspects constitutes only a tenuous link with the actual subject-matter of the decision. Whereas, when determining whether or not State aid is compatible with the common market, social aspects are liable to be taken into account by the Commission, but this will be done only as part of an overall assessment which includes a large number of considerations of various kinds, linked in particular to the protection of competition, regional development, the promotion of culture or again to the protection of the environment.[356]

(4) Anti-dumping cases

7–106 Measures of general application. Provisional and definitive anti-dumping duties are imposed by regulation pursuant to Art.14(1) of Regulation No 384/96.[357] What is involved is essentially a provision of general application, which applies to all economic entities concerned. Nevertheless, some parts of such a "regulation" or the extension of existing anti-dumping duties to like products or parts thereof are of individual concern to some persons[358] (see 7–069, *supra*).

7–107 Producers and exporters. Producers or exporters established outside the Community of products on which anti-dumping duties are imposed are individually concerned where information about their trading activities is used with a view to determining the duties. Generally speaking, this will be the case where manufacturing and exporting undertakings can establish that they were identified in measures adopted by the Commission or the

---

[355] ECJ, Case C–106/98 P *Comité d'entreprise de la Société française de production and Others v Commission* [2000] E.C.R. I–3659, para.45. See also CFI, Case T–69/96, *Hamburger Hafen-und Lagerhaus and Others v Commission* [2001] E.C.R. II–1037, para.50.

[356] ECJ, Case C–106/98 P *Comité d'entreprise de la Société française de production and Others v Commission* [2000] E.C.R. I–3659, paras 52–53. See also n.335, *supra*.

[357] Council Regulation (EC) No 384/96 of December 22, 1995 on protection against dumped imports from countries not members of the European Community ([1996] O.J. L56/1).

[358] For a survey, see Ress and Ukrow, "Direct Actions before the EC Court of Justice. The Case of EEC Anti-dumping Law", in Petersmann and Jaenicke (eds), *Adjudication of International Trade Disputes in International and National Economic Law* (University Press, Freiburg, 1992), at 159–260. See also, CFI, Joined Cases T–74/97 and T–75/97 *Büchel v Council and Commission* [2000] E.C.R. II–3067.

Council or concerned by the preliminary investigation.[359] Such a factor should have in some way prompted the intervention of the institutions or to have formed part of the *raison d'être* of the regulation itself.[360] An action for annulment is often the only legal remedy available to them against the imposition of such duties.[361] This argument provides support for the Community Court in finding that such an action is admissible.[362]

Manufacturing and exporting undertakings, however, are not individually concerned by an anti-dumping duty which is imposed on other undertakings by the same regulation. They are therefore not entitled to challenge such a duty.[363]

Complainants. Natural or legal persons or associations without legal **7–108** personality acting on behalf of the Community industry which lodge a complaint leading to a preliminary administrative procedure[364] are entitled to bring an action for annulment against a refusal by the Commission to initiate the actual anti-dumping procedure on the grounds that there is insufficient evidence.[365] Their particular legal position founded upon the procedural guarantees conferred by Regulation No 384/96[366] must be protected by the Community Court. A decision refusing to initiate a procedure may not undermine those procedural safeguards.

---

[359] ECJ, Joined Cases 239 and 275/82 *Allied Corporation v Commission* [1984] 1005, para.12. See, however, CFI, Case T–161/94 *Sinochem Heilongjiang v Council* [1996] E.C.R. II–695, paras 45–48, where the Court of First Instance held that the preliminary investigation had concerned the applicant undertaking, even though the Commission had decided not to make use of the information which it had provided: CFI, Case T–155/94 *Climax Paper v Council* [1996] E.C.R. II–873, paras 46–51; CFI, Case T–170/94 *Shanghai Bicycle v Council* [1997] F.C.R. II–1383, para.39; CFI, Case T–147/97 *Champion Stationery and Others v Council* [1998] E.C.R. II–4137, paras 30–38; CFI, Case T–597/97 *Euromin v Council* [2000] E.C.R. II–2419, para.45; CFI, Case T–598/97 *BSC Footwear Supplies and Others v Council* [2002] E.C.R. II–1155, para.45; ECJ, Case C–239/99 *Nachi Europe* [2001] E.C.R. I–1197, para.21. For an extensive discussion, see Coppieters, "Recente ontwikkelingen in de rechtspraak inzake het anti-dumpingbeleid van de EG ten aanzien van de Volksrepubliek China" (1997) S.E.W. 272–280.

[360] ECJ, Case C–75/92 *Gao Yao v Council* [1994] E.C.R. I–3141, paras 26–32; CFI, Case T–597/97 *Euromin v Council* [2000] E.C.R. II–2419, para.45.

[361] ECJ, Joined Cases 239 and 275/82 *Allied Corporation v Commission* [1984] 1005, para.13.

[362] But see 7–086, *supra*.

[363] ECJ, Case 240/84 *Toyo v Council* [1987] E.C.R. 1809, paras 4–7; ECJ, Case 258/84 *Nippon Seiko v Council* [1987] E.C.R. 1923, para.7; ECJ, Case C–156/87 *Gestetner Holdings v Council and Commission* [1990] E.C.R. I–781, para.12; ECJ, Case C–174/87 *Ricoh v Council* [1992] E.C.R. I–1335, paras 6–8.

[364] The "investigation" provided for by Art.6 of Regulation No 384/96.

[365] ECJ, Case 191/82 *Fediol v Commission* [1983] E.C.R. 2913, paras 15–33. See also Bellis, "Judicial Review of EEC Anti-dumping and Anti-subsidy Determinations after *Fediol*: The Emergence of a New Admissibility Test" (1984) C.M.L.Rev. 539, at 549, who argues that there should be generalised access to the Court of Justice (now the Court of First Instance) for any natural or legal person who participated in the administrative investigation into the dumping in question.

[366] The procedural guarantees conferred by the regulation are the right to lodge a complaint, the associated right that the complaint should be investigated with due care in accordance with the procedure laid down by the Commission and the right, upon written request, to inspect all information made available by any party to an investigation which is not confidential (Art.6(7)).

An action brought against the regulation imposing a definitive anti-dumping duty is available only to a complainant whose involvement in the adoption of the regulation extends further than simply lodging the complaint which initiated the anti-dumping procedure. Only where the complainant's observations were determinative of the course of the investigation or where its specific position on the market was taken into account, will the complainant be individually concerned by the regulation imposing a definitive anti-dumping duty.[367] The fact that the complaint was lodged by a trade association of which the applicant is a member does not detract from the undertaking's right to bring an action.[368] If the aforementioned conditions are fulfilled by both the trade association and the undertaking, both of them can bring an action for annulment.

7–109 **Importers.** *Importers associated with an exporter* are individually concerned by a regulation imposing an anti-dumping duty where their resale prices, and not the export prices, of the products in question are considered in order to determine whether dumping is taking place[369] or the level of the anti-dumping duty.[370] Where an importer brings an action for annulment against a regulation which, following circumvention, was extended to cover like products or parts thereof, an "importer" which is affected by the extension of the anti-dumping duty will be individually concerned only if the Commission took account of the undertaking's commercial activities in its investigation carried out following circumvention of the original anti-dumping duty or if the undertaking concerned participated in good time in the investigation.[371]

Generally speaking, *importers not associated with an exporter* are not individually concerned by a regulation imposing an anti-dumping duty.[372] The reason for this is that the imposition of the duty affects them in their

---

[367] ECJ, Case 264/82 *Timex v Council and Commission* [1985] E.C.R. 849, paras 8–17.
[368] *Ibid.*
[369] ECJ, Case 118/77 *ISO v Council* [1979] E.C.R. 1277; ECJ, Joined Cases 239 and 275/82 *Allied Corporation v Commission* [1984] E.C.R. 1005, para.15; ECJ, Case C–239/99 *Nachi Europe* [2001] E.C.R. I–1197, para.21.
[370] ECJ, Joined Cases C–305/86 and C–160/87 *Neotype Techmashexport v Commission and Council* [1990] E.C.R. I–2945, paras 20–21.
[371] CFI, Joined Cases T–74/97 and T–75/97 *Büchel v Council and Commission* [2000] E.C.R. II–3067, paras 50–68.
[372] ECJ, Case 307/81 *Alusuisse v Council and Commission* [1982] E.C.R. 3463; ECJ (order of July 8, 1987), Case 279/86 *Sermes v Commission* [1987] E.C.R. 3109; ECJ (order of July 8, 1987), Case 301/86 *Frimodt Pedersen v Commission* [1987] E.C.R. 3123. A regulation which is confined to accepting price undertakings offered by an exporter in an anti-dumping investigation in relation to products imported by the applicant is of individual concern only to the exporter in question. The importer—even if he is the sole importer—is necessarily not party to the undertakings given: ECJ (order of July 8, 1987), Case 295/86 *Garelly v Commission* [1987] E.C.R. 3117, para.14; CFI, Case T–598/97 *BSC Footwear Supplies and Others v Council* [2002] E.C.R. II–1155, paras 49–52. For a critical discussion, see Van Ginderachter, "Recevabilité des recours en matière de dumping" (1987) C.D.E. 635–666; see also ECJ (order of November 11, 1987), Case 205/87 *Nuova Ceam v Commission* [1987] E.C.R. 4427, para.14.

objective capacity as importers of the product subjected to an anti-dumping duty. Consequently, the regulation remains a regulation, even if independent importers were involved in the procedure which led to its adoption[373] or if their identity emerges from the regulation.[374] The existence of dumping is not normally determined by reference to importers' resale prices, but by reference to the actual prices paid or payable on export.[375]

The restrictive scope of the case-law relating to independent importers is mitigated by the fact that they can challenge the imposition of an anti-dumping duty in the national courts, which, in turn, may (or must) make a reference to the Court of Justice for a preliminary ruling on the validity of the regulation (see Ch.10, *infra*).

In exceptional circumstances, the Court of Justice has recognised the particular economic situation of an independent importer as a specific circumstance causing the importer to be individually concerned by a regulation imposing an anti-dumping duty.[376] The Court pointed out that the applicant was the largest importer of the product and that its business activities depended to a very large extent on imports, given that there was only one Community producer of the product, which, moreover, was its direct competitor and had strengthened its position considerably *vis-à-vis* the applicant as a result of the restriction of imports. It made no difference that its resale price was not taken into account in adopting the regulation.[377]

Original equipment manufacturers. An original equipment manufacturer (OEM)—an undertaking selling goods produced by other manufacturers under its own brand name[378]—will be individually concerned by a regulation imposing an anti-dumping duty where, in calculating the dumping margin, account was taken of the particular features of its business dealings with the manufacturers in respect of which anti-dumping duties are imposed by the regulation. An application by an OEM will be admissible only in so far as it seeks annulment of the specific anti-dumping duty imposed by the regu-   **7–110**

---

[373] *Alusuisse v Council and Commission*, cited in the preceding n., para.13.
[374] ECJ (order of July 8, 1987), Case 301/86 *Frimodt Pedersen v Commission* [1987] E.C.R. 3123, para.3.
[375] *Ibid.*, para.17.
[376] ECJ, Case C–358/89 *Extramet Industrie v Council* [1991] E.C.R. I–2501. See also CFI, Case T–597/97 *Euromin v Council* [2000] E.C.R. II–2419, paras 46 and 49–50. For an extensive commentary, see Brouwer and Carlin, "Qualité pour agir dans les procédures anti-dumping après *Extramet*" (1981) D.P.C.I. 243–267. For a critical note, see Arnull, "Challenging EC Anti-dumping Regulations: The Problem of Admissibility" (1992) E.Comp.L.Rev. 73, at 79.
[377] This case-law seems to be confined to anti-dumping. It appears from the *Buckl* case (ECJ, Joined Cases C–15 and 108/91 *Buckl and Others v Commission* [1992] E.C.R. I–6061) that the Court of Justice is limiting this "economic" approach to being individually concerned by a measure. See also CFI (order of September 6, 2004), Case T–213/02 *SNF v Commission*, not yet reported, paras 76–77.
[378] Consequently, an OEM falls somewhere between a producer/exporter, on the one hand, and an importer, on the other.

lation on the producer from which the OEM obtains the goods which it sells.[379]

(5) *Access to documents pursuant to Regulation No 1049/2001*

7-111 Decision addressed to another person. A legal person seeking the annulment of a decision addressed to another person refusing that person access to documents does not have standing before the Community Court. In such a case, the applicant cannot be considered to have an interest in seeking the annulment of such a decision, since it does not affect its own rights.[380]

(6) *Public contracts*

7-112 Competitors in a public tender procedure. Natural or legal persons who participate in a public tender procedure organised by the Community belong to a closed class. Each of them is individually concerned by a decision awarding the contract to one of their number.[381] The withdrawal or modification of a definitive decision awarding the contract is also of individual concern to the persons who participated in the public tender procedure.[382]

d. The requirement that there should be an interest in the annulment of the contested act

7-113 Concept. Natural or legal persons may bring an action for annulment only in so far as they can establish that they have an interest.[383] This means that

---

[379] ECJ, Joined Cases C–133 and C–150/87 *Nashua and Others v Commission and Council* [1990] E.C.R. I–719, paras 16–21; ECJ, Case C–156/87 *Gestetner Holdings v Council and Commission* [1990] E.C.R. I–781, paras 19–24.

[380] CFI, Case T–41/00 *British American Tobacco International v Commission* [2001] E.C.R. II–1301.

[381] ECJ, Case 135/81 *Groupement des Agences de Voyages v Commission* [1982] E.C.R. 3799; ECJ, Case C–496/99 P *Commission v CAS Succhi di Frutta* [2004] E.C.R. I–3801, paras 58–59.

[382] ECJ, Case 232/81 *Agricola Commerciale Olio and Others v Commission* [1984] E.C.R. 3881; ECJ, Case C–496/99 P *Commission v CAS Succhi di Frutta* [2004] E.C.R. I–3801, paras 58–61.

[383] CFI, Case T–183/97 *Micheli and Others v Commission* [2000] E.C.R. II–287, in which the lack of *locus standi* did not result in the application being declared inadmissible but in the finding that there was no need to adjudicate further on the case. *Cf.* CFI, Joined Cases T–204/97 and T–270/97 *EPAC v Commission* [2000] E.C.R. II–2267, paras 153–158, in which the Court of First Instance held that an action for annulment of a Commission decision in a State aid investigation calling on the Member State to suspend the aid pending the outcome of the investigation was to no purpose given that the Commission had reached a definitive decision in the course of the investigation, thereby depriving the provisional decision of any legal basis. As a result, the applicant had no interest in proceeding against the provisional decision. See also CFI, Case T–326/99 *Fern Olivieri v Commission* [2000] E.C.R. II–1985, paras 66–100, in which the Court of First Instance held that a specialist of

280

they must benefit from the annulment of the contested act.[384] That benefit consists in the elimination of the adverse repercussions on their legal position.[385]

As far as *State aid* is concerned, the conduct of the Member State to which the Commission decision is addressed does not have any bearing on the applicant's interest in the annulment of the Commission decision declaring the aid granted to the applicant unlawful and requiring the Member State to recover the aid, even though the Member State has fully complied with the contested decision and does not intend to reintroduce the aid scheme in question if the decision is annulled. The *rationale* is that the applicant may be able to put forward certain claims before the national authorities if the contested decision is found to be unlawful.[386]

As far as *merger control* is concerned, the fact that the addressees have complied with the Commission decision does not affect their interest in bringing proceedings. Where the Commission declares a concentration incompatible with the common market and orders it to be reversed, the undertakings involved in the concentration do not lose their interest in the annulment of the decision if they have complied with it and thereby brought the concentration irreversibly to an end.[387] Where a concentration has not been effectuated before the Commission takes its decision declaring it to be incompatible with the common market, an undertaking party to the intended concentration retains an interest in the annulment of the Commis-

---

worldwide repute in a particular illness had no *locus standi* to claim that a Commission decision granting a licence for the marketing of a medicinal product should be annulled on the ground that the product was ineffective for treating that illness. See, in general, Canedon, "L'intérêt à agir dans le recours en annulation du droit communautaire" [2000] R.T.D.E. 451–510.

[384] It suffices if the applicant has an interest in the annulment of the part of the act which is unfavourable to it (CFI, Case T–89/00 *Europe Chemi-Con v Council* [2002] E.C.R. II–3651, para.35). The legal sphere of an association of beneficiaries of a mutual provident association was held not to have been affected by a decision to close the file on its complaint. This was because it could derive no benefit from the annulment of the contested act (CFI, Case T–184/94 *ATM v Commission* [1997] E.C.R. II–2529, paras 62–63, upheld on appeal in ECJ (order of May 5, 1999), Case C–57/98 P *ATM v Commission*, not reported, para.41).

[385] Opinion of Advocate General G.F. Mancini in ECJ, Joined Cases 142 and 156/84 *British American Tobacco and R.J. Reynolds Industries v Commission* [1987] E.C.R. 4487. See also CFI, Case T–188/99 *Euroalliages v Commission* [2001] E.C.R. II–1757: an undertaking which had lodged a complaint against dumping prices of products imported into the Community was held to have an interest in the annulment of a decision by which the Commission terminated a review procedure carried out at the time when existing anti-dumping measures were to expire, without introducing new measures. This was because in the event of the annulment of that decision, the existing anti-dumping measures would have remained in force until such time as the Commission had taken a new decision completing the review procedure. Moreover, in the event of annulment, the Commission is obliged under Art.233 of the EC Treaty to take the necessary measures to comply with the judgment.

[386] CFI, Case T–9/98 *Mitteldeutsche Erdöl-Raffinerie v Commission* [2001] E.C.R. II–3367, paras 32–38.

[387] CFI, Case T–22/97 *Kesko v Commission* [1999] E.C.R. II–3775, paras 55–65.

sion decision also where the concentration can no longer take place, even in the event that the judgment of the Court of First Instance is in the applicant's favour, as a result of the disappearance of its contractual basis. The Court of First Instance takes account in particular of the existing and future legal consequences of annulment of such a decision by virtue of Art.233 of the EC Treaty and of the requirements of judicial review of the legality of Commission acts under the concentration regulation.[388]

On the same lines, in litigation concerning access to documents of Community institutions, the Court of First Instance has held that it was irrelevant that the documents to which access had been refused were already in the public domain. A person who is refused access to a document has a sufficient interest in the annulment of the decision refusing such access.[389]

Where necessary, the Court of Justice and the Court of First Instance will consider of their own motion whether the requirement to have an interest in bringing proceedings is satisfied.[390] They may have regard to the effect of the national law of a Member State when they consider the applicant's legal position in assessing its *locus standi*.[391]

7–114 **No interest in challenging act the adoption of which was sought by applicant.** Where a natural or legal person receives from the Commission an act which that person sought, the person in question has no interest in applying for the annulment of that act (or of certain grounds of that act) even if the grounds of the act contain a number of unfavourable passages. Accordingly, an undertaking which has notified a concentration has no interest in having the decision declaring it compatible with the common market annulled even if the decision finds that the undertaking concerned has a dominant position on a particular market.[392] Likewise, a Member

---

[388] CFI, Case T–102/96 *Gencor v Commission* [1999] E.C.R. II–753, paras 41–45. The same applies where the parties concerned withdraw from the merger before the Commission takes its decision, but the Commission nonetheless adopts a decision: CFI (judgment of September 28, 2004), Case T–310/00 *MCI v Commission*, not yet reported, paras 49–61.

[389] CFI, Case T–46/92 *Scottish Football Association v Commission* [1994] E.C.R. II–1039, paras 13–14; CFI, Case T–174/95 *Svenska Journalistenförbundet v Council* [1998] E.C.R. II–2289, paras 66–69.

[390] ECJ, Case 108/86 *D.M. v Council* [1987] E.C.R. 3933, para.10; CFI (order of March 10, 2005), Case T–273/00 *Unione degli industriali della provincia di Venezia v Commission*, not reported, para.15; CFI (order of March 10, 2005), Case T–269/00 *Baglioni Hotels and Sagar v Commission*, not reported, para.16.

[391] ECJ (order of May 5, 1999), Case C–57/98 P *ATM v Commission*, not reported, para.26.

[392] CFI, Joined Cases T–125/97 and T–127/97 *Coca-Cola v Commission* [2000] E.C.R. II–1733, paras 77–92. See also in this connection CFI, Case T–138/89 *NBV and NVB* [1992] E.C.R. II–2181, paras 32–34: undertakings which obtained at their request a declaration from the Commission pursuant to Art.2 of the former Regulation No 17 that their agreement was not in breach of Art.81(1) of the EC Treaty had no interest in having that declaration annulled, even though they considered that the decision contained considerations capable of damaging their interests. Since the undertakings had ended up in the legal position which they had requested of the Commission, they had no interest in having the decision annulled.

State or the recipient of aid have no interest in obtaining the annulment of a decision declaring aid notified by that State compatible with the common market.[393]

Personal interest. The interest must be personal to the applicant itself.[394] **7–115**
An applicant to which the contested act is not applicable cannot claim that it has a personal interest.[395]

Accordingly, an undertaking was held to have no legal interest in bringing proceedings for the annulment of a regulation which did not concern the product which it manufactured.[396]

As far as federated States are concerned, they will often have autonomous policy-making powers which are not subject to the control of the federal State. Consequently, such a federated State has an interest of its own, distinct from the interest of the federal or central authorities, in challenging a Community act which restricts its policy-making powers.[397]

Vested and present interest. The interest must be vested and present.[398] A **7–116**
hypothetical interest is therefore insufficient to ground an action for annulment.[399] However, an applicant may have an interest in the annulment of an act which is no longer in force.[400] The annulment of such a measure

---

[393] ECJ (order of January 24, 2004), Case C–164/02 *Netherlands v Commission* [2004] E.C.R. I–1177, paras 18–25; CFI (judgment of April 14, 2005), Case T–141/03 *Sniace v Commission*, not yet reported, paras 20–41.

[394] ECJ, Case 282/85 *DEFI v Commission* [1986] E.C.R. 2469, para.18; ECJ, Case 204/85 *Stroghili v Court of Auditors* [1987] E.C.R. 389, para.9; CFI, Case T–256/97 *BEUC v Commission* [2000] E.C.R. II–101, para.33.

[395] ECJ, Case 88/76 *Société pour l'Exportation des Sucres v Commission* [1977] E.C.R. 709, paras 18–19; CFI (order of April 30, 2001), Case T–41/00 *British American Tobacco International v Commission* [2001] E.C.R. II–1301, para.19.

[396] CFI, Case T–117/95 *Corman v Commission* [1997] E.C.R. II–95, paras 82–84. A Commission regulation protecting a geographical domination of origin which the applicant did not use was held not to affect its legal sphere with the result that it had no legal interest in obtaining its annulment (CFI (order of April 29, 1999), Case T–78/98 *Unione provinciale degli agricoltori di Firenze and Others v Commission* [1999] E.C.R. II–1377, paras 30–34).

[397] CFI, Case T–214/95 *Vlaams Gewest v Commission* [1998] E.C.R. II–717, para.30; CFI (order of April 29, 1999), Case T–78/98 *Unione provinciale degli agricoltori di Firenze and Others v Commission* [1999] E.C.R. II–1377, para.39; CFI, Case T–288/97 *Regione Autonoma Friuli Venezia Giulia v Commission* [1999] E.C.R. II–1871, para.34; CFI, Joined Cases T–132/96 and T–143/96 *Freistaat Sachsen and Others v Commission* [1999] E.C.R. II–3663, para.92.

[398] CFI (judgment of April 14, 2005), Case T–141/03 *Sniace v Commission*, not yet reported, para.25; CFI (order of February 10, 2000), Case T–5/99 *Andriotis v Commission and CEDEFOP* [2000] E.C.R. II–235, para.39: the Court of First Instance held that since the applicant had already achieved the result which he was pursuing, he had no legal interest in bringing proceedings.

[399] ECJ, Case 204/85 *Stroghili v Court of Auditors* [1987] E.C.R. 389, para.11; CFI (order of April 30, 2003), Case T–167/01 *Schmitz-Gotha Fahrzeugwerke v Commission* [2003] E.C.R. II–1873, para.58.

[400] ECJ, Case 53/85 *AKZO Chemie v Commission* [1986] E.C.R. 1965, para.21; ECJ, Case 207/86 *APESCO v Commission* [1988] E.C.R. 2151; CFI, Joined Cases T–191/96 and T–106/97 *CAS Succhi di Frutta v Commission* [1999] E.C.R. II–3181, paras 62–63 (7–004, *supra*).

has the effect of preventing its author from adopting a similar act in the future.[401] The applicant may also have an interest in bringing an action against a measure which has been implemented in full, the intention being for the defendant institution to do justice to the applicant, possibly by way of the payment of damages,[402] or for it to make the necessary amendments for the future to the legal system in the context of which the act was adopted.[403] Lastly, an applicant may have an interest in the annulment of a decision which has been repealed. The reason for this is that the repeal of a decision cannot invariably be equated with annulment by the Court since, by definition, it does not amount to recognition of the decision's illegality. Moreover, repeal generally takes effect *ex nunc*, whereas annulment within the meaning of Art.231 of the EC Treaty takes effect *ex tunc*. Accordingly, the judgment annulling a decision which has been withdrawn may put the originator of the act under an obligation to remove the effects of the illegal conduct found in the judgment by taking adequate steps to restore the applicant to its original position or to avoid the adoption of an identical measure.[404]

7–117 **Interest may disappear.** In order to obtain judgment on the substance, it is not enough that the applicant had an interest at the time when it brought its action.[405] The interest may disappear in the course of the

---

[401] If, however, the Court of First Instance finds that annulment of the act could not give rise to measures to comply with the judgment declaring the act void within the meaning of Art.233 of the EC Treaty, the applicant will have no interest in obtaining its annulment: see CFI (order of June 13, 1997), Case T–13/96 *TEAM and Kolprojekt v Commission* [1997] E.C.R. II–983, para.28.

[402] ECJ, Case C–496/99 P *Commission v CAS Succhi di Frutta* [2004] E.C.R. I–3801, para.83.

[403] ECJ, Case 92/78 *Simmenthal v Commission* [1979] E.C.R. 777, para.32; CFI, Joined Cases T–480 and T–483/93 *Antillean Rice Mills v Commission* [1995] E.C.R. II–2305, para.60; CFI (order of February 1, 1999), Case T–256/97 *BEUC v Commission* [1999] E.C.R. II–169, para.18.

[404] CFI, Joined Cases T–481 and T–484/93 *Exporteurs in Levende Varkens and Others v Commission* [1995] E.C.R. II–2941, paras 46–48; CFI, Case T–211/02 *Tideland Signal v Commission* [2002] E.C.R. II–3781, paras 48–49. However, the withdrawal of the contested decision may take effect *ex tunc* and also have the same consequences as a declaration of nullity. In such case, the Court of Justice or the Court of First Instance, as the case may be, may decide in an order that the action for annulment is devoid of purpose and that there is no need to proceed to judgment: ECJ (order of March 4, 1997), Case C–46/96 *Germany v Commission* [1997] E.C.R. I–1189; CFI (order of September 18, 1996), Case T–22/96 *Langdon v Commission* [1996] E.C.R. II–1009; CFI (order of March 14, 1997), Case T–25/96 *Arbeitsgemeinschaft Deutscher Luftfahrt-Unternehmen and Hapag Lloyd v Commission* [1997] E.C.R. II–363.

[405] Note, however, that the Court of First Instance has stressed that the applicant's interest in bringing proceedings must be determined "at the time when the application was lodged" and not assessed on the basis of a "future, hypothetical event" (CFI, Case T–16/96 *Cityflyer Express v Commission* [1998] E.C.R. II–757, para.30). In that State aid case, the Court of First Instance found that the matters on which the Commission had relied in order to argue that the competitor of the undertaking in receipt of the aid had no interest in bringing proceedings were purely speculative and hence could not affect the applicant's *locus standi*. See also CFI, Case T–509/93 *Glencore Grain v Commission* [2000] E.C.R. II–3697, para.39;

proceedings.[406] For instance, an undertaking which was declared bankrupt after bringing an application for annulment against a Commission decision authorising national aid to a competitor ceased to have any interest in bringing the proceedings since the competitive situation no longer existed as a result of the applicant's having been declared bankrupt and that situation could not have been affected by the aid since the applicant had been declared bankrupt before the aid was paid.[407] If the interest for bringing an action disappears in the course of the proceedings (for example, if the defendant institution revokes the contested act in all its aspects), it is for the applicant to discontinue the proceedings. If it fails to do so, it may be ordered to pay the costs.[408]

In a judgment given on appeal, the Court of Justice held that the Commission and a party which had intervened in the proceedings before the Court of First Instance still had an "interest" in bringing a cross-appeal against the judgment of the Court of First Instance declaring part of a Commission decision void even though that part of the decision would no longer have been applicable if the Court of First Instance had not annulled it. That court had annulled the provision of the Commission decision by which the addressee of the decision was prohibited from concluding

---

CFI (judgment of April 14, 2005), Case T–141/03 *Sniace v Commission*, not yet reported, para.25; CFI (order of September 20, 2005), Case T–258/99 *Makro Cash & Carry Nederland v Commission*, not reported, para.35. The Court of Justice has also held that the admissibility of an application must be assessed by reference to the situation prevailing at the time when it was lodged (ECJ, Joined Cases C–31/96, C–132/97, C–45/98, C–27/99, C–81/00 and C–22/01 *Spain v Council* [2002] E.C.R. I–3439, para.23). A party which brings an application for annulment against a Commission decision declaring a concentration incompatible with the common market and consequently prohibiting it pursuant to Art.8(3) of Regulation No 4064/89 maintains an interest in having that decision addressed to it annulled, even if the agreement concluded by the applicant as the basis for the proposed merger was rendered nugatory by the expiry of the contractual deadline by which the Commission had to approve the merger (CFI, Case T–102/96 *Gencor v Commission* [1999] E.C.R. II–753, paras 40–45). See also CFI, Case T–22/97 *Kesko v Commission* [1999] E.C.R. II–3775, paras 55–65, and CFI (judgment of September 28, 2004), Case T–310/00 *MCI v Commission*, not yet reported, paras 44–64, where it was held that an undertaking had an interest in challenging a Commission decision declaring a concentration incompatible with the common market even though it had withdrawn from the proposed merger. See also CFI, Case T–131/99 *Shaw and Falla v Commission* [2002] E.C.R. II–2023, paras 32–36, where the Court of First Instance held that an undertaking which had brought an action for annulment against a Commission decision declaring Art.81(1) of the EC Treaty inapplicable to a lease concluded by that undertaking had an interest in obtaining the annulment of the contested decision even after the lease had been terminated.

[406] CFI (order of October 17, 2005), Case T–28/02 *First Data and Others v Commission*, not yet reported, paras 34–53. It should be noted that it is only the action for annulment which becomes to no purpose if the applicant's interest disappears in the course of the proceedings. This does not mean, however, that an action for damages cannot subsequently be brought against the defendant institution which was late in giving satisfaction to the applicant: ECJ, Case 66/76 *CFDT v Council* [1977] E.C.R. 305, paras 9–10.

[407] CFI, Case T–443/93 *Casillo Grani v Commission* [1995] E.C.R. II–1375.

[408] ECJ, Case 243/78 *Simmenthal v Commission* [1980] E.C.R. 593, para.9 (where the Court of Justice dismissed the application); ECJ, Case 179/80 *Roquette Frères v Commission* [1982] E.C.R. 3623, paras 8–12 (where the Court of Justice declared that there was no need to proceed to judgment).

exclusive purchasing agreements up until December 31, 1997. Since the Court of Justice had not adjudicated on the cross-appeal by that date, the addressee of the decision, who had appealed, claimed that there was no need to adjudicate on the cross-appeal on the ground that it was to no purpose. The Court of Justice held, however, that the fact that the end-date for the prohibition had expired did "not make it any less desirable to settle definitively the dispute as to the legality and scope of [the relevant provision] of the contested decision with a view to determining its legal effects in the period up to the abovementioned date".[409] It would seem to us that the same reasoning would hold good in the case of an application for annulment of an act whose validity has expired. Thus, a Member State retains an interest in seeking the annulment of a decision to initiate the formal procedure under Art.88(2) of the EC Treaty at the time when the Commission has already adopted a final decision declaring the aid incompatible with the common market.[410]

7–118 **Flexible attitude taken by the Community Court.** Moreover, by and large the Court of Justice and the Court of First Instance are flexible about the requirement to establish an interest. Even if the contested decision finding an infringement of Art.81 and/or Art.82 of the EC Treaty does not impose a fine on the applicant, it nevertheless has an interest in having its legality reviewed.[411] In the event that, owing to the fact that bringing an action for annulment does not have suspensory effect, the applicant tailors its conduct to comply with the contested measure, that will not destroy its interest.[412] Neither does it have any effect on the applicant's interest that, in the event of annulment of the contested act, it will be impossible for the defendant institution to take all the measures necessary to comply with the judgment of the Court of Justice or the Court of First Instance.[413] The declaration of nullity can always constitute the basis for a damages claim.[414]

7–119 **Pleas solely in the interest of the law.** The applicant may adduce only pleas in law against the contested act which raise breaches of the law adversely affecting it—no matter how indirectly. Pleas *solely* raised in the interests of

---

[409] ECJ, Case C–279/95 P *Langnese-Iglo v Commission* [1998] E.C.R. I–5609, para.71.
[410] ECJ, Case C–400/99 *Italy v Commission* [2005] E.C.R. I–3657, paras 15–18. The Member State concerned had not attacked the final decision.
[411] ECJ, Case 77/77 *BP v Commission* [1978] E.C.R. 1513, para.13.
[412] ECJ, Joined Cases 172 and 226/83 *Hoogovens Groep v Commission* [1985] E.C.R. 2831, paras 18–19.
[413] ECJ, Case 76/79 *Könecke v Commission* [1980] E.C.R. 665, paras 8–9.
[414] ECJ, Joined Cases C–68/94 and C–30/95 *France and Others v Commission* [1998] E.C.R. I–1375, para.74; CFI, Case T–321/01 *Internationaler Hilfsfonds v Commission* [2003] E.C.R. II–3225, paras 36–37.

the law or of the institutions are inadmissible.[415] However, this does not prevent a party from raising a plea in an application for annulment which was not raised in any administrative proceedings prior to the adoption of the contested act.[416]

Different applicants. Where more than one applicants have brought one and the same action, a finding of admissibility in relation to one applicant means that there is no need to consider whether the other applicants are entitled to bring proceedings.[417]   **7–120**

III. SPECIAL CHARACTERISTICS

A. GROUNDS FOR ANNULMENT

Pleas which may be raised by the applicant. Under Art.230 of the EC Treaty or Art.146 of the EAEC Treaty, an act of a Community institution may be annulled on grounds of lack of competence, infringement of an essential procedural requirement, infringement of the Treaties or of any rule of law relating to their application, or misuse of powers. Consequently, the review exercised under those articles must be limited to the legality of the disputed measure and the Court of Justice and the Court of First Instance will not consider its expediency[418] or substitute their own reasoning for that of the author of the contested act.[419]   **7–121**

---

[415] ECJ, Case 85/82 *Schloh v Council* [1983] E.C.R. 2105, paras 13–14. This will arise only in extremely rare cases. Thus, even where an individual raises, as applicant, a breach of the division of powers as between the institutions or as between the Community and the Member States, or a breach of any procedural requirement in the course of the adoption of the contested act, he or she will never do so *exclusively* in the interests of the law or of the institutions, since all the superior rules of law in that connection are intended, *inter alia*, generally to protect individuals affected by acts of the institutions. See ECJ, Case 138/79 *Roquette Frères v Council* [1980] E.C.R. 3333, para.2; ECJ, Case 139/79 *Maizena v Council* [1980] E.C.R. 3393, para.2. A likely example of an inadmissible plea is where the applicant argues that the contested measure is discriminatory, while admitting that the discrimination operates only in his or her favour. Something somewhat similar arose moreover in *Schloh*: the applicant relied on the fact that the vacancy for the post for which his candidature had been rejected (which he was contesting) had not been brought to the notice of staff of Community institutions other than his own. Although that constituted a breach of the Staff Regulations, this had operated in the event only to the applicant's advantage, since there had been less competition for the post as a result.

[416] CFI, Case T–37/97 *Forges de Clabecq v Commission* [1999] E.C.R. II–859, para.94.

[417] ECJ, Case C–313/90 *CIRFS and Others v Commission* [1993] E.C.R. I–1125, para.31; CFI, Case T–266/94 *Skibsvaerftsforeningen and Others v Commission* [1996] E.C.R. II–1399, para.51; CFI (judgment of December 14, 2004), Case T–317/02 *FICF and Others v Commission*, not yet reported, para.40.

[418] ECJ, Case C–84/94 *United Kingdom v Council* [1996] E.C.R. I–5755, para.23.

[419] ECJ, Case C–164/98 P *DIR International Film and Others v Commission* [2000] E.C.R. I–447, para.38. Where the Community Court reviews the legality of a complicated economic assessment made by the Commission or another institution and the institution concerned

7–122   **Pleas which may be raised by the Court.** It appears from the case-law that the first three grounds for annulment may be subsumed under the heading of breach of superior law, since the rules on competence and essential procedural requirements form part of the Treaties or of general rules adopted pursuant thereto. This blurs the distinction between the different grounds for annulment. Yet the distinction is not without importance.[420] The Court of Justice and the Court of First Instance are bound to raise of their own motion[421] pleas alleging lack of competence[422] and infringement of an essential procedural requirement[423] in relation to the adoption of the

---

has a broad discretion, the review will be confined to whether the procedural requirements were complied with, whether the statement of reasons is sufficient, whether the facts are correctly reproduced and whether there was a manifestly wrong assessment or a misuse of power: ECJ, Joined Cases 142 and 156/84 *British American Tobacco and R.J. Reynolds Industries v Commission* [1987] E.C.R. 4487; ECJ, Joined Cases C–204/00 P, C–205/00 P, C–211/00 P, C–213/00 P, C–217/00 P and C–219/00 P *Aalborg Portland and Others v Commission* [2004] E.C.R. I–123, para.249; CFI, Case T–231/99 *Joynson v Commission* [2002] E.C.R. II–2085, para.36. An analysis of the review of the legality of discretionary acts of the institutions may be found in Ritleng, "Le juge communautaire de la légalité et le pouvoir discrétionnaire des institutions communautaires" (1999) A.J.D.A. 645–567.

[420] Opinion of Advocate General M. Lagrange in ECJ, Case 66/63 *Netherlands v High Authority* [1964] E.C.R. 533, at 553–554.

[421] ECJ, Case C–166/95 P *Commission v Daffix* [1997] E.C.R. I–983, para.24; ECJ, Case C–367/95 P *Commission v Sytraval and Brink's France* [1998] E.C.R. I–1719, para.67; ECJ, Case C–286/95 P *Commission v ICI* [2000] ECJ I–2341, para.55; ECJ, Case C–210/98 P *Salzgitter v Commission* [2000] E.C.R. I–5843, para.56. For further details, see Lenaerts, "Rechter en partijen in de rechtspleging voor Hof en Gerecht" (2002) S.E.W. 231–237.

[422] ECJ, Case 14/59 *Société des Fonderies de Pont-à-Mousson v High Authority* [1959] E.C.R. 215, at 229; CFI, Case T–182/94 *Marx Esser and Del Amo Martinez v European Parliament* [1996] E.C.R.-SC II–1197, para.44 (English abstract at I–A–411); CFI, Joined Cases T–12/99 and T–63/99 *UK Coal v Commission* [2001] E.C.R. II–2153, para.199; CFI, Case T–147/00 *Laboratoires Servier v Commission* [2003] E.C.R. II–85, paras 45–46; CFI (judgment of September 27, 2005), Joined Cases T–134/03 and T–135/03 *Common Market Fertilizers v Commission*, not yet reported, para.52.

[423] ECJ, Case 1/54 *France v High Authority* [1954 to 1956] E.C.R. 1, at 15; ECJ, Case 6/54 *Netherlands v High Authority* [1954 to 1956] E.C.R. 103, at 112; ECJ, Case 18/57 *Nold v High Authority* [1959] E.C.R. 41, at 51–52; ECJ, Case C–291/89 *Interhotel v Commission* [1991] E.C.R. I–2257, para.14; ECJ, Case 304/89 *Oliveira v Commission* [1991] E.C.R. I–2283, para.18; ECJ, Case C–265/97 P *VBA v Florimex and Others* [2000] E.C.R. I–2061, para.114; CFI, Case T–32/91 *Solvay v Commission* [1995] E.C.R. II–1825, para.43; CFI, Case T–106/95 *FFSA and Others v Commission* [1997] E.C.R. II–229, para.62; CFI, Case T–206/99 *Métropole Télévision v Commission* [2001] E.C.R. II–1057, para.43; CFI, Case T–231/99 *Joynson v Commission* [2002] E.C.R. II–2085, para.163; CFI (judgment of July 8, 2004), Case T–44/00 *Mannesmannröhren-Werke v Commission*, not yet reported, paras 126 and 210 (under appeal: Case C–411/04 P) (defective statement of reasons). The Court of First Instance may inquire of its own motion into whether essential procedural requirements, especially procedural safeguards conferred by Community law, have been infringed (CFI, Case T–154/98 *Asia Motor France and Others v Commission* [2000] E.C.R. II–3453, para.46). The Court of First instance may also consider of its own motion whether rights of the defence have been infringed during the administrative procedure (CFI, Joined Cases T–186/97, T–187/97, T–190/97 to T–192/97, T–210/97, T–211/97, T–216/97 to T–218/97, T–279/97, T–280/97, T–293/97 and T–147/99 *Kaufring and Others v Commission* [2001] E.C.R. II–1337, para.134. But see CFI (judgment of July 8, 2004), Joined Cases T–67/00, T–68/00, T–71/00 and T–78/00 *JFE Engineering and Others v Commission*, not yet reported, para.425, in which the Court of First Instance held that a breach of the rights of the defence, which

act (*la légalité externe*) in the light of the facts adduced.[424] Pleas alleging infringement of the Treaties or of any rules of law relating to their application, or misuse of powers, which relate to the content of the contested act (*la légalité interne*),[425] may only be considered by the Court of Justice or the Court of First Instance if they are raised by the applicant.[426] It is not necessary to that end for the grounds to be specified, it being "sufficient for the grounds for instituting the proceedings to be expressed in terms of their substance rather than the legal classification provided, however, that it is sufficiently clear from the application which of the grounds referred to in the Treaty is being invoked".[427]

Timeframe. The legality of an act is reviewed in the light of the facts and the state of the law at the time when it was adopted.[428] The content of the act being reviewed is determined as at that time also. Addenda and improvements effected by the institution subsequently are not capable of regularising the act and will not be taken into account.[429] Acts adopted after the adoption of the contested decision cannot affect the validity of that decision.[430]   **7–123**

---

by its nature is subjective, does not fall within the scope of an infringement of essential procedural requirements and therefore does not have to be raised by the Court of its own motion (under appeal: Joined Cases C–403/04 P and C–405/04 P).

[424] ECJ, Case C–235/92 P *Montecatini v Commission* [1999] E.C.R. I–4539, para.107. It should, however, be stressed that the Court cannot raise a plea of its own motion if the application, in the absence of such plea, is inadmissible (ECJ (judgment of December 13, 2005), Case C–78/03 P *Commission v Aktionsgemeinschaft Recht und Eigentum*, not yet reported).

[425] Vandersanden and Barav, *Contentieux communautaire*, at 187.

[426] ECJ, Case C–367/95 P *Commission v Sytraval and Brink's France* [1998] E.C.R. I–1719, para.67; ECJ, Case C–265/97 P *VBA v Florimex and Others* [2000] E.C.R. I–2061, para.114; ECJ (judgment of June 15, 2005), Case T–349/03 *Corsica Ferries France v Commission*, not yet reported, para.52.

[427] ECJ, Joined Cases 19 and 21/60, 2 and 3/61 *Société Fives Lille Cail and Others v High Authority* [1961] E.C.R. 281, at 295.

[428] ECJ, Joined Cases 9 and 11/71 *Compagnie d'Approvisionnement, de Transport et de Crédit and Others v Commission* [1972] E.C.R. 391, para.39; ECJ, Case 40/72 *Schroeder* [1973] E.C.R. 125, para.14; ECJ, Joined Cases 15 and 16/76 *France v Commission* [1979] E.C.R. 321, para.7; ECJ, Case C–449/98 P *IECC v Commission* [2001] E.C.R. I–3875, para.87; ECJ, Case C–277/00 *Germany v Commission* [2004] E.C.R. I–3925, para.39; CFI, Joined Cases T–79 and T–80/95 *SNCF and British Railways v Commission* [1996] E.C.R. II–1491, para.48; CFI, Case T–77/95 *SFEI and Others v Commission* [1997] E.C.R. II–1, para.74; CFI, Case T–115/94 *Opel Austria v Council* [1997] E.C.R. II–39, para.87; CFI, Joined Cases T–371/94 and T–394/94 *British Airways and Others v Commission* [1998] E.C.R. II–2405, para.81; CFI, Case T–63/98 *Transpo Maastricht and Ooms v Commission* [2000] E.C.R. II–135, para.55; CFI, Case T–395/94 *Atlantic Container Line and Others v Commission* [2002] E.C.R. II–875, para.252; CFI, Joined Cases T–127/99, T–129/99 and T–148/99, *Diputación Foral de Guipúzcoa and Others v Commission* [2002] E.C.R. II–1275, para.212.

[429] ECJ, Case 195/80 *Michel v European Parliament* [1981] E.C.R. 2861, para.22 (it seems from para.27 that addenda or improvements effected by the defendant institution before the period prescribed for bringing proceedings has expired may indeed regularise the act); ECJ, Case C–343/87 *Culin v Commission* [1990] E.C.R. I–225, para.15; CFI, Case T–331/94 *IPK-München v Commission* [2001] E.C.R. II–779, para.91.

[430] CFI, Case T–31/99 *ABB Asea Brown Boveri v Commission* [2002] E.C.R. II–1881, para.103.

7–124   **Competition cases.** In competition cases, too, the Court only inquires into the legality of the contested act.[431] The Court of First Instance will therefore consider whether the evidence adduced by the Commission in its decision, together with other factors, is sufficient to prove the existence of the alleged infringement.[432] The evidence must be convincing.[433] In the proceedings before the Court of First Instance, the Commission may not adduce new inculpatory evidence in support of the contested decision which is not contained in that decision.[434] Where there is doubt, the Court of First Instance must give the benefit of that doubt to the applicants. As a result, the Court of First Instance may not conclude that the Commission has established the existence of the infringement at issue to the requisite legal standard if it still entertains doubts on that point. This is because given the nature of the infringements in question and the nature and degree of severity of the ensuing penalties, the principle of the presumption of innocence (resulting in particular from Art.6(2) of the ECHR and Art.48 of the Charter of Fundamental Rights of the European Union) applies to competition procedures.[435]

1. Lack of competence

7–125   **Different aspects.** As a ground for annulment, lack of competence on the part of the defendant institution has several aspects, namely substantive, territorial and personal aspects.

---

[431] As far as State aid is concerned, see CFI, Case T–296/97 *Alitalia v Commission* [2000] E.C.R. II–3871, para.95. See also CFI (judgment of October 21, 2004), Case T–36/99 *Lenzing v Commission*, not yet reported, paras 127–162 (the Commission's assessment was wrong in that it held that the measure could not be regarded as being aid because it satisfied the private investor test). The legality of a decision concerning State aid is to be assessed in the light of the information available to the Commission when the decision was adopted (ECJ, Case 234/84 *Belgium v Commission* [1986] E.C.R. 2263, para.16; ECJ, Case C–241/94 *France v Commission* [1996] E.C.R. I–4551, para.33; ECJ, Case C–276/02 *Spain v Commission* [2004] E.C.R. I–8091, para.31).

[432] CFI, Joined Cases T–305/94, T–306/94, T–307/94, T–313/94 to T–316/94, T–318/94, T–325/94, T–328/94, T–329/94 and T–335/94 *Limburgse Vinyl Maatschappij and Others v Commission* [1999] E.C.R. II–931, para.891; CFI (judgment of July 8, 2004), Joined Cases T–67/00, T–68/00, T–71/00 and T–78/00 *JFE Engineering and Others v Commission*, not yet reported, paras 174–175.

[433] ECJ (judgment of February 15, 2005), Case C–12/03 P *Commission v Tetra Laval*, not yet reported, paras 37–51.

[434] In so far as the applicants seek to establish, on the basis of "new documents" produced to the Court of First Instance, that the Commission's position is based on inaccurate facts, the Commission is entitled to respond to their arguments by referring to the documents in question (CFI (judgment of July 8, 2004), Joined Cases T–67/00, T–68/00, T–71/00 and T–78/00 *JFE Engineering and Others v Commission*, not yet reported, paras 177–178).

[435] CFI (judgment of July 8, 2004), Joined Cases T–67/00, T–68/00, T–71/00 and T–78/00 *JFE Engineering and Others v Commission*, not yet reported, paras 177–178.

a. Substantive competence

Concept. The Community is empowered only to act in policy areas   **7–126**
assigned to it by the Treaties. A Community act which falls outside those
areas may be annulled.[436] That "external" lack of competence results, in
some commentators' view, in the act's being non-existent, and consequently
not within the compass of the grounds for annulment under discussion in
this section.[437]

Division of powers. The next question to be considered is the division of   **7–127**
powers in the context of Community decision-making. An example may be
found in the case-law on the seat of the European Parliament: the scope of
the Parliament's powers of internal organisation had to be delimited as
against the powers of the national governments under Art.77 of the ECSC
Treaty, Art.289 of the EC Treaty and Art.189 of the EAEC Treaty to
determine the seats of the institutions.[438]

Where an application for annulment is based on an alleged "lack of
competence" of a Community institution which has acted, the case will
generally consist of a dispute about the legal basis of the contested act.[439] If
the provision of superior law which is stated as being the legal basis for the
act is substantively insufficient to support its content, at the same time the
mode of decision-making laid down in that provision (including the powers
provided for therein for the various Community institutions), together with
the permitted legislative instruments (regulations, directives, decisions or
still other—albeit unspecified—instruments), will clearly have been used
unlawfully. In that sense, the institution which adopted the contested
measure will have exceeded its powers (even if it could have adopted the

---

[436] *Cf.* ECJ, Case 294/83 *Les Verts v European Parliament* [1986] E.C.R. 1339, paras 51–55.
[437] Joliet, *Le contentieux*, at 96; Vandersanden and Barav, *Contentieux communautaire*, at 213.
See also Bergerès, *Contentieux communautaire* (3rd ed., Presses Universitaires de France,
Paris, 1998), §204, at 226.
[438] ECJ, Case 230/81 *Luxembourg v European Parliament* [1983] E.C.R. 255, at 285–292; ECJ,
Case 108/83 *Luxembourg v European Parliament* [1984] E.C.R. 1945, at 1959–1960; ECJ,
Joined Cases 358/85 and 51/86 *France v European Parliament* [1988] E.C.R. 4821, at 4852–
4857. For a different example, see ECJ, Joined Cases 281, 283–285 and 287/85 *Germany,
and Others v Commission* [1987] E.C.R. 3203, paras 28–32; ECJ, Case C–57/95 *France v
Commission* [1997] E.C.R. I–1627, para.24.
[439] ECJ, Case C–376/98 *Germany v European Parliament and Council* [2000] E.C.R. I–8419,
paras 76–116; ECJ, Case C–211/01 *Commission v Council* [2003] E.C.R. I–8913, paras 38–
53; CFI (judgment of September 28, 2004), Case T–310/00 *MCI v Commission*, not yet
reported, para.107 (lack of power of the Commission to declare a merger incompatible with
the common market when the notifying parties had formally withdrawn their notification
and informed the Commission of the abandonment of the merger in the form envisaged in
the notification); CFI (judgment of September 21, 2005), Case T–306/01 *Yusuf and Al
Barakaat International Foundation v Council and Commission* not yet reported, paras 107–
171 (alleged lack of power of the Council to adopt resolutions imposing certain specific
restrictive measures directed against certain persons and entities associated with Osama bin
Laden, the Al-Qaida network and the Taliban).

same measure on the basis of some other provision of superior law).[440] So it would seem that in such cases the ground for nullity of lack of competence fuses almost entirely with the ground of infringement of the Treaties or of any rules of law relating to their application. From the procedural viewpoint, however, it is more a question of the correct application of the rules invoked as the legal basis for adopting a given act than a question purely of competence (or lack of it).[441]

b. Territorial competence

7–128 **Scope.** A Community act may apply to natural or legal persons established in areas outside the territorial scope of the Treaty.[442] It must, however, be applied in conformity with international law.[443] As far as competition law is concerned, it is enough that agreements concluded outside the Community are implemented in the territory of the Community.[444]

c. Delegation of powers

7–129 **Delegation of implementing powers.** In the Community legal order, an institution may, subject to certain conditions, delegate implementing powers[445] to itself or to other institutions,[446] to Member States,[447] to international organisations[448] or to agencies governed by public or private law not mentioned in the Treaty.[449]

---

[440] In this way, the Court of Justice held in ECJ, Case C–110/02 *Commission v Council* [2004] E.C.R. I–6333, paras 28–51, that where the Commission has declared in a decision that State aid is incompatible with the common market, the Council may no longer decide that that aid must be regarded as being compatible with the common market under the third para. of Art.88(2) of the EC Treaty. By adopting a decision to that effect the Council exceeded its powers.

[441] For an analysis of the concept of legal basis and its function in Community constitutional law, see Lenaerts and Van Nuffel, *Constitutional Law of the European Union*, § 5–009–§ 5–027, at 86–100.

[442] See EC Treaty, Art.299.

[443] ECJ, Case C–286/90 *Poulsen and Diva Navigation and Others* [1992] E.C.R. I–6019, paras 21–29.

[444] ECJ, Joined Cases 89, 104, 114, 116–117 and 125–129/85 *Ahlström and Others v Commission* [1988] E.C.R. 5193, paras 11–18. As far as merger control is concerned, see CFI, Case T–102/96 *Gencor v Commission* [1999] E.C.R. II–753.

[445] For a definition of "delegation" in the Community legal order and an extended discussion of this phenomenon, see Lenaerts (n.193, *supra*), at 23–49.

[446] ECJ, Case 25/70 *Köster* [1970] E.C.R. 1161, para.9.

[447] As a result of the first para.of Art.10 of the EC Treaty, it is implicit in every Community act that the Member States are under a duty to implement it, although the extent of the obligation and the detailed rules relating to it may also be expressly defined in the act itself (see ECJ, Case 5/77 *Tedeschi* [1977] E.C.R. 1555; ECJ, Joined Cases 213–215/81 *Norddeutsches Vieh- und Fleischkontor and Others* [1982] E.C.R. 3583).

[448] ECJ, Opinion 1/76 *Draft Agreement establishing a European laying-up fund for inland waterway vessels* [1977] E.C.R. 741, para.5.

[449] ECJ, Case 9/56 *Meroni v High Authority* [1957 and 1958] E.C.R. 133, at 151.

Implementation. The term "implementation" has to be given a broad   **7–130**
interpretation.[450] It is sufficient for the institution charged with a legislative
task to determine the "general objectives" of the policy in compliance with
the applicable mode of decision-making.[451] The execution of those general
objectives may be delegated to the institution itself (using a simplified
manner of decision-making), to another institution or to the Member
States, even if a measure of discretion is involved. The delegating institution, however, must always be able to supervise and, if necessary, correct
the exercise of the discretion.

On those terms, the Council has the right to delegate (important)
implementing powers to the Commission under the third indent of Art.202
and the last indent of Art.211 of the EC Treaty.[452] The delegation is often
subject to the requirement that specific committees must be involved.[453] In
implementing acts of the Council, the Commission must remain within the
limits of the implementing powers conferred upon it. If it does not respect
those limits, its decisions may be annulled for want of competence.[454]

In specific cases, the Council may exercise certain implementing powers
itself (delegation to itself pursuant to the third indent of Art.202 of the EC
Treaty). When it decides to do so, it must state in detail the grounds for its
decision.[455]

Delegation to international bodies. The Community is also empowered to   **7–131**
assign "powers of decision" to an international body.[456] Such a delegation
of powers, however, may not detract from the requirement for the
objectives of the Community to be attained by common action on the part
of the institutions, each one acting within the limits of the powers conferred
on it. If they did otherwise, it would constitute a surrender of the
independence of Community action in its external relations and a change in
the internal constitution of the Community as regards both the prerogatives
of the institutions and the position of the Member States *vis-à-vis* one
another.[457] Consequently, the possibility of delegating "powers of decision"
is confined to implementing powers.

---

[450] ECJ, Case 23/75 *Rey Soda* [1975] E.C.R. 1279, para.10.
[451] *Ibid.*, para.14.
[452] ECJ, Case C–240/90 *Germany v Commission* [1992] E.C.R. I–5383, paras 30–43.
[453] Council Decision 1999/468/EC of June 28, 1999 laying down the procedures for the exercise
of implementing powers conferred on the Commission ([1999] O.J. L184/23).
[454] *Cf.* ECJ, Case 22/88 *Vreugdenhil and Others* [1989] E.C.R. 2049; CFI (judgment of
September 21, 2005), Case T–306/01 *Yusuf and Al Barakaat International Foundation v
Council and Commission*, not yet reported, paras 172–176.
[455] ECJ, Case 16/88 *Commission v Council* [1989] E.C.R. 3457, para.10; ECJ, Case C–257/01
Commission v Council [2005] E.C.R. I–345, paras 49–61.
[456] ECJ, Opinion 1/76 *Draft Agreement establishing a European laying-up fund for inland
waterway vessels* [1977] E.C.R. 741, para.5.
[457] *Ibid.*, para.12.

7–132 **Delegation to agencies.** Lastly, agencies governed by public or private law may exceptionally be set up to carry out support tasks.[458] Such agencies must help to attain the objectives underlying the substantive Community competence pursuant to which they are set up.[459] In addition, the delegation of powers to such agencies may not detract from the balance of powers as between the institutions, which constitutes a safeguard against institutions' exceeding their powers.[460] Consequently, no discretionary power may be delegated. Moreover, an institution may not delegate powers broader than those which it itself derives from the Treaties.[461]

In exercising their powers, such agencies are subject to the same conditions as the delegating institution (in particular, as regards the duty to state reasons and judicial supervision of their acts). They carry out mainly preparatory or strictly executive work.[462]

7–133 **Delegation to a Member of the Commission.** The Commission may— provided that it does not detract from the principle of collective responsibility[463]—empower one or more of its Members to take, on its behalf and under its responsibility, clearly defined management or administrative measures.[464] Measures adopted pursuant to such a delegation of authority are still ascribed to the Commission, which, as a collegiate body, has the last word.[465] Members of the Commission who voluntarily resign retain their full powers until they are replaced.[466]

7–134 **Delegation to members of staff.** In so far as it is compatible with the intention behind the provision conferring a power on the Commission,[467] that institution may also delegate powers to its officials. In exceptional

---

[458] ECJ, Case 9/56 *Meroni v High Authority* [1957 and 1958] E.C.R. 133.

[459] *Ibid.*, at 151.

[460] *Ibid.*, at 152.

[461] *Ibid.*, at 150.

[462] For a survey of these agencies, see Lenaerts and Van Nuffel, *Constitutional Law of the European Union*, § 10–109–§10–110, at 472–476 and §14–062–§14–066, at 619–624.

[463] EC Treaty, Art.219: "The Commission shall act by a majority of the number of Members provided for in Art.213. A meeting of the Commission shall be valid only if the number of Members laid down in its Rules of Procedure is present."

[464] Art.11 of the Rules of Procedure of the Commission of November 29, 2000 ([2000] O.J. L308/26).

[465] ECJ, Case 5/85 *AKZO Chemie v Commission* [1986] E.C.R. 2585, paras 28–40; ECJ, Joined Cases 97–99/87 *Dow Chemical Ibérica and Others v Commission* [1989] E.C.R. 3165, paras 58–59.

[466] This is also the case when all the Members of the Commission voluntarily resign. The Commission retains its full powers until the new Members take office (CFI, Case T–219/99 *British Airways v Commission* [2003] E.C.R. II–5917, paras 46–58).

[467] ECJ, Case 35/67 *Van Eick v Commission* [1968] E.C.R. 329, at 344–345. In that case, the point at issue was whether the appointing authority was entitled to delegate to an official its duty under the third para.of Art.7 of Annex IX to the Staff Regulations to hear an official concerned by disciplinary proceedings before taking its decision in those proceedings. The Court of Justice held that the article in question constituted a peremptory legal requirement which did not authorise any delegation of powers. See also ECJ, Case C–249/02 *Portugal v Commission* [2004] E.C.R. I–10717, paras 44–47.

cases, a delegation of powers properly so called is involved where officials take decisions in the name of the Commission[468]; usually, however, what is involved is a delegation of signature, which, as a matter of the internal organisation of the institution, authorises an official to notify a decision taken by the Commission[469]; sometimes both aspects arise in the same case.[470] Where a delegation of powers properly so called is involved, the limits imposed on the Commission's ability to delegate powers to its Members apply *a fortiori* (see 7–133, *supra*).

2. Infringement of essential procedural requirements

Concept. An essential procedural requirement is a procedural rule intended to ensure that measures are formulated with due care, compliance with which may influence the content of the measure[471]; essential procedural requirements enable the legality of an act to be reviewed or may express a fundamental institutional rule. The fact that such a rule has been breached in the preparation or adoption of a measure will constitute a ground for its annulment only if the Court of Justice or the Court of First Instance finds that in the absence of the irregularity in question the contested measure might have been substantively different,[472] that the irregularity makes judicial review impossible,[473] or that, on account of the irregularity which it contains, the act in question breaches a fundamental institutional rule.[474] If a procedural provision is infringed but this does not prevent the aims of the provision from being achieved, no "substantial procedural defect" will be involved.[475] An express obligation to comply with

7–135

---

[468] ECJ, Case 48/70 *Bernardi v European Parliament* [1971] E.C.R. 175, paras 30–36. This arises in all institutions as far as decisions in staff matters are concerned.

[469] ECJ, Case 48/69 *ICI v Commission* [1972] E.C.R. 619, paras 11–15; ECJ, Case 8/72 *Vereeniging van Cementhandeleren v Commission* [1972] E.C.R. 977, paras 10–14; ECJ, Joined Cases 43 and 63/82 *VBVB and VBBB v Commission* [1984] E.C.R. 19, para.14; ECJ, Case C–220/89 *FUNOC v Commission* [1990] E.C.R. I–3669, para.14; CFI, Case T–450/93 *Lisrestal v Commission* [1994] E.C.R. II–1177, para.34.

[470] ECJ, Case C–200/89 *FUNOC v Commission* [1990] E.C.R. I–3669, paras 13–14.

[471] ECJ, Case 6/54 *Netherlands v High Authority* [1954 to 1956] E.C.R. 103, at 111–112.

[472] ECJ, Joined Cases 209–215 and 218/78 *Van Landewyck v Commission* [1980] E.C.R. 3125, para.47; ECJ, Case 150/84 *Bernardi v European Parliament* [1986] E.C.R. 1375, para.28. See also the Opinion of Advocate General G. Reischl in Joined Cases 275/80 and 24/81 *Krupp v Commission* [1981] E.C.R. 2489, at 2524.

[473] This is why the duty to give a statement of reasons is strictly enforced (7–145 to 7–148, *infra*). See also ECJ, Case C–137/92 P *Commission v BASF and Others* [1994] E.C.R. I–2555, paras 75–76, in which the Court of Justice held that authentication of a Commission decision is intended to guarantee legal certainty by ensuring that the text adopted by the college of Commissioners becomes fixed in the languages in which it is binding. Thus, in the event of a dispute, it can be verified that the texts notified or published correspond precisely to the text adopted by the college and so with the intention of the author. On those grounds, the Court held that authentication was an essential procedural requirement because failure to comply therewith makes judicial review impossible.

[474] ECJ, Case 138/79 *Roquette Frères v Council* [1980] E.C.R. 3333, para.33; ECJ, Case 139/79 *Maizena v Council* [1980] E.C.R. 3393, para.34.

[475] ECJ, Case 282/81 *Ragusa v Commission* [1983] E.C.R. 1245, para.22; ECJ, Case 207/81 *Ditterich v Commission* [1983] E.C.R. 1359, para.19.

certain procedural requirements when carrying out a particular act may not be extended to other acts by way of interpretation.[476] As has already been mentioned, the Court of Justice or the Court of First Instance will raise the issue of an infringement of an essential procedural requirement of its own motion (see 7–122, *supra*).[477]

a. Requirement to consult

7–136 **Duty to seek an opinion.** In the Community decision-making process, the body or institution adopting or implementing an act is sometimes under a duty (imposed by superior Community law) to seek the opinion of a body or institution before acting.[478] The requirement to consult constitutes an essential procedural requirement.[479] This is because consultation may affect the substance of the measure adopted.[480]

Furthermore, the Court of Justice has held that the consultation of the European Parliament required by the Treaty in certain cases constitutes a fundamental rule designed to guarantee the institutional balance intended by the Treaty, which reflects the fundamental democratic principle that the peoples should take part in the exercise of power through a representative assembly.[481]

7–137 **Timeframe and scope.** It is not sufficient merely to ask the body having to be consulted for its opinion; that body must have made its views known

---

[476] ECJ, Case 21/64 *Macchiorlati Dalmas & Figli v High Authority* [1965] E.C.R. 175, at 190–191; ECJ, Case 22/70 *Commission v Council* (the *AETR* case) [1971] E.C.R. 263, para.98.

[477] ECJ, Case 1/54 *France v High Authority* [1954 to 1956] E.C.R. 1, at 15; ECJ, Case 2/54 *Italy v High Authority* [1954 to 1956] E.C.R. 37, at 52; ECJ, Case 18/57 *Nold v High Authority* [1959] E.C.R. 41, at 51–52; ECJ, Joined Cases 73 and 74/63 *Internationale Crediet- en Handelsvereniging Rotterdam and Others* [1964] E.C.R. 1, at 13–14; ECJ, Case 185/85 *Usinor v Commission* [1986] E.C.R. 2079, para.19; ECJ, Case C–166/95 P *Commission v Daffix* [1997] E.C.R. I–983, para.24.

[478] In the case, for instance, of legislative action, the bodies or institutions concerned are the European Parliament, the European Economic and Social Committee and the Committee of the Regions under the EC Treaty; in the case of implementing action, they are the Advisory Committee on Restrictive Practices and Monopolies (Regulation No 1/2003, Art.14(1)) and the committees involved in the various procedures prescribed by Council Decision 1999/468/EC of June 28, 1999 laying down the procedures for the exercise of implementing powers conferred on the Commission ([1999] O.J. L184/23).

[479] ECJ, Case 1/54 *France v High Authority* [1954 to 1956] E.C.R. 1, at 15; ECJ, Case 2/54 *Italy v High Authority* [1954 to 1956] E.C.R. 37, at 52.

[480] ECJ, Case 165/87 *Commission v Council* [1988] E.C.R. 5545, para.20; see also Bradley, "Maintaining the Balance: the Role of the Court of Justice in Defining the Institutional Position of the European Parliament" (1987) C.M.L.Rev. 41, at 57.

[481] ECJ, Case 138/79 *Roquette Frères v Council* [1980] E.C.R. 3333, para.33; ECJ, Case 139/79 *Maizena v Council* [1980] E.C.R. 3393, para.34; ECJ, Case 1253/79 *Battaglia v Commission* [1982] E.C.R. 297, para.17; ECJ, Case C–417/93 *European Parliament v Council* [1995] E.C.R. I–1185, para.9; ECJ, Case C–21/94 *European Parliament v Council* [1995] E.C.R. I–1827, para.17.

before the act was adopted,[482] unless a derogating provision provides otherwise[483] or the body requesting the advice exhausted all possibilities of obtaining a preliminary opinion.[484] In addition, the draft instrument submitted to the consultative body must basically correspond to the instrument ultimately adopted, unless the amendments made to the draft are specifically intended to comply with the wishes expressed by the consultative body in its opinion.[485]

It is sufficient, however, that the opinion be delivered before the act is adopted. The institution seeking the opinion is not obliged to allow a certain period of time to elapse between receipt of the opinion and adoption of the act in order to be able better to consider the opinion. Consequently, a regulation which is adopted only a matter of days after the European Parliament delivered its opinion will be validly adopted.[486]

b. Requirement to hear the addressee

The right to be heard. Before an act adversely affecting a person is adopted, the addressee of the act or interested third parties must be heard by the institution concerned.[487] That obligation is prescribed either by the Treaty[488] or by secondary Community law[489] or arises out of the general legal principle that "a person whose interests are perceptibly affected by a decision taken by a public authority must be given the opportunity to make

7–138

---

[482] *Roquette Frères v Council*, para.34; *Maizena v Council*, para.35, both cases cited in the preceding n.

[483] ECJ, Case 128/86 *Spain v Commission* [1987] E.C.R. 4171, paras 22–26.

[484] ECJ, Case 138/79 *Roquette Frères v Council* [1980] E.C.R. 3333, para.36; ECJ, Case 139/79 *Maizena v Council* [1980] E.C.R. 3393, para.37.

[485] ECJ, Case 41/69 *ACF Chemiefarma v Commission* [1970] E.C.R. 661, paras 68–69; ECJ, Case 817/79 *Buyl v Commission* [1982] E.C.R. 245, paras 14–24; ECJ, Case 828/79 *Adam v Commission* [1982] E.C.R. 269, paras 18–25; ECJ, Case C–65/90 *European Parliament v Council* [1992] E.C.R. I–4593, whereby the Court of Justice annulled a Council regulation on the ground that the Council had not reconsulted the European Parliament whereas the regulation ultimately adopted by the Council departed substantially from the text on which the Parliament had originally been consulted; ECJ, Joined Cases C–13–16/92 *Driessen and Others* [1993] E.C.R. I–4751, para.23; ECJ, Case C–388/92 *European Parliament v Council* [1994] E.C.R. I–2067, para.10; ECJ, Case C–280/93 *Germany v Council* [1994] E.C.R. I–4973, para.38.

[486] ECJ, Case 114/81 *Tunnel Refineries v Council* [1982] E.C.R. 3189, para.18.

[487] ECJ, Case 17/74 *Transocean Marine Paint Association v Commission* [1974] E.C.R. 1063, para.15; ECJ, Joined Cases 209–215 and 218/78 *Van Landewyck v Commission* [1980] E.C.R. 3125, para.17. But see ECJ, Case C–111/92 P *European Parliament v Reynolds* [2004] E.C.R. I–5475, paras 57–60. For a discussion of the duty to hear parties in competition cases, see Kerse, "Procedures in EC Competition Cases: The Oral Hearing" (1994) E.Comp.L.Rev. 40–43; Joliet, *Le contentieux*, at 98–99.

[488] See, for example, EC Treaty, Art.88(2).

[489] See, for example, Art.27 of Regulation No 1/2003, Art.6(7) of Regulation No 384/96 (antidumping) and Art.18 of Regulation No 139/2004 (control of concentrations).

his point of view known".[490] This obligation is an essential procedural requirement.[491]

The person concerned must be informed in time,[492] effectively[493] and personally[494] of all the information in the file which might be useful for his or her defence[495] and of the grounds of the proposed act so that he or she is in a position to challenge it with full knowledge of the facts.[496]

7–139 **Infringement of the rights of the defence.** The rights of the defence are infringed where it is possible that the outcome of the administrative procedure conducted by the Commission may have been different as a result of an error committed by it.[497] An applicant undertaking establishes that there has been such an infringement where it adequately demonstrates, not that the Commission's decision would have been different in content, but rather that it would have been better able to ensure its defence had there been no error.[498]

7–140 **Application of Arts 81 and 82 of the EC Treaty.** The question whether the Commission has infringed the rights of the defence in competition proceedings through the non-disclosure of certain items in the file compiled during

---

[490] ECJ, Case 17/74 *Transocean Marine Paint Association v Commission* [1974] E.C.R. 1063, para.15. See to the same effect ECJ, Case 85/76 *Hoffmann-La Roche v Commission* [1979] E.C.R. 461, para.9; ECJ, Case C–462/98 P *Mediocurso v Commission* [2000] E.C.R. I–7183, para.36; CFI, Case T–50/96 *Primex Produkte Import-Export and Others v Commission* [1998] E.C.R. II–3773, para.59. However, the right of the person concerned to make his point of view known, is correlated to the exercise of discretion by the authority which is the author of the act at issue. Where the institutions have no discretion as to whether it is appropriate to adopt a certain act (*e.g.* where they are obliged to put into effect sanctions adopted by the UN Security Council), the institutions are not under an obligation to hear the person(s) concerned (see CFI (judgment of September 21, 2005), Case T–306/01 *Yusuf and Al Barakaat International Foundation v Council and Commission*, not yet reported, paras 327–331).

[491] ECJ, Case 31/69 *Commission v Italy* [1970] E.C.R. 25, para.13 (proceedings brought pursuant to Art.226 of the EC Treaty); CFI, Joined Cases T–186/97, T–187/97, T–190/97 to T–192/97, T–210/97, T–211/97, T–216/97 to T–218/97, T–279/97, T–280/97, T–293/97 and T–147/99 *Kaufring and Others v Commission* [2001] E.C.R. II–1337, para.134.

[492] ECJ, Case 55/69 *Cassella v Commission* [1972] E.C.R. 887, paras 13–15 (12 days' notice of the hearing did not jeopardise the defence).

[493] ECJ, Joined Cases 56 and 58/64 *Consten and Grundig v Commission* [1964] E.C.R. 299, at 338; CFI, Case T–7/89 *Hercules Chemicals v Commission* [1991] E.C.R. II–1711, paras 51–54; CFI, Joined Cases T–10–12 and T–15/92 *Cimenteries CBR and Others v Commission* [1992] E.C.R. II–2667, para.38; CFI, Case T–65/89 *BPB Industries and British Gypsum v Commission* [1993] E.C.R. II–389, paras 29–30.

[494] ECJ, Case C–176/99 P *ARBED v Commission* [2003] E.C.R. I–10687, paras 19–25 (a decision addressed to the parent company finding that it had committed an infringement of the competition rules of the ECSC Treaty was annulled on the ground that the statement of objections was addressed only to a subsidiary).

[495] CFI, Case T–36/91 *ICI v Commission* [1995] E.C.R. II–1847, paras 69–70; CFI, Case T–37/91 *ICI v Commission* [1995] E.C.R. II–1901, paras 49–50.

[496] ECJ, Case 121/76 *Moli v Commission* [1977] E.C.R. 1971, paras 19–20; ECJ, Case 75/77 *Mollet v Commission* [1978] E.C.R. 897, paras 18–21.

[497] ECJ, Case 30/78 *Distillers v Commission* [1980] E.C.R. 2229, para.26; ECJ, Case C–194/99 P *Thyssen Stahl v Commission* [2003] E.C.R. I–10821, para.31.

[498] ECJ, Case C–51/92 P *Hercules Chemicals v Commission* [1999] E.C.R. I–4235, para.81; ECJ, Case C–194/99 P *Thyssen Stahl v Commission* [2003] E.C.R. I–10821, para.31.

the administrative investigation has to be considered in the light of the specific circumstance of each particular case, since such an infringement depends chiefly on the objections raised by the Commission in order to determine the breach of competition law alleged against the undertaking concerned. The Commission infringes the rights of the defence if it appears that certain documents to which the undertaking concerned had no access could have been used in its defence having regard to the alleged breach of competition law.[499]

State aid cases. As far as State aid is concerned, the formal investigation **7–141** procedure is initiated in respect of the Member State responsible for granting the aid in the light of its Community obligations,.[500] Although all interested parties are invited to submit observations in the course of the formal investigation procedure, this procedure does not lead to an *inter partes* debate with the complainant or even with the recipient of the aid. Indeed, the comments received in the course of the formal investigation will be submitted only to the Member State concerned.[501] Only the Member State concerned can successfully raise a plea relating to a violation of its rights of defence in an annulment procedure before the Community courts.[502]

c. Duty of confidentiality

Concept and scope. Art.287 of the EC Treaty imposes an obligation not to **7–142** disclose information of the kind covered by the obligation of professional secrecy, in particular information about undertakings, their business rela-

---

[499] CFI, Joined Cases T–25/95, T–26/95, T–30/95, T–31/95, T–32/95, T–34/95, T–35/95, T–36/95, T–37/95, T–38/95, T–39/95, T–42/95, T–43/95, T–44/95, T–45/95, T–46/95, T–48/95, T–50/95, T–51/95, T–52/95, T–53/95, T–54/95, T–55/95, T–56/95, T–57/95, T–58/95, T–59/95, T–60/95, T–61/95, T–62/95, T–63/95, T–64/95, T–65/95, T–68/95, T–69/95, T–70/95, T–71/95, T–87/95, T–88/95, T–103/95 and T–104/95 *Cimenteries CBR and Others v Commission* [2000] E.C.R. II–491, paras 142–148, 156, 240, 241, 248, 284, 318, 323 and 364; for customs cases, see CFI, Case T–42/96 *Eyckeler & Malt v Commission* [1998] E.C.R. II–401, para.80; CFI, Joined Cases T–186/97, T–187/97, T–190/97 to T–192/97, T–210/97, T–211/97, T–216/97 to T–218/97, T–279/97, T–280/97, T–293/97 and T–147/99 *Kaufring and Others v Commission* [2001] E.C.R. II–1337, paras 151 and 179; for anti-dumping cases, see CFI (judgment of October 28, 2004), Case T–35/01 *Shanghai Teraoka Electronic v Council*, not yet reported, paras 287–290. See Lenaerts and Vanhamme, "Procedural Rights of Private Parties in the Community Administrative Process" (1997) C.M.L.Rev. 531–569. See also 7–028, *supra*.
[500] ECJ, Case 234/84 *Belgium v Commission (Meura)* [1986] E.C.R. 2263, para.29, and CFI, Case T–158/96 *Acciaierie di Bolzano v Commission* [1999] E.C.R. II–3927, para.81.
[501] ECJ, Case C–367/95 P *Commission v Sytraval and Brink's France* [1998] E.C.R. I–1719, para.59; CFI, Case T–613/97 *Ufex and Others v Commission* [2000] E.C.R. II–4055, paras 85–90; CFI (judgment of July 8, 2004), Case T–198/01 *Technische Glaswerke Ilmenau v Commission*, not yet reported, paras 193–198.
[502] ECJ, Case 234/84 *Belgium v Commission* [1986] E.C.R. 2263, para.30. Similarly, in the initial stage of the examination of a State aid measure under Art.88(3) of the EC Treaty, the Commission is never under an obligation to exchange views and arguments with interested parties other than the Member State concerned (see ECJ, Case C–367/95 P *Commission v Sytraval and Brink's France* [1998] E.C.R. I–1719, para.58). Even as regards the Member State concerned, the Court of Justice is reluctant to refer to a right to be heard during the initial stage of the investigation (see ECJ, Case C–400/99 *Italy v Commission* [2005] E.C.R. I–3657, paras 29–35).

tions or their cost components.[503] The question often arises in the Commission's administrative procedure for investigating infringements of competition law[504] or for determining dumping practices.[505] It is the institution to which the purportedly confidential information is made available itself which has to judge whether or not the duty of confidentiality is applicable after giving the party concerned the opportunity to state its views. In addition, before implementing its decision, the institution must give that party the opportunity of bringing an action before the Community Court with a view to having its assessments reviewed and to preventing disclosure.[506] Unlawful disclosure of confidential information in the course of the administrative procedure which led to the adoption of a decision finding an infringement of Art.81 and/or Art.82 of the EC Treaty will be regarded as an infringement of an essential procedural requirement only if it is shown that in the absence of such irregularity the contested decision might have been different. Consequently, it does not inevitably result in the act's being declared void.[507]

d. Internal procedural rules

7–143 **Concept and scope.** The institutions adopt internal procedural rules in their rules of procedure[508] and thereafter are obliged to comply with them.[509] Such rules may be categorised as essential procedural requirements. For instance, in one case the Court of Justice annulled a Council directive which was adopted in breach of Art.6 of the Council's Rules of Procedure.[510] The directive was adopted by the so-called written procedure,

---

[503] There are specific applications of this duty of confidentiality in regulations and directives: see, for example, Art.8(2) of Council Regulation No 288/82 on common rules for imports ([1982] O.J. L35/1).

[504] See Art.20(2) of Regulation No 17 in connection with the specific duty of confidentiality in competition cases, replaced by Arts. 27 and 28 of Council Regulation (EC) No 1/2003 of December 16, 2002 on the implementation of the rules on competition laid down in Arts 81 and 82 of the Treaty ([2003] O.J. L1/1). For an extensive discussion of the difficulty of reconciling the duty of confidentiality with the right to a fair hearing, see Joshua, "Balancing the Public Interests: Confidentiality, Trade Secret and Disclosure of Evidence in EC Competition Procedures" (1994) E.Comp.L.Rev. 68–80.

[505] See Art.19(5) of Regulation No 384/96 in relation to the duty of confidentiality in the investigation procedure for determining dumping practices ([1996] O.J. L56/1); ECJ, Case C–36/92 P *SEP v Commission* [1994] E.C.R. I–1911, paras 36–38.

[506] ECJ, Case 53/85 *AKZO Chemie v Commission* [1986] E.C.R. 1965, para.29. See also 1–029, *supra*.

[507] *Cf.* ECJ, Joined Cases 209–215 and 218/78 *Van Landewyck v Commission* [1980] E.C.R. 3125, para.47. Naturally, this does not preclude the person who has been disadvantaged by disclosure from bringing an action for damages against the institution responsible: ECJ, Case 145/83 *Adams v Commission* [1985] E.C.R. 3539, paras 34–44.

[508] See EC Treaty, Art.199 (European Parliament), Art.207(3) (Council) and Art.218(2) (Commission).

[509] Sometimes internal procedural rules are adopted in a different connection, *e.g.* in regard to staff matters, see ECJ, Case 282/81 *Ragusa v Commission* [1983] E.C.R. 1245, para.18.

[510] [1979] O.J. L268/1, now replaced by Council Decision 2002/682/EC, Euratom of July 22, 2002 adopting the Council's Rules of Procedure ([2002] O.J. L230/7).

even though two Member States had expressed objections to its use. Art.6 provides that recourse to a written vote on an urgent matter may be had only if all members of the Council agree.[511]

Protection for individuals. Natural or legal persons may plead infringe- **7–144** ment of internal procedural rules which confer rights on them and guarantee legal certainty.[512] This qualifies the view that internal procedural rules are intended to guarantee the sound functioning of internal decision-making while respecting the prerogatives of each of the Members of the institution, and that they are therefore not intended to ensure protection for individuals.[513]

e. Requirement to provide a statement of reasons

Concept and scope. The statement of reasons required by Art.253 of the **7–145** EC Treaty must disclose in a clear and unequivocal fashion the reasoning followed by the Community authority which adopted the measure in question in such a way as to make the persons concerned aware of the reasons for the measure and thus enable them to defend their rights and the Court to exercise its supervisory jurisdiction.[514] The reasoning must be logically compatible with the content of the measure.[515] A minimal, merely

---

[511] ECJ, Case 68/86 *United Kingdom v Council* [1988] E.C.R. 855, paras 40–49. For a case in which the Rules of Procedure of the Economic and Social Committee were invoked, yet no infringement was found, see ECJ, Case 307/85 *Gavanas v ESC and Council* [1987] E.C.R. 2435. For a case in which a Commission decision was annulled because a prior opinion was adopted in breach of the Rules of Procedure of the Standing Committee on Construction which assists the Commission in implementing a regulation in that a draft document was not sent to two addressees within the time-limit laid down and the vote was not postponed despite the request made to that effect by a Member State, see ECJ, Case C–263/95 *Germany v Commission* [1998] E.C.R. I–441, para.32. The Court of Justice declared void a Commission decision which was adopted without being authenticated as provided for in its Rules of Procedure (instruments adopted by the Commission in the course of a meeting have to be attached, in the authentic language or languages, in such a way that they cannot be separated, to the minutes of the meeting at which they were adopted and are to be authenticated by the signatures of the President and the Secretary-General on the first page of the minutes): ECJ, Case C–107/99 *Italy v Commission* [2002] E.C.R. I–1091, paras 47–48.

[512] ECJ, Case C–137/92 P *BASF and Others v Commission* [1994] E.C.R. I–2555, paras 72–78, in which the Court of Justice annulled a Commission decision on the ground that it infringed Art.12 of the Commission's Rules of Procedure; cf. CFI, Case T–32/91 *Solvay v Commission* [1995] E.C.R. II–1825, paras 46–54; see also ECJ, Case C–280/93 *Germany v Council* [1994] E.C.R. I–4973, para.36, from which it appears that in adopting acts which directly affect individuals, the procedural requirements applicable to such acts must be strictly complied with.

[513] ECJ, Case C–69/89 *Nakajima v Council* [1991] E.C.R. I–2069, paras 48–51.

[514] ECJ, Case C–350/88 *Delacre and Others v Commission* [1990] E.C.R. I–395, para.15; CFI (judgment of January 18, 2005), Case T–93/02 *Confédération Nationale du Crédit Mutuel v Commission*, not yet reported, para.68 (see also the case-law cited in those judgments); Cf. ECJ, Case 18/57 *Nold v High Authority* [1959] E.C.R. 41, at 51–52; ECJ, Case 24/62 *Germany v Commission* [1963] E.C.R. 63, at 68–69; ECJ, Case 294/81 *Control Data v Commission* [1983] E.C.R. 911, para.14.

[515] ECJ, Case 2/56 *Geitling v High Authority* [1957] E.C.R. 3, at 16.

formal statement of reasons is not enough, because it does not effectively enable interested parties[516] and the Court to verify the legality of the act.[517] However, the Community authority is not under a duty to go into all the arguments raised by interested parties during the administrative procedure which led to the adoption of the act.[518] It is sufficient if it sets out the facts and legal considerations having decisive importance in the context of the decision so as to enable its reasoning to be clearly understood.[519] It is therefore unnecessary to have a specific statement of reasons for each technical choice made.[520]

In any case, it is essential for the legal basis of the contested measure to be clearly indicated[521] or to be capable of being determined with certainty from other parts of the measure.[522]

In principle, the various relevant factual and legal aspects should be set out in the statement of reasons. There is a consistent line of cases, however, to the effect that this is not always necessary on the ground that, in considering whether the statement of reasons of an act satisfies the requirements of Art.253 of the EC Treaty, regard must be had not only to

---

[516] Interested parties comprise not only the addressee of an act, but also persons to whom the act is of direct and individual concern. The latters' interest in obtaining an explanation of the act should therefore be taken into account in determining the extent of the obligation to provide a statement of reasons: ECJ, Case 41/83 *Italy v Commission* [1985] E.C.R. 873, para.46; ECJ, Case C–367/95 P *Commission v Sytraval and Brink's France* [1998] E.C.R. I–1719, para.63; CFI, Case T–16/91 RV *Rendo and Others v Commission* [1996] E.C.R. II–1827, para.43; CFI (judgment of January 18, 2005), Case T–93/02 *Confédération Nationale du Crédit Mutuel v Commission*, not yet reported, para.68.

[517] ECJ, Case C–269/90 *Technische Universität München* [1991] E.C.R. I–5469, paras 26–27; *cf.*, however, the case of a decision ordering the repayment of unlawfully paid State aid: ECJ, Case C–75/97 *Belgium v Commission* [1999] E.C.R. I–3671, para.83.

[518] ECJ, Case 55/69 *Cassella v Commission* [1972] E.C.R. 887, para.22; ECJ, Case 56/69 *Hoechst v Commission* [1972] E.C.R. 927; ECJ, Joined Cases 209–215 and 218/78 *Van Landewyck v Commission* [1980] E.C.R. 3125, para.66; ECJ, Joined Cases 43 and 63/82 *VBVB and VBBB v Commission* [1984] E.C.R. 19, para.19; ECJ, Case 42/84 *Remia v Commission* [1985] E.C.R. 2545, para.26; ECJ, Joined Cases 240–242, 261, 262, 268 and 269/82 *Stichting Sigarettenindustrie v Commission* [1985] E.C.R. 3831, para.88; ECJ, Case C–41/93 *France v Commission* [1994] E.C.R. I–1829, para.36; CFI, Case T–8/89 *DSM v Commission* [1991] E.C.R. II–1833, para.257; CFI, Case T–9/89 *Hüls v Commission* [1992] E.C.R. II–499, para.332.

[519] CFI, Case T–44/90 *La Cinq v Commission* [1992] E.C.R. II–1, paras 40–44; CFI, Case T–7/92 *Asia Motor France and Others v Commission* [1993] E.C.R. II–669, para.31; *cf.* ECJ, Case 24/62 *Germany v Commission* [1963] E.C.R. 63, at 69.

[520] ECJ, Case C–168/98 *Luxembourg v European Parliament and Council* [2000] E.C.R. I–9131, para.62; ECJ, Case C–100/99 *Italy v Council and Commission* [2001] E.C.R. I–5217, paras 63–64; ECJ, Joined Cases C–27/00 and C–122/00 *Omega Air and Others* [2002] E.C.R. I–2569, para.47; ECJ, Case C–340/98 *Italy v Council* [2002] E.C.R. I–2663, para.59.

[521] ECJ, Case 203/86 *Spain v Council* [1988] E.C.R. 4563, para.37. Failure to indicate the legal basis also infringes the principle of legal certainty (ECJ, Case C–325/91 *France v Commission* [1993] E.C.R. I–3283, para.30).

[522] ECJ, Case 45/86 *Commission v Council* [1987] E.C.R. 1493, para.9.

its wording but also to its context and to all the legal rules governing the matter in question.[523]

The nature of the contested measure is one aspect of its context which goes to determine the extent of the obligation to provide a statement of reasons.[524] In the case of an act of general application, such as a regulation, it is enough for the circumstances which led to its adoption, together with its general objectives, to be mentioned.[525] If the need for the act is obvious from its content, additional reasoning is unnecessary.[526]

The degree of precision of the statement of reasons of an individual measure depends on the practical realities and the time and technical facilities available for drawing it up.[527] Furthermore, an individual measure which fits into a well-established line of decisions may be reasoned in a summary manner, for instance, by reference to the practice in question. If, in contrast, the measure deviates from previous practice, for example, by going appreciably further than previous decisions, the Community authority which adopted the measure must expressly explain why this is so.[528]

Lastly, the degree to which the addressee was involved in the process by which an act was drawn up has a bearing on the extent of the duty to provide a statement of reasons.[529] In addition, persons concerned by a

---

[523] ECJ, Case C–350/88 *Delacre and Others v Commission* [1990] E.C.R. I–395, para.16, and the case-law cited in that judgment; see also ECJ, Case 25/68 *Schertzer v European Parliament* [1977] E.C.R. 1729, para.39; ECJ, Case 35/80 *Denkavit Nederland* [1981] E.C.R. 45, para.33; ECJ, Case C–120/99 *Italy v Council* [2001] E.C.R. I–7997, paras 28–29; ECJ, Case C–310/99 *Italy v Commission* [2002] E.C.R. I–2289, para.48.

[524] CFI, Case T–26/90 *Finsider v Commission* [1992] E.C.R. II–1789, para.70. In the case of a decision reducing a Community financial aid for a project not carried out as specified, the statement of the reasons for such a measure must include an indication of the reasons for which the alterations taken into account have been judged to be unacceptable (CFI; Case T–241/00 *Le Canne v Commission* [2002] E.C.R. II–1251, para.55; CFI, Case T–180/00 *Astipesca v Commission* [2002] E.C.R. I–3985, para.126).

[525] ECJ, Case 5/67 *Beus* [1968] E.C.R. 83, at 95; ECJ, Case 244/81 *Klöckner-Werke v Commission* [1983] E.C.R. 1451, para.33.

[526] ECJ, Case 57/72 *Westzucker* [1973] E.C.R. 321, para.19.

[527] Settled case-law ever since ECJ, Case 16/65 *Schwarze* [1965] E.C.R. 877, at 888. For examples of the influence of "practical realities" on the obligation to provide a statement of reasons, see ECJ, Case 89/79 *Bonu v Council* [1980] E.C.R. 553, para.6; ECJ, Case 64/82 *Tradax v Commission* [1984] E.C.R. 1359, para.21.

[528] ECJ, Case 73/74 *Groupement des Fabricants de Papier Peints de Belgique and Others v Commission* [1975] E.C.R. 1491, para.31. A substantial change as compared with a previously adopted position of the institution concerned must be justified in the statement of reasons of the new decision containing the change (CFI, Case T–206/99 *Métropole Télévision v Commission* [2001] E.C.R. II–1057, para.53). The same stricter requirement to state reasons applies where an act derogates from a more general rule (ECJ, Case C–120/99 *Italy v Council* [2001] E.C.R. I–7997, para.53).

[529] ECJ, Case 13/72 *Netherlands v Commission* [1973] E.C.R. 27, paras 11–13; ECJ, Case 819/79 *Germany v Commission* [1981] E.C.R. 21, paras 15–21; ECJ, Case 1251/79 *Italy v Commission* [1981] E.C.R. 205, paras 20–21; ECJ, Case 347/85 *United Kingdom v Commission* [1988] E.C.R. 1749, para.60; ECJ, Case 14/88 *Italy v Commission* [1989] E.C.R. 3677, para.11. For decisions clearing EAGGF accounts, see ECJ, Case C–278/99 *Netherlands v Commission* [2001] E.C.R. I–1501, para.19. In staff cases, previous memoranda and

decision may be expected to make a certain effort to interpret the reasons if the meaning of the text is not immediately clear. The duty to give a statement of reasons is not infringed if it is possible to resolve ambiguities in the statement of reasons by means of such interpretation.[530]

7–146 **Material inaccuracy.** A shortcoming in the material accuracy of the statement of reasons, such as a factual inaccuracy or a wrong legal categorisation, is considered an infringement of the Treaty or of a rule relating to its application.[531]

7–147 **Timeframe.** A sufficient statement of reasons should be notified at the same time as the person concerned has notice of the act.[532] The absence of such a statement of reasons cannot be regularised after proceedings have been brought.[533]

---

staff notices influence the duty to provide a statement of reasons in the same way: ECJ, Case 61/76 *Geist v Commission* [1977] E.C.R. 1419, paras 21–26; ECJ, Case 86/77 *Ditterich v Commission* [1978] E.C.R. 1855, paras 34–42; ECJ, Joined Cases 36, 37 and 218/81 *Seton v Commission* [1983] E.C.R. 1789, paras 47–49; CFI, Case T–80/92 *Turner v Commission* [1993] E.C.R. II–1465, paras 62–63. The fact that an official was involved in the reorganisation of his department may justify a decision adversely affecting him or her having a summary statement of reasons: ECJ, Case 125/80 *Arning v Commission* [1981] E.C.R. 2539, para.14.

[530] CFI, Case T–16/91 RV *Rendo and Others v Commission* [1996] E.C.R. II–1827, para.46. *Cf.* CFI, Case T–331/94 *IPK-München v Commission* [2001] E.C.R. II–779, para.90.

[531] ECJ, Case 8/65 *Acciaierie e Ferriere Pugliesi v High Authority* [1966] E.C.R. 1, at 7–8; CFI, Case T–17/93 *Matra Hachette v Commission* [1994] E.C.R. II–595, para.57; *cf.* ECJ, Case 119/86 *Spain v Council and Commission* [1987] E.C.R. 4121, para.51. It is not always easy to draw a clear distinction in this connection, as can be seen from ECJ, Case C–360/92 *Publishers Association v Commission* [1995] E.C.R. I–23, paras 39–48; ECJ, Joined Cases C–329/93, C–62/95 and C–63/95 *Germany and Others v Commission* [1996] E.C.R. I–5151, paras 23–58; ECJ, Case C–367/95 P, *Commission v Sytraval and Brink's France* [1998] E.C.R. I–1719, paras 65–78; ECJ, Case C–172/01 P *International Power and Others v Commission* [2003] E.C.R. I–11421, paras 134–139.

[532] ECJ, Case 195/80 *Michel v European Parliament* [1981] E.C.R. 2861, para.22; ECJ, Case C–353/01 P *Mattila v Council and Commission* [2004] E.C.R. I–1073, para.32.

[533] ECJ, Case C–343/87 *Culin v Commission* [1990] E.C.R. I–225, para.15 (staff case); ECJ, Case C–353/01 P *Mattila v Council and Commission* [2004] E.C.R. I–1073, para.32 (access to documents); CFI, Case T–52/90 *Volger v European Parliament* [1992] E.C.R. II–121, paras 40–42, upheld by ECJ, Case C–115/92 P *European Parliament v Volger* [1993] E.C.R. I–6549, para.23; CFI (judgment of January 18, 2005), Case T–93/02 *Confédération Nationale du Crédit Mutuel v Commission*, not yet reported, paras 123–126 (State aid). At most, in staff cases the Court allows a concise statement of reasons to be completed in the course of the proceedings: ECJ, Case 111/83 *Picciolo v European Parliament* [1984] E.C.R. 2323, para.22; ECJ, Joined Cases 64, 71–73 and 78/86 *Sergio v Commission* [1988] E.C.R. 1399, para.52; CFI, Case T–37/89 *Hanning v European Parliament* [1990] E.C.R. II–463, para.42; CFI, Joined Cases T–160 and T–161/89 *Kalavros v Court of Justice* [1990] E.C.R. II–871, para.72; CFI, Case T–1/90 *Pérez-Mínguez Casariego v Commission* [1991] E.C.R. II–143, para.87; CFI, Case T–156/89 *Valverde Mordt v Court of Justice* [1991] E.C.R. II–407, paras 130–133; CFI, Case T–25/92 *Vela Palacios v ESC* [1993] E.C.R. II–201, para.26; ECJ, Case C–150/03 *Hectors v European Parliament* [2004] E.C.R. I–8691, para.50.

Pleas raised by the Court. The Court of Justice or the Court of First   7–148
Instance must raise of its own motion[534] the question as to whether the
requirement for a statement of reasons has been fulfilled (see 7–122,
supra).[535]

f. Publication and notification of the act

Irregularities in publication or notification. Irregularities in the publica-   7–149
tion or notification of an act are not classed as infringements of an essential
procedural requirement because they do not affect the act itself. Such
irregularities may at most prevent time from beginning to run for the
purposes of bringing proceedings.[536]

**3. Infringement of the Treaty or of any rule of law relating to its
application**

Scope. This ground for annulment encompasses any infringement of any   7–150
provision of superior Community law.[537]

Treaty. By "Treaty" is meant the Treaties establishing the Communities   7–151
(as amended), the Protocols annexed thereto[538] and the Accession Treaties
and Acts.[539] The pleas raised by the applicant do not necessarily have to be
confined to infringements of the Treaty on the basis of which the action is
brought. An action for annulment based on the EC Treaty may embody
admissible pleas referring to infringements of provisions of the EAEC
Treaty.[540]

Rule of law relating to the application of the Treaty. "Any rule of law   7–152
relating to [the] application [of the Treaty]" covers all other binding
provisions of the Community legal order. These include in the first place

---

[534] ECJ, Case C–166/95 P *Commission v Daffix* [1997] E.C.R. I–983, para.24; ECJ, Case C–367/95 P, *Commission v Sytraval and Brink's France* [1998] E.C.R. I–1719, para.67.
[535] ECJ, Case 18/57 *Nold v High Authority* [1959] E.C.R. 41; ECJ, Case 185/85 *Usinor v Commission* [1986] E.C.R. 2079, para.19; CFI, Case T–37/89 *Hanning v European Parliament* [1990] E.C.R. II–463, para.38; CFI, Case T 115/89 *González Holguera v European Parliament* [1990] E.C.R. II–831, para.37; CFI, Case T–61/89 *Dansk Pelsdyravlerforening v Commission* [1992] E.C.R. II–1931, para.129; CFI, Case T–534/93 *Grynberg v Commission* [1994] E.C.R.-SC II–595, para.59 (English abstract at [1994] E.C.R.-SC I–A-179); CFI, Case T–106/95 *FFSA and Others v Commission* [1997] E.C.R. II–229, para.62; CFI, Case T–4/96 *S. v Court of Justice* [1997] E.C.R. II–1125, para.53; CFI (judgment of July 8, 2004), T–44/00 *Mannesmannröhren-Werke v Commission*, not yet reported, paras 126 and 210 (under appeal: C–411/04 P).
[536] ECJ, Case 48/69 *ICI v Commission* [1972] E.C.R. 619, para.40; ECJ, Case 185/73 *König* [1974] E.C.R. 607, para.6.
[537] See, by way of example, ECJ, Case 92/78 *Simmenthal v Commission* [1979] E.C.R. 777, para.106. See also Boulouis, Darmon and Huglo, *Contentieux Communautaire* (2nd ed., Dalloz, Paris, 2001), §455–§463, at 209–212.
[538] EC Treaty, Art.311; EAEC Treaty, Art.207.
[539] ECJ, Case C–91/03 *Spain v Council* [2005] E.C.R. I–2267, paras 19–31.
[540] ECJ, Case C–62/88 *Greece v Council* [1990] E.C.R. I–1527, para.8.

provisions of international law, in particular provisions originating in treaties concluded by Member States before the EC Treaty was concluded,[541] agreements concluded by the Community itself[542] and customary international law.[543] Secondly, there is the group made up of the general principles of Community law,[544] such as the principle of proportionality,[545] the principle *nec bis in idem*[546] and the principle of reasonable time in administrative procedures.[547] Lastly, there are all valid, binding acts of Community institutions or bodies.[548]

---

[541] ECJ, Joined Cases 21–24/72 *International Fruit and Others* [1972] E.C.R. 1219, paras 6–7.

[542] EC Treaty, Art.300(7); ECJ, Case 181/73 *Haegeman* [1974] E.C.R. 449, para.5. For an example arising in connection with an action for annulment, see ECJ, Case 30/88 *Greece v Commission* [1989] E.C.R. 3711. The Court of Justice will review the legality of a Community measure in the light of the WTO rules only where the Community intended by means of that measure to implement a particular obligation assumed in the context of the WTO or where the measure refers expressly to the precise provisions of the WTO agreements (ECJ, Case C–149/96 *Portugal v Council* [1999] E.C.R. I–8395, paras 47–49).

[543] ECJ, Joined Cases 89, 104, 114, 116–117 and 125–129/85 *Ahlström and Others v Commission* [1988] E.C.R. 5193; CFI, Case T–115/94 *Opel Austria v Council* [1997] E.C.R. II–39, paras 87–95; CFI (judgment of September 21, 2005), Case T–306/01 *Yusuf and Al Barakaat International Foundation v Council and Commission* not yet reported, paras 281 and 282.

[544] ECJ, Case 4/73 *Nold v Commission* [1974] E.C.R. 491, para.13; ECJ, Case 114/76 *Bela Mühle* [1977] E.C.R. 1211, paras 5–7; ECJ, Case 224/82 *Meiko-Konservenfabrik* [1983] E.C.R. 2539, para.11; ECJ, Case C–325/91 *France v Commission* [1993] E.C.R. I–3283, para.30; CFI, Case T–65/98 *Van den Bergh Foods v Commission* [2003] E.C.R. II–4653, paras 197–198 (pleas based on infringement of the principles of subsidiarity, loyal cooperation and legal certainty dismissed).

[545] CFI, Case T–306/00 *Conserve Italia v Commission* [2003] E.C.R. II–5705, paras 127–151 (annulment of a Commission decision for infringing the principle of proportionality).

[546] ECJ (order of March 22, 2004), Case C–455/02 P *Sgaravatti Mediterranea*, not reported, paras. 45–46.

[547] Observation of a reasonable time in conducting administrative procedures in the sphere of competition policy is a general principle of Community law which the Community Court ensures is respected (ECJ, Case C–282/95 P *Guérin Automobiles v Commission* [1997] E.C.R. I–1503, paras 36–37; ECJ, Joined Cases C–238/99 P, C–244/99 P, C–245/99 P, C–247/99 P, C–250/99 P, C–252/99 P and C–254/99 P *Limburgse Vinyl Maatschappij and Others v Commission* [2002] E.C.R. I–8375, paras 167 and 171). It is set out, as part of the right to good administration, in Art.41(1) of the Charter of Fundamental Rights of the European Union promulgated at Nice on December 7, 2000 ([2000] O.J. C364/1): CFI, Case T–67/01 *JCB Service v Commission* [2004] E.C.R. II–49, para.36. An infringement of the reasonable-time principle justifies the annulment of a decision adopted at the end of the administrative procedure only when it also entails an infringement of the right of defence of the undertaking concerned. In the event that it is not proved that the undertaking could defend itself less effectively as a result of the excessively long period of time taken, the Commission's failure to respect the principle of reasonable time will have no effects on the validity of the administrative procedure in a competition case (CFI, Case T–67/01 *JCB Service v Commission* [2004] E.C.R. II–49, para.40, and the case-law cited therein); see also CFI, Case T–307/01 *François v Commission* [2004] E.C.R. II–1669, para.54, in which the plea—raised in a staff case—was declared well founded and the administrative procedure was held to be unlawful; CFI (judgment of July 13, 2005), Case T–242/02 *Sunrider v OHIM*, not yet reported, paras 51–55, in which the plea—raised in a trademark case—was rejected.

[548] As far as State aid cases are concerned, the Community Court may consider whether, in adopting the contested decision, the Commission complied with the rules which it laid down itself in guidelines and notices (see CFI, Case T–35/99 *Keller and Keller Meccanica v Commission* [2002] E.C.R. II–261, paras 74 and 77; CFI (judgment of November 18, 2004),

Infringement. The "infringement" of Community law for which annulment 7–153
is imposed under this head may consist equally of a misapplication of the
law (including an erroneous legal categorisation of the facts in question or a
misinterpretation of the applicable rule) or of an error in determining the
factual basis on which the application of Community law is founded.[549]

Margin of discretion. It is only in areas in which the institutions have a 7–154
broad discretion that the Court of Justice and the Court of First Instance
show reluctance in reviewing the assessment of economic facts and
circumstances which played a determinative role in the adoption of the
contested act.[550] In such a case, there will have to be a manifestly wrong

---

Case T–176/01 *Ferriere Nord v Commission*, not yet reported, para.134). This is because the
compatibility with the common market of planned aid has to be assessed in accordance
with the provisions of Art.87 of the EC Treaty and by reference to the Community
guidelines which the Commission has previously adopted for the purposes of such an
examination. The Commission is bound by the guidelines and notices that it issues in the
area of supervision of State aid where they do not depart from the rules in the Treaty and
are accepted by the Member States (ECJ, Case C–351/98 *Spain v Commission* [2002]
E.C.R. I–8031, para.53; CFI (judgment of November 18, 2004), Case T–176/01 *Ferriere
Nord v Commission*, not yet reported, para.134).

[549] ECJ, Case 18/62 *Barge v High Authority* [1963] E.C.R. 259, at 279–281. For an analytical
breakdown of those two aspects, see CFI, Case T–1/89 *Rhône-Poulenc v Commission* [1991]
E.C.R. II–867, paras 31–128; CFI, Case T–4/89 *BASF v Commission* [1991] E.C.R. II–1523,
paras 54–258; CFI, Case T–9/89 *Hüls v Commission* [1992] E.C.R. II–499, paras 90–328. It
also transpires from these judgments that the Court of First Instance thoroughly reviews
the findings of fact which the Commission regards as constituting an infringement of
Art.81(1) or Art.82 of the EC Treaty. See also CFI, Joined Cases T–68, T–77 and T–78/89
SIV and Others v Commission [1992] E.C.R. II–1403, paras 172–369. The Court effects its
review by inquiring into the correctness of the factual claims set out in the Commission
decision by testing it against the admissible evidence from the parties to the proceedings.

[550] *In agricultural cases*: ECJ, Case 138/79 *Roquette Frères v Council* [1980] E.C.R. 3333,
para.25, and ECJ, Case C–301/97 *Netherlands v Council* [2001] E.C.R. I–8853, para.105
(reluctance shown even with regard to determining the facts); *in competition cases*: ECJ,
Case 42/84 *Remia v Commission* [1985] E.C.R. 2545, para.34; ECJ, Joined Cases 142 and
156/84 *British American Tobacco and R.J. Reynolds Industries v Commission* [1987] E.C.R.
4487, para.62; ECJ, Joined Cases C–204/00 P, C–205/00 P, C–211/02 P, C–213/00 P, C–
217/00 P and C–219/00 P *Aalborg Portland and Others v Commission* [2004] E.C.R. I–2085,
para.279; CFI, Case T–44/90 *La Cinq v Commission* [1992] E.C.R. II–1, para.85; CFI, Case
T–7/92 *Asia Motor France and Others v Commission* [1993] E.C.R. II–669, para.33; CFI,
Joined Cases T–39 and T–40/92 *Groupement des Cartes Bancaires "CB" and Europay v
Commission* [1994] E.C.R. II–49, para.109; CFI, Case T–17/93 *Matra Hachette v Commis-
sion* [1994] E.C.R. II–595, para.104; *in anti-dumping cases*: ECJ, Case 240/84 *Toyo v
Council* [1987] E.C.R. 1809, para.19; ECJ, Case 187/85 *Fediol v Commission* [1988] E.C.R.
4155, para.6; ECJ, Case C–156/87 *Gestetner Holdings v Council and Commission* [1990]
E.C.R. I–781, para.63; ECJ, Case C–174/87 *Ricoh v Council* [1992] E.C.R. I–1335, para.68;
CFI, Case T–118/96 *Thai Bicycle v Council* [1998] E.C.R. II–2991, para.32; CFI (judgment
of October 28, 2004), Case T–35/01 *Shanghai Teraoka Electronic v Council*, not yet
reported, paras 48–49 (reluctance shown also to take account of "factual situations of a
legal and political nature in the [third] country concerned"); *in transport cases*: ECJ, Case
C–354/89 *Schiocchet v Commission* [1991] E.C.R. I–1775, para.14; *in State aid cases*: ECJ,
Case C–225/91 *Matra v Commission* [1993] E.C.R. I–3203, paras 24–25; but see, as regards
classifying a measure as aid, CFI, Case T–296/97 *Alitalia v Commission* [2000] E.C.R. II–
3871, para.95; CFI (judgment of October 21, 2004), Case T–36/99 *Lenzing v Commission*,

assessment or a misuse of power if the act is to be annulled (apart, of course, from any misapplication of Community law in some other respect).[551]

If, however, the institutions lay down guidelines with a view to specifying the criteria which they intend to apply in accordance with the Treaty in exercising their broad discretion, this will entail a self-imposed limitation on the exercise of the discretion in that they commit themselves to comply with their self-imposed guidelines.[552] In this context, it is for the Court of First Instance to consider whether the institutions have complied with those rules.[553]

4. Misuse of powers

7–155 **Concept.** An institution is said to misuse its powers when it uses them for a purpose other than that for which they were conferred (*détournement de pouvoir*).[554] An act may be annulled on that ground. The Court of Justice

---

not yet reported, paras 127–162 (Commission's assessment held to be wrong in that it held that the measure could not be regarded as being aid because it satisfied the private investor test); CFI (judgment of June 15, 2005), Case T–349/03 *Corsica Ferries France v Commission*, not yet reported, paras 137–138; *in concentration cases*: the review carried out by the Court of First Instance is broader: see, *e.g.* CFI, Case T–5/02 *Tetra Laval v Commission* [2002] E.C.R. II–4381. The Commission claimed on appeal that the Court of First Instance had not confined itself to a review of legality but also placed itself in the Commission's position. The appeal was rejected: ECJ, Case C–12/03 P *Commission v Tetra Laval* [2005] E.C.R. I–987, paras 37–51.

[551] ECJ, Case 29/77 *Roquette Frères* [1977] E.C.R. 1835, paras 19–20. In his Opinion of February 17, 2005 in Case C–40/03 P *Rica Foods v Commission*, not yet reported, paras 45 to 50, Advocate General P. Léger draws a distinction between discretion of a political nature (which corresponds to the political responsibilities which a Community provision confers on an institution) and discretion of a technical nature (discretion of an administrative authority justified by the technical, economic and legal complexity of the situations which it has to consider). The intensity of judicial review will be stronger where the act is the outcome of the exercise of discretion of a technical nature (*e.g.* in competition cases) than it is where the act is the result of the exercise of political discretion (*e.g.* in agricultural cases).

[552] Guidelines in connection with the assessment of State aid: see CFI, Case T–380/94 *AIUFFASS and AKT v Commission* [1996] E.C.R. II–2169, para.57; CFI, Case T–214/95 *Vlaams Gewest v Commission* [1998] E.C.R. II–717, para.89; CFI (judgment of December 1, 2004), Case T–27/02 *Kronofrance v Commission*, not yet reported, para.79. For guidelines regarding the fines which may be imposed for infringement of Arts 81 and 82 of the EC Treaty, see CFI (judgment of July 8, 2004), Case T– 44/00 *Mannesmannröhren-Werke v Commission*, not yet reported, paras 212 and 232.

[553] CFI, Case T–35/99 *Keller and Keller Meccanica v Commission* [2002] E.C.R. II–261, para.77; CFI (judgment of December 1, 2004), Case T–27/02 *Kronofrance v Commission*, not yet reported, para.79.

[554] ECJ, Case 8/55 *Fédération Charbonnière de Belgique v High Authority* [1954 to 1956] E.C.R. 292, at 303; ECJ, Case 15/57 *Compagnie des Hauts Fourneaux de Chasse v High Authority* [1957 and 1958] E.C.R. 211, at 230; ECJ, Case 92/78 *Simmenthal v Commission* [1979] E.C.R. 777, para.106; ECJ, Case 817/79 *Buyl v Commission* para.28; ECJ, Case C–400/99 *Italy v Commission* [2005] E.C.R. I–3657, para.38; CFI, Case T–38/89 *Hochbaum v Commission* [1990] E.C.R. II–43, para.22; CFI, Case T–108/89 *Scheuer v Commission* [1990]

has evolved from a subjective approach to an objective approach, principally in the context of the ECSC Treaty, of the concept of misuse of powers.[555] It is not always necessary to know the actual grounds which motivated the institution (subjective approach). When the outcome of the contested act diverges from the objectives for which the power was conferred, this can afford a sufficient basis for annulling the contested act for misuse of powers (objective approach).[556] Thus, the Court of Justice has equated with "disregard for the lawful aim" pursuing "objectively", through a serious lack of care or attention in the exercise of a power, purposes other than those for which the power was conferred.[557] An unlawful choice of a decision-making procedure in order to evade other procedures which would normally be applicable also constitutes a misuse of powers.[558]

Act pursuing authorised and unauthorised aims. An act which pursues both unauthorised and authorised aims may be annulled only if this detracts from the main aim for which the power was conferred[559] or if the unauthorised aim constitutes the main reason for exercising the power.[560] **7–156**

Proof. The Court subjects claims alleging misuse of powers to strict requirements as to proof. Only if the applicant proves, on the basis of objective, relevant and consistent facts, that the act was adopted for unauthorised purposes, will the Court of Justice or the Court of First **7–157**

E.C.R. II–411, para.49; CFI, Case T–46/89 *Pitrone v Commission* [1990] E.C.R. II–577, para.70. For an extensive discussion, see Schockweiler, "La notion de détournement de pouvoir en droit communautaire" (1990) A.J.D.A. 435.

[555] See Schockweiler (preceding n.), at 439–441.

[556] ECJ, Joined Cases 351 and 360/85 *Fabrique de Fer de Charleroi v Commission* [1987] E.C.R. 3639, paras 19 and 20; ECJ, Joined Cases 32, 52 and 57/87 *ISA v Commission* [1988] E.C.R. 3305, para.19; ECJ, Joined Cases 33, 44, 110, 226 and 285/86 *Stahlwerke Peine-Salzgitter and Others v Commission* [1988] E.C.R. 4309, paras 27–28.

[557] ECJ, Case 8/55 *Fédération Charbonnière de Belgique v High Authority* [1954 to 1956] E.C.R. 292, at 303; ECJ, Case 13/57 *Wirtschaftsvereinigung Eisen- und Stahlindustrie and Others v High Authority* [1957 and 1958] E.C.R. 265, at 282.

[558] ECJ, Case 2/57 *Compagnie des Hauts Fourneaux de Chasse v High Authority* [1957 and 1958] E.C.R. 199, at 207; ECJ, Joined Cases 140, 146, 221 and 226/82 *Walzstahl-Vereinigung and Thyssen v Commission* [1984] E.C.R. 951, paras 27 *et seq.*; ECJ, Joined Cases 32, 52 and 57/87 *ISA v Commission* [1988] E.C.R. 3305, para.19; ECJ, Joined Cases 33, 44, 110, 226 and 285/86 *Stahlwerke Peine-Salzgitter and Others v Commission* [1988] E.C.R. 4309, paras 27–28.

[559] ECJ, Case 1/54 *France v High Authority* [1954 to 1956] E.C.R. 1, at 16; ECJ, Case 8/55 *Fédération Charbonnière de Belgique v High Authority* [1954 to 1956] E.C.R. 292, at 301.

[560] ECJ, Case 2/57 *Compagnie des Hauts Fourneaux de Chasse v High Authority* [1957 and 1958] E.C.R. 199, at 232.

Instance entertain a claim of misuse of powers.[561] A misuse of powers cannot be presumed.[562]

7–158   Importance. In spite of the prominent role which this ground of nullity played in the ECSC Treaty, it is only seldom that the Court of Justice and the Court of First Instance declare an act void for misuse of powers.[563]

B. Conduct during the administrative procedure and admissibility of pleas in judicial proceedings

7–159   Acknowledgement of the facts in proceedings under Arts 81 and 82. An undertaking involved in an alleged infringement of Arts 81 and 82 of the EC Treaty may raise in its application any ground for annulment mentioned in Art.230 of the EC Treaty. Where the undertaking does not expressly acknowledge the facts, the Commission must prove the facts in its decision and the undertaking is free to put forward in the proceedings before the Court any plea in its defence which it deems appropriate. However, where the undertaking explicitly admits during the administrative procedure the substantive truth of the Commission's allegations made against it in the statement of objections, those facts must thereafter be regarded as established and the undertaking will be in principle estopped from disputing them during the proceedings before the Court.[564]

---

[561] ECJ, Joined Cases 18 and 35/65 *Gutmann v Commission* [1966] E.C.R. 103, at 117; ECJ, Case 69/83 *Lux v Court of Auditors* [1984] E.C.R. 2447, para.30; ECJ, Case 52/86 *Banner v European Parliament* [1987] E.C.R. 979, para.6; ECJ, Joined Cases 361 and 362/87 *Caturla-Poch and De la Fuente Pascual v European Parliament* [1989] E.C.R. 2471, para.21; ECJ, Case C–323/88 *Sermes* [1990] E.C.R. I–3027, para.33; ECJ, Case C–331/88 *Fedesa and Others* [1990] E.C.R. I–4023, para.24; ECJ, Case C–400/99 *Italy v Commission* [2005] E.C.R. I–3657, para.38; CFI, Case T–46/89 *Pitrone v Commission* [1990] E.C.R. II–577, para.71; CFI, Case T–23/91 *Maurissen v Court of Auditors* [1992] E.C.R. II–2377, para.28; CFI, Case T–80/92 *Turner v Commission* [1993] E.C.R. II–1465, para.70; CFI, Case T–109/92 *Lacruz Bassols v Court of Justice* [1994] E.C.R.-SC II–105, para.52 (English abstract at [1994] E.C.R.-SC I–A-31); CFI, Case T–46/93 *Michaël-Chiou v Commission* [1994] E.C.R.-SC II–929, para.35 (English abstract at [1994] E.C.R.-SC I–A-297); CFI, Case T–143/89 *Ferriere Nord v Commission* [1995] E.C.R. II–917, para.68; CFI, Joined Cases T–551/93, T–231, T–232, T–233 and T–234/94 *Industrias Pesqueras Campos and Others v Commission* [1996] E.C.R. II–247, para.168.

[562] ECJ, Case 23/76 *Pellegrini and Others v Commission* [1976] E.C.R. 1807, para.30, and the Opinion of Advocate General H. Mayras, at 1829–1830; CFI, Case T–146/89 *Williams v Court of Auditors* [1991] E.C.R. II–1293, para.89.

[563] ECJ, Joined Cases 18 and 35/65 *Gutmann v Commission* [1966] E.C.R. 103, at 117; ECJ, Case 105/75 *Giuffrida v Council* [1976] E.C.R. 1395, para.18; ECJ, Case 92/78 *Simmenthal v Commission* [1979] E.C.R. 777, para.106, at 811; ECJ, Joined Cases 59 and 129/80 *Turner v Commission* [1981] E.C.R. 1883, para.71, at 1920; ECJ, Joined Cases 33, 44, 110, 226 and 285/86 *Stahlwerke Peine-Salzitter and Others v Commission* [1988] E.C.R. 4309, para.28; CFI, Case T–106/92 *Frederiksen v European Parliament* [1995] E.C.R.-SC II–99, paras 46–60 (English abstract at [1995] E.C.R.-SC I–A-29).

[564] ECJ, Case C–297/98 P *SCA Holding v Commission* [2000] E.C.R. I–10101, para.37; CFI, Case T–224/00 *Archer Daniels Midland and Archer Daniels Midland Ingredients v Commis-*

State aid proceedings. A recipient of State aid or any other party 7–160
concerned may submit a plea against the final Commission decision which
was not submitted during the administrative procedure.[565] It should nevertheless be stressed that the legality of a Community measure falls to be
assessed on the basis of the elements of fact and of law existing at the time
when the measure was adopted. In particular, the assessments made by the
Commission must be examined solely on the basis of the information
available to the Commission at the time when those assessments were
made.[566] It follows that an applicant which took part in the investigation
procedure provided for in Art.88(2) of the EC Treaty cannot rely on factual
arguments which were not known to the Commission and which it did not
notify to the Commission during the investigation procedure.[567]

Nemo auditur. In proceedings before the Court of First Instance, a party 7–161
cannot rely on its own wrongful conduct in the administrative procedure.[568]
Similarly, a party cannot rely on the unlawful conduct of a person
authorised to act on its behalf in order to evade its own liability as a result
of actions performed by that person.[569]

C. LIMITATION PERIODS

Time-limit. Under Art.230 of the EC Treaty, annulment proceedings "shall 7–162
be instituted within two months of the publication of the measure, or its
notification to the plaintiff, or, in the absence thereof, of the day on which

---

sion [2003] E.C.R. II–2597, para.227 (under appeal: Case C–397/03 P); CFI, Joined Cases
T–236/01, T–239/01, T–244/01, T–246/01, T–251/01 and T–252/01 *Tokai Carbon and Others
v Commission* [2004] E.C.R. II–1181, para.108. However, inferences made by the Commission on the basis of declarations made during the administrative procedure may still be
challenged before the Court of First Instance (*Tokai Carbon*, para.109).
[565] CFI, Case T–16/96 *Cityflyer Express v Commission* [1998] E.C.R. II–757, para.39; CFI, Case
T–123/97 *Salomon v Commission* [1999] E.C.R. II–2925, para.55; CFI (judgment of May 11,
2005), Joined Cases T–111/01 and T–133/01 *Saxonia Edelmetalle and ZEMAG v Commission*, not yet reported, para.68.
[566] CFI, Joined Cases T–371/94 and T–394/94 *British Airways and Others v Commission* [1998]
E.C.R. II–2405, para.81; CFI, Case T–110/97 *Kneissl Dachstein v Commission* [1999] E.C.R.
II–2881, para.47; CFI (judgment of May 11, 2005), Joined Cases T–111/01 and T–133/01
Saxonia Edelmetalle and ZEMAG v Commission, not yet reported, para.67.
[567] CFI (judgment of May 11, 2005), Joined Cases T–111/01 and T–133/01 *Saxonia Edelmetalle
and ZEMAG v Commission*, not yet reported, para.68.
[568] CFI (judgment of January 18, 2005), Case T–141/01 *Entorn v Commission*, not yet reported,
para.121; see, by analogy, ECJ, Case 39/72 *Commission v Italy* [1973] E.C.R. 101, para.10,
and the Opinion of Advocate General J. Mischo in Case C–453/99 *Courage and Crehan*
[2001] E.C.R. I–6297, I–6300, para.39).
[569] CFI (judgment of January 18, 2005), Case T–141/01 *Entorn v Commission*, not yet reported,
para.121. In that case, a letter from the Commission intended to ensure the recipient its
right to be heard was sent to the wrong address. The Court of First Instance dismissed a
plea alleging infringement of the rights of the defence on the ground that the management
of the undertaking concerned deliberately misled the Commission as to its correct address.

it came to the knowledge of the latter, as the case may be".[570] It is settled case-law that the time-limit prescribed for bringing actions under Art.230 of the EC Treaty is a matter of public policy and not subject to the discretion of the parties or the Court, since it was established in order to ensure that legal positions are clear and certain and to avoid any discrimination or arbitrary treatment in the administration of justice.[571] The Community Courts will therefore consider of their own motion whether the time-limit for bringing an action has been respected.[572]

1. Publication

7–163   **Effects of publication.** Under Art.254(2) of the EC Treaty, regulations and directives addressed to all the Member States must be published in the *Official Journal of the European Union*.[573] Time for bringing proceedings against such acts starts to run from the fifteenth day after their publication in the *Official Journal*.[574] There is a rebuttable presumption that the date of publication is the date borne by the issue of the *Official Journal* containing the contested act.[575] Since publication is necessary in order for such acts to enter into effect,[576] time for bringing proceedings cannot start to run until they have been published in the *Official Journal*.[577] It makes no difference if the applicant became aware of the content of a regulation also in some other way. The same is true of acts which do not have to be published in order to enter into force where there is a consistent practice of publishing them. In those circumstances, the applicant is entitled to see the decision published in the *Official Journal* and the starting point of the period for

---

[570] For the method for calculating time-limits in general, which is also applicable to limitation periods, see 24–176 to 24–185, *infra*. This section deals only with factors determining the onset of the period for bringing an action for annulment. Examples of applications lodged out of time may be found in ECJ (order of January 11, 2000), Case C–295/98 *Italy v Commission* [2000] E.C.R. I–111 and CFI (order of May 27, 2005), Case T–485/04 *COBB v Commission*, not reported.

[571] ECJ, Case 152/85 *Misset v Council* [1987] E.C.R. 223, para.11; ECJ, Case C–246/95 *Coen* [1997] E.C.R. I–403, para.21; CFI, Joined Cases T–121/96 and T–151/96 *Mutual Aid Administration Services v Commission* [1997] E.C.R. II–1355, paras 38 and 39.

[572] See, *e.g.* CFI, Joined Cases T–142/01 and T–283/01 *OPTUC v Commission* [2004] E.C.R. II–329. See also 7–170, *infra*.

[573] The same applies to regulations, directives and decisions adopted in accordance with Art.251 (co-decision as between the Council and the European Parliament) by virtue of Art.254(1) of the EC Treaty.

[574] ECJ Rules of Procedure, Art.81(1); CFI Rules of Procedure, Art.102(1). This rule applies to *all* acts of Community institutions published in the *Official Journal of the European Union* and not only to those which enter into effect only after publication therein (see CFI (order of May 25, 2004), Case T–264/03 *Schmoldt and Others v Commission* [2004] E.C.R. II–1515, paras 51–62).

[575] ECJ, Case 98/78 *Racke* [1979] E.C.R. 69, paras 15–17; CFI, Case T–115/94 *Opel Austria v Council* [1997] E.C.R. II–39, para.127.

[576] ECJ, Case 185/73 *König* [1974] E.C.R. 607, para.6.

[577] *Cf.* Opinion of Advocate General K. Roemer in ECJ, Joined Cases 10 and 18/68 *"Eridania" Zuccherifici Nazionali and Others v Commission* [1969] E.C.R. 459, at 488–489.

instituting proceedings is the date of publication, regardless of whether the applicant had earlier notice by some other means of the existence and content of the act in question.[578]

Summary publication and Internet link. The fact that the Commission gave third parties full access to the text of a decision on its Internet site, combined with the publication of a succinct notice in the *Official Journal of the European Union* which enabled interested parties to identify the decision in question and brought their attention to the possibility of accessing it over the Internet must be regarded as constituting publication within the meaning of the fifth para. of Art.230 of the EC Treaty.[579] Such publication constitutes the starting point of the period for instituting proceedings.

7–164

2. Notification to the applicant

Effects of notification. Under Art.254(3) of the EC Treaty, all other directives and decisions take effect upon notification to the addressee. The period of time for commencing proceedings against such a measure runs from the day following the receipt by the person concerned of due notification,[580] where any delay in notification is not attributable to that person.[581] The person to whom the act is addressed cannot prevent time

7–165

---

[578] ECJ, Case C–122/95 *Germany v Council* [1998] E.C.R. I–973, paras 34–39, in which the Court of Justice held that there was a consistent practice for Council decisions embodying the conclusion of international agreements binding on the European Community to be published in the *Official Journal* (compare ECJ, Case C–309/95 *Commission v Council* [1998] E.C.R. I–655 for acts which are not published). See also CFI, Case T–110/97 *Kneissl Dachstein v Commission* [1999] E.C.R. II–2881, paras 40–44; CFI, Case T–123/97 *Salomon v Commission* [1999] E.C.R. II–2925, paras 40–45, in which the Court of First Instance held that the Commission has committed itself to publishing the complete text of decisions granting conditional authorisation for State aid taken at the end of the procedure provided for in Art.88(2) of the EC Treaty and that, for an undertaking to which the relevant decision was not notified, the period for commencing proceedings began to run from the day on which it was published in the *Official Journal*. See also CFI, Case T–296/97 *Alitalia v Commission* [2000] E.C.R. II–3871, paras 59–61. In recent case-law it is not even considered whether there is an established practice of publication. Time for beginning proceedings begins to run on notification or on the day of publication in the *Official Journal*. The subsidiary criterion of having notice of the act is relevant only where the act is neither notified nor published in the *Official Journal* (CFI (order of May 25, 2004), Case T–264/03 *Schmoldt and Others v Commission* [2004] E.C.R. II–1515, paras 51–61).
[579] CFI (judgment of June 15, 2005), Case T–17/02 *Olsen v Commission*, not yet reported, para.80; CFI (order of September 19, 2005), Case T–321/04 *Air Bourbon v Commission*, not yet reported, paras 34 and 37.
[580] However, a purely formal error in the notification (*e.g.* a mistake in the name of the addressee) does not prevent the time-limits laid down in the Treaty from applying, provided that the act in question actually reached the addressee and the latter realised that he or she actually was the addressee: ECJ (order of July 4, 1984), Case 82/84 *Metalgoi v Commission* [1984] E.C.R. 2585, at 2586; CFI (order of February 13, 1998), Case T–275/97 *Guérin Automobiles v Commission* [1998] E.C.R. II–253, para.14; CFI (order of February 13, 1998), Case T–276/97 *Guérin Automobiles v Commission* [1998] E.C.R. II–261, para.18.
[581] ECJ, Case 5/76 *Jänsch v Commission* [1976] E.C.R. 1027, para.9. ECJ Rules of Procedure, Art.80(1)(a); CFI Rules of Procedure, Art.101(1)(a). This rule is applicable to *all* acts of Community institutions which enter into force upon notification.

from starting to run by refusing to take cognisance of a properly notified act.[582]

Publication in the *Official Journal* of an act which takes effect upon notification to the addressee or the fact that the addressee has knowledge of its existence before notification has no effect on when time starts running.[583]

7–166 **Due notification.** Due notification requires that the act be communicated to the person to whom it is addressed[584] and should put that person in a position to take cognisance of its content and of the grounds on which it is based.[585] Registered mail with an acknowledgement slip is accepted as an appropriate means of notification, provided that the rules applicable to the delivery of mail are complied with,[586] since it enables the Court to determine with certainty when time started to run.[587] In such case, only unforeseen circumstances, *force majeure* or excusable error which prevented the applicant from actually taking cognisance of the act notified may justify exceeding the time-limit for instituting proceedings.[588]

---

[582] ECJ, Case 6/72 *Europemballage and Continental Can v Commission* [1973] E.C.R. 215, para.10.

[583] ECJ, Case 31/76 *Hebrant (née Macevicius) v European Parliament* [1977] E.C.R. 883, para.13.

[584] The notification to the Member State concerned of a decision declaring aid granted by a region incompatible with the common market has no effect on the period within which the region concerned has to bring an action for annulment (CFI, Case T–190/00 *Regione Siciliana v Commission* [2003] E.C.R. II–5015, paras 29–33). Moreover, notification causes time to run within the meaning of the fifth para. of Art.230 of the EC Treaty only where the act is notified to the person to whom the decision is addressed. If the Commission sends a copy of a State aid decision (addressed to the Member State) by e-mail to the undertaking which had lodged a complaint relating to the aid concerned, that communication does not start time running, but rather the subsequent publication of that act (see CFI (judgment of June 15, 2005), Case T–17/02 *Olsen v Commission*, not yet reported, paras 72–87).

[585] ECJ, Case 6/72 *Europemballage and Continental Can v Commission* [1973] E.C.R. 215, para.10; CFI, Case T–196/95 *H v Commission* [1997] E.C.R.-SC II–403, para.31 (English abstract at I–A-133). Consequently, to send only a brief summary of the contents of the act is not sufficient and will not start time running for the purposes of bringing proceedings: ECJ, Case C–143/95 P *Commission v Socurte and Others* [1997] E.C.R. I–1, para.32.

[586] CFI, Joined Cases T–374/94, T–375/94, T–384/94 and T–388/94 *European Night Services and Others v Commission* [1998] E.C.R. II–3141, paras 75–79. In that case, the Court of First Instance found that the first notification had been made to a person not authorised to take delivery of mail under the French postal rules and so this did not cause time to start running.

[587] ECJ, Joined Cases 32 and 33/58 *SNUPAT v High Authority* [1959] E.C.R. 127, at 136; ECJ, Case 224/83 *Ferriera Vittoria v Commission* [1984] E.C.R. 2349, para.9.

[588] ECJ, Joined Cases 220 and 221/78 *ALA and ALFER v Commission* [1979] E.C.R. 1693, para.9; ECJ (order of April 27, 1988), Case 352/87 *Farzoo and Kortmann v Commission* [1988] E.C.R. 2281, para.7; ECJ (order of February 5, 1992), Case C–59/91 *France v Commission* [1992] E.C.R. I–525, para.8. An excusable error can occur "when the conduct of the institution concerned has been, either alone or to a decisive extent, such as to give rise to pardonable confusion in the mind of a party acting in good faith and exercising all the diligence required of a normally well-informed person" (ECJ, Case C–193/01 P *Pitsiorlas v Council* [2003] E.C.R. I–48037, para.24).

Notification to an undertaking. If the act is addressed to a company, **7–167** notification to the registered office suffices. Companies have no right to require the Commission to give notice at a place other than the registered office or to a particular person.[589] In the case of companies, the rule is that measures addressed to the parent company may not be validly notified to subsidiaries.[590]

Burden of proof. The party alleging that the time-limit for bringing **7–168** proceedings has run out has to prove the date on which time started running.[591] When the time-limit for instituting proceedings is exceeded, the applicant will bear the burden of proving the existence of *force majeure* or excusable error. However, in order for legal certainty not to suffer too much, these exceptions are strictly interpreted.[592]

3. Date on which the applicant had notice of the act

Subsidiary criterion. The criterion of the day on which a measure came to **7–169** the knowledge of an applicant is subsidiary to the criteria of publication or notification of the measure.[593] This means that an individual who already has knowledge of the content of an act before it is published in the *Official Journal* is not obliged to bring proceedings within two months of the date when it came to his or her knowledge, but may wait until it is published.[594] The same applies where an act comes to the addressee's knowledge before it is officially notified to it.[595]

---

[589] ECJ, Case 42/85 *Cockerill-Sambre v Commission* [1985] E.C.R. 3749, paras 10–11.

[590] ECJ, Case 48/69 *ICI v Commission* [1972] E.C.R. 619, paras 34–38. In that case, however, the parent company had had full knowledge of the contested act and exercised the right to bring proceedings within the prescribed period. Consequently, the finding that notification might not have been properly effected had no bearing on the case: *ibid.*, paras 39–44.

[591] CFI, Joined Cases T–70 and T–71/92 *Florimex and VGB v Commission* [1997] E.C.R. II–693, para.74; CFI (order of April 13, 2000), Case T–263/97 *GAL Penisola Sorrentina v Commission* [2000] E.C.R. II–2041, para.48.

[592] ECJ, Case 284/82 *Busseni v Commission* [1984] E.C.R. 557, paras 11–12; ECJ, Case 224/83 *Ferriera Vittoria v Commission* [1984] E.C.R. 2349, para.13; ECJ, Case 209/83 *Valsabbia v Commission* [1984] E.C.R. 3089, paras 21–22; CFI, Case T–12/90 *Bayer v Commission* [1991] E.C.R. II–219; CFI, Joined Cases T–33 and T–74/89 *Blackman v European Parliament* [1993] E.C.R. II–249, paras 32–36; CFI, Case T–514/93 *Cobrecaf and Others v Commission* [1995] E.C.R. II–621, para.40.

[593] CFI, Case T–296/97 *Alitalia v Commission* [2000] E.C.R. II–3871, para.61.

[594] CFI, Case T–140/95 *Ryanair v Commission* [1998] E.C.R. II–3327, para.25; CFI, Case T–11/95 *B.P. v Commission* [1998] E.C.R. II–3235, paras 47–48; CFI, Case T–106/96 *Wirtschaftsvereinigung Stahl v Commission* [1999] E.C.R. II–2155, paras 28–31; CFI, Case T–89/96 *British Steel v Commission* [1999] E.C.R. II–2089, paras 33–36; CFI, Case T–14/96 *BAI v Commission* [1999] E.C.R. II–139, paras 33–37. For an extensive analysis of this case-law with reference to State aid, see Coulon and Cras, "Contentieux de la légalité dans le domaine des aides d'état: les récentes évolutions dans l'application des articles 173 et 175 du traité CE" (1999) C.D.E. 68–69.

[595] *Ibid.*

The period for commencing proceedings in the case of interested third parties seeking annulment of an act addressed to another person begins—except in the case of publication in the *Official Journal*—on the day on which that person acquired knowledge of the existence and the precise contents of the measure and of the reasons on which it is based in such a way as to enable him or her profitably to exercise his or her right of action.[596] If the act is published in the *Official Journal*[597] or in an official publication of a Member State[598] or if it is brought to the notice of interested third parties, this will constitute sufficient notice, with the result that time will start running.[599] However, whether an action for annulment brought by an interested third party against an act directed to another person is admissible does not depend on the fact of publication or notification. An application lodged before publication or notification will be admissible.[600]

A third party who acquires precise knowledge of the content of an act (not published in the *Official Journal*) must bring proceedings within two months of the moment at which it acquired that precise knowledge.[601] The expression "precise knowledge of the content of an act" does not mean knowledge of every aspect of the decision but of its essential contents.[602] It has been held that where the applicant had knowledge of the contested act from a letter of which the date of receipt could not be definitely established, the period for commencing proceedings began on the date on which the applicant itself referred to the act in a letter.[603]

---

[596] ECJ, Case 236/86 *Dillinger Hüttenwerke v Commission* [1988] E.C.R. 3761, para.14; ECJ, Case 378/87 *Top Hit Holzvertrieb v Commission* [1989] E.C.R. 1359, para.15.

[597] ECJ, Case 76/79 *Könecke v Commission* [1980] E.C.R. 665, para.7; CFI, Case T–380/94 *AIUFFASS and AKT v Commission* [1996] E.C.R. II–2169, para.42.

[598] ECJ, Joined Cases 31 and 33/62 *Wöhrmann and Others v Commission* [1962] E.C.R. 501, at 508.

[599] Time will start running irrespective as to whether or not the applicant had actual knowledge of the act which is published in the *Official Journal*. See CFI (order of July 27, 2004), Case T–238/04 *Raab and Others v European Parliament and Council*, not reported, paras 9–10.

[600] ECJ, Joined Cases 172 and 226/83 *Hoogovens Groep v Commission* [1985] E.C.R. 2831, para.8; CFI (judgment of June 15, 2005), Case T–17/02 *Olsen v Commission*, not yet reported, para.83.

[601] ECJ, Case C–309/95 *Commission v Council* [1998] E.C.R. I–655, paras 18–22. It could be inferred from the wording of this judgment that interested third parties invariably have to comply with this time-limit, irrespective as to whether or not the contested act has entered into force. But the objection to this interpretation is that if the act does not enter into force within two months of the time at which the third party acquired knowledge of it, the action would have to be brought against an act which does not yet produce any legal effects.

[602] CFI, Joined cases T–485/93, T–491/93, T–494/93 and T–61/98 *Dreyfus and Others v Commission* [2000] E.C.R. II–3659, para.49.

[603] CFI (order of April 28, 1994), Joined Cases T–452 and T–453/93 *Pevasa and Inpesca v Commission* [1994] E.C.R. II–229, paras 33–36.

However, a third party may not remain idle undefinitely until it acquires precise knowledge of the content of an act. Indeed, if interested parties are put on notice of the existence of an act, they are under an obligation to request the complete text of the act within a reasonable period.[604] So, where the applicant fails to ask for the full text of the act after it had had knowledge of its existence, its application will be held to be inadmissible if, at the time when it had cognisance of the content of the act, the reasonable time had expired.[605]

D. Examination *ex officio* of the conditions governing the admissibility of an action

Ex officio **examination.** The conditions governing the admissibility of an action are a matter of public policy. The Community Courts therefore examine of their own motion absolute bars to proceedings, which include bars relating to the time-limit for bringing an action,[606] to whether the contested measure is of a challengeable nature,[607] to the interest of the applicant in obtaining the annulment of the contested measure[608] and to

7–170

---

[604] ECJ, Case 59/84 *Tezi Textiel v Commission* [1986] E.C.R. 887, paras 9–11 (period of 14 months held to be reasonable); ECJ, Case C–180/88 *Wirtschaftsvereinigung Eisen- und Stahlindustrie v Commission* [1990] E.C.R. I–4413, para.22 (two years held to be unreasonable); ECJ (order of March 5, 1993), Case C–102/92 *Ferriere Acciaierie Sarde v Commission* [1993] E.C.R. I–801, paras 18–19 (two months held to be unreasonable); CFI (order of February 10, 1994), Case T–468/93 *Frinil v Commission* [1994] E.C.R. II–33, paras 33–34 (one year and 10 months held to be unreasonable); CFI, Case T–465/93 *Consorzio Gruppo di Azione Locale "Murgia Messapica" v Commission* [1994] E.C.R. II–361 (7.5 months held to be reasonable); CFI, Joined Cases T–432, T–433 and T–434/93 *Socurte and Others v Commission* [1995] E.C.R. II–503, para.49; CFI, Case T–109/94 *Windpark Groothusen v Commission* [1995] E.C.R. II–3007, paras 24–28 (7 months held to be unreasonable); CFI (order of September 30, 1997), Case T–151/95 *INEF v Commission* [1997] E.C.R. II–1541, para.48 (18 months held to be unreasonable); CFI (order of July 15, 1998), Case T–155/95 *LPN and GEOTA v Commission* [1998] E.C.R. I–2751, para.44 (6 months held to be unreasonable); CFI (order of May 27, 2005), Case T–485/04 *COBB v Commission*, not reported (4.5 months held to be unreasonable).

[605] CFI, Joined Cases T–191/96 and T–106/97 *CAS Succhi di Frutta v Commission* [1999] E.C.R. II–3181, paras 93–103; CFI (order of May 27, 2005), Case T–485/04 *COBB v Commission*, not reported.

[606] ECJ, Case 4/67 *Collignon v Commission* [1967] E.C.R. 365, at p. 372; ECJ, Case 108/79 *Belfiore v Commission* [1980] E.C.R. 1769, para.3; ECJ, Case 227/83 *Moussis v Commission* [1984] E.C.R. 3133, para.12; CFI, Case T–29/89 *Moritz v Commission* [1990] E.C.R. II–787, para.13; CFI, Joined Cases T–142/01 and T–283/01 *OPTUC v Commission* [2004] E.C.R. II–329, para.30.

[607] CFI (order of April 29, 2004), Case T–308/02 *SGL Carbon v Commission* [2004] E.C.R. II–1363; CFI (order of July 13, 2004), Case T–29/03 *Comunidad Autónoma de Andalucía v Commission*, not yet reported.

[608] See CFI (judgment of September 28, 2004), Case T–310/00 *MCI v Commission*, not yet reported, paras 44–45.

standing to bring proceedings.[609] The *lis pendens* objection will also be raised by the Community courts of their own motion.[610]

7–171 **Timeframe.** The admissibility of an action is judged by reference to the situation prevailing when the application was lodged.[611]

IV. CONSEQUENCES

A. RESULT OF AN APPLICATION FOR ANNULMENT

7–172 **Power of the Court limited to annulment.** If the action is well founded, the Court of Justice or the Court of First Instance will declare the contested act void.[612] If the application is not well founded, it will be dismissed.

The Court of Justice and the Court of First Instance may also declare part of the contested act void, either by annulling some of its provisions or by confining the declaration of nullity to some substantive or personal aspect.[613] The applicant may have sought partial annulment[614] or the Court of Justice or the Court of First Instance may itself take the view that only

---

[609] ECJ, Case C–298/00 P *Italy v Commission* [2004] E.C.R. I–4087, para.35; CFI, Case T–239/94 *EISA v Commission* [1997] E.C.R. II–1839, para.27; CFI (judgment of July 7, 2004), Joined Cases T–107/01 and T–175/01 *Société de Mines de Sacilor-Lormines v Commission*, not yet reported, paras 51–52; CFI (judgment of December 1, 2004), Case T–27/02 *Kronofrance v Commission*, not yet reported, para.30. See, however, with respect to a possible disappearance of an interest in bringing proceedings, 7–117, *supra*.

[610] ECJ, Joined Cases 45 and 49/70 *Bode v Commission* [1971] E.C.R. 465, para.11; ECJ, Case 75/72 *Perinciolo v Council* [1973] E.C.R. 511, para.5; CFI (order of March 10, 2005), Case T–288/00 *Gardena Hotels and Others v Commission*, not yet reported, para 30; CFI (order of July 14, 2005), Case T–79/05 *Gluiber v Commission*, not yet reported, para.7. This objection will be raised when more than one action is brought between the same parties seeking the annulment of the same act on the basis of the same submissions (see ECJ, Joined Cases 172 and 226/83 *Hoogovens Groep v Commission* [1985] E.C.R. 2831, para.9; ECJ, Joined Cases 358/85 and 51/86 *France v European Parliament* [1988] E.C.R. 4821, para.12; CFI (order of March 10, 2005), Joined Cases T–228/00, T–229/00, T–242/00, T–243/00, T–245/00 to T–248/00, T–250/00, T–252/00, T–256/00 to T–259/00, T–265/00, T–267/00, T–268/00, T–271/00, T–274/00 to T–276/00, T–281/00, T–287/00 to T–296/00 *Gruppo ormeggiatori del porto di Venezia and Others v Commission*, not yet reported, para.40; CFI (order of July 14, 2005), Case T–79/05 *Gluiber v Commission*, not yet reported, para.11.

[611] ECJ, Case 50/84 *Bensider and Others v Commission* [1984] E.C.R. 3991, para.8; CFI (order of February 15, 2005), Case T–229/02 *PKK and Others v Council*, not yet reported, para.30.

[612] EC Treaty, Art.231, first para.; EAEC Treaty, Art.147, first para. In an action for annulment, the applicant can claim only the annulment of the contested act (see CFI (order of February 28, 2005), Case T–108/03 *Von Pezold v Commission*, not yet reported, paras 56–58).

[613] See, by way of example, ECJ, Joined Cases 33, 44, 110, 226 and 285/86 *Stahlwerke Peine-Salzgitter and Others v Commission* [1988] E.C.R. 4309, point 1 of the operative part; CFI, Case T–26/90 *Finsider v Commission* [1992] E.C.R. II–1789, paras 52–57.

[614] If the applicant seeks only partial annulment of an act and the Court of Justice or the Court of First Instance considers that only annulment of the complete act is possible, it may not rule *ultra petita* (ECJ, Case 37/71 *Jamet v Commission* [1972] E.C.R. 483, para.12), but would have to declare the application inadmissible (see Joliet, *Le contentieux*, at 108).

some provisions of the contested act must be annulled.[615] However, partial annulment of a Community act is possible only if the elements to be annulled may be severed from the remainder of the act.[616] The requirement of severability is not satisfied where partial annulment of an act would have the effect of altering its substance.[617] This is because the Court of Justice and the Court of Justice cannot "revise" the contested act in annulment proceedings.

Ex tunc effect. The annulment of an act causes it to disappear from the Community legal order from the date on which it came into force (*ex tunc*), so that the parties to the proceedings are restored to the situation which they were in before it entered into force.[618]

7–173

The retroactive force of a declaration of nullity may be attenuated, pursuant to the second para. of Art.231 of the EC Treaty, in the light of the aim behind the action or on grounds of legal certainty.[619] Thus, the Court of Justice and the Court of First Instance may preserve the effects of the annulled act[620] or even declare that it is to remain in force until the

---

[615] ECJ, Case 27/76 *United Brands v Commission* [1978] E.C.R. 207, para.268.

[616] ECJ, Case 17/74 *Transocean Marine Paint Association v Commission* [1974] E.C.R. 1063, para.21; ECJ, Joined Cases C–68/94 and C–30/95 *France and Others v Commission* [1998] E.C.R. I–1375, paras 251–259; ECJ, Case C–29/99 *Commission v Council* [2002] E.C.R. I–11221, paras 45 and 46; ECJ, Case C–378/00 *Commission v European Parliament and Council* [2003] E.C.R. I–937, para.30; ECJ, Case C–239/01 *Germany v Commission* [2003] E.C.R. I–10333, para.33; ECJ, Case C 244/03 *France v European Parliament and Council* [2005] E.C.R. I–4021, para.12.

[617] ECJ, Case 34/86 *Council v European Parliament* [1986] E.C.R. 2155, paras 40–42; ECJ, Joined Cases C–68/94 and C–30/95 *France and Others v Commission* [1998] E.C.R. I–1375, para.257; ECJ, Case C–376/98 *Germany v European Parliament and Council* [2000] E.C.R. I–8419, para.117; ECJ, Case C–29/99 *Commission v Council* [2002] E.C.R. I–11221, para.46; ECJ, Case C–239/01 *Germany v Commission* [2003] E.C.R. I–10333, para.34; ECJ, Case C–244/03 *France v European Parliament and Council* [2004] E.C.R. I–4021, para.13. See also CFI, Joined Cases T–68, T–77 and T–78/89 *SIV and Others v Commission* [1992] E.C.R. II–1403, paras 318–339.

[618] ECJ, Case 22/70 *Commission v Council* (the *AETR* case) [1971] E.C.R. 263, paras 59–60; ECJ, Joined Cases 97, 193, 99 and 215/86 *Asteris and Others v Commission* [1988] E.C.R. 2181, para.30.

[619] The power of the Court of Justice to state which effects of the annulled regulation are to be considered as definitive has also been exercised with regard to other types of act: see ECJ, Case 92/78 *Simmenthal v Commission* [1979] E.C.R. 777, para.107—annulment of a decision; ECJ, Case 34/86 *Council v European Parliament* [1986] E.C.R. 2155, para.48—annulment of the act by which the President of the European Parliament declares the budget finally adopted; ECJ, Case C–295/90 *European Parliament v Council* [1992] E.C.R. I–4193, paras 22–27—annulment of a directive; ECJ, Case C–106/96 *United Kingdom v Commission* [1998] E.C.R. I–2729, paras 39–42—annulment of a decision pursuant to which contracts had been concluded under a Community action programme; ECJ, Case C–211/01 *Commission v Council* [2003] E.C.R. I–8913, paras 54–57—annulment of a Council decision concluding an international agreement between the EC and Bulgaria.

[620] ECJ, Case 45/86 *Commission v Council* [1987] E.C.R. 1493, para.23; ECJ, Case 51/87 *Commission v Council* [1988] E.C.R. 5459, para.22; ECJ, Case C–360/93 *European Parliament v Council* [1996] E.C.R. I–1195, paras 32–36; ECJ, Case C–271/94 *European Parliament v Council* [1996] E.C.R. I–1689, para.40; ECJ, Case C–22/96 *European Parliament v Council* [1998] E.C.R. I–3231, para.42.

competent institution has taken the necessary measures to give effect to the judgment annulling the act.[621]

B. AUTHORITY OF THE JUDGMENT

1. Declaration of nullity

7–174   *Erga omnes* **effect.** The declaration of nullity applies *erga omnes*. Consequently, an action for annulment of a measure which has already been declared void is to no purpose.[622] This is because the annulled act can no longer compromise the applicant's rights or interests.[623] In exceptional cases, the Court of Justice or the Court of First Instance may be prompted to curtail the general effect of the declaration of nullity on grounds of legal certainty.[624]

7–175   **Obligations for the institutions concerned.** The institution whose act has been declared void is required by the first para. of Art.233 of the EC Treaty to take the necessary measures to comply with the judgment.[625] The Court of Justice and the Court of First Instance have no power to indicate what measures should be taken.[626] The extent of the obligation to comply with the judgment is determined both by the operative part and by the grounds underlying the operative part.[627] The institution must comply with the

---

[621] ECJ, Case 81/72 *Commission v Council* [1973] E.C.R. 575, para.15; ECJ, Case 264/82 *Timex v Council and Commission* [1985] E.C.R. 849, para.32; ECJ, Case 275/87 *Commission v Council* [1989] E.C.R. 259, at 261; ECJ, Case C–295/90 *European Parliament v Council* [1992] E.C.R. I–4193, paras 22–27; ECJ, Case C–65/90 *European Parliament v Council* [1992] E.C.R. I–4593, paras 22–24; ECJ, Joined Cases C–164/97 and C–165/97 *European Parliament v Council* [1999] E.C.R. I–1139, paras 22–24; ECJ, Case C–211/01 *Commission v Council* [2003] E.C.R. I–8913, paras 54–57.

[622] ECJ, Case C–372/97 *Italy v Commission* [2004] E.C.R. I–3679, paras 33–38 (where the Court of First Instance has annulled a decision and an appeal against its judgment is dismissed, an action brought before the Court of Justice for the annulment of the same decision will be held to be to no purpose).

[623] ECJ, Case 3/54 *ASSIDER v High Authority* [1954 to 1956] E.C.R. 63, at 70.

[624] ECJ, Case 92/78 *Simmenthal v Commission* [1979] E.C.R. 777, para.107. See Bribosia and Rorive, "Le droit transitoire jurisprudentiel dans la pratique des juridictions européennes" (2002) R.D.ULB 125–152.

[625] Art.233 of the EC Treaty is not an autonomous remedy. As a result, a claim cannot be founded on that article. See CFI (order of April 21, 2005), Case T–28/03 *Holcim v Commission*, not yet reported, paras 27–40.

[626] ECJ, Case 53/85 *AKZO Chemie v Commission* [1986] E.C.R. 1965, para.23; ECJ, Case C–199/91 *Foyer Culturel du Sart-Tilman v Commission* [1993] E.C.R. I 2667, para.7; CFI, Case T–37/89 *Hanning v European Parliament* [1990] E.C.R. II–463, para.79; CFI, Case T–26/90 *Finsider v Commission* [1992] E.C.R. II–1789, para.65; CFI, Case T–75/95 *Günzler Aluminium v Commission* [1996] E.C.R. II–497, para.18; CFI (order of January 14, 2004), Case T–202/02 *Makedoniko Metro and Michaniki v Commission* [2004] E.C.R. II–181, para.53.

[627] ECJ, Joined Cases 97, 193, 99 and 215/86 *Asteris and Others v Commission* [1988] E.C.R. 2181, para.27; ECJ (order of July 13, 2000), Case C–8/99 P *Gòmez de Enterría y Sanchez v European Parliament* [2000] E.C.R. I–6031, paras 19–20; ECJ, Case C–458/98 P *Industrie des Poudres Sphériques v Council* [2000] E.C.R. I–8147, para.21; CFI, Case T–224/95 *Tremblay and Others v Commission* [1997] E.C.R. II–2215, para.72; CFI, Case T–154/98 *Asia Motor France and Others v Commission* [2000] E.C.R. II–3453, para.101.

judgment in good faith and may not take any measures liable to circumvent correct implementation of the judgment.[628]

However, the institution concerned is not required to consider whether, in the light of the reasoning of the judgment annulling the contested act, it needs to take measures in relation to persons for whom the partly annulled act remains in place.[629]

In addition, an institution which wishes to replace an annulled act may take up the decision-making procedure at the precise point where the illegality arose. This is because the annulment of the final decision does not necessarily affect the validity of the preparatory acts. The grounds of the judgment annulling the act set out precisely what the reasons are for the annulment pronounced in the operative part and the institution concerned must take account of them in replacing the annulled act.[630]

Compensation. The institution whose act is annulled may in addition be obliged, in complying with the judgment, to pay compensation for the damage originating in the illegality of the act annulled, provided that the all requirements for liability set out in the second para. of Art.288 of the EC Treaty are satisfied.[631] **7–176**

Time-limit. The institution has a reasonable time in which to comply with the judgment.[632] What constitutes a reasonable time depends on the nature of the measures having to be taken in order to carry out the judgment declaring the contested act void and on the attendant circumstances.[633] In the event that there are special difficulties in giving effect to the judgment annulling the contested act, the institution may comply with its obligation to give effect to the judgment by adopting any measure which fairly compensates for the disadvantage suffered by the applicant as a result of the unlawful conduct found.[634] Failure to comply with the judgment **7–177**

---

[628] See in a staff case: ECJ, Case C–153/99 P *Commission v Giannini* [2000] E.C.R. I–2891.

[629] ECJ, Case C–310/97 P *Commission v AssiDomän Kraft Products and Others* [1999] E.C.R. I–5363, paras 53–71, with a case note by Moloney (2000) C.M.L.Rev. 971–981; CFI, Case T–372/00 *Campolargo v Commission* [2002] E.C.R.-SC I–A–49, II–223, para.109 (as regards the duty to give effect to a judgment annulling an act which had already been carried out). See also ECJ, Case C–239/99 *Nachi Europe* [2001] E.C.R. I–1197, paras 24–26.

[630] ECJ, Case C–415/96 *Spain v Commission* [1998] E.C.R. I–6993, paras 30–32; CFI, Joined Cases T–305/94, T–306/94, T–307/94, T–313/94 to T–316/94, T–318/94, T–325/94, T–328/94, T–329/94 and T–335/94 *Limburgse Vinyl Maatschappij and Others v Commission* [1999] E.C.R. II–931, paras 183–193.

[631] CFI, Case T–220/97 *H & R Ecroyd v Commission* [1999] E.C.R. II–1677, para.56.

[632] ECJ, Case 266/82 *Turner v Commission* [1984] E.C.R. 1, para.5; CFI, Case T–120/89 *Stahlwerke Peine-Salzgitter v Commission* [1991] E.C.R. II–279, para.66; CFI, Case T–81/96 *Apostolidis and Others v Commission* [1997] E.C.R.-SC II–607, para.37 (English abstract at I–A–207).

[633] CFI, Case T–73/95 *Oliveira v Commission* [1997] E.C.R. II–381, para.41.

[634] CFI, Case T–91/95 *De Nil and Impens v Council* [1996] E..C.R.-SC II–959, para.34 (English abstract at I–A–327).

constitutes an infringement of Art.233 of the EC Treaty, which may cause the Community to incur liability.[635]

7–178 **Reimbursement of fines.** If the Court of Justice or the Court of First Instance annuls a decision finding an infringement of Art.81 and/or Art.82 of the EC Treaty and the undertakings concerned have already paid the fines imposed by the decision, the Commission is obliged, pursuant to Art.233 of the EC Treaty, to repay the fines plus interest to the undertakings which successfully brought the action for annulment.[636] If the Commission does not comply with this obligation, the undertaking concerned has the choice to either introduce an action for failure to act under Art.232 of the EC Treaty or an action for damages under Art.235 of the EC Treaty.[637] An explicit refusal on the part of the Commission to pay interest on the principal sum is itself a challengeable act.[638] The undertaking concerned may decide not to introduce an action for annulment of the Commission's refusal to pay interest, but bring a damages claim instead.[639]

Where, in contrast, the undertakings concerned have not paid the fine but furnished a bank guarantee, they are not entitled to claim the costs of that guarantee from the Commission. This is owing to the absence of any causal link between those costs and the unlawful act.[640]

Where the Court of Justice or the Court of First Instance annuls a decision finding an infringement of Art.81 and/or Art.82 of the EC Treaty, the Commission is not obliged to repay fines imposed by that decision to undertakings which did not bring an action for annulment. In the *AssiDomän* case, a number of Swedish woodpulp producers which had not brought an action for annulment of a Commission decision finding an infringement of Art.81(1) of the EC Treaty on account of concerted practices and imposing fines brought an action for annulment of a Commission decision rejecting their claim for repayment of the fines. The undertakings concerned had lodged a request for repayment with the Commission after the Court of Justice had annulled the original decision finding an infringement of Art.81(1) as far as the undertakings which had brought an action against

---

[635] CFI, Case T–11/00 *Hautem v EIB* [2000] E.C.R. II–4019, para.45. Art.223 of the EC Treaty does not, however, constitute an autonomous remedy. See CFI (judgment of April 21, 2005), Case T–28/03 *Holcim v Commission*, not yet reported, paras 27–40.

[636] CFI, Case T–171/99 *Corus UK v Commission* [2001] E.C.R. I–2967, paras 54–58.

[637] CFI (order of May 4, 2005), Case T–86/03 *Holcim v Commission*, not yet reported, paras 33–34.

[638] ECJ, Case C–123/03 P *Commission v Greencore* [2004] E.C.R. I–11647, para.47; CFI (order of May 4, 2005), Case T–86/03 *Holcim v Commission*, not yet reported, para.44. The mere fact that the fine has been repaid without interest cannot be regarded as a refusal to pay as far as the interest is concerned. Accordingly, the Commission's express refusal to pay interest in subsequent correspondence cannot be regarded as a confirmatory act against which an action for annulment will not lie (*ibid.*, paras 39–47).

[639] CFI (order of May 4, 2005), Case T–86/03 *Holcim v Commission*, not yet reported.

[640] CFI (order of April 21, 2005), Case T–28/03 *Holcim v Commission*, not yet reported, paras 119–132.

it were concerned. The Court of First Instance had held that it would be inconsistent with the principle of legality for the Commission not to have a duty to examine its initial position in relation to undertakings which had not brought an action for annulment of the original decision after the Court of Justice had held that the alleged concerted practice was not proved.[641] On appeal, however, the Court of Justice did not follow the lower court but relied on the principle that where the contested act is not challenged by its addressees within the time-limit prescribed by Art.230 of the EC Treaty, it becomes definitive *vis-à-vis* those addressees. Moreover, it held that the authority of a judgment annulling a measure cannot apply to the situation of persons who were not parties to the proceedings and with regard to whom the judgment cannot therefore have decided anything whatever.[642]

2. Dismissal of an application for annulment

Res judicata. After a judgment has been given dismissing an application for annulment, the applicant may not raise the same pleas in another action brought against the same act.[643] An action for annulment which is brought after a judgment dismissing an action brought between the same parties, has the same purpose and is based on the same submissions as the application which led to the first judgment will be inadmissible on the ground that the first judgment has the authority of *res judicata*.[644] But the principle of *res judicata* extends only to matters of fact and law actually or necessarily settled in the judicial decision in question.[645]

7–179

---

[641] CFI, Case T–227/95 *AssiDomän Kraft Products and Others v Commission* [1997] E.C.R. II–1185, para.72.

[642] ECJ, Case C–310/97 P *Commission v AssiDomän Kraft Products and Others* [1999] E.C.R. I–5363, paras 53–71, with a case note by Moloney (2000) C.M.L.Rev. 971–981.

[643] ECJ, Case 62/82 *Italy v Commission* [1983] E.C.R. 687, paras 17–18. It seems that any person is barred from raising the same pleas in another action for annulment or action for damages relating to the same act: CFI (judgment of October 19, 2005), Case T–415/03 *Cofradía de pescadores de "San Pedro" and Others v Council*, not yet reported, paras 66–67.

[644] ECJ (order of April 1, 1987), Joined Cases 159 and 267/84, 12 and 264/85 *Ainsworth v Commission* [1987] E.C.R. 1579, para.1; CFI, Joined Cases T–116/01 and T–118/01 *P & O European Ferries and Others v Commission* [2003] E.C.R. II–2957, paras 75–82, in which the Court of First Instance held that *res judicata* could not be pleaded in respect of an earlier judgment pronouncing annulment in new proceedings seeking to annul the decision taken to comply with that judgment. The reason was that the proceedings did not have the same subject-matter.

[645] ECJ (order of November 28, 1996), Case C–277/95 P *Lenz v Commission* [1996] E.C.R. I–6109, para.50. CFI, Case T–333/01 *Meyer v Commission* [2003] E.C.R. II–117, paras 22–27: *res judicata* did not mean that a first judgment in which the application was held inadmissible caused a second application between the same parties and having the same subject-matter to be inadmissible. This was because, in the first judgment, the Court of First Instance decided no point of fact or law by which it could be bound in the second proceedings.

V. THE CONSTITUTION

7–180 **General.** The changes which the Constitution is intended to introduce as regards annulment actions cover (i) the enlargement of the category of defendants against which annulment proceedings may be instituted, (ii) the inclusion of the Committee of the Regions in the category of "semi-privileged" applicants and (iii) the improvement of judicial protection for individuals.

A. ENLARGEMENT OF THE CATEGORY OF DEFENDANTS AGAINST WHICH AN ANNULMENT ACTION MAY BE BROUGHT

7–181 **Defendants.** Under the first para. of Art.230 of the EC Treaty, acts of the European Parliament, the Council, the Commission and the European Central Bank can, subject to certain conditions, be the subject of an action for annulment. Art.III-365(1) of the Constitution now provides that the Court can also review the legality of acts of the European Council and of acts of bodies, offices or agencies of the Union intended to produce legal effects *vis-à-vis* third parties. Since, under the provisions of the Constitution, the European Council is one of the institutions[646] of the Union which adopts acts intended to produce legal effects,[647] it was only logical to include its acts amongst those against which an action for annulment will lie insofar as they are intended to produce legal effects *vis-à-vis* third parties. As regards the acts of bodies, offices or agencies of the Union, their inclusion amongst the acts that may be challenged in an action for annulment does not constitute the mere incorporation of the existing *acquis* into the Constitution given that the question of the admissibility of annulment actions brought against acts of bodies, offices or agencies of the Community has not yet been settled by the Court of Justice.[648]

B. INCLUSION OF THE COMMITTEE OF THE REGIONS IN THE CATEGORY OF "SEMI-PRIVILEGED" APPLICANTS

7–182 **Committee of the Regions.** The EC Treaty already includes a category of "semi-privileged" applicants[649] which are entitled to challenge a Community act where the action is brought for the purpose of protecting their prerogatives. This category, which under the third para. of Art.230 of the EC Treaty is made up of the Court of Auditors and the European Central Bank, is extended by Art.III–365(3) of the Constitution to cover the

---

[646] Constitution, Art.I–19.
[647] See, for example, Art.I–20(2), second subpara., Art.I–24(3) and (4), and Art.I–26(6) of the Constitution.
[648] See 7–057, *supra*.
[649] See 7–063, *supra*.

Committee of the Regions. The former case-law developed when the European Parliament was still only a semi-privileged applicant will have a bearing on the assessment of the admissibility of future actions brought by the Committee of the Regions (as well as by the Court of Auditors and the European Central Bank).[650]

Violation of the principle of subsidiarity. In one specific situation, namely where the Committee of the Regions considers that a legislative act infringes the principle of subsidiarity, it will be entitled to bring an action for annulment even if the action is not brought for the purpose of protecting the Committee's prerogatives. Under the Protocol on the application of the principles of subsidiarity and proportionality,[651] the Court of Justice is to have jurisdiction in actions brought by the Committee of the Regions on grounds of infringement of the principle of subsidiarity by a European legislative act for the adoption of which the Constitution provides that it be consulted.[652] The action will be admissible regardless whether the Committee was actually consulted.[653]

7–183

C. IMPROVEMENT OF JUDICIAL PROTECTION FOR INDIVIDUALS

Acts of general application. As indicated above, the fourth para. of Art.230 of the EC Treaty seems totally to preclude individuals from bringing an action for annulment against measures of general application. The reason is that, in accordance with a literal reading of this provision, an individual may bring an action for annulment only against "genuine" decisions and "disguised" decisions, that is to say, decisions adopted in the form of regulations.[654] However, the case-law has evolved so that the only question to be determined in relation to the admissibility of proceedings brought by an individual against an act which is not addressed to that person is whether the act is of direct and individual concern to that person.[655] If this is the case, the action will be admissible even if the annulment of a measure of general application is sought.[656]

7–184

---

[650] *Ibid.*

[651] Art.8.

[652] If, in the context of one and the same action, the Committee of the Regions raises a plea relating to the infringement of the principle of subsidiarity as well as other pleas, it may be argued that the latter pleas will be admissible only if it can be shown that they are raised for the purpose of protecting the Committee's prerogatives.

[653] An action on the same grounds may also be brought by a Member State on behalf of their national Parliament or a chamber of it (Protocol on the application of the principles of subsidiarity and proportionality, Art.8).

[654] ECJ, Case 101/76 *Koninklijke Scholten Honig* [1977] E.C.R. 797, at 805.

[655] ECJ, Case C–309/89 *Codorníu v Council* [1994] E.C.R. I–1853, para.19; ECJ, Case C–452/98 *Nederlandse Antillen v Council* [2001] E.C.R. I–8973, para.55.

[656] See 7–070, *supra*. ECJ, Case C–309/89 *Codorníu v Council* [1994] E.C.R. I–1853; CFI, Case T–243/01 *Sony Computer Entertainment Europe v Commission* [2003] E.C.R. II–4189, paras 58–76.

Art.III-365(4) of the Constitution codifies this development in the case-law by providing that "[a]ny natural or legal person may [. . .] institute proceedings against an act addressed to that person or which is of direct and individual concern to him or her".[657]

Even if the general nature of the challenged act does not as such preclude the admissibility of the action for annulment, an individual will normally not be successful in demonstrating that he or she is individually concerned by such an act. Indeed, according to settled case-law, persons are individually concerned by an act only if that act affects them by reason of certain attributes which are peculiar to them, or by reason of factual circumstances which differentiate them from all other persons and thereby distinguish them individually in the same way as the person addressed.[658]

The *rationale* of this case-law lies in the fact that the possibility, or even the obligation,[659] for national courts to make a reference for a preliminary ruling to the Court of Justice is deemed to afford effective protection for the rights which individuals derive from Community law. This is because Community measures of general application are frequently implemented in the various Member States by national measures which can be challenged before national courts and those courts may—or must—refer a question to the Court of Justice on the validity of the Community act on which the national measure is based.

7–185 **Problem of effective judicial protection.** In some cases, it happens that an individual has no remedy in order to challenge the legality of a provision of Community law in a national court. This can occur in particular where a regulation does not require the Member States to adopt any implementing measures. Such a situation has already occurred in the cases of *Jégo-Quéré* and *Unión de Pequeños Agricultores*, to which reference has already been made.[660] However, the Court of Justice has refused to relax its interpretation of the concept of "individual concern", even where the result is that in certain cases individuals could not enjoy effective legal protection.[661] However, the Court of Justice did add that it is possible to envisage a system of judicial review of the legality of Community measures of general application different from that established by the EC Treaty, "but that it is for the Member States, if necessary, in accordance with Art.48 EU, to reform the system currently in force".[662]

---

657 See Cremer, "Der Rechtsschutz des Einzelnen gegen Sekundärrechtsakte der Union gem. Art.[III–365] Abs. 4 Konventsentwurf des Vertrags über eine Verfassung für Europa" (2004) Eu.GR.Z. 577–583.

658 See ECJ, Case 25/62 *Plaumann v Commission* [1963] E.C.R. 95, at 107; ECJ, Case C–321/95 P *Greenpeace Council and Others v Commission* [1998] E.C.R. I–1651, para.7.

659 See 7–086, *supra*.

660 CFI, Case T–177/01 *Jégo-Quéré v Commission* [2002] E.C.R. II–2365; CFI (order of November 20, 1999), Case T–173/98 *Unión de Pequeños Agricultores v Council* [1999] E.C.R. II–3357.

661 ECJ, Case C–50/00 P *Unión de Pequeños Agricultores v Council* [2002] E.C.R. I–6677; ECJ, Case C–263/02 P *Commission v Jégo-Quéré* [2004] E.C.R. I–3425.

662 Case C–50/00 P *Unión de Pequeños Agricultores v Council* [2002] E.C.R. I–6677, para.45.

Opening for regulatory acts which do not entail implementing measures. It is in this context that the new Art.III-365(4) of the Constitution should be understood.[663] It provides that "[a]ny natural or legal person may [. . .] institute proceedings against an act addressed to that person or which is of direct and individual concern to him or her, and against a regulatory act which is of direct concern to him or her and does not entail implementing measures". Art.III-365(4) recaptures the substance of the fourth para.Art.230 of the EC Treaty but relaxes the admissibility conditions—by deleting the "individually concerned" condition—for regulatory acts which do not require implementing measures.

7–186

Concept of "regulatory act". The concept of a "regulatory act" is not defined among the legal instruments referred to in Art.I-33 of the Constitution. It is apparent, however, from the *actes préparatoires*[664] that the authors of that provision had in mind non-legislative acts of general application or, in other words, regulations and decisions with no specific addressees.[665]

7–187

Extent of the opening. Once the provisions of the Constitution enter into force, an action for annulment brought by an individual against binding non-legislative acts of general application will be admissible if the individual successfully demonstrates that the act does not entail implementing measures and is of direct concern to him.[666]

7–188

It must be stressed, however, that the opening created by Art.III-365(4) of the Constitution is not as large as the one envisaged by the Court of First Instance in its judgment in *Jégo-Quéré*.[667] This is because the relaxation of the admissibility conditions in *Jégo-Quéré* would have covered both legislative and non-legislative acts of general application. In contrast, the opening created by Art.III-365(4) of the Constitution only covers non-legislative acts of general application. In other words, an action for annulment brought by an individual against a European law will be admissible only if the applicant successfully demonstrates that the act is of direct and *individual* (within the meaning of the *Plaumann* case law[668]) concern to him or her irrespective as

---

[663] CONV 734/03.

[664] CONV 734/03.

[665] If a third party challenges a decision addressed to a specific addressee (see Constitution, Art.I-33(1), fifth subpara.), he or she would have to satisfy the traditional test set out in the *Plaumann* case-law.

[666] As far as framework laws and regulations which entail implementing measures are concerned, the system of judicial protection will remain unchanged. An action for annulment brought by an individual against such an act will in principle be inadmissible, since the applicant will not be directly concerned by a Community act which still has to be implemented at national level (see, for example, CFI, Joined Cases T–172/98 and T–175/98 to T–177/98 *Salamander and Others v European Parliament and Council* [2000] E.C.R. II–2487, paras 52 and 71).

[667] CFI, Case T–177/01 *Jégo-Quéré v Commission* [2002] E.C.R. II–2365.

[668] ECJ, Case 25/62 *Plaumann v Commission* [1963] E.C.R. 95.

to whether the act in question requires further implementation at national level.

So, Art.III-365(4) does not improve the legal protection afforded to individuals with regard to European laws. Indeed, since individuals will be individually concerned by a European law only in very exceptional situations,[669] they will normally not be in a position to challenge such acts before the Court of First Instance by bringing an action for annulment.

---

[669] See 7–080 and 7–081, *supra*. For a wider discussion of the consequences of Art.III–365(4), see Corthaut, "An Effective Remedy For All? Paradoxes and Controversies in Respect of Judicial Protection in the Field of the CFSP under the European Constitution" (2005) Tilburg For.L.Rev. 110, at 131–136.

CHAPTER 8

THE ACTION FOR FAILURE TO ACT

I. SUBJECT-MATTER

A. GENERAL

Judicial review covers both action and inaction. The action for failure to 8–001
act is provided for in Art.232 of the EC Treaty and Art.148 of the EAEC
Treaty. Its object is a declaration on the part of the Court of Justice or the
Court of First Instance that the defendant institution acted unlawfully by
failing to take a decision.[670] Accordingly, the action for failure to act forms
part of the whole system of judicial review, which covers both action and
inaction on the part of Community institutions.

B. SUBJECT-MATTER OF AN ACTION FOR FAILURE TO ACT

Subject-matter. The subject-matter of the action is confined to an inquiry 8–002
into whether the omission to take a given decision was lawful.

Omission to take a decision. In the first place, the institution against which 8–003
the proceedings are brought must have failed to take a decision.[671] An
action for failure to act will be admissible only if the institution concerned
has first been called upon to act. If, within two months of being so called
upon, the institution concerned has not defined its position, the action may
be brought within a further period of two months.

The subject-matter of the action will cease to exist if the act to which it
relates is adopted after the action was brought but before judgment, since
then a declaration by the Court of Justice or the Court of First Instance
that the initial failure to act was unlawful can no longer bring about the
consequences prescribed by Art.233 of the EC Treaty.[672]

---

[670] ECJ, Case 377/87 *European Parliament v Council* [1988] E.C.R. 4017, para.9; ECJ, Case
383/87 *Commission v Council* [1988] E.C.R. 4051, para.9.
[671] Opinion of Advocate General J. Mischo in ECJ, Case 377/87 *European Parliament v
Council* [1988] E.C.R. 4017, at 4027. See also ECJ, Case 8/71 *Komponistenverband v
Commission* [1971] E.C.R. 705.
[672] ECJ, Case 377/87 *European Parliament v Council* [1988] E.C.R. 4017, para.10; ECJ, Case
383/87 *Commission v Council* [1988] E.C.R. 4051, para.10; ECJ, Joined Cases C–15 and C–

329

8–004 **Duty to act.** Furthermore, a failure to take a decision is unlawful only if the defendant institution was under a duty to act.[673] The duty to act must derive from superior Community law.[674] The reference in Art.232 of the EC Treaty to "this Treaty" does not mean that only a duty to act enshrined in an article of the Treaty may be enforced by means of an action for failure to act. In fact, an action will lie on the basis of any rule of Community law which is as such binding on the defendant institution and contains a duty to act.[675]

The Commission has no duty to institute infringement proceedings under Art.226 of the EC Treaty against a Member State which violates Community law. If the Commission leaves a complaint filed for that purpose

---

108/91 *Buckl and Others v Commission* [1992] E.C.R. I-6061, paras 13–18; ECJ, Case C–25/91 *Pesqueras Echebastar v Commission* [1993] E.C.R. I-1719, paras 11–12; ECJ (order of June 10, 1993), Case C–41/92 *Liberal Democrats v European Parliament* [1993] E.C.R. I-3153, para.4; CFI, Case T–28/90 *Asia Motor France and Others v Commission* [1992] E.C.R. II-2285, paras 34–38; CFI (order of November 29, 1993), Case T–56/92 *Koelman v Commission* [1993] E.C.R. II-1267, para.28; CFI, Case T–32/93 *Ladbroke Racing v Commission* [1994] E.C.R. II-1015, para.22; CFI (order of November 26, 1996), Case T–164/95 *Kuchlenz-Winter v European Parliament* [1996] E.C.R. II-1593, para.36; CFI (order of November 26, 1996), Case T–226/95 *Kuchlenz-Winter v Commission* [1996] E.C.R. II-1619, para.30; CFI, Case T–212/95 *Oficemen v Commission* [1997] E.C.R. II-1161, paras 65–68; CFI (order of November 26, 1997), Case T–39/97 *T. Port v Commission* [1997] E.C.R. II-2125, para.22; CFI, Case T–212/99 *Intervet International v Commission* [2002] E.C.R. II-1145, para.67; CFI, Joined Cases T–344/00 and T–345/00 *CEVA and Pharmacia Entreprises v Commission* [2002] E.C.R. II-1445, para.85; CFI, Joined Cases T–297/01 and T–298/01 *SIC v Commission* [2004] E.C.R. II–743, paras 57–58 (this also applies where the act concerned was not submitted within a reasonable time).

673 ECJ, Case 64/82 *Tradax v Commission* [1984] E.C.R. 1359, paras 22–23; CFI, Case T–277/94 *AITEC v Commission* [1996] E.C.R. II-351, paras 65-72 (as for the question whether an action should be brought in the Court of Justice, either under Art.226 or under Art.88(2) (concerning State aid), this depends on how the Commission uses its discretion; it does not entail any obligation which may be invoked by the applicant for the purposes of establishing a failure to act on the part of the defendant. Such a claim will be inadmissible); CFI (order of November 26, 1996), Case T–167/95 *Kuchlenz-Winter v Council* [1996] E.C.R. II-1607, para.24; CFI, Case T–334/02 *Viomichania Syskevasias Typopoiisis Kai Syntirisis Agrotikon Proïonton v Commission* [2003] E.C.R. II-5121, paras 42–44. But see CFI, Case T–17/96 *TF1 v Commission* [1999] E.C.R. II-1757, in which the Court of First Instance held that the applicant found itself in exceptional circumstances which allowed it to bring an action against the Commission for failure to adopt a decision under Art.86(3) of the EC Treaty even though the Commission has a wide discretion in this regard. It remains, however, to be seen whether this case-law is still good law in the light of ECJ, Case C–141/02 P *Commission v T–Mobile Austria* [2005] E.C.R. I-1283 (see 7–034, *supra*). See also Dony and Ronse, "Réflexions sur la spécificité du recours en carence" (2000) C.D.E. 596–636.

674 Such a duty can arise, for example, out of Art.233 of the EC Treaty. An action for failure to act is the appropriate means for obtaining a declaration that the failure by an institution to take the necessary measures to comply with a judgment of the Court of Justice or the Court of First Instance is unlawful (CFI, Joined Cases T–297/01 and T–298/01 *SIC v Commission* [2004] E.C.R. II–743, para.32).

675 ECJ, Joined Cases 10 and 18/68 *"Eridania" Zuccherifici Nationali and Others v Commission* [1969] E.C.R. 459, para.16, where the Court of Justice used the expression "provision of Community law".

unanswered, an action for failure to act will not lie (see 5–028, *supra*).[676] However, the Commission is under an obligation to act upon a complaint regarding a violation of competition rules.[677] But the earliest moment at which the Commission may be under an obligation to take a decision on a complaint is when it has been able to examine all the considerations of fact and law brought to its notice by the complainant.[678]

Identification of the act to be taken. The applicant must state what act the defendant institution has failed to adopt, failing which its application will be inadmissible.[679] It must also describe the act sufficiently precisely in order that the Court of Justice or the Court of First Instance may give a judgment which will enable the defendant institution to take the necessary measures to comply with it in accordance with Art.233 of the EC Treaty.[680]   **8–005**

The act must be capable of having legal effects. The duty to take a decision must give rise to an act which is capable of having legal effects.[681] The nature of the legal effects required, however, is not always the same.   **8–006**

If the action for failure to act is brought by a natural or legal person, the defendant institution must have failed to "address to that person any act other than a recommendation or an opinion" (EC Treaty, Art.232, third para.). It follows that where an action for failure to act is brought by a natural or legal person, it will be admissible only if it relates to the defendant institution's failure to adopt a binding act.[682]

If, in contrast, the action for failure to act is brought by a Member State or a Community institution, the act which was not performed does not

---

[676] CFI (order of February 19, 1997), Case T–117/96 *Intertronic v Commission* [1997] E.C.R. II–141, para.32; CFI (order of June 5, 2002), Case T–143/02 *Olive v Commission and Others*, not reported, para.11.

[677] For complaints alleging violation of Art.81 and/or Art.82 of the EC Treaty, see the case-law cited in 8–015, *infra*. In CFI, Case T–95/96 *Gestevisión Telecinco v Commission* [1998] E.C.R. II–3407, the Court held that the Commission's failure to deal with a complaint lodged by a competitor of a recipient of non-notified State aid constituted a failure to act. The Commission is likewise under an obligation to act where an undertaking lodges a complaint to the effect that a competitor is involved in a non-notified concentration falling within the scope of Regulation No 4064/89 (now Regulation No 139/2004) (ECJ, Case C–170/02 P *Schlüsselverlag J.S. Moser and Others v Commission* [2003] E.C.R. I–9889, paras 27–30). For the Commission's handling of a complaint relating to the grant of State aid to a producer of military goods and the application of Arts 296 and 298 of the EC Treaty, see CFI, Case T–26/01 *Fiocchi Munizioni v Commission* [2003] E.C.R. II–3951).

[678] CFI (order of July 6, 1998), Case T–286/97 *Goldstein v Commission* [1998] E.C.R. II–2629, paras 26–28; see also CFI (order of January 10, 2005), Case T–209/04 *Spain v Commission*, not yet reported, paras 41–44.

[679] ECJ (order of May 7, 1980), Joined Cases 114–117/79 *Fournier v Commission* [1980] E.C.R. 1529, at 1531.

[680] ECJ, Case 13/83 *European Parliament v Council* [1985] E.C.R. 1513, paras 35–37.

[681] Opinion of Advocate General J. Mischo in ECJ, Case 377/87 *European Parliament v Council* [1988] E.C.R. 4017, para.30, at 4029.

[682] Consequently, individuals cannot challenge an institution's failure to adopt a non-binding act, not even where the failure to act takes the form of an express refusal, see ECJ, Case 15/70 *Chevalley v Commission* [1970] E.C.R. 975.

necessarily have to be binding in order to have legal effects and so an action may be brought in this case too. For instance, an action may be brought against the Commission if it fails to submit a proposal for a legislative measure to the Council relating to a matter on which the Community is under an obligation to legislate.[683] The rationale is that the Commission proposal is necessary in order to enable the Council and the European Parliament to play their respective roles in the legislative process.[684]

C. RELATIONSHIP BETWEEN THE ACTION FOR ANNULMENT AND THE ACTION FOR FAILURE TO ACT

8–007 **No necessary link between the two forms of action.** The action for annulment and the action for failure to act provide for one and the same means of recourse. Indeed, the possibility for individuals to assert their rights should not depend upon whether the Union has acted or failed to act.[685]

There is, however, no necessary link between the action for annulment and the action for failure to act since the action for failure to act does not always enable the applicant to induce the adoption of a measure which can be the subject of an action for annulment.[686]

First, Member States or Community institutions may compel an institution to adopt a measure by means of an action for failure to act, even though no action for annulment would be available against the act in question. Accordingly, the European Parliament is entitled to a declaration from the Court of Justice that the Council's failure to lay before it a draft budget is unlawful. Yet once the draft budget has been adopted, no action for annulment will lie against it since it is a preparatory act.[687]

---

[683] ECJ (order of July 11, 1996), Case C–445/93 *European Parliament v Commission*, not reported (failure of the Commission to submit the necessary proposals pursuant to Arts 14 and 211 of the EC Treaty for the liberalisation of the movement of persons; on an application from the European Parliament, an order was given declaring that there was no need to proceed to judgment following the submission of the relevant proposal by the Commission). If the Council is not under a duty to legislate, the Commission cannot be obliged to submit a proposal for a legislative measure to the Council (Lauwaars, *Lawfulness and Legal Force of Community Decisions* (Sijthoff, Leyden, 1973), at 109). For a case in which the Council was under a duty to legislate, see ECJ, Case 13/83 *European Parliament v Council* [1985] E.C.R. 1513, paras 54–71.

[684] The same reasoning applies to decision-making in connection with the Community budget: ECJ, Case 377/87 *European Parliament v Council* [1988] E.C.R. 4017 (action brought against the Council for failure to act on the ground that it had failed to place before the European Parliament, in accordance with Art.272(4) of the EC Treaty, a draft general budget of the Community for the following financial year by no later than October 5).

[685] ECJ, Case 15/70 *Chevalley v Commission* [1970] E.C.R. 975, para.6; CFI, Case C–68/95 *T. Port* [1996] E.C.R. I–6065, para.59.

[686] ECJ, Case 302/87 *European Parliament v Council* [1988] E.C.R. 5615, para.16.

[687] *Ibid.*

Second, even if the applicant seeks the adoption of a binding act,[688] it happens that the defendant institution can put an end to its failure to act by adopting a non-binding act against which an action for annulment would not lie. Since the failure to act has been terminated, an action for failure to act will no longer lie, unless at a later stage a further failure to act on the part of the defendant institution can be established in the light of new circumstances (see 8–014 and 8–015, *infra*).

Annulment action will lie only against a binding act. Once the institution **8–008** adopts a binding act, an action will lie against it. The act in question may be a refusal to adopt the act sought[689] or the adoption of an act different from the one requested.[690] If, however, the failure to act is terminated by a definition of a position not constituting a binding act (see 8–014 and 8–015, *infra*), no action may be brought.[691]

The Court of Justice and the Court of First Instance will not tolerate any improper use of the action for failure to act. In the event that an institution has adopted a binding act, only an action for annulment will be available to challenge it. If the applicant has allowed the period for bringing an action to expire, it cannot provoke a failure to act by addressing a request to the institution concerned to revoke the measure adversely affecting it.[692] If the institution does not comply with such a request, moreover, it is not in breach of any obligation to act.

II. Identity of the Parties

A. Defendants

Institutions and the European Central Bank. Under Art.232 of the EC **8–009** Treaty, an action for failure to act may be brought against the Council,

---

[688] Unlike Member States and Community institutions, a natural or legal person can seek only the adoption of a binding act (*e.g.* a decision of the Commission finding an infringement of Arts 81 and 82 EC Treaty) under Art.232 of the EC Treaty. For natural and legal persons, "[t]he concept of a measure capable of giving rise to an action is identical in Arts 173 and 175*[now Arts 230 and 232]*" (ECJ, Case 15/70 *Chevalley v Commission* [1970] E.C.R. 975, para.6).

[689] ECJ, Case 42/71 *Nordgetreide v Commission* [1972] E.C.R. 105, para.4 (an action for annulment brought by an individual will then be admissible if the measure sought, constituting the subject-matter of the refusal, satisfies the conditions laid down in the fourth para. of Art.230 of the EC Treaty); ECJ, Case 44/81 *Germany v Commission* [1982] E.C.R. 1855, para.6.

[690] ECJ, Case 8/71 *Komponistenverband v Commission* [1971] E.C.R. 705, para.2.

[691] ECJ, Case 48/65 *Lütticke v Commission* [1966] E.C.R. 19, at 27; ECJ, Case 42/71 *Nordgetreide v Commission* [1972] E.C.R. 105.

[692] ECJ, Joined Cases 10 and 18/68 *"Eridania" Zurcherifici Nationali and Others v Commission* [1969] E.C.R. 459, para.17.

the Commission, the European Parliament[693] or the European Central Bank.

B. APPLICANTS

8–010 **Institutions and Member States.** Art.232 of the EC Treaty authorises "the Member States and the other institutions of the Community" to bring an action for failure to act. It confers that right of action on *all* the Community institutions.[694] The European Central Bank has the right to bring an action for failure to act "in the areas falling within [its] competence". Only the Court of Justice and the Court of First instance have no such right of action. This is because they are responsible for legal protection and do not themselves seek it.[695]

8–011 **Individual applicants.** Under the third para.of Art.232 of the EC Treaty, a natural or legal person may complain to the Court of First Instance that "an institution of the Community has failed to address to that person any act other than a recommendation or an opinion". An action brought by a natural or legal person can therefore relate only to a failure to adopt an act which has a direct influence on that person's legal position.[696]

The words "address to" preclude an applicant who is a natural or legal person from bringing an action for failure to adopt an act of general application.[697] On the other hand, in spite of the more stringent wording of the third para.of Art.232 by comparison with the fourth para.of Art.230 of the EC Treaty,[698] it is enough for a natural or legal person to be directly

---

[693] CFI (order of May 22, 2000), Case T–103/99 *Associazione delle Cantine Sociali Venete v European Ombudsman and European Parliament* [2000] E.C.R. II-4165, para.46 (the European Ombudsman is not a Community institution within the meaning of Art.232 of the EC Treaty).

[694] ECJ, Case 13/83 *European Parliament v Council* [1985] E.C.R. 1513, paras 17–18. Now that the Court of Auditors is an "institution" (EC Treaty, Art.7), it may also bring an action for failure to act.

[695] Opinion of Advocate General C.O. Lenz in ECJ, Case 13/83 *European Parliament v Council* [1985] E.C.R. 1513, at 1519.

[696] ECJ, Case 6/70 *Borromeo v Commission* [1970] E.C.R. 815; ECJ, Case 15/70 *Chevalley v Commission* [1970] E.C.R. 975; ECJ (order of October 17, 1984), Joined Cases 83 and 84/84 *NM v Commission and Council* [1984] E.C.R. 3571, para.10; ECJ (order of March 30, 1990), Case C–371/89 *Emrich v Commission* [1990] E.C.R. I-1555, para.6; CFI (order of May 27, 1994), Case T–5/94 *J v Commission* [1994] E.C.R. II-391, para.16; CFI (order of July 4, 1994), Case T–13/94 *Century Oils Hellas v Commission* [1994] E.C.R. II-431, para.13.

[697] ECJ, Case 15/71 *Mackprang v Commission* [1971] E.C.R. 797, para.4; ECJ, Case 134/73 *Holtz & Willemsen v Council* [1974] E.C.R. 1, para.5; ECJ, Case 90/78 *Granaria v Council and Commission* [1979] E.C.R. 1081, paras 12–15; ECJ (order of July 11, 1979), Case 60/79 *Fédération Nationale des Producteurs de Vins de Table et Vins de Pays v Commission* [1979] E.C.R. 2429, at 2433; CFI (order of November 26, 1996), Case T–167/95 *Kuchlenz-Winter v Council* [1996] E.C.R. II-1607, para.21; *cf.* McDonagh, "Pour un élargissement des conditions de recevabilité des recours en contrôle de la légalité par des personnes privées en droit communautaire: le cas de l'Art.175[now Art.232] du traité CE" (1994) C.D.E. 607–637.

[698] See also EC Treaty, Art.232, third para., of which the French and German versions are consistent in this regard: "de lui addresser un acte autre qu'une recommendation ou un avis"; "einen anderen Akt als eine Empfehlung oder eine Stellungnahme an sie zu richten".

and individually concerned by the act which the institution failed to adopt and which, formally, ought to have been addressed to another person (*e.g.* a Member State). This is because the Court of Justice has held that Arts 230 and 232 of the EC Treaty merely prescribe one and the same method of recourse.[699] Consequently, the subject-matter of the right of action of a natural or legal person is not confined to the defendant institution's failure expressly to address a particular act to the applicant.[700] The idea behind this is to underscore the parallel between the action for annulment and the action for failure to act as far as the measure at issue is concerned[701] on the ground that the possibility for individuals to assert their rights should not depend upon whether the institution concerned has acted or failed to act.[702]

III. Special Characteristics

A. Pre-litigation procedure

The duty to raise the matter. An action for failure to act is admissible only   8–012
if, before proceedings are brought, the defendant institution is requested to adopt the measure in question. The idea behind raising the matter with the institution in this way is to prompt it to adopt the measure within two months or at least to define its position in regard to the alleged failure to act.[703] The matter must be raised within a reasonable time after the

---

[699] ECJ, Case 15/70 *Chevalley v Commission* [1970] E.C.R. 975, para.6; ECJ, Case C–68/95 *T. Port v Commission* [1996] E.C.R. I-6065, para.59; CFI, Case T–17/96 *TF1 v Commission* [1999] E.C.R. II-1757, para.27; CFI (order of May 22, 2000), Case T–103/99 *Associazione delle Cantine Sociali Venete v European Ombudsman and European Parliament* [2000] E.C.R. II-4165, para.47.

[700] See ECJ, Case 134/73 *Holtz v Council* [1974] E.C.R. 1, para.5: "It appears that the action commenced by the applicant has the object of procuring a provision of a general regulatory character having the same legal scope as Regulation No 1336/72 and not an act concerning it directly and individually". An indirect interest which a natural or legal person might have in the adoption of the act requested is completely insufficient for him to be regarded as a potential addressee of the act, ECJ, Case 246/81 *Lord Bethell v Commission* [1982] E.C.R. 2277, para.16; *cf.* CFI (order of January 23, 1991), Case T–3/90 *Prodifarma v Commission* [1991] E.C.R. II-1, paras 35–45; CFI, Case T–32/93 *Ladbroke Racing v Commission* [1994] E.C.R. II-1015, paras 40–43.

[701] ECJ, Case 247/87 *Star Fruit v Commission* [1989] E.C.R. 291, para.13; ECJ (order of October 1, 2004), Case C–379/03 P *Pérez Escolar v Commission*, not reported, paras 15–26 (the fact that an individual lodged a complaint with the Commission with respect to an alleged violation of Arts 87 and 88 of the EC Treaty is—as such—not sufficient for that individual to have the standing to bring an action under Art.232 of the EC Treaty before the Court of First Instance. The person concerned will have to demonstrate that he or she is directly and individually concerned by the decision which the Commission failed to adopt).

[702] ECJ, Case C–68/95 *T. Port v Commission* [1996] E.C.R. I-6065, para.59.

[703] ECJ, Case 17/57 *De Gezamenlijke Steenkolenmijnen in Limburg v High Authority* [1959] E.C.R. 1, at 8; ECJ (order of 18 November, 1999), Case C–249/99 P *Pescados Congelados Jogamar v Commission* [1999] E.C.R. I-8333, para.18.

applicant initially finds that there has been a failure to act. An eighteen-month period is unreasonable.[704]

8–013 **What has to be raised.** The communication calling upon the defendant institution to act must make it clear that it is made pursuant to Art.232 of the EC Treaty.[705] In addition, it must indicate precisely what measure(s) of Community law the applicant expects the defendant to adopt.[706] Since only the person who calls upon the institution to act is entitled to bring an action, it is important that he or she should make his or her identity clear.

8–014 **Reaction of the institution put on notice.** In order to have brought the failure to act in question to an end, the defendant institution must have "defined its position" within two months of its having been called upon to act (EC Treaty, Art.232, second para.). Once the defendant institution has defined its position, an action for failure to act will be inadmissible.[707]

The reaction of the institution which has been called upon to act will be deemed to be a definition of a position within the meaning of the second para. of Art.232 of the EC Treaty only in so far as it explains the institution's stance with regard to the measure requested.[708] It is the content and not the form of the definition of a position which determines whether this condition has been met. Accordingly, the institution called upon to act may reject a request to adopt a particular measure by letter,[709] by telex[710] or impliedly by adopting a measure other than the one requested.

Although a definition of a position brings the failure to act to an end, thereby making it impossible to bring an action for failure to act any

---

[704] ECJ, Case 59/70 *Netherlands v Commission* [1971] E.C.R. 639, paras 12–24. See also ECJ, Case C–170/02 P *Schlüsselverlag J.S. Moser and Others v Commission* [2003] E.C.R. I-9889, paras 36–38 (where an action for failure to act in respect of the Commission's failure to respond to a complaint to the effect that an unnotified merger had a Community dimension was declared inadmissible. The Court of Justice held that since four months had elapsed since the national authorities' decision approving the merger, it was no longer possible to call on the Commission to act within a reasonable time).

[705] ECJ, Case 13/83 *European Parliament v Council* [1985] E.C.R. 1513, para.24; ECJ, Case 84/82 *Germany v Commission* [1984] E.C.R. 1451, para.23; CFI (order of April 30, 1999), Case T–311/97 *Pescados Congelados Jogamar v Commission* [1999] E.C.R. II-1407, para.37.

[706] ECJ, Case 25/85 *Nuovo Campsider v Commission* [1986] E.C.R. 1531, para.8; CFI, Case T–28/90 *Asia Motor France and Others v Commission* [1992] E.C.R. II-2285, para.28; CFI (order of April 30, 1999), Case T–311/97 *Pescados Congelados Jogamar v Commission* [1999] E.C.R. II-1407. For an instance in which the action was declared admissible only in part, see CFI, Case T–17/96 *TF1 v Commision* [1999] E.C.R. II-1757, paras 41–44.

[707] See, however, CFI (order of February 23, 2005), Case T–479/04, *Campailla v Commission*, not reported, in which the CFI found that such an action was manifestly lacking any foundation in law.

[708] A letter emanating from an institution, stating that examination of the questions raised is in progress, does not constitute a definition of position which brings to an end a failure to act (CFI, Case T–212/99 *Intervet International v Commission* [2002] E.C.R. II-1445, para.61; CFI, Joined Cases T–344/00 and T–345/00 *CEVA and Pharmacia Entreprises v Commission* [2003] E.C.R. II-229, para.80).

[709] ECJ, Case 125/78 *GEMA v Commission* [1979] E.C.R. 3173, paras 14–23.

[710] ECJ, Case 42/71 *Nordgetreide v Commission* [1972] E.C.R. 105, para.4.

more,[711] it is not always in the nature of a binding act against which an action for annulment will lie.[712]

This will, of course, be the case where the invitation to act is made by a Community institution or a Member State with a view to the adoption of a preparatory act needed for the purpose of the Community's decision-making procedure (see 7–020 to 7–022 and 8–006, *supra*). The only way in which the Court of Justice can secure legal protection for the applicant in such a situation is to be relatively exacting in adjudging whether the content of the definition of a position is such as to bring the failure to act to an end. The reason is that, since an action for annulment is ruled out in any event as a potential means of recourse, the only avenue remaining is an action for failure to act if the defendant institution is not fulfilling its obligations and so blocking the Community's decision-making process.[713]

Even where the invitation to act comes from a natural or legal person, who, in principle, therefore has in mind the adoption of a binding act against which an action for annulment will lie (see 8–006, *supra*), it is possible for the failure to act to be brought to an end by a non-binding definition of a position. The procedure for the investigation of complaints relating to infringements of Arts 81 and 82 of the EC Treaty affords an illustration.[714]

Complaint regarding infringement of Art.81 or Art.82 of the EC Treaty. A complaint is lodged in the hope that the Commission will find that there has been an infringement of Art.81 or Art.82 of the EC Treaty. But the complainant is not entitled to a definitive decision from the Commission on   **8–015**

---

[711] If the position defined by the institution concerned does not come up to the expectations of the person who requested the institution to act, that person may no longer challenge the position defined by means of an action for failure to act. This is because Art.232 of the EC Treaty refers to failure to take a decision or to define a position, and not to the adoption of a measure different from that desired or considered necessary by the person concerned: ECJ, Case 8/71 *Komponistenverband v Commission* [1971] E.C.R. 705, para.2; ECJ, Joined Cases 166 and 220/86 *Irish Cement v Commission* [1988] E.C.R. 6473, para.17; CFI (order of November 12, 1996), Case T–47/96 *SDDDA v Commission* [1996] E.C.R. II-1559, para.40; CFI (order of November 26, 1996), Case T–164/95 *Kuchlenz-Winter v European Parliament* [1996] E.C.R. II-1593, para.37; CFI (order of November 26, 1996), Case T–226/95 *Kuchlenz-Winter v Commission* [1996] E.C.R. II-1619, para.31; CFI, Case T–107/96 *Pantochim v Commission* [1998] E.C.R. II-311, para.30; CFI (order of March 11, 2002), Case T–3/02 *Schlüsselverlag J.S. Moser and Others v Commission* [2002] E.C.R. II-1473, para.27.

[712] *Cf.* Barav, "Considérations sur la spécificité du recours en carence en droit communautaire" (1975) R.T.D.E. 53, at 61.

[713] ECJ, Case 13/83 *European Parliament v Council* [1985] E.C.R. 1513, para.25; moreover, it was in an interinstitutional context that the Court of Justice held—in all likelihood for these reasons—that an express refusal to act does not put an end to a failure to act: ECJ, Case 302/87 *European Parliament v Council* [1988] E.C.R. 5615, para.17.

[714] For the Commission's handling of complaints relating to State aid, see CFI, Case T–95/96 *Gestevisión Telecinco v Commission* [1998] E.C.R. II-3407; CFI, Case T–17/96 *TF1 v Commission* [1999] E.C.R. II-1757; CFI, Joined Cases T–297/01 and T–298/01 *SIC v Commission* [2004] E.C.R. II–743.

the existence of the alleged infringement.[715] Yet it does have the right to a decision on the outcome which the Commission is to give to its complaint, so that, in the event that the complaint is rejected, it can be ensured of being able to bring an action against the decision rejecting the complaint and hence of securing judicial review by the Court of First Instance (and, possibly, the Court of Justice).[716] As we know, before the complaint is rejected, the Commission should send a letter to the complainant pursuant to Art.7 of Regulation No 773/2004 (formerly Art.6 of Regulation No 2842/98[717]) informing it of the reasons why it considers that on the basis of the information in its possession there are insufficient grounds for upholding the complaint and fixing a time-limit within which the complainant may make its views known in writing. Such a letter constitutes a definition of a position within the meaning of the second para. of Art.232 of the EC Treaty,[718] even though it is not a binding act against which an action for annulment will lie.[719]

If the complainant wishes to avail itself of the procedure provided for in Art.232 of the EC Treaty in order to induce the Commission to take a decision on the outcome of its complaint, it will call on the Commission to take that decision (which, moreover, the complainant hopes will be favourable to it).[720] Only if the Commission is planning to reject its complaint, will the complainant receive, under the normal procedure in such a case, a letter pursuant to Art.7 of Regulation No 773/2004, *i.e.* a definition of a position which is not a binding act.[721] This provisionally

---

[715] ECJ, Case 125/78 *GEMA v Commission* [1979] E.C.R. 3173, paras 17–18.

[716] CFI, Case T–7/92 *Asia Motor France and Others v Commission* [1993] E.C.R. II-669; *cf.* CFI (order of November 29, 1993), Case T–56/92 *Koelman v Commission* [1993] E.C.R. II-1267, paras 26–28 (action for failure to act held to be to no purpose because the Commission had definitively rejected the complaint) and CFI, Case T–575/93 *Koelman v Commission* [1996] E.C.R. II-1, in which the applicant sought the annulment of the definitive rejection of its complaint.

[717] Before the entry into force of Regulation No 2842/98, a similar obligation was imposed by Art.6 of Regulation No 99/63.

[718] ECJ, Case 125/78 *GEMA v Commission* [1979] E.C.R. 3173, para.21; ECJ, Case C–282/95 P *Guérin Automobiles v Commission* [1997] E.C.R. I-1503, para.30 (*cf.* the Opinion of Advocate General G. Tesauro in that case); CFI, Case T–186/94 *Guérin Automobiles v Commission* [1995] E.C.R. II-1753, para.26; CFI (order of October 19, 2001), Case T–121/01 *Piau v Commission*, not reported, para.14.

[719] CFI, Case T–64/89 *Automec v Commission* [1990] E.C.R. II-367, para.46; Case T–186/94 *Guérin Automobiles v Commission*, cited in the preceding n., para.41; CFI, Case T–38/96 *Guérin Automobiles v Commission* [1997] E.C.R. II-1223, para.31.

[720] CFI, Case T–28/90 *Asia Motor France and Others v Commission* [1992] E.C.R. II-2285, para.28.

[721] The fact that a complainant which requests that a decision be taken has to be satisfied in the first instance with an act which does not have the force of a decision, namely a definition of a position which does not bring the failure to act to an end, has to do with the Commission's obligation to take the intermediate step—designed to protect the complainant's interests—of notifying the draft decision, following which the complainant is entitled to submit observations. Sometimes, however, the decision is taken directly, whereupon an action for annulment will lie against it, see ECJ, Case C–39/93 P *SFEI and Others v Commission* [1994] E.C.R. I-2681, paras 24–33.

exhausts the complainant's possibilities of recourse, but not necessarily for long. This is because the initiative reverts to the complainant. If it submits written observations within the prescribed period, the Commission must take, within a reasonable time,[722] a final decision on the outcome of the complaint in the light of those observations.[723] If necessary, the complainant can call on the Commission pursuant to Art.232 of the EC Treaty to take the decision.[724] If the Commission rejects the complaint, the complainant may bring an action for annulment; if the Commission does nothing at all, an action for failure to act will lie.[725]

B. Procedure before the Court

Conditions for admissibility. The letter before action marks the starting point of the two-month period which the institution has in order to bring the failure to act to an end. The failure to act does not end on the day when the institution concerned defines its position, but instead on the date when the party which called on it to act received that position.[726] If, during that period, the institution persists in its failure to act, Member States, institutions or natural or legal persons who have called upon it to act may bring an action before the Court of Justice or the Court of First Instance "within a further period of two months".[727] In the event that the institution concerned defines its position before the action is brought, the action will be inadmissible.[728] If the act in question is adopted after the action for

8–016

---

[722] ECJ, Case C–282/95 P *Guérin Automobiles v Commission* [1997] E.C.R. I-1503, para.37. The call to act may not, however, be made at the same time as observations to a letter under Art.7 of Regulation No 773/2004. This is because the Commission must be given a reasonable period within which to examine the complainant's observations before being required to define its final position on the complaint (this can be inferred from the order for costs in a case where it was held that the action for failure to act was to no purpose at the time of the judgment: CFI, Case T–28/95 *IECC v Commission* [1998] E.C.R. II-3597, para.15). See also 8–004, *supra*.

[723] Art.7(2) of Regulation No 773/2004 provides: "If the complainant makes known its views within the time-limit set by the Commission and the written submissions made by the complainant do not lead to a different assessment of the complaint, the Commission shall reject the complaint by decision". According to Art.7(3), "[i]f the complainant fails to make known its views within the time-limit set by the Commission, the complaint shall be deemed to have been withdrawn".

[724] *Cf.* Opinion of Judge D.A.O. Edward, appointed to act as Advocate General, in CFI, Case T–24/90 *Automec v Commission* [1992] E.C.R. II-2223, para.23.

[725] An action for failure to act will not be held to have lost its purpose merely because the restriction of competition referred to in the complaint has been terminated following the intervention of the Commission, since that did not dispense the Commission from defining its position on the applicant's complaint. If, therefore, the Commission has failed to define its position on the complaint, the action does not lose its purpose in those circumstances: CFI, Case T–74/92 *Ladbroke Racing v Commission* [1995] E.C.R. II-115, paras 66–67.

[726] CFI, Joined Cases T–194/97 and T–83/98 *Branco v Commission* [2000] E.C.R. II-69, para.54.

[727] EC Treaty, Art.232, second para. For an action which was brought late, see CFI (Order of December 2, 2003), Case T–334/02 *Viomichania Syskevasias Typopoiisis Kai Syntirisis Agrotikon Proïonton v Commission* [2003] E.C.R. II-5121, paras 31–34.

[728] The Court will raise this question of inadmissibility of its own motion (CFI, Case T–26/01 *Fiocchi Munizioni v Commission* [2003] E.C.R. II-3951, paras 92–93).

failure to act has been brought but before judgment is given, the application becomes to no purpose (see 8–003, *supra*). In such a case, the defendant institution exposes itself to having an order for costs made against it.[729]

The letter before action also determines the subject-matter of the action. The action can relate only to a failure to act which has been previously so raised with the defendant institution.[730]

8–017 **Pleas in law.** Under Art.232 of the EC Treaty, the only plea open to the applicant is that the failure to act constitutes "an infringement of this Treaty". As has already been mentioned, the expression "infringement of the Treaty" covers any Community provision under which an obligation to act arises for the defendant institution (see 8–004, *supra*). Some commentators maintain that an action will lie also against the defendant institution's failure to exercise a discretionary power where that failure amounts to a misuse of powers.[731]

IV. CONSEQUENCES

8–018 **Limited scope of the judgment.** If the Court of First Instance or the Court of Justice finds that an institution has infringed the Treaty by failing to act, the institution is required under Art.233 of the EC Treaty to take the necessary measures to comply with the judgment. The scope of the judgment is limited. It merely reinforces the duty on the institution to act, but it does not take the place of the act which the institution failed to adopt. At most, the Court of Justice or the Court of First Instance may indicate what act is necessary in order to comply with its judgment.[732]

---

[729] ECJ, Case 377/87 *European Parliament v Council* [1988] E.C.R. 4017, paras 8–10; CFI, Case T–212/95 *Oficemen v Commission* [1997] E.C.R. II-1161, paras 72–75. See, however, CFI (order of November 26, 1997), Case T–39/97 *T. Port v Commission* [1997] E.C.R. II-2125, para.29.

[730] ECJ, Joined Cases 24 and 34/58 *Chambre Syndicale de la Sidérurgie de l'Est de la France and Others v High Authority* [1960] F.C.R. 281, at 299; ECJ, Joined Cases 41 and 50/59 *Hamborner Bergbau and Others v High Authority* [1960] E.C.R. 493; ECJ, Case 75/69 *Hake v Commission* [1970] E.C.R. 535, paras 8–9.

[731] Waelbroeck and Waelbroeck, *Répertoire du droit communautaire*, keyword: Carence (recours en), (Ed. Dalloz, Paris, 1994/1), § 28. The argument is that the defendant institution's obligation is to bring to an end the "misuse of powers" (brought about by its failure to exercise the power). In practice, this comes very close to reading into Art.232 of the EC Treaty the case which was expressly contemplated by the second para.of Art.35 of the ECSC Treaty.

[732] The Court does this in the body of the judgment, which helps to determine the scope of the operative part, *cf.* ECJ, Joined Cases 97, 193, 99 and 215/86 *Asteris and Others v Commission* [1988] E.C.R. 2181, paras 26–27.

V. THE CONSTITUTION

General. Since the action for annulment and the action for failure to act **8–019** provide for one and the same means of recourse,[733] the wording of Art.III-367 of the Constitution relating to the action for failure to act has therefore been brought into line with that of Art.III-365 relating to the action for annulment. Art.III-367 of the Constitution thus provides that an action for annulment may be brought not only against the institutions already mentioned in Art.232 of the EC Treaty,[734] but also against the European Council and the bodies, offices and agencies of the Union.

---

[733] ECJ, Case 15/70 *Chevalley v Commission* [1970] E.C.R. 975, para.6; CFI, Case C–68/95 *T. Port* [1996] E.C.R. I-6065, para.59.
[734] The Council, the Commission, the European Parliament and the European Central Bank (which, as a result of Art.I-30(3) of the Constitution, becomes an institution).

CHAPTER 9

THE OBJECTION OF ILLEGALITY

I. SUBJECT-MATTER

A. GENERAL

9–001 **Not an independent right of action.** The objection of illegality as provided for in Art.241 of the EC Treaty and Art.156 of the EAEC Treaty does not constitute an independent right of action.[735] It is an incidental plea in law[736] intended to avoid the application of unlawful Community acts of general application to the detriment of persons who are not—or no longer[737]— entitled to challenge them.[738]

9–002 **Essential function.** Art.241 of the EC Treaty "gives expression to a general principle conferring upon any party to proceedings the right to challenge, for the purpose of obtaining the annulment of a decision of direct and individual concern to that party, the validity of previous acts of the institutions which form the legal basis of the decision which is being attacked, if that party was not entitled under Art.230 of the Treaty to bring a direct action challenging those acts by which it was thus affected without having been in a position to ask that they be declared void".[739] It follows

---

[735] ECJ, Case 33/80 *Albini v Council and Commission* [1981] E.C.R. 2141, para.17; ECJ, Joined Cases 87 and 130/77, 22/83, 9 and 10/84 *Salerno and Others v Commission and Council* [1985] E.C.R. 2523, para.36.
[736] See Van Rijn, *Exceptie van onwettigheid en prejudiciële procedure inzake geldigheid van gemeenschapshandelingen* (Kluwer, Deventer, 1978), at 140–143; Smit and Herzog (now Campbell and Powers), *The Law of the European Community* (Matthew Bender & Co., New York, 1976), at 5–540–541; Brealey and Hoskins, *Remedies in E.C. Law*, at 331–332.
[737] For the question of who is entitled to raise an objection of illegality, see 9–006 to 9–009, *infra*.
[738] ECJ, Joined Cases 31 and 33/62 *Wöhrmann and Others v Commission* [1962] E.C.R. 501, at 507. See also Barav, "The Exception of Illegality in Community Law: A Critical Analysis" (1974) C.M.L.Rev. 366, at 368; Sinaniotis, "The Plea of Illegality in EC Law" (2001) E.Pub.L. 103–125; Vogt, "Bestandskraft von EG-Rechtsakten und Anwendungsbereich des Art.241 EGV" (2004) EuR. 618–636.
[739] ECJ, Case 92/78 *Simmenthal v Commission* [1979] E.C.R. 777, para.39. See also ECJ, Case 9/56 *Meroni v High Authority* [1957 and 1958] E.C.R. 133, at 140; ECJ, Case 10/56 *Meroni v High Authority* [1957 and 1958] E.C.R. 156, at 162–163; ECJ, Case 15/57 *Compagnie des Hauts Fourneaux de Chasse v High Authority* [1957 and 1958] E.C.R. 211, at 224–225; ECJ, Case 262/80 *Andersen v European Parliament* [1984] E.C.R. 195, para.6; CFI, Joined Cases

that the field of application of Art.241—according to which an objection of illegality may be raised only against a regulation—extends to "acts of the institutions which, although they are not in the form of a regulation, nevertheless produce similar effects and on those grounds may not be challenged under Art.230 by natural or legal persons other than Community institutions or Member States".[740] In so deciding, the Court of Justice intimated that the essential function of the objection of illegality is to enable natural and legal persons to have set aside an act against which they cannot bring an action for annulment under the fourth para.of Art.230 of the EC Treaty, in a case where they seek the annulment by the Court of First Instance of an implementing measure adopted by the Community on the basis of that act.

B. ACTS AGAINST WHICH AN OBJECTION OF ILLEGALITY MAY BE RAISED

"Regulation". Under Art.241 of the EC Treaty, an objection of illegality may be raised in respect of "a regulation of the Council, of the Commission, or of the ECB [European Central Bank]" or "a regulation adopted jointly by the European Parliament and the Council". But, as has already been mentioned, for the purposes of the application of Art.241, any measure having similar effects to a regulation will be treated as if it were a regulation provided that natural or legal persons cannot bring an action for annulment against it pursuant to the fourth para.of Art.230 of the EC Treaty (see 9-002, *supra*).[741]

9–003

In a recent case the Court of First Instance went even as far as allowing an objection of illegality to be raised against a resolution of the UN Security Council in an action for annulment brought against a Community regulation putting into effect, without the exercise of any discretion whatsoever, the said resolution of the Security Council.[742] Given the primacy of resolutions of the Security Council over Community law, the Court of First Instance considered that it had competence to review,

---

T–6 and T–52/92 *Reinarz v Commission* [1993] E.C.R. II-1047, para.56; CFI, Case T–64/92 *Chavane de Dalmassy and Others v Commission* [1994] E.C.R.-SC II-723, para.41 (English abstract at I-A-227); CFI, Case T–82/96 *ARAP and Others v Commission* [1999] E.C.R. II-1889, paras 46–48 (an applicant who has brought an action for annulment against a decision approving an individual aid measure may raise an objection of illegality against the measure approving the general aid measure pursuant to which the individual aid was granted).

[740] ECJ, Case 92/78 *Simmenthal v Commission*, cited in the preceding n., para.40; CFI, Joined Cases T–222/99, T–327/99 and T–329/99 *Martinez and Others v European Parliament* [2001] E.C.R. II-2823, para.134.

[741] Accordingly, an undertaking can plead the illegality of the Commission's guidelines on the method of setting fines imposed for a breach of the competition rules in an action for annulment brought against a decision imposing a fine : ECJ, Joined Cases C–189/02 P, C–202/02 P, C–205/02 P to C–208/02 P and C–213/02 P *Dansk Rørindustri and Others v Commission* [2005] E.C.R. I-5425, paras 212 and 213.

[742] The regulation imposed certain specific restrictive measures against certain persons and entities associated with Osama bin Laden, the Al-Qaeda network and the Taliban.

indirectly, the legality of the resolution of the Security Council in question having regard only to *jus cogens* (understood as a body of higher rules of public international law binding on all subjects of international law, including the bodies of the United Nations, from which no derogation is possible) but not to Community law.[743]

9–004 **Exclusion of decisions of which annulment could have been sought.** According to the case-law, a party to proceedings may not rely on Art.241 of the EC Treaty in order to challenge the legality of a decision addressed to it where it could have applied for the decision to be annulled under Art.230.[744] This is because legal certainty would be affected if a party could still challenge such a decision by means of an objection of illegality after the time-limit for bringing an action against it had expired.[745] The only exceptions are where the party concerned was entitled to entertain reasonable doubt as to the admissibility of an action for annulment[746] or in the exceptional case where the contested act contained such particularly serious and manifest defects that it could be deemed non-existent.[747]

9–005 **An act of general application must be "at issue".** Art.241 of the EC Treaty requires the "regulation" in respect of which the objection of illegality is raised to be "at issue". In the light of the essential function of the objection (see 9–002, *supra*), the case-law has interpreted that requirement as meaning that the general measure against which the objection is raised must constitute the legal basis of the individual measure which is being directly challenged.[748] The upshot is that, in principle, an objection of illegality may be raised only against the provisions of a general act which the individual act implements.[749] Nevertheless, other provisions of the general act may be affected by the objection if they are applicable to "the issue with which the application is concerned".[750]

---

[743] CFI (judgment of September 21, 2005), Case T–306/01 *Yusuf and Al Barakaat International Foundation v Council and Commission*, not yet reported, paras 226–254 and 260–283.

[744] ECJ, Case 156/77 *Commission v Belgium* [1978] E.C.R. 1881, para.20. See also 9–007 and 9–008, *infra*.

[745] *Ibid.*, para.21.

[746] CFI, Case T–343/02 *Schintgen v Commission* [2004] E.C.R.-SC II 605, para.26.

[747] ECJ, Case 223/87 *Commission v Greece* [1988] E.C.R. 3611, para.16.

[748] ECJ, Case 21/64 *Macchiorlati Dalmas & Figli v High Authority* [1965] E.C.R. 175, at 187–188 (where the Court of Justice referred to a "direct legal connection between the contested measure and the ... general decisions"); CFI, Joined Cases T–222/99, T–327/99 and T–329/99 *Martinez and Others v European Parliament* [2001] E.C.R. II-2823, para.136.

[749] ECJ, Joined Cases 275/80 and 24/81 *Krupp v Commission* [1981] E.C.R. 2489, para.32; CFI, Case T–120/99 *Kik v OHIM* [2001] E.C.R. II-2235, para.25. See in this connection the important case of *Chvatal* (ECJ, Joined Cases C–432/98 P and C–433/98 P *Council v Chvatal and Others* [2000] E.C.R. I-8535).

[750] ECJ, Case 32/65 *Italy v Council and Commission* [1966] E.C.R. 389, at 409; *cf.* ECJ, Case 18/62 *Barge v High Authority* [1963] E.C.R. 259, at 279–280; ECJ, Joined Cases 140, 146, 221 and 226/82 *Walzstahl-Vereinigung and Thyssen v Commission* [1984] E.C.R. 951, para.20; see also Van Rijn, (n.736, *supra*), at 194.

With the same concern to guarantee the essential function of the objection of illegality, it is considered in the case-law that such an objection may be raised against any act which cannot be contested for one reason or another, but whose content was nevertheless determinative in the adoption of individual acts which may be directly challenged.[751] Thus, an exception of illegality may be raised against the Commission's guidelines on the method of setting fines[752] in an annulment action brought against a decision imposing fines although the guidelines do not constitute the legal basis of the contested decision. Indeed, the guidelines determine, generally and abstractly, the method which the Commission has bound itself to use in assessing the fines imposed by the decision.[753] Similarly, the Court of Justice has assessed, via an objection of illegality, the lawfulness of a letter in which the High Authority gave directions for interpretation to a body which had to apply only articles of the Treaty and secondary Community legislation, after finding that the letter did not constitute an act against which an action would lie.[754] In practice, however, the inquiry into the legality of such directions for interpretation will generally coincide with the Court's interpretation of the provisions of Community law to which they relate. If the directions for interpretation are consistent with the Court's interpretation, they will be "lawful", otherwise not. The legality of the individual act therefore does not actually depend so much on the "legality" of the directions for interpretation, as on whether the interpretation of the provisions of Community law which they apply is or is not correct.

II. IDENTITY OF THE PARTIES

"Any party". Under Art.241 of the EC Treaty, "any party" may raise an objection of illegality.   9–006

Natural or legal persons. "Any party" covers, first, natural or legal persons who are unable to challenge before the Court of First Instance the act against which the objection is raised (see 9–004, *supra*). Natural or legal   9–007

---

[751] Waelbroeck therefore suggests that an objection of illegality should be allowed to be raised against any general act, such as decisions approving the budget or directives addressed to all the Member States (see *Commentaire Mégret*, at 389, together with the academic writings cited in support in n.738); see also the considerations put forward by Van Rijn (n.736, *supra*), at 167–186, who considers the availability of the objection of illegality against various sorts of acts in detail; in contrast, Lauwaars argues, on the basis of the clear wording of Art.241 of the EC Treaty, that objections of illegality should be able to be raised only against "regulations" (naturally in the substantive sense of the term) (Lauwaars (n.683, *supra*), at 276).

[752] [1998] O.J. C9/3.

[753] ECJ, Joined Cases C–189/02 P, C–202/02 P, C–205/02 P to C–208/02 P and C–213/02 P *Dansk Rørindustri a.o. v Commission* [2005] E.C.R. I–5425, paras 212 and 213; CFI, Case T–64/02 (judgment of November 29, 2005) *Heubach v Commission*, not yet reported, para.35.

[754] ECJ, Joined Cases 32 and 33/58 *SNUPAT v High Authority* [1959] E.C.R. 127, at 141.

persons may therefore raise an objection against regulations and other general acts which they could not reasonably challenge in an action for annulment before the Court of First Instance, provided, of course, that the act concerned applies to the issue with which the application is concerned.[755]

9–008 **Member States and Community institutions.** There is a school of thought in the literature to the effect that the fact that Member States and Community institutions may bring an action for annulment against *any* binding Community act precludes them from making use of the objection of illegality on the ground that, if they could, they would effectually be able to start time running again in breach of the principle of legal certainty.[756] But this view is not shared by all commentators. Some argue that Member States and Community institutions may also have recourse to Art.241 of the EC Treaty with a view to a finding that regulations and similar acts which are "at issue" are unlawful, even though they have not taken advantage of their right to bring an action for annulment against the acts in question within the period prescribed for bringing proceedings. This argument relies principally on the wording of Art.241 ("any party"), whilst referring at the same time to the ancillary function of the objection of illegality of avoiding the application of regulations and similar acts whose deficiencies and possible illegality become apparent to Member States or Community institutions after the time-limit for bringing proceedings has passed when they are implemented or raised in judicial proceedings.[757] The unlawful nature of an act may not in fact appear so much on its face as from the manner in which it is interpreted and applied.[758]

The following picture emerges from recent case-law of the Court of Justice. The Court accepts that a privileged applicant may invoke the

---

[755] However, an objection of illegality cannot be raised by an individual against a regulation in the exceptional case where the regulation has a dual nature and should be considered to constitute a decision as regards the individual so that that individual could undoubtedly have sought the annulment of the regulation under Art.230 of the EC Treaty (see ECJ, Case C–11/00 *Commission v ECB* [2003] E.C.R. I-7147, para.75: the Court of Justice cited by way of example regulations imposing anti-dumping duties. They have the dual nature of acts of a legislative nature and acts liable to be of direct and individual concern to certain traders).

[756] Bebr, "Judicial Remedy of Private Parties against Normative Acts of the European Communities: The Role of Exception of Illegality" (1966) C.M.L.Rev. 7, at 11–13; Usher, "The Interrelationship of Arts 173, 177 and 184 *[now Arts 230, 234 and 241]* EEC" (1979) E.L.Rev. 36, at 37; Joliet, *Le contentieux*, at 134 *et seq.*

[757] See to that effect Lauwaars (n.14, *supra*), at 277–279, who systematically refutes Bebr's arguments (n.87, *supra*). See also Barav (n.736, *supra*), at 371; Van Rijn (n.736, *supra*), at 160; Dubois, "L'exception d'illégalité devant la Cour de Justice des Communautés européennes" (1978) C.D.E. 407, at 411–413.

[758] See ECJ, Case C–11/00 *Commission v ECB* [2003] E.C.R. I-7147, para.73, in which the ECB contended that it had not brought an action for the annulment of Regulation No 1073/1999, in respect of which it subsequently raised an objection of illegality, because it believed that the regulation did not apply to it.

illegality of a regulation that it could have challenged under Art.230 of the EC Treaty.[759] The Court of Justice expressly confirmed this in its 2003 judgment in *Commission v ECB*.[760] In that case, the Commission applied, under Art.230 of the EC Treaty, for the annulment of Decision 1999/726/ EC of the European Central Bank of October 7, 1999 on fraud prevention.[761] In fact, the Commission considered that that decision was in breach of Regulation (EC) No 1073/1999 of the European Parliament and of the Council of May 25, 1999 concerning investigations conducted by the European Anti-Fraud Office (OLAF).[762] In the proceedings before the Court of Justice, the ECB objected, pursuant to Art.241 of the EC Treaty, that Regulation No 1073/1999 was unlawful. The Commission argued that that objection was inadmissible on the ground that the ECB had not brought an action for the annulment of the regulation within the two-month deadline prescribed by the fifth para. of Art.230 of the EC Treaty.

In its judgment of July 10, 2003, the Court of Justice made a clear distinction between decisions, on the one hand, and regulations of a genuinely legislative nature, on the other. As far as decisions are concerned, the Court pointed to its case-law to the effect that a decision which has not been challenged by its addressee within the time-limit laid down by the fifth para. of Art.230 of the EC Treaty becomes definitive as against that person.[763] This is because time-limits serve to ensure legal certainty by

---

[759] As long ago as 1966, the Court of Justice had implicitly accepted that Member States could raise an objection of illegality against provisions of a Council regulation and a Commission regulation in an action for the annulment of another Council regulation. Although it did not consider whether Member States were entitled to invoke Art.241, it did reject the objection on the ground that it was directed against provisions of regulations which were not applicable to the issue with which the application was concerned (ECJ, Case 32/65 *Italy v Council and Commission* [1966] E.C.R. 389).

[760] ECJ, Case C–11/00 *Commission v ECB* [2003] E.C.R. I-7147 (with a case note by Odudu (2004) C.M.L. Rev. 1073–1092). A number of Advocates General of the Court of Justice had earlier expressed the view in Opinions that the wording of Art.241 does not preclude Member States and Community institutions from raising an objection of illegality (Opinion of Advocate General K. Roemer in ECJ, Case 32/65 *Italy v Council and Commission* [1966] E.C.R. 389, at 414; Opinion of Advocate General Sir Gordon Slynn in ECJ, Case 181/85 *France v Commission* [1987] E.C.R. 689, at 702–703; Opinion of Advocate General G.F. Mancini in ECJ, Case 204/86 *Greece v Council* [1988] E.C.R. 5323, at 5343–5345). On this view, the possibility of Member States' or Community institutions' raising such an objection is not even subject to any limitation, because Art.241 does not so provide. Thus, a Member State does not have to show that there was a good reason why it did not act in time in bringing an action for annulment against the regulation or similar act at issue or that it was taken by surprise—after the time-limit for bringing an action for annulment had passed—by the interpretation given to the act, which raised doubts as to its legality (Opinion of Advocate General Sir Gordon Slynn in ECJ, Case 181/85 *France v Commission* [1987] E.C.R. 689, at 703).

[761] [1999] O.J. L291/36.

[762] [1999] O.J. L136/1.

[763] ECJ, Case C–11/00 *Commission v ECB* [2003] E.C.R. I-7147, para.74 (with a case note by Odudu (2004) C.M.L. Rev. 1073–1092). See also Case C–188/92 *TWD Textilwerke Deggendorf* [1994] E.C.R. I-833, para.13; ECJ, Case C–178/95 *Wiljo* [1997] E.C.R. I-585, paras 19–24; ECJ, Case C–239/99 *Nachi Europe* [2001] E.C.R. I-1197, paras 28–40; ECJ, Case C–241/01 *National Farmers' Union* [2002] E.C.R. I-9079, para.34; ECJ, Case C–194/01 *Commission v Austria* [2004] E.C.R. I-4579, paras 40–41; see also 5–060, *supra*.

preventing unlimited proceedings from being brought against Community acts which have legal effects.

However, the Court further observed that this case-law did not rule out the possibility of raising an objection of illegality against "genuine" regulations. The reason for this is that Art.241 of the EC Treaty provides expressly that any party may, in proceedings in which a regulation of the kind referred to in Art.241 is at issue, plead the grounds specified in the second para. of Art.230 of the EC Treaty in order to invoke before the Court of Justice the inapplicability of that regulation.[764] After finding that "the legislative nature of Regulation No 1073/1999 has not been challenged by any of the parties and that, more particularly, it has not been claimed that the regulation should be treated as a decision or that the ECB would, in such a case, be the addressee thereof", the Court declared the objection of illegality admissible.[765]

The possibility for Community institutions and Member States to raise an objection of illegality against regulations must be regarded as an exception based on a literal reading of the applicable provision of the Treaty. On the one hand, it is at odds with the principle of legal certainty to allow a privileged applicant which has not taken advantage of its right to apply for the annulment of an act within the prescribed time-limit a further opportunity to contest the legality of that act by raising an objection of illegality. On the other hand, Art.241 of the EC Treaty expressly provides that "any party"—hence also privileged applicants—can raise an objection against "regulations".[766]

The case-law has not extended the possibility of raising an objection of illegality to cover directives.[767] This is because that possibility is not provided for in any provision of the Treaty. In this connection, the Court of Justice has not made any distinction between directives addressed only to certain Member States and directives addressed to all Member States.[768]

---

[764] ECJ, Case C–11/00 *Commission v ECB* [2003] E.C.R. I-7147, para.76.

[765] *Ibid.*, paras 77–78. In his case note [(2004) C.M.L.Rev. 1073–1092], Odudu arrives at a restrictive interpretation of Art.241 of the EC Treaty. The author claims that "any party" will be considered to be circumventing the Art.230 time-limit, and thus prevented from raising the Art.241 plea of illegality, when it has notice both that a measure affects its interests and that it is able to challenge the measure.

[766] ECJ, Case C–11/00 *Commission v ECB* [2003] E.C.R. I-7147, para.76.

[767] Thus, the Commission cannot, in infringement proceedings, claim that a directive the provisions of which were complied with by the Member State concerned, is unlawful with a view to demonstrating the existence of an infringement by that Member State of a Treaty provision (ECJ, Case C–475/01 *Commission v Greece* [2004] E.C.R. I–8923, paras 17, 18, 24 and 25).

[768] Art.254(2) of the EC Treaty provides that directives which are addressed to all the Member States are to be published in the *Official Journal of the European Union* in the same way as regulations and are to enter into force, no longer upon notification to the Member States, but—again as in the case of regulations—on the twentieth day following that of their publication (unless they specify otherwise). What is involved therefore is directives of a general legislative character whose content and possible illegality might only become

Consequently, as far as the objection of illegality is concerned, directives share the same fate as decisions.[769]

Objection raised by the parties and exceptionally by the Court. Both applicants and defendants are entitled to raise an objection of illegality with a view to having a case decided in their favour.[770]   **9–009**

In principle, an objection of illegality must be raised by one of the parties. Nevertheless, exceptionally, the Court of Justice or the Court of First Instance may consider whether a general act constituting the basis for the measure contested in the proceedings is unlawful of its own motion.[771] The Court may do so in particular where the general act may possibly be unlawful for lack of competence or infringement of an essential procedural requirement (see 7–122, *supra*).

III. Special Characteristics

A. Requirements for admissibility

Action in connection with which the objection is raised must be admissible. An objection of illegality will be admissible only in so far as the direct action in connection with which it is raised is admissible.[772] The applicant's interest in successfully raising an objection of illegality against the general act on which the contested individual measure is based coincides with its interest in its succeeding with its application for the annulment of that   **9–010**

---

apparent—precisely as in the case of regulations and similar acts—after the time for bringing proceedings has run out, for example, when the Commission informs the Member States of the precise content of their obligations in terms of implementation. Nevertheless, an objection of illegality raised by a Member State against such a directive was declared inadmissible (see ECJ (judgment of July 15, 2004), Case C–118/03 *Commission v Germany*, not reported, para.7; ECJ (judgment of July 15, 2004), Case C–139/03 *Commission v Germany*, not reported, para.7).

[769] See to that effect ECJ, Case C–74/91 *Commission v Germany* [1992] E.C.R. I-5437, para.10; see also ECJ, Case C–241/01 *National Farmers' Union* [2002] E.C.R. I-9079, para.39, in which the Court held that a Member State which was an addressee of a Commission decision on emergency measures to protect against bovine spongiform encephalopathy and which had not challenged the legality of that decision within the time-limit laid down by the fifth para.of Art.230 of the EC Treaty did not have standing subsequently before a national court to invoke its unlawfulness in order to dispute the merits of an action brought against it. The decision was addressed to all the Member States and—despite its title—was legislative in nature.

[770] Waelbroeck and Waelbroeck, *Répertoire du droit communautaire*, key words: Exception d'illégalité (Ed. Dalloz, Paris, 1994/2). See ECJ, Case C–475/01 *Commission v Greece* [2004] E.C.R. I–8923, para.17.

[771] ECJ, Case 14/59 *Société des Fonderies de Pont-à-Mousson v High Authority* [1959] E.C.R. 215, at 230; CFI (judgment of September 27, 2005), Joined Cases T–134/03 and T–135/03 *Common Market Fertilizers v Commission*, not yet reported, paras 51–52.

[772] Opinion of Advocate General F. Capotorti in ECJ, Case 48/76 *Reinarz v Commission and Council* [1977] E.C.R. 291, at 301.

measure. If the general act is declared inapplicable, the individual measure loses its legal basis and the action for annulment of that measure will succeed. If the objection is raised by the defendant, its interest in obtaining a declaration that a Community act which it has allegedly infringed is inapplicable is likewise self-evident.

9–011 **Other conditions.** As already noted, an objection of illegality may be raised only in respect of a general act which is applicable to the issue with which the application is concerned (see 9–005, *supra*).[773] Furthermore, it must be raised in time, in principle in the application or the defence.[774]

An objection of illegality may be raised against general acts outside the time-limit for bringing an action for annulment against them. This follows from the essential nature of the objection[775]; it is also confirmed by Art.241 of the EC Treaty.

B. ACTIONS IN WHICH AN OBJECTION OF ILLEGALITY MAY BE RAISED

9–012 **Any direct action.** An objection of illegality may be raised after any direct action has been brought before the Court of Justice or the Court of First Instance. As we have already seen, objections of illegality are raised most often after an action for annulment has been brought.[776]

Such an objection may also be raised, however, in proceedings for failure to act, either by the defendant institution, where it asserts that the general act which—the applicant claims—gives rise to an obligation for it to act is unlawful, or by the applicant, where it argues that a general act which the defendant institution invokes in order to deny the existence of any obligation to act is unlawful.[777]

---

[773] It is not sufficient that the act should have the "label" of a general act. According to the Court of Justice, the general principle, to which Art.241 of the EC Treaty gives expression and which has the effect of ensuring that every person has or will have had the opportunity to challenge a Community measure which forms the basis of a decision adversely affecting him, does not in any way preclude a regulation from becoming definitive as against an individual in regard to whom it must be considered to be an individual decision. In this connection, the Court referred to regulations imposing anti-dumping duties by virtue of their dual nature (see ECJ, Case C–11/00 *Commission v ECB* [2003] E.C.R. I-7147, para.75, and ECJ, Case C–239/99 *Nachi Europe* [2001] E.C.R. I-1197, para.37).

[774] An objection of illegality expressly raised for the first time in the reply is admissible if it constitutes the expansion of a plea raised by implication in the application: CFI (judgment of November 18, 2004), Case T–176/01 *Ferriere Nord v Commission*, not yet reported, para.136.

[775] ECJ, Case 185/85 *Usinor v Commission* [1986] E.C.R. 2079, para.11.

[776] For an example in an action for annulment based on Regulation No 40/94, see CFI, Case T–120/99 *Kik v Commission* [2001] E.C.R. I-2235.

[777] ECJ, Joined Cases 32 and 33/58 *SNUPAT v High Authority* [1959] E.C.R. 127, at 139 (in that ECSC case, the action for failure to act was in fact an action to annul a tacit refusal). It is not as easy to raise an objection of illegality in proceedings for failure to act brought pursuant to Art.232 of the EC Treaty. Where the institution concerned has failed to act, the applicant can only presume on what general measure the failure to act is based. Once the institution indicates the general act on which its failure to act is based, it has defined its position and the action for failure to act becomes inadmissible, see Van Rijn (n.736, *supra*), at 151.

In addition, it should be possible for a Member State to defend itself against an action for failure to fulfil obligations by raising an objection of illegality against a regulation. It would appear that no such possibility exists in the case of directives (see 9–008, *supra*).

In principle, it is also possible to raise an objection of illegality after bringing an action for damages.[778] In practice, however, recourse to such an objection in this connection will be of little utility. The illegality of the general act against which the objection is raised admittedly results in the act being declared inapplicable, but it does not as such result in a determination that the Community has incurred liability, irrespective of whether the general act allegedly caused damage as a result of its direct effect or because it served as the legal basis for individual implementing measures.[779]

Lastly, an objection of illegality assumes importance in staff cases.[780]

Objection cannot be raised in preliminary proceedings. An objection of illegality *cannot* be raised before the Court of Justice in proceedings for a preliminary ruling. That procedure simply reflects a relationship of cooperation between the national courts and the Court of Justice. The national court determines the question(s) to be brought before the Court of Justice and the parties to the main proceedings are not entitled to alter their scope.[781] Yet, "according to a general principle of law which finds its expression in Art.241 of the EC Treaty", interested parties in the main proceedings must be able to plead the illegality of the Community act on which the national decision adopted in their regard was based.[782] If they do so, the national court may (or must) apply to the Court of Justice for a preliminary ruling on the validity of the Community act at issue (see Ch.10, *infra*). 9–013

C. PLEAS IN LAW

Reference to the action for annulment. By virtue of Art.241 of the EC Treaty, any party may plead "the grounds specified in the second para.of Art.230" in order to claim that an allegedly unlawful regulation is inapplicable. The pleas of lack of competence, infringement of an essential procedural requirement, infringement of the Treaty or of any rule of law relating to its application or misuse of powers (see 7–121 to 7–158, *supra*) are therefore potentially available in support of an objection of illegality. 9–014

---

[778] Lauwaars (n.14, *supra*), at 279.
[779] *Cf.* Dubois (n.88, *supra*), at 433.
[780] ECJ, Case 102/63 *Boursin v High Authority* [1964] E.C.R. 691; ECJ, Joined Cases 75 and 117/82 *Razzouk and Beydoun v Commission* [1984] E.C.R. 1509, paras 15–18; CFI, Case T–207/02 *Falcone v Commission* [2004] E.C.R.-SC II–1393, paras 18–25; CFI, Joined Cases T–219 and T–337/02 *Lutz Herrera v Commission* [2004] E.C.R.-SC II–1407, paras 38–50.
[781] ECJ, Case 44/65 *Singer* [1965] E.C.R. 965, at 970.
[782] ECJ, Case 216/82 *Universität Hamburg* [1983] E.C.R. 2771, para.10.

IV. CONSEQUENCES

9–015   **In principle *"inter partes"*.** If an objection of illegality is successfully raised, the general act to which it relates is declared inapplicable for the purposes of the proceedings in which the objection was raised. It is inapplicable only in relation to the parties involved in those proceedings.[783] The general act subsists as far as third parties are concerned.[784]

Nevertheless the institution which adopted the act declared inapplicable is under a duty to withdraw or adjust the act in order to eliminate the illegality found.[785]

V. THE CONSTITUTION

9–016   **Broader scope of the objection.** Art.III-378 of the Constitution provides: "Notwithstanding the expiry of the [two-month time limit for bringing an action for annulment], any party may, in proceedings in which an act of general application adopted by an institution, body, office or agency of the Union is at issue, plead the grounds specified in Art.III-365(2) in order to invoke before the Court of Justice of the European Union, the inapplicability of that act".

The wording of Art.III-378 of the Constitution is manifestly broader than the wording of the present Art.241 of the EC Treaty. It refers to acts of general application, which would undoubtedly cover the current category of directives under the EC Treaty (which, under the Constitution, will take the form either of a European framework law or of a European regulation).[786] It remains to be seen, however, how the Court of Justice will reconcile Art.III-378 with the requirement of legal certainty.

---

[783] ECJ, Joined Cases 15–33, 52–53, 57–109, 116–117, 123, 132 and 135–137/73 *Schots (née Kortner) and Others v Council and Others* [1974] E.C.R. 177, para.36; see also Van Rijn (n.736, *supra*), at 199–205.

[784] Nevertheless, the declaration that the act is inapplicable may have indirect effects on third parties. For example, if the implementation of the general act was determined by an individual act which was addressed to a number of persons, the annulment of the implementing measure on account of the non-applicability of the general act might also alter the legal position of persons to whom the implementing measure was addressed but who did not bring proceedings against it (Lauwaars (n.683, *supra*), at 283–284). In such an event, the Court of Justice or the Court of First Instance may of course restrict the effects of the declaration of nullity if such a step is necessary to protect the interests of third parties (see 7–173, *supra*); for an example, see ECJ, Case C–242/90 P *Commission v Albani and Others* [1993] E.C.R. I-3839, paras 13–16.

[785] Opinion of Advocate General M. Lagrange in ECJ, Case 14/59 *Société des Fonderies de Pont-à-Mousson v High Authority* [1959] E.C.R. 215, at 242, who refers to "the need—moral if not legal—to adopt a new decision", and in ECJ, Joined Cases 14, 16–17, 20, 24, 26–27/60 and 1/61 *Meroni and Others v High Authority* [1961] E.C.R. 161, at 174; Opinion of Advocate General K. Roemer in ECJ, Joined Cases 9 and 12/60 *Vloeberghs v High Authority* [1961] E.C.R. 197, at 227. Cf. ECJ, Joined Cases 75 and 117/82 *Razzouk and Beydoun v Commission* [1984] E.C.R. 1509, para.19.

[786] See Constitution, Art.I-33.

CHAPTER 10

DETERMINATION OF THE VALIDITY OF COMMUNITY ACTS BY REFERENCES FOR PRELIMINARY RULINGS

General. The Treaties confer jurisdiction on the Court of Justice to give **10–001** preliminary rulings (see Ch.2, *supra*) on the "validity" of Community acts ("acts of the institutions of the Communities and of the ECB [European Central Bank]": EC Treaty, Art.234, first para., indent (b); EAEC Treaty, Art.150, which has the same wording but makes no reference to the ECB). What this involves is a review of the validity of a given Community act as a step in proceedings before a national court in which the validity of that act is in issue, but the national court does not resolve that question itself, referring it instead to the Court of Justice for its assessment. Art.234 of the EC Treaty and Art.150 of the EAEC Treaty contain no obligation for national courts and tribunals to make a reference for a preliminary ruling in the case of courts and tribunals against whose decisions there is a "judicial remedy under national law" (see 2–046 and 2–047, *supra*) but, as already mentioned, the Court of Justice has decided that even these courts and tribunals have no jurisdiction themselves to declare that Community acts are invalid (see 2–056, *supra*). Consequently, they too are under an obligation to submit the question of validity to the Court of Justice whenever they regard a Community act as invalid.[787]

The subject-matter covered by the review of validity will now be considered, followed by its content and consequences.

I. SUBJECT-MATTER OF PRELIMINARY RULING PROCEEDINGS RELATING TO THE VALIDITY OF A COMMUNITY ACT

Acts excluded from review. The Treaties themselves and all other rules of **10–002** constitutional rank fall outside the ambit of preliminary rulings on the validity of Community acts. Those rules constitute in fact the yardstick against which the validity of such acts is reviewed.

---

[787] ECJ, Case 314/85 *Foto-Frost* [1987] E.C.R. 4199, paras 12–20. For an application in France, see Cassia, "Le juge administratif français et la validité des actes communautaires" (1999) R.T.D.E. 409–441.

In addition, the Court of Justice has held that "a preliminary ruling of the Court does not rank among the acts of the Community institutions whose validity is open to review in proceedings under Art.177 [*now Art.234*]".[788] Undoubtedly, that ruling must be extended to cover any judgment of the Court of Justice, which, as a result, remains outside the scope of review by way of preliminary rulings on validity. However, the fact that the Court of Justice has already given a preliminary ruling on the interpretation of an act does not preclude the Court from ruling on the validity of the same act in a later judgment.[789]

10–003 **International agreements.** A trickier question is whether the validity of international agreements concluded by the Community may be reviewed in preliminary ruling proceedings. Textbook writers have voiced great reservations,[790] chiefly on the ground that, in the event that it failed to give effect to such agreements, the Community might stand to incur liability at international level. Moreover, it was for that reason that the Treaty introduced a procedure whereby the Court of Justice gives a prior opinion on the compatibility of proposed international agreements with the provisions of the Treaties (which means in practice with Community constitutional law as a whole) (see Ch.12, *infra*). However, it is no simple matter to exclude international agreements concluded by the Community from the scope of the review of validity under the preliminary ruling procedure.

In the first place, this is because the Court of Justice has held that it has jurisdiction to give preliminary rulings on the interpretation of international agreements concluded by the Community (see 6–013, *supra*). Since indent (b) of the first para. of Art.234 of the EC Treaty draws no distinction between preliminary rulings on the validity of acts of the institutions as opposed to preliminary rulings on their interpretation, if the Court of Justice holds that it has jurisdiction to interpret international agreements by preliminary ruling, it creates the impression that it also has jurisdiction to review their validity.

What is more, a *dictum* of the Court of Justice has further reinforced this impression: "The question whether the conclusion of a given agreement is within the power of the Community and whether, in a given case, such power has been exercised in conformity with the provisions of the Treaty is, in principle, a question which may be submitted to the Court of Justice ... in accordance with the preliminary procedure".[791] This passage has been understood to mean that the Court of Justice should review the validity of

---

[788] ECJ (order of March 5, 1986), Case 69/85 *Wünsche v Germany* [1986] E.C.R. 947, para.16.
[789] ECJ, Joined Cases C–393/99 and C–394/99 *Hervein and Others* [2002] E.C.R. I-2829, para.27. Consequently, a judgment giving a preliminary ruling on interpretation does not therefore implicitly rule on the validity of the act interpreted.
[790] See Joliet, *Le contentieux*, at 198; *Commentaire Mégret*, at 214–215.
[791] ECJ, Opinion 1/75 *Draft understanding on a Local Cost Standard drawn up under the auspices of the OECD* [1975] E.C.R. 1355, at 1361.

the act whereby the Community purported to conclude the agreement, but not the validity of the agreement itself.[792] But that reading of the Court's case-law does not resolve the question of the possible liability of the Community at international level, since if the act by which the Community purported to conclude an international agreement is declared invalid, it will lose all binding force in the Community legal order, just as if the agreement itself was to be declared invalid.[793]

Yet this did not stop the Court of Justice in its 1994 judgment in *France v Commission* from declaring void "the act whereby the Commission of the European Communities sought to conclude the Agreement with the United States of America regarding the application of the competition laws of the European Communities and the United States, which was signed and entered into force on 23 September 1991"[794] (essentially on the ground that the Commission had disregarded the Council's powers under Art.300 of the EEC Treaty). Although "[i]n the event of non-performance of the Agreement by the Commission ... the Community could incur liability at international level",[795] the Court of Justice held that the action for annulment of the act whereby the Commission sought to conclude the agreement was admissible, on the ground that, "as is apparent from its actual wording, the Agreement [on which that act was based was] intended to produce legal effects" within the meaning of the *AETR* case-law.[796] In addition, it held that "[e]xercise of the powers delegated to the Community institutions in international matters cannot escape judicial review, under Art.173 [*now Art.230*] of the Treaty, of the legality of the acts adopted".[797]

Given that the Court of Justice considers the action for annulment and the preliminary ruling on validity to be two mechanisms in the same system of judicial review at Community level,[798] it would seem probable that the Court would not assess the legality of an act by which the Community sought to conclude an international agreement any differently if this question were to be raised by a national court in a reference for a preliminary ruling on the validity of that act.

Finally, the validity of a provision of an international agreement can indirectly be called into question in a reference for a preliminary ruling on

---

[792] Joliet, *Le contentieux*, at 59–60 and 198; Bebr, *Development of Judicial Control of the European Communities*, (Martinus Nijhoff, The Hague, 1981), at 469; Van Rijn (n.736, *supra*), at 236.

[793] *Commentaire Mégret*, at 214.

[794] ECJ, Case C–327/91 *France v Commission* [1994] E.C.R. I-3641. For a critical commentary, see Kaddous, "L'arrêt *France c. Commission* de 1994 (Accord concurrence) et le contrôle de la 'légalité' des accords externes en vertu de l'Art.173[*now Art.230*] CE: la difficile réconciliation de l'orthodoxie communautaire avec l'orthodoxie internationale" (1996) C.D.E. 613–633.

[795] *Ibid.*, para.25.

[796] ECJ, Case 22/70 *Commission v Council* (the *AETR* case) [1971] E.C.R. 263, paras 14–15.

[797] ECJ, Case C–327/91 *France v Commission* [1994] E.C.R. I-3641, para.16.

[798] ECJ, Case 112/83 *Société des Produits de Maïs* [1985] E.C.R. 719, para.17; ECJ, Case 294/83 *Les Verts v European Parliament* [1986] E.C.R. 1339, para.23; ECJ, Case 314/85 *Foto-Frost* [1987] E.C.R. 4199, para.16.

the interpretation of a provision of Community law. Thus, in *Tod's*, a question concerning the interpretation of Art.12 of the EC Treaty was referred to the Court of Justice in the proceedings before a national court relating to the application in the national legal order of a provision of the Berne Convention. It appears—indirectly—from the judgment given by the Court of Justice that the application of the relevant provision of the Berne Convention in the national legal order is invalid under Community law.[799]

10–004 **Acts of the institutions.** In principle, when it comes to reviewing the validity of "acts of the institutions" in preliminary ruling proceedings, the expression is to be given a broad interpretation in order to ensure that the system of legal protection is as "full" as possible.[800] Consequently, the validity of acts of the Council, the Commission, the European Parliament and the Court of Auditors, all institutions of the Community within the meaning of Art.7 of the EC Treaty, may unquestionably all be reviewed under the preliminary ruling procedure.[801] It goes without saying that this also applies to acts adopted jointly by the European Parliament and the Council under the co-decision procedure provided for in Art.251 of the EC Treaty. In addition, indent (b) of the first para.of Art.234 also makes acts of the European Central Bank (EC Treaty, Art.8) subject to review of their validity under the preliminary ruling procedure.

10–005 **Acts of bodies or agencies.** Acts of bodies or agencies set up by Community institutions to which powers of executive decision have been delegated by those institutions also come within the jurisdiction of the Court of Justice to give preliminary rulings on validity.[802] This is because the Court of Justice has made the compatibility with the Treaty of such a delegation of powers dependent upon its complying with the Treaty provisions to which the exercise of the powers by the delegating institution would have been subject, including the Treaty provisions on judicial supervision, had it exercised the powers itself.[803]

The question whether acts of a body established by an international agreement concluded by the Community may be subjected to a review of

---

[799] See ECJ, Case C–28/04 *Tod's and Tod's France* [2005] E.C.R I–5781.

[800] *Cf.* ECJ, Case 25/62 *Plaumann v Commission* [1963] E.C.R. 95, at 107: provisions of the Treaty regarding the right of interested persons to bring an action must not be interpreted restrictively.

[801] As far as the European Parliament is concerned, see Pescatore, "Reconnaissance et contrôle judiciaire des actes du Parlement européen" (1978) R.T.D.E. 581, at 590; for the Court of Auditors, see *Commentaire Mégret*, at 212.

[802] See Lauwaars, "Auxiliary Organs and Agencies in the EEC" (1979) C.M.L.Rev. 365, at 379–380.

[803] ECJ, Case 9/56 *Meroni v High Authority* [1957 and 1958] E.C.R. 133; see also Lenaerts, "Regulating the Regulatory Process: 'Delegation of Powers' in the European Community" (1993) E.L.Rev. 44–46. See in this respect also Art.III-369 of the Constitution, which provides that the "Court of Justice of the European Union shall have jurisdiction to give preliminary rulings concerning: [...] (b) the validity and interpretation of acts of the institutions, bodies, offices and agencies of the Union".

their validity under the preliminary ruling procedure is more difficult to answer. Also in the case of such bodies, the Court of Justice emphasises the need for a system of judicial supervision which provides effective legal protection for all individuals,[804] but so far has left it undecided whether the Court of Justice itself ought to provide the judicial protection in so far as the international agreement in question provides for no (or an insufficient) system of judicial supervision of the bodies which it establishes. Here too, the possibility of the Community incurring liability at international level counsels caution, but even so the requirement for a full system of judicial review is an argument in favour of allowing validity to be tested by references for preliminary rulings, especially since Community institutions contributed, within the framework of the bodies concerned, towards the adoption of the acts in question.[805]

Binding and non-binding acts. The validity of *all* acts of Community institutions and bodies may be reviewed in the context of a reference for a preliminary ruling irrespective as to what they are called[806] and whether or not they have direct effect.[807] The acts may be non-binding.[808] Reviewing the validity of non-binding acts in preliminary rulings can be of considerable interest: in the Court's words, such acts "cannot ... be regarded as having no legal effect. The national courts are bound to take recommendations[809] into consideration in order to decide disputes submitted to them, in particular where they cast light on the interpretation of national measures adopted in order to implement them or where they are designed to supplement binding Community provisions".[810] Sometimes it will be sufficient for the Court to interpret a non-binding act (*e.g.* a communication), thereby appraising its compatibility with the Community provisions which it is intended to elucidate.[811]

10–006

Acts of general application. Since the review of validity effected by means of a reference for a preliminary ruling is a species of review incidental to the main proceedings, some commentators have argued—by analogy with

10–007

---

[804] ECJ, Opinion 1/76 *Draft Agreement establishing a European laying-up fund for inland waterway vessels* [1977] E.C.R. 741, para.21.
[805] *Cf.* ECJ, Case C–192/89 *Sevince* [1990] E.C.R. I-3461, para.3.
[806] For the indirect review in a preliminary ruling of the validity of a Council resolution, see ECJ, Case 59/75 *Manghera and Others* [1976] E.C.R. 91, paras 19–22.
[807] The Court has jurisdiction to give preliminary rulings concerning the validity of a directive, regardless of whether it is directly applicable, even though the period for its implementation has not yet expired, provided that the question referred for a preliminary ruling is connected with a real dispute (ECJ, Case C–491/01 *British American Tobacco and Imperial Tobacco* [2002] E.C.R. I-11453, paras 32–38). See also Bebr, "Examen en validité au titre de l'Art.177 *[now Art.234]* du Traité CEE et cohésion juridique de la Communauté" (1975) C.D.E. 379, at 398–399.
[808] ECJ, Case C–322/88 *Grimaldi* [1989] E.C.R. 4407, para.8, where the Court of Justice compared the wording of Arts 230 and 234, reaching the conclusion that "all acts of the institutions of the Community without exception" are covered by Art.234.
[809] Recommendations are not binding as a result of Art.249 of the EC Treaty.
[810] ECJ, Case C–322/88 *Grimaldi* [1989] E.C.R. 4407, para.18.
[811] ECJ, Case C–94/91 *Wagner* [1992] E.C.R. I-2765, paras 16–17.

the objection of illegality (EC Treaty, Art.241)—that only acts of general application may be so reviewed.[812] The Court of Justice has also given the impression of acceding to that view by referring to the "complete system" of judicial review of acts of the institutions: "Where the Community institutions are responsible for the administrative implementation of . . . measures [of general application], natural or legal persons may bring a direct action before the Court against administrative measures which are addressed to them or which are of direct and individual concern to them and, in support of such an action, plead the illegality of the general measure on which they are based. Where implementation is a matter for the national authorities, such persons may plead the invalidity of general measures before the national courts and cause the latter to request the Court of Justice for a preliminary ruling".[813] It is clear, however, that while that passage correctly reproduces the *rationale* of judicial review of validity by means of the preliminary ruling procedure, it does not necessarily mean that such review may in no circumstances be carried out in respect of an individual act.[814]

10–008 **Individual acts.** What is actually behind the question whether it is possible to review by preliminary ruling the validity of an individual act of a Community institution often seems to arise under a different aspect, namely whether it is still possible for a party to the main proceedings to request the national court to apply to the Court of Justice for a preliminary ruling on the validity of an act where that party could have brought an action for annulment against the act in question within the prescribed time-limit (EC Treaty, Art.230, fifth para.), but neglected to do so.[815] The Court

---

[812] See, for instance, Lagrange, "L'action préjudicielle dans le droit interne des États membres et en droit communautaire" (1974) R.T.D.E. 268, at 281; Mertens de Wilmars, "La procédure suivant l'Art.177*[now Art.234]* CEE" (1965) S.E.W. 437, at 445.

[813] ECJ, Case 294/83 *Les Verts v European Parliament* [1986] E.C.R. 1339, para.23.

[814] See ECJ, Joined Cases 133–136/85 *Rau and Others* [1987] E.C.R. 2289, point 1 of the operative part: "The possibility of bringing a direct action under the [fourth] para.of Art.173*[now Art.230]* of the [EC] Treaty against a decision adopted by a Community institution does not preclude the possibility of bringing an action in a national court against a measure adopted by a national authority for the implementation of that decision on the ground that the latter decision is unlawful". That case was concerned with a Commission decision addressed to the Federal Republic of Germany within the meaning of the fourth para.of Art.189*[now Art.249]* of the EC Treaty; consequently an individual act, which a German authority had implemented with respect to the plaintiffs in the main proceedings, whereupon the plaintiffs brought an action for annulment of the Commission decision in the Court of Justice and an action for annulment of the German implementing decision in the national courts. It was in this context that the Court of Justice held that it had jurisdiction to conduct judicial review of an individual act of a Community institution in a preliminary ruling procedure on the basis of the *rationale* of that jurisdiction set out above. See, to the same effect, ECJ, Case C–70/97 P *Kruidvat v Commission* [1998] E.C.R. I-7183, paras 47–49 (relating to a Commission decision declaring Art.81(1) of the EC Treaty inapplicable to a selective distribution system pursuant to Art.81(3)).

[815] This goes back as far as Tomuschat, *Die gerichtliche Vorabentscheidung nach den Verträgen über die Europäischen Gemeinschaften* (Springer-Verlag, Berlin/Heidelberg/New York, 1964), at 89–92.

of Justice has answered this question in the negative[816]: a natural or legal person who undoubtedly has the right under Art.230 of the EC Treaty to seek the annulment of a Community act,[817] may not plead the illegality of that act in subsequent proceedings before the national courts. The same

---

[816] ECJ, Case C–188/92 *TWD Textilwerke Deggendorf* [1994] E.C.R. I-833: in this case, the Court of Justice held that a beneficiary of a scheme of aid in respect of which the Commission had taken a decision could have brought an action for annulment; ECJ, Case C–178/95 *Wiljo* [1997] E.C.R. I-585, paras 19–24: in this case the Court held that the validity of a Commission decision set out in a letter addressed to the undertaking concerned could no longer be challenged since the undertaking had failed to bring an action for annulment. The same principle applies where the validity of a regulation imposing a definitive anti-dumping levy is challenged by an undertaking which could undoubtedly have sought the annulment of the regulation before the Court of First Instance but failed to do so, even where the regulation has been declared null *vis-à-vis* other undertakings which did bring actions for annulment (ECJ, Case C–239/99 *Nachi Europe* [2001] E.C.R. I-1197, paras 28–40). *Cf.*, however, ECJ, Case C–390/98 *Banks* [2001] E.C.R. I-6117, paras 111–113. In two other cases, the Court of Justice held that a party could plead the illegality of a Community act in national proceedings on the ground that it was not obvious that an action for annulment pursuant to the fourth para. of Art.230 of the EC Treaty would have been admissible: in ECJ, Case C–241/95 *Accrington Beef* [1996] E.C.R. I-6699, para.15, where the applicants in the main proceedings alleged that a regulation was invalid, the Court found that, in view of the fact that the contested act was in the nature of a regulation, it was improbable that an action brought by the applicants for its annulment would have been declared admissible. A similar ruling, but relating to a directive, is contained in ECJ, Case C 408/95 *Eurotunnel and Others* [1997] E.C.R. I-6315, paras 29–30. See also CFI (order of March 10, 2005), Joined Cases T–228/00, T–229/00, T–242/00, T–243/00, T–245/00 to T–248/00, T–250/00, T–252/00, T–256/00 to T–259/00, T–265/00, T–267/00, T–268/00, T–271/00, T–274/00 to T–276/00, T–281/00 and T–287/00 to T–296/00 *Gruppo ormeggiatori del porto di Venezia and Others v Commission*, not yet reported, paras 24 and 30–32. For a critical analysis of the case-law, see Opinion of Advocate General D. Ruiz-Jarabo Colomer of April 28, 2005 in Joined Cases C–346/03 and C–529/03 *Atzeni and Others*, not yet reported, paras 86–98 (those cases concern the validity of a Commission decision declaring a general aid scheme incompatible with the common market).

[817] What comes to mind in the first place is the obvious case where a Community act is addressed to a natural or legal person or where in a specific area of Community law a natural or legal person is manifestly directly and individually concerned within the meaning of the fourth para. of Art.230 of the EC Treaty, such as a recipient of State aid which the Commission has found to be incompatible with the common market in a decision addressed to the Member State in question: ECJ, Case 730/79 *Philip Morris v Commission* [1980] E.C.R. 2671; for those reasons, the President of the Court of First Instance declared admissible an application for interim measures in respect of a Commission decision requiring the recovery of unlawful State aid and rejected the argument of the Commission (which claimed that the application was inadmissible) that application could still be made to the national court to suspend the national measure to recover the aid on the ground of the invalidity of the Commission decision (CFI (order of the President of April 4, 2002), Case T–198/01 R *Technische Glaswerke Ilmenau v Commission* [2002] E.C.R. II-2153, para.54, upheld in ECJ (order of the President of October 18, 2002), Case C–232/02 P(R) *Commission v Technische Glaswerke Ilmenau* [2002] E.C.R. I-8977, paras 32–33); see also ECJ, Case C–188/92 *TWD Textilwerke Deggendorf* [1994] E.C.R. I-833, paras 14 and 24. See also in this regard Pache, "Keine Vorlage ohne Anfechtung?" (1994) Eu.Z.W. 615–620. Where, in connection with the recovery of unlawful aid, the beneficiary undertaking has brought an action for annulment against the Commission decision obliging the aid to be recovered, Community law does not preclude the suspension by the national court of the

applies with regard to Member States and decisions addressed to them.[818] To have decided otherwise would have detracted excessively from the legal certainty which the limitation period prescribed by the fifth para.of Art.230 is intended to secure. The national courts must regard the act in question as valid *vis-à-vis* the party in question and therefore apply it in any event. As a result, there is no point in making a reference to the Court of Justice for a preliminary ruling or at least not with a view to protecting a party to the main proceedings who is no longer entitled to plead that the act is unlawful. Another party to the main proceedings which was not entitled to challenge the act in question pursuant to Art.230 may persuade the national court to make a reference for a preliminary ruling on the validity of the act. There is nothing to prevent the national court from inquiring into this question or from raising it with the Court of Justice of its own motion. If the Court then finds that the act is invalid, it will be for it to determine what consequences that finding should have for the party to the main proceedings for whom the act has become unappealable because of its failure to bring an action for annulment.[819]

10–009 **Failure to act.** In proceedings for a preliminary ruling the Court of Justice has no power to rule that a Community institution has failed to act.[820] Consequently, an action brought on the basis of Art.232 of the EC Treaty (see Ch.8, *supra*) is the only procedure for challenging an unlawful failure to act on the part of an institution.

II. SUBSTANCE OF THE REVIEW OF VALIDITY OF A COMMUNITY ACT IN PRELIMINARY RULING PROCEEDINGS

10–010 **Review of legality of Community acts reserved to the Court of Justice.** The review of the validity of a Community act by preliminary ruling, in common with the action for annulment, is a form of judicial review of the legality of

---

national measure executing the Commission decision (but see CFI (order of the President of December 3, 2002), Case T–181/02 R *Neue Erba Lautex v Commission* [2002] E.C.R. II-5081, para.108).

[818] ECJ, Case C–241/01 *National Farmers' Union* [2002] E.C.R. I-9079, paras 34–39, in which the Court of Justice held that a Member State which was an addressee of a Commission decision on emergency measures to protect against bovine spongiform encephalopathy and which had not challenged the legality of that decision within the time-limit laid down by the fifth para. of Art.230 of the EC Treaty did not have standing subsequently before a national court to invoke its unlawfulness in order to dispute the merits of an action brought against it. Since a Member State can raise an objection of illegality in respect of a regulation which it failed to challenge within the time-limit prescribed by the fifth para. of Art.230 of the EC Treaty (see 9–008, *supra*), it may be assumed that a Member State may also challenge the legality of a regulation before a national court even if it did not bring an action for the annulment of that regulation.

[819] Cf. *Commentaire Mégret*, at 210.

[820] ECJ, Case C–68/95 *T. Port v Commission* [1996] E.C.R. I-6065, para.53.

acts of Community institutions[821]: since Art.230 gives the Court of Justice exclusive jurisdiction to declare void an act of a Community institution, the coherence of the system requires that where the validity of a Community act is challenged before a national court, the power to declare the act invalid must also be reserved to the Court of Justice.[822] The Court, moreover, is "in the best position" to decide on the validity of Community acts, since "[u]nder Art.23 of the Protocol on the Statute of the Court of Justice of the [EC], Community institutions whose acts are challenged are entitled to participate in the proceedings in order to defend the validity of the acts in question".[823]

Differences compared with an action for annulment. The most important differences between the action for annulment and the review of validity in preliminary ruling proceedings are that the latter is not subject to any time-limit and cannot be "limited by the grounds on which the validity of [Community] measures may be contested"[824] and that the initiative for seeking a preliminary ruling on validity comes from the national court and not from interested natural or legal persons. In the main proceedings, the parties may try to move the national court to make a reference to the Court of Justice, but they cannot compel the Court to rule on the validity of a measure if the national court has not put a question to that effect.[825]   10–011

Grounds on which validity may be contested. The parties to the main proceedings or Community institutions and Member States submitting observations pursuant to Art.23 of the Statute cannot oblige the Court of Justice to appraise the validity of an act in the light of "submissions" or "grounds" of illegality not raised in the order for reference.[826] This does not mean, however, that the Court has no latitude at all in the matter.   10–012

The national court may request the Court of Justice merely to interpret a Community act, but the Court, having regard to the whole of the content of the order for reference, may consider the reference to be concerned with

---

[821] ECJ, Case 314/85 *Foto-Frost* [1987] E.C.R. 4199, para.16.

[822] *Ibid.*, para.17.

[823] *Ibid.*, para.18; the wording of this passage of the judgment is more consonant with the procedure in the case of a direct action, see Ch.24, *infra*, than with the formally non-contentious procedure of a reference for a preliminary ruling. The Court of Justice added that, furthermore, under the second para. of Art.24 of the Statute the Court may require the Member States and "institutions which are not participating in the proceedings" to supply all information which it considers necessary for the purposes of the case before it. It had done so on one occasion in order to enable the European Parliament, which was formerly not entitled to submit observations to the Court under Art.23, to defend its prerogatives in proceedings for a preliminary ruling on validity: ECJ, Case 20/85 *Roviello* [1988] E.C.R. 2805, at 2816.

[824] ECJ, Joined Cases 21–24/72 *International Fruit and Others* [1972] E.C.R. 1219, para.5; ECJ, Case C–162/96 *Racke* [1998] E.C.R. I-3655, para.26 (where the Court reviewed the validity of a Community act in the light of customary international law).

[825] ECJ, Case 44/65 *Singer* [1965] E.C.R. 965, at 970.

[826] ECJ, Joined Cases 50–58/82 *Dorca Marina and Others* [1982] E.C.R. 3949, para.13.

the validity of the act with a view to promoting the efficiency of judicial cooperation.[827] It is important in such a case that the order for reference may be construed as a request for a ruling on validity even though it is couched as a request for a ruling on interpretation. The reason for this is that only in such case may the parties to the main proceedings, the Commission, the Council and the European Parliament (if one of their acts is in issue) and the Member States correctly assess what the Court's ruling may cover and formulate their views thereon.[828]

Next, the Court of Justice may supplement the "submissions" or "grounds" of illegality of the Community act at issue as set forth in the order for reference in the light of matters which come to light in the course of legal argument before the Court itself.

One situation occurs where the national court raises the question of the validity of an act in general terms only. In such a case, the Court of Justice will answer that question in the light of an assessment of the submissions which are set out by the claimant in the main proceedings in its observations to the Court concerning the validity of the act[829] or which emerge from the statement of reasons of the order for reference.[830]

Secondly, the Court of Justice has held that it is empowered to find of its own motion infringements of essential procedural requirements by which an act is vitiated, thereby, if necessary, supplementing the submissions set out in the order for reference alleging that the act is invalid.[831] The case-law to this effect is related to the rule applicable to actions for annulment that the Court of Justice or the Court of First Instance will find infringements of essential procedural requirements of its own motion.[832] Lack of competence on the part of the institution which adopted the contested act should also perhaps be regarded as a peremptory plea, with the result that, as in the case of an infringement of an essential procedural requirement, it may be raised by the Court of its own motion in conducting judicial review of a contested act in preliminary ruling proceedings.[833]

10–013   **Finding of facts necessary to assess the legality of a given act.** In arriving at its preliminary ruling on the validity of a given act, the Court of Justice may go no deeper into the facts of the main proceedings than it may in the

---

[827] ECJ, Case 16/65 *Schwarze* [1965] E.C.R. 877, at 886.
[828] *Cf.* ECJ, Case 62/76 *Strehl* [1977] E.C.R. 211, at 217, where the Court of Justice held of its own motion that a provision of a regulation, of which only the interpretation had been sought, was invalid having regard to a decided case.
[829] ECJ, Joined Cases 103 and 145/77 *Royal Scholten Honig* [1978] E.C.R. 2037, paras 16 and 17.
[830] ECJ, Case 41/72 *Getreide-Import* [1973] E.C.R. 1, para.2.
[831] ECJ, Joined Cases 73 and 74/63 *Internationale Crediet- en Handelsvereniging Rotterdam and Others* [1964] E.C.R. 1, at 14.
[832] See ECJ, Case C–291/89 *Interhotel v Commission* [1991] E.C.R. I-2257, para.14; ECJ, Case C–304/89 *Oliveira v Commission* [1991] E.C.R. I-2283, para.18. See also 7–122, *supra*.
[833] See, to this effect, the Opinion of Advocate General J. Gand in ECJ, Case 5/67 *Beus* [1968] E.C.R. 83, at 108–109, who added that, in his view, the Court would not raise the question of misuse of powers of its own motion and that "there is doubt about the situation where there is a question of a breach of the Treaty or a rule of law".

case of a preliminary ruling on interpretation (see 6–021, *supra*).[834] There is a slight difference, however, in that the Court may make all the findings of fact necessary to assess the legality of the contested act.[835] In this respect, the Court's powers are no different if it reviews the legality of an act under Art.230 or Art.234 of the EC Treaty.[836] In this connection, it would be perfectly possible for measures of inquiry to be ordered pursuant to Art.45 of the ECJ Rules of Procedure.[837]

III. CONSEQUENCES OF THE REVIEW OF THE VALIDITY OF A COMMUNITY ACT IN PRELIMINARY RULING PROCEEDINGS

Ruling of the Court of Justice. Where the Court of Justice comes to the conclusion that the contested measure should not be declared invalid, the answer which it gives to the national court is not that the act is valid but as follows: "Examination of the question raised has revealed no factor of such a kind as to affect the validity of [the act]".[838] That answer does not preclude the court to which it is addressed from referring other questions to the Court of Justice which might call in question the validity of the same act.[839]

10–014

Where, in contrast, the Court of Justice declares the act in question invalid, its answer is binding on the national court to which it is made. It may no longer apply the act. The same applies to "any other national court" where there is "sufficient reason [for it] to regard that act as void for the purposes of a judgment which it has to give".[840] The effect *erga omnes* of the preliminary ruling on validity is justified as being the inevitable corollary of "particularly imperative requirements concerning legal certainty in addition to those concerning the uniform application of Community law. It follows from the very nature of such a declaration that a national court may not apply the act declared to be void without once more creating serious uncertainty as to the Community law applicable".[841]

---

[834] Joliet, *Le contentieux*, at 210.

[835] For an example, see ECJ, Case C–323/88 *Sermes* [1990] E.C.R. I-3027, paras 21–31.

[836] The parallel between the two procedures as adverted to by the Court in ECJ, Case 314/85 *Foto-Frost* [1987] E.C.R. 4199 emerges clearly here; for an example, see ECJ, Case C–16/90 *Nölle* [1991] E.C.R. I-5163, paras 17, 23 and 24.

[837] See as long ago as ECJ, Case 5/67 *Beus* [1968] E.C.R. 83, at 86.

[838] For an example, see ECJ, Case C–323/88 *Sermes* [1990] E.C.R. I-3027, operative part.

[839] ECJ, Case 8/78 *Milac* [1978] E.C.R. 1721, paras 4–9.

[840] ECJ, Case 66/80 *International Chemical* [1981] E.C.R. 1191, point 1 of the operative part.

[841] *Ibid.*, para.12, at 1215. For the effects in practice, see Bebr, "Direct and Indirect Judicial Control of Community Acts in Practice: the Relation Between Arts 173 and 177*[now Arts 230 and 234]* of the EEC Treaty" (1984) Mich.L.Rev. 1229, at 1239–1248; Harding, "The Impact of Art.177*[now Art.234]* of the EEC Treaty on the Review of Community Action" (1981) Y.E.L. 93, at 101–106.

10–015 **Definitive effect of a declaration of invalidity.** The declaration that an act is invalid is definitive, as in the case of a declaration of nullity (hence the Court's exclusive jurisdiction to declare an act void results in its also having exclusive jurisdiction to declare an act invalid[842]).

Nevertheless, the Court of Justice endeavours to reconcile the absolute effect of the declaration that a given act is invalid with the requirements of the preliminary ruling procedure as laid down by Art.234. Consequently, it acknowledges that the declaration of invalidity "does not mean ... that national courts are deprived of the power given to them by Art.234 of the Treaty and it rests with those courts to decide whether there is a need to raise once again a question which has already been settled by the Court where the Court has previously declared an act of a Community institution [invalid]".[843] The Court does not mean that the declaration of invalidity may be reversed, but that *any* national court (including the one which obtained the ruling that the act in question was invalid) may possibly have an interest in referring further questions for a preliminary ruling "if questions arise as to the grounds, the scope and possibly the consequences of the invalidity established earlier".[844]

10–016 **Consequences of invalidity in the national legal order.** It is for the national court to decide disputes concerning the consequences of the declaration that a Community act is invalid in accordance with its national law in so far as Community law does not provide otherwise. In principle, therefore, national law governs the formal and substantive requirements for the refund of amounts collected on behalf of the Community—on the basis of a regulation subsequently declared invalid—unless a rule of Community law specifically deals with such refunds.[845]

On a more general level, all national authorities in the Member States have to draw the necessary conclusions from a declaration that a Community measure is invalid. Action by the national authorities may no longer be based on that measure and any action previously taken on the basis of that measure must be withdrawn (and, where necessary, its consequences rectified).[846] However, the consequences which may be drawn in the national legal systems from such a ruling of invalidity depend directly on Community law as it stands in the light of that ruling.[847]

Sometimes the Court of Justice spells out the consequences of the declaration that an act is invalid in the national legal system, either in the judgment ruling that it is invalid or in a subsequent judgment following a request for an interpretation of the consequences of the declaration of invalidity.

---

[842] ECJ, Case 314/85 *Foto-Frost* [1987] E.C.R. 4199, para.16.
[843] ECJ, Case 66/80 *International Chemical* [1981] E.C.R. 1191, para.14.
[844] *Ibid.*
[845] ECJ, Case 199/86 *Raiffeisen* [1988] E.C.R. 1169, paras 12–19.
[846] ECJ, Case 23/75 *Rey Soda* [1975] E.C.R. 1279, paras 50–51.
[847] ECJ, Case C–127/94 *H. & R. Ecroyd and Rupert Ecroyd* [1996] E.C.R. I-2731, para.58.

The first scenario presented itself when an agricultural regulation which denied the benefit of exemption from a levy to a particular group of traders, thereby discriminating against them, was declared invalid. As far as the "scope of the preliminary ruling" was concerned, the Court of Justice inferred from that declaration that the Community legislature had to act upon the judgment by adopting such measures as might be appropriate in order to establish equal treatment for the traders concerned as regards the rules governing exemption from the levy.[848] In so doing, the Court implicitly applied Art.233 of the EC Treaty (governing the consequences of a declaration of nullity) by analogy to a declaration by way of preliminary ruling that an act of a Community institution was invalid. Next, the Court noted that, in the particular circumstances of the case, in which the discrimination did not arise from what the offending provision provided but from what it did not provide, a straightforward declaration that it was invalid would have had the result that, pending the adoption of new provisions, all exemptions would be precluded.[849] In order to avoid such a situation, the Court expressly held that the second para. of Art.231 of the EC Treaty[850] had to be applied "by analogy" for the same reasons of legal certainty which underlay that provision. Specifically, this meant that, pending such new provisions, "the competent authorities must continue to apply the exemption provided for in the provision declared invalid but they must also grant it to the operators affected by the discrimination found to exist".[851]

Next, there is the case where the national court comes back to the Court of Justice with a new request for a preliminary ruling for guidance on how it should react to the declaration of invalidity in deciding the case before it in the main proceedings. Such a request gives the Court of Justice an opportunity to give a precise indication of the consequences of its declaration of invalidity.[852]

Declaration of invalidity comparable to declaration of nullity. So it is clear   10–017
that the Court of Justice in fact attaches similar consequences to the declaration of invalidity and the declaration of nullity, especially as far as

---

[848] ECJ, Case 300/86 *Van Landschoot* [1988] E.C.R. 3443, para.22.
[849] *Ibid.*, para.23.
[850] "In the case of a regulation, however, the Court of Justice shall, if it considers this necessary, state which of the effects of the regulation which it has declared void shall be considered as definitive."
[851] ECJ, Case 300/86 *Van Landschoot* [1988] E.C.R. 3443, para.24; *cf.* ECJ, Case 264/82 *Timex v Council and Commission* [1985] E.C.R. 849, para.32.
[852] ECJ, Case 359/87 *Pinna* [1989] E.C.R. 585, at 612–616, where the Court explained the consequences of its declaration that Art.73(2) of Regulation No 1408/71 was invalid for "those authorities [which were obliged] to draw the inferences in their legal system from a declaration of invalidity made in the context of Art.177*[now Art.234]* of the Treaty" "so long as the Council has failed, following the judgment of the Court, to lay down new rules", *ibid.*, para.13; the earlier judgment containing the declaration of invalidity is reported at ECJ, Case 41/84 *Pinna* [1986] E.C.R. 1.

the application of the second para. of Art.231 and Art.233[853] of the EC
Treaty is concerned. The act which has been declared invalid may no longer
be applied by a national court or a national authority, the institution which
adopted the offending act must take appropriate steps to cure the illegality
and, if necessary, adopt a new measure, and the Court of Justice is
prepared in certain circumstances to maintain certain aspects of the act
which has been declared void in force until another measure has been
adopted.

10–018   **Temporal effects.** As far as temporal effects are concerned, the declaration
of invalidity and the declaration of nullity run on parallel lines. The Court
of Justice has held that "A judgment of the Court in proceedings for a
preliminary ruling declaring a Community act invalid in principle has
retroactive effect, like a judgment annulling an act".[854]

However, a problem may arise as a result of the fact that there is no
temporal restriction on a national court's requesting the Court of Justice to
declare a Community act invalid, in contrast to an action for annulment,
which has to be brought within the limitation period laid down. Consequently, the idea that the legal uncertainty resulting from the effect *ex tunc*
of a declaration of nullity (*i.e.* from the date on which the measure declared
void took effect) is mitigated by the relatively short period within which an
action for annulment must be brought has no relevance to a declaration of
invalidity. This may explain why the Court of Justice has inferred from
Art.234 the power to modulate the temporal effects of preliminary rulings
declaring Community acts invalid, depending on the case.[855] In order to
justify that power, the Court had recourse to the argument that the

---

[853] CFI, Case T–220/97 *H & R Ecroyd v Commission* [1999] E.C.R. II-1677, para.49.

[854] ECJ, Case C–228/92 *Roquette Frères* [1994] E.C.R. I-1445, para.17, from which it follows
that the national authorities must ensure the repayment of sums unduly charged on the
basis of Community regulations which are subsequently declared invalid by the Court, *ibid.*,
para.18; see also ECJ, Case 130/79 *Express Dairy Foods* [1980] E.C.R. 1887, para.14; *cf.*
Pescatore, "Art.177*[now Art.234]*", in Constantinesco et al. (eds), *Traité instituant la CEE.
Commentaire Art. par Art.* (Economica, Paris, 1992), No 70, at 1200–1121). See also Hyland,
"Temporal Limitation of the Effects of Judgments of the Court of Justice—A review of
recent case-law" (1995) Ir.J.E.L. 208–233; Isaac, "La modulation par la Cour de justice des
Communautés européennes des effets dans le temps de ses arrêts d'invalidité" (1987)
C.D.E. 444–470; Weiss, "Die Einschränkung der zeitlichen Wirkungen von Vora-
bentscheidungen nach Art.177 EGV" (1995) EuR. 377–397.

[855] ECJ, Case 112/83 *Société des Produits de Maïs* [1985] E.C.R. 719; for a case in which the
Court of Justice refused to restrict the effect *ex tunc* of a declaration of invalidity, see
Joined Cases C–363 and C–407-411/93 *Lancry and Others* [1994] E.C.R. I-3957, paras 40–
45. See also ECJ, Joined Cases C–177/99 and C–181/99 *Ampafrance and Sanofi Synthelabo*
[2000] E.C.R. I-7013, para.67 (in this case a Member State invoked for the first time the
principle of protection of legitimate expectations with a view to limiting the temporal
effects of a judgment declaring a decision invalid. The Court of Justice held that this was
not possible on the ground that to allow a Member State to do so would jeopardise the
possibility for individuals to be protected against conduct of the public authorities based on
unlawful rules) and ECJ, Case C–228/99 *Silos e Mangimi Martini* [2001] E.C.R. I-8401,
paras 35–38.

declaration of nullity and the declaration of invalidity were "two mechanisms provided for by the Treaty for reviewing the legality of acts of the Community institutions" and that the "necessary consistency" between the two mechanisms warranted interpreting the second para.of Art.231 of the EC Treaty as enabling the Court to impose "temporal limits on the invalidity of a Community regulation, whether under Art.230 or Art.234 ... in the interest of the uniform application of Community law throughout the Community" (in the event of the declaration's having full effect *ex tunc*, it would perhaps be impossible under the procedural law of some Member States to undo all the effects which the act declared invalid had already had, which would be at the expense of the uniform non-application of the act as far as the past was concerned).[856]

Limitation of temporal effects. As far as limiting the temporal effects of its judgments is concerned, the Court of Justice will decide "in each particular case" whether "an exception to that temporal limitation ... may be made in favour of the party who brought the action before the national court or of any other trader which took similar steps before the declaration of invalidity or whether, conversely, a declaration of invalidity applicable only to the future constitutes an adequate remedy".[857] In the latter case, the Court has in fact considered that the parties which took the initiative of challenging in the national courts the act ultimately declared invalid are sufficiently rewarded for their efforts by seeing the act eliminated from the legal system for the future.[858] That approach has come in for criticism on the ground that it effectively deprives the party who successfully pleaded the invalidity of the Community act of the benefit of his or her success, since that party only shares in the general benefit which anyone may have in an invalid Community act which is detrimental to his or her interests being no longer applied.[859] This is patently insufficient to act as a stimulus to setting judicial review in train.

The Court of Justice recognised this when it was faced with this question on a subsequent occasion and had to consider whether "an importer who, like the plaintiff in the main proceedings, has brought an administrative complaint followed by judicial proceedings, challenging a notice to pay MCAs [monetary compensatory amounts] on the ground that the Community regulation on the basis of which the notice was adopted was invalid, is entitled to rely for the purposes of those proceedings on the invalidity of

10–019

---

[856] *Société des Produits de Maïs*, cited in the preceding n., para.17.
[857] *Ibid.*, para.18.
[858] ECJ, Case 4/79 *Providence Agricole de la Champagne* [1980] E.C.R. 2823, paras 42–46; ECJ, Case 109/79 *Maïseries de Beauce* [1980] E.C.R. 2883, paras 42–46; ECJ, Case 145/79 *Roquette Frères* [1980] E.C.R. 2917, paras 50–53.
[859] See, among others, Vanavermaete, case note in (1982) S.E.W. 469; Labayle, "La Cour de justice des Communautés et les effets d'une déclaration d'invalidité" (1982) R.T.D.E. 484–510; Waelbroeck, "Le principe de la non-rétroactivité en droit communautaire à la lumière des arrêts 'isoglucose'" (1983) R.T.D.E. 363.

a regulation declared by the Court of Justice in the same proceedings".[860] If the Court were to have held that "a declaration of invalidity applicable only to the future is an adequate remedy even for that party", this would have meant that "the national court would dismiss the action brought against the notice in question, even though the regulation on the basis of which that notice was adopted had been declared invalid by the Court in the same proceedings".[861] The Court found that that outcome would be unacceptable: "An economic agent such as the plaintiff in the main proceedings would thereby be deprived of its right to effective judicial protection in the event of a breach of Community law by the institutions, and the practical effect of Art.234 of the Treaty would thereby be jeopardised".[862] Consequently, it came to the conclusion that "a trader who before the date of the present judgment has brought an action in a national court challenging a notice to pay MCAs adopted on the basis of a Community regulation declared invalid by the present judgment is entitled to rely on that invalidity in the national proceedings".[863] This meant not only the plaintiff in the main proceedings which had resulted in the reference to the Court of Justice, but also anyone who had brought judicial proceedings or "submitted an administrative complaint" before the date of the declaration of invalidity.[864]

Since the Court of Justice reached that decision sitting as the Full Court and it is based on the fundamental "right to effective judicial protection" and on guaranteeing the "practical effect [*effet utile*] of Art.234 of the Treaty", it seems unlikely that in future the Court will revert to the option, which still exists in theory, of holding that a declaration of invalidity is applicable to parties to the main proceedings and others whose position may be equated with theirs "only for the future".

---

[860] ECJ, Case C–228/92 *Roquette Frères* [1994] E.C.R. I-1445, para.24.
[861] *Ibid.*, paras 25 and 26.
[862] *Ibid.*, para.27.
[863] *Ibid.*, para.30.
[864] *Ibid.*; see also the earlier case ECJ, Case 41/84 *Pinna* [1986] E.C.R. 1, paras 29–30.

CHAPTER 11

THE ACTION FOR DAMAGES

I. SUBJECT-MATTER

A. GENERAL

Objective and conditions. An action for damages seeks to have the Community held non-contractually liable to make good any damage caused by its institutions or by its servants in the performance of their duties. The conditions for incurring liability are determined by the Court of Justice and the Court of First Instance "in accordance with the general principles common to the laws of the Member States" (EC Treaty, Art.288, second para.). The Court of Justice has drawn on those general principles—in so far as they could be identified—only as a source of inspiration with a view to developing an independent Community law on liability.[865] Liability on the part of the Community "presupposes the existence of a set of circumstances comprising actual damage, a causal link between the damage claimed and conduct alleged against the institution, and the illegality of such conduct".[866]

11–001

Exclusive jurisdiction. Art.235 of the EC Treaty confers on the Court of Justice exclusive jurisdiction to find the Community non-contractually liable.[867] This jurisdiction is now vested in the Court of First Instance by

11–002

---

[865] For an extensive discussion, see Fines, "Etude de la responsabilité extracontractuelle de la Communauté économique européenne", in *Bibliothèque de droit international* (Librairie générale de droit et de jurisprudence, Paris, 1990), Vol.101, 501 pp., and Brealey and Hoskins, *Remedies in E.C. Law*, at 350–372.

[866] ECJ, Case 4/69 *Lütticke v Commission* [1971] E.C.R. 325, para.10. For non-contractual liability under the former rules of the ECSC Treaty, see Arts 34 and 40 of that Treaty; see also CFI, Case T–120/89 *Stahlwerke Peine-Salzgitter v Commission* [1991] E.C.R. II–279, which should be compared with ECJ, Case C–220/91 P *Commission v Stahlwerke Peine-Salzgitter* [1993] E.C.R. I–2393.

[867] The Court has the same exclusive jurisdiction under Art.151 of the EAEC Treaty. The fact that the Court has exclusive jurisdiction also means that a national court has no competence to order, with respect to one of the institutions of the Community, proceedings for an expert report whose purpose is to determine the role of that institution in events alleged to have caused damage, for the purposes of subsequent proceedings against the European Community to establish its non-contractual liability (ECJ, Case C–275/00 *First and Franex* [2002] E.C.R. I–10943, paras 43–50). In contrast, the terms of a contract for

virtue of Art.225 of the EC Treaty.[868] The exclusive jurisdiction of the Court of First Instance—and of the Court of Justice on appeal—to find the Community non-contractually liable guarantees the Community's independence in so far as its acts are not reviewed in the light of national law by national courts; in addition, it has the advantage of ensuring that there are uniform rules on liability for unlawful acts of the Community.

B. INDEPENDENT NATURE OF THE ACTION FOR DAMAGES

11–003   **Independent form of action.** The question arises as to the extent to which the independent nature of the action for damages is influenced by the existence of other procedures which are available to an applicant in order to have the legality of an act causing damage reviewed by the Community Court. More specifically, the question is whether the action for damages is an independent form of action or whether the applicant may bring such proceedings only after it has been determined in some other proceedings that the act in question is unlawful.[869]

Originally, the case-law seemed to take the second of these two approaches in that actions for damages seemed to be regarded as admissible only if an action for the annulment of the contested act had been brought.[870] Shortly after, however, matters took a different turn when the Court of Justice described the action for damages as "an independent form of action with a particular purpose to fulfil within the system of actions and subject to conditions for its use, conceived with a view to its specific purpose".[871]

---

compensation concluded with an individual in the name and on behalf of the Council and the Commission by the competent national authority pursuant to Regulation No 2187/93, which gave so-called SLOM producers the possibility of obtaining flat-rate compensation following the judgment in *Mulder II*, were not categorised as non-contractual liability. They constituted contractual terms, which in the absence of an arbitration clause in favour of the Court of Justice within the meaning of Art.238 of the EC Treaty fell to be adjudicated by the national courts (ECJ, Joined Cases C–80/99 to C–82/99 *Flemmer and Others* [2001] E.C.R. I–7211). For a distinction between contractual and non-contractual liability, see also CFI, Case T–154/01 *Distilleria F. Palma v Commission* [2004] E.C.R. II–1493 paras 41–49.

[868] See Statute, Art.51.

[869] Mead, "The Relationship between an Action for Damages and an Action for Annulment: the Return of *Plaumann*", in Heukels and McDonnell (eds), *The Action for Damages in Community Law* (Kluwer Law International, The Hague/London/Boston, 1997), at 243–258.

[870] ECJ, Case 25/62 *Plaumann v Commission* [1963] E.C.R. 95, at 108: "An administrative measure which has not been annulled cannot of itself constitute a wrongful act on the part of the administration inflicting damage on those whom it affects". On this view, a finding of an unlawful failure to act or a declaration by way of preliminary ruling that a measure was invalid was to be equated with a declaration that the measure was void.

[871] ECJ, Case 4/69 *Lütticke v Commission* [1971] E.C.R. 325, at 336. See also ECJ (order of June 21, 1993), Case C–257/93 *Van Parijs and Others v Council and Commission* [1993] E.C.R. I–3335, para.14; ECJ, Case C–234/02 P *European Ombudsman v Lamberts* [2004] E.C.R. I–2803, para.59; CFI, Case T–170/00 *Förde-Reederei v Council and Commission* [2002] E.C.R. II–515, para.35. In his Opinion in ECJ, Joined Cases 9 and 11/71 *Compagnie d'Approvisionnement, de Transport et de Crédit and Others v Commission* [1972] E.C.R. 391,

Consequently, an action for damages will be admissible even if no prior action for annulment[872] or for failure to act[873] has been brought and if no preliminary ruling declaring the offending act invalid has been obtained. The purpose of an action for damages is solely to obtain financial compensation and, on that ground, differs from that of other forms of action.[874] What is more, the requirements in order for liability to be incurred are substantively very different from the criteria for reviewing the legality of an action or an alleged failure to act on the part of the Community.[875] The fact that an action for annulment of an act of a Community institution which at the same time is the subject of an action for damages is inadmissible does not necessarily make the claim for damages inadmissible.[876]

---

at 411, Advocate General A. Dutheillet de Lamothe argued cogently that the action for damages should be independent of any action for annulment. He pointed out that a declaration of nullity applies *erga omnes* and is retroactive. In his view, those far-reaching consequences explained why the authors of the Treaty had restricted individuals' access to the Court of Justice (now the Court of First Instance) on the basis of Art.230 of the EC Treaty and why the second para. of Art.231 of that Treaty had conferred on the Court of Justice the power to restrict the retroactive effect of a declaration of nullity. In contrast, the action for damages was an action for a declaration of subjective rights (*i.e.* rights appertaining to the applicant personally) and did not have the same far-reaching results. Consequently, the same stringent conditions as to admissibility ought not to apply. The argument that the authors of the Treaty had sought—irrespective of the type of dispute—to prevent the Court of Justice from ruling on the legality of a general act on an application from individuals was therefore misconceived. See also Cujo, "L'autonomie du recours en indemnité par rapport au recours en annulation" [1999] R.M.C. 414–420. For staff cases, see Ch.18, *infra*.

[872] ECJ, Case 5/71 *Zuckerfabrik Schöppenstedt v Council* [1971] E.C.R. 975, para.3. A party may bring a claim for damages without there being any provision requiring it also to claim annulment of the unlawful act which gave rise to the damage (CFI, Case T–178/98 *Fresh Marine v Commission* [2000] E.C.R. II–3331, para.49); there is also no requirement for the act which gave rise to the damage to be legally binding (CFI, Case T–209/00 *Lamberts v European Ombudsman* [2002] E.C.R. II–2203, para.58). The annulment of a decision does not have any effect on the limitation period for bringing an action for damages. Indeed, the infringement of Community law, which allegedly causes harm, exists before the annulment of the decision by the Community Court: CFI (judgment of April 21, 2005), Case T–28/03 *Holcim v Commission*, not yet reported, paras 66–67.

[873] ECJ, Case 4/69 *Lütticke v Commission* [1971] E.C.R. 325.

[874] See, for instance, the Opinion of Advocate General F. Capotorti in ECJ, Case 68/77 *IFG v Commission* [1978] E.C.R. 353, at 375.

[875] Consequently, a finding that an act is unlawful or that the Community has failed to act does not as such give rise to a right to compensation. But an action for damages which is brought together with an action for annulment and seeks compensation for damage allegedly caused solely by the unlawfulness of an act of an institution will be inadmissible if it appears from examination of the application for annulment that the act has no legal effects: ECJ (order of June 13, 1991), Case C–50/90 *Sunzest v Commission* [1991] E.C.R. I–2917, para.19; ECJ (order of October 4, 1991), Case C–117/91 *Bosman v Commission* [1991] E.C.R. I–4837, para.20; CFI (order of October 10, 1996), Case T–75/96 *Söktas v Commission* [1996] E.C.R. II–1689, para.49. The Court of First Instance also dismissed a damages claim after annulling the act which had allegedly caused the damage, stating that it could not rule on that claim without prejudging the substance of any new decision to be taken by the Commission to comply with its judgment pursuant to Art.233 of the EC Treaty (CFI, Case T–241/00 *Le Canne v Commission* [2002] E.C.R. I–1251, paras 61–64).

[876] ECJ, Case 175/84 *Krohn v Commission* [1986] E.C.R. 735, para.32; CFI, Case T–185/94

11–004 **Improper use of an action for damages.** However, an action for damages will be inadmissible where it is used improperly as an action for annulment or for failure to act. An applicant who seeks to use an action for damages in order to obtain the specific outcome sought by one of those forms of action will be denied access to the Community Court. To use an action for damages for that purpose would amount to an abuse of process. Accordingly, an action for damages may not be brought in order to avoid the consequences of time having run out for bringing an action for annulment against an act against which the applicant could have brought such an action. The covert, unlawful purpose of the action for damages will be inferred from the fact that the reparation sought coincides with the benefit which the applicant would have obtained as a result of the annulment of the contested Community act[877] or from the close connection between the damage which arose and the applicant's own failure to have recourse to another form of action.[878] No matter how comprehensible this case-law may be, textbook writers correctly point out that it detracts from the autonomous nature of the action for damages.[879]

II. IDENTITY OF THE PARTIES

A. APPLICANTS

11–005 **Any natural or legal person.** Any natural or legal person who claims to have been injured by acts or conduct of a Community institution or its officials or servants may bring an action for damages in the Court of First Instance.[880]

There is no requirement as to the applicant's nationality in the case of such an action.[881]

Geotronics v Commission [1995] E.C.R. II–2795, para.38; CFI, Case T–485/93 *Dreyfus v Commission* [1996] E.C.R. II–1101, para.67; CFI, Case T–491/93 *Richco v Commission* [1996] E.C.R. II–1131, para.64.

[877] ECJ, Case 59/65 *Schreckenberg v Commission* [1966] E.C.R. 543, at 550; *Krohn v Commission*, cited in the preceding n., para.33; ECJ, Joined Cases C–199 and C–200/94 P *Pevasa and Inpesca v Commission* [1995] E.C.R. I–3709, para.28; CFI, Case T–514/93 *Cobrecaf and Others v Commission* [1995] E.C.R. II–621, paras 59–60; *Dreyfus v Commission*, cited in the preceding n., para.68; *Richco v Commission*, cited in the preceding n., para.65; CFI (order of February 3, 1998), Case T–68/96 *Polyvios v Commission* [1998] E.C.R. II–153, paras 32–45; CFI, Case T–93/95 *Laga v Commission* [1997] E.C.R. II–195, paras 48–49; CFI, Case T–94/95 *Landuyt v Commission* [1997] E.C.R. II–213, paras 48–49; CFI, Case T–186/98 *Inpesca v Commission* [2001] E.C.R. II–557, paras 76–77; CFI, Case T–180/00 *Astipesca v Commission* [2002] E.C.R. II–3985, paras 139–147.

[878] ECJ, Case 4/67 *Muller (née Collignon) v Commission* [1967] E.C.R. 365, at 373.

[879] Waelbroeck and Waelbroeck, *Répertoire de droit communautaire*, key words: Responsabilité (de la Communauté) (Ed. Dalloz, Paris, 1994/3), 14. Note also ECJ, Case 153/73 *Holtz & Willemsen v Council and Commission* [1974] E.C.R. 675, paras 3–5; ECJ, Joined Cases 197–200, 243, 245 and 247/80 *Ludwigshafener Walzmühle and Others v Council and Commission* [1981] E.C.R. 3211, paras 4–5; ECJ, Case C–87/89 *SONITO and Others v Commission* [1990] E.C.R. I–1981, para.14.

[880] ECJ, Case 118/83 *CMC v Commission* [1985] E.C.R. 2325, para.31.

[881] *Cf.* ECJ, Case 119/77 *Nippon Seiko v Council and Commission* [1979] E.C.R. 1303; ECJ, Joined Cases 239 and 275/82 *Allied Corporation v Commission* [1984] E.C.R. 1005.

Injury must be personal. The injury for which the applicant seeks repara- **11–006**
tion must affect his or her own personal assets. Legal persons in particular
must show that the damage sustained affected their own separate assets and
not (exclusively) the personal assets of their members.[882] They may also not
claim compensation for the collective damage suffered by their members.[883]

Action by subrogation. Nevertheless, a person who suffers injury may **11–007**
assign his or her right which was infringed, together with his or her claim to
damages, to another person who will consequently be entitled to bring an
action by subrogation.[884] Once the injured party has assigned his or her
claim, that party ceases to have the right to bring an action.[885] If the
assignment is of a fraudulent nature—if the assignor and/or the assignee is
not in good faith—it may not be relied upon as against the defendant.[886]

Member States. Art.235 and the second para. of Art.288 of the EC Treaty **11–008**
do not preclude Member States from bringing an action for damages. To
date, no Member State has done so and hence there is no case-law
concerning the conditions that such an action has to satisfy.

B. Defendants

General. The Community may incur liability under the second para. of **11–009**
Art.288 of the EC Treaty as a result of damage caused by its institutions
(see 11–011, *infra*) or by its servants in the performance of their duties (see
11–012 to 11–014, *infra*). Community liability may also arise in conjunction
with liability on the part of the Member States (see 11–015 to 11–017,
infra). However, the Community cannot incur non-contractual liability for
an act of primary Community law (such as amendments to the Treaties),
since such an act cannot be imputed to a Community institution.[887]

---

[882] ECJ, Case 114/83 *Société d'Initiatives et de Coopération Agricoles v Commission* [1984]
E.C.R. 2589, paras 3–5; ECJ, Case 289/83 *GAARM v Commission* [1984] E.C.R. 4295, paras
4–5; CFI, Joined Cases T–481 and T–484/93 *Exporteurs in Levende Varkens and Others v
Commission* [1995] E.C.R. II–2941, para.76; CFI, Case T–149/96 *Coldiretti and Others v
Council and Commission* [1998] E.C.R. II–3841, paras 57–60; CFI (order of July 2, 2004),
Case T–9/03 *Coldiretti and Others v Commission*, not reported, para.47.
[883] ECJ, Case 72/74 *Union Syndicale and Others v Council* [1975] E.C.R. 401, para.21.
[884] ECJ, Case 238/78 *Ireks-Arkady v Council and Commission* [1979] E.C.R. 2955, para.5; ECJ,
Joined Cases 256–257, 265, 267/80, 5 and 51/81 and 282/82 *Birra Wührer and Others v
Council and Commission* [1984] E.C.R. 3693, para.12; CFI (order of July 2, 2004), Case T–
9/03 *Coldiretti and Others v Commission*, not reported, para.47.
[885] *Birra Wührer and Others v Council and Commission*, cited in the preceding n., para.7.
[886] ECJ, Case 250/78 *DEKA v EEC* [1983] E.C.R. 421.
[887] ECJ, Case 169/73 *Compagnie Continentale v Council* [1975] E.C.R. 117, para.16; ECJ,
Joined Cases 31 and 35/86 *LAISA and Others v Council* [1988] E.C.R. 2285, paras 19–22;
ECJ (order of July 8, 1999), Case C–95/98 P *Edouard Dubois and Fils v Council and
Commission* [1999] E.C.R. I–4835; CFI, Case T–113/96 *Edouard Dubois and Fils v Council
and Commission* [1998] E.C.R. II–125, para.47; CFI (order of June 26, 2000), Joined Cases

Similarly, acts of the Member States cannot cause the Community to incur liability.[888]

11–010 **Institution to which the harmful act is attributable.** Substantively, it is the Community which has to be regarded as being the defendant and not the institutions, since they have no legal personality.[889] Yet it is the Community institution to which the harmful act is attributable which has to be summoned before the Court of First Instance or the Court of Justice as representing the Community.[890] The Commission has no general right to represent the Community.[891] It is advisable for the applicant to specify the institution against which its action is brought in its application, even though the Court of Justice takes a flexible, non-formalistic approach in this regard.[892] If the damage was caused by more than one institution, they must all be brought into the proceedings.

1. Damage caused by institutions

11–011 **Broad interpretation.** The "institutions" which may cause the Community to incur liability under the second para. of Art.288 of the EC Treaty are not only those listed in Art.7(1) of that Treaty, but also all bodies and agencies active in the sphere of Community law, such as the European Central Bank,[893] the European Investment Bank[894] and the European Ombuds-

---

T–12/98 and T–13/98 *Argon and Others v Council and Commission* [2000] E.C.R. II–2473. The adoption (signature and ratification) of the Single European Act (or of any other Treaty amending the original EC Treaty) is an act of the Member States and cannot be ascribed to the Community (CFI (order of June 15, 2000), Case T–614/97 *Aduanas Pujol Rubio and Others v Council and Commission* [2000] E.C.R. II–2387).

[888] CFI (order of December 1, 2004), Case T–370/04 *Krahl-Seretna*, not reported.

[889] ECJ, Case 302/87 *European Parliament v Council* [1988] E.C.R. 5615, para.9. It does not follow that because an action was brought directly against a Community body it is inadmissible. Such an action must be deemed to be directed against the Community represented by that body: ECJ, Case 353/88 *Briantex and Di Domenico v Commission* [1989] E.C.R. 3623, para.7; CFI, Case T–209/00 *Lamberts v European Ombudsman* [2002] E.C.R. II–2203, para.48.

[890] ECJ, Joined Cases 63–69/72 *Werhahn Hansamuhle and Others v Council* [1973] E.C.R. 1229, para.7; Opinion of Advocate General C.O. Lenz in ECJ, Case 62/83 *Eximo v Commission* [1984] E.C.R. 2295, at 2317–2318.

[891] Art.282 of the EC Treaty is concerned only with the Community's power to act and its representation in the various Member States.

[892] ECJ, Case 106/81 *Kind v EEC* [1982] E.C.R. 2885; compare CFI, Case T–246/93 *Bühring v Council and Commission* [1998] E.C.R. II–171, para.26, in which the defendant institutions argued that the application was inadmissible on the ground that it designated the Council and the Commission as defendants and not the Community. The Court of First Instance held that this could not render the application inadmissible where it did not affect the rights of the defence.

[893] The third para. of Art.228 of the EC Treaty provides that the second para. of that article is to apply under the same conditions to damage caused by the European Central Bank or by its servants in the performance of their duties.

[894] ECJ, Case C–370/89 *SGEEM and Etroy v EIB* [1992] E.C.R. I–6211, para.16.

man.[895] This broad interpretation is designed to prevent the Community from escaping possible liability where it acts through bodies and agencies which are not institutions within the meaning of Art.7(1) of the EC Treaty,[896] since national courts have no jurisdiction to find the Community non-contractually liable.

In contrast, acts of the European Council cannot cause the Community to incur liability.[897]

---

[895] CFI, Case T–209/00 *Lamberts v European Ombudsman* [2002] E.C.R. II–2203, para.49: the Court of First Instance declared admissible an action for compensation for the damage which Mr Lamberts allegedly sustained as a result of negligence on the part of the European Ombudsman in the performance of his duties. The judgment was upheld on appeal (ECJ, Case C–234/02 *European Ombudsman v Lamberts* [2004] E.C.R. I–2803).

[896] Some bodies have legal personality. The Court of Justice or the Court of First Instance may hold that these bodies have incurred non-contractual liability pursuant to a specific provision in the decisions establishing them. See European Centre for the Development of Vocational Training: Art.17(2), first and second subparas, of Regulation (EEC) No 337/75 of the Council of February 10, 1975 establishing a European Centre for the Development of Vocational Training, [1975] O.J. L39/1; European Foundation for the Improvement of Living and Working Conditions: Art.21(2), first and second subparas, of Regulation (EEC) No 1365/75 of the Council of May 26, 1975 on the creation of a European Foundation for the Improvement of Living and Working Conditions, [1975] O.J. L139/1; European Agency for Cooperation: Art.18(2), first and second subparas, of Council Regulation (EEC) No 3245/81 of October 26, 1981 setting up a European Agency for Cooperation, [1981] O.J. L328/1; European Environment Agency and the European Environment Information and Observation Network: Art.18(2), first and second subparas, of Council Regulation (EEC) No 1210/90 of May 7, 1990 on the establishment of the European Environment Agency and the European Environment Information and Observation Network, [1990] O.J. L120/1; European Training Foundation: Art.15(2), first and second subparas, of Council Regulation (EEC) No 1360/90 of May 7, 1990 establishing a European Training Foundation, [1990] O.J. L131/1; European Monitoring Centre for Drugs and Drug Addiction: Art.16(2) of Council Regulation (EEC) No 302/93 of February 8, 1993 on the establishment of a European Monitoring Centre for Drugs and Drug Addiction, [1993] O.J. L36/1; European Agency for the Evaluation of Medicinal Products: Art.60(2) of Council Regulation (EEC) No 2309/93 of July 22, 1993 laying down Community procedures for the authorisation and supervision of medicinal products for human and veterinary use and establishing a European Agency for the Evaluation of Medicinal Products, [1993] O.J. L214/1; Office for Harmonisation in the Internal Market (Trade Marks and Designs): Art.114(3) and (4) of Council Regulation (EC) No 40/94 of December 20, 1993 on the Community trade mark, [1994] O.J. L11/1; European Agency for Safety and Health at Work: Art.21(2), first and second subparas, of Council Regulation (EC) No 2062/94 of July 18, 1994 establishing a European Agency for Safety and Health at Work, [1994] O.J. L216/1; Community Plant Variety Office: Art.33(3) and (4) of Council Regulation (EC) No 2100/94 of July 27, 1994 on Community plant variety rights, [1994] O.J. L227/1; Translation Centre for Bodies of the European Union: Art.18(2), first and second subparas, of Council Regulation (EC) No 2965/94 of November 28, 1994 setting up a Translation Centre for bodies of the European Union, [1994] O.J. L314/1; European Monitoring Centre on Racism and Xenophobia: Art.15(2) of Council Regulation (EC) No 1035/97 of June 2, 1997, [1997] O.J. L151/1. Other "bodies" include the European Economic and Social Committee (EC Treaty, Art.7(2)), the Committee of the Regions (EC Treaty, Art.7(2)) and the European Ombudsman (EC Treaty, Art.195(1)).

[897] CFI (order of December 17, 2003), Case T–346/03 *Krikorian and Others v European Parliament and Others* [2003] E.C.R. II–6037, para.17.

2. Damage caused by servants of institutions in the performance of their duties

11–012 **Acts carried out in performance of the servant's duties.** The Court of Justice has regarded only a limited class of acts of servants of the institutions as acts carried out "in the performance of their duties" which are potentially capable of causing the Community to incur liability. The Community may be held liable only for damage caused by acts which are the "necessary extension" of the tasks entrusted to the institution to which the staff member belongs.[898]

Where a servant drives his or her own car pursuant to a travel order, this does not satisfy that test, except in the case of *force majeure* or in exceptional circumstances of such overriding importance that the Community would otherwise have been unable to carry out the tasks entrusted to it. A servant who causes a road accident with his or her own car pursuant to a travel order issued by his or her institution therefore does not cause his or her institution to incur liability for the ensuing damage in the absence of *force majeure* or exceptional circumstances.[899]

11–013 **Other acts.** Servants are liable for acts not performed in pursuance of their duties. They are not immune from legal proceedings in respect of such acts under Art.12(a) of the Protocol on the Privileges and Immunities of the European Communities, since such immunity is limited to "acts performed by them in their official capacity, including their words spoken or written".

11–014 **Immunity of the servant and liability of the Community.** There is no parallel between the possible liability of the Community and the staff member's immunity from legal proceedings.[900] If the staff member's immunity is waived, this does not prevent the wrongful act from causing the Community to incur liability. Consequently, an act which cannot be regarded as having been performed by the staff member in an "official capacity" within the meaning of Art.12(a) of the Protocol may nevertheless be deemed an act carried out "in the performance of his duties" and imputed to the Community.[901] The idea behind this case-law is to avoid the

---

[898] ECJ, Case 9/69 *Sayag and Others* [1969] E.C.R. 329, para.7. The staff members concerned are the servants of any "institution" within the meaning of the second para. of Art.288 of the EC Treaty, including the European Central Bank (EC Treaty, Art.288, third para.).

[899] *Ibid.*, paras 8–13. Note that this judgment refers to Art.151 and the second para. of Art.188 of the EAEC Treaty, the provisions corresponding to Art.235 and the second para. of Art.288 of the EC Treaty.

[900] ECJ, Case 5/68 *Sayag and Others* [1968] E.C.R. 395, at 402.

[901] Schermers and Swaak suggest that a single concept of an "official act" should be used both for the scope of the immunity from legal proceedings and for determining the ambit of liability on the part of the Community. They argue that this concept should be given a broad interpretation so that the Community may be held liable for any official act, yet that

Community getting out of a claim all too easily by simply waiving the immunity of the staff member concerned, which would ultimately result in the injured party's risking coming up against an insolvent debtor—the staff member as opposed to the Community. As a result, concurrent claims against the Community (before the Court of First Instance) and against the staff member himself or herself (before the national courts) are not ruled out either.

3. Liability concurrent with that of Member States

Principle. The Member States make an extensive contribution to the implementation of Community law. If they act unlawfully in this connection, this may affect the assets of individuals.[902]

11–015

Sometimes the financial loss is exclusively ascribable to the Member State's infringing Community law in performing its executive task. But it may also arise because of the illegality of a Community act which was still regarded as valid at the time when it was implemented by the Member State. Lastly, the pecuniary loss may be the result of unlawful joint action on the part of the Community and a Member State.

In principle, the financial loss must be made good by the authority which caused it through its unlawful action. Accordingly, the Community must make good the financial loss caused by its institutions or by servants of its institutions in the performance of their duties, whilst the Member State will be liable for the financial loss caused by national authorities.[903]

Grounds on which an act may be attributed to the Community or a Member State. Having stated this principle, however, the question remains as to the grounds on which an unlawful act may be attributed to a

11–016

---

immunity should invariably be waived where this does not conflict with the interests of the Community. The injured party would virtually always be able to make a claim against both the Community and the staff member concerned and so the fear of the Court of Justice that the Community might escape liability by acting quickly to waive the staff member's immunity would be groundless: "Official Acts of Community Servants and Art.215*[now Art.288]*(4) EC", in Heukels and McDonnell (eds) (n.869, *supra*), at 167–178.

[902] For an extensive discussion, see Wils, "Concurrent Liability of the Community and a Member State" (1992) E.L.Rev. 191–206; Schockweiler, "Die Haftung der EG-Mitgliedstaaten gegenüber dem einzelnen bei Verletzung des Gemeinschaftsrechts" (1993) EuR. 107 *et seq.*. See also Goffin, "La recevabilité du recours en indemnité devant la Cour de justice des Communautés européennes" (1981) J.T. 1–5.

[903] ECJ, Case 175/84 *Krohn v Commission* [1986] E.C.R. 753, para.18; ECJ, Joined Cases 89 and 91/86 *Étoile Commerciale and CNTA v Commission* [1987] E.C.R. 3005, paras 16–21. See also Meij, "Art.215*[now Art.288]*(2) EC and Local Remedies", in Heukels and McDonnell (eds) (n.869, *supra*), at 273–284. The same principle applies in the event of financial loss arising where a non-member country (*e.g.* an ACP country) and the Community act jointly. The non-member country is liable for the financial loss attributable to its acts and the Community for the loss attributable to its acts: ECJ, Case 118/83 *CMC v Commission* [1985] E.C.R. 2325, para.31; ECJ, Case 33/82 *Murri Frères v Commission* [1985] E.C.R. 2759, paras 4–8; ECJ, Case 267/82 *Développement and Clemessy v Commission* [1986] E.C.R. 1907, paras 16–17; ECJ, Case C–370/89 *SGEEM and Etroy v EIB* [1993] E.C.R. I–2583, paras 29–31; CFI, Case T–52/99 *T. Port v Commission* [2001] E.C.R. II–981, para.26.

Community institution or a national authority. This is the central question. The answer determines the extent to which the Community may be held liable for financial loss arising as a result of illegality vitiating the application of a Community provision by a national authority.[904]

The decisive criterion appears to be the respective decision-making powers of the Community and the Member States.

In *Mulder*,[905] the Court of Justice held that, on the basis of Community law in force, the Member States did not have the power to carry out the act which individuals had claimed, namely allocation of a milk quota. The refusal to perform the act sought could not therefore be attributed to them. The ensuing financial loss was in fact the result of the illegality of the underlying Community act which had not provided for the grant of milk quota, even though the mere instrumental application of the act was entrusted to the Member States. The conclusion reached was that the loss of earnings had to be made good by the Community.

In *Etoile Commerciale*,[906] in contrast, the Court of Justice considered that the sole cause of the damage was a decision taken by a national authority pursuant to a general obligation imposed upon it by a Community regulation which did not, however, instruct it to take the specific decision that gave rise to the damage. Consequently, the national authority had in fact a genuine discretion in carrying out the general obligation imposed by the Community regulation and hence could have taken a different decision. The financial loss incurred therefore had to be made good by the Member State.[907] Moreover, the underlying Community regulation as a whole was not unlawful.

A Member State which follows an opinion given by the Commission at its request remains liable for any damage which may nevertheless ensue from any infringement of Community law. This is because opinions are not binding and hence do not restrict the Member State's discretion. Such cooperation cannot make the Community liable.[908]

---

[904] See, *e.g.* CFI, Case T–177/02 *Malagutti-Vezinhet v Commission* [2004] E.C.R. II–827, paras 26–31. See in this connection, De Visser, "The concept of Concurrent Liability and its Relationship with the Principle of Effectiveness: A One-way Ticket into Oblivion?" (2004) 11 M.J.E.C.L 1, at 47–70.

[905] ECJ, Joined Cases C–104/89 and C–37/90 *Mulder and Others v Council and Commission* [1992] E.C.R. I–3061, para.9; CFI, Case T–210/00 *Biret & Cie v Council* [2002] E.C.R. II–47, para.36.

[906] ECJ, Joined Cases 89 and 91/86 *Étoile Commerciale and CNTA v Commission* [1987] E.C.R. 3005, paras 16–21. See also CFI, Case T–261/94 *Schulte v Council and Commission* [2002] E.C.R. II–441, para.52.

[907] CFI, T–93/95 *Laga v Commission* [1998] E.C.R. II–195, para.47; CFI, Case T–94/95 *Landuyt v Commission* [1998] E.C.R. II–213, para.47; see also CFI, Case T–146/01 *DLD Trading v Council* [2003] E.C.R. II–6005, paras 80–82 and 91–97: after pointing out that the Member State had a genuine discretion in implementing the Community legislation in issue, the Court of First Instance held there was no direct causal link between the Council's conduct and the damage allegedly sustained by the applicant.

[908] ECJ, Case 133/79 *Sucrimex v Commission* [1980] E.C.R. 1299, para.22; ECJ, Case 217/81 *Interagra v Commission* [1982] E.C.R. 2233, paras 8–9; CFI, Case T–54/96 *Oleifici Italiani and Fratelli Rubino Industrie Olearie v Commission* [1998] E.C.R. II–3377, paras 66–67.

The position will be different only where, acting on the basis of a power conferred on it by Community law, the Commission imposes a requirement or a prohibition on a Member State, which has no choice other than to comply. Although, on the face of it, the financial loss results from the national "decision", it is really the outcome of the Commission's binding direction. The illegality on which the action for damages is based regards that direction alone and must therefore be attributed to the Commission, making an action for damages admissible.[909]

Genuine discretion of a Member State. Consequently, an infringement of Community law committed by a Member State which has a genuine discretion in implementing that law must be distinguished from a merely instrumental application by a Member State of an unlawful Community act where the Member State has no real discretion.

11–017

a. Pecuniary loss resulting from an infringement of Community law by a Member State

Member State's liability. The principle that a Member State will be liable for loss and damage caused to individuals as a result of breaches of Community law for which the State can be held responsible is inherent in the system of the Treaty. A further basis for the obligation of Member States to make good such loss and damage is to be found in Art.10 of the EC Treaty, under which the Member States are required to take all appropriate measures, whether general or particular, to ensure fulfilment of their obligations under Community law. Among these is the obligation to nullify the unlawful consequences of a breach of Community law.[910]

11–018

For those reasons, the Court of Justice has held that "it is a principle of Community law that the Member States are obliged to make good loss and damage caused to individuals by breaches of Community law for which they can be held responsible".[911] The action for damages must be brought in the national courts.[912] The conditions on which a Member State's liability under Community law will give rise to a right to damages are to be determined by national law, unless they have already been prescribed by Community law.[913] The applicable national law must result in effective legal redress and

---

[909] ECJ, Case 175/84 *Krohn v Commission* [1986] E.C.R. 753, paras 19–23.
[910] ECJ, Joined Cases C–6 and C–9/90 *Francovich and Others* [1991] E.C.R. I–5357, paras 35–36. See, in relation to Art.86 of the ECSC Treaty, ECJ, Case 6/60 *Humblet* [1960] E.C.R. 559. See also 3–041 to 3–047, *supra*.
[911] *Francovich and Others*, cited in the preceding n., para.37.
[912] ECJ (order of May 23, 1990), Case C–72/90 *Asia Motor France v Commission* [1990] E.C.R. I–2181, paras 14–15.
[913] For the procedural conditions, see Joined Cases C–6 and C–9/90 *Francovich and Others* [1991] E.C.R. I–5357, para.42; the basic conditions "depend on the nature of the breach of Community law giving rise to the loss and damage", *ibid.*, para.38, and the Court of Justice has specified them accordingly. They are designed to secure the full effect of the principle of State liability and hence the applicable national law must always satisfy them, *cf.* ECJ, Case 101/78 *Granaria* [1979] E.C.R. 623, paras 12–14.

the rules on liability for loss or damage ensuing from breaches of Community law must be at least equivalent to the rules governing liability for loss or damage resulting from breaches of domestic law (see 3–041 to 3–047, *supra*).

Obviously, the Community cannot incur liability for damage resulting from breaches of Community law which are ascribable exclusively to a Member State.[914]

b. Pecuniary loss resulting from the unlawfulness of the Community measure implemented

11–019 **Claim before the national court secures full compensation.** Where a Member State carries out an allegedly unlawful Community act,[915] an action for damages brought pursuant to Art.235 and the second para. of Art.288 will be inadmissible where the alleged damage can be made good by bringing a claim before the national courts. The Court of Justice has described the circumstances in which this is most likely to occur as follows: "Where an individual considers that he has been injured by the application of a Community legislative measure that he considers illegal, he may, when the implementation of the measure is left to the national authorities, contest the validity of the measure, when it is implemented, before a national court in an action against the national authorities. That court may, or even must, as provided for in Art.234, refer the question of the validity of the Community measure in dispute to the Court of Justice".[916] This means that, in order to decide on the admissibility of an action for damages brought before it, the Court of First Instance has to consider whether bringing a claim before the national courts would be capable of securing full compensation for the alleged damage. This will depend first on the type of pecuniary loss which purportedly constitutes the damage, together with the possibility that the declaration of the invalidity of the Community act in question by preliminary ruling will constitute a direct basis for the national courts to remedy the pecuniary loss suffered. This has to be considered in

---

[914] Failure to bring an action against a Member State for failure to fulfil obligations under Community law under Art.226 of the EC Treaty cannot cause the Community to incur liability. Liability attaches only to the Member State (ECJ (order of May 23, 1990), Case C–72/90 *Asia Motor France v Commission* [1990] E.C.R. I–2181, para.13; CFI (order of April 10, 2000), Case T–361/99 *Meyer v Commission* [2000] E.C.R. II–2031, para.13; CFI, Case T–209/00 *Lamberts v European Ombudsman* [2002] E.C.R. II–2203, para.53; CFI (order of January 14, 2004), Case T–202/02 *Makedoniko Metro and Michaniki v Commission* [2004] E.C.R. II–181, paras 42–47).

[915] If the act has already been annulled or declared invalid at the time when it is implemented by the Member State, the latter will be guilty of a breach of Community law and the question of compensation for any pecuniary loss will be dealt with in accordance with the previous section (see 11–018, *supra*).

[916] ECJ, Case 281/82 *Unifrex v Commission and Council* [1984] E.C.R. 1969, para.11; see also ECJ, Case 175/84 *Krohn v Commission* [1986] E.C.R. 753, para.27; ECJ, Case 81/86 *De Boer Buizen v Council and Commission* [1987] E.C.R. 3677, para.9.

the light of the particular circumstances. Only if, on account of the type of the alleged damage or of the limited extent of the consequences of any declaration of invalidity by way of preliminary ruling, compensation cannot be obtained from the national courts, will an action for damages lie against the Community institution from which the act implemented by the Member State originated.[917]

Undue payment to a national authority. First, it may be that the pecuniary loss simply stems from a payment which the individual concerned made to a national authority pursuant to what he or she considers to be an unlawful Community act. In order to recover the undue amount paid over, together with the applicable interest at the legal rate, the individual concerned must apply to the national courts.[918] Community law obliges the Member States to provide for legal proceedings enabling undue amounts paid to be recovered.[919] The national courts have no jurisdiction themselves to declare that the Community act on the basis of which payment was made is invalid, but if they consider that there are grounds for doubting whether the act is lawful, they must make a reference to the Court of Justice for a preliminary ruling on its validity.[920] If the Court of Justice declares the Community act at issue invalid, it provides the national court in principle with a sufficient basis for ordering restitution of the undue amount. Hence, it is not possible to bring an action for damages under Art.235 and the second para. of Art.288 of the EC Treaty in respect of this kind of pecuniary loss.[921] An action for damages under those provisions will lie only in the exceptional case where the Court of Justice limits the effects as regards the past of a preliminary ruling declaring an act invalid. In such case, the national court cannot order restitution of the undue payment. Since in such a case compensation for the alleged damage cannot be secured by bringing proceedings in the national courts, an action for damages may unquestionably be brought in the Court of First Instance against the institution in which the act in question originated.[922]

11–020

---

[917] CFI (judgment of November 23, 2004), Case T–166/98 *Cantina Sociale di Dolianova and Others v Commission*, not yet reported, paras 115–116.

[918] ECJ, Case 26/74 *Roquette Frères v Commission* [1976] E.C.R. 677, paras 11–12. See also ECJ, Case 96/71 *Haegeman v Commission* [1972] E.C.R. 1005, paras 15–16, and Arts 2 and 4 of Regulation No 1430/79 ([1979] O.J. L175/1), as amended by Regulation No 1854/89 ([1989] O.J. L186/1), in connection with the recovery of overpaid import and export levies.

[919] *Cf.* Tatham, "Restitution of Charges and Duties levied by the Public Administration in Breach of Community Law: a Comparative Analysis" (1994) E.L.Rev. 146–168.

[920] ECJ, Case 314/85 *Foto-Frost* [1987] E.C.R. 4199; see also 2–056 to 2–058, *supra*.

[921] Naturally, this does not mean that the Community does not have to bear the financial burden of repayment. Repayment occurs as a result of a preliminary ruling by the Court of Justice declaring the Community act in question invalid, which is binding on all Community institutions. For the question of settlement as between the Community and the Member States, see Oliver, "Joint Liability of the Community and the Member States", in Heukels and McDonnell (eds) (n.869, *supra*), at 285–310.

[922] ECJ, Case 20/88 *Roquette Frères v Commission* [1989] E.C.R. 1553, paras 18–20.

11–021 **National authority's unlawful refusal to effect a payment or to perform an act.** Secondly, the pecuniary loss may possibly be caused by a national authority's refusal to effect a payment or to perform some other act, whilst the individual concerned takes the view that the refusal is based on an unlawful Community act. In so far as individuals seek only reparation for the pecuniary loss resulting from the refusal, namely payment of what they maintain they are owed, or adoption of the act to which they consider they are entitled (*i.e.* compensation in kind), the only question arising in principle is whether the declaration by preliminary ruling of the Court of Justice that the Community act on which the refusal is based is invalid affords *in itself* the legal basis needed by the national court in order to order the payment requested or, as the case may be, the adoption of the act requested. If the answer to that question is in the affirmative, an action for damages brought in the Court of First Instance against the institution from which the act originated will be inadmissible.[923] If, in contrast, the answer to that question is in the negative, such an action for damages will be admissible.[924]

It should not come as a surprise in the light of the above that the admissibility of an action for damages should turn on a close analysis of the individual case. A degree of unpredictability of the outcome is therefore inevitable. For example, the importance of the time factor should not be underestimated. Even if a declaration of invalidity in preliminary ruling proceedings results in the national court's annulling the refusal to adopt the act requested (*e.g.* the grant of import licences), the loss of a number of years can no longer be made good. Consequently, an action for damages

---

[923] For examples, see ECJ, Case 99/74 *Société des Grands Moulins des Antilles v Commission* [1975] E.C.R. 1531; ECJ, Case 12/79 *Hans-Otto Wagner v Commission* [1979] E.C.R. 3657, paras 11–14; ECJ, Case C–119/88 *AERPO and Others v Commission* [1990] E.C.R. I–2189, 12–14. Here, too, the mechanism for settlement of the financial burden operates, see Oliver (n.921, *supra*).

[924] The examples in the case-law are generally concerned with cases in which the Community act was unlawful because it exhibited a *lacuna* which could be filled only by the necessary political decisions; on the basis of the mere finding that the act is invalid, the national court cannot order compensation to be paid for the "alleged damage" and hence the injured party will be entitled to bring proceedings in the Court of First Instance: see, for instance, ECJ, Joined Cases 9 and 11/71 *Compagnie d'Approvisionnement, de Transport et de Crédit and Others v Commission* [1972] E.C.R. 391; ECJ, Case 43/72 *Merkur Aussenhandels v Commission* [1973] E.C.R. 1055; ECJ, Case 153/73 *Holtz & Willemsen v Council and Commission* [1974] E.C.R. 675; ECJ, Case 281/82 *Unifrex v Council and Commission* [1984] E.C.R. 1969, para.12; ECJ, Case 81/86 *De Boer Buizen v Council and Commission* [1987] E.C.R. 3677, para.10; CFI (judgment of November 23, 2004), Case T–166/98 *Cantina Sociale di Dolianova and Others v Commission*, not yet reported, paras 112–113 and 115–116. More exceptionally, the Court itself will limit the effects of the declaration of invalidity by way of preliminary ruling, with the result that that ruling no longer constitutes a legal basis justifying the national court ordering reparation of the financial loss: see ECJ, Case 238/78 *Ireks-Arkady v Council and Commission* [1979] E.C.R. 2955, para.6; ECJ, Joined Cases 241–242, 245–250/78 *DGV v Council and Commission* [1979] E.C.R. 3017, para.6; ECJ, Joined Cases 261 and 262/78 *Interquell Stärke-Chemie and Diamalt v Council and Commission* [1979] E.C.R. 3045, para.6.

brought against the Community institution from which the act declared invalid originated will be admissible.[925]

Actual injury. Thirdly, the pecuniary loss may take the form of actual "injury", possibly alongside the financial loss resulting from an undue payment or from the fact that a payment or an act was unlawfully withheld. Examples include an undertaking becoming the subject of insolvency proceedings, a weakening of the undertaking's competitive position or the price of having at short notice to obtain credit. Compensation for such injury may be obtained only by bringing an action for damages in the Court of First Instance.[926]

11–022

The Court of First Instance and the Court of Justice have exclusive jurisdiction to find the Community liable to make good actual injury following actions brought pursuant to Art.235 and the second para. of Art.288 of the EC Treaty.[927] If the Court of Justice has found that the illegality of the Community provision at issue does not cause the Community to incur liability because the relevant requirements are not satisfied, that finding makes it impossible to bring a claim before the national courts for a declaration that the Member State which implemented that provision is liable on account of the same illegality.[928] The judgment of the Court of Justice does not preclude "an action on grounds other than the unlawfulness of the Community measure in issue in that judgment brought against the competent national authorities for damage caused to individuals by the national authorities, even where they were acting within the framework of Community law".[929] In other words, a claim may be brought against Member States only where the damage stemmed from a wrongful act or omission on their part and not where the act or omission consisted in the due implementation of a Community measure which was later declared invalid.

c. Pecuniary loss resulting from unlawful joint action on the part of the Community and a Member State

Unlawful joint action of the Community and a Member State. The Community and a Member State act jointly where they both contribute to the adoption of a measure through the exercise of their own discretion. An

11–023

---

[925] ECJ, Case 62/83 *Eximo v Commission* [1984] E.C.R. 2295, paras 15–17; ECJ, Case 175/84 *Krohn v Commission* [1986] E.C.R. 753, paras 27–28.

[926] For examples, see ECJ, Case 26/74 *Roquette Frères v Commission* [1976] E.C.R. 677, paras 15–25; ECJ, Joined Cases 116 and 124/77 *Amylum and Others v Council and Commission* [1979] E.C.R. 3479, para.9; CFI, Case T–167/94 *Nölle v Council and Commission* [1995] E.C.R. II–2589, paras 41–42; *cf.* Harding, "The Choice of Court Problem in Cases of Non-Contractual Liability under EEC Law" (1979) C.M.L.Rev. 389, at 392–397.

[927] ECJ, Case 101/78 *Granaria* [1979] E.C.R. 623, para.10.

[928] ECJ, Joined Cases 106–120/87 *Asteris and Others v Greece and EEC* [1988] E.C.R. 5515, paras 17–18.

[929] *Ibid.*, para.19.

example is where Member States adopt protective measures with the agreement of the Community.[930] If such action is unlawful, here again a distinction has to be drawn between the three types of pecuniary loss mentioned above (see 11–020 to 11–022, *supra*). As far as the first two types of pecuniary loss are concerned, that is to say recovery of an undue payment or a claim for a payment or for an act which was wrongfully refused, proceedings must in principle be brought before the national courts.[931] In contrast, where actual "injury" is involved, although an action brought against the Community will be admissible before national remedies have been exhausted, the extent of the Community's liability will not be determined until the national courts have determined the proportion of the liability to be borne by the Member State under national law. The Court of Justice has held in that connection that "[i]t is necessary to avoid the applicants' being insufficiently or excessively compensated for the same damage by the different assessment of two different courts applying different rules of law".[932]

III. SPECIAL CHARACTERISTICS

A. REQUIREMENTS FOR LIABILITY

11–024 Conditions. The classic requirements for liability—a wrongful Community act, loss or damage, and a causal connection between that act and the loss or damage—must be fulfilled if the Community is to be held liable (see 11–001, *supra*).[933]

1. The unlawful act

a. What test for unlawfulness?

11–025 Unlawfulness and fault. In the past the case-law was not always clear as to whether the unlawfulness of a Community act was based simply on the breach of a rule of superior law (objective or strict liability) or whether "fault" is also required on the part of the institution or person responsible for the act (subjective liability).[934]

11–026 Former ECSC Treaty. In the case of the ECSC Treaty, "fault" or "a wrongful act or omission on the part of the Community in the performance of its functions" (*faute de service*: maladministration) was required in order

---

[930] ECJ, Joined Cases 5, 7 and 13–24/66 *Kampffmeyer and Others v Commission* [1967] E.C.R. 245.
[931] *Ibid.*, at 263–264.
[932] *Ibid.*, at 226.
[933] ECJ, Case 153/73 *Holz & Willemsen v Council and Commission* [1974] E.C.R. 675, para.7.
[934] Hermann-Rodeville, "Un exemple de contentieux économique: le recours en indemnité devant la Cour de justice des Communautés européennes" (1986) R.T.D.E. 5, at 13–27.

for the Community to incur liability (see Arts 34 and 40). Such a requirement to show fault meant that actual "blame" had to attach to the act.[935] The criterion for determining blame was derived on an individual basis from the whole of the particular facts.[936] The complexity of the situations with which the institution had to deal, the difficulties in applying the Treaty provisions and the discretion which the institution had under those provisions were taken into account.[937] In addition, the fault had to be of a particular nature. Thus, only "unjustifiably bad administration"[938] or "a lack of adequate supervision"[939] might be regarded as constituting fault capable of causing the Community to incur liability. Consequently, the fact that a Community act was unlawful did not necessarily mean that it had to be regarded as constituting "fault" giving rise to Community liability.

EC Treaty. The second para. of Art.288 of the EC Treaty puts the Court of **11–027** Justice and the Court of First Instance under a duty to determine any liability incurred by the Community "in accordance with the general principles common to the laws of the Member States". In theory, that provision provides an opportunity for formulating a system of objective or strict liability, in which a generally applicable criterion of unlawfulness is determined in advance, without having regard to the particular circumstances surrounding the Community act at issue.[940] In that case, a breach of

---

[935] Heukels, "De niet-contractuele aansprakelijkheid van de Gemeenschap ex art. 215[now Art.288], lid 2, EEG: Dynamiek en continuïteit (1983–1991) (II)" (1992) S.E.W. 317–347.

[936] ECJ, Case C–220/91 P *Commission v Stahlwerke Peine-Salzgitter* [1993] E.C.R. I–2393, para.37. See also Lysén, "Three Questions on the Non-Contractual Liability of the EEC" (1985) 2 L.I.E.I. 108.

[937] ECJ, Joined Cases C–363 and C–364/88 *Finsider and Others v Commission* [1992] E.C.R. I–359, para.24 (these criteria for determining the type of fault which must have been committed in order for the Community to incur liability applied in connection with both Art.34 and Art.40 of the ECSC Treaty).

[938] ECJ, Joined Cases 14, 16–17, 20, 24, 26–27/60 and 1/61 *Meroni and Others v High Authority* [1961] E.C.R. 161, at 169.

[939] ECJ, Joined Cases 19 and 21/60, 2 and 3/61 *Société Fives Lille Cail and Others v High Authority* [1961] E.C.R. 281, at 297. See, to the same effect, ECJ, Joined Cases 29, 31, 36, 39–47, 50 and 51/63 *SA des Laminoirs, Hauts Fourneaux, Forges, Fonderies et Usines de la Providence and Others v High Authority* [1965] E.C.R. 911, at 937.

[940] Lysén (n.936, *supra*), at 109. See also van Gerven, "Non-Contractual Liability of Member States, Community Institutions and Individuals for Breaches of Community Law with a View to a Common Law for Europe" (1994) M.J.E.C.L. 6, at 28 and 37–38. This definition even affords room for objective, no-fault liability arising out of a lawful act which infringes the principle of *"egalité devant les charges publiques"* (a principle of French administrative law to the effect that public charges should be discharged equally). To date, the Court of Justice has not yet accepted that type of liability, but has also not ruled it out. *Cf.* ECJ, Joined Cases 9 and 11/71 *Compagnie d'Approvisionnement, de Transport et de Crédit and Others v Commission* [1972] E.C.R. 391, para.46; ECJ, Case 59/83 *Biovilac v EEC* [1984] E.C.R. 4057, para.28; ECJ, Case 267/82 *Développement and Clemessy v Commission* [1986] E.C.R. 1907, para.33; CFI, Case T–113/96 *Edouard Dubois and Fils v Council and Commission* [1998] E.C.R. II–125, para.42. The Court of First Instance has stated that liability for a lawful act could be incurred only if the damage alleged affects a particular circle of economic operators in a disproportionate manner by comparison with others

a superior rule of law would be sufficient in itself to cause the act to be regarded as unlawful and hence to cause the Community to incur liability, regardless as to whether the act was actually blameworthy and hence vitiated by fault.[941]

The concept of fault has not disappeared entirely from the system of liability founded upon the second para. of Art.288 of the EC Treaty.[942] The case-law has swung between mentioning fault[943] and not mentioning it,[944] but it is of course in the background whenever the mere unlawfulness of a Community act is insufficient to render the Community liable.[945]

(unusual damage) and exceeds the limits of the economic risks inherent in operating in the sector concerned (special damage), without the legislative measure that gave rise to the alleged damage being justified by a general economic interest (CFI, Case T–184/95 *Dorsch Consult v Council and Commission* [1998] E.C.R. II–667, para.80). See also CFI (December 14, 2005), Case T–69/00 *FIAMM and FIAMM Technologies v Council and Commission*, not yet reported, para.160; CFI (December 14, 2005), Case T–383/00 *Beamglow v European Parliament and Others*, not yet reported, para.174; CFI, Case T–196/99 *Area Cova and Others v Council and Commission* [2001] E.C.R. II–3597, para.171; CFI, Case T–170/00 *Förde-Reederei v Council and Commission* [2002] E.C.R. II–515, paras 56–57; CFI, Joined Cases T–64/01 and T–65/01 *Afrikanische Frucht-Compagnie and Others v Council and Commission* [2004] E.C.R. II–521, paras 150–156. See Bronkhorst, "The Valid Legislative Act as a Cause of Liability of the Communities", in Heukels and McDonnell (eds) (n.869, *supra*), at 153–165.

[941] ECJ, Case C–352/98 P *Bergaderm and Goupil v Commission* [2000] E.C.R. I–5291, paras 43–44.

[942] See CFI, Case T–120/89 *Stahlwerke Peine-Salzgitter v Commission* [1991] E.C.R. II–279, para.74, which reiterates the conditions having to be fulfilled before there can be "fault of such a nature as to render the Community liable under the second para. of Art.215*[now Art.288]* of the E[E]C Treaty". Academics are divided on this point. Some maintain that the Court has abandoned the requirement for fault, at least in the case of liability for legislative acts, and regards the illegality of the act at issue sufficient in certain circumstances to cause the Community to incur liability (Schockweiler, Wivines and Godart, "Le régime de la responsabilité extra-contractuelle du fait d'actes juridiques dans la Communauté européenne" (1990) R.T.D.E. 27–74). Others still adhere to the concept of fault, considering that it imposes requirements additional to the unlawful nature of the act at issue (see, *e.g.* Couzinet, "La faute dans le régime de la responsabilité non contractuelle des Communautés européennes" (1986) R.T.D.E. 367–390). The debate may perhaps be reduced to what is to be understood by "fault" and, to that extent, is purely epistemological (see, for example, Cornelis, "De extra-contractuele aansprakelijkheid van de Gemeenschap (1976–1982)" (1984) S.E.W. 5, at 11, who argues that the distinction between "fault" and "illegality" is superfluous on the ground that both concepts are objective, the concept of "fault" being based on the objective criterion of "a normal, prudent person"). See, however, 11–028, *infra*.

[943] See, for example, ECJ, Case 25/62 *Plaumann v Commission* [1963] 95, at 108; ECJ, Joined Cases 5, 7 and 13–24/66 *Kampffmeyer and Others v Commission* [1967] E.C.R. 245, at 262; ECJ, Case 30/66 *Becher v Commission* [1967] E.C.R. 285, at 296; ECJ, Case 16/67 *Labeyrie v Commission* [1968] E.C.R. 293, at 304; ECJ, Joined Cases 19–20, 25 and 30/69 *Richez-Parise and Others v Commission* [1970] E.C.R. 325, para.31; ECJ, Case 257/78 *Devred v Commission* [1979] E.C.R. 3767, para.22; ECJ, Case 137/79 *Kohl v Commission* [1980] E.C.R. 2601, para.14; CFI (order of December 17, 2003), Case T–346/03 *Krikorian and Others v European Parliament and Others* [2003] E.C.R. II–6037, para.23; CFI (order of February 20, 2004), Case T–319/03 *French and Others v Council and Commission* [2004] E.C.R. II–769, para.23.

[944] ECJ, Case 5/71 *Zuckerfabrik Schöppenstedt v Council* [1971] E.C.R. 975.

[945] See Mahieu, "Illégalité et responsabilité en droit communautaire", in *Mélanges Roger O.*

***Bergaderm* judgment.** The relevance of the question whether the test as to   **11–028**
unlawfulness is objective or subjective seems to have been blurred following
the judgment in *Bergaderm*.[946] In that case the Court of Justice aligned the
conditions which must be met in order for the Community to incur liability
on the conditions prescribed by Community law for a Member State to
incur liability for damage sustained by individuals as a result of an
infringement of Community law.

The case-law now requires there to have been a sufficiently serious
breach of a rule of law intended to confer rights on individuals. Where the
Community institution concerned has a discretion, a sufficiently serious
breach will be involved where the Community institution concerned
"manifestly and gravely" disregarded the limits on its discretion.[947] Where
the institution in question has only considerably reduced, or even no,
discretion, the mere infringement of Community law may be sufficient to
establish the existence of a sufficiently serious breach.

In this connection, the general or individual nature of the measure taken
by an institution is not a decisive criterion.[948] Furthermore, in both

---

Dalcq (Larcier, Brussels, 1994), 388, at 400–401. *Cf.* Fuss, "La responsabilité des Communautés européennes pour le comportement illégal de leurs organes" (1981) R.T.D.E. 1, at
14–15.

[946] ECJ, Case C–352/98 P *Bergaderm and Goupil v Commission* [2000] E.C.R. I–5291; for a
commentary, see Tridimas, "Liability for Breach of Community Law: Growing Up and
Mellowing Down?" (2001) C.M.L.Rev. 303–332. See also CFI, Case T–196/99 *Area Cova
and Others v Council and Commission* [2001] E.C.R. II–3597.

[947] For a commentary, see Hilson, "The role of discretion in EC law on non-contractual
liability" (2005) C.M.L.Rev. 677–695.

[948] The rules on liability set out in the judgment in *Bergaderm*, which formerly applied to a
comparable degree for legislative acts involving an economic policy choice, largely
correspond to the rule set forth in the *Schöppenstedt* judgment on liability for legislative
acts according to which, "[w]here legislative action involving measures of economic policy is
concerned", the Community will be liable only for damage suffered by individuals as a
consequence of that action where there has been "a sufficiently flagrant violation of a
superior rule of law for the protection of the individual" (ECJ, Case 5/71 *Zuckerfabrik
Schöppenstedt v Council* [1971] E.C.R. 975, para.11). That rule reflects the reluctance of the
Court of Justice and the Court of First Instance to assess the legality of acts which
inevitably involve choices made on the basis of considerations of expediency. The particular
nature of the role played by the courts means that they have to accept such choices. On
those grounds, moreover, the Member States have sharply curtailed or even ruled out
altogether State liability for action taken under "statute law". See ECJ, Joined Cases 83
and 94/76, 4, 15 and 40/77 *HNL and Others v Council and Commission* [1978] E.C.R. 1209,
paras 5 and 6: "This restrictive view is explained by the consideration that the legislative
authority, even where the validity of its measures is subject to judicial review, cannot always
be hindered in making its decisions by the prospect of applications for damages whenever it
has occasion to adopt legislative measures in the public interest which may adversely affect
the interests of individuals. It follows from these considerations that individuals may be
required, in the sectors coming within the economic policy of the Community, to accept
within reasonable limits certain harmful effects on their economic interests as a result of a
legislative measure without being able to obtain compensation from public funds even if
that measure has been declared null and void". See also Schockweiler, Wivines and Godart
(n.942, *supra*), at 54. On the other hand, the existence of rules governing such liability—no
matter how restrictive they may be—expresses a genuine concern to afford individuals the

situations, account must be taken of the complexity of the situations to be regulated and of difficulties in the application or interpretation of the texts.

Consequently, it appears that the test for liability applied by the Court of Justice will always contain a major "subjective" element, which is related to the discretion available to the institution concerned. The liability test laid down in *Bergaderm* requires the discretion of the institution concerned to be identified, a finding to be made that the higher-ranking rule of law which has been breached is intended to confer rights on individuals and that the infringement in question constitutes a sufficiently serious breach of Community law.[949]

11–029   **Liability on account of a failure to act.** Liability on the part of the Community on account of a failure to act must also be determined on the basis of the same criteria. Thus, the inaction of an institution may give rise to liability where it constitutes a clear and serious disregard of the limits imposed on the institution's discretion[950].

b. The discretion of the Community institution

11–030   **General or individual nature of the act is irrelevant.** The Court of First Instance and the Court of Justice have to determine the extent of the institution's discretion in the light of the legal context in which the measure at issue was adopted. It is irrelevant whether the measure is general or individual, normative (or legislative) or administrative (or implementing).[951]

---

widest possible legal protection in the absence of effective parliamentary control. See also the Opinion of Advocate General K. Roemer in ECJ, Case 5/71 *Zuckerfabrik Schöppenstedt v Council* [1971] E.C.R. 975, at 989.

[949] See also ECJ, Case C–312/00 P *Commission v Camar and Tico* [2002] E.C.R. I–11355, para.54; CFI, Case T–210/00 *Biret & Cie v Council* [2002] E.C.R. II–47, para.52; CFI, Case T–56/00 *Dole Fresh Fruit International v Council and Commission* [2003] E.C.R. II–577, para.71; CFI, Joined Cases T–64/01 and T–65/01 *Afrikanische Frucht-Compagnie and Others v Council and Commission* [2004] E.C.R. II–521, para.71.

[950] ECJ, Case 50/86 *Grands Moulins de Paris v Council and Commission* [1987] E.C.R. 4833, para.9; CFI (judgment of March 17, 2005), Case T–285/03 *Agraz and Others v Commission*, not yet reported, para.54; ECJ (judgment of July 12, 2005), Case C–198/03 P *Commission v CEVA Santé Animale and Pfizer Enterprises*, not yet reported, paras 63–69 and 73.

[951] ECJ, Case C–352/98 P *Bergaderm and Goupil v Commission* [2000] E.C.R. I–5291, para.46; CFI, Case T–155/99 *Dieckmann & Hansen v Commission* [2001] E.C.R. II–3143, paras 45–46. The distinction between legislation and implementation of legislation is not reflected in the Community legal order in a distinction between "authorities" or "institutions" charged with rule-making at the legislative or implementation levels. The distinction between "legislation" and "implementation" depends on the legal basis pursuant to which the act of the relevant Community institution is adopted. Any act which is based directly on an article of the Treaty will be a legislative act. Any act based on secondary legislation will be an implementing or executive act. It is to be expected that legislative acts will tend more often to be rule-making in comparison with implementing measures. For further particulars, see Lenaerts, "Regulating the Regulatory Process: 'Delegation of Powers' in the European Community" (1993) E.L.Rev., at 27–36. The type of measure involved may provide an indication of its discretionary nature. Regulations and directives are preeminently the legal

Discretion involves policy choices. It is critical whether the institution had   **11–031**
a discretion when it adopted the measure. There will be a discretion where
the Treaty provision or the provision of secondary Community law on
which the measure is based requires the institution to make a policy choice.

This is what the Court of First Instance held in *Dieckmann*,[952] which was
concerned with a Commission decision excluding a State from the list of
third counties from which importation of fishery products was authorised
and placing that act in the context of the common agricultural policy, a
policy area for which it had already been established that the Community
institutions had a discretion. Moreover, it appeared from the legislative acts
on which the Commission decision was based that the legislator had
expressly conferred a broad discretion on the Commission as regards
controlling the import of fisheries products.[953]

Also the fact that the institution has to reconcile divergent interests and
thus select options within the context of the policy choices which are its
own responsibility obviously points to the existence of a discretion.[954]

Case-by-case assessment. The fact, however, that an act was adopted in a   **11–032**
policy area that frequently involves (economic) policy choices does not
automatically lead to a finding that a discretion exists. The Community
judicature will always assess the margin of discretion in the light of the
specific circumstances. Thus, in the *Fresh Marine Company* case, the Court
of First Instance held that an act of the Commission by which an
undertaking on the part of the applicant (offer to avoid the imposition of
anti-dumping duties) was said to have been breached and anti-dumping

---

instruments which embody a legislative (and therefore often a discretionary) act. For
regulations, see, *e.g.* ECJ, Case 43/72 *Merkur Aussenhandels v Commission* [1973] E.C.R.
1055; ECJ, Joined Cases 63–69/72 *Werhahn Hansamuhle and Others v Council* [1973]
E.C.R. 1229; ECJ, Case 97/76 *Merkur v Commission* [1977] E.C.R. 1063. The fact that a
regulation is of direct and individual concern to a particular person within the meaning of
the fourth para. of Art.230 of the EC Treaty does not mean that it loses its legislative
nature for the purposes of an action for damages brought pursuant to the second para. of
Art.288 (see, for example, ECJ, Case C–152/88 *Sofrimport v Commission* [1990] E.C.R. I–
2477, at I–2510). See also CFI, Joined Cases T–480 and T–483/93 *Antillean Rice Mills and
Others v Commission* [1995] E.C.R. II–2305, paras 180–186, where the *Schöppenstedt* test
was applied. This approach was confirmed by the Court of Justice in ECJ, Case C–390/95 P
Antillean Rice Mills and Others v Commission [1999] E.C.R. I–769, paras 56–59, and
remains applicable in the context of the *Bergaderm* case-law. For directives, see ECJ, Case
C–63/89 *Assurances du Crédit v Council and Commission* [1991] E.C.R. I–1799, para.12.
[952] CFI, Case T–155/99 *Dieckmann & Hansen v Commission* [2001] E.C.R. II–3143, paras 48–
56.
[953] See also CFI, Case T–18/99 *Cordis v Commission* [2001] E.C.R. II–913, para.75 (the
Commission has a margin of discretion in the area of the common organisation of markets,
which involves constant adjustments to meet changes in the economic situation); CFI, Case
T–170/00 *Förde-Reederei v Council and Commission* [2002] E.C.R. II–515, para.46; CFI,
Case T–209/00 *Lamberts v European Ombudsman* [2002] E.C.R. II–2203, para.79.
[954] CFI, Case T–30/99 *Bocchi Food Trade International v Commission* [2001] E.C.R. II–943,
paras 91–93.

duties were imposed "did not involve any choices of economic policy". In that connection, the Commission had "only very little or no discretion".[955]

11–033 **European Ombudsman.** In order to determine whether there has been a sufficiently serious breach of Community law rendering the Community non-contractually liable owing to the conduct of the European Ombudsman, regard must be had to the specific nature of the latter's function. In that context, it should be borne in mind that the European Ombudsman is merely under an obligation to use his or her best endeavours and that he or she enjoys wide discretion.[956]

c. A superior rule of law intended to confer rights on individuals

11–034 **Hierarchy of norms.** Any judicial review of the legality of an act involves checking whether it conflicts with superior law. This necessitates ascertaining the rank of the measure at issue in the hierarchy of norms.[957]

11–035 **Superior rules of law.** The superior rules of law are the provisions of the Treaties, the general principles of law and the Community measures on which the contested act is based.

11–036 **Prior to the *Bergaderm* judgment.** The Treaty provisions which were already used before the judgment in *Bergaderm* to test the legality of an act include Art.12, Art.28, Art.29, Art.33(1) and Art.34(3) of the EC Treaty.[958]

---

[955] CFI, Case T–178/98 *Fresh Marine v Commission* [2000] E.C.R. II–3331, para.57, upheld on appeal: ECJ, Case C–472/00 P *Commission v Fresh Marine* [2003] E.C.R. I–7541; Wakefield, "Case C–472/00 P, *Commission v Fresh Marine AS*, Judgment of the Full Court of July 10, 2003" (2004) C.M.L.Rev. 235–244.

[956] ECJ, Case C–234/02 P *European Ombudsman v Lamberts* [2004] E.C.R. I–2803, para.50.

[957] The following hierarchy of norms obtains in the legal order of the European Community: at the top, the Treaties and the Acts of Accession, which constitute the basic constitutional charter (see ECJ, Case 294/83 *Les Verts v European Parliament* [1986] E.C.R. 1339, para.23). In addition, there is a series of decisions of a quasi-constitutional nature, such as the Decision on Own Resources (based on Art.269 of the EC Treaty) or the decision and the act concerning the direct election of the European Parliament (based on Art.190(3) of the EC Treaty). The general principles of law, including fundamental rights, constitute the unwritten constitutional norms, which are on an equal footing with the Treaties and the other written constitutional rules. Next come the rules of international law which permeate the legal order of the Community, *i.e.* agreements and customary international law. At the third level, there are acts of Community institutions directly based on Treaty provisions. Finally, there are acts of Community institutions implementing earlier acts. For further details, see Lenaerts and Van Nuffel, *Constitutional Law of the European Union*, §17–052–§17–055, at 703 –705.

[958] See, as regards Art.12 of the EC Treaty, ECJ, Joined Cases 71 and 72/84 *Surcouf and Vidou v EEC* [1985] E.C.R. 2925; as regards Arts 28 and 29 of the EC Treaty, ECJ, Case 265/85 *Van den Bergh and Jurgens v Commission* [1987] E.C.R. 1155; as regards Art.33(1) of the EC Treaty, ECJ, Case 27/85 *Vandemoortele v Commission* [1987] E.C.R. 1129, and, as regards Art.34(3) of the EC Treaty, ECJ, Case 281/82 *Unifrex v Council and Commission* [1984] E.C.R. 1969. Art.32(4) and Art.37(2) of the EC Treaty do not constitute superior rules of law for the protection of individuals: CFI, Case T–571/93 *Lefebvre and Others v Commission* [1995] E.C.R. II–2379, para.41.

The general rules of law which operated as superior rules of law included the principle of protection of legitimate expectation,[959] the principle of proportionality,[960] the principle of equal treatment (also known as the principle of equality or the prohibition of discrimination),[961] the principle of care,[962] the principle of proper administration,[963] and the prohibition of misuse of powers.[964] Fundamental rights, such as the right to property,[965]

---

[959] ECJ, Case 74/74 *CNTA v Commission* [1975] E.C.R. 533, at 548–550 (manifest infringement of the principle of protection of legitimate expectation); ECJ, Case C–152/88 *Sofrimport v Commission* [1990] E.C.R. I–2477, para.26 (manifest infringement of that principle); ECJ, Joined Cases C–104/89 and C–37/90 *Mulder and Others v Council and Commission* [1992] E.C.R. I–3061, para.15 (manifest infringement of that principle); CFI, Case T–472/93 *Campo Ebro Industrial and Others v Council* [1995] E.C.R. II–421, para.52 (no infringement of the principle of protection of legitimate expectation found); CFI, Joined Cases T–481/93 and T–484/93 *Exporteurs in Levende Varkens and Others v Commission* [1995] E.C.R. II–2941, paras 148–150 (no infringement of the principle of protection of legitimate expectation); CFI, Case T–521/93 *Atlanta and Others v EC* [1996] E.C.R. II–1707, paras 55–58 (no infringement of the principle of protection of legitimate expectation); CFI, Case T–105/96 *Pharos v Commission* [1998] E.C.R. II–285, paras 63–72 (no infringement of the principle of protection of legitimate expectation).

[960] ECJ, Joined Cases 63–69/72 *Werhahn Hansamuhle and Others v Council* [1973] E.C.R. 1229, paras 18–20; ECJ, Joined Cases 279–280, 285 and 286/84 *Rau v Commission* [1987] E.C.R. 1069, paras 33–37; ECJ, Case 27/85 *Vandemoortele v Commission* [1987] E.C.R. 1129, paras 30–34; ECJ, Case 265/85 *Van den Bergh and Jurgens v Commission* [1987] E.C.R. 1155, paras 30–34; CFI, Case T–152/95 *Petrides v Commission* [1997] E.C.R. II–2427, paras 48–53 (no infringement of the principle of proportionality).

[961] ECJ, Joined Cases 83 and 94/76, 4, 15 and 40/77 *HNL and Others v Council and Commission* [1978] E.C.R. 1209, para.5; ECJ, Joined Cases 64 and 113/76, 167 and 239/78, 27–28 and 45/79 *Dumortier Frères v Council* [1979] E.C.R. 3091, para.11; ECJ, Case 238/78 *Ireks-Arkady v Council and Commission* [1979] E.C.R. 2955, para.11; ECJ, Joined Cases 241–242, 245–250/78 *DGV v Council and Commission* [1979] E.C.R. 3017, para.11; ECJ, Joined Cases 261 and 262/78 *Interquell Stärke-Chemie and Diamalt v Council and Commission* [1979] E.C.R. 3045, para.14; ECJ, Case 106/81 *Kind v EEC* [1982] E.C.R. 2885, paras 22–25 (no infringement of the principle of equal treatment); ECJ, Case C–63/89 *Assurances du Crédit v Council and Commission* [1991] E.C.R. I–1799, paras 14–23 (no infringement of the principle of equal treatment); CFI, Case T–120/89 *Stahlwerke Peine-Salzgitter v Commission* [1991] E.C.R. II–279, para.92 (manifest infringement of the principle of equal treatment); CFI, Case T–489/93 *Unifruit Hellas v Commission* [1994] E.C.R. II–1201, paras 76–80 (no infringement of the principle of equal treatment); CFI, Case T–472/93 *Campo Ebro Industrial and Others v Commission* [1995] E.C.R. II–421, para.52; CFI, Joined Cases T–481 and T–484/93 *Exporteurs in Levende Varkens and Others v Commission* [1995] E.C.R. II–2941, para.102 (no infringement of the principle of equal treatment), CFI, Case T–152/95 *Petrides v Commission* [1997] E.C.R. II–2427, paras 54–60 (no infringement of the principle of equal treatment).

[962] CFI, Case T–167/94 *Nölle v Council and Commission* [1995] E.C.R. II–2589, para.76 (no infringement of the principle of care).

[963] CFI, Case T–105/96 *Pharos v Commission* [1998] E.C.R. II–285, paras 73–78 (no infringement of the principle of proper administration).

[964] ECJ, Case C–119/88 *AERPO and Others v Commission* [1990] E.C.R. I–2189, para.19; CFI, Joined Cases T–481 and T–484/93 *Exporteurs in Levende Varkens and Others v Commission* [1995] E.C.R. II–2941, paras 134–135 (no infringement of the prohibition of misuse of powers).

[965] ECJ, Case 59/83 *Biovilac v EEC* [1984] E.C.R. 4057, paras 21–22; ECJ, Case 281/84 *Zuckerfabrik Bedburg v Council and Commission* [1987] E.C.R. 49, paras 25–28.

the right to be heard (*audi alteram partem*)[966] and freedom to pursue an economic activity,[967] were also recognised as being superior rules of law.

11–037 **The *Bergaderm* judgment.** Since the judgment in *Bergaderm*, an infringement of a higher-ranking rule of law is capable of causing the Community to incur liability only where the higher-ranking rule of law is intended to confer rights on individuals.

That requirement appears to be based closely on the requirement laid down in the *Schöppenstedt* test that a superior rule of law intended to protect an interest peculiar to the person concerned must be involved.[968] This doctrine of the *Schutznorm*,[969] which originates in German law and may be found also in some other jurisdictions,[970] has the aim of limiting liability. In the past, however, it was applied flexibly. The Court of Justice did not rule out the possibility of superior rules of law protecting both general and individual interests.[971] Accordingly, the prohibition of discrimination laid down in Art.34(2) of the EC Treaty assists the common organisation of the agricultural markets and, at the same time, protects the interests of individual market participants.[972] In contrast, the requirement laid down by Art.253 of the EC Treaty for a statement of reasons is intended only to enable the Court of Justice or the Court of First Instance to review the legality of acts and does not serve any individual interest, with the result that an infringe-

---

[966] CFI, Joined Cases T–481 and T–484/93 *Exporteurs in Levende Varkens and Others v Commission* [1995] E.C.R. II–2941, para.154 (no infringement of the right to be heard).

[967] CFI, Case T–521/93 *Atlanta and Others v EC* [1996] E.C.R. II–1707, paras 62–64 (no infringement of the freedom to pursue an economic activity).

[968] This requirement was expressed for the first time in ECJ, Joined Cases 9 and 12/60 *Vloeberghs v High Authority* [1961] E.C.R. 197, at 217, where the Court of Justice dismissed a claim for damages brought under Art.40 of the ECSC Treaty on the ground that the article of the Treaty which the Commission had allegedly infringed had been adopted only in the interests of the Community. It seems, however, that the provision concerned does not have to have direct effect (*cf.* ECJ, Joined Cases C–6 and C–9/90 *Francovich and Others* [1991] E.C.R. I–5357, in which the applicant could not rely on the provision of the unimplemented directive because it did not have direct effect, but the directive was nevertheless regarded as a higher-ranking rule of law which conferred rights on individuals).

[969] Under German law, the public authorities are liable only if they cause damage and breach a "*Schutznorm*" protecting an individual right, not of individuals in general, but of a specific group to which the interested party belongs: see Arnull, "Liability for Legislative Acts under Art.215*[now Art.288]*(2) EC", in Heukels and McDonnell (eds) (n.869, *supra*), 129, at 136.

[970] See Schockweiler, Wivines and Godart (n.942, *supra*), at 53, who mention Denmark, Greece, Italy, the Netherlands and Portugal in this connection.

[971] ECJ, Joined Cases 5, 7 and 13–24/66 *Kampffmeyer and Others v Commission* [1967] E.C.R. 245, at 262–263.

[972] ECJ, Joined Cases 83 and 94/76, 4, 15 and 40/77 *HNL and Others v Council and Commission* [1978] E.C.R. 1209, para.5; ECJ, Case 238/78 *Ireks-Arkady v Council and Commission* [1979] E.C.R. 2955, para.11; ECJ, Joined Cases 241–242, 245–250/78 *DGV v Council and Commission* [1979] E.C.R. 3017, para.11; ECJ, Joined Cases 261 and 262/78 *Interquell Stärke-Chemie and Diamalt v Council and Commission* [1979] E.C.R. 3045, para.14.

ment of that requirement cannot make the Community liable.[973] The same is true of "the system of the division of powers between the various Community institutions", which is designed to "ensure that the balance between the institutions provided for in the [EC] Treaty is maintained, and not to protect individuals".[974] For those reasons, a declaration in a preliminary ruling that a provision which the Commission adopted *ultra vires* and hence in disregard of that system of institutional balance is invalid does not render the Community liable.

Examples of superior rules of law intended to confer rights on individuals. Since the judgment in *Bergaderm* the Community judicature has expressly (or sometimes indirectly) recognised as being higher-ranking rules of law conferring rights on individuals the principle of non-discrimination,[975] the principle of proportionality,[976] the principle of protection of legitimate expectation,[977] the right freely to exercise a trade or profession,[978] the duty of care,[979] the principle of the protection of property[980] and the prohibition of unjust enrichment.[981]

11–038

In contrast, the principle of relative stability and respect for traditional fisheries rights governs only relations between the Member States and does not confer on individuals rights whose infringement would ground a claim in damages.[982] The same applies to the principle of sound administration[983]

---

[973] ECJ, Case 106/81 *Kind v EEC* [1982] E.C.R. 2885, para.14; ECJ, Case C–119/88 *AERPO and Others v Commission* [1990] E.C.R. I–2189, para.20; ECJ, Case C–76/01 P *Eurocoton and Others v Council* [2003] E.C.R. I–10091, para.98; CFI, Case T–43/98 *Emesa Sugar v Council* [2001] E.C.R. II–3519, para.63; CFI, Joined Cases T–64/01 and T–65/01 *Afrikanische Frucht-Compagnie and Others v Council and Commission* [2004] E.C.R. II–521, para.128.

[974] ECJ, Case C–282/90 *Vreugdenhil v Commission* [1992] E.C.R. I 1937, paras 19–24; CFI, Joined Cases T–64/01 and T–65/01 *Afrikanische Frucht-Compagnie and Others v Council and Commission* [2004] E.C.R. II–521, para.116 (a possible unlawful delegation of powers by the Council to the Commission cannot cause the Community to incur non-contractual liability).

[975] CFI, Case T–56/00 *Dole Fresh Fruit International v Council and Commission* [2003] E.C.R. II–577, para.73.

[976] CFI, Case T–43/98 *Emesa Sugar v Council* [2001] E.C.R. II–3519, para.64.

[977] CFI, Case T–43/98 *Emesa Sugar v Council* [2001] E.C.R. II–3519, para.64; CFI, Case T–155/99 *Dieckmann & Hansen v Commission* [2001] E.C.R. II–3143, para.77 (no express recognition); CFI, Case T–210/00 *Biret & Cie v Council* [2002] E.C.R. II–47, para.57.

[978] CFI, Case T–30/99 *Bocchi Food Trade International v Commission* [2001] E.C.R. II–943, paras 79–83; CFI, Case T–52/99 *T. Port v Commission* [2001 E.C.R. II–981, para.81.

[979] CFI, Case T–178/98 *Fresh Marine v Commission* [2000] E.C.R. II–3331, para.63.

[980] CFI, Case T–52/99 *T. Port v Commission* [2001] E.C.R. II– 981, para.99.

[981] CFI (judgment of November 23, 2004), Case T–166/98 *Cantina Sociale di Dolianova and Others v Commission*, not yet reported, para.160.

[982] CFI, Case T–196/99 *Area Cova and Others v Council and Commission* [2001] E.C.R. II–3597, para.152; CFI (judgment of October 19, 2005), Case T–415/03 *Cofradía de pescadores de "San Pedro" and Others v Council*, not yet reported, paras 86–93.

[983] CFI, Case T–196/99 *Area Cova and Others v Council and Commission* [2001] E.C.R. II–3597, para.43, in which the Court of First Instance held that the principle of sound administration did not confer any rights on individuals. See, however, CFI, Case T–178/98

or Art.253[984] and Art.307[985] of the EC Treaty. In principle, the WTO Agreement and its annexes do not constitute—under Community law— rules of law which create rights for individuals.[986]

d. The requirement for a sufficiently serious breach

11–039 **Institution has a discretion.** The requirement for there to have been a sufficiently serious breach reflects once again the judiciary's reluctance to find the Community liable for loss or damage caused by acts involving policy choices. In these circumstances, there can have been a sufficiently serious breach of a superior rule of law only in the event that the Community institution in question manifestly and gravely disregarded the limits on the exercise of its powers.[987]

11–040 **Justifications.** Accordingly, the "breach" of a superior rule of law is sometimes justified, *inter alia*, on the ground that an important general interest takes precedence over the individual interest of the injured party[988]

Fresh Marine v Commission [2000] E.C.R. II–3331, para.63. In ECJ, Case C–222/02 *Paul and Others* [2004] E.C.R. I–9425, the Court of Justice ruled that Directives 94/19, 77/780, 89/299 and 89/646 do not confer rights on depositors in the event that their deposits are unavailable as a result of defective supervision on the part of the competent national authorities, if the compensation of depositors prescribed by Directive 94/19 is ensured. For a commentary, see Tison, "Do not attack the watchdog ! Banking supervisor's liability after *Peter Paul*" (2005) C.M.L.Rev. 639–675.

[984] ECJ, Case C–76/01 P *Eurocoton and Others v Council* [2003] E.C.R. I–10091, paras 98–99; CFI, Case T–43/98 *Emesa Sugar v Council* [2001] E.C.R. II–3519, para.63.

[985] CFI, Case T–2/99 *T. Port v Council* [2001] E.C.R. II–2093, para.83, and CFI, Case T–3/99 *Banatrading v Council* [2001] E.C.R. II–2123, para.78.

[986] CFI, Case T–52/99 *T. Port v Commission* [2001] E.C.R. II–981, para.51; CFI, Case T–2/99 *T. Port v Council* [2001] E.C.R. II–2093, para.51; CFI, Case T–18/99 *Cordis v Commission* [2001] E.C.R. II–913, para.46; CFI, Case T–30/99 *Bocchi Food Trade International v Commission* [2001] E.C.R. II–943, para.56; CFI, Case T–174/00 *Biret International v Council* [2002] E.C.R. II–417, para.61; ECJ, Case C–93/02 P *Biret International v Council* [2003] E.C.R. I–10497, para.52 (however, the Court of Justice does not rule out the possibility of reviewing the legality of Community acts in the light of the WTO rules in the event of a recommendation or ruling of the WTO Dispute Settlement Body against the Community (paras 57–64)). See also Snyder, "The gatekeepers: the European Courts and WTO Law" (2003) C.M.L.Rev. 313–367; Wiers, "One Day, You're Gonna Pay: The European Court of Justice in *Biret*" (2004) L.I.E.I. 143–151: Zonnekeyn, "EC liability for non-implementation of WTO Dispute Settlement Decisions—are the dice cast?" (2004) J.I.E.L. 483–490.

[987] For legislative acts, see ECJ, Joined Cases 83 and 94/76, 4, 15 and 40/77 *HNL and Others v Council and Commission* [1978] E.C.R. 1209, para.6; ECJ, Case 50/86 *Grand s Moulins de Paris v Council and Commission* [1987] E.C.R. 4833, para.8; ECJ, Case 20/88 *Roquette Frères v Commission* [1989] E.C.R. 1553, paras 23–26; ECJ, Case C–352/98 P *Bergaderm and Goupil v Commission* [2000] E.C.R. I–5291, para.43. For public tender procedures, see CFI (judgment of March 17, 2005), Case T–160/03 *AFCon Management Consultants and Others v Commission*, not yet reported, para.93.

[988] ECJ, Case 97/76 *Merkur v Commission* [1977] E.C.R. 1063, para.5; ECJ, Case 281/84 *Zuckerfabrik Bedburg v Council and Commission* [1987] E.C.R. 49, para.38; ECJ, Case 50/86 *Grand s Moulins de Paris v Council and Commission* [1987] E.C.R. 4833, para.21; CFI, Case T–56/00 *Dole Fresh Fruit International v Council and Commission* [2003] E.C.R. II–577, para.76.

or that the breach was the result of an erroneous, but excusable, approach to an unresolved legal question[989] or of the complexity of the situations to be regulated and the difficulties in the application or interpretation of the texts.[990] The absence of such justification raises a presumption that the Community institution acted "arbitrarily" as a result of which the breach of the relevant superior rule of law is deemed to be sufficiently serious.[991]

Extent of the loss or damage. The Court of Justice has also tackled the question as to whether the Community institution concerned manifestly and gravely disregarded its powers in the light of an appraisal of the loss or damage caused thereby.[992] The particular intensity of the damage and the fact that a limited or ascertainable number of persons were affected determine the matter.[993]   **11–041**

Institution does not have a discretion. Where the institution does not have a discretion, a serious breach will be involved where there is a mere infringement of Community law, in particular a finding of an error which an administrative authority exercising ordinary care and diligence[994] would not have committed in analogous circumstances.[995]   **11–042**

---

[989] CFI, Case T–120/89 *Stahlwerke Peine-Salzgitter v Commission* [1991] E.C.R. II–279, paras 108–118.

[990] CFI (judgment of April 21, 2005), Case T–28/03 *Holcim v Commission*, not yet reported, paras 100–101.

[991] ECJ, Joined Cases 116 and 124/77 *Amylum and Others v Council and Commission* [1979] E.C.R. 3497, para.19; ECJ, Case 106/81 *Kind v Commission* [1982] E.C.R. 2885, para.22.

[992] ECJ, Joined Cases 83 and 94/76, 4, 15 and 40/77 *HNL and Others v Council and Commission* [1978] E.C.R. 1209, para.7; CFI, Case T–56/00 *Dole Fresh Fruit International v Council and Commission* [2003] E.C.R. II–577, para.79.

[993] *Ibid.*, *cf.* CFI, Case T–120/89 *Stahlwerke Peine-Salzgitter v Commission* [1991] E.C.R. II–279, para.131 (ruling under the ECSC Treaty); see also ECJ, Case 50/86 *Grand s Moulins de Paris v Council and Commission* [1987] E.C.R. 4833, para.21. The fact that the number of persons involved was ascertainable in *Mulder* (ECJ, Joined Cases C–104/89 and C–37/90 *Mulder and Others v Council and Commission* [1992] E.C.R. I–3061) was not mentioned as a requirement for liability. See the case note by Heukels (1993) C.M.L.Rev. 368, at 381.

[994] CFI, Case T–178/98 *Fresh Marine v Commission* [2000] E.C.R. II–3331, para.61.

[995] CFI, Joined Cases T–198/95, T–171/96, T–230/97, T–174/98 and T–225/99 *Comafrica and Dole Fresh Fruit Europe/Commission* [2001] E.C.R. II–1975, para.144. Various shortcomings in the performance of administrative acts were held to constitute fault (before the judgment in *Bergaderm*). For a survey, see Schermers and Waelbroeck, *Judicial Protection*, §1089–§1100, at 541–545, and Heukels (n.935, *supra*), at 322–323. See also Van der Woude, "Liability for Administrative Acts under Art.215*[now Art.288]*(2) EC", in Heukels and McDonnell (eds) (n.869, *supra*), at 109–128. What was involved was the usual form taken by unlawful conduct attributed to the institutions: ECJ, Case C–55/90 *Cato v Commission* [1992] E.C.R. I–2533, para.18. The shortcomings in question included lack of care in exercising implementing powers: ECJ, Case 169/73 *Compagnie Continentale v Council* [1975] E.C.R. 117, para.21; CFI, Case T–514/93 *Cobrecaf and Others v Commission* [1995] E.C.R. II–621, paras 63–70 (by waiting fifteen months before rectifying a manifest error in paying a promised Community subsidy, the Commission exhibited an obvious lack of care); misuse of powers: ECJ, Joined Cases 5, 7 and 13–24/66 *Kampffmeyer and Others v Commission* [1967] E.C.R. 245, at 262; failure to adopt a required act: ECJ, Joined Cases 9

2. The loss or damage

11–043 **General.** The requirement for loss or damage is the second pillar on which Community liability is based. The requirement is satisfied when the existence and the extent of the damage have been proved.[996] In practice, these constituent aspects of the concept of damage—existence, extent, and proof—are merged. For the purposes of the following survey, they will be considered separately.

a. Existence and extent of the damage

11–044 **Existence of damage must be sufficiently certain.** The loss or damage caused by an unlawful Community act will found a claim for damages only if its existence is sufficiently certain,[997] in the form of a reduction in a person's assets (*damnum emergens*) or loss of earnings (*lucrum cessans*)[998] or else of future[999] or non-material[1000] damage.

---

and 12/60 *Vloeberghs v High Authority* [1961] E.C.R. 197, at 213; a defective system adopted by an authority which can be attributed to the Community: ECJ, Case 23/59 *FERAM v High Authority* [1959] E.C.R. 245, at 251–252 (system adopted held not defective); ECJ, Case 33/59 *Compagnie des Hauts Forneaux de Chasse v High Authority* [1962] E.C.R. 381, at 389 (system held not defective); ECJ, Joined Cases 46 and 47/59 *Meroni and Others v High Authority* [1962] E.C.R. 411, at 422–423; lack of supervision: ECJ, Joined Cases 19 and 21/60, 2 and 3/61 *Société Fives Lille Cail and Others v High Authority* [1961] E.C.R. 281, at 297; failure to rectify information in time once it became clear that the information provided was incorrect: ECJ, Joined Cases 19–20, 25 and 30/69 *Richez-Parise and Others v Commission* [1970] E.C.R. 325, paras 38–42; failure to comply with internal rules: ECJ, Joined Cases 10 and 47/72 *Di Pillo v Commission* [1973] E.C.R. 763, para.24; breach of the duty of confidentiality: ECJ, Case 145/83 *Adams v Commission* [1985] E.C.R. 3539, paras 28–44; principle of sound administration: the Commission infringed that principle by sending a fax to the persons responsible nationally for a PHARE programme funded by the Commission in which it cast doubt on the financial reliability of an undertaking which had managed several PHARE projects, without checking the data on which the fax was based or giving the undertaking concerned the opportunity to put over its views (CFI, Case T–231/97 *New Europe Consulting and Brown v Commission* [1999] E.C.R. II–2403, paras 38–45). Note that it was held in the judgment in *Area Cova* (CFI, Case T–196/99 *Area Cova and Others v Council and Commission* [2001] E.C.R. II–3597, para.43)—admittedly in connection with a discretionary legislative act—that the principle of sound administration is not intended to confer a right on individuals.

[996] Toth, "The Concepts of Damage and Causality as Elements of Non-contractual Liability", in Heukels and McDonnell (eds) (n.869, supra), at 179–198.

[997] See, for examples, ECJ, Joined Cases 19–20, 25 and 30/69 *Richez-Parise and Others v Commission* [1970] E.C.R. 325, para.31; CFI (judgment of March 17, 2005), Case T–285/03, *Agraz and Others v Commission*, not yet reported, paras 70–78 (existence of damage was not certain).

[998] Opinion of Advocate General F. Capotorti in ECJ, Case 238/78 *Ireks-Arkady v Council and Commission* [1979] E.C.R. 2955, at 2998–2999.

[999] Damage not yet sustained at the time when it is being appraised.

[1000] Such damage is not an actual reduction in assets, but the "reflection" of unreasonable inconvenience caused to an individual on account of an unlawful act or failure to act of a Community institution: CFI, Case T–231/97 *New Europe Consulting and Brown v Commission* [1999] E.C.R. II–2403, paras 53–55; CFI, Case T–11/00 *Hautem v EIB* [2000] E.C.R.

Loss of profit. As has already been mentioned, there are no objections in **11–045** principle to an award of damages for loss of profit.[1001] The applicant must show that it was legitimately entitled in all the circumstances to make the profit and was only frustrated by the unlawful act of the Community institution.[1002]

Future loss or damage. There has been a change as far as recovery of **11–046** future loss or damage is concerned. Originally, the Court of Justice held, with regard to the ECSC Treaty, that a claim for compensation for damage which had not yet materialised was inadmissible.[1003] It moderated its stance under the second para. of Art.288 of the EC Treaty when it held that a claim for compensation for damage which was to materialise only in the future, yet was foreseeable with sufficient certainty, was admissible.[1004] It reached this view on the grounds that it might prove necessary to prevent even greater damage to bring the matter before the Court of Justice as soon as the cause of damage was certain and that most Member States recognised an action for declaration of liability based on future damage which was sufficiently certain.

Non-material damage. Where non-material damage is found, equitable[1005] **11–047** or sometimes symbolic[1006] damages may be awarded.

II–4019, para.52, in which the Court of First Instance held that the unlawful conduct at issue (failure to comply with a judgment) had placed the applicant in a prolonged state of uncertainty and anxiety with regard to the recognition of his rights and his professional future, whilst the indeterminate nature of his work status had caused him difficulties in finding employment, which constituted non-material damage.

[1001] ECJ, Joined Cases 5, 7 and 13–24/66 *Kampffmeyer and Others v Commission* [1967] E.C.R. 245, at 266: the alleged loss must not be essentially speculative in nature; consequently, the Court of Justice held in that case that the intended transaction must at least have been begun to be performed. See also CFI (judgment of July 13, 2005), Case T–260/97 *Camar v Council and Commission*, not yet reported (award of damages for loss of profit).

[1002] ECJ, Case 74/74 *CNTA v Commission* [1975] E.C.R. 533, para.45; CFI, Case T–231//97 *New Europe Consulting and Brown v Commission* [1999] E.C.R. II–2403, paras 51–52.

[1003] ECJ, Joined Cases 9 and 25/64 *FERAM and Others v High Authority* [1965] E.C.R. 311, at 320–321.

[1004] ECJ, Joined Cases 56–60/74 *Kampffmeyer and Others v Commission and Council* [1976] E.C.R. 711, paras 6–8.

[1005] ECJ, Joined Cases 7/56 and 3–7/57 *Algera and Others v Common Assembly* [1957 and 1958] E.C.R. 39, at 66–67; ECJ, Case 110/63 *Willame v Commission* [1965] E.C.R. 649, at 667; ECJ, Joined Cases 10 and 47/72 *Di Pillo v Commission* [1973] E.C.R. 763, paras 23–25; ECJ, Case 75/77 *Mollet v Commission* [1978] E.C.R. 897, paras 27–29; ECJ, Case 207/81 *Ditterich v Commission* [1983] E.C.R. 1359, paras 28–29; ECJ, Joined Cases 169/83 and 136/84 *Leussink-Brummelhuis v Commission* [1986] E.C.R. 2801, para.18; CFI, Case T–13/92 *Moat v Commission* [1993] E.C.R. II–287, para.49; CFI, Case T–59/92 *Caronna v Commission* [1993] E.C.R. II–1129, para.107; CFI, Case T–203/96 *Embassy Limousines & Services v European Parliament* [1998] E.C.R. II–4239, para.109.

[1006] See, for example, CFI, Case T–18/93 *Marcato v Commission* [1994] E.C.R.-SC II–681, para.80 (English abstract at [1994] E.C.R.-SC I–A–215). The Court sometimes considers that the judgment itself, together with its reasoning, affords sufficient redress for the damage sustained (ECJ, Joined Cases 59 and 129/80 *Turner v Commission* [1981] E.C.R.

11–048   **Determination of the quantum.** The award of damages is intended to restore the injured party's financial situation to what it would have been in the absence of the unlawful act or as close as possible thereto.[1007] The quantum of the damage is therefore determined by comparing the actual assets of the person concerned with his notional assets in the event that he had not been affected by the wrongful act.

The damage must be quantifiable,[1008] since under Art.235 and the second para. of Art.288 of the EC Treaty, the Court of Justice and the Court of First Instance are empowered only to make an award of money. The damages are expressed in national currency or in euro. An "exact assessment" of the damage sustained is needed, but an approximate determination based on sufficiently reliable facts, preferably collected by an expert, will suffice if it is not possible to make an exact assessment.[1009]

The question of the determination of the quantum of the damages will be reserved in the event that the necessary information is not available at the time when the finding of liability is made.[1010] In that event, the Court will indicate as far as possible a number of calculation criteria and invite the parties to reach agreement on the amount of the damages within a specified period and to submit the result to it. If the parties fail to reach agreement, the Court will itself determine the amount of the damages. The following sections set out a number of general calculation criteria.

1883, at 1921). See also ECJ, Joined Cases 44, 77, 294 and 295/85 *Hochbaum and Rawes v Commission* [1987] E.C.R. 3259, para.22; CFI, Case T–37/89 *Hanning v European Parliament* [1990] E.C.R. II–463, para.83; CFI, Case T–158/89 *Van Hecken v ESC* [1991] E.C.R. II–1341, para.37; CFI, Case T–52/90 *Volger v European Parliament* [1992] E.C.R. II–121, para.46 (annulment of the contested decision constituted sufficient redress for the non-material damage sustained). But see ECJ, Case C–343/87 *Culin v Commission* [1990] E.C.R. I–225, para.29 (annulment of the contested decision held not to constitute appropriate and sufficient redress for non-material damage suffered); CFI, Case T–165/89 *Plug v Commission* [1992] E.C.R. II–367, para.118.

[1007] Opinion of Advocate General F. Capotorti in ECJ, Case 238/78 *Ireks-Arkady v Council and Commission* [1979] E.C.R. 2955, at 2999. Van Gerven (n.940, *supra*), at 31, points out that the principle of "full compensation" applies; ECJ (order of the President of December 19, 1990), Case C–358/90 R *Compagnia Italiana Alcool v Commission* [1990] E.C.R. I–4887, para.26. *Cf.* CFI, Case T–59/92 *Caronna v Commission* [1993] E.C.R. II–1129.

[1008] Toth (n.996, *supra*), at 27.

[1009] ECJ, Joined Cases 29, 31, 36, 39–47, 50 and 51/63 *SA des Laminoirs, Hauts Fourneaux, Forges, Fonderies et Usines de la Providence and Others v High Authority* [1965] E.C.R. 911, at 939.

[1010] ECJ, Joined Cases 95–98/74, 15 and 100/75 *Coopératives Agricoles de Céréales and Others v Commission and Council* [1975] E.C.R. 1615, para.5. The Court may find that liability exists in principle, indicating the wrongful act or omission, the type of damage and the causal connection between them, while deferring only the determination of the amount of damages (*SA des Laminoirs, Hauts Fourneaux, Forges, Fonderies et Usines de la Providence and Others v High Authority*, cited in the preceding n., at 940–941; see also ECJ, Case C–152/88 *Sofrimport v Commission* [1990] E.C.R. I–2477, para.30; ECJ, Joined Cases C–104/89 and C–37/90 *Mulder and Others v Council and Commission* [1992] E.C.R. I–3061, paras 37–38; CFI, Case T–120/89 *Stahlwerke Peine-Salzgitter v Commission* [1991] E.C.R. II–279, para.137; CFI, Case T–76/94 *Jansma v Council and Commission* [2001] E.C.R. II–243, paras 101–103). Initially, the Court may confine itself to the unlawful nature of the act at issue and defer finding the causal connection and the damage (ECJ, Case 90/78 *Granaria v Council and Commission* [1979] E.C.R. 1081, paras 4–6).

Damage in case of the unlawful collection of a charge or the withholding of   11–049
a payment. If the damage originated in the unlawful collection of a charge
or the unlawful withholding of a payment, the amount of the charge or
payment in question will form the basis for calculating the damages.[1011] The
fact that the amount of the damages coincides precisely with the charge or
payment at issue does not detract from the autonomous nature of the
action for damages. The payment of compensation is founded upon a legal
basis—the second para. of Art.288 of the EC Treaty—different from that of
the contested charge or payment.

Damage passed on to others. Loss or damage which the individual passes   11–050
or could pass on to others is not eligible for an award of damages.[1012] So, if
financial aid is withdrawn, a producer may recover his or her loss by
increasing the price of his or her products. In so far as that price increase
offsets the loss, it must be taken into account when quantifying the
damage.[1013] However, it must be certain that the producer concerned did
pass on the loss or could have done so.[1014]

Interests. Default interest, calculated at the normal legal rate as from the   11–051
date of judgment may be awarded.[1015] Interest is not due until the date of
judgment since the extent of the damage is also determined at that date,
which means that any increase in the damage from the time at which it
arose until the date of judgment is therefore taken into account.[1016] In staff

---

[1011] ECJ, Case 238/78 *Ireks-Arkady v Council and Commission* [1979] E.C.R. 2955, para.13;
ECJ, Joined Cases 64 and 113/76, 167 and 239/78, 27–28 and 45/79 *Dumortier Frères v
Council* [1982] E.C.R. 1733, paras 9–10.

[1012] *Ireks-Arkady v Council and Commission*, cited in the preceding n., para.14; ECJ, Case
256/81 *Pauls Agriculture v Council and Commission* [1983] E.C.R. 1707, paras 8–10; ECJ,
Joined Cases 256–257, 265, 267/80 and 51/81 and 282/82 *Birra Wührer and Others v Council
and Commission* [1984] E.C.R. 3693, paras 26–30. See, however, ECJ, Case 199/82 *San
Giorgio* [1983] E.C.R. 3595, para.15: "In a market economy based on freedom of
competition, the question whether, and to what extent, a fiscal charge imposed on an
importer has actually been passed on in subsequent transactions involves a degree of
uncertainty for which the person obliged to pay a charge contrary to Community law
cannot be systematically held responsible."

[1013] Toth (n.996, *supra*), at 189–190, sharply criticises this approach. His principal arguments
are that pricing policy depends on factors other than the withdrawal of financial aid and
that this approach places an unreasonable burden on the individual concerned inasmuch as
he or she has to pass on the loss to others, with the end result that the Community passes
on its duty to pay compensation to the community in general and consumers in particular.

[1014] Seemingly, there is an obligation on a prudent vendor to pass on the loss brought about by
an unlawful act of a public authority in his or her selling prices if market conditions so
permit.

[1015] ECJ, Case 238/78 *Ireks-Arkady v Council and Commission* [1979] E.C.R. 2955, para.20. A
claim for default interest does not have to be supported by specific reasons; see CFI ,
Joined Cases T–215/01, T–220/01 and T–221/01 *Calberson v Commission* [2004] E.C.R. II–
587, paras 90–91.

[1016] ECJ, Joined Cases 64 and 113/76, 167 and 239/78, 27–28 and 45/79 *Dumortier Frères v
Council* [1982] E.C.R. 1733, para.11; Opinion of Advocate General G.F. Mancini in ECJ,

cases, interest is due from the date on which the staff member lodged his complaint with the administration concerned pursuant to Art.90(2) of the Staff Regulations or from the date on which a debt not paid by the administration became payable if that date occurred after the day on which the complaint was lodged.[1017]

11–052 **Exchange rate.** The exchange rate for an award of damages expressed is that ruling on the date of judgment.[1018]

11–053 **Effect of other "*Bergaderm*" conditions.** The extent of the compensation awarded also depends on the manner in which the requirement for there to be a causal connection between the unlawful Community act and the loss or damage is fulfilled (see 11–057 to 11–060, *infra*).

Furthermore, as has already been mentioned, in the case of an act involving policy choices the extent and the specific characteristics of the damage suffered play a particular role with a view to determining whether the relevant breach of a superior rule of law was sufficiently serious (see 11–041, *supra*).[1019]

b. Proof of damage

11–054 **Applicant bears the burden of proof.** The burden of proof has to be discharged by the applicant.[1020] He or she has to convince the Court of the existence of the damage and of its extent. The defendant may adduce factual evidence which casts doubt on the existence and extent of the

---

Case 256/81 *Pauls Agriculture v Council and Commission* [1983] E.C.R. 1707, at 1723–1729; ECJ, Joined Cases 256–257, 265, 267/80 and 51/81 and 282/82 *Birra Wührer and Others v Council and Commission* [1984] E.C.R. 3693, para.37; ECJ, Case C–152/88 *Sofrimport v Commission* [1990] E.C.R. I–2477, para.32; ECJ, Joined Cases C–104/89 and C–37/90 *Mulder and Others v Council and Commission* [1992] E.C.R. I–3061, para.35. The award of interest, however, may be a means of assessing the total amount of the damage at the date of judgment. In that case, it is due from the day on which the damage materialised (ECJ, Case 185/80 *Garganese v Commission* [1981] E.C.R. 1785, paras 19–21).

[1017] ECJ, Joined Cases 75 and 117/82 *Razzouk and Beydoun v Commission* [1984] E.C.R. 1509, para.19; ECJ, Case 158/79 *Roumengous Carpentier v Commission* [1985] E.C.R. 39, para.11; ECJ, Joined Cases 532, 534, 567, 600, 618, 660/79 and 543/79 *Amesz and Others v Commission* [1985] E.C.R. 55, para.14; ECJ, Case 737/79 *Battaglia v Commission* [1985] E.C.R. 71, para.10.

[1018] ECJ, Joined Cases 64 and 113/76, 167 and 239/78, 27–28 and 45/79 *Dumortier Frères v Council* [1982] E.C.R. 1733, para.12.

[1019] For an application, see CFI, Joined Cases T–480/93 and T–483/93 *Antillean Rice Mills and Others v Commission* [1995] E.C.R. II–2305, paras 200–208.

[1020] ECJ, Case 26/74 *Roquette Frères v Commission* [1976] E.C.R. 677, paras 22–24. A head of damage (such as the payment of bank interest) which is incidental in relation to another head of damage and is not sufficiently proved does not qualify for compensation (CFI, Case T–1/99 *T. Port v Commission* [2001] E.C.R. II–465, para.74).

damage.[1021] As a public authority, the defendant may sometimes be compelled to disclose information to which it alone has access.[1022]

Factual evidence. If the applicant does not succeed in proving that damage occurred and its extent, the application will be inadmissible[1023] or, albeit declared admissible, will be dismissed.[1024] The application must indicate the nature and extent of the damage sufficiently precisely.[1025] For example, it is not sufficient for the applicant to allege that he or she suffered "serious damage". He or she must at least adduce factual evidence on the basis of which the nature and the extent of the damage may be assessed. The Court of Justice recognises that to hold an action inadmissible on this ground requires an assessment of the facts, in particular of whether the appellant has sufficiently proved the amount of compensation claimed by it in the application and the reply. It lies beyond the jurisdiction of the Court of Justice on appeal to rule on whether the assessment made by the Court of First Instance was well founded.[1026]

11–055

Uncertainty about the extent of the damage. Uncertainty about the *extent* of the damage does not mean that the application will be declared inadmissible, provided that the case discloses a real possibility that damage has been suffered.[1027] Mention has already been made (see 11–048, *supra*) of the fact that where the Court finds the Community liable in an interlocutory judgment, it can set the parties a time within which they are to agree on the amount of damages. If they do not succeed and, in addition, the applicant does not adduce sufficiently precise evidence of the extent of the damage within the prescribed period, the application will be dismissed.[1028]

11–056

[1021] See the cases on passing on the loss (see 11–050, *supra*). The defendant has to show that the loss was actually passed on. The applicant may counter the defendant's evidence by showing that the loss was not passed on or that a price increase was attributable to other factors.

[1022] Opinion of Advocate General M. Lagrange in ECJ, Joined Cases 29, 31, 36, 39–47, 50 and 51/63 *SA des Laminoirs, Hauts Fourneaux, Forges, Fonderies et Usines de la Providence and Others v High Authority* [1965] E.C.R. 911, at 943–944.

[1023] ECJ, Case 68/63 *Luhleich v Commission* [1965] E.C.R. 581, at 605; CFI, Case T–64/89 *Automec v Commission* [1990] E.C.R. II–367, paras 72–75; CFI, Case T–461/93 *An Taisce and WWF UK v Commission* [1994] E.C.R. II–733, paras 42–43.

[1024] ECJ, Case 10/55 *Mirossevich v High Authority* [1954 to 1956] E.C.R. 333, at 344–345; ECJ, Joined Cases 14, 16–17, 20, 24, 26–27/60 and 1/61 *Meroni and Others v High Authority* [1961] E.C.R. 161, at 171; ECJ, Case 15/63 *Lassalle v European Parliament* [1964] E.C.R. 31, at 39; ECJ, Case 26/74 *Roquette Frères v Commission* [1976] E.C.R. 677; ECJ, Case 49/79 *Pool v Council* [1980] E.C.R. 569, para.12. For further particulars, see Toth (n.996, *supra*), at 184–185.

[1025] ECJ, Case 5/71 *Zuckerfabrik Schöppenstedt v Council* [1971] E.C.R. 975, para.9; CFI, Case T–64/89 *Automec v Commission* [1990] E.C.R. II–367, para.73; CFI (order of November 21, 1996), Case T–53/96 *Syndicat des Producteurs de Viand e Bovine and Others v Commission* [1996] E.C.R. II–1579, paras 22–23; CFI, Case T–149/96 *Coldiretti v Council and Commission* [1998] E.C.R. II–3841, paras 47–51; CFI, Case T–277/97 *Ismeri Europa v Court of Auditors* [1999] E.C.R. II–1825, paras 65 and 81.

[1026] ECJ, Case C–209/94 P *Buralux and Others v Council* [1996] E.C.R. I–615, para.21.

[1027] ECJ, Case 74/74 *CNTA v Commission* [1975] E.C.R. 533; ECJ, Case 90/78 *Granaria v Council and Commission* [1979] E.C.R. 1081, paras 4–6.

[1028] ECJ, Case 74/74 *CNTA v Commission* [1976] E.C.R. 797.

3. The causal connection

11–057 **Damage must be a direct consequence of unlawful act.** The Community will be liable only for damage which is a direct consequence of its unlawful acts.[1029] The principle is reflected in the Treaties[1030] and links up with the law of the Member States. It is for the applicant to prove the causal connection.[1031]

11–058 **Case-by-case assessment.** Whether or not the damage was a direct consequence of the Community act will depend on various circumstances.

Damage which is a consequence of damage caused in the first place by the Community act does not flow directly from that act and hence is too remote. Accordingly, loss suffered by members of the family of a member of the Commission's staff on account of the personal injuries and psychological *sequelae* suffered by that person as a result of a road accident attributable to careless maintenance of the car on the part of the Commission could not be indemnified.[1032]

11–059 **Chain of causation may be broken.** The person concerned may also break the chain of causation if he or she contributed to the damage arising.[1033] He or she is under a duty to take all such measures within his or her sphere as may help to obviate the damage or limit its extent. Only damage arising to

---

[1029] ECJ, Case 18/60 *Worms v High Authority* [1962] E.C.R. 195, at 206; Opinion of Advocate General A. Dutheillet de Lamothe in ECJ, Case 4/69 *Lütticke v Commission* [1971] E.C.R. 325, at 346; ECJ, Joined Cases 64 and 113/76, 167 and 239/78, 27–28 and 45/79 *Dumortier Frères v Council* [1979] E.C.R. 3091, para.21; CFI, Case T–175/94 *International Procurement Services v Commission* [1996] E.C.R. II–729, para.55; CFI, Case T–7/96 *Perillo v Commission* [1997] E.C.R. II–1061, para.41; CFI, Joined Cases T–213/95 and T–18/96 *SCK and FNK v Commission* [1997] E.C.R. II–1739, paras 94–98; CFI, Case T–13/96 *TEAM v Commission* [1998] E.C.R. II–4073, paras 68 and 74; CFI, Case T–196/99 *Area Cova and Others v Council and Commission* [2001] E.C.R. II–3597, para.152; CFI (order of December 17, 2003), Case T–346/03 *Krikorian and Others v European Parliament and Others* [2003] E.C.R. II–6037, para.23.

[1030] The second para. of Art.288 of the EC Treaty provides that the Community is liable to make good any damage "*caused* by its institutions or by its servants in the performance of their duties" (italics supplied); CFI, Case T–277/97 *Ismeri Europa v Court of Auditors* [1999] E.C.R. II–1825, para.100.

[1031] ECJ, Joined Cases 197–200, 243, 245 and 247/80 *Ludwigshafener Walzmühle and Others v Council and Commission* [1981] E.C.R. 3211, paras 51–56; ECJ, Case 310/81 *EISS v Commission* [1984] E.C.R. 1341, paras 16–17; CFI, Case T–146/01 *DLD Trading v Council* [2003] E.C.R. II–6005, para.73; CFI (order of December 17, 2003), Case T–346/03 *Krikorian and Others v European Parliament and Others* [2003] E.C.R. II–6037, para.23.

[1032] ECJ, Joined Cases 169/83 and 136/84 *Leussink-Brummelhuis v Commission* [1986] E.C.R. 2801, para.22; see also the Opinion of Advocate General Sir Gordon Slynn, at 2819.

[1033] An undertaking cannot claim compensation for the costs it incurred relating to the provision of a bank guarantee when the Court of First Instance subsequently annuls the decision in which the Commission found that the undertaking concerned had infringed Art.81 and/or Art.82 of the EC Treaty. This is because the damage suffered is the consequence of the undertaking's own decision not to comply with its obligation to pay the fine: CFI (judgment of April 21, 2005), Case T–28/03 *Holcim v Commission*, not yet reported, para.123.

the detriment of a person who showed normal prudence is recoverable from the Community.[1034] If the person concerned did not show reasonable prudence, the Community will either not be liable[1035] or liable only for part of the damage suffered.[1036]

Damage must be attributable to the Community. The Community will not be answerable for damage which is attributable exclusively to action by a Member State[1037] or action by an institution of a third country.[1038] The Commission's failure to bring an action against a Member State for failure to fulfil obligations under Community law under Art.226 of the EC Treaty cannot cause the Community to incur liability. The reason for this is that the damage caused by the infringement of Community law is attributable only to the Member State concerned.[1039] However, express Community approval of a national measure which is in breach of Community law may be regarded as the direct cause of any damage flowing from that measure.[1040]

11–060

B. LIMITATION PERIOD

1. Commencement and duration

Period of five years. A claim against the Community for non-contractual liability becomes time-barred after a period of five years from the occurrence of the event giving rise thereto.[1041]

11–061

[1034] ECJ, Case 36/62 *Société des Aciéries du Temple v High Authority* [1963] E.C.R. 289, at 296.
[1035] ECJ, Joined Cases 14, 16–17, 20, 24, 26–27/60 and 1/61 *Meroni and Others v High Authority* [1961] E.C.R. 161, at 171; ECJ, Case 4/67 *Muller (née Collignon) v Commission* [1967] E.C.R. 365, at 373 (application inadmissible); ECJ, Case 169/73 *Compagnie Continentale v Council* [1975] E.C.R. 117, paras 22–32; ECJ, Case 58/75 *Sergy v Commission* [1976] E.C.R. 1139, paras 46–47; ECJ, Case 26/81 *Oleifici Mediterranei v EEC* [1982] E.C.R. 3057, para.24; ECJ, Joined Cases C–104/89 and C–37/90 *Mulder and Others v Council and Commission* [1992] E.C.R. I–3061, para.33, and the Opinion of Advocate General W. van Gerven, at I–3122–3123.
[1036] ECJ, Case 145/83 *Adams v Commission* [1985] E.C.R. 3539, paras 53–55; ECJ, Case C–308/87 *Grifoni v Commission* [1990] E.C.R. I–1203, paras 16–17; CFI, Case T–178/98 *Fresh Marine v Commission* [2000] E.C.R. II–3331, paras 84–92.
[1037] ECJ, Case 132/77 *Société pour l'Exportation des Sucres v Commission* [1978] E.C.R. 1061, para.27; CFI, Case T–146/01 *DLD Trading v Council* [2003] E.C.R. II–6005, paras 80–82 and 91–97. See also CFI (judgment of November 30, 2005), Case T–250/02 *Autosalone Ispra v EAEC*, not yet reported.
[1038] CFI, Case T–220/96 *EVO v Council and Commission* [2002] E.C.R. II–2265, paras 41–48.
[1039] ECJ (order of May 23, 1990), Case C–72/90 *Asia Motor France v Commission* [1990] E.C.R. I–2181, para.13; CFI, Case T–361/99 *Meyer v Commission and EIB* [2000] E.C.R. II–2031, para.13; CFI, Case T–209/00 *Lamberts v European Ombudsman* [2002] E.C.R. II–2203, para.53; CFI (order of January 14, 2004), Case T–202/02 *Makedoniko Metro and Michaniki v Commission* [2004] E.C.R. II–181, paras 42–47.
[1040] ECJ, Joined Cases 5, 7 and 13–24/66 *Kampffmeyer and Others v Commission* [1967] E.C.R. 245, at 260 *et seq.*
[1041] Statute, Art.46. For an application, see CFI, Case T–143/97 *Van den Berg v Council and Commission* [2001] E.C.R. II–277. For an extensive discussion, see Broberg, "The calculation of the period of limitation in claims against the European Community for non-contractual liability" (2001) E.L.Rev. 275–290.

11–062 Materialisation of the damage causes time to start running. The event that causes the claim to arise is the materialisation of the damage.[1042] It is not until that time that all the conditions for liability to be incurred are fulfilled.[1043] It is then that time starts running.

If the full extent of the damage does not materialise immediately but only over a period of time, the damages claim will be admissible only for compensation for the damage which arose during the period starting five years before the date on which the action was brought.[1044]

The possibility of bringing a claim for compensation for future damage or damage which has not yet been assessed does not influence when time starts to run. Time under the limitation period always starts to run when the damage materialises and not from the time when it became possible to bring an action for damages. If that were not the case, the claim for damages could be time-barred before the damage had actually materialised.[1045]

11–063 Legislative acts. The limitation period for Community liability for unlawful legislative acts also does not begin until the resulting damage materialises.[1046] Neither notification of the act nor its entry into force as such causes the limitation period to begin running.

11–064 Unawareness of the event giving rise to the damage. Expiry of the limitation period cannot be pleaded against an applicant who was not aware in time of the event which gave rise to the damage and therefore did not have a reasonable time before the limitation period ran out in order to

---

[1042] ECJ, Joined Cases 46 and 47/59 *Meroni and Others v High Authority* [1962] E.C.R. 411, at 420. The lodging of an action for annulment of a decision does not interrupt the limitation period for bringing an action for damages related to the harm caused by that decision. It is the alleged infringement of Community law in the contested decision which causes damage and not the finding of such infringement by the Court of First Instance: CFI (judgment of April 21, 2005), Case T–28/03 *Holcim v Commission*, not yet reported, paras 63–66.

[1043] CFI, Case T–152/97 *Petrides v Commission* [1997] E.C.R. II–2427, paras 25–31: the applicant has to show that there is a link between the allegedly unlawful act and time when the damage arose. If it fails to do so the claim will be inadmissible in any event in so far as it is based on an act which took place more than five years before the application was lodged.

[1044] CFI, Case T–571/93 *Lefebvre and Others v Commission* [1995] E.C.R. II–2379, para.26; CFI, Case T–210/00 *Biret & Cie v Council* [2002] E.C.R. II–47, paras 44–45; CFI, Case T–174/00 *Biret International v Council* [2002] E.C.R. II–417, para.41.

[1045] Cornelis (n.942, *supra*), at 9–10; ECJ, Joined Cases 56–60/74 *Kampffmeyer and Others v Commission and Council* [1976] E.C.R. 711.

[1046] ECJ, Joined Cases 256–257, 265 and 267/80 and 5/81 *Birra Wührer and Others v Council and Commission* [1982] E.C.R. 85, paras 9–12; ECJ, Case 51/81 *De Francheschi v Council and Commission* [1982] E.C.R. 117, paras 9–11; ECJ, Joined Cases 256–257, 265, 267/80, 5 and 51/81 and 282/82 *Birra Wührer and Others v Council and Commission* [1984] E.C.R. 3693, para.15; for an example of how to calculate the limitation period, see how it was done for each of the applicants in the 1984 *Birra Wührer* case, *ibid.*, paras 16–24; CFI, Case T–20/94 *Hartmann v Council and Commission* [1997] E.C.R. II–595, para.107.

bring a claim.[1047] The fact that the applicant was unaware must be excusable.[1048] This means that a normally prudent person who had done everything possible to become apprised of the facts which resulted in the damage would not have been in a position in the same circumstances to have been aware of the event which led to the damage.[1049]

Expiry of the limitation period must be raised by the defendant. As in most Member States, expiry of the limitation period cannot be raised by the Court of its own motion.[1050]

11–065

2. Interruption of the limitation period

Art.46 of the Statute. Art.46 of the Statute of the Court of Justice provides that the period of limitation is to be interrupted if proceedings are instituted before the Court of Justice (or the Court of First Instance)[1051] or if prior to such proceedings an application is made by the aggrieved party to the relevant Community institution. In the latter event, proceedings must be instituted within the two-month period provided for in Art.230; the provisions of the second para. of Art.232 apply where appropriate.

11–066

Reference to Arts 230 and 232 is made solely in connection with the possibility of interrupting the five-year limitation period prescribed by the first sentence of Art.46 of the Statute. This reference is not intended to shorten the five-year limitation period, but simply to protect interested parties by preventing certain periods from being taken into account in calculating that limitation period. Its aim is merely "to postpone the expiration of the period of five years when proceedings instituted or a prior application made within this period start time to run in respect of the periods provided for in Art.230 or Art.232".[1052]

[1047] ECJ, Case 145/83 *Adams v Commission* [1985] E.C.R. 3539, para.50. See, however, ECJ (order of July 18, 2002), Case C–136/01 P *Autosalone Ispra dei Fratelli Rossi v Commission* [2002] E.C.R. I–6565, paras 30–31 (the fact that the person who sustained the damage was not aware at that time of the precise cause of the damage held to be irrelevant for the purposes of establishing the moment when time started to run); CFI, Case T–76/94 *Jansma v Council and Commission* [2001] E.C.R. I–243, para.76.

[1048] Opinion of Advocate General G.F. Mancini in ECJ, Case 145/83 *Adams v Commission* [1985] E.C.R. 3539, at 3550.

[1049] Heukels and McDonnell, "Limitation of the Action for Damages against the Community: Considerations and New Developments, in Heukels and McDonnell (eds) (n. 869, *supra*), 217, at 225–229.

[1050] ECJ, Case 20/88 *Roquette Frères v Commission* [1989] E.C.R. 1553, para.12. See also Goffin, "La Cour de justice: Recours en indemnité", in *Les Novelles: Droit des Communautés européennes* (Larcier, Brussels, 1969), 333, at 337.

[1051] The institution of proceedings before the national courts does not constitute an act interrupting the limitation period under Art.46 of the Statute: ECJ (order of July 18, 2002), Case C–136/01 P *Autosalone Ispra dei Fratelli Rossi v Commission* [2002] E.C.R. I–6565, para.57; CFI, Case T–246/93 *Bühring v Council and Commission* [1998] E.C.R. II–171, para.72.

[1052] ECJ, Joined Cases 5, 7 and 13–24/66 *Kampffmeyer and Others v Commission* [1967] E.C.R. 245, at 260; CFI (judgment of April 21, 2005), Case T–28/03 *Holcim v Commission*, not yet reported, paras 72–74.

If a prior application is addressed by the aggrieved party to the institution concerned, interruption will occur only if that application is followed by an application to the Court within the time-limits determined by reference to Arts 230 and 232 of the EC Treaty.[1053] If the aggrieved party does not bring proceedings within those time-limits, the initial five-year limitation period continues to run in spite of the application made to the defendant institution. On the other hand, the limitation period is not reduced as a result.[1054]

IV. CONSEQUENCES

A. JUDGMENT HOLDING THE COMMUNITY LIABLE

11–067 **Obligation to pay compensation.** If the Court of Justice or the Court of First Instance finds the Community liable, the Community will be obliged under the second para. of Art.288 of the EC Treaty to pay the necessary damages to the person concerned.

11–068 **Judgment is enforceable.** By virtue of Arts 244 and 256 of the EC Treaty, judgments of the Court of Justice and of the Court of First Instance are enforceable.[1055] Enforcement is carried out in accordance with the law of the Member State on whose territory it takes place. However, the property and assets of the Communities shall not be the subject of any administrative or legal measure of constraint without the authorisation of the Court of Justice.[1056]

B. JUDGMENT DISMISSING THE ACTION FOR DAMAGES

11–069 **Effect inter partes.** A judgment dismissing an application for damages does not take effect erga omnes.[1057] Its force as res judicata extends only to the parties to the proceedings: they are no longer entitled to bring the same

---

[1053] ECJ, Case 11/72 Giordano v Commission [1973] E.C.R. 417, para.6; CFI, Case T–222/97 Steffens v Council and Commission [1998] E.C.R. II–4175, paras 35–41; CFI, Case T–76/94 Jansma v Council and Commission [2001] E.C.R. II–243, para.81; CFI (order of September 19, 2001), Case T–332/99 Jestädt v Council and Commission [2001] E.C.R. II–2561, para.47. For an exhaustively reasoned, specific application in the context of the Mulder cases, see, inter alia, CFI, Case T–143/97 Van den Berg v Council and Commission [2001] E.C.R. II–277, paras 58–74; CFI, Case T–187/94 Rudolph v Council and Commission [2002] E.C.R. II–367, paras 49–65; CFI, Case T–201/94 Kustermann v Council and Commission [2002,] E.C.R. II–415, paras 61–77.

[1054] ECJ, Case 11/72 Giordano v Commission [1973] E.C.R. 417, para.7; CFI, Case T–167/94 Nölle v Council and Commission [1995] E.C.R. II–2589, para.30.

[1055] Judgments of the Court of First Instance are enforceable even if an appeal has been brought before the Court of Justice. Appeals do not have suspensory effect (Statute, Art.60, first para.). Yet the Court of Justice may order application of the judgment of the Court of First Instance to be suspended for the duration of the appeal proceedings pursuant to Arts 242 and 243 of the EC Treaty.

[1056] Art.1 of the Protocol on the Privileges and Immunities of the European Communities. See Ch.14, infra.

[1057] Plouvier, Les décisions de la Cour de Justice des Communautés européennes et leurs effets juridiques (Bruylant, Brussels, 1975), at 147.

claim before the Court on the basis of the same facts. Other persons wishing to bring an action for damages on the basis of the same facts may indeed do so.

V. THE CONSTITUTION

General. The Constitution merges the EC Treaty with the non-Community **11–070** actions of the Union under what were the second and third pillars in the European Union, which is to have legal personality.[1058] In this context, it is logical that Art.III-431 of the Constitution should provide that the Union shall, in accordance with the general principles common to the laws of the Member States, make good any damage caused by its institutions or by its servants in the performance of their duties.[1059] It may be regretted, however, that that article contains no reference to bodies, offices or agencies of the Union, even though the principle that the Union is responsible for acts committed by such bodies, offices or agencies is clearly established.[1060]

[1058] Constitution, Art.I–6.
[1059] Since the ECB has legal personality (Constitution, Art.I–30, third para.), the ECB itself—and not the Union—will have to make good damage caused by it or by its servants in the performance of their duties in accordance with the general principles common to the laws of the Member States (Constitution, Art.III–431, third para.).
[1060] ECJ, Case C–370/89 *SGEEM and Etroy v EIB* [1992] E.C.R. I–6211, para.16; CFI, Case T–209/00, *Lamberts v European Ombudsman*, [2002] E.C.R. II–2203, para.49, upheld by ECJ, Case C–234/02 P *European Ombudsman v Lamberts* [2004] E.C.R. I–2803, paras 43–52.

CHAPTER 12

APPLICATION FOR AN OPINION ON THE COMPATIBILITY WITH THE PROVISIONS OF THE EC TREATY OF AN INTERNATIONAL AGREEMENT TO BE CONCLUDED BY THE COMMUNITY

I. Subject-Matter

A. General

12–001   **Objective.** The jurisdiction of the Court of Justice to give opinions under Art.300(6) of the EC Treaty is intended to avoid potential complications arising out of legal disputes concerning the compatibility with provisions of the EC Treaty of international agreements concluded by the Community.[1061] The Court has described such complications in the following terms: "[A] possible decision of the Court to the effect that such an agreement is, either by reason of its content or of the procedure adopted for its conclusion, incompatible with the provisions of the Treaty could not fail to provoke, not only in the Community context but also in that of international relations, serious difficulties and might give rise to adverse consequences for all interested parties, including third countries".[1062] Consequently, such opinions perform a preventive function.[1063] The Court of Justice has described the procedure as "a special procedure of collaboration between the Court of Justice on the one hand and the other Community institutions and the Member States on the other whereby, at a stage prior to conclusion of an agreement which is capable of giving rise to a dispute

---

[1061] The Court of Justice also has the power to give opinions under Art.103 of the EAEC Treaty (see ECJ, Ruling 1/78 *Draft Convention of the International Energy Agency on the Physical Protection of Nuclear Materials, Facilities and Transports* [1978] E.C.R. 2151).

[1062] ECJ, Opinion 1/75 *Draft Understanding on a Local Cost Standard drawn up under the auspices of the OECD* [1975] E.C.R. 1355, at 1360–1361.

[1063] For further details see Kovar, "La compétence consultative de la Cour de justice et la procédure de conclusion des accords internationaux par la Communauté économique européenne", in *Mélanges offerts à P. Reuter* (Pedone, Paris, 1981), at 357–377; Gattinara, "La compétence consultative de la Cour de justice après les avis 1/00 et 2/00" (2003) R.D.U.E., 3, 687–741.

concerning the legality of a Community act which concludes, implements or applies it, the Court is called upon to ensure, in accordance with Art.164 *[now Art.220]* of the Treaty, that in the interpretation and application of the Treaty the law is observed".[1064] The existence of this judicial procedure, however, does not mean that the Court of Justice will not conduct judicial review *ex post* of the act by which a Community institution intended to conclude an international agreement.[1065] In other words, whilst the procedure for obtaining the opinion of the Court of Justice is intended to obviate the adoption of unlawful acts, if it does not succeed in this, the usual channels for judicial review of the acts in question remain open.[1066] To date, the Court has given a limited number of opinions.[1067]

B. THE EXPRESSION "AGREEMENT ENVISAGED"

Agreement. The term "agreement" in Art.300(6) refers to any undertaking entered into by entities subject to international law which has binding force, whatever its formal designation.[1068] Provided that it is a "'standard' [norm], that is to say a rule of conduct, covering a specific field, determined by precise provisions, which is binding upon the participants", the Court of Justice has jurisdiction to give an opinion on its compatibility with the provisions of the EC Treaty.[1069]

12–002

[1064] ECJ, Opinion 2/94 *Accession by the Communities to the Convention for the Protection of Human Rights and Fundamental Freedoms* [1996] E.C.R. I–1759, para.6.

[1065] ECJ, Case C–327/91 *France v Commission* [1994] E.C.R. I–3641, paras 15–17.

[1066] For the action for annulment, see 7–011 and 7–014, *supra*; for the preliminary ruling on validity, see 10–003, *supra*.

[1067] See ECJ, Opinion 1/75 *Draft Understanding on a Local Cost Standard drawn up under the auspices of the OECD* [1975] E.C.R. 1355; ECJ, Opinion 1/76 *Draft Agreement establishing a European laying-up fund for inland waterway vessels* [1977] E.C.R. 741; ECJ, Opinion 1/78 *International Agreement on Natural Rubber* [1979] E.C.R. 2871; ECJ, Opinion 1/91 *Draft Agreement between the Community, on the one hand, and the countries of the European Free Trade Association, on the other, relating to the creation of the European Economic Area* [1991] E.C.R. I–6079; ECJ, Opinion 1/92 *Draft Agreement between the Community, on the one hand, and the countries of the European Free Trade Association, on the other, relating to the creation of the European Economic Area* [1992] E.C.R. I–2821; ECJ, Opinion 2/91 *Convention No 170 of the International Labour Organisation concerning safety in the use of chemicals at work* [1993] E.C.R. I–1061; ECJ, Opinion 1/94 *Agreement establishing the World Trade Organisation* [1994] E.C.R. I–5267; ECJ, Opinion 2/92 *Competence of the Community or one of its institutions to participate in the Third Revised Decision of the OECD on national treatment* [1995] E.C.R. I–521; ECJ, Opinion 3/94 *GATT—WTO—Framework Agreement on Bananas* [1995] E.C.R. I–4577; ECJ, Opinion 2/94 *Accession by the Communities to the Convention for the Protection of Human Rights and Fundamental Freedoms* [1996] E.C.R. I–1759; ECJ, Opinion 2/00 *Cartagena Protocol* [2001] E.C.R. I–9713; ECJ, Opinion 1/00 *Proposed Agreement between the European Community and non-Member States on the establishment of a European Common Aviation Area* [2002] E.C.R. I–3493. ECJ (February 7, 2006), Opinion 1/03 *New Lugano Convention*, not yet reported.

[1068] ECJ, Opinion 1/75 *Draft Understanding on a Local Cost Standard drawn up under the auspices of the OECD* [1975] E.C.R. 1355, at 1359–1360.

[1069] *Ibid.*, at 1360.

12–003 Participation of the Community. Since the Court's power to give opinions is provided for in Art.300 of the EC Treaty, which lays down the Community decision-making procedure with regard to the conclusion of international agreements, the power extends only to agreements in which the Community proposes to participate.[1070] This relates to the aim of the opinion procedure, which is "to forestall . . . legal disputes concerning the compatibility with the Treaty of international agreements binding upon the Community".[1071] By the same token, the Court of Justice is entitled to give opinions on the compatibility with the Treaty of mixed agreements to which both the Community and some or all Member States are parties.[1072]

II. IDENTITY OF THE APPLICANTS

12–004 Applicants. The European Parliament,[1073] the Council, the Commission or a Member State may request the Court of Justice to deliver an opinion.[1074]

12–005 No obligation. It is optional whether a request for an opinion is made. The Community can validly conclude an international agreement without seeking the opinion of the Court.[1075]

[1070] One commentator considers that it can be inferred from the vague wording of Opinion 2/91 that all "agreements", including those concluded by Member States, may be submitted to the Court of Justice for its opinion (see case note by Neuwahl in (1993) C.M.L.Rev. 1185, at 1190–1191). The possibility has to be ruled out. Unlike Art.103 of the EAEC Treaty, the EC Treaty affords no textual basis therefor. What is more, such agreements are not binding on the Community and hence, if they are subsequently found to be incompatible with the Treaty, there will be no likelihood of the Community incurring liability under international law. In contrast, in the case of mixed agreements, the Court of Justice is entitled to test Member States' obligations against the requirements of Art.10 of the EC Treaty, see Kovar (n.1063, *supra*), at 366.

[1071] ECJ, Opinion 1/75 *Draft Understanding on a Local Cost Standard drawn up under the auspices of the OECD* [1975] E.C.R. 1355, at 1360.

[1072] See, for instance, ECJ, Opinion 1/76 *Draft Agreement establishing a European laying-up fund for inland waterway vessels* [1977] E.C.R. 741.

[1073] The European Parliament has had this power since the entry into force of the Treaty of Nice. For the former position of the European Parliament, see Barents, "The Court of Justice and the EEA Agreement: Between Constitutional Values and Political Realities", in Stuyck and Looijestijn-Clearie (eds), *The European Economic Area EC–EFTA: Institutional Aspects and Financial Services* (Kluwer, Deventer, 1994), 57, at 58.

[1074] To date, all requests for opinions have been made by the Commission with the exception of ECJ, Opinion 2/92 *Competence of the Community or one of its institutions to participate in the Third Revised Decision of the OECD on national treatment* [1995] E.C.R. I–521 (Belgium); ECJ, Opinion 2/94 *Accession by the Communities to the Convention for the Protection of Human Rights and Fundamental Freedoms* [1996] E.C.R. I–1759 (the Council); ECJ, Opinion 3/94 *GATT—WTO—Framework Agreement on Bananas* [1995] E.C.R. I–4577 (Germany); ECJ (February 7, 2006), Opinion 1/03 *New Lugano Convention*, not yet reported (the Council).

[1075] *Cf.* Christianos, "La compétence consultative de la Cour de justice à la lumière du traité sur l'Union européenne" (1994) R.M.C.U.E. 37, at 39.

III. SPECIAL CHARACTERISTICS

A. EXTENT OF THE JURISDICTION TO GIVE OPINIONS

Scope of review. The Court of Justice has interpreted its jurisdiction to review "whether an agreement envisaged is compatible with the provisions of the [EC] Treaty" in the sense that its judgement may depend not only on provisions of substantive law but also on those concerning the powers, procedure or organisation of the institutions of the Community.[1076] This approach is also expressed in Art.107(2) of the ECJ Rules of Procedure.[1077]

12–006

Review limited to the compatibility of the agreement with the Treaty. The Court's review is limited, however, to the envisaged agreement's compatibility with the Treaty. The requirements imposed upon the Community by international law are not covered. Thus, the Court did not inquire into the provisions establishing the International Labour Organisation to see whether the Community was entitled to join that organisation.[1078] The opinion procedure is also not intended to solve difficulties associated with implementation of an envisaged agreement which falls within shared Community and Member State competence.[1079] In addition, the review as to compatibility covers only the legal aspects of the envisaged agreement. Judicial review does not extend to political expediency. As a result of the broad compass of the Court's review, conflicting powers often form the basis of requests for opinions.

12–007

Review may be limited to parts of the agreement. Alongside the question as against what provisions the Court of Justice reviews the compatibility of an envisaged agreement with the Treaty, the question arises as to whether

12–008

[1076] ECJ, Opinion 1/75 *Draft Understanding on a Local Cost Standard drawn up under the auspices of the OECD* [1975] E.C.R. 1355; ECJ, Opinion 1/76 *Draft Agreement establishing a European laying-up fund for inland waterway vessels* [1977] E.C.R. 741; ECJ, Opinion 1/78 *International Agreement on Natural Rubber* [1979] E.C.R. 2871, para.30; ECJ, Opinion 2/91 *Convention No 170 of the International Labour Organisation concerning safety in the use of chemicals at work* [1993] E.C.R. I–1061, para.3; ECJ, Opinion 2/94 *Accession by the Communities to the Convention for the Protection of Human Rights and Fundamental Freedoms* [1996] E.C.R. I–1759, para.9; ECJ, Opinion 2/00 *Cartagena Protocol* [2001] E.C.R. I–9713, para.3, in which the Court of Justice held that its opinion may be obtained in particular on questions concerning the division between the Community and the Member States of competence to conclude a given agreement with non-member countries.

[1077] Art.107(2) of the ECJ Rules of Procedure provides as follows: "The Opinion may deal not only with the question whether the envisaged agreement is compatible with the provisions of the EC Treaty but also with the question whether the Community or any Community institution has the power to enter into that agreement." See also in this connection ECJ (February 7, 2006), Opinion 1/03 *New Lugano Convention*, not yet reported.

[1078] ECJ, Opinion 2/91 *Convention No 170 of the International Labour Organisation concerning safety in the use of chemicals at work* [1993] E.C.R. I–1061, para.4.

[1079] ECJ, Opinion 2/00 *Cartagena Protocol* [2001] E.C.R. I–9713, para.17.

in the case of a given request the Court must examine the whole agreement or simply part of it. In Opinion 1/91, the Court, at the Commission's request, considered only the provisions of the envisaged EEA Agreement which related to the system of judicial supervision provided for therein.[1080] In Opinion 1/92, the Court confined its review to those provisions of the EEA Agreement which had been amended following Opinion 1/91 finding the Agreement incompatible with the Treaty, despite the request made by the European Parliament in its observations submitted to the Court that it should consider the influence of the EEA Agreement on the role and powers of the Parliament.[1081] In Opinion 1/00, the Court assessed the compatibility with the Treaty of the system of judicial supervision established by an agreement on a European Common Aviation Area. In determining the scope of the assessment requested, the Court considered all the language versions in which the request had been made.[1082]

B. Time-limit

12–009 **Preventive nature.** Art.300(6) sets no time-limit. Nevertheless, the preventive nature of these judicial proceedings and the extent of the Court's jurisdiction to give opinions place restrictions on the time within which a request may be made to the Court.[1083]

12–010 **Subject-matter of the envisaged agreement must be known.** First, a request for an opinion may be made to the Court only as from the time when the subject-matter of the envisaged agreement is known.[1084] It is hard to conceive that the Court would be requested to give an opinion at a time when the subject-matter of the envisaged agreement was still uncertain. But as soon as the subject-matter is known, the Court's opinion may be sought, even before the negotiations have started.[1085] From that time, the Court is in a position to adjudge whether the Community is competent to conclude the agreement in question. Indeed, in the event of any conflicts of jurisdiction it is of essential importance for the Community, the Member

---

[1080] ECJ, Opinion 1/91 *Draft Agreement between the Community, on the one hand, and the countries of the European Free Trade Association, on the other, relating to the creation of the European Economic Area* [1991] E.C.R. I–6079, para.1.

[1081] ECJ, Opinion 1/92 *Draft Agreement between the Community, on the one hand, and the countries of the European Free Trade Association, on the other, relating to the creation of the European Economic Area* [1992] E.C.R. I–2821, para.1.

[1082] ECJ, Opinion 1/00 *Proposed Agreement between the European Community and non-Member States on the establishment of a European Common Aviation Area* [2002] E.C.R. I–3493, para.1.

[1083] See Karagiannis, "L'expression 'accord envisagé' dans l'Art.228[now Art.300]", 6 du traité CE" (1998) C.D.E. 105–136.

[1084] ECJ, Opinion 1/78 *International Agreement on Natural Rubber* [1979] E.C.R. 2871, paras 32–34.

[1085] ECJ, Opinion 2/94 *Accession by the Communities to the Convention for the Protection of Human Rights and Fundamental Freedoms* [1996] E.C.R. I–1759, paras 11–12.

States and third countries or international organisations concerned to be certain about the precise powers of the parties at the beginning of the negotiations.

But the Court will not be in a position to give its opinion on the compatibility of an envisaged agreement so long as it does not have sufficient information about the content and institutional machinery of the agreement. Consequently, a request for an opinion raising the question of the compatibility of an envisaged agreement with the Treaty will be admissible only in so far as the Court can have access to such information.[1086]

Community must not yet be bound by the agreement. Secondly, a request **12–011** may be made to the Court only in so far as the Community is not yet bound by the agreement.[1087] Failing this, the opinion would not play its preventive role.[1088] It makes no difference in this connection at what stage in the process of concluding the international agreement the opinion is sought, provided that the Community is not yet bound by it. Accordingly, an opinion may be obtained from the Court before the Commission has made any recommendations to the Council pursuant to Art.300(1) of the EC Treaty with a view to opening negotiations and before the Council has given it the necessary authorisation. The Court's opinion may also be sought after the negotiations have closed, but before the Council concludes the agreement pursuant to Art.300(2) of the EC Treaty.[1089]

If, however, the envisaged agreement is concluded after the request for an opinion was submitted but before the Court has given its opinion, the request becomes devoid of purpose. The preventive intent of the procedure provided for in Art.300(6) of the EC Treaty requires the "envisaged" agreement to be still only envisaged at the time when the Court gives its opinion. Moreover, if the Court were to give an adverse opinion on the compatibility with the Treaty of an agreement which had already been concluded, that opinion would not be capable of having the legal effect prescribed by the second sentence of Art.300(6), namely that, if the Court has given an adverse opinion, the agreement may enter into force only after the Treaty has been amended in accordance with the procedure provided for in Art.48 of the EU Treaty (see 12–014, *infra*). In those circumstances the Court will not respond to the request for an opinion.[1090]

[1086] *Ibid.*

[1087] Kovar (n.1063, *supra*), at 362; Christianos (n. 1075, *supra*), at 40–41.

[1088] An opinion dealing with the compatibility with the Treaty of an international agreement which has already entered into force may be given where the Community is not yet bound by it, but is considering acceding to it.

[1089] ECJ, Opinion 1/94 *Agreement establishing the World Trade Organisation* [1994] E.C.R. I–5267, para.12. The Commission requested Opinion 2/00 (ECJ, Opinion 2/00 *Cartagena Protocol* [2001] E.C.R. I–9713) after the Protocol had been signed by the Council, but before the Commission had submitted a proposal to the Council for the conclusion of the Protocol.

[1090] ECJ, Opinion 3/94 *GATT—WTO—Framework Agreement on Bananas* [1995] E.C.R. I–4577.

C. Procedure before the Court

12–012   **Special procedure.** Since a request for an opinion pursuant to Art.300(6) of the EC Treaty does not introduce normal contentious proceedings, the decision is reached in the Court of Justice in accordance with a special procedure held behind closed doors. It is traced out in Arts 107 and 108 of the ECJ Rules of Procedure. The request for an opinion has to be lodged with the registry. If it is lodged by the European Parliament, it has to be served on the Council, the Commission and the Member States. If it is lodged by the Council, it has to be served on the Commission and the European Parliament.[1091] If the request is lodged by the Commission, it must be served on the Council, the European Parliament and the Member States. If a Member State requests an opinion, the request has to be served on the Council, the Commission, the European Parliament and the other Member States.[1092] The President of the Court prescribes a period within which the Member States which have been served with the request may submit written observations.[1093] It is not possible to apply the expedited procedure in the case of a request for an opinion made pursuant to Art.300(6) of the EC Treaty.[1094]

12–013   **Reasoned opinion.** The Court, sitting in closed session, delivers its reasoned opinion after hearing all the Advocates General.[1095] No provision is made for a hearing, although the Court may hear the institutions and Member States.[1096] The opinion is signed by the President, by the Judges who took part in the deliberations and by the Registrar, following which it is served on the Council, the Commission, the European Parliament and the Member States.[1097]

IV. Consequences

12–014   **Adverse opinion.** An agreement on which the Court of Justice has given an adverse opinion may enter into effect only if the conditions set out in Art.48 of the EU Treaty are complied with. This means first that the EC Treaty must be amended in accordance with the applicable procedure (EC

[1091] The Member States, as "members" of the Council, are always apprised of the fact that a request is to be lodged.

[1092] ECJ Rules of Procedure, Art.107(1).

[1093] ECJ Rules of Procedure, Art.107(1), second subpara.

[1094] ECJ (order of the President of April 29, 2004), Opinion 1/04 *Proposed Agreement between the European Community and the United States of America on the processing and transfer of Passanger Name Record data*, not reported. For the expedited procedure, see 24–057 to 24–059, *infra*.

[1095] ECJ Rules of Procedure, Art.108(2).

[1096] Christianos (n.1075, *supra*), at 41.

[1097] ECJ Rules of Procedure, Art.108(3).

Treaty, Art.300(6)).[1098] Naturally, it is also possible for the envisaged agreement to be amended in consultation with the third countries and international organisations concerned in order to meet the objections raised by the Court.[1099]

Favourable opinion. A favourable opinion leaves the way free for the Community to enter into the agreement, but naturally does not compel it to do so. However, the opinion does not prevent the legality of the act by which the Community concludes the agreement from being raised in some other judicial proceedings, especially where the opinion considered the compatibility of the agreement with the Treaty only from a clearly specified point of view (see also 12–008, *supra*). **12–015**

V. THE CONSTITUTION

General. Art.III-325, para.11, of the Constitution provides: "A Member State, the European Parliament, the Council or the Commission may obtain the opinion of the Court of Justice as to whether an agreement envisaged is compatible with the Constitution. Where the opinion of the Court of Justice is adverse, the agreement envisaged may not enter into force unless it is amended or the Constituition is revised". **12–016**

[1098] For further details, see Kheitmi, "La fonction consultative de la Cour de justice des Communautés européennes" (1967) R.T.D.E. 553, at 576; Gray, "Advisory Opinions and the European Court of Justice" (1983) E.L.Rev. 24, at 36, who argues that there are only procedural differences between an opinion and a declaratory judgment.
[1099] See, for example, the EEA Agreement: the proposed system of judicial supervision was amended following Opinion 1/91: *cf.* Opinions 1/91 and 1/92 (n.1067, *supra*).

PART IV

SPECIAL FORMS OF PROCEDURE

CHAPTER 13

PROCEEDINGS FOR INTERIM MEASURES BEFORE THE COURT OF JUSTICE AND THE COURT OF FIRST INSTANCE

I. SUBJECT-MATTER

General. Actions brought before the Court of Justice or the Court of First Instance do not have suspensory effect.[1] As a result of the time which elapses between the bringing of proceedings and judgment, that principle may detract from the effectiveness of legal protection. Consequently, interim measures which the Court may impose as necessary in interlocutory proceedings are intended, *inter alia*, to secure full effect for the application in the event that the dispute is decided in the applicant's favour.[2]

13–001

A. TYPES OF MEASURES

Suspension of the operation of the contested act. First, under Art.242 of the EC Treaty, the Court may order that application of the contested act be suspended. Only the operation of "enforceable" measures may be suspended.[3] On that ground an administrative authority's refusal to grant a request made to it may not be suspended, generally speaking, unless, as such, it alters the applicant's legal position.[4] The Judge dealing with

13–002

---

[1] EC Treaty, Art.242 first sentence; EAEC Treaty, Art.157, first sentence.
[2] ECJ (order of the President of May 3, 1996), Case C–399/95 R *Germany v Commission* [1996] E.C.R. I–2441, para.46; CFI (order of the President of January 31, 2005), Case T–447/04 R *Capgemini Nederland v Commission*, not yet reported, para.89.
[3] CFI (order of the President of June 7, 1991), Case T–19/91 R *Vichy v Commission* [1991] E.C.R. II–265, para.20; Van Ginderachter, "Le référé en droit communautaire" (1993) R.D.ULB 113, at 118.
[4] Joliet, Bertrand and Nihoul, "Protection juridictionnelle provisoire et droit communautaire" (1992) Riv.D.E. 253, at 258, take the view that suspension of operation may be granted only if the decision rejecting the request is "enforceable", as in ECJ (order of the President of March 23, 1988), Case 76/88 R *La Terza v Court of Justice* [1988] E.C.R. 1741, in which the decision rejecting the applicant's request for an extension of her authorisation to work part time was suspended. The decision rejecting her request meant that she had to start working full time with immediate effect, which altered her legal position as an official.

applications for interim relief must not encroach upon the domain of the "executive".[5] If he or she did so, suspension of the operation of the rejection of a request would be tantamount to performing the act requested, which would entail the Judge acting in place of the administrative authority. At the same time, the purpose of the main action would disappear in that the applicant would obtain the act which it sought to obtain by means of its action for failure to act.[6]

13–003 **Other interim measures.** In some cases, suspension of the operation of the contested act does not suffice in order to prevent irreparable damage from occurring. Consequently, under Art.243 of the EC Treaty, the Court may prescribe "any necessary interim measures".[7] The range of possible measures is not predetermined,[8] but the Judge who imposes them may not exercise a power which is vested first and foremost in another institution as this would jeopardise the balance between the institutions.[9]

13–004 **Interim relief is tailored to the case.** The interim measure imposed by the Court is tailored to the case. Consequently, suspension of operation may be ordered of only part of the contested act or may be made subject to specific

---

In principle, suspension of the operation of a negative administrative decision is impossible, however, since suspension would not be capable of effecting any change in the applicant's situation: ECJ (order of the President of April 30, 1997), Case C–89/97 P(R) *Moccia Irme v Commission* [1997] E.C.R. I–2327, para.45; CFI (order of the President of January 16, 2004), Case T–369/03 R *Arizona Chemical and Others v Commission* [2004] E.C.R. II–205, para.62; ECJ (order of the President of April 29, 2005), Case C–404/04 P-R *Technische Glaswerke v Commission* [2005] E.C.R. I–3539, para.13.

[5] See the Opinion of Advocate General J. Gand in ECJ (order of October 5, 1969), Case 50/69 R *Germany v Commission* [1969] E.C.R. 449, at 454–455.

[6] ECJ (order of the President of October 15, 1976), Case 91/76 R *De Lacroix v Court of Justice* [1976] E.C.R. 1561, para.2; in general, Judges hearing applications for interim relief may not grant measures which cause the main action to become nugatory: ECJ (order of the President of September 26, 1986), Case 231/86 R *Breda-Geomineraria v Commission* [1986] E.C.R. 2639, para.18; CFI (order of the President of March 3, 1998), Case T–610/97 R *Carlsen and Others v Council* [1998] E.C.R. II–485, para.56. For further particulars, see Boulouis, Darmon and Huglo, *Contentieux communautaire* (2nd ed., Dalloz, Paris, 2001), § 299, at 142–143.

[7] See also EAEC Treaty, Art.158.

[8] See, by way of example, CFI (order of the President of July 16, 1992), Case T–29/92 R *SPO and Others v Commission* [1992] E.C.R. II–2161; see also *Commentaire Mégret*, at 406–407; Joliet, Bertrand and Nihoul, (n.4, *supra*), at 261; Borchardt, "The Award of Interim Measures by the European Court of Justice" (1985) C.M.L.Rev. 203, at 226–229.

[9] ECJ (order of the President of October 22, 1975), Case 109/75 R *National Carbonising v Commission* [1975] E.C.R. 1193, para.8. For the Commission's power to impose interim measures during an investigation into infringements of the competition rules, see Art.8 of Regulation No 1/2003; see also ECJ (order of January 17, 1980), Case 792/79 R *Camera Care v Commission* [1980] E.C.R. 119; CFI, Case T–44/90 *La Cinq v Commission* [1992] E.C.R. II–1; CFI (order of the President of December 2, 1994), Case T–322/94 R *Union Carbide v Commission* [1994] E.C.R. II–1159, paras 26–27; CFI (order of the President of October 26, 2001), Case T–184/01 R *IMS Health v Commission* [2001] E.C.R. II–3193; see further Ferry, "Interim Relief under the Rome Treaty—The European Commission's Powers" (1980) E.I.P.Rev. 330–335; Piroche, "Les mesures provisoires de la Commission des Communautés européennes dans le domaine de la concurrence" (1989) R.T.D.E. 439–469.

conditions.[10] Sometimes security may be required to be lodged.[11] The Judge hearing applications for interim relief may also remind a party to comply with existing provisions where this may provisionally ensure appropriate protection of the applicant's rights.[12]

B. THE ANCILLARY NATURE OF PROCEEDINGS FOR INTERIM MEASURES

Ancillary to the main proceedings. The ancillary nature of proceedings for interim measures clearly emerges from Art.242 of the EC Treaty, which merely permits application of the "contested act" to be suspended, and from Art.243 of that Treaty, which provides only for interim measures in cases before the Court of Justice or the Court of First Instance.[13]

13-005

Accordingly, the Rules of Procedure of the two courts provide that an application to suspend the operation of a measure shall be admissible only if the applicant is challenging it in main proceedings[14] and that an

---

[10] For examples, see ECJ (order of the President of October 15, 1974), Cases 71/74 R and RR *Fruit- en Groentenimporthandel and Frubo v Commission* [1974] E.C.R. 1031, at 1034; ECJ (order of the President of March 31, 1982), Joined Cases 43 and 63/82 R *VBVB and VBBB v Commission* [1982] E.C.R. 1241, para.11; CFI (order of the President of June 16, 1992), Joined Cases T–24 and T–28/92 R *Langnese-Iglo and Schöller Lebensmittel v Commission* [1992] E.C.R. II–1839.

[11] ECJ Rules of Procedure, Art.86(2); CFI Rules of Procedure, Art.107(2); for applications, see ECJ (order of the President of May 7, 1982), Case 86/82 R *Hasselblad v Commission* [1982] E.C.R. 1555; CFI (order of the President of October 26, 1994), Joined Cases T–231/94 R, T–232/94 R and T–234/94 R *Transacciones Marítimas and Others v Commission* [1994] E.C.R. II–885, para.46.

[12] CFI (order of the President of December 12, 1995), Case T–203/95 R *Connolly v Commission* [1995] E.C.R. II–2919, para.25.

[13] See also ECJ Rules of Procedure, Art.83(1); CFI Rules of Procedure, Art.104(1). See further Cruz Vilaĺca, "La procédure en référé comme instrument de protection juridiction-nelle des particuliers en droit communautaire", in *Scritti in onore di Giuseppe Federico Mancini* (Giuffrè editore, Milan, 1998), Vol.II, 257, at 265–269.

[14] ECJ Rules of Procedure, Art.83(1), first subpara.; CFI Rules of Procedure, Art.104(1), first subpara.These requirements are not always interpreted in a strictly formalistic manner. For instance, the applicant may seek suspension of the operation of an act which is not the immediate subject-matter of the main proceedings, but the consequence of the act challenged in those proceedings: ECJ (order of the President of April 8, 1965), Case 18/65 R *Gutmann v Commission* [1966] E.C.R. 135, at 136–137; but see ECJ (order of the President of July 16, 1963), Joined Cases 35/62 and 16/63 R *Leroy v High Authority* [1963] E.C.R. 213, at 215. See also Pastor and Van Ginderachter, "La procédure en référé" (1989) R.T.D.E. 561, at 567. But generally the Courts do adopt a formalistic approach: see, for example, CFI (order of the President of November 22, 1995), Case T–395/94 R II *Atlantic Container and Others v Commission* [1995] E.C.R. II–2893, para.39, in which the President of the Court of First Instance rejected an application for an interim order forestalling the application of an (as yet untaken) Commission decision withdrawing immunity from fines in respect of a notified agreement pursuant to Art.15(6) of Regulation No 17. The action in the main proceedings was directed against a Commission decision finding an earlier version of the agreement to be contrary to Art.81(1) of the EC Treaty. An amended version of the agreement had since been notified to the Commission. It was with regard to that new agreement that the Commission had communicated its intention to adopt a decision pursuant to Art.15(6) of Regulation No 17. See also CFI (order of the President of July 2, 2004), Case T–422/03 R II *Enviro Tech Europe and Others v Commission*, not yet reported, paras 48 and 56 (the President raised the question of admissibility of his own motion).

421

application for any other interim measure must be made by a party to a pending case and must relate to that case.[15] Where an applicant seeks pursuant to Art.243 of the EC Treaty an interim measure which essentially seeks the same result as an application for suspension of operation under Art.242 of the EC Treaty, the application will be declared admissible only if the applicant is challenging the same act in the main proceedings.[16]

In principle, an application for interim measures may be made after any direct action has been brought.[17] However, the interim relief sought may not make the claim in the main proceedings nugatory.

13–006 **Judge may not assume the role of the defendant institution.** If the application aims at the adoption of a measure which would be contrary to Community law, the application will be dismissed.[18] Consequently, an application for a measure amounting to the Judge's assuming the role of the defendant institution, not merely reviewing its activity, may not be granted unless the application contains evidence from which the Judge hearing the interim application can find that there are exceptional circumstances justifying the adoption of the measure requested.[19]

13–007 **Interim relief in the context of an action for failure to act.** There would seem to be little chance of successfully applying for suspension of operation in connection with an action for failure to act, since the very object of that

---

[15] ECJ Rules of Procedure, Art.83(1), second subpara.; CFI Rules of Procedure, Art.104(1), second subpara. For examples of applications for interim measures held not to be related to the relevant case before the Court, see ECJ (order of the President of October 19, 1976), Case 88/76 R *Société pour l'Exportation des Sucres* [1976] E.C.R. 1585, at 1587; ECJ (order of the President of November 3, 1980), Case 186/80 R *Suss v Commission* [1980] E.C.R. 3501, paras 15–16; ECJ (order of the President of December 16, 1980), Case 258/80 R *Rumi v Commission* [1980] E.C.R. 3867, paras 20–22; ECJ (order of the President of May 17, 1991), Case C–313/90 R *CIRFS and Others v Commission* [1991] E.C.R. I–2557, para.23, in which the applicants sought, by way of interim measure, an order requiring repayment of allegedly unlawful aid, whilst in the main proceedings they had applied for annulment of the Commission decision declaring that there was no obligation for prior notification of the aid in question under Art.88(3) of the EC Treaty. The President of the Court pointed out that annulment of the contested decision would not result in the contested aid being unlawful. Consequently, the application for repayment of the aid exceeded the scope of the application in the main proceedings. See also CFI (order of the President of December 14, 1993), Case T–543/93 R *Gestevisión Telecinco v Commission* [1993] E.C.R. II–1411, para.25; CFI (order of the President of December 2, 1994), Case T–322/94 R *Union Carbide v Commission* [1994] E.C.R. II–1159, para.28; CFI (order of the President of February 27, 1996), Case T–235/95 R *Goldstein v Commission*, not reported, para.38; CFI (order of the President of March 29, 2001), Case T–18/01 R *Goldstein v Commission*, not reported, para.32.
[16] ECJ (order of the President of December 13, 2004), Case C–380/04 *Bactria v Commission*, not reported, paras 13–18.
[17] *Commentaire Mégret*, at 395 and 405; Mertens de Wilmars, "Het kort geding voor het Hof van Justitie van de Europese Gemeenschappen" (1986) S.E.W. 32, at 40.
[18] CFI (order of the President of October 21, 1996), Case T–107/96 R *Pantochim v Commission* [1996] E.C.R. II–1361, paras 41–42.
[19] CFI (order of the President of July 12, 1996), Case T–52/96 R *Sogecable v Commission* [1996] E.C.R. II–797, paras 38–41, and the case-law cited therein; CFI (order of the President of February 1, 2001), Case T–350/00 R *Free Trade Foods v Commission* [2001] E.C.R. II–493, para.48.

action is to procure the adoption of a measure.[20] An application for other interim measures would normally make the action in the main proceedings devoid of purpose and would therefore be inadmissible.[21]

Interim relief in the context of an action for damages. The question whether, in connection with an action for damages, suspension of the operation of the act which allegedly caused the damage may be sought remains for the present an open question.[22] In any event, it is now clear that it is not possible "to rule out in advance, in a general and abstract manner, that payment, by way of advance, even of an amount corresponding to that sought in the main application, may be necessary in order to ensure the practical effect of the judgment in the main action and may, in certain cases, appear justified with regard to the interests involved".[23]

13–008

Interim relief in the context of infringement actions. The Court of Justice may order the adoption of interim measures under Art.243 of the EC Treaty in the context of an action for failure to fulfil obligations.[24] The interim relief most often sought is—full or partial, conditional or unconditional—suspension of the operation of a contested national measure.[25] The fact that the judgment finding the failure to fulfil obligations is declaratory in nature does not preclude the imposition of interim measures. The Court's interlocutory order does not derive its binding force from the Court's power to give judgment in the main proceedings. If a contested national measure threatens to cause irreparable damage to one of the parties, the Judge hearing the application for interim relief must be able to

13–009

---

[20] Nevertheless, it is not impossible. See ECJ, Case C–319/97 *Kortas* [1999] E.C.R. I–3143, para.37.

[21] But see CFI (order of the President of April 27, 2005), Case T–34/05 R *Makhteshim-Agan Holding and Others v Commission*, not yet reported (application dismissed because the action for failure to act in the main proceedings was inadmissible).

[22] ECJ (order of the President of May 23, 1990), Joined Cases C–51 and C–59/90 R *Comos-Tank and Others v Commission* [1990] E.C.R. I–2167, para.33; CFI (order of the President of October 15, 2004), Case T–193/04 R *Tillack v Commission*, not yet reported, paras 52–63 (no *prima facie* case).

[23] ECJ (order of the President of January 29, 1997), Case C–393/96P(R) *Antonissen v Council and Commission* [1997] E.C.R. I–441, para.37; for the opposite view, see CFI (order of the President of November 29, 1996), Case T–179/96 R *Antonissen v Council and Commission* [1996] E.C.R. II–1641, para.30. For a commentary, see Pijnacker Hornijk and Geurts, "Het kort geding voor de communautaire rechter" (1997) S.E.W. 254, at 257, first column.

[24] ECJ (order of May 21, 1977), Cases 31 and 53/77 R *Commission v United Kingdom* [1977] E.C.R. 921; ECJ (order of May 22, 1977), Case 61/77 R *Commission v Ireland* [1977] E.C.R. 937; ECJ (order of July 13, 1977), Case 61/77 R II *Commission v Ireland* [1977] E.C.R. 1411; ECJ (order of the President of October 2, 2003), Case C–320/03 R *Commission v Austria* [2003] E.C.R. I–11665. For a commentary, see Wainwright, "Art.186*[now Art.243]* EEC: Interim Measures and Member States" (1977) E.L.Rev. 349–354.

[25] ECJ (order of the President of October 25, 1985), Case 293/85 R *Commission v Belgium* [1985] E.C.R. 3521; ECJ (order of the President of October 2, 2003), Case C–320/03 R *Commission v Austria* [2003] E.C.R. I–11665.

order the necessary measures to secure the full effectiveness of the action in the main proceedings. This view is firmly established in the case-law.[26]

13–010 **Interim relief in the context of preliminary ruling proceedings.** The Court of Justice takes the view that it is not empowered to order interim measures in preliminary ruling procedures. However, in the judgments in *Factortame I,*[27] *Zuckerfabrik*[28] and *Atlanta Fruchthandelsgesellschaft*[29] it provided indications as to the interim relief which the national courts are under a duty to provide following the bringing of proceedings relating to the application of Community law (see 3–051 to 3–055, *supra*).

13–011 **Interim relief in the context of appeals.** A party who has brought an appeal may apply for interim measures in the form of suspension of the operation of the judgment of the Court of First Instance or other interim relief. The application must be made to the Court of Justice under Art.60 of the Statute of the Court of Justice.[30] When the Court of First Instance has dismissed an application to annul an act of a Community institution, an order of the President of the Court of Justice to suspend the judgment of the Court of First Instance would be to no avail to the applicant. In order to grant effective judicial protection to such an applicant, the President of the Court of Justice may, in the context of an appeal, suspend the application of the act which had been challenged before the lower court.[31]

C. THE PROVISIONAL NATURE OF INTERIM MEASURES

13–012 **Interim measures apply for a limited period of time.** Interim measures are only provisional. There are two aspects to this[32]: the measures are valid only for a limited period and may not prejudice the judgment in the main proceedings. The period of time for which the measures are to apply may be expressly specified in the order.[33] If no time-limit is mentioned in the

---

[26] See all the orders cited in this chapter in connection with actions for failure to fulfil obligations.

[27] ECJ, Case C–213/89 *Factortame and Others (Factortame I)* [1990] E.C.R. I–2433 .

[28] ECJ, Joined Cases C–143/88 and C–92/89 *Zuckerfabrik Süderdithmarschen and Zuckerfabrik Soest* [1991] E.C.R. I–415.

[29] ECJ, Case C–465/93 *Atlanta Fruchthandelsgesellschaft and Others* [1995] E.C.R. I–3761.

[30] See CFI (order of the President of November 22, 1991), Case T–77/91 R *Hochbaum v Commission* [1991] E.C.R. II–1285, paras 19–22; ECJ (order of the President of May 8, 2003), Case C–39/03 P-R *Commission v Artegodan and Others* [2003] E.C.R. I–4485, para.36.

[31] ECJ (order of the President of April 29, 2005), Case C–404/04 P-R *Technische Glaswerke v Commission* [2005] E.C.R. I–3539, paras 13–14.

[32] Statute, Art.39, third para.

[33] ECJ (order of the President of April 8, 1965), Case 18/65 R *Gutmann v Commission* [1966] 135, at 138; ECJ (order of the President of July 5, 1983), Case 78/83 R *Usinor v Commission* [1983] E.C.R. 2183, para.9; ECJ (order of the President of July 16, 1984), Case 160/84 R *Oryzomyli Kavallas v Commission* [1984] E.C.R. 3217, para.9; ECJ (order of the President of March 17, 1986), Case 23/86 R *United Kingdom v European Parliament* [1986] E.C.R. 1085, operative part; CFI (order of the President of April 2, 1993), Case T–12/93 R *CCE de Vittel and Others v Commission* [1993] E.C.R. II–449, para.33; CFI (order of the President of January 12, 1994), Case T–554/93 R *Abbott Trust v Council and Commission* [1994] E.C.R. II–1, para.19.

order, the order will expire when judgment is given in the main proceedings. At the request of one of the parties[34] or by order given by the Court of its own motion,[35] interim measures may at any time be varied, extended[36] or cancelled on account of a change in circumstances.[37]

Interim measures may not prejudice the decision to be given in the main **13–013** **proceedings.** The order giving interim relief may not prejudice the decision to be given in the main proceedings.[38] It may not decide disputed points of law or fact or neutralise in advance the consequences of the decision to be taken subsequently on the substance.[39] The Judge hearing applications for interim relief may not order measures which are irrevocable and would confront the Judges responsible for the substantive decision with an irreversible situation[40] or which would make the main application devoid of purpose.[41] Indeed, proceedings for interim relief do not lend themselves to an in-depth investigation of the facts and the parties' pleas. In addition, an excessively far-reaching pronouncement would completely reverse the relationship between interim measures and the main proceedings, which is not the intention behind interim relief.[42] Sometimes, however, interim measures unavoidably create an irreversible situation, which the Judges hearing the main case have to accept.[43]

---

[34] ECJ Rules of Procedure, Art.87; CFI Rules of Procedure, Art.108.

[35] ECJ Rules of Procedure, Art.84(2); CFI Rules of Procedure, Art.105(2).

[36] ECJ (order of the President of July 8, 1974), Case 20/74 R II *Kali-Chemie v Commission* [1974] E.C.R. 787; CFI (order of the President of September 29, 1999) Case T–44/98 R II *Emesa Sugar v Commission* [1999] E.C.R. II–2815.

[37] ECJ (order of the President of June 12, 1992), Case C 272/91 R *Commission v Italy* [1992] E.C.R. I–3929, paras 7–8.

[38] ECJ (order of the President of June 25, 1963), Case 65/63 R *Prakash v Commission* [1965] E.C.R. 576, at 579; ECJ (order of the President of July 7, 1981), Joined Cases 60 and 190/81 R *IBM v Commission* [1981] E.C.R. 1857, para.4; ECJ (order of the President of March 17, 1986), Case 23/86 R *United Kingdom v European Parliament* [1986] E.C.R. 1085, para.32 *et seq.*; ECJ (order of the President of April 30, 1986), Case 62/86 R *AKZO Chemie v Commission* [1986] E.C.R. 1503, para.18; ECJ (order of the President of March 26, 1987), Case 46/87 R *Hoechst v Commission* [1987] E.C.R. 1549, paras 29–31; CFI (order of the President of June 3, 1996), Case T–41/96 R *Bayer v Commission* [1996] E.C.R. II–381, para.13.

[39] ECJ (order of the President of February 26, 1981), Case 20/81 R *Arbed v Commission* [1981] E.C.R. 721, para.13; ECJ (order of the President of July 20, 1981), Case 206/81 R *Alvarez v European Parliament* [1981] E.C.R. 2187, para.6.

[40] ECJ (order of the President of May 28, 1975), Case 44/75 R *Könecke v Commission* [1975] E.C.R. 637, para.4.

[41] ECJ (order of the President of October 15, 1976), Case 91/76 R *De Lacroix v Court of Justice* [1976] E.C.R. 1561, para.2.

[42] Opinion of Advocate General F. Capotorti in ECJ (order of March 28, 1988), Joined Cases 24 and 97/80 R *Commission v France* [1980] E.C.R. 1319, at 1338–1339.

[43] ECJ (order of January 17, 1980), Case 792/79 R *Camera Care v Commission* [1980] E.C.R. 119, in which the Court of Justice recognised the Commission's power to adopt interim measures.

II. IDENTITY OF THE PARTIES

A. THE APPLICANT

13–014 **General.** The ancillary nature of interim measures also determines the identity of the parties who may apply to the Court for such relief. An application for suspension of the operation of an act may be made only by the party who is challenging that measure in proceedings before the Court.[44] Other interim measures may be sought by any party to the main proceedings.[45]

13–015 **Interveners.** Textbook writers are divided over the question whether a party intervening in the main proceedings is entitled to apply for interim measures regardless of the stance taken by the party in support of whose submissions it has intervened.[46] It is perhaps preferable not to grant interveners a right of their own to apply for interim measures, since if they were given such a right they might obtain the initiative in the litigation, something which Art.40 of the Statute of the Court of Justice sought specifically to avoid by allowing them only to intervene in support of the submissions of one of the parties. However, they may join in proceedings for interim measures provided that they show a sufficient interest.[47] If they satisfy that requirement, it appears even to be unnecessary for them to have already intervened in the main proceedings.[48] In such case, the view of the Judge hearing the application for interim relief as to whether leave should be granted to intervene in those proceedings would not be binding on the

---

[44] ECJ Rules of Procedure, Art.83(1), first subpara.; CFI Rules of Procedure, Art.104(1), first subpara. See CFI (order of the President of September 21, 2004), Case T–310/03 R *Kreuzer Medien v European Parliament and Council*, not yet reported, paras 15–22 (application by intervener held to be inadmissible).

[45] ECJ Rules of Procedure, Art.83(1), second subpara.; CFI Rules of Procedure, Art.104(1), second subpara.

[46] See in this connection CFI (order of the President of September 21, 2004), Case T–310/03 R *Kreuzer Medien v European Parliament and Council*, not yet reported, paras 15–22: the Court did not have to rule on this question, since the application based on Art.243 of the EC Treaty had to be regarded as an application for the suspension of the operation of a Community act based on Art.242 of the EC Treaty. Since the intervener had not brought an action for the annulment of the act in question, the application for interim measures was inadmissible. See Statute, Art.40. *In favour of this proposition*: *Commentaire Mégret*, at 407; Pastor and Van Ginderachter (n.14, *supra*), at 577, who tie in the intervener's status with the distinction between suspension—which may be sought only by the applicant—and other interim measures, for which any party may apply. They argue that suspension is in fact far too drastic a measure for the purposes of safeguarding the intervener's interests, whereas other interim measures might well be appropriate to this end. *Against the proposition*: Mertens de Wilmars (n.17, *supra*), at 38.

[47] For examples, see CFI (order of the President of July 7, 2004), Case T–37/04 R *Autonomous Region of the Azores v Council*, not yet reported, paras 57–71; CFI (order of the President of July 26, 2004), T–201/04 R *Microsoft v Commission*, not yet reported.

[48] See, by implication, CFI (order of the President of May 13, 1993), Case T–24/93 R *CMBT v Commission* [1993] E.C.R. II–543, paras 14–16.

Judges hearing the main application. A party which has been given leave to intervene in proceedings for interim measures may seek relief different from that applied for by the party which it is supporting.[49]

Interest. A party may request interim measures only in order to protect his or her own interests,[50] not in order to avoid disadvantages which the failure to grant the relief would cause third parties to suffer.[51]

13–016

B. The Defendant

Opponent in the main proceedings. The defendant in proceedings for interim measures is the opponent in the main proceedings of the party which lodged the application for interim relief. There has been one wholly exceptional case in which the Commission was obliged to comply with an interim measure addressed to it in the context of proceedings concerning the Community's budget which were brought by the United Kingdom against the European Parliament.[52]

13–017

III. Special Characteristics

A. Competent Judge

President. The President of the Court of Justice or the President of the Court of First Instance, depending on the court before which the main proceedings have been brought, is empowered to rule on applications for interim measures.[53] The President of the Court of Justice may refer the application to his or her respective court for decision.[54] Such a reference will generally be made on the ground of the difficulty or exceptional interest of the case.[55] If the application is so referred, the Court of Justice has to give it priority over all other cases.[56] By contrast, before the Court of

13–018

---

[49] Mertens de Wilmars (n.17, *supra*), at 38.
[50] ECJ (order of the President of May 4, 1964), Case 12/64 R *Ley v Commission* [1965] E.C.R. 132, at 134.
[51] ECJ (order of the President of February 25, 1975), Case 22/75 *Küster v European Parliament* [1975] E.C.R. 277, paras 6–8; CFI (order of the President of November 10, 2004), Case T–316/04 R *Wam v Commission*, not yet reported, para.28.
[52] ECJ (order of the President of March 17, 1986), Case 23/86 R *United Kingdom v European Parliament* [1986] E.C.R. 1085, paras 23–24. *Cf.*, however, ECJ (order of the President of June 25, 1987), Case 133/87 R *Nashua v Commission* [1987] E.C.R. 2883, para.8; CFI (order of the President of December 14, 1993), Case T–543/93 R *Gestevisión Telecinco v Commission* [1993] E.C.R. II–1411, para.25.
[53] Statute, Art.39, first para. It follows from that provision read together with the second and third paras of Art.57 of the Statute, that the President of the Court of Justice is empowered to rule on appeals brought against orders given by the President of the Court of First Instance in applications for interim relief.
[54] ECJ Rules of Procedure, Art.85, first para.
[55] See Pastor and Van Ginderachter (n.14, *supra*), at 579, and the cases cited therein.
[56] ECJ Rules of Procedure, Art.85, third para.

First Instance, only the President will hear actions for interim relief. However, when the latter is absent or prevented from dealing with such actions, the Judge specifically designated for this purpose[57] will hear actions for interim relief.[58]

B. PROCEDURE BEFORE THE COURT

13–019 **Summary procedure.** An application for interim relief is adjudicated upon "by way of summary procedure".[59] The application is served on the opposite party; the President of the Court of Justice or the Court of First Instance, as the case may be, prescribes a short period within which that party may submit written or oral observations.[60] The President may grant the application even before the observations of the opposite party have been submitted.[61] In most cases, a hearing is held at which the parties put their case and the President puts questions.[62] If necessary a preparatory inquiry may be ordered in so far as this is compatible with the objectives of the interim proceedings.[63]

C. OTHER REQUIREMENTS FOR ADMISSIBILITY

1. Admissibility of the application in the main proceedings

13–020 **Manifest inadmissibility of the main action.** Again on account of the ancillary nature of proceedings for interim relief, whether an application for interim measures is admissible will be contingent upon the admissibility of

---

[57] See, *e.g.* [2005] O.J. C205/16.
[58] CFI Rules of Procedure, Art.106.
[59] Statute, Art.39. See also Pastor and Van Ginderachter (n.14, *supra*), at 581–583.
[60] ECJ Rules of Procedure, Art.84(1); CFI Rules of Procedure, Art.105(1). The applicant does not have the right to present a rejoinder; if the President of the Court of First Instance refuses to give the applicant the possibility to submit a rejoinder or to take measures of inquiry as requested, no infringement of the rights of the defence ensues (ECJ (order of September 30, 2003), Case C–348/03 P(R) *Asian Institute of Technology v Commission*, not reported, paras 23–24).
[61] ECJ Rules of Procedure, Art.84(2), second para.; CFI Rules of Procedure, Art.105(2) second para.; it is provided therein that the decision may be varied or cancelled even without any application being made by any party. For an example, see ECJ (order of the President of June 28, 1990), Case C–195/90 R *Commission v Germany* [1990] E.C.R. I–2715, followed by ECJ (order of July 12, 1990), Case C–195/90 R *Commission v Germany* [1990] E.C.R. I–3351; CFI (order of the President of August 10, 2001), Case T–184/01 R *IMS Health v Commission* [2001] E.C.R. II–2349, followed by CFI (order of the President of October 26, 2001), Case T–184/01 R *IMS Health v Commission* [2001] E.C.R. II–3193; CFI (order of the President of October 14, 2005), Case T–376/05 R *TEA CEGOS and STG v Commission*, not reported, paras 1–3.
[62] If the Judge hearing applications for interim relief considers that the case-file contains all the information which is required to make a pronouncement, he or she may lawfully dispense with oral explanations from the parties: ECJ (order of the President of January 29, 1997), Case C–393/96 P(R) *Antonissen v Council and Commission* [1997] E.C.R. I–441, para.24; CFI (order of the President of November 14, 2003), Case C–393/03 R *Austria v Commission* [2003] E.C.R. I–13593, para.57; CFI (order of the President of July 2, 2004), Case T–422/03 R II *Enviro Tech Europe and Others v Commission*, not yet reported, para.49.
[63] ECJ Rules of Procedure, Art.84(2), first subpara.; CFI Rules of Procedure, Art.105(2), first subpara. See, *e.g.* CFI (order of the President of July 27, 2004), Case T–148/04 R *TQ3 Travel Solutions Belgium v Commission*, not yet reported, paras 60–63.

the application in the main proceedings.[64] Proceedings for interim relief would acquire an impermissible degree of autonomy if interim measures could be ordered in connection with an inadmissible application in the main proceedings. This requirement faces the Judge hearing the application for interim relief with a dilemma: because of the provisional nature of such relief he or she may not prejudge in any way the final judgment, yet in order to determine the admissibility of the application for interim measures, he or she must make a reasonably accurate determination of whether the main application will be declared admissible.

Consequently, the Judge hearing the application for interim relief takes a cautious approach to this question. It has been consistently held that the issue of the admissibility of the main application should not be examined in proceedings relating to an application for interim measures in order not to prejudice the substantive proceedings.[65] Yet where the opposite party contends that the main application is manifestly inadmissible, it will be necessary nevertheless for the Judge hearing the application for interim relief to establish whether there are any grounds for concluding *prima facie* that the main application is admissible.[66] He or she will always take care

---

[64] ECJ (order of the President of May 23, 1990), Case C–68/90 R *Blot and Front National v European Parliament* [1990] E.C.R. I–2177, paras 4–5; ECJ (order of the President of June 27, 1991), Case C–117/91 R *Bosman v Commission* [1991] E.C.R. I–3353, para.6; ECJ (order of the President of July 6, 1993), Case C–257/93 R *Van Parijs and Others v Council and Commission* [1993] E.C.R. I–3917, para.4; ECJ (order of the President of July 9, 1993), Case C–64/93 R *Donatab and Others v Commission* [1993] E.C.R. I–3955, para.4; ECJ (order of the President of July 16, 1993), Case C–107/93 R *AEFMA v Commission* [1993] E.C.R. I–4177, para.4.

[65] ECJ (order of the President of November 21, 1962), Case 25/62 R *Plaumann v Commission* [1963] E.C.R. 126, at 129; ECJ (order of the President of July 7, 1965), Case 28/65 R *Fonzi v Commission* [1966] E.C.R. 508, at 509; ECJ (order of the President of November 30, 1972), Case 75/72 R *Perinciolo v Council* [1972] E.C.R. 1201, para.7; ECJ (order of the President of November 3, 1980), Case 186/80 R *Suss v Commission* [1980] E.C.R. 3501, paras 13–14; ECJ (order of the President of March 17, 1986), Case 23/86 R *United Kingdom v European Parliament* [1986] E.C.R. 1085, para.21; ECJ (order of the President of April 22, 1986), Case 351/85 R *Fabrique de Fer de Charleroi v Commission* [1986] E.C.R. 1307, para.13; ECJ (order of the President of October 16, 1986), Case 221/86 R *Group of the European Right and National Front Party v European Parliament* [1986] E.C.R. 2969, para.19; ECJ (order of the President of April 8, 1987), Case 65/87 R *Pfizer v Commission* [1987] E.C.R. 1691, para.15; CFI (order of the President of November 28, 2003), Case T–264/03 R *Schmoldt and Others v Commission* [2003] E.C.R. II–5089, para.55.

[66] See, for example, ECJ (order of the President of August 5, 1983), Case 118/83 R *CMC v Commission* [1983] E.C.R. 2583, para.37; ECJ (order of the President of May 8, 1987), Case 82/87 R *Autexpo v Commission* [1987] E.C.R. 2131, paras 15–16; ECJ (order of the President of August 10, 1987), Case 209/87 R *EISA v Commission* [1987] E.C.R. 3453, para.10; ECJ (order of the President of August 10, 1987), Case 214/87 R *Cockerill Sambre v Commission* [1987] E.C.R. 3463, para.10; ECJ (order of the President of August 10, 1987), Case 223/87 R *ASSIDER v Commission* [1987] E.C.R. 3473, para.10; ECJ (order of the President of July 13, 1988), Case 160/88 R *Fédération Européenne de la Santé Animale and Others v Council* [1988] E.C.R. 4121, para.22; ECJ (order of the President of June 27, 1991), Case C–117/91 R *Bosman v Commission* [1991] E.C.R. I–3353, para.7; ECJ (order of the President of October 12, 1992), Case C–295/92 R *Landbouwschap v Commission* [1992] E.C.R. I–5069; CFI (order of the President of March 23, 1992), Joined Cases T–10–12/92 R

that the Judges hearing the main case retain their latitude. The assessment made by the Judge hearing applications for interim relief does not preclude interim measures being granted following the bringing of an action which is subsequently declared inadmissible,[67] but it does avoid an application which is manifestly inadmissible giving rise to proceedings for interim relief which enable the application or effects of a Community act to be temporarily averted.[68]

The Judge hearing applications for interim measures takes the view that the application in the main proceedings may be admissible where he or she finds that that application discloses *prima facie* grounds for concluding that there is a certain probability that it is admissible.[69] Such grounds will be lacking where, in the light of settled case-law, the main application is manifestly inadmissible. For instance, an application for annulment of the Commission's refusal to initiate proceedings for failure to fulfil obligations is manifestly inadmissible (see 5–027 and 5–028, *supra*). Accordingly, an application for interim measures brought in connection with such an action will also be inadmissible.[70] Other examples of manifest inadmissibility of the main application are when the applicant has failed to comply with certain formal requirements[71] or to lodge the application within the prescribed time-limit[72] and where individuals have brought an action against an act which is unmistakeably of general application[73] or against an act which

---

and T–14–15/92 R *Cimenteries CBR and Others v Commission* [1992] E.C.R. II–1571, para.44; CFI (order of the President of December 15, 1992), Case T–96/92 R *CCE de la Société Générale des Grandes Sources and Others v Commission* [1992] E.C.R. II–2579, para.31; CFI (order of the President of March 2, 1998), Case T–310/97 R *Netherlands Antilles v Council* [1998] E.C.R. II–455, paras 30–37; CFI (order of the President of November 28, 2003), Case T–264/03 R *Schmoldt and Others v Commission* [2003] E.C.R. II–5089, para.55.

[67] For an example, see ECJ (order of the President of October 25, 1985), Case 293/85 R *Commission v Belgium* [1985] E.C.R. 3521, followed by ECJ, Case 293/85 *Commission v Belgium* [1988] E.C.R. 305.

[68] ECJ (order of the President of January 27, 1988), Case 376/87 R *Distrivet v Council* [1988] E.C.R. 209, para.22; CFI (order of the President of April 28, 1999), Case T–11/99 R *Van Parijs and Others v Commission* [1999] E.C.R. II–1355, para.51. This also applies to the requirement for a *prima facie* case (see 13–027 and 13–028), *infra*.

[69] ECJ (order of the President of February 1, 1984), Case 1/84 R *Ilford v Commission* [1984] E.C.R. 423, paras 6–7; CFI (order of the President of April 2, 1993), Case T–12/93 R *CCE de Vittel and Others v Commission* [1993] E.C.R. II–449, paras 20–26; CFI (order of the President of May 13, 1993), Case T–24/93 R *CMBT v Commission* [1993] E.C.R. II–543, paras 27–30.

[70] ECJ (order of the President of May 5, 1994), Case C–97/94 P-R *Schulz v Commission* [1994] E.C.R. I–1701, paras 12–15.

[71] ECJ (order of the President of February 26, 1981), Case 10/81 *Farrall v Commission* [1981] E.C.R. 717 (application not lodged by a lawyer).

[72] ECJ (order of the President of May 23, 1984), Case 50/84 R *Bensider v Commission* [1984] E.C.R. 2247, para.24.

[73] ECJ (order of the President of July 13, 1988), Case 160/88 R *Fédération Européenne de la Santé Animale and Others v Council* [1988] E.C.R. 4121, paras 23–30.

produces no legal effects.[74] An action brought by individuals against a decision addressed to a Member State which the Judge hearing applications for interim relief finds, *prima facie*, not to be of individual concern to them will be held to be manifestly inadmissible.[75]

2. Time-limits

General. An application for interim measures will be admissible only as from the time when the application in the main proceedings has been brought.[76] As long as the main action is pending, an application for interim measures can in principle be made.[77] Nevertheless, the Judge hearing applications for interim relief will not hold an application admissible if it is lodged after the written and oral procedures in the main case have been concluded and only a matter of weeks before final judgment is given.[78] In addition, the applicant should take care that its decision as to the time when it submits an application for interim measures does not prejudice its chance of the measures being granted. If the applicant delays too long, there is a danger that the Judge hearing the application for interim relief will draw inferences detracting from the urgency of the measures sought.[79]

13–021

Staff cases. In staff cases, an application may be made for interim measures from the time when the applicant lodges his or her complaint with the appointing authority. At the same time, the main action must have

13–022

---

[74] CFI (order of the President of August 26, 1996), Case T–75/96 R *Söktas v Commission* [1996] E.C.R. II–859, paras 16–30; CFI (order of the President of October 14, 1996), Case T–137/96 R *Valio v Commission* [1996] E.C.R. II–1327, paras 27–37; CFI (order of the President of October 15, 2004), Case T–193/04 R *Tillack v Commission*, not yet reported, paras 38–48, confirmed on appeal ECJ (order of the President of April 19, 2005), Case C–521/04P(R) *Tillack v Commission* [2005] E.C.R. I–3103, paras 35–41: the finding of the manifest inadmissibility of the main action in an order regarding an application for interim measures does not violate the principle of effective judicial protection.

[75] CFI (order of the President of December 22, 1995), Case T–219/95 R *Danielsson and Others v Commission* [1995] E.C.R. II–3051, paras 66–76.

[76] ECJ Rules of Procedure, Art.83(1), first subpara.; CFI Rules of Procedure, Art.104(1), first subpara.

[77] An application for interim relief is to no purpose once the Court of Justice or the Court of First Instance has given judgment in the main proceedings (ECJ (order of the President of September 13, 2004), Case C–18/04 P(R) *Krikorian v European Parliament, Council and Commission*, not reported, paras 6–7).

[78] ECJ (order of the President of April 11, 1960), Joined Cases 3–16, 18 and 25–26/58 R *Barbara Erzbergbau and Others v High Authority* [1960] E.C.R. 220, at 223–224.

[79] ECJ (order of the President of April 22, 1994), Case C–87/94 R *Commission v Belgium* [1994] E.C.R. I–1395, paras 38 and 42. In this order, the President of the Court of Justice held that the Commission had not displayed the diligence to be expected of a party lodging an application for interim measures who relied on the urgency of the measures sought. On October 29, 1993, the Commission received a complaint from the bus manufacturer Van Hool alleging irregularities in the choice of suppliers of new buses by the Walloon regional transport company (*Société régionale wallonne de transport*). The Commission did not announce its intention to seek interim measures until its reasoned opinion of February 8, 1994. The President held that this was too late. For a commentary, see Mattera, "L'ordonnance du 22 avril 1994 sur les 'bus wallons'" (1994) R.M.U.E. 161–171.

been brought before the Court of First Instance.[80] The proceedings in the principal action are then suspended until such time as an express or implied decision rejecting the complaint is taken.[81]

3. Requirement for a separate application

13–023 **Separate document.** Under Art.83(3) of the ECJ Rules of Procedure and Art.104(3) of the CFI Rules of Procedure, an application for interim measures must be made by a separate document and in accordance with the formal requirements applying to procedural documents in general and applications in particular.[82] A request for interim relief contained in the application initiating the main proceedings will be inadmissible.[83] Applications for interim measures must state the subject-matter of the proceedings, the circumstances giving rise to urgency and the pleas of fact and law establishing a *prima facie* case for the interim measures applied for.[84] Pleas not set out in this way in the application will not be taken into consideration in adjudicating on the application.[85] It is therefore not sufficient for the application for interim measures merely to refer to the pleas set out in the application in the main proceedings without setting forth the actual pleas in the application for interim measures.[86]

13–024 **Modification of the application.** The application may be "varied" in the course of the oral procedure if the variation falls within the framework of the measures requested in the application for interim relief and has less of an effect on the defendant.[87] If those requirements are not fulfilled and the varied application substantially differs in kind from the original application,

---

[80] In principle, an application to the Court of First Instance will be admissible in staff cases only after the administrative phase has run its course: the official lodges a complaint with his or her appointing authority, which then has four months to take a decision. If no decision is taken within that four-month period, the complaint is deemed to have been impliedly refused (Staff Regulations, Art.90(2)).

[81] Staff Regulations, Art.91(4).

[82] ECJ Rules of Procedure, Arts 37 and 38; CFI Rules of Procedure, Arts 43 and 44.*infra*).

[83] ECJ, Case 108/63 *Merlini v High Authority* [1965] E.C.R. 1, at 9; ECJ, Case 32/64 *Italy v Commission* [1965] E.C.R. 365, at 372; CFI (order of June 19, 1995), Case T–107/94 *Kik v Council and Commission* [1995] E.C.R. II–1717; CFI, Case T–140/94 *Gutiérrez de Quijano y Llorens v European Parliament* [1996] E.C.R.-SC II–689, para.32 (English abstract at I–A-241); CFI, Case T–146/95 *Bernardi v European Parliament* [1996] E.C.R. II–769, para.30; CFI (order of September 29, 1997), Case T–4/97 *D'Orazio and Hublau v Commission* [1997] E.C.R. II–1505, para.14.

[84] ECJ Rules of Procedure, Art.83(2); CFI Rules of Procedure, Art.104(2).

[85] CFI (order of the President of January 15, 2001), Case T–236/00 R *Stauner and Others v European Parliament and Commission* [2001] E.C.R. II–15; CFI (order of the President of May 7, 2002), Case T–306/01 R *Aden and Others v Council and Commission* [2002] E.C.R. II–2387, para.54.

[86] CFI (order of the President of May 8, 2001), Case T–95/01 R *Coget and Others v Court of Auditors* [2001] E.C.R.-SC IA-191, II–879, paras 8–12.

[87] ECJ (order of June 29, 1993), Case C–280/93 R *Germany v Council* [1993] E.C.R. I–3667, para.15.

the application to vary the initial request for interim measures will be inadmissible.[88]

D. SUBSTANTIVE REQUIREMENTS

General. All the following three requirements[89] have to be met if the application for interim measures is to be granted: (1) the application must establish a *prima facie* case, which means that the application in the main proceedings with which it is associated must, at first sight, have a reasonable chance of succeeding (*fumus boni juris*); (2) the application must be urgent, and (3) the applicant's interest in the imposition of interim measures must outweigh the other interests at stake in the proceedings.[90] The first two requirements arise under Art.83(2) of the ECJ Rules of Procedure and Art.104(2) of the CFI Rules of Procedure. The third has come out of the case-law, sometimes in connection with the determination whether the application in the main proceedings is potentially well founded or with the urgency of the application for interim relief.

13–025

Requirements of equal importance. The order in which the Judge hearing applications for interim relief considers these substantive requirements is of little consequence.[91] Once one of the requirements is not satisfied, interim measures may not be imposed. In practice, the determination of the urgency of the measures sought is often decisive and the other requirements do not have to be considered.[92] Nevertheless, the Judge hearing applications for interim relief must proceed with the necessary care, in particular where the institution concerned has a discretion. According to the Court of Justice, the mere fact that a discretionary power is vested in the institution which adopted the contested act cannot in itself, in the absence of any consideration whether there is a *prima facie* case and of any balancing of the interests involved, determine requirements relating to the condition of urgency. To take a different approach would mean excluding or at least restricting legal protection in proceedings for interim relief where the act at issue was adopted pursuant to a broad discretionary power. The result could, in particular, be that provisional measures necessary to secure the effectiveness of the judgment in the main proceedings would be

13–026

[88] *Ibid.*, para.16.
[89] ECJ (order of the President of December 17, 1998), Case C–364/98 P (R) *Emesa Sugar v Commission* [1998] E.C.R. I–8815, para 47.
[90] CFI (order of the President of December 15, 1999), Case T–191/98 R II *Cho Yang Shipping v Commission* [1999] E.C.R. II–3909, para.46.
[91] ECJ (order of the President of July 19, 1995), Case C–149/95 P (R) *Commission v Atlantic Container Line and Others* [1995] E.C.R. I–2165, para 23; ECJ (order of the President of December 17, 1998), Case C–364/98 P (R) *Emesa Sugar v Commission* [1998] E.C.R. I–8815, para 44.
[92] ECJ (order of the President of July 25, 2002), Case C–198/02 P(R) *De Nicola*, not reported, para.45.

refused on the sole ground that the urgency was not indisputable in cases where there was a particularly strong *prima facie* case and the balance of interests was in favour of the party applying for the interim measures.[93]

It may be noted in this connection that the Judge hearing the application for interim relief is not required to reply explicitly to all the points of law and fact raised in the course of the interlocutory proceedings. It is sufficient that the reasons given validly justify the order given in the light of the circumstances of the case.[94]

1. Prima facie case

13–027 **Objective.** The requirement for a *prima facie* case to be made out (also referred to as *fumus boni juris*) is designed—just as in the case of the determination that the main application is not manifestly inadmissible—to prevent improper use being made of applications for interim relief (see 13–020, *supra*).

13–028 **Evolution towards *fumus non mali juris*.** The main case must have a reasonable chance of succeeding. Since the Judge hearing applications for interim relief may not prejudge the decision in the proceedings on the substance his or her assessment in this regard will be confined to whether the arguments put forward by the applicant in the main proceedings are, *prima facie*, basically sound or are certainly doomed to fail.[95] The application for interim measures must describe the pleas raised in the main proceedings sufficiently precisely to enable the Judge hearing the application to assess whether there is a *prima facie* case.[96] The case-law, which is influenced greatly by the particular circumstances, exhibits in practice quite considerable subtle differences in its interpretation of this requirement.

---

[93] ECJ (order of the President of December 17, 1998), Case C–364/98 P (R) *Emesa Sugar v Commission* [1998] E.C.R. I–8815, paras 50–51.

[94] ECJ (order of the President of September 10, 1997), Case C–248/97 P(R) *Chaves Fonseca Ferrão v Office for Harmonisation in the Internal Market (Trade Marks and Designs)* [1997] E.C.R. I–4729, para.20. In exceptional circumstances, the Judge hearing applications for interim relief may order the suspension of the contested act or part of it pending additional information which will enable him or her to assess the basic requirements for the grant of interim measures. Such suspension by way of "intermediate order" is valid until such time as a decision is given terminating the proceedings for interim relief: CFI (order of the President of December 15, 1999), Case T–191/98 R II *Cho Yang Shipping v Commission* [1999] E.C.R. II–3909; CFI (order of the President of October 14, 2005), Case T–376/05 R *TEA CEGOS and STG v Commission*, not reported, paras 1–3.

[95] See, for example, CFI (order of the President of April 5, 1993), Case T–21/93 *Peixoto v Commission* [1993] E.C.R. II–463, para.27, where it was found that the arguments advanced provided a "firm basis" for the applicant's claims in the main proceedings. *Cf.* CFI (order of the President of May 26, 1998), Case T–60/98 R *Ecord Consortium v Commission* [1998] E.C.R. II–2205, where the President clearly held that the plea alleging infringement of the principle of protection of legitimate expectation appeared unfounded.

[96] If this is not done, the application for interim relief will be inadmissible (see CFI (order of the President of June 9, 2004), Case T–91/04 R *Just v Commission*, not yet reported, paras 17–18).

Sometimes the Judge hearing applications for interim relief holds that there should be "a strong presumption that the application in the main action is well founded".[97] In other cases, it is found that there is substantial *prima facie* evidence that the applicant is in the right,[98] or that the legality of the contested act is, to say the least, doubtful.[99] In other—more recent— cases, the Judge hearing applications for interim relief takes the opposite approach and finds that there are no grounds for holding that the substantive application is manifestly without foundation.[100] That formula expresses the view of the Judge hearing the application that the arguments put forward by the person seeking the interim measures cannot be rejected at that stage of the proceedings in the absence of an in-depth consideration of the case.[101] Thus *fumus boni juris* is slowly but surely turning into *fumus non mali juris*. It would therefore seem that the Judge hearing interim applications is no longer required to be of the opinion that the main action will succeed in order to grant the measures requested, merely having to be persuaded that the main application is reasonable.[102]

---

[97] ECJ (order of the President of October 20, 1959), Joined Cases 43, 44 and 45/59 R *Von Lachmüller and Others v Commission* [1960] E.C.R. 489, at 492. See, to the same effect, ECJ (order of the President of June 25, 1963), Case 65/63 R *Prakash v Commission* [1965] E.C.R. 576, at 578, in which the President dismissed the application for interim measures on the ground that he did not have sufficient information to assess whether the main application was *prima facie* well founded.

[98] ECJ (order of March 4, 1982), Case 42/82 R *Commission v France* [1982] E.C.R. 841, paras 13–14.

[99] ECJ (order of the President of August 21, 1981), Case 232/81 R *Agricola Commerciale Olio and Others v Commission* [1981] E.C.R. 2193, para.5.

[100] ECJ (order of the President of January 16, 1975), Case 3/75 R *Johnson & Firth Brown v Commission* [1975] E.C.R. 1, para.1; CFI (order of the President of July 7, 1998), Case T–65/98 R *Van den Bergh Foods v Commission* [1998] E.C.R. II–2641, para.61 ("In view of all of the foregoing, the pleas in law put forward by the applicants cannot be held *prima facie* to lack any foundation"); CFI (order of the President of October 31, 2000), Case T–83/00 R I *Hänseler v Commission* [2000] E.C.R. II–3563, para.32 ("the pleas raised by the applicant do not *prima facie* appear to be entirely unfounded"); CFI (order of the President of October 15, 2004), Case T–193/04 R *Tillack v Commission*, not yet reported, paras 52–63 (the applicant had not shown that his application in the main proceedings was not manifestly unfounded; there was therefore a *fumus mali juris*).

[101] ECJ (order of the President of June 13, 1989), Case 56/89 R *Publishers Association v Commission* [1989] E.C.R. 1693, para.33; ECJ (order of the President of October 10, 1989), Case 246/89 R *Commission v United Kingdom* [1989] E.C.R. 3125, para.33; ECJ (order of the President of June 28, 1990), Case C–195/90 R *Commission v Germany* [1990] E.C.R. I–2715, para.19; ECJ (order of the President of January 31, 1992), Case C–272/91 R *Commission v Italy* [1992] E.C.R. I–457, para.24; ECJ (order of the President of June 29, 1993), Case C–280/93 R *Germany v Council* [1993] E.C.R. I–3667, para.21; ECJ (order of the President of July 19, 1995), Case C–149/95 P(R) *Commission v Atlantic Container Line and Others* [1995] E.C.R. I–2165, para.26.

[102] See cases cited in n.100. See also ECJ (order of the President of January 31, 1992), Case C–272/91 R *Commission v Italy* [1992] E.C.R. I–457, paras 19–24: the President of the Court of Justice set forth the Commission's and Italy's arguments alongside each other before holding that the Commission's application did not appear to be without substance; CFI (order of the President of April 15, 1991), Case T–13/91 R *Harrison v Commission* [1991] E.C.R. II–179, para.26: the President found first that the pleas adduced in support of the

If the application in the main proceedings raises questions of legal principle which the Court of Justice has not yet had occasion to determine and the pleas adduced relate to those questions, the application will be regarded as not being manifestly unfounded and the Judge hearing the application for interim relief will hold that the requirement for a *prima facie* case has been made out.[103]

2. Urgent nature of the application for interim measures

13–029 **Urgency relates to damage liable to arise.** An application for interim relief is urgent where the absence of the judgment in the main proceedings threatens to cause the person seeking the relief serious and irreparable damage. The urgent nature of the interim application is therefore determined by the nature of the damage which is liable to arise as a result of the duration of the main proceedings.[104] It was therefore not by chance that the serious and irreparable nature of the damage has emerged in the case-law as the yardstick for determining the urgency of an application for interim measures. That two-fold criterion is intended to restrict the grant of interim measures to cases in which the judgment in the main proceedings would not afford any legal redress in the absence of the interim relief sought.[105] The case-law does not provide any conclusive definitions of the two terms. Moreover, the seriousness and the irreparable nature of the alleged damage are not always considered separately.[106] Although the damage must be both serious and irreparable,[107] the case-law seems to attach the most importance to the question of irreparability.[108]

---

application in the main proceedings did not bear out the applicant's claims, before going on to hold that "the applicant has failed to make out a *prima facie* case suggesting that his main application is well founded".

[103] ECJ (order of the President of January 31, 1991), Case C–345/90 P-R *European Parliament v Hanning* [1991] E.C.R. I–231, paras 29–30.

[104] ECJ (order of the President of July 25, 2000), Case C–377/98 R *Netherlands v European Parliament and Council* [2000] E.C.R. I–6229, para.45: it is not enough to allege infringement of fundamental rights in the abstract for the purposes of establishing that the harm which could result would necessarily be irreparable.

[105] ECJ (order of the President of November 28, 1966), Case 29/66 R *Gutmann v Commission* [1967] E.C.R. 241, at 242.

[106] See the Opinion of Advocate General F. Capotorti in ECJ (order of March 28, 1980), Joined Cases 24 and 97/80 R *Commission v France* [1980] E.C.R. 1319, at 1341–1342, who equated irreparable with serious. In ECJ (order of the President of June 26, 1959), Case 31/59 R *Acciaieria e Tubificio di Brescia v High Authority* [1960] E.C.R. 98, at 99, the requirement for urgency was defined in terms of the applicant's having to show that the implementation of the contested measure would cause "irreparable or at least serious damage".

[107] ECJ (order of the President of January 13, 1978), Case 4/78 R *Salerno v Commission* [1978] E.C.R. 1, para.11.

[108] CFI (order of the President of January 31, 2005), Case T–447/04 R *Capgemini Nederland v Commission*, not yet reported, para.89: it is for the party applying for interim measures to adduce proof that it cannot await the outcome of the main action without suffering serious and irreparable damage.

Serious and irreparable damage. The damage is irreparable where it will   **13–030**
not be eliminated by a judgment in the main proceedings in favour of the
applicant.[109] Financial loss is in principle regarded as irreparable damage
only in the event that it would not be fully compensated if the applicant in
the main proceedings were to be successful. This may be so, for instance,
where the alleged damage threatens the existence of the undertaking
concerned or where the damage, even when it occurs, cannot be quan-
tified.[110] In addition, the damage must be serious, which gives a relative

---

[109] The high liability threshold which applies in the cases of acts of Community institutions
(see Ch.11, *supra*) may have the result that the financial loss sustained by a individual on
account of a possibly unlawful act of a Community institution must be regarded as
constituting irreparable damage in proceedings for interim relief: CFI (order of the
President of August 1, 2001), Case T–132/01 R *Euroalliages v Commission* [2001] E.C.R. II–
2307. Joliet, Bertrand and Nihoul (n.4, *supra*), at 269, reject the view that damage is
irreparable only if compensation may not be given therefor (for this view, see *Commentaire
Mégret*, at 399). They argue that the fiction that any damage may be made good applies only
to damage which has already arisen. In contrast, the Judge hearing applications for interim
relief has to forestall the damage. He or she must therefore regard as irreparable damage
for which the applicant would have to claim compensation in separate proceedings after a
judgment in his or her favour in the main proceedings on the ground of the illegal aspects
found in that judgment. Nevertheless, the principle remains that pure financial loss which
may be awarded in full pursuant to the judgment in the main proceedings (*e.g.* recovery of
an unlawfully imposed levy or grant of a subsidy) cannot be regarded as irreparable: see
ECJ (order of the President of July 19, 1983), Case 120/83 R *Raznoimport v Commission*
[1983] E.C.R. 2573, para.15; CFI (order of the President of November 23, 1990), Case T–
45/90 R *Speybrouck v European Parliament* [1990] E.C.R. II–705, para.23; CFI (order of the
President of August 1, 1991), Case T–51/91 R *Hoyer v Commission* [1991] E.C.R. II–679,
para 19; CFI (order of the President of March 23, 1993), Case T–115/92 R *Hogan v
European Parliament* [1993] E.C.R. II–339, para.17; CFI (order of the President of
September 29, 1993), Case T–497/93 R II *Hogan v Court of Justice* [1993] E.C.R. II–1005,
para.17.
[110] ECJ (order of the President of October 25, 1990), Case C–257/90 R *Italsolar v Commission*
[1990] E.C.R. I–3841, para.15; ECJ (order of the President of May 23, 1990), Joined Cases
C–51 and C–59/90 R *Comos-Tank and Others v Commission* [1990] E.C.R. I–2167, para.24;
CFI (order of the President of March 21, 1997), Case T–41/97 R *Antillean Rice Mills v
Council* [1997] E.C.R. II–447, para.47; CFI (order of the President of April 30, 1999), Case
T–44/98 R II *Emesa Sugar v Commission* [1999] E.C.R. II–1427, para.131; CFI (order of
the President of October 31, 2000), Case T–137/00 R *Cambridge Healthcare Supplies v
Commission* [2000] E.C.R. II–3653, Summ. pub., paras 43–44, in which the President
accepted that the fact that it would be impossible to restore consumer confidence, even if
the contested Commission decision prohibiting sales of the product in question were to be
annulled, had to be regarded as irreparable damage. See also CFI (order of the President
of October 31, 2000), Case T–84/00 R *Roussel and Roussel Diamant v Commission* [2000]
E.C.R. II–3591, para.43. *Cf.* CFI (order of the President of June 28, 2000), Case T–74/00 R
Artegodan v Commission [2000] E.C.R. II–2583, para.46. For an instance in which it was
accepted that there was a threat to the continued existence of the business, see CFI (order
of the President of April 4, 2002), Case T–198/01 R *Technische Glaswerke Ilmenau v
Commission* [2002] E.C.R. II–2153, paras 96–109. In inquiring into the precarious financial
situation, account may be taken of the group to which the applicant belongs, since the
objective interests of the undertaking concerned cannot be regarded in isolation from the
interests of the persons who control the undertaking: CFI (order of the President of
October 22, 2001), Case T–141/01 R *Entorn v Commission* [2001] E.C.R. II–3123, paras 51–
52; CFI (order of the President of December 7, 2001), Case T–192/01 R *Lior v Commission*
[2001] E.C.R. II–3657, paras 54–54 (and the case-law cited therein). As for associations,

aspect to the urgency of an application for interim relief. Thus, a small undertaking has less of an ability to bear financial or economic burdens than a multinational or a Member State.[111] In addition, the requirement for the damage to be serious prevents interim measures being imposed in order to avert irreparable, but negligible, damage.[112] The impending damage does not necessarily have to be financial.[113] Thus, the excessive burden caused by the increasing number of heavy goods vehicles transiting through a country was held to constitute irreparable damage.[114] Lastly, in assessing the seriousness of the damage and the related urgency of the measures requested, the Judge may take account of the stance adopted by the applicant. Accordingly, the European Parliament was held not to be entitled to maintain that to give immediate effect to a judgment of the Court of First Instance annulling the appointment of an official would cause it serious damage, since it had left the post vacant for some six months.[115]

13–031 **Objective is to avoid damage from arising.** The purpose of interim proceedings is not to secure reparation of damage but to guarantee the full effectiveness of the judgment on the substance.[116] Interim measures serve

---

account is taken of the financial situation of the members: CFI (order of the President of January 21, 2004), Case T–217/03 R *FNCBV v Commission* [2004] E.C.R. II–239, para.78.

[111] ECJ (order of the President of February 26, 1981), Case 20/81 R *Arbed v Commission* [1981] E.C.R. 721, para.14; ECJ (order of the President of September 24, 1986), Case 214/86 R *Greece v Commission* [1986] E.C.R. 2631, para.20; ECJ (order of the President of December 17, 1986), Case 294/86 R *Technointorg v Commission* [1986] E.C.R. 3979, para.28; ECJ (order of the President of August 10, 1987), Case 223/87 R *ASSIDER v Commission* [1987] E.C.R. 3473, para.22; ECJ (order of the President of May 6, 1988), Case 111/88 R *Greece v Commission* [1988] E.C.R. 2591, para.18; ECJ (order of the President of June 10, 1988), Case 152/88 R *Sofrimport v Commission* [1988] E.C.R. 2931, paras 31–32; CFI (order of the President of July 12, 2000), Joined Cases T–94/00 R and T–110/00 R *Rica Foods and Others v Commission*, not reported, para.115.

[112] This concern is very much to the fore in the case of the third substantive requirement that the applicant's interest must outweigh the interest of the opposite party/third parties (see 13–033 and 13–034, *infra*).

[113] CFI (order of the President of October 30, 2003), Joined Cases T–125/03 R and T–253/03 R *Akzo Nobel and Others v Commission* [2003] E.C.R. II–4771, paras 162–169: a breach of professional confidentiality may result in irreparable damage. In that case, the Commission wished to have cognisance of documents containing notes made by a member of staff of an undertaking following a meeting with a lawyer. The President of the Court of Justice annulled the relevant paragraphs of this order: (ECJ (order of the President of September 29, 2004), Case C–7/04 P (R) *Commission v Akzo Nobel and Others* [2004] E.C.R. I–8739). The President of the Court of Justice considered that the breach of professional confidentiality did not in itself establish the urgency of the application for interim measures since the Commission had undertaken not to disclose the relevant documents to third parties (*ibid.*, paras 41–42).

[114] ECJ (order of February 23, 2001), Case C–445/00 R *Austria v Council* [2001] E.C.R. I–1461, para.106.

[115] ECJ (order of the President of April 3, 1992), Case C–35/92 P-R *European Parliament v Frederiksen* [1992] E.C.R. I–2399, para.20. *Cf.* CFI (order of the President of April 11, 2003), Case T–392/02 R *Solvay Pharmaceuticals v Council* [2003] E.C.R. II–1825, para.100.

[116] CFI (order of the President of January 31, 2005), Case T–447/04 R *Capgemini Nederland v Commission*, not yet reported, para.89.

only to avoid damage from arising. This requirement is considered separately.[117] If the Judge hearing the application for interim relief finds that the contested act has been completely implemented and produced all its effects, damage can no longer be averted by imposing interim measures. If that is so, the application for interim measures is to no purpose.[118] It may happen that a measure which had already produced damage before the application for interim measures was brought is continuing to cause damage, in which case interim measures may be imposed to prevent any increase in the damage.

Furthermore, the threat of damage must be a real one; which means that it must be foreseeable with a sufficient degree of probability.[119] Indefinite potential damage does not suffice.[120] The Judge hearing the application for interim measures may have regard, in assessing the imminence of damage, whether or not effective relief is available from the national courts.[121] The fact that both material and non-material damage is imminent may result in the grant of interim measures.[122] Nevertheless as far as non-material damage is concerned, urgency cannot be established where the interim measure would not remedy the damage any more than any judgment in the main proceedings.[123]

---

[117] ECJ (order of the President of August 28, 1978), Case 166/78 R *Italy v Council* [1978] E.C.R. 1745, para.14.

[118] CFI (order of the President of October 30, 2003), Joined Cases T–125/03 R and T–253/03 R *Akzo Nobel and Others v Commission* [2003] E.C.R. II–4771, paras 170–178.

[119] CFI (order of the President of October 31, 2000), Case T–83/00 R I *Hänseler v Commission* [2000] E.C.R. II–3563, para.41; CFI (order of the President of December 8, 2000), Case T–237/99 R *BP Nederland and Others v Commission* [2000] E.C.R. II–3849, paras 49 and 56.

[120] ECJ (order of the President of June 15, 1987), Case 142/87 R *Belgium v Commission* [1987] E.C.R. 2589, para.25: indefinite potential damage cannot be regarded as serious and irreparable damage; ECJ (order of the President of July 16, 1993), Case C–296/93 R *France v Commission* [1993] E.C.R. I–4181, para.26; CFI (order of the President of June 7, 1991), Case T–19/91 R *Vichy v Commission* [1991] E.C.R. II–265, para.19; CFI (order of the President of May 13, 1993), Case T–24/93 R *CMBT v Commission* [1993] E.C.R. II–543, para.34. However, the threat of damage does not have to be proved with absolute certainty. It is sufficient for the damage to be foreseeable with a sufficient degree of probability: CFI (order of the President of December 15, 1999), Case T–191/98 R II *Cho Yang Shipping v Commission* [1999] E.C.R. II–3909, para.40.

[121] ECJ (order of the President of June 15, 1987), Case 142/87 R *Belgium v Commission* [1987] E.C.R. 2589, para.26.

[122] This may be inferred from ECJ (order of the President of June 26, 1959), Case 31/59 R *Acciaieria e Tubificio di Brescia v High Authority* [1960] E.C.R. 98, at 100, and CFI (order of the President of November 30, 1993), Case T–549/93 R *D v Commission* [1993] E.C.R. II–1347, para.44.

[123] CFI (order of the President of May 7, 2002), Case T–306/01 R *Aden and Others v Council and Commission* [2002] E.C.R. II–2387, paras 116–117, in which the President held that suspension of the operation of the contested regulation could not remedy the alleged non-material damage sustained any more than would annulment of that regulation in the future when the main action was decided. See to like effect CFI (order of the President of October 18, 2001), Case T–196/01 R *Aristoteleio Panepistimio Thessalonikis v Commission* [2001] E.C.R. II–3107, para 36 (and the case-law cited therein).

13–032   **Imminent damage must affect the applicant personally.** The applicant for interim relief must show that damage affecting him or her personally is imminent.[124] A Member State may rely on damage allegedly suffered by a domestic industrial sector[125] on the ground that it is the guardian of national economic and social interests.[126] Furthermore, by virtue of its participation in the exercise of legislative and budgetary powers and contribution to the Community budget, a Member State may rely on the damage which would arise from expenditure being incurred contrary to the rules governing the powers of the Community and its institutions.[127] All the same, it does not appear sufficient for a Member State to refer to damage specifically suffered by an individual undertaking.[128] In connection with an action for failure to fulfil obligations, the Commission is entitled to adduce evidence of damage to its own interests as guardian of Community law[129] or to the interests of nationals of other Member States[130] or even of the Member State concerned.[131]

3. Balance of interests

13–033   **Concept.** Even where the Judge hearing the application for interim relief has found that the application in the main proceedings is *prima facie* not unreasonable and that the interim measures sought are urgent, he or she is

---

[124] ECJ (order of the President of May 6, 1988), Case 111/88 R *Greece v Commission* [1988] E.C.R. 2591, para.15; ECJ (order of the President of May 6, 1988), Case 112/88 R *Crete Citron Producers Association v Commission* [1988] E.C.R. 2597, para.20. Damage to the personal reputation of employees and members of the board of directors of an undertaking seeking interim relief may not be taken into consideration in the proceedings for interim relief unless the undertaking succeeds in showing that such damage is likely to cause serious harm to its own reputation: CFI (order of the President of December 20, 2001), Case T–214/01 R *Bank für Arbeit und Wirtschaft v Commission* [2001] E.C.R. II–3993, para.69. See also CFI (order of the President of November 10, 2004), Case T–316/04 R *Wam v Commission*, not yet reported, para.28.

[125] ECJ (order of the President of August 28, 1978), Case 166/78 R *Italy v Council* [1978] E.C.R. 1745: Italy sought to protect the interests of its domestic cereal starch industry. The application for interim measures was dismissed on the ground that Italy had not established the imminence of damage. No objection of admissibility was raised on account of the fact that the alleged damage was not imminent for the Italian State as such. See, to the same effect, ECJ (order of the President of July 16, 1993), Case C–296/93 R *France v Commission* [1993] E.C.R. I–4181; ECJ (order of the President of July 16, 1993), Case C–307/93 R *Ireland v Commission* [1993] E.C.R. I–4191.

[126] ECJ (order of the President of June 29, 1993), Case C–280/93 R *Germany v Council* [1993] E.C.R. I–3667, para.27.

[127] ECJ (order of the President of September 24, 1996), Joined Cases C–239 and C–240/96 R *United Kingdom v Commission* [1996] E.C.R. I–4475, para.66.

[128] ECJ (order of the President of June 15, 1987), Case 142/87 R *Belgium v Commission* [1987] E.C.R. 2589, paras 23–24; ECJ (order of the President of May 8, 1991), Case C–356/90 R *Belgium v Commission* [1991] E.C.R. I–2423, para.23.

[129] Pastor and Van Ginderachter (n.14, *supra*), at 600.

[130] ECJ (order of the President of July 13, 1977), Case 61/77 R II *Commission v Ireland* [1977] E.C.R. 1411, para.14; ECJ (order of the President of October 25, 1985), Case 293/85 R *Commission v Belgium* [1985] E.C.R. 3521.

[131] ECJ (order of June 7, 1985), Case 154/85 R *Commission v Italy* [1985] E.C.R. 1753, para.19.

not obliged to give an order imposing those measures. He or she will withhold consent if the applicant's interest does not outweigh the possible effects of the measures on the interests of the opposite party[132] or third parties[133] or the public interest.[134] The exercise of weighing those interests against each other may sometimes result in interim measures different from those sought being imposed.[135] This exercise provides yet another illustration of the cautious approach taken by Judges hearing applications for interim relief. Since they conduct only a "marginal review" of the application in the main proceedings, it is not certain that the applicant will win his or her case and therefore not unreasonable to have regard to the possible impact of the interim measures sought on others' interests.

Applications. The interest of the opposite party or of a third party sometimes weighs so heavily in the balance that interim measures are not granted even though there has been a manifest infringement of Community law. Thus, the President of the Court of Justice considered that the interests of the inhabitants of Dundalk in having sound water supplies as soon as possible outweighed the Commission's interest in having the relevant Community rules applied to the grant of a public contract for the construction of a water main to carry water from the river to the treatment plant. Notwithstanding the manifest infringement of Community law and the urgency of the interim measures sought, the Commission's application

13-034

---

[132] In staff cases, the interests of the service are weighed against the applicant's interests. See, for instance, ECJ (order of the President of July 11, 1988), Case 176/88 R *Hanning v European Parliament* [1988] E.C.R. 3915, para.14.

[133] ECJ (order of the President of January 16, 1975), Case 3/75 R *Johnson & Firth Brown v Commission* [1975] E.C.R. 1; ECJ (order of the President of May 22, 1978), Case 92/78 R *Simmenthal v Commission* [1978] E.C.R. 1129, para.18; ECJ (order of the President of June 13, 1989), Case 56/89 R *Publishers Association v Commission* [1989] E.C.R. 1693, para.35; CFI (order of the President of July 6, 1993), Case T–12/93 R *CCE de Vittel and Others v Commission* [1993] E.C.R. II–785, paras 19–20. The balance of interests may, of course, also be used to reinforce other arguments on the basis of which the application for interim measures is rejected, see CFI (order of the President of September 26, 1997), Case T–183/97 R *Micheli and Others v Commission* [1997] E.C.R. II–1473, para.75; CFI (order of the President of April 30, 1999), Case T–44/98 RII *Emesa Sugar v Commission* [1999] E.C.R. II–1427, paras 137–146. In principle, the interest of protection of public health takes precedence over economic interests: CFI (order of the President of June 15, 2001), Case T–339/00 R *Bactria v Commission* [2001] E.C.R. II–1721, paras 112–113.

[134] CFI (order of the President of December 15, 1992), Case T–96/92 R *CCE de la Société des Grandes Sources and Others v Commission* [1992] E.C.R. II–2579, para.39. The individual interest of a Member of the European Parliament in being able to continue to exercise his or her mandate prevails over the general interest of the European Parliament in the maintenance of the application of the applicant's disqualification from holding office (pursuant to national law): CFI (order of the President of January 26, 2001), Case T–353/00 R *Le Pen v European Parliament* [2001] E.C.R. II–125, paras 101–103.

[135] ECJ (order of the President of January 16, 1975), Case 3/75 R *Johnson & Firth Brown v Commission* [1975] E.C.R. 1, para.7; CFI (order of the President of June 16, 1992), Joined Cases T–24 and T–28/92 R *Langnese-Iglo and Schöller Lebensmittel v Commission* [1992] E.C.R. II–1839; CFI (order of the President of July 16, 1992), Case T–29/92 R *SPO v Commission* [1992] E.C.R. II–2161.

for the suspension of the award of any construction contract until judgment had been given in the main proceedings was rejected.[136]

An interest originating in an omission or shortcoming on the part of a party in principle carries little weight.[137] It does not prevent the Judge hearing the application for interim relief nevertheless from recognising the parallel interest of third parties and allowing the balance to be tilted in favour of the party which showed negligence in that way. In *Commission v Belgium*,[138] Belgium invoked its interest in the speedy replacement of a very old bus fleet as a defence against an application from the Commission for suspension, by way of interim measure, of the implementation of contracts for the supply of new buses. The President found that Belgium (more specifically the Walloon regional transport company) had been guilty of a gross failure to replace the bus fleet in due time, but nevertheless caused the balance of interests to tip in Belgium's favour on the ground that the dilapidated state of the vehicles constituted a danger to the safety of staff and customers. The decision of the Judge hearing the application for interim relief could not perpetuate that situation.

IV. CONSEQUENCES

13–035 **Provisional nature.** The decision on the application takes the form of a reasoned order. It is served on the parties[139] and is enforceable.[140] The interim measure lapses when final judgment is delivered or on the date fixed by the order.[141] On application by a party, the order may at any time be varied or cancelled on account of a change in circumstances.[142] Rejection

---

[136] ECJ (order of the President of March 13, 1987), Case 45/87 R *Commission v Ireland* [1987] E.C.R. 1369, para.33.

[137] ECJ (order of the President of September 27, 1988), Case 194/88 R *Commission v Italy* [1988] E.C.R. 5647, para.16.

[138] ECJ (order of the President of April 22, 1994), Case C–87/94 R *Commission v Belgium* [1994] E.C.R. I–1395, paras 39–42.

[139] ECJ Rules of Procedure, Art.86(1); CFI Rules of Procedure, Art.107(1).

[140] Enforcement of the order may be made conditional on the applicant's lodging security, of an amount and nature to be fixed in the light of the circumstances: ECJ Rules of Procedure, Art.86(2); CFI Rules of Procedure, Art.107(2). See also 13–004, *supra*. In *R v Secretary of State for Transport, ex parte Factortame Ltd* [1997] Eu L.R. 475, at 523G, the English Divisional Court stated that an order of the Court of Justice is an order "which is expressed in mandatory terms and which takes immediate effect. Under Community law, the Order of the President has the same force and direct effect as any other order of the court or provision of Community law. It must immediately be complied with by the party to which it is addressed . . . and failure to do so is a breach of Community law".

[141] ECJ Rules of Procedure, Art.86(3); CFI Rules of Procedure, Art.107(3).

[142] ECJ Rules of Procedure, Art.87; CFI Rules of Procedure, Art.108. See ECJ (order of February 14, 2002), Case C–440/01 P(R) *Commission v Artegodan* [2002] E.C.R. I–1489, para.62: in this case the President of the Court of First Instance had considered that the expression "change in circumstances" had to be interpreted restrictively (CFI (order of the President of September 5, 2001), Case T–74/00 R *Artegodan v Commission* [2001] E.C.R.

of an application for an interim measure does not bar the party who made it from making a further application on the basis of new facts. The Judge hearing the application for interim relief will then consider whether the new facts justify the grant of the measures sought.[143]

Costs. In general, the costs in proceedings for interim measures are reserved for the decision on the substance. Usually, costs follow the event in the main proceedings,[144] even if the successful party did not obtain the interim relief which it sought. Unless one of the parties raises the issue of the distribution of costs as between the proceedings for interim relief and the main proceedings (in which case the Court of Justice or the Court of First Instance, as the case may be, will have to rule thereon), the order to pay the costs covers both the costs of the proceedings for interim measures and of the main proceedings.[145]
    13–036

Appeal. An appeal will lie to the Court of Justice against interim orders of the Court of First Instance within two months of their notification. Appeals are dealt with by way of summary procedure.[146]
    13–037

II–2367, paras 77–99). He decided that the annulment on appeal of the orders given in parallel cases could not be regarded as a change in circumstances, especially since the Commission had failed to appeal against the order whose cancellation was sought. In those circumstances, the cancellation or variation of the earlier order would be in breach of the principle of legal certainty. However, the President of the Court of Justice annulled the order, referring to the difference between the legal force of an order given in proceedings for interim relief and that of a final judgment or of an order bringing proceedings to an end. Accordingly, the annulment on appeal of an order given by the President of the Court of First Instance could constitute a circumstance warranting the variation of an earlier order which had not been the subject of appeal. See also CFI (order of the President of April 4, 2002), Case T–198/01 R *Technische Glaswerke Ilmenau v Commission* [2002] E.C.R. II–2153, para.123.

[143] ECJ Rules of Procedure, Art.88; CFI Rules of Procedure, Art.109. See ECJ (order of the President of July 10, 1979), Case 51/79 RII *Buttner v Commission* [1979] E.C.R. 2387, para.1; CFI (order of the President of December 11, 1996), Case T–235/95 RII *Goldstein v Commission*, not reported, para.27; CFI (order of the President of July 19, 2004), Case T–439/03 R II *Eppe v European Parliament*, not reported, paras 29–31.

[144] CFI, Joined Cases T–191/96 and T–106/97 *CAS Succhi di Frutta v Commission* [1999] E.C.R. II–3181, provides an example of a case in which a party which was successful in the main proceedings nevertheless was ordered to pay its own costs in relation to the proceedings for interim relief, in which its application for interim measures was refused for want of urgency.

[145] CFI (order of October 11, 1990), Case T–50/89 *Sparr v Commission* [1990] E.C.R. II–539, para.9.

[146] Statute, Art.57, second and third paras.

CHAPTER 14

PROCEEDINGS FOR AUTHORISATION TO SERVE A GARNISHEE ORDER ON THE COMMUNITIES

I. SUBJECT-MATTER

14–001 **Principle and purpose.** Where a debtor fails to pay the sums owed, the creditor may seek to claim the funds owed by a third party to its debtor. However, where that third party is the European Communities, account should be taken of Art.1 of the Protocol on the Privileges and Immunities of the European Communities (the "Protocol") which provides that "[t]he property and assets of the Community shall not be the subject of any administrative or legal measure of constraint without the authorisation of the Court of Justice". The purpose of that provision is to ensure that there is no interference with the functioning and independence of the Communities.[147] Therefore a garnishee order can be served on the Communities only after prior authorisation of the Court of Justice.

14–002 **Competent court.** The competent court is always the Court of Justice, since Art.225(1) of the EC Treaty does not confer jurisdiction on the Court of First Instance with respect to actions brought under Art.1 of the Protocol.

II. IDENTITY OF THE PARTIES

14–003 **Applicants.** Proceedings for authorisation to serve a garnishee order on a Community institution are brought by a natural or legal person in relation to the amounts owed by the institution to the party's debtor.

Nothing precludes a Member State from bringing an application for authorisation to serve a garnishee order on the Community. However, to date no Member State has done so.

---

[147] ECJ (order of April 11, 1989), Case 1/88 SA *Générale de Banque v Commission* [1989] E.C.R. 857, para.2; ECJ (order of May 29, 2001), Case C–1/00 SA *Cotecna Inspection v Commission* [2001] E.C.R. I–4219, para.9; ECJ (order of March 27, 2003), Case 1/02 SA *Antippas v Commission* [2003] E.C.R. I–2893, para.12; ECJ (order of December 14, 2004), Case C–1/04 SA *Tertir-Terminais de Portugal v Commission* [2004] E.C.R. I–11931, para.10; ECJ (order of October 13, 2005), Case C–1/05 SA *Intek v Commission*, not reported, para.13.

Defendants. It is the Community institution or body which owes sums to   **14–004**
the applicant's debtor which will be summoned before the Court of Justice.
To date all applications have been brought against the Commission.

III. SPECIAL CHARACTERISTICS

Automatic immunity. The immunity provided for in Art.1 of the Protocol   **14–005**
is automatic. There is no need for the Community institution concerned to
rely expressly on Art.1 of the Protocol, in particular by giving notice to the
person who caused the order to be issued. Under those circumstances, it is
for the latter to seek authorisation from the Court to waive the immunity.
However, if the institution concerned states that it has no objection to the
measure of constraint, the application for authorisation is devoid of
purpose and need not be considered by the Court.[148]

Limited jurisdiction. It is neither the object nor the effect of Art.1 of the   **14–006**
Protocol to substitute review by the Court of Justice for that exercised by
the national court having jurisdiction to determine whether all the conditions for a garnishee order are actually satisfied. Thus, the determination of
the question of the garnishee's indebtedness to the debtor does not fall
within the jurisdiction of the Court of Justice but within that of the
competent national court.[149] Consequently, the jurisdiction with respect to
garnishee orders is confined to considering whether such measures are
likely, in view of the effects which they have under the applicable national
law, to interfere with the proper functioning and the independence of the
European Communities.[150] However, the Court can make such an assessment only if the indebtedness is not contested by the institution concerned
or has been found in a prior judgment of a national court.[151]

Applications. The Court has repeatedly held that the functioning of the   **14–007**
Communities may be hampered by measures of constraint affecting the
financing of common policies or the implementation of the action programmes established by the Communities.[152] Since an application for

---

[148] ECJ, Case C–182/91 *Forafrique Burkinabe v Commission* [1993] E.C.R. I–2161, para.12;
ECJ (order of October 13, 2005), Case C–1/05 SA *Intek v Commission*, not reported,
para.13.

[149] ECJ (order of March 27, 2003), Case 1/02 SA *Antippas v Commission* [2003] E.C.R. I–2893,
para.13.

[150] ECJ (order of June 17, 1987), Case 1/87 SA *Universe Tankship v Commission* [1987] E.C.R.
2807, para.2; ECJ (order of May 29, 2001), Case C–1/00 SA *Cotecna Inspection v
Commission* [2001] E.C.R. I–4219, para.10; ECJ (order of March 27, 2003), Case 1/02 SA
Antippas v Commission [2003] E.C.R. I–2893, para.14.

[151] ECJ (order of October 13, 2005), Case C–1/05 SA *Intek v Commission*, not reported, paras
15–22.

[152] ECJ (order of April 11, 1989), Case 1/88 SA *Générale de Banque v Commission* [1989]
E.C.R. 857, para.13; ECJ (order of May 29, 2001), Case C–1/00 SA *Cotecna Inspection v
Commission* [2001] E.C.R. I–4219, para.12; ECJ (order of March 27, 2003), Case C–1/02
SA *Antippas v Commission* [2003] E.C.R. I–2893, para.15; ECJ (order of December 14,
2004), Case C–1/04 SA *Tertir-Terminais de Portugal v Commission* [2004] E.C.R. I–11931,
para.14.

authorisation to serve a garnishee order on the Communities normally concerns funds which the Commission decided to allocate to the financing of a common policy[153] or the implementation of a specific action programme,[154] such application will only rarely be successful.[155]

[153] ECJ (order of December 14, 2004), Case C–1/04 SA *Tertir-Terminais de Portugal v Commission* [2004] E.C.R. I–11931 (fisheries).

[154] ECJ (order of May 29, 2001), Case C–1/00 SA *Cotecna Inspection v Commission* [2001] E.C.R. I–4219; ECJ (order of March 27, 2003), Case C–1/02 SA *Antippas v Commission* [2003] E.C.R. I–2893. Both cases concerned the financing of action programmes in the field of development aid.

[155] For a successful application, see ECJ (order of April 11, 1989), Case 1/88 SA *Générale de Banque v Commission* [1989] E.C.R. 857.

CHAPTER 15

UNLIMITED JURISDICTION OF THE COURT OF JUSTICE AND THE COURT OF FIRST INSTANCE IN RESPECT OF ACTIONS RELATING TO SANCTIONS

I. GENERAL

Legal basis. Regulations adopted by the Council pursuant to the provisions of the EC Treaty may give the Court of Justice and the Court of First Instance unlimited jurisdiction with regard to sanctions provided for in such regulations.[156]

    As far as the EAEC Treaty is concerned, the Commission is empowered to impose sanctions by virtue of Art.83. Art.144(b) confers on the Court of Justice and the Court of First Instance unlimited jurisdiction in proceedings instituted against such sanctions.[157]

15–001

Objective. Sometimes an action for annulment is too narrow to be used in order to contest an act imposing a fine. This is because, in annulment proceedings, the Court has jurisdiction only to review the legality of the act

15–002

---

[156] EC Treaty, Art.229. The relevant regulations are as follows:

    (a) Regulation No 11 of June 27, 1960 concerning the abolition of discrimination in transport rates and conditions, in implementation of Art.79[now Art.75](3) of the Treaty establishing the European Economic Community ([1959–1962] O.J. English Spec. Ed. I, 60; Art.25);

    (b) Council Regulation (EEC) No 2299/89 of July 24, 1989 on a code of conduct for computerised reservation systems (air transport) ([1989] O.J. L220/1; Art.17);

    (c) Council Regulation (EC) No 2532/98 of November 23, 1998 concerning the powers of the European Central Bank to impose sanctions ([1998] O.J. L318/4; Art.5);

    (d) Council Regulation (EC) No 1/2003 of December 16, 2002 on the implementation of the rules on competition laid down in Arts 81 and 82 of the Treaty ([2003] O.J. L1/1; Art.31);

    (e) Council Regulation (EC) No 139/2004 of January 20, 2004 on the control of concentrations between undertakings (the EC Merger Regulation) ([2004] O.J. L1/1; Art.16).

[157] Art.144(a) of the EAEC Treaty also confers unlimited jurisdiction on the Court of Justice and the Court of First Instance in proceedings instituted under Art.12 of that Treaty to have the appropriate terms fixed for the granting by the Commission of licences or sub-licences. In addition, the Court of Justice or the Court of First Instance may have unlimited jurisdiction under an arbitration clause (EC Treaty, Art.238) or a special agreement (EC Treaty, Art.239) or under Art.91(1) of the Staff Regulations in disputes of a financial character.

in the light of pleas raised in the application or by the Court of its own motion. If the act is found to be unlawful, it may only be annulled entirely or in part. In the event that the act is partly annulled, the sanction imposed may become unreasonable having regard to the breach of Community law remaining extant. Moreover, a "lawful" act may possibly impose a sanction not consonant with what is considered to be just for reasons peculiar to the person on whom the penalty is imposed or relating to the particular circumstances of the case which may not be taken into account in the judicial review of the legality of the act. Accordingly, for example, the amount of a fine imposed by the Commission for infringement of the competition rules may be reduced by the Community Court on the ground that the calculation was based on defective data provided by the relevant undertaking, without any blame attaching to the Commission.[158]

15–003 **Two views.** The precise scope of the Court's "unlimited jurisdiction"[159] in actions brought against sanctions has not yet been definitively determined.

There is no dispute that "unlimited jurisdiction" enlarges the Court's powers in two ways. First, it enables the Court to determine the individual or "subjective" rights of the parties to the proceedings, which means that it is no longer confined to inquiring into the objective legality of the contested act. In this way, the Court may take into account matters to which it would not be entitled to have regard in straightforward judicial review proceedings of the legality of the contested act.[160] Secondly, where the Court has unlimited jurisdiction it has a more extensive arsenal of sanctions than in proceedings in which only the legality of the contested act is in issue.

Opinions differ, however, as to how far unlimited jurisdiction extends. The broad view of unlimited jurisdiction regards it as an "autonomous" procedure[161] under which the Court may amend or cancel sanctions even though the measure imposing them is not tainted by any illegality. Accordingly, the Court of First Instance described the exercise of unlimited

---

[158] CFI, Case T–156/94 *Aristrain v Commission* [1999] E.C.R. II–645, para.586.

[159] French: *"pleine juridiction"*; German *"Verfahren mit unbeschränkter Ermessens-nachprüfung"*.

[160] Opinion of Advocate General M. Lagrange in ECJ, Joined Cases 2 and 3/60 *Niederrheinische Bergwerks-Aktiengesellschaft and Unternehmensverband des Aachener Steinkohlenbergbaues v High Authority* [1961] E.C.R. 133, at 152; see also, as regards the full jurisdiction conferred on the Court of Justice in the case of an action for failure to fulfil obligations by Art.88 of the ECSC Treaty, ECJ, Case 20/59 *Italy v High Authority* [1960] E.C.R. 325, at 339: "unlimited jurisdiction allowing any submission to be made based not only on legality but on any reasons justifying failure to act".

[161] However, as far as the allocation of jurisdiction between the Court of Justice and the Court of First Instance is concerned, neither Art.225 of the EC Treaty nor Art.51 of the Statute of the Court of Justice refers to Art.229 of the EC Treaty, which indicates that a separate legal procedure is not involved. See in this regard CFI (order of November 9, 2004), Case T–252/03 *FNICGV v Commission*, not yet reported, paras 20–26, in which the Court found on this ground that unlimited jurisdiction is not an autonomous form of action. The time limits laid down by Art.230 of the EC Treaty apply to an action in which recourse is made to Art.229 of the EC Treaty.

jurisdiction as an "exhaustive examination" of a sanction imposed by a decision adopted under the ECSC Treaty and referred to the Report of the French Delegation on the ECSC Treaty in which it was stated, in regard to appeals provided for by the Treaty in which the Court has unlimited jurisdiction, that "special safeguards had to be provided for the persons concerned, [since] the normal rules governing actions for annulment were not appropriate. It is for that reason that provision was made for an appeal in which the Court has unlimited jurisdiction not only to appraise the facts but also to cancel or amend the fine as it sees fit".[162] On this view, unlimited jurisdiction denotes a procedure in which the contested measure is tested more extensively. It is claimed, on the other hand, that unlimited jurisdiction embraces all the sanctions which are available to the Court in other procedures. Thus, where the Court has unlimited jurisdiction, it may annul an act or award damages as well as order any other form of redress.[163] However, the Community Court has no power to issue directions, for instance to order repayment of a fine which has been paid.[164]

In contrast, the narrow view of unlimited jurisdiction links it with other proceedings.[165] On this view, unlimited jurisdiction enables the Court to attach to its pronouncement consequences which it could not impose by virtue of its normal jurisdiction in the proceedings in question. Thus, it is argued, where the Court annuls part of the contested act, it may adjust the sanctions imposed if they no longer seem commensurate with the breach of Community law remaining after that partial annulment.

II. SCOPE OF REVIEW

Review of the sanction. Whichever of the two views of unlimited jurisdiction is preferred, the Court is empowered to review the legality of the sanction imposed by the contested act. On the view that unlimited jurisdiction enables an all-embracing review to be carried out, this review of the legality of the contested act forms part of the Court's unlimited jurisdiction; on the narrower view, the review is part of the proceedings with which unlimited jurisdiction is coupled. In practice, it makes no difference, since in any case the applicant may adduce submissions for the annulment of the contested act which are targeted exclusively against the sanction, alleging, for instance, that the amount of the sanction is such that

15–004

---

[162] CFI, Case T–156/94 *Aristrain v Commission* [1999] E.C.R. II–645, paras 115–116.

[163] For a fuller formulation of this view, see *Commentaire Mégret*, at 89–95; Plouvier, "Le contentieux de pleine juridiction devant la Cour de justice des Communautés européennes" (1973) R.M.C. 365–379. See, *e.g.* CFI, Case T–10/02 *Girardot v Commission* [2004] E.C.R.-SC II–483, para.89.

[164] ECJ, C–5/93 P *DSM v Commission* [1999] E.C.R. I–4695, para.36; CFI (order of January 14, 2004), Case T–202/02 *Makedoniko Metro and Michaniki v Commission* [2004] E.C.R. II–181, para.53.

[165] See n.157, *supra*.

it is in breach of the principle of equal treatment or proportionality, or that the reasoning for the sanction is insufficient.[166]

15–005 **Reasonableness of the sanction.** The most important difference between the broad and the narrow views of unlimited jurisdiction relates to the assessment of the sanction in so far as it is not unlawful. On the broad view, the Court is entitled to assess the reasonableness of the sanction even where the act imposing it is not tainted by any illegality.[167] On the narrow view, the Court is entitled to do this only if the act is tainted by illegality.

15–006 **Criteria.** The gravity and the duration of the infringement of Community law are the most important criteria which go to determine the amount of the sanction. In addition, consideration has to be given to the particular circumstances of the case and to the context in which the infringement took place.[168]

III. FORCE OF UNLIMITED JURISDICTION

15–007 **Reduction or increase in a fine.** Under the EC Treaty, the substance of the Court's unlimited jurisdiction is determined by the regulations which provide for such jurisdiction: the Court may cancel, reduce or increase the

---

[166] For examples, see CFI, Case T–9/89 *Hüls v Commission* [1992] E.C.R. II–499; CFI, Case T–10/89 *Hoechst v Commission* [1992] E.C.R. II–629, at II–738–753; CFI, Case T–11/89 *Shell v Commission* [1992] E.C.R. II–757, at II–891–903; CFI, Case T–12/89 *Solvay v Commission* [1992] E.C.R. II–907, at II–1007–1017; CFI, Case T–14/89 *Montedipe v Commission* [1992] E.C.R. II–1155, at II–1259–1272; CFI, Case T–15/89 *Chemie Linz v Commission* [1992] E.C.R. II–1275, at II–1385–1399. Pursuant to its unlimited jurisdiction, the Court of First Instance is empowered to amend the contested measure, even if it does not annul it, in order to amend the amount of the fine imposed (CFI (judgment of July 8, 2004), Joined Cases T–67/00 T–68/00, T–71/00 and T–78/00 *JFE Engineering and Others v Commission*, not yet reported, para.577).

[167] ECJ, Joined Cases 6 and 7/73 *Instituto Chemioterapico Italiano and Commercial Solvents v Commission* [1974] E.C.R. 223, paras 51–52; CFI, Case T–13/89 *ICI v Commission* [1992] E.C.R. II–1021, paras 389–394. If an undertaking asks the Court of Justice on appeal to vary the amount of a fine imposed by the Commission on the basis of arguments put forward on appeal, without also setting aside the judgment of the Court of First Instance for infringing the law, the Court has no jurisdiction to reconsider this matter. This is because it is not for the Court of Justice, where it is deciding questions of law in the context of an appeal, to substitute, on grounds of fairness, its own appraisal for that of the Court of First Instance adjudicating, in the exercise of its unlimited jurisdiction, on the amount of a fine imposed on an undertaking by reason of its infringement of Community law (ECJ, Case C–320/92 P *Finsider v Commission* [1994] E.C.R. I–5697, paras 45–46).

[168] ECJ, Case 41/69 *ACF Chemiefarma v Commission* [1970] E.C.R. 661, paras 172–189; ECJ, Case 45/69 *Boehringer Mannheim v Commission* [1970] E.C.R. 769, paras 53–61; ECJ, Joined Cases 6 and 7/73 *Instituto Chemioterapico Italiano and Commercial Solvents v Commission* [1974] E.C.R. 223, para.51; ECJ, Joined Cases 100–103/80 *Musique Diffusion Française and Others v Commission* [1983] E.C.R. 1825, para.106; ECJ, Case 322/81 *Michelin v Commission* [1983] E.C.R. 3461, paras 106–114; ECJ, Case 183/83 *Krupp v Commission* [1985] E.C.R. 3609, para.42; CFI, Case T–12/89 *Solvay v Commission* [1992] E.C.R. II–907, para.309; CFI, Case T–14/89 *Montedipe v Commission* [1992] E.C.R. II–1155, para.346; CFI, Joined Cases T–39 and T–40/92 *Groupement des Cartes Bancaires "CB" and Europay v Commission* [1994] E.C.R. II–49, para.143. For an extensive discussion, see CFI, Case T–43/92 *Dunlop Slazenger v Commission* [1994] E.C.R. II–441, paras 133–179.

fine or penalty payment imposed.[169] Even if the applicant has not expressly claimed that the fine should be cancelled or reduced, the Court may do so of its own motion if it can infer such a claim indirectly from another claim.[170] As for the possibility of increasing the amount of a fine or penalty payment, it must be considered whether this would be *ultra petita*.[171] Where the Court of First Instance finds that an undertaking has had a fine imposed upon it which infringes the principle of equal treatment on the ground that the fines imposed on other undertakings which participated in the same way in the same infringement were lower, the Court logically has two ways of bringing the infringement of that principle to an end. It can either reduce the fine imposed on the first undertaking or increase the fines imposed on the other undertakings. The latter eventuality is contingent on the other undertakings' also having brought an application before the Court. In the *JFE Engineering* case, the Court opted, reluctantly, for the first option, that is to say, of reducing the fine. In the Court's view, the fines imposed on the other undertakings could not be increased because the Commission had not claimed such an increase and the other undertakings had therefore not been given the possibility to express their views on this question in the proceedings before the Court.[172]

---

[169] For the references of the relevant provisions, see n.156, *supra*. The substance of unlimited jurisdiction is not precisely specified in the case of the EAEC Treaty. It further appears from the case-law that the award of default interest in staff cases under Art.91(1), second sentence, of the Staff Regulations also falls within the unlimited jurisdiction of the Court of First Instance and, where appropriate, the Court of Justice: ECJ, Case C–90/95 P *De Compte v European Parliament* [1997] E.C.R. I–1999, para.45.

[170] ECJ, Case 8/56 *ALMA v High Authority* [1957 and 1958] E.C.R. 95, at 99–100; CFI, Case T–65/89 *BPB Industries and British Gypsum v Commission* [1993] E.C.R. II–389, para.162.

[171] *Commentaire Mégret*, at 95. In CFI, Case T–66/99 *Minoan Lines v Commission* [2003] E.C.R. II–5515, paras 356–359, the Court of First Instance dismissed the Commission's application for an increase in a fine, not on the ground that the Court had no power to make such an increase, but because there were no grounds in the case in question for granting it. In CFI, Joined Cases T–236/01, T–239/01, T–244/01 to T–246/01, T–251/01 and T–252/01 *Tokai Carbon and Others v Commission* [2004] E.C.R. II–1181, paras 107–113, the Court of First Instance granted for the first time an increase in a fine requested by the Commission. The Court considered that the undertaking had called in question facts which it had conceded during the administrative procedure on the grounds of which the Commission had granted it a reduction in the fine.

[172] CFI (judgment of July 8, 2004), Joined Cases T–67/00, T–68/00, T–71/00 and T–78/00 *JFE Engineering and Others v Commission*, not yet reported, paras 566–579 (in particular paras 576 and 579).

CHAPTER 16

APPEALS

I. SUBJECT-MATTER

A. GENERAL

16–001 **Two-tier legal protection.** The fact that an appeal is possible against judicial decisions means that they have to be scrupulously reasoned. A system of two-tier legal protection enhances the legitimacy of judicial decisions and the quality of legal protection.[173]

Under Art.113(1) of the ECJ Rules of Procedure, an appeal may seek to set aside, in whole or in part, the decision of the Court of First Instance or request the same form of order, in whole or in part, as that sought at first instance.[174] As far as decisions of the European Union Civil Service Tribunal are concerned, an appeal may be brought before the Court of First Instance.[175]

B. APPEALS ARE CONFINED TO POINTS OF LAW

16–002 **Errors of law.** An appeal brought before the Court of Justice against a decision of the Court of First Instance is *not* an appeal on the facts and the law. Appeals are confined to points of law,[176] irrespective of the type of decision of the Court of First Instance against which they are brought.[177] The Court's jurisdiction to hear appeals is thus confined to reviewing the legality of decisions of the Court of First Instance in order to remedy errors

---

[173] *Cf.* Waelbroeck, "Le transfert des recours directs au Tribunal de première instance des Communautés européennes—vers une meilleure protection judiciaire des justiciables?", in *La réforme du système juridictionnel communautaire* (Éditions de l'Université de Bruxelles, Brussels, 1994), at 87–97.

[174] A new form of order may not be sought.

[175] Statute, Annex I, Art.9; CFI Rules of Procedure, Arts 113–149. On this subject, see also 1–037, *supra*, and 18–021, *infra*.

[176] EC Treaty, Art.225(1); Statute, Art.58. See also ECJ, Case C–136/92 P *Commission v Brazzelli Lualdi and Others* [1994] E.C.R. I–1981, para.29.

[177] ECJ (order of the President of July 11, 1996), Case C–148/96 P(R) *Goldstein v Commission* [1996] E.C.R. I–3883, para.22. Consequently, an appeal against an interim order or an order dismissing an application to intervene may be based only on the pleas listed in Art.58 of the Statute: ECJ (order of the President of July 19, 1995), Case C–149/95 P(R) *Commission v Atlantic Container Line and Others* [1995] E.C.R. I–2165, paras 17–18.

of law and hence guarantee the necessary coherence of the Community legal order[178] and the uniform interpretation of Community law.[179] This avoids the Court of Justice having to inquire into findings of fact already made by the Court of First Instance, which satisfies the dual aim of lightening the workload of the Court of Justice and improving the legal protection of individuals in direct actions.

An error of law may have been committed by the Court of First Instance in its appraisal of a particular plea or argument raised before it. The omission of the Court of First Instance to examine a plea of law raised before it or a form of order sought by the applicant also constitutes an error of law which may lead to the annulment of the decision of the Court of First Instance.[180]

The Court of Justice has no jurisdiction to make findings of fact. The fact that appeals are confined to points of law means that the Court of First Instance has sole jurisdiction to make findings as to the facts underlying the proceedings at first instance.[181] Parties are not entitled on appeal to contest the factual findings of the Court of First Instance[182] or to offer to adduce evidence of facts which were not found by the Court of First Instance.[183] This is because, if they were so entitled, it would oblige the Court of Justice to make a determination of the facts, which it is not competent to do on appeal.[184] Consequently, the Court of Justice must leave out of account in reviewing the decision of the Court of First Instance any new facts raised.

16–003

Appraisal of evidence by the Court of First Instance. Finding certain facts may be straightforward. For example, parties may agree that a particular event occurred on a particular date or that an uncontested fact appears

16–004

---

[178] Opinion of Advocate General G. Tesauro in ECJ, Case C–132/90 P *Schwedler v European Parliament* [1991] E.C.R. I–5745, at I–5757; ECJ, Case C–49/92 P *Commission v Anic Partecipazioni* [1999] E.C.R. I–4125, paras 70–71.

[179] Fifth recital in the preamble to Council Decision 88/591 (cited in 1–028, n.95, *supra*).

[180] ECJ, Case C–123/03 P *Commission v Greencore* [2004] E.C.R. I–11647, paras 40–41; see also ECJ (order of June 3, 2005), Case C–396/03 P *Killinger v Germany, Council and Commission* [2005] E.C.R.–4967, paras 11–13.

[181] Joliet and Vogel, "Le Tribunal de première instance des Communautés européennes" (1989) R.M.C. 423, at 430. A survey of the points of law which have been considered by the Court of Justice on appeal may be found in Rideau and Picod, "Le pourvoi sur les questions de droit" (1995) R.M.C.U.E. 584, at 594–599.

[182] ECJ (order of March 20, 1991), Case C–115/90 P *Turner v Commission* [1991] E.C.R. I–1423, paras 13–14; ECJ, Case C–283/90 P *Vidrányi v Commission* [1991] E.C.R. I–4339, paras 11–13; ECJ, Case C–132/90 P *Schwedler v European Parliament* [1991] E.C.R. I–5745, paras 9–12; ECJ, Case C–378/90 P *Pitrone v Commission* [1992] E.C.R. I–2375, paras 12–13; ECJ, Case C–346/90 P *F v Commission* [1992] E.C.R. I–2691, para.7; ECJ, Case C–326/91 P *De Compte v European Parliament* [1994] E.C.R. I–2091, para.29; ECJ (order of October 17, 1995), Case C–62/94 P *Turner v Commission* [1995] E.C.R. I–3177, para.25; ECJ, Case C–1/98 P *British Steel v Commission* [2000] E.C.R. I–10349, para.53.

[183] ECJ, Case C–396/93 P *Henrichs v Commission* [1995] E.C.R. I–2611, para.14.

[184] Opinion of Advocate General W. van Gerven in ECJ, Case C–137/92 P *Commission v BASF and Others* [1994] E.C.R. I–2555, at I–2565-2566; ECJ, Case C–320/93 P *Finsider v Commission* [1994] E.C.R. I–5697, para.41.

from a decision contested (on other grounds) before the Court of First Instance. However, often the finding of facts by the Court of First Instance has to be preceded by an appraisal of the evidence.

On appeal the Court of Justice has no jurisdiction to make findings of fact or, in principle, to inquire into the evidence on the basis of which the Court of First Instance made its findings of fact.[185] Where the evidence has been properly obtained and the general principles of law and the rules of procedure in relation to the burden of proof and the taking of evidence have been observed, it is for the Court of First Instance alone to assess the value which should be attached to the evidence produced to it.[186]

Consequently, an appeal brought against decisions of the Court of First Instance concerning the assessment of evidence adduced before it will be inadmissible, unless the Court of First Instance has committed an error of law.[187] Accordingly, the person bringing the appeal—the appellant[188]—may argue that evidence was not lawfully obtained or that the Court of First Instance failed to respect the legal rules and general principles relating to the burden of proof or the procedural rules of evidence.[189] As a result, the

---

[185] ECJ, Case C–53/92 P *Hilti v Commission* [1994] E.C.R. I–667, para.42; ECJ, Case C–7/95 P *John Deere v Commission* [1998] E.C.R. I–3111, paras 21–22; ECJ, Case C–185/95 P *Baustahlgewebe v Commission* [1998] E.C.R. I–8417, para.24; ECJ, Joined Cases C–24/01 P and C–25/01 P *Glencore and Compagnie Continentale v Commission* [2002] E.C.R. I–10119, para.65; ECJ, Joined Cases C–204/00 P, C–205/00 P, C–211/00 P, C–213/00 P, C–217/00 P and C–219/00 P *Aalborg Portland and Others v Commission* [2004] E.C.R. I–123, paras 48–49. But see ECJ, Case C–32/95 P *Commission v Lisrestal and Others* [1996] E.C.R. I–5373, para.40, in which the Court held that "the assessment made by the Court of First Instance of the tenor and wording" of letters produced as evidence could be considered on appeal. The Court cited in support of this view of the scope of its power of review on appeal the judgment in ECJ, Case C–39/93 P *SFEI and Others v Commission* [1994] E.C.R. I–2681, para.26), in which it held that, where the Court of First Instance not only assessed the facts but also assigned a classification to them, that categorisation could be reviewed on appeal. This is logical, since the categorisation of a letter which the Commission sent as the response to a complaint pursuant to Art.3(2) of Regulation No 17 (now Art.7(2) of Regulation No 1/2003) is nothing other than a legal categorisation of a fact in the light of Regulation No 99/63 (now Regulation No 773/2004), which determines the applicant's procedural rights. It is plain that such a legal categorisation of a fact can be reviewed by the Court of Justice on appeal. Yet in *Lisrestal* no legal categorisation of facts was involved, merely the question as to whether the Court of First Instance had correctly assessed the evidence adduced, which is an entirely different matter.

[186] ECJ, Case C–7/95 P *John Deere v Commission* [1998] E.C.R. I–3111, paras 21–22; ECJ, C–185/95 P *Baustahlgewebe v Commission* [1998] E.C.R. I–8417, para.24; ECJ, Case C–24/01 P and C–25/01 P *Glencore and Compagnie Continentale v Commission* [2002] E.C.R. I–10119, para.65.

[187] ECJ (order of September 30, 1992), Case C–294/91 P *Sebastiani v European Parliament* [1992] E.C.R. I–4997, para.13; ECJ, Case C–53/92 P *Hilti v Commission* [1994] E.C.R. I–667, para.42; ECJ, Case C–143/95 P *Commission v Socurte and Others* [1997] E.C.R. I–1, para.36; ECJ (order of November 11, 2003), Case C–488/01 P *Martinez v European Parliament* [2003] E.C.R. I–13355, para.53.

[188] ECJ Rules of Procedure, Art.112(1)(a).

[189] ECJ (order of January 11, 1996), Case C–89/95 P *D v Commission* [1996] E.C.R. I–53, para.14; ECJ (order of September 17, 1996), Case C–19/95 P *San Marco v Commission* [1997] E.C.R. I–4435, para.39; ECJ (order of October 6, 1997), Case C–55/97 P *AIUFFASS and AKT v Commission* [1997] E.C.R. I–5383, para.25; ECJ (order of October 16, 1997), Case C–140/96 P *Dimitriadis v Court of Auditors* [1997] E.C.R. I–5635, para.27; ECJ, Case C–401/96 P *Somaco v Commission* [1998] E.C.R. I–2587, para.54.

Court of First Instance must respect the parties' right to be heard.[190] Yet this does not mean that the Court of First Instance (and the Community judicature generally) has to incorporate in full in its decision all the submissions put forward by each party. The Court, after listening to the submissions of the parties and assessing the evidence, has to decide whether or not to grant the relief sought in the application and give reasons for its decision.[191]

Distortion of the evidence or of the content of the contested act. It is not   16–005
always straightforward to distinguish between "points of law" in relation to the interpretation and application of Community law and questions of fact which come solely within the purview of the Court of First Instance.[192] It appears from the case-law that in exceptional circumstances a wrong finding of fact by the Court of First Instance may nevertheless produce a point of law which can be reviewed by the Court of Justice on appeal.[193] This will be the case where it is manifest from the documents in the case remitted to the Court of First Instance that it made a wrong finding of fact.[194]

---

[190] Whether the Court of First Instance acted in breach of the rights of the defence is a question of law (ECJ, Case C–82/01 P *Aéroports de Paris* [2002] E.C.R. I–9297, para.38). See also 15–008, *infra*.

[191] ECJ, Case C–221/97 P *Schröder and Others v Commission* [1998] E.C.R. I 8255, para.24. If the appellant can show that the failure by the Court of First Instance to consider certain parts of its arguments affected the outcome of the proceedings and so adversely affected its interests, this may possibly constitute a breach of the right to be heard. *Cf.* ECJ, Case C–237/98 P *Dorsch Consult v Council and Commission* [2000] E.C.R. I 4549, para.51, in which the Court of Justice held that the Court of First Instance cannot be required to give express reasons for its assessment of the value of each piece of evidence presented to it, in particular where it considers that that evidence is unimportant or irrelevant to the outcome of the dispute. See also ECJ, Case C–330/00 P *AICS v European Parliament* [2001] E.C.R. I–4805, para.37.

[192] De Gryse and Duk, "De Europese Cassatierechter" (1998) S.E.W. 368–380; Honorat, "Plaider un pourvoi devant la Cour de justice", in Christianos (ed.), *Evolution récente du droit judiciaire communautaire* (European Institute of Public Administration, Maastricht, 1994), Vol.I, 21, at 28–34; Sonelli, "Appeals on Points of Law in the Community System—A Review" (1998) C.M.L.Rev. 871–900.

[193] The national courts to which jurisdiction in cassation has been conferred consider that they have a general power to quash decisions of inferior courts where it appears that their assessment of the facts does not square with reality as perceived by a normal observer. Such a manifestly wrong assessment of the facts is regarded as an infringement of the law (case-law or statute law). If the Court of Justice were to put itself in a position in which findings of fact could be reviewed, this would undermine the objectives of setting up the Court of First Instance, because the former power of the Court of Justice to take cognisance of certain categories of cases necessitating an inquiry into complicated facts was transferred to the Court of First Instance. In this way, the Court of Justice can concentrate on its essential task, which is guaranteeing uniformity in the interpretation of Community law, and can maintain efficient and effective legal protection in the Community legal order.

[194] ECJ, Case C–136/92 P *Commission v Brazzelli Lualdi and Others* [1994] E.C.R. I–1981, para.49; ECJ, Case C–390/95 P *Antillean Rice Mills and Others v Commission* [1999] E.C.R. I–769, para.29; ECJ, Case C–284/98 P *European Parliament v Bieber* [2000] E.C.R. I–1527, para.31; ECJ, Joined Cases C–2/01 P and C–3/01 P *BAI and Commission* [2004] E.C.R.

It may thus happen that the Court of First Instance makes a wrong reading of the contested decision.[195] According to the Court of Justice, this error constitutes a question of law because the Court of First Instance read something into the contested decision which was not there and thereby infringed the law by substituting its own reasoning for that set out in the contested decision.[196]

Similarly, it may be apparent from the presentation of evidence in the decision of the Court of First Instance that the Court of First Instance interpreted the evidence adduced in a way that is at odds with its wording.[197] Where the Court of First Instance thus wrongly presents the evidence adduced or distorts it,[198] this will constitute a question of law which the Court of Justice may review.[199] It should, however, be stressed

---

I–23, para.47; ECJ, Joined Cases C–204/00 P, C–205/00 P, C–211/00 P, C–213/00 P, C–217/00 P and C–219/00 P *Aalborg Portland and Others v Commission* [2004] E.C.R. I–123, para.48.

[195] ECJ, Case C–164/98 P *DIR International Film and Others v Commission* [2000] E.C.R. I–447, paras 44–48; ECJ, Case C–197/99 P *Belgium v Commission* [2003] E.C.R. I–8461, paras 58–67; ECJ, Joined Cases C–172/01 P, C–175/01 P, C–176/01 P and C–180/01 P *International Power v Commission* [2003] E.C.R. I–11421, para.156; ECJ, Joined Cases C–204/00 P, C–205/00 P, C–211/00 P, C–213/00 P, C–217/00 P and C–219/00 P *Aalborg Portland and Others v Commission* [2004] E.C.R. I–123, paras 381–385.

[196] ECJ, Case C–164/98 P *DIR International Film and Others v Commission* [2000] E.C.R. I–447, paras 43–48. But see ECJ, Joined Cases C–204/00 P, C–205/00 P, C–211/00 P, C–213/00 P, C–217/00 P and C–219/00 P *Aalborg Portland and Others v Commission* [2004] E.C.R. I–123, paras 381–385: in its *cement judgment*, the Court of First Instance found that it was uncontested that an undertaking formed part of a particular group at the time of the infringement, whereas it was clear from the contested decision itself that that was not the case. The Court of Justice held that "the Court of First Instance . . . made a *manifest error* which could be detected upon reading a document such as the Cement Decision" (para.383, emphasis added).

[197] See in this connection the Opinion of Advocate General M. Mischo in ECJ, Case C–433/97 P *IPK v Commission* [1999] E.C.R. I–6795, para.36, at I–6797, where he stated as follows: "According to settled case-law, a finding of fact by the Court of First Instance cannot, *prima facie*, be reopened on appeal. There is, however, an exception to this principle where the finding is vitiated by a manifest error of assessment. This occurs, in particular, where a finding of fact by the Court of First Instance is contradicted by the case documents".

[198] De Gryse and Duk rightly observe that the French expression "*dénaturation*" better describes this plea on appeal. For a fuller account, see De Gryse and Duk, "De Europese Cassatierechter" (1998) S.E.W. 371–372 and the case-law cited therein.

[199] ECJ, Case C–53/92 P *Hilti v Commission* [1994] E.C.R. I–667, para.42; ECJ, Case C–390/95 P *Antillean Rice Mills and Others v Commission* [1999] E.C.R. I–769, para.29; ECJ, Joined Cases C–280/99 P and C–282/99 P *Moccia Irme and Others v Commission* [2001] E.C.R. I–4717, para.78; ECJ, Case C–197/99 P *Belgium v Commission* [2003] E.C.R. I–8461, para.122; ECJ (order of November 11, 2003), Case C–488/01 P *Martinez v European Parliament* [2003] E.C.R. I–13355, para.53; ECJ, Joined Cases C–204/00 P, C–205/00 P, C–211/00 P, C–213/00 P, C–217/00 P and C–219/00 P *Aalborg Portland and Others v Commission* [2004] E.C.R. I–123, para.49; ECJ, Joined Cases C–2/01 P and C–3/01 P *BAI and Commission* [2004] E.C.R. I–23, para.47. For a practical application, see the Opinion of Advocate General P. Léger in ECJ, Case C–197/99 P *Belgium v Commission* [2003] E.C.R. I–8461, paras 105–120: the Court of First Instance had given a distorted picture of the evidence in so far as it had left some evidence out of account in assessing the facts. The Court of Justice did not follow its Advocate General in this respect (see paras 121–124 of the judgment) because the evidence that the Court of First Instance had left out of account

that the actual assessment of the evidence by the Court of First Instance is to be regarded as definitive (see 15–004, *supra*).

Evidence on which the parties were not heard at first instance. The question whether the Court of First Instance can found its dismissal of the appellants' case on factual evidence on which the appellants were not heard is a question of law on appeal. Furthermore, in such case the Court of Justice may also examine whether the contested decision of the Court of First Instance is in fact based on such evidence. This is because that examination is directed to the procedure followed before the Court of First Instance and is not an examination of the facts relating to the substance of the case.[200]   **16–006**

Legal categorisation of facts. In addition, the fact that appeals are confined to points of law does not preclude the Court of Justice from reviewing the legal categorisation of facts found by the Court of First Instance.[201] This is because infringements of Community law do not always occur in the form of a wrong interpretation of the Community rule which has been applied or not applied, but also in that of a wrong categorisation of a given situation of fact, as a result of which the rule at issue is wrongly applied—or, conversely, not applied—in a particular case.[202] In this way, the identification of the relevant product market for the purpose of determining whether a given undertaking is in a dominant position within the meaning of Art.82 of the EC Treaty is a conclusion of law. Accordingly, the Court of Justice is entitled to examine whether the Court of First Instance took account of all the relevant factors. If relevant factors were not taken into consideration,   **16–007**

---

had not been brought to the Commission's attention during the administrative procedure.
[200] ECJ, Case C–480/99 P *Plant and Others v Commission and South Wales Small Mines Association* [2002] E.C.R. I–265, para.20; ECJ (order of September 27, 2004), Case C–470/02P *UER v Commission*, not reported, para.75.
[201] ECJ (order of July 11, 1996), Case C–325/94 P *An Taisce and WWF UK v Commission* [1996] E.C.R. I–3727, paras 28 and 30; ECJ (order of September 17, 1996), Case C–19/95 P *San Marco v Commission* [1996] E.C.R. I–4435, para.39; ECJ, Case C–278/95 P *Siemens v Commission* [1997] E.C.R. I–2507, para.44; ECJ, Case C–154/99 P *Politi v European Training Foundation* [2000] E.C.R. I–5019, para.11; ECJ, Joined Cases C–2/01 P and C–3/01 P *BAI and Commission* [2004] E.C.R. I–23, para.47. The question whether a "fact" on which an application for revision can be regarded as a "new fact" within the meaning of Art.44 of the Statute is a question of law which is amenable to appeal (ECJ, Case C–2/98 P *De Compte v European Parliament* [1999] E.C.R. I–1787, paras 15–23; ECJ, Case C–5/93 P *DSM v Commission* [1999] E.C.R. I–4695, paras 30–33).
[202] Opinion of Advocate General W. van Gerven in ECJ, Case C–145/90 P *Costacurta v Commission* [1991] E.C.R. I–5449, at I–5459; ECJ, Case C–132/90 P *Schwedler v European Parliament* [1991] E.C.R. I–5745, paras 13–25; ECJ, Case C–255/90 P *Burban v European Parliament* [1992] E.C.R. I–2253, para.5; ECJ, Case C–322/93 P *Peugeot v Commission* [1994] E.C.R. I–2727, para.34; ECJ (order of January 21, 1997), Case C–156/96 P *Williams v Court of Auditors* [1997] E.C.R. I–239, para.27; see also Mongin, "Les pourvois devant la Cour: un premier bilan", in *Tendances actuelles et évolution de la jurisprudence de la Cour de justice des Communautés européennes* (European Institute of Public Administration, Maastricht, 1993), 231, at 235–237.

the Court of First Instance will have erred in law by basing its conclusions on insufficient reasoning.[203]

16–008 **Extent of the duty to provide a statement of reasons.** The extent of the duty to provide a statement of reasons is a point of law.[204] In any event, the judgment of the Court of First Instance must be sufficiently reasoned to enable the Court of Justice to review it.[205] The obligation on the Court of First Instance to give reasons for its decisions does not go so far as to require it to respond in detail to every single argument advanced by the appellant, particularly if the argument was not sufficiently clear and precise and was not adequately supported by evidence.[206] However, the Court of First Instance is obliged to respond to all pleas raised by an applicant.[207] The Court of First Instance must have taken account of the requirement to state reasons also in assessing purely factual matters (for instance, in determining the amount of damage sustained) because the Court of Justice must be in a position to check that the lower court has not breached the law in assessing the facts.

16–009 **Assessment of damages.** In an appeal against a judgment given in an action for damages, the Court of First Instance has the last word on whether there has been loss or damage or an event causing damage, except where there is

---

[203] For an application, see ECJ, Case C–82/01 P *Aéroports de Paris* [2002] E.C.R. I–9297, paras 84–97 (with regard to the correct delimitation of the relevant market) and paras 98–102 (with the regard to the existence of a dominant position). See also the Opinion of Advocate General F.G. Jacobs in ECJ, Case C–53/92 P *Hilti v Commission* [1994] E.C.R. I–667, para.28.

[204] ECJ, Case C–166/95 P *Commission v Daffix* [1997] E.C.R. I–983 and ECJ, Case C–188/96 P *Commission v V.* [1997] E.C.R. I–6561, para.24. The question whether the grounds of a judgment of the Court of First Instance (or of any other decision amenable to appeal) are contradictory is a question of law (see ECJ, Case C–401/96 P *Somaco v Commission* [1998] E.C.R. I–2587, para.53; ECJ, Case C–446/00 P *Cubero Vermurie v Commission* [2001] E.C.R. I–10315, para.20; ECJ (order of June 5, 2002), Case C–217/00 P *Buzzi Unicem v Commission*, not reported, para.125.

[205] ECJ, Case C–259/96 P *Council v De Nil and Impens* [1998] E.C.R. I–2915, para.32; ECJ, Case C–197/99 P *Belgium v Commission* [2003] E.C.R. I–8461, paras 80–83 and 126–130. If the Court of First Instance refers in its judgment to an earlier judgment of that court, it necessarily integrates the grounds of the earlier judgment into the contested judgment (ECJ, Case C–248/99 P *France v Monsanto and Commission* [2002] E.C.R. I–1, para.35).

[206] ECJ, Case C–274/99 P *Connolly v Commission* [2001] E.C.R. I–1611, para.121; ECJ, Case C–197/99 P *Belgium v Commission* [2003] E.C.R. I–8461, para.81.

[207] ECJ, Joined Cases C–238/99 P, C–244/99 P, C–245/99 P, C–247/99 P, C–250/99 P, C–251/99 P, C–252/99 P and C–254/99 P *Limburgse Vinyl Maatschappij and Others v Commission* [2002] E.C.R. I–8375, paras 416–428; ECJ, Case C–197/99 P *Belgium v Commission* [2003] E.C.R. I–8461, para.82. An implicit statement of reasons may be sufficient (ECJ, Joined Cases C–204/00 P, C–205/00 P, C–211/00 P, C–213/00 P, C–217/00 P and C–219/00 P *Aalborg Portland and Others v Commission* [2004] E.C.R. I–123, para.372). Where the Court of First Instance incorrectly presents the undertaking's pleas, the judgment will contain an incorrect statement of reasons and will be annulled (ECJ (judgment of July 14, 2005), Case C–57/02 P *Acerinox v Commission*, not yet reported, paras 33–39).

a wrong presentation or a distortion (*"dénaturation"*) of evidence.[208] The question whether, in an action for damages, the amount of compensation has been sufficiently proven in the application and the reply is exclusively part of the assessment of the facts[209] and cannot be raised on appeal.

Exercise by Court of First Instance of its unlimited jurisdiction. On appeal the Court of Justice is not empowered to substitute, on grounds of fairness, its own assessment for that of the Court of First Instance exercising its unlimited jurisdiction to rule on the amount of fines imposed on undertakings for infringements of Community law.[210] The only review which the Court of Justice may conduct in this connection consists of considering whether the Court of First Instance responded to a sufficient legal standard[211] or in accordance with the principle of equality[212] to all the arguments raised with a view to having the fine abolished or reduced.

16–010

C. Against what decisions of the Court of First Instance will an appeal lie?

Final decisions. Under Art.56 of the Statute of the Court of Justice, an appeal may be brought against final decisions of the Court of First Instance and against decisions of that Court disposing of substantive issues in part only or disposing of a procedural issue concerning a plea of lack of competence or inadmissibility.[213] An appeal will not lie against the part of a judgment of the Court of First Instance in which it considers that it is unnecessary to rule on an objection of inadmissibility since the claims have

16–011

---

[208] ECJ, Case C–362/95 P *Blackspur DIY and Others v Council and Commission* [1997] E.C.R. I–4775, paras 28–29; ECJ, Case C–62/01 P *Campogrande v Commission* [2002] E.C.R. I–3793, para.24.

[209] ECJ, Case C–209/94 P *Buralux and Others v Council* [1996] E.C.R. I–615, para.21.

[210] ECJ, Case C–310/93 P *BPB Industries and British Gypsum v Commission* [1995] E.C.R. I–865, para.34; ECJ, Case C–199/92 P *Hüls v Commission* [1999] E.C.R. I–428, para.197.

[211] ECJ, Case C–219/95 P *Ferriere Nord v Commission* [1997] E.C.R. I–4411, para.31; ECJ, Case C–185/95 P *Baustahlgewebe v Commission* [1998] E.C.R. I–8417, para.128; ECJ, Case C–283/98 P *Mo och Domsjö v Commission* [2000] E.C.R. I–9855, para.24.

[212] ECJ, Case C–291/98 P *Sarrió v Commission* [2000] E.C.R. I–9991, paras 96–97.

[213] See CFI, Case T–60/92 *Noonan v Commission* [1993] E.C.R. II–911, para.18, in which the Court of First Instance only declared the application admissible (confirmed on appeal in ECJ, Case C–448/93 P *Commission v Noonan* [1995] E.C.R. I–2321). See also Millett, *The Court of First Instance of the European Communities* (Butterworths, London-Edinburgh, 1990), at 56; Vaughan and Lasok (eds), *Butterworths European Court Practice*, (Butterworths, London, 1993), at 245. An appeal seeking to have an order made by the Court of First Instance set aside is inadmissible where the order under appeal instructs a party to produce documents (ECJ (order of October 4, 1999), Case C–349/99 P *Commission v ADT Projekt* [1999] E.C.R. I–6467). If the Court of First Instance stays proceedings on the ground that a case pending before the Court of Justice concerns the same subject-matter, no appeal will lie against that decision: ECJ (order of November 26, 2003), Joined Cases C–366/03 P to C–368/03 P, C–390/03 P, C–391/03 P and C–394/03 P *Associazione Bancaria Italiana and Others v Commission*, not reported.

in any event to be dismissed on the merits. This is because that decision makes the objection to no purpose.[214]

An appeal will also lie against decisions of the Court of First Instance dismissing an application to intervene.[215] Decisions of the Court of First Instance relating to applications for interim relief may also be the subject of an appeal (EC Treaty, Arts 242–243), together with decisions suspending the operation of Council or Commission decisions imposing a financial obligation on natural or legal persons (EC Treaty, Art.256, fourth para.).[216]

16–012   **Appeal regarding costs.** Under the second para. of Art.58 of the Statute of the Court of Justice, no appeal shall lie regarding only the amount of the costs or the party ordered to pay them. In addition, where all the other pleas put forward in an appeal have been rejected, any plea challenging the decision of the Court of First Instance on costs must be rejected as inadmissible by virtue of that provision.[217]

II. IDENTITY OF THE PARTIES

16–013   **Unsuccessful party at first instance.** An appeal may be brought by any party which has been unsuccessful, in whole or in part, in its submissions made before the Court of First Instance,[218] provided that the appeal, if

---

[214] ECJ, Case C–23/00 P *Council v Boehringer* [2002] E.C.R. I–1973, para.51. The position is different in the case of a judgment where the main application is rejected after the Court of First Instance has also rejected an objection of inadmissibility. An appeal directed only against the rejection of the objection of inadmissibility will lie in that event (ECJ, Case C–73/97 P *France v Comafrica and Others* [1999] E.C.R. I–185).

[215] Statute, Art.57, first para. For an application, see ECJ (order of the President of June 17, 1997), Joined Cases C–151/97 P and C–157/97 P(I) *National Power and PowerGen v British Coal and Commission* [1997] E.C.R. I–3491.

[216] Statute, Art.57, second para.; see ECJ (order of the President of May 5, 1994), Case C–97/94 P-R *Schulz v Commission* [1994] E.C.R. I–1701; ECJ (order of the President of October 21, 2003), Case C–365/03 P(R) *Industrias Químicas del Vallés v Commission* [2003] E.C.R. I–12389.

[217] ECJ (order of January 13, 1995), Case C–253/94 P *Roujansky* [1995] E.C.R. I–7, paras 12–14; ECJ (order of January 13, 1995), Case C–264/94 P *Bonnamy* [1995] E.C.R. I–15, paras 12–14; ECJ, Case C–396/93 P *Henrichs v Commission* [1995] E.C.R. I–2611, paras 65–66; ECJ (order of March 6, 1997), Case C–303/96 P *Bernardi v European Parliament* [1997] E.C.R. I–1239, para.49; ECJ, Case C–301/02 P *Tralli v ECB* [2005] E.C.R. I–4071, para.88.

[218] Statute, Art.56, second para.; ECJ, Case C–383/99 P *Procter & Gamble v OHIM* [2001] E.C.R. I–6251, paras 16–27, in which the Court of Justice held that the appellant had an interest in appealing notwithstanding the fact that the Court of First Instance had (partially) annulled the decision contested by it (a refusal by the OHIM to register a trade mark pursuant to Art.7(3) of Regulation No 40/94). The Court of Justice held that the Court of First Instance had refused to uphold the claim to annul the OHIM's decision to refuse registration in so far as it was based on Art.7(1)(b) and (c) of Regulation No 40/94. See also ECJ (order of June 28, 2004), Case C–445/02 P *Glaverbel v OHIM* [2004] E.C.R. I–6267. It remains an open question whether a party to the proceedings before the board of appeal of the OHIM may lodge an appeal against a judgment of the Court of First Instance

successful, is likely to procure an advantage to the party bringing it.[219] A cross-appeal may therefore be brought only if both parties have been unsuccessful—at least in part—before the Court of First Instance.[220] The Court of Justice may of its own motion raise the objection that a party has no interest in bringing or maintaining an appeal on the ground that an event subsequent to the judgment of the Court of First Instance removes its prejudicial effect as regards the appellant.[221]

Interveners. Persons who have been refused leave to intervene may appeal against that decision of the Court of First Instance.[222]

16–014

Another question is whether persons who have intervened before the Court of First Instance may appeal against that Court's final decision. As far as concerns interveners who are not Member States or Community institutions, an appeal will lie only if their situation is directly affected by the decision of the Court of First Instance.[223] The interest which an intervener, other than a Member State or a Community institution, must establish in order to be able to bring an appeal is, in principle, the same as it had to establish in order to obtain leave to intervene at first instance (Statute, Art.40, second para.), but the Court of Justice has, in the decision of the Court of First Instance, a more concrete basis for testing that interest than the Court of First Instance has when appraising the interest of a would-be intervener before any decision on the substance has been taken. It is therefore quite possible that the intervener at first instance will be refused leave to appeal.

---

if that party has not intervened in the proceedings before the Court of First Instance (see, however, implicitly ECJ (order of January 18, 2005), Case C–325/03 P *Zuazaga Meabe v OHIM* [2005] E.C.R. I–403.

[219] ECJ, Case C–19/93 P *Rendo and Others v Commission* [1995] E.C.R. I–3319, para.13.

[220] Cross-appeals are possible under Art.116(1) of the ECJ Rules of Procedure. The Court of Justice will examine the cross-appeal even if the main appeal is dismissed (see, *e.g.* ECJ, Case C–234/02 P *European Ombudsman v Lamberts* [2004] E.C.R.I–2803). It also happens that the Court of Justice examines first the cross appeal and then decides that there is no longer any need to adjudicate on the main appeal (ECJ, Case C–486/01 P *Front National v European Parliament* [2004] E.C.R. I–6289: the Court of First Instance had dismissed the application of the *Front National* on the merits and the *Front National* appealed against that judgment; the European Parliament, in its cross appeal, successfully alleged that the action brought before the Court of First Instance should have been declared inadmissible. In these circumstances there was no longer need to adjudicate on the main appeal).

[221] ECJ, Case C–19/93 P *Rendo and Others v Commission* [1995] E.C.R. I–3319, para.23.

[222] Statute, Art.57, first para.

[223] ECJ, Case C–200/92 P *ICI v Commission* [1999] E.C.R. I–4399, paras 22–33; ECJ, Joined Cases C–172/01 P, C–175/01 P, C–176/01 P and C–180/01 P *International Power v Commission* [2003] E.C.R. I–11421, paras 49–53.

16–015 Institutions and Member States. In contrast, institutions and Member States may invariably appeal,[224] even if the decision of the Court of First Instance does not affect them directly and if they did not intervene in the proceedings at first instance,[225] with the exception, in the latter case, of staff cases.[226]

III. Special Characteristics

16–016 Pleas. Appeals must be based on pleas alleging lack of competence of the Court of First Instance, a breach of procedure before it which adversely affects the interests of the appellant,[227] or infringement of Community law by the Court of First Instance.[228] A plea which merely takes issue with a factual appraisal made by the Court of First Instance will be inadmissible.[229]

---

[224] Statute, Art.56, third para. For an example, see ECJ, Case C–73/97 P *France v Comafrica and Others* [1999] E.C.R. I–185. Friden, "Quelques réflexions sur la recevabilité d'un pourvoi contre un arrêt du Tribunal de première instance" (2000) R.A.E. 231–238.

[225] Statute, Art.56, third para. See, by way of example, the appeal brought by France against CFI, Case T–70/94 *Comafrica and Dole Fresh Fruit Europe v Commission* [1996] E.C.R. II–1741 (Case C–73/97 P).

[226] ECJ, Case C–434/98 P *Council v Busacca and Others* [2000] E.C.R. I–8577, para.21.

[227] For an extensive discussion, see Lenaerts, "Le Tribunal de première instance des communautés européennes: regard sur une décennie d'activités et sur l'apport du double Degré d'instance au droit communautaire" (2000) C.D.E. 323–411. For instance, the Court of First Instance is bound by the general principle of Community law derived from Art.6 § 1 of the ECHR that everyone is entitled to legal process within a reasonable period in the context of proceedings brought against a Commission decision imposing fines on an undertaking for infringement of competition law. In *Baustahlgewebe* (ECJ, Case C–185/95 P *Baustahlgewebe v Commission* [1998] E.C.R. I–8417), the Court of Justice held (three years after the appeal had been brought) that the Court of First Instance had not respected that requirement on the ground that 32 months had elapsed between the end of the written procedure and the decision to open the oral procedure and 22 months had elapsed between the close of the oral procedure and the delivery of the judgment of the Court of First Instance. That amount of time was not reasonable in the light of the circumstances of the case, not even having regard to the particular attention that the Court of First Instance must pay to investigating actions calling for a close examination of complex facts. See further ECJ, Case C–199/99 P *Corus UK v Commission* [2003] E.C.R. I–11177, paras 41–56.

[228] Statute, Art.58, first para.; ECJ, Case C–283/90 P *Vidrányi v Commission* [1991] E.C.R. I–4339, paras 11–13; ECJ, Case C–346/90 P *F. v Commission* [1992] E.C.R. I–2691, paras 6–7; ECJ, Case C–53/92 P *Hilti v Commission* [1994] E.C.R. I–667, para.10; ECJ, Case C–136/92 P *Commission v Brazzelli Lualdi and Others* [1994] E.C.R. I–1981, para.48; ECJ, Joined Cases C–204/00 P, C–205/00 P, C–211/00 P, C–213/00 P, C–217/00 P and C–219/00 P *Aalborg Portland and Others v Commission* [2004] E.C.R. I–123, para.47. See also Schermers, "The European Court of First Instance" (1988) C.M.L.Rev. 541, at 554–555.

[229] ECJ (order of March 20, 1991), Case C–115/90 P *Turner v Commission* [1991] E.C.R. I–1423, paras 13–14; ECJ, Case C–283/90 P *Vidrányi v Commission* [1991] E.C.R. I–4339, paras 11–13; ECJ, Case C–132/90 P *Schwedler v European Parliament* [1991] E.C.R. I–5745, paras 9–12; ECJ, Case C–378/90 P *Pitrone v Commission* [1992] E.C.R. I–2375, paras 12–13; ECJ, Case C–346/90 P *F v Commission* [1992] E.C.R. I–2691, para.7; ECJ, Case C–326/91 P *De Compte v European Parliament* [1994] E.C.R. I–2091, para.29; ECJ, Case C–1/98 P *British Steel v Commission* [2000] E.C.R. I–10349, para.53. See also 15–003, *supra*.

Appeal must clearly indicate errors of law. The appellant must clearly state   **16–017**
which aspects of the contested decision of the Court of First Instance it is
criticising and indicate the contested parts of the judgment,[230] together with
the legal arguments supporting those complaints.[231] A complaint which is
not explained will be manifestly inadmissible and rejected.[232] Consequently,
it is not enough for the appellant to support a plea by merely referring back
to arguments raised in connection with another plea.[233] It is also not
permitted in an appeal simply to repeat pleas already raised in the Court of
First Instance, since to interpret an appeal in that way would be no more
than an attempt to have the case re-tried and no provision is made for
retrials by the Court of Justice.[234] Consequently, a plea declared inadmissible by the Court of First Instance cannot be raised afresh by the appellant,
although the latter may challenge on specific grounds the lower court's

---

[230] If the appellant fails to do so, the plea will be declared inadmissible (ECJ, Case C–248/99 P
France v Monsanto and Commission [2002] E.C.R. I–1, para.69). However, an appeal, or a
plea in support of an appeal, does not have to refer to all the points of the contested
judgment containing all the reasons which led the Court of First Instance to adopt a
position on a question. The fact that an appeal, or a plea in support of an appeal, takes up
some points containing only some of the reasons given by the Court of First Instance will
not result in its being declared inadmissible (ECJ, Case C–458/98 P *Industrie des Poudres
Sphériques v Council* [2000] E.C.R. I–8147, para.67).

[231] ECJ (order of April 26, 1993), Case C–244/92 P *Kupka-Floridi v ESC* [1993] E.C.R. I–2041,
para.9. The Court of Justice will sometimes particularise the pleas adduced by the appellant
(ECJ, Case C–283/90 P *Vidrányi v Commission* [1991] E.C.R. I 4339, para.29; ECJ, Case
C–255/90 P *Burban v European Parliament* [1992] E.C.R. I–2253, paras 4–5; ECJ (order of
October 17, 1995), Case C–62/94 P *Turner v Commission* [1995] E.C.R. I–3177, para.16;
ECJ (order of March 6, 1997), Case C–303/96 P *Bernardi v European Parliament* [1997]
E.C.R. I–1239, paras 37–40; ECJ, Case C–138/95 P *Campo Ebro Industrial and Others v
Council* [1997] E.C.R. I–2027, paras 60–61.) Where the appellant alleges a wrong
presentation or distortion of the evidence by the Court of First Instance, that party must
indicate precisely the evidence alleged to have been distorted by that Court and show the
errors of appraisal which led to that distortion (ECJ, Joined Cases C–204/00 P, C–205/00 P,
C–211/00 P, C–213/00 P, C–217/00 P and C–219/00 P *Aalborg Portland and Others v
Commission* [2004] E.C.R. I–123, para.50; ECJ (order of December 16, 2004) Case C–
222/03P *APOL and AIPO v Commission*, not reported, para.40).

[232] ECJ (order of December 12, 1996), Case C–49/96 P *Progoulis v Commission* [1996] E.C.R.
I–6803, para.24; ECJ, Joined Cases C–280/99 P, C–281/99 P and C–282/99 P *Moccia Irme
and Others v Commission* [2001] E.C.R. I–4717, paras 35–36.

[233] ECJ (order of February 5, 1997), Case C–51/95 P *Unifruit Hellas v Commission* [1997]
E.C.R. I–727, para.33.

[234] ECJ (order of April 26, 1993), *Kupka-Floridi v ESC* [1993] E.C.R. I–2041, para.10; ECJ
(order of March 7, 1994), Case C–338/93 P *De Hoe v Commission* [1994] E.C.R. I–819,
paras 17–19 and 26; ECJ (order of September 26, 1994), Case C–26/94 P *X v Commission*
[1994] E.C.R. I–4379, para.13; ECJ (order of October 17, 1995), Case C–62/95 P *Turner v
Commission* [1995] E.C.R. I–3177, para.17; ECJ (order of March 14, 1996), Case C–31/95 P
Del Plato v Commission [1996] E.C.R. I–1443, para.20, ECJ (order of November 12, 1999),
Case C–453/98 P *Branco v Commission* [1999] E.C.R. I–8037, para.96; ECJ, Joined Cases
C–280/99 P, C–281/99 P and C–282/99 P *Moccia Irme and Others v Commission* [2001]
E.C.R. I–4717, para.67; ECJ (order of June 28, 2001), Case C–351/99 P *Eridania and Others
v Council* [2001] E.C.R. I–5007, para.36; ECJ, Joined Cases C–204/00 P, C–205/00 P, C–
211/00 P, C–213/00 P, C–217/00 P and C–219/00 P *Aalborg Portland and Others v
Commission* [2004] E.C.R. I–123, para.51; ECJ, Case C–499/03 P *Biegi Nahrungsmittel and
Commonfood v Commission* [2005] E.C.R. I–1751, paras 37–38.

finding that the plea is inadmissible.[235] The appellant must raise arguments in this connection establishing that the Court of First Instance has erred in law.[236]

However, where an appellant submits that the Court of First Instance did not respond to a plea, its submission cannot be challenged, in terms of the admissibility of the ground of appeal, on the basis that it does not cite any passage or part of the contested judgment as the specific object of its complaint. Such submission can also not be challenged on the ground that it simply repeats or reproduces the plea raised at first instance.[237]

16–018 **No change in the subject-matter of the proceedings.** The limited range of pleas which may be raised on appeal against a decision of the Court of First Instance precludes any change in the subject-matter of the proceedings as compared with the proceedings before the Court of First Instance.[238] Parties are not entitled to seek a new form of order—*i.e.* relating to pleas not raised before the Court of First Instance.[239] The reason for this is that such a plea would involve the Court of Justice, not in reviewing the decision of the Court of First Instance, but in carrying out an additional substantive inquiry, thereby changing the subject-matter of the proceedings.[240] Pleas withdrawn by a party in the proceedings before the Court of First Instance are also inadmissible on appeal.[241] This is because the Court's jurisdiction is confined to a review of the findings of law on the pleas argued at first instance.[242] A party who tolerates the rejection of a plea raised at first

---

[235] This may be inferred from ECJ, Case C–354/92 P *Eppe v Commission* [1993] E.C.R. I–7027, para.13.

[236] ECJ (order of February 5, 1998), Case C–30/96 P *Abello and Others v Commission* [1998] E.C.R. I–377, para.45.

[237] ECJ, Joined Cases C–238/99 P, C–244/99 P, C–245/99 P, C–247/99 P, C–250/99 P and C–251/99 P, C–252/99 P and C–254/99 P *Limburgse Vinyl Maatschappij and Others v Commission* [2002] E.C.R. I–8375, paras 416–428.

[238] This bar applies both to the appeal itself (ECJ Rules of Procedure, Art.113(2)) and to the response lodged by the respondent (ECJ Rules of Procedure, Art.116(2)).

[239] ECJ Rules of Procedure, Arts 113(1) and 116(1). See also ECJ (order of April 26, 1993), Case C–244/92 P *Kupka-Floridi v ESC* [1993] E.C.R. I–2041, paras 12-20; ECJ, Case C–53/92 P *Hilti v Commission* [1994] E.C.R. I–667, para.49; *cf.* ECJ, Case C–76/93 P *Scaramuzza v Commission* [1994] E.C.R. I–5173, paras 15–19; ECJ (order of September 17, 1996), Case C–19/95 P *San Marco v Commission* [1996] E.C.R. I–4435, para.49; ECJ (order of June 11, 1998), Case C–291/97 P *H v Commission* [1998] E.C.R. I–3577, para.25; ECJ, Case C–155/98 P *Alexopoulou v Commission* [1999] E.C.R. I–4069, para.41; ECJ, Case C–1/98 P *British Steel v Commission* [2000] E.C.R. I–10349, para.47; ECJ, Case C–450/98 P *IECC v Commission* [2001] E.C.R. I–3947, para.36; ECJ, Joined Cases C–24/01 P and C–25/01 P *Glencore and Compagnie Continentale v Commission* [2002] E.C.R. I–10119, para.62.

[240] *Cf.* the Opinion of Advocate General C.O. Lenz in ECJ, Case C–348/90 P *European Parliament v Virgili-Schettini* [1991] E.C.R. I–5211, at I–5222; ECJ, Case C–279/95 P *Langnese-Iglo v Commission* [1998] E.C.R. I–5609, para.55.

[241] ECJ, Case C–354/92 P *Eppe v Commission* [1993] E.C.R. I–7027, para.13.

[242] ECJ (order of December 12, 1996), Case C–49/96 P *Progoulis v Commission* [1996] E.C.R. I–6803, para.32; ECJ, Case C–153/96 P *De Rijk v Commission* [1997] E.C.R. I–2901, para.18; Case C–450/98 P *IECC v Commission* [2001] E.C.R. I–3947, para.36.

instance before the lower court by not contesting the point in question of the decision of the Court of First Instance in the pleas set out in its appeal cannot contest the lower court's decision on this point for the first time in the reply. It cannot rely on a new plea based on a new matter within the meaning of Art.42(2) of the ECJ Rules of Procedure of the Court of Justice which is inescapably and directly linked to a plea which the Court of First Instance rejected. If such a plea were admissible, this would be tantamount to allowing the appellant to challenge for the first time at the stage of the reply the dismissal by the Court of First Instance of a plea which it had raised before that court, whereas nothing prevented it from submitting such a plea at the time of its application to the Court of Justice.[243]

Inoperative pleas. A plea alleging that the grounds of a judgment are unlawful is inoperative and will therefore be rejected where those grounds had no effect on the judgment.[244]   **16–019**

Pleas of public interest. The bar on raising new pleas on appeal and hence on changing the subject-matter of the proceedings does not prevent pleas relating to a matter of public interest (*moyens d'ordre public*) from being raised for the first time on appeal if the Court of First Instance has failed to raise such pleas, since the Court of Justice can do so of its own motion. It is, however, difficult to distinguish admissible pleas relating to a matter of public interest from ordinary inadmissible new pleas.[245]   **16–020**

Injury suffered as a result of the bringing of the appeal. In the response, the respondent may not claim damages for injury allegedly suffered as a result of the bringing of the appeal. As a result of Art.116(1) and (2) of the ECJ Rules of Procedure, such a claim is inadmissible.[246]   **16–021**

---

[243] ECJ, Case C–104/97 P *Atlanta v EC* [1999] E.C.R. I–6983, paras 17–23.

[244] ECJ, Joined Cases C–302/99 P and C–308/99 P *Commission and France v TF1* [2001] E.C.R. I–5603, paras 26–29. In this case (decided by the Full Court) the Commission had appealed against a judgment of the Court of First Instance in which an action for failure to act under Art.86 of the EC Treaty was declared admissible in the grounds of the judgment. In the operative part of the judgment, the Court of First Instance decided, however, that it did not have to adjudicate on the claim because, as it pointed out elsewhere in the grounds, the Commission had defined its position and for that reason the action was to no purpose. See also ECJ (order of October 28, 2004), Case C–236/03 P *Commission v CMA CGM and Others*, not reported, paras 25–27.

[245] Lenaerts, "Le Tribunal de première instance des Communautés européennes: genèse et premiers pas" (1990) J.T. 409, at 414. See the grounds for annulling a measure which the Court of Justice and the Court of First Instance may raise of their own motion and certain requirements for admissibility which the Court of Justice and the Court of First Instance may inquire into of their own motion, such as whether the time-limits prescribed for bringing certain actions have been complied with. But see ECJ, Case C–121/01 P *O'Hannrachain v European Parliament* [2003] E.C.R. I–5539, para.9, in which the Court of Justice held that a plea relating to the insufficient reasoning of the decision contested before the Court of First Instance was inadmissible on the ground that it had not been raised at first instance (notwithstanding the fact that such a plea may—or even must—be raised by the Court of First Instance of its own motion; see ECJ, Case C–367/95 P *Commission v Sytraval and Brink's France* [1998] E.C.R. I–1719, para.67).

[246] ECJ, Case C–35/92 P *European Parliament v Frederiksen* [1993] E.C.R. I–991, paras 33–36.

16–022   Measures of inquiry. The limitation of appeals to questions of law also means that the Court of Justice cannot order measures of inquiry in order to determine in what way the Community institution adopted the act contested before the Court of First Instance. Such measures of inquiry would necessarily lead the Court of Justice to decide questions of fact and, as a result, to go beyond its competence in appeals.[247] The Court of First Instance is the sole judge of any need for the information available to it concerning the cases before it to be supplemented through measures of inquiry.[248] In these circumstances a plea relating to the refusal of the Court of First Instance to order the production of a document, which had been explicitly requested by a party, will only be successful if it is apparent that the Court of First Instance was not in a position to rule on the correctness of the allegations made by that party without ordering the measure of inquiry concerned.[249]

16–023   Time-limits. An appeal must be lodged within two months of notification of the decision appealed against.[250]

Appeals against decisions of the Court of First Instance refusing leave to intervene must be brought within two weeks of notification of the decision dismissing the application.[251] Cross-appeals must be brought within two months of service on the respondent of notice of appeal[252]—that is to say, within the time-limit for lodging the response.[253]

IV. CONSEQUENCES

16–024   No suspensory effect. Appeals do not have suspensory effect, but the parties are entitled under Arts 242 and 243 of the EC Treaty to apply for suspension of the operation of the decision of the Court of First Instance

---

[247] ECJ, Case C–234/92 P *Shell v Commission* [1999] E.C.R. I–4501, paras 70–73.

[248] ECJ, Case C–315/99 P *Ismeri v Court of Auditors* [2001] E.C.R. I–5281, para.19; ECJ, Joined Cases C–24/01 P and C–25/01 P *Glencore and Compagnie Continentale v Commission* [2002] E.C.R. I–10119, para.77; ECJ (judgment of October 14, 2004), Case C–279/02 P *Antas de Campos v European Parliament*, not reported, paras 34 and 35; ECJ (order of December 7, 2004), Case C–521/03 P *Internationaler Hilfsfonds v Commission*, not reported, paras 37–38. The question of the allocation of the burden of proof, although it may have an impact on the findings of fact by the Court of First Instance, is a question of law (ECJ, Joined Cases C–2/01 P and C–3/01 P *BAI and Commission* [2004] E.C.R. I–23, para.61).

[249] See ECJ, Case C–119/97 P *Ufex and Others v Commission* [1999] E.C.R. I–1341, paras 107–112; ECJ (judgment of October 14, 2004), Case C–279/02 P *Antas de Campos v European Parliament*, not reported, paras 34–35; ECJ (judgment of April 14, 2005), Case C–243/04 P *Gaki-Kakouri v Court of Justice*, not reported, paras 52–55.

[250] Statute, Art.56, first para. Time starts to run on the date when the contested decision is received (ECJ (order of April 30, 1999), Case C–7/99 P *Campoli v Commission* [1999] E.C.R. I–2679, para.6).

[251] Statute, Art.57, first para.

[252] ECJ, Case C–136/92 P *Commission v Brazzelli Lualdi and Others* [1994] E.C.R. I–1981, paras 70–73.

[253] ECJ Rules of Procedure, Art.115(1).

and for interim measures.[254] If, however, the contested decision of the Court of First Instance declares a regulation invalid, the decision takes effect only as from the date of expiry of the period for lodging an appeal or, if an appeal is brought within that period, as from the date of the dismissal of the appeal.[255]

Dismissal of the appeal. If the appeal is unfounded, it will be dismissed. In the event that the reasoning of the contested decision of the Court of First Instance contains an infringement of Community law, but its operative part is nevertheless lawful, the appeal will likewise be dismissed. In that event, the Court of Justice sets out the "correct" grounds in its judgment, but does not set aside the judgment of the Court of First Instance (substitution of grounds).[256] The Court of Justice may also find that the operative part of the judgment of the Court of First Instance is correct in law and dismiss the appeal on a legal ground different from the ground or grounds put forward by the Court of First Instance, without pronouncing on the "legality" of the grounds of the lower court's judgment. In such case, the pleas put forward

16–025

---

[254] Statute, Art.60, first para. For examples, see ECJ (order of the President of November 27, 1990), Case C–242/90 P-R *Commission v Albani and Others* [1990] E.C.R. I–4329, para.3: ECJ (order of the President of January 31, 1991), Case C–345/90 P-R *European Parliament v Hanning* [1991] E.C.R. I–231, paras 24–26; ECJ (order of the President of April 3, 1992), Case C–35/92 P-R *European Parliament v Frederiksen* [1992] E.C.R. I–2399, paras 17–18; ECJ (order of the President of July 6, 1995), Case C–166/95 P-R *Commission v Duffix* [1995] E.C.R. I–1955, para.17; ECJ (order of the President of September 15, 1995), Case C–254/95 P-R *European Parliament v Innamorati* [1995] E.C.R. I–2707, paras 14–19. An application for suspension of the operation of the decision of the Court of First Instance against which an appeal has been brought must be made to the Court of Justice: CFI (order of the President of November 22, 1991), Case T–77/91 R *Hochbaum v Commission* [1991] E.C.R. II–1285, paras 21–22.

[255] Statute, Art.60, second para. Under Arts 242 and 243 of the EC Treaty, a party may also request the Court of Justice to suspend the operation of the regulation declared void or to grant any other interim measures.

[256] ECJ, Case C–30/91 P *Lestelle v Commission* [1992] E.C.R. I–3755, para.28; ECJ, Case C–36/92 P *SEP v Commission* [1994] E.C.R. I–1911, para.33; ECJ, Case C–320/92 P *Finsider v Commission* [1994] E.C.R. I–5697, para.37; ECJ, Case C–150/98 P *ESC v E* [1999] E.C.R. I–8877, paras 17–18; ECJ, Case C–49/92 P *Commission v Anic Partecipazioni* [1999] E.C.R. I–4125, para.120; ECJ, Case C–210/98 *Salzgitter v Commission* [2000] E.C.R. I–5843, para.58; ECJ, Case C–280/98 P *Weig v Commission* [2000] E.C.R. I–9757, para.49; ECJ, Case C–282/98 P *Enso Española v Commission* [2000] E.C.R. I–9817, para.47; ECJ, Case C–312/00 P *Commission v Camar and Tico* [2002] E.C.R. I–11355, para.57; ECJ, Case C–93/02 P *Biret International v Council* [2003] E.C.R.I–10497, para.60; ECJ, Case C–164/01 P *van den Berg v Council and Commission* [2004] E.C.R. I–10225, para.95; ECJ (order of June 3, 2005), Case C–396/03 *Killinger v Germany, Council and Commission* [2005] E.C.R. I–4967, para.12. Where, in contrast, a fresh appraisal of the facts of the case is required by reason of the adoption of other legal grounds, the Court of Justice may carry out that appraisal only after setting aside the decision of the Court of First Instance. It then gives final judgment on the ground that the state of the proceedings permits it to do so. In this way, the Court of Justice may set aside a judgment of the Court of First Instance and then produce an operative part identical to that set out in the judgment at first instance after making its own assessment of the law and the facts. See ECJ, Case C–298/93 P *Klinke v Court of Justice* [1994] E.C.R. I–3009, in which the Court of Justice set aside a decision of the Court of First Instance and then set out an identical operative part.

on appeal will not be considered.[257] Furthermore, a plea directed against a superabundant ground of the decision of the Court of First Instance will be nugatory and cannot affect the legality of the decision.[258]

16–026 **Successful appeal.** An appeal will be well founded if at least one of the appellant's pleas succeeds. In that event, the Court of Justice will set aside the contested decision. The decision may be set aside in its entirety or only in part. A decision may be set aside in part, not only if the contested decision determines a number of claims made in a single action—the decision on one claim being quashed, for example, and the appeal dismissed as regards the others[259]—but apparently also if the decision of the Court of First Instance relates only to a single claim. In that case, the Court of Justice will confine itself to quashing one or more grounds of the decision.[260]

16–027 **Consequences of a successful appeal.** In the event that it sets aside a decision of the lower court, the Court of Justice may itself give final judgment in the matter if the state of the proceedings so permits, but is not obliged to do so, or else refer the case back to the Court of First Instance for judgment.[261]

The subject-matter of the proceedings concluded by the Court of Justice or the Court of First Instance after a judgment setting a decision aside depends on various factors. It appears from the wording of the first para. of Art.61 of the Statute and Art.119 of the CFI Rules of Procedure that the judgment setting aside the decision of the first-instance court does not extend to the written and/or oral procedure which preceded that decision.

---

257 ECJ (order of December 3, 1992), Case C–32/92 P *Moat v Commission* [1992] E.C.R. I–6379, para.11; ECJ, Case C–480/93 P *Zunis Holding and Others v Commission* [1996] E.C.R. I–1, paras 15–16; ECJ, Case C–170/02 P *Schlüsselverlag J.S. Moser and Others v Commission* [2003] E.C.R. I–9889, paras 25–39.
258 ECJ, Case C–35/92 P *European Parliament v Frederiksen* [1993] E.C.R. I–991, para.31; ECJ, Case C–244/91 P *Pincherle v Commission* [1993] E.C.R. I–6965, para.31; ECJ (order of March 25, 1996), Case C–137/95 P *SPO and Others v Commission* [1996] E.C.R. I–1611, para.47; ECJ, Case C–264/95 P *Commission v UIC* [1997] E.C.R. I–1287, para.48; ECJ, Case C–395/95 P *Geotronics v Commission* [1997] E.C.R. I–2271, para.23.
259 ECJ, Case C–18/91 P *V v European Parliament* [1992] E.C.R. I–3997; ECJ, Case C–19/93 P *Rendo and Others v Commission* [1995] E.C.R. I–3319.
260 ECJ, Case C–294/95 P *Ojha v Commission* [1996] E.C.R. I–5863, para.62; see also the Opinion of Advocate General P. Léger in that case, points 178–191.
261 Statute, Art.61, first para.; for examples, see ECJ, Case C–404/92 P *X. v Commission* [1994] E.C.R. I–4737, para.25 (case dispatched by the Court of Justice); ECJ, Case C–254/95 P *European Parliament v Innamorati* [1996] E.C.R. I–3423 (case dispatched by the Court of Justice); ECJ, Case C–188/96 P *V v Commission* [1997] E.C.R. I–6561, paras 32–33 (referred to the Court of First Instance); ECJ, Case C–353/01 P *Mattila v Council and Commission* [2004] E.C.R. I–1073, paras 35–28 (case dispatched by the Court of Justice). *Cf.* Mongin (n.202, *supra*), at 238. The first para. of Art.61 of the Statute is also applicable to appeals brought under the second para. of Art.57, of the Statute: ECJ (order of the President of January 29, 1997), Case C–393/96 P(R) *Antonissen v Council and Commission* [1997] E.C.R. I–441, para.45.

What is annulled is therefore determined in the first place by the form of order sought and the pleas put forward by the parties in the pleadings which they originally lodged with the Court of First Instance. Consequently, the judgment setting aside the original decision does not enable them to seek a new form of order or to raise new pleas and to have completely new proceedings determined by the Court of First Instance or the Court of Justice, as the case may be, except where a new plea is based on a new fact within the meaning of Art.48(2) of the CFI Rules of Procedure and Art.42(2) of the ECJ Rules of Procedure.[262] In the second place, regard must be had to the extent to which the judgment of the Court of Justice annulled the decision of the lower court. This can be determined from close consideration of the judgment on appeal. It is clear from earlier case-law that in order to comply with a judgment and to implement it fully, regard must be had not only to the operative part but also to the grounds which led to the judgment and constitute its essential basis, in so far as they are necessary to determine the exact meaning of what is stated in the operative part.[263] Depending on the reasoning of the judgment of the Court of Justice, the assessment made by the Court of First Instance of all the pleas submitted may be rejected or the Court of Justice may reject the assessment of one or more pleas and accept the remainder of the lower court's reasoning.[264] Thirdly, the content of the decision of the Court of First Instance which is set aside influences the way in which the case is finally dispatched.

Where the Court of First Instance dismisses an application, having considered all the pleas raised, and the Court of Justice then sets aside the decision on account of an error of law in assessing one of the pleas, it will be unlikely that in order to wind up the case the Court of Justice or the Court of First Instance will pronounce (again) on the assessment of the pleas that the decision on appeal leaves unaffected. The proceedings will be confined in that event to a re-examination of the plea which the Court of First Instance wrongly rejected, having regard to the determination made by the Court of Justice of the point of law at issue.[265] Where, in contrast, the Court of First Instance grants the application—for instance, in the case of an action for annulment of an act of an institution—on the basis of a plea without considering the other pleas raised and the Court of Justice sets aside its decision on appeal, it would appear that, in order to wind up the

---

[262] Where a case is referred back to the Court of First Instance after the latter's judgment has been set aside, the parties may not present any facts which were not brought before the Court when it first considered the case (CFI, Case T–36/96 *Gaspari v European Parliament* [1999] E.C.R.-SC I–A–135, II–729, para.77).

[263] ECJ, Joined Cases 97, 193, 99 and 215/86 *Asteris and Others v Commission* [1988] E.C.R. 2181, para.27.

[264] For an example, see CFI, Case T–16/91 RV *Rendo and Others v Commission* [1996] E.C.R. II–1827, para.28.

[265] See the Opinion of Advocate General P. Léger in ECJ, Case C–294/95 P *Ojha v Commission* [1996] E.C.R. I–5863, paras 184–189.

case, not only the plea which wrongly succeeded will have to be re-examined, but consideration will also have to be given to those pleas which the Court of First Instance did not examine in its original decision,[266] although it is possible that the case may be able to be dispatched by upholding only one of the pleas raised.

16–028 **Court of Justice gives final judgment.** The Court of Justice will give final judgment in the matter where it finds that all the appellant's claims can be rejected because the Community act in issue was lawfully adopted.[267] Advocate General Jacobs argues that, where the Court of Justice gives final judgment in a matter, a respondent ought to be entitled, in his response, to raise an issue which was raised against the contested Community act before, but not addressed by the Court of First Instance because it granted his or her claims on other grounds. The Advocate General bases that view on the fact that the Court of Justice has the entire case-file at its disposal[268] and on the fact that Arts 115 and 116 of the ECJ Rules of Procedure do not preclude such a course of action. He further maintains that this would serve the interest of procedural economy.[269] As a corollary, Advocate General Jacobs suggests that when the Court of First Instance gives judgment on one ground in favour of an applicant, it should make the necessary findings of fact relevant to any other grounds on which the applicant has relied and on which, in the event of an appeal, the applicant might seek to rely as respondent.[270]

16–029 **Referral to the Court of First Instance.** The Court of Justice will refer the case back to the Court of First Instance for final judgment where the case has not been completely decided and additional findings of fact are needed or a fresh look has to be taken at those already made.[271] Where a case is referred back to the Court of First Instance, that Court is bound by the decision of the Court of Justice on points of law.[272]

16–030 **Effects of a successful appeal brought by a Member State or an institution.** Where an appeal brought by a Member State or a Community institution which did not intervene in the proceedings before the Court of

---

[266] CFI, Case T–43/89 RV *Gill v Commission* [1993] E.C.R. II–303.
[267] ECJ, Case C–345/90 P *European Parliament v Hanning* [1992] E.C.R. I–949, paras 35–38.
[268] ECJ Rules of Procedure, Art.111(2).
[269] If such issues could not be taken into account, it would invariably be necessary to refer the case back to the Court of First Instance in order to avoid the risk of injustice. That would result in further proceedings, additional costs and possibly a further appeal.
[270] Opinion of Advocate General F.G. Jacobs in ECJ, Case C–185/90 P *Commission v Gill* [1991] E.C.R. I–4779, at I–4803 (nevertheless, after quashing the contested judgment, the Court referred the case back to the Court of First Instance for final judgment). It may be seen from CFI, Joined Cases T–371/94 and T–394/94 *British Airways and Others v Commission* [1998] E.C.R. I–2405, that the Court of First Instance sometimes adopts this approach.
[271] ECJ, Case C–68/91 P *Moritz v Commission* [1992] E.C.R. I–6849, paras 41–42.
[272] Statute, Art.61, second para. For examples, see CFI, Case T–43/89 RV *Gill v Commission* [1993] E.C.R. II–303; CFI, Case T–20/89 RV *Moritz v Commission* [1993] E.C.R. II–1423.

First Instance is well founded, the Court of Justice may, if it considers it necessary, state which of the effects of the decision of the Court of First Instance which has been set aside are to be considered definitive in respect of the other parties to the litigation.[273]

---

[273] Statute, Art.61, third para.

CHAPTER 17

THE REVIEW PROCEDURE

17–001 **Exceptional review.** From the point of view of the parties concerned, the Member States and the institutions, neither decisions of the Court of First Instance in appeals brought against decisions of judicial panels nor its decisions on preliminary references are open to be challenged. Exceptionally, however, such decisions may be subject to review by the Court of Justice where there is a serious risk of the unity or consistency of Community law being affected.[274] Only the First Advocate General of the Court of Justice can take the initiative for a review of decisions of the Court of First Instance when he or she considers that such a risk exists.[275] The review should therefore be distinguished from an appeal, which, in principle, is brought by one of the parties to the case[276] and may be based on any error of law which the Court of First Instance or judicial panel may have committed in the judgment under appeal.[277]

17–002 **Initiation of the review.** The proposal of the First Advocate General must be made within one month of delivery of the decision of the Court of First Instance, and the Court of Justice must decide within one month of receiving the proposal whether or not the decision should be reviewed.[278]

17–003 **Procedure.** The Court of Justice will give a ruling on the questions which are subject to review by means of an urgent procedure on the basis of the file forwarded to it by the Court of First Instance.[279]

---

[274] EC Treaty, Arts 225(2), second subpara., and 225(3), third subpara. In preliminary ruling proceedings the Court of First Instance may avoid a review by referring a case which falls under its jurisdiction to the Court of Justice. This is because Art.225(3), second para., of the EC Treaty provides that "[w]here the [Court of First Instance] considers that the case requires a decision of principle likely to affect the unity or consistency of Community law, it may refer the case to the Court of Justice for a ruling". In this connection, see Fardet "Le 'réexamen' des décisions du Tribunal de première instance" (2004) R.M.C.U.E. 184-193.

[275] Statute, Art.62, first para.

[276] With the exception of cases relating to disputes between the Communities and their servants, an appeal may also be brought by Member States and institutions of the Communities which did not intervene in the proceedings before the Court of First Instance (Statute, Art.56).

[277] EC Treaty, Art.225(1).

[278] Statute, Art.62.

[279] Statute, Art.62a, first para.

The review procedure does not constitute a mere appeal in the interest of the law.[280] Indeed, the parties to the decision under review and, in the case of a preliminary ruling, all interested parties within the meaning of Art.23 of the Statute are entitled to lodge statements or written observations with the Court of Justice relating to the questions which are subject to review.[281] The Court of Justice may decide to open the oral procedure before giving a ruling.[282]

If the review concerns a decision given upon appeal by the Court of First Instance, the procedure will not have suspensory effect.[283] By contrast, a preliminary ruling of the Court of First Instance takes effect only as from the date of expiry of the period for opening a review procedure or, if a review procedure is initiated within that period, as from the end of such review procedure, unless the Court of Justice decides otherwise.[284] The review procedure concerning a preliminary ruling of the Court of First Instance will thus in principle have suspensory effect.

Effects of review. If the decision of the Court of First Instance is reviewed, the effects of such review will be as follows. In preliminary proceedings the "new" interpretation of the Court of Justice will be binding on the national court. Indeed, the answer given by the Court of Justice will be substituted for that given by the Court of First Instance.[285] **17–004**

As regards a decision given upon appeal by the Court of First Instance which has been reviewed by the Court of Justice, after having given a correct interpretation of the law, the Court of Justice will refer the case back to the Court of First Instance. The Court of First Instance will be bound by the decision of the Court of Justice on points of law. If necessary, the Court of Justice will state which of the effects of the decision of the Court of First Instance are to be considered as definitive in respect of the parties to the litigation.[286] Alternatively, the Court of Justice may itself give final judgment where the outcome of the case is obvious from the facts on which the decision of the Court of First Instance is based.[287]

---

[280] It was already apparent from Declaration No 13 annexed to the Nice Treaty that the parties concerned were to be involved in the review procedure.

[281] Statute, Art.62a, second para.

[282] Statute, Art.62a, third para.

[283] However, interim relief can be granted (see Statute, Art.62b, first para.).

[284] Statute, Art.62b, second para.

[285] Statute, Art.62b, second para.

[286] Statute, Art.62b, first para.

[287] When the appeal before the Court of First Instance is limited to points of law (as is the case with respect to decisions of the European Union Civil Service Tribunal), the facts on which the decision of the Court of First Instance is based will necessarily be the facts on which the decision of the judicial panel was based.

CHAPTER 18

PROCEEDINGS BROUGHT BY OFFICIALS AND OTHER SERVANTS OF THE COMMUNITIES (STAFF CASES)

I. SUBJECT-MATTER

A. GENERAL

18–001   **Disputes between the Community and its staff.** The relationship between the Community and its servants is governed by the "Staff Regulations of officials of the European Communities" and the "Conditions of employment of other servants of the European Communities".[288] Every Community act regarding staff policy must comply with the provisions of the Staff Regulations or Conditions of Employment. Disputes between the Community and its staff within the limits and under the conditions set down in the Staff Regulations or Conditions of Employment are brought before the European Union Civil Service Tribunal.[289] Until December 12, 2005 this jurisdiction was exercised by the Court of First Instance, *i.e.* the date of publication in the *Official*

---

[288] Regulation (EEC, Euratom, ECSC) No 259/68 of the Council of February 29, 1968 laying down the Staff Regulations of Officials and the Conditions of Employment of Other Servants of the European Communities and instituting special measures temporarily applicable to officials of the Commission, [1968] O.J. Spec. Ed. I, 30, as reformed by Council Regulation (EC, Euratom) No 723/2004 of March 22, 2004 amending the Staff Regulations of officials of the European Communities and the Conditions of Employment of other servants of the European Communities, [2004] O.J. L124/1; *corrigendum* in [2005] l51/28. The Conditions of Employment indicate the provisions of the Staff Regulations which apply to categories of Community staff other than officials (temporary staff, auxiliary staff, contract staff, local staff, special advisers). These staff members are engaged by contract.

[289] Art.236 in conjunction with Art.255 of the EC Treaty and Annex I to the Statute of the Court of Justice. The European Union Civil Service Tribunal was established by Council Decision 2004/752/EC, Euratom of November 2, 2004 ([2004] O.J. L333/7). The Court of Justice has special jurisdiction with regard to members of some institutions. For instance, the third subpara. of Art.213(2) of the EC Treaty provides that the Council or the Commission may apply to the Court of Justice where Members or former Members of the Commission have breached their obligation not to engage in any other occupation, whether gainful or not, or their undertaking that, both during and after their term of office, they will respect the obligations arising therefrom and in particular their duty to behave with integrity and discretion as regards the acceptance, after they have ceased to hold office, of certain appointments or benefits. For an application, see Council Decision 1999/494/EC, ECSC, Euratom of July 9, 1999 on the referral of the case of Mr Bangemann to the Court of Justice ([1999] O.J. L192/55). See also Case C–432/04 *Commission v Cresson*, pending.

Journal of the European Union of the Decision of the President of the Court of Justice recording that the European Union Civil Service Tribunal has been constituted in accordance with law ([2005] O.J. L325/1).

Art.91(1) of the Staff Regulations. The jurisdiction of the Community judicature is delineated in Art.91(1) of the Staff Regulations. It has jurisdiction in any dispute between the Communities and any person to whom the Staff Regulations apply regarding the legality of an act adversely affecting such a person either because the appointing authority has taken a decision or because it has not adopted a measure which it was under a duty to adopt under the Staff Regulations.[290] In the case of disputes of a financial nature, the Community judicature has unlimited jurisdiction.[291]   18–002

B. AGAINST WHAT MEASURES WILL AN ACTION LIE?

Act must have adverse effect. An action will lie only against an act adversely affecting the person concerned.[292] The expression "act having adverse effect" has two aspects: (1) the act must have legal effects as far the applicant is concerned and (2) those legal effects must be unfavourable to the staff member, with the result that he or she can establish a personal interest in a judgment granting his or her claims.[293]   18–003

1. What measures constitute acts having adverse effect?

Binding act. An act having adverse effect is one which directly affects the applicant's legal position.[294] This concept is very similar to the expression "binding act" which has been discussed in connection with actions for annulment (see 7–007, *supra*).[295]   18–004

---

[290] This chapter deals only with the basic features of staff cases. More detailed discussions can be found in *Commentaire Mégret*, at 335–371; Dubouis, "Fonctionnaires et agents des Communautés européennes" (1965) R.T.D.E. 666–686; (1966) R.T.D.E. 511–522; (1969) R.T.D.E. 648–664; (1970) R.T.D.E. 120–144; (1972) R.T.D.E. 376–394; (1975) R.T.D.E. 280–307; (1978) R.T.D.E. 469–515; (1981) R.T.D.E. 710–763; (1983) R.T.D.E. 86–146; (1990) R.T.D.E. 127–169; (1994) R.T.D.E. 237–276; and Rogalla, *Dienstrecht der Europäischen Gemeinschaften* (Carl Heymanns Verlag KG, Cologne/Berlin/Bonn/Munich, 1992), 328 pp.

[291] Accordingly, the Court of First Instance (now the European Union Civil Service Tribunal) can award damages to the applicant of its own motion where the applicant seeks the annulment of a particular decision yet protecting the interests of third parties precludes the annulment of the decision (CFI, Case T–10/02 *Girardot v Commission* [2004] E.C.R.-SC II–483, para.89).

[292] This also applies to proceedings brought against the ECB: see CFI, Case T–320/02 *Esch-Leonhardt and Others v EIB* [2004] E.C.R.-SC II–79, paras 36–37.

[293] The fact that a decision adversely affects an official and he or she can bring an action against it does not automatically mean that the appointing authority was under an obligation to give him or her a proper hearing before adopting the decision at issue (ECJ, Case C–111/02 P *European Parliament v Reynolds* [2004] E.C.R. I–5475, para.57).

[294] ECJ, Case 26/63 *Pistoj v Commission* [1964] E.C.R. 341, at 352; ECJ, Case 32/68 *Graselli v Commission* [1969] E.C.R. 505, para.4; CFI, Case T–213/99 *Verheyden v Commission* [2000] E.C.R.-SC IA-297, II–1355, para.20. For some recent cases, see CFI (order of February 2, 2001), Case T–97/00 *Vakalopoulou v Commission* [2001] E.C.R.-SC I–A-23, II–91, para.13;

18–005 **Measures of a general nature.** Where an applicant challenges a "measure of a general nature" (Staff Regulations, Art.90(2), first indent), the application will be admissible only in so far as he or she shows that the act adversely affects him or her.[296] This means that the measure of a general nature must directly affect his or her legal position.[297] If this is not the case, no action will lie against the measure in question, but subsequently an objection of illegality may be raised against it if that measure is used as the basis for an act adversely affecting the applicant.[298]

18–006 **Acts not performed by the appointing authority.** Some authorities argue that it may be inferred from the wording of Arts 90 and 91 of the Staff Regulations that a decision will be capable of having adverse effect only if it is taken by the appointing authority.[299] Frequently, decisions of the appointing authority are prepared by a lower-ranking official or in an advisory body. Such preparatory measures are not acts having adverse effect, because they do not affect the applicant's legal position.[300] In some cases, however, acts not performed by the appointing authority actually do have adverse effect. One example is the finding by an invalidity committee that a staff member is not suffering from invalidity, which is an act having adverse effect on the person concerned because it is the act which actually terminates the invalidity procedure.[301] Another is a selection board's decision, taken in the course of a recruitment competition, to eliminate the applicant from the further stages of the competition.[302]

CFI, Case T–51/01 *Fronia v Commission* [2002] E.C.R.-SC I–A-43, II–187, paras 24–35.

[295] See, *e.g.* ECJ, Case 346/87 *Bossi v Commission* [1989] E.C.R. I–303, para.23; ECJ (order of March 9, 2004), Case C–159/03 *Pflugradt v ECB*, not reported, para.17. For further details see *Commentaire Mégret*, at 335–353; Van Raepenbusch, "Le contentieux de la fonction publique européenne", in *Tendances actuelles et évolution de la jurisprudence de la Cour de justice des Communautés européennes* (European Institute of Public Administration, Maastricht, 1993), 95, at 111–115.

[296] See also ECJ, Case 125/87 *Brown v Court of Justice* [1988] E.C.R. 1619, para.17; CFI, (judgment of April 12, 2005), Case T–191/02 *Lebedef v Commission*, not yet reported, paras 49–54 and 90–95.

[297] See, *inter alia*, ECJ, Case 78/63 *Huber v Commission* [1964] E.C.R. 367, at 375; CFI, Case T–135/89 *Pfloeschner v Commission* [1990] E.C.R. II–153, para.11; CFI (order of July 4, 1991), Case T–47/90 *Herremans v Commission* [1991] E.C.R. II–467, para.22. In so far as the conditions set out in a notice of vacancy exclude a person from applying for the post in question, that person will be adversely affected by the notice. See, by way of example, ECJ, Case 79/74 *Küster v European Parliament* [1975] E.C.R. 725, para.6; ECJ, Case 25/77 *De Roubaix v Commission* [1978] E.C.R. 1081, para.8.

[298] See CFI, Case T–47/91 *Auzat v Commission* [1992] E.C.R. II–2536, para.11; CFI (order of May 6, 2004), Case T–34/03 *Hecq v Commission* [2004] E.C.R.-SC II–1371, paras 32–39.

[299] See Van Raepenbusch (n.295, *supra*), at 115. The appointing authority differs depending upon the level of the official or staff member in the hierarchy (Staff Regulations, Art.2).

[300] The award of promotion points by an official's superior is, however, a decision having adverse effect, since it directly affects the official's legal position (CFI, Case T–323/02 *Breton v Court of Justice* [2003] E.C.R.-SC IA-325, II–1587, paras 44–46).

[301] CFI, Case T–54/89 *V v European Parliament* [1990] E.C.R. II–659, para.45; ECJ, Case C–18/91 P *V v European Parliament* [1992] E.C.R. I–3997, para.26.

[302] CFI, Case T–37/93 *Stagakis v European Parliament* [1994] E.C.R.-SC I–A-137, at I–A-138–139; CFI (judgment of May 31, 2005), Case T–294/03 *Gibault v Commission*, not yet reported, para.22.

2. The requirement for an interest

Personal interest. Applicants are entitled to challenge a decision which has **18–007** implications for their legal position only in so far as that decision adversely affects that legal position. In other words, there must be an advantage for the applicant personally in a judgment granting his or her claims. Accordingly, an applicant has no interest in the annulment of an appointment to a post to which he or she personally is ineligible for appointment.[303]

Consequently, the applicant is entitled only to adduce grievances which affect him or her personally. He or she may not bring an action in the interests of the law or of the institutions.[304] Furthermore, the applicant's interest must be legitimate, present and vested.[305] In addition, the applicant may only make submissions which genuinely serve his or her interest.[306] A plea criticising a defect in the contested act will therefore be inadmissible if the defect was incapable of disadvantaging the applicant.[307]

II. IDENTITY OF THE PARTIES

A. APPLICANTS

Any member of staff. Any person whose relationship with the Community is **18–008** determined by the Staff Regulations or the Conditions of Employment may bring a dispute concerning the application of the Staff Regulations or the Conditions of Employment before the European Union Civil Service Tribunal.[308] Only "local staff"—staff engaged in places outside the European Union according to local practice for manual or service duties—must, under Art.122 of the Conditions of Employment, bring any dispute between them and the institution concerned before the arbitral body indicated in their contract for employment.

Persons taking part in recruitment procedures are also among those deriving rights under the Staff Regulations or the Conditions of Employment,[309] together with the legal successors of persons whose relationship with

---

[303] See, *inter alia*, CFI, Case T–20/89 *Moritz v Commission* [1990] E.C.R. II–769, para.16; CFI, Case T–51/90 *Moretti v Commission* [1992] E.C.R. II–487, para.22.

[304] ECJ, Case 85/82 *Schloh v Council* [1983] E.C.R. 2105, para.14; CFI, Case T–163/89 *Sebastiani v European Parliament* [1991] E.C.R. II–715, para.24.

[305] ECJ, Case 17/78 *Deshormes v Commission* [1979] E.C.R. 189, para.9; CFI (order of December 14, 1989), Case T–119/89 *Teisonnière v Commission* [1990] E.C.R. II–7, para.19.

[306] ECJ, Case 90/74 *Deboeck v Commission* [1975] E.C.R. 1123, para.12.

[307] *Ibid.*, paras 13–16. The plea must also be able to be inferred from the content of the complaint (see 18–017, *infra*).

[308] Staff Regulations, Art.91(1); Conditions of Employment, Art.46 (temporary staff), Art.73 (auxiliaries), Art.117 (contract staff) and Art.124 (special advisers). See, however, as regards "local staff" and the application of national law to their employment relationship, ECJ, Case C–165/01 *Betriebsrat der Vertretung der Europäischen Kommission in Österreich* [2003] E.C.R. I–7683.

[309] ECJ, Case 23/64 *Vandevyvere v European Parliament* [1965] E.C.R. 157, at 163–164.

LIVERPOOL JOHN MOORES UNIVERSITY
LEARNING SERVICES

the Community was governed by the Staff Regulations or the Conditions of Employment.[310]

18–009 **Staff of bodies and agencies.** Members of staff of Community bodies and agencies with legal personality may also bring actions in the European Union Civil Service Tribunal where it appears from the regulation establishing the relevant body or agency that its staff are in a legal position equivalent to that of servants of Community institutions.[311]

18–010 **Trade unions and staff associations of employees.** Trade unions and staff associations of employees of the Community which have legal personality are not entitled to bring proceedings pursuant to Art.236 of the EC Treaty because the procedure for complaint and appeal established by Arts 90 and 91 of the Staff Regulations is designed to deal exclusively with individual disputes.[312] Consequently, they must satisfy the requirements of the fourth para. of Art.230 of the EC Treaty in order to bring an action for annulment and of Art.235 and the second para. of Art.288 of that Treaty in order to bring an action for damages. In addition, they may intervene in support of the form of order sought by a party in proceedings instituted under Art.236 of the EC Treaty.[313]

---

[310] ECJ, Case 18/70 *Duraffour v Council* [1971] E.C.R. 515; ECJ, Case 24/71 *Meinhardt (née Forderung) v Commission* [1972] E.C.R. 269, para.2; CFI, Case T–65/92 *Arauxo-Dumay v Commission* [1993] E.C.R. II–597.

[311] The Community judicature has jurisdiction to hear and determine disputes between the European Investment Bank and its servants: see ECJ, Case 110/75 *Mills v EIB* [1976] E.C.R. 955, para.14; CFI, Case T–192/99 *Dunnett and Others v EIB* [2001] E.C.R. II–813, para.46. As far as the ECB is concerned, Art.36.2 of the Protocol on the Statute of the European System of Central Banks and of the European Central Bank provides that "The Court of Justice shall have jurisdiction in any dispute between the ECB and its servants within the limits and under the conditions laid down in the conditions of employment." The ECB argued that, under that provision, not the Court of First Instance (now the European Union Civil Service Tribunal), but the Court of Justice was the competent court to hear and determine disputes between the ECB and its staff. The Court of First Instance held, however, that the interpretation of that provision should not conflict with the general and uniform system of legal remedies for servants of the Community laid down by Decision 88/591 and based on Art.225 of the EC Treaty. The term "the Court of Justice" was therefore to be interpreted as referring to the Community judicature as a whole within the meaning of Art.7 of the EC Treaty and thus as including the Court of First Instance. Consequently, the Court of First Instance had jurisdiction to hear the dispute (CFI, Case C–333/99 *X v ECB* [2001] E.C.R.-SC I–A 199, II–921, paras 36–44). See concerning the European Aviation Safety Agency, CFI (judgment of May 4, 2005), T–30/04 *Sena v EASA*, not yet reported. The jurisdiction of the Court of First Instance may also extend to a "third pillar" body: see ECJ, Case C–160/03 *Spain v Eurojust* [2005] E.C.R. I–2077, para.42; CFI (judgment of March 1, 2005), Case T–143/03 *Smit v Europol*, not yet reported.

[312] ECJ, Case 175/73 *Union Syndicale, and Others v Council* [1974] E.C.R. 917, para.19; ECJ, Case 18/74 *Syndicat Général du Personnel des Organismes Européens v Commission* [1974] E.C.R. 933, para.15; ECJ, Joined Cases 193 and 194/87 *Maurissen and European Public Service Union v Court of Auditors* [1989] E.C.R. 1045, para.29; CFI (order of December 4, 1991), Case T–78/91 *Moat and TAO/AFI v Commission* [1991] E.C.R. II–1387, para.7.

[313] In accordance with the second para. of Art.40 of the Statute. See, by way of example, CFI, Case T–84/91 *Meskens v European Parliament* [1992] E.C.R. II–1565, para.9: trade-union organisations are widely allowed to intervene in staff cases where the decision is likely to affect a collective interest.

B. Defendants

Institutions. Actions are brought against the institution from which the act at issue emanated.[314] **18–011**

Body or agency. A staff member employed by a body or agency with legal personality in its own right has to bring his or her claim against that body or agency, not against a Community institution.[315] **18–012**

III. Special Characteristics

A. The requirement for a pre-litigation procedure

1. Course and time-limits

Complaints. Under Art.91(2) of the Staff Regulations, an appeal to the European Union Civil Service Tribunal will lie only if the applicant has previously submitted a complaint within the prescribed period to the appointing authority about the act allegedly adversely affecting him or her, and the complaint has been rejected by express or implied decision.[316] The aim of this pre-litigation procedure is to enable the dispute to be settled amicably. Consequently, the complaint must put the appointing authority in a position to know in sufficient detail the applicant's criticisms of the contested act.[317] **18–013**

The question whether the pre-litigation procedure was lawfully conducted may be inquired into by the European Union Civil Service Tribunal of its

---

[314] ECJ, Case 18/63 *Wollast (née Schmitz) v EEC* [1964] E.C.R. 85, at 96. *Cf.* CFI, Case T–177/94 *Altmann and Others v Commission* [1994] E.C.R.-SC II–969, paras 32–45 (action held inadmissible in so far as it was brought against JET, a joint undertaking within the meaning of Arts 46, 47 and 49 of the EAEC Treaty, and the JET Council).

[315] See n.311, *supra*.

[316] See, *e.g.* CFI (order of July 9, 2004), Case T–132/04 *Bonnet v Court of Justice*, not reported, paras 11–17. However, there is no obligation to submit a prior complaint against a decision of a selection board for a competition since the appointing authority has no power to annul or vary such a decision (see, *inter alia*, ECJ, Case 44/71 *Marcato v Commission* [1972] E.C.R. 427, paras 4–9; CFI, Case T–49/03 *Schumann v Commission* [2004] E.C.R.-SC II–1371, para.25). If the applicant nevertheless submits a prior complaint against a decision, it cannot be objected that his application is inadmissible for being out of time. An action against an act which is connected to another act against which the applicant lodged a complaint is admissible, even though the applicant did not submit a prior complaint in respect of the related act (ECJ, Case 806/79 *Gerin v Commission* [1980] E.C.R. 3515, at 3524).

[317] See, *inter alia*, ECJ, Case 58/75 *Sergy v Commission* [1976] E.C.R. 1139, para.32; ECJ, Case 133/88 *Del Amo Martinez v European Parliament* [1989] E.C.R. 689, para.9; CFI, Case T–57/89 *Alexandrakis v Commission* [1990] E.C.R. II–143, para.8. A "complaint" is an act whereby an official or servant specifically challenges an administrative measure which adversely affects him or her. It is necessary to give priority to the content of the document rather than its form or title (ECJ, Case C–154/99 P *Politi v European Training Foundation* [2000] E.C.R. I–5019, para.17). See also CFI (judgment of February 16, 2005), Case T–354/03 *Reggimenti v European Parliament*, not yet reported, paras 43 and 44. See also 18–017, *infra*.

own motion in considering whether the application made to it is admissible.[318] In this way the Tribunal will examine whether the time-limits prescribed by Arts 90 and 91 of the Staff Regulations were complied with in the course of the pre-litigation procedure and whether the complaint and the application to the Tribunal are consistent with each other.[319]

18–014 **Requests.** If a person to whom the Staff Regulations apply seeks to challenge an omission to take a decision relating to him or her, he or she must first submit a request to the appointing authority pursuant to Art.90(1) of the Staff Regulations for the decision in question to be taken.[320] The appointing authority then has four months, starting from the date on which the request was made, to notify the person concerned of its reasoned decision. If at the end of that period no reply to the request has been received, this will be deemed to constitute an implied decision rejecting the request. A complaint may be submitted against such a decision, just as in the case of a decision whose content is unfavourable to the person concerned.[321] The complaint

---

[318] *Alexandrakis v Commission*, cited in the preceding n., para.8; CFI (order of July 8, 2004), Case T–200/02 *Tsarnavas v Commission*, not reported, para.41.

[319] For an example relating to time-limits, see CFI (order of July 9, 1991), Case T–48/91 *Minic v Court of Auditors* [1991] E.C.R. II–479; as for whether the complaint and the application are consistent with each other, see CFI, Case T–57/89 *Alexandrakis v Commission* [1990] E.C.R. II–143, para.8.

[320] If he or she submits a "complaint" at the same time and then brings an action before the Court of First Instance (now the European Union Civil Service Tribunal) when it is rejected, that action will be inadmissible for infringing Art.90(1) and (2) of the Staff Regulations, see CFI (order of February 25, 1992), Case T–64/91 *Marcato v Commission* [1992] E.C.R. II–243, paras 31–46. If a person covered by the Staff Regulations wishes to bring an action for damages and the damage is caused by a decision adversely affecting him or her, he or she must submit a complaint pursuant to Art.90(2) of the Staff Regulations. If, in contrast, the damage originated in an administrative act which cannot be characterised as an act having adverse effect, the pre-litigation procedure must commence with a request, under Art.90(1) of the Staff Regulations, for compensation, which, if rejected, will have to be followed by a complaint against the rejection of the request: CFI, Case T–391/94 *Baiwir v Commission* [1996] E.C.R.-SC II–787, paras 45–48 (English abstract at I–A–269); CFI, Case T–500/93 *Y. v Court of Justice* [1996] E.C.R.-SC II–977 (English abstract at I–A–355). The request must be lodged within a reasonable time (see, in this connection, CFI, Case T–45/01 *Sanders v Commission* [2004] E.C.R.-SC II–1183, paras 59–85, and CFI, Case T–144/02 *Eagle and Others v Commission* [2004] E.C.R.-SC II–1231, paras 57–84). If there is a close link between an action for annulment and a claim for compensation, the compensation claim will be admissible as ancillary to the action for annulment and does not have to be preceded by a request to the appointing authority to make good the alleged damage, followed by a complaint directed against the implied or express rejection of that complaint: CFI, Case T–27/90 *Latham v Commission* [1991] E.C.R. II–35; CFI, Case T–44/93 *Saby v Commission* [1995] E.C.R.-SC II–541, para.31 (English abstract at I–A–175); CFI, Case T–140/94 *Gutiérrez de Quijano y Llorens v European Parliament* [1996] E.C.R.-SC II–689, para.54 (English abstract at I–A–241); CFI, Case T–238/02 *Barbosa Goncalves v Commission* [2004] E.C.R.-SC II–473, para.26.

[321] If the appointing authority has already taken a decision adversely affecting the official concerned, that official may no longer commence the pre-litigation procedure by submitting a request for a decision under Art.90(1) of the Staff Regulations, but must directly submit a complaint pursuant to Art.90(2): CFI, Case T–113/95 *Mancini v Commission* [1996] E.C.R.-SC II–543, para.28 (English abstract at I–A–239).

must be submitted to the appointing authority within three months. When time starts to run depends on the type of measure against which the complaint is brought.[322] The appointing authority then has four months from the date on which the complaint was lodged to notify its reasoned decision to the person concerned. If at the end of that period no reply to the complaint has been received, this will be deemed to constitute a decision rejecting the complaint. An action may be brought in the European Union Civil Service Tribunal against such a decision, just as in the case of an express rejection of a complaint.[323] This will only be the case, however, if an action will lie against the act in respect of which the complaint was submitted. The express or implied rejection of a complaint is in fact only confirmation of the "act" (express or implied) about which the person concerned complained and is, *per se*, not a challengeable act.[324]

2. Formal requirements

No requirement as to form. Requests for decisions and complaints are not subject to any requirement as to form.[325] Art.90 c of the Staff Regulations provides that requests and complaints must be lodged with the appointing authority entrusted with the exercise of powers. The institutions themselves may lay down procedures for the submission and processing of requests and complaints.[326]

18–015

3. Effects

Action before the European Union Civil Service Tribunal. If the pre-litigation procedure does not bring the dispute to an end, an action ("appeal") will lie to the European Union Civil Service Tribunal.[327] The

18–016

---

[322] Art.90(2) of the Staff Regulations determines when time starts running in each case. Failure to comply with the time-limit for submitting a complaint will inevitably result in a subsequent action being declared inadmissible: CFI (order of July 14, 1993), Case T–55/92 *Knijff v Court of Auditors* [1993] E.C.R. II–823. The question of admissibility will be raised by the Community judicature of its own motion (CFI, Case T–14/03 *Di Marzio v Commission* [2004] E.C.R.-SC II–167, para.37).

[323] Staff Regulations, Art.90(2), second subpara., and Art.91.

[324] ECJ, Joined Cases 33 and 75/79 *Kuhner v Commission* [1980] E.C.R. 1677, para.9; ECJ (order of June 16, 1988), Case 371/87 *Progoulis v Commission* [1988] E.C.R. 3081, para.17; CFI (order of June 7, 1991), Case T–14/91 *Weyrich v Commission* [1991] E.C.R. II–235, para.43; CFI, Case T–4/93 *André v Commission* [1994] E.C.R.-SC II–471, para.21 (English abstract at I–A–145); CFI, Case T–14/03 *Di Marzio v Commission* [2004] E.C.R.-SC II–167, para.54.

[325] ECJ, Case 54/77 *Herpels v Commission* [1978] E.C.R. 585, para.47; CFI, Case T–506/93 *Moat v Commission* [1995] E.C.R.-SC II–147, para.18; CFI, Case T–192/94 *Maurissen v Court of Auditors* [1996] E.C.R.-SC II–1229, para.31 (English abstract at I–A–425).

[326] *Commentaire Mégret*, at 322.

[327] Under Art.91(4) of the Staff Regulations, an applicant may bring an action before the European Union Civil Service Tribunal without awaiting the reply from the appointing authority, provided that he or she applies for interim measures at the same time. The proceedings in the principal action are then suspended until such time as the appointing authority has responded to the complaint.

action must be brought within three months.[328] Time starts running on the date of notification of the decision taken in response to the complaint or, in the case of an implied decision rejecting the complaint, on the date of expiry of the period of fourth months after the complaint was lodged.[329]

18–017 **Parallelism between the complaint and the application.** The prior complaint defines the subject-matter of the action to a negative extent only. The action may not extend the purpose or the subject-matter of the complaint, but may curtail them. Consequently, the subject-matter of the action is defined solely by the application, provided that it remains within the limits laid down by the complaint.[330] Generally, the complaint will not be drawn up by a lawyer and will be very informal, since it aims at achieving an amicable resolution of the dispute.[331] Consequently, it is sufficient if the pleas set out in the application emerge implicitly from the complaint[332] or are closely linked thereto if they do not appear as such in the complaint.[333] Provided that the subject-matter

---

[328] The question of admissibility will be raised by the Community judicature of its own motion (CFI, Case T–14/03 *Di Marzio v Commission* [2004] E.C.R.-SC II–167, para.37).

[329] Art.91(3) provides as follows: where a complaint is rejected by express decision after being rejected by implied decision but before the period for lodging an appeal to the Court of First Instance has expired, time for bringing court proceedings starts to run afresh (the date of adoption of the decision is relevant in this respect, not the date of its notification: CFI (order of December 6, 2004), Case T–55/02 *Finch v Commission* [2004] E.C.R.-SC II–1621, paras 46–49). That provision may not be invoked to the detriment of an applicant where the latter has already brought an action and the defendant institution seeks to remedy, by means of a late, reasoned rejection of the complaint, the fact that the act adversely affecting the applicant entirely lacked any statement of reasons, see CFI, Case T–52/90 *Volger v European Parliament* [1992] E.C.R. II–121, paras 31–42, upheld by ECJ, Case C–115/92 P *European Parliament v Volger* [1993] E.C.R. I–6549, paras 22–24. Where an express decision rejecting a complaint is taken after the period for lodging an appeal has run out, time does not start running afresh; although the express decision makes it clear why the complaint was rejected, it constitutes merely confirmation of the implied decision rejecting the complaint: ECJ (order of June 25, 1998), Case C–312/97 P *Fichtner v Commission* [1998] E.C.R. I–4135, paras 16–17, dismissing an appeal against CFI (order of July 9, 1997), Case T–63/96 *Fichtner v Commission* [1997] E.C.R. II–563 (English abstract at I-A–189). Where the applicable rules of a functionally autonomous body—such as the EIB—lay down no time-limit for bringing actions relating to disputes between staff and that body, the Court of First Instance has decided that actions must be brought within a reasonable time having regard to the rules laid down in the Staff Regulations. In reaching this conclusion, the Court of First Instance weighed the entitlement of those subject to its jurisdiction to effective protection by the courts, which implies that such persons must have a sufficient period of time available to them, against the need for legal certainty which requires that, after a certain time, measures taken by Community bodies become definitive (CFI, Case T–192/99 *Dunnett and Others v EIB* [2001] E.C.R. II–813, paras. 44–58).

[330] CFI, Case T–134/89 *Hettrich and Others v Commission* [1990] E.C.R. II–565, para.16; CFI (judgment of May 4, 2005), Case T–144/03 *Schmit v Commission*, not yet reported, paras 90–93.

[331] However, the complaint may be lodged by a lawyer acting on behalf of his or her client, see CFI, Case T–139/89 *Virgili-Schettini v European Parliament* [1990] E.C.R. II–535.

[332] ECJ, Case 184/80 *Van Zaanen v Court of Auditors* [1981] E.C.R. 1951, para.13.

[333] See, *inter alia*, ECJ, Case 133/88 *Del Amo Martinez v European Parliament* [1989] E.C.R. 689, para.10; CFI, Case T–57/89 *Alexandrakis v Commission* [1990] E.C.R. II–143, para.9; CFI, Case T–2/90 *Ferreira de Freitas v Commission* [1991] E.C.R. II–103, para.41; CFI, Case T–312/02 *Gussetti v Commission* [2004] E.C.R.-SC II–547, para.47.

and the grounds of the complaint are not altered, the application and the pleas adduced in support of it will be admissible.[334] The test is whether an open-minded assessment of the complaint carried out by the appointing authority would have enabled it to know the heads of complaint set out in the application to the Court in order to reach an amicable settlement of the dispute.[335] If the heads of complaint, from the point of view of their subject-matter and purpose, remain the same in the complaint and the application, the application will be admissible, even if those heads of complaint are given a more legal character in pleas and arguments which were not raised as such in the complaint.[336]

Furthermore, according to the case-law, a claim for compensation for damage arising out of the contested act may be made even if no mention was made of it in the complaint. This flexible approach is attributable to the close link between such a claim and the complaint made against the contested act.[337]

B. PRIORITY OF AN ACTION BROUGHT UNDER ART.236 OF THE EC TREATY

Exclusive jurisdiction. Any dispute arising out of the employment relation-   **18–018**
ship bctwccn a person and the Community must if necessary be brought
before the Community judicature in accordance with the conditions prescribed by Art.236 of the EC Treaty and Arts 90 and 91 of the Staff
Regulations. No other judicial procedure may be used for this purpose.[338]

---

[334] ECJ, Joined Cases 75 and 117/82 *Razzouk and Beydoun v Commission* [1984] E.C.R. 1509, para.9.

[335] See, *e.g.*, CFI, Case T–312/02 *Gussetti v Commission* [2004] E.C.R.-SC II–547, para.47. A plea which the Community judicature can raise of its own motion (such as lack of a statement of reasons) will always be admissible even if it is not raised in the complaint (CFI, Case T–325/02 *Soubies v Commission* [2004] E.C.R.-SC II–1067, para.30).

[336] For a case in which this condition was not satisfied at least as regards one of the pleas raised, see CFI, Case T–4/92 *Vardakas v Commission* [1993] E.C.R. II–357, paras 16–17. See also CFI, Case T–588/93 *G v Commission* [1994] E.C.R.-SC II–875, paras 27–30 (English abstract at I–A-277); CFI, Case T–361/94 *Weir v Commission* [1996] E.C.R.-SC II–381, para.32 (English abstract at I–A-121).

[337] ECJ, Case 224/87 *Koutchoumoff v Commission* [1989] E.C.R. 99; ECJ, Case 126/87 *Del Plato v Commission* [1987] E.C.R. 643; CFI, Case T–44/93 *Saby v Commission* [1995] E.C.R.-SC II–541, para.28 (English abstract at I–A-175); CFI, Case T–238/02 *Barbosa Goncalves v Commission* [2004] E.C.R.-SC II–473, para.26.

[338] ECJ, Case 9/75 *Meyer-Burckhardt v Commission* [1975] E.C.R. 1171, para.7; CFI (order of July 11, 1996), Case T–30/96 *Gomes de Sá Pereira v Council* [1996] E.C.R. II–785, paras 24–26. Even if the legality of a recruitment procedure initiated by a Community institution may depend on whether certain acts of the national authorities, to which that institution has turned, are themselves lawful (where, for instance, the Community institution asks the Member State concerned to present suitable candidates for appointment as members of the temporary staff), it is for the person aggrieved to exercise, within the time-limits laid down by the Staff Regulations, the remedies provided for in the Staff Regulations, even if only as a precautionary measure: ECJ, Case C–246/95 *Coen* [1997] E.C.R. I–403, para.22. *Cf.* CFI (order of the President of June 21, 1999), Case T–107/99 R *García Retortillo v Council* [1999] E.C.R. II–1939, IA-107, II–591, para.45. The President of the Court of First Instance held

The subject-matter of the application determines whether it has to be regarded as a "staff case".[339] Accordingly, an action brought by members of an official's family pursuant to Arts 235 and 288 of the EC Treaty for compensation for damage suffered by them personally as a result of effects of "the conduct of an institution" on the career of the official in question will be inadmissible on the ground that the official himself was "in a position to avail himself of the opportunities afforded by the Treaty to challenge any decision of the institution concerned".[340]

IV. CONSEQUENCES

18–019 **Decision of the European Union Civil Service Tribunal.** Depending upon the purpose and outcome of the proceedings, the European Union Civil Service Tribunal may dismiss the application, annul the contested act, award damages—together, in a proper case, with default interest—and, in disputes of a financial nature, impose such measures as it may grant in the exercise of its unlimited jurisdiction. However, the Tribunal may not substitute itself for the institution party to the proceedings; at the most, it may provide "guidance" as to the measures to be taken in order to comply with its judgment.[341] At the same time, it must make sure that the scope of the operative part of its judgment emerges clearly from the grounds in conjunction with which it must be read. This is a corollary of the obligation weighing on the Community judicature to state reasons for its decisions.[342]

18–020 **Costs.** The European Union Civil Service Tribunal rules on the costs. Subject to the specific provisions of the Rules of Procedure, the unsuccessful party will be ordered to pay the costs.[343] It remains to be seen whether the European Union Civil Service Tribunal will incorporate in its Rules of Procedure a provision similar to Art.88 of the CFI Rules of Procedure, which

---

that an action brought under Art.236 of the EC Treaty against Council Decision 1999/307 integrating the Schengen secretariat into the general secretariat of the Council was manifestly inadmissible on the ground that the applicant was neither an official nor a temporary official and therefore ought to have brought her action under Art.230 of the EC Treaty.

[339] See, in this connection, CFI, Case T–45/01 *Sanders v Commission* [2004] E.C.R.-SC II–1183, paras 42–54; CFI, Case T–144/02 *Eagle and Others v Commission* [2004] E.C.R.-SC II–1231, paras 40–52; CFI (judgment of March 8, 2005), Case T–277/03 *Vlachaki v Commission*, not yet reported, paras 29–39.

[340] ECJ (order of May 7, 1980), Joined Cases 114–117/79 *Fournier v Commission* [1980] E.C.R. 1529, at 1531. See also CFI (order of June 14, 1995), Joined Cases T–462, T–464 and T–470/93 *Lenz v Commission*, not reported, paras 55–59.

[341] ECJ, Case 225/82 *Verzyck v Commission* [1983] E.C.R. 1991, paras 19–20; CFI, Case T–37/89 *Hanning v European Parliament* [1990] E.C.R. II–463, para.79; CFI, Case T–588/93 *G v Commission* [1994] E.C.R.-SC II–875, para.26; *cf.* CFI, Case T–73/89 *Barbi v Commission* [1990] E.C.R. II–619, para.38.

[342] Opinion of Advocate General W. van Gerven in ECJ, Case C–242/90 P *Commission v Albani and Others* [1993] E.C.R. I–3839, at I–3861–3862.

[343] Statute, Annex I, Art.7(5).

provides that, in proceedings between the Communities and their servants, the institutions are to bear their own costs, irrespective of the outcome.[344]

Appeal. An appeal, limited to points of law, may be brought before the Court of First Instance, within two months of notification of the decision appealed against, against final decisions of the European Union Civil Service Tribunal and decisions of that Tribunal disposing of the substantive issues in part only or disposing of a procedural issue concerning a plea of lack of jurisdiction or inadmissiblity. Such an appeal may be brought by any party which has been unsuccessful, in whole or in part, in its submissions. However, interveners other than the Member States and the institutions of the Communities may bring such an appeal only where the decision of the European Union Civil Service Tribunal directly affects them.[345]   **18–021**

Review. Decisions taken by the Court of First Instance upon appeal in cases for which the European Union Civil Service Tribunal has jurisdiction at first instance may, exceptionally, be reviewed by the Court of Justice where there is a serious risk of the unity or consistency of Community law being affected.[346]   **18–022**

V. THE CONSTITUTION

General. Art.III–372 of the Constitution reproduces virtually verbatim Art.236 of the EC Treaty by providing that "[t]he Court of Justice of the European Union shall have jurisdiction in any dispute between the Union and its servants within the limits and under the conditions laid down in the Staff Regulations of Officials and the Conditions of Employment of other servants of the Union".   **18–023**

---

[344] The applicant, however, may be ordered to pay the institution's costs which he or she unreasonably or vexatiously caused it to incur: see CFI (judgment of October 5, 2005), Case T–203/03 *Rasmussen v Commission*, not yet reported, paras 88–89. For costs in appeals against decisions of the Court of First Instance in staff cases in the period before the European Union Civil Service Tribunal was established, see Art.122, second para., of the ECJ Rules of Procedure: if the official (or the person treated as an official) unsuccessfully appeals, he or she will in principle have to pay the respondent institution's costs. For examples, see ECJ (order of March 20, 1991), Case C–115/90 P *Turner v Commission* [1991] E.C.R. I–1423, para.15; ECJ, Case C–283/90 P *Vidrányi v Commission* [1991] E.C.R. I–4339, para.34.

[345] EC Treaty, Art.225(2), first subpara.; Statute, Annex I, Arts 9 and 10; CFI Rules of Procedure, Arts 113–149.

[346] EC Treaty, Art.225(2), second subpara.; see Ch.17, *supra*.

CHAPTER 19

JURISDICTION OF THE COMMUNITY COURT TO GIVE JUDGMENT PURSUANT TO AN ARBITRATION CLAUSE OR A SPECIAL AGREEMENT

I. ART.238 OF THE EC TREATY

A. SUBJECT-MATTER

1. General

19–001 **Arbitration clause.** Under Art.282 of the EC Treaty, the Community, which has legal personality,[347] enjoys the most extensive legal capacity accorded to legal persons under national law. The Community's participation in legal transactions may give rise to disputes having to be decided judicially. Art.238 of the EC Treaty authorises the Community and parties contracting with it to confer jurisdiction over such disputes on the Community Court pursuant to an arbitration clause contained in a contract governed by private or public law concluded by or on behalf of the Community.[348] In the absence of such a clause, the national courts have jurisdiction under national law to settle any disputes.[349]

---

[347] EC Treaty, Art.281.

[348] See also EAEC Treaty, Art.153.

[349] EC Treaty, Art.240. In the absence of an arbitration clause, the Court of Justice or the Court of First Instance lacks jurisdiction to rule on any liability in contract where one of the parties brings an action for non-contractual liability under Art.235 of the EC Treaty. In that event, the fact that the parties have brought their dispute before the Court of Justice or the Court of First Instance cannot be regarded as an expression of their intention to confer on the Court jurisdiction over disputes arising out of an agreement: CFI (order of July 18, 1997), Case T–180/95 *Nutria v Commission* [1997] E.C.R. II–1317, paras 37–40. Moreover, a party cannot unilaterally circumvent the division of jurisdiction between the Community Court and the national courts by causing the Community institution concerned to reject its request for compensation and then describing that rejection as a decision within the meaning of Art.230 of the EC Treaty: CFI (order of July 18, 1997), Case T–44/96 *Oleifici Italiani v Commission* [1997] E.C.R. II–1331, para.44; CFI (order of October 3, 1997), Case T–186/96 *Mutual Aid Administration Services v Commission* [1997] E.C.R. II–1633, para.44; CFI (order of May 10, 2004) Joined Cases T–314/03 and T–378/03 *Musée Grévin v Commission* [2004] E.C.R. II–1421, paras 79–89. *Cf.*, however, CFI, Case T–26/00 *Lecureur*

As from June 1, 2004, all claims brought under Art.238 of the EC Treaty are to be brought before the Court of First Instance (see 19–008, *infra*).

Objective. There are a number of grounds which may prompt the conclu-   **19–002** sion of an arbitration clause. The Court of First Instance constitutes the meeting place of a number of legal cultures, as a result of which it may be regarded as suitable forum for determining a dispute relating to an international contract. What is more, an arbitration clause is a means of avoiding a national court's adjudicating on a dispute in which important Community interests are at stake. The Community may also want to bring any disputes before its natural court under a procedure with which it is familiar.[350]

2. What contracts are concerned?

Contract concluded by or on behalf of the Community. As has already   **19–003** been noted, the Community Court may have jurisdiction to give judgment pursuant to an arbitration clause "contained in a contract concluded by or on behalf of the Community, whether that contract be governed by public or private law". Decided cases have not yet made it clear what is meant by a public-law contract in this context. What may be meant is agreements concluded by the Community with Member States, with third countries or with international organisations (whether or not in the form of a convention) and administrative agreements concluded with individuals.[351] Private-law contracts comprise all contracts into which the Community enters as a party to normal legal transactions.

Institutions or bodies. The stipulation that the contracts may be concluded   **19–004** "on behalf of the Community" undoubtedly means that entities which are not institutions or bodies of the Community may nevertheless include an arbitration clause in a contract concluded by them on behalf of the Community.[352]

---

v Commission [2001] E.C.R. II–2623, paras 37–39, in which the Court of First Instance held that Art.24 of Regulation (EC) No 2519/97, which provides that the Court of Justice is to be competent to resolve any dispute resulting from the implementation or the non-implementation or from the interpretation of the rules governing supply operations carried out in accordance with that regulation, formed an integral part of the supply contract concluded on the basis of that regulation and therefore had to be regarded as an arbitration clause. See to the same effect CFI, Joined Cases T–215/01, T–220/01 and R–221/01 *Calberson v Commission* [2004] E.C.R. II–587, paras 11 and 81–88; CFI (order of June 9, 2005), Case T–265/03 *Helm Düngemittel v Commission*, not yet reported, para 46.

[350] Kremlis, "De quelques clauses d'élection de for et de droit applicable stipulées dans des contrats de droit privé conclus par les Communautés européennes dans le cadre de leurs activités d'emprunt et de prêt" (1986) Diritto comunitario e degli scambi internazionali 777.

[351] For further details, see Bleckmann, "Die öffentlichrechtlichen Verträge der EWG" (1978) N.J.W. 464–467.

[352] *Cf. Commentaire Mégret*, at 377.

3. Nature and extent of the Court's jurisdiction pursuant to an arbitration clause

19–005   **Term is misleading.** The expression "arbitration clause" employed in Art.238 of the EC Treaty is misleading. Where the Court of First Instance gives judgment pursuant to an "arbitration clause", it acts, not as an arbitrator, but as a court giving judgments which may be directly enforced.

19–006   **Powers of national courts.** The arbitration clause may or may not give the Community Court exclusive jurisdiction. If the clause confers an exclusive right on the Court to hear and determine disputes, courts in Member States must decline jurisdiction by reason of the primacy of Community law (*i.e.* compliance with the arbitration clause concluded pursuant to Art.238 of the EC Treaty). If a number of courts, including the Court of First Instance, are entitled to determine disputes under the arbitration clause, a problem of *lis alibi pendens* may arise. No specific rules exist for resolving this problem.

19–007   **Extent of jurisdiction of the Court of First Instance.** The extent of the Court's jurisdiction emerges from the arbitration clause itself.[353] Because that jurisdiction is conferred by derogation from the ordinary rules of law, it must be construed very narrowly.[354] Only claims and pleas arising from the contract containing the arbitration clause or directly connected therewith may be entertained.[355] Consequently, a claim based on the other party's having been unduly enriched inevitably falls outside the scope of the contractual relations between the parties. This means that the Court of First Instance has no jurisdiction to entertain such a claim pursuant to an

---

[353] See, by way of example, ECJ, Case 1/56 *Bourgaux v Common Assembly* [1954 to 1956] E.C.R. 361, at 367. The Court may inquire into whether the contract incorporating the arbitration clause has been rescinded under the law applicable to the contract (ECJ, Case C–274/97 *Commission v Coal Products* [2000] E.C.R. I–3175, paras 17–18).

[354] ECJ, Case C–114/94 *IDE v Commission* [1997] E.C.R. I–803, para.82.

[355] ECJ, Case 426/85 *Commission v Zoubek* [1986] E.C.R. 4057, para.11; ECJ, Case C–337/96 *Commission v IRACO* [1998] E.C.R. I–7943, para.49. It is possible that the Court would take cognisance of a cluster of contracts concluded by the parties on the basis of an arbitration clause contained in only one (or some) of the contracts. In *Porta v Commission*, the applicant had concluded contracts, each for a term of one year, over a number of years with the director of the Community's research centre in Ispra to teach at the centre's school. Initially, the contract was only oral, but subsequently it was reduced to writing, whereupon an arbitration clause was added. The Court of Justice held that that arbitration clause entitled it to have regard to all the contracts entered into between Mrs Porta and the Commission; see ECJ, Case 109/81 *Porta v Commission* [1982] E.C.R. 2469, para.10. The Court may adjudicate under an arbitration clause on a claim for damages for non-performance of the contract based on the law applicable to the contract which provides for such compensation (ECJ, Case C–69/97 *Commission v SNUA* [1999] E.C.R. I–2363, paras 35–36).

arbitration clause.[356] In contrast, counterclaims made by the defendant which are directly based on the contract are admissible.[357]

B. IDENTITY OF THE PARTIES

Any party to the contract. Any party bound by the contract embodying the arbitration clause has the right to bring a dispute before the Community Court.[358] Before June 1, 2004, the situation was that, in the case of a contract concluded between the Community and a natural or legal person, disputes could be brought before either the Court of Justice or the Court of First Instance depending on whether the applicant was the Community or an individual. The Court of Justice had jurisdiction if the Community initiated the proceedings[359]; the Court of First Instance if they were brought by an individual.[360] This split jurisdiction had the result that a private party which was a defendant in proceedings brought before the Court of Justice by the Community pursuant to an arbitration clause had only one chance of putting over its defence, whereas if the Community was the defendant in

19–008

---

[356] ECJ, Case C–330/88 *Grifoni v EAEC* [1991] E.C.R. I–1045, para.20. The President of the Court of First Instance held that that court had no jurisdiction to entertain proceedings relating to the termination by the Commission of a contract concluded with an organisation which included a term conferring jurisdiction over disputes relating to the performance of the contract on the courts of Brussels. The applicant argued that the jurisdiction of the courts of Brussels concerned only disputes relating to the performance of the contract, not the Commission's decision to terminate the contract itself. The President of the Court of First Instance dismissed this argument on the ground that there was a direct connection between the contract and the dispute: CFI (order of the President of July 20, 2000), Case T–149/00 R *Innova v Commission* [2000] E.C.R. II–2941, para.21.

[357] ECJ, Case C–114/94 *IDE v Commission* [1997] E.C.R. I–803, paras 82–83. In CFI (order of November 25, 2003), Case T–85/01 *IAMA Consulting v Commission* [2003] E.C.R. II–4973, para.62, the Court of First Instance (which at that time could only hear actions brought by natural and legal persons) referred a counterclaim brought by the Commission to the Court of Justice after the Court of First Instance had determined that the applicant's main claim was inadmissible. However, the Court of Justice referred the case back to the Court of First Instance (ECJ (order of May 27, 2004), Case C–517/03 *IAMA Consulting v Commission*, not reported. It did this on the ground that it is implicit in the jurisdiction of the Court of First Instance to entertain the main claim that it also has jurisdiction to entertain a counterclaim.

[358] There is nothing to prevent a party to a contract from assigning his or her rights to a successor. For an example, see ECJ, Case C–209/90 *Commission v Feilhauer* [1992] E.C.R. I–2613, para.5.

[359] ECJ, Case C–356/99 *Commission v Hitesys* [2000] E.C.R. I–9517.

[360] An application brought in the Court of Justice by an individual pursuant to an arbitration clause was referred by that court to the Court of First Instance: see CFI, Case T–10/98 *E-Quattro v Commission* [1999] E.C.R. II–1811, paras 8–9. Where, with regard to the same contract, the Community brought proceedings in the Court of Justice and the individual concerned brought proceedings in the Court of First Instance, the Court of Justice referred the case before it to the Court of First Instance as a counterclaim. See, however, ECJ (order of November 21, 2003), Case C–280/03 *Commission v European Economic Interest Grouping Lior and Others*, not reported, para.9, in which the Court of Justice did not regard the Commission's claim as a counterclaim on the grounds that it had been lodged two years after the proceedings had been initiated in the Court of First Instance and that the claim brought before the Court of Justice was directed not only against the applicant in the proceedings before the Court of First Instance but also against other undertakings.

proceedings brought by a natural or legal person, it might have a second chance, if it lost, by appealing against the decision of the Court of First Instance. This lack of symmetry in contracting parties' position as litigants was brought to an end by the entry into force of Council Decision 2004/407/ EC, Euratom of April 26, 2004, which amended Art.51 of the Statute of the Court of Justice.[361] All claims brought under Art.238 of the EC Treaty are henceforward to be brought before the Court of First Instance.[362]

19–009 **Legal capacity of the parties.** An action against a company is inadmissible if, when the action is brought, that company had neither the legal capacity nor the standing to be a party to legal proceedings. An action brought against a dissolved company will thus be inadmissible. Similarly, an action brought against a party against which insolvency proceedings have been instituted will also be inadmissible.[363]

C. SPECIAL CHARACTERISTICS

1. Requirements relating to validity

19–010 **Assessment of validity.** The Treaty does not lay down any particular wording to be used in an arbitration clause. Accordingly, any wording which indicates that the parties intend to remove any dispute between them from the purview of the national courts and to submit them to the Community courts must be regarded as sufficient to give the latter jurisdiction under Art.238 of the EC Treaty.[364]

The validity of the arbitration clause is adjudged exclusively on the basis of Art.238 of the EC Treaty and Art.44(5a) of the CFI Rules of Procedure, under which the application must be accompanied by a copy of the arbitration clause. The Court pays no regard to special requirements laid down by the national law applicable to the contract.[365] For the same reason, a court or an administrative authority in a Member State cannot refuse to give effect to the judgment of the Court of First Instance on the ground that the Court's jurisdiction is based on an arbitration clause which is invalid under national law.

2. Applicable law

19–011 **Choice of parties.** In the absence of a Community applicable law, the Community Court must identify the applicable law of its own authority. The Court respects the parties' choice of applicable law, whether express or

---

[361] See 1–051, *supra*.
[362] EC Treaty, Art.225(1), and Statute, Art.51.
[33] ECJ, Case C–294/02 *Commission v AMI Semiconductor Belgium and Others* [2005] E.C.R. I– 2175, paras 60 and 66–72.
[364] *Ibid.*, para.50.
[365] ECJ, Case 23/76 *Pellegrini and Others v Commission* [1976] E.C.R. 1807, paras 8–10; ECJ, Case C–209/90 *Commission v Feilhauer* [1992] E.C.R. I–2613, paras 12–14; ECJ, Case C–299/93 *Bauer v Commission* [1995] E.C.R. I–839, para.11 (Art.153 of the EAEC Treaty applied in the same way).

implied,[366] provided that this does not detract from the scope and effectiveness of Community law.[367] In the absence of such a choice, the Rome Convention of June 19, 1980 on the law applicable to contractual obligations is a possible source of inspiration, apart from the general private international law of the Member States.

3. Procedure before the Court

Procedure relating to direct actions. The procedure ordinarily applied to direct actions is used for the determination of disputes under an arbitration clause.

19–012

D. CONSEQUENCES

Judgment is enforceable. A judgment given by the Court of First Instance pursuant to Art.238 of the EC Treaty is enforceable under Arts 244 and 256 of that Treaty in the same way as any other judgment. An appeal may be brought before the Court of Justice.

19–013

E. THE CONSTITUTION

General. Art.III–374 of the Constitution reproduces virtually verbatim Art.238 of the EC Treaty by providing that "[t]he Court of Justice of the European Union shall have jurisdiction to give judgment pursuant to any arbitration clause contained in a contract concluded by or on behalf of the Union, whether that contract be governed by public or private law".

19–014

II. ART.239 OF THE EC TREATY

Disputes between Member States. Art.239 of the EC Treaty[368] allows Member States to conclude a special agreement to refer any dispute between them relating to the subject-matter of the Treaty to the Court of Justice. To date, the Member States have not availed themselves of this facility.

19–015

Art.239 *juncto* Art.292 of the EC Treaty. In the light of Art.292 of the EC Treaty,[369] which puts Member States under an obligation not to submit a dispute concerning the interpretation or application of that Treaty to any

19–16

---

[366] ECJ, Case 318/81 *Commission v CO.DE.MI.* [1985] E.C.R. 3693, paras 18–22; ECJ, Case 220/85 *Fadex v Commission* [1986] E.C.R. 3387, para.10; *Commission v Feilhauer*, cited in the preceding n., para.3, and para.16.
[367] ECJ, Joined Cases C–80/99 to C–82/99 *Flemmer and Others* [2001] E.C.R. I–7211, para.57.
[368] Constitution, Art.III–375(3), reproduces virtually verbatim Art.239 of the EC Treaty.
[369] Constitution, Art.III–375(2), reproduces virtually verbatim Art.292 of the EC Treaty.

method of settlement other than those provided for therein,[370] Art.239 is not an optional provision. Once a dispute arises relating to "the interpretation or application" of the Treaty which the Member States have no other way of bringing before the Court of Justice, Art.292 obliges them to conclude a special agreement within the meaning of Art.239 which confers jurisdiction on the Court to resolve the dispute.[371]

---

[370] The only example to date is pending Case C–459/03 *Commission v Ireland*, in which the Commission argues that, by submitting a dispute with the United Kingdom to an arbitrator outside the Community legal order, Ireland is in breach of the exclusive jurisdiction of the Court of Justice laid down in Art.292 of the EC Treaty. The Commission submits that Ireland initiated the procedure against the UK without taking account of the fact that the European Community is a party to the United Nations Convention on the Law of the Sea. It is also submitted that the provisions of the Convention relied on by Ireland together with a number of Community acts are provisions of Community law ([2004] O.J. C7/24).

[371] *Commentaire Mégret*, at 381; see also Cazala, "La contestation de la compétence exclusive de la Cour de Justice des Communautés européennes" (2004) R.T.D.E. 521–524.

CHAPTER 20

JURISDICTION OF THE COMMUNITY COURT OVER DISPUTES RELATING TO INTELLECTUAL PROPERTY RIGHTS

I. Subject-Matter

Community intellectual property rights. The Community created Community intellectual property rights by three regulations adopted on the basis of Art.308 of the EC Treaty. The Community trade mark was introduced by Council Regulation (EC) No 40/94 of December 20, 1993, as amended by Council Regulation (EC) No 422/2004 of February 19, 2004.[372] Community plant variety rights were introduced by Council Regulation (EC) No 2100/94 of July 27, 1994, as amended by Council Regulation (EC) No 2506/95 of October 25, 1995.[373] Community designs were introduced by Council Regulation (EC) No 6/2002 of December 12, 2001.[374]

20–001

These intellectual property rights are conferred by Community bodies especially set up for the purpose. Community trade marks are granted by the Office for Harmonisation in the Internal Market (Trade Marks and Designs) (OHIM), whilst Community plant variety rights are conferred by the Community Plant Variety Office. The two Offices may also declare intellectual property rights falling within their jurisdiction null and void or cancel them and take decisions on observations or objections submitted by third parties.

---

[372] 1994 O.J. L11/1; 2004 O.J. L70/1.

[373] 1994 O.J. L227/1; 1995 O.J. L258/3; the amendment relates to Art.73 of the original regulation, which governs the system of actions brought in the Court of Justice against decisions of the Boards of Appeal. According to the third recital in the preamble to Regulation No 2506/95, the amendment is intended to "ensure coherence of the system of appeal procedures to the Community jurisdiction in the different fields of industrial and commercial property". To this end, Regulation No 2506/95 aligns the rules on actions which may be brought against decisions of the Community Plant Variety Office with those provided for by Regulation No 40/94 on the Community trade mark (Art.63 of the latter regulation is essentially identical to the new Art.73 of Regulation No 2100/94, as amended by Regulation No 2506/95).

[374] Council Regulation (EC) No 6/2002 of December 12, 2001 on Community designs (2002 O.J. L3/1). See Kaesmacher and Duez, "Le nouveau règlement (C.E.) n° 6/2002 sur les dessins ou modèles communautaires" (2002) J.T.D.E. 185–191.

493

20–002 **System of legal protection.** Each of those regulations introduces a specific system of legal protection which safeguards the rights of parties affected by the Offices' decisions and takes account of the specific characteristics of intellectual property rights. One or more Boards of Appeal have been set up at the two Offices to which appeals may be brought against the decisions of other authorities of the relevant Office.[375] Accordingly, as far as the Community trade mark is concerned, an appeal may be brought before the Boards of Appeal[376] against decisions of the examiners (who are responsible for taking decisions in relation to an application for registration of a Community trade mark)[377], decisions of the Opposition Divisions (which are responsible for taking decisions on an opposition to an application to register a Community trade mark)[378], decisions of the Administration of Trade Marks and Legal Division (which is responsible for matters not attributed to other divisions, in particular relating to the particulars to be included in the registry of Community trade marks[379]) and decisions of the Cancellation Divisions (which are responsible for taking decisions in relation to an application for the revocation or declaration of invalidity of a Community trade mark[380]). An appeal may be brought against decisions of the Boards of Appeal in the Court of First Instance.[381]

20–003 **Jurisdiction to annul or alter the contested decision.** The Court of First Instance may annul or alter a contested decision.[382] As a result, in addition to its power to annul a decision of a Board of Appeal, the Court of First

---

[375] Under Art.67 of Regulation No 2100/94, appeals will lie against a declaration that a Community plant variety right is null and void (Art.20), the cancellation of such a right (Art.21), decisions concerning objections lodged against the grant of such a right (Art.59), the refusal of applications for a right (Art.61), the grant of a Community plant variety right (Art.62), the approval and amendment of a variety denomination (Arts 63 and 66), decisions concerning the fees payable under Art.83 and costs under Art.85, the registration and deregistration of particulars in the registers under Art.87 and public inspection under Art.88. The Office may grant compulsory exploitation rights under Art.29 and may in certain circumstances grant exploitation rights to a person not being the holder of the relevant plant variety right under Art.100(2). Decisions under Arts 29 and 100(2) may also be challenged before the Boards of Appeal or be the subject of a direct appeal to the Court of First Instance under Art.74(1).

Under Arts 55 and 106 of Regulation No 6/2002, an appeal will lie from decisions of the examiners (Art.103 empowers the examiners to take decisions in relation to an application for registration of a Community design), the Administration of Trade Marks and Designs and Legal Division and Invalidity Divisions (responsible under Art.104(2) for taking those decisions which do not fall within the competence of an examiner or an Invalidity Division) and the Invalidity Division (responsible under Art.105 for taking decisions in relation to applications for declarations of invalidity of registered Community designs).

[376] Regulation No 40/94, Art.57.
[377] Regulation No 40/94, Art.126.
[378] Regulation No 40/94, Art.127.
[379] Regulation No 40/94, Art.128.
[380] Regulation No 40/94, Art.129.
[381] Art.63 of Regulation No 40/94, Art.73 of Regulation No 2100/94 and Art.61 of Regulation No 6/2002. Those provisions confer jurisdiction on the "Court of Justice". By virtue of Art.225(1) of the EC Treaty and Art.51 of the Statute, this jurisdiction is to be exercised by the Court of First Instance.
[382] *Ibid.*

Instance is vested with a form of unlimited jurisdiction to alter the Board's decision and replace it with its own.[383] When exercising its power to amend a decision of the Office for Harmonisation in the Internal Market, the Court of First Instance may annul, not only the contested decision, but also the decision of the Opposition Division.[384]

Limits to the Court's jurisdiction. The Court of First Instance may exercise its jurisdiction to annul or alter only where the Office has taken a decision.[385] Where the Office has not processed a claim or a application, the Court of First Instance is not empowered to consider whether the claim is well founded for the first time.[386] Accordingly, the Court is not empowered to consider whether a trade mark applied for has distinctive character in consequence of the use which has been made of it[387] where that argument was not raised before the Board of Appeal.[388]   **20–004**

II. IDENTITY OF THE PARTIES

A. THE DEFENDANT

The Office is the defendant. As has already been mentioned, an appeal will lie to the Court of First Instance against decisions of the Offices' Boards of Appeal. Nevertheless, the Boards of Appeal of these Community agencies are not the defendants in proceedings before the Court, rather the Offices themselves. It should be noted in this connection that although the members of the Boards of Appeal are independent and not bound by any instructions, they constitute an integral part of the relevant Office and hence a decision of a Board of Appeal is ascribed to the Office to which it   **20–005**

---

[383] For cases in which the contested decision was altered, see CFI, Case T–292/01 *Philips-Van Heusen v OHIM* [2003] E.C.R. II–4335; CFI (judgment of June 15, 2005), Case T–7/04 *Shaker di L. Laudato & C. Sas v OHIM*, not yet reported.

[384] CFI (judgment of July 8, 2004), Case T–334/01 *MFE Marienfelde v OHIM*, not yet reported.

[385] Decisions may be annulled or altered only where they contain a substantive or procedural irregularity: see CFI, Case T–247/01 *eCopy v OHIM* (ECOPY) [2002] E.C.R. II–5301, para.46; CFI (judgment of November 23, 2004), Case T–360/03 *Frischpack v OHIM*, not yet reported, para.25.

[386] CFI, Case T–323/00 *SAT.1 v OHIM (SAT.2)* [2002] E.C.R. II–2839, para.18, where the Court of First Instance held that the possibility to alter the contested decision is, in principle, restricted to situations in which the case has reached a stage permitting final judgment. That is not so where the Board of Appeal has failed to rule on the merits of an entire head of claim.

[387] Regulation No 40/94, Art.7(3).

[388] CFI, Case T–30/00 *Henkel v OHIM (Representation of detergent)* [2001] E.C.R. II–2663, para.66; CFI, Case T–337/99 *Henkel v OHIM (Red and white round tablet)* [2001] E.C.R. II–2597, para.62.

belongs in the course of proceedings before the Court.[389] A Board of Appeal therefore cannot be regarded as being a "court or tribunal".[390]

20–006 **Forms of order which may be sought by the Office.** In the judgment of December 12, 2002 in *Vedial*, the Court of First Instance held that the Office was not entitled to ask the Court to alter or annul a contested decision of a Board of Appeal.[391] The Court of First Instance referred in this connection to the fact that the Boards of Appeal formed an integral part of the Office and that the Office did not have the right to appeal against a decision of one of the Boards. In addition, the CFI Rules of Procedure designated the Office as sole defendant.[392] In a subsequent judgment of June 30, 2004 in the *GE Betz* case, the Court of First Instance specified that there was nothing to prevent the Office from endorsing a head of claim of an applicant or from simply leaving the decision to the discretion of the Court, while putting forward all the arguments that it considered appropriate for giving guidance to the Court.[393] This judgment seems hard to reconcile with the judgment of December 12, 2002 in *Vedial*. In *GE Betz* the Office had claimed that the Court should "grant the applicant's claim for annulment of the contested decision".[394] The distinction between an admissible claim by which the Office asks the Court to grant the applicant's claim for annulment of the contested decision and an inadmissible claim by which the Office asks the Court to annul the contested decision does not seem convincing. Nevertheless it is now established case-law that the Office may claim that the form of order sought by the applicant or another party be granted and put forward arguments in support of the pleas in law advanced by that party. However, it cannot independently seek an order for annulment or put forward pleas for annulment which have not been raised by other parties.[395]

---

[389] See Art.130(1) of the CFI Rules of Procedure, under which "[s]ubject to the special provisions of this Title the provisions of these Rules of Procedure shall apply to proceedings brought against the Office for Harmonisation in the Internal Market (Trade Marks and Designs) and against the Community Plant Variety Office" and Art.133(2), which provides that the application initiating the proceedings is to be served on the Office "as defendant". See Mengozzi, "Le contrôle des décisions de l'OHMI par le Tribunal de première instance et la Cour de justice dans le contentieux relatif aux droits de la propriété industrielle" (2002) R.D.U.E. 315–333.

[390] CFI, Case T–63/01 *Procter & Gamble v OHIM (Shape of a tablet of soap)* [2002] E.C.R. II–5255, para.20.

[391] CFI, Case T–110/01 *Vedial v OHIM (HUBERT)* [2002] E.C.R. II–5275, paras 16–25.

[392] *Ibid.*

[393] CFI, Case T–107/02 *GE Betz v OHIM* [2004] E.C.R. II–1845, paras 29–37.

[394] *Ibid.*, para.27.

[395] CFI (judgment of May 4, 2005), Case T–22/04 *Reemark Gesellschaft für Markenkooperation v OHIM*, not yet reported, paras 16–18; CFI (judgment of October 25, 2005), Case T–379/03 *Peek & Cloppenburg v OHIM*, not yet reported, paras 22–29. Where the OHIM requests the Court of First Instance to dismiss the application, its pleas and arguments should support this request. Where the pleas and arguments of the OHIM seek in reality

B. THE APPLICANT

Any party adversely affected by the contested decision. Art.63(4) of **20–007**
Regulation No 40/94, Art.73(4) of Regulation No 2100/94 and Art.61(4) of
Regulation No 6/2002 provide that an action may be brought by any party
to proceedings before the Board of Appeal adversely affected by its
decision in whole or in part.[396] The other parties to the proceedings before
the Board of Appeal may participate, as interveners, in the proceedings
before the Court of First Instance and have the same procedural rights as
the main parties.[397] This means that, unlike "ordinary" interveners in direct
actions,[398] they can present an autonomous form of order sought and
autonomous pleas in law.

An application will be admissible only in so far as the applicant has an
interest in annulment. This means that annulment of the measure of itself
must be capable of having legal consequences.[399] A decision may therefore
only be the subject of an application for annulment in so far as it denies the
applicant's claims.[400]

---

the annulment of the decision of the Board of Appeal, the request to dismiss the
application will be inadmissible in the absence of pleas and arguments in support of the
request (CFI (judgment of July 7, 2005), Case T–385/03 *Miles Handelsgesellschaft International v OHIM*, not yet reported, paras 11–13).

[396] The identity of parties to proceedings before a Board of Appeal depends on the type of
decision against which an appeal has been brought before the Board. Art.58 of Regulation
No 40/94 provides that any party to proceedings adversely affected by a decision may
appeal to a Board. Any other parties to the proceedings are parties to the appeal by
operation of law.

[397] CFI Rules of Procedure, Art.134(1) and (2) (see, *e.g.* CFI (judgment of May 11, 2005),
Joined Cases T–160/02-T–162/02 *Naipes Heraclio Fournier v OHIM*, not yet reported, paras
17–18). Where the trade mark is assigned after the decision of the Board of Appeal and
after proceedings have been brought in the Court of First Instance, the new trade mark
holder can take the place of the former holder in the proceedings before the Court (see
CFI (judgment of June 28, 2005), Case T–301/03 *Canali Ireland v OHIM*, not yet reported,
paras 18–20). If the original trade mark holder agrees to this substitution, the new trade
mark holder will be regarded as an intervener within the meaning of Art.134 of the CFI
Rules of Procedure. If the original trade mark holder objects, the new holder can be
admitted to the proceedings only as an "ordinary" intervener pursuant to Art.40 of the
Statute: CFI (order of March 5, 2004), Case T–94/02 *Hugo Boss v OHIM* [2004] E.C.R. II–
813. It remains an open question whether a party to the proceedings before a Board of
Appeal may lodge an appeal against a judgment of the Court of First Instance if that party
has not intervened in the proceedings before the Court of First Instance (see, however,
implicitly ECJ (order of January 18, 2005), Case C–325/03 P *Zuazaga Meabe v OHIM*
[2005] E.C.R. I–403.

[398] Statute, Art.40. See 24–093 to 24–110, *infra*.

[399] CFI, Case T–129/00 *Procter & Gamble v OHIM (Rectangular tablet with inlay)* [2001] E.C.R.
II–2793, para.12.

[400] CFI, Case T–30/00 *Henkel v OHIM (Representation of detergent)* [2001] E.C.R. II–2663,
para.15; CFI (judgment of September 16, 2004), Case T–342/02 *Metro-Goldwyn-Mayer Lion
v OHIM*, not yet reported, paras 36–50.

III. Special Characteristics

A. Pleas in law

20–008 **Parallelism with Art.230 of the EC Treaty.** An action for annulment or alteration brought under Regulation No 40/94 (Art.63(2)), Regulation No 2100/94 (Art.73(2)) or Regulation No 6/2002 (Art.61(2)) may be brought on grounds of lack of competence, infringement of an essential procedural requirement,[401] infringement of the Treaty, of the relevant regulation or of any rule of law relating to their application or misuse of power. These grounds approximate to the pleas which may be raised in an action for annulment brought under Art.230 of the EC Treaty (see 7–121 to 7–158, *supra*).[402]

20–009 **Review of the contested decision.** The legality of the decision falls to be assessed on the basis of the elements of fact and of law existing at the time when the measure was adopted.[403] A procedural irregularity will entail the annulment of a decision in whole or in part only if it is shown that had it not been for the irregularity the contested decision might have been substantively different.[404]

---

[401] Infringement of the requirement to state reasons is a matter of public policy and must be raised by the Court of its own motion (CFI, Case T–129/00 *Procter & Gamble v OHIM (Rectangular tablet with inlay)* [2001] E.C.R. II–2793, para.72). The Board of Appeal will infringe an essential procedural requirement if it applies absolute grounds of refusal of its own motion without according the applicant an opportunity to express its view thereon (CFI, Case T–122/99 *Procter & Gamble v OHIM* [2000] E.C.R. II–265, para.47; CFI, Case T–34/00 *Eurocool Logistik v OHIM (EUROCOOL)* [2002] E.C.R. II–683, para.22; CFI, Case T–79/00 *Rewe-Zentral v OHIM (LITE)* [2002] E.C.R. II–705, paras 16–19; CFI (judgment of July 8, 2004), Case T–289/02 *Telepharmacy Solutions v OHIM*, not yet reported, paras 22–30).

[402] By virtue of the principle of continuity of functions between the examiners and the Boards of Appeal, the Boards can re-examine the application without limiting themselves to the reasoning of the examiner (CFI, Case T–122/99 *Procter & Gamble v OHIM* [2000] E.C.R. II–265, para.17; CFI, Case T–198/00 *Hershey Foods v OHIM (Kiss Device with plume)* [2002] E.C.R. II–2567, para.25). This case-law may also be applied to relations between the other authorities of the OHIM which can give rulings at first instance, such as the Opposition and Cancellation Divisions and the Boards of Appeal (CFI, Case T–308/01 *Henkel v OHIM* [2003] E.C.R. II–3253, para.25). If, in taking his or her decision, the examiner infringes the right to be heard, that defect may be remedied by the Board of Appeal given the continuity which exists in terms of their functions (CFI, Case T–16/02 *Audi v OHIM* [2003] E.C.R. II–5167, paras 80–82). In addition, because of the principle of continuity of functions the Board of Appeal cannot leave out of account a particular fact which was raised before it for the first time and not raised before the authority which ruled at first instance (CFI (judgment of November 10, 2004), Case T–164/02 *Kaul and Bayer v OHIM* not yet reported, paras 25–30).

[403] CFI, Case T–247/01 *eCopy v OHIM (ECOPY)* [2002] E.C.R. II–5301, para.46.

[404] CFI (judgment of June 8, 2005), Case T–315/03 *Wilfer v OHIM* not yet reported, para.33. A violation of the rules governing the language of proceedings will lead to the annulment of the decision of the Board of Appeal only if the procedural irregularities violated the applicant's rights of the defence (CFI (judgment of July 13, 2005), Case T–242/02 *Sunrider v OHIM*, not yet reported, paras 39–45).

Pleas must relate to a decision of a Board of Appeal. Since by virtue of   **20–010**
Art.63(1) of Regulation No 40/94, actions may be brought before the
Community judicature only against decisions of the Boards of Appeal, only
pleas directed against the decision of the Board of Appeal itself are
admissible. As a result pleas relating to a decision of the Opposition
Division will be inadmissible.[405]

Pleas must not change the subject-matter of the proceedings. Art.135(4) of   **20–011**
the CFI Rules of Procedure provides that the parties' pleadings may not
change the subject-matter of the proceedings before the Board of
Appeal.[406] On that ground, claims not put forward by a party before the
Board of Appeal but in its application (or at a later stage) in the
proceedings before the Court of First Instance will be inadmissible.[407]

Consequently, the review by the Court of First Instance must not exceed
the factual and legal context of the dispute as it was brought before the
Office.[408] Facts raised for the first time before the Court of First Instance
cannot affect the legality of the Office's decision unless the Office should
have taken them into account itself of its own motion.[409] It must be stressed
in this connection that in proceedings concerning relative grounds for
refusal, the Office is not obliged to review facts of its own motion. This is
because Art.74 of Regulation No 40/94 confines review by the Office as

---

[405] CFI (judgment of June 7, 2005), Case T–303/03 *Lidl Stiftung v OHIM*, not yet reported, paras 59–60.
[406] CFI (judgment of November 23, 2004), Case T–360/03 *Frischpack v OHIM*, not yet reported, paras 30–35; CFI (judgment of May 31, 2005), Case T–373/03 *Solo Italia v OHIM*, not yet reported, paras 25–26.
[407] CFI, Case T–24/00 *Sunrider v OHIM (VITALITE)* [2001] E.C.R. II–449, para.13; CFI (judgment of October 5, 2005), Case T–423/04 *Bunker & BKR v OHIM*, not yet reported, paras 17–22). But it should be noted that the party bringing an appeal before a Board of Appeal has to determine only the subject-matter and not the extent of the examination which the Board of Appeal must conduct. The extent of the examination which the Board of Appeal must conduct is not determined by the grounds relied on by the party who has brought the appeal. Even if the party who has brought the appeal has not raised a specific ground of appeal, the Board of Appeal is none the less bound to examine whether or not, in the light of all the relevant matters of fact and of law, a new decision with the same operative part as the decision under appeal may be lawfully adopted at the time of the appeal ruling (CFI, Case T–308/01 *Henkel v OHIM* [2003] E.C.R. II–3253, paras 29–30 and 34).
[408] CFI, Case T–194/01 *Unilever v OHIM* (Oval tablet) [2003] E.C.R. II–383, para.16; CFI, Case T–66/03 *Koffiebranderij en Theehandel "Drie Mollen sinds 1818" v OHIM*, [2004] E.C.R. II–1765, paras 40–49.
[409] CFI (judgment of July 13, 2004), Case T–115/03 *Samar v OHIM*, not yet reported, paras 13–15; CFI, Case T–185/02 *Ruiz-Picasso and Others v OHIM*, [2004] E.C.R. II–1739, paras 27–32; CFI (judgment of November 10, 2004), Case T–396/02 *Storck v OHIM*, not yet reported, para.24 (it is not the function of the Court to re-examine the facts in the light of documents submitted for the first time before it).

regards relative grounds for refusal to the facts, evidence and arguments adduced by the parties.[410]

Arguments raised for the first time before the Court of First Instance will be inadmissible where their assessment (such as the assessment of the reputation of an older mark) would be based on factual data not adduced in the course of the proceedings before the Office.[411] Evidence sought to be adduced for the first time before the Court of First Instance in support of inadmissible facts and arguments will also be inadmissible.[412]

As far as the inadmissibility of new facts, evidence and arguments is concerned, the same rules apply for the applicant, the Office and the interveners participating in the proceedings before the Court pursuant to Art.134 of the CFI Rules of Procedure. The principle of equality of arms requires that all parties before the Court of First Instance have the same means at their disposal.[413]

20–012 **Plea of illegality.** When seeking the annulment or alteration of a decision of the Office, a party may raise a plea of illegality notwithstanding the fact that Regulation No 40/94 does not expressly mention such a plea as a collateral legal remedy which persons bringing actions may use before the Court of First Instance.[414]

B. Time-limits

20–013 **Two months.** An action has to be brought within two months of the date of notification of the decision of the Board of Appeal.[415]

IV. Consequences

20–014 **Successful action.** If the Court of First Instance upholds the claim, it may annul or alter the decision of the Board of Appeal. Annulment has the same characteristics as a declaration of nullity made pursuant to Art.230 of

---

[410] CFI (judgment of July 13, 2004), Case T–115/03 *Samar v OHIM*, not yet reported, paras 13–15; CFI, Case T–185/02 *Ruiz-Picasso and Others v OHIM* [2004] E.C.R. II–1739, paras 27–32; CFI (judgment of November 10, 2004), Case T–396/02 *Storck v OHIM*, not yet reported, para.24; CFI (judgment of February 1, 2005), Case T–57/03 *SPAG v OHIM*, not yet reported, paras 17–35 (extensive survey of the applicable case-law).

[411] CFI, Case T–66/03 *Koffiebranderij en Theehandel "Drie Mollen sinds 1818" v OHIM* [2004] E.C.R. II–1765, para.46; CFI (judgment of February 1, 2005), Case T–57/03 *SPAG v OHIM*, not yet reported, paras 30–32: a plea concerning the reputation of an older mark which is raised for the first time before the Court of First Instance will be inadmissible. In contrast, the assessment of the intrinsically distinctive character does not presuppose any matter of fact which is up to the parties to establish. Accordingly, an argument in that regard raised for the first time in the Court of First Instance will be admissible.

[412] CFI (judgment of February 15, 2005), Case T–296/02 *Lidl Stiftung v OHIM*, not yet reported, paras 36–37.

[413] CFI (judgment of February 1, 2005), Case T–57/03 *SPAG v OHIM*, not yet reported, para.23.

[414] CFI, Case T–120/99 *Kik v OHIM* [2001] E.C.R. II–2235, para.21.

[415] Regulation No 40/94, Art.63(5), Regulation No 2100/94, Art.73(5), Regulation 6/2002, Art.61(5).

the EC Treaty. If the Court alters the Board's decision, the Court's decision replaces that of the Board. In either case, the Office is required to take the necessary steps to comply with the Court's judgment.[416] The Court of First Instance is not entitled to issue directions to the Office in relation thereto,[417] although the Office is obliged to draw the necessary conclusions from the operative part and the grounds of the judgment.[418] However, the Court does consider that it is competent to remit the case back to the examiner.[419] The reason for this is that, by remitting the case to the examiner, the Court would not be imposing on the Office any obligation to take action or refrain from doing so and would not therefore be issuing directions to the Office.[420]

Action dismissed. If the appeal is dismissed,[421] the Board's decision stands.   **20–015**

Appeal. An appeal will lie against the decision of the Court of First   **20–016**
Instance to the Court of Justice (see Ch.16, *supra*).

---

[416] Regulation No 40/94, Art.63(6), Regulation No 2100/94, Art.73(6), Regulation 6/2002, Art.61(6).

[417] CFI, Case T–247/01 *eCopy v OHIM (ECOPY)* [2002] E.C.R. II–5301, para.13; CFI, Case T–39/01 *Kabushiki Kaisha Fernandes v OHIM* [2002] E.C.R. II–5233, para.18; CFI, Case T–216/02 *Fieldturf v OHIM (LOOKS LIKE GRASS)* [2004] E.C.R. II–1023, para.15.

[418] CFI, Case T–163/98 *Procter & Gamble v OHIM (BABY DRY)* [1999] E.C.R. II–2383, para.53; CFI, Case T–331/99 *Mitsubishi HiTec Paper Bielefeld v OHIM (Giroform)* [2001] E.C.R. II–433, para.33; CFI, Case T–359/99 *DKV v OHIM (EuroHealth)* [2001] E.C.R. II–1645; CFI (judgment of September 27, 2005), Case T–123/04 *Cargo Partner v OHIM*, not yet reported, para.32.

[419] CFI, Case T–106/00 *Streamserve v OHIM (STREAMSERVE)* [2002] E.C.R. II–723, paras 17–19. In the case in question, the Court considered that the applicant's interests were sufficiently secured by annulment of the contested decision.

[420] The Court refers in this connection to the fact that remission of the case to the examiner may be ordered by the Board of Appeal under Art.62(1) of Regulation No 40/94. It therefore falls within the measures which may be taken by the Court of First Instance in the exercise of its power to amend decisions, as provided for in Art.63(3) of Regulation No 40/94 (CFI, Case T–106/00 *Streamserve v OHIM (STREAMSERVE)* [2002] E.C.R. II–723, para.19).

[421] The Court of First Instance may declare in a reasoned order that an application is manifestly inadmissible (see CFI (order of December 8, 1999), Case T–79/99 *Euro-Lex v OHIM (EU-LEX)* [1999] E.C.R. II–3555) or manifestly lacks any foundation in law (CFI (order of November 17, 2003), Case T–235/02 *Strongline v OHIM* [2003] E.C.R. II–4903; CFI (order of December 10, 2004), Case T–261/03 *Euro Style '94 v OHIM*, not reported).

CHAPTER 21

JURISDICTION OF THE COURT OF JUSTICE UNDER CONVENTIONS CONCLUDED BY THE MEMBER STATES

I. SUBJECT-MATTER

A. GENERAL

21–001 **Conventions may confer jurisdiction on the Court of Justice.** Both the EC Treaty and the EU Treaty expressly empower the Member States to conclude agreements with each other in certain areas. In the resulting conventions or in protocols annexed thereto, additional jurisdiction is often conferred on the Court of Justice.[422] That jurisdiction is generally a special

---

[422] The following conventions and protocols are involved (the instruments marked with an asterisk are in force):
1. Agreement establishing an Association between the EEC and Turkey, Art.25 (J.O. 3687/64; English text published in [1973] O.J. C113).*
2. Protocol of June 3, 1971 on the interpretation by the Court of Justice of the Convention of September 27, 1968 on jurisdiction and the enforcement of judgments in civil and commercial matters (consolidated version in [1998] O.J. C27/1).*
3. Protocol on the interpretation by the Court of Justice on the Convention of February 29, 1968 on the mutual recognition of companies and bodies corporate, signed at Luxembourg on June 3, 1971 (not published in the O.J., see [1971] Bull.EC Suppl.4).
4. First Protocol of December 19, 1988 on the interpretation by the Court of Justice of the European Communities of the Convention on the law applicable to contractual obligations (consolidated version in [1998] O.J. C27/47).*
5. Second Protocol of December 19, 1988 on the interpretation by the Court of Justice of the European Communities of the Convention on the law applicable to contractual obligations (consolidated version in [1998] O.J. C27/52).*
6. Agreement relating to Community patents—Done at Luxembourg on December 15,1989, Arts 2–4 ([1998] O.J. L401/1).
7. Agreement on the European Economic Area—Protocol 34 on the possibility for courts and tribunals of EFTA States to request the Court of Justice of the European Communities to decide on the interpretation of EEA rules corresponding to EC rules ([1994] O.J. L1/204).*
8. Convention defining the Statute of the European Schools, Art.26 ([1994] O.J. L212/3).*
9. Council Act of July 24, 1996 drawing up the Protocol on the interpretation, by way of preliminary rulings, by the Court of Justice of the European Communities of the Convention on the establishment of a European Police Office ([1996] O.J. C299/1).*
10. Council Act of September 27, 1996 drawing up a Protocol to the Convention on the protection of the European Communities' financial interests, Art.8 ([1996] O.J. C313/1).*

power to give preliminary rulings not based on Art.234 of the EC Treaty. In addition, conventions which the Member States have concluded in the area of cooperation in the field of justice and home affairs (*i.e.* the original "third pillar" of the Union) often provide for a direct action which may be brought in the Court of Justice in order to resolve disputes relating to the application or interpretation of the relevant convention which arise as between Member States or one or more Member States and the Commission.

B. WHAT CONVENTIONS ARE INVOLVED?

The Brussels Convention. Art.293 of the EC Treaty requires Member 21–002
States, as far as is necessary, to enter into negotiations with each other with a view to removing barriers in certain areas to the sound functioning of the

11. Council Act of November 29, 1996 drawing up the [First] Protocol on the interpretation, by way of preliminary rulings, by the Court of Justice of the European Communities of the Convention on the protection of the European Communities' financial interests ([1996] O.J. C151/1).*

12. Council Act of November 29, 1996 drawing up the Protocol on the interpretation, by way of preliminary rulings, by the Court of Justice of the European Communities of the Convention on the use of information technology for customs purposes ([1997] O.J. C151/15).

13. Council Act of May 26, 1997 drawing up the Convention on the fight against corruption involving officials of the European Communities or officials of Member States of the European Union, Art.12 ([1997] O.J. C195/1).

14. Council Act of June 19, 1997 drawing up the Second Protocol on the interpretation, by way of preliminary rulings, by the Court of Justice of the European Communities of the Convention on the protection of the European Communities' financial interests, Arts 13–15 ([1997] O.J. C221/11).

15. Council Act of December 18, 1997 drawing up the Convention on mutual assistance and cooperation between customs administrations, Art.26 ([1998] O.J. C24/1).

16. Council Act of June 17, 1998 drawing up the Convention on Driving Disqualifications, Art.14 ([1998] O.J. C216/1).

17. Internal agreement between the representatives of the governments of the Member States, meeting within the Council, on measures to be taken and procedures to be followed for the implementation of the ACP-EC Partnership Agreement, Art.6 ([2000] O.J. L317/376).*

18. Agreement between the Federal Republic of Germany and the Republic of Austria for the avoidance of double taxation in the sphere of income and wealth tax, Art.25 (Deutscher Bundestag—14. Wahlperiode—Drucksache 14/7040, p.7).*

19. Agreement between the European Community and the Swiss Confederation on Air Transport, Art.20 ([2002] O.J. L114/73).* See ECJ (order of July 14, 2005), Case C–70/04 *Swiss Confederation v Commission*, not reported, on the question as to whether an action for annulment should be brought before the Court of Justice or the Court of First Instance.

20. Monetary Agreement between the Government of the French Republic, on behalf of the European Community, and the Government of His Serene Highness the Prince of Monaco, Art.13 ([2002] O.J. L142/59).*

21. Agreement between the European Community and the Kingdom of Denmark on jurisdiction and the recognition and enforcement of judgments in civil and commercial matters, Art.6 ([2005] O.J. L299/62).*

22. Agreement between the European Community and the Kingdom of Denmark on the service of judicial and extrajudicial documents in civil or commercial matters, Art.7 ([2005] O.J. L300/55).*

common market. It was pursuant to that provision that the Convention of September 27, 1968 on jurisdiction and the enforcement of judgments in civil and commercial matters came about ("the Brussels Convention").[423] Since the Brussels Convention contributes towards the attainment of the common market, it is essential that, just like Community law in the narrow sense,[424] it is applied uniformly in the Member States. To that end, the Protocol of June 3, 1971 confers on the Court of Justice jurisdiction to interpret the Brussels Convention by preliminary ruling at the request of certain national courts.[425] In the meantime, the Council adopted Regulation (EC) No 44/2001 of December 22, 2000 on jurisdiction and the recognition and enforcement of judgments in civil and commercial matters.[426] The regulation is based on Art.61(c) and Art.67(1) of the EC Treaty. As a result, the jurisdiction of the Court of Justice to give preliminary rulings is based on Art.68(1) of the EC Treaty (and no longer on the Protocol).[427] The regulation entered into force on March 1, 2002. Under Art.68 of Regulation No 44/2001, as between the Member States, the regulation supersedes the Brussels Convention, except as regards the territories of the Member States which fall within the territorial scope of that Convention and which are excluded from the regulation pursuant to Art.299 of the EC Treaty. The regulation does not apply to relations between Denmark and

---

[423] On September 16, 1988 the Member States of the Community concluded with the member countries of the European Free Trade Association (EFTA) the Lugano Convention on jurisdiction and the enforcement of judgments in civil and commercial matters, which contains rules on jurisdiction and enforcement similar to those of the Brussels Convention ([1988] O.J. L319/9). However, the Court of Justice has no power to interpret that convention. Yet the Contracting Parties did sign a Protocol setting up an information-exchange system providing for the centralisation of judgments of the Court of Justice and courts of last instance in the Contracting Parties with a view to uniform interpretation. See Jung, "The Brussels and Lugano Conventions: The European Court's Jurisdiction; its Procedures and Methods" (1992) Civil Justice Quarterly 38–51; Tebbens, Kennedy, Kohler (eds), *Civil Jurisdiction and Judgments in Europe* (Butterworths, London, 1992), 402 pp.; Van Houtte and Pertegás Sender (eds), *Europese IPR-verdragen* (Acco, Leuven, 1997), 410 pp.

[424] The Court of Justice has observed that the Brussels Convention was concluded on the basis of the fourth indent of Art.293 of the EC Treaty, whose purpose is to facilitate the working of the common market through the adoption of rules of jurisdiction and through the elimination, as far as possible, of difficulties concerning the enforcement of judgments in the territory of the Contracting States. It is for these reasons that the provisions of the Brussels Convention and also the national provisions to which the Convention refers are linked to the EC Treaty: ECJ, Case C–398/92 *Mund & Fester* [1994] E.C.R. I–467, paras 11–12.

[425] Protocol on the interpretation by the Court of Justice of the Convention of September 27, 1968 on jurisdiction and the enforcement of judgments in civil and commercial matters, which entered into force on September 1, 1975. The original protocol has been adjusted each time new Member States have acceded to the Community (a consolidated version of the Brussels Convention and the Protocol is to be found in [1998] O.J. C27/1, which lists the publication references of the successive official versions of the Convention and the Protocol). The Protocol may be found in Sch.2 to the Civil Jurisdiction and Judgments Act 1982.

[426] [2001] O.J. L12/1; *corrigendum* in [2001] O.J. L307/38.

[427] See 22–002, *infra*.

the other Member States, to which the Brussels Convention and the Protocol continued to apply until the Agreement between the European Community and the Kingdom of Denmark on jurisdiction and the recognition and enforcement of judgments in civil and commercial matters entered into force.[428]

The Rome Convention. Furthermore, the Member States have concluded   21–003
the Convention of June 19, 1980 on the law applicable to contractual obligations ("the Rome Convention"), even though this subject is not specifically mentioned in Art.293 of the EC Treaty. Yet it does link up with the aims underlying that provision of the Treaty. It is most probably for that reason that the First Protocol of December 19, 1988 confers on the Court of Justice jurisdiction to interpret the Rome Convention by preliminary ruling at the request of certain national courts.[429]

Conventions based on the EU Treaty. Even before the Treaty of Amster-   21–004
dam entered into effect, the Member States concluded conventions under the first and third sub-subparas of Art.K.3(2)(c) of the EU Treaty which conferred on the Court of Justice, in some cases by separate protocols, jurisdiction not based on Art.234 of the EC Treaty to interpret them and sometimes to rule on disputes between Member States or between one or more Member States and the Commission regarding their application and interpretation in a direct action brought by a Member State or the Commission.[430]

---

[428] [2005] O.J. L299/62. See, *e.g.* ECJ, Case C–39/02 *Maersk Olie & Gas* [2004] E.C.R. I–9657.

[429] The First Protocol entered into effect on August 1, 2004. For a consolidated version of the Rome Convention and the First Protocol (incorporating all changes consequential upon the accession of new Member States), see [1998] O.J. C27/34.

[430] The following conventions have been concluded pursuant to the former Art.K.3(2) of the EU Treaty:
— Convention on simplified extradition procedures between the Member States of the European Union, drawn up by Council Act of March 10, 1995 ([1995] O.J. C78/1; no jurisdiction conferred on the Court of Justice);
— Convention relating to extradition between the Member States of the European Union, drawn up by Council Act of September 27, 1996 ([1996] O.J. C313/11). This Convention does not confer jurisdiction on the Court of Justice, but in a declaration appended to the Convention on the follow-up thereto the Council states that it will consider, one year after the entry into force of the Convention, whether jurisdiction should be given to the Court of Justice;
— Convention on the establishment of a European Police Office (Europol Convention), drawn up by Council Act of July 26, 1995 ([1995] C361/1; as far as dispute settlement is concerned, see Art.40 of the Declaration made by all the Member States with the exception of the United Kingdom [1995] O.J. C316/32). By Council Act of July 23, 1996 drawn up on the basis of the former Art.K.3 of the EU Treaty, a Protocol was added on the interpretation, by way of preliminary rulings, by the Court of Justice of the European Communities of the Convention on the establishment of a European Police Office ([1996] O.J. C299/1). It was signed on July 24, 1996. By Council Act of June 19, 1997, a protocol was drawn up on the privileges and immunities of Europol, the members of its organs, the Deputy Directors and employees of Europol pursuant to the former Art.K.3 of the EU

II. SURVEY OF THE COURT'S POWERS

A. JURISDICTION TO GIVE PRELIMINARY RULINGS

21–005   **Different rules.** Different rules govern the jurisdiction to give preliminary rulings on the interpretation of these Conventions and Protocols. The differences have to do with limiting the number of courts which are entitled to make references to the Court of Justice.

Treaty and Art.41(3) of the Europol Convention ([1997] O.J. C221/1, for dispute settlement, see Art.13). The Europol Convention entered into force on October 1, 1998;
— Convention on the use of information technology for customs purposes, drawn up by Council Act of July 26, 1995 ([1995] O.J. C316/33; for the powers of the Court of Justice, see Art.27). By Council Act of November 29, 1996, a Protocol, drawn up on the basis of the former Art.K.3 of the EU Treaty, was annexed to the Convention on the interpretation, by way of preliminary rulings, by the Court of Justice of the European Communities of the Convention on the use of information technology for customs purposes ([1997] O.J. C151/15);
— Convention on the protection of the European Communities' financial interests, drawn up by Council Act of July 26, 1995 ([1995] O.J. C316/ 48; for the jurisdiction of the Court of Justice, see Art.8). By Council Act of September 27, 1996, a First Protocol was adopted to that convention ([1996] O.J. C313/1; for the jurisdiction of the Court of Justice, see Art.8). Subsequently, by Council Act of November 29, 1996, a Protocol was drawn up, on the basis of the former Art.K.3 of the EU Treaty, on the interpretation by way of preliminary rulings, by the Court of Justice of the European Communities of the Convention on the protection of the European Communities' financial interests (Under Art.2(1) the Court's powers extend to interpreting both the Convention and the First Protocol) ([1997] O.J. C151/1). By Council Act of June 19, 1997, a Second Protocol was annexed to the Convention ([1997] O.J. C221/11; for the jurisdiction of the Court of Justice, see Arts 13, 14 and 15).
— Convention on the fight against corruption involving officials of the European Communities or officials of Member States of the European Union, drawn up by Council Act of May 26, 1997 ([1997] O.J. C195/1; for the jurisdiction of the Court of Justice, see Art.12);
— Convention on the service in the Member States of the European Union of judicial and extrajudicial documents in civil or commercial matters, drawn up by Council Act of May 26, 1997 ([1997] O.J. C261/1; for the interpretative jurisdiction of the Court of Justice, see Art.17). Also by Council Act of May 26, 1977, a Protocol was drawn up on the interpretation, by the Court of Justice of the European Communities of the Convention on the service in the Member States of the European Union of judicial and extrajudicial documents in civil or commercial matters ([1997] O.J. C261/17, including explanatory reports at pp.26 and 38);
— Convention on mutual assistance and cooperation between customs administrations, drawn up by Council Act of December 18, 1997 ([1998] O.J. C24/1; with an explanatory report in [1998] O.J. C189/1; for the jurisdiction of the Court of Justice, see Art.26);
— Convention on Jurisdiction and the Recognition and Enforcement of Judgments in Matrimonial Matters, drawn up by Council Act of May 28, 1998 ([1998] O.J. C221/1; for the interpretative jurisdiction of the Court of Justice, see Art.45). A Protocol on the interpretation, by the Court of Justice of the European Communities of the Convention on Jurisdiction and the Recognition and Enforcement of Judgments in Matrimonial Matters was appended to this Convention by Council Act of the same date ([1998] O.J. C221/19, with explanatory reports at pp.27 and 65);
— Convention on Driving Disqualifications, drawn up by Council Act of June 17, 1998 ([1998] O.J. C216/1; for the jurisdiction of the Court of Justice, see Art.14).

The Brussels and Rome Conventions. Under the Protocols annexed to the **21–006** Brussels Convention[431] and the Rome Convention, only a limited number of courts are entitled to make a reference to the Court of Justice for a preliminary ruling. Only those mentioned in Art.2(1) of the Protocol of June 3, 1971 and in Art.2(a) of the First Protocol of December 19, 1988— for the United Kingdom, the House of Lords and, for Ireland, the Supreme Court—and appellate courts may request a ruling.[432] A similar restriction is contained in Art.2(1)(a) (the "highest courts"—the House of Lords in the United Kingdom; the Supreme Court in the case of Ireland) and Art.2(1)(b) (courts sitting in an appellate capacity)[433] of the Protocol of May 26, 1997 (service of judicial and extrajudicial documents in civil or commercial matters)[434] and Art.2(2)(a) (the "highest courts"—the Judicial Committee of the House of Lords in the United Kingdom; the Supreme Court in the case of Ireland) and Art.2(2)(b) (courts sitting in an appellate capacity) of the Protocol of May 28, 1998 (jurisdiction and the recognition and enforcement of judgments in matrimonial matters)[435]. This restriction was introduced out of concern lest too many questions might be referred in all sorts of private-law disputes. In addition, it was thought that no more heed should be given to differences of interpretation of these Conventions by inferior courts in applying them than was paid to differences as between decided cases of lower courts in a given Member State. Lastly, there was a concern that the Court of Justice should only be required to give preliminary rulings where it was "fully informed", so as to allow stable case-law to develop.[436]

Art.2(1) of the Protocol of May 28, 1998 is novel, in comparison with the 1971, 1988 and 1997 Protocols, in that it allows each Member State to restrict by declaration the courts empowered to make references for preliminary rulings to the highest courts. The reason for this is that judgments on matters covered by the Convention (divorce, legal separation, marriage annulment, parental responsibility for children of a marriage)

---

[431] Now replaced as between the Member States by Council Regulation (EC) No 44/2001 of December 22, 2000 on jurisdiction and the recognition and enforcement of judgments in civil and commercial matters, ([2001] O.J. L21/1; *corrigendum* in [2004] O.J. L307/28. See 21–001, *supra*, and 22–002, *infra*.

[432] ECJ (order of November 9, 1983), Case 80/83 *Habourdin International and Others* [1983] E.C.R. 3639; ECJ (order of March 18, 1984), Case 56/84 *Von Gallera* [1984] E.C.R. 1769; ECJ, Case C–69/02 *Reichling* [2002] E.C.R. I–3393; ECJ, Case C–24/02 *Marseille Fret* [2002] E.C.R. I–3383.

[433] For an application, see ECJ, Case C–38/98 *Renault* [2000] E.C.R. I–2973, paras 17–23.

[434] Now replaced by Council Regulation (EC) No 1348/2000 of May 29, 2000 on the service in the Member States of judicial and extrajudicial documents in civil or commercial matters ([2000] O.J. L160/37). See 22–002, *infra*.

[435] Now replaced by Council Regulation (EC) No 2201/2003 of November 27, 2003 concerning jurisdiction and the recognition and enforcement of judgments in matrimonial matters and the matters of parental responsibility, repealing Regulation (EC) No 1347/2000 ([2003] O.J. L338/1). See 22–002, *infra*.

[436] See the Jenard Report ((1979) O.J. C59/68). But see Ras, "Een nieuwe taak voor het Hof van Justitie E.G." (1975) N.J.B. 1117, at 1180.

need to be given as promptly as possible in order not to prejudice the interests of individuals.[437]

A court which, under Art.37 of the Brussels Convention, has to decide on an appeal against a decision authorising enforcement of a judicial decision given in another Member State[438] may under Art.2(3) of the Protocol of June 3, 1971 also refer questions to the Court of Justice for a preliminary ruling. A court which, pursuant to Art.40 of the Brussels Convention, has to give judgment on an appeal against a refusal to grant an application for enforcement may make a reference for a preliminary ruling under the general provision contained in Art.2(2) of the Protocol of June 3, 1971.[439]

The aforementioned four Protocols also provide that the "competent authority of a Contracting State" may request the Court of Justice to give a ruling on a question of interpretation of the relevant Convention if judgments given by courts of that State conflict with the interpretation given either by the Court of Justice or in a judgment of one of the courts of a Contracting State which is entitled to make references for preliminary rulings.[440] The Procurators-General of the Courts of Cassation of the Contracting States constitute a competent authority, but the Contracting States may designate any other authority.[441] This means of obtaining a ruling from the Court of Justice after final judgment has been given is inspired by the appeal in cassation in the interests of the law. It affords an opportunity of limiting the effects of an anomalous application of the Convention by means of an interpretation from the Court of Justice which is binding for the future.[442] To date, no "competent authority" has referred such a question.

21–007 **Conventions based on the EU Treaty.** Member States have to accept the Court's jurisdiction to give preliminary rulings pursuant to other Conventions[443] and Protocols[444] drawn up on the basis of the former Art.K.3 of the

---

[437] Explanatory report ([1998] O.J. C 221/66, point 4).
[438] Art.37 of the Brussels Convention sets out the courts in which an appeal may be brought against a decision authorising enforcement of a judgment given in another Member State (in the United Kingdom, the High Court and the Magistrates' Court (in the case of a maintenance judgment)). The court granting an enforcement order does so in the absence of the person against whom enforcement is sought (Brussels Convention, Art.34).
[439] ECJ, Case 178/83 Firma P. [1984] E.C.R. 3033.
[440] Art.4 of the Protocol of June 3, 1971; Art.3 of the First Protocol of December 19, 1988; Art.4 of the Protocol of May 26, 1997; Art.6 of the Protocol of May 28, 1998.
[441] Art.4(3) of the Protocol of June 3, 1971; Art.3(3) of the First Protocol of December 19, 1988; Art.4(3) of the Protocol of May 26, 1997; Art.6(3) of the Protocol of May 28, 1998.
[442] The interpretation given by the Court of Justice following such a request does not affect the judgments which give rise to the request for interpretation (Art.4(2) of the Protocol of June 3, 1971; Art.3(2) of the First Protocol of December 19, 1988; Art.4(2) of the Protocol of May 26, 1997; Art.6(2) of the Protocol of May 28, 1998).
[443] Art.12(3) to (5) of the Convention of May 26, 1997 on the fight against corruption involving officials of the European Communities or officials of Member States of the European Union; Art.26(3) to (8) of the Convention of December 18, 1997 on mutual assistance and

508

EU Treaty (see 21–004, *supra*) by means of a declaration, either that any national court or tribunal against whose decisions there is no judicial remedy under national law may make a reference for a preliminary ruling if the court or tribunal in question considers it to be necessary in order to give judgment or that any national court or tribunal may request a preliminary ruling.[445] Courts or tribunals which may request a preliminary ruling are not

cooperation between customs administrations (Art.26(8) limits the Court's jurisdiction in precisely the same way as Art.35(5) of the EU Treaty, see 22–004, *infra*): the Court "shall not have jurisdiction to check the validity or proportionality of operations carried out by competent law enforcement agencies under this Convention nor to rule on the exercise of responsibilities which devolve upon Member States for maintaining law and order and for safeguarding internal security"); Art.14(2) to (4) of the Convention of June 17, 1998 on Driving Disqualifications.

[444] Protocol of July 24, 1996 (Europol); Protocol of November 29, 1996 (use of information technology for customs purposes); Protocol of November 29, 1996 (protection of the Communities' financial interests), the applicability of which was extended by Art.13(2) of the Second Protocol of June 19, 1997.

[445] The following Member States have declared in respect of the Protocol indicated that only national courts or tribunals against whose decisions there is no judicial remedy under national law may make a reference for a preliminary ruling (for the *O.J.* references of the Protocols, see n.422, *supra*):
— Protocol of July 24, 1996 (Europol): France and Ireland;
— Protocol of November 29, 1996 (use of information technology for customs purposes): Ireland and Portugal;
— Protocol of November 29, 1996 (protection of financial interests): France, Ireland and Portugal (a Member State may declare that a declaration made under the Protocol of November 29, 1996 does not apply to the Second Protocol of June 19, 1997; see Art.13(3) of the Second Protocol).
The following Member States have declared that any national court or tribunal may seek a preliminary ruling from the Court of Justice (for the *O.J.* references of the Protocols, see n.422, *supra*):
— Protocol of July 24, 1996 (Europol): Austria, Belgium, Finland, Germany, Greece, Italy, Luxembourg, the Netherlands, Portugal and Sweden (as far as Sweden is concerned, see [1997] O.J. C100/1). In addition, Austria, Belgium, Germany, Greece, Italy, Luxembourg, the Netherlands and Portugal reserved the right to make provision in their national law to the effect that, where a question relating to the interpretation of the Convention or the Protocol is raised in a case pending before a national court or tribunal against whose decision there is no judicial remedy under national law, that court or tribunal will be required to refer the matter to the Court of Justice.
— Protocol of November 29, 1996 (use of information technology for customs purposes): Austria, Finland, France, Germany, Greece, the Netherlands and Sweden. In addition, Austria, Germany, Greece and the Netherlands reserved the right to make provision in their national law to the effect that, where a question relating to the interpretation of the Convention or the Protocol is raised in a case pending before a national court or tribunal against whose decision there is no judicial remedy under national law, that court or tribunal will be required to refer the matter to the Court of Justice.
— Protocol of November 29, 1996 (protection of financial interests): Austria, Finland, Germany, Greece, the Netherlands and Sweden (a Member State may declare that a declaration made under the Protocol of November 29, 1996 does not apply to the Second Protocol of June 19, 1997; see Art.13(3) of the Second Protocol). In addition, Austria, Germany, Greece and the Netherlands reserved the right to make provision in their national law to the effect that, where a question relating to the interpretation of the Convention or the First Protocol is raised in a case pending before a national court or tribunal against whose decision there is no judicial remedy under national law, that court or tribunal will be required to refer the matter to the Court of Justice.

obliged to do so, even if they consider such a ruling to be necessary in order to give judgment.

B. Direct Actions

21–008 **Disputes between Member States.** A direct action under Conventions concluded on the basis of Art.K.3 of the EU Treaty may be brought in the Court of Justice in the event of a dispute on the "interpretation or application" of the Convention in question.

In an initial stage, such disputes are to be discussed by the Council with the aim of finding a settlement. If the dispute is not settled within six months, one of the parties may submit it to the Court of Justice.[446]

21–009 **Disputes between the Commission and Member States.** The Commission or one or more Member States may bring a dispute between that institution and one or more Member States on the "application" of a Convention directly before the Court of Justice if it cannot be settled through negotiation.[447]

21–010 **Convention on the Protection of the European Communities' financial interests.** Lastly, Art.14 of the Second Protocol to the Convention on the protection of the European Communities' financial interests declares the second para. of Art.288 and Art.235 of the EC Treaty to be applicable. Art.15 of that Protocol gives the Court of First Instance (and, on appeal,

---

[446] Art.27(1) of the Convention on the use of information technology for customs purposes; Art.8(1) of the Convention on the protection of the European Communities' financial interests (see also Art.8(1) of the First Protocol and Art.13(1) of the Second Protocol); Art.12(1) of the Convention on the fight against corruption involving officials of the European Communities or officials of Member States of the European Union; Art.26(1) of the Convention on mutual assistance and cooperation between customs administrations; Art.14(1) of the Convention on Driving Disqualifications. Art.40(2) of the Europol Convention provides that if such disputes are not settled within six months, the Member States party to the dispute are to decide, by agreement amongst themselves, the modalities according to which they are to be settled. It appears from a declaration on Art.40(2) annexed to the Convention that all the Member States, with the exception of the United Kingdom, agree that in such cases they will systematically submit the dispute to the Court of Justice. For the question of the involvement or non-involvement of the Court of Justice, see Curtin and Pouw, "Samenwerking op het gebied van justitie en binnenlandse zaken in de Europese Unie: pre-Maastricht-nostalgie? (1995) S.E.W. 579, at 591–596.

[447] Art.27(2) of the Convention on the use of information technology for customs purposes; Art.8(2) of the Convention on the protection of the European Communities' financial interests (see also Art.8(2) of the First Protocol and Art.13(2) of the Second Protocol); Art.12(2) of the Convention on the fight against corruption involving officials of the European Communities or officials of Member States of the European Union (this article restricts the bringing of disputes directly before the Court of Justice to a few articles of the Convention and then only in so far as they concern a question of Community law or the Communities' financial interests or involve members or officials of Community institutions or bodies set up in accordance with the Treaties establishing the European Communities); Art.26(2) of the Convention on mutual assistance and cooperation between customs administrations; Art.14(1) of the Convention on Driving Disqualifications.

the Court of Justice) jurisdiction in proceedings instituted by any natural or legal person for annulment of a decision of the Commission which is addressed to that person or of direct and individual concern to that person, or for interim measures, on the ground of infringement of Art.8 of the Protocol (infringement of the duty to provide a level of protection of personal data equivalent to that set out in Directive 95/46/EC) or any rule adopted pursuant thereto or misuse of powers in connection with the exchange of information between the Member States and the Commission in connection with combating fraud, active and passive corruption and money laundering.[448]

III. PROCEDURE BEFORE THE COURT

Preliminary references. The Statute and the Rules of Procedure of the Court of Justice are applicable in so far as the relevant Convention or Protocol do not provide otherwise.[449] Consequently, the procedure applicable to requests for preliminary rulings generally applies.   **21–011**

Direct actions. It is as yet unclear what procedure will apply to proceedings for resolving disputes between Member States or between Member States and the Commission on the interpretation and application of a number of Conventions concluded pursuant to the former Art.K.3(2)(c) of the EU Treaty. In the absence of any specific provisions in the Rules of Procedure, the most likely procedure is that employed for direct actions and also employed for cases brought pursuant to an arbitration clause under Art.238 of the EC Treaty.   **21–012**

IV. CONSEQUENCES

Preliminary references. Judgments given by the Court of Justice pursuant to the Conventions and Protocols discussed above have the same consequences as preliminary rulings generally (see 6–027 to 6–034, *supra*).   **21–013**

Direct actions. Judgments given in direct actions probably have the same effects as judgments given pursuant to an arbitration clause (see Ch.19, *supra*).   **21–014**

---

[448] Second Protocol, Art.7(2).
[449] Art.5 of the Protocol of June 3, 1971; Art.1(1) of the Second Protocol conferring on the Court of Justice of the European Communities certain powers to interpret the Convention on the law applicable to contractual obligations, opened for signature in Rome on June 19, 1980 ([1989] O.J. L48/18); Art.3 of the Protocol of July 24, 1996; Art.3 of the two Protocols of November 29, 1996; Art.5 of the Protocol of May 26, 1997; Arts 5 and 7 of the Protocol of May 28, 1998; Art.12(6) of the Convention on the fight against corruption involving officials of the European Communities or officials of Member States of the European Union; Art.26(6) and (7) of the Convention on mutual assistance and cooperation between customs administrations; Art.14(4) of the Convention on Driving Disqualifications.

CHAPTER 22

JURISDICTION OF THE COURT OF JUSTICE WITH REGARD TO THE AREA OF FREEDOM, SECURITY AND JUSTICE

22–001 **General.** The Council is to adopt measures with a view to the gradual establishment of an area of freedom, security and justice based on Title IV of the EC Treaty ("Visas, asylum, immigration and other policies related to free movement of persons") and Title VI of the EU Treaty ("Provisions on police and judicial cooperation in criminal matters"), the so-called third pillar of the EU Treaty. Specific provisions apply as regards the jurisdiction of the Court of Justice in this area.

I. VISAS, ASYLUM, IMMIGRATION AND OTHER POLICIES RELATED TO FREE MOVEMENT OF PERSONS

22–002 **Art.68 of the EC Treaty.** Measures based on Title IV of the EC Treaty are in principle subject to the normal judicial supervision provided for in Arts 220 to 245 of the EC Treaty. However, Art.68 of the EC Treaty lays down a number of specific provisions with regard to preliminary rulings. In the first place, Art.68(1) restricts the possibility to make references for preliminary rulings to the Court of Justice to courts and tribunals "against whose decisions there is no judicial remedy under national law".[450] Secondly, Art.68(3) of the EC Treaty provides for a species of preliminary ruling procedure to be brought, not by a national court, but by the Council, the Commission or a Member State in so far as it states that "the Council, the Commission or a Member State may request the Court of Justice to give a ruling on a question of interpretation of [Title IV of the EC Treaty] or of acts of the institutions of the Community based on this title".[451]

---

[450] See, *e.g.* ECJ (order of March 18, 2004), Case C–45/03 *Dem' Yanenko*, not reported, paras 41–43; ECJ (order of March 31, 2004), Case C–51/03 *Georgescu* [2004] E.C.R. I–3203, para. 29; ECJ (order of June 10, 2004), Case C–555/03 *Warbecq* [2004] E.C.R. I–6041, paras 11–16 (reference for a preliminary ruling from a lower court declared inadmissible).

[451] For this subject, see Cheneviere, "L'article 68 CE—Rapide survol d'un renvoi préjudiciel mal compris" (2004) C.D.E. 567–589.

Lastly, Art.68(2) of the EC Treaty limits the jurisdiction of the Community judicature by providing that with respect to measures taken with a view to ensuring the absence of any controls on persons when crossing internal borders,[452] the Court of Justice does not have jurisdiction to rule on any measure relating to the maintenance of law and order and the safeguarding of internal security. This restriction seems to be aimed at all the judicial procedures provided for in the Treaty and not only at the preliminary ruling procedure.

As has already been mentioned, a number of matters of private international law have recently been "communitarised" by regulations based on Title IV of the EC Treaty. In this way, the Brussels Convention (including the Protocol of June 3, 1971) has been replaced by Council Regulation (EC) No 44/2001 of December 22, 2000 on jurisdiction and the recognition and enforcement of judgments in civil and commercial matters.[453] The Protocols of May 26, 1997 and May 28, 1998 have now been replaced by the provisions of, respectively, Council Regulation (EC) No 1348/2000 of May 29, 2000 on the service in the Member States of judicial and extrajudicial documents in civil or commercial matters[454] and Council Regulation (EC) No 2201/2003 of November 27, 2003 concerning jurisdiction and the recognition and enforcement of judgments in matrimonial matters and the matters of parental responsibility, repealing Regulation (EC) No 1347/2000.[455] These regulations were all adopted on the basis of Art.61(c) and Art.67(1) of the EC Treaty.[456] As a result, the competence of the Court of Justice to give preliminary rulings is now founded upon Art.68(1) of the EC Treaty and no longer upon the aforementioned Protocols. That article restricts the possibility of referring a question to the Court of Justice for a preliminary ruling to courts and tribunals "against whose decisions there is no judicial remedy under national law".[457] This constitutes a step backwards as compared with the former Protocols, which afforded this possibility also to appellate courts. The highest courts are obliged to seek a preliminary ruling on interpretation—as under Art.234 of the EC Treaty—where they consider that a decision on the question is necessary to enable them to give judgment.

---

[452] Measures taken pursuant to Art.62(1) of the EC Treaty.

[453] [2001] O.J. L12/1; *corrigendum* in [2001] O.J. L307/28.

[454] [2000] O.J. L160/37. See in this connection ECJ (judgment of November 8, 2005), Case C–443/03 *Leffler*, not yet reported.

[455] [2003] O.J. L338/1.

[456] In addition, mention should also be made of Council Regulation (EC) No 1346/2000 of May 29, 2000 on insolvency proceedings ([2000] O.J. L160/1) and Council Regulation (EC) No 1206/2001 of May 28, 2001 on cooperation between the courts of the Member States in the taking of evidence in civil or commercial matters ([2001] O.J. L174/1).

[457] See, *e.g.* ECJ (order of March 18, 2004), Case C–45/03 *Dem' Yanenko*, not reported, paras 41–43; ECJ (order of March 31, 2004), Case C–51/03 *Georgescu* [2004] E.C.R. I–3203, para.29; ECJ (order of June 10, 2004), Case C–555/03 *Warbecq* [2004] E.C.R. I–6041, paras 11–16 (reference for a preliminary ruling from an inferior court declared inadmissible). It is not always clear whether or not a national court or tribunal is ruling in last instance.

22–003 **Schengen Convention.** Mention should also be made of the Schengen Convention. Upon the entry into effect of the Amsterdam Treaty, all EU Member States, with the exception of Ireland and the UK,[458] were parties to the Schengen Convention. That Treaty provided for the incorporation of the Schengen *acquis* into the European Union. A protocol to the EU Treaty and the EC Treaty thus empowers the Member States involved in Schengen cooperation to integrate the whole of that cooperation within the framework of the European Union: existing provisions or decisions could be converted and developed as Community law under Title IV of the EC Treaty or as "Union law" under Title VI of the EU Treaty.[459] On May 20, 1999 the Council determined the—Community or non-Community—legal basis for each of the provisions or decisions which constitute the Schengen *acquis*.[460] Depending upon the choice of legal basis, the Court of Justice has jurisdiction conferred upon it either by the EC Treaty[461] or by the EU Treaty.[462] Schengen cooperation continues on the basis of the provisions of Title IV of the EC Treaty and Title VI (third pillar) of the EU Treaty as appropriate.

II. POLICE AND JUDICIAL COOPERATION IN CRIMINAL MATTERS

22–004 **Art.35 of the EU Treaty.** The jurisdiction of the Court of Justice in the field of police and judicial cooperation in criminal matters is set out in Art.35 of the EU Treaty.[463] It may be subdivided into three heads.

---

[458] Denmark has an exceptional status. See Lenaerts and Van Nuffel, *Constitutional Law of the European Union*, § 5–165, at 223–224.

[459] See *ibid.*, § 5–164, at 221–223.

[460] Council Decision 1999/436/EC of May 20, 1999 determining, in conformity with the relevant provisions of the Treaty establishing the European Community and the Treaty on European Union, the legal basis for each of the provisions or decisions which constitute the Schengen *acquis* ([1999] O.J. L176/17; *corrigendum* in [2000] L9/31).

[461] Accordingly, Art.68(1) of the EC Treaty restricts preliminary references in connection with Schengen measures to national courts and tribunals ruling at last instance.

[462] For a first example, see ECJ, Joined Cases C–187/01 and C–385/01 *Gözütok and Brügge* [2003] E.C.R. I–1345 (with a case note by Vervaele (2004) C.M.L.Rev. 795–812). That case was concerned with the interpretation of Art.54 of the Convention implementing the Schengen Agreement of June 14, 1985 between the Governments of the States of the Benelux Economic Union, the Federal Republic of Germany and the French Republic on the gradual abolition of checks at their common borders ([2000] O.J. L239/19) (Schengen implementation agreement), signed at Schengen (Luxembourg) on June 19, 1990. In accordance with Council Decision 1999/436/EC of May 20, 1999 determining, in conformity with the relevant provisions of the Treaty establishing the European Community and the Treaty on European Union, the legal basis for each of the provisions or decisions which constitute the Schengen *acquis* ((1999) O.J. L176/17), the legal basis for Art.54 of the Schengen implementation agreement is Arts 31 and 34 of the EU Treaty. See also ECJ, Case C–469/03 *Miraglia* [2005] E.C.R. I–2009.

[463] See Art.46(b) of the EU Treaty, which refers to Art.35 of that Treaty. In addition, Art.46(d) of the EU Treaty provides that acts of the institutions over which the Court of Justice has jurisdiction under the EU Treaty may be reviewed in the light of fundamental rights as defined in Art.6(2) of the EU Treaty.

Under Art.35(1) of the EU Treaty, the Court is empowered to give preliminary rulings on the validity and interpretation of framework decisions and decisions (for these acts, see Art.34(2)(b) and (c)), on the interpretation of conventions established under Title VI and on the validity and interpretation of measures implementing them (for such measures, see Art.34(2)(d)).[464]

That jurisdiction has to be expressly accepted by Member States by declaration.[465] In such declaration, the Member State may elect to allow either any court or tribunal against whose decisions there is no judicial remedy under national law[466] or any court or tribunal to request a preliminary ruling from the Court.[467]

Under Art.35(5) of the EU Treaty, however, the Court of Justice has no jurisdiction to review the "validity or proportionality of operations carried out by the police or other law enforcement services of a Member State or the exercise of the responsibilities incumbent upon Member States with regard to the maintenance of law and order and the safeguarding of internal security".

In addition to that specific power to give preliminary rulings, the Court has jurisdiction in direct actions brought under Art.35(6) of the EU Treaty to review the legality of framework decisions and decisions.[468] This procedure resembles in some respects the action for annulment provided for in Art.230 of the EC Treaty (see Ch.7, *supra*), except that an action may be

---

[464] For a first example of a reference for a preliminary ruling on the interpretation of a framework decision, see ECJ, Case C–105/03 *Pupino* [2005] E.C.R. I–5285. In that case the Court ruled that the principle of interpretation in conformity with Community law is binding in relation to framework decisions adopted in the context of Title VI of the EU Treaty. When applying national law, a national court which is called upon to interpret it must do so as far as possible in the light of the wording and purpose of the framework decision in order to attain the result which it pursues and thus comply with Art.34(2)(b) of the EU Treaty (*ibid.*, para. 43).

[465] EU Treaty, Art.35(2). However, irrespective as to whether a Member State has or has not accepted the Court's jurisdiction under Art.35(1), it may submit statements of case or written observations to the Court in cases arising under that provision (see EU Treaty, Art.35(4)).

[466] EU Treaty, Art.35(3)(a). Spain and Hungary have accepted the Court's jurisdiction on these terms, see [2005] O.J. L327/19; [2005] O.J. C318/1 (and further citations therein).

[467] EU Treaty, Art.35(3)(b). A declaration to this effect has been lodged by Austria, Belgium, the Czech Republic, Finland, France, Germany, Greece, Italy, Luxembourg, the Netherlands, Portugal and Sweden, see [2005] O.J. L327/19; [2005] O.J. C318/1 (and further citations therein). Upon lodging such a declaration, Member States may reserve the right to make provision in their national law to the effect that a national court or tribunal against whose decisions there is no remedy under national law is *required* to make a reference to the Court of Justice: Declaration (No 10) *ad* Art.35 of the EU Treaty, [1997] O.J. C340/133. In their declarations, Austria, Belgium, the Czech Republic, France, Germany, Italy, Luxembourg, the Netherlands, and Spain reserved that right. See Fennelly, "The area of 'Freedom, Security and Justice', and the European Court of Justice—A Personal View" (2000) (1) I.C.L.Q 8–12; Knapp, "Die Garantie des effektiven Rechtsschutzes durch den EuGH im 'Raum der Freiheit, der Sicherheit und des Rechts'" (2001) D.ö.V. 13–14.

[468] See ECJ (judgment of September 13, 2005), Case C–176/03 *Commission v Council*, not yet reported.

515

brought only by a Member State or the Commission and not by any other institution or natural or legal persons. The pleas which may be raised are lack of competence, infringement of an essential procedural requirement, infringement of the EU Treaty or of any rule of law relating to its application and misuse of powers. An action must be brought within two months of publication of the measure challenged.[469]

Lastly, under Art.35(7) of the EU Treaty, the Court of Justice has jurisdiction to rule on any dispute between Member States regarding the interpretation or the application of acts adopted under Art.34(2) whenever such dispute cannot be settled by the Council within six months of its being referred to that institution by one of its members. This procedure bears a resemblance to the action which a Member State may bring before the Court against another Member State under Art.227 of the EC Treaty for failure to fulfil an obligation (see 5–029, *supra*).

Art.35(7) also confers jurisdiction on the Court of Justice to "rule on any dispute between Member States and the Commission regarding the interpretation or the application of conventions established under Art.34(2)(d)" of the EU Treaty. This procedure resembles the action for failure to fulfil obligations which the Commission may bring against a Member State under Art.226 of the EC Treaty (see 5–025, *supra*).

22–005 **No other jurisdiction for the Court of Justice.** Apart from the actions provided for in Art.35(1), (6) and (7) of the EU Treaty, the Court of Justice has no jurisdiction to review acts of the institutions of the Union in the field of police and judicial cooperation.[470] Actions for damages brought by natural and legal persons alleging that they have sustained damage as a result of such action on the part of the Union have been declared inadmissible.[471] In order to obviate the choice of an incorrect legal basis wrongly resulting in the exclusion of any legal redress, the Community judicature will closely consider whether the Union was justified in basing its action on a provision of Title VI of the EU Treaty.[472]

---

[469] See ECJ (judgment of September 13, 2005), Case C–176/03 *Commission v Council*, not yet reported, in which the Commission obtained the annulment of Council Framework Decision 2003/80/JHA of January 27, 2003 on the protection of the environment through criminal law ([2003] O.J. L29/55). The aim of the framework decision was to protect the environment through the imposition of criminal sanctions for environmental offences, which corresponded to the Community competences set forth, in particular, in Title XIX (Arts 174 to 176) and Art.6 of the EC Treaty.

[470] See ECJ, Case C–160/03 *Spain v Eurojust* [2005] E.C.R. I–2077, paras 35–44.

[471] CFI (order of June 7, 2004), Case T–333/02 *Gestoras Pro-Amnistia and Others v Council*, not reported, paras 32–34; CFI (order of June 7, 2004), Case T–338/02 *Segi and Others v Council* [2004] E.C.R. II–1647, paras 32–34.

[472] CFI (order of June 7, 2004), Case T–333/02 *Gestoras Pro-Amnistia and Others v Council*, not reported, paras 41–42; CFI (order of June 7, 2004), Case T–338/02 *Segi and Others v Council* [2004] E.C.R. II–1647, paras 41–42. See also ECJ (judgment of September 13, 2005), Case C–176/03 *Commission v Council*, not yet reported.

III. Enhanced Cooperation in the Context of Police and Judicial Cooperation in Criminal Matters

General. The jurisdiction of the Court of Justice in regard to enhanced   22–006
cooperation between Member States wishing to engage in it within the area
of the third pillar is dealt with in Art.40(3) of the EU Treaty.[473]

The mechanism of legal protection provided for in Art.35 of the EU
Treaty as outlined above applies in full to such enhanced cooperation by
virtue of Art.40(2), which provides that the provisions of Arts 29 to 39,
including therefore Art.35, are to apply to enhanced cooperation.

Under Art.40(3) of the EU Treaty, however, the Court of Justice has all
its powers under the EC Treaty in order to enforce the conditions which
have to be respected in order to achieve enhanced cooperation as laid down
in Arts 40a and 40b, which also refer to the obligation to comply with Arts
43, 44 and 45.

IV. The Constitution

Extension of the Community model. The extension of the Community   22–007
model to the old third pillar (police and judicial cooperation in criminal
matters) is reflected in the suppression of restrictions on the exercise by the
Court of Justice of its competences in matters concerning freedom, security
and justice. The only reservation lies nevertheless in the fact that, under
with Art.III–377 of the Constitution, the Court should, in relation to police
and judicial cooperation in criminal matters, abstain from reviewing "the
validity or proportionality of operations carried out by the police or the
other law-enforcement services of a Member State or the exercise of the
responsibilities incumbent upon Member States with regard to the maintenance of law and order and the safeguarding of internal security".[474]

Jurisdiction no longer dependent upon declarations of Member   22–008
States. The generalisation of the Community model to the third pillar
signifies that the power of national courts to refer preliminary questions on
the interpretation and the validity of the law will no longer depend on a
declaration of the Member States to that effect, as is the present situation
for police and judicial cooperation in criminal matters. All national courts
(without restriction) will be empowered to make a reference for a
preliminary ruling with regard to all measures of the Union taken in the

---

[473] No specific procedures are provided for to deal with enhanced cooperation in the context
of the EC Treaty (pursuant to Arts 11 and 11a of the EC Treaty). Arts 220 to 245 of the
EC Treaty apply unreservedly.
[474] See also Constitution, Art.III–262.

field of freedom, security and justice. Similarly, actions for annulment and infringement actions will no longer be subject to the restrictions laid down in Art.35 of the EU Treaty.

PART V

PROCEDURE BEFORE THE COURT OF JUSTICE AND THE COURT OF FIRST INSTANCE

CHAPTER 23

INTRODUCTION

The different types of jurisdiction of the Court of Justice and the Court of   **23–001**
First Instance give rise to six sorts of procedures: the procedure in the case
of direct actions, which is followed where an applicant brings a case before
the Court of Justice or the Court of First Instance against a named
defendant (irrespective of the type of case); the procedure in the case of a
reference for a preliminary ruling pursuant to Art.234 of the EC Treaty; the
procedure where the Council, the Commission or a Member State makes a
reference for a preliminary ruling pursuant to Art.68(3) of the EC Treaty
on the interpretation of Title VI of the EC Treaty (Visas, asylum,
immigration and other policies related to free movement of persons) or on
acts of the Community institutions based on that title[1]; the procedure
applicable to dispute resolution under Art.35 of the EU Treaty[2]; the
procedure in the case of an appeal against a decision of the Court of First
Instance and, lastly, the procedure for review of a decision of the Court of
First Instance.[3]

The procedure is governed by the Statute of the Court of Justice, whose   **23–002**
provisions have the same legal force as Treaty articles, even though the
rules contained therein (with the exception of those relating to the Status of
Judges and Advocates General (Title 1)) may be amended by the Council,
acting unanimously at the request of the Court of Justice and after
consulting the Commission and the European Parliament[4] or at the request
of the Commission and after consulting the European Parliament and the
Court of Justice. The rules set out in the Statutes are expanded upon in the
Rules of Procedure of the Court of Justice and the Court of First Instance,
which are adopted by the Court of Justice and the Court of First Instance
in agreement with the Court of Justice, respectively, and approved by the
Council by a qualified majority vote.[5] There are also the Supplementary

---

[1] The rules for this procedure are set out in Art.109a of the ECJ Rules of Procedure and will
not be further discussed hereinafter.
[2] ECJ, Rules of Procedure, Art.109b; this procedure will not be further discussed hereinafter.
[3] As far as review is concerned, see Ch.17, *supra*.
[4] EC Treaty, Art.245, second para.; EAEC Treaty, Art.160, second para.
[5] Court of Justice: see EC Treaty, Art.223, sixth para.; EAEC Treaty, Art.160, third para.
Court of First Instance: see EC Treaty, Art.224, fifth para.; EAEC Treaty, Art.140, fifth
para. For a brief article on the working methods of the Court of Justice which is well worth
reading, see Edward, "How the Court of Justice Works" (1995) E.L.Rev. 539–558.

Rules[6] and the Instructions to the Registrar[7] and the Practice Directions for parties,[8] the Information Note on references from national courts for a preliminary ruling[9] and the Notes for the guidance of Counsel.[10] All relevant texts relating to procedure can be consulted at the website of the Court of Justice (*www.curia.eu.int*).

---

[6] Done at Luxembourg on December 4, 1974 ([1974] O.J. L350/29), last amended on February 21, 2006 ([2006] O.J. L72/1).

[7] Done at Luxembourg on December 4, 1974 ([1974] O.J. L350/33), last amended on October 3, 1986 ([1986] O.J. C286/4). The CFI Instructions to the Registrar were done at Luxembourg on March 3, 1994 ([1994] O.J. L78/32) and amended on March 29, 2001 ([2001] O.J. L119) and June 5, 2002 ([2002] O.J. L160).

[8] As far as the Court of Justice is concerned, see the Practice Directions relating to direct actions and appeals ([2004] O.J. L361/15). For the Court of First Instance, see the Practice Directions to parties ([2002] O.J. L87/48). See also *www.curia.eu.int*.

[9] See *www.curia.eu.int*.

[10] Notes for the guidance of Counsel for the Court of Justice and Notes for the guidance of Counsel before for the Court of First Instance for the oral procedure (see *www.curia.eu.int*).

CHAPTER 24

PROCEDURE IN THE CASE OF DIRECT ACTIONS

General. The procedure in the case of direct actions consists of two parts, the written procedure and the oral procedure.[11] The case closes with a judicial decision (judgment or order), unless the parties discontinue the proceedings, the applicant withdraws its claims or the Court of Justice or the Court of First Instance, as the case may be, decides that there is no need to proceed to judgment. Exceptionally, judgments of either court may be contested by means of exceptional review procedures. Furthermore, appeals may be brought against decisions "at first instance" of the Court of First Instance[12] and a review procedure can be initiated against decisions "at last instance" of the latter Court.[13] Lastly, parties may apply to the Court of Justice or the Court of First Instance for interpretation of a judgment, rectification of clerical mistakes or rectification of an omission to give a decision.

24-001

I. THE WRITTEN PROCEDURE

Objective. The purpose of the written procedure is to define the subject-matter of the action and to put before the Court of Justice or the Court of First Instance all the claims of the parties.

24-002

A. THE APPLICATION

1. Lodging an application

Lodging of application. A case is brought before the Court of Justice or the Court of First Instance by addressing an application to the Registrar.[14]

The application may be handed in to the registry or sent by post, by fax or by e-mail.[15] In the event that it is sent by e-mail, only a scanned copy of

24-003

---

[11] Statute, Art.20.
[12] See Ch.16, *supra*.
[13] See Ch.17, *supra*.
[14] Statute, Art.21, first para.
[15] Fax number of the ECJ: (352) 4337 66; e-mail address of the ECJ: *ECJ.Registry@curia.eu.int*. Fax number of the CFI: (352) 4303 2100; e-mail address of the CFI: *CFI.Registry@curia.eu.int*.

the signed original will be accepted.[16] The original, accompanied by all annexes referred to therein, must be lodged together with five copies for the Court of Justice/Court of First Instance and a copy for every other party to the proceedings. Copies must be certified by the party lodging them (in this case the applicant).[17]

24–004 **Application must be signed.** The original of the application must be signed by the agent[18] or lawyer representing the applicant (see 24–186 to 24–191, *infra*).[19] If it is not so signed, it will not be registered by the Registrar[20] and will be returned to the applicant.[21] The obligation for individuals to have each pleading signed by a lawyer is designed to ensure that what is submitted to the Court of Justice or the Court of First Instance consists of only legal opinions and explanations of fact which are considered by a lawyer to be fit to be put forward.[22] A pleading which was drafted by the party himself and merely formally signed by his lawyer may be regarded, in the light of all the circumstances, as being an inadmissible pleading.[23]

---

[16] Documents should be scanned at a resolution of 300 DPI and wherever possible, in PDF format (images plus text), using Acrobat or Readiris 7 Pro software (see ECJ Practice Directions, point 1; CFI Practice Directions, point I,1). Documents sent by e-mail may not exceed 4 megabites, or approximately 30 pages. Documents exceeding this maximum size will be automatically returned to sender and may not be processed (see "Lodging of documents" on *www.curia.eu.int*).

[17] ECJ Rules of Procedure, Art.37(1); CFI Rules of Procedure, Art.43(1).

[18] See for the organisation of the representation of the UK, Collins, "Representation of a Member State before the Court of Justice of the European Communities: practice in the UK" (2002) E.L.Rev. 359–364.

[19] Statute, Art.19, third para.; see also ECJ Rules of Procedure, Art.37(1); CFI Rules of Procedure, Art.43(1). For an application, see CFI, Case T–158/99 *Thermenhotel Stoiser Franz and Others v Commission* [2004] E.C.R. II–1, paras 41–46.

[20] Art.16 of the ECJ Rules of Procedure and Art.24 of the CFI Rules of Procedure require the respective Registrars to keep a register in which all pleadings and supporting documents have to be entered.

[21] ECJ, Joined Cases 220 and 221/78 *ALA and ALFER v Commission* [1979] E.C.R. 1693, paras 3–5; CFI (order of November 29, 1993), Case T–56/92 *Koelman v Commission* [1993] E.C.R. II–1267, para.1.

[22] This suggestion was put forward by Advocate General K. Roemer in ECJ, Case 108/63 *Merlini v High Authority* [1965] E.C.R. 1, at 16. For those reasons, the lawyer signing the application must be a "third party" collaborating in the administration of justice and being required to provide, in full independence and in the overriding interests of justice, such legal assistance as his or her client needs. An application which is signed by a lawyer who is also a director of the company submitting the application will be inadmissible on the ground that since the lawyer is an organ of the company, he or she cannot be regarded as being an independent third party (CFI (order of December 8, 1999), Case T–79/99 *Euro-Lex v OHIM (EU-LEX)* [1999] E.C.R. II–3555).

[23] Judgment in *Merlini v High Authority*, cited in the preceding n., at 9. The Court of Justice seems to have gone further than its Advocate General, who considered the merely formal signature of a pleading by a lawyer only as "negligence by the lawyer in his conduct of the proceedings" which might perhaps be considered incompatible with the dignity of the Court (ECJ Rules of Procedure, Art.35(1); CFI Rules of Procedure, Art.41(1)). All the same, this precedent should be approached with some caution given that the Court of Justice held that the pleading drafted by the applicant itself, which the lawyer had signed and lodged as the

Application must be dated. The application must be dated, but for the   **24–005**
purposes of the reckoning of time-limits for taking steps in proceedings,
only the date of lodgment at the registry is taken into account (*i.e.* the date
on which the application arrives at the registry).[24] Where, however, the
application is received by the registry together with the schedule of
documents by telefax or other technical means of communication available
to the Court of Justice or the Court of First Instance (e-mail), the date of
lodgment for the purposes of compliance with the time-limits for taking
steps in proceedings is deemed to be the date of receipt, provided that the
signed original[25] of the pleading, accompanied by the annexes and copies is
lodged at the registry no later than 10 days thereafter.[26]

2. Content

Requirements. The identity of the parties, the subject-matter of the   **24–006**
proceedings and the pleas in law adduced are determined by the application.[27] In the course of the procedure, the application may not, or only
exceptionally, be modified in these respects.

The following must appear at the beginning of each application:
- the applicant's name and address;
- the name and capacity of the applicant's agent or lawyer;
- the identity of the party or parties against whom the action is
  brought;
- the address for service in Luxembourg and/or agreement to service
  by telefax or any other technical means of communication.[28]

---

reply, should not only be rejected as being in breach of Art.20 of the ECSC Statute and
Art.37 of the ECJ Rules of Procedure, but also because it "rais[ed] fresh submissions and
arguments" (*ibid.*).

[24] ECJ Rules of Procedure, Art.37(3); CFI Rules of Procedure, Art.43(3). A party has the
right to lodge a document instituting legal proceedings at any time up to the last working
day of the period set by the Statute. This means that, prior to the expiry of that period, he
or she must be allowed to withdraw a first document instituting legal proceedings in order to
replace it, within the same period, by a new version of that document (ECJ, Case C–274/00
P *Simon v Commission* [2002] E.C.R. I–5999, para.30)

[25] According to ECJ Rules of Procedure, Art.37(6) and CFI Rules of Procedure, Art.43(7),
the Court "may by decision determine the criteria for a procedural document sent to the
registry by electronic means to be deemed to be the original of that document. That
decision shall be published in the *Official Journal of the European Union*".

[26] ECJ, Rules of Procedure, Art.37(6); CFI Rules of Procedure, Art.43(6). In the event of any
discrepancy between the signed original and the copy previously lodged, only the date of
lodgment of the signed original will be taken into consideration ECJ Practice Directions,
point 3, CFI Practice Directions, point I.3). For an application, see CFI (order of May 8,
2003), Case T–63/03 *El Corte Inglés v OHIM*, not reported: application inadmissible because
the original was not lodged with the registry in time.

[27] Art.37 of the ECJ Rules of Procedure and Art.43 of the CFI Rules of Procedure set out
general conditions with which every pleading must comply. For the Court of First Instance's
desiderata as to the structure and layout of the application, see Notes for the guidance of
counsel (n.10, *supra*); ECJ and CFI Practice Directions (n.8, *supra*).

[28] ECJ Rules of Procedure, Art.38(1); CFI Rules of Procedure, Art.44(1); ECJ Practice
Directions, point 10; CFI Practice Directions, point III, 2.

The application must also state:
- the subject-matter of the proceedings and a summary of the pleas in law on which the application is based;
- the form of order sought by the applicant;
- where appropriate, the nature of any evidence offered in support.[29]

a. Name and address of the applicant

24–007 **General.** This requirement raises few problems. Nevertheless, the Court of First Instance was once faced with the question whether the applicant's details could be altered at the request of the defendant. The latter contended that the partnership which had brought the action had no capacity to bring proceedings and asked the Court to designate the two sole partners as applicants. The Court joined the partners as applicants after finding that they had signed the authority of the lawyer acting in the case.[30]

An application may be lodged on behalf of several parties,[31] provided that it has the same subject-matter and raises the same pleas in law as regards each of them.[32] An applicant's successors are entitled to continue proceedings started by the deceased.[33] If there are no successors or if the successors decline the succession the proceedings will become devoid of purpose.[34] A legal person resulting from the merger of legal persons who have brought proceedings before the Court of First Instance—or an appeal before the Court of Justice—may continue the proceedings where that person has acquired the rights and obligations of the original applicants/appellants.[35]

24–008 **Address for service in Luxembourg.** The applicant should in principle have an address for service in Luxembourg at which all pleadings may be served. To this end, the application must state the name of the person who is authorised and has expressed willingness to accept all service.[36] However, in addition to, or instead of, specifying an address for service as referred to in

---

[29] ECJ Rules of Procedure, Art.38(1); CFI Rules of Procedure, Art.44(1).

[30] CFI (order of March 30, 1994), Case T–482/93 *Weber v Commission*, not reported, para.4. See also CFI, Case T–174/95 *Svenska Journalistförbundet v Council* [1998] E.C.R. II–2289, paras 33–44; CFI, Case T–185/02 *Ruiz-Picasso and Others v OHIM* [2004] E.C.R. II–1739, paras 19–22.

[31] The unintentional omission of the name of one of the applicants can be subsequently remedied if the defendant does not object: see ECJ, Case 21/58 *Felten und Guilleaume Carlswerk Eisen- und Stahl and Walzwerke v High Authority* [1959] E.C.R. 99, at 101.

[32] ECJ, Case 13/57 *Wirtschaftsvereinigung Eisen- und Stahlindustrie and Others v High Authority* [1957 and 1958] E.C.R. 265, at 277.

[33] ECJ, Case 92/82 *Gutmann v Commission* [1983] E.C.R. 3127.

[34] CFI (order of July 14, 2004), Case T–360/02 *Yorck von Wartenburg v Commission* not reported, paras 5–10.

[35] ECJ, Case 294/83 *Les Verts v European Parliament* [1986] E.C.R. 1339, paras 15–18.

[36] ECJ Rules of Procedure, Art.38(2), first subpara.; CFI Rules of Procedure, Art.44(2), first subpara.

the first subpara., the application may state that the lawyer or agent agrees that service is to be effected on him by telefax or other technical means of communication (e-mail).[37]

If these requirements are not satisfied, all service on the applicant for the purpose of the proceedings will be effected by registered letter addressed to the agent or lawyer of the party. Service is then deemed to be duly effected by the lodging of the registered letter at the post office in Luxembourg.[38] Any procedural time-limits applicable start to run as from the said deemed service, which means that the entire risk of delay in the post is borne by the applicant in the event that he has neglected to provide a more reliable address for service in Luxembourg.[39] In this context, it would even be hard to argue that a postal strike constitutes *force majeure*.

b. Designation of the party against whom the application is made

General. The requirement that the application state the name of the party against whom it is made is satisfied if it is sufficiently clear from the application as a whole against whom the action is being brought. The omission of the defendant's name by an oversight does not necessarily mean that the application is inadmissible, provided that the rights of the defence are not impaired.[40] It is sufficient for the judgment to designate the defendant correctly.[41] The defendant's identity may also emerge from the contested act.[42] However, it is not possible to extend the application to include a defendant who is not designated in the application and whose identity does not emerge therefrom.[43]   24–009

Staff cases. Actions relating to disputes between "the Community" and its servants[44] must be brought against the institution in which the applicant is or was employed, in which his or her predecessor was employed or where   24–010

---

[37] ECJ Rules of Procedure, Art.38(2), second subpara.; CFI Rules of Procedure, Art.44(2), second subpara. See also ECJ Practice Directions, point 4; CFI Practice Directions, point 1, 4.

[38] ECJ Rules of Procedure, Art.38(2), second subpara.; CFI Rules of Procedure, Art.44(2), second subpara.

[39] Formerly, the stricter sanction of holding the application to be inadmissible applied: ECJ (order of January 29, 1986), Case 297/84 *Sahinler v Commission* [1986] E.C.R. 443.

[40] ECJ (order of July 3, 1986), Case 85/86 *Commission v EIB* [1986] E.C.R. 2215 (the application, which stated that the defendant was the "European Investment Bank" instead of the "Board of Governors of the European Investment Bank", was declared admissible on the ground that it appeared from that pleading that the action brought under Art.237(b) of the E[E]C Treaty was directed against the EIB's Board of Governors).

[41] Opinion of Advocate General G. Reischl in ECJ, Case 44/76 *Milch-, Fett- und Eier-Kontor v Council and Commission* [1977] E.C.R. 393, at 413. See also CFI (order of July 12, 2005), Case T–163/04 *Schäfer v OHIM*, not reported, para.23.

[42] ECJ, Joined Cases C–184/02 and C–223/02 *Spain and Finland v European Parliament and Council* [2004] E.C.R. I–7789, para.17.

[43] ECJ (order of November 10, 1977), Case 90/77 *Stimming v Commission* [1977] E.C.R. 2113.

[44] EC Treaty, Art.236.

he or she took part in a recruitment procedure.[45] As regards the non-contractual liability of "the Community",[46] actions for damages must be brought against the institution whose conduct gave rise to the alleged liability.[47]

c. Subject-matter of the proceedings and summary of the pleas in law on which the application is based

24–011 **General.** The application must set out a brief summary of the facts and the subject-matter of the proceedings. This means that both its purpose and, where appropriate, the act against which the proceedings are brought must be specified. In addition, the application must contain a summary of the pleas in fact and law on which the application is based.

24–012 **Subject-matter and pleas must be clearly stated.** The Court of Justice and the Court of First Instance require the subject-matter of the proceedings and the pleas raised to be stated clearly and precisely in order that the defendant may prepare its defence and the Court give judgment without having to have further particulars.[48] In order to secure legal certainty and the sound administration of justice, the essential facts and law on which the application is based must be set out—at least summarily—in the text of the application itself in a coherent and comprehensible manner.[49] If the

---

[45] See, for example, ECJ, Case 18/63 *Wollast (née Schmitz) v EEC* [1964] E.C.R. 85, at 96: ECJ, Case 27/63 *Raponi v Commission* [1964] E.C.R. 129, at 135–136; ECJ, Joined Cases 79 and 82/63 *Reynier and Erba v Commission* [1964] E.C.R. 259, 265; CFI, Case T–497/93 *Hogan v Court of Justice* [1995] E.C.R. II–703, para.31.

[46] EC Treaty, Art.288, second para.

[47] See 11–010, *supra*.

[48] ECJ, Case 281/82 *Unifrex v Council and Commission* [1984] E.C.R. 1969, para.15; CFI, Case T–21/90 *Generlich v Commission* [1991] E.C.R. II–1323, paras 31–32; CFI (order of April 28, 1993), Case T–85/92 *De Hoe v Commission* [1993] E.C.R. II–523, para.20, upheld by ECJ (order of March 7, 1994), Case C–338/93 P *De Hoe v Commission* [1994] E.C.R. I–819, para.29; CFI (order of November 29, 1993), Case T–56/92 *Koelman v Commission* [1993] E.C.R. II–1267, para.21; CFI, Case T–575/93 *Koelman v Commission* [1996] E.C.R. II–1, para.33; CFI, Case T–84/96 *Cipeke v Commission* [1997] E.C.R. II–2081, paras 30–31; CFI, Case T–5/97 *Industrie des Poudres Sphériques v Commission* [2000] E.C.R. II–3755, paras 192–195. For an action for damages, see CFI (order of May 14, 1998), Case T–262/97 *Goldstein v Commission* [1998] E.C.R. II–2175, paras 19–30; CFI, Case T–13/96 *TEAM v Commission* [1998] E.C.R. II–4073, para.29 (an application initiating an action for damages must contain particulars which make it possible to determine what conduct the applicant attributes to the institution, the grounds for which the applicant considers that there is a causal link between that conduct and the alleged damage and the nature and extent of the damage. As far as the damage is concerned, it is sufficient for the application to provide sufficient evidence on the basis of which its nature and extent can be assessed and so as to allow the defendant institution to prepare its defence. The applicant must supplement this information in its reply by figures, thereby enabling the defendant to discuss them in its rejoinder and at the hearing.) See in addition as regards actions for damages: CFI, Joined Cases T–215/01, T–220/01 and T–221/01 *Calberson v Commission* [2004] E.C.R. II–587, paras 176–180; CFI (order of February 20, 2004), Case T–319/03 *French and Others v Council and Commission* [2004] E.C.R. II–769, paras 11–25.

[49] CFI (order of March 26, 1992), Case T–35/92 TO 2 *Buggenhout and Others*, not reported, paras 16–17; CFI, Case T–338/99 *Schuerer v Council* [2000] E.C.R. II–2571, ECR-SC I-A-131, II–599, para.19.

application fails to provide details of the underlying facts and circumstances, it will be inadmissible on the ground that the Court is unable to rule on it.[50] The text of the application may be elucidated by references to passages in documents appended to it, but a general reference to such documents cannot constitute a statement of the essential facts and law on which the action is based.[51] Furthermore, information may not be provided at the hearing in order to fill gaps in the application.[52] The degree of precision required of an application varies from case to case.[53] The Court of Justice and the Court of First Instance may not go so far in specifying the subject-matter of the application as to impair the rights of the defence or of interested third parties.[54]

Court is bound by the subject-matter of the case. The Court is bound by 24–013 the subject-matter of the case as stated in the application.[55] A dispute between the applicant and the defendant about the demarcation of the subject-matter of the litigation will not have any bearing on the admissibility of the application so long as the Court is able to define the subject-matter of the action precisely on the basis of the application.[56]

Presentation of pleas. As far as concerns the requirement for a summary of 24–014 the pleas in law on which the application is based, it must be possible to identify from the text of the application what the applicant's specific complaints are and the legal and factual particulars on which they are based.[57] The resulting exposition must enable the defendant to protect its

---

[50] ECJ, Case C–52/90 *Commission v Denmark* [1992] E.C.R. I–2187, paras 17–18; ECJ (judgment of October 14, 2004), Case C–55/03 *Commission v Spain*, not reported, paras 24–29; ECJ (order of November 11, 2004), Case C–114/03 P *Rocco Piscioneri v European Parliament*, not reported, paras 7–9; CFI (order of November 25, 2003), Case T–85/01 *IAMA Consulting v Commission* [2003] E.C.R. II–4973, paras 58–59; CFI (judgment of July 13, 2004), Case T–115/02 *AVEX v OHIM*, not reported, para.11 (trade mark case); CFI (order of July 2, 2004), Case T–256/03 *Bundesverband der Nahrungsmittel- und Speiseresteverwertung and Kloh v Commission*, not yet reported, paras 29–30.

[51] CFI (order of November 29, 1993), Case T–56/92 *Koelman v Commission* [1993] E.C.R. II–1267, para.21; CFI, Case T–84/96 *Cipeke v Commission* [1997] E.C.R. II–2081, paras 33–34; CFI, Case T–127/02 *Concept-Anlagen v OHIM* [2004] E.C.R. II–1113, paras 17–21.

[52] CFI, Case T–195/95 *Guérin Automobiles v Commission* [1997] E.C.R. II–679, para.26; CFI, Case T–247/01 *eCopy v OHIM (ECOPY)* [2002] E.C.R. II–5301, para.17.

[53] See *Commentaire Mégret*, at 422. For an example, see CFI, Case T–20/94 *Hartmann v Council and Commission* [1997] E.C.R. II–595, para.37.

[54] ECJ, Case 30/68 *Lacroix v Commission* [1970] E.C.R. 301, paras 21–28.

[55] ECJ, Case 232/78 *Commission v France* [1979] E.C.R. 2729, para.3.

[56] ECJ, Case 168/78 *Commission v France* [1980] E.C.R. 347, paras 17–25; ECJ, Case 270/83 *Commission v France* [1986] E.C.R. 273, at 300–301; CFI (order of June 19, 1995), Case T–107/94 *Kik v Council and Commission* [1995] E.C.R. II–1717, para.29.

[57] ECJ, Case 111/63 *Lemmerz-Werke v High Authority* [1965] E.C.R. 677, at 696; ECJ, Joined Cases 26 and 86/79 *Forges de Thy-Marcinelle and Monceau v Commission* [1980] E.C.R. 1083, para.4; ECJ, Case C–347/88 *Commission v Greece* [1990] E.C.R. I–4747, para.28; ECJ, Case C–52/90 *Commission v Denmark* [1992] E.C.R. I–2187, para.17; CFI (order of April 28, 1993), Case T–85/92 *De Hoe v Commission* [1993] E.C.R. II–523, para.22; CFI (order of

interests and the Court to carry out judicial review. The applicant is not bound to set out its pleas in any particular way.[58] It is also unnecessary for express reference to be made to the provision of Community law which has allegedly been breached or for a legal categorisation to be given to the pleas raised in the application,[59] provided that the pleas emerge sufficiently clearly from the application.[60] Even an error in citing the provision of Community law on which a plea is based will not cause that plea to be inadmissible.

A mere enumeration of pleas does not suffice. The application must set out the facts and reasoning on which each plea is based.[61] A reference to pleas raised in another case, even if the two cases are linked, does not constitute a sufficient statement of the pleas in law on which the application is based.[62] Such a reference, however, will not render the application

---

March 28, 1994), Case T–515/93 *B v Commission* [1994] ECR-SC II–379, para.12; CFI (order of February 4, 2005), Case T–20/04 *Aguar Fernandez and Others v Commission*, not reported, paras 44–47. It is possible that the summary of some pleas satisfy this condition and the summary of others does not. In this event, the Community judicature will declare inadmissible only those pleas which are not sufficiently defined and not the application as a whole (CFI, Joined Cases T–9/96 and T–211/96 *Européenne Automobile v Commission* [1999] E.C.R. II–3639, para.57; CFI, Case T–251/97 *T. Port v Commission* [2000] E.C.R. II–1775, paras 90–92).

[58] CFI, Case T–145/98 *ADT Projekt v Commission* [2000] E.C.R. II–387, para.67.

[59] ECJ, Joined Cases 19 and 21/60, 2 and 3/61 *Société Fives Lille Cail and Others v High Authority* [1961] E.C.R. 281, at 295; CFI, Case T–35/93 *Cucchiara and Others v Commission* [1994] ECR-SC II–413, paras 26–27 (English abstract at I–A–126).

[60] ECJ, Joined Cases 7/56 and 3–7/57 *Algera and Others v Common Assembly* [1957 and 1958] E.C.R. 39, at 64–65; ECJ, Joined Cases 2–10/63 *Società Industriale Acciaerie San Michele and Others v High Authority* [1963] E.C.R. 327, at 341; ECJ, Case 62/65 *Serio v Commission* [1966] E.C.R. 561, at 568 (it must be sufficiently clear from the application as a whole what legal principles the applicant considers have been breached); CFI, Case T–18/90 *Jongen v Commission* [1991] E.C.R. II–187, para.13. But see CFI, Case T–224/95 *Tremblay and Others v Commission* [1997] E.C.R. II–2215, paras 79–82, in which the Court of First Instance held that the claim that the defendant had "infringed the Treaty", which was only briefly enlarged upon in general terms in the application, did not enable it to determine the subject-matter of the proceedings sufficiently precisely and so did not enable the Commission effectively to defend itself.

[61] ECJ, Joined Cases 19 and 21/60, 2 and 3/61 *Société Fives Lille Cail and Others v High Authority* [1961] E.C.R. 281, at 295; ECJ, Case C–52/90 *Commission v Denmark* [1992] E.C.R. I–2187, para.18. An application by which an action for damages is brought must contain the following particulars: the evidence from which the conduct alleged against the institution can be identified, the reasons for which the applicant considers that there is a causal link between the conduct and the damage it claims to have suffered, and the nature and extent of that damage: CFI, Case T–64/89 *Automec v Commission* [1990] E.C.R. II–367, para.73; CFI, Case T–167/94 *Nölle v Council and Commission* [1995] E.C.R. II–2589, para.32; CFI, Case T–38/96 *Guérin Automobiles v Commission* [1997] E.C.R. II–1223, para.42; CFI, Case T–277/97 *Ismeri Europa v Court of Auditors* [1999] E.C.R. II–1825, paras 28–30, 65 and 81; CFI, Case T–210/00 *Biret & Cie v Council* [2002] E.C.R. II–47, para.34.

[62] ECJ, Case 9/55 *Société des Charbonnages de Beeringen and Others v High Authority* [1954 to 1956] E.C.R. 311, at 325; ECJ, Joined Cases 19 and 65/63 *Prakash v Commission* [1965] E.C.R. 533, at 546. But see CFI, Case T–37/91 *ICI v Commission* [1995] E.C.R. II–1901, para.47, in which the Court of First Instance accepted a reference made in one case to another on account of the specific circumstances; namely a close link existed between two

inadmissible if, leaving aside that reference, the application contains all the necessary particulars.[63]

New pleas. New pleas—that is to say, pleas not raised in the application— may not be introduced in the course of the proceedings unless they are based on matters of law or of fact which come to light in the course of the proceedings.[64] An amendment, in the course of proceedings, of the

24–015

---

cases which had not been joined (the parties, the agents and the lawyers were the same, the actions had been brought before the Court on the same day, the cases had been assigned to the same Chamber and the same Judge-Rapporteur and the contested decisions related to aspects of competition on the same market).

[63] ECJ, Case 4/69 *Lütticke v Commission* [1971] E.C.R. 325, paras 2–4.

[64] ECJ Rules of Procedure, Art.42(2); CFI Rules of Procedure, Art.48(2). The fact that the applicant became aware of a factual matter during the course of the procedure before the Court of First Instance or the Court of Justice does not mean that that element constitutes a matter of fact coming to light in the course of the procedure. A further requirement is that the applicant was not in a position to be aware of that matter previously (CFI, Case T–139/99 *AICS v European Parliament* [2000] E.C.R. II–2849, para.62; CFI, Case T–76/02 *Messina v Commission* [2003] E.C.R. II–3203, paras 36–37). For instances in which a new plea was not admitted, see ECJ, Case 11/81 *Dürbeck v Commission* [1982] E.C.R. 1251, paras 13–15; ECJ, Case 108/81 *Amylum v Council* [1982] E.C.R. 3107, paras 23–26; ECJ, Case 59/83 *Biovilac v EEC* [1984] E.C.R. 4057, paras 24–25; ECJ, Case 5/85 *AKZO Chemie v Commission* [1986] E.C.R. 2585, paras 13–17; ECJ, Joined Cases 279–280, 285 and 286/84 *Rau v Commission* [1987] E.C.R. 1069, para.38; CFI, Case T–521/93 *Atlanta and Others v EC* [1996] E.C.R. II–1707, paras 39–40; CFI, Case T–252/97 *Dürbeck v Commission* [2000] E.C.R. II–3031, para.44. A judgment which merely confirms law which ought to have been known to the applicant when it brought an action cannot be regarded as a new matter allowing a fresh plea to be raised: ECJ, Case 11/81 *Dürbeck v Commission* [1982] E.C.R. 1251, para.17; CFI, Case T–106/95 *FFSA and Others v Commission* [1997] E.C.R. II–229, para.57; CFI (order of July 25, 2000), Case T–110/98 *RJB Mining v Commission* [2000] E.C.R. II–2971, para.36; CFI, Case T–3/99 *Bananatrading v Council* [2001] E.C.R. II–2123, para.49. In the course of an action for damages, a submission which changes the very basis of liability constitutes a new plea in law which cannot be introduced in the course of proceedings. Accordingly, the applicant cannot submit for the first time in its reply that the Community is liable for a duly lawful regulatory act, even if the plea, in common with the alleged liability for an unlawful act of the application, is based on Art.288 of the EC Treaty (ECJ, Case C–104/97 P *Atlanta v EC* [1999] E.C.R. I–6983, para.27; ECJ, Joined Cases 279/84, 280/84, 285/84 and 286/84 *Rau and Others v Commission* [1987] E.C.R. 1069, para.38). Considerations relating to economy of procedure or respect for the rights of the defence cannot justify extending the exceptions to the rule which prevents new pleas in law beyond those expressly provided for in the Rules of Procedure (Case C–104/97 P *Atlanta*, para.28). For cases in which a new plea was admitted, see ECJ, Case 14/81 *Alpha Steel v Commission* [1982] E.C.R. 749, para.8; CFI, Case T–43/89 RV *Gill v Commission* [1993] E.C.R. II–303, paras 47–49; CFI, Case T–22/92 *Weißenfels v European Parliament* [1993] E.C.R. II–1095, paras 33–35; CFI, Case T–109/92 *Lacruz Bassols v Court of Justice* [1994] ECR-SC II–105, para.67 (English abstract at I–A-31); CFI, Case T–508/93 *Mancini v Commission* [1994] ECR-SC II–761, paras 33–34 (English abstract at I–A-239); CFI, Case T–32/91 *Solvay v Commission* [1995] E.C.R. II–1825, paras 35–42. It is also possible for only part of a new plea to be declared admissible where, following a measure of organisation of procedure by which all the applicants are granted access to the file (also those which did not enter a plea alleging infringement of their right of access to the file), a party introduces a new plea based on documents of which they had cognisance only in the course of the proceedings: ECJ, Joined Cases C–238/99 P, C–244/99 P, C–245/99 P, C–247/99 P, C–250/99 P, C–251/99 P, C–252/99 P and C–254/99 P *Limburgse Vinyl Maatschappij and Others v*

contested decision constitutes a new factor which allows the applicant to amend its pleas and the form of order sought.[65]

Given the absence of express, unequivocal rules on the matter, a new plea does not have to be submitted immediately, or within a particular period, after the matters of fact or law to which it refers come to light, in order to avoid being time-barred.[66]

24–016 **Elaboration of pleas raised in the application.** The rule that, in principle, new pleas may not be entered does not mean to say, however, that pleas adduced in the application may not subsequently be enlarged upon.[67] Even pleas only raised impliedly may be extended in this way.[68] Accordingly, the applicant is entitled to raise additional arguments in the reply in support of pleas raised in the application.[69] This means that the Court will often have to make a subtle distinction between a new plea and a new argument.[70] In addition, the applicant may clarify in the reply the factual basis on which its pleas are based.[71] Obviously, however, the applicant may "clarify" only pleas which have already been raised in the application.

The rule that—in principle—no new pleas may be raised applies only to the parties, not to the Court of First Instance or the Court of Justice.[72] Accordingly, the rule does not prevent the Court of First Instance and the Court of Justice from raising pleas of their own motion.[73]

Commission [2002] E.C.R. I–8375, paras 366–375; CFI, Case T–19/95 *Adia Interim v Commission* [1996] E.C.R. II–321, paras 22–24.

[65] CFI (judgment of October 21, 2004), Case T–36/99 *Lenzing v Commission*, not yet reported, para.54.

[66] *Solvay v Commission*, cited in the preceding n.64, para.40.

[67] ECJ, Joined Cases 9 and 12/60 *Vloeberghs v High Authority* [1961] E.C.R. 197, at 215; ECJ, Case 18/60 *Worms v High Authority* [1962] E.C.R. 195, at 203. Pleas can be amended when, in the course of proceedings, the contested decision is amended (CFI (judgment of October 21, 2004), Case T–36/99 *Lenzing v Commission*, not yet reported, para.54).

[68] ECJ, Case 306/81 *Verros v European Parliament* [1983] E.C.R. 1755, paras 9–10; CFI, Case T–37/89 *Hanning v European Parliament* [1990] E.C.R. II–463, para.38; CFI, Case T–216/95 *Moles García Ortúzar v Commission* [1997] ECR-SC II–1083, para.87 (English abstract at I–A-403); CFI, Case T–217/95 *Passera v Commission* [1997] ECR-SC II–1109, para.87 (English abstract at I–A-413); CFI, Case T–204/99 *Mattila v Council and Commission* [2001] E.C.R. II–2265, para.32.

[69] ECJ, Case 2/54 *Italy v High Authority* [1954 to 1956] E.C.R. 37, at 51.

[70] See, *e.g.* ECJ (judgment of September 15, 2005), Case C–37/03 P *BioID v OHIM*, not yet reported, paras 56–58. For a somewhat sceptical view—expressed already in the very early days of the Community—see Wijckerheld Bisdom, "Enige bijzonderheden over de rechtsgang van het Hof van Justitie van de Europese Gemeenschappen", in *Individuele rechtsbescherming in de Europese Gemeenschappen* (Kluwer, Deventer/Antwerp, 1964), at 61.

[71] ECJ, Case 74/74 *CNTA v Commission* [1975] E.C.R. 533, para.4; CFI, Case T–21/90 *Generlich v Commission* [1991] E.C.R. II–1323, para.32; CFI, Case T–109/92 *Lacruz Bassols v Court of Justice* [1994] ECR-SC II–105, para.67 (English abstract at I–A-30); CFI, Case T–35/93 *Cucchiara and Others v Commission* [1994] ECR-SC II–413, paras 26–29 (English abstract at I–A-127); ECJ Case C–456/03 *Commission v Italy* [2005] E.C.R. I–5335, paras 32–34.

[72] ECJ, Case C–252/96 P *European Parliament v Gutiérrez de Quijano y Lloréns* [1998] E.C.R. I–7421, para.30.

[73] See 7–122, *supra*.

d. Form of order sought by the applicant

Form of order sought must be unequivocal. The form of order sought (also **24–017** referred to as "conclusions" or "claims") sets out the decision which the applicant is claiming that the Court should give.[74] It generally takes the form of the operative part of a judgment or order. However, the Court may also infer that a particular form of order is sought from the wording of the application.[75]

The form of order sought must be unequivocal and set out at the beginning or the end of the application[76] so that the Court is spared from either giving judgment *ultra petita* or from failing to give judgment on one of the heads of the form of order sought. This also protects the rights of the defence.[77] A head of claim set out in the form of order sought which is unclear will be regarded as inadmissible.[78] Since the form of order sought flows from the subject-matter of the proceedings and the pleas in law which have to be summarised in the application, it may not be amended in the course of the proceedings.[79] The applicant is not even entitled to amend the form of order sought where new matters of law or fact have come to light in the course of the proceedings, allowing it to introduce new pleas in law. Accordingly, it cannot alter the nature of the proceedings by amending the form of order sought.[80] However, the applicant can "clarify" the form of order sought in its reply or at the hearing,[81] for instance, by restricting the scope of its claims in an action for annulment.[82]

---

[74] ECJ, Case 55/64 *Lens v Court of Justice* [1965] E.C.R. 837, at 841.
[75] ECJ, Case 8/56 *ALMA v High Authority* [1957 and 1958] E.C.R. 95, at 99–100; ECJ, Case 80/63 *Degreef v Commission* [1964] E.C.R. 391, at 408; ECJ (order of February 7, 1994), Case C–388/93 *PIA HiFi v Commission* [1994] E.C.R. I–387, para.10.
[76] ECJ Practice Directions, point 13; CFI Practice Directions, point III, 3.
[77] ECJ, Joined Cases 46 and 47/59 *Meroni and Others v High Authority* [1962] E.C.R. 411, at 419.
[78] ECJ, Case 188/73 *Grassi v Council* [1974] E.C.R. 1099, paras 5–9; CFI (order of June 7, 2001), Case T–202/00 *Costacurta v Commission*, not reported, para.54. But see CFI (judgment of September 27, 2005), Case T–123/04 *Cargo Partner v OHIM*, not yet reported, para.34: the applicant formally asked for the case to be sent back to the OHIM. The form of order was considered to be admissible since it was clear from the application that the applicant sought, in substance, the annulment of the contested decision.
[79] ECJ, Case 232/78 *Commission v France* [1979] E.C.R. 2729, paras 2–4; ECJ, Case 124/81 *Commission v United Kingdom* [1983] E.C.R. 203, paras 5–7; CFI, Case T–398/94 *Kahn Scheepvaart v Commission* [1996] E.C.R. II–477, para.20; CFI, Case T–24/00 *Sunrider v OHIM (VITALITE)* [2001] E.C.R. II–449, para.12; CFI (judgment of April 21, 2005), Case T–28/03 *Holcim v Commission*, not yet reported, paras 41–46. A form of order sought which is unsupported by any plea will be inadmissible (CFI, Case T–310/02 *Theodorakis v Council* [2004] E.C.R.–SC II–427, paras 21–22).
[80] ECJ, Case 125/78 *GEMA v Commission* [1979] E.C.R. 3173, para.26; CFI, Case T–28/90 *Asia Motor France and Others v Commission* [1992] E.C.R. II–2285, paras 43–44.
[81] CFI, Joined Cases T–178/00 and T–341/00 *Pflugradt v ECB* [2002] E.C.R. II–4035, para.34; ECJ, Case C–456/03 *Commission v Italy*, [2005] E.C.R. I–5335, paras 39–40.
[82] CFI (order of May 11, 2001), Case T–178/96 *Eridania and Others v Council*, not reported, para.42; CFI (judgment of June 2, 2005), Case T–177/03 *Strohm v Commission*, not yet

24–018 **Contested act replaced by a new act.** In the exceptional circumstance where the institution concerned replaces the contested act by an act which does not essentially diverge from it, the applicant may adjust its form of order sought accordingly. It would not be in the interests of the proper administration of justice or of the requirements of procedural economy to oblige the applicant to make a fresh application to the Court against the new act. This is because the actual subject-matter of the proceedings is not changed.[83] It is also possible for the applicant to amend the form of order sought in this way where a contested implied decision is replaced by an express decision with the same content.[84] However, the act against which the original application was brought must be an act against which an action would lie. If that is not so and the original act is replaced by a challengeable act, the form of order sought may not be amended because that would change the subject-matter of the proceedings contrary to Art.21 of the Statute of the Court of Justice.[85]

e. Supporting evidence

24–019 **Application must set out the necessary evidence.** The applicant must adduce, where appropriate, evidence in support of its pleas. It is apparent from the expression "where appropriate" that the application does not necessarily have to contain offers of evidence.[86] The only sanction concerning offers of evidence is that they may be rejected on account of delay if they are submitted for the first time, and without justification, at the reply or rejoinder stage.[87]

All evidence offered in support must be expressly and accurately indicated, in such a way as to show clearly the facts to be proved[88]:

---

reported, para.21. The subject-matter of the proceedings is not extended where the Commission, after alleging that a Member State has failed to transpose a directive at all, specifies in its reply that the transposition pleaded for the first time by the Member State concerned in its defence is in any event incorrect or incomplete so far as certain provisions of the directive are concerned. Such a complaint is necessarily included in the complaint alleging a complete failure to transpose and is subsidiary to that complaint (ECJ, Case C–456/03 *Commission v Italy* [2005] E.C.R. I–5335, para.40).

[83] ECJ, Case 14/81 *Alpha Steel v Commission* [1982] E.C.R. 749, para.8; ECJ, Joined Cases 351 and 360/85 *Fabrique de Fer de Charleroi v Commission* [1987] E.C.R. 3639, paras 8–11; CFI (judgment of October 21, 2004), Case T–36/99 *Lenzing v Commission*, not yet reported, para.54; CFI (order of February 15, 2005), Case T–229/02 *PKK and Others v Council*, not yet reported, para.29; CFI (judgment of September 21, 2005), Case T–306/01 *Yusuf and Al Barakaat International Foundation v Council and Commission*, not yet reported, paras 72–76.

[84] ECJ, Case 103/85 *Stahlwerke Peine-Salzgitter v Commission* [1988] E.C.R. 4131, paras 11–12.

[85] CFI, Case T–64/89 *Automec v Commission* [1990] E.C.R. II–367, paras 68–69.

[86] CFI (judgment of February 3, 2005), Case T–19/01 *Chiquita Brands International and Others v Commission*, not yet reported, para.71.

[87] *Ibid.* and CFI Rules of Procedure, Art.48(1) and ECJ Rules of Procedure, Art.42(2). See, however, the case-law cited in n.89, *infra*.

[88] CFI Practice Directions, point III, 9.

- documentary evidence offered in support must refer to the relevant document number in a schedule of annexed documents.[89] Alternatively, if a document is not in the possession of the party concerned, the pleading must clearly indicate where and how the document may be obtained,

- where oral testimony is sought to be given, each proposed witness or person from whom information is to be obtained must be clearly identified.[90]

As already indicated, if evidence is offered in the course of the proceedings rather than in the application, reasons must be given for the delay in tendering it.[91]

f. Accompanying documents

General. Certain documents must accompany the application in order for the action to be validly brought. **24–020**

Certificate of the lawyer. The lawyer assisting or representing the applicant must lodge at the registry a certificate that he or she is entitled to practise before a court of a Member State or of a State party to the EEA Agreement.[92] He or she must provide evidence of the authority conferred on him or her by the client.[93] **24–021**

Contested act. If the annulment of an act is sought, the application must be accompanied by the contested act.[94] If the application is for failure to act, documentary evidence must be provided of the date on which the relevant institution was requested to act.[95] An application pursuant to an arbitration clause contained in a contract must be accompanied by a copy of the contract which contains that clause.[96] **24–022**

---

[89] ECJ Rules of Procedure, Art.37(4) and CFI, Rules of Procedure, Art.43(4) provide "[t]o every pleading there shall be annexed a file containing the documents relied on in support of it, together with a schedule listing them". The case-law shows that non-compliance with that obligation may entail the inadmissibility of the action if it is of such a kind as to hamper the other parties in the preparation of their arguments. See, in this respect, CFI, Case T–293/01 *Ineichen v Commision* [2003] ECR-SC I–A-83, II–441, para.29 *et seq.*; CFI (judgment of February 3, 2005), Case T–19/01 *Chiquita Brands International and Others v Commission*, not yet reported, para 72.

[90] CFI Practice Directions, point III, 9.

[91] ECJ Rules of Procedure, Art.42(1); CFI Rules of Procedure, Art.48(1). See, *e.g.* CFI, Case T–172/01 *M v Court of Justice* [2004] E.C.R. II–1075, paras 43–46.

[92] ECJ Rules of Procedure, Art.38(3); CFI Rules of Procedure, Art.44(3). A university teacher who, albeit not a practitioner, has rights of audience in his or her Member State is deemed to be a "lawyer" for this purpose. Statute, Art.19, seventh para.

[93] See 24–187 and 24–188, *infra*.

[94] Statute, Art.21, second para.; ECJ Rules of Procedure, Art.38(4); CFI Rules of Procedure, Art.44(4).

[95] *Ibid.*

[96] ECJ Rules of Procedure, Art.38(6); CFI Rules of Procedure, Art.44(5a).

24–023 **Documents relating to legal persons.** If the applicant is a legal person governed by private law, the application must be accompanied by proof of its "existence in law". Such proof consists of the instrument or instruments constituting or regulating that legal person or a recent extract from the register of companies, firms or associations or any other proof.[97] The fact that the legal person is governed by private law is determined by the law of its country of origin. At the same time, the applicant must adduce proof that the authority granted to its lawyer has been properly conferred on him or her by someone authorised for the purpose.[98]

24–024 **Disputes relating to intellectual property rights.** An application bringing a dispute relating to intellectual property before the Court of First Instance[99] in the form of an action against the Office for Harmonisation in the Internal Market (Trade Marks and Designs) or against the Community Plant Variety Office must also contain the names of all the parties to the proceedings before the Board of Appeal and the addresses which they had given for the purposes of the notifications to be effected in the course of the proceedings before the Board of Appeal.[100] In addition, the contested decision has to be appended to the application and the date on which the applicant was notified of it must be indicated.[101]

24–025 **Summary for publication.** The Court of Justice and the Court of First Instance require each application to be accompanied by a summary (not more than two pages long) of the pleas in law and main arguments relied on designed to facilitate publication of the notice in the *Official Journal of the European Union*.[102]

3. Consequences

24–026 **Case becomes pending.** The lodging of the application at the registry causes the case to become pending before the Court of Justice or the Court of First Instance, as the case may be. The Registrar enters the case in the register and gives it a serial number reflecting the order in which it was lodged. The case numbers of the Court of Justice are preceded by the letter "C", those of the Court of First Instance by the letter "T" (for the French

---

[97] ECJ Rules of Procedure, Art.38(5)(a); CFI Rules of Procedure, Art.44(5)(a).
[98] ECJ Rules of Procedure, Art.38(5)(b); CFI Rules of Procedure, Art.44(5)(b).
[99] Art.63 of Council Regulation (EC) No 40/94 of December 20, 1993 on the Community trade mark, [1994] O.J. L11/1; Art.73, as amended, of Council Regulation (EC) No 2100/94 of July 27, 1994 on Community plant variety rights, (1994) L227/1. See Ch.20, *supra*.
[100] CFI Rules of Procedure, Art.132(1), first subpara.
[101] CFI Rules of Procedure, Art.132(1), second subpara.
[102] This is a requirement in the Court of First Instance (see CFI Practice Directions, Point III, 5); it is recommended in the Court of Justice (ECJ Practice Directions, point 12).

"Tribunal") and those of the European Union Civil Service Tribunal by the letter "F".[103]

Role of the registry. The Registrar[104] serves the application on the defen-   **24–027**
dant[105] by dispatch of a copy by registered post with a form for acknowledgement of receipt or by personal delivery against a receipt[106] and, in
disputes relating to intellectual property, on the relevant Office and on all
parties to the proceedings before the Board of Appeal, after determining
the language of the case in accordance with Art.131(1) of the CFI Rules of
Procedure.[107] The Registrar ensures that notice is given in the *Official
Journal of the European Union* of the date of registration of the application
initiating proceedings, the names and addresses of the parties, the subject-
matter of the proceedings, the form of order sought by the applicant and a
summary of the pleas in law and of the main supporting arguments.[108] The
purpose of the notice in the C series of the *Official Journal* is to put
Community institutions, Member States and natural and legal persons on
notice of the proceedings, giving them the opportunity of intervening.
Where the Council or the Commission is not a party to the case, the
Registrar sends them copies of the application and of the defence, without
the annexes thereto, to enable them to assess whether the inapplicability of
one of its acts is being invoked under Art.241 of the EC Treaty or Art.156
of the EAEC Treaty. Copies of the application are likewise sent to the
European Parliament, to enable it to assess whether the inapplicability of
an act adopted jointly by that institution and by the Council is being
invoked under Art.241 of the EC Treaty.[109]

Regularisation of the application. If the application does not comply with   **24–028**
certain requirements or if the requisite accompanying documents are not
appended to it, the Registrar prescribes a reasonable period within which
the applicant is to comply with requirements either by putting the
application in order or by producing any documents missing.[110] If the

---

[103] In *Gluiber* (CFI (order of the President of July 11, 2001), Case T–154 AJ *Gluiber*, not
reported, the President rejected an application for legal aid referring to an order of the
Court of First Instance directing the Registrar not to enter in the registry applications
having the same subject-matter as sixteen other similar applications. The Court of First
Instance regarded lodgment of such a large number of applications as an abuse.
[104] ECJ Rules of Procedure, Art.17(1); CFI Rules of Procedure, Art.25(1).
[105] ECJ Rules of Procedure, Art.39; CFI Rules of Procedure, Art.45.
[106] ECJ Rules of Procedure, Art.79; CFI Rules of Procedure, Art.100.
[107] CFI Rules of Procedure, Art.132(1).
[108] ECJ Rules of Procedure, Art.16(6); CFI Rules of Procedure, Art.24(6).
[109] ECJ Rules of Procedure, Art.16(7); CFI Rules of Procedure, Art.24(7). The CFI Rules of
Procedure do not provide for these documents to be sent to the European Parliament.
[110] ECJ Rules of Procedure, Art.38(7); CFI Rules of Procedure, Art.44(6). The requirements
in question are those set out in Art.38(3) to (6) of the ECJ Rules of Procedure and in
Art.44(3) to (5) of the CFI Rules of Procedure. See also CFI Rules of Procedure,
Art.132(2).

applicant fails to comply with the Registrar's directions, the Court of Justice or the Court of First Instance, as the case may be, decides whether this renders the application formally inadmissible.[111]

Service of the application on the defendant will be effected as soon as the application has been put in order or the Court has declared it admissible notwithstanding the failure to observe the formal requirements in question.[112]

B. THE DEFENCE

1. Lodging the defence

a. General

24–029 **Time-limit.** The defendant has one or two months following service upon it of the application in which to lodge a defence.[113] The President of the Court of Justice or the Court of First Instance, as the case may be, may extend this time-limit on a reasoned application by the defendant, which must be lodged before the original time-limit runs out.[114]

24–030 **Defence must be signed and dated.** As a pleading, the defence is subject to the same formal requirements as the application initiating the proceedings (see 24–003 to 24–005, *supra*). It must thus be signed by an agent or a lawyer (see, 24–186 to 24–191 *infra*). Inobservance of this requirement leads to the inadmissibility of the defence.[115]

24–031 **Disputes relating to intellectual property rights.** In disputes relating to intellectual property rights, the Office, as defendant, and interveners within the meaning of Art.134(1) of the CFI Rules of Procedure may submit

---

[111] *Ibid.*; ECJ (order of July 10, 1984), Case 289/83 *GAARM v Commission* [1984] E.C.R. 2789; CFI (order of February 8, 1993), Case T–101/92 *Stagakis v European Parliament* [1993] E.C.R. II–63; CFI (order of June 22, 1995), Case T–101/95 *Zedelmaier v Council and Commission*, not reported.

[112] ECJ Rules of Procedure, Art.39; CFI Rules of Procedure, Art.45.

[113] ECJ Rules of Procedure, Art.40(1) (one month); CFI Rules of Procedure, Art.46(1) (two months). In ECJ, Case C–59/99 *Commission v Pereira Roldão & Filhos and Others* [2001] E.C.R. I–8499, para.19, the Court of Justice found that the application could not be served on one of the defendants. The applicant then informed the Court that the proceedings were to be pursued in relation to the other two defendants, thereby implicitly abandoning the proceedings so far as the untraceable party was concerned.

[114] ECJ Rules of Procedure, Art.40(2); CFI Rules of Procedure, Art.46(3) (since a two-month period applies at the Court of First Instance an extension will be granted only in exceptional circumstances). The fact that the defendant applies for an extension of time for lodging its defence does not prevent it from raising an objection of inadmissibility pursuant to Art.114 of the CFI Rules of Procedure on the basis of facts which were already known at the time when the extension was applied for. This does not render the application for an extension an abuse (CFI (order of July 10, 2002), Case T–387/00 *Comitato organizzatore del convegno internazionale v Commission* [2002] E.C.R. II–3031, para.359).

[115] The applicant may then apply for the form of order sought to be granted by default: see ECJ (judgment of February 24, 2005), Case C–279/03 *Commission v Implants*, not reported, paras 22–23.

responses to the application within a period of two months from the service of the application.[116] Since, in such disputes, interveners may apply for a form of order and put forward pleas in law not applied for or put forward by the main parties, the other parties to the proceedings may, within two months of service of the responses, submit replies or rejoinders, in response to the form of order sought and pleas in law put forward by an intervener for the first time. The President may extend the time-limit.[117]

b. Judgments by default and applications to set them aside

Default judgment. If, despite the fact that the originating application was duly served on the defendant, the latter fails to lodge a defence in the proper form within the time prescribed, the applicant may apply for the form of order sought to be granted.[118] The Court of Justice or the Court of First Instance may then give judgment by default.[119]   **24–032**

The application is served on the defendant.[120] No special formal requirements apply, although the application must comply with the general requirements laid down for pleadings.[121]

Before giving judgment by default, the Court of Justice/Court of First Instance, after hearing the Advocate General, considers whether the application initiating proceedings is admissible, whether the appropriate formalities have been complied with, and whether the application appears well founded.[122]

The Court of Justice or the Court of First Instance, as the case may be, may decide to open the oral procedure relating to the application to grant the applicant's claims. Naturally, only the applicant will be heard. The Court of Justice and the Court of First Instance may also order a preparatory inquiry.[123]

---

[116] CFI Rules of Procedure, Art.135(1).
[117] CFI Rules of Procedure, Art.135(3).
[118] The applicant may waive the right to avail itself of the procedure for judgment by default (ECJ, Case C–32/02 *Commission v Italy* [2003] E.C.R. I–12063, paras 11–12).
[119] ECJ Rules of Procedure, Art.94(1), first subpara.; CFI Rules of Procedure, Art.122(1), first subpara.; for disputes relating to intellectual property rights, see CFI Rules of Procedure, Art.134(4). See ECJ, Case C–274/93 *Commission v Luxembourg* [1996] E.C.R. I–2019, para.9; CFI, Case T–42/89 *Yorck von Wartenburg v European Parliament* [1990] E.C.R. II–31; ECJ, Case C–285/96 *Commission v Italy* [1998] E.C.R. I–5935, para.13; ECJ, Case C–172/97 *Commission v SIVU and Hydro-Réalisations* [1999] E.C.R. I–3363, para.16; ECJ, Case C–356/99 *Commission v Hitesys* [2000] E.C.R. I–9517, para.18; ECJ, Case C–365/99 *Portugal v Commission* [2001] E.C.R. I–5645, para.13; ECJ, Case C–77/99 *Commission v Oder-Plan Architektur and Others* [2001] E.C.R. I–7355, para.25; ECJ, Case C–59/99 *Commission v Pereira Roldão & Filhos and Others* [2001] E.C.R. I–8499, para.18; ECJ, Case C–29/03 *Commission v ITEC* [2003] E.C.R. I–12205, paras 18–20; CFI, Case T–85/94 *Branco v Commission* [1995] E.C.R. II–45, para.19; CFI (judgment of October 14, 2004), Case T–44/02 *Dresdner Bank v Commission*, not reported, paras 40–42.
[120] ECJ Rules of Procedure, Art.94(1), second subpara.; CFI Rules of Procedure, Art.122(1), second subpara.
[121] ECJ Rules of Procedure, Art.37; CFI Rules of Procedure, Art.43.
[122] ECJ Rules of Procedure, Art.94(2); CFI Rules of Procedure, Art.122(2).
[123] ECJ Rules of Procedure, Art.94(2); CFI Rules of Procedure, Art.122(2).

A judgment by default is enforceable, although the Court of Justice or the Court of First Instance, as the case may be, may grant a stay of execution until the Court has given its decision on any application to set it aside, or it may make execution subject to the provision of security. In the latter case, the security will be released if no application to set the default judgment aside is made or if such an application fails.[124]

24–033 **Application to set aside a default judgment.** Application to set aside a judgment by default must be made within one month of service of the judgment. It must be made in the form prescribed for applications initiating proceedings (see 24–003 to 24–006, *supra*).[125] After the application has been served, the President prescribes a period within which the other party may submit written observations.[126] After a possible preparatory inquiry, the oral procedure takes place. Lastly, the Court gives judgment. No application may be made to have that judgment set aside.[127]

24–034 **Consequences.** If an application to set aside a default judgment is rejected, the default judgment remains in place.[128] Conversely, if the application is successful, the judgment setting aside the judgment by default takes its place.[129]

2. Content

24–035 **Requirements.** In addition to the case-number and the applicant's name, the following must appear at the beginning of each defence:

- the defendant's name and address;

- the name and capacity of the defendant's agent or lawyer;

- an address for service in Luxembourg and/or agreement to service by telefax or other technical means of communication.[130]

The defence further contains:

- the arguments of fact and law relied on;

---

[124] ECJ Rules of Procedure, Art.94(3); CFI Rules of Procedure, Art.122(3).
[125] ECJ Rules of Procedure, Art.94(4); CFI Rules of Procedure, Art.122(4).
[126] ECJ Rules of Procedure, Art.94(5); CFI Rules of Procedure, Art.122(5).
[127] ECJ Rules of Procedure, Art.94(6), first subpara.; CFI Rules of Procedure, Art.122(6).
[128] ECJ, Case C–172/97 OP *SIVU* [2001] E.C.R. I–6699; CFI, Case T–42/89 OPPO *European Parliament v Yorck von Wartenburg* [1990] E.C.R. II–299; CFI, Case T–85/94 OPPO *Commission v Branco* [1995] E.C.R. II–2993.
[129] ECJ, Case C–172/97 OP *SIVU* [2001] E.C.R. I–6699 (by which the default judgment was partially annulled).
[130] ECJ Rules of Procedure, Art.40(1), first subpara.; CFI Rules of Procedure, Art.46(1), first subpara.; ECJ Practice Directions, point 17; CFI Practice Directions, point II, 11).

- the form of order sought by the defendant;
- the nature of any evidence offered by him.[131]

a. Name and address of the defendant

General. The defence is subject to the same requirements as the appli- **24–036**
cation, for instance as regards the address for service, assistance or
representation by a lawyer and proof of the existence in law of a legal
person governed by private law[132] (see 24–007 to 24–008, *supra*).

b. Arguments of fact and law relied on

Pleas and arguments must be clearly set out. The arguments of fact and **24–037**
law relied on must be clearly set out in the defence.[133] If any fact alleged by
the applicant is contested it must be clearly indicated and the basis on
which it is challenged must be stated explicitly.[134]

New pleas. The defendant is limited to pleas set out in the defence. In **24–038**
subsequent pleadings, the defendant may introduce new pleas in law only if
they are based on matters of law or of fact which come to light in the course
of the proceedings.[135] Consequently, "new pleas" have the same standing for
both the applicant and the defendant[136] in order to secure observance of the
principle *audi alteram partem*. If the defendant could keep its defence pleas
undisclosed until it lodged the rejoinder or, *a fortiori*, until the hearing, the
applicant would lose any chance of making a "reply" and of preparing its
counter-arguments for the hearing, which would jeopardise proper debate,
with both parties putting forward pleas and counter-pleas.

The defence has to take issue only with pleas raised by the applicant. A
counter-claim may be made provided that it is related to the applicant's
claim.[137]

---

[131] ECJ Rules of Procedure, Art.40(1), first subpara.; CFI Rules of Procedure, Art.46(1), first
subpara.

[132] ECJ Rules of Procedure, Art.40(1), second subpara.; CFI Rules of Procedure, Art.46(1),
second subpara. The defendant may be a person governed by private law where a
Community institution asserts a claim against such a person pursuant to an arbitration
clause within the meaning of Art.238 of the EC Treaty (see Ch.19, *supra*).

[133] Vaughan and Lasok (eds), *Butterworths European Court Practice* (Butterworths, London,
1993), at 96.

[134] ECJ Practice Directions, point 20; CFI Practice Directions, point III, 14.

[135] ECJ Rules of Procedure, Art.42(2); CFI Rules of Procedure, Art.48(2). See ECJ, Case C–
136/92 P *Commission v Brazzelli and Others* [1994] E.C.R. I–1981, para.58; CFI, Case T–
81/97 *Regione Toscana v Commission* [1998] E.C.R. II–2889, para.41.

[136] The German version of the provisions cited accordingly refers to *"Angriffs- und Ver-
teidigungsmittel"*. For an example, see ECJ, Case C–471/98 *Commission v Belgium* [2002]
E.C.R. I–9681, paras 41–43.

[137] ECJ, Case 250/78 *DEKA v EEC* [1983] E.C.R. 421: in this case, the Commission sought to
set off against compensation which the Community had to pay the applicant a claim which
had been assigned to the Commission for repayment of an amount which had been wrongly
paid to the applicant by way of export refunds and monetary compensatory amounts for
exports of maize gritz. As a "defence plea", the claim for repayment of the amounts
wrongly paid was apparently admissible.

c. Form of order sought by the defendant

24–039 **Form of order sought must be unequivoqual** Generally, the form of order sought by the defendant, which must be precisely specified at the beginning or the end of the defence,[138] will claim that the application and the claims set out therein should be dismissed and the applicant ordered to pay the costs. The claim for a costs order is very important, since both the Court of Justice and the Court of First Instance will order the unsuccessful party to pay the costs only "if they have been applied for in the successful party's pleadings".[139] This means that the defendant, too, should not omit to ask the Court to make a costs order against the applicant in case—as it naturally hopes—it is successful in its defence on the substance (see also 24–124, *infra*).

d. Any evidence offered in support

24–040 **Defence must set out the necessary evidence.** At the first possible opportunity, *i.e.* in the defence, the defendant should tender any supporting evidence. If, subsequently, the defendant offers further evidence in the rejoinder or at the hearing, it must give reasons for the delay in tendering it.[140] In this respect, too, the positions of the defendant and the applicant are parallel. Once again, it is the quality of debate before the Court which necessitates each party putting forward supporting evidence at a time when the other can still effectively put forward a counter-argument.

e. Accompanying documents

20–041 **General.** Just as in the case of the application, documents may have to be submitted with the defence (see 24–020 to 24–025, *supra*).

3. The objection of inadmissibility

24–042 **Objection by separate act.** Instead of lodging a defence, the defendant can apply, by separate act, to the Court of Justice or the Court of First Instance (within the time prescribed for lodging a defence) for a decision on an objection of inadmissibility without a ruling on the substance of the case.[141] In that event, the President prescribes a period within which the opposite party may lodge a document containing a statement of the form of order sought by that party and its pleas in law.

---

[138] ECJ Practice Directions, point 18; CFI Practice Directions, point III, 12.
[139] ECJ Rules of Procedure, Art.69(2), first subpara.; CFI Rules of Procedure, Art.87(2), first subpara.
[140] ECJ Rules of Procedure, Art.42(1); CFI Rules of Procedure, Art.48(1). See, *e.g.* CFI, Case T–172/01 *M v Court of Justice* [2004] E.C.R. II–1075, paras 36–42; CFI (order of May 26, 2004), Case T–266/03 *Groupement des Cartes Bancaires "CB" v Commission*, not yet reported, paras 15–19.
[141] ECJ Rules of Procedure, Art.91(1); CFI Rules of Procedure, Art.114(1).

Separate decision or decision reserved for final judgment. When it   24–043
receives the objection and the response to it, the Court decides at an
administrative meeting, on a proposal from the Judge-Rapporteur and after
hearing the Advocate General, whether to decide on the application for a
decision on the preliminary objection or to reserve its decision for final
judgment.[142]

If the Court decides to reserve its decision, the President prescribes new
time-limits for the further steps in the proceedings (in practice, this means
that the defendant is given a new time-limit for lodging the defence and
hence for the resumption of the written procedure on the substance).

If the Court decides to rule on the objection of inadmissibility, it is dealt
with orally in principle and a date is fixed for a hearing, unless the Court of
Justice or the Court of First Instance, as the case may be, decides
differently.[143] If the action is clearly inadmissible, there is a tendency to
uphold the objection without holding a hearing. In such a case, the Court,
after hearing the Advocate General, declares the action inadmissible by
reasoned order.[144]

If, after a hearing, a judgment is given refusing the application on the
preliminary objection and declaring the action admissible, the President
prescribes new time-limits for the further steps in the proceedings.[145]

Absolute bar to proceeding or action devoid of purpose. In addition, the   24–044
Court of Justice and the Court of First Instance may at any time, after
hearing the parties, decide whether there exists any absolute bar to
proceeding with an action or declare that the action has become devoid of
purpose and that there is no need to adjudicate on it.[146] The admissibility of

---

[142] ECJ Rules of Procedure, Art.91(2), (3) and (4), first subpara.; CFI Rules of Procedure, Art.114(2), (3) and (4), first subpara.

[143] CFI (order of May 4, 2005), Case T–86/03 *Holcim v Commission*, not yet reported: objection dismissed without an oral hearing.

[144] ECJ Rules of Procedure, Art.92(1); CFI Rules of Procedure, Art.111. For examples, see ECJ (orders of September 26, 1994), Case 216/83 *Les Verts v Commission and Council* [1984] E.C.R. 3325; Case 296/83 *Les Verts v European Parliament* [1984] E.C.R. 3335; Case 297/83 *Les Verts v Council* [1984] E.C.R. 3339; ECJ, Case C–224/03 *Italy v Commission* [2003] E.C.R. I–14751; CFI (order of November 26, 1993), Case T–460/93 *Tête and Others v EIB* [1993] E.C.R. II–1257; CFI (order of December 14, 1993), Case T–29/93 *Calvo Alonso-Cortés v Commission* [1993] E.C.R. II–1389; CFI (order of July 20, 1994), Case T–45/93 *Branco v Court of Auditors* [1994] ECR-SC II–641, para.21 (English abstract at I–A-197); ECJ (order of October 29, 2004), Case C–360/02 P *Ripa di Meana v European Parliament* [2004] E.C.R. I–10339, para.35 (no obligation for the Court of First Instance to organise an oral hearing).

[145] ECJ Rules of Procedure, Art.91(4), second subpara.; CFI Rules of Procedure, Art.114(4), second subpara. Nevertheless, sometimes the admissibility of the application is determined by order without joining this question to the main proceedings (see CFI (order of July 13, 1998), Case T–293/97 *Eltatronic v Commission*, not reported).

[146] ECJ Rules of Procedure, Art.92(2); CFI Rules of Procedure, Art.113. See ECJ, Case C–298/00 P *Italy v Commission* [2004] E.C.R. I–4087, para.35 (examination *ex officio* by the Court of Justice of the question whether the applicant was individually concerned by the

an action is judged by reference to the situation prevailing when the application was lodged.[147]

24–045 **CFI Rules of Procudure, Art.111.** Under Art.111 of the CFI Rules of Procedure, the Court of First Instance may decide by reasoned order without taking further steps in the proceedings and without hearing the parties that it has no jurisdiction to take cognisance of the action or that the application is manifestly inadmissible or manifestly lacking any foundation in law.[148] It is not clear whether the defendant can raise an objection by which it calls on the Court to declare, by order, that an action is manifestly ill-founded in law.[149]

C. THE REPLY AND THE REJOINDER

24–046 **General.** After the defence has been lodged, the applicant may supplement its application by lodging a reply within a time-limit prescribed by the President of the Court. The defendant may then lodge a rejoinder on the same terms.[150]

Either party may apply to the President for an extension of time.[151] The parties are not obliged to lodge a reply and a rejoinder. If a party allows the

---

contested measure); CFI, Joined Cases T–142/01 and T–283/01 *OPTUC v Commission* [2004] E.C.R. II–329 (examination *ex officio* by Court of First Instance of the expiration of the time-limit for bringing an action); CFI (judgment of December 1, 2004), Case T–27/02 *Kronofrance v Commission,* not yet reported, para.30 (examination *ex officio* by the Court of First Instance of the question whether the applicant was individually concerned by the contested measure); CFI (judgment of March 15, 2005), Case T–29/02 *GEF v Commission,* not yet reported, para.72 (examination *ex officio* by the Court of First Instance of its jurisdiction to hear the case); CFI (order of March 10, 2005), Joined Cases T–228/00, T–229/00, T–242/00, T–243/00, T–245/00 to T–248/00, T–250/00, T–252/00, T–256/00 to T–259/00, T–265/00, T–267/00, T–268/00, T–271/00, T–274/00 to T–276/00, T–281/00, T–287/00 to T–296/00 *Gruppo ormeggiatori del porto di Venezia and Others v Commission,* not yet reported, paras 38–40 (*exceptio litis pendentis* examined *ex officio* by the Court of First Instance).

[147] ECJ, Case 50/84 *Bensider and Others v Commission* [1984] E.C.R. 3991, para.8; CFI (order of February 15, 2005), Case T–229/02 *PKK and Others v Council,* not yet reported, para.30.

[148] The words "or manifestly lacking any foundation in law" were added to Art.111 of the CFI Rules of Procedure in order to make it clear that the Court of First Instance cannot deal with a case under that provision where the outcome of the proceedings depends on an assessment of the facts.

[149] Art.114(1) of the CFI Rules of Procedure does not seem to afford any basis for the defendant's doing so since it expressly provides that the Court is to rule on an application made in this way which does not "go to the substance of the case". Of course, the defendant may claim at any time in its defence that the application is manifestly ill-founded in law and ask the Court to rule on that claim without taking further steps in the written procedure. For examples, see CFI (order of December 10, 1997), Case T–334/96 *Smets v Commission* [1997] E.C.R. II–2333, para.16; CFI (order of April 29, 1998), Case T–367/94 *British Coal v Commission* [1998] E.C.R. II–705, paras 22–26; CFI (order of October 28, 1998), Case T–100/98 *Goldstein v Commission* [1998] E.C.R. II–4063.

[150] ECJ Rules of Procedure, Art.41(1) and (2); CFI Rules of Procedure, Art.47(1) and (2).

[151] If no extension of time is requested, a rejoinder lodged out of time will not be joined to the file (CFI, Case T–208/01 *Volkswagen v Commission* [2003] E.C.R. II–5141, para.11).

relevant period to expire without lodging such a pleading or if it waives its right to do so, the proceedings continue.[152]

In proceedings before the Court of First Instance, the Court may decide, after hearing the Advocate General, that a second exchange of pleadings is unnecessary because the documents before it are sufficiently comprehensive to enable the parties to elaborate their pleas and arguments in the course of the oral procedure.[153] However, the Court of First Instance may authorise the parties to supplement the documents if the applicant presents a reasoned request to that effect within two weeks from the notification of that decision. The President fixes the time-limits within which these pleadings are to be lodged.

Formal requirements. No specific formal requirements are laid down for replies and rejoinders, although they do have to comply with the general requirements which pleadings have to satisfy.[154]   24–047

Objective. The reply and the rejoinder afford each party an opportunity to supplement the application and the defence, respectively, in the light of its opponent's observations. They may contain supplementary arguments supporting or clarifying the pleas raised by the parties. As already noted, if a party offers further evidence in the reply or the rejoinder (or possibly even at a later stage in the proceedings), reasons must be given for the delay in tendering it.[155] However, parties may tender evidence in rebuttal and the amplification of the offers of evidence submitted in response to evidence in rebuttal contained in the defence or reply of the other party. Naturally they do not have to give further reasons for this.[156]   24–048

No new pleas. As has also already been observed, neither the reply nor the rejoinder may raise new pleas, unless they are based on matters of law or of fact which have come to light in the course of the proceedings[157] or constitute pleas which the Community courts have to examine of their own motion.[158] This will not be the case where, although the party raising the new plea was not previously aware of a matter of fact on which the new substantive plea is based, it could have known of it at the time when the   24–049

---

[152] ECJ Rules of Procedure, Art.44(1), third subpara.; CFI Rules of Procedure, Art.52(2), second subpara.

[153] CFI Rules of Procedure, Art.47(1). See, *e.g.* CFI (judgment of March 8, 2005), Case T–277/03 *Vlachaki v Commission*, not yet reported, para.23.

[154] ECJ Rules of Procedure, Art.37; CFI Rules of Procedure, Art.43.

[155] ECJ Rules of Procedure, Art.42(1); CFI Rules of Procedure, Art.48(1); See, *e.g.* CFI, Case T–172/01 *M v Court of Justice* [2004] E.C.R. II–1075, paras 39–40 (admissible evidence) and paras 43–46 (inadmissible evidence).

[156] ECJ, Case C–185/95 P *Baustahlgewebe v Commission* [1998] E.C.R. I–8417, para.72.

[157] ECJ Rules of Procedure, Art.42(2); CFI Rules of Procedure, Art.48(2). See, *e.g.* ECJ, Case C–471/98 *Commission v Belgium* [2002] E.C.R. I–9681, paras 41–43.

[158] CFI (judgment of December 1, 2004), Case T–27/02 *Kronofrance v Commission*, not yet reported, para 30.

application or the defence, as the case may be, was lodged.[159] If, in contrast, a matter of fact is mentioned for the first time in the defence, the applicant is entitled to raise a plea based thereon in the reply.[160] Lastly, new claims made in the reply or the rejoinder are inadmissible.[161]

24–050 **Improper use of procedural documents.** Parties may not make improper use of procedural documents to which they have access in the course of the proceedings. They may use such documents only for the purpose of pursuing their own case. If a party uses some of the procedural documents of other parties for other purposes, such as for provoking public criticism of the other parties' arguments as a result of the disclosure of the documents in question, it infringes a general principle of the due administration of justice according to which parties have the right to defend their interests free of external influences and particularly from influences on the part of the public. Such an abuse of process may be penalised in the order for costs.[162] However, a party may join an application by which another party has brought other proceedings as a document to its own application if the third party agrees. This is because there is no rule or provision to prevent parties from disclosing their pleadings to third parties.[163]

24–051 **Disputes relating to intellectual property rights.** In disputes relating to intellectual property rights, parties may submit replies and rejoinders only if the President, on a reasoned application made within two weeks of service of responses or replies, considers such further pleading necessary and allows it in order to enable the party concerned to put forward its point of view.[164]

D. DIRECTIONS FOR PREPARING PLEADINGS AND OTHER PROCEDURAL DOCUMENTS

24–052 **General.** Pleadings and other procedural documents lodged by the parties must be submitted in a form which can be processed electronically by the Court of Justice or the Court of First Instance and which, in particular, makes it possible to scan documents and to use character recognition.[165] For that purpose, the following requirements must be complied with:

- the paper must be white, unlined and A4 size, with text on one side of the page only;

---

[159] ECJ, Case 110/81 *Roquette Frères v Council* [1982] E.C.R. 3159, para.31.
[160] ECJ, Joined Cases 12 and 29/64 *Ley v Commission* [1965] E.C.R. 107, at 118–119.
[161] CFI, Case T–22/92 *Weißenfels v European Parliament* [1993] E.C.R. II–1095, para.27; CFI, Case T–146/95 *Bernardi v European Parliament* [1996] E.C.R. II–769, para.31.
[162] CFI, Case T–174/95 *Svenska Journalistförbundet v Council* [1998] E.C.R. II–2289, paras 135–139, where the applicant published the Council's defence on the Internet, requesting the public to inform the Council of their comments.
[163] ECJ (order of April 3, 2000), Case C–376/98 *Germany v European Parliament and Council* [2000] E.C.R. I–2247, para.10.
[164] CFI Rules of Procedure, Art.135(2).
[165] ECJ Practice Directions, point 5; CFI Practice Directions, point II, 1.

- pages of pleadings and annexes, if any, must be assembled in such a way as to be easily separable (they must not be bound together or permanently attached by means such as glue or staples);
- the text must be in a commonly-used font (such as Times New Roman, Courier or Arial), in at least 12 pt in the body of the text and at least 10 pt in the footnotes, with one and a half line spacing and upper, lower, left and right margins of at least 2.5 cm;
- the pages of the pleading must be numbered consecutively in the top right-hand corner. That numbering must also cover all the pages of any annexes to the pleading, so as to make it possible to check that all the pages of the annexes have been duly scanned.

First page. The following information must appear on the first page of the pleading[166]:

24–053

- the title of the pleading (application, appeal, defence, response, reply, rejoinder, application for leave to intervene, statement in intervention, observations on the statement in intervention, objection of inadmissibility, etc.);
- the case number, if it has already been notified by the registry;
- the names of the applicant (appellant) and defendant (respondent) and on appeal, the identification of the decision under appeal and the parties before the Court of First Instance;
- the names of the applicant and of the defendant and, on appeal, the contested decision and the names of the parties to the proceedings before the Court of First Instance;
- the name of the party on whose behalf the pleading is lodged.

Paragraphs need to be numbered. Each paragraph of the pleading must be numbered. The signature of the agent or lawyer acting for the party concerned must appear at the end of the pleading.[167]

24–054

Brief submissions. The pleadings should be as short as possible in order to expedite the disposal of the case. It is the experience of the Court of Justice that, save in exceptional circumstances, effective pleadings need not exceed 10 or 15 pages and replies, rejoinders and responses can be limited to 5 to 10 pages.[168]

24–055

In its *Practice Directions*, the Court of First Instance lays down the maximum number of pages for a series of pleadings. The maximum number

---

[166] ECJ Practice Directions, point 6; CFI Practice Directions, point II, 2.
[167] ECJ Practice Directions, points 7–8; CFI Practice Directions, point II, 3 and 4.
[168] ECJ Practice Directions, point 43.

of pages for an application and a defence should not, in principle, exceed 20 to 50. The corresponding figures are 10 to 25 for the reply and the rejoinder, 10 to 25 for the reply and the rejoinder, 10 to 20 for an objection of inadmissibility and observations thereon and 10 to 20 pages for statements in intervention. These limits may be exceeded in cases involving particularly complex legal or factual issues.[169]

24–056 **Appendices.** Only those documents mentioned in the actual text of a pleading which are necessary in order to prove or illustrate its contents may be submitted as annexes.[170]

Annexes will be accepted only if they are accompanied by a schedule indicating, for each document annexed: the number of the annex, a short description of the document (*e.g.* "letter"), followed by its date, author and addressee and its number of pages, the page reference and paragraph number in the pleading where the document is mentioned and its relevance is described.[171] Where annexes are documents which themselves contain annexes, they must be arranged and numbered in such a way as to avoid all possibility of confusion.[172]

Where, for the convenience of the Court of Justice or the Court of First Instance, copies of judgments, legal writings or legislation are annexed to a pleading, they must be appended separately from the other annexes and must not be listed in the appendix of annexes.[173]

Each reference to a document lodged must state the relevant annex number as given in the schedule of annexes in which it appears and indicate the pleading to which it is annexed. In appeal proceedings, where the document has already been produced before the Court of First Instance, the identification used for that document before the Court of First Instance must also be given.[174]

---

[169] CFI Practice Directions, point V. Non-compliance with these Practice Directions can lead to an unfavourable costs order for the party concerned: see CFI, Joined Cases T–191/98, T–212/98 to T–214/98 *Atlantic Container Line and Others v Commission* [2003] E.C.R. II–3275, paras 1645–1647.

[170] ECJ Practice Directions, point 33; CFI Practice Directions, point IV, 1.

[171] ECJ Practice Directions, point 34; CFI Practice Directions, point IV, 2 and 3. For the Court of First Instance, an annex should also be numbered in such a way as to identify the pleading in which it is produced (thus, for example, Annex A.1, A.2, etc. in an application; Annex B.1, B.2, etc. in a defence; Annex C.1, C.2, etc. in a reply; Annex D.1, D.2, etc. in a rejoinder). Where a pleading contains more than 10 annexes, the schedule of annexes must be accompanied by an appendix identifying and setting out the relevant passages in each annex on which the party wishes to rely, save in the case of documents not exceeding three pages in length.

[172] CFI Practice Directions, point IV. 6.

[173] ECJ Practice Directions, point 35; CFI Practice Directions, point IV, 5.

[174] ECJ Practice Directions, point 42; CFI Practice Directions, point IV, 7.

E. THE EXPEDITED PROCEDURE

General. On application by the applicant or the defendant, the President of   **24–057**
the Court of Justice (on the basis of a recommendation by the Judge-
Rapporteur and after hearing the other party and the Advocate General) or
the President of the Court of First Instance (after hearing the other parties
and the Advocate General), may decide that a case is to be determined
pursuant to an expedited procedure where the particular urgency of the
case requires the Court to give its ruling with the minimum of delay.[175]

Separate document. An application for a case to be decided under an   **24–058**
expedited procedure must be made by a separate document lodged at the
same time as the application initiating the proceedings or the defence, as
the case may be.[176] The party concerned must briefly state the reasons for
the special urgency of the case.[177] The application may state that certain
pleas in law or arguments or certain passages of the application initiating
the proceedings or the defence are raised only in the event that the case is
not decided under an expedited procedure.[178]

Importance of the oral procedure. The Court of Justice and the Court of   **24–059**
First Instance are not bound to accept such an application.[179] If the
application is accepted, in principle the parties may not lodge a reply, a
rejoinder or a statement in intervention unless the Court of Justice or the
Court of First Instance, as the case may be, considers this to be necessary.[180]
The key point here is the oral procedure in the course of which parties may
supplement their arguments and offer evidence (reasons must be given for

---

[175] ECJ Rules of Procedure, Art.62a(1), first subpara.; CFI Rules of Procedure, Art.76a(1),
first subpara.
[176] ECJ Rules of Procedure, Art.62a(1), first subpara.; CFI Rules of Procedure, Art.76a(1),
first subpara.The Court of First Instance has directed that an application in respect of
which the expedited procedure is requested must not in principle (depending on the nature
of the issues and the circumstances of the case) exceed a maximum of 10 to 25 pages (CFI
Practice Directions, point VI, 3). As far as the Court of Justice is concerned, such pleadings
must not, "save in exceptional circumstances", exceed 10 pages." (ECJ Practice Directions,
point 46).
[177] ECJ Practice Directions, point 45; CFI Practice Directions, point VI, 1. The ECJ Practice
Directions state that, "save in exceptional circumstances", the application for a case to be
decided under an expedited procedure must not exceed five pages.
[178] CFI Rules of Procedure, Art.76a(1).
[179] For a case in which such an application was rejected, see ECJ (order of the President of
February 10, 2004), Case C–540/03 *European Parliament v Council*, not reported. The
Court of Justice considered that that case, in which the annulment was sought of a directive
which had to be implemented by the Member States only 22 months following lodgment of
the application was not particularly urgent. The Court further held that the fact that a large
number of persons would be affected by the provisions of the directive did not in itself
warrant recourse to the expedited procedure.
[180] ECJ Rules of Procedure, Art.62a(2); CFI, Rules of Procedure, Art.76a(2). Under an
expedited procedure, the period for lodging the defence is one month.

any delay in tendering it).[181] In practice, where an application for the expedited procedure is accepted, the Court of Justice and the Court of First Instance reach a final decision within an average period of six to nine months.

F. THE PRELIMINARY REPORT

24–060   **General.** After the rejoinder has been lodged or the parties have refrained from lodging a reply or a rejoinder, or the Court of First Instance has decided that the application and the defence do not need supplementing, the written procedure is at an end and the President fixes the date on which the Judge-Rapporteur is to present his preliminary report to the Court of Justice or the Court of First Instance, as the case may be.[182] The preliminary report is not published. It is intended for the administrative meeting of the Court of Justice (the Judges, the Advocates General and the Registrar) or for the competent Chamber of the Court of First Instance a(the Judges and the Registrar). Where necessary, it proposes measures of organisation of procedure[183] or measures of inquiry.[184]

---

[181] This procedure has recently been followed in Case C–27/04 *Commission v Council* relating to the measures taken by the Council in connection with the excessive budget deficits of two Member States (ECJ, Case C–27/04 *Commission v Council*, [2004] E.C.R. I–6649). A decision of the Court of Justice was necessary within the shortest possible period for the purposes of the sound operation of Economic and Monetary Union (see ECJ (order of the President of February 13, 2004), Case C–27/04 *Commission v Council*, not yet reported). The Court of Justice had already applied the expedited procedure in one appeal case (ECJ, Case C–39/03 P *Commission v Artegodan* [2003] E.C.R. I–7885) and in a reference for a preliminary ruling (ECJ, Case C–189/01 *Jippes and Others* [2001] E.C.R. I–5689). It is not possible to use the expedited procedure in the case of an application for an opinion pursuant to Art.300(6) of the EC Treaty (ECJ (order of the President of April 29, 2004), *Opinion 1/04*, not reported). The Court of First Instance applies the expedited procedure more frequently than the Court of Justice. See in particular CFI, Joined Cases T–195/01 and T–207/01 *Gibraltar v Commission* [2002] E.C.R. II–2309; CFI, Case T–211/02 *Tideland Signal v Commission* [2002] E.C.R. II–3781; CFI, Case T–310/01 *Schneider Electric v Commission* [2002 E.C.R. II–4071; CFI, Case T–5/02 *Tetra Laval v Commission* [2002] E.C.R. II–4381; CFI, Case T–114/02 *BaByliss v Commission* [2003] E.C.R. II–1279; CFI, Joined Cases T–346/02 and T–347/02 *Cableuropa and Others v Commission* [2003] E.C.R. II–4251; CFI (order of January 10, 2005), Case T–209/04 *Spain v Commission*, not yet reported (in relation to an action for failure to act). In the *Solvay Pharmaceuticals* case (CFI (order of the President of April 11, 2003), Case T–392/02 R *Solvay Pharmaceuticals v Council* [2003] E.C.R. II–1825, para.104), the President of the Court of First Instance held that the fact that the Court had rejected an application for the expedited procedure did not mean that an application for interim measures would also have to be rejected for want of urgency.

[182] ECJ Rules of Procedure, Art.44(1); CFI Rules of Procedure, Art.52(1).

[183] See CFI Rules of Procedure, Art.64.

[184] ECJ Rules of Procedure, Arts 45–46; CFI Rules of Procedure, Arts 65–67 (see 24–076 to 24–085, *infra*). For a distinction between these two measures, see CFI (judgment of January 18, 2005), Case T–141/01 *Entorn v Commission*, not yet reported, paras 129 and 130: the purpose of measures of organisation of procedure is in particular to ensure efficient conduct of the written and oral procedure and to facilitate the taking of evidence, and also to determine the points on which the parties must present further argument or which call for measures of inquiry; measures of inquiry are intended to prove the veracity of the facts alleged by one of the parties in support of its pleas in law.

In proceedings before the Court of Justice, the Judge-Rapporteur invariably proposes the formation which will deal with the case (three- or five-Judge Chamber, Grand Chamber or the Full Court). In contrast, before the Court of First Instance a case will normally be handled by the three-judge chamber of which the Judge-Rapporteur is a member. The Judge-Rapporteur will deal with the question of the formation only where it is desirable to have an extended composition or to have the case decided by a single Judge.

The Court of Justice and the Court of First Instance decide on the Judge-Rapporteur's proposals, after hearing the Advocate General.[185] They may decide to open the oral proceedings without proceeding to measures of organisation of procedure or measures of inquiry. If so, the President fixes the opening date.[186] If not, the preparatory measures requested by the Advocate General or the Judge-Rapporteur[187] and the measures of organisation of procedure or inquiry decided upon have to have been completed before the President fixes the date for the opening of the oral procedure.[188] After the inquiry, the Court of Justice or the Court of First Instance, as the case may be, may prescribe a time-limit within which the parties are to submit written observations. The oral procedure follows after that time-limit has expired. In addition, during the oral procedure measures of organisation of procedure or measures of inquiry may still be prescribed.[189]

II. THE ORAL PROCEDURE

A. OPENING OF THE ORAL PROCEDURE

Timing. The President fixes the date for the opening of the oral procedure,[190] after any measures of organisation of procedure or measures of inquiry have been carried out. The Court of Justice and the Court of First Instance take cognisance of cases brought before them in order, depending on when the inquiry was completed. If the preparatory inquiries in several cases are completed simultaneously, the order in which they are dealt with

24–061

---

[185] This is invariably the case for the Court of Justice, only exceptionally for the Court of First Instance where a Judge is designated to act as Advocate General.

[186] ECJ Rules of Procedure, Art.44(2), second subpara.; CFI Rules of Procedure, Art.53. Where the expedited procedure applies before the Court of Justice, the President of the Court fixes the date of the hearing almost immediately after the defence has been lodged or at the time when the decision is taken to have recourse to the expedited procedure where that decision is taken after lodgment of the defence (ECJ Rules of Procedure, Art.62a(3)).

[187] ECJ Rules of Procedure, Art.54a.

[188] ECJ Rules of Procedure, Art.54; CFI Rules of Procedure, Art.54.

[189] For an example, see CFI, Joined Cases T–79, T–84–86, T–89, T–91–92, T–94, T–96, T–98, T–102 and T–104/89 *BASF and Others v Commission* [1992] E.C.R. II–315, para.25.

[190] ECJ Rules of Procedure, Art.54; CFI Rules of Procedure, Arts 53–54.

is determined by the dates of entry in the register of the initiating applications.[191] In special circumstances, the President may order that a case be given priority over others.[192] He or she may do so of his or her own motion, although parties may request him or her to do so. Furthermore, the President may in special circumstances, after hearing the parties and the Advocate General, either on his or her own initiative or at the request of one of the parties, defer a case to be dealt with at a later date. On a joint application by the parties the President may directly order that a case be deferred.[193]

Under Art.44a of the ECJ Rules of Procedure,[194] the Court of Justice may decide a case without an oral procedure. The Court may decide not to hear oral argument where none of the parties has applied to be heard. Such application must be made within a period of three weeks from notification to the party of the closure of the written procedure. In practice, it is rare for a hearing to be organised in the absence of such an application.

24–062 **Application for oral hearing.** The application must specify why the party wishes to be heard. That reasoning must be based on a real assessment of the benefit of a hearing to the party in question and must indicate the documentary elements or arguments which that party considers it necessary to develop or disprove more fully at a hearing. It is not sufficient to provide a general statement of reasons referring to the importance of the case or of the questions to be decided.[195]

There is no equivalent article in the CFI Rules of Procedure. Proceedings before the Court of First Instance therefore always include a hearing, unless the Court dismisses the case as manifestly inadmissible or manifestly unfounded (in law).[196]

B. COURSE OF THE ORAL PROCEDURE

24–063 **General.** Before the hearing begins the agents or lawyers are called to a short meeting with the relevant formation of the Court of Justice or the Court of First Instance, as the case may be, in order to plan the hearing. At that point the Judge-Rapporteur and the Advocate General may indicate the matters they wish to hear developed in the arguments.[197]

---

[191] ECJ Rules of Procedure, Art.55(1); CFI Rules of Procedure, Art.55(1).
[192] ECJ Rules of Procedure, Art.55(2), first subpara.; CFI Rules of Procedure, Art.55(2), first subpara.
[193] ECJ Rules of Procedure, Art.55(2), second subpara.; CFI Rules of Procedure, Art.55(2), second subpara.
[194] The corresponding provision for appeals is Art.120 of the ECJ Rules of Procedure.
[195] ECJ Practice Directions, point 48. In principle, the Court of Justice will make use of this possibility where the pleas and arguments of the parties, together with the evidence of the facts relied on, have emerged sufficiently during the written procedure and a hearing cannot make any further contribution.
[196] See 24–042 to 24–045, *supra*.
[197] ECJ Practice Directions, point 49.

The proceedings are opened and directed by the President.[198] In principle, they are open to the public, unless the Court of Justice or the Court of First Instance decides, of its own motion or on application by the parties, otherwise for serious reasons.[199]

Report for the hearing. The report for the hearing is sent to the parties a few weeks before the hearing. At the beginning of the sitting, the President mentions that the report has been sent out and invites comments.

24–064

The report for the hearing sets out the facts, an outline of the procedure up to the date of the hearing and a summary of the forms of order sought and of the parties' pleas and arguments. The judgment of the Court of Justice or of the Court of First Instance will be largely based on the report for the hearing and so it is important for the parties that its contents are accurate.[200] Since January 1, 1994, the report for the hearing has no longer been printed in the European Court Reports except in special cases.

Oral argument. Oral argument is then heard from the parties and any interveners (see 24–093 to 24–110, *infra*).[201] Each party may address the Court of Justice for 30 minutes or for 15 minutes in a case heard by a Chamber of three Judges. Before any formation the presentation of an intervener's argument is limited to 15 minutes maximum.[202] Before the Court of First Instance, speaking time is generally restricted to 15 minutes. This time may be extended by parties' making a reasoned application to the registry at least 14 days before the hearing. Oral argument is intended to clarify the pleas and arguments raised during the written procedure, of which the Judges are already apprised, and to touch on certain aspects of them. In pleading before the Court, the parties may not raise any new pleas unless they are based on matters of law or of fact which have come to light in the course of the proceedings[203] or it is a question of pleas which the Community Courts have to raise of their own motion.[204] In contrast, new evidence may be presented at the hearing, although an explanation must be given as to why it was not tendered during the written procedure.[205]

24–065

Questions. After the parties have presented their oral arguments, the President, the Judges and the Advocate General may put questions to the agents, advisers or lawyers of the parties.[206] This affords an opportunity to

24–066

---

[198] ECJ Rules of Procedure, Art.56(1); CFI Rules of Procedure, Art.56.
[199] Statute, Art.31; some proceedings must be held *in camera* (see EC Treaty, Art.298).
[200] Schermers and Waelbroeck, *Judicial Protection*, §1364, at 676, §1466 and §1467, at 731.
[201] Very frequently the Judges and Advocate General will listen to oral argument via simultaneous interpretation. In order to make that interpretation possible, agents and lawyers should speak at a natural and unforced pace and use short sentences of simple structure (ECJ Practice Directions, point 52).
[202] ECJ Practice Directions, point 50.
[203] ECJ Rules of Procedure, Art.42(2); CFI Rules of Procedure, Art.48(2).
[204] CFI (judgment of December 1, 2004), Case T–27/02 *Kronofrance v Commission*, not yet reported, para 30.
[205] ECJ Rules of Procedure, Art.42(1); CFI Rules of Procedure, Art.48(1).
[206] ECJ Rules of Procedure, Art.57; CFI Rules of Procedure, Art.58.

elucidate any aspects of the case-file remaining unclear and may result in measures of inquiry being repeated or expanded, this being ordered by the Court of Justice or the Court of First Instance after hearing the Advocate General.

24–067 **Closure of the oral procedure.** The oral stage of the procedure is closed by the President after the Advocate General has presented his Opinion. The Advocate General reads out his or her proposal for the operative part generally a few weeks after the hearing.[207] In the case of the Court of First Instance, where an Advocate General has not been designated in a case, the President declares the oral procedure closed at the end of the hearing.[208] The President also declares the oral proceedings closed where an Advocate General has been designated in a case and he or she delivers his or her Opinion in writing by lodging it at the registry.[209]

24–068 **No right to respond to the Advocate General's Opinion.** The parties do not have the possibility of submitting written observations in response to the Advocate-General's Opinion.[210]

C. REOPENING OF THE ORAL PROCEDURE

24–069 **Objective.** The Court of Justice or the Court of First Instance may, after hearing the Advocate General, order the reopening of the oral procedure.[211] It will do so if an apparently determinative matter only becomes

---

[207] Where it considers that the case raises no new point of law, the Court of Justice may decide, after hearing the Advocate General, that the case shall be determined without a submission from the Advocate General (Statute, Art.20, fifth para.). A document which is lodged after the Advocate General has read out his or her proposal for the operative part will be inadmissible. However, the Court of Justice may decide to reopen the oral proceedings (ECJ, Case C–380/01 *Schneider* [2004] E.C.R. I–1389, paras 14 and 19).

[208] CFI Rules of Procedure, Art.60.

[209] CFI Rules of Procedure, Art.61.

[210] See ECJ (order of February 4, 2000), Case C–17/98 *Emesa Sugar* [2000] E.C.R. I–665. Having regard to both the organic and the functional link between the Advocate General and the Court, the Court considered that the fact that it was impossible for a party to submit written observations in response to the Advocate General's Opinion did not violate the right to adversarial proceedings.

[211] ECJ Rules of Procedure, Art.61; CFI Rules of Procedure, Art.62. The Court of Justice ordered the oral procedure to be reopened (in preliminary ruling proceedings) after the Advocate General had delivered an Opinion in which he criticised very severely another judgment of the Court which had been given after the end of the oral procedure. In the order re-opening the oral procedure, the Court asked the parties and the institutions and Member States concerned to concentrate their oral observations on a number of specific questions (ECJ (order of June 18, 2002) Case C–280/00 *Altmark Trans and Regierungspräsidium Magdeburg*, not reported; see also ECJ (order of September 17, 1999), Case C–35/98 *Verkooijen*, not reported). In contrast, in *Wouters* the Court of Justice refused to reopen the oral procedure as applied for by the applicant in the main proceedings on the ground that it was in possession of all the necessary facts, observing that those facts had been the subject of argument at the hearing (ECJ, Case C–309/99 *Wouters and Others*

apparent after the oral procedure has been closed or, even more generally, if the Court needs further clarification on a certain point.[212] If the procedure is reopened, the parties may make further written submissions,[213] additional measures of inquiry may be ordered and, following further oral argument, the Advocate General may deliver a supplementary Opinion.[214]

Request for reopening. In refusing to reopen the oral procedure after the judgment in the *PVC* cases,[215] the Court of First Instance equated the circumstances in which a request to that effect might be granted with the conditions which have to be met in order to obtain revision of a judgment. On appeal, the Court of Justice confirmed that this is the case.[216] The oral procedure will be reopened only if the applicant or the defendant adduces a fact or reasonable evidence of a fact of which neither it nor the Court could have been aware at the time of the hearing and which possibly had a decisive bearing on the case. Naturally, the fact must be connected with the case in issue. Indications of a general nature or declarations made in other proceedings are not sufficient.[217] Consequently, the deliberations will be only upset for serious reasons in the same way as the authority of a judgment as *res judicata* may be revised only very exceptionally (see 24–145 to 24–153, *infra*).

24–070

Absence during initial hearing. In addition, a party may apply to have the oral procedure reopened if it was not present when it was originally held. Such an application will be granted if the party in question proves that its

24–071

[2002] E.C.R. I–1577, paras 40–43). See also ECJ, Case C–184/01 P *Hirschfeldt v European Environment Agency* [2002] E.C.R. I–10173, paras 29–32, and ECJ, Case C–273/00 *Sieckmann* [2002] E.C.R. I–11737, para.22. The Court of Justice may reopen the oral procedure before the Advocate General has delivered his or her Opinion, see ECJ, Case 56/77 *Agence Européenne d'Intérims v Commission* [1978] E.C.R. 2215, at 2230.

[212] ECJ (order of October 21, 2005), Case C–475/03 *Banca popolare di Cremona*, not yet reported.

[213] *Ibid.*

[214] For examples, see ECJ, Case 383/85 *Commission v Belgium* [1989] E.C.R. 3069, at 3077–3078; ECJ, Case C–2/90 *Commission v Belgium* [1992] E.C.R. I–4431.

[215] CFI, Case T–9/89 *Hüls v Commission* [1992] E.C.R. II–499, paras 382–385; CFI, Case T–10/89 *Hoechst v Commission* [1992] E.C.R. II–629, paras 372–375; CFI, Case T–11/89 *Shell v Commission* [1992] E.C.R. II–757, paras 372–374; CFI, Case T–12/89 *Solvay v Commission* [1992] E.C.R. II–907, paras 345–347; CFI, Case T–13/89 *ICI v Commission* [1992] E.C.R. II–1021, paras 399–401; CFI, Case T–14/89 *Montedipe v Commission* [1992] E.C.R. II–1155, paras 389–391; CFI, Case T–15/89 *Chemie Linz v Commission* [1992] E.C.R. II–1275, paras 393–395. See also ECJ, Case 77/70 *Prelle v Commission* [1971] E.C.R. 561, para.7; ECJ, Case C–415/93 *Bosman* [1995] E.C.R. I–4921, para.53; CFI, Joined Cases T–236/01, T–239/01, T–244/01 to T–246/01, T–251/01 and T–252/01 *Tokai Carbon and Others v Commission* [2004] E.C.R. II–1181 para.484.

[216] See, *inter alia*, ECJ, Case C–199/92 P *Hüls v Commission* [1999] E.C.R. I–4287, para.127; ECJ, Case C–200/92 P *ICI v Commission* [1999] E.C.R. I–4399, para.61 (the Court of First Instance is probably obliged to order the procedure to be reopened when these conditions are met); ECJ, Case C–235/92 *Montecatini v Commission* [1999] E.C.R. I–4539, para.102.

[217] See, *inter alia*, ECJ, Case C–199/92 P *Hüls v Commission* [1999] E.C.R. I–4287, para.130; ECJ, Case C–235/92 *Montecatini v Commission* [1999] E.C.R. I–4539, para.105.

absence was due to *force majeure*, which, according to settled case-law, means abnormal difficulties, independent of the will of the party concerned and apparently inevitable, even if all due care is taken.[218] If the person providing the address for service in Luxembourg for the absent party forgets to forward the summons to attend the hearing, this does not constitute a sufficient ground for ordering the oral procedure to be reopened.[219]

III. MEASURES OF ORGANISATION OF PROCEDURE AND MEASURES OF INQUIRY

A. BURDEN OF PROOF ON THE PARTIES AND ROLE PLAYED BY THE COURT IN FACT-FINDING

24–072 **General.** Fact-finding is the outcome of a complex interplay between the parties and between the parties and the Court.[220]

24–073 **Active role played by the Judge.** The classic apportionment of the burden of proof, whereby each party proves the facts on which its claim or defence is based, applies also in Community law. The Court may adjust this by means of presumptions designed to mitigate the substantive inequality between the parties in terms of their ability to prove the necessary facts.[221] For this reason too, a party not having to discharge the burden of proof may nevertheless be obliged to release information to which only it has access, in order to enable its opponent to provide the necessary evidence.[222]

The Court may further play an active role in fact-finding provided, however, that the parties have been able to define their position as regards the facts on which the Court grounds its judgment.[223] This involvement in

---

[218] CFI, Case T–12/90 *Bayer v Commission* [1991] E.C.R. II–219, para.44.

[219] CFI, Case T–235/94 *Galtieri v European Parliament* [1996] ECR-SC II–129, para.17 (English abstract at I-A–43).

[220] For a more extensive discussion, see Berger, "Beweisaufname vor dem Europäischen Gerichtshof", in Gottwald and Roth (eds), *Festschrift für Ekkehard Schumann zum 70. Geburtstag* (Mohr Siebeck, Tübingen, 2001), at 27–41; Lenaerts, "Rechter en partijen in de rechtspleging voor Hof en Gerecht" (2002) S.E.W. 231–237, in particular the part relating to the passive role played by the Court of Justice and the Court of First Instance.

[221] ECJ, Case 10/55 *Mirossevich v High Authority* [1954 to 1956] E.C.R. 333, at 343–344.

[222] ECJ, Case 45/64 *Commission v Italy* [1965] E.C.R. 857, at 867; pursuant to Art.10 of the EC Treaty, Member States are under a duty to provide the Commission with the information necessary in order for it to monitor whether Community law is being complied with. If a Member State fails to comply with that duty, this in itself is enough to justify proceedings under Art.226 of the EC Treaty. In the course of such proceedings, the Court of Justice may put questions to Member States and order measures of inquiry, see ECJ, Case 96/81 *Commission v Netherlands* [1982] E.C.R. 1791 and ECJ, Case 97/81 *Commission v Netherlands* [1982] E.C.R. 1819.

[223] ECJ (order of September 27, 2004), Case C–470/02 P *UER v Commission*, not reported, paras 63–74.

fact-finding originates in the mission of the Court of Justice and the Court of First Instance of ensuring that the law is observed.[224] They may do so only if the facts on which the application of the law is based accord with reality. At the same time, the decisions of the Court of Justice and the Court of First Instance often affect the general interest alongside the individual interest of the parties concerned. The potential ramifications of their decisions may prompt the Court of Justice and the Court of First Instance to prescribe measures of inquiry. Lastly, sometimes the facts and the law are so closely intertwined that it is difficult to make a hard and fast distinction between fact-finding and making determinations of law.[225] The allocation of duties as between the Court and the parties which is encapsulated in the maxim *da mihi factum, dabo tibi jus* cannot be unqualifiedly applied. Moreover, the jurisdiction transferred from the Court of Justice to the Court of First Instance was primarily to hear and determine cases requiring a thorough investigation of complex facts, the aim being to relieve the Court of Justice of the time-consuming task of making findings of fact. For its part, the Court of First Instance incorporated in its Rules of Procedure provisions specifically designed to facilitate greater interaction between the Court and the parties with a view to this task. What is involved is the so-called "measures of organisation of procedure" (Art.64). The Court of First Instance makes avid use of such measures, acting in a more inquisitorial manner than the Court of Justice formerly did.[226]

Parties must prove their assertions. The fact that the Court has the power to order measures of organisation of procedure to be carried out does not release the parties from their obligation to prove their assertions. This is because the judicial contribution to fact-finding is only optional and complementary. Evidence offered in support by the parties[227] must make out a plausible case for their allegations and so constitute at least *prima facie* evidence. This means, for instance, where a party asks the Court to order the opposite party to produce documents in its possession, that the party requesting production must identify the documents requested[228] and provide at least minimum information indicating the utility of those documents for the purposes of the proceedings.[229] It is only if the evidence

24–074

---

[224] EC Treaty, Art.220.

[225] Lenaerts, "Le Tribunal de première instance des Communautés européennes: genèse et premiers pas" (1990) J.T. 409, at 413.

[226] Vesterdorf, "The Court of First Instance of the European Communities after Two Full Years in Operation" (1992) C.M.L.Rev. 897, at 912–915.

[227] ECJ Rules of Procedure, Art.38(1); CFI Rules of Procedure, Art.44(1) as regards the application; ECJ Rules of Procedure, Art.40(1); CFI Rules of Procedure, Art.46(1) as regards the defence; ECJ Rules of Procedure, Art.93(5); CFI Rules of Procedure, Art.115(4) as regards statements in intervention.

[228] See CFI (judgment of April 26, 2005), Joined Cases T–110/03, T–150/03 and T–405/03 *Sison v Council*, not yet reported, para.29.

[229] ECJ, Case C–185/95 P *Baustahlgewebe v Commission* [1998] E.C.R. I–8417, para.93; CFI (judgment of January 18, 2005), Case T–141/01 *Entorn v Commission*, not yet reported, para.132.

satisfies those conditions that the Court will decide, in an appropriate case, to investigate the allegations further by means of measures of organisation of procedure or measures of inquiry.[230] Whether the Court does so decide will be largely determined by the context of the proceedings. In this way, the Court's decision to take particular measures will be influenced by the fact that one party has difficulty, by comparison with its opponent, in obtaining evidence or by the fact that the parties agree on the existence of certain facts. Furthermore, the Community judicature is obliged to order measures of inquiry where this is necessary in order to be able to rule on whether a plea is well founded.[231]

24–075 **Inadmissible means of proof.** Community law does not lay down any specific rules on the use of evidence. All means of proof are admissible, except for evidence obtained improperly[232] and internal documents, such as an opinion of the legal service of an institution. Internal documents should not be disclosed in the framework of proceedings before the Community Courts unless such production has been authorised by the institution concerned or ordered by the Courts.[233] However, it may happen that an applicant adduces as evidence internal and/or confidential documents which were not lawfully obtained. If the Community judicature finds, having regard to the subject-matter and the particular nature of the action brought, that such documents are manifestly relevant for determining the dispute, it will order that the documents must remain in the case-file. In that event, an application from the defendant to remove the documents from the file and return them to it will be rejected.[234]

---

[230] For an example, see CFI (order of November 21, 1996), Case T–53/96 *Syndicat des Producteurs de Viande Bovine and Others v Commission* [1996] E.C.R. II–1579, para.26; CFI (order of February 4, 2005), Case T–20/04 *Aguar Fernandez and Others v Commission*, not reported, para.36. For an extensive discussion, see Brealey, "The Burden of Proof before the European Court" (1985) E.L.Rev. 250–262.

[231] For an example in which the Court of Justice held that the Court of First Instance had wrongly rejected a party's request for the production of documents, see ECJ, Case C–119/97 P *Ufex and Others v Commission* [1999] E.C.R. I–1341, para.111.

[232] ECJ, Joined Cases 197–200, 243, 245 and 247/80 *Ludwigshafener Walzmühle and Others v Council and Commission* [1981] E.C.R. 3211, para.16; CFI (order of May 26, 2004), Case T–266/03 *Groupement des Cartes Bancaires "CB" v Commission*, not yet reported, para.19; CFI (judgment of January 18, 2005), Case T–141/01 *Entorn v Commission*, not yet reported, paras 37–39 (evidence will be admissible if applicant could have obtained the evidence properly).

[233] ECJ (order of October 23, 2002), Case C–445/00 *Austria v Council* [2002] E.C.R. I–9151, para.12; CFI (order of January 10, 2005), Case T–357/03 *Gollnisch and Others v European Parliament*, not yet reported, para.34.

[234] ECJ, Case 232/84 *Commission v Tordeur* [1985] E.C.R. 3027; ECJ (order of October 15, 1986), Case 31/86 *LAISA v Council*, not reported; CFI, Case T–192/99 *Dunnett and Others v EIB* [2001] E.C.R. II–813, paras 32–34. *Cf.*, however, CFI, Joined Cases T–228/99 and T–233/99 *Westdeutsche Landesbank Girozentrale v Commission* [2003] E.C.R. II–435, paras 90–91.

B. Measures of Organisation of Procedure

General. Art.64 of the CFI Rules of Procedure enables the Court of First   **24–076**
Instance to prescribe measures in order to ensure that "cases are prepared
for hearing, procedures carried out and disputes resolved under the best
possible conditions". Although such measures do not form part of an
inquiry prescribed by the Court, they may nevertheless assist in finding the
facts of the case.[235]

The measures include putting questions to the parties, inviting them to
make written or oral submissions on certain aspects of the proceedings,
asking them or third parties for information or particulars, asking for
documents or any papers relating to the case to be produced, and
summoning the parties' agents or the parties in person to meetings.[236]

Measures of organisation of procedure are relatively informal. They do
not have the compelling nature of measures of inquiry and—unlike such
measures—are not prescribed by order, but notified to the parties by letter
from the Registrar. Any party may, at any stage of the procedure, propose
the adoption or modification of measures of organisation of procedure. The
other parties must be heard before any measures are prescribed. If a
request for measures of organisation of procedure is intended to obtain
new factual evidence and is made at a stage in the procedure when the
production of new evidence is in principle no longer allowed,[237] it is
necessary in particular for the party requesting those measures to set out
the reasons why the request could not have been made earlier.[238]

Where the procedural circumstances so require, the Registrar has to
inform the parties of the measures envisaged by the Court of First Instance
and to give them an opportunity to submit comments orally or in writing.[239]
The Judge-Rapporteur may be given the task of putting the measures into
effect.[240] The Court of First Instance makes frequent use of this type of
measure in order to streamline somewhat the processing of large or
complex case-files.[241] The Court of First Instance may, without infringing
Art.48(2) of its Rules of Procedure, base its judgment or order on matters
which came to its knowledge from replies to questions put to the parties as

---

[235] For a list of the specific purposes of measures of organisation of procedure, see Art.64(2)
of the CFI Rules of Procedure. Note that they include "to facilitate the amicable settlement
of proceedings".
[236] CFI Rules of Procedure, Art.64(3).
[237] See, 24–019 and 24–040, *supra*.
[238] CFI (judgment of January 18, 2005), Case T–141/01 *Entorn v Commission*, not yet reported,
para.132.
[239] CFI Rules of Procedure, Art.64(4).
[240] CFI Rules of Procedure, Art.64(5).
[241] Biancarelli, "Le règlement de procédure du Tribunal de première instance des Communautés européennes: le perfectionnement dans la continuité" (1991) R.T.D.E. 543–564. For
an example, see CFI, Case T–68, T–77 and T–78/89 *SIV and Others v Commission* [1992]
E.C.R. II–1403, paras 40–51.

measures of organisation of procedure on which the parties had the opportunity to state their views in the course of the proceedings.[242]

C. MEASURES OF INQUIRY

24–077   **General.** Measures of inquiry are intended to prove the veracity of the facts alleged by one of the parties in support of its pleas in law.[243] Such measures of inquiry as the Court of Justice or the Court of First Instance should deem necessary are prescribed by order. The order sets out the facts to be established. Before prescribing such measures, the Court hears the Advocate General and, where it proposes to hear oral testimony, may commission an expert's report or inspect a place or a thing, the parties likewise.[244] The order is served on the parties. The Court of Justice or the Court of First Instance, as the case may be, may entrust the undertaking of the inquiry to the Judge-Rapporteur.[245] During the inquiry, evidence may be submitted in rebuttal and further evidence may be adduced.[246] The parties may be present at measures of inquiry.[247]

The following measures of inquiry may be adopted: personal appearance of the parties; a request for information and production of documents; oral testimony; the commissioning of an expert's report, and an inspection of a place or a thing.[248]

1. Personal appearance of the parties

24–078   **Purpose.** The Court of Justice and the Court of First Instance may summon parties to appear personally in order to provide explanations about the case or answer questions.[249] Unlike experts and witnesses, they are not heard under oath.[250] A party who does not comply with a summons

---

[242] ECJ, Case C–259/96 P *Council v De Nil and Impens* [1998] E.C.R. I–2915, para.31.
[243] CFI, Case T–175/97 *Bareyt and Others v Commission* [2000] ECR-SC I–A–229 and II–1053, para.90; CFI (judgment of January 18, 2005), Case T–141/01 *Entorn v Commission*, not yet reported, para.130.
[244] ECJ Rules of Procedure, Art.45(1); CFI Rules of Procedure, Art.66(1). Where a party makes an application for measures of inquiry after the oral procedure is closed, such a request may be admitted only if it relates to facts which may have a decisive influence on the outcome of the case and which the party concerned could not put forward *before* the close of the oral procedure (ECJ, Case C–200/92 *ICI v Commission* [1999] E.C.R. I–4399, para.60).
[245] ECJ Rules of Procedure, Art.45(3); CFI Rules of Procedure, Art.67(1).
[246] ECJ Rules of Procedure, Art.45(4); CFI Rules of Procedure, Art.66(2). See also CFI (judgment of January 18, 2005), Case T–141/01 *Entorn v Commission*, not yet reported, para.130.
[247] ECJ Rules of Procedure, Art.46(3); CFI Rules of Procedure, Art.67(2).
[248] ECJ Rules of Procedure, Art.45(2); CFI Rules of Procedure, Art.65.
[249] It is not because parties may "plead" only through their representatives (Statute, Art.29) that they themselves may not even address the Court in an inquiry based on the appearance of the parties. For an example, see CFI (order of December 6, 1989), Case T–59/89 *Yorck von Wartenburg v European Parliament*, not reported.
[250] Statute, Art.28.

from the Court of Justice or the Court of First Instance may not be fined, unlike a witness. As in the case of any hearing, minutes are kept, in which the appearance of parties is recorded. The President and the Registrar sign the minutes.[251]

2. Requests for information and production of documents

Information and documents relevant to the case. The Court of Justice and the Court of First Instance have the power to require parties—and even Member States and Community institutions not parties to the proceedings—to produce all documents and to supply all information which the Court considers desirable.[252] The Court of Justice and the Court of First Instance may request only the production of documents which are relevant, having regard to the subject-matter of the proceedings.[253] Formal note is taken of any refusal.[254] No formal sanctions attach to a refusal to provide information or to produce documents but this may possibly affect the outcome of the case.[255]

24–079

That a document produced is allegedly confidential[256] puts the Court under a duty to exercise care in putting it into *inter partes* proceedings.[257] It may do so, after carefully weighing the interests at stake, only where the document is genuinely necessary in order for it to decide the case[258] or in order the respect the rights of defence.[259]

---

[251] ECJ Rules of Procedure, Art.53(1); CFI Rules of Procedure, Art.76(1).

[252] Statute, Art.21. For examples, see CFI, Case T–2/90 *Ferreira de Freitas v Commission* [1991] E.C.R. II–103, paras 20–21; CFI (order of the President of May 7, 2000), Case T–306/01 R *Aden and Others v Council and Commission* [2002] E.C.R. II–2387, para.34.

[253] CFI (order of November 18, 1997), Case T–367/94 *British Coal v Commission* [1997] E.C.R. II–2103, para.24; CFI, Case T–192/99 *Dunnett and Others v EIB* [2001] E.C.R. II–813, paras 38–39. Internal documents of the institutions are not to be communicated to the applicants, unless the circumstances of the case are exceptional and the applicants make out a plausible case for the need to do so (CFI, Case T–9/99 *HFB and Others v Commission* [2002] E.C.R. II–1487, para.40). Where, however, the Commission spontaneously joins internal documents to the case-file, the other parties cannot prevent it from doing so (CFI (order of May 26, 2004), Case T–266/03 *Groupement des Cartes Bancaires "CB" v Commission*, not yet reported, para.19).

[254] Statute, Art.24.

[255] See, *e.g.* Case 155/78 *M v Commission* [1980] E.C.R. 1797, paras 20–21.

[256] A document may be confidential on grounds, for instance, of State security (EC Treaty, Art.296(1)(a)) or professional or business secrecy.

[257] Under Art.67(3), first subpara., of the CFI Rules of Procedure, the Court of First Instance is to take into consideration only those documents which have been made available to the lawyers and agents of the parties and on which they have been given an opportunity of expressing their views. However, if the Court of First Instance has to review the confidentiality of a document that may be relevant for the determination of a dispute, that document will not be disclosed to the parties at the stage of the review. In addition, the Court of First Instance may consider the substantive accuracy of a non-confidential summary of a confidential document without disclosing the confidential document to the party with respect to which that document is confidential (see CFI, Case T–5/02 *Tetra Laval v Commission* [2002] E.C.R. II–4381, paras 78 and 116–117).

[258] For an extensive discussion, see *Commentaire Mégret*, at 437–438; Vaughan and Lasok, *Butterworths European Court Practice* (n.133, *supra*), at 130–133.

[259] ECJ (order of September 9, 2005), Case C–432/04 *Commission v Cresson*, not reported.

Where a document to which access has been denied by a Community institution has been produced before the Court of First Instance in proceedings relating to the legality of that denial, that document will not be communicated to the other parties.[260]

3. Oral testimony and experts' reports

24–080   **Witnesses.** Occasionally, the Court of Justice or the Court of First Instance may, either of its own motion or on an application by a party, order that certain facts be proved by witnesses.[261] The Court's order sets out the facts about which the witness is to be examined.[262] Witnesses give their main evidence, after which the President, the Judges, the Advocate General and, subject to the control of the President, the parties' representatives may put questions to them.[263] The hearing may be in open court or, on application, *in camera*.[264] After giving his or her main evidence, the witness takes the oath, although he or she may be released from this requirement.[265] The Registrar takes minutes in which the evidence is reproduced. The minutes are checked by the witness and signed by him or her, the President or the Judge-Rapporteur responsible for conducting the examination of the witness and the Registrar. On penalty of a fine, a witness who has been duly summoned must attend the hearing, give evidence and take the oath.[266] Proceedings for perjury are taken at the instance of the Court in the competent court of the Member State concerned.[267] Member States are obliged to treat any violation of an oath by witnesses as if the offence had been committed before one of its courts with jurisdiction in civil proceedings.[268]

---

[260] CFI Rules of Procedure, Art.67(3), third subpara. For an application, see CFI (order of February 19, 2001), Case T–111/00 *British American Tobacco International v Commission*, not reported.

[261] ECJ Rules of Procedure, Art.47(1); CFI Rules of Procedure, Art.68(1). A party applying for a witness to be heard must state precisely about what facts and for what reasons the witness should be examined, failing which the Court of First Instance may decline the request without considering whether it is appropriate to hear the person in question (CFI, Case T–9/99 *HFB and Others v Commission* [2002] E.C.R. II–1487, paras 34–38).

[262] For the full content of such an order, see Art.47(2) of the ECJ Rules of Procedure and Art.68(2) of the CFI Rules of Procedure.

[263] ECJ Rules of Procedure, Art.47(4); CFI Rules of Procedure, Art.68(4).

[264] Statute, Art.31. See, *e.g.* CFI, Case T–172/01 *M v Court of Justice* [2004] E.C.R. II–1075, para.29 (*in camera*).

[265] ECJ Rules of Procedure, Art.47(5); CFI Rules of Procedure, Art.68(5). Art.71 of the CFI Rules of Procedure provides that witnesses may take the oath in a manner laid down by their national law (para.2) or by solemn affirmation equivalent to an oath as well as or instead of taking an oath, where this is provided for by the national law (para.3, first subpara.).

[266] ECJ Rules of Procedure, Art.48; CFI Rules of Procedure, Art.69.

[267] Statute, Art.30; Supplementary Rules, Arts 6 and 7.

[268] *Ibid.*

Experts. The Court of Justice and the Court of First Instance may also order that an expert's report be obtained.[269] The order appointing the expert defines his or her task and sets a time-limit within which the report is to be made.[270] After making his or her report, the expert is sworn in,[271] unless exempted from taking an oath. The provisions on oaths apply. The Court may order that the expert be examined.[272]   **24–081**

Compensation. Witnesses and experts are entitled to reimbursement of their travel and subsistence expenses.[273] In addition, witnesses are entitled to compensation for loss of income, experts to fees.[274]   **24–082**

Objection to a witness or an expert. Parties may object to a witness or an expert on the ground that he or she is not a competent or a proper person to act as such or for any other reason.[275] An objection to a witness or an expert must be raised within two weeks after service of the order summoning the witness or appointing the expert; the statement of objection must set out the grounds of objection and indicate the nature of any evidence offered.[276] The Court of Justice or the Court of First Instance, as the case may be, decides on the objection.   **24–083**

Letters rogatory. In order to obtain a statement from witnesses or experts who cannot appear before the Court of Justice or the Court of First Instance, letters rogatory may be issued for the purpose of having them examined.[277] The competent national authority obtains the statements and sends the resulting documents to the Registrar of the Court of Justice or the Court of First Instance, as appropriate.   **24–084**

4. Inspections of the place or thing in question

Inspections are exceptional. To date, the Court of Justice has only undertaken two inspections of a place.[278] The Rules of Procedure contain no specific provisions on the conduct of a visit.   **24–085**

---

[269] Olivier, "L'expertise devant les juridictions communautaires" (1994) Gazette du Palais 2–6; For examples, see ECJ, Joined Cases C–89, C–104, C–114, C–116–117 and C–125–129/85 *Åhlström and Others v Commission* [1993] E.C.R. I–1307, paras 31–32; CFI, Case T–169/89 *Frederiksen v European Parliament* [1991] E.C.R. II–1403, paras 38–48; CFI, Case T–90/95 *Gill v Commission* [1997] ECR-SC II–1231.

[270] ECJ Rules of Procedure, Art.49(1); CFI Rules of Procedure, Art.70(1).

[271] ECJ Rules of Procedure, Art.49(6); CFI Rules of Procedure, Art.70(6).

[272] ECJ Rules of Procedure, Art.49(5); CFI Rules of Procedure, Art.70(5).

[273] ECJ Rules of Procedure, Art.51(1); CFI Rules of Procedure, Art.74(1).

[274] ECJ Rules of Procedure, Art.51(2); CFI Rules of Procedure, Art.74(2).

[275] ECJ Rules of Procedure, Art.50(1); CFI Rules of Procedure, Art.73(1).

[276] ECJ Rules of Procedure, Art.50(2); CFI Rules of Procedure, Art.73(2).

[277] Statute, Art.29; ECJ Rules of Procedure, Art.52; Supplementary Rules, Arts 1–3.

[278] ECJ, Case 14/59 *Société des Fonderies de Pont-à-Mousson v High Authority* [1959] E.C.R. 215, at 224; ECJ, Joined Cases 42 and 49/59 *SNUPAT v High Authority* [1961] E.C.R. 53.

D. PREPARATORY MEASURES

24–086 **General.** Under Art.54a of the ECJ Rules of Procedure, the Judge-Rapporteur and the Advocate General may request the parties to submit within a specified period all such information relating to the facts, and all such documents or other particulars, as they may consider relevant. This power serves to facilitate the preparation of the Opinion and the judgment. There is no equivalent provision in the CFI Rules of Procedure.

IV. JOINDER OF CASES

24–087 **Connection between cases.** The President of the Court of Justice or of the Court of First Instance[279] may, at any time after hearing the parties and the Advocate General (if an Advocate General has been assigned), order that two or more cases concerning the same subject-matter be joined, on account of the connection between them, for the purposes of the written or oral procedure or of the final judgment.[280] The President may refer the decision to the Court of Justice or the Court of First Instance, as the case may be.

Cases will be regarded as sufficiently connected, *inter alia*, where they contest the same act[281] using the same submissions[282] or where the same parties are involved in different proceedings based on similar facts.[283]

Although, in theory there is no reason why a reference for a preliminary ruling should not be joined with a direct action, it is improbable given the differences in the respective procedures.[284]

---

[279] This power was conferred on the President in order to speed up proceedings, see Christianos and Picod, "Les modifications récentes du règlement de la Cour de justice des Communautés européennes" (1991) Rec. Dalloz, Chronique, at 278–282.

[280] ECJ Rules of Procedure, Art.43; CFI Rules of Procedure, Art.50. CFI Rules of Procedure, Art.50(2) provides that "the agents, advisers or lawyers of all the parties to the joined cases, including interveners, may examine at the registry the pleadings served on the parties in the other cases concerned" and adds that the "President may [..] on application by a party, exclude secret or confidential documents from that consultation".

[281] ECJ, Joined Cases 19 and 20/74 *Kali & Salz and Kali-Chemie v Commission* [1975] E.C.R. 499, para.2; CFI, Case T–1/89 *Rhône-Poulenc v Commission* [1991] E.C.R. II–867, para.232.

[282] ECJ, Joined Cases 112, 144 and 145/73 *Campogrande and Others v Commission* [1974] E.C.R. 957, para.5.

[283] ECJ, Joined Cases 7 and 9/54 *Groupement des Industries Sidérurgiques Luxembourgeoises v High Authority* [1954 to 1956] E.C.R. 175.

[284] Schermers and Waelbroeck, *Judicial Protection*, § 1440, at 716, cite two cases, which were not joined, yet in which the Court of Justice had regard in deciding one case to arguments put forward in the other. The Court observed that the parties' rights had been respected since all the parties to the case had submitted observations in the other. See ECJ, Case 61/77 *Commission v Ireland* [1978] E.C.R. 417, paras 19–22, and ECJ, Case 88/77 *Minister for Fisheries v Schonenberg and Others* [1978] E.C.R. 473, paras 10–13. For another example, see ECJ, Case C–204/90 *Bachmann v Belgium* [1992] E.C.R. I–249; ECJ, Case 300/90 *Commission v Belgium* [1992] E.C.R. I–305; CFI, Case T–27/90 *Latham v Commission* [1991] E.C.R. II–35; CFI, Case T–63/89 *Latham v Commission* [1991] E.C.R. II–19.

Objective. Cases are joined in order to facilitate the processing of cases by   **24–088**
avoiding unnecessary repetition of procedural acts. Joinder has sometimes
been justified on the ground that it avoids conflicting interpretations of
judgments.[285]

Effect. In principle, joinder has no effects on the parties' legal position.[286] It   **24–089**
does not preclude separate examination of the cases in the judgment.[287]
Furthermore, it is possible for one of the cases to be declared inadmissible
after joinder. The arguments put forward in the case declared inadmissible
may be taken into account in determining the second or other cases joined.[288]
    The President may at any time disjoin cases.[289]

V. Preliminary Issues

General. A party may always make an application to the Court of Justice   **24–090**
or the Court of First Instance, as the case may be, under Art.91 of the ECJ
Rules of Procedure or Art.114 of the CFI Rules of Procedure for a decision
on a preliminary objection or other preliminary plea which relates to the
course of the proceedings but does not go to the substance of the case. This
possibility is frequently used by the defence in order to raise an objection of
inadmissibility or of want of jurisdiction (see 24–042 to 24–045, *supra*), but
any other application may also be made,[290] such as a request by a party for
measures of inquiry[291] or for documents to be excluded from the proceedings[292] or to be treated as confidential,[293] a request that the Court declare

---

[285] ECJ, Joined Cases 36–38 and 40/59 *Präsident Ruhrkohlen-Verkaufsgesellschaft and Others v High Authority* [1960] E.C.R. 423, at 438.
[286] Consequently, after joinder, the Court may not rely, as against one party, on documents from the case-file of another party to which the first party did not have access. See ECJ, Case C–480/99 P *Plant and Others v Commission and South Wales Small Mines Association* [2002] E.C.R. I–265, paras 24–34.
[287] ECJ, Joined Cases 7 and 9/54 *Groupement des Industries Sidérurgiques Luxembourgeoises v High Authority* [1954 to 1956] E.C.R. 175, at 188.
[288] ECJ, Joined Cases 26 and 86/79 *Forges de Thy-Marcinelle and Monceau v Commission* [1980] E.C.R. 1083, para.4.
[289] ECJ Rules of Procedure, Art.43; CFI Rules of Procedure, Art.50. For examples, see ECJ, Case 261/78 *Interquell Stärke-Chemie v EEC* [1982] E.C.R. 3271, para.4; ECJ (order of the President of November 17, 2004), Joined Cases C–131/03 P and C–146/03 P *Reynolds Tobacco Holdings and Others v Commission*, not reported, para 8.
[290] See Louterman and Febvre, "Les incidents de procédure au sens de l'Art.91 du Règlement de procédure de la Cour de justice des Communautés européennes" (1989) Gazette du Palais (doctrine) 276 *et seq*.
[291] See, for example, ECJ (order of June 2, 1960), Joined Cases 33, 46 and 47/59 *Compagnie des Hauts Fourneaux de Chasse and Others v High Authority*, not reported; ECJ (order of June 20, 1960), Joined Cases 24 and 34/58 *Chambre Syndicale de la Sidérurgie de l'Est de la France v High Authority*, not reported.
[292] ECJ (order of March 10, 1966), Case 28/65 *Fonzi v Commission* [1966] E.C.R. 506; CFI, Case T–62/99 *Sodima v Commission* [2001] E.C.R. II–655, paras 22–25, where the

that there is no need to proceed to judgment (see 24–169, *infra*) or a request to remedy alleged procedural defects.[294]

24–091 **Separate document.** The application must be made by separate document and state the pleas of fact and law relied on, together with the form of order sought. Any supporting documents must be annexed to it.[295] As soon as the application has been lodged, the President prescribes a period during which the opposite party may lodge a document containing its pleas and the form of order sought.[296] The remainder of the proceedings is oral, unless the Court of Justice or the Court of First Instance, as the case may be, decides to reach its determination on the basis of the documents submitted by the parties. The Court will decide on the application by order or reserve its decision for the final judgment.[297]

24–092 **Decision by the Court of its own motion.** Furthermore, the Court of Justice and the Court of First Instance may at any time, of its own motion, decide, after having heard the parties, whether there exists any absolute bar to proceeding with an action or declare, after hearing the parties, that the action has become devoid of purpose and that there is no need to adjudicate on it.[398]

VI. INTERVENTION

A. AIM AND MANNER OF INTERVENTION

24–093 **Objective.** The outcome of proceedings before one of the two Courts may affect both Community institutions and natural or legal persons even though they are not parties. Intervention allows them to join voluntarily in the proceedings on the side of one of the parties. This enables the Court to take their interests into account in deciding the case.[299]

24–094 **Pleas which an intervener may raise.** Intervention does not constitute a means for third parties to enter the proceedings by the back door as parties thereto. In the first place, interveners' submissions must be limited to

---

Commission successfully applied to the Court of First Instance to have an internal document accidentally communicated to a third party in another case removed from the file.
[293] See, for example, ECJ (order of March 20, 1985), Case 260/84 *Minebea v Council*, not reported; CFI (order of April 4, 1990), Case T–30/89 *Ililti v Commission* [1990] E.C.R. II–163; CFI (order of November 15, 1990), Joined Cases T–1-T–4 and T–6-T–15/89 *Rhône-Poulenc and Others v Commission* [1990] E.C.R. II–637.
[294] CFI (order of December 14, 1992), Case T–47/92 *Lenz v Commission* [1992] E.C.R. II–2523.
[295] ECJ Rules of Procedure, Art.91(1); CFI Rules of Procedure, Art.114(1).
[296] ECJ Rules of Procedure, Art.91(2); CFI Rules of Procedure, Art.114(2).
[297] ECJ Rules of Procedure, Art.91(4); CFI Rules of Procedure, Art.114(4).
[398] ECJ Rules of Procedure, Art.92(2); CFI Rules of Procedure, Art.113.
[299] See also Dauses and Henkel, "Streithilfe durch natürliche oder juristische Personen in Verfahren vor dem EuGH und EuG" (2000) Eu.Z.W. 581–585.

supporting the form of order sought by one of the parties (see 24–017, 24–018 and 24–039, *supra*).[300] The intervener can therefore only raise pleas and arguments in support of this form of order.[301] Whilst an intervener cannot submit claims which go beyond those in support of which it makes its intervention, it can support those claims only partly.[302]

The intervener is at liberty to put forward its own (different) arguments. Indeed if it were not able to do so, intervention would serve no purpose as the intervener would have to confine itself to repeating the arguments put forward by the party which it supported.[303] Thus, an intervener is not bound to discuss the whole of the argument underlying the application.[304] However, an intervener is not entitled to raise an objection of inadmissibility not raised by the defendant[305]; the reason for this is that

---

[300] Statute, Art.40, fourth para. The Court of Justice seems to interpret this provision flexibly. If it appears from the statement in intervention as a whole and from the context that the intervener intends to cast further light on the dispute and so contribute to the success of the claim of the party which it is supporting, the "form of order sought" set out in the statement in intervention is intended to support the party in favour of whom intervention is made, even if its literal wording seems to refer to another aim (ECJ, Case C–377/98 *Netherlands v European Parliament and Council* [2001] E.C.R. I–7079). In other cases, the ECJ takes a stricter approach: see, *e.g.* ECJ (judgment of January 13, 2005), Case C–38/03 *Commission v Belgium*, not reported, paras 7–9.

[301] ECJ, Case C–155/91 *Commission v Council* [1993] E.C.R. I–939, paras 22–25. A party which intervenes on appeal and was not a party to the proceedings before the Court of First Instance cannot therefore claim that the annulment pronounced by that court in the contested judgment should apply equally to it: ECJ, Case C–245/95 P *Commission v NTN Corporation and Koyo Seiko* [1998] E.C.R. I–401, para.24; CFI, Joined Cases T–125/96 and T–152/96 *Boehringer v Council and Commission* [1999] E.C.R. II–3427, para.183.

[302] CFI (judgment of June 15, 2005), Case T–171/02 *Regione Autonoma della Sardegna v Commission*, not yet reported, para.193.

[303] ECJ, Case 30/59 *De Gezamenlijke Steenkolenmijnen in Limburg v High Authority* [1961] E.C.R. 1, at 18; ECJ, Case C–155/98 P *Alexopoulou v Commission* [1999] E.C.R. I–4069; ECJ, Case C–248/99 P *France v Monsanto and Commission* (appeal brought by France) [2002] E.C.R. I–1, para.56; CFI, Case T–459/93 *Siemens v Commission* [1995] E.C.R. II–1675, paras 21–23; CFI, Case T–37/97 *Forges de Clabecq v Commission* [1999] E.C.R. II–859, para.93.

[304] ECJ, Case C–156/93 *European Parliament v Commission* [1995] E.C.R. I–2019; CFI, Case T–459/93 *Siemens v Commission* [1995] E.C.R. II–1675, paras 21–23.

[305] ECJ, Case C–313/90 *CIRFS and Others v Commission* [1993] E.C.R. I–1125, paras 19–22; ECJ, Case C–225/91 *Matra v Commission* [1993] E.C.R. I–3203, paras 11–12; *cf.* ECJ, Joined Cases 42 and 49/59 *SNUPAT v High Authority* [1961] E.C.R. 53, at 75 (where an objection of inadmissibility not raised by the defendant was allowed to be raised on the ground that it sought the rejection of the form of order sought by the applicant). The broad wording employed in that judgment was qualified in ECJ, Joined Cases C–305/86 and C–160/87 *Neotype Techmashexport v Commission and Council* [1990] E.C.R. I–2945, para.18. The Court of Justice left it undecided whether an intervener is entitled to raise a plea of inadmissibility not raised by the party it is supporting because it held that the objection was one based on public policy which the Court could raise of its own motion. The Court held that the objection *was to be* raised of its own motion under Art.92 of the ECJ Rules of Procedure, even though, according to the wording of that Art., the Court only *may* at any time of its own motion consider whether there exists any absolute bar to proceeding with a case (*i.e.* an objection based on public policy). In both the *CIRFS* and the *Matra* cases, the Court refused to entertain the possibility that the intervener could raise an objection of inadmissibility, but then considered the plea of its own motion on the ground that it

submissions in an application to intervene must be limited to supporting the submissions of one of the parties[306] and that the intervener must accept the case as it finds it at the time of its intervention.[307] This means that the intervener is bound by any acts which have already been carried out in the course of the proceedings and that new arguments adduced by it are admissible only in so far as they do not alter the framework of the dispute as defined by the applicant.[308] Consequently, in principle an intervener cannot raise new pleas.[309]

---

involved public policy considerations. See also ECJ, Case C–107/99 *Italy v Commission* [2002] E.C.R. I–1091, para.29; *cf.* ECJ, Case C–13/00 *Commission v Ireland* [2002] E.C.R. I–2943, paras 3–6, in which in proceedings for failure to fulfil obligations the UK submitted that the Court should declare that it had no jurisdiction to rule in the dispute. This was held to be inadmissible since the defendant Member State, Ireland, accepted that it had failed to fulfil an obligation and had not contested the Court's jurisdiction. See also CFI, Case T–266/94 *Skibsværftsforeningen and Others v Commission* [1996] E.C.R. II–1399, paras 38–39; CFI, Case T–19/92 *Leclerc v Commission* [1996] E.C.R. II–1851, paras 50–51; CFI, Case T–174/95 *Svenska Journalistförbundet v Council* [1998] E.C.R. II–89, paras 77–78. See further CFI, Case T–184/97 *BP Chemicals v Commission* [2000] E.C.R. II–3145, para.39, in which the Court of First Instance rejected an objection of inadmissibility raised by France on the ground that it went further than the form of order sought by the Commission and there was no reason for which the Court should consider of its own motion the admissibility of the application as regards the whole of the contested decision (in fact the Court held the application to be partially inadmissible).

[306] Statute, Art.40, fourth para.

[307] ECJ Rules of Procedure, Art.93(4); CFI Rules of Procedure, Art.116(3).

[308] ECJ, Case C–195/02 *Commission v Spain* [2004] E.C.R. I–7857, paras 26–32: the arguments of the intervener (in support of the defendant) which differed in part from those put forward by the Spanish Government purported to show that the Commission's application should be dismissed and were therefore admissible; CFI, Joined Cases T–447/93, T–448/93 and T–449/93 *AITEC and Others v Commission* [1995] E.C.R. II–1971, para.122: the intervener stepped outside the framework of the dispute by contesting that a measure constituted State aid within the meaning of Art.87 of the EC Treaty whereas the applicant had not questioned its nature as State aid; CFI, Case T–243/94 *British Steel v Commission* [1997] E.C.R. II–1887, paras 70–73: an argument based on the EEA Agreement raised by the intervener was held to be inadmissible because the applicant had not alleged that the Agreement had been breached. Consequently, the argument fell outside the framework of the dispute. See also Joined Cases T–125/96 and T–152/96 *Boehringer v Council and Commission* [1999] E.C.R. II–3427, paras 183–184. Arguments raised by an intervener supporting the form of order sought by the Commission (dismissal of an action for annulment) which would permit a finding that the contested decision is unlawful are inadmissible since consideration by the Court of such arguments would have the effect of altering the framework of the dispute as defined in the application and the defence: CFI (judgment of April 13, 2005), Case T–2/03 *Verein für Konsumenteninformation v Commission*, not yet reported, paras 49–53.

[309] CFI, Case T–114/02 *BaByliss v Commission* [2003] E.C.R. II–1279, paras 416–419, and the case-law cited therein. An intervener may raise new arguments. The distinction between a new argument and a new plea is not always very clear (see ECJ, Case C–185/00 *Commission v Finland* [2003] E.C.R. I–14189, paras 91–92). Recently, however, the Court of First Instance ruled that the intervener has the right to set out arguments as well as pleas independently. But since the new pleas have to be connected with a plea already raised by the party supported by the intervener, this case-law confirms that only new arguments can be invoked by the intervener. Indeed, the framework of the dispute as defined in the application and the defence cannot be altered by the intervener (CFI (judgment of June 15, 2005), Case T–171/02 *Regione Autonoma della Sardegna v Commission*, not yet reported,

In proceedings for interim relief, in which the urgency of an application for interim measures is assessed in the light of the extent to which they are necessary in order to avoid serious and irreparable damage, the intervener may assert its interests, but cannot widen the subject-matter of the dispute by laying claim to a personal right to interim legal protection.[310]

B. SUBSTANTIVE REQUIREMENTS

Who can intervene? Community institutions and Member States are entitled to intervene in cases before the Court of Justice or the Court of First Instance. The same right is "open to any other person establishing an interest in the result of any case submitted to the Court".[311] The term "case" refers only to contentious procedures before the Court of Justice or the Court of First Instance, designed to settle a dispute. Consequently, an application by a natural or legal person to intervene—pursuant to Art.40 of the Statute—in order to submit written observations in a preliminary ruling procedure pending before the Court of Justice will be inadmissible.[312]   **24–095**

"Any other person". The expression "any other person" covers both natural and legal persons. Entities not formally having legal personality may be given leave to intervene if they have the ability, however circumscribed, to undertake autonomous action and to assume liability. This is because those characteristics constitute the basis for legal personality.[313] Consequently, a body which takes decisions which have legal effects only within the institution of which it constitutes a part has no autonomy *vis-à-vis* third parties and hence does not possess characteristics such as to entitle it to intervene.[314]   **24–096**

Privileged interveners. Community institutions[315] and Member States are privileged interveners and do not have to establish an interest in the outcome of the case.[316]   **24–097**

---

paras 152–153).
[310] ECJ (order of the President of November 18, 1999), Case C–329/99 P (R) *Pfizer Animal Health v Council* [1999] E.C.R. I–8343, paras 93–94.
[311] Statute, Art.40, second para.
[312] ECJ (order of the President of February 26, 1996), Case C–181/95 *Biogen* [1996] E.C.R. I–717, para.4; ECJ (order of the President of March 30, 2004), Case C–453/03 *ABNA and Others*, not reported, paras 13–16; ECJ (order of the President of May 25, 2004), Case C–458/03 *Parking Brixen and Others*, not reported, paras 5–8.
[313] ECJ (order of December 11, 1973), Joined Cases 41, 43–48, 50, 111, 113 and 114/73 *Générale Sucrière and Others v Commission* [1973] E.C.R. 1465, para.3.
[314] See, in connection with the staff committee of the European Parliament, ECJ (order of November 14, 1963), Case 15/63 *Lassalle v European Parliament* [1964] E.C.R. 31, at 36, and the Opinion of Advocate General M. Lagrange, at 52–57.
[315] The European Economic and Social Committee is not an institution and therefore not a privileged intervener (ECJ (order of the President of March 17, 2004), Case C–176/03 *Commission v Council*, not reported, paras 9–10).
[316] ECJ, Case 138/79 *Roquette Frères v Council* [1980] E.C.R. 3333, paras 17–21; ECJ, Case 139/79 *Maizena v Council* [1980] E.C.R. 3393, paras 17–21: if the institutions' right to intervene were to be restricted it would adversely affect their institutional position.

24–098 **Non-privileged interveners.** Any other person must make out a reasonable case that he or she has an interest in the result of a case brought before the Court of Justice or the Court of First Instance.[317]

Such an interest will exist if the intervener's legal position or economic situation[318] might actually be directly affected by the operative part of the decision to be taken by the Court of Justice or the Court of First Instance.[319] In addition, the interest must be safeguarded by the form of order sought by the party in support of whom the intervener seeks to join in the proceedings.[320] It is not sufficient for the intervener to be in a similar situation to one of the parties to the proceedings and for it to maintain on that ground that it has an indirect interest in the grounds of the decision to

---

[317] Statute, Art.40, second para. A party which has already been given leave to intervene in support of party in the main action has in principle an interest in supporting the form of order sought by the latter in interim proceedings: CFI (order of the President of December 14, 2000), Case T–5/00 R *Nederlandse Federatieve Vereniging voor de Groothandel op Elektrotechnisch Gebied v Commission* [2000] E.C.R. II–4121, para.25.

[318] CFI (order of May 29, 1997), Case T–89/96 *British Steel v Commission* [1997] E.C.R. II–835, paras 20–21; CFI (order of the President of July 11, 2001), Case T–339/00 *Bactria v Commission*, not reported, paras 12–14, in which the President recognised that a party had an interest in intervening in so far as the decision in the pending case would considerably affect the substantive situation, rules and procedures on the basis of which it marketed its products. In CFI (order of the President of June 26, 2002), Case T–210/01 *General Electric v Commission*, not reported, paras 28–29, the President recognised that competitors of undertakings which had brought an action against a Commission decision declaring a merger incompatible with the common market had an interest in intervening in support of the Commission.

[319] ECJ (order of October 4, 1979), Case 40/79 *P v Commission* [1979] E.C.R. 3299. See also CFI (order of March 26, 1992), Case T–35/89 TO 1 *Ascasibar Zubizarreta and Others* [1992] E.C.R. II–1599, paras 32–35, in which an application seeking to initiate third-party proceedings was dismissed as inadmissible because the applicants could have intervened. By the same token, an undertaking which is the subject of a complaint made to the Commission for infringing Art.82 of the EC Treaty has an interest to intervene in proceedings for failure to act (EC Treaty, Art.232) brought by the person who made the complaint against the Commission for failing to take any action. This is because the intervener has an interest in the complaint not causing the Commission to take binding measures against it and therefore in the Court of Justice or the Court of First Instance not declaring the Commission's failure to act contrary to Community law: CFI (order of May 13, 1993), Case T–74/92 *Ladbroke Racing v Commission* [1993] E.C.R. II–535, paras 8–9. Conversely, an undertaking which has lodged a complaint which has resulted in the Commission's initiating a procedure and adopting a decision finding an infringement of competition law has an interest in the outcome of proceedings brought against the Commission by undertakings to which the decision is addressed. It therefore may intervene in support of the Commission: CFI (order of November 28, 1991), Case T–35/91 *Eurosport v Commission* [1991] E.C.R. II–1359, paras 1–6. For examples of the interest required for an individual to intervene in appeal proceedings, see ECJ, Case C–200/92 ICI *v Commission* [1999] E.C.R. I–4399, para.25; ECJ, Joined Cases C–172/01 P, C–175/01 P, C–176/01 P and C–180/01 P *International Power and Others v Commission* [2003] E.C.R. I–11421, paras 49–53.

[320] ECJ (order of November 25, 1964), Case 111/63 *Lemmerz-Werke v High Authority* [1965] E.C.R. 716, at 717–718; ECJ (order of April 12, 1978), Joined Cases 116, 124 and 143/77 *Amylum and Others v Council and Commission* [1978] E.C.R. 893, para.7.

be given by the Court of Justice or the Court of First Instance.[321] A person's interest in one of the pleas raised by a party to the proceedings succeeding or failing is insufficient if the operative part of the decision to be taken by the Court has no bearing on that party's legal position or economic situation.[322]

Intervention within the framework of an action for damages. In the context of an action for damages, it is therefore difficult for a person in a similar situation to the applicant to show that he or she has a "direct and continuing" interest. Since the form of order sought by the applicant in such an action is directed only towards obtaining compensation for the damage sustained by it, a would-be intervener does not have a direct interest in the outcome of the application, but at the most an indirect interest in a judgment whose grounds might influence the manner in which the defendant institution(s) would deal with the intervener's own situation. Such an interest is insufficient.[323]   24–099

Intervention within the framework of an annulment action. A natural or legal person to whom a decision is addressed—*e.g.* a decision finding an infringement of Art.81 of the EC Treaty—has an interest in intervening in annulment proceedings brought by another addressee of the decision.[324] A person having an independent right of action must be considered as having an interest in the result of a case brought by another addressee.[325] A competitor of an undertaking which allegedly violated Art.82 of the EC Treaty has an interest in intervening in support of the form of order sought by the Commission.[326] This is because such an undertaking has indeed a direct interest that the decision finding an abuse of a dominant position and   24–100

---

[321] ECJ (order of the President of March 6, 2003), Case C–186/02 P *Ramondín and Others v Commission* [2003] E.C.R. I–2415, paras 14–17; CFI (order of December 8, 1993), Case T–87/92 *Kruidvat v Commission* [1993] E.C.R. II–1375, paras 12–13.

[322] ECJ (order of the President of June 17, 1997), Joined Cases C–151 and C–157/97 P(I) *National Power and PowerGen v British Coal and Commission* [1997] E.C.R. I–3491, para.57.

[323] CFI (order of the President of July 17, 1995), Case T–517/93 *Van Parijs v Council and Commission*, not reported, paras 8–13; CFI (order of March 7, 1997), Case T–184/95 *Dorsch Consult v Council and Commission* [1997] E.C.R. II–351, paras 15–21. But see ECJ (order of March 20, 1985), Case 253/84 *GAEC de la Ségaude v Council and Commission*, not reported.

[324] ECJ (order of February 14, 1996), Case C–245/95 P *Commission v NTN Corporation* [1996] E.C.R. I–559, para.9; CFI (order of November 28, 1991), Case T–35/91 *Eurosport v Commission* [1991] E.C.R. II–1359, para.15: the individual may intervene in support of the applicant. His or her interest is not defeated by the fact that he or she did not bring an action to annul the decision. But he or she may only act as intervener, *i.e.* only support the form of order sought by the applicant.

[325] *Ibid.*. However, an addressee of a decision regarding the application of Art.81 cannot intervene to support the form of order sought by the Commission (CFI (order of December 16, 2004), Case T–410/03 *Hoechst v Commission*, not yet reported).

[326] CFI (order of the President of July 26, 2004), Case T–201/04 R *Microsoft v Commission*, not yet reported, para.91.

obliging the addressee of the decision to put an end to the abuse be upheld. In contrast, where the prospective intervener only establishes an interest in the result of the case by reason of similarities between his situation and that of one of the parties in the main proceedings, his application will be dismissed.[327] This will be the case, for instance, where a local authority refers only to the similarity of an aid regime applicable in its region to that applicable in another region in an action for annulment of a Commission decision finding the latter aid regime incompatible with the common market.[328]

After granting a party leave to intervene, the Court of Justice or the Court of First Instance may consider the admissibility of the application afresh if the circumstances warrant this.[329]

24–101   Associations. Associations have the right to intervene if the outcome of the proceedings is liable to affect the collective interest defended by the association in question.[330] Thus, an association of undertakings which did not participate in the prior administrative procedure before the Commission for the application of the competition rules may be given leave to intervene only if (1) it represents an appreciable number of the undertakings active in the sector concerned, (b) its objects include that of protecting its members' interests, (3) the case may raise questions of principle affecting the functioning of the sector concerned and (4) the interests of its members may therefore be affected to an appreciable extent by the forthcoming judgment.[331] Unlike in the case of individuals applying to

---

[327] CFI (order of June 15, 1993), Joined Cases T–97 and T–111/92 *Rijnoudt and Hocken v Commission* [1993] E.C.R. II–587; CFI (order of December 8, 1993), Case T–87/92 *Kruidvat v Commission* [1993] E.C.R. II–1375, paras 12–13; CFI (order of September 18, 1995), Case T–375/94 *European Passenger Services v Commission*, not reported, paras 20–26; CFI (order of March 20, 1998), Case T–191/96 *CAS Succhi di Frutta v Commission* [1998] E.C.R. II–573, paras 31–32. See also ECJ (order of the President of July 23, 1998), Case C–155/98 P *Alexopoulou v Commission* [1998] E.C.R. I–4935; ECJ (order of the President of March 6, 2003), Case C–186/02 P *Ramondín and Others v Commission* [2003] E.C.R. I–2415, paras 14–17.

[328] ECJ (order of the President of March 6, 2003), Case C–186/02 P *Ramondín and Others v Commission* [2003] E.C.R. I–2415, paras 14–17. However, where an aid scheme in a region has a direct and present effect on the economic situation of a neighbouring region, either by causing the relocation of some undertakings or by adversely affecting the competitive position of other undertakings, the authorities of the neighbouring region have a direct, present interest in seeing the form of order sought by the Commission granted (*ibid.*, para.9).

[329] CFI, Case T–158/96 *Acciaierie di Bolzano v Commission* [1999] E.C.R. II–3927, para.33.

[330] ECJ (order of October 24, 1962), Joined Cases 16 and 17/62 *Confédération Nationale des Producteurs de Fruits et Légumes and Others v Council* [1962] E.C.R. 487, at 488–489; ECJ (order of December 11, 1973), Joined Cases 41, 43–48, 50, 111, 113 and 114/73 *Générale Sucrière and Others v Commission* [1973] E.C.R. 1465, paras 7–9; CFI (order of December 8, 1993), Case T–87/92 *Kruidvat v Commission* [1993] E.C.R. II–1363, para.10; CFI (order of December 8, 1993), Case T–87/92 *Kruidvat v Commission* [1993] E.C.R. II–1369, paras 12–14; CFI (order of March 18, 1997), Case T–135/96 *UEAPME v Council* [1997] E.C.R. II–373, para.9.

[331] CFI (order of December 8, 1993), Case T–87/92 *Kruidvat v Commission* [1993] E.C.R. II–

intervene, associations therefore do not have to show that their own legal position or economic situation is likely to be affected by the outcome of the case. An association will be regarded as having an interest in intervening if it coincides with that of its members in a context in which the association's intervention will enable the Court of Justice or the Court of First Instance better to assess the background to the case.[332] This somewhat more flexible approach with regard to the interest required to be established by an association wishing to intervene makes up to some extent for the strict approach taken to applications by individuals for leave to intervene.

Individuals. Finally, individuals are not entitled to intervene in cases   **24–102** between Member States, between Community institutions or between Member States and Community institutions[333] unless a provision of Community law specifically entitles a person to intervene in such proceedings.[334]

C. FORMAL REQUIREMENTS

Timing and requirements. An application to intervene must be made   **24–103** within six weeks of publication in the *Official Journal of the European Union* of the notice "of the date of registration of an application initiating proceedings, the names and addresses of the parties, the subject-matter of the proceedings, the form of order sought by the applicant and a summary of the pleas in law and of the main supporting arguments"[335] or, after the

---

1375, para.14; CFI (order of May 28, 1997), Case T–120/96 *Lilly Industries v Commission*, not reported, para.24; ECJ (order of the President of September 28, 1998), Case C–151/98 P *Pharos v Commission* [1998] E.C.R. I–5441, para.6; CFI (order of the President of March 23, 1998), Case T–18/97 *Atlantic Container Line und Others v Commission* [1998] E.C.R. II–589, paras 10–19 (no interest in intervening in an action for annulment of a Commission decision withdrawing immunity from fines under Art.15(6) of Regulation No 17); CFI (order of the President of July 26, 2004), Case T–201/04 R *Microsoft v Commission*, not yet reported, para.37.

[332] In the context of an application for the partial suspension of a Regulation governing, *inter alia*, fishing activities within Azorean waters, the President of the Court of First Instance gave leave to Porto de Abrigo—a cooperative defending the interests of fishermen active in the Azores—to intervene in the proceedings but rejected the request of the WWF on the ground that its interests were too wide and general to be significantly affected by the outcome of the proceedings (CFI (order of the President of July 7, 2004), Case T–37/04 R *Autonomous Region of the Azores v Council*, not yet reported, paras 57–71).

[333] Statute, Art.40, second para. For an example, see ECJ (order of the President of February 26, 1996), Case C–181/95 *Biogen* [1996] E.C.R. I–717.

[334] See in this respect Art.47(1) of Regulation (EC) No 45/2001 of the European Parliament and of the Council of December 18, 2000 on the protection of individuals with regard to the processing of personal data by the Community institutions and bodies and on the free movement of such data ([2001] O.J. L8/1) and ECJ (order of March 17, 2005), Case C–317/04 *European Parliament v Council* [2005] E.C.R. I–2457; ECJ (order of March 17, 2005), Case C–318/04 *European Parliament v Commission* [2005] E.C.R. I–2467 (with respect to the European data protection controller who was given leave to intervene). See by contrast ECJ (order of the President of March 17, 2004), Case C–176/03 *Commission v Council*, not reported: the European Economic and Social Committee was not given leave to intervene.

[335] ECJ Rules of Procedure, Art.93(1); CFI Rules of Procedure, Art.115(1). See also ECJ Rules of Procedure, Art.16(6); CFI Rules of Procedure, Art.24(6).

expiry of this six-week period, before the decision to open the oral procedure.[336] An application to intervene in support of the defendant may be lodged before the defence is lodged. In that case, the intervener runs the risk of supporting a form of order sought whose content is still unknown to it.[337]

24–104 **Non-member States.** States party to the Agreement on the European Economic Area (EEA), not being Member States of the European Union, and the EFTA Surveillance Authority may intervene in cases before the Court of Justice or the Court of First Instance where one of the fields of application of that Agreement is concerned.[338]

24–105 **Disputes relating to intellectual property rights.** Finally, it should be noted that in the case of disputes concerning intellectual property rights in which a decision of the Office for Harmonisation in the Internal Market (Trade Marks and Designs) or of the Community Plant Variety Office is brought before the Court of First Instance, special rules on intervention apply as regards parties other than the applicant or the defendant Office who were involved in the proceedings before the relevant Board of Appeal. Such parties may take part as interveners in the proceedings before the Court of First Instance.[339] They have the same procedural rights as the main parties.[340] In addition, they may, unlike "ordinary" interveners, apply for a form of order and put forward pleas in law independently of those applied for and put forward by the main parties.[341]

24–106 **General requirements applicable to pleadings.** Applications to intervene have to comply with the general requirements applicable to pleadings.[342] Each application has to contain a description of the case, a description of the parties, the intervener's name and address, the intervener's address for service in Luxembourg, the form of order sought in support of which the intervener is applying for leave to intervene and, except in the case of applications made by Member States or Community institutions, a statement of reasons establishing the intervener's interest in the result of the case.[343]

---

[336] Where the six-week period has expired and there is no oral procedure (where, for instance, the case is dispatched by order), the application to intervene will be inadmissible (ECJ (order of the President of June 28, 2004), Case C–445/02 P *Glaverbel v OHIM* [2004] E.C.R. I–6267).

[337] CFI (order of December 11, 2000), Case T–158/00 *ARD v Commission*, not reported, paras 5–8.

[338] Statute, Art.40, third para.See also CFI, Case T–115/94 *Opel Austria v Council* [1997] E.C.R. II–39, para.29, and para.138; CFI, Joined Cases T–371/94 and T–394/94 *British Airways and Others v Commission* [1998] E.C.R. II–2405, para.27.

[339] CFI Rules of Procedure, Art.134(1).

[340] CFI Rules of Procedure, Art.134(2), first subpara.

[341] CFI Rules of Procedure, Art.134(1), second subpara.

[342] See ECJ Rules of Procedure, Art.37; CFI Rules of Procedure, Art.43.

[343] ECJ Rules of Procedure, Art.93(1); CFI Rules of Procedure, Art.115(2).

Language. Applications to intervene are to be lodged in the language of **24–107** the case (see 24–170, *infra*).[344] Member States, however, are always entitled to use their official language.[345]

Application to intervene is served on the parties. The application to **24–108** intervene is served on the parties, who are given the opportunity to submit written or oral observations. The President decides on the application by order. He or she may refer the application to the Court of Justice or the Court of First Instance, as the case may be, which then decides by order.[346] If the application is rejected, the order will be reasoned.[347] A decision granting leave to intervene does not prevent the Court of Justice or the Court of First Instance, as the case may be, from reconsidering the admissibility of the application to intervene in the final judgment and declaring it wholly or partially inadmissible.[348]

Leave to intervene is granted. If the application to intervene is made **24–109** within six weeks of publication in the *Official Journal of the European Union* of the notice that the case is pending at the Court of Justice or the Court of First Instance (see 24–103, *supra)* and provided that leave is granted to intervene, the President prescribes a period within which the intervener may submit a statement in intervention. The statement in intervention has to contain a statement of the form of order sought by the intervener, the pleas in law and arguments relied on by the intervener and, where appropriate, the nature of any evidence offered.[349] With a view to expediting the proceedings, the statement should be as short as possible.[350] The

---

[344] Art.6(5), second subpara., of the Instructions to the Registrar of the Court of First Instance (n.7, *supra*) provides, however, that where an application to intervene originating from a third party other than a Member State is not drawn up in the language of the case, the Registrar shall require the application to be put in order before it is placed on the file and served on the parties. If, however, a version of such an application drawn up in the language of the case is lodged within the period prescribed for this purpose by the Registrar, the date on which the first version, not in the language of the case, was lodged shall be taken as the date on which the document was lodged for the purposes of registration.

[345] ECJ Rules of Procedure, Art.29(3), fourth subpara.; CFI Rules of Procedure, Art.35(3), fourth para.

[346] ECJ Rules of Procedure, Art.93(2), third subpara.; CFI Rules of Procedure, Art.116(1), third subpara. For examples, see ECJ (order of April 8, 1981), Joined Cases 197–200, 243, 245 and 247/80 *Ludwigshafener Walzmühle and Others v Council and Commission* [1981] E.C.R. 1041; CFI (order of November 28, 1991), Case T–35/91 *Eurosport v Commission* [1991] E.C.R. II–1359.

[347] This is specifically prescribed by Art.116(1), third subpara., of the CFI Rules of Procedure, since an appeal may lie against the order (see 16–011, *supra*). In fact, all decisions concerning applications to intervene are reasoned.

[348] ECJ, Case C–199/92 P *Hüls v Commission* [1999] E.C.R. I–4287, para.52; ECJ, Case C–200/92 P *ICI v Commission* [1999] E.C.R. I–4399, para.25; ECJ, Case C–235/92 *Montecatini v Commission* [1999] E.C.R. I–4539, para.75.

[349] ECJ Rules of Procedure, Art.93(5); CFI Rules of Procedure, Art.116(4).

[350] For the Court of Justice, 10–15 pages (ECJ Practice Directions, point 44), for the Court of First Instance, 10–20 pages (CFI Practice Directions, point V).

intervener receives a copy of every document served on the parties. However, in its observations on an application to intervene, a party may ask the Court of Justice/Court of First Instance to treat certain documents in the case as confidential and not send them to the intervener.[351] An application for confidential treatment must accurately identify the particulars or passages to be excluded and briefly state the reasons for which each of those particulars or passages is regarded as confidential. Such an application must be strictly limited to material which is genuinely confidential and may not cover the entirety of a pleading. The application must be accompanied by a non-confidential version of each pleading or document concerned with the confidential material deleted.[352]

If the request for confidential treatment is not granted, the party concerned may ask for certain documents to be removed from the case-file but that request will not necessarily be granted.[353]

Where an application to intervene is made after the expiry of the period of six weeks after publication of the notice in the *Official Journal*, the intervener may, on the basis of the Report for the Hearing communicated

---

[351] ECJ Rules of Procedure, Art.93(3); CFI Rules of Procedure, Art.116(2). To this end, it is necessary for the Court of Justice or the Court of First Instance to ascertain, in respect of each document on the Court' s file for which confidential treatment is claimed, the extent to which a reconciliation will in fact be effected between the applicant's legitimate concern to prevent substantial damage to its business interests and the interveners' equally legitimate concern to have the necessary information for the purpose of being fully in a position to assert their rights and to state their case before the Court: CFI (order of April 4, 1990), Case T–30/89 *Hilti v Commission* [1990] E.C.R. II–163, para.11; CFI (order of May 29, 1997), Case T–89/96 *British Steel v Commission* [1997] E.C.R. II–835, para.23. If documents in the case-file contain confidential information about natural or legal persons who are not parties to the proceedings, such persons have the right, in principle, to have the confidential nature of that information protected unless they have business relations with the intervener or the information is known to third parties: CFI (order of March 19, 1996), Case T–24/93 *CMBT and Others v Commission*, not reported, para.7. In proceedings for interim relief, it is sufficient for the information for which confidential treatment is sought to appear, at first sight, to comprise business secrets: see CFI (order of the President of May 13, 1993), Case T–24/93 R *CMBI v Commission* [1993] E.C.R. II–543, para.17; CFI (order of the President of July 7, 1998), Case T–65/98 R *Van den Bergh Foods v Commission* [1998] E.C.R. II–2641, para.32; CFI (order of the President of July 15, 1998), Case T–73/98 R *Prayon-Rupel v Commission* [1998] E.C.R. II–2769, para.18; CFI (order of the President of March 22, 1999), Case T–13/99 R *Pfizer Animal Health v Council*, not reported. Because the assessment of whether items in the case-file are or are not confidential is relatively onerous, the Court of First Instance now proceeds as follows. The party claiming confidentiality is asked to put together a non-confidential file. This is communicated to the intervener. If the intervener then contests the confidentiality of certain documents, the Court of First Instance will determine by order (of the President of the Chamber concerned) whether or not the contested documents are confidential (see CFI (order of the President of October 15, 2002), Case T–203/01 *Michelin v Commission*, not reported, CFI (order of the President of March 4, 2005), Case T–289/03 *BUPA and Others v Commission*, not reported).

[352] CFI Practice Directions, Point VIII.

[353] ECJ (order of March 28, 1979), Case 30/78 *Distillers v Commission*, referred to in the report for the hearing in Case 30/78 *Distillers v Commission* [1980] E.C.R. 2229, at 2237.

to it, only submit oral observations (if an oral procedure takes place). In proceedings before the Court of First Instance the intervener will prepare its observations on the basis of the report for the hearing. In proceedings before the Court of Justice, the intervener will receive a copy of every document served on the parties.[354]

Reply to the statement in intervention. Parties may reply to the statement in intervention. The President prescribes a time-limit for making such a reply.[355]

  24–110

VII. The Closure of Proceedings

A. The judgment or order

1. Meaning of the term and how it comes about

General. The decision of the Court of Justice or of the Court of First Instance which brings the proceedings to an end takes the form of a judgment or order. Occasionally, however, a judgment is given which determines only some of the issues. Examples are a judgment merely declaring the action admissible[356] or one finding the Community liable but not making any determination of the amount of damages to be paid.[357]

  24–111

Orders. Orders are given when the Court of Justice or the Court of First Instance decide—without having recourse to an oral hearing—that a case is manifestly inadmissible[358] or, as far as the Court of First Instance is concerned, that a case manifestly lacks any foundation in law.[359] When a case is clearly unfounded, the Court of Justice is only allowed in appeal proceedings to dismiss the case by reasoned order.[360]

  24–112

---

[354] ECJ Rules of Procedure, Art.93(3) and (7); CFI Rules of Procedure, Art.116(6). See CFI, Joined Cases T–142/01 and T–283/01 *OPTUC v Commission* [2004] E.C.R. II–329, para.24: a statement lodged by the intervener was not joined to the file: This was because the intervener was only allowed to make its observations orally at the hearing. Where there is no hearing (for instance, where a case is dispatched by order), the application to intervene will be inadmissible (order of the President of June 28, 2004), Case C–445/02 P *Glaverbel v OHIM* [2004] E.C.R. I–6267. Even if unforeseeable circumstances or *force majeure* prevented the intervener from making its application to intervene within six weeks of the publication in the *Official Journal of the European Union* of the notice of initiation of the action, he will not be allowed to file written submissions (CFI (order of the President of April 28, 2005), Case T–201/04 *Microsoft v Commission*, not yet reported, paras 19–20 and 46–47).

[355] ECJ Rules of Procedure, Art.93(6); CFI Rules of Procedure, Art.116(5).

[356] ECJ, Case C–70/88 *European Parliament v Council* [1990] E.C.R. I–2041, operative part.

[357] ECJ, Case C–152/88 *Sofrimport v Commission* [1990] E.C.R. I–2477, operative part.

[358] CFI Rules of Procedure, Art.111; ECJ Rules of Procedure, Art.92(1).

[359] CFI Rules of Procedure, Art.111.

[360] ECJ Rules of Procedure, Art.119.

24–113 **Timing.** There is no principle of immediacy in Community law on the basis of which the Court of First Instance and the Court of Justice are bound to give judgment shortly after the hearing. This is because no provision of the Rules of Procedure or the Statute provides that the judgments of the Court of First Instance must be delivered within a specified period after the oral procedure. Nevertheless the general principle of Community law, derived from Art.6(1) of the ECHR, that everyone is entitled to fair legal process applies and so the two courts have to give judgment within a reasonable period.[361]

24–114 **Deliberations.** The Court of Justice and the Court of First Instance alike deliberate in closed session.[362] Only those Judges who were present at the oral proceedings may take part in the deliberations.[363] They are not assisted by interpreters—French is the working language of both Courts and is used in the deliberations—or by other members of staff. The deliberations take place on the basis of a draft judgment drawn up by the Judge-Rapporteur. The judgment ultimately arrived at reflects the views of at least the majority of the Judges who took part in the deliberations and may certainly not be regarded as the decision of the Judge-Rapporteur. Every Judge taking part in the deliberations is to state his or her opinion and the reasons for it.[364] Pains are taken to reach a consensus among the Judges. If a consensus cannot be reached, the decision is taken by a majority vote.[365] It is for this reason that an uneven number of Judges always take part in the deliberations: it prevents a tied vote. Where, by reason of a Judge being absent or prevented from attending, there is an even number of Judges, the most junior Judge (where there is equal seniority in office, the younger) is to abstain from taking part in the deliberations unless he or she is the Judge-Rapporteur. In that case, the Judge immediately senior to him or her is to abstain from taking part in the deliberations.[366] The Judges cast their votes

---

[361] ECJ, Case C–185/95 P *Baustahlgewebe v Commission* [1998] E.C.R. I–8417, paras 21 and 52; ECJ (order of June 5, 2002), Case C–217/00 P *Buzzi Unicem v Commission*, not reported, para.86 (no infringement of that principle) and in particular para.91, in which the Court of Justice held that that principle was concerned not so much with the passage of time but with any unjustified delay in the proceedings which could be attributed to the Community judicature; ECJ, Joined Cases C–238/99 P, C–244/99 P, C–245/99 P, C–247/99 P, C–250/99 P, C–251/99 P, C–252/99 P and C–254/99 P *Limburgse Vinyl Maatschappij and Others v Commission* [2002] E.C.R. I–8375, paras 179 and 208–222—see also para.229, in which the Court of Justice did not give any ruling on the question whether in assessing reasonable time regard had to be had to the total duration of both the administrative procedure and the proceedings before the Courts, including the appeal proceedings before the Court of Justice. See also Cras, "Het arrest Baustahlgewebe: de "redelijke termijn" in Luxemburg" (1999) N.T.E.R., 82–90.

[362] ECJ Rules of Procedure, Art.27(1); CFI Rules of Procedure, Art.33(1).

[363] ECJ Rules of Procedure, Art.27(2); CFI Rules of Procedure, Art.33(2).

[364] ECJ Rules of Procedure, Art.27(3); CFI Rules of Procedure, Art.33(3).

[365] ECJ Rules of Procedure, Art.27(5); CFI Rules of Procedure, Art.33(5).

[366] ECJ Rules of Procedure, Art.26(1); CFI Rules of Procedure, Art.32(1). For an example, see CFI, Joined Cases T–70 and T–71/92 *Florimex and VGB v Commission* [1997] E.C.R. II–693, para.60.

in reverse order to the order of precedence established by their seniority.[367] The aim is that the judgement of Judges with less seniority should not be swayed by the view taken by more experienced colleagues.[368]

2. Content and formal requirements

Content. Judgments and orders of the Court of Justice and the Court of First Instance consist of three parts: the introductory part, the grounds for the decision and the operative part.[369]

There are no dissenting opinions as there are, for instance, in the House of Lords, the European Court of Human Rights or the International Court of Justice. Even the Judges who voted against the decision ultimately adopted sign the judgment.

24–115

Language. The judgment or order is given in the language of the case.[370] The judgment or order in that language is the only authentic version[371] and it is translated into the other official languages of the Community in the *European Court Reports*.[372]

24–116

Judgment is delivered in open court. The judgment is delivered in open court, the parties being given notice to attend to hear it.[373] The original of the judgment, signed by the President, by the Judges who took part in the deliberations and by the Registrar, is sealed and deposited at the registry, the parties being served with certified copies.[374]

24–117

3. Legal force

Binding nature. A judgment or order of the Court of Justice is binding from the date of its delivery.[375] A judgment or order of the Court of First Instance also has binding force from the date of delivery, unless it annuls a regulation. In that case, the judgment takes effect only as from the date of the expiry of the period for bringing an appeal or, if an appeal is lodged

24–118

---

[367] ECJ Rules of Procedure, Art.27(5); CFI Rules of Procedure, Art.33(5).
[368] Schermers and Waelbroeck, *Judicial Protection*, § 1477, at 735–736.
[369] ECJ Rules of Procedure, Art.63; CFI Rules of Procedure, Art.81. For further details, see Vaughan and Lasok, *Butterworths European Court Practice* (n.133, *supra*), at 163 *et seq.*
[370] ECJ Rules of Procedure, Art.29(3), first subpara.; CFI Rules of Procedure, Art.35(3), first subpara.
[371] CFI (order of February 5, 2001), Case T–334/00 *Goldstein v Court of Justice*, not reported, para.6.
[372] As far as the Court of Justice is concerned, judgments given by Chambers of three Judges are not longer published. The same applies to judgments given by Chambers of five Judges without an Advocate General's Opinion. In contrast, judgments in preliminary ruling cases are always published.
[373] ECJ Rules of Procedure, Art.64(1); CFI Rules of Procedure, Art.82(1).
[374] ECJ Rules of Procedure, Art.64(2); CFI Rules of Procedure, Art.82(2).
[375] ECJ Rules of Procedure, Art.65.

within that period, as from the date of dismissal of the appeal.[376] Apart from this, a request for leave to appeal has no suspensory effect (see 16–024, *supra*).

24–119 **Judgments are enforceable.** The fact that the judgment is binding means that anyone to whom it applies is bound to take the necessary steps to comply with it. That obligation stems from the Treaty articles which specify the effects of judgments.[377] On a more general level, it also arises because of the function performed by judicial pronouncements.[378] The principle of *res judicata* extends only to matters of fact and law actually or necessarily settled by the judicial decision in question.[379]

Judgments imposing a pecuniary obligation on natural or legal persons are enforceable *per se*.[380] They have an order for enforcement appended to them by the competent national authority without any review as to their substance[381] and are enforced in accordance with domestic law, if necessary with the cooperation of the competent judicial and other authorities.[382]

---

[376] CFI Rules of Procedure, Art.83; Statute, Art.60, second para.To date, the Court of First Instance has annulled a number of regulations: CFI, Joined Cases T–163/94 and T–165/94 *NTN Corporation and Koyo Seiko v Council* [1995] E.C.R. II–1381 and CFI, Case T–115/94 *Opel Austria v Council* [1997] E.C.R. II–39; CFI, Joined Cases T–32/98 and T–41/98 *Nederlandse Antillen v Commission* [2000] E.C.R. II–201. The latter judgment was annulled by the Court of Justice: ECJ, Case C–142/00 P *Commission v Nederlandse Antillen* [2003] E.C.R. I–3483; CFI, Case T–243/01 *Sony Computer Entertainment Europe v Commission* [2003] E.C.R. II–4189.

[377] See, *inter alia*, Arts 228, 233, 244 and 256 of the EC Treaty; Schockweiler, "L'exécution des arrêts de la Cour", in *Du droit international au droit de l'intégration—Liber amicorum Pierre Pescatore* (Nomos, Baden-Baden, 1987), at 613–635; Toth, "The Authority of Judgments of the European Court of Justice: Binding Force and Legal Effects" (1984) Y.E.L. 1, at 44–68. Díez-Hochleitner, "Le traité de Maastricht et l'inexécution des arrêts de la Cour de justice par les Etats membres" (1994) R.M.U.E. 111–139.

[378] Toth (n.377, *supra*), at 1.

[379] ECJ, Joined Cases C–238/99 P, C–244/99 P, C–245/99 P, C–247/99 P, C–250/99 P, C–251/99 P, C–252/99 P and C–254/99 P *Limburgse Vinyl Maatschappij and Others v Commission* [2002] E.C.R. I–8375, para.44.

[380] Art.244 of the EC Treaty, under which Art.256 applies to judgments of the Court of Justice and the Court of First Instance.

[381] In the United Kingdom, application to append to a judgment the order for enforcement is made to the Secretary of State. The person concerned then applies to the High Court in England or Wales or in Northern Ireland or the Court of Session in Scotland for the judgment to be registered, and that court must register the judgment forthwith (European Communities (Enforcement of Community Judgments) Order 1972, SI 1972/1590, Art.3(1); see also European Communities Act, s.3(3)). Once registered, the judgment has for all purposes of execution, the same force and effect as if it had been a judgment or order given by the High Court or Court of Session on the date of registration; proceedings may be taken on it and any sum payable under it carries interest as if it had been such a judgment or order (*ibid.*, Art.4).

[382] Art.256 of the EC Treaty provides that enforcement may be suspended only by a decision of the Court of Justice. In *Comune di Montorio al Vomano v Commission* (ECJ (order of the President of May 30, 2001), Case C–334/97 R-EX *Comune di Montorio al Vomano v Commission* [2001] E.C.R. I–4229, paras 20–21), the President of the Court of Justice rejected an application made by the municipality of Montorio on the basis of Arts 244 and

4. Costs

Decision in the judgment or order. The order for costs is contained in the   24–120
final judgment or order which closes the proceedings.[383]

a. What costs are recoverable?

Proceedings are free of charge. Proceedings before the Court of Justice or   24–121
the Court of First Instance are free of charge. Exceptionally, a party may be
ordered to refund avoidable costs which it has caused the Court of Justice
or the Court of First Instance to incur, or to pay for, in respect of excessive
copying or translation work carried out at the party's request.[384]

Recoverable costs. Recoverable costs are sums payable to witnesses and   24–122
experts and expenses necessarily incurred by the parties for the purposes of
the proceedings, in particular travel and subsistence expenses, the
remuneration of agents, advisers or lawyers[385] and office costs.[386]
   The costs must have been caused by bringing the proceedings before the
Court of Justice or the Court of First Instance. This means that costs
incurred during the pre-litigation stage of a staff case or during the
administrative investigation into a purported infringement of competition
law are not recoverable, since they are not related to the judicial proceedings.[387] The expense of paying a litigation insurance premium is not
considered to be an indispensable expense unless in exceptional circumstances the party concerned can prove that it would not have been able to
bring its action without such an insurance policy.[388] In intellectual property

---

256 of the EC Treaty for suspension of the enforcement of the Court's judgment of June
   10, 1999 (ECJ, Case C–334/97 *Commission v Comune di Montorio al Vomano* [1999] E.C.R.
   I–3387).
[383] ECJ Rules of Procedure, Art.69(1); CFI Rules of Procedure, Art.87(1). For a general
   discussion, see Klinke, "Introduction au régime des dépens et à celui de l'assistance
   judiciaire gratuite", in Christianos (ed.), *Evolution récente du droit judiciaire communautaire*
   (European Institute of Public Administration, Maastricht, 1994), Vol.I, 137.
[384] ECJ Rules of Procedure, Art.72; CFI Rules of Procedure, Art.90.
[385] ECJ Rules of Procedure, Art.73; CFI Rules of Procedure, Art.91.
[386] ECJ (order of January 6, 2004), Case C–104/89 DEP *Mulder and Others v Council and
   Commission* [2004] E.C.R. I–1, para.70 (the office costs were set at a flat rate of 50% of the
   fees).
[387] ECJ (order of October 21, 1970), Case 75/69 *Hake v Commission* [1970] E.C.R. 901, para.1;
   ECJ (order of November 30, 1994), Case C–294/90 DEP *British Aerospace v Commission*
   [1994] E.C.R. I–5423, para.12. See, however, Fiebig, "The Indemnification of Costs in
   Proceedings before the European Courts" (1997) C.M.L.Rev. 89, at 116–118, who argues
   that non-recoverable costs connected with the administrative procedure before the
   Commission may be included in the claim in an action for damages. However, this point of
   view was dismissed by the Court of First Instance in a case relating to the costs of a
   procedure before the European Ombudsman (see CFI (order of July 11, 2005), Case T–
   294/04 *Internationaler Hilfsfonds v Commission*, not yet reported, paras 50–55). A party
   cannot, by way of an action for damages, seek to recover costs which are in principle not
   recoverable.
[388] CFI (order of November 27, 2000), Case T–78/99 (92) *Elder v Commission* [2000] E.C.R.
   II–3717, paras 17–18.

cases, costs necessarily incurred by the parties for the purposes of the proceedings before the Board of Appeal and costs incurred for the purposes of the production of translations of pleadings or other documents into the language of the case[389] are regarded as recoverable costs.[390]

All costs incurred for the purposes of the judicial proceedings, including the costs of any interlocutory proceedings, may be recoverable on condition, of course, that they were necessary.[391] Fees relating to the period after the oral procedure (such as lawyers' fees for considering the Advocate General's Opinion) cannot be regarded in principle as being necessary costs incurred in connection with the proceedings.[392]

The salaries of officials who represent a Community institution before the Court of Justice or the Court of First Instance does not constitute recoverable costs since a salary is in law paid, not as a fee for representing the institution, but for the purposes of fulfilling an obligation imposed on the institution concerned by the Staff Regulations. However, the travel and subsistence expenses of such officials are recoverable, as is the fee payable to a practitioner assisting the institution.

24–123 **Disputes about the amount of the recoverable costs.** The party concerned may bring a dispute about the amount of recoverable costs before the Chamber dealing with the case. The Chamber decides by order against which no appeal will lie, after hearing the opposite party.[393] Such an

---

[389] Pursuant to CFI Rules of Procedure, Art.131(4), second subpara.

[390] CFI Rules of Procedure, Art.136(2). For examples, see CFI, Case T–32/00 *Messe München v OHIM (electronica)* [2000] E.C.R. II–3829, paras 10–12; CFI, Case T–135/99 *Taurus-Film v OHIM (Cine Action)* [2001] E.C.R. II–379, para.36; CFI, Case T–136/99 *Taurus-Film v OHIM (Cine Comedy)* [2001] E.C.R. II–397, para.35; CFI, Case T–34/00 *Eurocool Logistik v OHIM (EUROCOOL)* [2002] E.C.R. II–683, paras 54–56; CFI (order of December 15, 2004), Case T–129/01 DEP *Alejandro v OHIM*, not reported, paras 7–20.

[391] CFI (order of September 17, 1998), Case T–271/94 (92) *Branco v Commission* [1998] E.C.R. II–3761.

[392] ECJ (order of January 6, 2004), Case C–104/89 DEP *Mulder and Others v Council and Commission* [2004] E.C.R. I–1, paras 48–50: fees relating to negotiations conducted by the parties in order to establish the amount of damages payable by agreement where the Court of Justice itself expressly called upon the parties in the operative part of an interlocutory judgment to inform it of the amount of such damages within a specific period dating from the date of delivery of the judgment may not be excluded from the category of necessary costs. Where, in the interests of procedural economy, the Court of Justice itself does not rule on the amounts due but calls on the parties to reach agreement on them, the successful party would be placed at a disadvantage if the recovery of the costs incurred because of those negotiations was not taken into account.

[393] ECJ Rules of Procedure, Art.74(1); in the Court of Justice, the Advocate General is also heard; CFI Rules of Procedure, Art.92(1). If the parties cannot agree on the amount of the recoverable costs, the interested party must bring the dispute before the Court of Justice or the Court of First Instance, as the case may be. A party cannot enforce the payment of such costs by offsetting in the event that the other party refuses to pay them: CFI, Case T–214/00 *X v Commission* [2001] ECR-SC I–A–143, II–663.

application for the taxation of costs is admissible only if it genuinely relates to a dispute about the amount of recoverable costs.[394] An application for an order for costs to be reviewed does not constitute a dispute about the amount of recoverable costs.[395] If the dispute relates to the amount of a lawyer's fees, the Court of Justice or the Court of First Instance, as the case may be, does not rule on whether the fees were appropriate, but only on the extent to which they are recoverable.[396] In so doing, it takes account of the subject-matter and the character of the proceedings,[397] the importance of the dispute from the point of view of Community law, the volume of work involved for the lawyer[398] and the economic importance of the case for the parties concerned.[399] In general, the fees for one lawyer will be accepted as being recoverable costs, but in complex cases the fees of more than one lawyer will be recoverable within reasonable limits.[400] However, if lawyers of

---

[394] The application becomes devoid of purpose when it concerns only the costs of the (initial) procedure before the Court of First Instance in the event that the Court of Justice annuls the judgment of the Court of First Instance and refers the case back to the Court of First Instance. In such case the Court of Instance will have to take in its final judgment a new decision with respect to the costs taking into account the proceedings both before the Court of First Instance and the Court of Justice: see CFI (order of December 7, 2004), Case T–237/00 DEP *Reynolds v European Parliament*, not reported, paras 10–17.

[395] CFI (order of July 15, 1993), Joined Cases T–33 and T–74/89 DEPE *Blackman v European Parliament* [1993] E.C.R. II–837, paras 5–6.

[396] CFI (order of November 28, 1996), Case T–447/93 DEPE *AITEC v Commission* [1996] E.C.R. II–1631, para.19; CFI (order of March 7, 2000), Case T–2/95 (92) *Industries des Poudres Sphériques v Council* [2000] E.C.R. II–463, para.34.

[397] Whether a case raises questions already raised in other cases may have a bearing on this: see CFI (order of July 11, 1995), Cases T–23/90 (92) and T–9/92 (92) *Peugeot v Commission* [1995] E.C.R. II–2057, para.30; CFI (order of December 13, 1995), Case T–138/95 (92) *Engelking v Council and Commission*, not reported, para.14.

[398] As regards costs incurred by an intervener, see CFI (order of January 24, 2005), Joined Cases T–346/02 and T–347/02 DEP *Cableuropa and Others v Commission*, not reported, paras 28 and 32.

[399] ECJ (order of October 21, 1970), Case 75/69 *Hake v Commission* [1970] E.C.R. 901, para.2; ECJ (order of November 26, 1985), Case 318/82 *Leeuwarder Papierwarenfabriek v Commission* [1985] E.C.R. 3727; ECJ (order of January 6, 2004), Case C–104/89 DEP *Mulder and Others v Council and Commission* [2004] E.C.R. I–1, para.51; CFI (order of February 25, 1992), Joined Cases T–18 and T–24/89 *Tagaras v Court of Justice* [1992] E.C.R. II–153, para.13; CFI (order of June 9, 1993), Case T–78/89 DEPE *PPG Industries Glass v Commission* [1993] E.C.R. II–573, para.36; CFI (order of July 15, 1993), Case T–84/91 DEPE *Meskens v European Parliament* [1993] E.C.R. II–757.

[400] CFI (order of November 8, 1996), Case T–120/89 (92) *Stahlwerke Peine-Salzgitter v Commission* [1996] E.C.R. II–1547, para.31; CFI (order of November 28, 1996), Case T–447/93 DEPE *AITEC v Commission* [1996] E.C.R. II–1631, para.23; CFI (order of October 30, 1998), Case T–290/94 (92) *Kaysersberg v Commission* [1998] E.C.R. II–4105, para.20 (this order also gives an insight into the recovery of costs by an intervener); ECJ (order of January 6, 2004), Case C–104/89 DEP *Mulder and Others v Council and Commission* [2004] E.C.R. I–1, para.62. As far as the involvement of a barrister and a solicitor in proceedings before the Court of First Instance are concerned, see CFI (order of June 28, 2004), T–342/99 DEP *Airtours v Commission* [2004] E.C.R. II–1785, paras 40–53. The VAT paid by a VAT taxable person on lawyers' and experts' fees cannot be regarded as a cost (in view of the possibility to deduct VAT provided for in the Sixth VAT Directive) and is therefore not recoverable (CFI (order of June 28, 2004), Case T–342/99 DEP *Airtours v Commission*

different law firms are appointed, the coordination costs for the joint preparation of the pleadings will not be recoverable.[401]

The Community Court is not bound by national scales of lawyers' fees[402] or by any agreement concluded by the applicant with its lawyer.[403] Where the contested Commission decision is largely based on economic considerations, the involvement of one or more economic advisers or experts may sometimes prove necessary and entail recoverable costs in proceedings before the Court of First Instance.[404]

As far as the costs of the proceedings for the taxation of costs are concerned, the Court of Justice and the Court of First Instance do not take a separate decision thereon. The reason for this is that, in determining the recoverable costs, the courts take account of all the circumstances of the case up to the time of their decision on the taxation of costs.[405] As the right to recover costs has its basis in the order of Court of Justice or the Court of First Instance fixing the amount recoverable, interest thereon is payable only from the date of that order.[406]

[2004] E.C.R. II–1785, para.79). See in contrast CFI (order of July 8, 2004), Joined Cases T–7/98 and T–208/98 DEP and T–109/99 DEP *De Nicola v EIB*, [2004] E.C.R.–SC II–973, para.37, as regards non VAT taxable persons. An appeal procedure will normally not justify the recourse to more than one counsel. This is because an appeal is limited to points of law (ECJ (order of July 8, 2004), Case C–286/95 P-DEP *ICI v Commission* [2004] E.C.R. I–6469, para.26).

[401] CFI (order of October 29, 2004), Case T–77/02 DEP *Schneider Electric v Commission*, not reported, para.61.

[402] CFI (order of January 20, 1995), Case T–124/93 *Werner v Commission* [1995] E.C.R. II–91, para.10, CFI (order of June 5, 1996), Case T–228/94 (92) *Rusp v Council and Commission*, not reported, para.11; CFI (order of November 8, 2001), Case T–65/96 DEP *Kish Glass v Commission* [2001] E.C.R. II–3261, para.19. A rate of 210 euro per hour was deemed to be acceptable and recoverable in CFI (order of December 20, 2004), Case T–123/00 DEP *Thomae v Commission*, not reported, para.37.

[403] CFI (order of December 7, 2000), Case T–77/95 DEP *Ufex and Others v Commission*, not reported, para.29. In a merger case, an hourly rate of 400 euro was held to be recoverable: CFI (order of October 29, 2004), Case T–77/02 DEP *Schneider Electric v Commission*, not reported, para.62.

[404] CFI (order of June 28, 2004) Case T–342/99 DEP *Airtours v Commission* [2004] E.C.R. II–1785, paras 55–61; CFI (order of October 29, 2004), Case T–77/02 DEP *Schneider Electric v Commission*, not reported, para.69.

[405] ECJ (order of January 6, 2004), Case C–104/89 DEP *Mulder and Others v Council and Commission* [2004] E.C.R. I–1, para.87; CFI (order of December 20, 2004), Case T–123/00 DEP *Thomae v Commission*, not reported, para.37; ECJ (order of February 4, 2004), C–77/99 DEP *Commission v Oder-Plan Architektur and Others* [2004] E.C.R. I–1267, paras 24 and 25 (the recoverable costs relating to the taxation were estimated at 400 euro).

[406] ECJ (order of April 18, 1975), Case 6/72 *Europemballage and Continental Can v Commission* [1975] E.C.R. 495, para.5; CFI (order of June 9, 1993), Case T–78/89 DEPE *PPG Industries Glass v Commission* [1993] E.C.R. II–573, paras 25–29; ECJ (order of January 6, 2004), Case C–104/89 DEP *Mulder and Others v Council and Commission* [2004] E.C.R. I–1, para.86.

b. Who has to pay the costs?

Principle. In principle, the Court of Justice or the Court of First Instance   **24–124**
orders the unsuccessful party to pay the costs if they have been applied for
in the successful party's pleadings.[407] It is possible to apply for costs for the
first time at the stage of the oral procedure.[408]

Other possibilities. An order may be made that the costs be shared or that   **24–125**
the parties bear their own costs where each party succeeds on some and
fails on other heads or where the Court so decides on specific grounds[409] or
for reasons of equity.[410] In addition, Art.136(1) of the CFI Rules of
Procedure provides that where an action against a decision of a Board of
Appeal is successful, the Court of First Instance may order the Office to
bear only its own costs. In such a case, the Court of First Instance may
order the intervener to pay the applicant's costs.[411]

---

[407] ECJ Rules of Procedure, Art.69(2); CFI Rules of Procedure, Art.87(2). See ECJ, Joined
Cases 23–24 and 52/63 *Usines Emile Henricot and Others v High Authority* [1963] E.C.R.
217, at 225; ECJ, Joined Cases 188–190/80 *France and Others v Commission* [1982] E.C.R.
2545, para.39. But see ECJ, Joined Cases 40–48, 50, 54–56, 111, 113 and 114/73 *Suiker Unie
and Others v Commission* [1975] E.C.R. 1663, para.627. An application that the other party
be ordered to pay the costs must be made without ambiguity: see, *e.g.* CFI (judgment of
March 8, 2005), Case T–277/03 *Vluchaki v Commission*, not yet reported, para.97.

[408] ECJ, Case 113/77 *NTN Toyo Bearing v Council* [1979] E.C.R. 1185, Opinion of Advocate
General J.-P. Warner, at 1274, who took the view that omission by a party to ask for costs
under Art.69(2) of the ECJ Rules of Procedure does not debar the Court from awarding
them under Art.69(1); CFI, Case T–64/89 *Automec v Commission* [1990] E.C.R. II–367,
para.79; CFI, Case T–13/92 *Moat v Commission* [1993] E.C.R. II–287, para.50; CFI
(judgment of October 5, 2005), Case T–423/04 *Bunker & BKR v OHIM*, not yet reported,
para.84. See, however, ECJ, Case 298/83 *CICCE v Commission* [1985] E.C.R. 1105, para.32,
where costs were claimed in the rejoinder and this was considered to be too late and
therefore the claim was inadmissible. This shows a tolerance of the Community Court *vis-
à-vis* private parties. In the judgment in *CICCE*, the private party lost its case and would
therefore have had to pay the costs. In *Moat*, the individual was successful and his claim
was not regarded as having been made too late.

[409] ECJ Rules of Procedure, Art.69(3), first subpara.; CFI Rules of Procedure, Art.87(3), first
subpara. For examples, see *Commentaire Mégret*, at 458; CFI, Case T–38/96 *Guérin
Automobiles v Commission* [1997] E.C.R. II–1223, paras 48–50; CFI, Joined Cases T–
191/98, T–212/98 to T–214/98 *Atlantic Container Line and Others v Commission* [2003]
E.C.R. II–3275, paras 1645–1647 (the application was too voluminous; by their conduct the
applicants substantially added to the burden of dealing with the case, thus needlessly
adding in particular to the costs of the defendant).

[410] See CFI Rules of Procedure, Art.97(4) which provides: "Where the recipient of [legal] aid
is unsuccessful, the Court of First Instance may, in its decision, as to costs, closing the
proceedings, if equity so requires, order that one or more parties should bear their own
costs or that those costs should be borne, in whole or in part, by the cashier of the Court of
First Instance by way of legal aid".

[411] See Mengozzi, "Le contrôle des décisions de l'OHIM par le Tribunal de première instance
et la Cour de justice dans le contentieux relatif aux droits de la propriété industrielle"
[2002] R.D.U.E. 315–333.

24–126 **Unreasonable or vexatious procedure.** The successful party may be ordered to pay costs which the Court considers it to have unreasonably or vexatiously caused the other party to bear.[412] Thus, where within the framework of infringement proceedings, the defendant Member State fails to provide all the relevant information to the Commission in the pre-litigation procedure, the Court of Justice will order the Member State to bear (part of) the costs. This is because in such circumstances, it cannot be held against the Commission that it brought an infringement action before the Court of Justice, even though the action is ill-founded.[413]

24–127 **Staff cases.** In proceedings between the Communities and their servants, the institutions bear their own costs in any event,[414] unless they were caused unreasonably or vexatiously.[415] Thus, where the representative of the servant does not appear at the oral hearing without any notice, the servant will have to support the cost incurred of the defendant institution as a result of its attending the hearing.[416]

24–128 **Interveners.** As interveners, Member States, institutions, EEA States and the EFTA Supervisory Authority bear their own costs.[417] Other interveners may also be ordered to bear their own costs, even if they intervened in support of the successful party.[418] Generally, however, an intervener which intervened in support of the successful party will recover its costs from the unsuccessful party.[419] An intervener which supported the form of order sought by the unsuccessful party may be ordered to pay the costs together with that party. In particular, the Court of Justice and the Court of First

---

412 ECJ Rules of Procedure, Art.69(3), second subpara.; CFI Rules of Procedure, Art.87(3), second subpara. For examples, see ECJ, Joined Cases 35/62 and 16/63 *Leroy v High Authority* [1963] E.C.R. 197, at 208; ECJ, Joined Cases 23–24 and 52/63 *Usines Emile Henricot and Others v High Authority* [1963] E.C.R. 217, at 225; ECJ, Case 148/79 *Korter v Council* [1981] E.C.R. 615, paras 19–20; ECJ, Case 263/81 *List v Commission* [1983] E.C.R. 103, paras 30–31; CFI (order of the President of January 23, 2001), Joined Cases T–63/00 and T–90/00 *Rasmussen v Commission*, not reported; CFI, Case T–311/00 *British American Tobacco v Commission* [2002] E.C.R. II–2781, paras 62–67; CFI, Case T–40/01 *Scan Office Design v Commission* [2002] E.C.R. II–5043, paras 123–125.

413 ECJ, Case C–456/03 *Commission v Italy* [2005] E.C.R. I–5335, paras 110–115.

414 ECJ Rules of Procedure, Art.70; CFI Rules of Procedure, Art.88.

415 For an example, see CFI (order of December 15, 1995), Case T–131/95 *Progoulis v Commission* [1995] ECR-SC II–907, paras 52–55 (English abstract at I-A–297).

416 CFI, Joined Cases T–120/01 and T–300/01 *De Nicola v EIB* [2004] E.C.R.-SC II–1671, para.331; CFI (judgment of May 4, 2005), Case T–398/03 *Castets v Commission*, not yet reported, paras 39–40.

417 ECJ Rules of Procedure, Art.69(4), first and second subparas; CFI Rules of Procedure, Art.87(4), first and second subparas.

418 ECJ Rules of Procedure, Art.69(4), third subpara.; CFI Rules of Procedure, Art.87(4), third subpara.

419 CFI, Case T–2/93 *Air France v Commission* [1994] E.C.R. II–323, para.106.

Instance may allow the successful party to recover the costs it incurred as a result of the intervention of the intervener.[420]

Proceedings which are discontinued. If a party discontinues or withdraws **24–129** from proceedings (see 24–167 and 24–168, *infra*), that party will be ordered to pay the costs if they have been applied for in the other party's observations on the discontinuance or withdrawal. However, the party discontinuing or withdrawing from proceedings may apply for an order for costs against the other party if this appears justified by that party's conduct.[421] Where the parties have come to an agreement on costs, the decision on costs will be in accordance with that agreement. If costs are not claimed, the parties bear their own costs.[422]

Action becomes devoid of purpose. Where a case does not proceed to **24–130** judgment, the costs are in the discretion of the Court.[423]

5. Legal aid

General. A party who is wholly or in part unable to meet the costs of the **24–131** proceedings may at any time apply for legal aid.[424] The application, which need not be made through a lawyer,[425] has to be accompanied by evidence of the applicant's need of assistance, in particular by a document from the

---

[420] See, for example, the 1979 ball bearing cases: ECJ, Case 113/77 *NTN Toyo Bearing v Council* [1979] E.C.R. 1185, para.31; ECJ, Case 118/77 *ISO v Council* [1979] E.C.R. 1277, para.62; ECJ, Case 119/77 *Nippon Seiko v Council and Commission* [1979] E.C.R. 1303, para.38; ECJ, Case 120/77 *Koyo Seiko v Council and Commission* [1979] E.C.R. 1337, para.63; ECJ, Case 121/77 *Nachi Fujikoshi v Council* [1979] E.C.R. 1363, para.29.

[421] Where the Commission discontinues proceedings for failure to fulfil obligations because the Member State has brought the infringement to an end, it will normally claim that the Member State concerned be ordered to pay the costs. For examples, see ECJ (order of July 11, 2000), Case C–271/99 *Commission v Belgium*, not reported, para.4; ECJ (order of October 21, 2003), Case C–80/03 *Commission v Netherlands*, not reported, paras 3–4. Where the Commission withdraws the contested decision, the action becomes devoid of purpose; in that case the Commission will have to bear the costs (CFI (order of September 2, 2004), Case T–291/02 *González y Diéz v Commission*, not reported, paras 17–23).

[422] ECJ Rules of Procedure, Art.69(5); CFI Rules of Procedure, Art.87(5). For examples, see CFI (order of October 16, 1995), Case T–561/93 *Tiercé Ladbroke v Commission* [1995] E.C.R. II–2755; CFI (order of October 22, 1996), Case T–19/96 *Carvel and Guardian Newspapers v Council* [1996] E.C.R. II–1519.

[423] ECJ Rules of Procedure, Art.69(6); CFI Rules of Procedure, Art.87(6). For an example, see CFI, Case T–56/92 *Koelman v Commission* [1993] E.C.R. II–1267, paras 29–32.

[424] For a more extensive discussion, see Kennedy, "Paying the Piper: Legal Aid in Proceedings Before the Court of Justice" (1988) C.M.L.Rev. 559–591. A party to proceedings in England and Wales who is legally aided is entitled to have the legal aid order extended to cover the proceedings before the Court of Justice: *R v Malborough Street Magistrates, ex parte Bouchereau* [1977] 1 W.L.R. 414.

[425] Application for legal aid may be made without the assistance of a lawyer not only before proceedings have been brought, but also after the application has been lodged by a lawyer: see CFI Rules of Procedure, Art.95(1); see also CFI (order of February 19, 1997), Case T–157/96 *Affatato v Commission* [1997] E.C.R. II–155.

competent authority under national law certifying his or her lack of means.[426] Before the Court of First Instance only natural persons quality for legal aid.[427]

24–132   **Application may be made prior to proceedings.** An application for legal aid may be made prior to proceedings which the applicant wishes to commence. If such an application is made, it must briefly state the subject of the proceedings.[428] In principle, lodging an application for legal aid has no effect on the calculation or running of time for initiating proceedings.[429] The time for lodging the main application will be extended only if the applicant shows that exceptional circumstances attributable to unforeseen circumstances or *force majeure* prevented him or her from bringing the main application within the time-limit laid down in the Statute.[430]

However, in order to improve access to justice, the Court of First Instance recently amended its Rules of Procedure, which now expressly state that the introduction of an application for legal aid suspends the period prescribed for the bringing of the action until the date of notification of the decision of the Court with respect to the legal aid.[431]

24–133   **Decision of the Court.** The Court of Justice, on the Judge Rapporteur's proposal and after hearing the Advocate General, refers the application to a formation of the Court which will decide whether legal aid should be granted in full or in part or whether it should be refused. It considers, *inter alia*, whether the application lodged or to be lodged is not manifestly inadmissible or unfounded.[432] Orders of the Court of First Instances relating to legal aid are not amenable to appeal.[433] If the application for legal aid is

---

[426] ECJ Rules of Procedure, Art.76(1) and (2), second subpara.; CFI Rules of Procedure, Art.95 (2). See, *e.g.* ECJ (order of November 16, 2004), Case C–374/03 AJ *Gürol*, not reported: legal aid was granted to a party with a monthly income of 700 euros.

[427] CFI Rules of Procedure, Art.94(2). See by contrast ECJ Rules of Procedure, Art.76(1), which allows "a party" to make such request.

[428] ECJ Rules of Procedure, Art.76(2), first subpara.; CFI Rules of Procedure, Art.95(2), second subpara.

[429] CFI (order of November 24, 1999), Case T–109/98 *A.V.M. v Commission* [1999] E.C.R. II–3383, para 25. See, however, CFI (order of January 14, 1993), Case T–92/92 AJ *Lallemand-Zeller v Commission* [1993] E.C.R. II–31: an application for legal aid is made by a—genuinely—impecunious applicant without the assistance of a lawyer. The application is made during the period prescribed for bringing an action. This prevents time from running until the date on which the order ruling on the application for legal aid is served on the applicant.

[430] CFI (order of November 24, 1999), Case T–109/98 *A.V.M. v Commission* [1999] E.C.R. II–3383, paras 27–28.

[431] CFI Rules of Procedure, Art.96(4). The ECJ Rules of Procedure do not contain a similar provision.

[432] For examples see CFI (order of the President of May 6, 1999), Case T–92/99 AJ *Carvalho Lopes v Commission*, not reported; CFI (order of the President of November 6, 2003), Case T–356/03 AJ *Alvarez Sagrario v Commission*, not reported; CFI (order of the President of March 17, 2005), Case T–102/05 AJ *Petit v Commission*, not reported.

[433] CFI Rules of Procedure, Art.96(6).

refused, the order will state the reasons fur such refusal.[434] If circumstances alter during the proceedings, the Court may at any time, either of its own motion or on application, withdraw legal aid.[435] In the Court of First Instance, the President decides whether legal aid should be granted.[436]

Legal aid is granted. If legal aid is granted, the cashier of the Court of Justice/Court of First Instance advances the necessary funds. An order granting legal aid may specify an amount to be paid to the lawyer appointed to act for the person concerned or fix a limit which the lawyer's fees and disbursements may not, in principle, exceed.[437] Subsequently the Court may recover these costs from the opposite party if a costs order is made against it.[438]   **24–134**

Necessity. The principal reason why legal aid must be available is that individuals must invariably be represented before the Court of Justice or the Court First Instance by a lawyer. In the event that they were unable to pay lawyer's fees, they would have no access to the Community Court if no-one were prepared to pay the costs of legal representation. This is why the budget of the Court of Justice contains an item covering legal aid.   **24–135**

6. Exceptional review procedures

a. Third-party proceedings

(1) Subject-matter

General. Judgments may be prejudicial to the rights of third parties. Notwithstanding the force of *res judicata*, third parties are therefore entitled in exceptional circumstances to contest such judgments.   **24–136**

(2) Substantive requirements and time-limits

Third parties. Third-party proceedings may be brought by Member States, Community institutions and natural or legal persons "to contest a judgment rendered without their being heard, where the judgment is prejudicial to their rights".[439]   **24–137**

---

[434] ECJ Rules of Procedure, Art.76(3); CFI Rules of Procedure, Art.96(2).
[435] ECJ Rules of Procedure, Art.76(4); CFI Rules of Procedure, Art.96 (5).
[436] CFI Rules of Procedure, Art.96(2), third subpara. He or she may, however, refer the matter to the Court of First Instance.
[437] CFI Rules of Procedure, Art.96 (3).
[438] ECJ Rules of Procedure, Art.76(5); CFI Rules of Procedure, Art.97. CFI, Case T–11/00 *Hautem v EIB* [2000] ECR-SC II–4019, I–A-283, II–1295, para.60. Under normal circumstances, legal aid does not cover the expenses of the other party. Since the risk for the impecunious party of having to bear the other party's costs in the event that he or she loses the case may in itself constitute an impediment to access to justice, the Court of First Instance inserted Art.97(4) in its Rules of Procedure, which provides: "Where the recipient of the aid is unsuccessful, the Court of First Instance may, in its decision as to costs, closing the proceedings, if equity so requires, order that one or more parties should bear their own costs or that those costs should be borne, in whole or in part, by the cashier of the Court of First Instance by way of legal aid".
[439] Statute, Art.42.

Consequently, an application to bring third-party proceedings on the part of an intervener will be inadmissible. Third-party proceedings instituted by interested third parties who did not have good reasons for failing to intervene in the original proceedings will also be inadmissible.[440] The notice published in the *Official Journal of the European Union* setting out the subject-matter of the proceedings, the form of order sought and the pleas in law and main supporting arguments[441] is specifically intended to enable third parties to intervene in proceedings whose outcome may be prejudicial to their rights. Only careful third parties who were unable to suspect on the basis of that notice that their rights might be affected can claim that they were not put on notice. An application to bring third-party proceedings by such a party will therefore be admissible.[442] The duty of care is assessed in the light of the circumstances of the case and with due concern not to detract unnecessarily from the authority as *res judicata* of the contested judgment in the interests of legal certainty. The hurdle is therefore set very high. Accordingly, a decision on the part of an interested third party not to intervene in the original proceedings does not satisfy the duty of care where that decision was based on the party's own assessment of the probable outcome of the case based on the information as to the facts and law known at the time when the action was started. This is because further facts may emerge in the course of the proceedings to influence the outcome of the dispute. Moreover, the Court may depart from settled case-law.[443]

24–138   **Third parties which could have taken part in the main proceedings.** Third-party proceedings may be brought only by parties who could—at least in theory—have taken part in the main proceedings. Since natural or legal persons are not entitled to intervene in proceedings brought under Arts 226–227 of the EC Treaty, they may not bring third-party proceedings against a judgment closing such proceedings.[444]

24–139   **Judgment must be prejudicial to the rights of the third party.** The contested judgment must be prejudicial to the *rights* of the third party. It is not enough that the third party has a legitimate interest to protect.[445] The

---

[440] ECJ, Joined Cases 42 and 49/59 Third-party proceedings *Breedband v Société des Aciéries du Temple and Others* [1962] E.C.R. 145.
[441] ECJ Rules of Procedure, Art.16(6); CFI Rules of Procedure, Art.24(6).
[442] ECJ, Joined Cases 9 and 12/60 Third-party proceedings *Belgium v Vloeberghs and High Authority* [1962] E.C.R. 171, at 182.
[443] CFI (order of March 26, 1992), Case T–35/89 TO 1 *Ascasibar Zubizarreta and Others v Albani* [1992] E.C.R. II–1599, paras 33–35.
[444] ECJ (order of the President of December 6, 1989), Case C–147/86 TO 1 *POIFXG and Others v Greece and Commission* [1989] E.C.R. 4103; ECJ (order of the President of December 6, 1989), Case C–147/86 TO 2 *PALSO and Others v Greece and Commission* [1989] E.C.R. 4111; ECJ (order of the President of December 6, 1989), Case C–147/86 TO 3 *PSIITENSM v Greece and Commission* [1989] E.C.R. 4119.
[445] ECJ Rules of Procedure, Art.97(1)(b); CFI Rules of Procedure, Art.123(1)(b); ECJ (order of September 22, 1987), Case 292/84 TO *Bolognese and Others v Scharf and Commission* [1987] E.C.R. 3563, para.7.

prejudice to the third party's rights must ensue from the operative part or the grounds[446] of the judgment itself.[447] The alleged prejudice may be material or non-material.[448]

Timing. Third-party proceedings must be brought within two months of   **24–140**
publication of the contested judgment in the *Official Journal of the European Union*.[449]

Third-party proceedings and appeal. Where an appeal before the Court of   **24–141**
Justice and an application initiating third-party proceedings before the Court of First Instance contest the same judgment of the latter court, the Court of First Instance may, after hearing the parties, stay proceedings until the Court of Justice has delivered its judgment.[450] However, the Court of Justice may defer hearing the appeal until such time as the Court of First Instance has dealt with the application for third-party proceedings.[451]

(3) Formal requirements

General requirements. The application initiating third-party proceedings   **24–142**
must comply with the general requirements applicable to pleadings and with the specific requirements relating to applications.[452] In addition, the application must specify the contested judgment, state how the judgment is prejudicial to the rights of the third party and indicate the reasons for which the third party was unable to take part in the original case.[453]

Application addressed to the parties to the original case. The application   **24–143**
is addressed to all the parties to the original case. If the contested judgment is varied, the variation may be relied upon against all the parties to the original proceedings since they were summoned to the third-party proceedings.

(4) Consequences

Successful action. In so far as the third-party proceedings are successful,   **24–144**
the contested judgment will be varied.

---

[446] ECJ, Joined Cases 9 and 12/60 Third-party proceedings *Belgium v Vloeberghs and High Authority* [1962] E.C.R. 171, at 183–184.

[447] See *Commentaire Mégret*, at 465, where it is pointed out that an individual may bring third-party proceedings against a judgment annulling a regulation, since the alleged prejudice then ensues from the judgment, but not against a judgment rejecting an application for the annulment of a regulation, since in that case the alleged prejudice results from the regulation and not from the judgment.

[448] ECJ, Joined Cases 9 and 12/60 Third-party proceedings *Belgium v Vloeberghs and High Authority* [1962] E.C.R. 171, at 183–184, and the Opinion of Advocate General K. Roemer, at 190.

[449] ECJ Rules of Procedure, Art.97(1), third subpara.; CFI Rules of Procedure, Art.123(1), third subpara.

[450] CFI Rules of Procedure, Art.123(4).

[451] It would do so pursuant to Art.54 of the Statute.

[452] ECJ Rules of Procedure, Arts 37 and 38; CFI Rules of Procedure, Arts 43 and 44.

[453] ECJ Rules of Procedure, Art.97(1); CFI Rules of Procedure, Art.123(1).

The original of the judgment in the third-party proceedings is annexed to the original of the contested judgment. A note of the judgment in the third-party proceedings is made in the margin of the original judgment.[454]

b. Revision

24–145 **General.** Revision affords an opportunity of varying a judgment after a "new fact" has come to light.[455]

(1) Substantive requirements and time-limits

24–146 **New fact.** Under the first para. of Art.44 of the Statute of the Court of Justice, an application for revision of a judgment of the Court of Justice or of the Court of First Instance may be made on discovery of a fact which is of such a nature as to be a decisive factor and which, when the judgment was given, was unknown to the Court and to the party claiming revision.[456] Consequently, revision is not a form of appeal, but an exceptional review procedure that allows an applicant to call in question the authority of *res judicata* attaching to a final judgment on the basis of the findings of fact relied upon by the Court. In order for revision proceedings to be admissible, a number of conditions have to be satisfied: (1) matters of a factual nature which existed prior to the judgment must have been discovered; (2) those matters must have been unknown at that time to the Court which delivered the judgment as well as to the party applying for revision, and (3) the matters must be such that, if the Court had been able to take them into consideration, they might have led it to a different determination of the proceedings.[457]

---

[454] ECJ Rules of Procedure, Art.97(3); CFI Rules of Procedure, Art.123(3).

[455] Statute, Art.44. It is not possible, however, to seek revision of a preliminary ruling since there are no parties to the proceedings and Arts 41 to 44 of the Statute relating to exceptional pleas are not applicable: ECJ (order of April 28, 1998), Case C–116/96 Rev *Reisebüro Binder* [1998] E.C.R. I–1889, paras 6–9.

[456] The Court of Justice has extended this provision of the Statute to cover orders producing the same effects as a judgment (ECJ, Joined Cases C–199/94 P and C–200/94 P-Rev *Inpesca v Commission and Perasa* [1998] E.C.R. I–831, para.16). Accordingly, it is possible to obtain the revision of an order declaring an appeal partially inadmissible or partially unfounded because such an order has the same effects as a judgment declaring an appeal partially inadmissible or partially unfounded (ECJ (judgment of November 7, 2002), Case C–301/00 P-Rev. *Meyer v Commission*, not reported, paras 19 and 20).

[457] ECJ (order of February 25, 1992), Case C–185/90 P-Rev. *Gill v Commission* [1992] E.C.R. I–993, paras 11–12. In that case, the application for revision of a judgment given by the Court of Justice on appeal setting aside a judgment of the Court of First Instance was held to be manifestly inadmissible. In its judgment on appeal, the Court of Justice had given a decision on points of law only and did not adopt a view on the facts as found by the Court of First Instance. Moreover, the Court of Justice had referred the case back to the Court of First Instance and hence the new fact could have been raised before that court. See also CFI (order of March 26, 1992), Case T–4/89 Rev. *BASF v Commission* [1992] E.C.R. II–1591, paras 8–9. Naturally, an application for revision which makes no mention of any new

Late discovery not attributable to applicant. The late discovery of the new   **24–147**
fact must not be attributable to the applicant for revision. Accordingly,
where the applicant was aware of the existence of a given report but not of
its content at the time of the original proceedings, the report in question
did not constitute a new fact.[458] This was because the party's failure to ask
for the content of the report to be communicated to it or to apply to the
Court for measures of inquiry was part of the reason why the applicant was
not apprised of the content of the report before judgment was delivered.
The Court of Justice or the Court of First Instance, as the case may be,
must also not have been aware of the allegedly "new" fact at the time when
judgment was delivered. Accordingly, the Court is aware of the content of a
document produced before the end of the oral procedure even though it
was not drawn up in the language of the case but in another official
language of the Community. There is an irrebuttable presumption that the
Court of Justice and the Court of First Instance master all the official
languages, and hence they may have cognisance of such a document.[459]

Fact had already occurred when judgment was given. As has been   **24–148**
mentioned, the fact on which the application for revision is based must
have already occurred at the time when judgment was given.[460] The fact
must have been in existence—yet unknown—at that time.[461] For that
reason, subsequent case-law of the Court of Justice or the Court of First
Instance cannot be regarded as a new fact for the purposes of Art.44 of the
Statute of the Court of Justice.[462]

---

fact will be inadmissible, see ECJ, Case C–295/90 Rev. *Council v European Parliament and
Others* [1992] E.C.R. I–5299; see also ECJ, Case 13/69 *Van Eick v Commission* [1970]
E.C.R. 3, para.33; ECJ, Case C–130/91 Rev. *ISAE/VP and Interdata v Commission* [1995]
E.C.R. I–407; CFI, Case T–8/89 Rev. *DSM v Commission* [1992] E.C.R. II–2399, para.14;
CFI, Case T–14/89 Rev. *Montecatini v Commission* [1992] E.C.R. II–2409, para.10; CFI,
Case T–77/99 Rev. *Ojha v Commission* [2002] ECR-SC I–A–29, II–131, para.12 (and the
case-law cited therein).
[458] ECJ, Case 56/70 Rev. *Mandelli v Commission* [1971] E.C.R. 1.
[459] ECJ, Case 1/60 *FERAM v High Authority* [1960] E.C.R. 165, at 169–170.
[460] ECJ, Case C–130/91 Rev. II *ISAE/VP and Interdata v Commission* [1996] E.C.R. I–65,
para.6.
[461] ECJ, Case 116/78 Rev. *Bellintani v Commission* [1980] E.C.R. 23, para.2. Assertions or
personal opinions which have no official authority relating to facts which might possibly be
classified as new facts cannot in themselves constitute such facts (ECJ, Case C–2/98 P *De
Compte v European Parliament* [1999] E.C.R. I–1787, para.32).
[462] ECJ, Case C–403/85 Rev. *Ferrandi v Commission* [1991] E.C.R. I–1215, para.13; CFI (order
of March 26, 1992), Case T–4/89 Rev. *BASF v Commission* [1992] E.C.R. II–1591, para.12.
Cf. ECJ, Case 56/75 *Elz v Commission* [1977] E.C.R. 1617, para.7, where the Court of
Justice held with regard to a judgment of a national court that "[t]he mere fact that the
judgment of the Tribunal was subsequent to the judgment of the Court [of Justice] cannot
of itself prevent the first-mentioned judgment from being considered as the discovery of a
new fact". However, the national court's judgment merely confirmed earlier judgments of a
lower court which were known to the Court of Justice and to the parties, and "drew the
foreseeable legal consequences from that confirmation". As a result, the national court's
judgment was not a "new fact" and the application for revision was declared inadmissible.

24–149 **Decisive factor for the outcome of the case.** Lastly, the fact must be of such a nature as to be a decisive factor for the outcome of the case.[463] The new fact must potentially form the basis for amending the operative part of the contested judgment. A new fact which is relevant only to an additional ground, but cannot shake the judgment itself, does not satisfy that requirement.[464]

The application for revision must contest the determination made in the judgment, not the order for costs or any measures taken in order to give effect to the judgment.[465]

24–150 **Timing.** An application for revision of a judgment must be made within three months of the date on which the facts on which the application is based came to the applicant's knowledge.[466] No application for revision may be made after the lapse of 10 years from the date of the judgment.[467]

(2) Formal requirements

24–151 **General requirements.** The application must be made against all parties to the case in which the contested judgment was given.[468]

An application for revision must comply with the general requirements for pleadings and the specific requirements for applications.[469] In addition, it must specify the judgment contested, indicate the points on which the judgment is contested, set out the facts on which the application is based, and indicate the nature of the evidence to show that there are facts justifying revision of the judgment, and that the applicable time-limit has been observed.

24–152 **Procedure.** Without prejudice to its decision on the substance, the Court of Justice or the Court of First Instance, as the case may be, decides on the admissibility of the application after hearing the Advocate General and having regard to the written observations of the parties.[470] If the application is admissible, normal proceedings, resulting in delivery of a judgment, ensue.[471] The Court of Justice mentions that this division of the procedure

---

[463] ECJ, Case 28/64 Rev. *Müller v Council* [1967] E.C.R. 141, at 144; ECJ, Case 37/71 Rev. *Jamet v Commission* [1973] E.C.R. 295, para.3; ECJ, Case 107/79 Rev. *Schuerer v Commission* [1983] E.C.R. 3805; ECJ, Case 285/81 Rev. I and II *Geist v Commission* [1984] E.C.R. 1789; ECJ, Case 267/80 Rev. *Riseria Modenese v Council, and Others* [1985] E.C.R. 3499, para.12; ECJ, Case C–119/94 P Rev. *Coussios v Commission*, not reported, para.10.
[464] ECJ, Case 40/71 *Richez-Parise v Commission* [1972] E.C.R. 73, para.21; CFI (order of July 1, 1994), Case T–106/89 Rev. *Norsk Hydro v Commission* [1994] E.C.R. II–419, para.14.
[465] ECJ, Case 235/82 Rev. *Ferriere San Carlo v Commission* [1986] E.C.R. 1799, para.9.
[466] ECJ Rules of Procedure, Art.98; CFI Rules of Procedure, Art.125.
[467] Statute, Art.44, third para.
[468] ECJ Rules of Procedure, Art.99(2); CFI Rules of Procedure, Art.126(2).
[469] ECJ Rules of Procedure, Arts 37 and 38; CFI Rules of Procedure, Arts 43 and 44.
[470] ECJ Rules of Procedure, Art.100(1); CFI Rules of Procedure, Art.127(2).
[471] ECJ Rules of Procedure, Art.100(2); CFI Rules of Procedure, Art.127(3).

into two stages is due to the strict conditions applying to revision. This is understandable having regard to the fact that such a plea affects the principle of *res judicata*.[472]

Successful action. The original of the revising judgment is annexed to the original of the judgment revised. A note of the revising judgment is made in the margin of the original of the judgment revised.[473]   **24–153**

7. Procedural measures after giving of judgment: the interpretation of judgments, rectification of clerical errors or of the omission to give a decision

a. The interpretation of judgments

General. If the meaning or scope of a judgment is in doubt, application may be made to the Court of Justice or the Court of First Instance, as the case may be, to construe it.[474]   **24–154**

An application for interpretation of a judgment must seek only to resolve an obscurity or ambiguity relating to the determination made in the judgment. Questions concerning the implications of the judgment for other disputes or the content of measures needed in order to give effect to it or points not decided by the judgment do not constitute questions of interpretation for this purpose and hence are inadmissible.[475] Such questions, however, might form the subject-matter of new proceedings.

(1) Who can bring an application for interpretation?

Applicant. An application for interpretation of a judgment may be made by any party to the proceedings.[476] An intervener in the original proceedings may make an application, irrespective as to the stance taken by the party in whose support it intervened.[477]   **24–155**

---

[472] ECJ, Case 116/78 *Bellintani and Others v Commission* [1980] E.C.R. 23, para.3, ECJ, Case C–5/93 P *DSM v Commission* [1999] E.C.R. I–4695, paras 66–67.

[473] ECJ Rules of Procedure, Art.100(3); CFI Rules of Procedure, Art.127(4).

[474] Statute, Art.43.

[475] ECJ, Case 70/63 A *High Authority v Cllotti and Court of Justice* [1965] E.C.R. 275, at 279; ECJ, Case 110/63 A *Willame v Commission* [1966] E.C.R. 287, at 292; ECJ (order of September 29, 1983), Case 9/81-Interpretation *Court of Auditors v Williams* [1983] E.C.R. 2859; ECJ (order of September 29, 1983), Case 206/81 A *Alvarez v European Parliament* [1983] E.C.R. 2865, para.8; ECJ (order of December 11, 1986), Case 25/86 *Suss v Commission* [1986] E.C.R. 3929, para.9; ECJ (order of April 20, 1988), Joined Cases 146 and 431/85-Interpretation *Maindiaux and Others v ESC* [1988] E.C.R. 2003, para.6; CFI (order of July 14, 1993), Case T–22/91 INT *Raiola-Denti and Others v Council* [1993] E.C.R. II–817, para.6.

[476] Statute, Art.43.

[477] ECJ (order of April 20, 1988), Joined Cases 146 and 431/85-Interpretation *Maindiaux and Others v ESC* [1988] E.C.R. 2003, para.4; ECJ, Case C–245/95 P-INT *NSK and Others v Commission* [1999] E.C.R. I–1, para.15.

In the case of parallel proceedings, based on the same complaints, in which judgment is given in one or more cases by reference to a judgment in an initial case, all parties involved are entitled to apply for an interpretation of that judgment, even if they were not parties to those particular proceedings.[478] In contrast, an application for interpretation of a judgment which is concerned merely to define the consequences of an earlier judgment constitutes an application to interpret that initial judgment and so only parties to those proceedings are entitled to bring an application for interpretation.[479]

24–156 **Special position of institutions.** A Community institution which establishes an interest in having a judgment interpreted may bring an application for interpretation even if it was not a party to the proceedings which culminated in the judgment whose interpretation is sought.[480]

(2) Substantive and formal requirements

24–157 **Doubt as regards the meaning or the scope of a judgment.** In order for there to be a doubt as to the meaning or scope of a judgment within the meaning of Art.43 of the Statute, it is sufficient that parties give differing meanings to it.[481]

The doubt must relate to an issue determined by the judgment. It must therefore attach to the operative part or to one of the grounds determining it. An application for interpretation may not be made to the Court of Justice or the Court of First Instance for interpretation of an ancillary matter which supplements or explains those basic grounds.[482]

Lastly, there must be a real obscurity or ambiguity in the judgment.[483] The applicant must expressly identify that obscurity or ambiguity.

24–158 **General requirements.** The application for interpretation must comply with the general requirements for pleadings and with the specific requirements for applications.[484] It must also specify the judgment in question and the passages of which interpretation is sought.[485]

The application must be made against all the parties to the case in which the original judgment was given.[486]

---

[478] ECJ, Case 5/55 *ASSIDER v High Authority* [1954 to 1956] E.C.R. 135, at 141–142.
[479] ECJ, Case 24/66 bis *Gesellschaft für Getreidehandel v Commission* [1973] E.C.R. 1599, para.3.
[480] Statute, Art.43.
[481] ECJ, Case 5/55 *ASSIDER v High Authority* [1954 to 1956] E.C.R. 135, at 142.
[482] *Ibid.*, at 142.
[483] Observations of Advocate General P. VerLoren van Themaat in ECJ (order of September 29, 1983), Case 206/81 A *Alvarez v European Parliament* [1983] E.C.R. 2865, at 2876; CFI (order of July 14, 1993), Case T–22/91 INT *Raiola-Denti and Others v Council* [1993] E.C.R. II–817, paras 7–10.
[484] ECJ Rules of Procedure, Arts 37 and 38; CFI Rules of Procedure, Arts 43 and 44.
[485] ECJ Rules of Procedure, Art.102(1); CFI Rules of Procedure, Art.129(1).
[486] ECJ Rules of Procedure, Art.102(1), second subpara.; CFI Rules of Procedure, Art.129(1), second subpara.

No time-limit. No time-limit is prescribed for bringing an application for **24–159** interpretation.

(3) Procedure before the Court and judgment

Procedure. The Court of Justice or the Court of First Instance, as the case **24–160** may be, gives its decision in the form of a judgment after having given the parties an opportunity to submit their observations and after hearing the Advocate General.[487]

Effect. The original of the interpreting judgment is annexed to the original **24–161** of the judgment interpreted and a note of the interpreting judgment is made in the margin of the judgment interpreted. The interpreting judgment is binding not only on all parties to the proceedings in which the interpreted judgment was given, but also on parties to proceedings in which a judgment was given containing a passage exactly similar to the passage interpreted.[488]

b. Rectification of clerical errors

General. Clerical mistakes, errors in calculation and obvious slips in the **24–162** judgment may be rectified by the Court of Justice or the Court of First Instance by order setting out the rectified text.[489]

Procedure. The Court may take this step of its own motion or on **24–163** application by a party (including an intervener) within two weeks after delivery of the judgment.

The parties are entitled to lodge prior written observations. The Court of Justice or the Court of First Instance takes its decision in closed session after hearing the Advocate General.

Effect. The original of the rectification order is annexed to the original of **24–164** the rectified judgment and a note of the order is made in the margin of the rectified judgment.

---

[487] ECJ Rules of Procedure, Art.102(2); CFI Rules of Procedure, Art.129(2). Of course, if the application for interpretation is manifestly inadmissible, the Court may dismiss it by order (ECJ Rules of Procedure, Art.92(1); CFI Rules of Procedure, Art.111). For an example, see CFI (order of July 14, 1993), Case T–22/91 INT *Raiola-Denti and Others v Council* [1993] E.C.R. II–817.

[488] ECJ, Joined Cases 41, 43 and 44/73-Interpretation *Générale Sucrière and Others v Commission* [1977] E.C.R. 445, para.29.

[489] ECJ Rules of Procedure, Art.66; CFI Rules of Procedure, Art.84. For examples, see ECJ (order of December 10, 2003), Joined Cases C–328/99 and C–399/00 *Italy and SIM 2 Multimedia v Commission*, not reported; ECJ (order of July 14, 2004) Case C–278/02 *Handlbauer*, not yet reported; CFI (order of September 15, 1995), Joined Cases T–466, T–469, T–473, T–474 and T–477/93 *O'Dwyer and Others v Council*, not reported.

c. Rectification in the event of an omission to give a decision

24–165 **General.** If the Court of Justice or the Court of First Instance should omit to give a decision on a specific head of claim or on costs, the omission can be rectified on application by any party.[490]

24–166 **Procedure.** The application must be lodged within one month after service of the judgment in question; it is served on the opposite party and the President prescribes a period within which that party may lodge written observations. After that, the Court decides both on the admissibility and on the substance of the application after hearing the Advocate General.[491]

B. DISCONTINUANCE

24–167 **Settlement of the dispute.** If, before the Court of Justice or the Court of First Instance has given its decision, the parties notify the Court in question that they have reached a settlement of their dispute and that they have abandoned their claims, the President orders the case to be removed from the register and gives a decision as to the costs.[492] Where parties to proceedings for interim measures reach an amicable settlement whereby the applicant declares that it will withdraw its application for interim relief, the Judge hearing the application must of his or her own motion order the application to be removed from the register if the applicant does not honour the undertaking given in the amicable settlement. This is because the amicable settlement is legally binding and, as such, must be enforced by the Judge.[493]

---

[490] ECJ Rules of Procedure, Art.67; CFI Rules of Procedure, Art.85. The omission of the Court of First Instance to examine a form of order sought by the applicant also constitutes an error of law which may lead to the annulment of the decision of the Court of First Instance (ECJ (order of June 3, 2005), Case C–396/03 P *Killinger v Germany, Council and Commission* [2005] E.C.R. I–4967, paras 11–13).

[491] For an example, see CFI (order of October 11, 1990), Case T–50/89 *Sparr v Commission* [1990] E.C.R. II–539.

[492] ECJ Rules of Procedure, Art.77, first para.; CFI Rules of Procedure, Art.98, first para. Those provisions do not apply to proceedings under Arts 230 and 232 of the EC Treaty or Arts 146 and 148 of the EAEC Treaty. The decision on costs is taken in accordance with Art.69(5) of the ECJ Rules of Procedure or Art.87(5) of the CFI Rules of Procedure, as the case may be. For the active role played by the Court of First Instance and the Court of Justice in this connection, see Schønberg, "Coping with Judicial Over-Load: the Role of Mediation and Settlement in Community Court Litigation" (2001) C.M.L.Rev. 333–357; Schønberg and Stockwell, "Juges, médiateurs ou négociateurs? Le rôle du règlement amiable des conflits au sein des juridictions communautaires" (2003) R.T.D.E. 415–440.

[493] CFI (order of the President of August 12, 1998), Case T–42/98 R *Sabbatucci v European Parliament* [1998] E.C.R. II–3043, para.30.

Unilateral discontinuance. The applicant may also discontinue proceedings **24–168** without the agreement of the opposite party.[494] It does so by informing the Court of Justice or the Court of First Instance, as the case may be, in writing. In this case, too, the President orders the case to be removed from the register and decides as to the costs.[495]

C. No need to proceed to judgment

General. The Court of Justice or the Court of First Instance, as the case **24–169** may be, may decide that there is no need to proceed to judgment on the ground that there is no purpose to the proceedings.[496] If the Court makes a finding to this effect, this closes the proceedings.[497]

Where the Court decides that there is no need to give judgment in an action which has ceased to have any purpose, it is not necessary for it to examine the admissibility of that action.[498]

VIII. General Remarks

A. Use of languages

Language of the case. The case may be conducted in any of the following **24–170** twenty-one languages: Czech, Danish, Dutch, English, Estonian, Finnish, French, German, Greek, Hungarian, Irish, Italian, Latvian, Lithuanian,

---

[494] ECJ Rules of Procedure, Art.78; CFI Rules of Procedure, Art.99. The defendant cannot object to the other party's discontinuing the proceedings: see ECJ (order of the President of March 19, 1996), Case C–120/94 *Commission v Greece* [1996] E.C.R. I–1513. The applicant may also partly discontinue proceedings: ECJ, Case C–331/94 *Commission v Greece* [1996] E.C.R. I–2675, paras 5–6.

[495] Again, the decision on costs is taken in accordance with Art.69(5) of the ECJ Rules of Procedure or Art.87(5) of the CFI Rules of Procedure, as the case may be.

[496] This is borne out indirectly by Art.69(6) of the ECJ Rules of Procedure and Art.87(6) of the CFI Rules of Procedure.

[497] For examples, see ECJ, Case 377/87 *European Parliament v Council* [1988] E.C.R. 4017, paras 10–12; CFI, Case T–140/89 *Della Pietra v Commission* [1990] E.C.R. II–717. Where the applicant dies and his or her successors do not take over the proceedings, the application becomes to no purpose: CFI (order of December 6, 1999), Case T–81/98 *Boyes v Commission* [1999] E.C.R. II–3501. Exceptionally, proceedings can become to no purpose as a result of the passiveness of the applicant, in particular where he or she repeatedly fails to lodge certain procedural documents: CFI (order of March 1, 2004), Case T–210/99 *Gankema v Commission* [2004] E.C.R. II–781; CFI (order of May 26, 2004), Case T–165/02 *Lloris Maeso v Commission*, not reported.

[498] ECJ, Joined Cases C–15/91 and C–108/91 *Buckl and Others v Commission* [1992] E.C.R. I–6061, paras 14–17; ECJ (order of June 10, 1993), Case C–41/92 *Liberal Democrats v European Parliament* [1993] E.C.R. I–3153, para.4; ECJ, Joined Cases C–302/99 P and C–308/99 P *Commission and France v TF 1* [2001] E.C.R. I–5603, para.28. But see CFI (order of May 22, 2000), Case T–103/99 *Associazione delle Cantine Sociali Venete v European Ombudsman and European Parliament* [2000] E.C.R. II–4165, para.41, in which the Court of First Instance held that it can rule on whether the application is to no purpose only after it has determined that the application is admissible.

Maltese, Polish, Portuguese, Slovak, Slovenian, Spanish and Swedish.[499] In principle, the applicant chooses the language of the case. However, where the defendant is a Member State or a natural or legal person having the nationality of a Member State,[500] the language of the case will be the official language of that State; where the State has more than one official language, the applicant may choose between them.[501] Exceptionally, the President of the Court of Justice or the Court of First Instance may authorise another Community language to be used for all or part of the proceedings at the joint request of the parties. If, at the request of one of the parties and after the opposite party and the Advocate General have been heard, the President of the Court of Justice or of the Court of First Instance wishes to give such authorisation but all the parties do not agree, he or she must refer the request to the Court of Justice or the Court of First Instance, as the case may be.[502] A request for leave to derogate from the rule on the use of the language of the case must be accompanied by a detailed and specific statement of reasons, *a fortiori* where the request is made by the applicant, who has to justify a departure from the initial choice made by itself.[503] Institutions may not make such a request.

24–171 **Disputes relating to intellectual property rights.** The language of the case in proceedings relating to intellectual property rights is determined in accordance with a special procedure laid down in Art.131(2) of the CFI Rules of Procedure on account of the fact that the disputes concerned involve individuals. The language of the case is the language, chosen from amongst the official languages, in which the application is drafted where the applicant was the only party to the proceedings before the Board of Appeal or if no other party objects. If, within a period following lodgment of the application determined by the Registrar, the parties agree to use an official language other than the one used in the application, that language will become the language of the case. However, if a party objects to the language used in the application being the language of the case and the

---

[499] ECJ Rules of Procedure, Art.29(1); CFI Rules of Procedure, Art.35(1). Although the Welsh Courts Act 1942 provides that the Welsh language may be used in any court in Wales and the Welsh Language Act 1967 states that in any legal proceedings in Wales or Monmouthshire, the Welsh language may be spoken by any person who desires to use it, Art.29(1) of the ECJ Rules of Procedure and Art.35(1) of the CFI Rules of Procedure do not allow for the use of Welsh as the language of a case. But note that witnesses and experts may use a language not capable of being a language of the case, ECJ Rules of Procedure, Art.29(4); CFI Rules of Procedure, Art.35(5); see 24–173, *infra*.

[500] This may occur where a Community institution brings proceedings against a natural or legal person pursuant to an arbitration clause within the meaning of Art.238 of the EC Treaty.

[501] ECJ Rules of Procedure, Art.29(2)(a); CFI Rules of Procedure, Art.35(2)(a).

[502] ECJ Rules of Procedure, Art.29(2)(b) and (c); CFI Rules of Procedure, Art.35(2)(b) and (c).

[503] CFI (order of May 13, 1993), Case T–74/92 *Ladbroke Racing v Commission* [1993] E.C.R. II–535, para.14; CFI (order of January 24, 1997), Case T–121/95 *EFMA v Council* [1997] E.C.R. II–87, para.10.

parties cannot agree on the choice of language, the language in which the application for registration in question was filed at the Office becomes the language of the case,[504] unless the President or the Court of First Instance, on the matter being referred to it, finds that the use of that language would not enable all parties to the proceedings before the Board of Appeal to follow the proceedings and defend their interests. In that case, the President of the Court may designate another official language as the language of the case after receipt of a reasoned request by any party and after hearing the other parties.

Written and oral pleadings. The language of the case is used "in the written and oral pleadings of the parties and in supporting documents, and also in the minutes and decisions of the Court". The language of the case remains the same in any appeal proceedings. Any supporting documents expressed in another language must be accompanied by a translation into the language of the case.[505] This means that, if an intervener is not a Member State (see 24–0175, *infra*), it must in principle produce a translation in the language of the case of all documents and annexes which it produces.[506] If, however, lengthy documents are involved, extracts may be submitted, unless the Court of Justice or the Court of First Instance, as the case may be, calls for a complete or fuller translation of its own motion or at the request of a party.[507] Generally, a request to use a language other than the language of the case during the oral procedure will be granted.[508]   **24–172**

Witnesses and experts. A witness or expert who is unable adequately to express himself or herself in the language of the case, may use another language, even a language not included among the list of possible languages which may be used before the Court. The Registrar arranges for translation into the language of the case.[509]   **24–173**

Members of the Court. The President, the Judges and the Advocate General are entitled to use a language other than the language of the case, in particular in conducting oral proceedings, in putting questions and, as far   **24–174**

---

[504] CFI, Case T–292/01 *Philips-Van Heusen v OHIM*, [2003] E.C.R. I–4335, paras 15–17; CFI (judgment of October 6, 2004), Case T–356/02 *Vitakraft-Werke Wührmann & Sohn v OHIM*, not yet reported, para.13.

[505] ECJ Rules of Procedure, Art.29(3), first subpara.; CFI Rules of Procedure, Art.35(3), first subpara.

[506] CFI Rules of Procedure, Art.35(3), second subpara.; for an example, see CFI (order of June 26, 1996), Case T–11/95 *BP Chemicals v Commission* [1996] E.C.R. II–599.

[507] ECJ Rules of Procedure, Art.29(3), third subpara.; CFI Rules of Procedure, Art.35(3), third subpara.

[508] CFI (order of June 12, 1995), Case T–371/94 *British Airways and Others v Commission*, not reported, para.13, and CFI (order of June 12, 1995), Case T–394/94 *British Midland Airways v Commission*, not reported, para.13; CFI (order of August 16, 1995), Case T–290/94 *Kaysersberg v Commission* [1995] E.C.R. II–2247, para.8; CFI (order of November 17, 1995), Case T–330/94 *Salt Union v Commission* [1995] E.C.R. II–2881, paras 25–28. However, see also n.503, *supra*, and accompanying text.

[509] ECJ Rules of Procedure, Art.29(4); CFI Rules of Procedure, Art.35(4).

as the Advocate General is concerned, in delivering his or her Opinion. Here, too, the Registrar is responsible for arranging for translation into the language of the case.[510]

24–175 **Member State.** A Member State intervening in a case is entitled to use its official language (or one of its official languages at its election) both during the written procedure and at the hearing. Here again, it is the Registrar who has to arrange for translation into the language of the case.[511] EEA States not being Member States of the European Union may be authorised by the Registrar to use an official language other than the language of the case where they intervene in proceedings pending before the Court of Justice or the Court of First Instance or take part in preliminary ruling proceedings.[512]

B. CALCULATION OF TIME-LIMITS

24–176 **General.** The procedural time-limits prescribed by the EC Treaty, the EAEC Treaty, the Statute of the Court of Justice and the Rules of Procedure of the Court of Justice and the Court of First Instance are reckoned in a uniform manner.

24–177 *Dies a quo.* As far as the day from which time starts running (*dies a quo*) is concerned, the following is important. Time-limits calculated from the moment at which an event occurs or an action takes place start to run on the day after the event occurs or the action takes place.[513]

24–178 **Starting point in case of publication.** This principle is further specified as regards actions for annulment:

"Where the period of time allowed for commencing proceedings against a measure adopted by an institution runs from the publication of that measure, that period shall be calculated . . . from the end of the 14th day after publication thereof in the *Official Journal of the European Union*".[514]

---

[510] ECJ Rules of Procedure, Art.29(5); CFI Rules of Procedure, Art.35(5).
[511] ECJ Rules of Procedure, Art.29(3), fourth subpara.; CFI Rules of Procedure, Art.35(3), fourth subpara.
[512] ECJ Rules of Procedure, Art.29(3), fifth subpara.; CFI Rules of Procedure, Art.35(3) fifth subpara.
[513] ECJ Rules of Procedure, Art.80(1)(a); CFI Rules of Procedure, Art.101(1)(a).
[514] ECJ Rules of Procedure, Art.81(1); CFI Rules of Procedure, Art.102(1). This rule applies to all acts published in the *Official Journal of the European Union* and not only to acts whose publication is necessary in order for them to enter into effect (see CFI (order of May 25, 2004), Case T–264/03 *Schmoldt and Others v Commission* [2004] E.C.R. II–1515, paras 51–62). The *Official Journal of the European Union* is normally available on the day of issue. In that case, time would start running on the 15th day following the day of issue of the *Official Journal* publishing the contested act. For examples, see ECJ (order of May 17, 2002), Case C–406/01 *Germany v European Parliament and Council* [2002] E.C.R. I–4561;

Extension on account of distance. As far as the *running* and *duration* of the period are concerned, it should first be noted that Saturdays, Sundays, official holidays and judicial vacations count towards the period.[515] In addition, *all* procedural time-limits are subject to a standard extension on account of distance of ten days.[516] These extensions also apply to Community institutions.[517] Formerly there were different extensions on account of distance for different countries. The idea behind this was that, even though procedural documents were validly served at the parties' address for service in Luxembourg, an extension of time was necessary for parties who resided or were established a long way away so as to give all the parties the same time in which to prepare for their participation in the proceedings before the Court. Now that use can be made of modern means of communication (such as e-mail) for the service of documents, that differentiation is no longer necessary. The extension on account of distance is not to be regarded as separate from the procedural time-limit but merely as a prolongation of it.[518]

24–179

Dies ad quem. As far as the day on which time stops running (*dies ad quem*) is concerned, two aspects must be borne in mind. First, there is the rule that if the period would otherwise end on a Saturday, Sunday or an official holiday, it is extended until the end of the first following working day.[519] Secondly, the last day of the period is determined as follows: "A

24–180

CFI, Joined Cases T–142/01 and T–283/01 *OPTUC v Commission* [2004] E.C.R. II–329. If the *Official Journal* is not available on the date appearing on the issue, the period will start running 15 days after the day on which the *Official Journal* was actually published, see ECJ, Case 98/78 *Racke* [1979] E.C.R. 69, para.15. The date of publication is the date on which the *Official Journal* is available at the Publications Office in Luxembourg in all the official language versions. It is therefore not necessary that the *Official Journal* be available at that time in all the official language versions at the applicant's place of residence or establishment for time to start running (CFI (order of the President of June 26, 2002), Case T–210/01 R *General Electric v Commission*, not reported, paras 11–16).

[515] ECJ Rules of Procedure, Art.80(1)(d) and (e); CFI Rules of Procedure, Art.101(1)(d) and (e). For a list of holidays, see the Decision of the ECJ of June 10, 2003, ([2003] O.J. C172/12, as amended and annexed to the ECJ Rules of Procedure).

[516] ECJ Rules of Procedure, Art.81(2); CFI Rules of Procedure, Art.102(2).

[517] ECJ Case C–137/92 P *Commission v BASF and Others* [1994] E.C.R. I–2555, paras 40–41; ECJ, Case C–245/95 P *Commission v NTN Corporation and Koyo Seiko* [1998] E.C.R. I–401, paras 19–23.

[518] CFI (order of November 20, 1997), Case T–85/97 *Horeca-Wallonie v Commission* [1997] E.C.R. II–2113, para.26. Consequently, the last day of the time-limit is the day on which the procedural time-limit, together with the time on account of distance, runs out. This is important in order to determine whether the time-limit may be extended because the last day is a Saturday, a Sunday or an official holiday (see 24–180, *infra*). In the *Horeca-Wallonie* case, the applicant argued that the procedural time-limit, the "last" day of which fell on Easter Monday—an official holiday—had to be extended, after which time on account of distance started to run. The Court of First Instance rejected this argument. See also CFI (order of January 19, 2001), Case T–126/00 *Confindustria and Others v Commission* [2001] E.C.R. II–85, para.18. For an example of the calculation of the time for intervening, see CFI (order of the President of July 11, 2001), Case T–339/00 *Bactria v Commission*, not reported, para.10.

[519] ECJ Rules of Procedure, Art.80(2), first subpara.; CFI Rules of Procedure, Art.101(2), first subpara.

period expressed in weeks, months or in years shall end with the expiry of whichever day in the last week, month or year is the same day of the week, or falls on the same date as *the day during which the event or action from which the period is to be calculated occurred or took place*. If, in a period expressed in months or in years, the day on which it should expire does not occur in the last month, the period shall end with the expiry of the last day of that month; where a period is expressed in months and days, it shall first be reckoned in months, then in days".[520] It should be noted that the key day for determining the last day of a period is the actual day corresponding to the one on which the event or action occurred which caused time to start running, and not the day after, even though that is the day on which time actually started to run. Although this may appear contradictory, it is in fact quite logical, as the following example shows: if the period for bringing an action for annulment starts running as a result of notification of the contested act on April 3, then the two months within which the action must be brought run from April 4 at 0 hours (*i.e.* the *dies a quo*, being the day after notification) to June 3 at midnight (*i.e.* the *dies ad quem*, that it to say, the day which falls on the same date as "the day during which the event or action from which the period is to be calculated occurred or took place", namely the date of notification). Thus, the period amounts to precisely two months.

24–181 **Applications.** Let us take a further example to illustrate the rules set out above: a Commission decision is notified to an undertaking established in the Netherlands on October 15, 2002. The usual two-month time-limit ends at midnight on December 15, 2002, but is extended by ten days on account of distance, *i.e.* to midnight on December 25, 2002, an official holiday, which produces a further extension to the first working day, *i.e.* midnight on Monday December 27, 2002.[521]

Another example comes from the case-law. An application for annulment was lodged on June 21, 2001 against a Commission regulation published in the *Official Journal of the European Union* on March 27, 2001. The Court of First Instance held first, however, that time for bringing proceedings began to run from the end of the fourteenth day after publication, i.e. April 10, 2001. As a result, the two-month period laid down by Art.230(5) of the EC Treaty ran out on Sunday June 10, 2001, but was extended by time on account of distance to Wednesday June 20, 2001. Accordingly the application served on June 21 was out of time. In this connection, it was

---

[520] ECJ Rules of Procedure, Art.80(1)(b) and (c); CFI Rules of Procedure, Art.101(1)(b) and (c) (emphasis added). These provisions on the *dies ad quem* codify the rule in *Misset* which used to be applied alongside Arts 80–82 of the ECJ Rules of Procedure (which have now been amended using that very form of words). See ECJ, Case 152/85 *Misset v Council* [1987] E.C.R. 223, para.8; ECJ, Joined Cases 281, 283–285 and 287/85 *Germany and Others v Commission* [1987] E.C.R. 3203, paras 5–6.
[521] This is because December 26 is an official holiday.

irrelevant that the "original" deadline expired on a Sunday. This is because time on account of distance forms part of the complete limitation period, which ran out on a normal working day.[522]

The Court is never closed. On a practical note, documents may be handed   **24–182**
in at the entrance of the Court of Justice and the Court of First Instance at any time of the day or night; the security guard will note the exact time of receipt and this will be decisive evidence.

Lodgment at the registry. Under Art 37(3) of the ECJ Rules of Procedure   **24–183**
and Art.43(3) of the CFI Rules of Procedure, the day to be taken into account for calculating procedural time-limits is the date on lodgment at the registry. The date of which a pleading or other document is registered at the registry is therefore not determinative.[523]

Lodgment by telefax or e-mail. Where a pleading is lodged with the   **24–184**
appropriate registry by telefax or other technical means of communication available to the Court of Justice or the Court of First Instance (e-mail) the date of receipt is deemed to be the date of lodgment provided that the signed original of the pleading is lodged at the registry no later than ten days thereafter.[524]

Unforeseeable circumstances or *force majeure*. Lastly, it should be men-   **24–185**
tioned that the expiry of a time-limit cannot be pleaded if the other party proves the existence of unforeseen circumstances or *force majeure*.[525] This exceptional rule is applicable to any procedural time-limit, but both the Court of Justice and the Court of First Instance take an extremely strict view. The typical case of a clerical error made by the representative of one of the parties is not enough to bring the rule into play. In circumstances such as a post strike which objectively would have taken a careful party by surprise (the strike breaks out suddenly and lasts three weeks, as a result of which the document dispatched in plenty of time arrives a day too late at

---

[522] CFI, Joined Cases T–142/01 and T–283/01 *OPTUC v Commission* [2004] E.C.R. II–329, paras 36–42.

[523] CFI, Case T–145/98 *ADT Projekt v Commission* [2000] E.C.R. II–387, para.80.

[524] ECJ Rules of Procedure, Art.37(6); CFI Rules of Procedure, Art.43(6). The period of ten days is not a procedural time-limit and cannot be extended by the period on account of distance (see 24–179, *supra*). In the event of any discrepancy between the signed original and the copy previously lodged, only the date of lodgment of the signed original will be taken into consideration (ECJ Practice Directions, point 3; CFI Practice Directions, point I,3). For an example, see CFI (order of May 8, 2003), Case T–63/03 *El Corte Inglés v OHIM*, not reported: the application was inadmissible because the original was not lodged with the registry within ten days.

[525] Statute, Art.45.

the registry) may suffice. But to rely on this rule remains a great—and hence unwarranted—risk.[526]

C. REPRESENTATION OF THE PARTIES

24–186 **Agents.** Community institutions, Member States and EEA States which are not Member States of the Union as well as the EFTA Surveillance Authority are represented by an agent, who has to lodge an authority with the registry of the Court of Justice or the Court of First Instance, as the case may be. An agent may be assisted by an adviser or by a lawyer entitled to practise before a court of a Member State.[527]

24–187 **Lawyers.** All other parties must be represented by a lawyer entitled to practise before a court of a Member State[528] or of an EEA State not being a Member State of the European Union or by a university teacher who is a national of a Member State whose law accords him or her a right of audience (that is to say, as a university teacher and not as, say, a member of the Bar), even if the applicant is a lawyer with rights of audience before a national court or tribunal.[529] The lawyer representing the party cannot be an officer of the applicant (for example the director of the applicant company).[530] The requirement to use a "third party" as one's lawyer is based on

---

[526] See ECJ (order of May 7, 1998), Case C–239/97 *Ireland v Commission* [1998] E.C.R. I–2655, in which the fact that a courier service had not been able to deliver the application to the registry on time because of technical difficulties was not considered to constitute *force majeure*, particularly since the applicant had waited until the day before time was due to run out (including time on account of distance) before sending the application from Ireland. See also CFI (order of March 21, 2002), Case T–218/01 *Laboratoire Monique Rémy v Commission* [2002] E.C.R. II–2139, in which the application was sent by registered post a few days before time ran out but was not delivered to the registry of the Court of First Instance until after time had run out; ECJ (order of January 18, 2005), Case C–325/03 P *Zuazaga Meabe v OHIM* [2005] E.C.R. I–403, paras 21–28.

[527] Statute, Art.19, first para.

[528] It does not suffice that the person who signs the application is entitled to plead before a national court of a Member State. He or she has to be a member of the Bar (see, *e.g.* CFI (order of February 28, 2005), Case T–445/04 *Energy Technologies v OHIM*, not yet reported, paras 1–3). The lawyer who signs the original of each pleading must be entitled to practise before a court of a Member State, even where he or she signs a pleading "on behalf of" another lawyer who satisfies this requirement and represents the party concerned (CFI (order of February 24, 2000), Case T–37/98 *FTA and Others v Council* [2000] E.C.R. II–373, paras 26–32: the Court of First Instance declared the application inadmissible on the ground that the lawyer who had signed the pleading on behalf of his colleague was not entitled to practise before a court of a Member State); CFI (order of September 9, 2004), Case T–14/04 *Alto de Casablanca v OHIM*, not yet reported, para.11, and CFI (judgment of June 8, 2005), Case T–315/03 *Wilfer v OHIM*, not yet reported, paras 10–11 (patent and trade mark agents are not authorised to represent parties in proceedings before the Court of First Instance even if they are entitled to represent parties in certain actions before national courts).

[529] ECJ (order of December 5, 1996), Case C–174/96 P *Lopes v Court of Justice* [1996] E.C.R. I–6401, para.10, and Case C–175/96 P [1996] E.C.R. I–6409, para.10; CFI (order of February 23, 2005), Case T–454/04 *Correia de Matos v Commission*, not reported, paras 10–13.

[530] CFI (order of December 8, 1999), Case T–79/99 *Euro-Lex v OHIM* [1999] E.C.R. II–3555, paras 23–31; CFI (order of January 13, 2005), Case T–184/04 *Sulvida v Commission*, not yet reported, paras 8–9.

a conception of the lawyer's role as collaborating in the administration of justice and as being required to provide, in full independence and in the overriding interests of justice, such legal assistance as his client needs.[531] The lawyer must lodge a certificate that he or she is entitled to practise before a court of a Member State or of a non-EU EEA State and an authority from the party which he or she represents[532] (see 24–021 and 24–041, *supra*).

Representation of legal persons. If the applicant is a legal person governed by private law, the lawyer must ensure that the application contains proof that the authority granted to him or her has been properly conferred on him or her by someone authorised for the purpose.[533]　　**24–188**

Regularisation. If necessary, the authority and proof in question may be furnished within a "reasonable time" to be prescribed by the Registrar. The sanction for failing to produce them within the time prescribed is that the Court of Justice or the Court of First Instance will decide, after hearing the Advocate General (only in the case of the Court of Justice), whether non-compliance renders the application formally inadmissible.[534] The same conditions apply to the defence.[535]　　**24–189**

Intermediaries. The agents, advisers and lawyers are intermediaries representing the parties. Only the person, Member State or institution represented are parties to the proceedings.[536]　　**24–190**

Immunity. Agents, advisers and lawyers enjoy immunity in respect of words spoken or written by them concerning the case or the parties.[537] An adviser or lawyer must conduct himself or herself in a way which is compatible with the dignity of the Court of Justice/Court of First Instance and with the requirements of the proper administration of justice. Any adviser or lawyer whose conduct towards the Court is incompatible with the dignity of the Court, or who uses his rights for purposes[538] other than those for which they were granted, may be excluded from the proceedings.　　**24–191**

---

[531] CFI (order of February 28, 2005), Case T–445/04 *Energy Technologies v OHIM*, not yet reported, para 9.

[532] ECJ Rules of Procedure, Art.38(3); CFI Rules of Procedure, Art.44(3).

[533] ECJ Rules of Procedure, Art.38(5); CFI Rules of Procedure, Art.44(5). For examples, see CFI, Case T–145/98 *ADT Projekt v Commission* [2000] E.C.R. II–387, paras 50–54; CFI, Case T–180/00 *Astipesca v Commission* [2002] E.C.R. II–3985, paras 41–46.

[534] ECJ Rules of Procedure, Art.38(7); CFI Rules of Procedure, Art.44(6).

[535] ECJ Rules of Procedure, Art.40(1), second subpara.; CFI Rules of Procedure, Art.46(1), second subpara.

[536] CFI (order of June 8, 2005), Case T–151/03 *Nuova Agricast v Commission*, not yet reported, para.29.

[537] ECJ Rules of Procedure, Art.32(1); CFI Rules of Procedure, Art.38(1).

[538] ECJ Rules of Procedure, Art.35(1); CFI Rules of Procedure, Art.41(1). See also CFI (order of the President), Case T–302/00 R *Goldstein v Commission* [2001] E.C.R. II–1127, paras 40–42.

CHAPTER 25

PROCEDURE IN THE CASE OF A REFERENCE FOR A PRELIMINARY RULING

25–001 **Order for reference made by a national court.** The order for reference is to be sent by the national court directly to the Court of Justice by registered post.[539] Upon arrival, it will be registered at the registry. This is when the case receives its serial number.

Notice is given of the request for a preliminary ruling in the *Official Journal of the European Union*.[540]

The registry requests the national court to lodge the whole of the case-file in order that the Court of Justice may be better placed to give a useful answer (see 2–019 to 2–026, *supra*).

25–002 **Content of the order for reference.** The decision by which a national court or tribunal refers a question to the Court of Justice for a preliminary ruling may be in any form allowed by national law as regards procedural steps. The order for reference must be succinct but sufficiently complete and contain all the relevant information to give the Court and the parties entitled to submit observations a clear understanding of the factual and legal context of the main proceedings. In particular, the order for reference must:

– include a brief account of the subject-matter of the dispute and the relevant findings of fact, or, at least, set out the factual situation on which the question referred is based;

– set out the tenor of any applicable national provisions and identify, where necessary, the relevant national case-law, giving in each case precise references (*e.g.* the page of an Official Journal or specific law report, with any internet reference);

– identify the Community provisions relevant to the case as accurately as possible;

---

[539] Information note on references from national courts for a preliminary ruling ([2005] O.J. C143/01), point 29. It should be addressed to the registry of the Court of Justice of the European Communities, L–2925 Luxembourg, telephone number: +352–4303–1.
[540] By analogy with the ECJ Rules of Procedure, Art.16(6).

– explain the reasons which prompted the national court to raise the question of the interpretation or validity of the Community provisions, and the relationship between those provisions and the national provisions applicable to the main proceedings;

– include, where appropriate, a summary of the main arguments of the parties.[541]

Length of the order for reference. The reference should in principle not 25–003 exceed ten pages. The question or questions themselves should appear in a separate and clearly identified section of the order for reference, generally at the beginning or the end. It must be possible to understand them without referring to the statement of the grounds for the reference[542].

Notification of the order for reference. The order for reference is immedi- 25–004 ately translated into the other official languages of the Community.[543] The Registrar of the Court of Justice notifies it to the parties to the main proceedings (*i.e.* to all "parties" to the case, including any interveners), the Member States (a copy of the original order for reference and a translation in an official language of the Member State in question) and the Commission.[544] Notice is given by registered letter with a form for acknowledgement of receipt, addressed to the lawyers of the parties to the main proceedings or, if the parties are not represented, to their personal address as set out in the order for reference; notice is given to the Member States by registered letter with a form for acknowledgment of receipt, addressed to the Ministry of Foreign Affairs (with a copy to the Permanent Representation in Brussels). There is in fact no form of address for service whatsoever in Luxembourg in the case of references for preliminary rulings.

Notification to the Council, the European Parliament and the European 25–005 **Central Bank.** The Registrar of the Court of Justice further notifies the order for reference to the Council or the European Central Bank "if the act the validity or interpretation of which is in dispute originates from one of them" and to the European Parliament and the Council "if the act the validity or interpretation of which is in dispute was adopted jointly by those two institutions".[545] In exceptional cases, the order for reference is also notified to the European Parliament if the Court of Justice wishes to obtain information from it (*e.g.* if the preliminary question has a bearing on the

---

[541] Information note on references from national courts for a preliminary ruling, point 22.
[542] Information note on references from national courts for a preliminary ruling points 22 and 24.
[543] But see 25–006, *infra.*
[544] Statute, Art.23, first para.; *cf.* Art.103(3), first subpara., of the ECJ Rules of Procedure in conjunction with Art.35(1) of the EU Treaty.
[545] Statute, Art.23.

Parliament's prerogatives).[546] The Registrar also notifies the order for reference to the States, other than Member States, which are parties to the EEA Agreement and to the EFTA Surveillance Authority.

25–006 **Notification to the Member States.** The Member States are notified by service of a copy of the original version of the decisions of national courts and tribunals, accompanied by a translation in the official language of the recipient Member State.[547] Where appropriate on account of the length of the national court's decision, such translation is replaced by the translation into the official language of the State to which it is addressed of a summary of the decision, which will serve as a basis for the position to be adopted by that State.[548] States party to the EEA Agreement which are not Member States and the EFTA Supervisory authority receive a copy of the original version and a translation of the decision, or where appropriate of a summary, in the official language of their choice.[549]

25–007 **Written observations.** The parties to the main proceedings, the Member States,[550] the Commission and, where appropriate, the European Parliament, the Council and the European Central Bank are entitled to submit statements of case or observations within two months of notification of the order for reference.[551] States party to the EEA Agreement which are not Member States and the EFTA Supervisory Authority may likewise submit statements of case or observations within two months if the national court's decision concerns one of the fields of application of the EEA Agreement.[552]

Where an agreement relating to a specific subject-matter, concluded by the Council and one or more non-member States, provides that those States are to be entitled to submit statements of case or written observations where a court or tribunal of a Member State refers to the Court of Justice for a preliminary ruling a question falling within the scope of the agreement, the decision of the national court or tribunal containing that question shall also be notified to the non-member States concerned. Within

---

[546] Such a request for information is based on Art.24 of the Statute. For an example, see ECJ, Case 20/85 *Roviello* [1988] E.C.R. 2805.

[547] ECJ Rules of Procedure, Art.104(1), first subpara.

[548] *Ibid*. The summary includes the full text of the question or questions referred for a preliminary ruling. It also contains, in so far as that information appears in the national court's decision, the subject-matter of the main proceedings, the essential arguments of the parties in the main proceedings, a succinct presentation of the reasoning in the reference for a preliminary ruling and the case-law and the provisions of Community and domestic law relied on.

[549] ECJ Rules of Procedure, Art.104(1), second subpara.

[550] For the involvement of Member States in preliminary ruling procedures, see Granger, "When governments go to Luxembourg . . . : the influence of governments on the Court of Justice" (2004) E.L.Rev. 3–31.

[551] Statute, Art.23, second para.

[552] Statute, Art.23, third para.

two months of such notification, those States may lodge at the Court statements of case or written observations.[553]

Calculation of the two-month period. The two-months period is calculated in the same way as for direct actions, including time on account of distance (see 24–176 to 24–185, *supra*). Time starts to run as from notification, which is determined from the form for acknowledgment of receipt attached to the registered letter sent by the Court. The two-month period may be extended only in the event of "unforeseeable circumstances or *force majeure*" within the meaning of Art.45 of the Statute.   25–008

No second exchange of observations. The written procedure consists solely of this opportunity to submit observations to the Court. The observations received are sent to all those to whom the order for reference was notified. There is no "reply" as between those who have submitted observations should they disagree with each other's views. This follows from the fact that the preliminary ruling procedure is not, formally speaking, a dispute between "parties".   25–009

No intervention. A request by an individual to be joined to preliminary ruling proceedings—pursuant to Art.40 of the Statute—in order to submit observations is inadmissible.[554] This is because a preliminary ruling procedure is not a "case before the Court" within the meaning of Art.40 of the Statute.   25–010

Preliminary report. After the written observations have been submitted or none have been received within the prescribed period, the Judge-Rapporteur draws up the "preliminary report" for submission to the administrative meeting of the Court. From that point onwards, the procedure—from the oral procedure to delivery of judgment by the Court of Justice—is the same as in the case of direct actions.   25–011

Special characteristics. Nevertheless, some aspects warrant specific attention.   25–012

Formation. A preliminary reference may be assigned to a three- or five-Judge Chamber, to the Grand Chamber or to the Full Court (see 1–011, *supra*).   25–013

---

[553] Statute, Art.23, fourth para. According to ECJ Rules of Procedure, Art.104 (1), third subpara., the original version of the decision of the national court or tribunal will be communicated to it together with a translation of the decision, or where appropriate of a summary, into one of the languages mentioned in ECJ Rules of Procedure, Art.29 (1).

[554] ECJ (order of the President of February 26, 1996), Case C–181/95 *Biogen* [1996] E.C.R. I–717, para.4; ECJ (order of the President of March 30, 2004), Case C–453/03 *ABNA and Others*, not reported, paras 13–16; ECJ (order of the President of May 25, 2004), Case C–458/03 *Parking Brixen and Others*, not reported, paras 5–8.

25–014 **Oral observations.** The Court of Justice also allows parties who have not exercised their right to submit written observations to take part in the hearing. This signifies in fact that a failure to make use of the time-limit for submitting written observations does not mean that there is no right to state one's case orally and answer any questions put by the Court.

This is important since generally the so-called non-contentious nature of preliminary-ruling proceedings appears to be no more than a fiction. Indeed, note should be taken, for instance, of the case where a Member State submits written observations or a statement of case contending that a part of its national law is compatible with Community law[555] or where a party to the main proceedings seeks implementation of an agreement whilst the other party claims that the agreement is contrary to Community law.[556]

Even if written observations are lodged by all involved, the oral procedure affords a full opportunity for explanations and counter-argument to be presented.

The Court may after hearing the Advocate General order the reopening of the oral procedure of its own motion[557] if it considers that it is insufficiently informed or that the case should be decided on the basis of an argument on which no discussion has taken place between the parties.[558]

25–015 **Cases in which no hearing is held.** The Court may answer the question referred for a preliminary ruling without a hearing by reasoned order where the question is identical[559] to a question on which the Court has already ruled, where the answer to such a question may be clearly deduced from existing case-law or where the answer to the question referred admits of no reasonable doubt. The Court will then refer to an earlier judgment or to the relevant case-law.[560]

---

[555] See, for example, ECJ, Case 26/62 *Van Gend & Loos* [1963] E.C.R. 1; ECJ, Case 293/83 *Gravier* [1985] E.C.R. 593.

[556] See, for example, ECJ, Case 261/81 *Rau* [1982] E.C.R. 3961.

[557] ECJ Rules of Procedure, Art.61. For examples, see ECJ (order of June 18, 2002), Case C–280/00 *Altmark Trans and Regierungspräsidium Magdeburg*, not reported; ECJ (order of September 17, 1999), Case C–35/98 *Verkooijen*, not reported.

[558] ECJ (order of February 4, 2000), Case C–17/98 *Emesa Sugar* [2000] E.C.R. I–665, para.18; ECJ, Case C–309/99 *Wouters and Others* [2002] E.C.R. I–1577, para.42; ECJ (judgment of November 13, 2003), Case C–209/01 *Schilling and Fleck-Schilling* [2003] E.C.R. I–13389, para.19; ECJ (order of October 21, 2005), Case C–475/03 *Banca popolare di Cremona*, not yet reported.

[559] The wording used need not be identical. It is enough for the questions to be essentially identical: ECJ (order of June 8, 2004), Joined Cases C–250/02 to C–253/02 and C–256/02 *Telecom Italia Mobile*, not reported, paras 9–10.

[560] ECJ Rules of Procedure, Art.104(3). See also 6–032, *supra*. For applications, see ECJ (order of October 20, 2000), Case C–242/99 *Vogler* [2000] E.C.R. I–9083; ECJ (order of April 5, 2001), Case C–518/99 *Gaillard* [2001] E.C.R. I–2771; ECJ (order of May 2, 2001), Case C–307/99 *OGT Fruchthandelsgesellschaft* [2001] E.C.R. I–3159 (question not identical but the answer was sufficiently clear from the case-law); ECJ (order of November 22, 2001), Case C–80/01 *Michel* [2001] E.C.R. I–9141 (answer sufficiently clear from the case-law); ECJ (order of July 24, 2003), Case C–166/02 *Messejana Viegas*, not reported (answer

Where the question is identical to a question on which the Court has already ruled, or where the answer to such question may be clearly deduced from existing case-law, the Court may at any time give its decision by reasoned order, after hearing the Advocate General. Where the answer to the question admits of no reasonable doubt, the Court must before rendering its decision first inform the national court which referred the question to it and hear the Advocate General as well as the persons referred to in Art.23 of the Statute.[561]

The Court of Justice may dispense with a hearing if no-one who has the right to submit written observations has submitted an application setting out the reasons for which it wishes to be heard.[562] Finally, the case will be decided by order—without oral hearing—where the Court has no jurisdiction to take cognisance of the reference or where the action is manifestly inadmissible.[563]

Accelerated procedure. At the request of the national court, the President   **25–016** may exceptionally decide, on a proposal from the Judge-Rapporteur and after hearing the Advocate General, to apply an accelerated procedure where the circumstances referred to establish that a ruling on the question put to the Court is a matter of exceptional urgency.[564]

The accelerated procedure differs from the ordinary procedure. The President immediately fixes the date for the hearing and the period (not less than 15 days) within which parties and other interested persons may lodge statements of case or written observations.[565]

---

sufficiently clear from the case-law); ECJ (order of January 27, 2004), Case C–428/01 *Fratelli Costanzo and Others*, not reported (identical question); ECJ (order of January 27, 2004), Case C–259/02 *La Mer Technology and Others* [2004] E.C.R. I–1159 (answer to all the questions—with the exception of the last—sufficiently clear from the case-law; there was no reasonable doubt about the answer to the last question). Where the Court of Justice manifestly lacks jurisdiction (*e.g.* where the question is not raised by a court or tribunal) it gives an order on the basis of Art.92(1) of the ECJ Rules of Procedure (see ECJ (order of July 11, 2003), Case C–161/03 *CAFOM and Samsung Electronics France*, not reported, paras 10–17).

[561] ECJ Rules of Procedure, Art.104(3).
[562] ECJ Rules of Procedure, Art.104(4). Such an application has to be made within a period of three weeks from service on the party or person of the written statements of case or written observations which have been lodged by the other parties mentioned in Art.23 of the Statute. See, *e.g.* ECJ, Case C–17/92 *Federación de Distribuidores Cinematográficos* [1993] E.C.R. I–2239; ECJ, Case C–126/04 *Heineken Brouwerijen* [2005] E.C.R. I–331.
[563] Where the Court has no jurisdiction (*e.g.* where the reference was not made by a national court or tribunal) or where the reference is manifestly inadmissible, the Court grounds its order on the Rules of Procedure, Art.92(1) (ECJ (order of July 11, 2003), Case C–161/03 *CAFOM and Samsung Electronics France*, not reported, paras 10–17; ECJ (order of February 11, 2004), Joined Cases C–438/03, C–439/03, C–509/03 and C–2/04 *Cannito and Others* [2004] E.C.R. I–1605, paras 9–13).
[564] ECJ Rules of Procedure, Art.104a.
[565] For a first application, see ECJ, Case C–189/01 *Jippes and Others* [2001] E.C.R. I–5689,

25–017   **Measures of inquiry.** In principle, the Court of Justice will not prescribe measures of inquiry in preliminary ruling proceedings, since it is for the national court to make the findings of fact in relation to the main proceedings and to draw the necessary conclusions for the purposes of reaching its decision.[566] Neither may the Court of Justice verify the facts placed before it.[567] However, the Court may, after hearing the Advocate General, request clarification from the national court.[568]

25–018   **Representation.** As far as representation of the parties to the main proceedings and their attendance at the Court are concerned, the Court has regard to the rules applicable to the court hearing the main case. Consequently, parties do not have to be represented by a lawyer (unlike the position in the case of a direct action (see 24–187, *supra*) where a party may validly be otherwise represented before the national court (*e.g.* by a representative of a representative trade union in employment disputes in some jurisdictions) or where a party is entitled to plead as a litigant in person.[569]

25–019   **Costs.** The question of the costs incurred by the parties to the main proceedings on account of the reference for a preliminary ruling—in practice, lawyers' fees and expenses, since the actual procedure before the Court of Justice is free of charge—is a matter for the national court.[570] The

---

with a case note by Spaventa (2002) C.M.L.Rev. 1159–1170. For cases in which leave to apply the accelerated procedure was refused, see ECJ (order of the President of April 1, 2004), Case C–81/04 *Richert*, not reported (possible pecuniary loss did not require exceptional urgency); ECJ (order of the President of May 7, 2004), Joined Cases C–154/04 and C–155/04 *Alliance for Natural Health and Others*, not reported (no exceptional urgency where the directive whose validity is contested will enter into effect 17 months after the reference for a preliminary ruling and the undertakings concerned have to make substantial investments in order to comply with the directive); ECJ (orders of the President of August 23, 2004 and March 18, 2005), Case C–300/04 *Eman and Sevinger*, not reported (application for the accelerated procedure based on considerations not directly connected with the main proceedings).

[566] ECJ, Case 17/81 *Pabst & Richarz* [1982] E.C.R. 1331, para.12. See 2–025, 2–026 and 6–021, *supra*.

[567] ECJ, Case 104/77 *Oehlschläger* [1978] E.C.R. 791, para.4. See 2–025, 2–026 and 6–021, *supra*; ECJ, Case C–418/01 *IMS Health and Others* [2004] E.C.R. I–5039, para.18.

[568] ECJ Rules of Procedure, Art.104(5). For an example, see ECJ (order of March 12, 2004), Case C–54/03 *Austroplant-Arzneimittel*, not reported, para.14.

[569] For an example, see ECJ, Case C–293/93 *Houtwipper* [1994] E.C.R. I–4249.

[570] ECJ Rules of Procedure, Art.104(6), first subpara. Arts 69–75 of the ECJ Rules of Procedure are concerned with costs of contentious proceedings brought before the Court of Justice. In view of the essential difference between contentious proceedings and proceedings under Art.234 of the EC Treaty, which are only a step in the proceedings before the national court, those provisions do not cover the recovery of costs and the recoverability of expenses incurred in the main proceedings in connection with a reference for a preliminary ruling. The applicable national provisions must be applied to determine how the costs are to be allocated in such a case: ECJ, Case 62/72 *Bollmann* [1973] E.C.R. 269, paras 5–6. In *R v Intervention Board for Agricultural Produce, ex parte Fish Producers' Organisation Ltd*

Court of Justice merely adverts to this in its judgment. In addition, in special circumstances the Court of Justice may "grant, by way of legal aid, assistance for the purpose of facilitating the representation or attendance of a party", which operates in practice in the same way as the grant of legal aid in the context of a direct action (see 25–131 to 25–135, *supra*).[571] The costs incurred by Member States and Community institutions as a result of their intervention in preliminary ruling proceedings are not recoverable.[572]

Language of the case. The language of the case is the language of the court which made the reference for a preliminary ruling. Written observations must be drawn up and the parties have to plead in that language, subject to the proviso that Member States may use their official language or one of their official languages.[573] The use of languages by the President, Judges and the Advocate General is dealt with in the same way as in the case of direct actions (see 24–174, *supra*).   **25–020**

No appeal. No appeal will lie from parties to the main proceedings, Member States or Community institutions against a preliminary ruling, since it is only for national courts and tribunals to decide whether to make a reference and, if so, what its subject-matter should be.[574] Consequently, they decide whether they have received sufficient clarification from the preliminary ruling and whether they consider it necessary to make a further reference to the Court of Justice.[575] The parties to the main proceedings may urge the national court to make an additional reference, but they have no right to apply to the Court of Justice directly.   **25–021**

[1993] 1 C.M.L.R. 707, the Court of Appeal held that the normal English rule that costs follow the event applies to preliminary ruling procedures. Costs which under national procedural rules have to be borne by a successful party to the main proceedings may not be the subject of a claim for damages brought against the Community, even though the judgment in the main proceedings was based on a declaration made in a preliminary ruling that an act of a Community institution was invalid. This is because to hold the Community liable in damages on this head would place in question the existence and exercise of the exclusive jurisdiction which national courts enjoy in the matter of the costs of the reference for a preliminary ruling under Art.104(5), first para., of the ECJ Rules of Procedure: CFI, Case T–167/94 *Nölle v Council and Commission* [1995] E.C.R. II–2589, paras 37–39.

[571] ECJ Rules of Procedure, Art.104(6), second subpara. See ECJ (order of November 16, 2004), Case C–374/03 AJ *Gürol*, not reported (the Court examined whether the legal aid granted under national law also covered the procedure before the Court of Justice; legal aid was granted to a party with a monthly income of 700 euros); see also ECJ (order of October 7, 2004), Case C–350/03 AJ *Schulte*, not reported.

[572] Mortelmans, "Observations in the Cases governed by Art.177*[now Art.234]* of the EEC Treaty: Procedure and Practice" (1979) C.M.L.Rev. 557, at 568.

[573] ECJ Rules of Procedure, Art.29(2) and (3).

[574] ECJ (order of May 16, 1968), Case 13/67 *Becher* [1968] E.C.R. 196, at 197.

[575] *Ibid.*; see also ECJ (order of October 18, 1979), Case 40/70 *Sirena* [1979] E.C.R. 3169; ECJ (order of March 5, 1986), Case 69/85 *Wünsche* [1986] E.C.R. 947; ECJ (order of April 28, 1998), Case C–116/96 Rev. *Reisebüro Binder* [1998] E.C.R. I–1889, paras 6–9.

25–022   **EEA Agreement.** Special features of the procedure followed in preliminary ruling proceedings brought before the Court of Justice pursuant to Art.1 of Protocol No 34 to the EEA Agreement are prescribed in Art.123b of the ECJ Rules of Procedure.

CHAPTER 26

PROCEDURE IN THE CASE OF AN APPEAL AGAINST A DECISION OF THE COURT OF FIRST INSTANCE

General. The procedure before the Court of Justice in the case of an appeal brought against a decision of the Court of First Instance consists of a written and an oral part. The language of the case is the language of the decision against which the appeal is brought.[576]   **26–001**

Appeal. The written part of the proceedings is limited in principle to two documents, the appeal and the response. The appeal must be lodged at the registry of the Court of Justice or of the Court of First Instance.[577] The appeal has to be brought before the Court of Justice, within two months of the notification of the decision appealed against.[578]   **26–002**

It has to comply with the requirements generally applying to applications.[579] The following must appear at the beginning of each appeal: the appellant's name and address; the name and capacity of the appellant's agent or lawyer; the identification of the decision of the Court of First

---

[576] ECJ Rules of Procedure, Art.110.

[577] ECJ Rules of Procedure, Art.111(1).

[578] Art.56 of the Statute of the Court of Justice. Service shall then be deemed to have been effected on the addressee by registered post on the tenth day following the lodging of the registered letter at the post office of the place where the Court of First Instance has its seat, unless it is shown by the acknowledgement of receipt that the letter was received on a different date or the addressee informs the Registrar, within three weeks of being advised by telefax or other technical means of communication, that the document to be served has not reached him (see ECJ (order of October 29, 2004), Case C–360/02 P *Ripa di Meana v European Parliament* [2004] E.C.R. I–10339, paras 23–24).

[579] ECJ Rules of Procedure, Art.112(1), second subpara., which refers to ECJ Rules of Procedure, Arts 37 and 38(2) and (3). A clerical error in an application, for instance, an incorrect reference to a provision of the Statute as constituting the basis for an appeal, which has no incidence on the subsequent course of the proceedings is not a ground for finding the appeal inadmissible: ECJ (order of the President of July 19, 1995), Case C–149/95 P(R) *Commission v Atlantic Container Line and Others* [1995] E.C.R. I–2165, para.14. The fact that the appeal is not accompanied—in accordance with Art.37(1), second subpara., and Art.4 of the ECJ Rules of Procedure (to which Art.112(1) and (2) refers)—by the documents and decisions appealed against does not result in the appeal being inadmissible. The Court of Justice found that no evidence had been adduced to show that the parties had been prejudiced by the fact that the documents to which the appeal referred were not annexed to it.

Instance appealed against (type of decision, formation of the Court, date and number of the case) and the names of the parties before the Court of First Instance; the date on which the decision of the Court of First Instance was notified to the appellant, and an address for service in Luxembourg and/or agreement to service by telefax or other technical means of communication.[580] The appeal should be accompanied by a summary of the grounds of appeal and main arguments relied on.[581] The decision appealed against must be attached to the appeal.[582] If the appeal complies with those requirements, it will be served on all the parties to the proceedings before the Court of First Instance.[583] An appeal must indicate precisely the contested elements of the judgment which the appellant seeks to have set aside, and also the legal arguments specifically advanced in support of the appeal.[584] An appeal which confines itself to repeating or reproducing word for word the pleas in law and arguments previously submitted to the Court of First Instance does not satisfy that requirement.[585]

26–003　**Response.** Within a period of two months after service of the appeal, which may not be extended, any of the parties to the proceedings before the Court of First Instance may lodge a response. The following heads must appear at the beginning of the response: the name and address of the party lodging it; the name and capacity of the agent or lawyer acting for that party; the date on which notice of the appeal was served on the party and an address for service in Luxembourg and/or agreement to service by telefax or any other technical means of communication, together with the pleas and arguments and the form of order sought.[586]

---

[580] ECJ Rules of Procedure, Art.112(1), first subpara.; ECJ Practice Directions, point 24. If the Court of Justice finds that the appeal was lodged within the prescribed period starting from the date on which the Court of First Instance gave judgment, failure to mention the date on which the judgment was notified in the appeal does not make the appeal inadmissible: ECJ, Case C–91/95 P *Tremblay and Others v Commission* [1996] E.C.R. I–5547, paras 10–11. Mention in the appeal of a wrong address is not "so substantial" an irregularity as to make the appeal inadmissible where the correct address can be found from other documents in the case file, such as the contested judgment annexed to the appeal: ECJ, Case C–161/97 P *Kernkraftwerke Lippe-Ems v Commission* [1999] E.C.R. I–2057, para.55.

[581] ECJ, Rules of Procedure, Art.112(1), first subpara.

[582] ECJ Rules of Procedure, Art.112(2).

[583] ECJ Rules of Procedure, Art.114.

[584] ECJ (order of November 11, 2003), Case C–488/01 P *Martinez v European Parliament* [2003] E.C.R. I–13355, paras 40–41.

[585] ECJ, Case C–48/96 P *Windpark Groothusen v Commission* [1998] E.C.R. I–2873, para.56; ECJ (order of July 16, 1998) Case C–252/97 N v Commission [1998] E.C.R. I–4871, paras 17–19; ECJ, Case C–221/97 P *Schröder and Others v Commission* [1998] E.C.R. I–8255, para.35; ECJ (order of December 12, 2003), *Case C–258/02 P Bactria Industriehygiene-Service v Commission* [2003] E.C.R. I–15105, para.31; ECJ, Case C–499/03 P *Biegi Nahrungsmittel and Commonfood v Commission* [2005] E.C.R. I–1751, paras 37–38.

[586] ECJ Rules of Procedure, Art.115(2). See also ECJ Practice Directions, point 31.

Cross-appeal. If the response seeks an order setting aside, in whole or in part, the decision of the Court of First Instance on a plea in law not raised in the appeal, that fact must be indicated in the title of the pleading (Response and Cross-appeal).[587]

26–004

Reply and rejoinder. The appeal and the response may be supplemented by a reply and a rejoinder where the President, on application made by the appellant within seven days of service of the response, considers such further pleading necessary and expressly allows the submission of a reply in order to enable the appellant to put forward his or her point of view or in order to provide a basis for the decision on the appeal. The President prescribes the date by which the reply is to be submitted and, upon service of that pleading, the date by which the rejoinder is to be submitted.[588]

26–005

In principle, an application to lodge a reply to an application must not exceed 2 to 3 pages and must be confined to summarising the precise reasons for which, in the appellant's opinion, a reply is necessary. The request must be comprehensible in itself without any need to refer to the appeal or the response.[589]

However, the appellant has the right to submit a reply, without making a specific request to the President of the Court, where a party makes a cross-appeal in its response. It may deal only with the relevant plea and must be submitted within two months of the service of the response in question. If a party wishes to respond to such a reply in writing, it must obtain the leave of the President of the Court.[590]

Cases in which no hearing is held. Where an appeal is, in whole or in part, clearly inadmissible or clearly unfounded, the Court of Justice may at any time, acting on a report from the Judge-Rapporteur and after hearing the Advocate General, by reasoned order dismiss the appeal in whole or in part.[591]

26–006

Lastly, at the end of the written part of the procedure, the Court may, acting on a report from the Judge-Rapporteur and after hearing the

---

[587] ECJ Practice Directions, point 33.
[588] ECJ Rules of Procedure, Art.117(1).
[589] ECJ Practice Directions, point 47.
[590] ECJ Rules of Procedure, Art.117(2).
[591] ECJ Rules of Procedure, Art.119(1). For examples, see ECJ (order of February 27, 1991), Case C–126/90 P *Bocos Viciano v Commission* [1991] E.C.R. I–781; ECJ (order of March 20, 1991), Case C–115/90 P *Turner v Commission* [1991] E.C.R. I–1423; ECJ (order of January 24, 1994), Case C–275/93 P *Boessen v ESC* [1994] E.C.R. I–159. See ECJ (order of June 5, 2002), Case C–211/00 P *Ciments Français v Commission*, not reported, and other orders given on the same day in the "cement case", by which the Court dismissed by order a number of pleas which were manifestly inadmissible or manifestly unfounded. The Court may also declare arguments inadmissible which are raised in connection with pleas that are admissible *per se*, for instance where the arguments do not contest the legal assessment but rather the findings of fact made by the Court of First Instance on the basis of the documents submitted as evidence (ECJ, Case C–449/99 *EIB v Hautem* [2001] E.C.R. I–6733, paras 46–49).

Advocate General and the parties, decide to dispense with the oral part of the procedure unless one of the parties submits an application setting out the reasons for which he wishes to be heard.[592] If the Court gives judgment without a hearing, the Advocate General delivers his or her Opinion in open court at a date determined by the President. The Judge-Rapporteur has to make a recommendation in his or her preliminary report as to whether the appeal may be dealt with without a hearing.[593]

26–007 **Rules regarding direct actions in general.** A series of provisions of the Rules of Procedure is stated to be applicable to the procedure before the Court of Justice on appeals from the Court of First Instance.[594] The provisions relate to the bar on introducing new pleas in the course of the proceedings (Art.42(2)), the joinder of cases (Art.43), the Judge-Rapporteur's preliminary report (Art.44), the oral procedure (Arts 55 to 62), the expedited procedure (Art.62a),[595] judgments (Arts 63 to 68), costs (Arts 69 to 75; see also Art.122), legal aid (Art.76), time on account of distance (Art.76), discontinuance (Arts 77 and 78), service (Art.79), time-limits (Arts 80, 81 and 82), stays of proceedings (Art.82a), interim measures (Arts 83 to 90), intervention (Art.93; see also Art.123[596]), assignment of cases to Chambers (Art.95), third-party proceedings (Art.97), revision (Arts 98, 99 and 100) and interpretation of judgments (Art.102). As a result, the rules applicable to these matters are the same as for direct actions.[597]

26–008 **No measures of inquiry.** The Court of Justice cannot order measures of inquiry in appeal proceedings. Measures of inquiry would necessarily exceed the bounds of an appeal since it is limited to questions of law and is based on the facts as found by the Court of First Instance.[598]

26–009 **Dismissal of the appeal does not affect any cross-appeal.** Dismissal of the main appeal has no effect on the treatment of any cross-appeal.[599]

---

[592] ECJ Rules of Procedure, Art.120. The application must be submitted within a period of three weeks from notification to the party of the closure of the written procedure. For an example, see ECJ (order of March 9, 2000), Case C–291/98 P *Sarrió v Commission* [2000] E.C.R. I–1213, in which the appellant had spontaneously forgone applying for leave to submit a reply so that it was hard for it to argue that the written procedure had not enabled it to defend its point of view in full.

[593] Statute, Art.59; ECJ Rules of Procedure, Arts 120 and 121. For examples, see ECJ, Case C–354/92 P *Eppe v Commission* [1993] E.C.R. I–7027, at I–7034; ECJ (order of March 23, 2001), Case C–7/01 P (R) *FEG v Commission* [2001] E.C.R. I–2559, para.28.

[594] ECJ Rules of Procedure, Art.118.

[595] See, *e.g.* ECJ Case C–39/03 P *Commission v Artegodan* [2003] E.C.R. I–7885.

[596] For examples of the interest having to be shown by an individual in order to intervene in appeal proceedings, see ECJ, Case C–200/92 P *ICI v Commission* [1999] E.C.R. I–4399, para.25; ECJ, Joined Cases C–172/01 P, C–175/01 P, C–176/01 P and C–180/01 P *International Power and Others v Commission* [2003] E.C.R. I–11421, paras 49–53.

[597] For the matters concerned, see Ch.24, *supra*.

[598] ECJ, Case C–199/92 P *Hüls v Commission* [1999] E.C.R. I–4287, paras 90–91; ECJ, Case C–235/92 P *Montecatini v Commission* [1999] E.C.R. I–4539, paras 109–110.

[599] See, *e.g.* ECJ, Case C–234/02 P *European Ombudsman v Lamberts* [2004] E.C.R. I–2803, paras 72–94.

Procedure when a case is referred back to Court of First Instance. The   26–010
procedure followed where the Court of Justice sets aside a judgment or an
order of the Court of First Instance and refers the case back to that Court
is set forth in Arts 117 to 121 of the CFI Rules of Procedure.

Where the written procedure before the Court of First Instance has been
completed when the judgment referring the case back to it is delivered, the
course of the procedure is as follows:

(a) Within two months from the service upon him or her of the judgment
of the Court of Justice the applicant may lodge a statement of written
observations.

(b) In the month following the communication to him or her of that
statement, the defendant may lodge a statement of written observations. The time allowed to the defendant for lodging it may in no
case be less than two months from the service upon him or her of the
judgment of the Court of Justice.

(c) In the month following the simultaneous communication to the
intervener of the observations of the applicant and the defendant, the
intervener may lodge a statement of written observations. The time
allowed to the intervener for lodging it may in no case be less than
two months from the service upon him or her of the judgment of the
Court of Justice.

Where the written procedure before the Court of First Instance has not
been completed when the judgment referring the case back to the Court of
First Instance was delivered, it is to be resumed, at the stage which it had
reached, by means of measures of organisation of procedure adopted by the
Court of First Instance.

The Court of First Instance decides on the costs relating to the
proceedings instituted before it and to the proceedings on the appeal
before the Court of Justice.[600]

---

[600] CFI Rules of Procedure, Art.121. See CFI (judgment of September 14, 2004), Case T–
156/94 *Siderúrgica Aristrain Madrid v Commission*, not reported, paras 45–52.

Appendix A

Articles 220 to 245 of the EC Treaty

Article 220

A1–001

The Court of Justice and the Court of First Instance, each within its jurisdiction, shall ensure that in the interpretation and application of this Treaty the law is observed.

In addition, judicial panels may be attached to the Court of First Instance under the conditions laid down in Article 225a in order to exercise, in certain specific areas, the judicial competence laid down in this Treaty.

Article 221

The Court of Justice shall consist of one judge per Member State.

The Court of Justice shall sit in chambers or in a Grand Chamber, in accordance with the rules laid down for that purpose in the Statute of the Court of Justice.

When provided for in the Statute, the Court of Justice may also sit as a full Court.

Article 222

The Court of Justice shall be assisted by eight Advocates-General. Should the Court of Justice so request, the Council, acting unanimously, may increase the number of Advocates-General.

It shall be the duty of the Advocate-General, acting with complete impartiality and independence, to make, in open court, reasoned submissions on cases which, in accordance with the Statute of the Court of Justice, require his involvement.

Article 223

The Judges and Advocates-General of the Court of Justice shall be chosen from persons whose inde-pendence is beyond doubt and who possess the qualifications required for appointment to the highest judicial offices in their respective countries or who are jurisconsults of recognised competence; they shall be appointed by common accord of the governments of the Member States for a term of six years.

Every three years there shall be a partial replacement of the Judges and Advocates-General, in accordance with the conditions laid down in the Statute of the Court of Justice.

The Judges shall elect the President of the Court of Justice from among their number for a term of three years. He may be re-elected.

Retiring Judges and Advocates-General may be reappointed.

The Court of Justice shall appoint its Registrar and lay down the rules governing his service.

The Court of Justice shall establish its Rules of Procedure. Those Rules shall require the approval of the Council, acting by a qualified majority.

Article 224

The Court of First Instance shall comprise at least one judge per Member State. The number of Judges shall be determined by the Statute of the Court of Justice.

The Statute may provide for the Court of First Instance to be assisted by Advocates-General.

The members of the Court of First Instance shall be chosen from persons whose independence is beyond doubt and who possess the ability required for appointment to high judicial office. They shall be appointed by common accord of the governments of the Member States for a term of six years. The membership shall be partially renewed every three years. Retiring members shall be eligible for reappointment.

The Judges shall elect the President of the Court of First Instance from among their number for a term of three years. He may be re-elected.

The Court of First Instance shall appoint its Registrar and lay down the rules governing his service.

The Court of First Instance shall establish its Rules of Procedure in agreement with the Court of Justice. Those Rules shall require the approval of the Council, acting by a qualified majority.

Unless the Statute of the Court of Justice provides otherwise, the provisions of this Treaty relating to the Court of Justice shall apply to the Court of First Instance.

Article 225

1. The Court of First Instance shall have jurisdiction to hear and determine at first instance actions or proceedings referred to in Articles 230, 232, 235, 236 and 238, with the exception of those assigned to a judicial panel and those reserved in the Statute for the Court of Justice. The Statute may provide for the Court of First Instance to have jurisdiction for other classes of action or proceeding.

Decisions given by the Court of First Instance under this paragraph may be subject to a right of appeal to the Court of Justice on points of law only, under the conditions and within the limits laid down by the Statute.

2. The Court of First Instance shall have jurisdiction to hear and determine actions or proceedings brought against decisions of the judicial panels set up under Article 225a.

Decisions given by the Court of First Instance under this paragraph may exceptionally be subject to review by the Court of Justice, under the conditions and within the limits laid down by the Statute, where there is a serious risk of the unity or consistency of Community law being affected.

3. The Court of First Instance shall have jurisdiction to hear and determine questions referred for a preliminary ruling under Article 234, in specific areas laid down by the Statute.

Where the Court of First Instance considers that the case requires a decision of principle likely to affect the unity or consistency of Community law, it may refer the case to the Court of Justice for a ruling.

Decisions given by the Court of First Instance on questions referred for a preliminary ruling may exceptionally be subject to review by the Court of Justice, under the conditions and within the limits laid down by the Statute, where there is a serious risk of the unity or consistency of Community law being affected.

Article 225a

The Council, acting unanimously on a proposal from the Commission and after consulting the European Parliament and the Court of Justice or at the request of the Court of Justice and after consulting the European Parliament and the Commission, may create judicial panels to hear and determine at first instance certain classes of action or proceeding brought in specific areas.

The decision establishing a judicial panel shall lay down the rules on the organisation of the panel and the extent of the jurisdiction conferred upon it.

Decisions given by judicial panels may be subject to a right of appeal on points of law only or, when provided for in the decision establishing the panel, a right of appeal also on matters of fact, before the Court of First Instance.

The members of the judicial panels shall be chosen from persons whose independence is beyond doubt and who possess the ability required for appointment to judicial office. They shall be appointed by the Council, acting unanimously.

The judicial panels shall establish their Rules of Procedure in agreement with the Court of Justice. Those Rules shall require the approval of the Council, acting by a qualified majority.

Unless the decision establishing the judicial panel provides otherwise, the provisions of this Treaty relating to the Court of Justice and the provisions of the Statute of the Court of Justice shall apply to the judicial panels.

Article 226

If the Commission considers that a Member State has failed to fulfil an obligation under this Treaty, it shall deliver a reasoned opinion on the matter after giving the State concerned the opportunity to submit its observations.

If the State concerned does not comply with the opinion within the period laid down by the Commission, the latter may bring the matter before the Court of Justice.

Article 227

A Member State which considers that another Member State has failed to fulfil an obligation under this Treaty may bring the matter before the Court of Justice.

Before a Member State brings an action against another Member State for an alleged infringement of an obligation under this Treaty, it shall bring the matter before the Commission.

The Commission shall deliver a reasoned opinion after each of the States concerned has been given the opportunity to submit its own case and its observations on the other party's case both orally and in writing.

If the Commission has not delivered an opinion within three months of the date on which the matter was brought before it, the absence of such opinion shall not prevent the matter from being brought before the Court of Justice.

Article 228

1. If the Court of Justice finds that a Member State has failed to fulfil an obligation under this Treaty, the State shall be required to take the necessary measures to comply with the judgment of the Court of Justice.

2. If the Commission considers that the Member State concerned has not taken such measures it shall, after giving that State the opportunity to submit its observations, issue a reasoned opinion specifying the points on which the Member State concerned has not complied with the judgment of the Court of Justice.

If the Member State concerned fails to take the necessary measures to comply with the Court's judgment within the time-limit laid down by the Commission, the latter may bring the case before the Court of Justice. In so doing it shall specify the amount of the lump sum or penalty payment to be paid by the Member State concerned which it considers appropriate in the circumstances.

If the Court of Justice finds that the Member State concerned has not complied with its judgment it may impose a lump sum or penalty payment on it.

This procedure shall be without prejudice to Article 227.

Article 229

Regulations adopted jointly by the European Parliament and the Council, and by the Council, pursuant to the provisions of this Treaty, may give the Court of Justice unlimited jurisdiction in regard to the penalties provided for in such regulations.

Article 229a

Without prejudice to the other provisions of this Treaty, the Council, acting unanimously on a proposal from the Commission and after consulting the European Parliament, may adopt provisions to confer jurisdiction, to the extent that it shall determine, on the Court of Justice in disputes relating to the application of acts adopted on the basis of this Treaty which create Community industrial property rights. The Council shall recommend those provisions to the Member States for adoption in accordance with their respective constitutional requirements.

Article 230

The Court of Justice shall review the legality of acts adopted jointly by the European Parliament and the Council, of acts of the Council, of the Commission and of the ECB, other than recommendations and opinions, and of acts of the European Parliament intended to produce legal effects vis-à-vis third parties.

It shall for this purpose have jurisdiction in actions brought by a Member State, the European Parliament, the Council or the Commission on grounds of lack of competence, infringement of an essential procedural requirement, infringement of this Treaty or of any rule of law relating to its application, or misuse of powers.

The Court of Justice shall have jurisdiction under the same conditions in actions brought by the European Parliament, by the Court of Auditors and by the ECB for the purpose of protecting their prerogatives.

Any natural or legal person may, under the same conditions, institute proceedings against a decision addressed to that person or against a decision which, although in the form of a regulation or a decision addressed to another person, is of direct and individual concern to the former.

The proceedings provided for in this Article shall be instituted within two months of the publication of the measure, or of its notification to the plaintiff, or, in the absence thereof, of the day on which it came to the knowledge of the latter, as the case may be.

Article 231

If the action is well founded, the Court of Justice shall declare the act concerned to be void.

In the case of a regulation, however, the Court of Justice shall, if it considers this necessary, state which of the effects of the regulation which it has declared void shall be considered as definitive.

Article 232

Should the European Parliament, the Council or the Commission, in infringement of this Treaty, fail to act, the Member States and the other institutions of the Community may bring an action before the Court of Justice to have the infringement established.

The action shall be admissible only if the institution concerned has first been called upon to act. If, within two months of being so called upon, the institution concerned has not defined its position, the action may be brought within a further period of two months.

Any natural or legal person may, under the conditions laid down in the preceding paragraphs, complain to the Court of Justice that an institution of the Community has failed to address to that person any act other than a recommendation or an opinion.

The Court of Justice shall have jurisdiction, under the same conditions, in actions or proceedings brought by the ECB in the areas falling within the latter's field of competence and in actions or proceedings brought against the latter.

Article 233

The institution or institutions whose act has been declared void or whose failure to act has been declared contrary to this Treaty shall be required to take the necessary measures to comply with the judgment of the Court of Justice.

This obligation shall not affect any obligation which may result from the application of the second paragraph of Article 288.

This Article shall also apply to the ECB.

Article 234

The Court of Justice shall have jurisdiction to give preliminary rulings concerning

(a) the interpretation of this Treaty;

(b) the validity and interpretation of acts of the institutions of the Community and of the ECB;

(c) the interpretation of the statutes of bodies established by an act of the Council, where those statutes so provide.

Where such a question is raised before any court or tribunal of a Member State, that court or tribunal may, if it considers that a decision on the question is necessary to enable it to give judgment, request the Court of Justice to give a ruling thereon.

Where any such question is raised in a case pending before a court or tribunal of a Member State, against whose decisions there is no judicial remedy under national law, that court or tribunal shall bring the matter before the Court of Justice.

Article 235

The Court of Justice shall have jurisdiction in disputes relating to compensation for damage provided for in the second paragraph of Article 288.

Article 236

The Court of Justice shall have jurisdiction in any dispute between the Community and its servants within the limits and under the conditions laid down in the Staff Regulations or the Conditions of Employment.

Article 237

The Court of Justice shall, within the limits hereinafter laid down, have jurisdiction in disputes concerning:

(a) the fulfilment by Member States of obligations under the Statute of the European Investment Bank. In this connection, the Board of Directors of the Bank shall enjoy the powers conferred upon the Commission by Article 226;

627

(b) measures adopted by the Board of Governors of the European Investment Bank. In this connection, any Member State, the Commission or the Board of Directors of the Bank may institute proceedings under the conditions laid down in Article 230;

(c) measures adopted by the Board of Directors of the European Investment Bank. Proceedings against such measures may be instituted only by Member States or by the Commission, under the conditions laid down in Article 230, and solely on the grounds of non-compliance with the procedure provided for in Article 21(2), (5), (6) and (7) of the Statute of the Bank.

(d) the fulfilment by national central banks of obligations under this Treaty and the Statute of the ESCB. In this connection the powers of the Council of the ECB in respect of national central banks shall be the same as those conferred upon the Commission in respect of Member States by Article 226. If the Court of Justice finds that a national central bank has failed to fulfil an obligation under this Treaty, that bank shall be required to take the necessary measures to comply with the judgment of the Court of Justice.

Article 238

The Court of Justice shall have jurisdiction to give judgment pursuant to any arbitration clause contained in a contract concluded by or on behalf of the Community, whether that contract be governed by public or private law.

Article 239

The Court of Justice shall have jurisdiction in any dispute between Member States which relates to the subject-matter of this Treaty if the dispute is submitted to it under a special agreement between the parties.

Article 240

Save where jurisdiction is conferred on the Court of Justice by this Treaty, disputes to which the Community is a party shall not on that ground be excluded from the jurisdiction of the courts or tribunals of the Member States.

Article 241

Notwithstanding the expiry of the period laid down in the fifth paragraph of Article 230, any party may, in proceedings in which a regulation adopted jointly by the European Parliament and the Council, or a regulation of the Council, of the Commission, or of the ECB is at issue, plead the grounds specified in the second paragraph of Article 230 in order to invoke before the Court of Justice the inapplicability of that regulation.

Article 242

Actions brought before the Court of Justice shall not have suspensory effect. The Court of Justice may, however, if it considers that circumstances so require, order that application of the contested act be suspended.

Article 243

The Court of Justice may in any cases before it prescribe any necessary interim measures.

Article 244

The judgments of the Court of Justice shall be enforceable under the conditions laid down in Article 256.

Article 245

The Statute of the Court of Justice shall be laid down in a separate Protocol.

The Council, acting unanimously at the request of the Court of Justice and after consulting the European Parliament and the Commission, or at the request of the Commission and after consulting the European Parliament and the Court of Justice, may amend the provisions of the Statute, with the exception of Title I.

Appendix B

Statute of the Court of Justice[1]

Article 1

B1–001   The Court of Justice shall be constituted and shall function in accordance with the provisions of the Treaty on European Union (EU Treaty), of the Treaty establishing the European Community (EC Treaty), of the Treaty establishing the European Atomic Energy Community (EAEC Treaty) and of this Statute.

TITLE 1

Judges and Advocates General

Article 2

Before taking up his duties each Judge shall, in open court, take an oath to perform his duties impartially and conscientiously and to preserve the secrecy of the deliberations of the Court.

Article 3

The Judges shall be immune from legal proceedings. After they have ceased to hold office, they shall continue to enjoy immunity in respect of acts performed by them in their official capacity, including words spoken or written.

The Court, sitting as a full Court, may waive the immunity.

Where immunity has been waived and criminal proceedings are instituted against a Judge, he shall be tried, in any of the Member States, only by the court competent to judge the members of the highest national judiciary.

Articles 12 to 15 and Article 18 of the Protocol on the privileges and immunities of the European Communities shall apply to the Judges, Advocates General, Registrar and Assistant Rapporteurs of the Court, without prejudice to the provisions relating to immunity from legal proceedings of Judges which are set out in the preceding paragraphs.

---

[1] Protocol on the Statute of the Court of Justice annexed to the Treaty on European Union, to the Treaty establishing the European Community and to the Treaty establishing the European Atomic Energy Community, in accordance with Art. 7 of the Treaty of Nice, amending the Treaty on European Union, the Treaties establishing the European Communities and certain related acts, signed at Nice on February 26, 2001 ([2001] O.J. C80/1), as amended by Council Decision of July 15, 2003 ([2003] O.J. L188/1), by Art.13(2) of the Act concerning the conditions of accession of April 16, 2003 ([2003] O.J. L236/37), Council Decisions of April 19 and 26, 2004 ([2004] O.J. L132/1 and 5 and [2004] O.J. L194/3 (corrigendum)) and Council Decision of November 2, 2004 establishing the European Union Civil Service Tribunal ([2004] O.J. L 333/37), and by Council Decision of October 3, 2005 ([2005] O.J. L266/60).

Article 4

The Judges may not hold any political or administrative office.

They may not engage in any occupation, whether gainful or not, unless exemption is exceptionally granted by the Council.

When taking up their duties, they shall give a solemn undertaking that, both during and after their term of office, they will respect the obligations arising therefrom, in particular the duty to behave with integrity and discretion as regards the acceptance, after they have ceased to hold office, of certain appointments or benefits.

Any doubt on this point shall be settled by decision of the Court.

Article 5

Apart from normal replacement, or death, the duties of a Judge shall end when he resigns.

Where a Judge resigns, his letter of resignation shall be addressed to the President of the Court for transmission to the President of the Council. Upon this notification a vacancy shall arise on the bench.

Save where Article 6 applies, a Judge shall continue to hold office until his successor takes up his duties.

Article 6

A Judge may be deprived of his office or of his right to a pension or other benefits in its stead only if, in the unanimous opinion of the Judges and Advocates General of the Court, he no longer fulfils the requisite conditions or meets the obligations arising from his office. The Judge concerned shall not take part in any such deliberations.

The Registrar of the Court shall communicate the decision of the Court to the Presidents of the European Parliament and of the Commission and shall notify it to the President of the Council.

In the case of a decision depriving a Judge of his office, a vacancy shall arise on the bench upon this latter notification.

Article 7

A Judge who is to replace a member of the Court whose term of office has not expired shall be appointed for the remainder of his predecessor's term.

Article 8

The provisions of Articles 2 to 7 shall apply to the Advocates General.

TITLE II

Organisation

Article 9

When, every three years, the Judges are partially replaced, 13 and 12 Judges shall be replaced alternately.

When, every three years, the Advocates General are partially replaced, four Advocates General shall be replaced on each occasion.

Article 10

The Registrar shall take an oath before the Court to perform his duties impartially and conscientiously and to preserve the secrecy of the deliberations of the Court.

Article 11

The Court shall arrange for replacement of the Registrar on occasions when he is prevented from attending the Court.

Article 12

Officials and other servants shall be attached to the Court to enable it to function. They shall be responsible to the Registrar under the authority of the President.

Article 13

On a proposal from the Court, the Council may, acting unanimously, provide for the appointment of Assistant Rapporteurs and lay down the rules governing their service. The Assistant Rapporteurs may be required, under conditions laid down in the Rules of Procedure, to participate in preparatory inquiries in cases pending before the Court and to cooperate with the Judge who acts as Rapporteur.

The Assistant Rapporteurs shall be chosen from persons whose independence is beyond doubt and who possess the necessary legal qualifications; they shall be appointed by the Council. They shall take an oath before the Court to perform their duties impartially and conscientiously and to preserve the secrecy of the deliberations of the Court.

Article 14

The Judges, the Advocates General and the Registrar shall be required to reside at the place where the Court has its seat.

Article 15

The Court shall remain permanently in session. The duration of the judicial vacations shall be determined by the Court with due regard to the needs of its business.

Article 16

The Court shall form chambers consisting of three and five Judges. The Judges shall elect the Presidents of the chambers from among their number. The Presidents of the chambers of five Judges shall be elected for three years. They may be re-elected once.

The Grand Chamber shall consist of thirteen Judges. It shall be presided over by the President of the Court. The Presidents of the chambers of five Judges and other Judges appointed in accordance with the conditions laid down in the Rules of Procedure shall also form part of the Grand Chamber.

The Court shall sit in a Grand Chamber when a Member State or an institution of the Communities that is party to the proceedings so requests.

The Court shall sit as a full Court where cases are brought before it pursuant to Article 195(2), Article 213(2), Article 216 or Article 247(7) of the EC Treaty or Article 107d(2), Article 126(2), Article 129 or Article 160b(7) of the EAEC Treaty.

Moreover, where it considers that a case before it is of exceptional importance, the Court may decide, after hearing the Advocate General, to refer the case to the full Court.

Article 17

Decisions of the Court shall be valid only when an uneven number of its members is sitting in the deliberations.

Decisions of the chambers consisting of either three or five Judges shall be valid only if they are taken by three Judges.

Decisions of the Grand Chamber shall be valid only if nine Judges are sitting.

Decisions of the full Court shall be valid only if fifteen Judges are sitting.

In the event of one of the Judges of a chamber being prevented from attending, a Judge of another chamber may be called upon to sit in accordance with conditions laid down in the Rules of Procedure

Article 18

No Judge or Advocate General may take part in the disposal of any case in which he has previously taken part as agent or adviser or has acted for one of the parties, or in which he has been called upon to pronounce as a member of a court or tribunal, of a commission of inquiry or in any other capacity.

If, for some special reason, any Judge or Advocate General considers that he should not take part in the judgment or examination of a particular case, he shall so inform the President. If, for some special reason, the President considers that any Judge or Advocate General should not sit or make submissions in a particular case, he shall notify him accordingly.

Any difficulty arising as to the application of this Article shall be settled by decision of the Court.

A party may not apply for a change in the composition of the Court or of one of its chambers on the grounds of either the nationality of a Judge or the absence from the Court or from the chamber of a Judge of the nationality of that party.

TITLE III

Procedure

Article 19

The Member States and the institutions of the Communities shall be represented before the Court by an agent appointed for each case; the agent may be assisted by an adviser or by a lawyer.

The States, other than the Member States, which are parties to the Agreement on the European Economic Area and also the EFTA Surveillance Authority referred to in that Agreement shall be represented in same manner.

Other parties must be represented by a lawyer.

Only a lawyer authorised to practise before a court of a Member State or of another State which is a party to the Agreement on the European Economic Area may represent or assist a party before the Court.

Such agents, advisers and lawyers shall, when they appear before the Court, enjoy the rights and immunities necessary to the independent exercise of their duties, under conditions laid down in the Rules of Procedure.

As regards such advisers and lawyers who appear before it, the Court shall have the powers normally accorded to courts of law, under conditions laid down in the Rules of Procedure.

University teachers being nationals of a Member State whose law accords them a right of audience shall have the same rights before the Court as are accorded by this Article to lawyers.

633

Article 20

The procedure before the Court shall consist of two parts: written and oral.

The written procedure shall consist of the communication to the parties and to the institutions of the Communities whose decisions are in dispute, of applications, statements of case, defences and observations, and of replies, if any, as well as of all papers and documents in support or of certified copies of them.

Communications shall be made by the Registrar in the order and within the time laid down in the Rules of Procedure.

The oral procedure shall consist of the reading of the report presented by a Judge acting as Rapporteur, the hearing by the Court of agents, advisers and lawyers and of the submissions of the Advocate General, as well as the hearing, if any, of witnesses and experts.

Where it considers that the case raises no new point of law, the Court may decide, after hearing the Advocate General, that the case shall be determined without a submission from the Advocate General.

Article 21

A case shall be brought before the Court by a written application addressed to the Registrar. The application shall contain the applicant's name and permanent address and the description of the signatory, the name of the party or names of the parties against whom the application is made, the subject-matter of the dispute, the form of order sought and a brief statement of the pleas in law on which the application is based.

The application shall be accompanied, where appropriate, by the measure the annulment of which is sought or, in the circumstances referred to in Article 232 of the EC Treaty and Article 148 of the EAEC Treaty, by documentary evidence of the date on which an institution was, in accordance with those Articles, requested to act. If the documents are not submitted with the application, the Registrar shall ask the party concerned to produce them within a reasonable period, but in that event the rights of the party shall not lapse even if such documents are produced after the time-limit for bringing proceedings.

Article 22

A case governed by Article 18 of the EAEC Treaty shall be brought before the Court by an appeal addressed to the Registrar. The appeal shall contain the name and permanent address of the applicant and the description of the signatory, a reference to the decision against which the appeal is brought, the names of the respondents, the subject-matter of the dispute, the submissions and a brief statement of the grounds on which the appeal is based.

The appeal shall be accompanied by a certified copy of the decision of the Arbitration Committee which is contested.

If the Court rejects the appeal, the decision of the Arbitration Committee shall become final.

If the Court annuls the decision of the Arbitration Committee, the matter may be re-opened, where appropriate, on the initiative of one of the parties in the case, before the Arbitration Committee. The latter shall conform to any decisions on points of law given by the Court.

Article 23

In the cases governed by Article 35(1) of the EU Treaty, by Article 234 of the EC Treaty and by Article 150 of the EAEC Treaty, the decision of the court or tribunal

634

of a Member State which suspends its proceedings and refers a case to the Court shall be notified to the Court by the court or tribunal concerned. The decision shall then be notified by the Registrar of the Court to the parties, to the Member States and to the Commission, and also to the Council or to the European Central Bank if the act the validity or interpretation of which is in dispute originates from one of them, and to the European Parliament and the Council if the act the validity or interpretation of which is in dispute was adopted jointly by those two institutions.

Within two months of this notification, the parties, the Member States, the Commission and, where appropriate, the European Parliament, the Council and the European Central Bank, shall be entitled to submit statements of case or written observations to the Court.

In the cases governed by Article 234 of the EC Treaty, the decision of the national court or tribunal shall, moreover, be notified by the Registrar of the Court to the States, other than the Member States, which are parties to the Agreement on the European Economic Area and also to the EFTA Surveillance Authority referred to in that Agreement which may, within two months of notification, where one of the fields of application of that Agreement is concerned, submit statements of case or written observations to the Court.

Where an agreement relating to a specific subject-matter, concluded by the Council and one or more non-member States provides that those States are to be entitled to submit statements of case or written observations where a court or tribunal of a Member State refers to the Court of Justice for a preliminary ruling a question falling within the scope of the agreement, the decision of the national court or tribunal containing that question shall also be notified to the non-member States concerned. Within two months from such notification, those States may lodge at the Court statements of case or written observations.

Article 24

The Court may require the parties to produce all documents and to supply all information which the Court considers desirable. Formal note shall be taken of any refusal.

The Court may also require the Member States and institutions not being parties to the case to supply all information which the Court considers necessary for the proceedings.

Article 25

The Court may at any time entrust any individual, body, authority, committee or other organisation it chooses with the task of giving an expert opinion.

Article 26

Witnesses may be heard under conditions laid down in the Rules of Procedure.

Article 27

With respect to defaulting witnesses the Court shall have the powers generally granted to courts and tribunals and may impose pecuniary penalties under conditions laid down in the Rules of Procedure.

Article 28

Witnesses and experts may be heard on oath taken in the form laid down in the Rules of Procedure or in the manner laid down by the law of the country of the witness or expert.

Article 29

The Court may order that a witness or expert be heard by the judicial authority of his place of permanent residence.

The order shall be sent for implementation to the competent judicial authority under conditions laid down in the Rules of Procedure. The documents drawn up in compliance with the letters rogatory shall be returned to the Court under the same conditions.

The Court shall defray the expenses, without prejudice to the right to charge them, where appropriate, to the parties.

Article 30

A Member State shall treat any violation of an oath by a witness or expert in the same manner as if the offence had been committed before one of its courts with jurisdiction in civil proceedings. At the instance of the Court, the Member State concerned shall prosecute the offender before its competent court.

Article 31

The hearing in court shall be public, unless the Court, of its own motion or on application by the parties, decides otherwise for serious reasons.

Article 32

During the hearings the Court may examine the experts, the witnesses and the parties themselves. The latter, however, may address the Court only through their representatives.

Article 33

Minutes shall be made of each hearing and signed by the President and the Registrar.

Article 34

The case list shall be established by the President.

Article 35

The deliberations of the Court shall be and shall remain secret.

Article 36

Judgments shall state the reasons on which they are based. They shall contain the names of the Judges who took part in the deliberations.

Article 37

Judgments shall be signed by the President and the Registrar. They shall be read in open court.

Article 38

The Court shall adjudicate upon costs.

Article 39

The President of the Court may, by way of summary procedure, which may, in so far as necessary, differ from some of the rules contained in this Statute and which shall be laid down in the Rules of Procedure, adjudicate upon applications to suspend execution, as provided for in Article 242 of the EC Treaty and Article 157 of the EAEC Treaty, or to prescribe interim measures in pursuance of Article 243 of the EC Treaty or Article 158 of the EAEC Treaty, or to suspend enforcement in accordance with the fourth paragraph of Article 256 of the EC Treaty or the third paragraph of Article 164 of the EAEC Treaty.

Should the President be prevented from attending, his place shall be taken by another Judge under conditions laid down in the Rules of Procedure.

The ruling of the President or of the Judge replacing him shall be provisional and shall in no way prejudice the decision of the Court on the substance of the case.

Article 40

Member States and institutions of the Communities may intervene in cases before the Court.

The same right shall be open to any other person establishing an interest in the result of any case submitted to the Court, save in cases between Member States, between institutions of the Communities or between Member States and institutions of the Communities.

Without prejudice to the second paragraph, the States, other than the Member States, which are parties to the Agreement on the European Economic Area, and also the EFTA Surveillance Authority referred to in that Agreement, may intervene in cases before the Court where one of the fields of application that Agreement is concerned.

An application to intervene shall be limited to supporting the form of order sought by one of the parties.

Article 41

Where the defending party, after having been duly summoned, fails to file written submissions in defence, judgment shall be given against that party by default. An objection may be lodged against the judgment within one month of it being notified. The objection shall not have the effect of staying enforcement of the judgment by default unless the Court decides otherwise.

Article 42

Member States, institutions of the Communities and any other natural or legal persons may, in cases and under conditions to be determined by the Rules of Procedure, institute third-party proceedings to contest a judgment rendered without their being heard, where the judgment is prejudicial to their rights.

Article 43

If the meaning or scope of a judgment is in doubt, the Court shall construe it on application by any party or any institution of the Communities establishing an interest therein.

Article 44

An application for revision of a judgment may be made to the Court only on discovery of a fact which is of such a nature as to be a decisive factor, and which, when the judgment was given, was unknown to the Court and to the party claiming the revision.

The revision shall be opened by a judgment of the Court expressly recording the existence of a new fact, recognising that it is of such a character as to lay the case open to revision and declaring the application admissible on this ground.

No application for revision may be made after the lapse of 10 years from the date of the judgment.

Article 45

Periods of grace based on considerations of distance shall be determined by the Rules of Procedure.

No right shall be prejudiced in consequence of the expiry of a time-limit if the party concerned proves the existence of unforeseeable circumstances or of force majeure.

Article 46

Proceedings against the Communities in matters arising from non-contractual liability shall be barred after a period of five years from the occurrence of the event giving rise thereto. The period of limitation shall be interrupted if proceedings are instituted before the Court or if prior to such proceedings an application is made by the aggrieved party to the relevant institution of the Communities. In the latter event the proceedings must be instituted within the period of two months provided for in Article 230 of the EC Treaty and Article 146 of the EAEC Treaty; the provisions of the second paragraph of Article 232 of the EC Treaty and the second paragraph of Article 148 of the EAEC Treaty, respectively, shall apply where appropriate.

TITLE IV

The Court of First Instance of the European Communities

Article 47

Articles 2 to 8, Articles 14 and 15, the first, second, fourth and fifth paragraphs of Article 17 and Article 18 shall apply to the Court of First Instance and its members. The oath referred to in Article 2 shall be taken before the Court of Justice and the decisions referred to in Articles 3, 4 and 6 shall be adopted by that Court after hearing the Court of First Instance.

The fourth paragraph of Article 3 and Articles 10, 11 and 14 shall apply to the Registrar of the Court of First Instance mutatis mutandis.

Article 48

The Court of First Instance shall consist of 25 Judges.

Article 49

The members of the Court of First Instance may be called upon to perform the task of an Advocate General.

It shall be the duty of the Advocate General, acting with complete impartiality and independence, to make, in open court, reasoned submissions on certain cases brought before the Court of First Instance in order to assist the Court of First Instance in the performance of its task.

The criteria for selecting such cases, as well as the procedures for designating the Advocates General, shall be laid down in the Rules of Procedure of the Court of First Instance.

A member called upon to perform the task of Advocate General in a case may not take part in the judgment of the case.

Article 50

The Court of First Instance shall sit in chambers of three or five Judges. The Judges shall elect the Presidents of the chambers from among their number. The Presidents of the chambers of five Judges shall be elected for three years. They may be re-elected once.

The composition of the chambers and the assignment of cases to them shall be governed by the Rules of Procedure. In certain cases governed by the Rules of Procedure, the Court of First Instance may sit as a full court or be constituted by a single Judge.

The Rules of Procedure may also provide that the Court of First Instance may sit in a Grand Chamber in cases and under the conditions specified therein.

Article 51

By way of derogation from the rule laid down in Article 225(1) of the EC Treaty and Article 140a(1) of the EAEC Treaty, jurisdiction shall be reserved to the Court of Justice in the actions referred to in Articles 230 and 232 of the EC Treaty and in Articles 146 and 148 of the EAEC Treaty when they are brought by a Member State:

(a) against an act of or failure to act by the European Parliament or the Council, or by those institutions acting jointly, except for:

- decisions taken by the Council under the third subparagraph of Article 88(2) of the EC Treaty;
- acts of the Council adopted pursuant to a Council regulation concerning measures to protect trade within the meaning of Article 133 of the EC Treaty;
- acts of the Council by which it exercises implementing powers in accordance with the third indent of Article 202 of the EC Treaty;

(b) against an act of or failure to act by the Commission under Article 11a of the EC Treaty.

Jurisdiction shall also be reserved to the Court of Justice in the actions referred to in the same articles when they are brought by an institution of the Communities or the European Central Bank against an act of or failure to act by the European Parliament, the Council, both those institutions acting jointly, the Commission, or brought by an institution of the Communities against an act of or failure to act by the European Central Bank.

Article 52

The President of the Court of Justice and the President of the Court of First Instance shall determine, by common accord, the conditions under which officials and other servants attached to the Court of Justice shall render their services to the Court of First Instance to enable it to function. Certain officials or other servants shall be responsible to the Registrar of the Court of First Instance under the authority of the President of the Court of First Instance.

Article 53

The procedure before the Court of First Instance shall be governed by Title III.

Such further and more detailed provisions as may be necessary shall be laid down in its Rules of Procedure. The Rules of Procedure may derogate from the fourth paragraph of Article 40 and from Article 41 in order to take account of the specific features of litigation in the field of intellectual property.

Notwithstanding the fourth paragraph of Article 20, the Advocate General may make his reasoned submissions in writing.

Article 54

Where an application or other procedural document addressed to the Court of First Instance is lodged by mistake with the Registrar of the Court of Justice, it shall be transmitted immediately by that Registrar to the Registrar of the Court of First Instance; likewise, where an application or other procedural document addressed to the Court of Justice is lodged by mistake with the Registrar of the Court of First Instance, it shall be transmitted immediately by that Registrar to the Registrar of the Court of Justice.

Where the Court of First Instance finds that it does not have jurisdiction to hear and determine an action in respect of which the Court of Justice has jurisdiction, it shall refer that action to the Court of Justice; likewise, where the Court of Justice finds that an action falls within the jurisdiction of the Court of First Instance, it shall refer that action to the Court of First Instance, whereupon that Court may not decline jurisdiction.

Where the Court of Justice and the Court of First Instance are seised of cases in which the same relief is sought, the same issue of interpretation is raised or the validity of the same act is called in question, the Court of First Instance may, after hearing the parties, stay the proceedings before it until such time as the Court of Justice has delivered judgment. In the same circumstances, the Court of Justice may also decide to stay the proceedings before it; in that event, the proceedings before the Court of First Instance shall continue.

Where a Member State and an institution of the Communities are challenging the same act, the Court of First Instance shall decline jurisdiction so that the Court of Justice may rule on those applications.

Article 55

Final decisions of the Court of First Instance, decisions disposing of the substantive issues in part only or disposing of a procedural issue concerning a plea of lack of competence or inadmissibility, shall be notified by the Registrar of the Court of First Instance to all parties as well as all Member States and the institutions of the Communities even if they did not intervene in the case before the Court of First Instance.

Article 56

An appeal may be brought before the Court of Justice, within two months of the notification of the decision appealed against, against final decisions of the Court of First Instance and decisions of that Court disposing of the substantive issues in part only or disposing of a procedural issue concerning a plea of lack of competence or inadmissibility.

Such an appeal may be brought by any party which has been unsuccessful, in whole or in part, in its submissions. However, interveners other than the Member States and the institutions of the Communities may bring such an appeal only where the decision of the Court of First Instance directly affects them.

With the exception of cases relating to disputes between the Communities and their servants, an appeal may also be brought by Member States and institutions of the Communities which did not intervene in the proceedings before the Court of First Instance. Such Member States and institutions shall be in the same position as Member States or institutions which intervened at first instance.

Article 57

Any person whose application to intervene has been dismissed by the Court of First Instance may appeal to the Court of Justice within two weeks from the notification of the decision dismissing the application.

The parties to the proceedings may appeal to the Court of Justice against any decision of the Court of First Instance made pursuant to Article 242 or Article 243 or the fourth paragraph of Article 256 of the EC Treaty or Article 157 or Article 158 or the third paragraph of Article 164 of the EAEC Treaty within two months from their notification.

The appeal referred to in the first two paragraphs of this Article shall be heard and determined under the procedure referred to in Article 39.

Article 58

An appeal to the Court of Justice shall be limited to points of law. It shall lie on the grounds of lack of competence of the Court of First Instance, a breach of procedure before it which adversely affects the interests of the appellant as well as the infringement of Community law by the Court of First Instance.

No appeal shall lie regarding only the amount of the costs or the party ordered to pay them.

Article 59

Where an appeal is brought against a decision of the Court of First Instance, the procedure before the Court of Justice shall consist of a written part and an oral part. In accordance with conditions laid down in the Rules of Procedure, the Court of Justice, having heard the Advocate and the parties, may dispense with the oral procedure.

Article 60

Without prejudice to Articles 242 and 243 of the EC Treaty or Articles 157 and 158 of the EAEC Treaty, an appeal shall not have suspensory effect.

By way of derogation from Article 244 of the EC Treaty and Article 159 of the EAEC Treaty, decisions of the Court of First Instance declaring a regulation to be void shall take effect only as from the date of expiry of the period referred to in the first paragraph of Article 56 of this Statute or, if an appeal shall have been brought within that period, as from the date of dismissal of the appeal, without prejudice, however, to the right of a party to apply to the Court of Justice, pursuant to Articles 242 and 243 of the EC Treaty or Articles 157 and 158 of the EAEC Treaty, for the suspension of the effects of the regulation which has been declared void or for the prescription of any other interim measure.

Article 61

If the appeal is well founded, the Court of Justice shall quash the decision of the Court of First Instance. It may itself give final judgment in the matter, where the state of the proceedings so permits, or refer the case back to the Court of First Instance for judgment.

Where a case is referred back to the Court of First Instance, that Court shall be bound by the decision of the Court of Justice on points of law.

When an appeal brought by a Member State or an institution of the Communities, which did not intervene in the proceedings before the Court of First Instance, is well founded, the Court of Justice may, if it considers this necessary, state which of the effects of the decision of the Court of First Instance which has been quashed shall be considered as definitive in respect of the parties to the litigation.

Article 62

In the cases provided for in Article 225(2) and (3) of the EC Treaty and Article 140a(2) and (3) of the EAEC Treaty, where the First Advocate General considers that there is a serious risk of the unity or consistency of Community law being affected, he may propose that the Court of Justice review the decision of the Court of First Instance.

The proposal must be made within one month of delivery of the decision by the Court of First Instance. Within one month of receiving the proposal made by the First Advocate General, the Court of Justice shall decide whether or not the decision should be reviewed.

Article 62a

The Court of Justice shall give a ruling on the questions which are subject to review by means of an urgent procedure on the basis of the file forwarded to it by the Court of First Instance.

Those referred to in Article 23 of this Statute and, in the cases provided for in Article 225(2) of the EC Treaty and in Article 140a(2) of the EAEC Treaty, the parties to the proceedings before the Court of First Instance shall be entitled to lodge statements or written observations with the Court of Justice relating to questions which are subject to review within a period prescribed for that purpose.

The Court of Justice may decide to open the oral procedure before giving a ruling.

Article 62b

In the cases provided for in Article 225(2) of the EC Treaty and in Article 140a(2) of the EAEC Treaty, without prejudice to Articles 242 and 243 of the EC Treaty, proposals for review and decisions to open the review procedure shall not have suspensory effect. If the Court of Justice finds that the decision of the Court of First Instance affects the unity or consistency of Community law, it shall refer the case back to the Court of First Instance which shall be bound by the points of law decided by the Court of Justice; the Court of Justice may state which of the effects of the decision of the Court of First Instance are to be considered as definitive in respect of the parties to the litigation. If, however, having regard to the result of the review, the outcome of the proceedings flows from the findings of fact on which the decision of the Court of First Instance was based, the Court of Justice shall give final judgment.

In the cases provided for in Article 225(3) of the EC Treaty and Article 140a(3) of the EAEC Treaty, in the absence of proposals for review or decisions to open the review procedure, the answer(s) given by the Court of First Instance to the questions submitted to it shall take effect upon expiry of the periods prescribed for that purpose in the second paragraph of Article 62. Should a review procedure be opened, the answer(s) subject to review shall take effect following that procedure, unless the Court of Justice decides otherwise. If the Court of Justice finds that the decision of the Court of First Instance affects the unity or consistency of

Community law, the answer given by the Court of Justice to the questions subject to review shall be substituted for that given by the Court of First Instance.

TITLE IVA

Judicial panels

Article 62c

The provisions relating to the jurisdiction, composition, organisation and procedure of the judicial panels established under Article 225a of the EC Treaty and Article 140b of the EAEC Treaty are set out in an Annex to this Statute.

TITLE V

Final provisions

Article 63

The Rules of Procedure of the Court of Justice and of the Court of First Instance shall contain any provisions necessary for applying and, where required, supplementing this Statute.

Article 64

Until the rules governing the language arrangements applicable at the Court of Justice and the Court of First Instance have been adopted in this Statute, the provisions of the Rules of Procedure of the Court of Justice and of the Rules of Procedure of the Court of First Instance governing language arrangements shall continue to apply. Those provisions may only be amended or repealed in accordance with the procedure laid down for amending this Statute.

ANNEX

The European Union Civil Service Tribunal

Article 1*

The European Union Civil Service Tribunal (hereafter "the Civil Service Tribunal") shall exercise at first instance jurisdiction in disputes between the Communities and their servants referred to in Article 236 of the EC Treaty and Article 152 of the EAEC Treaty, including disputes between any all bodies or agencies and their servants in respect of which jurisdiction is conferred on the Court of Justice.

Article 2

The Civil Service Tribunal shall consist of seven judges. Should the Court of Justice so request, the Council, acting by a qualified majority, may increase the number of judges.

---

* Under the second paragraph of Article 4 of Council Decision 2004/752 establishing the European Union Civil Service Tribunal (OJ 2004 L 333, p. 7), Article 1 of the Annex is to enter into force on the day of the publication in the *Official Journal of the European Union* of the decision of the President of the Court of Justice recording that the European Union Civil Service Tribunal has been constituted in accordance with law.

The judges shall be appointed for a period of six years. Retiring judges may be reappointed.

Any vacancy shall be filled by the appointment of a new judge for a period of six years.

Article 3

1. The judges shall be appointed by the Council, acting in accordance with the fourth paragraph of Article 225a of the EC Treaty and the fourth paragraph of Article 140b of the EAEC Treaty, after consulting the committee provided for by this Article. When appointing judges, the Council shall ensure a balanced composition of the Tribunal on as broad a geographical basis as possible from among nationals of the Member States and with respect to the national legal systems represented.

2. Any person who is a Union citizen and fulfils the conditions laid down in the fourth paragraph of Article 225a of the EC Treaty and the fourth paragraph of Article 140b of the EAEC Treaty may submit an application. The Council, acting by a qualified majority on a recommendation from the Court, shall determine the conditions and the arrangements governing the submission and processing of such applications.

3. A committee shall be set up comprising seven persons chosen from among former members of the Court of Justice and the Court of First Instance and lawyers of recognised competence. The committee's membership and operating rules shall be determined by the Council, acting by a qualified majority on a recommendation by the President of the Court of Justice.

4. The committee shall give an opinion on candidates' suitability to perform the duties of judge at the Civil Service Tribunal. The committee shall append to its opinion a list of candidates having the most suitable high-level experience. Such list shall contain the names of at least twice as many candidates as there are judges to be appointed by the Council.

Article 4

1. The judges shall elect the President of the Civil Service Tribunal from among their number for a term of three years. He may be re-elected.

2. The Civil Service Tribunal shall sit in chambers of three judges. It may, in certain cases determined by its rules of procedure, sit in full court or in a chamber of five judges or of a single judge.

3. The President of the Civil Service Tribunal shall preside over the full court and the chamber of five judges. The Presidents of the chambers of three judges shall be designated as provided in paragraph 1. If the President of the Civil Service Tribunal is assigned to a chamber of three judges, he shall preside over that chamber.

4. The jurisdiction of and quorum for the full court as well as the composition of the chambers and the assignment of cases to them shall be governed by the rules of procedure.

Article 5

Articles 2 to 6, 14, 15, the first, second and fifth paragraphs of Article 17, and Article 18 of the Statute of the Court of Justice shall apply to the Civil Service Tribunal and its members.

The oath referred to in Article 2 of the Statute shall be taken before the Court of Justice, and the decisions referred to in Articles 3, 4 and 6 thereof shall be adopted by the Court of Justice after consulting the Civil Service Tribunal.

Article 6

1. The Civil Service Tribunal shall be supported by the departments of the Court of Justice and of the Court of First Instance. The President of the Court of Justice

644

or, in appropriate cases, the President of the Court of First Instance, shall determine by common accord with the President of the Civil Service Tribunal the conditions under which officials and other servants attached to the Court of Justice or the Court of First Instance shall render their services to the Civil Service Tribunal to enable it to function. Certain officials or other servants shall be responsible to the Registrar of the Civil Service Tribunal under the authority of the President of that Tribunal.

2. The Civil Service Tribunal shall appoint its Registrar and lay down the rules governing his service. The fourth paragraph of Article 3 and Articles 10, 11 and 14 of the Statute of the Court of Justice shall apply to the Registrar of the Tribunal.

Article 7

1. The procedure before the Civil Service Tribunal shall be governed by Title III of the Statute of the Court of Justice, with the exception of Articles 22 and 23. Such further and more detailed provisions as may be necessary shall be laid down in the rules of procedure.

2. The provisions concerning the Court of First Instance's language arrangements shall apply to the Civil Service Tribunal.

3. The written stage of the procedure shall comprise the presentation of the application and of the statement of defence, unless the Civil Service Tribunal decides that a second exchange of written pleadings is necessary. Where there is such second exchange, the Civil Service Tribunal may, with the agreement of the parties, decide to proceed to judgment without an oral procedure.

4. At all stages of the procedure, including the time when the application is filed, the Civil Service Tribunal may examine the possibilities of an amicable settlement of the dispute and may try to facilitate such settlement.

5. The Civil Service Tribunal shall rule on the costs of a case. Subject to the specific provisions of the Rules of Procedure, the unsuccessful party shall be ordered to pay the costs should the court so decide.

Article 8

1. Where an application or other procedural document addressed to the Civil Service Tribunal is lodged by mistake with the Registrar of the Court of Justice or Court of First Instance, it shall be transmitted immediately by that Registrar to the Registrar of the Civil Service Tribunal. Likewise, where an application or other procedural document addressed to the Court of Justice or to the Court of First Instance is lodged by mistake with the Registrar of the Civil Service Tribunal, it shall be transmitted immediately by that Registrar to the Registrar of the Court of Justice or Court of First Instance.

2. Where the Civil Service Tribunal finds that it does not have jurisdiction to hear and determine an action in respect of which the Court of Justice or the Court of First Instance has jurisdiction, it shall refer that action to the Court of Justice or to the Court of First Instance. Likewise, where the Court of Justice or the Court of First Instance finds that an action falls within the jurisdiction of the Civil Service Tribunal, the Court seised shall refer that action to the Civil Service Tribunal, whereupon that Tribunal may not decline jurisdiction.

3. Where the Civil Service Tribunal and the Court of First Instance are seised of cases in which the same issue of interpretation is raised or the validity of the same act is called in question, the Civil Service Tribunal, after hearing the parties, may stay the proceedings until the judgment of the Court of First Instance has been delivered.

Where the Civil Service Tribunal and the Court of First Instance are seised of cases in which the same relief is sought, the Civil Service Tribunal shall decline jurisdiction so that the Court of First Instance may act on those cases.

645

Article 9

An appeal may be brought before the Court of First Instance, within two months of notification of the decision appealed against, against final decisions of the Civil Service Tribunal and decisions of that Tribunal disposing of the substantive issues in part only or disposing of a procedural issue concerning a plea of lack of jurisdiction or inadmissibility.

Such an appeal may be brought by any party which has been unsuccessful, in whole or in part, in its submissions. However, interveners other than the Member States and the institutions of the Communities may bring such an appeal only where the decision of the Civil Service Tribunal directly affects them.

Article 10

1. Any person whose application to intervene has been dismissed by the Civil Service Tribunal may appeal to the Court of First Instance within two weeks of notification of the decision dismissing the application.

2. The parties to the proceedings may appeal to the Court of First Instance against any decision of the Civil Service Tribunal made pursuant to Article 242 or Article 243 or the fourth paragraph of Article 256 of the EC Treaty or Article 157 or Article 158 or the third paragraph of Article 164 of the EAEC Treaty within two months of its notification.

3. The President of the Court of First Instance may, by way of summary procedure, which may, insofar as necessary, differ from some of the rules contained in this Annex and which shall be laid down in the rules of procedure of the Court of First Instance, adjudicate upon appeals brought in accordance with paragraphs 1 and 2.

Article 11

1. An appeal to the Court of First Instance shall be limited to points of law. It shall lie on the grounds of lack of jurisdiction of the Civil Service Tribunal, a breach of procedure before it which adversely affects the interests of the appellant as well as the infringement of Community law by the Tribunal.

2. No appeal shall lie regarding only the amount of the costs or the party ordered to pay them.

Article 12

1. Without prejudice to Articles 242 and 243 of the EC Treaty or Articles 157 and 158 of the EAEC Treaty, an appeal before the Court of First Instance shall not have suspensory effect.

2. Where an appeal is brought against a decision of the Civil Service Tribunal, the procedure before the Court of First Instance shall consist of a written part and an oral part. In accordance with conditions laid down in the rules of procedure, the Court of First Instance, having heard the parties, may dispense with the oral procedure.

Article 13

1. If the appeal is well founded, the Court of First Instance shall quash the decision of the Civil Service Tribunal and itself give judgment in the matter. It shall refer the case back to the Civil Service Tribunal for judgment where the state of the proceedings does not permit a decision by the Court.

2. Where a case is referred back to the Civil Service Tribunal, the Tribunal shall be bound by the decision of the Court of First Instance on points of law.

Appendix C

Procedure before the Court of Justice

Rules of Procedure of the Court of Justice[1]

Interpretation

Article 1

In these Rules:

C1–001

-"Union Treaty" means the Treaty on European Union,

-"EC Treaty" means the Treaty establishing the European Community,

-"EAEC Treaty" means the Treaty establishing the European Atomic Energy Community,

-"Statute" means the Protocol on the Statute of the Court of Justice,

-"EEA Agreement" means the Agreement on the European Economic Area.

For the purposes of these Rules:

-"institutions" means the institutions of the Communities and bodies which are established by the Treaties, or by an act adopted in implementation thereof, and which may be parties before the Court,

-"EFTA Surveillance Authority" means the surveillance authority referred to in the EEA Agreement.

TITLE 1

ORGANISATION OF THE COURT

Chapter 1

Judges and Advocates General

Article 2

The term of office of a Judge shall begin on the date laid down in his instrument of appointment. In the absence of any provisions regarding the date, the term shall begin on the date of the instrument.

---

[1] This edition consolidates the Rules of Procedure of the Court of Justice of the European Communities of June 19, 1991, [1991] O.J. L176/7, and [1992] O.J. L383/117 (corrigenda), as amended on February 21, 1995 ([1995] O.J. L44/61), on March 11, 1997 ([1997] O.J. L103/1, and [1997] O.J. L351/72 (corrigenda)), on May 16, 2000 ([2000] O.J. L122/43), on November 28, 2000 ([2000] O.J. L322/1), on April 3, 2001 ([2001] O.J. L119/1), on September 17, 2002 ([2002] O.J. L272/24, and [2002] O.J. L281/24 (corrigenda)), on April 8, 2003 ([2003] O.J. L147/17), on July 10, 2003 ([2003] O.J. L172/12), on April 19, 2004 ([2004] O.J. L132/2), on April 20, 2004 ([2004] O.J. L127/107), on July 12, 2005 ([2005] O.J. L203/19), and on October 18, 2005 ([2005] O.J. L288/51).

Article 3

1. Before taking up his duties, a Judge shall at the first public sitting of the Court which he attends after his appointment take the following oath:
"I swear that I will perform my duties impartially and conscientiously; I swear that I will preserve the secrecy of the deliberations of the Court".
2. Immediately after taking the oath, a Judge shall sign a declaration by which he solemnly undertakes that, both during and after his term of office, he will respect the obligations arising therefrom, and in particular the duty to behave with integrity and discretion as regards the acceptance, after he has ceased to hold office, of certain appointments and benefits.

Article 4

When the Court is called upon to decide whether a Judge no longer fulfils the requisite conditions or no longer meets the obligations arising from his office, the President shall invite the Judge concerned to make representations to the Court, in closed session and in the absence of the Registrar.

Article 5

Articles 2, 3 and 4 of these Rules shall apply to Advocates General.

Article 6

Judges and Advocates General shall rank equally in precedence according to their seniority in office.
Where there is equal seniority in office, precedence shall be determined by age.
Retiring Judges and Advocates General who are reappointed shall retain their former precedence.

Chapter 2

Presidency of the Court and Constitution of the Chambers

Article 7

1. The Judges shall, immediately after the partial replacement provided for in Article 223 of the EC Treaty, and Article 139 of the EAEC Treaty, elect one of their number as President of the Court for a term of three years.
2. If the office of the President of the Court falls vacant before the normal date of expiry thereof, the Court shall elect a successor for the remainder of the term.
3. The elections provided for in this Article shall be by secret ballot. If a Judge obtains an absolute majority he shall be elected. If no Judge obtains an absolute majority, a second ballot shall be held and the Judge obtaining the most votes shall be elected. Where two or more Judges obtain an equal number of votes the oldest of them shall be deemed elected.

Article 8

The President shall direct the judicial business and the administration of the Court; he shall preside at hearings and deliberations.

Article 9

1. The Court shall set up Chambers of five and three Judges in accordance with Article 16 of the Statute and shall decide which Judges shall be attached to them.

The assignment of Judges to Chambers shall be published in the *Official Journal of the European Union*.

2. As soon as an application initiating proceedings has been lodged, the President shall designate a Judge to act as Rapporteur.

3. For cases assigned to a formation of the Court in accordance with Article 44(3), the word 'Court' in these Rules shall mean that formation.

4. In cases assigned to a Chamber of five or three Judges, the powers of the President of the Court shall be exercised by the President of the Chamber.

Article 10

1. The Judges shall, immediately after the election of the President of the Court, elect the Presidents of the Chambers of five Judges for a term of three years.

The Judges shall elect the Presidents of the Chambers of three Judges for a term of one year.

The Court shall appoint for a period of one year the First Advocate General.

The provisions of Article 7(2) and (3) shall apply.

The elections and appointment made in pursuance of this paragraph shall be published in the *Official Journal of the European Union*.

2. The First Advocate General shall assign each case to an Advocate General as soon as the Judge-Rapporteur has been designated by the President. He shall take the necessary steps if an Advocate General is absent or prevented from acting.

Article 11

When the President of the Court is absent or is prevented from attending or when the office of President is vacant, the functions of President shall be exercised by a President of a Chamber of five Judges according to the order of precedence laid down in Article 6 of these Rules

When the President of the Court and the Presidents of the Chambers of five Judges are all absent or prevented from attending at the same time, or their posts are vacant at the same time, the functions of President shall be exercised by one of the Presidents of the Chambers of three Judges according to the order of precedence laid down in Article 6 of these Rules.

If the President of the Court and all the Presidents of Chambers are all absent or prevented from attending at the same time, or their posts are vacant at the same time, the functions of President shall be exercised by one of the other Judges according to the order of precedence laid down in Article 6 of these Rules.

Chapter 2a

Formations of the Court

Article 11a

The Court shall sit in the following formations:

- the full Court, composed of all the Judges;

- the Grand Chamber, composed of 13 Judges in accordance with Article 11b,

- Chambers composed of five or three Judges in accordance with Article 11c.

Article 11b

1. For each case the Grand Chamber shall be composed of the President of the Court, the Presidents of the Chambers of five Judges, the Judge-Rapporteur and the

number of Judges necessary to reach 13. The lastmentioned Judges shall be designated from the list referred to in paragraph 2, following the order laid down therein. The starting-point on that list, in every case assigned to the Grand Chamber, shall be the name of the Judge immediately following the last Judge designated from the list for the preceding case assigned to that formation of the Court.

2. After the election of the President of the Court and of the Presidents of the Chambers of five Judges, a list of the other Judges shall be drawn up for the purposes of determining the composition of the Grand Chamber. That list shall follow the order laid down in Article 6 of these Rules, alternating with the reverse order: the first Judge on that list shall be the first according to the order laid down in that Article, the second Judge shall be the last according to that order, the third Judge shall be the second according to that order, the fourth Judge the penultimate according to that order, and so on.

The list shall be published in the *Official Journal of the European Union*.

3. In cases which are assigned to the Grand Chamber between the beginning of a year in which there is a partial replacement of Judges and the moment when that replacement has taken place, two substitute Judges shall also sit. Those substitute Judges shall be the two Judges appearing in the list referred to in the previous paragraph immediately after the last Judge designated for the composition of the Grand Chamber in the case.

The substitute Judges shall replace, in the order of the list referred to in the previous paragraph, such Judges as are unable to take part in the decision on the case.

Article 11c

1. The Chambers of five Judges and three Judges shall, for each case, be composed of the President of the Chamber, the Judge-Rapporteur and the number of Judges required to attain the number of five and three Judges respectively. Those last-mentioned Judges shall be designated from the lists referred to in paragraph 2 and following the order laid down in them. The starting-point in those lists, for every case assigned to a Chamber, shall be the name of the Judge immediately following the last Judge designated from the list for the preceding case assigned to the Chamber concerned.

2. For the composition of the Chambers of five Judges, after the election of the Presidents of those Chambers lists shall be drawn up including all the Judges attached to the Chamber concerned, with the exception of its President. The lists shall be drawn up in the same way as the list referred to in Article 11b(2).

For the composition of the Chambers of three Judges, after the election of the Presidents of those Chambers lists shall be drawn up including all the Judges attached to the Chamber concerned, with the exception of its President. The lists shall be drawn up according to the order laid down in Article 6 of these Rules.

The lists referred to in this paragraph shall be published in the *Official Journal of the European Union*.

Article 11d

1. Where the Court considers that several cases must be heard and determined together by one and the same formation of the Court, the composition of that formation shall be that fixed for the case in respect of which the preliminary report was first examined.

2. Where a Chamber to which a case has been assigned refers the case back to the Court under Article 44(4), in order that it may be reassigned to a formation composed of a greater number of Judges, that formation shall include the members of the Chamber which has referred the case back.

Article 11e

When a member of the formation determining a case is prevented from attending, he shall be replaced by a Judge according to the order of the lists referred to in Article 11b(2) or 11c(2).

When the President of the Court is prevented from attending, the functions of the President of the Grand Chamber shall be exercised in accordance with the provisions of Article 11.

When the President of a Chamber of five Judges is prevented from attending, the functions of President of the Chamber shall be exercised by a President of a Chamber of three Judges, where necessary according to the order laid down in Article 6 of these Rules or, if that Chamber does not include a President of a Chamber of three Judges, by one of the other Judges according to the order laid down in Article 6.

When the President of a Chamber of three Judges is prevented from attending, the functions of President of the Chamber shall be exercised by a Judge of that Chamber according to the order laid down in Article 6 of these Rules.

Chapter 3

Registry

Section 1—The Registrar and Assistant Registrars

Article 12

1. The Court shall appoint the Registrar. Two weeks before the date fixed for making the appointment, the President shall inform the Members of the Court of the applications which have been made for the post.

2. An application shall be accompanied by full details of the candidate's age, nationality, university degrees, knowledge of any languages, present and past occupations and experience, if any, in judicial and international fields.

3. The appointment shall be made following the procedure laid down in Article 7(3) of these Rules.

4. The Registrar shall be appointed for a term of six years. He may be reappointed.

5. The Registrar shall take the oath in accordance with Article 3 of these Rules.

6. The Registrar may be deprived of his office only if he no longer fulfils the requisite conditions or no longer meets the obligations arising from his office; the Court shall take its decision after giving the Registrar an opportunity to make representations.

7. If the office of Registrar falls vacant before the normal date of expiry of the term thereof, the Court shall appoint a new Registrar for a term of six years.

Article 13

The Court may, following the procedure laid down in respect of the Registrar, appoint one or more Assistant Registrars to assist the Registrar and to take his place in so far as the Instructions to the Registrar referred to in Article 15 of these Rules allow.

Article 14

Where the Registrar and the Assistant Registrars are absent or prevented from attending or their posts are vacant, the President shall designate an official or other servant to carry out temporarily the duties of Registrar.

Article 15

Instructions to the Registrar shall be adopted by the Court acting on a proposal from the President.

Article 16

1. There shall be kept in the Registry, under the control of the Registrar, a register in which all pleadings and supporting documents shall be entered in the order in which they are lodged.

2. When a document has been registered, the Registrar shall make a note to that effect on the original and, if a party so requests, on any copy submitted for the purpose.

3. Entries in the register and the notes provided for in the preceding paragraph shall be authentic.

4. Rules for keeping the register shall be prescribed by the Instructions to the Registrar referred to in Article 15 of these Rules.

5. Persons having an interest may consult the register at the Registry and may obtain copies or extracts on payment of a charge on a scale fixed by the Court on a proposal from the Registrar.

The parties to a case may on payment of the appropriate charge also obtain copies of pleadings and authenticated copies of judgments and orders.

6. Notice shall be given in the *Official Journal of the European Union* of the date of registration of an application initiating proceedings, the names and addresses of the parties, the subject-matter of the proceedings, the form of order sought by the applicant and a summary of the pleas in law and of the main supporting arguments.

7. Where the Council or the Commission is not a party to a case, the Court shall send to it copies of the application and of the defence, without the annexes thereto, to enable it to assess whether the inapplicability of one of its acts is being invoked under Article 241 of the EC Treaty, or Article 156 of the EAEC Treaty. Copies of that act shall likewise be sent to the European Parliament, to enable it to assess whether the inapplicability of an act adopted jointly by that institution and by the Council is being invoked under Article 241 of the EC Treaty.

Article 17

1. The Registrar shall be responsible, under the authority of the President, for the acceptance, transmission and custody of documents and for effecting service as provided for by these Rules.

2. The Registrar shall assist the Court, the President and the Presidents of Chambers and the Judges in all their official functions.

Article 18

The Registrar shall have custody of the seals. He shall be responsible for the records and be in charge of the publications of the Court.

Article 19

Subject to Articles 4 and 27 of these Rules, the Registrar shall attend the sittings of the Court and of the Chambers.

Section 2—Other departments

Article 20

1. The officials and other servants of the Court shall be appointed in accordance with the provisions of the Staff Regulations.

2. Before taking up his duties, an official shall take the following oath before the President, in the presence of the Registrar:

"I swear that I will perform loyally, discreetly and conscientiously the duties assigned to me by the Court of Justice of the European Communities."

Article 21

The organisation of the departments of the Court shall be laid down, and may be modified, by the Court on a proposal from the Registrar.

Article 22

The Court shall set up a translating service staffed by experts with adequate legal training and a thorough knowledge of several official languages of the Court.

Article 23

The Registrar shall be responsible, under the authority of the President, for the administration of the Court, its financial management and its accounts; he shall be assisted in this by an administrator.

Chapter 4

Assistant Rapporteurs

Article 24

1. Where the Court is of the opinion that the consideration of and preparatory inquiries in cases before it so require, it shall, pursuant to Article 13 of the Statute, propose the appointment of Assistant Rapporteurs.

2. Assistant Rapporteurs shall in particular assist the President in connection with applications for the adoption of interim measures and assist the Judge-Rapporteurs in their work.

3. In the performance of their duties the Assistant Rapporteurs shall be responsible to the President of the Court, the President of a Chamber or a Judge-Rapporteur, as the case may be.

4. Before taking up his duties, an Assistant Rapporteur shall take before the Court the oath set out in Article 3 of these Rules.

Chapter 5

The Working of the Court

Article 25

1. The dates and times of the sittings of the Grand Chamber and of the full Court shall be fixed by the President.

2. The dates and times of the sittings of the Chambers of five and three Judges shall be fixed by their respective Presidents.

3. The Court may choose to hold one or more sittings in a place other than that in which the Court has its seat.

Article 26

1. Where, by reason of a Judge being absent or prevented from attending, there is an even number of Judges, the most junior Judge within the meaning of Article 6 of these Rules shall abstain from taking part in the deliberations unless he is the Judge-Rapporteur. In that case the Judge immediately senior to him shall abstain from taking part in the deliberations.

2. If after the Grand Chamber or full Court has been convened it is found that the quorum referred to in the third or fourth paragraph of Article 17 of the Statute has not been attained, the President shall adjourn the sitting until there is a quorum.

3. If in any Chamber of five or three Judges the quorum referred to in the second paragraph of Article 17 of the Statute has not been attained and it is not possible to replace the Judges prevented from attending in accordance with Article 11e, the President of that Chamber shall so inform the President of the Court who shall designate another Judge to complete the Chamber.

Article 27

1. The Court shall deliberate in closed session.

2. Only those Judges who were present at the oral proceedings and the Assistant Rapporteur, if any, entrusted with the consideration of the case may take part in the deliberations.

3. Every Judge taking part in the deliberations shall state his opinion and the reasons for it.

4. Any Judge may require that any questions be formulated in the language of his choice and communicated in writing to the Court before being put to the vote.

5. The conclusions reached by the majority of the Judges after final discussion shall determine the decision of the Court. Votes shall be cast in reverse order to the order of precedence laid down in Article 6 of these Rules.

6. Differences of view on the substance, wording or order of questions or on the interpretation of the voting shall be settled by decision of the Court.

7. Where the deliberations of the Court concern questions of its own administration, the Advocates General shall take part and have a vote. The Registrar shall be present, unless the Court decides to the contrary.

11. Where the Court sits without the Registrar being present it shall, if necessary, instruct the most junior Judge within the meaning of Article 6 of these Rules to draw up minutes. The minutes shall be signed by that Judge and by the President.

Article 28

1. Subject to any special decision of the Court, its vacations shall be as follows:

- from 18 December to 10 January,

- from the Sunday before Easter to the second Sunday after Easter,

- from 15 July to 15 September.

During the vacations, the functions of President shall be exercised at the place where the Court has its seat either by the President himself, keeping in touch with the Registrar, or by a President of Chamber or other Judge invited by the President to take his place.

2. In a case of urgency, the President may convene the Judges and the Advocates General during the vacations.

3. The Court shall observe the official holidays of the place where it has its seat.

4. The Court may, in proper circumstances, grant leave of absence to any Judge or Advocate General.

Chapter 6

Languages

Article 29

1. The language of a case shall be Czech, Danish, Dutch, English, Estonian, Finnish, French, German, Greek, Hungarian, Irish, Italian, Latvian, Lithuanian, Maltese, Polish, Portuguese, Slovak, Slovene, Spanish or Swedish.

2. The language of a case shall be chosen by the applicant, except that:

(a) where the defendant is a Member State or a natural or legal person having the nationality of a Member State, the language of the case shall be the official language of that State; where that State has more than one official language, the applicant may choose between them;

(b) at the joint request of the parties, the use of another of the languages mentioned in paragraph 1 for all or part of the proceedings may be authorised;

(c) at the request of one of the parties, and after the opposite party and the Advocate General have been heard, the use of another of the languages mentioned in paragraph 1 as the language of the case for all or part of the proceedings may be authorised by way of derogation from subparagraphs (a) and (b); such a request may not be submitted by an institution of the European Communities.

In cases to which Article 103 of these Rules applies, the language of the case shall be the language of the national court or tribunal which refers the matter to the Court. At the duly substantiated request of one of the parties to the main proceedings, and after the opposite party and the Advocate General have been heard, the use of another of the languages mentioned in paragraph 1 may be authorised for the oral procedure.

Requests as above may be decided on by the President; the latter may, and where he wishes to accede to a request without the agreement of all the parties, must, refer the request to the Court.

3. The language of the case shall in particular be used in the written and oral pleadings of the parties and in supporting documents, and also in the minutes and decisions of the Court.

Any supporting documents expressed in another language must be accompanied by a translation into the language of the case.

In the case of lengthy documents, translations may be confined to extracts. However, the Court may, of its own motion or at the request of a party, at any time call for a complete or fuller translation.

Notwithstanding the foregoing provisions, a Member State shall be entitled to use its official language when intervening in a case before the Court or when taking part in any reference of a kind mentioned in Article 103. This provision shall apply both to written statements and to oral addresses. The Registrar shall cause any such statement or address to be translated into the language of the case.

The States, other than the Member States, which are parties to the EEA Agreement, and also the EFTA Surveillance Authority, may be authorised to use one of the languages mentioned in paragraph 1, other than the language of the case, when they intervene in a case before the Court or participate in preliminary ruling proceedings envisaged by Article 23 of the Statute. This provision shall apply both to written statements and oral addresses. The Registrar shall cause any such statement or address to be translated into the language of the case.

Non-member States taking part in proceedings for a preliminary ruling pursuant to the fourth paragraph of Article 23 of the Statute may be authorised to use one of the languages mentioned in paragraph (1) of this Article other than the language of the case. This provision shall apply both to written statements and to oral statements. The Registrar shall cause any such statement or address to be translated into the language of the case.

4. Where a witness or expert states that he is unable adequately to express himself in one of the languages referred to in paragraph (1) of this Article, the Court may authorise him to give his evidence in another language. The Registrar shall arrange for translation into the language of the case.

5. The President of the Court and the Presidents of Chambers in conducting oral proceedings, the Judge-Rapporteur both in his preliminary report and in his report for the hearing, Judges and Advocates General in putting questions and Advocates General in delivering their opinions may use one of the languages referred to in paragraph 1 of this Article other than the language of the case. The Registrar shall arrange for translation into the language of the case.

Article 30

1. The Registrar shall, at the request of any Judge, of the Advocate General or of a party, arrange for anything said or written in the course of the proceedings before the Court to be translated into the languages he chooses from those referred to in Article 29(1).

2. Publications of the Court shall be issued in the languages referred to in Article 1 of Council Regulation No 1.

Article 31

The texts of documents drawn up in the language of the case or in any other language authorised by the Court pursuant to Article 29 of these Rules shall be authentic.

Chapter 7

Rights and Obligations of Agents, Advisers and Lawyers

Article 32

1. Agents, advisers and lawyers appearing before the Court or before any judicial authority to which the Court has addressed letters rogatory, shall enjoy immunity in respect of words spoken or written by them concerning the case or the parties.

2. Agents, advisers and lawyers shall enjoy the following further privileges and facilities:

(a) papers and documents relating to the proceedings shall be exempt from both search and seizure; in the event of a dispute the customs officials or police may seal those papers and documents; they shall then be immediately forwarded to the Court for inspection in the presence of the Registrar and of the person concerned;

(b) agents, advisers and lawyers shall be entitled to such allocation of foreign currency as may be necessary for the performance of their duties;

(c) agents, advisers and lawyers shall be entitled to travel in the course of duty without hindrance.

Article 33

In order to qualify for the privileges, immunities and facilities specified in Article 32, persons entitled to them shall furnish proof of their status as follows:

(a) agents shall produce an official document issued by the party for whom they act, and shall forward without delay a copy thereof to the Registrar;

(b) advisers and lawyers shall produce a certificate signed by the Registrar. The validity of this certificate shall be limited to a specified period, which may be extended or curtailed according to the length of the proceedings.

Article 34

The privileges, immunities and facilities specified in Article 32 of these Rules are granted exclusively in the interests of the proper conduct of proceedings.

The Court may waive the immunity where it considers that the proper conduct of proceedings will not be hindered thereby.

Article 35

1. If the Court considers that the conduct of an adviser or lawyer towards the Court, a Judge, an Advocate General or the Registrar is incompatible with the dignity of the Court or with the requirements of the proper administration of justice, or that such adviser or lawyer is using his rights for purposes other than those for which they were granted, it shall inform the person concerned. If the Court informs the competent authorities to whom the person concerned is answerable, a copy of the letter sent to those authorities shall be forwarded to the person concerned.

On the same grounds, the Court may at any time, having heard the person concerned and the Advocate General, exclude the person concerned from the proceedings by order. That order shall have immediate effect.

2. Where an adviser or lawyer is excluded from the proceedings, the proceedings shall be suspended for a period fixed by the President in order to allow the party concerned to appoint another adviser or lawyer.

3. Decisions taken under this Article may be rescinded.

Article 36

The provisions of this Chapter shall apply to university teachers who have a right of audience before the Court in accordance with Article 19 of the Statute.

TITLE II

PROCEDURE

Chapter 1

Written Procedure

Article 37

1. The original of every pleading must be signed by the party's agent or lawyer.

The original, accompanied by all annexes referred to therein, shall be lodged together with five copies for the Court and a copy for every other party to the proceedings. Copies shall be certified by the party lodging them.

2. Institutions shall in addition produce, within time-limits laid down by the Court, translations of all pleadings into the other languages provided for by Article 1 of Council Regulation No 1. The second subparagraph of paragraph 1 of this Article shall apply.

3. All pleadings shall bear a date. In the reckoning of time-limits for taking steps in proceedings, only the date of lodgment at the Registry shall be taken into account.

4. To every pleading there shall be annexed a file containing the documents relied on in support of it, together with a schedule listing them.

5. Where in view of the length of a document only extracts from it are annexed to the pleading, the whole document or a full copy of it shall be lodged at the Registry.

6. Without prejudice to the provisions of paragraphs 1 to 5, the date on which a copy of the signed original of a pleading, including the schedule of documents referred to in paragraph 4, is received at the Registry by telefax or other technical means of communication available to the Court shall be deemed to be the date of lodgment for the purposes of compliance with the time-limits for taking steps in proceedings, provided that the signed original of the pleading, accompanied by the annexes and copies referred to in the second subparagraph of paragraph 1 above, is lodged at the Registry no later than 10 days thereafter. Article 81(2) shall not be applicable to this period of 10 days.

7. Without prejudice to the first subparagraph of paragraph 1 or to paragraphs 2 to 5, the Court may by decision determine the criteria for a procedural document sent to the Registry by electronic means to be deemed to be the original of that document. That decision shall be published in the *Official Journal of the European Union*.

Article 38

1. An application of the kind referred to in Article 21 of the Statute shall state:

   (a) the name and address of the applicant;

   (b) the designation of the party against whom the application is made;

   (c) the subject-matter of the proceedings and a summary of the pleas in law on which the application is based;

   (d) the form of order sought by the applicant;

(e) where appropriate, the nature of any evidence offered in support.

2. For the purpose of the proceedings, the application shall state an address for service in the place where the Court has its seat and the name of the person who is authorised and has expressed willingness to accept service.

In addition to, or instead of, specifying an address for service as referred to in the first subparagraph, the application may state that the lawyer or agent agrees that service is to be effected on him by telefax or other technical means of communication.

If the application does not comply with the requirements referred to in the first and second subparagraphs, all service on the party concerned for the purpose of the proceedings shall be effected, for so long as the defect has not been cured, by registered letter addressed to the agent or lawyer of that party. By way of derogation from Article 79(1), service shall then be deemed to be duly effected by the lodging of the registered letter at the post office of the place where the Court has its seat.

3. The lawyer acting for a party must lodge at the Registry a certificate that he is authorised to practise before a court of a Member State or of another State which is a party to the EEA Agreement.

4. The application shall be accompanied, where appropriate, by the documents specified in the second paragraph of Article 21 of the Statute.

5. An application made by a legal person governed by private law shall be accompanied by:

(a) the instrument or instruments constituting or regulating that legal person or a recent extract from the register of companies, firms or associations or any other proof of its existence in law;

(b) proof that the authority granted to the applicant's lawyer has been properly conferred on him by someone authorised for the purpose.

6. An application submitted under Articles 238 and 239 of the EC Treaty—and Articles 153 and 154 of the EAEC Treaty shall be accompanied by a copy of the arbitration clause contained in the contract governed by private or public law entered into by the Communities or on their behalf, or, as the case may be, by a copy of the special agreement concluded between the Member States concerned.

7. If an application does not comply with the requirements set out in paragraphs 3 to 6 of this Article, the Registrar shall prescribe a reasonable period within which the applicant is to comply with them whether by putting the application itself in order or by producing any of the abovementioned documents. If the applicant fails to put the application in order or to produce the required documents within the time prescribed, the Court shall, after hearing the Advocate General, decide whether the non-compliance with these conditions renders the application formally inadmissible.

Article 39

The application shall be served on the defendant. In a case where Article 38(7) applies, service shall be effected as soon as the application has been put in order or the Court has declared it admissible notwithstanding the failure to observe the formal requirements set out in that Article.

Article 40

1. Within one month after service on him of the application, the defendant shall lodge a defence, stating:

(a) the name and address of the defendant;

(b) the arguments of fact and law relied on;

(c) the form of order sought by the defendant;

(d) the nature of any evidence offered by him.

The provisions of Article 38(2) to (5) of these Rules shall apply to the defence.

2. The time-limit laid down in paragraph 1 of this Article may be extended by the President on a reasoned application by the defendant.

Article 41

1. The application initiating the proceedings and the defence may be supplemented by a reply from the applicant and by a rejoinder from the defendant.

2. The President shall fix the time-limits within which these pleadings are to be lodged.

Article 42

1. In reply or rejoinder a party may offer further evidence. The party must, however, give reasons for the delay in offering it.

2. No new plea in law may be introduced in the course of proceedings unless it is based on matters of law or of fact which come to light in the course of the procedure.

If in the course of the procedure one of the parties puts forward a new plea in law which is so based, the President may, even after the expiry of the normal procedural time-limits, acting on a report of the Judge-Rapporteur and after hearing the Advocate General, allow the other party time to answer on that plea.

The decision on the admissibility of the plea shall be reserved for the final judgment.

Article 43

The Court may, at any time, after hearing the parties and the Advocate General, if the assignment referred to in Article 10(2) has taken place, order that two or more cases concerning the same subject-matter shall, on account of the connection between them, be joined for the purposes of the written or oral procedure or of the final judgment. The cases may subsequently be disjoined. The President may refer these matters to the Court.

Chapter 1a

The Preliminary Report and Assignment of Cases to Formations

Article 44

1. The President shall fix a date on which the Judge-Rapporteur is to present his preliminary report to the general meeting of the Court, either:

(a) after the rejoinder has been lodged, or

(b) where no reply or no rejoinder has been lodged within the time-limit fixed in accordance with Article 41(2), or

(c) where the party concerned has waived his right to lodge a reply or rejoinder, or

(d) where the expedited procedure referred to in Article 62a is to be applied, when the President fixes a date for the hearing.

2. The preliminary report shall contain recommendations as to whether a preparatory inquiry or any other preparatory step should be undertaken and as to the formation to which the case should be assigned. It shall also contain the Judge-Rapporteur's recommendation, if any, as to whether to dispense with a hearing as provided for in Article 44a and as to whether to dispense with an Opinion of the Advocate General pursuant to the fifth subparagraph of Article 20 of the Statute.

The Court shall decide, after hearing the Advocate General, what action to take upon the recommendations of the Judge-Rapporteur.

3. The Court shall assign to the Chambers of five and three Judges any case brought before it in so far as the difficulty or importance of the case or particular circumstances are not such as to require that it should be assigned to the Grand Chamber.

However, a case may not be assigned to a Chamber of five or three Judges if a Member State or an institution of the Communities, being a party to the proceedings, has requested that the case be decided by the Grand Chamber. For the purposes of this provision, "party to the proceedings" means any Member State or any institution which is a party to or an intervener in the proceedings or which has submitted written observations in any reference of a kind mentioned in Article 103. A request such as that referred to in this subparagraph may not be made in proceedings between the Communities and their servants.

The Court shall sit as a full Court where cases are brought before it pursuant to the provisions referred to in the fourth paragraph of Article 16 of the Statute. It may assign a case to the full Court where, in accordance with the fifth paragraph of Article 16 of the Statute, it considers that the case is of exceptional importance.

4. The formation to which a case has been assigned may, at any stage of the proceedings, refer the case back to the Court in order that it may be reassigned to a formation composed of a greater number of Judges.

5. Where a preparatory inquiry has been opened, the formation determining the case may, if it does not undertake it itself, assign the inquiry to the Judge-Rapporteur.

Where the oral procedure is opened without an inquiry, the President of the formation determining the case shall fix the opening date.

Article 44a

Without prejudice to any special provisions laid down in these Rules, the procedure before the Court shall also include an oral part. However, after the pleadings referred to in Article 40(1) and, as the case may be, in Article 41(1) have been lodged, the Court, acting on a report from the Judge-Rapporteur and after hearing the Advocate General, and if none of the parties has submitted an application setting out the reasons for which he wishes to be heard, may decide otherwise. The application shall be submitted within a period of three weeks from notification to the party of the close of the written procedure. That period may be extended by the President.

Chapter 2

Preparatory Inquiries and Other Preparatory Measures

Section 1—Measures of inquiry

Article 45

1. The Court, after hearing the Advocate General, shall prescribe the measures of inquiry that it considers appropriate by means of an order setting out the facts to be proved. Before the Court decides on the measures of inquiry referred to in paragraph 2(c), (d) and (e) the parties shall be heard.

The order shall be served on the parties.

2. Without prejudice to Articles 24 and 25 of the Statute, the following measures of inquiry may be adopted:

    (a) the personal appearance of the parties;

    (b) a request for information and production of documents;

    (c) oral testimony;

    (d) the commissioning of an expert's report;

    (e) an inspection of the place or thing in question.

3. The Advocate General shall take part in the measures of inquiry.

4. Evidence may be submitted in rebuttal and previous evidence may be amplified.

Article 46

1. A Chamber to which a preparatory inquiry has been assigned may exercise the powers vested in the Court by Articles 45 and 47 to 53 of these Rules; the powers vested in the President of the Court may be exercised by the President of the Chamber.

2. Articles 56 and 57 of these Rules shall apply to proceedings before the Chamber.

3. The parties shall be entitled to attend the measures of inquiry.

Section 2—The summoning and examination of witnesses and experts

Article 47

1. The Court may, either of its own motion or on application by a party, and after hearing the Advocate General, order that certain facts be proved by witnesses. The order of the Court shall set out the facts to be established.

The Court may summon a witness of its own motion or on application by a party or at the instance of the Advocate General.

An application by a party for the examination of a witness shall state precisely about what facts and for what reasons the witness should be examined.

2. The witness shall be summoned by an order of the Court containing the following information:

(a) the surname, forenames, description and address of the witness;

(b) an indication of the facts about which the witness is to be examined;

(c) where appropriate, particulars of the arrangements made by the Court for reimbursement of expenses incurred by the witness, and of the penalties which may be imposed on defaulting witnesses.

The order shall be served on the parties and the witnesses.

3. The Court may make the summoning of a witness for whose examination a party has applied conditional upon the deposit with the cashier of the Court of a sum sufficient to cover the taxed costs thereof; the Court shall fix the amount of the payment.

The cashier shall advance the funds necessary in connection with the examination of any witness summoned by the Court of its own motion.

4. After the identity of the witness has been established, the President shall inform him that he will be required to vouch the truth of his evidence in the manner laid down in these Rules.

The witness shall give his evidence to the Court, the parties having been given notice to attend. After the witness has given his main evidence the President may, at the request of a party or of his own motion, put questions to him.

The other Judges and the Advocate General may do likewise.

Subject to the control of the President, questions may be put to witnesses by the representatives of the parties.

5. After giving his evidence, the witness shall take the following oath:

"I swear that I have spoken the truth, the whole truth and nothing but the truth."

The Court may, after hearing the parties, exempt a witness from taking the oath.

6. The Registrar shall draw up minutes in which the evidence of each witness is reproduced.

The minutes shall be signed by the President or by the Judge-Rapporteur responsible for conducting the examination of the witness, and by the Registrar. Before the minutes are thus signed, witnesses must be given an opportunity to check the content of the minutes and to sign them.

The minutes shall constitute an official record.

Article 48

1. Witnesses who have been duly summoned shall obey the summons and attend for examination.

2. If a witness who has been duly summoned fails to appear before the Court, the Court may impose upon him a pecuniary penalty not exceeding EUR 5 000[1] and may order that a further summons be served on the witness at his own expense.

The same penalty may be imposed upon a witness who, without good reason, refuses to give evidence or to take the oath or where appropriate to make a solemn affirmation equivalent thereto.

3. If the witness proffers a valid excuse to the Court, the pecuniary penalty imposed on him may be cancelled. The pecuniary penalty imposed may be reduced at the request of the witness where he establishes that it is disproportionate to his income.

---

[1] See Article 2 of Council Regulation EC No 1103/97 (OJ L 162 of 19.6.1997, p. 1).

4. Penalties imposed and other measures ordered under this Article shall be enforced in accordance with Articles 244 and 256 of the EC Treaty—and Articles 159 and 164 of the EAEC Treaty.

Article 49

1. The Court may order that an expert's report be obtained. The order appointing the expert shall define his task and set a time-limit within which he is to make his report.

2. The expert shall receive a copy of the order, together with all the documents necessary for carrying out his task. He shall be under the supervision of the Judge-Rapporteur, who may be present during his investigation and who shall be kept informed of his progress in carrying out his task.

The Court may request the parties or one of them to lodge security for the costs of the expert's report.

3. At the request of the expert, the Court may order the examination of witnesses. Their examination shall be carried out in accordance with Article 47 of these Rules.

4. The expert may give his opinion only on points which have been expressly referred to him.

5. After the expert has made his report, the Court may order that he be examined, the parties having been given notice to attend.

Subject to the control of the President, questions may be put to the expert by the representatives of the parties.

6. After making his report, the expert shall take the following oath before the Court:

"I swear that I have conscientiously and impartially carried out my task."

The Court may, after hearing the parties, exempt the expert from taking the oath.

Article 50

1. If one of the parties objects to a witness or to an expert on the ground that he is not a competent or proper person to act as witness or expert or for any other reason, or if a witness or expert refuses to give evidence, to take the oath or to make a solemn affirmation equivalent thereto, the matter shall be resolved by the Court.

2. An objection to a witness or to an expert shall be raised within two weeks after service of the order summoning the witness or appointing the expert; the statement of objection must set out the grounds of objection and indicate the nature of any evidence offered.

Article 51

1. Witnesses and experts shall be entitled to reimbursement of their travel and subsistence expenses. The cashier of the Court may make a payment to them towards these expenses in advance.

2. Witnesses shall be entitled to compensation for loss of earnings, and experts to fees for their services. The cashier of the Court shall pay witnesses and experts their compensation or fees after they have carried out their respective duties or tasks.

Article 52

The Court may, on application by a party or of its own motion, issue letters rogatory for the examination of witnesses or experts, as provided for in the supplementary rules mentioned in Article 125 of these Rules.

Article 53

1. The Registrar shall draw up minutes of every hearing. The minutes shall be signed by the President and by the Registrar and shall constitute an official record.

2. The parties may inspect the minutes and any expert's report at the Registry and obtain copies at their own expense.

Section 3—Closure of the preparatory inquiry

Article 54

Unless the Court prescribes a period within which the parties may lodge written observations, the President shall fix the date for the opening of the oral procedure after the preparatory inquiry has been completed.

Where a period had been prescribed for the lodging of written observations, the President shall fix the date for the opening of the oral procedure after that period has expired.

Section 4—Preparatory Measures

Article 54a

The Judge-Rapporteur and the Advocate General may request the parties to submit within a specified period all such information relating to the facts, and all such documents or other particulars, as they may consider relevant. The information and/or documents provided shall be communicated to the other parties.

Chapter 3

Oral Procedure

Article 55

1. Subject to the priority of decisions provided for in Article 85 of these Rules, the Court shall deal with the cases before it in the order in which the preparatory inquiries in them have been completed. Where the preparatory inquiries in several cases are completed simultaneously, the order in which they are to be dealt with shall be determined by the dates of entry in the register of the applications initiating them respectively.

2. The President may in special circumstances order that a case be given priority over others.

The President may in special circumstances, after hearing the parties and the Advocate General, either on his own initiative or at the request of one of the parties, defer a case to be dealt with at a later date. On a joint application by the parties the President may order that a case be deferred.

Article 56

1. The proceedings shall be opened and directed by the President, who shall be responsible for the proper conduct of the hearing.

2. The oral proceedings in cases heard *in camera* shall not be published.

Article 57

The President may in the course of the hearing put questions to the agents, advisers or lawyers of the parties.

The other Judges and the Advocate General may do likewise.

Article 58

A party may address the Court only through his agent, adviser or lawyer.

Article 59

1. The Advocate General shall deliver his opinion orally at the end of the oral procedure.
2. After the Advocate General has delivered his opinion, the President shall declare the oral procedure closed.

Article 60

The Court may at any time, in accordance with Article 45(1), after hearing the Advocate General, order any measure of inquiry to be taken or that a previous inquiry be repeated or expanded. The Court may direct the Judge-Rapporteur to carry out the measures so ordered.

Article 61

The Court may after hearing the Advocate General order the reopening of the oral procedure.

Article 62

1. The Registrar shall draw up minutes of every hearing. The minutes shall be signed by the President and by the Registrar and shall constitute an official record.
2. The parties may inspect the minutes at the Registry and obtain copies at their own expense.

Chapter 3a

Expedited Procedures

Article 62a

1. On application by the applicant or the defendant, the President may exceptionally decide, on the basis of a recommendation by the Judge-Rapporteur and after hearing the other party and the Advocate General, that a case is to be determined pursuant to an expedited procedure derogating from the provisions of these Rules, where the particular urgency of the case requires the Court to give its ruling with the minimum of delay.

An application for a case to be decided under an expedited procedure shall be made by a separate document lodged at the same time as the application initiating the proceedings or the defence, as the case may be.

2. Under the expedited procedure, the originating application and the defence may be supplemented by a reply and a rejoinder only if the President considers this to be necessary.

An intervener may lodge a statement in intervention only if the President considers this to be necessary.

3. Once the defence has been lodged or, if the decision to adjudicate under an expedited procedure is not made until after that pleading has been lodged, once

that decision has been taken, the President shall fix a date for the hearing, which shall be communicated forthwith to the parties. He may postpone the date of the hearing where the organisation of measures of inquiry or of other preparatory measures so requires.

Without prejudice to Article 42, the parties may supplement their arguments and offer further evidence in the course of the oral procedure. They must, however, give reasons for the delay in offering such further evidence.

4. The Court shall give its ruling after hearing the Advocate General.

Chapter 4

Judgments

Article 63

The judgment shall contain:

- a statement that it is the judgment of the Court,
- the date of its delivery,
- the names of the President and of the Judges taking part in it,
- the name of the Advocate General,
- the name of the Registrar,
- the description of the parties,
- the names of the agents, advisers and lawyers of the parties,
- a statement of the forms of order sought by the parties,
- a statement that the Advocate General has been heard,
- a summary of the facts,
- the grounds for the decision,
- the operative part of the judgment, including the decision as to costs.

Article 64

1. The judgment shall be delivered in open court; the parties shall be given notice to attend to hear it.

2. The original of the judgment, signed by the President, by the Judges who took part in the deliberations and by the Registrar, shall be sealed and deposited at the Registry; the parties shall be served with certified copies of the judgment.

3. The Registrar shall record on the original of the judgment the date on which it was delivered.

Article 65

The judgment shall be binding from the date of its delivery.

Article 66

1. Without prejudice to the provisions relating to the interpretation of judgments the Court may, of its own motion or on application by a party made within two

667

weeks after the delivery of a judgment, rectify clerical mistakes, errors in calculation and obvious slips in it.

2. The parties, whom the Registrar shall duly notify, may lodge written observations within a period prescribed by the President.

3. The Court shall take its decision in closed session after hearing the Advocate General.

4. The original of the rectification order shall be annexed to the original of the rectified judgment. A note of this order shall be made in the margin of the original of the rectified judgment.

Article 67

If the Court should omit to give a decision on a specific head of claim or on costs, any party may within a month after service of the judgment apply to the Court to supplement its judgment.

The application shall be served on the opposite party and the President shall prescribe a period within which that party may lodge written observations.

After these observations have been lodged, the Court shall, after hearing the Advocate General, decide both on the admissibility and on the substance of the application.

Article 68

The Registrar shall arrange for the publication of reports of cases before the Court.

Chapter 5

Costs

Article 69

1. A decision as to costs shall be given in the final judgment or in the order which closes the proceedings.

2. The unsuccessful party shall be ordered to pay the costs if they have been applied for in the successful party's pleadings.

Where there are several unsuccessful parties the Court shall decide how the costs are to be shared.

3. Where each party succeeds on some and fails on other heads, or where the circumstances are exceptional, the Court may order that the costs be shared or that the parties bear their own costs.

The Court may order a party, even if successful, to pay costs which the Court considers that party to have unreasonably or vexatiously caused the opposite party to incur.

4. The Member States and institutions which intervene in the proceedings shall bear their own costs.

The States, other than the Member States, which are parties to the EEA Agreement, and also the EFTA Surveillance Authority, shall bear their own costs if they intervene in the proceedings.

The Court may order an intervener other than those mentioned in the preceding subparagraphs to bear his own costs.

5. A party who discontinues or withdraws from proceedings shall be ordered to pay the costs if they have been applied for in the other party's observations on the discontinuance. However, upon application by the party who discontinues or

withdraws from proceedings, the costs shall be borne by the other party if this appears justified by the conduct of that party.

Where the parties have come to an agreement on costs, the decision as to costs shall be in accordance with that agreement.

If costs are not claimed, the parties shall bear their own costs.

6. Where a case does not proceed to judgment the costs shall be in the discretion of the Court.

Article 70

Without prejudice to the second subparagraph of Article 69(3) of these Rules, in proceedings between the Communities and their servants the institutions shall bear their own costs.

Article 71

Costs necessarily incurred by a party in enforcing a judgment or order of the Court shall be refunded by the opposite party on the scale in force in the State where the enforcement takes place.

Article 72

Proceedings before the Court shall be free of charge, except that:

(a) where a party has caused the Court to incur avoidable costs the Court may, after hearing the Advocate General, order that party to refund them;

(b) where copying or translation work is carried out at the request of a party, the cost shall, in so far as the Registrar considers it excessive, be paid for by that party on the scale of charges referred to in Article 16(5) of these Rules.

Article 73

Without prejudice to the preceding Article, the following shall be regarded as recoverable costs:

(a) sums payable to witnesses and experts under Article 51 of these Rules;

(b) expenses necessarily incurred by the parties for the purpose of the proceedings, in particular the travel and subsistence expenses and the remuneration of agents, advisers or lawyers.

Article 74

1. If there is a dispute concerning the costs to be recovered, the formation of the Court to which the case has been referred shall, on application by the party concerned and after hearing the opposite party and the Advocate General, make an order.

2. The parties may, for the purposes of enforcement, apply for an authenticated copy of the order.

Article 75

1. Sums due from the cashier of the Court and from its debtors shall be paid in euro.

2. Where costs to be recovered have been incurred in a currency other than the euro or where the steps in respect of which payment is due were taken in a country of which the euro is not the currency, conversions of currency shall be made at the European Central Bank's official rates of exchange on the day of payment.

Chapter 6

Legal Aid

Article 76

1. A party who is wholly or in part unable to meet the costs of the proceedings may at any time apply for legal aid.

The application shall be accompanied by evidence of the applicant's need of assistance, and in particular by a document from the competent authority certifying his lack of means.

2. If the application is made prior to proceedings which the applicant wishes to commence, it shall briefly state the subject of such proceedings.

The application need not be made through a lawyer.

3. The President shall designate a Judge to act as Rapporteur. The Court, on the Judge-Rapporteur's proposal and after hearing the Advocate General, shall refer the application to a formation of the Court which shall decide whether legal aid should be granted in full or in part, or whether it should be refused. That formation shall consider whether there is manifestly no cause of action.

The formation of the Court shall give its decision by way of order. Where the application for legal aid is refused in whole or in part, the order shall state the reasons for that refusal.

4. The formation of the Court may at any time, either of its own motion or on application, withdraw legal aid if the circumstances which led to its being granted alter during the proceedings.

5. Where legal aid is granted, the cashier of the Court shall advance the funds necessary to meet the expenses.

In its decision as to costs the Court may order the payment to the cashier of the Court of the whole or any part of amounts advanced as legal aid.

The Registrar shall take steps to obtain the recovery of these sums from the party ordered to pay them.

Chapter 7

Discontinuance

Article 77

If, before the Court has given its decision, the parties reach a settlement of their dispute and intimate to the Court the abandonment of their claims, the President shall order the case to be removed from the register and shall give a decision as to costs in accordance with Article 69(5), having regard to any proposals made by the parties on the matter.

This provision shall not apply to proceedings under Articles 230 and 232 of the EC Treaty—and Articles 146 and 148 of the EAEC Treaty.

Article 78

If the applicant informs the Court in writing that he wishes to discontinue the proceedings, the President shall order the case to be removed from the register and shall give a decision as to costs in accordance with Article 69(5).

Chapter 8

Service

Article 79

1. Where these Rules require that a document be served on a person, the Registrar shall ensure that service is effected at that person's address for service either by the dispatch of a copy of the document by registered post with a form for acknowledgement of receipt or by personal delivery of the copy against a receipt.

The Registrar shall prepare and certify the copies of documents to be served, save where the parties themselves supply the copies in accordance with Article 37(1) of these Rules.

2. Where, in accordance with the second subparagraph of Article 38(2), the addressee has agreed that service is to be effected on him by telefax or other technical means of communication, any procedural document other than a judgment or order of the Court may be served by the transmission of a copy of the document by such means.

Where, for technical reasons or on account of the nature or length of the document, such transmission is impossible or impracticable, the document shall be served, if the addressee has failed to state an address for service, at his address in accordance with the procedures laid down in paragraph 1 of this article. The addressee shall be so advised by telefax or other technical means of communication. Service shall then be deemed to have been effected on the addressee by registered post on the tenth day following the lodging of the registered letter at the post office of the place where the Court has its seat, unless it is shown by the acknowledgement of receipt that the letter was received on a different date or the addressee informs the Registrar, within three weeks of being advised by telefax or other technical means of communication, that the document to be served has not reached him.

Chapter 9

Time-Limits

Article 80

1. Any period of time prescribed by the Union Treaty, the EC Treaty and the EAEC Treaty, the Statute of the Court or these Rules for the taking of any procedural step shall be reckoned as follows:

(a) where a period expressed in days, weeks, months or years is to be calculated from the moment at which an event occurs or an action takes place, the day during which that event occurs or that action takes place shall not be counted as falling within the period in question;

(b) a period expressed in weeks, months or in years shall end with the expiry of whichever day in the last week, month or year is the same day of the week, or falls on the same date, as the day during which the event or action from which the period is to be calculated occurred or took place. If, in a period expressed in months or in years, the day on which it should expire does not occur in the last month, the period shall end with the expiry of the last day of that month;

671

(c) where a period is expressed in months and days, it shall first be reckoned in whole months, then in days;

(d) periods shall include official holidays, Sundays and Saturdays;

(e) periods shall not be suspended during the judicial vacations.

2. If the period would otherwise end on a Saturday, Sunday or an official holiday, it shall be extended until the end of the first following working day.

A list of official holidays drawn up by the Court shall be published in the *Official Journal of the European Union.*

Article 81

1. Where the period of time allowed for initiating proceedings against a measure adopted by an institution runs from the publication of that measure, that period shall be calculated, for the purposes of Article 80(1)(a), from the end of the 14th day after publication thereof in the *Official Journal of the European Union.*

2. The prescribed time-limits shall be extended on account of distance by a single period of 10 days.

Article 82

Any time-limit prescribed pursuant to these Rules may be extended by whoever prescribed it.

The President and the Presidents of Chambers may delegate to the Registrar power of signature for the purpose of fixing time-limits which, pursuant to these Rules, it falls to them to prescribe or of extending such time-limits.

Chapter 10

Stay of Proceedings

Article 82a

1. The proceedings may be stayed:

(a) in the circumstances specified in the third paragraph of Article 54 of the Statute, by order of the Court, made after hearing the Advocate General;

(b) in all other cases, by decision of the President adopted after hearing the Advocate General and, save in the case of references for a preliminary ruling as referred to in Article 103, the parties.

The proceedings may be resumed by order or decision, following the same procedure.

The orders or decisions referred to in this paragraph shall be served on the parties.

2. The stay of proceedings shall take effect on the date indicated in the order or decision of stay or, in the absence of such indication, on the date of that order or decision.

While proceedings are stayed time shall cease to run for the purposes of prescribed time-limits for all parties.

3. Where the order or decision of stay does not fix the length of stay, it shall end on the date indicated in the order or decision of resumption or, in the absence of such indication, on the date of the order or decision of resumption.

From the date of resumption time shall begin to run afresh for the purposes of the time-limits.

TITLE III

SPECIAL FORMS OF PROCEDURE

Chapter 1

Suspension of Operation of Enforcement and Other Interim Measures

Article 83

1. An application to suspend the operation of any measure adopted by an institution, made pursuant to Article 242 of the EC Treaty or Article 157 of the EAEC Treaty, shall be admissible only if the applicant is challenging that measure in proceedings before the Court.

An application for the adoption of any other interim measure referred to in Article 243 of the EC Treaty or Article 158 of the EAEC Treaty shall be admissible only if it is made by a party to a case before the Court and relates to that case.

2. An application of a kind referred to in paragraph 1 of this Article shall state the subject-matter of the proceedings, the circumstances giving rise to urgency and the pleas of fact and law establishing a prima facie case for the interim measures applied for.

3. The application shall be made by a separate document and in accordance with the provisions of Articles 37 and 38 of these Rules.

Article 84

1. The application shall be served on the opposite party, and the President shall prescribe a short period within which that party may submit written or oral observations.

2. The President may order a preparatory inquiry.

The President may grant the application even before the observations of the opposite party have been submitted. This decision may be varied or cancelled even without any application being made by any party.

Article 85

The President shall either decide on the application himself or refer it to the Court.

If the President is absent or prevented from attending, Article 11 of these Rules shall apply.

Where the application is referred to it, the Court shall postpone all other cases, and shall give a decision after hearing the Advocate General. Article 84 shall apply.

Article 86

1. The decision on the application shall take the form of a reasoned order, from which no appeal shall lie. The order shall be served on the parties forthwith.

2. The enforcement of the order may be made conditional on the lodging by the applicant of security, of an amount and nature to be fixed in the light of the circumstances.

3. Unless the order fixes the date on which the interim measure is to lapse, the measure shall lapse when final judgment is delivered.

4. The order shall have only an interim effect, and shall be without prejudice to the decision of the Court on the substance of the case.

Article 87

On application by a party, the order may at any time be varied or cancelled on account of a change in circumstances.

Article 88

Rejection of an application for an interim measure shall not bar the party who made it from making a further application on the basis of new facts.

Article 89

The provisions of this Chapter shall apply to applications to suspend the enforcement of a decision of the Court or of any measure adopted by another institution, submitted pursuant to Articles 244 and 256 of the EC Treaty or Articles 159 and 164 of the EAEC Treaty.

The order granting the application shall fix, where appropriate, a date on which the interim measure is to lapse.

Article 90

1. An application of a kind referred to in the third and fourth paragraphs of Article 81 of the EAEC Treaty shall contain:

   (a) the names and addresses of the persons or undertakings to be inspected;

   (b) an indication of what is to be inspected and of the purpose of the inspection.

2. The President shall give his decision in the form of an order. Article 86 of these Rules shall apply.

If the President is absent or prevented from attending, Article 11 of these Rules shall apply.

Chapter 2

Preliminary Issues

Article 91

1. A party applying to the Court for a decision on a preliminary objection or other preliminary plea not going to the substance of the case shall make the application by a separate document.

The application must state the pleas of fact and law relied on and the form of order sought by the applicant; any supporting documents must be annexed to it.

2. As soon as the application has been lodged, the President shall prescribe a period within which the opposite party may lodge a document containing a statement of the form of order sought by that party and its pleas in law.

3. Unless the Court decides otherwise, the remainder of the proceedings shall be oral.

4. The Court shall, after hearing the Advocate General, decide on the application or reserve its decision for the final judgment.

If the Court refuses the application or reserves its decision, the President shall prescribe new time-limits for the further steps in the proceedings.

Article 92

1. Where it is clear that the Court has no jurisdiction to take cognisance of an action or where the action is manifestly inadmissible, the Court may, by reasoned order, after hearing the Advocate General and without taking further steps in the proceedings, give a decision on the action.

2. The Court may at any time of its own motion, after hearing the parties, decide whether there exists any absolute bar to proceeding with a case or declare that the action has become devoid of purpose and that there is no need to adjudicate on it; it shall give its decision in accordance with Article 91(3) and (4) of these Rules.

Chapter 3

Intervention

Article 93

1. An application to intervene must be made within six weeks of the publication of the notice referred to in Article 16(6) of these Rules.
   The application shall contain:

(a) the description of the case;

(b) the description of the parties;

(c) the name and address of the intervener;

(d) the intervener's address for service at the place where the Court has its seat;

(e) the form of order sought, by one or more of the parties, in support of which the intervener is applying for leave to intervene;

(f) a statement of the circumstances establishing the right to intervene, where the application is submitted pursuant to the second or third paragraph of Article 40 of the Statute.

The intervener shall be represented in accordance with Article 19 of the Statute.
   Articles 37 and 38 of these Rules shall apply.

2. The application shall be served on the parties.
   The President shall give the parties an opportunity to submit their written or oral observations before deciding on the application.
   The President shall decide on the application by order or shall refer the application to the Court.

3. If the President allows the intervention, the intervener shall receive a copy of every document served on the parties. The President may, however, on application by one of the parties, omit secret or confidential documents.

4. The intervener must accept the case as he finds it at the time of his intervention.

5. The President shall prescribe a period within which the intervener may submit a statement in intervention.
   The statement in intervention shall contain:

(a) a statement of the form of order sought by the intervener in support of or opposing, in whole or in part, the form of order sought by one of the parties;

(b) the pleas in law and arguments relied on by the intervener;

(c) where appropriate, the nature of any evidence offered.

6. After the statement in intervention has been lodged, the President shall, where necessary, prescribe a time-limit within which the parties may reply to that statement.

7. Consideration may be given to an application to intervene which is made after the expiry of the period prescribed in paragraph 1 but before the decision to open the oral procedure provided for in Article 44(3). In that event, if the President allows the intervention, the intervener may submit his observations during the oral procedure, if that procedure takes place.

Chapter 4

Judgments by Default and Applications to Set Then Aside

Article 94

1. If a defendant on whom an application initiating proceedings has been duly served fails to lodge a defence to the application in the proper form within the time prescribed, the applicant may apply for judgment by default.

The application shall be served on the defendant. The Court may decide to open the oral procedure on the application.

2. Before giving judgment by default the Court shall, after hearing the Advocate General, consider whether the application initiating proceedings is admissible, whether the appropriate formalities have been complied with, and whether the application appears well founded. The Court may order a preparatory inquiry.

3. A judgment by default shall be enforceable. The Court may, however, grant a stay of execution until the Court has given its decision on any application under paragraph 4 to set aside the judgment, or it may make execution subject to the provision of security of an amount and nature to be fixed in the light of the circumstances; this security shall be released if no such application is made or if the application fails.

4. Application may be made to set aside a judgment by default.

The application to set aside the judgment must be made within one month from the date of service of the judgment and must be lodged in the form prescribed by Articles 37 and 38 of these Rules.

5. After the application has been served, the President shall prescribe a period within which the other party may submit his written observations.

The proceedings shall be conducted in accordance with Article 44 et seq. of these Rules.

6. The Court shall decide by way of a judgment which may not be set aside.

The original of this judgment shall be annexed to the original of the judgment by default. A note of the judgment on the application to set aside shall be made in the margin of the original of the judgment by default.

Chapter 5

Article 95

(repealed)

Article 96

(repealed)

Chapter 6

Exceptional Review Procedures

Section 1—Third-party proceedings

Article 97

1. Articles 37 and 38 of these Rules shall apply to an application initiating third-party proceedings. In addition such an application shall:

(a) specify the judgment contested;

(b) state how that judgment is prejudicial to the rights of the third party;

(c) indicate the reasons for which the third party was unable to take part in the original case.

The application must be made against all the parties to the original case.

Where the judgment has been published in the *Official Journal of the European Union*, the application must be lodged within two months of the publication.

2. The Court may, on application by the third party, order a stay of execution of the judgment. The provisions of Title III, Chapter I, of these Rules shall apply.

3. The contested judgment shall be varied on the points on which the submissions of the third party are upheld.

The original of the judgment in the third-party proceedings shall be annexed to the original of the contested judgment. A note of the judgment in the third-party proceedings shall be made in the margin of the original of the contested judgment.

Section 2—Revision

Article 98

An application for revision of a judgment shall be made within three months of the date on which the facts on which the application is based came to the applicant's knowledge.

Article 99

1. Articles 37 and 38 of these Rules shall apply to an application for revision. In addition such an application shall:

(a) specify the judgment contested;

(b) indicate the points on which the judgment is contested;

(c) set out the facts on which the application is based;

(d) indicate the nature of the evidence to show that there are facts justifying revision of the judgment, and that the time-limit laid down in Article 98 has been observed.

2. The application must be made against all parties to the case in which the contested judgment was given.

Article 100

1. Without prejudice to its decision on the substance, the Court, in closed session, shall, after hearing the Advocate General and having regard to the written observations of the parties, give in the form of a judgment its decision on the admissibility of the application.
2. If the Court finds the application admissible, it shall proceed to consider the substance of the application and shall give its decision in the form of a judgment in accordance with these Rules.
3. The original of the revising judgment shall be annexed to the original of the judgment revised. A note of the revising judgment shall be made in the margin of the original of the judgment revised.

Chapter 7

Appeals Against Decisions of the Arbitration Committee

Article 101

1. An application initiating an appeal under the second paragraph of Article 18 of the EAEC Treaty shall state:

(a) the name and address of the applicant;

(b) the description of the signatory;

(c) a reference to the arbitration committee's decision against which the appeal is made;

(d) the description of the parties;

(e) a summary of the facts;

(f) the pleas in law of and the form of order sought by the applicant.

2. Articles 37(3) and (4) and 38(2), (3) and (5) of these Rules shall apply.
A certified copy of the contested decision shall be annexed to the application.
3. As soon as the application has been lodged, the Registrar of the Court shall request the arbitration committee registry to transmit to the Court the papers in the case.
4. Articles 39, 40 and 55 et seq. of these Rules shall apply to these proceedings.
5. The Court shall give its decision in the form of a judgment. Where the Court sets aside the decision of the arbitration committee it may refer the case back to the committee.

Chapter 8

Interpretation of Judgments

Article 102

1. An application for interpretation of a judgment shall be made in accordance with Articles 37 and 38 of these Rules. In addition it shall specify:

(a) the judgment in question;

(b) the passages of which interpretation is sought.

The application must be made against all the parties to the case in which the judgment was given.

2. The Court shall give its decision in the form of a judgment after having given the parties an opportunity to submit their observations and after hearing the Advocate General.

The original of the interpreting judgment shall be annexed to the original of the judgment interpreted. A note of the interpreting judgment shall be made in the margin of the original of the judgment interpreted.

Chapter 9

Preliminary Rulings and Other References for Interpretation

Article 103

1. In cases governed by Article 23 of the Statute, the procedure shall be governed by the provisions of these Rules, subject to adaptations necessitated by the nature of the reference for a preliminary ruling.

2. The provisions of paragraph 1 shall apply to the references for a preliminary ruling provided for in the Protocol concerning the interpretation by the Court of Justice of the Convention of 29 February 1968 on the mutual recognition of companies and legal persons and the Protocol concerning the interpretation by the Court of Justice of the Convention of 27 September 1968 on jurisdiction and the enforcement of judgments in civil and commercial matters, signed at Luxembourg on 3 June 1971, and to the references provided for by Article 4 of the latter Protocol.

The provisions of paragraph 1 shall apply also to references for interpretation provided for by other existing or future agreements.

Article 104

1. The decisions of national courts or tribunals referred to in Article 103 shall be communicated to the Member States in the original version, accompanied by a translation into the official language of the State to which they are addressed. Where appropriate on account of the length of the national court's decision, such translation shall be replaced by the translation into the official language of the State to which it is addressed of a summary of the decision, which will serve as a basis for the position to be adopted by that State. The summary shall include the full text of

the question or questions referred for a preliminary ruling. That summary shall contain, in particular, in so far as that information appears in the national court's decision, the subject-matter of the main proceedings, the essential arguments of the parties in the main proceedings, a succinct presentation of the reasoning in the reference for a preliminary ruling and the case-law and the provisions of Community and domestic law relied on.

In the cases governed by the third paragraph of Article 23 of the Statute, the decisions of national courts or tribunals shall be notified to the States, other than the Member States, which are parties to the EEA Agreement and also to the EFTA Surveillance Authority in the original version, accompanied by a translation of the decision, or where appropriate of a summary, into one of the languages mentioned in Article 29(1), to be chosen by the addressee of the notification.

Where a non-Member State has the right to take part in proceedings for a preliminary ruling pursuant to the fourth paragraph of Article 23 of the Statute, the original version of the decision of the national court or tribunal shall be communicated to it together with a translation of the decision, or where appropriate of a summary, into one of the languages mentioned in Article 29(1), to be chosen by the non-Member State concerned.

2. As regards the representation and attendance of the parties to the main proceedings in the preliminary ruling procedure the Court shall take account of the rules of procedure of the national court or tribunal which made the reference.

3. Where a question referred to the Court for a preliminary ruling is identical to a question on which the Court has already ruled, or where the answer to such a question may be clearly deduced from existing case-law, the Court may, after hearing the Advocate General, at any time give its decision by reasoned order in which reference is made to its previous judgment or to the relevant case-law.

The Court may also give its decision by reasoned order, after informing the court or tribunal which referred the question to it, hearing any observations submitted by the persons referred to in Article 23 of the Statute and after hearing the Advocate General, where the answer to the question referred to the Court for a preliminary ruling admits of no reasonable doubt.

4. Without prejudice to paragraph (3) of this Article, the procedure before the Court in the case of a reference for a preliminary ruling shall also include an oral part. However, after the statements of case or written observations referred to Article 23 of the Statute have been submitted, the Court, acting on a report from the Judge-Rapporteur, after informing the persons who under the aforementioned provisions are entitled to submit such statements or observations, may, after hearing the Advocate General, decide otherwise, provided that none of those persons has submitted an application setting out the reasons for which he wishes to be heard. The application shall be submitted within a period of three weeks from service on the party or person of the written statements of case or written observations which have been lodged. That period may be extended by the President.

5. The Court may, after hearing the Advocate General, request clarification from the national court.

6. It shall be for the national court or tribunal to decide as to the costs of the reference.

In special circumstances the Court may grant, by way of legal aid, assistance for the purpose of facilitating the representation or attendance of a party.

Article 104a

At the request of the national court, the President may exceptionally decide, on a proposal from the Judge-Rapporteur and after hearing the Advocate General, to apply an accelerated procedure derogating from the provisions of these Rules to a reference for a preliminary ruling, where the circumstances referred to establish that a ruling on the question put to the Court is a matter of exceptional urgency.

In that event, the President may immediately fix the date for the hearing, which shall be notified to the parties in the main proceedings and to the other persons referred to in Article 23 of the Statute when the decision making the reference is served.

The parties and other interested persons referred to in the preceding paragraph may lodge statements of case or written observations within a period prescribed by the President, which shall not be less than 15 days. The President may request the parties and other interested persons to restrict the matters addressed in their statement of case or written observations to the essential points of law raised by the question referred.

The statements of case or written observations, if any, shall be notified to the parties and to the other persons referred to above prior to the hearing.

The Court shall rule after hearing the Advocate General.

Chapter 10

Special Procedures under Articles 103 to 105 of the EAEC Treaty

Article 105

1. Four certified copies shall be lodged of an application under the third paragraph of Article 103 of the EAEC Treaty. The Commission shall be served with a copy.

2. The application shall be accompanied by the draft of the agreement or contract in question, by the observations of the Commission addressed to the State concerned and by all other supporting documents.

The Commission shall submit its observations to the Court within a period of 10 days, which may be extended by the President after the State concerned has been heard.

A certified copy of the observations shall be served on that State.

3. As soon as the application has been lodged the President shall designate a Judge to act as Rapporteur. The First Advocate General shall assign the case to an Advocate General as soon as the Judge-Rapporteur has been designated.

4. The decision shall be taken in closed session after the Advocate General has been heard.

The agents and advisers of the State concerned and of the Commission shall be heard if they so request.

Article 106

1. In cases provided for in the last paragraph of Article 104 and the last paragraph of Article 105 of the EAEC Treaty, the provisions of Article 37 et seq. of these Rules shall apply.

2. The application shall be served on the State to which the respondent person or undertaking belongs.

Chapter 11

Opinions

Article 107

1. A request by the European Parliament for an opinion pursuant to Article 300 of the EC Treaty shall be served on the Council, on the Commission and on the

Member States. Such a request by the Council shall be served on the Commission and on the European Parliament. Such a request by the Commission shall be served on the Council, on the European Parliament and on the Member States. Such a request by a Member State shall be served on the Council, on the Commission, on the European Parliament and on the other Member States.

The President shall prescribe a period within which the institutions and Member States which have been served with a request may submit their written observations.

2. The Opinion may deal not only with the question whether the envisaged agreement is compatible which the provisions of the EC Treaty but also with the question whether the Community or any Community institution has the power to enter into that agreement.

Article 108

1. As soon as the request for an Opinion has been lodged, the President shall designate a Judge to act as Rapporteur.

2. The Court sitting in closed session shall, after hearing the Advocates General, deliver a reasoned Opinion.

3. The Opinion, signed by the President, by the Judges who took part in the deliberations and by the Registrar, shall be served on the Council, the Commission, the European Parliament and the Member States.

Article 109

(repealed)

Chapter 12

Requests for Interpretation under Article 68 of the EC Treaty

Article 109a

1. A request for a ruling on a question of interpretation under Article 68(3) of the EC Treaty shall be served on the Commission and the Member States if the request is submitted by the Council, on the Council and the Member States if the request is submitted by the Commission and on the Council, the Commission and the other Member States if the request is submitted by a Member State.

The President shall prescribe a time-limit within which the institutions and the Member States on which the request has been served are to submit their written observations.

2. As soon as the request referred to in paragraph 1 has been submitted, the President shall designate the Judge-Rapporteur. The First Advocate General shall thereupon assign the request to an Advocate General.

3. The Court shall, after the Advocate General has delivered his Opinion, give its decision on the request by way of judgment.

The procedure relating to the request shall include an oral part where a Member State or one of the institutions referred to in paragraph 1 so requests.

Chapter 13

Settlement of the Disputes Referred to in Article 35 of the Union Treaty

Article 109b

1. In the case of disputes between Member States as referred to in Article 35(7) of the Union Treaty, the matter shall be brought before the Court by an application by

a party to the dispute. The application shall be served on the other Member States and on the Commission.

In the case of disputes between Member States and the Commission as referred to in Article 35(7) of the Union Treaty, the matter shall be brought before the Court by an application by a party to the dispute. The application shall be served on the other Member States, the Council and the Commission if it was made by a Member State. The application shall be served on the Member States and on the Council if it was made by the Commission.

The President shall prescribe a time-limit within which the institutions and the Member States on which the application has been served are to submit their written observations.

2. As soon as the application referred to in paragraph 1 has been submitted, the President shall designate the Judge-Rapporteur. The First Advocate General shall thereupon assign the application to an Advocate General.

3. The Court shall, after the Advocate General has delivered his Opinion, give its ruling on the dispute by way of judgment.

The procedure relating to the application shall include an oral part where a Member State or one of the institutions referred to in paragraph 1 so requests.

4. The same procedure shall apply where an agreement concluded between the Member States confers jurisdiction on the Court to rule on a dispute between Member States or between Member States and an institution.

Title IV

APPEALS AGAINST DECISIONS OF THE COURT OF FIRST INSTANCE

Article 110

Without prejudice to the arrangements laid down in Article 29(2)(b) and (c) and the fourth subparagraph of Article 29(3) of these Rules, in appeals against decisions of the Court of First Instance as referred to in Articles 56 and 57 of the Statute, the language of the case shall be the language of the decision of the Court of First Instance against which the appeal is brought.

Article 111

1. An appeal shall be brought by lodging an application at the Registry of the Court of Justice or of the Court of First Instance.

2. The Registry of the Court of First Instance shall immediately transmit to the Registry of the Court of Justice the papers in the case at first instance and, where necessary, the appeal.

Article 112

1. An appeal shall contain:

(a) the name and address of the appellant;

(b) the names of the other parties to the proceedings before the Court of First Instance;

(c) the pleas in law and legal arguments relied on;

(d) the form or order sought by the appellant.

Article 37 and Article 38(2) and (3) of these Rules shall apply to appeals.

2. The decision of the Court of First Instance appealed against shall be attached to the appeal. The appeal shall state the date on which the decision appealed against was notified to the appellant.

3. If an appeal does not comply with Article 38(3) or with paragraph 2 of this Article, Article 38(7) of these Rules shall apply.

Article 113

1. An appeal may seek:

- to set aside, in whole or in part, the decision of the Court of First Instance;
- the same form of order, in whole or in part, as that sought at first instance and shall not seek a different form of order.

2. The subject-matter of the proceedings before the Court of First Instance may not be changed in the appeal.

Article 114

Notice of the appeal shall be served on all the parties to the proceedings before the Court of First Instance. Article 39 of these Rules shall apply.

Article 115

1. Any party to the proceedings before the Court of First Instance may lodge a response within two months after service on him of notice of the appeal. The time-limit for lodging a response shall not be extended.

2. A response shall contain:

(a) the name and address of the party lodging it;

(b) the date on which notice of the appeal was served on him;

(c) the pleas in law and legal arguments relied on;

(d) the form of order sought by the respondent.

Article 37 and Article 38(2) and (3) of these Rules shall apply.

Article 116

1. A response may seek:

- to dismiss, in whole or in part, the appeal or to set aside, in whole or in part, the decision of the Court of First Instance;
- the same form of order, in whole or in part, as that sought at first instance and shall not seek a different form of order.

2. The subject-matter of the proceedings before the Court of First Instance may not be changed in the response.

Article 117

1. The appeal and the response may be supplemented by a reply and a rejoinder where the President, on application made by the appellant within seven days of service of the response, considers such further pleading necessary and expressly allows the submission of a reply in order to enable the appellant to put forward his point of view or in order to provide a basis for the decision on the appeal. The President shall prescribe the date by which the reply is to be submitted and, upon service of that pleading, the date by which the rejoinder is to be submitted.

2. Where the response seeks to set aside, in whole or in part, the decision of the Court of First Instance on a plea in law which was not raised in the appeal, the appellant or any other party may submit a reply on that plea alone within two months of the service of the response in question. Paragraph 1 shall apply to any further pleading following such a reply.

Article 118

Subject to the following provisions, Articles 42(2), 43, 44, 55 to 90, 93, 95 to 100 and 102 of these Rules shall apply to the procedure before the Court of Justice on appeal from a decision of the Court of First Instance.

Article 119

Where the appeal is, in whole or in part, clearly inadmissible or clearly unfounded, the Court may at any time, acting on a report from the Judge-Rapporteur and after hearing the Advocate General, by reasoned order dismiss the appeal in whole or in part.

Article 120

After the submission of pleadings as provided for in Article 115(1) and, if any, Article 117(1) and (2) of these Rules, the Court, acting on a report from the Judge-Rapporteur and after hearing the Advocate General and the parties, may decide to dispense with the oral part of the procedure unless one of the parties submits an application setting out the reasons for which he wishes to be heard. The application shall be submitted within a period of three weeks from notification to the party of the close of the written procedure. That period may be extended by the President.

Article 121

The report referred to in Article 44(2) shall be presented to the Court after the pleadings provided for in Article 115(1) and where appropriate Article 117(1) and (2) of these Rules have been lodged. Where no such pleadings are lodged, the same procedure shall apply after the expiry of the period prescribed for lodging them.

Article 122

Where the appeal is unfounded or where the appeal is well founded and the Court itself gives final judgment in the case, the Court shall make a decision as to costs.
  In proceedings between the Communities and their servants:

  - Article 70 of these Rules shall apply only to appeals brought by institutions;
  - by way of derogation from Article 69(2) of these Rules, the Court may, in appeals brought by officials or other servants of an institution, order the parties to share the costs where equity so requires.

If the appeal is withdrawn Article 69(5) shall apply.

When an appeal brought by a Member State or an institution which did not intervene in the proceedings before the Court of First Instance is well founded, the Court of Justice may order that the parties share the costs or that the successful appellant pay the costs which the appeal has caused an unsuccessful party to incur.

Article 123

An application to intervene made to the Court in appeal proceedings shall be lodged before the expiry of a period of one month running from the publication referred to in Article 16(6).

Title V

PROCEDURES PROVIDED FOR BY THE EEA AGREEMENT

Article 123a

1. In the case governed by Article 111(3) of the EEA Agreement,[2] the matter shall be brought before the Court by a request submitted by the Contracting Parties to the dispute. The request shall be served on the other Contracting Parties, on the Commission, on the EFTA Surveillance Authority and, where appropriate, on the other persons to whom a reference for a preliminary ruling raising the same question of interpretation of Community legislation would be notified.

The President shall prescribe a period within which the Contracting Parties and the other persons on whom the request has been served may submit written observations.

The request shall be made in one of the languages mentioned in Article 29(1). Paragraphs 3 to 5 of that Article shall apply. The provisions of Article 104(1) shall apply *mutatis mutandis*.

2. As soon as the request referred to in paragraph 1 of this Article has been submitted, the President shall appoint a Judge-Rapporteur. The First Advocate General shall, immediately afterwards, assign the request to an Advocate General.

The Court shall, after hearing the Advocate General, give a reasoned decision on the request in closed session.

3. The decision of the Court, signed by the President, by the Judges who took part in the deliberations and by the Registrar, shall be served on the Contracting Parties and on the other persons referred to in paragraph 1.

Article 123b

In the case governed by Article 1 of Protocol 34 to the EEA Agreement, the request of a court or tribunal of an EFTA State shall be served on the parties to the case, on the Contracting Parties, on the Commission, on the EFTA Surveillance Authority and, where appropriate, on the other persons to whom a reference for a preliminary ruling raising the same question of interpretation of Community legislation would be notified.

---

[2] OJ L 1 of 3.1.1994, p. 27.

686

If the request is not submitted in one of the languages mentioned in Article 29(1), it shall be accompanied by a translation into one of those languages.

Within two months of this notification, the parties to the case, the Contracting Parties and the other persons referred to in the first paragraph shall be entitled to submit statements of case or written observations.

The procedure shall be governed by the provisions of these Rules, subject to the adaptations called for by the nature of the request.

Miscellaneous provisions

Article 124

1. The President shall instruct any person who is required to take an oath before the Court, as witness or expert, to tell the truth or to carry out his task conscientiously and impartially, as the case may be, and shall warn him of the criminal liability provided for in his national law in the event of any breach of this duty.

2. The witness shall take the oath either in accordance with the first subparagraph of Article 47(5) of these Rules or in the manner laid down by his national law.

Where his national law provides the opportunity to make, in judicial proceedings, a solemn affirmation equivalent to an oath as well as or instead of taking an oath, the witness may make such an affirmation under the conditions and in the form prescribed in his national law.

Where his national law provides neither for taking an oath nor for making a solemn affirmation, the procedure described in paragraph 1 shall be followed.

3. Paragraph 2 shall apply *mutatis mutandis* to experts, a reference to the first subparagraph of Article 49(6) replacing in this case the reference to the first subparagraph of Article 47(5) of these Rules.

Article 125

Subject to the provisions of Article 223 of the EC Treaty and Article 139 of the EAEC Treaty and after consultation with the Governments concerned, the Court shall adopt supplementary rules concerning its practice in relation to:

(a) letters rogatory;

(b) applications for legal aid;

(c) reports of perjury by witnesses or experts, delivered pursuant to Article 30 of the Statute.

Article 125a

The Court may issue practice directions relating in particular to the preparation and conduct of the hearings before it and to the lodging of written statements of case or written observations.

Article 126

These Rules replace the Rules of Procedure of the Court of Justice of the European Communities adopted on 4 December 1974 (OJ L 350 of 28 December 1974, p. 1), as last amended on 15 May 1991.

Article 127

These Rules, which are authentic in the languages mentioned in Article 29(1) of these Rules, shall be published in the *Official Journal of the European Union* and shall enter into force on the first day of the second month following their publication.

ANNEX

DECISION ON OFFICIAL HOLIDAYS

THE COURT OF JUSTICE OF THE EUROPEAN COMMUNITIES,
  having regard to Article 80(2) of the Rules of Procedure, which requires the Court to draw up a list of official holidays;
DECIDES:

Article 1

For the purposes of Article 80(2) of the Rules of Procedure the following shall be official holidays:

 – New Year's Day;

 – Easter Monday;

 – 1 May;

 – Ascension Day;

 – Whit Monday;

 – 23 June;

 – 15 August;

 – 1 November;

 – 25 December;

 – 26 December.

The official holidays referred to in the first paragraph hereof shall be those observed at the place where the Court of Justice has its seat.

Article 2

Article 80(2) of the Rules of Procedure shall apply only to the official holidays mentioned in Article 1 of this Decision.

Article 3

This Decision, which shall be annexed to the Rules of Procedure, shall enter into force on the day of their publication in the *Official Journal of the European Union*.

Information note on references from national courts for a preliminary ruling

1. The preliminary ruling system is a fundamental mechanism of European Union law aimed at enabling national courts to ensure uniform interpretation and application of that law in all the Member States.   **C2–001**
2. The Court of Justice of the European Communities has jurisdiction to give preliminary rulings on the interpretation of the law of the European Union and on the validity of acts of secondary legislation. That general jurisdiction is conferred on it by Article 234 of the EC Treaty and, in certain specific cases, by other provisions.
3. The preliminary ruling procedure being based on cooperation between the Court and national courts, it may be helpful, in order to ensure that that cooperation is effective, to provide the national courts with the following information.
4. This practical information, which is in no way binding, is intended to provide guidance to national courts as to whether it is appropriate to make a reference for a preliminary ruling and, should they proceed, to help them formulate and submit questions to the Court.

The role of the Court in the preliminary ruling procedure

5. Under the preliminary ruling procedure, the Court's role is to give an interpretation of Community law or to rule on its validity, not to apply that law to the factual situation underlying the main proceedings, which is the task of the national court. It is not for the Court to decide issues of fact raised in the main proceedings or to resolve differences of opinion on the interpretation or application of rules of national law.
6. In ruling on the interpretation or validity of Community law, the Court makes every effort to give a reply which will be of assistance in resolving the dispute, but it is for the referring court to draw the appropriate conclusions from that reply, if necessary by disapplying the rule of national law in question.

The decision to submit a question to the Court

The originator of the question

7. Under Article 234 of the EC Treaty and Article 150 of the EAEC Treaty, any court or tribunal of a Member State, in so far as it is called upon to give a ruling in proceedings intended to arrive at a decision of a judicial nature, may as a rule refer a question to the Court for a preliminary ruling. The status of that court or tribunal is interpreted by the Court as a self-standing concept of Community law.
8. However, in the specific sphere of acts of the institutions in Title IV of Part Three of the EC Treaty on visa, asylum, immigration and other policies related to free movement of persons—in particular jurisdiction and the recognition and enforcement of judicial decisions—a reference may be made only by courts or tribunals against the decisions of which there is no appeal, in accordance with Article 68 of the EC Treaty.
9. Likewise, under Article 35 of the Treaty on European Union, acts of the institutions in the area of police and judicial cooperation in criminal matters may be the subject of a reference for a preliminary ruling only from courts in the Member States which have accepted the jurisdiction of the Court, each

689

Member State specifying whether that right of referral to the Court applies to any court or tribunal of that State or only to those against the decisions of which there is no appeal.

10. It is not necessary for the parties in the case to raise the question; the national court may do so of its own motion.

References on interpretation

11. Any court or tribunal **may** refer a question to the Court on the interpretation of a rule of Community law if it considers it necessary to do so in order to resolve a dispute brought before it.

12. However, courts or tribunals against whose decisions there is no judicial remedy under national law **must**, as a rule, refer such a question to the Court, unless the Court has already ruled on the point (and there is no new context that raises any serious doubt as to whether that case-law may be applied), or unless the correct interpretation of the rule of Community law is obvious.

13. Thus, a court or tribunal against whose decisions there is a judicial remedy may, in particular when it considers that sufficient clarification is given by the case-law of the Court, itself decide on the correct interpretation of Community law and its application to the factual situation before it. However, a reference for a preliminary ruling may prove particularly useful, at an appropriate stage of the proceedings, when there is a new question of interpretation of general interest for the uniform application of Community law throughout the Union, or where the existing case-law does not appear to be applicable to a new set of facts.

14. It is for the national court to explain why the interpretation sought is necessary to enable it to give judgment.

References on determination of validity

15. Although national courts may reject pleas raised before them challenging the validity of Community acts, the Court has exclusive jurisdiction to declare such acts invalid.

16. All national courts **must** therefore refer a question to the Court when they have doubts about the validity of a Community act, stating the reasons for which they consider that the Community act may be invalid.

17. If a national court has serious doubts about the validity of a Community act on which a national measure is based, it may exceptionally suspend application of that measure temporarily or grant other interim relief with respect to it. It must then refer the question of validity to the Court of Justice, stating the reasons for which it considers the Community act to be invalid.

The stage at which to submit a question for a preliminary ruling

18. A national court or tribunal may refer a question to the Court of Justice for a preliminary ruling as soon as it finds that a ruling on the point or points of interpretation or validity is necessary to enable it to give judgment; it is the national court which is in the best position to decide at what stage of the proceedings such a question should be referred.

19. It is, however, desirable that a decision to seek a preliminary ruling should be taken when the proceedings have reached a stage at which the national court is able to define the factual and legal context of the question, so that the Court has available to it all the information necessary to check, where appropriate, that Community law applies to the main proceedings. It may also be in the interests of justice to refer a question for a preliminary ruling only after both sides have been heard.

The form of the reference for a preliminary ruling

20. The decision by which a national court or tribunal refers a question to the Court of Justice for a preliminary ruling may be in any form allowed by national law as

regards procedural steps. It must however be borne in mind that it is that document which serves as the basis of the proceedings before the Court and that it must therefore contain such information as will enable the latter to give a reply which is of assistance to the national court. Moreover, it is only the actual reference for a preliminary ruling which is notified to the parties entitled to submit observations to the Court, in particular the Member States and the institutions, and which is translated.

21. Owing to the need to translate the reference, it should be drafted simply, clearly and precisely, avoiding superfluous detail.

22. A maximum of about ten pages is often sufficient to set out in a proper manner the context of a reference for a preliminary ruling. The order for reference must be succinct but sufficiently complete and must contain all the relevant information to give the Court and the parties entitled to submit observations a clear understanding of the factual and legal context of the main proceedings. In particular, the order for reference must:

- include a brief account of the subject-matter of the dispute and the relevant findings of fact, or, at least, set out the factual situation on which the question referred is based;

- set out the tenor of any applicable national provisions and identify, where necessary, the relevant national case-law, giving in each case precise references (e.g. page of an official journal or specific law report, with any internet reference);

- identify the Community provisions relevant to the case as accurately as possible;

- explain the reasons which prompted the national court to raise the question of the interpretation or validity of the Community provisions, and the relationship between those provisions and the national provisions applicable to the main proceedings;

- include, where appropriate, a summary of the main arguments of the parties.

In order to make it easier to read and refer to the document, it is helpful if the different points or paragraphs of the order for reference are numbered.

23. Finally, the referring court may, if it considers itself to be in a position to do so, briefly state its view on the answer to be given to the questions referred for a preliminary ruling.

24. The question or questions themselves should appear in a separate and clearly identified section of the order for reference, generally at the beginning or the end. It must be possible to understand them without referring to the statement of the grounds for the reference, which however provides the necessary background for a proper assessment.

The effects of the reference for a preliminary ruling on the national proceedings

25. A reference for a preliminary ruling in general calls for the national proceedings to be stayed until the Court has given its ruling.

26. However, the national court may still order protective measures, particularly in a reference on determination of validity (see point 17 above).

Costs and legal aid

27. Proceedings for a preliminary ruling before the Court are free of charge and the Court does not rule on the costs of the parties to the main proceedings; it is for the national court to rule on those costs.

28. If a party has insufficient means and where possible under national rules, the national court may grant that party legal aid to cover the costs, including those of lawyers' fees, which it incurs before the Court. The Court itself may also grant legal aid.

Communication between the national court and the Court of Justice

29. The order for reference and the relevant documents (including, where applicable, the case file or a copy of the case file) are to be sent by the national court directly to the Court of Justice, by registered post (addressed to the Registry of the Court of Justice of the European Communities, L-2925 Luxembourg, telephone + 352–4303–1).
30. The Court Registry will stay in contact with the national court until a ruling is given, and will send it copies of the procedural documents.
31. The Court will send its ruling to the national court. It would welcome information from the national court on the action taken upon its ruling in the national proceedings and, where appropriate, a copy of the national court's final decision.

Practice Directions
relating to direct actions and appeals

THE COURT OF JUSTICE OF THE EUROPEAN COMMUNITIES,
Pursuant to Article 125a of its Rules of Procedure,
Whereas:

(1) It is in the interest of the efficient conduct of proceedings in direct actions and **C3–001** appeals that practice directions should be issued to agents and lawyers representing parties before the Court, dealing with the submission of pleadings and the preparation and conduct of hearings;

(2) The present directions reflect, explain and complement provisions in the Rules of Procedure and are designed to enable agents and lawyers to take account of the constraints under which the Court operates, particularly as regards the electronic processing of procedural documentation and translation and interpretation requirements;

(3) The Rules of Procedure and the Instructions to the Registrar require the Registrar to receive procedural documents, to ensure that they comply with the provisions of the Rules of Procedure and to assist the Court and Chambers, in particular in the organisation of hearings. In carrying out his duties, the Registrar must satisfy himself that the agents and lawyers comply with these practice directions, requiring them to make good any irregularities of form in documents lodged which do not comply with those provisions or requesting the agent or lawyer concerned to comply therewith;

(4) The views of representatives of the agents of the Member States and the institutions acting in proceedings before the Court, and of the Council of the Bars and Law Societies of the European Community (CCBE), have been heard on the drafting of these practice directions;

HEREBY ADOPTS THE FOLLOWING PRACTICE DIRECTIONS:

USE OF TECHNICAL MEANS OF COMMUNICATION
1. A copy of the signed original of a procedural document may be transmitted to the Registry in accordance with Article 37(6) of the Rules of Procedure either:

   – by telefax (to fax number: + 352 43 37 66);

   or

   – as an attachment to an electronic mail (e-mail address: ecj.registry@curia.eu.int).

2. Where transmission is by electronic mail, only a scanned copy of the signed original will be accepted. An ordinary electronic file or one bearing an electronic signature or a computer-generated facsimile signature will not be treated as complying with Article 37(6) of the Rules of Procedure.

   Documents should be scanned at a resolution of 300 DPI and, wherever possible, in PDF format (images plus text), using Acrobat or Readiris 7 Pro software.

3. A document lodged by telefax or electronic mail will be treated as complying with the relevant time-limit only if the signed original itself reaches the Registry

693

within ten days following such lodgment, as specified in Article 37(6) of the Rules of Procedure. The signed original must be sent without delay, immediately after the despatch of the copy, without any corrections or amendments, even of a minor nature. In the event of any discrepancy between the signed original and the copy previously lodged, only the date of lodgment of the signed original will be taken into consideration.

4. Where, in accordance with Article 38(2) of the Rules of Procedure, a party agrees to be notified by telefax or other technical means of communication, the statement to that effect must specify the telefax number and/or the electronic mail address to which the Registry may send that party documents to be served. The recipient's computer must be equipped with suitable software (for example, Acrobat or Readiris 7 Pro) for reception and display of communications from the Registry, which will be transmitted in PDF format.

PRESENTATION OF PLEADINGS

5. Pleadings and other procedural documents lodged[1] by the parties must be submitted in a form which can be processed electronically by the Court and which, in particular, makes it possible to scan documents and to use character recognition.

For that purpose, the following requirements must be complied with:

(1) The paper must be white, unlined and A4 size, with text on one side of the page only.

(2) Pages of pleadings and annexes, if any, must be assembled in such a way as to be easily separable. They must not be bound together or permanently attached by means such as glue or staples.

(3) The text must be in a commonly-used font (such as Times New Roman, Courier or Arial), in at least 12 pt in the body of the text and at least 10 pt in the footnotes, with 1.5 line spacing and upper, lower, left and right margins of at least 2.5 cm.

(4) The pages of the pleading must be numbered consecutively in the top right-hand corner. That numbering must also cover all the pages of any annexes to the pleading, so as to make it possible to check that all the pages of the annexes have been duly scanned.

6. The following information must appear on the first page of the pleading:

(1) the title of the pleading (application, appeal, defence, response, reply, rejoinder, application for leave to intervene, statement in intervention, observations on the statement in intervention, objection of inadmissibility, etc.);

where a response seeks an order setting aside in whole or in part the decision of the Court of First Instance on a plea in law not raised in the appeal, the title of the pleading must indicate that the document is a response and cross-appeal.

(2) the case number (C–.../..), if it has already been notified by the Registry;

(3) the names of the applicant (appellant) and defendant (respondent) and, in appeals, the identification of the decision under appeal and the parties before the Court of First Instance;

---

[1] – The Court's postal address is:
Court of Justice of the European Communities
L-2925 LUXEMBOURG

(4) the name of the party on whose behalf the pleading is lodged.

7. Each paragraph of the pleading must be numbered.
8. The signature of the agent or lawyer acting for the party concerned must appear at the end of the pleading.

FORM AND CONTENT OF THE PRINCIPAL TYPES OF PLEADING

A. Direct actions

Application initiating proceedings

9. An application must contain the statements prescribed by Article 38(1) and (2) of the Rules of Procedure.
10. The following must appear at the beginning of each application:

   (1) the applicant's name and address;

   (2) the name and capacity of the applicant's agent or lawyer;

   (3) the identity of the party or parties against whom the action is brought;

   (4) the statements referred to in Article 38(2) of the Rules of Procedure (address for service in Luxembourg and/or agreement to service by telefax or any other technical means of communication).

11. In the case of an application for annulment, a copy of the contested measure must be annexed to the application and identified as such.
12. Each application should be accompanied by a summary of the pleas in law and main arguments relied on, intended to facilitate publication in the Official Journal of the notice prescribed by Article 16(6) of the Rules of Procedure, which will be prepared by the Registry. The summary in question must not be more than two pages long.
13. precise wording of the forms of order sought by the applicant must be specified either at the beginning or the end of the application.
14. introductory part of the application must be followed by a brief account of the facts giving rise to the dispute.
15. structure of the legal argument must reflect the pleas in law relied upon. After the account of the facts giving rise to the dispute, a summary outline of those pleas in law should be given.

Defence

16. The defence must contain the statements prescribed by Article 40(1) of the Rules of Procedure.
17. In addition to the case-number and the applicant's name, the following must appear at the beginning of each defence:

   (1) the defendant's name and address;

   (2) the name and capacity of the defendant's agent or lawyer;

   (3) an address for service in Luxembourg and/or agreement to service by telefax or other technical means of communication (second subparagraph of Article 40(1) of the Rules of Procedure).

695

18. The precise wording of the forms of order sought by the defendant must be specified either at the beginning or at the end of the defence.
19. The structure of the legal argument must, so far as is possible, reflect that of the pleas in law put forward in the application.
20. The factual and legal background is to be recapitulated in the defence only in so far as its presentation in the application is disputed or calls for further particulars. If any fact alleged by the other party is contested it must be clearly indicated and the basis on which it is challenged must be stated explicitly.

Reply and rejoinder

21. The reply and rejoinder must not recapitulate the factual and legal background except in so far as its presentation in the previous pleadings is disputed or, exceptionally, calls for further particulars. If any fact alleged by the other party is contested it must be clearly indicated and the basis on which it is challenged must be stated explicitly.

Statement in intervention

22. The statement in intervention must develop no arguments that are not new in relation to those put forward by the main party. It may be confined to a mere reference to the other arguments.
   The statement in intervention must not recapitulate the factual and legal background except in so far as its presentation in the previous pleadings is disputed or, exceptionally, calls for further particulars. If any fact alleged by the other party is contested it must be clearly indicated and the basis on which it is challenged must be stated explicitly.

B. Appeals

The appeal

23. An appeal must contain the statements prescribed by Article 112(1) of Rules of Procedure.
24. The following must appear at the beginning of each appeal:

   (1) the appellant's name and address;

   (2) the name and capacity of the appellant's agent or lawyer;

   (3) the identification of the decision of the Court of First Instance appealed against (type of decision, formation of the Court, date and number of the case) and the names of the parties before the Court of First Instance;

   (4) the date on which the decision of the Court of First Instance was notified to the appellant;

   (5) an address for service in Luxembourg and/or agreement to service by telefax or other technical means of communication.

23. A copy of the decision of the Court of First Instance appealed against must be annexed to the appeal.
26. The appeal should be accompanied by a summary of the grounds of appeal and main arguments relied on, intended to facilitate publication in the Official Journal of the notice prescribed by Article 16(6) of the Rules of Procedure. The summary in question must not be more than two pages long.
27. The precise wording of the forms of order sought by the appellant must be specified either at the beginning or at the end of the appeal (Article 113(1) of Rules of Procedure).

28. It is not generally necessary to set out the background to the dispute or its subject-matter; it will be sufficient to refer to the decision of the Court of First Instance.

29. The structure of the legal arguments must reflect the grounds, in particular errors of law, relied upon in support of the appeal. A summary outline of those grounds should be given at the beginning of the appeal.

Response

30. A response must contain the statements prescribed by Article 115(1) of the Rules of Procedure.

31. The following must appear at the beginning of each response, in addition to the case number and the appellant's name:

    (1) the name and address of the party lodging it;

    (2) the name and capacity of the agent or lawyer acting for that party;

    (3) the date on which notice of the appeal was served on the party;

    (4) an address for service in Luxembourg and/or agreement to service by telefax or any other technical means of communication.

32. The precise wording of the forms of order sought by the party lodging the response must be specified either at the beginning or at the end of the response.

33. If the response seeks an order setting aside, in whole or in part, the decision of the Court of First Instance on a plea in law not raised in the appeal, that fact must be indicated in the title of the pleading ('Response and Cross-appeal').

34. The structure of the legal arguments must, so far as is possible, reflect the grounds of appeal put forward by the appellant and/or, as appropriate, the grounds put forward by way of cross-appeal.

35. Since the factual and legal background has already been set out in the judgment under appeal, it is to be recapitulated in the response only quite exceptionally, in so far as its presentation in the appeal is disputed or calls for further particulars. Any fact challenged must be clearly indicated, and the point of fact or law in question indicated explicitly.

Reply and rejoinder

36. As a rule, the reply and rejoinder will not recapitulate any more the factual and legal background. Any fact challenged must be clearly indicated, and the point of fact or law in question indicated explicitly.

Statement in intervention

37. The statement in intervention must develop no arguments that are not new in relation to those put forward by the main party. It may be confined to a mere reference to the other arguments.

    The statement in intervention must not recapitulate the factual and legal background except in so far as its presentation in the previous pleadings is disputed or, exceptionally, calls for further particulars. Any fact challenged must be clearly indicated, and the point of fact or law in question indicated explicitly.

ANNEXES TO PLEADINGS

38. Legal argument submitted for consideration by the Court must appear in the pleadings and not in the annexes.

39. Only documents mentioned in the actual text of a pleading and necessary in order to prove or illustrate its contents may be submitted as annexes.

40. Annexes will be accepted only if they are accompanied by a schedule of annexes (Article 37(4) of the Rules of Procedure). That schedule must indicate for each document annexed:

   (1) the number of the annex;

   (2) a short description of the document (e.g. "letter", followed by its date, author and addressee and its number of pages);

   (3) a reference to the page and paragraph in the pleading at which the document is mentioned and from which the need to produce it is apparent.

41. If, for the convenience of the Court, copies of judgments, legal writings or legislation are annexed to a pleading, they must be separate from the other annexes.

42. Each reference to a document lodged must state the relevant annex number as given in the schedule of annexes in which it appears and indicate the pleading to which it is annexed. In appeal proceedings, where the document has already been produced before the Court of First Instance, the identification used for that document before the Court of First Instance must also be given.

DRAFTING AND LENGTH OF PLEADINGS

43. With a view to avoiding delay in proceedings, when drafting pleadings the following points in particular must be taken into consideration:

   • the case is examined on the basis of the pleadings; in order to facilitate that examination, documents must be structured and concise and must avoid repetition;

   • pleadings will, as a general rule, be translated; in order to facilitate translation and to make it as accurate as possible sentences should be simple in structure and vocabulary should be simple and precise;

   • the time needed for translation and for examination of the case-file is proportionate to the length of the pleadings lodged, so that the shorter the pleadings, the swifter the disposal of the case.

44. It is the Court's experience that, save in exceptional circumstances, effective pleadings need not exceed 10 or 15 pages and replies, rejoinders and responses can be limited to 5 to 10 pages.

APPLICATIONS FOR EXPEDITED PROCEDURE

45. A party applying by separate document under Article 62a of the Rules of Procedure for a case to be decided by the Court by expedited procedure must briefly state the reasons for the special urgency of the case. Save in exceptional circumstances, that application must not exceed 5 pages.

46. As the expedited procedure is largely oral, the pleading of the party requesting it must be confined to a summary of the pleas relied upon. Such pleadings must not, save in exceptional circumstances, exceed 10 pages.

APPLICATIONS FOR LEAVE TO LODGE A REPLY IN APPEAL PROCEEDINGS

47. The President may, on application, allow a reply to be lodged if it is necessary in order to enable the appellant to defend its point of view or in order to provide a

basis for the decision on the appeal.

Save in exceptional circumstances such an application must not exceed 2 to 3 pages and must be confined to summarising the precise reasons for which, in the appellant's opinion, a reply is necessary. The request must be comprehensible in itself without any need to refer to the appeal or the response.

APPLICATIONS FOR HEARING OF ORAL ARGUMENT

48. The Court may decide not to hear oral argument where none of the parties has applied to be heard (Articles 44a and 120 of the Rules of Procedure). In practice, it is rare for a hearing to be organised in the absence of such an application.

The application must specify why the party wishes to be heard. That reasoning must be based on a real assessment of the benefit of a hearing to the party in question and must indicate the documentary elements or arguments which that party considers it necessary to develop or disprove more fully at a hearing. It is not sufficient to provide a general statement of reasons referring to the importance of the case or of the questions to be decided.

PREPARATION AND CONDUCT OF HEARINGS

49. Before the hearing begins the agents or lawyers are called to a short meeting with the relevant formation of the Court, in order to plan the hearing. At that point the Judge-Rapporteur and the Advocate General may indicate the matters they wish to hear developed in the arguments.

50. Oral argument is limited to 30 minutes *maximum* before the full Court, the Grand Chamber or a chamber of five Judges and to 15 minutes *maximum* before a Chamber of three Judges. Before any formation the presentation of an intervener's argument is limited to 15 minutes *maximum*.

Speaking time may exceptionally be extended beyond those limits on application made to the President of the formation concerned together with a detailed statement of reasons. The application must reach the Court as soon as possible and, in order to be taken into consideration, at the latest two weeks before the date of the hearing.

The notification of the hearing asks the agents and lawyers to inform the Registry of the likely duration of their oral arguments. The information supplied is used in the planning of the business of the Court and the Chambers, and it is not possible to exceed the speaking time requested.

51. Having read the written pleadings, the Judges and the Advocate General are already familiar with the case, its subject-matter and the pleas in law and arguments put forward by the parties. The purpose of oral argument is not to present a party's point of view afresh but to clarify any matters which the agent or lawyer regards as particularly important, especially those referred to in the application for a hearing (see paragraph 42 above). Repetition of what has already been stated in the written pleadings must be avoided; if necessary, a reference to the pleadings during the course of the oral argument will suffice.

Oral submissions should begin by outlining the plan to be followed.

52. Very frequently the Judges and Advocate General will listen to oral argument via simultaneous interpretation. In order to make that interpretation possible, agents and lawyers should speak at a natural and unforced pace and use short sentences of simple structure.

It is inadvisable to read out a text prepared in advance. It is preferable to speak on the basis of properly structured notes. If the oral argument is, nevertheless, prepared in writing, account should be taken in drafting the text of the fact that it is to be delivered orally and ought therefore to come as close as

possible to oral exposition. To facilitate interpretation, agents and lawyers are requested to send the text or written outline of their oral argument by fax in advance to the Interpretation Division (fax + 352 43 03 36 97).
Done at Luxembourg, 15 October 2004

Notes for the guidance of Counsel[1]

Introduction

Two factors distinguish proceedings before the Court of Justice from those before certain national supreme courts. Firstly, proceedings before the Court of Justice are governed by strict rules of law contained in the Treaties, the Protocol on the Statute of the Court and its Rules of Procedure. The Court is thus not in a position to make exceptions to them. Secondly, proceedings before the Court are subject to rules on the use of languages appropriate to a multilingual Community, a fact which influences the nature and purpose of both the written and the oral procedure (see A.3 and C.4 below).

C4–001

Accordingly, this guide is designed to explain to Counsel the purpose of proceedings before the Court, in order to enhance the quality of judicial protection within the Community legal order and ensure the rapid and effective conduct of cases.

This guide should therefore be seen as a working tool intended to enable Counsel to present their written and oral pleadings in the form which the Court of Justice considers most fitting. At the same time, attention will be drawn to the Court's procedural practice. However, this guide is intended neither to lay down legal rules in itself nor to override the relevant provisions in force.

In these notes, references to "Article . . . EC", "Article . . . of the Statute" and "Article . . . of the RP" are respectively references to articles of the EC Treaty, of the Statute of the Court of Justice and of the Rules of Procedure of the Court. The version of the Rules of Procedure at present in force was adopted on 19 June 1991 (Official Journal 1991 L 176, p. 1) and was amended on 21 February 1995 (OJ 1995 L 44, p. 61), 11 March 1977 (OJ 1997 L 103, p. 1) and 16 May 2000 (OJ 2000 L 122, p. 43) and on 28 November 2000 (OJ 2000 L 322, p. 1). A consolidated version of the Rules of Procedure was published in OJ C 34 of 1 February 2001. Since then, five amendments have been made to the Rules of Procedure, on 3 April 2001 (OJ 2001 L 119, p. 1), on 17 September 2002 (OJ 2002 L 272, p. 24), on 8 April 2003 (OJ 2003 L 147, p. 17), on 19 April 2004 (OJ 2004 L 132, p. 2) and on 20 April 2004 (OJ 2004 L 127, p. 107).

A. General points

1. The various stages of proceedings before the Court of Justice

Proceedings before the Court comprise a written phase followed by an oral phase (see the first paragraph of Article 20 of the Statute).

The oral procedure includes the presentation of oral argument at the hearing and the Advocate General's Opinion, which is delivered in open court. In accordance with the Rules of Procedure, the Court may dispense with a hearing of oral

---

[1] The word "Counsel" is used in a non technical sense so as to include all those appearing before the Court and acting as advocate, whatever their capacity or professional status.

argument (see C.7 below) and, in accordance with the Statute, it may, where it considers that the case raises no new point of law and after hearing the Advocate General, decide to proceed to judgment without an Opinion from the Advocate General (fifth paragraph of Article 20 of the Statute).

The active participation of Counsel for parties to the proceedings concludes with the hearing at which oral argument is presented. Without prejudice to the possibility of the procedure being reopened for exceptional reasons, no observations of the parties following the Opinion may be included in the file.

2. Representation of the parties

a. The rule

The requirement that parties be represented is laid down in Article 19 of the Statute. Apart from Member States, EEA States and Community institutions, which are represented by their Agents, parties must be represented in all proceedings by a lawyer entitled to practise before a court of a Member State or other EEA State. The requirement of representation by a lawyer does not apply to applications for legal aid (see A.4.b. below), and, in certain circumstances, preliminary-ruling proceedings (see b. below).

University professors who are nationals of Member States whose law allows them to plead before courts are treated as Counsel by virtue of the seventh paragraph of Article 19 of the Statute.

Pursuant to Article 38(3) of the RP, Counsel are required, when lodging an application, to attach a certificate as to their right of audience before the courts of one of the Member States or another EEA State. A copy of the Lawyer's Professional Identity Card (issued by the CCBE) is accepted for this purpose.

b. Representation in preliminary ruling proceedings

The requirement of representation differs slightly in preliminary ruling proceedings (Article 104(2) of the RP). Any person empowered to represent or assist a party in the proceedings before the national court may also do so before the Court of Justice. Consequently, if the rules of procedure applicable to proceedings before the national court do not require parties to be represented, the parties to those proceedings are entitled to submit their own written and oral observations.

3. Use of languages

A clear distinction must be drawn between the **language of the case**, which is governed by Article 29 et seq. of the RP, and the **working language** used within the Court.

All the official languages of the Member States of the E.C. can be the language of the case. However, each case has its "own" language. Only one language may therefore be chosen as the language of the case. An exception is made to this rule where cases are joined and the language of the case is different for each: in such circumstances each language used is a language of the case.

The provisions of Article 29 of the RP concerning that choice are very detailed but can be summarised in three sentences.

- In **direct actions**, the applicant has the right to choose the language of the case unless the defendant is a Member State or a natural or legal person who is a national of a Member State; in such cases, the language of the case is the official language (or one of the official languages where there are more than one) of that State.

702

- In **preliminary rulings**, the language of the case is always that of the national court making the reference.

- The Member States may use their own language where they intervene in a direct action or take part in preliminary-ruling proceedings.

The Judges and Advocates General are not required to use the language of the case. They are therefore at liberty to ask questions at the hearing in any of the official languages of the Communities even if it is not the language of the case.

The **working language of the Court** is the language used by the Members of the Court and its staff for day to day internal communication and work produced jointly. At present, the working language is French. Consequently, pleadings submitted in a language other than French are translated into French for the Court's internal purposes.

4. Costs and legal aid

a. Costs

Proceedings before the Court are free, in that no charge or fee of any kind is payable to the Court.

The costs referred to in Article 69 et seq. of the RP are only those costs which are described as "recoverable", namely lawyers' fees, payments to witnesses, post and telephone costs, and so forth, incurred by the parties themselves.

The rule concerning the **award of costs** is simple: the unsuccessful party is ordered to pay the costs and thus bears its own costs and those of the other parties, except Member States and institutions, which, when intervening, bear their own costs. For costs to be awarded on that basis, a request to that effect must be included as one of the orders sought ("conclusions")—if no such request is made the parties bear their own costs.

However, the Court may, according to the circumstances of the case, either order that the parties bear their own costs wholly or in part or even award costs against the successful party.

Special conditions apply to proceedings brought by officials (see Article 70 of the RP).

The Court gives a decision on costs in the judgment or order which brings the proceedings to an end.

With regard to costs incurred in preliminary ruling cases, the Court's decision incorporates a standard form of words referring to the final decision to be taken by the national court which made the reference to the Court of Justice. Institutions, Member States and other EEA States which submit observations bear their own costs.

b. Legal aid

Article 76 of the RP provides for legal aid. The Court has a limited budget for that purpose.

Any party may at any time apply for legal aid if he is "wholly or in part unable to meet the costs of the proceedings". The right to make such an application is not conditional upon the nature of the action or procedure. Thus, legal aid may also be applied for in a preliminary ruling case. However, in such a case, the party concerned must first seek legal aid from the competent authorities in his own country. In order to establish his lack of means, the person concerned must provide the Court with all relevant information, in particular a certificate from the competent authority to that effect.

Where legal aid is applied for before the commencement of proceedings, the party must give a brief description of the subject matter of the application in order to enable the Court to consider whether the application is not manifestly unfounded.

The obligation to be represented by Counsel does not apply to applications for legal aid.

An order granting or withholding legal aid does not state the reasons on which it is based and is not subject to appeal.

It must be emphasised that the grant of legal aid does not mean that the recipient of it cannot, if appropriate, be ordered to pay the costs. Moreover, the Court may take action to recover sums disbursed by way of legal aid.

B. The written procedure

1. The purpose of the written procedure

Regardless of the nature of the proceedings concerned (direct action, reference for a preliminary ruling, appeal), the purpose of the written procedure is always the same, namely to put before the Court, the Judges and the Advocate General, an exhaustive account of the facts, pleas and arguments of the parties and the forms of order sought.

In that connection, it is important to note that the entire procedure before the Court, in particular the written phase, is governed by the principle whereby new pleas may not be raised in the course of the proceedings, with the sole exception of those based on matters of law and fact which come to light in the course of the procedure.

The procedure before the Court does not therefore have the same flexibility as that allowed by certain national rules of procedure.

2. The conduct of the written procedure

The course of the written procedure differs according to the nature of the proceedings.

a. Direct actions

In direct actions, each litigant may submit two sets of pleadings: the application and the reply in the case of the applicant and the defence and rejoinder in the case of the defendant.

b. Appeals

In an appeal against a decision of the Court of First Instance, the parties may, in principle, submit only one set of pleadings, the application or response, depending on their respective roles. The possibility of a reply is subject to express authorisation from the President of the Court of Justice (see B.8.c. below).

c. Preliminary-ruling proceedings

In preliminary ruling proceedings, the persons referred to in Article 23 of the Statute may, within a mandatory period of two months after notification of the order for reference, submit their written observations (see B.9. below).

3. The lodgement of pleadings

All pleadings must be sent to the Registry of the Court in order to be registered in accordance with Article 37 of the RP. The original must be signed by Counsel for the party concerned. Copies must be certified by the party lodging them.

All documents relied on must be annexed to the relevant pleading, which must be accompanied by a schedule listing them.

In direct actions, the original pleading and all the annexes to it must be lodged together with five copies for the Court and, for the purposes of notification (see B.4. below), a copy for every other party to the proceedings.

Any pleading may be delivered by hand to the Court Registry or, outside the working hours of the Registry, to the security officer on duty at the main entrance to the Court building (Boulevard Konrad Adenauer, Plateau du Kirchberg). The Court building is open 24 hours a day.

If pleadings are sent by post, the envelope must bear the following address and nothing else:

Court of Justice of the European Communities
– Registry –
L–2925 Luxembourg

4. Notification
a. The addressees

In direct actions, the following, inter alia, are notified to the parties concerned: applications, appeals, defences, replies, rejoinders, applications for interim measures and applications for leave to intervene.

References for a preliminary ruling from national courts, and the observations of those entitled to submit them under Article 23 of the Statute, are notified to the parties to the proceedings, to the Member States, to the Commission and, if appropriate, to the Council, or to the Council, the European Parliament and the European Central Bank, and to the other EEA States and the EFTA Supervisory Authority.

In all cases, the Report for the Hearing (if a hearing of oral argument takes place), the Opinion of the Advocate General, where delivered, and the judgment are notified to those taking part in the proceedings before the Court.

b. Address for service and consent to notification by fax or e-mail

In the case of direct actions, Article 38(2) of the RP provides that parties are to give an address for service in Luxembourg; the address given may be that of any natural person residing in Luxembourg, with the exception of officials of the Court of Justice. In such cases, due notification is deemed to take place upon receipt of the document in question by the person whose address has been given as the address for service.

As well as, or instead of, giving an address for service, the lawyer or agent for a party may consent to service by fax or any other technical means of communication. In such cases, procedural documents, other than judgments and orders, will be notified by fax or e-mail and shall be deemed to have been duly served when such means are used.

However, where for technical reasons or on account of the nature or length of the document concerned transmission by fax or e-mail is not feasible, it will be sent to the party's address for service in Luxembourg or, if no address for service has been given, by registered post with a form for acknowledgment of receipt to the address of the party's lawyer or agent. The lawyer or agent will be informed by fax or e-mail that the document has been sent by that means and the postal dispatch shall be deemed to have been delivered to its addressee on the tenth day following the day on which it was lodged at the Luxembourg post office, unless it is shown by the acknowledgment of receipt that it was received on another date or the addressee informs the Registrar, within three weeks of being advised of the dispatch, that it has not reached its addressee (Article 79(2) of the RP).

A lawyer or agent who consents to service by fax or any other technical means of communication must indicate his fax number or e-mail address.

If no address for service in Luxembourg is given of if a party's lawyer or agent consents to service by fax or any other technical means of communication, procedural documents shall be sent by registered post to the address of the lawyer or agent in question and, in such cases, due service shall be deemed to have been effected by the lodging of the dispatch at the Luxembourg post office.

In the case of preliminary ruling proceedings, as there is no obligation to give an address for service, service is effected by registered post with a form for acknowledgement of receipt. A party may, however, expressly consent to service by fax or any other technical means of communication. In such cases, service will be effected in accordance with the procedures indicated above.

5. Procedural time limits

Procedural time limits are calculated in accordance with Article 80 et seq. of the RP. It must be emphasised that certain of those time limits cannot be extended—in particular, the time-limit for instituting proceedings (Articles 230 (formerly Article 173) and 232 (formerly Article 175) EC), the time-limit for applications for leave to intervene (Articles 93 and 123 of the RP), the time-limit for lodging a response (Article 115 of the RP) and the time-limit for lodging written observations in preliminary-ruling proceedings (Article 23 of the Statute).

a. Calculation of time-limits

A period which starts with the service of a pleading is reckoned from the time when the document is received at the address for service in Luxembourg, from the time when the document is received by the addressee when it is sent by registered post to the addressee or from the time of its transmission by fax or e-mail where the lawyer or agent has consented to service by those means of communication.

The day on which the document is received or sent is not included within the time limit (Article 80(1) of the Rules of Procedure).

b. Extension of time-limits on account of distance

Time limits are extended on account of distance by a fixed period of 10 days regardless of the place of establishment or habitual residence of the person concerned.

c. Curtailment of time-limits

The period within which a pleading must be lodged stops running when the original thereof is lodged.

However, the date on which a copy of the signed original of a procedural document, including where appropriate a list of the annexures to it, reaches the Registry by fax or by any other technical means of communication available to the Court (e-mail) shall be taken into account for the purpose of verifying compliance with time-limits, including those which cannot be extended, provided that the signed original of the document, accompanied by the annexures to it and the requisite copies, is lodged at the Registry within the ten days following that date. For transmission by e-mail, this means that a scanned version of the signed original of the document must be sent.

Transmission must without fail be directed either to the Registry fax number (+352) 433766 or to the e-mail address of the Registry: ecj.registry@curia.eu.int.

d. Extension of time-limits for other reasons

Certain time limits laid down by the Rules of Procedure may be extended under Article 82 thereof, such as the period within which a defence must be lodged. An application for any such extension must be made in every case by the party concerned. The application must be made a reasonable time before the prescribed period has expired and reasons for the application must be given. For that purpose, it is helpful if the consent of the opposite party is lodged at the same time as the application for extension.

Applications for extensions may be submitted by fax.

6. Originating applications

a. The application in direct actions

The originating application must be submitted in accordance with Articles 37 and 38 of the RP. It is important to note that Article 38(1) of the RP is strictly applied (see Article 38(7) of the RP). Failure to observe mandatory conditions may, in certain cases, render the application formally inadmissible.

In principle, the language of the case is chosen by the applicant (Article 29 of the RP).

b. Applications initiating appeal proceedings

The conditions applicable to applications initiating appeal proceedings are laid down in Article 112 of the RP. Article 112(1) of the RP is strictly applied (see Article 112(3) of the RP).

The language of the case is that of the decision of the Court of First Instance against which the appeal is brought (see Article 110 of the RP).

c. The purpose common to all originating applications

Originating applications must place before the Court all matters of fact and law which justify the commencement of proceedings. At the same time, the application defines the scope of the proceedings—in principle, it is not permitted to raise new issues or add to the forms of order sought in the course of the proceedings (see also B.13.a. below).

d. Summary of pleas and arguments

It is desirable for all pleadings to be accompanied by a summary, comprising no more than two pages, of the pleas and arguments put forward. The summary ensures that the pleas and arguments relied upon are clearly identified for the purpose, in particular, of preparation of the Report for the Hearing by the Judge Rapporteur.

7. References for preliminary rulings

In preliminary rulings, proceedings before the Court are set in motion by the national court's decision to stay the proceedings before it and submit questions on Community law. The litigants before the national court are not entitled to make a reference to the Court of Justice on their own initiative, nor are they under any obligation to take any action before they are served with a copy of the order for reference by the Registry of the Court of Justice (see B.2.c. and B.4. above).

The order for reference, the form of which is governed by the rules of the national jurisdiction, is forwarded to the Court of Justice either by the registry of the national court or by the Judge himself. The Court of Justice has drawn up guidance notes for the use of national courts when submitting requests for preliminary rulings.

If Counsel propose the text of the order for reference, it is important that they give a clear account of the factual and legislative background so that the meaning of the questions is clear.

707

8. The other documents submitted in direct actions and appeals

a. The defence

The substantive conditions governing the defence are set out in Article 40 of the RP. In view of the prohibition of putting forward new pleas in law, which applies to all stages of the proceedings, the defendant must set out all matters of law and of fact available to him when drafting the defence.

b. The reply and the rejoinder

The reply is intended merely to respond to the pleas and arguments raised in the defence. All unnecessary repetition must be avoided.

Similarly, the sole purpose of the rejoinder is to respond to the pleas and arguments put forward in the reply.

Both replies and rejoinders are subject to the requirements of Article 42 of the RP and may not, in principle, put forward new pleas in law.

The lodgement of a reply or rejoinder is purely optional. With a view to expediting the written procedure, the parties are requested seriously to consider the possibility of waiving the right to lodge them.

An extension of the time allowed for lodging replies and rejoinders is granted only in exceptional circumstances.

c. The response, reply and rejoinder in appeal proceedings

The response to an appeal must fulfil the requirements of Article 115 of the RP. A reply may be lodged only with the express prior consent of the President following an application from the person concerned. That application must without fail be lodged within a period of seven days as from notification of the response. With a view to completion of the written procedure within the shortest possible time, parties are requested as far as possible to refrain from making such applications. A rejoinder may be lodged following a reply.

d. Summaries of pleas in law and arguments

It is desirable for the defence and other pleadings to be accompanied, in the same way as originating applications, by a summary, not exceeding two pages in length, of the pleas in law and arguments put forward.

9. Written observations in preliminary ruling proceedings

After receiving a copy from the Court Registry of the request for a preliminary ruling, the "interested parties"—the litigants before the national court, the Member States, the Commission and, if appropriate, the Council, the Parliament and the European Central Bank and, in some cases, the other EEA States and the EFTA Supervisory Authority—may submit a document, referred to as written observations, within a period of two months (extended on account of distance by a period of 10 days in all cases). This time limit is mandatory and cannot therefore be extended.

The purpose of the written observations is to suggest the answers which the Court should give to the questions referred to it, and to set out succinctly, but completely, the reasoning on which those answers are based. It is important to bring to the attention of the Court the factual circumstances of the case before the national court and the relevant provisions of the national legislation at issue.

It must be emphasised that none of the parties is entitled to reply in writing to the written observations submitted by the others. Any response to the written observations of other parties must be made orally at the hearing. For that purpose, the written observations are notified to all the parties once the written procedure is completed and the necessary translations have been made.

The submission of written observations is strongly recommended since the time allowed for oral argument at the hearing is strictly limited. However, any party who has not submitted written observations retains the right to present oral argument, in particular his responses to the written arguments, at the hearing, if a hearing is held.

10. Stay of proceedings

Pursuant to Article 82a of the RP, the proceedings may be stayed:

- in the circumstances specified in Article 54 of the Statute where the Court of Justice and the Court of First Instance are called on to adjudicate at the same time on the same subject matter; the decision to stay the proceedings is a matter for the Court of Justice and the parties will not necessarily be given an opportunity to express their views;

- in all other cases, by decision of the President. The decision is taken after the views of the Advocate General have been heard and, save in the case of references for a preliminary ruling, those of the parties.

Whilst the proceedings are suspended, no period prescribed for any procedural steps by the parties will expire.

11. Applications for interim measures

a. Applications made directly to the Court of Justice

Applications for interim measures can be entertained only if they are made by a party to proceedings pending before the Court of Justice and relate to those proceedings. Notwithstanding that connection with the main proceedings, the application for interim measures must always be made in a separate document and must meet the conditions laid down by Article 83 of the RP. It may be presented at the same time as the originating application.

In view of the fact that applications for interim measures are made as a matter of urgency and of the need for rapid translation, applicants are requested to set out succinctly in their applications the pleas in fact and law on which their application is based. The application for interim measures should itself provide all the details needed to enable the President or the Court, as the case may be, to decide whether there are good grounds for the requested measures to be granted.

Once the application for interim measures has been served on him, the other party is traditionally allowed to submit written observations within a brief period, approximately one month.

It is only after those observations have been lodged that the President, with the Judge Rapporteur and Advocate General in attendance in some cases, hears the parties concerned (in public) and makes an order.

In cases of extreme urgency, the President may make an order immediately, that is to say within three or four days after the application for interim measures is made and without awaiting written observations from the other party. In such cases, the order is provisional, in that it does not bring the procedure on the interlocutory application to an end. The other party is then invited to submit written observations. The final stage, after the hearing, is a (second) order concluding the interlocutory proceedings which confirms or amends the first (provisional) order.

b. Appeals against interim orders made by the Court of First Instance

An appeal, limited to points of law, may be brought under Article 57 of the Statute against interim orders made by, in particular, the President of the Court of First

Instance. Such appeals are subject to the same procedure as applications for the adoption of interim measures made directly to the Court of Justice.

12. Expedited procedures

In direct actions, where it is inappropriate to issue interim measures and the particular urgency of a case is such that the Court must give final judgment with a minimum of delay, Article 62a of the Rules of Procedure provides that exceptionally, by decision of the President, a case may be determined pursuant to an expedited procedure.

An application for a case to be decided under an expedited procedure must be made in a separate document lodged at the same time as the application initiating the proceedings or the defence, as the case may be.

Under the expedited procedure, the oral procedure takes on greater significance. The written procedure is normally limited to the application and the defence. It is recommended that those documents be kept as short and concise as possible.

The date of the hearing, which is mandatory under the expedited procedure, will be fixed once the defence has been lodged or, if the decision to adjudicate under an expedited procedure is not made until after the defence has been lodged, once that decision has been taken.

An expedited procedure is also available for preliminary-ruling proceedings (Article 104a of the RP). Application of that procedure may be requested only by the national court from which the order for reference emanates.

13. Intervention

Intervention is allowed only in direct actions and appeals. The forms of order sought in the application to intervene must be limited to supporting the submissions of one or other of the parties. It must be borne in mind that the intervener is required to accept the case as it stands at the time of intervention.

The intervention procedure is twofold, comprising: (a) the action taken in order to obtain leave to intervene and (b) the actual participation of the intervener in the proceedings.

a. Action taken to obtain leave to intervene

A person wishing to intervene in a direct action must submit an application to intervene. The application must be submitted within a period of six weeks after publication of the notice in the Official Journal. An application lodged outside that time-limit may nevertheless be taken into account (see paragraph b. below). That document must contain all the information needed to enable the President or, in certain cases, the Court to make an order granting leave to intervene. Before the Court or the President makes an order, the original litigants are invited to submit written observations, and in exceptional cases even oral observations, as to whether or not intervention is admissible and appropriate. At the same time, they are asked to inform the Court whether they intend availing themselves of the right of confidentiality. If leave to intervene is granted, the party concerned is invited to lodge non confidential versions of its observations.

The application to intervene need not be in the language of the case.

b. The intervener's participation in the proceedings

Once leave to intervene has been granted, the intervener submits a statement in intervention. At that stage, the language of the case must be used, unless the intervener is a Member State.

The statement in intervention may be followed by observations from the parties.

However, if the application to intervene is lodged outside the normal time-limit for such applications, but before the decision to open the oral procedure has been taken, the intervener may submit his observations only orally at the hearing, if a hearing is held.

If a case is to be dealt with under the expedited procedure, an intervener may only make his submissions orally at the hearing.

14. Practical advice

a. The drafting and scheme of pleadings

There are no formal requirements applicable to pleadings (subject to compliance with rules laid down elsewhere); but they must be clear, concise and complete.

In view of the translation workload, in particular, and the time involved in translation, repetition must be avoided. The Court should be able, on a single reading, to apprehend the essential matters of fact and law.

Since in most cases pleadings will be read by the Judges and the Advocate General in a language other than that in which they are drafted, Counsel must always bear in mind that, if the meaning of a text is obscure in the original language, there is a risk that the translation will deepen the obscurity. That risk is aggravated by the fact that it is not always possible, in the transition from one language to another, to find a satisfactory, or even accurate, translation of the "legal jargon" which may be used before national courts.

Counsel should also remember the strict rule concerning the introduction of fresh pleas in law (see B.1, B.6.c and B.8.a above); they are not entitled to "reserve", even conditionally, pleas or arguments for subsequent pleadings or the hearing.

Ideally, the structure of pleadings should be clear and logical and they should be divided into separate parts with titles and paragraph numbers. In addition to a summary of the pleas in law and arguments, a table of contents may be useful in complex cases.

The pattern of originating applications may be outlined as follows:

- Details of the type of dispute involved, and of the kind of decision sought: action for annulment, application for interim measures, and so on.

- A brief account of the relevant facts.

- All the pleas in law on which the application is based.

- The arguments in support of each plea in law. They must include relevant references to the case law of the Court.

- The forms of order sought, based on the pleas in law and arguments.

In appeals, the forms of order sought are limited by Article 113 of the RP.

It is desirable for the defence and similar documents to follow closely the structure of the reasoning set out in the pleadings to which they constitute a response.

Written observations in preliminary rulings must set out:

- the relevant facts and the relevant provisions of national law,

- legal argument, including references to the case law of the Court,

- proposals for answers to be given by the Court to the questions submitted by the national court.

However, if the party concerned accepts the facts of the case as set out in the order for reference, he need merely say so.

b. Documents annexed to pleadings

It must be borne in mind that, pursuant to Article 37 of the RP, documents relied on by the parties must be annexed to pleadings. Unless there are exceptional circumstances and the parties consent, the Court will not take account of documents submitted outside the prescribed time limits or produced at the hearing.

Only relevant documents, on which the parties base their arguments, must be annexed to pleadings. Where documents are of some length, it is not only permissible, but indeed desirable, for the relevant extracts only to be annexed to the pleading and for a copy of the complete document to be lodged at the Registry.

Since annexes are not translated by the Court unless a Member of the Court so requests, the relevance of every document must be clearly indicated in the body of the pleading to which it is annexed.

The Court does not accept notes on which oral argument is to be based for inclusion in the file on the case (See C.4. below regarding the forwarding to the Interpretation Division of notes on which oral submissions are to be based.)

However, Counsel may in all cases send unofficial translations of pleadings and annexes, although, by virtue of Article 31 of the RP, such translations are not authentic.

c. Facts and evidence

The initial pleadings must indicate all evidence in support of each of the points of fact at issue. However, new evidence may be put forward subsequently (in contrast to the rule excluding new pleas in law), provided that adequate reasons are given to justify the delay.

The various forms of evidence upon which parties may rely are set out in Article 45(2) of the RP.

d. Citations

Counsel are requested, when citing a judgment of the Court, to give full details, including the names of the parties or, at least, the name of the applicant. In addition, when citing a passage from a judgment of the Court or from an Opinion of an Advocate General, they are requested to specify the page number and the number of the paragraph in which the passage in question is to be found.

To facilitate its work, the Court suggests as an appropriate form of citation that used in the judgments of the Court, for example: "judgment in Case 152/85 [1987] ECR 223, paragraph . . ."

C. Oral procedure

1. Preparation for the main hearing

Once the written procedure is completed and the necessary translations have been made, the Judge Rapporteur places the preliminary report before the general meeting, in which all the Members of the Court take part. At that meeting, the Judge Rapporteur, in consultation with the Advocate General, proposes any procedural or preparatory measures to be taken by the Court.

In most cases, the Court, at the suggestion of the Judge Rapporteur, decides to open the oral procedure without any preparatory inquiries. The exact date is fixed by the President.

a. Preparatory measures

At the same time, the Court decides on any preparatory measures to be taken, on a proposal from the Judge Rapporteur in consultation with the Advocate General. Accordingly, in some cases the parties may be asked, before the hearing, either to provide better particulars of the forms of order sought by them and of their pleas in law in order to clarify obscure points, or to examine in greater detail issues which have not been adequately canvassed, or to concentrate their pleadings on the decisive issues or to commence their oral submissions by answering certain questions put to them by the Court. The parties' replies to those questions should be given either in writing before the hearing within a period laid down for that purpose, or in writing on the date of the hearing or orally during the hearing. Exceptionally, preparatory measures may be decided upon at a later stage by the Judge Rapporteur and the Advocate General in consultation with the presiding Judge, but within a reasonable period, before Counsel have prepared their oral submissions.

A situation sometimes arises where the Court considers it appropriate to request coordination of oral submissions by several Counsel who are putting forward essentially the same views or of those of the Counsel called on to put forward the same views several times at the same hearing (for example in a direct action and related preliminary ruling proceedings).

Counsel are requested in all cases to take the initiative themselves to coordinate their oral submissions with a view to limiting the duration of the oral procedure.

b. The Report for the Hearing

A Report for the Hearing is prepared when the procedure in the case includes a hearing of oral argument (see C.7 below as regards dispensing with a hearing of oral argument). About three weeks before the hearing, the Report for the Hearing is sent to Counsel for the parties, interested parties and the other participants in the proceedings.

That Report, drawn up by the Judge Rapporteur, comprises, for direct actions and appeals, a brief description of the relevant facts and applicable law, a note of the forms of order sought by the parties and the pleas in law relied upon, with, as a rule, the arguments put forward in support of the pleas being recorded only in summary form. For references for a preliminary ruling, the Report comprises a description of the legal and factual background to the case, a note of the questions referred and the answers proposed in the written observations lodged, with the arguments put forward in support of the proposed answers being, as a rule, not recorded.

After receiving the Report for the Hearing, the parties are invited to satisfy themselves that there are no errors in the information contained in the Report. If Counsel consider that errors are present, they are requested to inform the Registrar before the hearing—and to suggest such amendments as they consider appropriate. It must, however, be emphasised that the Report for the Hearing is, by its very nature, a report presented by the Judge Rapporteur to the other Members of the Court and that it is for him to decide whether it need be amended.

2. The purpose of the oral procedure

In all cases (both direct actions and preliminary rulings)—except where a case is dealt with under the expedited procedure—the purpose of the oral procedure is:

- to answer the questions put by the Court;
- to recall, if necessary, by way of a highly condensed summary, the positions taken by the parties, with emphasis on the essential submissions in support of which written argument has been presented;

– to submit any new arguments prompted by recent events occurring after the close of the written procedure which, for that reason, could not be set out in the pleadings;

– to explain and expound the more complex points and those which are more difficult to grasp, and to highlight the most important points.

In preliminary rulings, the oral procedure enables lawyers to reply briefly to the main arguments set out in other written observations.

The oral procedure must, however, be seen as supplementing the written procedure and should involve no repetition of what has already been stated in writing.

3. Conduct of the oral procedure

Before the sitting commences, the Court invites Counsel to a brief private meeting in order to settle arrangements for the hearing. In some cases, at this early stage, the Judge Rapporteur or the Advocate General, or both, may indicate the matters which they would like to be developed in the oral observations.

As a rule, the hearing starts with oral argument from Counsel for the parties. This is followed by questions put to Counsel by the Members of the Court. The hearing concludes with brief responses from those Counsel who wish to make them.

The Members of the Court frequently interrupt Counsel when they are speaking in order to clarify points which appear to them to be of particular relevance.

4. The constraints of simultaneous interpretation

The Members of the Court do not necessarily follow the oral submissions in the language in which they are made but often listen to the simultaneous interpretation. This imposes certain constraints to which Counsel should, in their own interests, be attentive in order to ensure that what they say is perfectly understood by the Members of the Court. Counsel must therefore regard the interpreters as essential partners in presentation of their argument.

In the first place, it is highly inadvisable to read a text prepared in advance. The reason for this is that an address prepared in writing is made up of longer and more complicated sentences and is delivered at greater speed than one which is largely extemporaneous. It is preferable to speak on the basis of well-structured notes, using simple terms and short sentences.

In cases where Counsel prefers to follow a text, the same advice applies: simple terms and short sentences should be used and the text should be read at normal talking speed.

For the same reasons, it is desirable for Counsel to give details of the proposed structure of their submissions before dealing with any matter in detail.

Before attending the hearing, the interpreters carefully study the entire file on the case. If, as soon as possible, Counsel forward all relevant information concerning the probable content of their oral submissions (possibly the notes on which they are to be based), the interpreters will be able to complete their preparatory work, give a better rendering of the oral submissions and ensure that they are not disconcerted by technical terms, citations of texts or figures.

It is preferable to send such information, addressed to the Interpretation Division of the Court, by fax (Luxembourg (352) 4303 3697). Needless to say, the confidentiality of texts will be preserved. To obviate any misunderstanding, the name of the party must be indicated in the text.

Finally, it should be borne in mind that Counsel will not be heard unless they speak directly into the microphone.

5. Time allowed for addressing the Court

As a general rule, the period initially allowed to each main party is limited to a maximum of 30 minutes, limited, however, to a maximum of 15 minutes before Chambers composed of three Judges. The time allowed to interveners is limited to a maximum of 15 minutes. (This limitation applies only to oral argument properly so called and does not include the time taken to reply to questions put by Members of the Court).

Exceptions to this rule may be allowed by the Court in order to put the parties on an equal footing. For that purpose, an application must be sent to the Registrar of the Court, giving a detailed explanation and indicating the time considered necessary. In order to be taken into account, such applications must reach the Court at least 15 days before the date of the hearing. The decision on the application will be notified to the applicant at least one week before the hearing.

Any party who indicates that a shorter period will be sufficient must keep to the period allowed.

Where a party is represented by more than one Counsel, no more than two of them may present oral argument and their combined speaking time must not exceed the time limits indicated above. The answers to the questions put by Members of the Court and replies to the observations of other Counsel may however be given by Counsel other than those who addressed the Court.

Where several parties defend the same point of view before the Court (a situation which arises particularly where there are interventions or cases are joined), their Counsel are invited to confer with each other before the hearing so as to avoid any repetition.

The President of the Court or Chamber hearing the case will seek to ensure observance of the principles set out above, as regards both the purpose of the oral procedure, that is to say the actual content of the oral submissions, and the time allowed for addressing the Court.

6. The need for oral submissions

It is for each Counsel to judge, in the light of the purpose of the oral procedure, as defined above, whether oral argument is really necessary or whether a simple reference to the written observations or pleadings would suffice. The Court would like to stress that if a party refrains from presenting oral argument, this will never be construed as constituting acquiescence in the oral argument presented by another party.

In that connection, it goes without saying that the Court takes account of the procedural constraints inherent in preliminary ruling cases, in which only the oral procedure gives the parties an opportunity to respond to the written observations of another "interested party" and, if necessary, to take a position regarding new developments.

7. Omission of the hearing

The Rules of Procedure allow the oral procedure to be dispensed with unless one of the litigants or, in preliminary-ruling proceedings, an interested party taking part in the procedure has lodged a request for a hearing to be held, giving the reasons for which that litigant or interested party wishes to be heard.

A request for a hearing of the kind referred to above must, under the Rules of Procedure (Article 44a, Article 104(4) and Article 120) be lodged within one month after the person concerned has been notified of the conclusion of the written procedure or, in the case of preliminary-ruling proceedings, notification to the litigants and other interested parties of the written observations submitted. Reference to the necessity of lodging such an application to avoid possible omission of a hearing will be made in the letter from the Registry giving notice of conclusion of the written procedure or, in the case of preliminary-ruling proceedings, forwarding the written observations submitted. The period of one month for submitting such an application may be extended in response to a duly reasoned request.

8. The hearing of applications for interim measures

Before an order granting interim measures is made, the views of the parties concerned may be heard by the President, with the Judge Rapporteur and the Advocate General in attendance in some cases. The hearing is public and takes place about two to four weeks before the President, or, where appropriate, the Court, makes an order on the application. Such hearings are much less formal than the main hearing. In practice, the President starts by summarising, orally, the difficulties involved in the case. He then invites the parties to express their views on those difficulties. The hearing ends with questions put to the parties.

Where the matter is referred to the Court, the hearing before the formation dealing with the case follows the usual procedure.

It must be borne in mind that such hearings are not intended to enable the parties to address the merits of the case.

9. Practical advice

a. Postponement of hearings

The Court grants requests for postponement only for compelling reasons.

b. Entrance to the building

As a security measure, access to the Court building is controlled. Counsel are therefore requested kindly to produce their professional card, identity card, passport or some other means of identification.

c. Dress

Except at hearings of applications for interim measures, lawyers are required to appear before the Court in their robes. The Court always has a number of plain robes available to help out those who have forgotten their own.

Appendix D

Procedure before the Court of First Instance

Rules of Procedure of the Court of First Instance[1]

INTERPRETATION

Article 1(2)(7)

In these Rules:

D1–001

— "EC Treaty" means the Treaty establishing the European Community;

"EAEC Treaty" means the Treaty establishing the European Atomic Energy Community (Euratom);

— "Statute of the Court of Justice" means the Protocol on the Statute of the Court of Justice;

— "EEA Agreement" means the Agreement on the European Economic Area.

For the purposes of these Rules:

— "institutions" means the institutions of the Communities and bodies which are established by the Treaties, or by an act adopted in implementation thereof, and which may be parties before the Court of First Instance;

— "EFTA Surveillance Authority" means the surveillance authority referred to in the EEA Agreement.

TITLE 1

ORGANISATION OF THE COURT OF FIRST INSTANCE

Chapter 1

President and Members of the Court of First Instance

Article 2

1. Every Member of the Court of First Instance shall, as a rule, perform the function of Judge.

---

[1] This edition consolidates the Rules of Procedure of the Court of First Instance of the European Communities of May 2, 1991, [1991] O.J. L136/1, and [1991] O.J. L317/34 (corrigenda), as amended on September 15, 1994 ([1994] O.J. L249/17), on February 17, 1995 ([1995] O.J. L44/64), on July 6, 1995 ([1995] O.J. L172/3), on March 12, 1997 ([1997] O.J. L103/6, and [1997] O.J. L351/72 (corrigenda)), on May 17, 1999 ([1999] O.J. L135/92), on December 6, 2000 ([2000] O.J. L322/4), on May 21, 2003 ([2003] O.J. L147/22), on April 19, 2004 ([2004] O.J. L132/3), on April 21, 2004 ([2004] O.J. L127/108), and on October 12, 2005 ([2005] O.J. L298/1).

Members of the Court of First Instance are hereinafter referred to as "Judges".

2. Every Judge, with the exception of the President, may, in the circumstances specified in Articles 17 to 19, perform the function of Advocate General in a particular case.

References to the Advocate General in these Rules shall apply only where a Judge has been designated as Advocate General.

Article 3

The term of office of a Judge shall begin on the date laid down in his instrument of appointment. In the absence of any provision regarding the date, the term shall begin on the date of the instrument.

Article 4

1. Before taking up his duties, a Judge shall take the following oath before the Court of Justice of the European Communities:

"I swear that I will perform my duties impartially and conscientiously; I swear that I will preserve the secrecy of the deliberations of the Court."

2. Immediately after taking the oath, a Judge shall sign a declaration by which he solemnly undertakes that, both during and after his term of office, he will respect the obligations arising therefrom, and in particular the duty to behave with integrity and discretion as regards the acceptance, after he has ceased to hold office, of certain appointments and benefits.

Article 5(6)

When the Court of Justice is called upon to decide, after consulting the Court of First Instance, whether a Judge of the Court of First Instance no longer fulfils the requisite conditions or no longer meets the obligations arising from his office, the President of the Court of First Instance shall invite the Judge concerned to make representations to the Court of First Instance, in closed session and in the absence of the Registrar.

The Court of First Instance shall state the reasons for its opinion.

An opinion to the effect that a Judge of the Court of First Instance no longer fulfils the requisite conditions or no longer meets the obligations arising from his office must receive the votes of a majority of the Judges of the Court of First Instance. In that event, particulars of the voting shall be communicated to the Court of Justice.

Voting shall be by secret ballot; the Judge concerned shall not take part in the deliberations.

Article 6

With the exception of the President of the Court of First Instance and of the Presidents of the Chambers, the Judges shall rank equally in precedence according to their seniority in office.

Where there is equal seniority in office, precedence shall be determined by age.

Retiring Judges who are reappointed shall retain their former precedence.

Article 7(2)(6)(7)(10)

1. The Judges shall, immediately after the partial replacement provided for in Article 224 of the EC Treaty and Article 140 of the EAEC Treaty, elect one of their number as President of the Court of First Instance for a term of three years.

2. If the office of President of the Court of First Instance falls vacant before the normal date of expiry thereof, the Court of First Instance shall elect a successor for the remainder of the term.

3. The elections provided for in this Article shall be by secret ballot. If a Judge obtains an absolute majority he shall be elected. If no Judge obtains an absolute majority, a second ballot shall be held and the Judge obtaining the most votes shall be elected. Where two or more Judges obtain an equal number of votes the oldest of them shall be deemed elected.

Article 8(7)

The President of the Court of First Instance shall direct the judicial business and the administration of the Court of First Instance. He shall preside at plenary sittings and deliberations.

The President of the Court of First Instance shall preside over the Grand Chamber.

If the President of the Court of First Instance is assigned to a Chamber of three or of five Judges, he shall preside over that Chamber.

Article 9(10)

When the President of the Court of First Instance is absent or prevented from attending or when the office of President is vacant, the functions of President shall be exercised by a President of a Chamber according to the order of precedence laid down in Article 6.

If the President of the Court of First Instance and the Presidents of the Chambers are all absent or prevented from attending at the same time, or their posts are vacant at the same time, the functions of President shall be exercised by one of the other Judges according to the order of precedence laid down in Article 6.

Chapter 2

Constitution of the Chambers and Designation of Judge-Rapporteurs and Advocates General

Article 10(7)(9)

1. The Court of First Instance shall set up Chambers of three and of five Judges and a Grand Chamber of thirteen Judges and shall decide which Judges shall be attached to them.

2. The decision taken in accordance with this Article shall be published in the *Official Journal of the European Union*.

Article 11(5)(7)

1. Cases before the Court of First Instance shall be heard by Chambers composed of three or of five Judges in accordance with Article 10.

Cases may be heard by the Court of First Instance sitting in plenary session or by the Grand Chamber under the conditions laid down in Articles 14, 51, 106, 118, 124, 127 and 129.

Cases may be heard by a single Judge where they are delegated to him under the conditions specified in Articles 14 and 51 or assigned to him pursuant to Articles 124, 127(1) or 129(2).

2. In cases coming before a Chamber, the term "Court of First Instance" in these Rules shall designate that Chamber. In cases delegated or assigned to a single Judge the term "Court of First Instance" in these Rules shall designate that Judge.

Article 12(1)(7)

1. The Court of First Instance shall lay down criteria by which cases are to be allocated among the Chambers.
   The decision shall be published in the *Official Journal of the European Union*.

Article 13

1. As soon as the application initiating proceedings has been lodged, the President of the Court of First Instance shall assign the case to one of the Chambers.
   2. The President of the Chamber shall propose to the President of the Court of First Instance, in respect of each case assigned to the Chamber, the designation of a Judge to act as Rapporteur; the President of the Court of First Instance shall decide on the proposal.

Article 14(5)(7)

1. Whenever the legal difficulty or the importance of the case or special circumstances so justify, a case may be referred to the Court of First Instance sitting in plenary session, to the Grand Chamber or to a Chamber composed of a different number of Judges.
   2. (1) The following cases assigned to a Chamber composed of three Judges may be heard and determined by the Judge-Rapporteur sitting as a single Judge where, having regard to the lack of difficulty of the questions of law or fact raised, to the limited importance of those cases and to the absence of other special circumstances, they are suitable for being so heard and determined and have been delegated under the conditions laid down in Article 51:

   (a) cases brought pursuant to Article 236 of the EC Treaty and to Article 152 of the EAEC Treaty;
   (b) cases brought pursuant to the fourth paragraph of Article 230, the third paragraph of Article 232 and Article 235 of the EC Treaty, to the second paragraph of Article 33, Article 35 and the first and second paragraphs of Article 40 of the ECSC Treaty and to the fourth paragraph of Article 146, the third paragraph of Article 148 and Article 151 of the EAEC Treaty that raise only questions already clarified by established case-law or that form part of a series of cases in which the same relief is sought and of which one has already been finally decided;
   (c) cases brought pursuant to Article 238 of the EC Treaty, Article 42 of the ECSC Treaty and Article 153 of the EAEC Treaty.

   (2) Delegation to a single Judge shall not be possible:

   (a) in cases which raise issues as to the legality of an act of general application;
   (b) in cases concerning the implementation of the rules:

   — on competition and on control of concentrations,
   — relating to aid granted by States,
   — relating to measures to protect trade,
   — relating to the common organisation of the agricultural markets, with the exception of cases that form part of a series of cases in which the same relief is sought and of which one has already been finally decided;

   (c) in the cases referred to in Article 130(1).

   (3) The single Judge shall refer the case back to the Chamber if he finds that the conditions justifying its delegation are no longer satisfied.

3. The decisions to refer or to delegate a case which are provided for in paragraphs 1 and 2 shall be taken under the conditions laid down in Article 51.

Article 15(7)

1. The Judges shall elect from amongst themselves, pursuant to the provisions of Article 7(3), the Presidents of the Chambers composed of three and of five Judges.

2. The Presidents of Chambers of five Judges shall be elected for a term of three years. Their term of office shall be renewable once.

The election of the Presidents of Chambers of five Judges shall take place immediately after the election of the President of the Court of First Instance as provided for in Article 7(1).

3. The Presidents of Chambers of three Judges shall be elected for a defined term.

4. If the office of the President of a Chamber falls vacant before the normal date of expiry thereof, a successor shall be elected as President of the Chamber for the remainder of the term.

5. The results of those elections shall be published in the *Official Journal of the European Union*.

Article 16(5)

In cases coming before a Chamber the powers of the President shall be exercised by the President of the Chamber.

In cases delegated or assigned to a single Judge, with the exception of those referred to in Articles 105 and 106, the powers of the President shall be exercised by that Judge.

Article 17

When the Court of First Instance sits in plenary session, it shall be assisted by an Advocate General designated by the President of the Court of First Instance.

Article 18

A Chamber of the Court of First Instance may be assisted by an Advocate General if it is considered that the legal difficulty or the factual complexity of the case so requires.

Article 19

The decision to designate an Advocate General in a particular case shall be taken by the Court of First Instance sitting in plenary session at the request of the Chamber before which the case comes.

The President of the Court of First Instance shall designate the Judge called upon to perform the function of Advocate General in that case.

Chapter 3

Registry

Section 1—The Registrar

Article 20

1. The Court of First Instance shall appoint the Registrar.

Two weeks before the date fixed for making the appointment, the President of the Court of First Instance shall inform the Judges of the applications which have been submitted for the post.

2. An application shall be accompanied by full details of the candidate's age, nationality, university degrees, knowledge of any languages, present and past occupations and experience, if any, in judicial and international fields.

3. The appointment shall be made following the procedure laid down in Article 7(3).

4. The Registrar shall be appointed for a term of six years. He may be reappointed.

5. Before he takes up his duties the Registrar shall take the oath before the Court of First Instance in accordance with Article 4.

6. The Registrar may be deprived of his office only if he no longer fulfils the requisite conditions or no longer meets the obligations arising from his office; the Court of First Instance shall take its decision after giving the Registrar an opportunity to make representations.

7. If the office of Registrar falls vacant before the usual date of expiry of the term thereof, the Court of First Instance shall appoint a new Registrar for a term of six years.

Article 21

The Court of First Instance may, following the procedure laid down in respect of the Registrar, appoint one or more Assistant Registrars to assist the Registrar and to take his place in so far as the Instructions to the Registrar referred to in Article 23 allow.

Article 22

Where the Registrar is absent or prevented from attending and, if necessary, where the Assistant Registrar is absent or so prevented, or where their posts are vacant, the President of the Court of First Instance shall designate an official or servant to carry out the duties of Registrar.

Article 23

Instructions to the Registrar shall be adopted by the Court of First Instance acting on a proposal from the President of the Court of First Instance.

Article 24(2)(6)(7)(10)

1. There shall be kept in the Registry, under the control of the Registrar, a register in which all pleadings and supporting documents shall be entered in the order in which they are lodged.

2. When a document has been registered, the Registrar shall make a note to that effect on the original and, if a party so requests, on any copy submitted for the purpose.

3. Entries in the register and the notes provided for in the preceding paragraph shall be authentic.

4. Rules for keeping the register shall be prescribed by the Instructions to the Registrar referred to in Article 23.

5. Persons having an interest may consult the register at the Registry and may obtain copies or extracts on payment of a charge on a scale fixed by the Court of First Instance on a proposal from the Registrar.

The parties to a case may on payment of the appropriate charge also obtain copies of pleadings and authenticated copies of orders and judgments.

6. Notice shall be given in the *Official Journal of the European Union* of the date of registration of an application initiating proceedings, the names and addresses of the parties, the subject-matter of the proceedings, the form of order sought by the applicant and a summary of the pleas in law and of the main supporting arguments.

7. Where the Council or the Commission is not a party to a case, the Court of First Instance shall send to it copies of the application and of the defence, without the annexes thereto, to enable it to assess whether the inapplicability of one of its acts is being invoked under Article 241 of the EC Treaty, the third paragraph of Article 36 of the ECSC Treaty or Article 156 of the EAEC Treaty.

Article 25

1. The Registrar shall be responsible, under the authority of the President, for the acceptance, transmission and custody of documents and for effecting service as provided for by these Rules.

2. The Registrar shall assist the Court of First Instance, the President and the Judges in all their official functions.

Article 26

The Registrar shall have custody of the seals. He shall be responsible for the records and be in charge of the publications of the Court of First Instance.

Article 27

Subject to Articles 5 and 33, the Registrar shall attend the sittings of the Court of First Instance.

Section 2—Other Departments

Article 28

The officials and other servants whose task is to assist directly the President, the Judges and the Registrar shall be appointed in accordance with the Staff Regulations. They shall be responsible to the Registrar, under the authority of the President of the Court of First Instance.

Article 29

The officials and other servants referred to in Article 28 shall take the oath provided for in Article 20(2) of the Rules of Procedure of the Court of Justice before the President of the Court of First Instance in the presence of the Registrar.

Article 30

The Registrar shall be responsible, under the authority of the President of the Court of First Instance, for the administration of the Court of First Instance, its financial management and its accounts; he shall be assisted in this by the departments of the Court of Justice.

Chapter 4

The Working of the Court of First Instance

Article 31

1. The dates and times of the sittings of the Court of First Instance shall be fixed by the President.

2. The Court of First Instance may choose to hold one or more sittings in a place other than that in which the Court of First Instance has its seat.

Article 32(4)(5)(7)(10)

1. Where, by reason of a Judge being absent or prevented from attending, there is an even number of Judges, the most junior Judge within the meaning of Article 6 shall abstain from taking part in the deliberations unless he is the Judge-Rapporteur. In this case, the Judge immediately senior to him shall abstain from taking part in the deliberations.

Where, following the designation of an Advocate General pursuant to Article 17, there is an even number of Judges in the Court of First Instance sitting in plenary session, the President of the Court shall designate, before the hearing and in accordance with a rota established in advance by the Court of First Instance and published in the *Official Journal of the European Union*, the Judge who will not take part in the judgment of the case.

2. If after the Court of First Instance has been convened in plenary session, it is found that the quorum of nine Judges has not been attained, the President of the Court of First Instance shall adjourn the sitting until there is a quorum.

3. If in any Chamber of three or of five Judges, the quorum of three Judges has not been attained, the President of that Chamber shall so inform the President of the Court of First Instance who shall designate another Judge to complete the Chamber.

The quorum of the Grand Chamber shall be nine Judges. If that quorum has not been attained, the President of the Court of First Instance shall designate another Judge to complete the Chamber.

If in the Grand Chamber or in any Chamber of five Judges the number of Judges provided for by Article 10(1) is not attained by reason of a Judge's being absent or prevented from attending before the date of the opening of the oral procedure, the President of the Court of First Instance shall designate a Judge to complete that Chamber in order to restore the number of Judges provided for.

4. If in any Chamber of three or five Judges the number of Judges assigned to that Chamber is higher than three or five respectively, the President of the Chamber shall decide which of the Judges will be called upon to take part in the judgment of the case.

5. If the single Judge to whom the case has been delegated or assigned is absent or prevented from attending, the President of the Court of First Instance shall designate another Judge to replace that Judge.

Article 33

1. The Court of First Instance shall deliberate in closed session.

2. Only those Judges who were present at the oral proceedings may take part in the deliberations.

3. Every Judge taking part in the deliberations shall state his opinion and the reasons for it.

4. Any Judge may require that any question be formulated in the language of his choice and communicated in writing to the other Judges before being put to the vote.

5. The conclusions reached by the majority of the Judges after final discussion shall determine the decision of the Court of First Instance. Votes shall be cast in reverse order to the order of precedence laid down in Article 6.

6. Differences of view on the substance, wording or order of questions, or on the interpretation of a vote shall be settled by decision of the Court of First Instance.

7. Where the deliberations of the Court of First Instance concern questions of its own administration, the Registrar shall be present, unless the Court of First Instance decides to the contrary.

8. Where the Court of First Instance sits without the Registrar being present it shall, if necessary, instruct the most junior Judge within the meaning of Article 6 to draw up minutes. The minutes shall be signed by this Judge and by the President.

Article 34

1. Subject to any special decision of the Court of First Instance, its vacations shall be as follows:

— from 18 December to 10 January,

— from the Sunday before Easter to the second Sunday after Easter,

— from 15 July to 15 September.

During the vacations, the functions of President shall be exercised at the place where the Court of First Instance has its seat either by the President himself, keeping in touch with the Registrar, or by a President of Chamber or other Judge invited by the President to take his place.

2. In a case of urgency, the President may convene the Judges during the vacations.

3. The Court of First Instance shall observe the official holidays of the place where it has its seat.

4. The Court of First Instance may, in proper circumstances, grant leave of absence to any Judge.

Chapter 5

Languages

Article 35(2)(4)(8)

1. The language of a case shall be Czech, Danish, Dutch, English, Estonian, Finnish, French, German, Greek, Hungarian, Irish, Italian, Latvian, Lithuanian, Maltese, Polish, Portuguese, Slovak, Slovene, Spanish or Swedish.

2. The language of the case shall be chosen by the applicant, except that:

(a) where the defendant is a Member State or a natural or legal person having the nationality of a Member State, the language of the case shall be the official language of that State; where that State has more than one official language, the applicant may choose between them;

(b) at the joint request of the parties, the use of another of the languages mentioned in paragraph 1 for all or part of the proceedings may be authorised;

(c) at the request of one of the parties, and after the opposite party and the Advocate General have been heard, the use of another of the languages

LIVERPOOL JOHN MOORES UNIVERSITY
Aldham Robarts L.R.C.
TEL. 0151 231 3701/3634

mentioned in paragraph 1 as the language of the case for all or part of the proceedings may be authorised by way of derogation from subparagraph (**b**); such a request may not be submitted by an institution.

Requests as above may be decided on by the President; the latter may and, where he proposes to accede to a request without the agreement of all the parties, must refer the request to the Court of First Instance.

3. The language of the case shall be used in the written and oral pleadings of the parties and in supporting documents, and also in the minutes and decisions of the Court of First Instance.

Any supporting documents expressed in another language must be accompanied by a translation into the language of the case.

In the case of lengthy documents, translations may be confined to extracts. However, the Court of First Instance may, of its own motion or at the request of a party, at any time call for a complete or fuller translation.

Notwithstanding the foregoing provisions, a Member State shall be entitled to use its official language when intervening in a case before the Court of First Instance. This provision shall apply both to written statements and to oral addresses. The Registrar shall cause any such statement or address to be translated into the language of the case.

The States, other than the Member States, which are parties to the EEA Agreement, and also the EFTA Surveillance Authority, may be authorised to use one of the languages mentioned in paragraph 1, other than the language of the case, when they intervene in a case before the Court of First Instance. This provision shall apply both to written statements and oral addresses. The Registrar shall cause any such statement or address to be translated into the language of the case.

4. Where a witness or expert states that he is unable adequately to express himself in one of the languages referred to in paragraph 1 of this Article, the Court of First Instance may authorise him to give his evidence in another language. The Registrar shall arrange for translation into the language of the case.

5. The President in conducting oral proceedings, the Judge-Rapporteur both in his preliminary report and in his report for the hearing, Judges and the Advocate General in putting questions and the Advocate General in delivering his opinion may use one of the languages referred to in paragraph 1 of this Article other than the language of the case. The Registrar shall arrange for translation into the language of the case.

Article 36

1. The Registrar shall, at the request of any Judge, of the Advocate General or of a party, arrange for anything said or written in the course of the proceedings before the Court of First Instance to be translated into the languages he chooses from those referred to in Article 35(1).

2. Publications of the Court of First Instance shall be issued in the languages referred to in Article 1 of Council Regulation No 1.

Article 37

The texts of documents drawn up in the language of the case or in any other language authorised by the Court of First Instance pursuant to Article 35 shall be authentic.

Chapter 6

Rights and Obligations of Agents, Advisers and Lawyers

Article 38(2)

1. Agents, advisers and lawyers, appearing before the Court of First Instance or before any judicial authority to which it has addressed letters rogatory, shall enjoy

immunity in respect of words spoken or written by them concerning the case or the parties.

2. Agents, advisers and lawyers shall enjoy the following further privileges and facilities:

(a) papers and documents relating to the proceedings shall be exempt from both search and seizure; in the event of a dispute the customs officials or police may seal those papers and documents; they shall then be immediately forwarded to the Court of First Instance for inspection in the presence of the Registrar and of the person concerned;

(b) agents, advisers and lawyers shall be entitled to such allocation of foreign currency as may be necessary for the performance of their duties;

(c) agents, advisers and lawyers shall be entitled to travel in the course of duty without hindrance.

Article 39(2)

In order to qualify for the privileges, immunities and facilities specified in Article 38, persons entitled to them shall furnish proof of their status as follows:

(a) agents shall produce an official document issued by the party for whom they act and shall forward without delay a copy thereof to the Registrar;

(b) advisers and lawyers shall produce a certificate signed by the Registrar. The validity of this certificate shall be limited to a specified period, which may be extended or curtailed according to the length of the proceedings.

Article 40

The privileges, immunities and facilities specified in Article 38 are granted exclusively in the interests of the proper conduct of proceedings.

The Court of First Instance may waive the immunity where it considers that the proper conduct of proceedings will not be hindered thereby.

Article 41(10)

1. If the Court of First Instance considers that the conduct of an adviser or lawyer towards the Court of First Instance, the President, a Judge or the Registrar is incompatible with the dignity of the Court of First Instance or with the requirements of the proper administration of justice, or that such adviser or lawyer uses his rights for purposes other than those for which they were granted, it shall so inform the person concerned. The Court of First Instance may inform the competent authorities to whom the person concerned is answerable; a copy of the letter sent to those authorities shall be forwarded to the person concerned.

On the same grounds the Court of First Instance may at any time, having heard the person concerned, exclude that person from the proceedings by order. That order shall have immediate effect.

2. Where an adviser or lawyer is excluded from the proceedings, the proceedings shall be suspended for a period fixed by the President in order to allow the party concerned to appoint another adviser or lawyer.

3. Decisions taken under this Article may be rescinded.

Article 42(2)(7)

The provisions of this Chapter shall apply to university teachers who have a right of audience before the Court of First Instance in accordance with Article 19 of the Statute of the Court of Justice.

TITLE 2

PROCEDURE

Chapter 1

Written Procedure

Article 43(6)(10)

1. The original of every pleading must be signed by the party's agent or lawyer.

The original, accompanied by all annexes referred to therein, shall be lodged together with five copies for the Court of First Instance and a copy for every other party to the proceedings. Copies shall be certified by the party lodging them.

2. Institutions shall in addition produce, within time-limits laid down by the Court of First Instance, translations of all pleadings into the other languages provided for by Article 1 of Council Regulation No 1. The second subparagraph of paragraph 1 of this Article shall apply.

3. All pleadings shall bear a date. In the reckoning of time-limits for taking steps in proceedings only the date of lodgment at the Registry shall be taken into account.

4. To every pleading there shall be annexed a file containing the documents relied on in support of it, together with a schedule listing them.

5. Where in view of the length of a document only extracts from it are annexed to the pleading, the whole document or a full copy of it shall be lodged at the Registry.

6. Without prejudice to the provisions of paragraphs 1 to 5, the date on which a copy of the signed original of a pleading, including the schedule of documents referred to in paragraph 4, is received at the Registry by telefax or other technical means of communication available to the Court of First Instance shall be deemed to be the date of lodgment for the purposes of compliance with the time-limits for taking steps in proceedings, provided that the signed original of the pleading, accompanied by the annexes and copies referred to in the second subparagraph of paragraph 1, is lodged at the Registry no later than ten days thereafter. Article 102(2) shall not be applicable to this period of ten days.

7. Without prejudice to the first subparagraph of paragraph 1 or to paragraphs 2 to 5, the Court of First Instance may by decision determine the criteria for a procedural document sent to the Registry by electronic means to be deemed to be the original of that document. That decision shall be published in the *Official Journal of the European Union*.

Article 44(1)(2)(6)(7)

1. An application of the kind referred to in Article 21 of the Statute of the Court of Justice shall state:

(a) the name and address of the applicant;

(b) the designation of the party against whom the application is made;

(c) the subject-matter of the proceedings and a summary of the pleas in law on which the application is based;

(d) the form of order sought by the applicant;

(e) where appropriate, the nature of any evidence offered in support.

2. For the purposes of the proceedings, the application shall state an address for service in the place where the Court of First Instance has its seat and the name of the person who is authorised and has expressed willingness to accept service.

In addition to or instead of specifying an address for service as referred to in the first subparagraph, the application may state that the lawyer or agent agrees that service is to be effected on him by telefax or other technical means of communication.

If the application does not comply with the requirements referred to in the first and second subparagraphs, all service on the party concerned for the purposes of the proceedings shall be effected, for so long as the defect has not been cured, by registered letter addressed to the agent or lawyer of that party. By way of derogation from the first paragraph of Article 100, service shall then be deemed to have been duly effected by the lodging of the registered letter at the post office of the place where the Court of First Instance has its seat.

3. The lawyer acting for a party must lodge at the Registry a certificate that he is authorised to practise before a Court of a Member State or of another State which is a party to the EEA Agreement.

4. The application shall be accompanied, where appropriate, by the documents specified in the second paragraph of Article 21 of the Statute of the Court of Justice.

5. An application made by a legal person governed by private law shall be accompanied by:

(a) the instrument or instruments constituting and regulating that legal person or a recent extract from the register of companies, firms or associations or any other proof of its existence in law;

(b) proof that the authority granted to the applicant's lawyer has been properly conferred on him by someone authorised for the purpose.

5a. An application submitted under Article 238 of the EC Treaty, Article 42 of the ECSC Treaty or Article 153 of the EAEC Treaty pursuant to an arbitration clause contained in a contract governed by public or private law, entered into by the Community or on its behalf, shall be accompanied by a copy of the contract which contains that clause.

6. If an application does not comply with the requirements set out in paragraphs 3 to 5 of this Article, the Registrar shall prescribe a reasonable period within which the applicant is to comply with them whether by putting the application itself in order or by producing any of the above-mentioned documents. If the applicant fails to put the application in order or to produce the required documents within the time prescribed, the Court of First Instance shall decide whether the non-compliance with these conditions renders the application formally inadmissible.

Article 45

The application shall be served on the defendant. In a case where Article 44(6) applies, service shall be effected as soon as the application has been put in order or the Court of First Instance has declared it admissible notwithstanding the failure to observe the formal requirements set out in that Article.

Article 46(10)

Within two months after service on him of the application, the defendant shall lodge a defence, stating:

(a) the name and address of the defendant;

(b) the arguments of fact and law relied on;

(c) the form of order sought by the defendant;

(d) the nature of any evidence offered by him.

The provisions of Article 44(2) to (5) shall apply to the defence.

2. In proceedings between the Communities and their servants the defence shall be accompanied by the complaint within the meaning of Article 90(2) of the Staff Regulations of Officials and by the decision rejecting the complaint together with the dates on which the complaint was submitted and the decision notified.

3. The time-limit laid down in paragraph 1 of this Article may, in exceptional circumstances, be extended by the President on a reasoned application by the defendant.

Article 47(6)

1. The application initiating the proceedings and the defence may be supplemented by a reply from the applicant and by a rejoinder from the defendant unless the Court of First Instance, after hearing the Advocate General, decides that a second exchange of pleadings is unnecessary because the documents before it are sufficiently comprehensive to enable the parties to elaborate their pleas and arguments in the course of the oral procedure. However, the Court of First Instance may authorise the parties to supplement the documents if the applicant presents a reasoned request to that effect within two weeks from the notification of that decision.

2. The President shall fix the time-limits within which these pleadings are to be lodged.

Article 48

1. In reply or rejoinder a party may offer further evidence. The party must, however, give reasons for the delay in offering it.

2. No new plea in law may be introduced in the course of proceedings unless it is based on matters of law or of fact which come to light in the course of the procedure.

If in the course of the procedure one of the parties puts forward a new plea in law which is so based, the President may, even after the expiry of the normal procedural time-limits, acting on a report of the Judge-Rapporteur and after hearing the Advocate General, allow the other party time to answer on that plea.

Consideration of the admissibility of the plea shall be reserved for the final judgment.

Article 49

At any stage of the proceedings the Court of First Instance may, after hearing the Advocate General, prescribe any measure of organisation of procedure or any measure of inquiry referred to in Articles 64 and 65 or order that a previous inquiry be repeated or expanded.

Article 50(4)(10)

1. The President may, at any time, after hearing the parties and the Advocate General, order that two or more cases concerning the same subject-matter shall, on account of the connection between them, be joined for the purposes of the written or oral procedure or of the final judgment. The cases may subsequently be disjoined. The President may refer these matters to the Court of First Instance.

2. The agents, advisers or lawyers of all the parties to the joined cases, including interveners, may examine at the Registry the pleadings served on the parties in the other cases concerned. The President may, however, on application by a party,

without prejudice to Article 67(3), exclude secret or confidential documents from that consultation.

Article 51(1)(5)(7)

1. In the cases specified in Article 14(1), and at any stage in the proceedings, the Chamber hearing the case or the President of the Court First Instance may, either on its or his own initiative or at the request of one of the parties, propose to the Court of First Instance sitting in plenary session that the case be referred to the Court of First Instance sitting in plenary session, to the Grand Chamber or to a Chamber composed of a different number of Judges. The Court of First Instance sitting in plenary session shall, after hearing the parties and the Advocate General, decide whether or not to refer a case.

The case shall be decided by a Chamber composed of at least five Judges where a Member State or an institution of the European Communities which is a party to the proceedings so requests.

2. The decision to delegate a case to a single Judge in the situations specified in Article 14(2) shall be taken, after the parties have been heard, unanimously by the Chamber composed of three Judges before which the case is pending.

Where a Member State or an institution of the European Communities which is a party to the proceedings objects to the case being heard by a single Judge the case shall be maintained before or referred to the Chamber to which the Judge-Rapporteur belongs.

Article 52(6)(7)

1. Without prejudice to Article 49, the President shall,

(a) after the rejoinder has been lodged, or

(b) where no reply or no rejoinder has been lodged within the time-limit fixed in accordance with Article 47(2), or

(c) where the party concerned has waived his right to lodge a reply or rejoinder, or

(d) where the Court of First Instance has decided that there is no need, in accordance with Article 47(1), to supplement the application and the defence by a reply and a rejoinder, or

(e) where the Court of First Instance has decided that it is appropriate to adjudicate under an expedited procedure in accordance with Article 76a(1),

fix a date on which the Judge-Rapporteur is to present his preliminary report to the Court of First Instance.

2. The preliminary report shall contain recommendations as to whether measures of organisation of procedure or measures of inquiry should be undertaken and whether the case should be referred to the Court of First Instance sitting in plenary session, to the Grand Chamber or to a Chamber composed of a different number of Judges.

The Court of First Instance shall decide, after hearing the Advocate General, what action to take upon the recommendations of the Judge-Rapporteur.

Article 53

Where the Court of First Instance decides to open the oral procedure without undertaking measures of organisation of procedure or ordering a preparatory inquiry, the President of the Court of First Instance shall fix the opening date.

731

Article 54

Without prejudice to any measures of organisation of procedure or measures of inquiry which may be arranged at the stage of the oral procedure, where, during the written procedure, measures of organisation of procedure or measures of inquiry have been instituted and completed, the President shall fix the date for the opening of the oral procedure.

Chapter 2

Oral Procedure

Article 55(10)

1. The Court of First Instance shall deal with the cases before it in the order in which the preparatory inquiries in them have been completed. Where the preparatory inquiries in several cases are completed simultaneously, the order in which they are to be dealt with shall be determined by the dates of entry in the register of the applications initiating them respectively.

2. The President may in special circumstances order that a case be given priority over others.

The President may in special circumstances, after hearing the parties and the Advocate General, either on his own initiative or at the request of one of the parties, defer a case to be dealt with at a later date. On a joint application by the parties the President may order that a case be deferred.

Article 56

The proceedings shall be opened and directed by the President, who shall be responsible for the proper conduct of the hearing.

Article 57

The oral proceedings in cases heard *in camera* shall not be published.

Article 58

The President may in the course of the hearing put questions to the agents, advisers or lawyers of the parties.

The other Judges and the Advocate General may do likewise.

Article 59

A party may address the Court of First Instance only through his agent, adviser or lawyer.

Article 60

Where an Advocate General has not been designated in a case, the President shall declare the oral procedure closed at the end of the hearing.

Article 61

1. Where the Advocate General delivers his opinion in writing, he shall lodge it at the Registry, which shall communicate it to the parties.

2. After the delivery, orally or in writing, of the opinion of the Advocate General the President shall declare the oral procedure closed.

Article 62

The Court of First Instance may, after hearing the Advocate General, order the reopening of the oral procedure.

Article 63

1. The Registrar shall draw up minutes of every hearing. The minutes shall be signed by the President and by the Registrar and shall constitute an official record.

2. The parties may inspect the minutes at the Registry and obtain copies at their own expense.

Chapter 3

Measures of Organisation of Procedure and Measures of Inquiry

Section 1—Measures of organisation of procedure

Article 64(10)

1. The purpose of measures of organisation of procedure shall be to ensure that cases are prepared for hearing, procedures carried out and disputes resolved under the best possible conditions. They shall be prescribed by the Court of First Instance, after hearing the Advocate General.

2. Measures of organisation of procedure shall, in particular, have as their purpose:

(a) to ensure efficient conduct of the written and oral procedure and to facilitate the taking of evidence;

(b) to determine the points on which the parties must present further argument or which call for measures of inquiry;

(c) to clarify the forms of order sought by the parties, their pleas in law and arguments and the points at issue between them;

(d) to facilitate the amicable settlement of proceedings.

3. Measures of organisation of procedure may, in particular, consist of:

(a) putting questions to the parties;

(b) inviting the parties to make written or oral submissions on certain aspects of the proceedings;

(c) asking the parties or third parties for information or particulars;

(d) asking for documents or any papers relating to the case to be produced;

(e) summoning the parties' agents or the parties in person to meetings.

4. Each party may, at any stage of the procedure, propose the adoption or modification of measures of organisation of procedure. In that case, the other parties shall be heard before those measures are prescribed.

Where the procedural circumstances so require, the Registrar shall inform the parties of the measures envisaged by the Court of First Instance and shall give them an opportunity to submit comments orally or in writing.

5. If the Court of First Instance sitting in plenary session or as the Grand Chamber decides to prescribe measures of organisation of procedure and does not undertake such measures itself, it shall entrust the task of so doing to the Chamber to which the case was originally assigned or to the Judge-Rapporteur.

If a Chamber prescribes measures of organisation of procedure and does not undertake such measures itself, it shall entrust the task to the Judge-Rapporteur.

The Advocate General shall take part in measures of organisation of procedure.

Section 2—Measures of inquiry

Article 65(2)(7)

Without prejudice to Articles 24 and 25 of the Statute of the Court of Justice, the following measures of inquiry may be adopted:

(a) the personal appearance of the parties;

(b) a request for information and production of documents;

(c) oral testimony;

(d) the commissioning of an expert's report;

(e) an inspection of the place or thing in question.

Article 66

1. The Court of First Instance, after hearing the Advocate General, shall prescribe the measures of inquiry that it considers appropriate by means of an order setting out the facts to be proved. Before the Court of First Instance decides on the measures of inquiry referred to in Article 65(c), (d) and (e) the parties shall be heard.

The order shall be served on the parties.

2. Evidence may be submitted in rebuttal and previous evidence may be amplified.

Article 67(6)(10)

1. Where the Court of First Instance sitting in plenary session or as the Grand Chamber orders a preparatory inquiry and does not undertake such an inquiry itself, it shall entrust the task of so doing to the Chamber to which the case was originally assigned or to the Judge-Rapporteur.

Where a Chamber orders a preparatory inquiry and does not undertake such an inquiry itself, it shall entrust the task of so doing to the Judge-Rapporteur.

The Advocate General shall take part in the measures of inquiry.

2. The parties may be present at the measures of inquiry.

3. Subject to the provisions of Article 116(2) and (6), the Court of First Instance shall take into consideration only those documents which have been made available to the lawyers and agents of the parties and on which they have been given an opportunity of expressing their views.

Where it is necessary for the Court of First Instance to verify the confidentiality, in respect of one or more parties, of a document that may be relevant in order to rule in a case, that document shall not be communicated to the parties at the stage of such verification.

Where a document to which access has been denied by a Community institution has been produced before the Court of First Instance in proceedings relating to the legality of that denial, that document shall not be communicated to the other parties.

Section 3—The summoning and examination of witnesses and experts

Article 68

1. The Court of First Instance may, either of its own motion or on application by a party, and after hearing the Advocate General and the parties, order that certain facts be proved by witnesses. The order shall set out the facts to be established.

The Court of First Instance may summon a witness of its own motion or on application by a party or at the instance of the Advocate General.

An application by a party for the examination of a witness shall state precisely about what facts and for what reasons the witness should be examined.

2. The witness shall be summoned by an order containing the following information:

(a) the surname, forenames, description and address of the witness;

(b) an indication of the facts about which the witness is to be examined;

(c) where appropriate, particulars of the arrangements made by the Court of First Instance for reimbursement of expenses incurred by the witness, and of the penalties which may be imposed on defaulting witnesses.

The order shall be served on the parties and the witnesses.

3. The Court of First Instance may make the summoning of a witness for whose examination a party has applied conditional upon the deposit with the cashier of the Court of First Instance of a sum sufficient to cover the taxed costs thereof; the Court of First Instance shall fix the amount of the payment.

The cashier of the Court of First Instance shall advance the funds necessary in connection with the examination of any witness summoned by the Court of First Instance of its own motion.

4. After the identity of the witness has been established, the President shall inform him that he will be required to vouch the truth of his evidence in the manner laid down in paragraph 5 of this Article and in Article 71.

The witness shall give his evidence to the Court of First Instance, the parties having been given notice to attend. After the witness has given his main evidence the President may, at the request of a party or of his own motion, put questions to him.

The other Judges and the Advocate General may do likewise.

Subject to the control of the President, questions may be put to witnesses by the representatives of the parties.

5. Subject to the provisions of Article 71, the witness shall, after giving his evidence, take the following oath:

"I swear that I have spoken the truth, the whole truth and nothing but the truth."

The Court of First Instance may, after hearing the parties, exempt a witness from taking the oath.

6. The Registrar shall draw up minutes in which the evidence of each witness is reproduced.

The minutes shall be signed by the President or by the Judge-Rapporteur responsible for conducting the examination of the witness, and by the Registrar. Before the minutes are thus signed, witnesses must be given an opportunity to check the content of the minutes and to sign them.

The minutes shall constitute an official record.

Article 69(2)(6)(7)

1. Witnesses who have been duly summoned shall obey the summons and attend for examination.

2. If a witness who has been duly summoned fails to appear before the Court of First Instance, the latter may impose upon him a pecuniary penalty not exceeding EUR 5 000 and may order that a further summons be served on the witness at his own expense.

The same penalty may be imposed upon a witness who, without good reason, refuses to give evidence or to take the oath or where appropriate to make a solemn affirmation equivalent thereto.

3. If the witness proffers a valid excuse to the Court of First Instance, the pecuniary penalty imposed on him may be cancelled. The pecuniary penalty imposed may be reduced at the request of the witness where he establishes that it is disproportionate to his income.

4. Penalties imposed and other measures ordered under this Article shall be enforced in accordance with Articles 244 and 256 of the EC Treaty and Articles 159 and 164 of the EAEC Treaty.

Article 70

1. The Court of First Instance may order that an expert's report be obtained. The order appointing the expert shall define his task and set a time-limit within which he is to make his report.

2. The expert shall receive a copy of the order, together with all the documents necessary for carrying out his task. He shall be under the supervision of the Judge-Rapporteur, who may be present during his investigation and who shall be kept informed of his progress in carrying out his task.

The Court of First Instance may request the parties or one of them to lodge security for the costs of the expert's report.

3. At the request of the expert, the Court of First Instance may order the examination of witnesses. Their examination shall be carried out in accordance with Article 68.

4. The expert may give his opinion only on points which have been expressly referred to him.

5. After the expert has made his report, the Court of First Instance may order that he be examined, the parties having been given notice to attend.

Subject to the control of the President, questions may be put to the expert by the representatives of the parties.

6. Subject to the provisions of Article 71, the expert shall, after making his report, take the following oath before the Court of First Instance:

"I swear that I have conscientiously and impartially carried out my task."

The Court of First Instance may, after hearing the parties, exempt the expert from taking the oath.

Article 71

1. The President shall instruct any person who is required to take an oath before the Court of First Instance, as witness or expert, to tell the truth or to carry out his task conscientiously and impartially, as the case may be, and shall warn him of the criminal liability provided for in his national law in the event of any breach of this duty.

2. Witnesses and experts shall take the oath either in accordance with the first subparagraph of Article 68(5) and the first subparagraph of Article 70(6) or in the manner laid down by their national law.

3. Where the national law provides the opportunity to make, in judicial proceedings, a solemn affirmation equivalent to an oath as well as or instead of taking an oath, the witnesses and experts may make such an affirmation under the conditions and in the form prescribed in their national law.

Where their national law provides neither for taking an oath nor for making a solemn affirmation, the procedure described in the first paragraph of this Article shall be followed.

Article 72

1. The Court of First Instance may, after hearing the Advocate General, decide to report to the competent authority referred to in Annex III to the Rules supplementing the Rules of Procedure of the Court of Justice of the Member State whose courts have penal jurisdiction in any case of perjury on the part of a witness or expert before the Court of First Instance, account being taken of the provisions of Article 71.

2. The Registrar shall be responsible for communicating the decision of the Court of First Instance. The decision shall set out the facts and circumstances on which the report is based.

Article 73

1. If one of the parties objects to a witness or to an expert on the ground that he is not a competent or proper person to act as witness or expert or for any other reason, or if a witness or expert refuses to give evidence, to take the oath or to make a solemn affirmation equivalent thereto, the matter shall be resolved by the Court of First Instance.

2. An objection to a witness or to an expert shall be raised within two weeks after service of the order summoning the witness or appointing the expert; the statement of objection must set out the grounds of objection and indicate the nature of any evidence offered.

Article 74

1. Witnesses and experts shall be entitled to reimbursement of their travel and subsistence expenses. The cashier of the Court of First Instance may make a payment to them towards these expenses in advance.

2. Witnesses shall be entitled to compensation for loss of earnings, and experts to fees for their services. The cashier of the Court of First Instance shall pay witnesses and experts their compensation or fees after they have carried out their respective duties or tasks.

Article 75

1. The Court of First Instance may, on application by a party or of its own motion, issue letters rogatory for the examination of witnesses or experts.

2. Letters rogatory shall be issued in the form of an order which shall contain the name, forenames, description and address of the witness or expert, set out the facts on which the witness or expert is to be examined, name the parties, their agents, lawyers or advisers, indicate their addresses for service and briefly describe the subject-matter of the proceedings.

Notice of the order shall be served on the parties by the Registrar.

3. The Registrar shall send the order to the competent authority named in Annex I to the Rules supplementing the Rules of Procedure of the Court of Justice of the Member State in whose territory the witness or expert is to be examined. Where necessary, the order shall be accompanied by a translation into the official language or languages of the Member State to which it is addressed.

The authority named pursuant to the first subparagraph shall pass on the order to the judicial authority which is competent according to its national law.

The competent judicial authority shall give effect to the letters rogatory in accordance with its national law. After implementation the competent judicial authority shall transmit to the authority named pursuant to the first subparagraph the order embodying the letters rogatory, any documents arising from the implementation and a detailed statement of costs. These documents shall be sent to the Registrar.

The Registrar shall be responsible for the translation of the documents into the language of the case.

4. The Court of First Instance shall defray the expenses occasioned by the letters rogatory without prejudice to the right to charge them, where appropriate, to the parties.

Article 76

1. The Registrar shall draw up minutes of every hearing. The minutes shall be signed by the President and by the Registrar and shall constitute an official record.

2. The parties may inspect the minutes and any expert's report at the Registry and obtain copies at their own expense.

Chapter 3a (6)

Expedited Procedures

Article 76a(10)

1. The Court of First Instance may, on application by the applicant or the defendant, after hearing the other parties and the Advocate General, decide, having regard to the particular urgency and the circumstances of the case, to adjudicate under an expedited procedure.

An application for a case to be decided under an expedited procedure shall be made by a separate document lodged at the same time as the application initiating the proceedings or the defence. That application may state that certain pleas in law or arguments or certain passages of the application initiating the proceedings or the defence are raised only in the event that the case is not decided under an expedited procedure, in particular by enclosing with the application initiating the proceedings and a list of the annexes which are to be taken into consideration only if the case is decided under an expedited procedure

By way of derogation from Article 55, cases on which the Court of First Instance has decided to adjudicate under an expedited procedure shall be given priority.

2. By way of derogation from Article 46(1), where the applicant has requested, in accordance with paragraph 1 of this Article, that the case should be decided under an expedited procedure, the period prescribed for the lodging of the defence shall be one month. If the Court of First Instance decides not to allow the request, the defendant shall be granted an additional period of one month in order to lodge or, as the case may be, supplement the defence. The time-limits laid down in this subparagraph may be extended pursuant to Article 46(3).

Under the expedited procedure, the pleadings referred to in Articles 47(1) and 116(4) and (5) may be lodged only if the Court of First Instance, by way of measures of organisation of procedure adopted in accordance with Article 64, so allows.

3. Without prejudice to Article 48, the parties may supplement their arguments and offer further evidence in the course of the oral procedure. They must, however, give reasons for the delay in offering such further evidence.

4. The decision of the Court of First Instance to adjudicate under an expedited procedure may prescribe conditions as to the volume and presentation of the pleadings of the parties; the subsequent conduct of the proceedings or as to the pleas in law and arguments on which the Court of First Instance will be called upon to decide.

If one of the parties does not comply with any one of those conditions, the decision to adjudicate under an expedited procedure may be revoked. The proceedings shall then continue in accordance with the ordinary procedure.

Chapter 4

Stay of Proceedings and Declining of Jurisdiction by the Court of First Instance

Article 77(2)(7)

Without prejudice to Article 123(4), Article 128 and Article 129(4), proceedings may be stayed:

(a) in the circumstances specified in the third paragraph of Article 54 of the Statute of the Court of Justice;

(b) where an appeal is brought before the Court of Justice against a decision of the Court of First Instance disposing of the substantive issues in part only, disposing of a procedural issue concerning a plea of lack of competence or inadmissibility or dismissing an application to intervene;

(c) at the joint request of the parties.

Article 78(4)

The decision to stay the proceedings shall be made by order of the President after hearing the parties and the Advocate General; the President may refer the matter to the Court of First Instance. A decision ordering that the proceedings be resumed shall be adopted in accordance with the same procedure. The orders referred to in this Article shall be served on the parties.

Article 79

1. The stay of proceedings shall take effect on the date indicated in the order of stay or, in the absence of such an indication, on the date of that order.

While proceedings are stayed time shall, except for the purposes of the time-limit prescribed in Article 115(1) for an application to intervene, cease to run for the purposes of prescribed time-limits for all parties.

2. Where the order of stay does not fix the length of the stay, it shall end on the date indicated in the order of resumption or, in the absence of such indication, on the date of the order of resumption.

From the date of resumption time shall begin to run afresh for the purposes of the time-limits.

Article 80(2)(7)

Decisions declining jurisdiction in the circumstances specified in the third paragraph of Article 54 of the Statute of the Court of Justice shall be made by the Court of First Instance by way of an order which shall be served on the parties.

Chapter 5

Judgments

Article 81

The judgment shall contain:

— a statement that it is the judgment of the Court of First Instance,

— the date of its delivery,

— the names of the President and of the Judges taking part in it,

— the name of the Advocate General, if designated,

— the name of the Registrar,

— the description of the parties,

— the names of the agents, advisers and lawyers of the parties,

— a statement of the forms of order sought by the parties,

— a statement, where appropriate, that the Advocate General delivered his opinion,

— a summary of the facts,

— the grounds for the decision,

— the operative part of the judgment, including the decision as to costs.

Article 82

1. The judgment shall be delivered in open court; the parties shall be given notice to attend to hear it.

2. The original of the judgment, signed by the President, by the Judges who took part in the deliberations and by the Registrar, shall be sealed and deposited at the Registry; the parties shall be served with certified copies of the judgment.

3. The Registrar shall record on the original of the judgment the date on which it was delivered.

Article 83(2)(7)

Subject to the provisions of the second paragraph of Article 60 of the Statute of the Court of Justice, the judgment shall be binding from the date of its delivery.

Article 84

1. Without prejudice to the provisions relating to the interpretation of judgments, the Court of First Instance may, of its own motion or on application by a party made within two weeks after the delivery of a judgment, rectify clerical mistakes, errors in calculation and obvious slips in it.

2. The parties, whom the Registrar shall duly notify, may lodge written observations within a period prescribed by the President.

3. The Court of First Instance shall take its decision in closed session.

4. The original of the rectification order shall be annexed to the original of the rectified judgment. A note of this order shall be made in the margin of the original of the rectified judgment.

Article 85

If the Court of First Instance should omit to give a decision on costs, any party may within a month after service of the judgment apply to the Court of First Instance to supplement its judgment.

The application shall be served on the opposite party and the President shall prescribe a period within which that party may lodge written observations.

After these observations have been lodged, the Court of First Instance shall decide both on the admissibility and on the substance of the application.

Article 86

The Registrar shall arrange for the publication of cases before the Court of First Instance.

Chapter 6

Costs

Article 87(2)(4)

1. A decision as to costs shall be given in the final judgment or in the order which closes the proceedings.

2. The unsuccessful party shall be ordered to pay the costs if they have been applied for in the successful party's pleadings.

Where there are several unsuccessful parties the Court of First Instance shall decide how the costs are to be shared.

3. Where each party succeeds on some and fails on other heads, or where the circumstances are exceptional, the Court of First Instance may order that the costs be shared or that each party bear its own costs.

The Court of First Instance may order a party, even if successful, to pay costs which it considers that party to have unreasonably or vexatiously caused the opposite party to incur.

4. The Member States and institutions which intervened in the proceedings shall bear their own costs.

The States, other than the Member States, which are parties to the EEA Agreement, and also the EFTA Surveillance Authority, shall bear their own costs if they intervene in the proceedings.

The Court of First Instance may order an intervener other than those mentioned in the preceding subparagraph to bear his own costs.

5. A party who discontinues or withdraws from proceedings shall be ordered to pay the costs if they have been applied for in the observations of the other party on the discontinuance. However, upon application by the party who discontinues or withdraws from proceedings, the costs shall be borne by the other party if this appears justified by the conduct of that party.

Where the parties have come to an agreement on costs, the decision as to costs shall be in accordance with that agreement.

If costs are not applied for, the parties shall bear their own costs.

6. Where a case does not proceed to judgment, the costs shall be in the discretion of the Court of First Instance.

Article 88

Without prejudice to the second subparagraph of Article 87(3), in proceedings between the Communities and their servants the institutions shall bear their own costs.

741

Article 89

Costs necessarily incurred by a party in enforcing a judgment or order of the Court of First Instance shall be refunded by the opposite party on the scale in force in the State where the enforcement takes place.

Article 90

Proceedings before the Court of First Instance shall be free of charge, except that:

(a) where a party has caused the Court of First Instance to incur avoidable costs, the Court of First Instance may order that party to refund them;

(b) where copying or translation work is carried out at the request of a party, the cost shall, in so far as the Registrar considers it excessive, be paid for by that party on the scale of charges referred to in Article 24(5).

Article 91

Without prejudice to the preceding Article, the following shall be regarded as recoverable costs:

(a) sums payable to witnesses and experts under Article 74;

(b) expenses necessarily incurred by the parties for the purpose of the proceedings, in particular the travel and subsistence expenses and the remuneration of agents, advisers or lawyers.

Article 92

1. If there is a dispute concerning the costs to be recovered, the Court of First Instance hearing the case shall, on application by the party concerned and after hearing the opposite party, make an order, from which no appeal shall lie.

2. The parties may, for the purposes of enforcement, apply for an authenticated copy of the order.

Article 93

1. Sums due from the cashier of the Court of First Instance and from debtors of the Court of First Instance shall be paid in euro.

2. Where expenses to be refunded have been incurred in a currency other than the euro or where the steps in respect of which payment is due were taken in a country of which the euro is not the currency, conversions of currency shall be made at the official rates of exchange of the European Central Bank on the day of payment.

Chapter 7(4)(10)

Legal Aid

Article 94

1. In order to ensure effective access to justice, legal aid shall be granted for proceedings before the Court of First Instance in accordance with the following rules.

Legal aid shall cover, in whole or in part, the costs involved in legal assistance and representation by a lawyer in proceedings before the Court of First Instance. The cashier of the Court of First Instance shall be responsible for those costs.

2. Any natural person who, because of his economic situation, is wholly or partly unable to meet the costs referred to in paragraph 1 shall be entitled to legal aid.

The economic situation shall be assessed, taking into account objective factors such as income, capital and the family situation.

3. Legal aid shall be refused if the action in respect of which the application is made appears to be manifestly inadmissible or manifestly unfounded.

Article 95

1. An application for legal aid may be made before or after the action has been brought.

The application need not be made through a lawyer.

2. The application for legal aid must be accompanied by all information and supporting documents making it possible to assess the applicant's economic situation, such as a certificate issued by the competent national authority attesting to his economic situation.

If the application is made before the action has been brought, the applicant must briefly state the subject-matter of the proposed action, the facts of the case and the arguments in support of the action. The application must be accompanied by supporting documents in that regard.

3. The Court of First Instance may provide, in accordance with Article 150, for the compulsory use of a form in making an application for legal aid

Article 96

1. Before giving its decision on an application for legal aid, the Court of First Instance shall invite the other party to submit its written observations unless it is already apparent from the information produced that the conditions laid down in Article 94(2) have not been satisfied or that those laid down in Article 94(3) have been satisfied.

2. The decision on the application for legal aid shall be taken by the President by way of an order. He may refer the matter to the Court of First Instance.

An order refusing legal aid shall state the reasons on which it is based.

3. In any order granting legal aid a lawyer shall be designated to represent the person concerned.

If the person has not indicated his choice of lawyer or if his choice is unacceptable, the Registrar shall send a copy of the order granting legal aid and a copy of the application to the competent authority of the Member State concerned mentioned in Annex II to the Rules supplementing the Rules of Procedure of the Court of Justice. The lawyer instructed to represent the applicant shall be designated having regard to the suggestions made by that authority.

An order granting legal aid may specify an amount to be paid to the lawyer instructed to represent the person concerned or fix a limit which the lawyer's disbursements and fees may not, in principle, exceed. It may provide for a contribution to be made by the person concerned to the costs referred to in Article 94(1), having regard to his economic situation.

4. The introduction of an application for legal aid shall suspend the period prescribed for the bringing of the action until the date of notification of the order making a decision on that application or, in the cases referred to in the second subparagraph of paragraph 3, of the order designating the lawyer instructed to represent the applicant.

5. If the circumstances which led to the grant of legal aid should alter during the proceedings, the President may at any time, on his own motion or on application,

withdraw legal aid, having heard the person concerned. He may refer the matter to the Court of First Instance.

An order withdrawing legal aid shall contain a statement of reasons.

6. No appeal shall lie from orders made under this article.

Article 97

1. Where legal aid is granted, the President may, on application by the lawyer of the person concerned, decide that an amount by way of advance should be paid to the lawyer.

2. Where, by virtue of the decision closing the proceedings, the recipient of legal aid has to bear his own costs, the President shall fix the lawyer's disbursements and fees which are to be paid by the cashier of the Court of First Instance by way of a reasoned order from which no appeal shall lie. He may refer the matter to the Court of First Instance.

3. Where, in the decision closing the proceedings, the Court of First Instance has ordered another party to pay the costs of the recipient of legal aid, that other party shall be required to refund to the cashier of the Court of First Instance any sums advanced by way of aid.

In the event of challenge or if the party does not comply with a demand by the Registrar to refund those sums, the President shall rule by way of reasoned order from which no appeal shall lie. The President may refer the matter to the Court of First Instance.

4. Where the recipient of the aid is unsuccessful, the Court of First Instance may, in its decision, as to costs, closing the proceedings, if equity so requires, order that one or more parties should bear their own costs or that those costs should be borne, in whole or in part, by the cashier of the Court of First Instance by way of legal aid.

Chapter 8

Discontinuance

Article 98(2)(6)(7)

If, before the Court of First Instance has given its decision, the parties reach a settlement of their dispute and intimate to the Court of First Instance the abandonment of their claims, the President shall order the case to be removed from the register and shall give a decision as to costs in accordance with Article 87(5) having regard to any proposals made by the parties on the matter.

This provision shall not apply to proceedings under Articles 230 and 232 of the EC Treaty and Articles 146 and 148 of the EAEC Treaty.

Article 99

If the applicant informs the Court of First Instance in writing that he wishes to discontinue the proceedings, the President shall order the case to be removed from the register and shall give a decision as to costs in accordance with Article 87(5).

Chapter 9

Service

Article 100(6)

1. Where these Rules require that a document be served on a person, the Registrar shall ensure that service is effected at that person's address for service either by the

744

dispatch of a copy of the document by registered post with a form for acknowledge-ment of receipt or by personal delivery of the copy against a receipt.

The Registrar shall prepare and certify the copies of documents to be served, save where the parties themselves supply the copies in accordance with Article 43(1).

2. Where, in accordance with the second subparagraph of Article 44(2), the addressee has agreed that service is to be effected on him by telefax or other technical means of communication, any procedural document other than a judgment or order of the Court of First Instance may be served by the transmission of a copy of the document by such means.

Where, for technical reasons or on account of the nature or length of the document, such transmission is impossible or impracticable, the document shall be served, if the addressee has failed to state an address for service, at his address in accordance with the procedures laid down in paragraph 1. The addressee shall be so advised by telefax or other technical means of communication. Service shall then be deemed to have been effected on the addressee by registered post on the tenth day following the lodging of the registered letter at the post office of the place where the Court of First Instance has its seat, unless it is shown by the acknowledgement of receipt that the letter was received on a different date or the addressee informs the Registrar, within three weeks of being advised by telefax or other technical means of communication, that the document to be served has not reached him.

Chapter 10

Time-Limits

Article 101(2)(7)

1. Any period of time prescribed by the EC and EAEC Treaties, the Statute of the Court of Justice or these Rules for the taking of any procedural step shall be reckoned as follows:

(a) Where a period expressed in days, weeks, months or years is to be calculated from the moment at which an event occurs or an action takes place, the day during which that event occurs or that action takes place shall not be counted as falling within the period in question;

(b) A period expressed in weeks, months or in years shall end with the expiry of whichever day in the last week, month or year is the same day of the week, or falls on the same date, as the day during which the event or action from which the period is to be calculated occurred or took place. If, in a period expressed in months or in years, the day on which it should expire does not occur in the last month, the period shall end with the expiry of the last day of that month;

(c) Where a period is expressed in months and days, it shall first be reckoned in whole months, then in days;

(d) Periods shall include official holidays, Sundays and Saturdays;

(e) Periods shall not be suspended during the judicial vacations.

2. If the period would otherwise end on a Saturday, Sunday or official holiday, it shall be extended until the end of the first following working day.

The list of official holidays drawn up by the Court of Justice and published in the *Official Journal of the European Union* shall apply to the Court of First Instance.

Article 102(4)(6)(7)

1. Where the period of time allowed for commencing proceedings against a measure adopted by an institution runs from the publication of that measure, that

period shall be calculated, for the purposes of Article 101(1)(a), from the end of the 14th day after publication thereof in the *Official Journal of the European Union*.

2. The prescribed time-limits shall be extended on account of distance by a single period of ten days.

Article 103

1. Any time-limit prescribed pursuant to these Rules may be extended by whoever prescribed it.

2. The President may delegate power of signature to the Registrar for the purpose of fixing time-limits which, pursuant to these Rules, it falls to the President to prescribe, or of extending such time-limits.

TITLE 3

SPECIAL FORMS OF PROCEDURE

Chapter 1

Suspension of Operation or Enforcement and Other Interim Measures

Article 104(2)(6)(7)

1. An application to suspend the operation of any measure adopted by an institution, made pursuant to Article 242 of the EC Treaty and Article 157 of the EAEC Treaty, shall be admissible only if the applicant is challenging that measure in proceedings before the Court of First Instance.

An application for the adoption of any other interim measure referred to in Article 243 of the EC Treaty, the third paragraph of Article 39 of the ECSC Treaty and Article 158 of the EAEC Treaty shall be admissible only if it is made by a party to a case before the Court of First Instance and relates to that case.

2. An application of a kind referred to in paragraph 1 of this Article shall state the subject-matter of the proceedings, the circumstances giving rise to urgency and the pleas of fact and law establishing a prima facie case for the interim measures applied for.

3. The application shall be made by a separate document and in accordance with the provisions of Articles 43 and 44.

Article 105

1. The application shall be served on the opposite party, and the President of the Court of First Instance shall prescribe a short period within which that party may submit written or oral observations.

2. The President of the Court of First Instance may order a preparatory inquiry.

The President of the Court of First Instance may grant the application even before the observations of the opposite party have been submitted. This decision may be varied or cancelled even without any application being made by any party.

Article 106(7)

A Judge, designated for the purpose in the decision adopted by the Court of First Instance in accordance with Article 10, shall replace the President of the Court of First Instance in deciding an application in the event that the President is absent or prevented from dealing with it.

Article 107

1. The decision on the application shall take the form of a reasoned order. The order shall be served on the parties forthwith.

2. The enforcement of the order may be made conditional on the lodging by the applicant of security, of an amount and nature to be fixed in the light of the circumstances.

3. Unless the order fixes the date on which the interim measure is to lapse, the measure shall lapse when final judgment is delivered.

4. The order shall have only an interim effect, and shall be without prejudice to the decision on the substance of the case by the Court of First Instance.

Article 108

On application by a party, the order may at any time be varied or cancelled on account of a change in circumstances.

Article 109

Rejection of an application for an interim measure shall not bar the party who made it from making a further application on the basis of new facts.

Article 110(2)(6)(7)

The provisions of this Chapter shall apply to applications to suspend the enforcement of a decision of the Court of First Instance or of any measure adopted by another institution, submitted pursuant to Articles 244 and 256 of the EC Treaty and Articles 159 and 164 of the EAEC Treaty.

The order granting the application shall fix, where appropriate, a date on which the interim measure is to lapse.

Chapter 2

Preliminary Issues

Article 111(4)

Where it is clear that the Court of First Instance has no jurisdiction to take cognisance of an action or where the action is manifestly inadmissible or manifestly lacking any foundation in law, the Court of First Instance may, by reasoned order, after hearing the Advocate General and without taking further steps in the proceedings, give a decision on the action.

Article 112(2)(7)

The decision to refer an action to the Court of Justice, pursuant to the second paragraph of Article 54 of the Statute of the Court of Justice, shall, in the case of manifest lack of competence, be made by reasoned order and without taking any further steps in the proceedings.

Article 113(4)(10)

The Court of First Instance may at any time, of its own motion, after hearing the parties, decide whether there exists any absolute bar to proceeding with an action or declare that the action has become devoid of purpose and that there is no need to adjudicate on it; it shall give its decision in accordance with Article 114(3) and (4).

Article 114(10)

1. A party applying to the Court of First Instance for a decision on admissibility, on lack of competence or other preliminary plea not going to the substance of the case shall make the application by a separate document.

The application must contain the pleas of fact and law relied on and the form of order sought by the applicant; any supporting documents must be annexed to it.

2. As soon as the application has been lodged, the President shall prescribe a period within which the opposite party may lodge a document containing the form of order sought and the arguments of fact and law relied on.

3. Unless the Court of First Instance otherwise decides, the remainder of the proceedings shall be oral.

4. The Court of First Instance shall, after hearing the Advocate General, decide on the application or reserve its decision for the final judgment. It shall refer the case to the Court of Justice if the case falls within the jurisdiction of that Court.

If the Court of First Instance refuses the application or reserves its decision, the President shall prescribe new time-limits for further steps in the proceedings.

Chapter 3

Intervention

Article 115(2)(6)(7)

1. An application to intervene must be made either within six weeks of the publication of the notice referred to in Article 24(6) or, subject to Article 116(6), before the decision to open the oral procedure as provided for in Article 53.

2. The application shall contain:

(a) the description of the case;

(b) the description of the parties;

(c) the name and address of the intervener;

(d) the intervener's address for service at the place where the Court of First Instance has its seat;

(e) the form of order sought, by one or more of the parties, in support of which the intervener is applying for leave to intervene;

(f) a statement of the circumstances establishing the right to intervene, where the application is submitted pursuant to the second or third paragraph of Article 40 of the Statute of the Court of Justice.

Articles 43 and 44 shall apply.

3. The intervener shall be represented in accordance with Article 19 of the Statute of the Court of Justice.

Article 116(6)

1. The application shall be served on the parties.

The President shall give the parties an opportunity to submit their written or oral observations before deciding on the application.

748

The President shall decide on the application by order or shall refer the decision to the Court of First Instance. The order must be reasoned if the application is dismissed.

2. If an intervention for which application has been made within the period of six weeks prescribed in Article 115(1) is allowed, the intervener shall receive a copy of every document served on the parties. The President may, however, on application by one of the parties, omit secret or confidential documents.

3. The intervener must accept the case as he finds it at the time of his intervention.

4. In the cases referred to in paragraph 2 above, the President shall prescribe a period within which the intervener may submit a statement in intervention.

The statement in intervention shall contain:

(a) a statement of the form of order sought by the intervener in support of or opposing, in whole or in part, the form of order sought by one of the parties;

(b) the pleas in law and arguments relied on by the intervener;

(c) where appropriate, the nature of any evidence offered.

5. After the statement in intervention has been lodged, the President shall, where necessary, prescribe a time-limit within which the parties may reply to that statement.

6. Where the application to intervene is made after the expiry of the period of six weeks prescribed in Article 115(1), the intervener may, on the basis of the Report for the Hearing communicated to him, submit his observations during the oral procedure.

Chapter 4

Judgments of the Court of First Instance Delivered After its Decision Has Been Set Aside and the Case Referred Back to it

Article 117

Where the Court of Justice sets aside a judgment or an order of the Court of First Instance and refers the case back to that Court, the latter shall be seised of the case by the judgment so referring it.

Article 118(5)(7)

1. Where the Court of Justice sets aside a judgment or an order of a Chamber, the President of the Court of First Instance may assign the case to another Chamber composed of the same number of Judges.

2. Where the Court of Justice sets aside a judgment delivered or an order made by the Court of First Instance sitting in plenary session or by the Grand Chamber, the case shall be assigned to that Court or that Chamber as the case may be.

2a. Where the Court of Justice sets aside a judgment delivered or an order made by a single Judge, the President of the Court of First Instance shall assign the case to a Chamber composed of three Judges of which that Judge is not a member.

3. In the cases provided for in paragraphs 1, 2 and 2a of this Article, Articles 13(2), 14(1) and 51 shall apply.

Article 119

1. Where the written procedure before the Court of First Instance has been completed when the judgment referring the case back to it is delivered, the course of the procedure shall be as follows:

(a) Within two months from the service upon him of the judgment of the Court of Justice the applicant may lodge a statement of written observations;

(b) In the month following the communication to him of that statement, the defendant may lodge a statement of written observations. The time allowed to the defendant for lodging it may in no case be less than two months from the service upon him of the judgment of the Court of Justice;

(c) In the month following the simultaneous communication to the intervener of the observations of the applicant and the defendant, the intervener may lodge a statement of written observations. The time allowed to the intervener for lodging it may in no case be less than two months from the service upon him of the judgment of the Court of Justice.

2. Where the written procedure before the Court of First Instance had not been completed when the judgment referring the case back to the Court of First Instance was delivered, it shall be resumed, at the stage which it had reached, by means of measures of organisation of procedure adopted by the Court of First Instance.

3. The Court of First Instance may, if the circumstances so justify, allow supplementary statements of written observations to be lodged.

Article 120

The procedure shall be conducted in accordance with the provisions of Title II of these Rules.

Article 121

The Court of First Instance shall decide on the costs relating to the proceedings instituted before it and to the proceedings on the appeal before the Court of Justice.

Chapter 5

Judgments by Default and Applications to Set Them Aside

Article 122(4)

1. If a defendant on whom an application initiating proceedings has been duly served fails to lodge a defence to the application in the proper form within the time prescribed, the applicant may apply to the Court of First Instance for judgment by default.

The application shall be served on the defendant. The Court of First Instance may decide to open the oral procedure on the application.

2. Before giving judgment by default the Court of First Instance shall consider whether the application initiating proceedings is admissible, whether the appropriate formalities have been complied with, and whether the application appears well founded. It may order a preparatory inquiry.

3. A judgment by default shall be enforceable. The Court of First Instance may, however, grant a stay of execution until it has given its decision on any application under paragraph 4 of this Article to set aside the judgment, or it may make execution subject to the provision of security of an amount and nature to be fixed in the light of the circumstances; this security shall be released if no such application is made or if the application fails.

4. Application may be made to set aside a judgment by default.

The application to set aside the judgment must be made within one month from the date of service of the judgment and must be lodged in the form prescribed by Articles 43 and 44.

5. After the application has been served, the President shall prescribe a period within which the other party may submit his written observations.

The proceedings shall be conducted in accordance with the provisions of Title II of these Rules.

6. The Court of First Instance shall decide by way of a judgment which may not be set aside. The original of this judgment shall be annexed to the original of the judgment by default. A note of the judgment on the application to set aside shall be made in the margin of the original of the judgment by default.

Chapter 6

Exceptional Review Procedures

Section 1—Third-party proceedings

Article 123(7)

1. Articles 43 and 44 shall apply to an application initiating third-party proceedings. In addition such an application shall:

(a) specify the judgment contested;

(b) state how that judgment is prejudicial to the rights of the third party;

(c) indicate the reasons for which the third party was unable to take part in the original case before the Court of First Instance.

The application must be made against all the parties to the original case.

Where the judgment has been published in the *Official Journal of the European Union*, the application must be lodged within two months of the publication.

2. The Court of First Instance may, on application by the third party, order a stay of execution of the judgment. The provisions of Title III, Chapter 1, shall apply.

3. The contested judgment shall be varied on the points on which the submissions of the third party are upheld.

The original of the judgment in the third-party proceedings shall be annexed to the original of the contested judgment. A note of the judgment in the third-party proceedings shall be made in the margin of the original of the contested judgment.

4. Where an appeal before the Court of Justice and an application initiating third-party proceedings before the Court of First Instance contest the same judgment of the Court of First Instance, the Court of First Instance may, after hearing the parties, stay the proceedings until the Court of Justice has delivered its judgment.

Article 124(5)

The application initiating third-party proceedings shall be assigned to the Chamber which delivered the judgment which is the subject of the application; if the Court of First Instance sitting in plenary session or the Grand Chamber of the Court of First Instance delivered the judgment, the application shall be assigned to it. If the judgment has been delivered by a single Judge, the application initiating third-party proceedings shall be assigned to that Judge.

Section 2—Revision

Article 125(2)(7)

Without prejudice to the period of ten years prescribed in the third paragraph of Article 44 of the Statute of the Court of Justice, an application for revision of a judgment shall be made within three months of the date on which the facts on which the application is based came to the applicant's knowledge.

Article 126

1. Articles 43 and 44 shall apply to an application for revision. In addition such an application shall:

   (a) specify the judgment contested;

   (b) indicate the points on which the application is based;

   (c) set out the facts on which the application is based;

   (d) indicate the nature of the evidence to show that there are facts justifying revision of the judgment, and that the time-limits laid down in Article 125 have been observed.

2. The application must be made against all parties to the case in which the contested judgment was given.

Article 127(5)(7)

1. The application for revision shall be assigned to the Chamber which delivered the judgment which is the subject of the application; if the Court of First Instance sitting in plenary session or the Grand Chamber of the Court of First Instance delivered the judgment, the application shall be assigned to it. If the judgment has been delivered by a single Judge, the application for revision shall be assigned to that Judge.

2. Without prejudice to its decision on the substance, the Court of First Instance shall, after hearing the Advocate General, having regard to the written observations of the parties, give its decision on the admissibility of the application.

3. If the Court of First Instance finds the application admissible, it shall proceed to consider the substance of the application and shall give its decision in the form of a judgment in accordance with these Rules.

4. The original of the revising judgment shall be annexed to the original of the judgment revised. A note of the revising judgment shall be made in the margin of the original of the judgment revised.

Article 128

Where an appeal before the Court of Justice and an application for revision before the Court of First Instance concern the same judgment of the Court of First Instance, the Court of First Instance may, after hearing the parties, stay the proceedings until the Court of Justice has delivered its judgment.

Section 3—Interpretation of judgments

Article 129(5)(7)

1. An application for interpretation of a judgment shall be made in accordance with Articles 43 and 44. In addition it shall specify:

   (a) the judgment in question;

   (b) the passages of which interpretation is sought.

The application must be made against all the parties to the case in which the judgment was given.

2. The application for interpretation shall be assigned to the Chamber which delivered the judgment which is the subject of the application; if the Court of First Instance sitting in plenary session or the Grand Chamber of the Court of First Instance delivered the judgment, the application shall be assigned to it. If the judgment has been delivered by a single Judge, the application for interpretation shall be assigned to that Judge.

3. The Court of First Instance shall give its decision in the form of a judgment after having given the parties an opportunity to submit their observations and after hearing the Advocate General.

The original of the interpreting judgment shall be annexed to the original of the judgment interpreted. A note of the interpreting judgment shall be made in the margin of the original of the judgment interpreted.

4. Where an appeal before the Court of Justice and an application for interpretation before the Court of First Instance concern the same judgment of the Court of First Instance, the Court of First Instance may, after hearing the parties, stay the proceedings until the Court of Justice has delivered its judgment.

Title IV (3)

PROCEEDINGS RELATING TO INTELLECTUAL PROPERTY RIGHTS

Article 130(3)

1. Subject to the special provisions of this Title, the provisions of these Rules of Procedure shall apply to proceedings brought against the Office for Harmonisation in the Internal Market (Trade Marks and Designs) and against the Community Plant Variety Office (both hereinafter referred to as "the Office"), and concerning the application of the rules relating to an intellectual property regime.

2. The provisions of this Title shall not apply to actions brought directly against the Office without prior proceedings before a Board of Appeal.

Article 131(3)

1. The application shall be drafted in one of the languages described in Article 35(1), according to the applicant's choice.

2. The language in which the application is drafted shall become the language of the case if the applicant was the only party to the proceedings before the Board of Appeal or if another party to those proceedings does not object to this within a period laid down for that purpose by the Registrar after the application has been lodged.

If, within that period, the parties to the proceedings before the Board of Appeal inform the Registrar of their agreement on the choice, as the language of the case, of one of the languages referred to in Article 35(1), that language shall become the language of the case before the Court of First Instance.

In the event of an objection to the choice of the language of the case made by the applicant within the period referred to above and in the absence of an agreement on the matter between the parties to the proceedings before the Board of Appeal, the language in which the application for registration in question was filed at the Office shall become the language of the case. If, however, on a reasoned request by any party and after hearing the other parties, the President finds that the use of that language would not enable all parties to the proceedings before the Board of Appeal to follow the proceedings and defend their interests and that only the use of another language from among those mentioned in Article 35(1) makes it possible to remedy that situation, he may designate that other language as the language of the case; the President may refer the matter to the Court of First Instance.

3. In the pleadings and other documents addressed to the Court of First Instance and during the oral procedure, the applicant may use the language chosen by him in accordance with paragraph 1 and each of the other parties may use a language chosen by that party from those mentioned in Article 35(1).

4. If, by virtue of paragraph 2, a language other than that in which the application is drafted becomes the language of the case, the Registrar shall cause the application to be translated into the language of the case.

Each party shall be required, within a reasonable period to be prescribed for that purpose by the Registrar, to produce a translation into the language of the case of the pleadings or documents other than the application that are lodged by that party in a language other than the language of the case pursuant to paragraph 3. The party producing the translation, which shall be authentic within the meaning of Article 37, shall certify its accuracy. If the translation is not produced within the period prescribed, the pleading or the procedural document in question shall be removed from the file.

The Registrar shall cause everything said during the oral procedure to be translated into the language of the case and, at the request of any party, into the language used by that party in accordance with paragraph 3.

Article 132(3)

1. Without prejudice to Article 44, the application shall contain the names of all the parties to the proceedings before the Board of Appeal and the addresses which they had given for the purposes of the notifications to be effected in the course of those proceedings.

The contested decision of the Board of Appeal shall be appended to the application. The date on which the applicant was notified of that decision must be indicated.

2. If the application does not comply with paragraph 1, Article 44(6) shall apply.

Article 133(3)

1. The Registrar shall inform the Office and all the parties to the proceedings before the Board of Appeal of the lodging of the application. He shall arrange for service of the application after determining the language of the case in accordance with Article 131(2).

2. The application shall be served on the Office, as defendant, and on the parties to the proceedings before the Board of Appeal other than the applicant. Service shall be effected in the language of the case.

Service of the application on a party to the proceedings before the Board of Appeal shall be effected by registered post with a form of acknowledgment of receipt at the address given by the party concerned for the purposes of the notifications to be effected in the course of the proceedings before the Board of Appeal.

3. Once the application has been served, the Office shall forward to the Court of First Instance the file relating to the proceedings before the Board of Appeal.

Article 134(3)

1. The parties to the proceedings before the Board of Appeal other than the applicant may participate, as interveners, in the proceedings before the Court of First Instance.

2. The interveners referred to in paragraph 1 shall have the same procedural rights as the main parties.

They may support the form of order sought by a main party and they may apply for a form of order and put forward pleas in law independently of those applied for and put forward by the main parties.

3. An intervener, as referred to in paragraph 1, may, in his response lodged in accordance with Article 135(1), seek an order annulling or altering the decision of the Board of Appeal on a point not raised in the application and put forward pleas in law not raised in the application.

Such submissions seeking orders or putting forward pleas in law in the intervener's response shall cease to have effect should the applicant discontinue the proceedings.

4. In derogation from Article 122, the default procedure shall not apply where an intervener, as referred to in paragraph 1 of this Article, has responded to the application in the manner and within the period prescribed.

Article 135(3)

1. The Office and the interveners referred to in Article 134(1) may submit responses to the application within a period of two months from the service of the application.

Article 46 shall apply to the responses.

2. The application and the responses may be supplemented by replies and rejoinders by the parties, including the interveners referred to in Article 134(1), where the President, on a reasoned application made within two weeks of service of the responses or replies, considers such further pleading necessary and allows it in order to enable the party concerned to put forward its point of view.

The President shall prescribe the period within which such pleadings are to be submitted.

3. Without prejudice to the foregoing, in the cases referred to in Article 134(3), the other parties may, within a period of two months of service upon them of the response, submit a pleading confined to responding to the form of order sought and the pleas in law submitted for the first time in the response of an intervener. That period may be extended by the President on a reasoned application from the party concerned.

4. The parties' pleadings may not change the subject-matter of the proceedings before the Board of Appeal.

Article 136(3)

1. Where an action against a decision of a Board of Appeal is successful, the Court of First Instance may order the Office to bear only its own costs.

2. Costs necessarily incurred by the parties for the purposes of the proceedings before the Board of Appeal and costs incurred for the purposes of the production, prescribed by the second subparagraph of Article 131(4), of translations of pleadings or other documents into the language of the case shall be regarded as recoverable costs.

In the event of inaccurate translations being produced, the second subparagraph of Article 87(3) shall apply.

TITLE 5(10)

APPEALS AGAINST DECISIONS OF THE EUROPEAN UNION CIVIL SERVICE TRIBUNAL

Article 137

1. An appeal shall be brought by lodging a notice of appeal at the Registry of the Court of First Instance or of the Civil Service Tribunal.

2. The Registry of the Civil Service Tribunal shall immediately transmit to the Registry of the Court of First Instance the papers in the case at first instance and, where necessary, the appeal.

Article 138

1. The notice of appeal shall contain:

   (a) the name and address of the appellant;

   (b) the names of the other parties to the proceedings before the Civil Service Tribunal;

   (c) the pleas in law and legal arguments relied on;

   (d) the form of order sought by the appellant.

   Article 43 and Article 44(2) and (3) shall apply to appeals.
   2. The decision of the Civil Service Tribunal appealed against shall be attached to the notice. The notice shall state the date on which the decision appealed against was notified to the appellant.
   3. If a notice of appeal does not comply with Article 44(3) or with paragraph (2) of this Article, Article 44(6) shall apply.

Article 139

1. An appeal may seek:

   (a) to set aside, in whole or in part, the decision of the Civil Service Tribunal;

   (b) the same form of order, in whole or in part, as that sought at first instance and shall not seek a different form of order.

   2. The subject matter of the proceedings before the Civil Service Tribunal may not be changed in the appeal.

Article 140

The notice of appeal shall be served on all the parties to the proceedings before the Civil Service Tribunal. Article 45 shall apply.

Article 141

1. Any party to the proceedings before the Civil Service Tribunal may lodge a response within two months after service on him of the notice of appeal. The time limit for lodging a response shall not be extended.
   2. A response shall contain:

   (a) the name and address of the respondent;

   (b) the date on which notice of the appeal was served on the respondent;

   (c) the pleas in law and legal arguments relied on;

   (d) the form of order sought by the respondent.

   Article 43 and Article 44(2) and (3) shall apply.

Article 142

1. A response may seek:

(a) to dismiss, in whole or in part, the appeal or to set aside, in whole or in part, the decision of the Civil Service Tribunal;

(b) the same form of order, in whole or in part, as that sought at first instance and shall not seek a different form of order.

2. The subject-matter of the proceedings before the Civil Service Tribunal may not be changed in the response.

Article 143

1. The notice of appeal and the response may be supplemented by a reply and a rejoinder where the President, on application made by the appellant within seven days of service of the response, considers such further pleading necessary and expressly allows the submission of a reply in order to enable the appellant to put forward his point of view or in order to provide a basis for the decision on the appeal. The President shall prescribe the date by which the reply is to be submitted and, upon service of that pleading, the date by which the rejoinder is to be submitted.

2. Where the response seeks to set aside, in whole or in part, the decision of the Civil Service Tribunal on a plea in law which was not raised in the appeal, the appellant or any other party may submit a reply on that plea alone within two months of the service of the response in question. Paragraph 1 shall apply to any further pleading following such a reply.

Article 144

Subject to the provisions of Articles 144 to 149 inclusive, Articles 48(2) and Articles 49, 50, 51(1), 52, 55 to 64, 76a to 110, 115(2) and (3), 116, 123 to 127 and 129 shall apply to the procedure before the Court of First Instance on appeal from a decision of the Civil Service Tribunal.

Article 145

Where the appeal is, in whole or in part, clearly inadmissible or clearly unfounded, the Court of First Instance may at any time, acting on a report from the Judge Rapporteur and after hearing the Advocate General, by reasoned order dismiss the appeal in whole or in part.

Article 146

After the submission of pleadings as provided for in Article 141(1) and, if applicable, Article 143(1) and (2), the Court of First Instance, acting on a report from the Judge Rapporteur and after hearing the Advocate General and the parties, may decide to rule on the appeal without an oral procedure unless one of the parties submits an application setting out the reasons for which he wishes to be heard. The application shall be submitted within a period of one month from notification to the party of the closure of the written procedure. That period may be extended by the President.

Article 147

The preliminary report referred to in Article 52 shall be presented to the Court of First Instance after the pleadings provided for in Article 141(1) and where appropriate Article 143(1) and (2) have been lodged. Where no such pleadings are lodged, the same procedure shall apply after the expiry of the period prescribed for lodging them.

Article 148

Where the appeal is unfounded or where the appeal is well founded and the Court of First Instance itself gives judgment in the case, the Court of First Instance shall make a decision as to costs.

Article 88 shall apply only to appeals brought by institutions;

By way of derogation from Article 87(2), the Court of First Instance may, in appeals brought by officials or other servants of an institution, decide to apportion the costs between the parties where equity so requires.

If the appeal is withdrawn Article 87(5) shall apply.

Article 149

An application to intervene made to the Court in appeal proceedings shall be lodged before the expiry of a period of one month running from the date of the publication of the notice referred to in Article 24(6)

Final provisions

Article 150(10)

The Court of First Instance may issue practice directions relating, in particular, to the preparations for and conduct of hearings before it and to the lodging of written pleadings or observations.

Article 151(3)(7)(10)

These Rules, which are authentic in the languages mentioned in Article 35(1), shall be published in the *Official Journal of the European Union*. They shall enter into force on the first day of the second month from the date of their publication.

Court of First Instance Practice Directions to parties

THE COURT OF FIRST INSTANCE OF THE EUROPEAN COMMUNITIES,
Pursuant to Article 136a of its Rules of Procedure,
Whereas:

(1) It is in the interests of the efficient conduct of proceedings before the Court **D2–001** of First Instance (hereinafter "the Court") and the expeditious processing of cases that practice directions should be issued to the lawyers and agents of parties, dealing with the manner in which pleadings and other procedural documents relating to the written procedure are to be submitted;

(2) The present directions reflect, explain and complement provisions in the Court's Rules of Procedure and are designed to enable lawyers and agents to allow for the constraints under which the Court operates, and particularly those attributable to translation requirements and the electronic processing of procedural documentation;

(3) The Instructions to the Registrar dated March 3, 1994 (OJ L 78 of March 22, 1994, p. 32), as amended on March 29, 2001 (OJ L 119 of April 27, 2001, p. 2), require the Registrar to ensure that documents placed on a case-file comply with the provisions of the Statutes of the Court of Justice, the Rules of Procedure and any Practice Directions of the Court, together with the Instructions to the Registrar, and, in particular, oblige him to require that any irregularities of form in documents lodged be made good and, in default of such regularisation, that he refuse, where appropriate, to accept them if they do not comply with the provisions of the Statutes of the Court of Justice or the Rules of Procedure;

(4) Compliance with these Practice Directions will assure lawyers and agents that the pleadings and documents lodged by them may properly be processed by the Court and will not, with respect to the matters dealt with in these Practice Directions, entail the application of Article 90(a) of the Rules of Procedure;

(5) These Practice Directions have been drawn up following consultations with the agents of the Member States and the institutions acting in proceedings before the Court, and with the Council of the Bars and Law Societies of the European Community (CCBE), and take account of the observations made by them;

(6) In addition, lawyers and agents are strongly advised to have regard to the Notes for the Guidance of Counsel for the written procedure and for the oral procedure, as issued by the Registrar,

hereby adopts the following Practice Directions:

I. Use of technical means of communication

1. A copy of the signed original of a procedural document may be transmitted to the Registry in accordance with Article 43(6) of the Rules of Procedure either:

— by telefax (to fax number: 00 352 4303 2100);

or

— by electronic mail (electronic mail address: cfi.registry@curia.eu.int).

2. In the case of transmission by electronic mail, only a scanned copy of the signed original will be accepted. A document despatched in the form of an ordinary electronic file which is unsigned or bears an electronic signature or a facsimile signature generated by computer will not be treated as complying with Article 43(6) of the Rules of Procedure. No correspondence relating to a case which is received by the Court in the form of an ordinary electronic mail message will be taken into consideration.

In order to enable scanned documents to be uploaded to the Court's electronic archives, such documents should be scanned at a resolution of 300 DPI and in PDF format (images plus text), using Acrobat or Readiris 7 Pro software.

3. The lodgment of a document by telefax or electronic mail will be treated as complying with the relevant time-limit only if the signed original thereof reaches the Registry prior to the expiry of the period of ten days following such lodgment, as specified in Article 43(6) of the Rules of Procedure. The signed original must be sent without delay, immediately after the despatch of the copy, without any corrections or amendments, even of a minor nature, being made thereto. In the event of any divergence between the signed original and the copy previously lodged, only the date of lodgment of the signed original will be taken into consideration.

4. Where, in accordance with Article 44(2) of the Rules of Procedure, a party consents to be served by telefax or other technical means of communication, the statement to that effect must specify the telefax number and/or the electronic mail address to which the Registry may send that party documents to be served. The recipient's computer must be equipped with suitable software (for example, Acrobat or Readiris 7 Pro) enabling communications from the Registry, which will be transmitted in PDF format, to be read.

II. Lodgment of pleadings

1. Pleadings and other procedural documents lodged by the parties must be submitted in such a way as to enable them to be processed electronically by the Court, in particular by means of document scanning and character recognition.

In order to permit the use of such technology, the following requirements must be complied with:

(1) The paper must be white, unlined and A4 size, with the text appearing on one side of the page only.

(2) Pages of pleadings and annexes, if any, must be placed together in such a way as to enable them to be easily undone. They must not be bound together or fixed to each other by any other means (e.g. glued or stapled).

(3) The text must appear in characters of a current type (such as Times New Roman, Courier or Arial), in at least 12 pt in the body of the text and at least 10 pt in the footnotes, with one-and-a-half line spacing and upper, lower, left and right margins of at least 2.5 cm.

(4) The pages of the pleading must be numbered consecutively in the top right-hand corner. Such consecutive page numbering must also cover all the pages of the annexes to the pleading, so as to make it possible to ensure, by means of a page count, that all the pages of the annexes have been duly scanned.

2. The following information must appear on the first page of the pleading:

(1) the title of the pleading (application, defence, reply, rejoinder, application for leave to intervene, statement in intervention, objection of inadmissibility, observations on . . ., replies to questions, etc.);
(2) the case number (T–. . ./. .), where it has already been notified by the Registry;
(3) the names of the applicant and of the defendant;
(4) the name of the party on whose behalf the pleading is lodged.

3. Each paragraph of the pleading must be numbered.

4. The signature of the lawyer or agent acting for the party concerned must appear at the end of the pleading.

III. The form and content of the application and of the defence

1. All applications initiating proceedings must contain the statements prescribed by Article 44(1) and (2) of the Rules of Procedure.

2. The following must appear at the beginning of each application:

(1) the name and address of the applicant;
(2) the name and capacity of the applicant's lawyer or agent;
(3) the identity of the party against whom the application is made;
(4) the statements referred to in Article 44(2) of the Rules of Procedure (statement of an address for service or agreement to service by technical means of communication).

3. The application must contain, either at the beginning or at the end, the precise wording of the form of order sought in the decision of the Court (such as an order annulling an identified measure or awarding a sum by way of damages).

4. In the case of an application for annulment, a copy of the contested measure must be annexed to the application and identified as such.

5. Each application must be accompanied by a summary of the pleas in law and main arguments relied on, designed to facilitate publication of the notice prescribed by Article 24 of the Rules of Procedure, which will be prepared by the Registry. The summary in question must not be more than two pages long.

6. Together with the application, but separately from the documents annexed in support thereof, the documents referred to in Article 44(3) and (5)(a) and (b) of the Rules of Procedure must be produced.

7. The introductory part of the application must be followed by a brief account of the facts giving rise to the dispute.

8. Legal arguments must be set forth and grouped by reference to the particular pleas in law to which they relate, and ideally each argument or group of arguments should be preceded by a summary statement of the relevant plea.

9. All evidence offered in support must be expressly and accurately indicated, in such a way as to show clearly the facts to be proved:

— Documentary evidence offered in support must refer to the relevant document number in a schedule of annexed documents. Alternatively, if a document is not in the possession of the party concerned, the pleading must clearly indicate where and how the document may be obtained.

— Where oral testimony is sought to be given, each proposed witness or person from whom information is to be obtained must be clearly identified.

10. Each defence must contain the statements prescribed by Article 46(1) of the Rules of Procedure.

11. In addition to the case-number and a statement of the name of the applicant, the following must appear at the start of each defence:

   (1) the name and address of the defendant;
   (2) the name and capacity of the defendant's lawyer or agent;
   (3) the statements referred to in Article 44(2) of the Rules of Procedure (specification of an address for service or to which documents to be served by technical means of communication may be sent).

12. The precise wording of the form of order sought by the defendant in the decision of the Court must be specified either at the beginning or at the end of the defence.

13. Points 6, 8 and 9 above shall apply to the defence.

14. Any fact alleged by the other party which is contested must be accurately indicated and the basis on which it is contested must be stated explicitly.

IV. Annexes to pleadings

1. Only those documents mentioned in the actual text of a pleading and which are necessary in order to prove or illustrate its contents may be submitted as annexes.

2. Annexes will be accepted only if they are accompanied by a schedule indicating, for each document annexed:

   (1) the number of the annex;
   (2) a short description of the document (e.g. "letter"), followed by its date, author and addressee and its number of pages;
   (3) the page reference and paragraph number in the pleading where the document is mentioned and its relevance is described.

   An annex should also be numbered in such a way as to identify the pleading in which it is produced (thus, for example, Annex A.1, A.2, etc. in an application; Annex B.1, B. 2, etc. in a defence; Annex C.1, C.2, etc. in a reply; Annex D.1, D.2, etc. in a rejoinder).

3. Where a pleading contains more than 10 annexes, the schedule of annexes must be accompanied by an appendix identifying and setting out the relevant passages in each annex on which the party wishes to rely, save in the case of documents not exceeding three pages in length.

4. The actual annexes, as such, should follow the appendix in order, as per the numbering of the schedule.

5. Where, for the convenience of the Court, copies of judgments, legal writings or legislation are annexed to a pleading, they must be appended separately from the other annexes and must not be listed in the appendix of annexes.

6. Where annexes are documents which themselves contain annexes, they must be arranged and numbered in such a way as to avoid all possibility of confusion and should where necessary be separated by dividers.

7. Each reference in the text of the pleading to a document lodged must state the relevant annex number as given in the schedule of annexes and indicate the pleading with which the annex has been lodged, in the manner described at point IV.2 above.

V. Length of pleadings

1. In the interests both of the parties themselves and of the proper administration of justice, pleadings must concentrate on essential matters and be as brief as possible. Excessively lengthy pleadings complicate consideration of the case-file and are a prime cause of delay in the disposal of cases.

2. Depending on the nature of the issues and the circumstances of the case, the maximum number of pages should not in principle exceed:

   — 20–50 pages for the application and the defence;
   — 10–25 pages for the reply and the rejoinder;
   — 10–20 pages for an objection of inadmissibility and for observations thereon;
   — 10–20 pages for statements in intervention.

   Pleadings should wherever possible be shorter than the maxima indicated above. In cases involving particularly complex legal or factual issues, those maxima may be exceeded.

VI. Applications for expedited procedure

1. A party applying by separate document under Article 76a of the Rules of Procedure for a case to be decided by expedited procedure must briefly state the reasons for the special urgency of the case.

2. As the expedited procedure is largely oral, such an application will be granted only if the pleading (application or defence) of the party requesting expedition is confined to a summary of the pleas relied upon and where its annexes are limited in number.

3. An application in respect of which expedited procedure is requested must not in principle—depending on the nature of the issues and the circumstances of the case—exceed a maximum of 10 to 25 pages.

VII. Applications for suspension of operation or enforcement and other interim measures

1. The application must be made by a separate document. It must be intelligible in itself, without necessitating reference to the application lodged in the main proceedings.

2. An application for suspension of operation or enforcement or for other interim measures must state, with the utmost concision, the subject-matter of the proceedings, the pleas of fact and law on which the main action is based—establishing a *prima facie* case on the merits in that action—and the circumstances giving rise to urgency. It must specify the measure(s) applied for. Sections III and IV above shall apply.

3. Because an application for interim measures requires the existence of a *prima facie* case to be assessed for the purposes of a summary procedure, it

must not, under any circumstances, set out in full the text of the application in the main proceedings.

4. In order that an application for interim measures may be dealt with urgently, the number of pages it contains must not in principle—depending on the nature of the issues and the circumstances of the case—exceed a maximum of between 10 and 25.

VIII. Applications for confidential treatment

1. An application pursuant to Article 116(2) of the Rules of Procedure for the exclusion on grounds of confidentiality of any part of the contents of the case-file from the documents to be furnished to an intervener shall be made by a separate document.

2. Such an application must be strictly limited to material which is genuinely confidential. It may not in any event cover the entirety of a pleading and may only exceptionally extend to the entirety of an annexed document. It should usually be feasible to furnish a non-confidential version in which passages, words or figures have been deleted without harming the interest sought to be protected. An application which is inadequately detailed will not be considered.

3. An application must accurately identify the particulars or passages to be excluded and briefly state the reasons for which each of those particulars or passages is regarded as confidential.

4. The application must be accompanied by a non-confidential version of each pleading or document concerned with the confidential material deleted.

5. Where a party, despite a request in that regard from the Registrar, fails to put an application for confidential treatment into proper form to enable it to be considered, all the procedural documents concerned will be furnished to the intervener in accordance with Article 116(2) of the Rules of Procedure.

Done at Luxembourg, March 14, 2002

H. Jung   B. Vesterdorf
Registrar   President

Notes for the guidance of Counsel before the Court of First Instance for the oral procedure

These notes are intended to explain to Counsel appearing before the Court of First **D3–001** Instance the purpose of the oral procedure before it and the manner in which it is organized. The underlying concern is to reconcile in the best way possible the aim of maintaining the quality of judicial protection in the Community legal order and the need for proceedings to be conducted expeditiously and efficiently.

I. The purpose of the oral procedure

When the stage of the oral procedure is reached, the bench hearing the case and the Member of the Court performing the function of Advocate General, if one has been designated, will already have a good knowledge of the case and will have carefully studied the formal claims, pleas and arguments of the parties. There is therefore little point in repeating orally everything that has been set out in writing or even in commenting on the pleadings or written observations.

The purpose of the oral procedure is:

— where necessary, to reiterate in condensed form the position taken by the parties, emphasizing the key submissions advanced in writing;

— to clarify, if necessary, certain arguments advanced during the written procedure and to submit any new arguments based on recent events which arose after the close of the written procedure and which could not therefore be set out in the pleadings;

— to reply to any questions put by the Court.

II. The hearing of oral argument

1. Usefulness of oral submissions

It is for Counsel for each party to judge, in the light of the purpose of the oral procedure as defined above, whether there is any real point in presenting oral submissions or whether it would be sufficient simply to refer to the pleadings or written observations. The oral procedure can then concentrate on the replies to questions put by the Court. If Counsel does consider it necessary to address the Court, he may always confine himself to making specific points and referring to the pleadings in relation to other points.

The Court would emphasize that if a party decides not to present oral argument this will never be construed as acquiescence in another party's oral argument if the argument in point has already been rebutted in writing, nor will such silence prevent that party from replying to an oral submission put forward by the other party.

In some cases, the Court may consider it preferable to start the oral procedure with questions put by its Members to Counsel for the parties. In that case, Counsel are requested to take this into account if they then wish to make a brief address.

2. Presentation and structure of oral submissions

In the interests of clarity and in order to enable the Members of the Court to understand oral submissions better, it is generally preferable for Counsel to speak freely on the basis of notes rather than to read out a written text. The reading of a written text makes simultaneous interpretation of oral submissions more difficult.

Counsel for the parties are also requested to simplify their presentation of the case as far as possible: a series of short sentences will always be preferable to a long, complicated sentence. It would also assist the Court if Counsel could structure their oral argument and indicate, before developing it, the structural plan they intend to adopt.

3. *The constraints of simultaneous interpretation*

Counsel are reminded that, depending on the case being heard, only some of the Members of the bench will be following the oral argument in the language in which it is being presented: the other Members will be listening to the simultaneous interpretation. Although the interpreters are highly qualified, their task is a difficult one and in the interests of the better conduct of the proceedings Counsel are strongly advised to speak slowly and directly into the microphone.

If Counsel intend to cite verbatim passages from certain texts or documents, particularly passages not appearing in the documents before the Court, it would be helpful if they would indicate the passages concerned to the interpreters before the hearing. Similarly, it may be helpful to draw the interpreters' attention to any terms which may be difficult to translate.

As the courtrooms are equipped with an automatic sound amplification system, Counsel must press the button on the microphone in order to switch it on and wait for the light to come on before starting to speak. The button should not be pressed whilst a Member of the Court or another person is speaking so as not to cut off their microphone.

4. *Duration of oral submissions*

The Court is well aware that the time taken in presenting oral submissions may vary, depending on the complexity of the case and on whether or not new facts have arisen. However, having regard to the purpose of the oral procedure, there is generally little to be gained in allowing proceedings to exceed a certain length of time.

Counsel are therefore requested to limit their oral submissions to 15 minutes or thereabouts for each party unless the Registry has indicated otherwise. This limitation, applies, of course, only to the presentation of oral argument itself and not to time spent in answering questions put at the hearing.

If circumstances so require, a request for leave to exceed the speaking time normally allowed, giving reasons and indicating the speaking time considered necessary, may be made to the Registry at least 15 days before the date fixed for the hearing. When such requests are made, Counsel for the parties will be informed of the time which they will each have for presenting their oral submissions.

Where a party is represented by more than one Counsel, no more than two of them may normally present argument and their combined speaking time must not exceed the time-limits indicated above. However, Counsel other than those who addressed the Court may reply to questions from Members of the Court and gives replies to the observations of other Counsel.

Where two or more parties are advancing the same argument before the Court (a situation which may occur where, in particular, there are interventions or where cases have been joined), their Counsel are requested to confer with each other before the hearing so as to avoid any repetition.

III. Miscellaneous

1. *Report for the Hearing*

The Report for the Hearing is drawn up by the Judge-Rapporteur and provides an objective summary of the case. It does not set out every single detail of the parties' arguments but is meant to enable the parties to check that their pleas and arguments have been properly understood and to facilitate study of the trial documents by the other Members of the bench hearing the case.

The Court will make every effort to ensure that Counsel for the parties receive the Report for the Hearing at least three weeks before the date of the hearing. As far as the Court is concerned, the sole purpose of this document is to prepare the hearing for the oral procedure; the Court will not refer to it in its judgment and it will not form part of its judgment.

If the Report for the Hearing contains factual errors, Counsel are requested to notify them to the Registry in writing before the hearing. Similarly, if it does not correctly convey the essence of a party's argument, Counsel for that party may propose the amendments he considers appropriate.

If at the hearing Counsel submit oral observations on the Report for the Hearing, they should subsequently resubmit those observations in writing to the Registry.

2. Citing judgments

When citing a judgment of the Court of Justice or of the Court of First Instance, Counsel are requested to give all the references, including the names of the parties, and to state the number of the page of the ECR on which the passage in question appears.

3. Documents

Article 43 of the Rules of Procedure of the Court of First Instance provides that documents relied on by the parties must be annexed to a pleading. Save in exceptional circumstances and with the consent of the parties, the Court of First Instance will not accept documents produced after the procedural time-limits have expired, including documents submitted at the hearing.

Since all oral argument is recorded, the Court does not allow notes of oral argument to be lodged.

INDEX